KALTE BUFFETS

Kalte Buffets

Vegetarische Küche
Regionale und klassische Küche
Exotische Küche

Von
Karin Lilienthal
Rolf Schürmann
Wolfgang Markloff
Markus Haxter

Förderungsgesellschaft für das Hotel-
und Gaststättengewerbe mbH

Verlag Glückauf GmbH · Essen 1998

Impressum

Herausgeber	Förderungsgesellschaft für das Hotel- und Gaststättengewerbe mbH, Abteilung Bildung, Coesfeld
Verlag	Verlag Glückauf GmbH, VGE cuisine, Essen
Autoren	Karin Lilienthal, Rolf Schürmann, Wolfgang Markloff, Markus Haxter
Zeichnungen	Wolfgang Markloff
Fotos	Matthias Ibeler
Redaktion	Elisabeth Frahling, Förderungsgesellschaft für das Hotel- und Gaststättengewerbe mbH
Verlagsleistungen:	
Lektorat	Bernd Litke
Gestaltung, Layout, Herstellung	Kurt Klein
Desktop publishing	Kurt Klein, Herbert Stimper
Reproduktionen	repro contact studio, Stadtlohn
Druck, Verarbeitung	B.o.s.s Druck und Medien GmbH, Kleve

Dieses Werk ist urheberrechtlich geschützt. Jede Verwertung außerhalb der Grenzen des Urheberrechts ist ohne schriftliche Genehmigung des Verlags Glückauf unzulässig. Dies gilt auch für herkömmliche Vervielfältigungen (darunter Fotokopien, Nachdruck), Übersetzungen, Aufnahme in Mikrofilmarchive, elektronische Datenbanken und Mailboxes sowie für Vervielfältigungen auf CD-ROM oder anderen digitalen Datenträgern.

© Copyright 1998 Verlag Glückauf GmbH, Essen

ISBN 3-7739-1200-5

Inhaltsverzeichnis

Vegetarische Küche
Karin Lilienthal

Präsident Guido Dellwig	11
Vorbemerkung	12
Vorschlag für ein Frühlingsbuffet	14
Frühlingssalat mit Bulgur, Grünkern und Wildreis	15
Frischkäseterrine	16
Gänseblumen-Vinaigrette	17
Olivenpaste	18
Knoblauchcreme mit gerösteten Walnußkernen und Kräutern	19
Kürbiskern-Dip	19
Süß-saure Gemüse mit Winzeressig und Kandiszucker vollendet	20
Gekochte Eier in kaltem Thymian-Rosmarin-Sud	21
Roggenfladen	22
Raukebutter	22
Walnußbaguette	23
Sesamzöpfe	23
Wurzelrübencreme mit Blattpetersilie und dickem Schmand	24
Cassoulet von Lauch und schwarzem Pfeffer mit Käse gratiniert, gebratene Plätzchen von der Sandmöhre	25
Gebratene Plätzchen von der Sandröhre	26
Linsen-Dinkelbratlinge auf dreierlei Paprikamark	27
Rot-grün-gelbes Paprikamark	28
Gebackene Blüten vom Mai-Holunder auf einer Mascarpone-Aprikosen-Sauce	30
Drei-Käsecreme-Torte mit Gartenerdbeeren	31
Früchte mit Ahorndip	32
Verschiedene Käse aus dem Graskorb	33
Vorschlag für ein Sommer-/Herbstbuffet	35
Quark-Gemüse-Terrine an sommerlichen Blattsalaten mit Borretsch-Vinaigrette	36
Sommerliche Gemüse-Gelee-Variationen	38
Eingelegte, gehobelte Zwergkürbisse mit einer Edelpilzcreme und Walnußbaguette	39
Bauernsalat mit mariniertem Tofu und geröstetem Sesam	40
Tofu-Mayonnaise und Soja-Knoblauch-Dip	41
Püree von Artischocken mit geräuchertem Knoblauch	41
Kalte Tomatensauce mit Basilikum und Chili	42
Eingelegter Fenchel mit Sherryessig	43
Marinierte Paprika	44
Pikante Cremechampignons	44
Vollkorn-Croissants	45
Knoblauch-Kräuterbutter „nach meiner Art"	45
Mandelbrot	46
Schafskäsecreme mit frischen Gartenkräutern	46
Schmand-Brötchen	47
Kaltes Süppchen von Gartengurken mit Schwedenmilch und geröstetem Knoblauch	48

Wähe von Eierfrüchten (Auberginen) und Herbstpilzen
mit einem Zwiebel-Minz-Mus 49
Belag: Auberginenröllchen 50
Belag: Pfifferlinge 51
Zwiebel-Minz-Mus 51
Crêpes von Kichererbsen, mit Weißschimmelkäse gefüllten Äpfeln
und Mascarpone-Joghurt 52
Gedünstete Äpfel mit Weißschimmelkäse, Staudensellerie
und Pinienkernen gefüllt 53
Sesamsauce mit Mascarpone-Joghurt 53
In Vollkorn gebackene Aprikosen mit Marzipanfüllung und Orangenblütenhonig ... 54
Champagnertörtchen mit marinierten blauen Feigen in Orangenlikör 55
Traubenkompott 56
Eingelegte Minimozzarella 56
Halbgefrorenes vom Ahornsirup in der Williamsbirne
mit Himbeermark und Luzernesprossen 57
Eßbare Dekorationsblüten 58

Vorschlag für ein Winterbuffet 60

Vollkornwindbeutel mit Avocadomus auf einem Salat von roten Linsen 62
Avocadomus 63
Salat von roten Linsen 63
Sellerietaler mit Cheddarcreme und Feldsalat 64
Buntes Gemüse süß-sauer eingelegt 65
Gemüse-Terrine im Auberginenmantel 66
Rote Tofucreme 67
Sojabohnen-Dip mit Lauchzwiebeln und Knoblauch 67
Tofu-Sauerrahm 68
Crème fraîche mit Chili-Linsen 68
Öl vom Zitronen-Thymian mit Lavendelblüten 68
Salat von Gartengemüsen mit Öl vom Zitronen-Thymian
und Lavendelblüten, geröstetes Mandelbrot und Raukebutter 69
Weißkohlsalat mit Möhren und Mango 70
Artischockenherzen mit Strauchtomaten 71
Rübli-Brötchen mit Grünkern 72
Sesambutter 72
G'rissene Thübingerle 73
Vollkorn-Knäckebrot 73
Suppe von Cox-Orange-Äpfeln mit Ceylon-Zimt und Mandelsplittern 74
Falscher Hase vom Grünkern mit eingelegten Ebereschenbeeren,
dazu Kartoffeln aus dem Tontopf 75
Eingelegte Ebereschenbeeren 76
Maispflanzerln mit Sojasprossen 77
Kräutersauce 77
Schwarzwurzelgemüse 77
Gratin von Kartoffeln, Kohlrabi und Tomaten 78
Ricotta-Zimtschaum mit Gelee-Nocken vom Boskopapfel 79
Mandelkuchen mit Cabua-Kakao 80
Frische Datteln mit Stiltoncreme 81
Pikante Vollkornplätzchen mit Thymian 82
Käse-Kräuter-Kugeln mit Walnußkernen 82
Plätzchen mit saurer Sahne, Mohn, Sesam und Leinsamen 83

Regionale und klassische Küche

Rolf Schürmann · Wolfgang Markloff

Vorbemerkung	84
Vorschlag für ein Frühlingsbuffet in der Oster-, Kommunions- und Konfirmationszeit	86
Schaumbrot von geräuchertem Fisch mit Zucchiniplätzchen und Tomaten-Crème fraîche	87
Zucchinplätzchen	88
Kalte Quarkschaum-Gemüseterrine im Rauchschinkenmantel	89
Gebeizte sauerländische Bachforellen	90
Apfelmeerrettich	90
Meerrettichmayonnaise	92
Rote Bete-Sauce	92
Zuckerschoten-Matjes-Salat	93
Fenchel-Orangen-Salat	93
Spargel-Artischocken-Salat	94
Orangen-Pfeffer-Butter	94
Bleichselleriecreme mit Räucherfischnocken	95
Räucherfischnocken	96
Schweinefiletscheiben in der Spargelhülle, Sauerampferbuttersauce, neue Kartoffeln	96
Sauerampferbuttersauce	97
Moorlammrückenfilet mit Zucchinipiccata, geschmelzten Tomaten und Kartoffelnudeln	98
Kartoffelnudeln	98
Marinierte Erdbeeren in Florentinerschalen mit einer Cognac-Vanillecreme	100
Grießplätzchen in einer Haselnußkruste mit Rhabarber-Apfel-Grütze	102
Rhabarber-Apfel-Grütze	103
Frischkäse im Pumpernickelmantel	104
Vorschlag für ein Sommer-/Herbstbuffet	105
Terrine von Rotzungenfilets und Lachsforellen mit Spargelkohl und einer leichten Limettencreme	106
Limettencreme	107
Gemüsegelee mit gepökelter Schweineschulter im geriebenen Teig	108
Geriebener Pastetenteig	109
Putenvögerl in Tomaten-Kräuter-Püree mit einer Geflügelterrine im Linsenmantel	110
Geflügelterrine im Linsenmantel	111
Eingelegter Tafelspitz mit saurem Paprikagemüse	112
Fenchel-Honig-Sauce	113
Brunnenkresse-Sauce	113
Käse-Obst-Salat	114
Lauch-Mais-Salat	114
Käsebutter	115
Räucherfisch-Butter	115
Kalte Kartoffelrahmsuppe	116
Warmer tannenhonig-gebeizter Lachs auf Knisterfinken mit Gemüse-Kartoffel-Törtchen	118
Knisterfinken	118
Gemüse-Kartoffel-Törtchen	119
Sauerländer Seildrehermahl	120
Erdbeer-Riesling-Gelee mit Zitronenjoghurt und Eierlikörsauce	122

Eierlikörsauce — 123
Pistazien-Quarktaschen mit Pflaumen-Mirabellen-Kompott — 124
Pflaumen-Mirabellen-Kompott — 125

Vorschlag für ein Winter-/Weihnachtsbuffet — 126
Sauerländer Bauernpastete und Leberkranz mit einer Sauce von
Wiesenchampignons und frischem Estragon auf Linsensalat — 127
Leberkranz — 128
Sauce von Wiesenchampignons und frischem Estragon — 129
Linsensalat — 130
Rehrückenfilet mit einer Kaninchen-Pfifferling-Sülze und Schlehensauce — 131
Herstellung von Wildbrühe für Wildgelee — 132
Schlehensauce — 133
Gefüllte Kalbsröllchen mit Herbsttrompeten,
mariniertem Fenchel und Winterlauch — 134
Marinierter Fenchel — 136
Eingelegter Winterlauch — 137
Kalte Hagebuttensauce — 138
Buttermilch-Estragon-Sauce — 138
Roquefortbutter — 139
Petersilien-Schnittlauch-Butter — 139
Wirsingsalat — 140
Salat von Fisch und winterlichen Gemüsen — 141
Rotkohl-Johannisbeeren-Suppe mit Stutenklößchen — 142
Stutenklößchen — 142
Frico von Kaninchen und Schwein im Mangoldblatt serviert,
Sherry-Gemüse-Sauce und Kartoffel-Möhren-Hucke — 144
Sherry-Gemüse-Sauce — 145
Kartoffel-Möhren-Hucke — 146
Perlhuhnbrust im Rohschinkenmantel mit gerösteten Nüssen,
Apfel-Essig-Sauce und Sauerländer Nudelpickert — 147
Apfel-Essig-Sauce — 148
Sauerländer Nudelpickert — 149
Geeister Altenaer Weihnachtskuchen mit eingelegten Kornbirnen
und Punschsauce — 150
Eingelegte Kornbirnen — 151
Punschsauce — 151
Mandelcreme mit Weißwein-Zimt-Apfel und Zitronenmelissenschaum — 152
Weißwein-Zimt-Apfel — 153
Zitronenmelissenschaum — 153
Herzhafter Käserettich — 154

20 Menügänge — 156
Gebeizte Entenbrust in Altbiergelee, dazu Gemüsevinaigrette — 158
Gebratene Hirschnüßchen in Wacholder-Preiselbeermarinade,
Salat von Winterendivien und Topinambur — 159
Warme Hechtterrine auf Kürbis-Korianderkompott und Rotkohlsalat — 160
Kürbis-Korianderkompott — 160
Rotkohlsalat — 161
Westfälischer Kartoffelsalat von Kaninchen und Flußkrebsen,
dazu Estragon-Buttersauce — 162

Warm geräuchertes Filet vom Kirschdöbel auf marinierter Rauke,
mit glacierten Zuckermöhrchen und einer grünen Sauce -------------------------- 163
Grüne Kräutersauce nach Frankfurter Art -- 164
Meerrettichsüppchen mit Walnußschöberln -- 165
Kaltes Liebstöckelsüppchen, Radieschenstreifen ---------------------------------- 166
Gebratenes Ems-Zanderfilet auf Rieslingkraut mit glacierten Trauben,
geröstetem Rauchfleisch und Stutenwürfeln, Butterkartoffeln -------------------- 167
Rieslingkraut --- 167
Gebratenes Karpfenfilet unter der Haferflockenkruste,
geschmorter Lattich, Kartoffel-Plinsen -- 168
Geschmorter Lattich --- 168
Kartoffel-Plinsen --- 169
Arm und Reich – Kalbsmedaillon und Blutwurst
auf Apfel-Meerrettichgemüse, Schwarzbrot-Struwen ------------------------------ 170
Apfel-Meerrettichgemüse -- 170
Schwarzbrot-Struwen -- 171
Westfälischer Pumpernickel-Schinkenpfannkuchen
mit gebratenen Schweinefiletblättchen in Braunbiersauce, geröstete Baumpilze,
Kopfsalat in Kräuterschmanddressing -- 172
Braunbiersauce -- 172
Kräuterschmanddressing -- 173
Gefülltes Stubenküken in Apfelmost gegart auf Knisterfinken ---------------------- 174
Spanisches Frico vom Weideochsen im Strudelteig gebacken,
Karotten-Zwiebelgemüse --- 176
Gebratenes Rückenstück vom Weidelamm
mit Salbei, Zitronensauce, Blattspinat und Butternocken -------------------------- 178
Süße Reibekuchen mit hausgemachtem Vanilleeis,
Rübenkraut und Doppelrahm -- 180
Apfelplätzchen mit Muskat-Pflaumen und Vanillebuttermilch -------------------- 182
Muskat-Pflaumen -- 182
Münsterländer Stippmilch mit Zimt und Zucker,
dazu Blaubeergefrorenes und Kassebetten --- 184
Hausgemachtes Hagebuttenrahmeis mit Pfannbirnen und Brombeerschmand -- 185
Westfälischer Welfenhut --- 186

Exotische Küche

Markus Haxter

Vorbemerkung	188
Vorschlag für ein exotisches Buffet	**190**
Früchtespieße auf Papaya-Sauce mit Bananenblütensalat	191
Papaya-Sauce	192
Bananenblütensalat	192
Gemüse-Sushi	194
Jakobsmuschel- und Seeteufelspieß, Limetten-Meerrettich-Sauce und Salat von Chayoten	196
Tandoori-Marinade	197
Tandooripaste	197
Garam masala	197
Salat von Chayoten mit Macadamia-Nußöl-Dressing	198
Limetten-Meerrettich-Sauce	198
Rinderfilet-Garnelen-Spieße mit Guacamole und Reissalat	199
Guacamole	199
Rum-Gewürzmischung	200
Teriyaki-Gewürzmischung	200
West-Indies-Gewürzmischung	200
Reissalat mit Chilis und Ananas	201
Tandoori-Hähnchen	202
Jerk Poulardenbrust	202
Ananas-Chutney	203
Tomatensalsa	204
Erdnußsauce	204
Barbarie-Entenbrust mit Palmzucker und »Fünf Gewürzen« karamelisiert, Sansibar-Salat	205
Sansibar-Salat	206
Tempura-Garnelen auf Linsen-Ananas-Curry	207
Linsen-Ananas-Curry	208
Bohnensalat	209
Zitrusgebeizter Lachs	210
Lachs-Frühlingszwiebel-Salat	211
Glasnudelsalat mit Rinderfiletstreifen	212
Kokosbrioche	213
Erntedank-Brot	214
Zwiebel-Rosmarin-Brot	214
Tomatenbutter	215
Salak-Zwiebelschmalz	215
Quinoa-Plätzchen	216
Mais- und Paprikacreme	217
Spare-ribs	218
Curry-Brätlinge	218
Gemüse aus dem Wok	219
Rinderfilet im griechischen Blätterteig, schwarze Bohnensauce	220
Bohnensauce	221
Bonito im Bananenblatt	222
Paprika-Ananas-Gemüse	224
Maisfritter	224
Kokos-Maispudding mit Tamarillosauce	225
Tamarillosauce	226
Bananen-Rum-Parfait	227
Mozzarella-Cheddar-Wonton	228
Nashibirne mit Gorgonzola	228
Register	**230**
Mengen, Zeiten, Abkürzungen, Richtwerte	**232**

Immer wieder verlangen gastgewerbliche Betriebe, aber auch Hobbyköche und Seminarleiter ein Kochbuch, das keine Wünsche offenläßt.
„Kalte Buffets" vermittelt deshalb eine Vielzahl von Angeboten, die nicht nur meisterlich inszeniert, sondern auch von der Autorin und den Autoren sehr verständlich beschrieben wurden.
Die einzelnen Schwerpunktthemen vegetarische, regionale klassische und exotische Küche werden nicht nur bei Fachexperten und Kochbuchautoren Anerkennung finden. Der optischen Aufbereitung wurde durch die besondere Gestaltung und die großzügige Bebilderung größte Aufmerksamkeit gewidmet. Alle Rezepte sind in der Praxis erprobt und fordern die Leserinnen und Leser zur Nachahmung auf.
Ich möchte die Gelegenheit nutzen, der Autorin Karin Lilienthal und den Autoren Rolf Schürmann, Wolfgang Markloff und Markus Haxter zu danken.

GUIDO DELLWIG

Dieses Fachbuch wird in der Abteilung Bildung, bei einer Vielzahl von Seminaren und bei den Gastgewerblichen Bildungszentren ein positives Echo hervorrufen. Es wird auch denen Freude bereiten, die es zu einem besonderen Anlaß geschenkt bekommen.
Mit freundlicher Unterstützung der Porzellanmanufaktur Villeroy & Boch AG, Mettlach, sowie der Württembergischen Metallwarenfabrik AG WMF, Geislingen/Steige, konnten die schönsten Kompositionen auch für die Augen, die ja bekanntlich mitessen, ansprechend präsentiert werden.
Ich hoffe, daß dieses Fachbuch ein bedeutender Ratgeber sein wird. Ich bin mir sicher, daß die Auswahl und die Zubereitung kalter/warmer Platten zukünftig nicht nur leichter von der Hand gehen werden – es soll natürlich auch Freude bereiten!

Herbst 1998

Guido Dellwig
Präsident des Hotel- und Gaststättenverbands Westfalen e.V.

VEGETARISCHE KÜCHE

KARIN LILIENTHAL

Drei jahreszeitlich orientierte Buffets hat Karin Lilienthal nach Kriterien der vegetarischen Küche komponiert. Rezepte und Illustrationen stehen
➤ ab Seite 15 für ein Frühlingsbuffet,
➤ ab Seite 36 für ein Sommer-/Herbstbuffet und
➤ ab Seite 62 für ein Winterbuffet.

Es handelt sich um abwechslungsreiche Offerten aus Getreiden, Hülsenfrüchten, Gemüse, Obst, Eiern und Milchprodukten. Veganer sind also nicht die Zielgruppe dieses Kapitels. Dafür ist diejenige Küche angesprochen, die ohne Fleisch und Fisch auskommen und im übrigen sehr gezielt saisonale Frischwaren verwenden will.

Karin Lilienthal ist Hauswirtschaftsmeisterin und Fachdozentin für Ernährungslehre. Sie arbeitet für die Förderungsgesellschaft für das Hotel- und Gaststättengewerbe in Coesfeld.

Vorschlag für ein Frühlingsbuffet

Frühlingssalat mit Bulgur, Grünkern und Wildreis

Frischkäseterrine mit Blattsalaten nach Saison und einer Gänseblumen-Vinaigrette

Rohkost von Gartengemüsen, dazu:
Olivenpaste
Knoblauchcreme mit gerösteten Walnußkernen und Kräutern
Kürbiskern-Dip

Süß-saure Gemüse mit Winzeressig und Kandiszucker vollendet

Gekochte Eier in kaltem Thymian-Rosmarin-Sud

Roggenfladen
Raukebutter
Walnußbaguette
Sesamzöpfe

Wurzelrübencreme mit Blattpetersilie und dickem Schmand

Cassoulet von Lauch und schwarzem Pfeffer mit Käse gratiniert, gebratene Plätzchen von der Sandmöhre

Linsen-Dinkelbratlinge auf dreierlei Paprikamark
Gebackene Blüten vom Mai-Holunder auf einer Mascarpone-Aprikosen-Sauce

Drei-Käsecreme-Torte mit Gartenerdbeeren

Früchte mit Ahorndip

Verschiedene Käse aus dem Graskorb

Frühlingssalat mit Bulgur, Grünkern und Wildreis

ZUTATEN

125 g	Bulgur
100 g	Grünkern
50 g	Wildreis
500 ml	Gemüsebrühe
2 Bd.	Frühlingszwiebeln
2 Bd.	Radieschen
200 g	Möhren
1	Knoblauchzehe
1 Bd.	glatte Petersilie
1 Topf	Minzblätter
1	Limette
	Salz, Pfeffer, Kreuzkümmel
30 ml	Olivenöl, vergine extra

ZUBEREITUNG

1 Getreide in Brühe aufkochen und 30 Minuten quellen lassen.

2 Die Frühlingszwiebeln putzen und in feine Ringe schneiden, Radieschen in Stifte schneiden, Möhren grob raffeln, Knoblauch hacken.

3 Petersilie und Minze von den Stielen zupfen, etwas zum Garnieren beiseite legen, den Rest grob hacken.

4 Kräuter und Gemüse unter das gegarte Getreide mischen, mit Limettensaft, Salz, Pfeffer und Kreuzkümmel würzen.

5 Anschließend Olivenöl untermischen und den Salat gut durchziehen lassen.

Vorbereitungszeit: 45 Minuten
Zubereitungszeit: 20 Minuten

WUSSTEN SIE SCHON?

Bulgur
Vorgekochter, geschälter, grob gemahlener Weizen. Wird wie Reis zu süßen und salzigen Speisen verwendet. Die Kochzeit beträgt 10 bis 12 Minuten.

Kreuzkümmel
Cumin, ein dem Kümmel ähnlicher Samen.

Frischkäseterrine

ZUTATEN

400 g Doppelrahmfrischkäse
500 g Schmand
6 TL Agar-Agar
(ersatzweise 6 Blatt klare Gelatine)
1 rote Paprika
2 Bd. Kräuter
2 Knoblauchzehen
30 g Paprikagewürzpaste
1 EL rote Paprikawürfel
Salz, Pfeffer
2-l-Kastenform

Vorbereitungszeit: 45 Minuten
Zubereitungszeit: ca. 30 Minuten
Zeit des Auskühlens:
mind. 1 Stunde

ZUBEREITUNG

1 Frischkäse und Schmand verrühren, mit Salz und Pfeffer würzen.

2 Die Masse dritteln. Einen Teil mit durchgedrücktem Knoblauch würzen, den zweiten Teil mit pürierten Kräutern verfeinern, den letzten Teil mit Paprikagewürzpaste sowie kleinen roten Paprikawürfeln und Salz abschmecken.

3 Jede Portion mit 2 Teelöffeln Agar-Agar (mit 8 Eßlöffeln kaltem Wasser verrühren, quellen lassen, aufkochen, 2 Minuten kochen, bis sich alles gelöst hat, etwas abkühlen lassen) und mit der Käsemasse glattrühren.

4 Eine Kastenform mit Klarsichtfolie auslegen, damit man die Terrine nach dem Erstarren leicht stürzen kann.

5 Nun schichtweise die weiße, rote und grüne Masse einfüllen und im Kühlschrank erstarren lassen.

6 Stürzen und mit gehackten Kräutern bestreuen.

TIP

Bereiten Sie die Terrine einen Tag vor dem Verzehr vor.

WUSSTEN SIE SCHON?

Agar-Agar ist ein Geliermittel, das aus Algen hergestellt wird.

1 Teelöffel Agar-Agar entspricht etwa der Bindefähigkeit von 6 Blatt Gelatine.

Nachteil: Agar-Agar muß immer aufgekocht werden.

Wenn Sie öfter mit Agar-Agar gelieren und ein Mikrowellengerät besitzen, sollte Agar-Agar auf Vorrat zubereitet werden. 500 ml Wasser mit 25 g Agar-Agar zwei Minuten unter kräftigem Rühren aufkochen. Das noch flüssige Gel abkühlen lassen, in ein Schraubglas füllen und kühl aufbewahren. Bei Bedarf entsprechende Menge Agar-Agar-Gel in der Mikrowelle verflüssigen und mit der zu gelierenden Speise verrühren. Sie braucht nicht mehr aufgekocht zu werden. Man benötigt für 500 g gelierende Masse etwa 30 g Agar-Agar-Gel.

Quelle: Gewürzmühle Brecht

Gänseblumen-Vinaigrette

ZUTATEN
(für ca. 500 ml)

3 EL gehackte Kräuter (Kerbel, Zitronenmelisse, Sauerampfer und Blüten von Gänseblumen)
1 TL grüner Pfeffer, gehackt
2 Frühlingszwiebeln
100 ml Sherryessig
150 ml Olivenöl
100 ml Gemüsebrühe
Salz, Pfeffer, Zucker

ZUBEREITUNG

1 Essig und Gemüsebrühe gut verrühren.

2 Frühlingszwiebeln in feine Ringe schneiden und mit den Kräutern und dem Pfeffer gut mischen.

3 Mit Salz, Pfeffer und Zucker abschmecken und das Öl dazugeben.

4 Als letztes die Gänseblümchen untermischen.

Vorbereitungszeit: 10 Minuten
Zubereitungszeit: 10 Minuten

Olivenpaste

ZUTATEN
(für ca. 600 ml)

500 g schwarze Oliven
90 ml Olivenöl
2 geschälte Knoblauchzehen
1 kleines Bd. Basilikum
Zitronensaft
schwarzer Pfeffer aus der Mühle

ZUBEREITUNG

1 Oliven – wenn nötig – entsteinen, mit Olivenöl, Knoblauch, Basilikum und Zitronensaft in einer Küchenmaschine grob pürieren.

2 Nach Belieben abschmecken.

Vorbereitungszeit: 15 Minuten
Zubereitungszeit: 10 Minuten

TIP

In der provenzalischen Küche Frankreichs nennt man die Paste „Olivenkaviar".

Knoblauchcreme mit gerösteten Walnußkernen und Kräutern

ZUTATEN
(für ca. 500 ml)
100 g Knoblauchzehen
200 g Walnußkerne
20 ml Armagnac
250 ml Olivenöl, vergine extra
jodiertes Salz
frisch gemahlener Pfeffer
50 g frische Kräuter
(Kerbel, Thymian, Ysop, Basilikum, Petersilie)

ZUBEREITUNG

1 Abgezogene Knoblauchzehen, geröstete Walnußkerne und Armagnac zu einer glatten Creme verarbeiten und mit Salz und Pfeffer abschmecken.

2 Langsam das Öl unterrühren.

3 Kräuter hacken und unter die Sauce ziehen.

Vorbereitungszeit: 15 Minuten
Zubereitungszeit: 10 Minuten

> **TIP**
>
> Anstelle von Walnüssen eignen sich auch Mandeln, Pinienkerne oder Haselnüsse.

Kürbiskern-Dip

ZUTATEN
(für ca. 500 ml)
100 g Kürbiskerne
2 Eier, hart gekocht
1/2 Knoblauchzehe
1/2 EL Zitronensaft
60 ml Kürbiskernöl
250 ml Sahne
Jodsalz

ZUBEREITUNG

1 Gemahlene Kürbiskerne und Eigelbe mit Knoblauch und Zitronensaft in einem Mixgerät pürieren.

2 Erst das Kürbiskernöl löffelweise, dann nach und nach die geschlagene Sahne unterziehen.

3 Mit Salz abrunden und kühl stellen.

Vorbereitungszeit: 15 Minuten
Zubereitungszeit: 10 Minuten

> **TIP**
>
> Das beste Kürbiskernöl kommt in Europa aus Tirol.

Süß-saure Gemüse mit Winzeressig und Kandiszucker vollendet

ZUTATEN

500 g	Paprikaschoten, rot und gelb
500 g	Porree
500 g	Zucchini
500 ml	trockener Kerner
60 ml	Winzeressig „Kerner Auslese"
20 g	brauner Kandis
2	Lorbeerblätter
2	Knoblauchzehen
1	Zwiebel
15 g	Salz
	frisch gemahlener Pfeffer
450 ml	Olivenöl, vergine extra

Vorbereitungszeit: ca. 60 Minuten
Zubereitungszeit: ca. 30 Minuten

WUSSTEN SIE SCHON?

Die Weinbauern bieten aus Traubenmost hergestellten Winzeressig von milder ausgereifter Qualität an.

TIP

Bereits 1 Tag vorher zubereiten.

Das Gemüse hält sich verschlossen und im Kühlschrank 14 Tage.

Kombinieren Sie Gemüse nach Saison.

ZUBEREITUNG

1 Paprikaschoten, Porree und Zucchini vorbereiten und in gleichmäßige Stücke schneiden.

2 Knoblauchzehen halbieren, Zwiebeln in Scheiben schneiden und mit Wein, Essig, Salz, Pfeffer, Kandis und Lorbeerblättern aufkochen.

3 Das vorbereitete Gemüse – jede Sorte getrennt – im Sud bißfest garen, in ein großes Glas schichten, mit dem Sud und Olivenöl übergießen.

4 Das Gemüse muß gut mit Öl bedeckt sein.

Gekochte Eier in kaltem Thymian-Rosmarin-Sud

ZUTATEN

10 Eier
Zwiebelschalen
(von 3 Zwiebeln)
1 Zweig Rosmarin
2 Zweige Thymian
5 Chilischoten, rot-grün
3 Knoblauchzehen
Salz, Pfefferkörner, Lorbeerblatt

ZUBEREITUNG

1 Die Eier anstechen.

2 Wasser mit Zwiebelschalen kochen lassen, bis das Wasser braune Farbe annimmt.

3 Den Sud passieren.

4 Die Eier in braungefärbtem Wasser 10 Minuten kochen, abschrekken und kalt werden lassen.

5 1 Liter Wasser mit 2 Eßlöffeln Salz aufkochen und abkühlen lassen.

6 Die Eier etwas anschlagen, damit die Schalen kleine Risse bekommen.

7 Gewürze wie Rosmarin, Thymian, Chilischoten, Knoblauchzehen (in Scheiben), Pfefferkörner und Lorbeerblatt in ein hohes Glasgefäß füllen. Eier einlegen und mit Salzlake übergießen.

8 Mindestens 2 Tage durchziehen lassen.

9 Entweder pur oder – wie Soleier – mit verschiedenen Saucen und Gewürzen essen.

Vorbereitungszeit: 30 Minuten
Zubereitungszeit: 30 Minuten
Ruhezeit: 2 Tage zum Durchziehen

Roggenfladen

ZUTATEN
(für ca. 20 Stück)

1 kg Roggen, fein gemahlen
42 g frische Hefe
700 ml Wasser
90 g Sauerteig (als Fertigprodukt im Bio-Laden oder im Reformhaus erhältlich)
20 g Salz
100 g Butter

TIP

Bestreuen Sie die Fladen mit Kräutern wie Thymian und Rosmarin; auch Kümmel und Koriander passen gut.

ZUBEREITUNG

1 Hefe mit etwas lauwarmem Wasser verrühren, mit allen Zutaten gut kneten und 30 Minuten ruhen lassen.

2 Den Teig noch einmal gut durchkneten und in 20 Portionen teilen.

3 Jedes Teigstück zu einem Fladen formen und noch einmal 15 Minuten ruhen lassen.

4 Mit lauwarmem Wasser bestreichen und bei 220 Grad C etwa 15 Minuten mit Dampf backen.

Vorbereitungszeit: ca. 15 Minuten
Zeit zum Gehenlassen: ca. 45-60 Minuten
Backzeit: 15-20 Minuten

Raukebutter

ZUTATEN

1 Bd. Rauke
1 Limette
250 g weiche Butter
Salz, Pfeffer aus der Mühle

Vorbereitungszeit: 15 Minuten
Zubereitungszeit: 10 Minuten

TIP

Raukebutter paßt hervorragend zu allen Nußbroten.

ZUBEREITUNG

1 Butter schaumig rühren.

2 Rauke waschen, trockenschleudern und sehr fein hacken.

3 Limettenschale sehr dünn abreiben, Frucht auspressen.

4 Mit 1 Eßlöffel Limettensaft und der Rauke unter die weiche Butter rühren.

5 Mit Salz und Pfeffer abschmecken.

WUSSTEN SIE SCHON?

Rauke ist eine einjährige mediterrane Ölpflanze mit einem leicht nussigen Geschmack.

Die Blätter sind ähnlich dem Löwenzahn und verleihen Blattsalaten ein besonderes Aroma.

Walnußbaguette

ZUTATEN
FÜR 4 BAGUETTES

400 g Weizenvollkornmehl, ausgesiebt
100 g Roggenvollkornmehl, ausgesiebt
30 g Hefe
10 g Salz
250 ml Buttermilch
50 g weiche Butter
200 g Walnußkerne, grob gehackt

Für die Bleche:
Fett oder Backtrennpapier
Zum Bestreichen:
Milch
Backzeit:
220 Grad C, etwa 35 Minuten

ZUBEREITUNG

1 Mehl mit Hefe und Salz mischen, Buttermilch, weiche Butter zufügen und alles von Hand 20 Minuten lang gut durchkneten.

2 Zuletzt die Nüsse einkneten.

3 Den Teig mit einem feuchten Tuch abdecken und ca. 30 Minuten gehen lassen.

4 Den Hefeteig nochmals durchkneten, in vier gleich große Stücke teilen und diese wiederum in je zwei Teile portionieren.

5 Auf bemehlter Arbeitsfläche die einzelnen Teigstücke zu Rollen von 30 bis 40 cm Länge formen und immer 2 Rollen miteinander verschlingen.

6 Die 4 Baguettes auf ein Backblech legen, noch einmal kurz gehen lassen und knusprig backen.

7 5 Minuten vor Ende der Backzeit die Brote mit etwas Milch bestreichen.

Vorbereitungszeit: 30 Minuten
Zeit zum Gehenlassen: insgesamt ca. 1 Stunde
Zubereitungszeit: 30 Minuten

Sesamzöpfe

ZUTATEN
(für ca. 16 Stück)

1 kg Dinkel, fein gemahlen
400 g Rahm
300 g Wasser
84 g frische Hefe
15 g Salz
Rahm zum Bestreichen
geschälter Sesam zum Bestreuen

ZUBEREITUNG

1 Hefe in lauwarmem Wasser auflösen, mit den angegebenen Zutaten kräftig verkneten und 30 Minuten gehen lassen.

2 Anschließend den Hefeteig nochmals gut durcharbeiten und in 16 Portionen teilen.

3 Jedes Teigstück dreiteilen, Stränge von 20 Zentimetern Länge formen und zu Zöpfen flechten, diese mit Sahne bestreichen und mit Sesam bestreuen.

4 15 Minuten gehen lassen, dann bei 250 Grad C 15 Minuten mit Dampf backen.

Vorbereitungszeit: 15 Minuten
Zeit zum Gehenlassen: 30-45 Minuten
Zubereitungszeit: 60 Minuten
Backzeit: ca. 15-20 Minuten

Wurzelrübencreme mit Blattpetersilie und dickem Schmand

ZUTATEN
(für ca. 10 Portionen)

1,5 kg Pastinaken
200 g Zwiebeln
200 g Lauch
2 Knoblauchzehen
Butter
3 l Gemüsebrühe
125 ml Sahne
1 frisches Lorbeerblatt
2 Nelken
Salz, Pfeffer, Muskat
Schmand
glatte Petersilie

ZUBEREITUNG

1 Vorbereitetes Gemüse, Zwiebeln und Knoblauch würfeln, in Butter andünsten und mit Brühe auffüllen. Gewürze zugeben, leicht köcheln lassen.

2 Lorbeer und Nelken entfernen und die Suppe pürieren. Mit Salz, Pfeffer, Muskat und Sahne abschmecken.

3 Schmand und Petersilienblättchen als Garnitur in die Suppe geben.

Vorbereitungszeit:
20-30 Minuten
Zubereitungszeit:
30 Minuten

TIP

Statt Pastinaken können Sie auch Petersilienwurzeln, Möhren oder Wirsing verwenden.

Ein Teil vom Gemüse kann mit Kartoffeln ausgetauscht werden.

Rote Bete ist für diese Art von Suppenzubereitung ebenfalls sehr gut geeignet. Dann Dill statt Petersilie verwenden.

WUSSTEN SIE SCHON?

Wurzelrüben nennt man auch Hammelmöhren oder Pastinaken. Sie sind größer als Möhren und gelb- bis weißfleischig. Wurzelrüben haben ein ausgeprägtes Aroma und sind sehr nährstoffreich. Besonders in Osteuropa findet man die Anbaugebiete für dieses Gemüse.

Schmand ist eine alte bäuerliche Bezeichnung für Sahne. Allgemein wird Schmand als löffelfester Sauerrahm mit mindestens 20 % Fett angeboten.

Cassoulet von Lauch und schwarzem Pfeffer mit Käse gratiniert, gebratene Plätzchen von der Sandmöhre

ZUTATEN
(für ca. 10 Portionen)
2 kg Lauch
70 g Butter
70 g Dinkelvollkornmehl
500 ml Milch
70 g Gorgonzola
30 g Ricotta
Vollmeersalz
schwarzer Pfeffer, Muskat

Vorbereitungszeit: 30 Minuten
Zubereitungszeit: 30 Minuten

TIP

Halb Lauch, halb Kartoffeln oder Möhren verwenden.

ZUBEREITUNG

1 Lauch putzen, das Helle in 3 cm lange Stücke schneiden und in Salzwasser 5 Minuten blanchieren. Das Gemüse sollte noch Biß haben.

2 Aus Butter, Mehl und Milch eine Béchamel herstellen, mit Salz, Pfeffer und Muskat würzen.

3 Eine Auflaufform fetten, Lauch einschichten und mit Béchamel bedecken.

4 Gorgonzola und Ricotta durch ein Sieb streichen, auf die Sauce streuen und überbacken.

Gebratene Plätzchen von der Sandmöhre

ZUTATEN
(für ca. 20 Stück)

500 g Sandmöhren
200 g Knollensellerie
700 g Kartoffeln, mehligkochend
4 Eier
1 Bd. glatte Petersilie
jodiertes Salz, Pfeffer
Butterschmalz

ZUBEREITUNG

1 Sandmöhren, Sellerie und Kartoffeln schälen und sehr fein raspeln.

2 Petersilie fein schneiden und mit den Eiern unter das Gemüse rühren.

3 Pikant abschmecken.

4 Dünne Plätzchen in Butterschmalz braten.

Vorbereitungszeit: 20 Minuten
Zubereitungszeit: 10 Minuten

TIP
Die Möhrenplätzchen mit Räucherlachs und Kaperndip als kleine Vorspeise reichen.

Linsen-Dinkelbratlinge auf dreierlei Paprikamark

ZUTATEN

(für ca. 20 Stück)

- 500 g rote Linsen
- 1,2 l Gemüsebrühe
- 100 g Zwiebeln
- 100 g Möhren
- 1 Bd. Kräuter (Majoran, Thymian, Basilikum)
- 4 Eier
- 100 g Greyerzer
- 100 g Dinkelvollkornmehl
- 100 g feine Haferflocken
- Kräutersalz, Pfeffer
- Olivenöl

Vorbereitungszeit: 30 Minuten
Zubereitungszeit: 20 Minuten

ZUBEREITUNG

1 Linsen in Gemüsebrühe weich kochen.

2 Käse raspeln. Zwiebeln und Möhren fein würfeln und in Olivenöl bißfest dünsten.

3 Kräuter hacken, mit dem Gemüse, den Eiern, Dinkelmehl und Käse unter die Linsen rühren, kräftig abschmecken.

4 Kleine flache Bratlinge aus der Masse formen und von beiden Seiten goldbraun braten.

WUSSTEN SIE SCHON?

Die rote Linse ist eine in Indien und in der Türkei angebaute kleine Linsenart mit lilafarbener Schale und einem leuchtend orangeroten Kern, die bei uns geschält im Handel erhältlich ist.

Rote Linsen kochen innerhalb kürzester Zeit zu Brei. Nach dem Garen nehmen die Linsen eine gelbe Farbe an.

Greyerzer, auch Gruyère genannt, ist ein Schweizer Hartkäse, der aus Rohmilch hergestellt wird. Das Aroma ist kräftig.

In der Küche ist Greyerzer ideal zum Gratinieren, für Saucen und Fondues.

TIP

Statt Käse können Sie auch Schmand in die Masse geben. Die fertigen Bratlinge mit Käsescheiben belegen und gratinieren. Ideal als kleiner Imbiß.

Rot-grün-gelbes Paprikamark

ZUBEREITUNG

1 Paprikaschoten aufschneiden, entkernen und grob würfeln.

2 Nach Farbe getrennt in Salzwasser blanchieren, anschließend in Eiswasser abschrecken.

3 Sehr fein pürieren, durch ein Sieb streichen und mit Salz und Pfeffer abschmecken.

4 Das Püree zu den Linsen-Dinkelbratlingen servieren.

Vorbereitungszeit: 30 Minuten
Zubereitungszeit: 20 Minuten

ZUTATEN
(für ca. 10 Portionen)

500 g rote Paprikaschoten
500 g grüne Paprikaschoten
500 g gelbe Paprikaschoten
jodiertes Salz, weißer Pfeffer

Gebackene Blüten vom Mai-Holunder auf einer Mascarpone-Aprikosen-Sauce

ZUTATEN

10 Holunderblüten
100 g Dinkelvollkornmehl
120 ml Milch
4 Eier
Salz
Sonnenblumenkernöl
300 g getrocknete Aprikosen, ungeschwefelt
200 ml Orangensaft
1 kg Mascarpone
400 ml Milch
Aprikosenlikör

ZUBEREITUNG

1 Aprikosen fein würfeln und in Orangensaft einweichen, danach pürieren.

2 Mascarpone mit Milch glattrühren, Aprikosenmus unterziehen und abschmecken.

3 Holunderblüten vorsichtig waschen und abtropfen lassen.

4 Aus Mehl, Milch und Eigelb eine geschmeidige Masse rühren, mit Salz würzen.

5 Eiklar steif schlagen und unter die Masse heben.

6 Holunderblüten in den Teig tauchen und in Öl ausbacken.

7 Gebackene Holunderblüten an Mascarpone-Aprikosen-Sauce servieren.

Vorbereitungszeit: 30-40 Minuten
Zubereitungszeit: 15 Minuten

WUSSTEN SIE SCHON?

Dinkel ist eine Spelzenweizenart. Farbe und Geschmack sind kräftiger als beim Weizen. Wegen des hohen Klebereiweißanteils besitzt Dinkel besonders gute Backeigenschaften. Sie erhalten Dinkel in gut sortierten Lebensmittelgeschäften.

Mascarpone ist ein italienischer Doppelrahmfrischkäse ohne Salz.

TIP

Der Holunder blüht Ende Mai bis Ende Juni.

Drei-Käsecreme-Torte mit Gartenerdbeeren

ZUTATEN

(für eine Tarteform von 24 cm Durchmesser)

200 g Löffelbiskuit
125 g Butter
200 g Ricotta
400 g Doppelrahmfrischkäse
100 g Schmand
40 g Puderzucker
1 Zitrone
Grand Marnier
250 g Gartenerdbeeren
Waldmeister

Vorbereitungszeit: ca. 15 Minuten
Zubereitungszeit: ca. 60 Minuten

WUSSTEN SIE SCHON?

Biobin ist ein pflanzliches Bindemittel auf Johannisbrotkernmehl-Basis.

Sie erhalten es im Reformhaus.

TIP

Sie können dieses Dessert je nach Jahreszeit mit Früchten der Saison variieren.

Erscheint die Creme zu flüssig, mit Biobin andicken.

ZUBEREITUNG

1 Ricotta in einem Tuch ausdrücken, Butter schaumig rühren.

2 Löffelbiskuit fein zerbröseln, unter die Butter rühren, damit die Tarteform auskleiden und kalt stellen.

3 Ricotta, Doppelrahmfrischkäse und Schmand glattrühren. Zitronenschale fein reiben und mit Puderzucker unter die Käsecreme rühren, etwas Grand Marnier hebt den Geschmack.

4 Den durchgekühlten Tarteboden mit der Creme füllen und die vorbereiteten Erdbeeren darauf verteilen.

5 Mit Waldmeisterblättchen dekorieren.

Früchte mit Ahorndip

ZUTATEN

1 Ananas
1 Netzmelone
500 g Erdbeeren
2 Pfirsiche
2 Nektarinen
200 g kernlose Trauben
2 Bananen
2 Limetten

ZUTATEN DIP

300 g Frischkäse
2 EL Ahornsirup
1 Limette

ZUBEREITUNG

1 Den Frischkäse mit Ahornsirup und geriebener Limettenschale verrühren.

2 Ananas halbieren, aushöhlen, das Fruchtfleisch in Stücke schneiden.

3 Die ausgehöhlten Fruchthälften beiseite stellen.

4 Die übrigen Früchte in gleichmäßige Stücke schneiden und in einer Schüssel mit den Ananasstücken im Limettensaft wenden, damit sich das Obst nicht verfärbt.

5 Die ausgehöhlte Ananashälfte mit den Früchten füllen und auf einer großen Platte mit dem Ahorndip und kleinen Holzstäbchen servieren.

Vorbereitungszeit: ca. 30 Minuten
Zubereitungszeit: ca. 15 Minuten

WUSSTEN SIE SCHON?

Ahornsirup wird aus dem Saft des Zuckerahorns gewonnen und wird wegen seines besonderen Geschmacks im Dessertbereich eingesetzt.

TIP

Sie können auch anderes Obst – je nach Jahreszeit – verwenden.

Verschiedene Käse aus dem Graskorb

Eine Auswahl von internationalen Käsesorten ist ein „Muß" auf jedem Buffet.

Neben Hart-, Schnitt-, Frisch- und Sauermilchkäse sollten auch noch selbsthergestellte Käsespezialitäten wie Käseterrinen, Cremes und eingelegter Käse angeboten werden.

BEKANNTE KÄSESORTEN

Hartkäse

Emmentaler „Schweizer original"

Mildes bis süßlich-nussiges Aroma bei jungen, kräftig-pikantes Aroma bei älteren (4 bis 5 Monate alten) Käsen.

Allgäuer Bergkäse (deutscher Rohmilchkäse)

Nach Emmentaler Art hergestellter, delikater, aromatischer Käse.

Comte (Frankreich)

Schmeckt durch Schmierebehandlung sehr aromatisch.

Schnittkäse

Gouda (Holland)

Oft wird der milde bis kräftig-pikante Geschmack durch geschmacksgebende Zusätze ergänzt, zum Beispiel durch Brennessel, frische Kräuter, Knoblauch oder Kreuzkümmel.

Wilstermarsch (Holstein/Deutschland)

Dieser Käse ähnelt dem Tilsiter und hat einen aromatischen Geschmack.

Halbfester Schnittkäse

Esrom (Dänemark)

Ein sehr aromatischer, halbfester Schnittkäse, der auch mit besonderen Zutaten wie Kümmel, Pfeffer, Kräutern der Provence und Paprika angeboten wird.

Schwäbischer Landkäse (Deutschland)

Junge Käse haben einen mild-säuerlichen Geschmack, ältere sind aromatisch-würzig.

Steinbuscher (Deutschland)

Steinbuscher hat eine rötlich-braune Haut und ist mild-würzig im Geschmack.

Weichkäse

Limburger, Romadur, Weinkäse

Diese Käsesorten sind durch bakteriell hervorgerufene Oberflächenschmiere kräftig im Geschmack.

Munster (Elsaß)

Die Oberfläche bildet eine orange-rote Schmiere, die Haut ist feucht. Munster hat ein ausgeprägt kräftiges Aroma.

Camembert (Frankreich)

Camembert ist eine Spezialität aus der Normandie, die je nach Reifegrad einen milden bis herzhaften Geschmack entwickelt.

Brie (Frankreich)

Brie ist dem Camembert ähnlich, hat ein feines Schimmelaroma mit mildem bis dezent-würzigem Geschmack.

Brie wird auch mit Alpenkräutern und mit Pfeffer angeboten.

Frischkäse

Frischkäse sind Käse ohne Reifung, die durch Zusatz von verschiedenen Rohstoffen wie zum Beispiel Pfeffer, Kräutern und Gewürzen in vielen Geschmacksvarianten im Handel erhältlich sind.

Sauermilchkäse

Unter dem Begriff „Sauermilchkäse" versteht man in Deutschland aus Magermilch mit Hilfe von Milchsäurebakterien hergestellten Käse.

Wir kennen zwei Gruppen: den Gelbkäse und den Edelschimmelkäse.

Harzer

Harzer ist ein pikanter Gelbkäse, voll und kräftig im Geschmack, bekannt auch als Handkäse.

Vienenburger

Vienenburger ist ein Sauermilchkäse mit Schimmelbildung, mild und leicht würzig im Geschmack.

Vorschlag für ein Sommer-/Herbstbuffet

Quark-Gemüse-Terrine an sommerlichen Blattsalaten mit Borretsch-Vinaigrette
Sommerliche Gemüse-Gelee-Variationen
Eingelegte, gehobelte Zwergkürbisse mit einer Edelpilzcreme und Walnußbaguette
Bauernsalat mit mariniertem Tofu und geröstetem Sesam
Rohkostspieße, dazu:
Soja-Knoblauch-Dip
Püree von Artischocken mit geräuchertem Knoblauch

Kalte Tomatensauce mit Basilikum und Chili
Eingelegter Fenchel mit Sherryessig
Marinierte Paprika
Pikante Cremechampignons

Vollkorn-Croissants
Knoblauch-Kräuterbutter „nach meiner Art"
Mandelbrot
Westfälische Schafskäsecreme mit frischen Gartenkräutern
Schmand-Brötchen

Kaltes Süppchen von Gartengurken mit Schwedenmilch und geröstetem Knoblauch
Wähe von Eierfrüchten und Herbstpilzen mit einem Zwiebel-Minz-Mus
Beläge: Auberginenröllchen, Pfifferlinge, Zwiebel-Minz-Mus
Crêpes von Kichererbsen, mit Weißschimmelkäse gefüllten Äpfeln und Mascarpone-Joghurt

In Vollkorn gebackene Aprikosen mit Marzipanfüllung und Orangenblütenhonig
Champagnertörtchen mit marinierten blauen Feigen in Orangenlikör
Traubenkompott
Eingelegte Minimozzarella
Halbgefrorenes vom Ahornsirup in der Williamsbirne mit Himbeermark und Luzernesprossen
Eßbare Dekorationsblüten

Quark-Gemüse-Terrine an sommerlichen Blattsalaten mit Borretsch-Vinaigrette

ZUTATEN
FÜR DIE SPINATFÜLLUNG

400 g	frischer Spinat
2 TL	Agar-Agar
10 ml	Gemüsebrühe
60 g	Quark (40 %)
	Salz, Pfeffer
1 TL	gehackter Salbei

ZUTATEN
FÜR DIE SELLERIEFÜLLUNG

100 g	Knollensellerie
2 TL	Agar-Agar
10 ml	Gemüsebrühe
60 g	Quark (40 %)
	Salz, Pfeffer, Muskat
1 TL	gehackter Salbei

ZUTATEN
FÜR DIE KAROTTENFÜLLUNG

500 g	Möhren
10 g	Zucker
10 g	Koriandergrün
2 TL	Agar-Agar
10 ml	Gemüsebrühe
60 g	Quark (40 %)
	Salz, Pfeffer

TIP

Durch die Klarsichtfolie kann man die Terrine nach dem Erkalten gut stürzen.

Die Gemüseterrine kann – je nach Saison – mit verschiedenen Gemüsen zubereitet werden.

Dazu reicht man eine Vinaigrette, abgeschmeckt mit fein gehacktem Borretsch und Blüten an einem Getreidesalat.

ZUBEREITUNG DER SPINATFÜLLUNG

1 Spinat waschen und ohne Zugabe von Flüssigkeit dünsten, bis er zusammenfällt. Gut auspressen und pürieren.

2 Agar-Agar in Gemüsebrühe aufkochen, unter das Spinatpüree mischen und auskühlen lassen.

3 Den Quark unterrühren, mit Salz, Pfeffer und Salbei abschmecken.

ZUBEREITUNG DER SELLERIEFÜLLUNG

1 Die Sellerieknollen schälen, würfeln, in Salzwasser garen, abtropfen lassen und noch warm pürieren.

2 Agar-Agar in Gemüsebrühe aufkochen, abkühlen lassen und zufügen.

3 Quark unterziehen, mit Salz, Pfeffer und Muskat abschmecken.

ZUBEREITUNG DER KAROTTENFÜLLUNG

1 Die Möhren schälen, würfeln und in Salzwasser garen, bis sie weich sind.

2 Zucker, Koriandergrün, Salz, Pfeffer und das in Gemüsebrühe aufgekochte Agar-Agar zugeben.

3 Pürieren und abgekühlt den Quark unterziehen.

ZUBEREITUNG TERRINE

Eine Form von 1,5 Liter Inhalt mit Klarsichtfolie auskleiden und die drei Pürees nacheinander einfüllen. Gut abdecken und im Kühlschrank 5 bis 6 Stunden fest werden lassen.

Vorbereitungszeit: 60 Minuten
Zubereitungszeit: 60 Minuten
Kühlzeit: ca. 12 Stunden

Sommerliche Gemüse-Gelee-Variationen

Rezept zum Foto: Seite 71

Eingelegte, gehobelte Zwergkürbisse mit einer Edelpilzcreme und Walnußbaguette

ZUTATEN FÜR DIE EINGELEGTEN ZWERGKÜRBISSE

200 g Zwergkürbisse	
Walnußöl	
Olivenöl, vergine extra	
1 Limette	
grobes Salz aus der Mühle	
schwarzer Pfeffer aus der Mühle	
100 g Gorgonzola	
200 g Frischkäse	
2 Bd. Schnittlauch	
150 g Walnußkerne	

Vorbereitungszeit: 20 Minuten
Zubereitungszeit: 20 Minuten

WUSSTEN SIE SCHON?

Zwergkürbisse nennt man auch Zucchetti oder Courgettes.

TIP

Statt Walnußkerne geröstete Pinienkerne verwenden und Baguette ohne Walnußkerne dazu reichen.

ZUBEREITUNG

1 Walnußkerne grob hacken und ohne Fett leicht rösten.

2 Zwergkürbisse in dünne Scheiben hobeln, mit Limettensaft, Walnußöl, Olivenöl, Salz und Pfeffer marinieren.

3 Gorgonzola durch ein Sieb passieren, mit Frischkäse glattrühren.

4 Schnittlauch in feine Ringe schneiden und unterrühren.

5 Die marinierten Zwergkürbisscheiben auf einer Platte anrichten und in die Mitte die Käsecreme häufen.

6 Mit gerösteten Walnußkernen bestreuen und Scheiben vom Walnußbaguette *(siehe Seite 23)* dazu reichen.

Bauernsalat mit mariniertem Tofu und geröstetem Sesam

ZUTATEN
(für ca. 10 Portionen)

- 250 g Tofu
- 8 Knoblauchzehen, zerdrückt
- 100 ml Olivenöl, vergine extra
- 100 ml Sesamöl, hell
- 50 ml Weißweinessig
- Salz
- 1 kg Paprikaschoten, rot, grün und gelb
- 250 g rote Zwiebeln
- 500 g Tomaten
- 100 g Kidney-Bohnen, gekocht
- 100 g grüne Oliven ohne Stein
- Senf
- 1 Bd. glatte Petersilie
- 2 EL gerösteter Sesam

Vorbereitungszeit: ca. 30 Minuten
Zeit des Marinierens: 1-2 Stunden
Zubereitungszeit: ca. 10 Minuten

ZUBEREITUNG

1 Tofu würfeln (1 cm Kantenlänge) und mehrere Stunden in einer Marinade aus Öl, 25 ml Essig, 4 zerdrückten Knoblauchzehen und Salz einlegen.

2 Paprikaschoten vorbereiten, in Streifen und die Zwiebeln in Ringe schneiden.

3 Tomaten achteln.

4 Aus dem restlichen Essig, Salz, Senf, Knoblauch und Öl ein Dressing bereiten und mit den Gemüsen mischen.

5 Oliven in Scheiben schneiden, Petersilie hacken und mit den Tofuwürfeln und Sesam auf dem Salat verteilen.

WUSSTEN SIE SCHON?

In der natürlichen Küche zieht man die Haut von Paprikaschoten und Tomaten nicht ab. Ballaststoffe!

Tofu-Mayonnaise und Soja-Knoblauch-Dip

ZUTATEN
(für ca. 500 ml)

400 g Tofu
80 ml Öl
etwas Sojamilch

ZUBEREITUNG

1 Tofu zerkleinern und mit dem Öl pürieren.

2 Die Sojamilch nur zufügen, wenn die Mayonnaise nicht cremig ist.

3 Wie herkömmliche Mayonnaise weiterverarbeiten.

Zubereitungszeit: ca. 10 Minuten

Die Mayonnaise mit 10 pürierten Knoblauchzehen mischen und mit Salz und Zitronensaft abschmecken.

Zubereitungszeit: ca. 10 Minuten

Püree von Artischocken mit geräuchertem Knoblauch

ZUTATEN
(für ca. 500 ml)

500 g Artischockenherzen
2 geräucherte Knoblauchzehen
1 Limette
30 ml Olivenöl, vergine extra
Salz, Pfeffer
Paprikapulver, edelsüß

Zubereitungszeit: 10-15 Minuten

ZUBEREITUNG

1 Knoblauch schälen und mit den Artischokkenherzen pürieren.

2 Olivenöl unter das Püree rühren, mit Salz, Pfeffer und Limettensaft abschmecken.

3 Vor dem Servieren mit Olivenöl beträufeln und mit Paprika bestäuben.

WUSSTEN SIE SCHON?

Die Artischocke ist der Blütenkopf einer distelartigen Staude. Die faustgroßen Blütenköpfe sind rundlich oder zylindrisch und wiegen 100-500 g.

Kalte Tomatensauce mit Basilikum und Chili

ZUTATEN

(für ca. 500 ml)

500 g Fleischtomaten
50 g Zwiebeln
1 Chilischote, mittelscharf
1 Limette, Saft
1 Bd. Basilikum
Salz, Pfeffer, Zucker

Zubereitungszeit: ca. 30 Minuten

ZUBEREITUNG

1 Die Tomaten häuten, entkernen und fein würfeln.

2 Zwiebeln schälen, fein würfeln und unter die Tomaten mischen.

3 Die Chilischoten aufschlitzen, entkernen und sehr fein würfeln.

4 Mit dem Limettensaft zu den übrigen Zutaten geben und mit Salz, Pfeffer und einer Prise Zucker abschmecken.

5 Basilikum fein schneiden und unterziehen.

6 Tomatensauce kalt stellen.

Foto: Rohkostspieße

TIP

Diese Sauce kann auch von gelben Tomaten hergestellt werden.

Eingelegter Fenchel mit Sherryessig

ZUTATEN

Olivenöl, vergine extra
Sherryessig
4 Fenchelknollen
3 feste Tomaten
Salz, Pfeffer, Knoblauch, Zucker

GARNITUR

Fenchelgrün, Dill

Vorbereitungszeit: ca. 30 Minuten
Zubereitungszeit: ca. 30 Minuten

ZUBEREITUNG

1 Die äußeren Fenchelblätter schälen und in 2 bis 3 cm große Streifen schneiden.

2 Restlichen Fenchel in Scheiben schneiden und in Olivenöl goldbraun braten. Mit gehacktem Knoblauch, Sherryessig, Salz, Pfeffer und Zucker abschmecken.

3 Fenchel erkalten lassen und nochmals abschmecken.

4 Tomaten kurz blanchieren, abschrecken, Haut abziehen, entkernen und in Streifen schneiden.

5 Fenchel mit Tomatenstreifen, Fenchelgrün und Dill ausgarnieren.

Marinierte Paprika

ZUTATEN

1 rote Paprika
1 grüne Paprika
1 gelbe Paprika
2 Knoblauchzehen
1 Zweig Rosmarin
Salz, Zucker
Pfeffer
aus der Mühle
50 ml Weißweinessig
50 ml Olivenöl

ZUBEREITUNG

1 Paprika waschen, halbieren und entkernen, in gleichmäßige Stücke von etwa 2 cm schneiden.

2 In heißem Öl kurz anbraten.

3 Die geschälten und fein gehackten Knoblauchzehen, Rosmarinzweig, Weißweinessig, Salz, Zucker und Pfeffer dazugeben und gut schwenken.

4 Olivenöl unterziehen und abkühlen lassen.

Vorbereitungszeit: 30 Minuten
Zubereitungszeit: 15 Minuten

Pikante Cremechampignons

ZUTATEN

500 g kleine
Cremechampignons
Sonnenblumenöl

ZUTATEN FÜR DIE MARINADE

250 ml Weißweinessig
500 ml Gemüsebrühe
2 Lorbeerblätter
20 Pfefferkörner
(rot, schwarz und weiß)
1 TL Senfkörner
10 Wacholderbeeren
5 Körner Piment
20 g Salz
20 g Zucker
Saft 1/2 Zitrone
1 Bd. Schnittlauch, fein geschnitten

ZUBEREITUNG

1 Pilze reinigen.

2 Die Zutaten – außer Schnittlauch – für die Marinade 15 Minuten kochen.

3 Öl erhitzen, Pilze kurz anschwitzen.

4 Pilze mit der Marinade in Gläser füllen, verschließen.

5 48 Stunden marinieren.

6 Fein geschnittenen Schnittlauch zugeben.

Vorbereitungszeit: 30 Minuten
Zubereitungszeit: 30 Minuten
Zeit des Marinierens: 48 Stunden

Vollkorn-Croissants

ZUTATEN
(für ca. 10 Stück)

350 g Weizen- oder
Dinkelvollkornmehl, ausgesiebt
1 P. Trockenhefe
100 g geriebene Mandeln
50 g Butter
200 ml Sahne
3 EL Honig
1 Prise Salz

**Vorbereitungszeit: 30 Minuten
Zeit zum Gehenlassen:
ca. 60 Minuten
Zubereitungszeit: 30 Minuten
Backzeit: 25-30 Minuten**

ZUBEREITUNG

1 Mehl, Trockenhefe, geriebene Mandeln, Honig und Salz in einer Schüssel mischen.

2 Erwärmte Sahne und Butter zugeben und den Teig ca. 10 Minuten kneten.

3 Zugedeckt gehen lassen, bis er sich verdoppelt hat.

4 Der Teig muß locker und weich sein, sonst noch etwas Sahne unterkneten.

5 Teig in 3 Portionen auswellen. Dreiecke schneiden, Hörnchen rollen, zugedeckt 30 Minuten ruhen lassen.

6 Bei 200 Grad C etwa 25 bis 30 Minuten backen.

Knoblauch-Kräuterbutter „nach meiner Art"

ZUTATEN

1 kg Butter
30 ml Weißwein
1 EL Zitronensaft
15 ml Worcestershiresauce
5 Schalotten
1 TL französischer Senf
4 Knoblauchzehen
1 EL Salz
Pfeffer
reichlich Kräuter
nach Geschmack

**Vorbereitungszeit: 30 Minuten
Zubereitungszeit: 15 Minuten**

ZUBEREITUNG

1 Butter mit Senf, Worcestershiresauce und Zitronensaft cremig rühren.

2 Schalotten sehr fein hacken, Knoblauch pressen, in Weißwein dünsten und auskühlen.

3 Kräuter sorgfältig waschen, gut trocknen (die Kräuterbutter hält dann länger) und fein hacken.

4 Alle Zutaten mit der Butter vermischen und mit Salz und Pfeffer abrunden.

TIP

Die Knoblauch-Kräuterbutter gut durchziehen lassen.

Sie läßt sich auch gut einfrieren. Dazu formt man die Butter in Rollen und wickelt sie in Folie.

Mandelbrot

ZUTATEN
(für ein Brot von 1 kg)

150 g Mandeln
(100 g gemahlen, 50 g gehackt)
500 g Dinkelvollkornmehl
15 g Jodsalz
1 Würfel Hefe
1 TL Honig
150 g saure Sahne
Fett für das Blech
Mehl für das Blech
und zum Bestäuben

ZUBEREITUNG

1 Die gemahlenen Mandeln in einer Pfanne ohne Fett goldbraun rösten, mit Mehl und Salz mischen.

2 Die Hefe mit dem Honig in 200 ml lauwarmem Wasser auflösen und unter die Mandel-Mehl-Mischung kneten.

3 Saure Sahne zugeben und zu einem glatten Teig verarbeiten.

4 Den Teig gehen lassen, bis er sein Volumen verdoppelt hat.

5 Gehackte Mandeln goldbraun rösten und unter den Teig kneten.

6 Das Blech fetten und mit Mehl bestäuben. Den Teig zu einem Laib formen, mit etwas Mehl bestäuben und leicht einritzen. Nochmals 15 Minuten ruhen lassen.

7 Im vorgeheizten Backofen bei 200 Grad C 50 Minuten backen.

Vorbereitungszeit: 60 Minuten
Zeit zum Gehenlassen: ca. 1 Stunde
Backzeit: ca. 50 Minuten

ZUTATEN
(für ca. 10 Portionen)

200 g große schwarze Oliven, ohne Kern
2 geräucherte Knoblauchzehen
1 rote Chilischote
400 g milder westfälischer Schafskäse
200 g Frischkäse
1 kleiner Zweig Rosmarin
1 Zweig frischer Thymian
Kapuzinerkresseblätter

Schafskäsecreme mit frischen Gartenkräutern

ZUBEREITUNG

1 Oliven fein würfeln.

2 Knoblauch mit Salz zerdrücken.

3 Rosmarinnadeln fein hacken.

4 Thymian abribbeln.

5 Chilischote entkernen und in feine Ringe schneiden.

6 Schafskäse pürieren und mit Frischkäse verrühren.

7 Alle Zutaten untermischen und abschmecken.

8 Mit Hilfe eines Eisportionierers Kugeln formen und auf Kapuzinerkresseblättern anrichten und zu lauwarmem Fladenbrot servieren.

Vorbereitungszeit: 30 Minuten
Zubereitungszeit: 10 Minuten

Schmand-Brötchen

ZUTATEN
(für ca. 12 Stück)

550 g Weizenvollkornmehl, fein geschrotet
oder Weizenmehl Type 1050
1 TL Honig
30 g Hefe
150 ml Wasser
Vollmeersalz
100 g saure Sahne
50 g Kürbiskerne
Mehl zum Bestäuben
1 Eiweiß

ZUBEREITUNG

1 Weizenmehl in eine Schüssel sieben, eine Mulde eindrücken, Honig und Hefe in lauwarmem Wasser auflösen und in die Mulde gießen, etwas Mehl vom Rand darüber streuen, Salz und saure Sahne auf den Mehlrand geben.

2 Die Kürbiskerne bis auf einen Eßlöffel in einer Pfanne ohne Fett goldgelb rösten, ebenfalls auf den Rand streuen, alles zu einem elastischen Teig verkneten, diesen mit Mehl bestäuben und zugedeckt etwa 20 Minuten gehen lassen.

3 Anschließend auf einer mit Mehl bestäubten Arbeitsfläche kurz durchkneten, eine Rolle formen und diese in 12 Stücke schneiden.

4 Aus den Stücken längliche Rollen formen und auf das mit Mehl bestäubte Backblech setzen.

5 Eiweiß mit einem Teelöffel Wasser verquirlen, die Brötchen damit bestreichen, restliche Kürbiskerne und Mehl darüber streuen.

6 Die Brötchen bei 200 Grad C ca. 20 Minuten backen.

7 Dann eventuell unter dem Grill 3 bis 5 Minuten nachbräunen.

Vorbereitungszeit: ca. 45 Minuten
Zeit zum Gehenlassen: 20-30 Minuten
Backzeit: ca. 20 Minuten

TIP

Brötchen rund formen und in einer Pizza-Form dicht zusammensetzen, vor dem Backen mit Wasser bestreichen und mit Mohn, Sesam- oder Sonnenblumenkernen bestreuen, ergibt ein Partyrad.

Kaltes Süppchen von Gartengurken mit Schwedenmilch und geröstetem Knoblauch

ZUTATEN

1 kg Gartengurken
1,5 l Schwedenmilch
60 g Olivenöl, vergine extra
jodiertes Salz, weißer Pfeffer
2 Knoblauchzehen
300 g milder Schafskäse
Dill

ZUBEREITUNG

1 Gurken schälen, halbieren, entkernen und pürieren, dabei für die Dekoration eine halbe Gurke beiseite legen.

2 Das Püree kalt stellen.

3 Knoblauch hacken und leicht rösten.

4 Schafskäse und Gurke würfeln, Dill hacken.

5 Schwedenmilch, Olivenöl, Gurkenpüree und Knoblauch verrühren, würzen und kalt stellen.

6 Mit Gurkenwürfeln, Schafskäse und Dill anrichten.

Vorbereitungszeit:
20 Minuten
Zubereitungszeit:
20 Minuten
Zeit des Kühlens:
ca. 2 Stunden

WUSSTEN SIE SCHON?

Schwedenmilch, auch Sauermilch, wird mit einer besonderen Milchsäurebakterienkultur hergestellt.

Der Geschmack ist mild, die Konsistenz ist sämig.

Sie erhalten Schwedenmilch im Reformhaus.

Wähe von Eierfrüchten (Auberginen) und Herbstpilzen mit einem Zwiebel-Minz-Mus

ZUTATEN
FÜR 1 KG GERIEBENEN TEIG

500 g Dinkelvollkornmehl, ausgesiebt
250 g Butter
250 ml Wasser
10 g Salz
für 2 Springformen Ø 26 cm

ZUTATEN
FÜR DEN GUSS

2 Eier
500 ml saure Sahne
Salz
1 Prise Cayennepfeffer

Vorbereitungszeit: 30 Minuten
Zubereitungszeit: 45 Minuten

TIP

Ersetzen Sie bei gleicher Teigzubereitung die Hälfte des Vollkornmehls durch Auszugsmehl.

Beim Guß können Sie die Eier durch 3 Eßlöffel Sojamehl austauschen. Bei den 500 ml saurer Sahne kann die Hälfte durch Quark ausgetauscht werden.

ZUBEREITUNG

1 Butter in Flocken zum gesiebten Mehl geben und verreiben, mit Salzwasser rasch zu einem glatten Teig verarbeiten.

2 1 Stunde kühl ruhen lassen.

3 Den Teig ausrollen und 2 Springformen auslegen.

4 Einen 2 Zentimeter hohen Rand formen und den Teigboden mehrmals einstechen, 15 Minuten vorbacken.

5 Den vorgebackenen Teig mit gefüllten Eierfrüchten und Pilzen füllen.

6 Die Zutaten für den Guß verrühren, mit Salz und Cayennepfeffer würzen, über die vorbereitete Wähe gießen und in 40 Minuten fertig backen.

Belag: Auberginenröllchen

ZUTATEN

- 600 g gleich große Auberginen
- 4 Knoblauchzehen
- 200 g Walnußkerne
- 150 ml Olivenöl, vergine extra
- 50 ml Walnußöl
- 1 Bd. glatte Petersilie
- 1 Bd. Basilikum
- 50 g Pecorino romana
- Salz, Pfeffer, Olivenöl

für 2 Springformen Ø 26 cm

ZUBEREITUNG

1 Auberginen längs in 1/2 cm dicke Scheiben schneiden und in heißem Öl kurz anbraten und abtropfen lassen.

2 Knoblauch zerdrücken, Walnußkerne mahlen, Käse reiben, Petersilie und Basilikum feinhacken.

3 Alle Zutaten mit dem Öl zu einer Paste rühren, auf die vorbereiteten Auberginenscheiben streichen und aufrollen.

Vorbereitungszeit: 30 Minuten
Zubereitungszeit: 15 Minuten

WUSSTEN SIE SCHON?

Eierfrüchte oder Auberginen sind glänzend dunkelviolette, auch weiße, ovale oder tropfenförmige Beerenfrüchte der Eierfruchtpflanze.

Pecorino romana ist ein aus Italien stammender Hartkäse mit Ursprungsschutz.

Unter Verwendung von Schafsmilch und Lämmermagenlab entsteht das charakteristische pikante Aroma.

Pecorino-Käse gibt es in vielen Variationen. Ausschlaggebend ist die Milchart, beziehungsweise die Mischung aus Kuh-, Schafs- und Ziegenmilch.

Belag: Pfifferlinge

ZUTATEN
300 g frische Pfifferlinge
100 g Zwiebeln
Butter
Salz, Pfeffer
1 Bd. glatte Petersilie

ZUBEREITUNG

1 Pfifferlinge vorbereiten, Zwiebeln würfeln, Petersilie fein hacken.

2 Zwiebelwürfel in Butter andünsten, Pilze zugeben und offen braten.

3 Mit Salz und Pfeffer abschmecken, Petersilie untermischen.

Vorbereitungszeit: 20 Minuten
Zubereitungszeit: 15 Minuten

Zwiebel-Minz-Mus

ZUTATEN
500 g rote Zwiebeln
100 ml trockener Weißwein
1 Bd. Apfelminze
Öl

ZUBEREITUNG

1 Zwiebeln schälen, würfeln und in Öl glasig dünsten. Wein angießen, die Zwiebelwürfel weich garen, pürieren und erkalten lassen.

2 Mit Salz würzen.

3 Minze fein hacken und unter das Mus mischen.

Vorbereitungszeit: 20 Minuten
Zubereitungszeit: 30 Minuten

> **TIP**
>
> Wenn Sie es süßlich-pikant möchten, geben Sie auf diese Menge 1 Eßlöffel Mintjelly und etwas Worcestershiresauce hinzu.

Crêpes von Kichererbsen, mit Weißschimmelkäse gefüllten Äpfeln und Mascarpone-Joghurt

ZUTATEN

FÜR DIE KICHERERBSENCRÊPES
(für ca. 10 Stück)

- 400 g Kichererbsen
- 1,6 l Gemüsebrühe
- 4 Knoblauchzehen
- 100 g Zwiebeln
- 50 g Weizenvollkornmehl
- 2 Eier
- Olivenöl
- Koriandersamen, gemahlen
- Paprika edelsüß
- Kreuzkümmel
- Muskatnuß
- Salz

Einweichzeit: ca. 12 Stunden
Vorbereitungszeit: 30 Minuten
Zubereitungszeit: 15 Minuten

ZUBEREITUNG

1 Kichererbsen in der Gemüsebrühe über Nacht einweichen, dann kochen, bis die gesamte Flüssigkeit von den Kichererbsen aufgenommen worden ist (etwa 1 Stunde).

2 Zwiebeln fein würfeln, Knoblauch zerdrücken und beides in Olivenöl dünsten.

3 Die Kichererbsen pürieren, mit Vollkornmehl, Eigelben und Zwiebel-Knoblauch-Mischung zu einer Masse verarbeiten und mit den Gewürzen pikant abschmecken.

4 Eiklar steif schlagen und unter die Masse ziehen. Kleine Plätzchen formen und goldbraun braten.

WUSSTEN SIE SCHON?

Kichererbsen sind die haselnußgroßen, beige-gelben, kantig-unregelmäßig geformten Samen einer Erbsensorte, die in Portugal, Afrika und Südamerika angepflanzt wird. Es gibt sie getrocknet, als Mehl oder als Naßkonserve zu kaufen.

Gedünstete Äpfel mit Weißschimmelkäse, Staudensellerie und Pinienkernen gefüllt

ZUTATEN

10 Äpfel, Cox Orange
250 g Weißschimmelkäse
50 g Bleichsellerie
50 g Pinienkerne
200 ml Gemüsebrühe
100 g Butter
Salz, Pfeffer

WUSSTEN SIE SCHON?

Verwenden Sie einen Weißschimmelkäse mit gut entwickeltem, feinaromatischem Weißschimmel, gleichmäßig durchgereift.

Bleichsellerie, auch Staudensellerie genannt, wächst in Büscheln und entwickelt keine Knollen.

Bleichsellerie hat fleischige, gelbliche bis hellgrüne saftige Stengel und zarte Blätter.

ZUBEREITUNG

1 Bleichsellerie schälen und würfeln. Käse würfeln.

2 Pinienkerne ohne Fett goldbraun rösten und mit den Sellerie- und Weißschimmelkäse-Würfeln mischen.

3 Von den Äpfeln einen Deckel abschneiden und beiseite legen. Die Kerngehäuse aus den Äpfeln lösen und mit der Käse-Sellerie-Nußmischung füllen. Deckel aufsetzen, mit Butterflöckchen belegen, in eine feuerfeste Form setzen, Brühe angießen und im Backofen 15 Minuten garen.

Vorbereitungszeit: 30 Minuten
Zubereitungszeit: 20 Minuten

Sesamsauce mit Mascarpone-Joghurt

ZUTATEN
(für ca. 500 ml)

250 g Mascarpone
150 g Joghurt
50 g Tahin
50 g geschälte Sesamsaat
4 Knoblauchzehen
Salz

WUSSTEN SIE SCHON?

Tahin ist eine Paste aus gemahlenem Sesam. Sie wird in der vegetarischen Küche zum Würzen von Salatsaucen, Gemüsen und Obstspeisen eingesetzt.

ZUBEREITUNG

1 Sesamsaat ohne Fett goldbraun rösten und abkühlen lassen.

2 Mascarpone mit Joghurt und Tahin verrühren.

3 Knoblauch fein pürieren und mit der gerösteten Sesamsaat unter die Sauce rühren.

4 Mit Salz abschmecken und zu den Kichererbsencrêpes reichen.

Vorbereitungszeit: 15 Minuten
Zubereitungszeit: 10 Minuten

In Vollkorn gebackene Aprikosen mit Marzipanfüllung und Orangenblütenhonig

ZUTATEN
(für ca. 10 Stück)

250 ml	Wasser
50 g	Butter
1 Msp.	Salz
150	Dinkelvollkornmehl, sehr fein gemahlen
4	Eier
10	kleine Aprikosen
100 g	Marzipan
50 g	Walnußkerne, gemahlen
50 g	Orangenblütenhonig
	Zimt

Vorbereitungszeit: ca. 20 Minuten
Zubereitungszeit: ca. 45 Minuten

ZUBEREITUNG

1 Brandteig herstellen *(siehe Vollkornwindbeutel, Seite 62)*.

2 Den Teig in 10 gleich große Portionen teilen, flach drücken. Aus den Aprikosen den Stein lösen und mit Marzipan füllen. Aprikosen mit Teig umhüllen und auf ein vorbereitetes Backblech setzen.

3 10 Minuten bei 220 Grad C anbacken. Je nach Größe etwa 15 bis 25 Minuten bei 170 Grad C fertig backen.

4 Die fertigen Bällchen mit Orangenblütenhonig beträufeln, mit gemahlenen Walnüssen bestreuen und mit wenig Zimt bestäuben.

Champagnertörtchen mit marinierten blauen Feigen in Orangenlikör

ZUTATEN
(für ca. 10 Portionen)
100 ml Weißwein
2 TL Agar-Agar
150 g Orangenblütenhonig
16 Eier
400 ml Champagner
2 Limette
80 ml Orangenlikör
250 ml Orangensaft
1 Orange
10 blaue Feigen

Vorbereitungszeit: 30 Minuten
Zubereitungszeit: 10 Minuten

TIP

Stechen Sie die Feigen kurz von allen Seiten mit einer Nadel ein und marinieren Sie sie mit Orangenlikör. Servieren Sie die Feigen anschließend geviertelt oder halbiert in der Schale.

ZUBEREITUNG

1 Agar-Agar in Weißwein auflösen, 2 Minuten kochen und abkühlen lassen.

2 Eigelbe und Champagner über heißem Wasserbad zur Rose aufschlagen.

3 Abgekühlte Agar-Agar-Mischung dazurühren, kalt rühren.

4 Steifgeschlagene Sahne unterheben.

5 In kleine Förmchen füllen und erstarren lassen.

6 Orangensaft und Honig auf die Hälfte einreduzieren, mit Limettensaft, Orangenschale und Orangenlikör parfümieren.

7 Feigen halbieren, vierteln oder in Scheiben schneiden und als Garnitur anrichten.

8 Champagnertörtchen stürzen und mit Feigen und Sauce servieren.

Trauben-kompott

ZUTATEN

500 g blaue Trauben	
500 g helle Trauben	
20 g Speisestärke	
1/2 l roter Traubensaft	
50 g Zucker	
4 cl Grappa	

ZUBEREITUNG

1 Trauben waschen, gut abtropfen lassen, halbieren und entkernen.

2 Traubensaft mit Zucker aufkochen, mit Stärke binden und etwa 3 bis 4 Minuten kochen.

3 Trauben unterheben und erkalten lassen.

4 Grappa – nach Geschmack – unter das kalte Kompott rühren.

Vorbereitungszeit: 30 Minuten
Zubereitungszeit: 10 Minuten
Kühlzeit: ca. 2 Stunden

TIP

Wohlschmeckende, reife Trauben eignen sich am besten.

Dazu empfiehlt sich Walnußeis.

Eingelegte Minimozzarella

ZUTATEN

500 g Minimozzarella	
3 Knoblauchzehen	
3 Zweige Thymian	
1 Zitrone, unbehandelt	
1 Peperoni	
3 EL Weißweinessig	
250 ml Olivenöl	
1 Lorbeerblatt	

ZUBEREITUNG

1 Zitronenzesten herstellen.

2 Peperoni halbieren und entkernen.

3 Alle Zutaten in ein Glas füllen, mit Essig und Öl marinieren.

4 Im Kühlschrank aufbewahren.

Zubereitungszeit: 20 Minuten
Zeit des Marinierens: 2 Tage

TIP

Hält sich 1 Woche.

Halbgefrorenes vom Ahornsirup in der Williamsbirne mit Himbeermark und Luzernesprossen

ZUTATEN
(für ca. 10 Portionen)

- 5 Williamsbirnen
- 1 Vanillestange
- Riesling
- Vanille-Ahornsirup-Eis
- 500 g Himbeeren
- Luzernesprossen

ZUTATEN FÜR DAS VANILLE-AHORNSIRUP-EIS

- 60 g Ahornsirup
- 2 Eier
- 1 Vanillestange
- 500 ml Sahne

Vorbereitungszeit: 30 Minuten
Tiefkühlzeit: 12 Stunden
Zubereitungszeit: 1 Stunde

WUSSTEN SIE SCHON?

Ahornsirup ist der Saft des Zuckerahorns. Wegen seines besonderen Aromas wird er gern zum Süßen von Desserts verwendet.

Luzerne ist ein Kleegewächs, das besonders reich an Mineralstoffen, Vitaminen und Chlorophyll ist.

Luzerne enthält ein sehr hochwertiges pflanzliches Eiweiß. Der Geschmack erinnert an frische Erbsen und ist leicht herb. Sie erhalten Luzerne im Großhandel.

TIP

Statt Vanille mit 150 g gehackten Nüssen, 100 g Kakao oder mit Zimtpulver würzen.

ZUBEREITUNG EIS

1 Eigelb mit Ahornsirup cremig rühren und mit dem Mark der Vanillestange würzen.

2 Sahne und Eiklar steif schlagen, unter die Eicreme rühren und tiefkühlen.

ZUBEREITUNG HIMBEERMARK

Himbeeren pürieren und durch ein Haarsieb streichen.

ZUBEREITUNG BIRNEN

1 Birnen schälen, halbieren, entkernen und kurz in Riesling mit Vanillemark bißfest dünsten und auskühlen lassen.

2 Birnenhälften mit Vanille-Ahornsirup-Eis füllen, mit Himbeerpüree auf Luzernesprossen servieren.

Eßbare Dekorationsblüten

BÄLLIS · GÄNSEBLÜMCHEN · Weiß bis rosa gefärbte Randblätter mit gelbem Zentrum / *Blütezeit:* Das ganze Jahr

BORRETSCH · Himmelblaue, rosa, selten weiße Blüten, fünfblättrig, sterngleich mit auffälligen schwarzen Staubgefäßen / *Blütezeit*: Spätsommer

TIP Sollen die Blüten kandiert werden, faßt man die Staubgefäße an und trennt die Blüte vorsichtig vom Stengel.

EIBISCH · Rosa oder weiße Blüten, 4 cm breit, mit dunkelroten Staubgefäßen / *Blütezeit*: Spätsommer bis Frühherbst

GARTENNELKE · Einfache gefüllte, weiße, rosa, dunkelrote Blüten / *Blütezeit*: Sommer

TIP Bitteren weißen Ansatz entfernen.

GERANIEN · Weiße, rosa oder rote Blüten / *Blütezeit:* Sommer / Herbst

GEMEINE SCHARFGABE · Kleine, mattweiße und rosafarbene flache Büschel / *Blütezeit:* Sommer / Herbst

GELBDOLDE · Grünlichgelbe, nektarreiche Blüten / *Blütezeit:* Frühjahr bis Hochsommer

TIP Lassen sich gut in Fett ausbacken.

HOPFEN · Gelbgrüne, konische weibliche Blüten / *Blütezeit:* Spätsommer

KAPUZINER KRESSE · Rote, gelbe, orangefarbene, trichterförmige Blüten / *Blütezeit:* Hochsommer / Herbst

KÖNIGSKERZE · Hellgelbe, stiellose Blüten / *Blütezeit:* Hochsommer bis Frühherbst

LAVENDEL · Hellblaue, rosa, weiße oder rote Blüten / *Blütezeit:* Sommer

MÄDESÜSS · Cremefarbene Büschel winziger Blüten mit Mandelduft / *Blütezeit:* Sommer

MÄRZ-VEILCHEN · Violette oder weiße Blüten / *Blütezeit:* Spätwinter bis Frühjahr

MONARDE · Zottige Köpfe, bestehend aus gedrängten büschelröhrenförmigen roten bis weich-rosa Blüten / *Blütezeit:* Spätsommer

MYRTE · Reinweiße Blüten mit goldenen Staubfäden / *Blütezeit:* Sommer / Herbst

NACHTVIOLE · Violette, lila und weiße Blüten / *Blütezeit:* Sommer

PYRETHRUM (CHOP SUEY KRAUT) · Ähnlich wie Gänseblümchen, mit langen weißen zugespitzten Blütenblättern und flachem gelbem Zentrum / *Blütezeit:* Hochsommer

ROSMARIN · Weiße, manchmal lavendelartig geäderte, hellblaue und rosa Blüten / *Blütezeit:* Frühjahr

RINGELBLUME · Goldgelbe und orangefarbene Blütenblätter, mit dunklem Zentrum / *Blütezeit:* Sommer bis Spätherbst

ROSEN · Große Farbenvielfalt / *Blütezeit:* Sommer / Herbst

TIP Duftende Blätter verwenden. Den bitteren, weißen Ansatz entfernen.

SCHLÜSSELBLUME ODER KISSENPRIMEL · Goldene Blütenblätter mit orangefarbenem Fleck an der Basis / *Blütezeit:* Frühjahr

SALBEI · Tiefkehlige, zweilippige, blaulila Blüten / *Blütezeit:* Sommer

SCHNITTLAUCH · Runde lila Blütenköpfe / *Blütezeit:* Sommer

WEGWARTE · Klarblaue zugespitzte Blütenblätter. 2 bis 3 Blüten an jeder Blattachsel / *Blütezeit:* Sommer / Herbst

YSOP · Tiefblaue Lippenblüten, in Büscheln an den Blattachseln auf einer Seite der Stengel stehend / *Blütezeit:* Spätsommer

BLUMENBEIGABEN FÜR SALATE · Borretsch, Ringelblume, Kapuzinerkresse, Schlüsselblume, Rosenblätter, Nachtviole, Veilchen, Schnittlauchblüten

BLUMENBEIGABEN FÜR DESSERTS · Bergamottenblüten, Ringelblume, Lavendelblüten, Veilchen, duftende Geranienblüten

BLÜTEN ZUM KANDIEREN · Borretsch, Schlüsselblume, Lavendel, Flieder, Nelken, Rosenblätter, Rosmarin und Salbei

Vorschlag für ein Winterbuffet

Vollkornwindbeutel mit Avocadomus auf einem Salat von roten Linsen

Sellerietaler mit Cheddarcreme und Feldsalat

Buntes Gemüse süß-sauer eingelegt

Gemüse-Terrine im Auberginenmantel

Rote Tofucreme
Sojabohnen-Dip mit Lauchzwiebeln und Knoblauch
Tofu-Sauerrahm
Crème fraîche mit Chili-Linsen
Öl vom Zitronen-Thymian mit Lavendelblüten

Salat von Gartengemüsen mit Öl vom Zitronen-Thymian und Lavendelblüten, geröstetes Mandelbrot und Raukebutter

Weißkohlsalat mit Möhren und Mango

Artischockenherzen mit Strauchtomaten

Rübli-Brötchen mit Grünkern
Sesambutter
G'rissene Thübingerle
Vollkorn-Knäckebrot

Suppe von Cox-Orange-Äpfeln mit Ceylon-Zimt und Mandelsplittern

Falscher Hase vom Grünkern mit eingelegten Ebereschenbeeren

Maispflanzerln mit Sojasprossen

Kräutersauce

Schwarzwurzelgemüse

Gratin von Kartoffeln, Kohlrabi und Tomaten

Ricotta-Zimtschaum mit Gelee-Nocken vom Boskopapfel

Mandelkuchen mit Cabua-Kakao

Frische Datteln mit Stiltoncreme

Pikante Vollkornplätzchen mit Thymian

Käse-Kräuter-Kugeln mit Walnußkernen

Plätzchen mit saurer Sahne, Mohn, Sesam und Leinsamen

Vollkornwindbeutel mit Avocadomus auf einem Salat von roten Linsen

ZUTATEN
FÜR DIE WINDBEUTEL
(für ca. 20 Stück)

- 250 ml Wasser
- 1 Msp. Salz
- 50 g Butter
- 150 g Dinkelvollkornmehl
- 4 Eier

ZUBEREITUNG

1 Wasser, Butter und Salz aufkochen.

2 Mehl auf einmal in die Flüssigkeit schütten, zu einem glatten Kloß rühren, bis sich ein weiß-grauer Belag am Topfboden bildet, und von der Kochstelle nehmen.

3 Nach und nach die Eier unterarbeiten. Der Teig ist gut, wenn er glänzt und so vom Löffel abreißt, daß lange Spitzen hängenbleiben.

4 Auf ein gefettetes, bemehltes Backblech walnußgroße Brandteigrosetten spritzen.

5 Bei 220 Grad C 10 Minuten anbacken und je nach Größe 15-25 Minuten bei 170 Grad C fertig backen.

6 Sofort nach dem Backen die Deckel abschneiden, damit die Feuchtigkeit entweichen kann.

7 Ein Windbeutel ist dann gegart, wenn er leicht wird! Alle schweren Teile sind noch nicht gebacken.

Vorbereitungszeit:	30 Minuten
Backzeit:	35 Minuten
Fertigstellung:	10 Minuten

62

Avocadomus

ZUTATEN

200 g Fleischtomaten
100 g Zwiebel
1 frische Chilischote
4 reife Avocados
2 Limetten
1 Bd. glatte Petersilie
Salz, Pfeffer
1 TL Agar-Agar

Vorbereitungszeit: 30 Minuten
Ruhezeit: 1 Stunde
Zubereitungszeit: 20 Minuten

ZUBEREITUNG

1 Tomaten häuten, entkernen und fein hacken.

2 Zwiebeln schälen und sehr fein würfeln.

3 Chili aufschlitzen, entkernen und fein schneiden. Vorsicht scharf!

4 Avocados halbieren, Kern entfernen und das Fruchtfleisch aus der Schale lösen und mit Limettensaft pürieren.

5 Das Avocadopüree mit Tomaten, Zwiebeln, Chili und fein gehackter Petersilie mischen und mit Salz und Pfeffer abschmecken.

6 Agar-Agar in 50 ml Wasser rühren, 2 Minuten kochen, abkühlen lassen, unter das Avocadomus rühren und fest werden lassen.

7 Die Windbeutel mit dem Mus füllen.

Salat von roten Linsen

ZUTATEN

400 ml Gemüsebrühe
350 g rote Linsen
Salz, Pfeffer
150 ml Öl
250 g rote Zwiebeln
40 g Pistazienkerne
75 ml Obstessig
30 ml Birnendicksaft
500 g Birnen

WUSSTEN SIE SCHON?

Birnendicksaft ist ein Sirup aus Birnensaft und ist hervorragend zum Süßen von Fruchtdesserts geeignet.

Sie erhalten ihn im Naturkostladen.

ZUBEREITUNG

1 Linsen in Gemüsebrühe bei milder Hitze 10 bis 12 Minuten im offenen Topf garen.

2 Die Zwiebel pellen, längs halbieren und in dünne Scheiben schneiden.

3 Die Pistazien grob hacken.

4 Essig mit Salz und Pfeffer, Birnendicksaft und Öl verrühren.

5 Die Birnen schälen, halbieren, von den Kerngehäusen befreien und längs in dünne Scheiben schneiden und mit den Zwiebeln in die Salatsauce geben.

6 Die Linsen in einem Durchschlag abtropfen lassen und noch warm unter die Salatsauce rühren. Mit Pistazien bestreuen.

Vorbereitungszeit: 30 Minuten
Zubereitungszeit: 15 Minuten

Sellerietaler mit Cheddarcreme und Feldsalat

ZUTATEN

	100 g Cheddar
	125 g Schlagsahne
	2 Eigelb
	500 g Sellerieknolle
	2 EL Zitronensaft
	200 g Feldsalat
	80 g Butter
	10 Walnußkernhälften

Vorbereitungszeit:
ca. 30 Minuten
Zubereitungszeit:
ca. 5-10 Minuten

ZUBEREITUNG

1 Den Cheddar reiben, Schlagsahne bis auf einen Eßlöffel mit dem Eigelb verquirlen (Liaison), Rest zum Kochen bringen, Cheddar unterrühren und auflösen.

2 Sahne-Käse-Mischung mit der Liaison verrühren, abkühlen lassen und mit Butter zur Creme aufrühren.

3 Geschälten und gewaschenen Sellerie in 1/2 cm dicke Scheiben schneiden, diese in Wasser und Zitronensaft gar kochen (12 Minuten), herausnehmen und 10 Taler (5 cm Durchmesser) ausstechen.

4 Feldsalat waschen, Blätter einzeln ablösen.

5 Sellerietaler mit Feldsalat belegen, die Käsecreme auf die Taler dressieren.

6 Zum Schluß mit Walnüssen ausgarnieren.

TIP

Richten Sie dieses Gericht, kurz bevor Ihre Gäste kommen, an, da der Feldsalat bei längerer Wartezeit sehr sensibel reagiert!

Buntes Gemüse süß-sauer eingelegt

ZUTATEN
(für ca. 10 Portionen)

300 g kleine Gurken
500 g Blumenkohl
300 g Karotten
300 g kleine Zwiebeln
150 g rote Paprika
6 Knoblauchzehen

ZUTATEN
FÜR DIE MARINADE

600 ml Kräuteressig
2 EL Zucker
1 TL Pfefferkörner (schwarz und weiß)
2 cm Ingwerwurzel
2 rote Chilis
2 Lorbeerblätter
1/2 TL Senfsamen

TIP

Je länger das Gemüse mariniert wird, desto herzhafter der Geschmack.

Auch andere Gemüse können so zubereitet werden, zum Beispiel Rote Bete, Kürbis, Zucchini.

Rote Bete nur mit Zwiebeln verwenden. Kürbis und Zucchini können auch noch mit zu dem Gemüse gegeben werden.

ZUBEREITUNG

1 Salatgurken halbieren und mit einem Löffel die Kerne entfernen.

2 Das Gemüse in gleichmäßige Stücke oder Streifen schneiden.

3 Blumenkohl in Röschen teilen und blanchieren.

4 Zwiebeln und Knoblauch schälen und eventuell halbieren, Ingwer fein hacken.

5 Zutaten für die Marinade aufkochen. Das Gemüse in die kochende Flüssigkeit geben, abkühlen lassen und für mindestens 24 Stunden marinieren.

Vorbereitungszeit: ca. 1 Stunde
Zeit des Marinierens: mindestens 24 Stunden

Gemüse-Terrine im Auberginenmantel

ZUTATEN
(für ca. 10 Portionen)

- 700 g gleichgroße Auberginen
- 250 g Zucchini
- 250 g Staudensellerie
- 200 g Zwiebeln
- 250 g rote Paprikaschoten
- 250 g grüne Paprikaschoten
- 500 g Tomaten
- Olivenöl, vergine extra
- 1 TL Thymian, gekerbelt
- 1/2 TL Rosamarinnadeln
- 1 Bund glatte Petersilie
- 3 EL Agar-Agar
- Salz, Pfeffer
- 1 Kugelform von 2 Litern Inhalt
- Klarsichtfolie

ZUBEREITUNG

1 Auberginen der Länge nach in dünne Scheiben schneiden. Unregelmäßige Scheiben würfeln und beiseite stellen.

2 Die Auberginenscheiben in Salzwasser blanchieren, abschrecken und gut abtropfen lassen. Die Kugelform mit Klarsichtfolie auskleiden und mit Auberginenscheiben überlappend belegen.

3 Für die Füllung die Gemüse vorbereiten, in gleichgroße Würfel schneiden und bei milder Hitze in Olivenöl bißfest garen.

4 Mit Kräutern, Salz und Pfeffer abschmecken. Tomaten häuten, entkernen und würfeln. Agar-Agar unter das Gemüse rühren und alles 5 Minuten köcheln lassen.

5 Das fertig gegarte Gemüse in die vorbereitete Form füllen und glattstreichen.

6 Mindestens 3 Stunden kühl stellen, danach stürzen.

7 Zu dieser Terrine reichen Sie Baguette mit Kräuterbutter.

Vorbereitungszeit: 30 Minuten
Zubereitungszeit: 30 Minuten
Zeit des Kühlens: mind. 3 Stunden

TIP

Schneiden Sie die Terrine mit einem Wellenschliff-Messer oder Elektro-Messer.

Rote Tofucreme

ZUTATEN
(für ca. 500 ml)

360 g Tofu-Mayonnaise *(Seite 41)*

140 g Ketchup

(eventuell Hot-Ketchup)

Salz, weißer Pfeffer

Cayennepfeffer oder Tabasco

Orangen- und Zitronensaft

Schnittlauch

ZUBEREITUNG

1 Mayonnaise und Ketchup glattrühren.

2 Mit Salz, weißem Pfeffer, Cayennepfeffer oder Tabasco und mit Orangen- und Zitronensaft abschmecken. Den gehackten Schnittlauch unterheben.

Sojabohnen-Dip mit Lauchzwiebeln und Knoblauch

ZUTATEN
(für ca. 500 ml)

250 g Frischkäse

80 ml Tofu-Mayonnaise *(Seite 41)*

80 ml Tofu-Sauerrahm *(Seite 68)*

2 Lauchzwiebeln

2 EL Dill

1 TL Worcestershiresauce

Knoblauch

Salz, weißer Pfeffer

Zitronensaft

ZUBEREITUNG

1 Frischkäse, Mayonnaise und Sauerrahm glattrühren.

2 Lauchzwiebeln sehr fein schneiden und zugeben, mit den Gewürzen abschmecken und mit Dill verfeinern.

Vorbereitungszeit: 5 Minuten
Zubereitungszeit: 5 Minuten

Tofu-Sauerrahm

ZUTATEN
(für ca. 500 ml)

350 g weicher Tofu
80 ml Öl
60 ml Weißweinessig oder Zitronensaft
1/2 TL Honig
1/2 TL jodiertes Salz

ZUBEREITUNG

Tofu und die restlichen Zutaten in einer Küchenmaschine pürieren.

Vorbereitungszeit: 5 Minuten
Zubereitungszeit: 10 Minuten

Crème fraîche mit Chili-Linsen

ZUTATEN
(für ca. 500 ml)

120 g rote Linsen
1 Knoblauchzehe
80 g Schalottenwürfel
1 rote Chilischote
120 ml Haselnußöl
80 g Frischkäse
100 g Crème fraîche
Kräuter: Petersilie, Schnittlauch
Salz, Pfeffer

ZUBEREITUNG

1 Die roten Linsen in Salzwasser weichkochen.

2 Linsen, Knoblauch und Chili in einer Küchenmaschine fein pürieren und nach und nach das Haselnußöl zugeben.

3 Frischkäse und Crème fraîche unterarbeiten.

4 Die Masse in eine Schüssel geben und die fein geschnittenen Schalotten und die gehackten Kräuter zufügen.

5 Mit Salz und Pfeffer abschmecken.

Vorbereitungszeit: ca. 15 Minuten
Zubereitungszeit: ca. 5 Minuten

Öl vom Zitronen-Thymian mit Lavendelblüten

ZUTATEN

1 l Olivenöl, vergine extra
6 Stiele Zitronen-Thymian
2 Stiele Lavendel mit Blüten

ZUBEREITUNG

1 Thymian und Lavendel gut abspülen und antrocknen lassen.

2 Die abgetrockneten Zweige in eine sterile Flasche legen, mit Öl auffüllen und gut verschließen.

3 Das Würzöl wenigstens 8 Tage kühl und dunkel ziehen lassen.

Vorbereitungszeit: 10 Minuten
Zeit des Ziehenlassens: 8 Tage

Salat von Gartengemüsen mit Öl vom Zitronen-Thymian und Lavendelblüten, geröstetes Mandelbrot und Raukebutter

ZUTATEN
FÜR DEN SALAT

300 g Zwiebeln
4 Knoblauchzehen
600 g Auberginen
600 g Zucchini
800 g gelbe, grüne, rote Paprikaschoten
600 g Tomaten
1 Zweig Estragon
3 Zweige Basilikum
Zitronen-Thymian-Öl mit Lavendelblüten
200 ml trockener Weißwein
Salz, schwarzer Pfeffer
100 ml Balsamico-Essig

Vorbereitungszeit: 30–45 Minuten
Zubereitungszeit: 30 Minuten

ZUBEREITUNG

1 Knoblauch fein hacken. Zwiebeln, Auberginen, Zucchini, Paprikaschoten und enthäutete Tomaten in 1 cm große Würfel schneiden.

2 Zwiebelwürfel in Olivenöl glasig dünsten, Auberginenwürfel zugeben und kurz mitbraten. Paprikawürfel und Knoblauch dazugeben. Das Gemüse scharf anbraten. Zuletzt die Zucchiniwürfel unterheben und mitdünsten.

3 Weißwein angießen, Tomatenwürfel zugeben und mit Salz und Pfeffer würzen.

4 Kräuter hacken, untermischen und die Gemüsemischung abkühlen lassen.

5 Das abgekühlte Gemüse mit Balsamico-Essig abschmecken.

6 Mit Kräuterzweigen garnieren und zum Mandelbrot *(siehe Seite 46)* mit Raukebutter *(siehe Seite 22)* servieren.

TIP

In einer Menüfolge servieren Sie zu diesem Salat Lammfilet im Sesammantel oder einfach Reispuffer.

Weißkohlsalat mit Möhren und Mango

ZUTATEN
(für ca. 500 g)
150 g Möhren
150 g Weißkohl
3 EL Zitronensaft
3 EL Öl
1 TL Honig
1 TL Senf
Salz, weißer Pfeffer
2 cm frischer Ingwer
1 Mango
2 Frühlingszwiebeln
Saft einer Orange
50 g Cashew-Kerne

Vorbereitungszeit: 30 Minuten
Zubereitungszeit: 10 Minuten

TIP

Alternativ zu Cashew-Kernen eignen sich gehobelte Mandeln.

ZUBEREITUNG

1 Weißkohl putzen, waschen, sehr fein hobeln.

2 Weißkohl mit Zitronensaft in einer Schüssel kneten, damit er weich wird.

3 Möhren waschen, schälen, in feine Streifen schneiden und mit Öl, Honig, Weißkohl und Senf untermischen und mit Salz, fein gewürfeltem Ingwer und Orangensaft abschmecken.

4 Die Mango in Würfel, Frühlingszwiebeln in feine Ringe schneiden und unter den Salat heben.

5 Cashew-Kerne goldbraun rösten, grob hacken und über den Salat streuen.

Artischockenherzen mit Strauchtomaten

ZUTATEN
(für ca. 10 Portionen)

- 10 Artischockenherzen (Konserve)
- 3 Schalotten
- 60 ml Olivenöl, vergine extra
- 125 ml trockener Weißwein
- 1/2 Zitrone
- 1 Zweig Thymian
- 1 Zweig Rosmarin
- 1 Lorbeerblatt
- 1 Knoblauchzehen
- Salz, frisch gemahlener Pfeffer
- 3 Strauchtomaten
- 20 ml Weißweinessig

TIP
Sofern Sie frische Artischocken verwenden, geben Sie in das Kochwasser schon einige Grundzutaten und etwas Essig.

ZUBEREITUNG

1 Artischockenherzen halbieren.

2 Schalottenwürfel in etwas Olivenöl anschwitzen, mit Wein und Zitronensaft ablöschen.

3 Kräuter und Gewürze dazugeben und 5 Minuten ziehen lassen.

4 Tomaten häuten, entkernen und würfeln.

5 Die Marinade über das Artischocken- und Tomatenwürfelgemisch geben.

6 Zum Schluß mit Weißweinessig abschmecken.

Vorbereitungszeit: ca. 30 Minuten
Zubereitungszeit: ca. 10-15 Minuten

Rübli-Brötchen mit Grünkern

ZUTATEN
(für ca. 10 Brötchen)

10 g Grünkern (ganze Körner, über Nacht eingeweicht)
40 g Hefe
1 TL Honig
100 g Grünkernmehl, fein
250 g Weizenvollkornmehl
100 g Möhren, fein geraffelt
1 TL jodiertes Salz

ZUBEREITUNG

1 Zerbröckelte Hefe mit Honig in 1/4 Liter lauwarmem Wasser auflösen und mit beiden Mehlsorten verrühren.

2 Die geraffelten Möhren, die Körner und Salz unterkneten, Teig zu einer Kugel formen und etwa 45 Minuten gehen lassen.

3 Nochmals gut durchkneten, zu einer Rolle formen, in 10 Stücke schneiden, jedes Stück rund formen und auf bemehltem Brett weitere 10 Minuten gehen lassen.

4 Die Oberflächen mit Wasser bestreichen und bei 200 Grad C etwa 20 Minuten backen.

Vorbereitung: Grünkern über Nacht einweichen
Zubereitungszeit: ca. 1-2 Stunden
Backzeit: 20 Minuten

Sesambutter

ZUTATEN

250 g weiche Butter
50 g Sesamsamen
50 g Tahin
jodiertes Salz, weißer Pfeffer
Knoblauch nach Geschmack

ZUBEREITUNG

1 Sesamsamen in einer trockenen Pfanne leicht anrösten.

2 Butter und Tahin cremig rühren, ausgekühlten Sesam unterrühren, mit Jodsalz, wenig Pfeffer und nach Geschmack mit einem Hauch Knoblauch würzen.

Vorbereitungszeit: ca. 10 Minuten
Zubereitungszeit: ca. 5 Minuten

> **TIP**
>
> Gekühlt aufbewahrt, hält sich die Sesambutter mehrere Tage.

G'rissene Thübingerle

ZUTATEN

1 kg Weizenvollkornmehl, mittelgrob geschrotet

800 ml Wasser

5 g Hefe

15 g Salz

TIP

Vollkornmehl läßt sich einfacher verarbeiten, wenn man es etwas aussiebt.

ZUBEREITUNG

1 Alle Zutaten ca. 10 Minuten miteinander gut kneten, zudecken und mindestens 3 Stunden stehen lassen.

2 Auf naß abgespülter Fläche Teig mit Handfläche breit drücken.

3 Mit nasser Handkante 2 Zentimeter breite Stücke abstechen, auf ein gefettetes, nasses Blech legen.

4 Bei 250 Grad C etwa 15 Minuten backen.

5 G'rissene Thübingerle schmecken lauwarm am besten. Man kann sie auch gut in der Mikrowelle noch einmal aufbacken.

Vorbereitungszeit:	ca. 15 Minuten
Zeit zum Gehenlassen:	mind. 3 Stunden
Zubereitungszeit:	15 Minuten
Backzeit:	15 Minuten

Vollkorn-Knäckebrot

ZUTATEN

(für ca. 30 Stück)

250 g Weizenschrot

30 g Ölsamen, zum Beispiel Leinsamen, Sesam, Kürbiskerne, Sonnenblumenkerne, Mohn

4 EL Pflanzenöl, zum Beispiel Sonnenblumenkernöl

1 TL Vollmeersalz

100 ml Wasser

eventuell Gewürze oder Kräutersalz

ZUBEREITUNG

1 Die Kürbis- und Sonnenblumenkerne grob hacken.

2 Aus den Zutaten einen Teig kneten.

3 Teig auf einem gefetteten Blech dünn ausrollen und in Quadrate schneiden.

4 Die einzelnen Teile mit der Gabel mehrmals einstechen, sonst wölbt sich das Gebäck auf dem Blech. Bei 225 Grad C etwa 20 Minuten backen.

Vorbereitungszeit:
ca. 30 Minuten
Backzeit:
20 Minuten

TIP

Knäckebrot stets kühl und trocken lagern.

Suppe von Cox-Orange-Äpfeln mit Ceylon-Zimt und Mandelsplittern

ZUTATEN
FÜR DIE SUPPE
(für ca. 10 Portionen)

- 50 g Lauch
- Butter
- 200 g Kartoffeln, mehlig kochend
- 150 g Cox-Orange-Äpfel
- 200 ml Vollmilch
- 200 ml Apfelsaft, naturtrüb
- 1 l Gemüsebrühe
- 15 g Madrascurry
- Meersalz, Pfeffer
- Macisblüte
- Ceylon-Zimt

ZUTATEN
FÜR DIE EINLAGE

- 100 g Äpfel
- Butter
- 200 ml Sahne
- gemischte Kräuter
- Mandelsplitter

ZUBEREITUNG

1 Das Helle vom Lauch vorbereiten und in Streifen schneiden, Kartoffeln und Äpfel würfeln.

2 Alles in Butter anschwitzen und Curry unterrühren, mit Milch, Gemüsebrühe und Apfelsaft löschen und im geschlossenen Topf garen.

3 Suppe fein pürieren und mit Salz, Pfeffer, Macisblüte und Zimt abschmecken.

4 Mandelsplitter ohne Fett leicht bräunen.

5 Kräuter fein hacken.

6 Äpfel würfeln und kurz in Butter dünsten.

7 Die Sahne angießen, aufkochen und die Kräuter zugeben.

8 Vor dem Servieren die Apfel-Sahne-Mischung zur Suppe geben und abschmecken.

9 Mit Sahnehaube und gebräunten Mandelsplittern garniert reichen.

Vorbereitungszeit: 30 Minuten
Zubereitungszeit: 30-40 Minuten

WUSSTEN SIE SCHON?

Madrascurry hat einen besonders pikanten Geschmack.

Falscher Hase vom Grünkern mit eingelegten Ebereschenbeeren dazu Kartoffeln aus dem Tontopf

ZUTATEN

(für ca. 10 Portionen)

- 150 g Zwiebeln
- 200 g Lauch
- 200 g Zucchini
- 200 g Möhren
- 1 Bd. Estragon
- 1 Bd. frischer Thymian
- 500 g Grünkernschrot, mittelfein
- 1 l Gemüsebrühe
- Butter
- 5 Eier
- 200 g Emmentaler
- 100 g Sonnenblumenkerne
- 50 g Mandelblätter
- Vollmeersalz, Pfeffer, Muskat
- bei Bedarf: Grieß

ZUBEREITUNG

1 Zwiebeln und Möhren schälen und klein würfeln. Zucchini ebenfalls würfeln, und alles in Butter dünsten.

2 Grünkernschrot zugeben und kurz mitdünsten. Mit heißer Gemüsebrühe ablöschen, aufkochen und 30 Minuten zugedeckt quellen.

3 In die abgekühlte Grünkernmasse die Eier rühren.

4 Käse reiben, Estragon und Thymian hacken, unter die Masse kneten.

5 Mit Salz, Pfeffer und Muskat abschmecken.

6 Die Masse zu einem länglichen Laib formen, auf ein gefettetes Backblech setzen, mit Mandelblättern bestreuen und bei 175 Grad C etwa 45 Minuten backen.

7 Den ausgetretenen Bratensaft mit dem Ebereschenbeeren-Kompott *(siehe Seite 76)* verrühren und abschmecken. Als Beilage empfehlen wir Möhrenplätzchen *(siehe Seite 26)*.

Vorbereitungszeit: ca. 45-60 Minuten
Backzeit: ca. 45-50 Minuten

TIP

Aus dieser Masse können Sie auch Bratlinge formen.

Wenn man sie vor dem Braten in Paniermehl wendet, werden die Bratlinge besonders knusprig.

Als Sauce eignet sich ein Knoblauch-Kräuter-Quark.

Ist die Konsistenz zu dünn, kann etwas Grieß untergearbeitet werden.

WUSSTEN SIE SCHON?

Grünkern ist das im halbreifen Zustand geerntete, gedarrte Korn des Dinkels und wird zu Graupen, Grünkernmehl, Grünkerngrieß und Grünkernflocken verarbeitet.

Grünkern gibt Suppen und Saucen eine grüngelbliche Farbe und einen würzigen Geschmack.

Eingelegte Ebereschenbeeren

ZUTATEN

2 kg Ebereschenbeeren
1 l Obstessig
1 l Wasser
1 kg feiner Zucker
3 Nelken
3 cm Zimtstange
2 Lorbeerblätter
10 g Salz
Einweckgläser

TIP

So sterilisieren Sie im Backofen:

Gefüllte Gläser verschließen, in die 1 Zentimeter hoch mit Wasser gefüllte Fettfangschale des Backofens stellen, dabei dürfen sich die Gläser nicht berühren. Die Temperatur auf 200 Grad C einstellen. Steigen Luftblasen vom Boden der Gläser auf, Backofen ausschalten und 1/2 Stunde lang sterilisieren.

Nach Beendigung die Gläser aus dem heißen Wasser nehmen.

ZUBEREITUNG

1 Ebereschenbeeren entstielen, mit kochendem Wasser überbrühen, abgießen und in vorbereitete Gläser füllen.

2 Essig, Wasser, Zucker und Gewürze aufkochen und über die Beeren gießen.

3 Die Gläser verschließen und sterilisieren.

Vorbereitungszeit: ca. 30 Minuten
Zeit der Sterilisation: ca. 45-60 Minuten

WUSSTEN SIE SCHON?

Die Eberesche wird auch Vogelbeerbaum oder Krammetsbeerbaum genannt.

Die Früchte sind leuchtend rot, der Geschmack ist leicht herb.

Maispflanzerln mit Sojasprossen

ZUTATEN
(für ca. 20 Stück)

500 g Maiskörner, gegart
2 Eigelb
2 Eiklar
20 g Mehl
200 g Sojasprossen
50 g Haferflocken
1 EL glatte Petersilie
Butterschmalz
Salz, Pfeffer

ZUBEREITUNG

1 Maiskörner leicht ausrücken, 250 Gramm fein pürieren, mit Eigelb, Mehl und Haferflocken verrühren und mit Salz und Pfeffer würzen.

2 Petersilie fein hacken, Sojasprossen grob zerschneiden und mit den ganzen Maiskörnern unter die Masse rühren.

3 Eiklar steif schlagen und vorsichtig unter die Masse heben.

4 Kleine flache Taler formen, in Butterschmalz goldbraun braten.

Vorbereitungszeit: ca. 30 Minuten
Zubereitungszeit: ca. 30 Minuten

Kräutersauce

ZUTATEN
(für ca. 1 l Sauce)

100 g Schalotten
Butter
500 ml Sahne
500 ml Gemüsebrühe
4 Eigelbe, ersatzweise Eierersatz *(Reformhaus)*
3 Bd. Kräuter, gemischt
Salz, Pfeffer, Muskat

ZUBEREITUNG

1 Schalotten fein würfeln und in Butter glasig dünsten.

2 Gemüsebrühe und 300 ml Sahne zugießen, etwas reduzieren.

3 Kräuter sehr fein hacken und mit der restlichen Sahne und den Eigelben verrühren. In die reduzierte Flüssigkeit geben, kurz erhitzen und abschmecken.

Vorbereitungszeit: ca. 30 Minuten
Zubereitungszeit: 5 Minuten

Schwarzwurzelgemüse

ZUTATEN
(für ca. 10 Portionen)

2 kg Schwarzwurzeln
100 ml Weißweinessig
Wasser
Salz
Butter

ZUBEREITUNG

1 Schwarzwurzeln unter fließendem Wasser schälen, in 3 cm lange Stücke schneiden und in Essigwasser legen.

2 In leicht gesalzenem Wasser bißfest garen.

3 Vor dem Servieren in Butter schwenken.

Vorbereitungszeit: 30 Minuten
Zubereitungszeit: 10 Minuten

Gratin von Kartoffeln, Kohlrabi und Tomaten

ZUTATEN
(für ca. 10 Portionen)

1,5 kg Kartoffeln, festkochend
1,5 kg Kohlrabi
1,5 kg Fleischtomaten
2 Lauchzwiebeln
2 Knoblauchzehen
1 frischer Bund Majoran
600 ml Rahm
600 ml Milch
Salz
Pfeffer
Muskat
100 g grob gehackte Kürbiskerne
100 g frisch geriebener Appenzeller

Vorbereitungszeit: ca. 30 Minuten
Zubereitungszeit: ca. 60 Minuten

ZUBEREITUNG

1 Kartoffeln und Kohlrabi schälen, Tomaten häuten.

2 Die Gemüse in feine Scheiben schneiden und dachziegelartig auf ein gefettetes Backblech schichten.

3 Lauchzwiebeln putzen, in Ringe schneiden, Knoblauch pellen, fein hacken, Majoranblättchen von den Stielen zupfen.

4 Die vorbereiteten Zutaten mit dem Käse und den Kürbiskernen über die geschichteten Kartoffeln, Kohlrabi und Tomaten streuen.

5 Rahm und Milch vorrühren, mit Salz, Pfeffer und Muskat würzen und an das Gratin gießen.

6 Bei 200 Grad C etwa 45 Minuten garen.

Ricotta-Zimtschaum mit Gelee-Nocken vom Boskopapfel

ZUTATEN

2 kg Boskopäpfel	
100 g Heidehonig	
1 Limette	
1 l Apfelsaft, naturtrüb	
Calvados	
3 TL Agar-Agar	
500 g Ricotta, ungereift und ungesalzen	
300 ml Milch	
40 g Heidehonig	
1 Vanilleschote	
200 g Marzipanrohmasse	
1 TL Zimtpulver	
1 Prise Macisblüte	

Vorbereitungszeit: 30 Minuten
Zeit des Kühlens: 12 Stunden
Zubereitungszeit: 20 Minuten

ZUBEREITUNG

1 Äpfel schälen, entkernen und würfeln.

2 Vom Apfelsaft 100 ml abnehmen und mit Agar-Agar verrühren.

3 Im restlichen Apfelsaft mit Limettenschale und Honig die Apfelwürfel 10 Minuten dünsten, in den letzten 2 Minuten angerührtes Agar-Agar dazugeben.

4 Mit Calvados abschmecken und über Nacht fest werden lassen.

5 Ricotta, Milch, Honig und Vanillemark glattrühren.

6 Marzipanrohmasse zerkleinern und unterrühren, mit Zimt und Macisblüte abschmecken.

7 Geleenocken abstechen und auf dem Saucenspiegel servieren.

TIP

Statt Agar-Agar Gelatine verwenden.

Mandelkuchen mit Cabua-Kakao

ZUTATEN

(für eine Tarteform von 28 cm Durchmesser)

100 g Butter
150 g Rohrzucker
1 Vanilleschote
2 Eier
45 g Cabua-Kakao
125 g Mehl
2 TL Weinsteinbackpulver
50 g gehackte Mandeln
2 cl Kakaolikör

Vorbereitungszeit: 30 Minuten
Zubereitungszeit: ca. 20 Minuten

TIP

Zu diesem Dessert schmeckt halbsteif geschlagene Sahne, gewürzt mit Zimt und Kakaolikör.

ZUBEREITUNG

1 Tarteform gut fetten.

2 Mandeln ohne Fett hell rösten, abkühlen lassen.

3 Butter schaumig rühren, nach und nach Zucker, Vanillemark und die Eier unterrühren.

4 Kakao, Mehl und Backpulver mischen und mit den Mandeln unter die Creme rühren, mit Likör abschmecken.

5 Teig in die Tarteform füllen, glattstreichen und bei 175 Grad C 20 Minuten backen.

Frische Datteln mit Stiltoncreme

ZUTATEN
(für ca. 20 Datteln)

500 g frische Datteln
150 g Stilton
150 g Doppelrahmfrischkäse
50 g Pistazien, ungesalzen

Vorbereitungszeit: 15 Minuten
Zubereitungszeit: 15 Minuten

ZUBEREITUNG

1 Datteln längs einschneiden und den Kern entfernen.

2 Stilton und Doppelrahmfrischkäse cremig rühren und mit einem Spritzbeutel in die Datteln dressieren.

3 Pistazien hacken und auf die Creme streuen.

WUSSTEN SIE SCHON?

Stilton, ein Edelpilzkäse aus England, kommt in Zylindern von 6-8 kg in den Handel.

Seine Rinde sollte faltig, leicht schuppig und braun-weiß gefärbt sein. Das Aroma ist mild, rein und doch pikant.

Da er ein Saisonkäse ist, kauft man ihn am besten zwischen November und April. Er ist ein typischer Dessertkäse.

TIP

Zu dem „Blue Stilton" schmecken Datteln besonders herzhaft, wenn sie vorher 1-2 Stunden in weißem Portwein eingelegt werden.

Pikante Vollkornplätzchen mit Thymian

ZUTATEN

(für ca. 100 Plätzchen)

250 g Dinkel-Vollkornmehl
250 g Roggen-Vollkornmehl
1 EL gemahlener Kümmel
6 g Salz
15 g Weinsteinbackpulver
1 TL Thymian, getrocknet
2 Eier
1 Eiklar
300 g Butter
1 Eigelb
grobes Salz

Vorbereitungszeit: 30 Minuten
Kühlzeit: 30 Minuten
Backzeit: 20 Minuten

ZUBEREITUNG

1 Mehl, Kümmel, Thymian, Salz und Backpulver mischen.

2 In die Mitte eine Mulde drücken, Eier und Eiklar hineingeben und mit etwas Mehl verrühren.

3 Butter in kleinen Würfeln daraufgeben, alles zu einem glatten Teig verkneten und kühl stellen.

4 Anschließend den Teig 2 Millimeter dick ausrollen, Plätzchen ausstechen und auf ein gefettetes Backblech legen. Eigelb mit Wasser verquirlen und die Plätzchen damit bestreichen und mit Thymian und grobem Salz bestreuen.

5 Bei 200 Grad C 15 Minuten goldbraun backen.

WUSSTEN SIE SCHON?

Weinsteinbackpulver ist besonders zu empfehlen, da es als Säureträger natürliche Weinsteinsäure (aus Holzweinfässern) enthält.

Käse-Kräuter-Kugeln mit Walnußkernen

ZUTATEN

(für ca. 500 g)

200 g Gorgonzola
100 g Butter
100 g Quark
80 g Parmesan
je 1/2 Bd. glatte Petersilie
und Kerbel
Meersalz
1/2 TL Schabziger Klee
1/2 TL weißer Pfeffer
Öl
Walnußkerne

ZUBEREITUNG

1 Gorgonzola fein zerdrücken.

2 Zuerst die weiche Butter, dann den Quark unterrühren.

3 Hartkäse reiben, Walnußkerne hacken, Kerbel und Petersilie wiegen und mit dem Käse unter die Creme mengen.

4 Mit Salz, Klee und Pfeffer abschmecken und Kugeln formen.

Zubereitungszeit: ca. 30 Minuten

WUSSTEN SIE SCHON?

Schabziger Klee oder Bisamklee ist eine einjährige Steinkleeart, die in der Schweiz und in Deutschland als Würzpflanze angebaut wird. Mit Vorsicht würzen!

Plätzchen mit saurer Sahne, Mohn, Sesam und Leinsamen

ZUTATEN

(für ca. 200 Plätzchen)

400 g Dinkelvollkornmehl
200 g Butter
300 g saure Sahne
1 TL Salz

Zum Bestreichen:
Eigelb mit Wasser

Zum Bestreuen:
Mohn, Sesam, Leinsamen

ZUBEREITUNG

1 Mehl und Butter verreiben und mit der sauren Sahne und dem Salz zu einem glatten Teig verkneten.

2 Eine halbe Stunde ruhen lassen.

3 Danach den Teig 1/2 cm dick ausrollen, verschiedene Formen ausstechen, mit verquirltem Eigelb bestreichen und mit Samen bestreuen.

Vorbereitungszeit: ca. 10 Minuten
Zubereitungszeit: ca. 60 Minuten
Backzeit: ca. 10 Minuten

REGIONALE UND KLASSISCHE KÜCHE

ROLF SCHÜRMANN

WOLFGANG MARKLOFF

Saisonal wie im ersten Drittel der „Kalten Buffets" – im Gegensatz dazu unter Verwendung von Fisch und Fleisch – teilt zunächst Rolf Schürmann seine Vorschläge ein. Rezepte und Illustrationen stehen
➤ ab Seite 87 für ein Frühlingsbuffet in der Oster-, Kommunions- und Konfirmationszeit,
➤ ab Seite 106 für ein Sommer-/Herbstbuffet und
➤ ab Seite 127 für ein Winter-/Weihnachtsbuffet.

Die klassische Menüfolge, die auch warme Gänge enthält, strukturiert seine Rezepte in kalte Vorspeisen, Suppen, warme Vorspeisen, Fisch- und Fleisch-Hauptgänge sowie Desserts.
Rolf Schürmann ist Küchenmeister, Fachdozent und Jurymitglied von Kochwettbewerben.

Vervollkommnet wird dieses Kapitel mit Rezepten für zwanzig raffinierte Menügänge
➤ ab Seite 158, die untereinander kombinierbar sind, von Wolfgang Markloff.
Besondere Aufmerksamkeit wurde dabei auf Garnituren und Speisenplazierungen gelegt.
Nicht allein die Küche, sondern auch der Service erhält Tips.
Wolfgang Markloff ist Küchenmeister und Fachdozent mit Auszeichnungen und Medaillen zahlreicher Kochkunstwettbewerbe. 1995 wurde er als kulinarischer „Botschafter des Landes Nordrhein-Westfalen" ausgezeichnet. Er arbeitet wie Rolf Schürmann auch für die Förderungsgesellschaft für das Hotel- und Gaststättengewerbe in Coesfeld.

Vorschlag für ein Frühlingsbuffet in der Oster-, Kommunions- und Konfirmationszeit

Schaumbrot von geräuchertem Fisch mit Zucchiniplätzchen und Tomaten-Crème fraîche

Kalte Quarkschaum-Gemüseterrine im Rauchschinkenmantel

Gebeizte sauerländische Bachforellen

Apfelmeerrettich

Meerrettichmayonnaise

Rote Bete-Sauce

Zuckerschoten-Matjes-Salat

Fenchel-Orangen-Salat

Spargel-Artischocken-Salat

Orangen-Pfeffer-Butter

Bleichselleriecreme mit Räucherfischnocken

Schweinefiletscheiben in der Spargelhülle, Sauerampferbuttersauce, neue Kartoffeln

Moorlammrückenfilet mit Zucchinipiccata, geschmelzten Tomaten und Kartoffelnudeln

Marinierte Erdbeeren in Florentinerschalen mit einer Cognac-Vanillecreme

Grießplätzchen in einer Haselnußkruste mit Rhabarber-Apfel-Grütze

Frischkäse im Pumpernickelmantel

Schaumbrot von geräuchertem Fisch mit Zucchiniplätzchen und Tomaten-Crème fraîche

ZUTATEN
(für ca. 4-6 Portionen)

120 g Forellenfilet, geräuchert
120 g Welsfilet, ohne Haut, geräuchert
4 Blatt Gelatine
30 g feine Schalottenwürfel
etwas Öl zum Anschwitzen
100 ml Fischbrühe (Fond)
50 ml trockener Weißwein oder Noilly Prat
125 ml Sahne
Salz, Cayennepfeffer
Saft einer 1/4 Zitrone
1 Msp. Zucker zum Abrunden
1 kleines Bd. Kerbel
1/4 Lorbeerblatt

TOMATEN-CRÈME FRAÎCHE

Tomaten
1/4 l Fischgrundsauce
etwas Zitronensaft
150 g Crème fraîche
30 ml Sahne
etwas Salbei, gehackt
Salz, Cayennepfeffer
Tomatensaft

Vorbereitungszeit: 120 Minuten
Zubereitungszeit: 60 Minuten

TIP
Man kann die Sauce glatt oder mit einigen abgezogenen Tomatenstückchen servieren.

ZUBEREITUNG

1 Die Schalotten in Öl glasig schwitzen, mit etwas Fischfond ablöschen und trockenen Weißwein zugeben. Alles durchköcheln und danach kühl stellen.

2 Nach 20 Minuten die Schalotten in der Küchenmaschine pürieren und durch ein Küchensieb streichen (passieren).

3 Alle Fischfilets mit der Schalottenmasse und der Fischbrühe in der Küchenmaschine mixen, bis eine cremige Masse ensteht.

4 Die eingeweichte Gelatine ausdrücken und im lauwarmen Wasserbad auflösen. Anschließend etwas Fischmasse zur Gelatine geben, glattrühren und nun alles zusammen vermengen.

5 Wenn man möchte, kann man einen Teil der Räucherfische auch als Filet oder Würfel in das Schaumbrot geben – dann vorher beiseitelegen.

6 Nachdem die Masse mit Gelatine gebunden wurde, gibt man sofort die geschlagene Sahne hinzu und schmeckt mit den Gewürzen ab. Alles möglichst rasch in eine ausgekleidete Form einfüllen und 12 Stunden durchkühlen lassen.

7 Die Fischgrundsauce mit den Tomaten aufkochen, den Zitronensaft und die Gewürze zugeben. Alles nach ca. 10 Minuten Kochzeit mit dem Mixstab pürieren. Danach durch ein Sieb streichen und, wenn nötig, die Sauce mit etwas trockenem Weißwein und Sahne leicht strecken. Nochmals aufkochen und nachschmecken. Danach auskühlen lassen.

8 Die Sauce mit etwas Tomatensaft, Crème fraîche und Sahne in kaltem Zustand mit dem Pürierstab aufschäumen und zum Schaumbrot servieren.

WUSSTEN SIE SCHON?

Das Wort „Schaumbrot" wird im Französischen als „Mousse" bezeichnet. Es handelt sich hierbei um feine Pürees aus Fisch, Fleisch oder Gemüse, die mit Gelatine und geschlagener Sahne verarbeitet und anschließend gekühlt werden.

Zucchiniplätzchen

ZUTATEN

300 g Zucchini
100 g Mehl
50 ml Sahne
2 Eier
Knoblauch
Salz
bunte, eingelegte Pfefferkörner
50 g Bratfett

Vorbereitungszeit: 10 Minuten
Zubereitungszeit: 15 Minuten

TIP

Eine gleichmäßige Form erhalten Sie, wenn Sie einen runden Ausstecher benutzen.

ZUBEREITUNG

1 Die Zucchini grob raffeln und mit etwas Salz vermengen.

2 Aus Mehl, Sahne, Eiern und Gewürzen sowie Pfefferkörnern einen Teig herstellen.

3 Die zerkleinerten Zucchini mit einem Passiertuch ausdrücken, damit die überschüssige Flüssigkeit entfernt wird, anschließend unter den Teig geben.

4 Im Bratfett zu kleinen Plätzchen ausbacken.

5 Die Plätzchen vor dem Servieren auf einem Küchenkrepp abtropfen.

Kalte Quarkschaum-Gemüseterrine im Rauchschinkenmantel

ZUTATEN
(für ca. 4 Portionen)

500 g	Speisequark
150 g	Sahne
14-15 Blatt	Gelatine, im Sommer 17 Blatt
je 15 g	Petersilie und Schnittlauch
50 g	Karotten
	etwas flüssige Sahne
1	Zitrone
12 dünne Scheiben	Rauchschinken
	Salz und Pfeffer
1 Kissen	rote Kresse
1 Kissen	grüne Kresse

Vorbereitungszeit: ca. 30 Minuten
Zubereitungszeit: 10 Minuten

ZUBEREITUNG

1 Den Speisequark mit etwas flüssiger Sahne glattrühren und mit den Gewürzen abschmecken. Die fein geschnittenen Kräuter, die fein geraspelte Karotte und die gehackte Kresse unterheben. Etwas Zitronenabrieb und, wenn notwendig, einige Spritzer Zitronensaft zum Vollenden zugeben.

2 Die Blattgelatine in kaltem Wasser einweichen, gut ausdrücken und im heißen Wasserbad in einer Schüssel zerlaufen lassen. Etwas Quarkmasse damit anrühren, mit dem restlichen Quark glattrühren und die geschlagene Sahne zügig unterheben.

3 Eine Terrinenform mit Klarsichtfolie auskleiden und rundherum mit Schinken-Scheiben auslegen.

4 Die Quarkmasse einfüllen.

5 6 Stunden kühl stellen.

Gebeizte sauerländische Bachforellen

ZUTATEN
(für ca. 8 Portionen)

4 Bachforellenfilets mit Haut
(à ca. 100 g)
1 Bd. Dill
1 Bd. glatte Petersilie
1 EL Walnußöl
4 zerdrückte Wacholderbeeren
20 g Salz, grob
5 g Zucker
schwarzer Pfeffer, grob
1 EL Brandy

ZUBEREITUNG

1 Die Kräuter mit Stielen waschen, abtrocknen und fein hacken.

2 Mit Öl, Salz, Zucker, Pfeffer und Wacholderbeeren mischen.

3 Forellenfilets entgräten und mit der Hautseite nach unten in eine Schale legen.

4 Kräuterbeize gleichmäßig auf der Oberseite der Forellenfilets verteilen, mit Brandy beträufeln und 6 Stunden beizen.

5 Beizrückstände von den Forellenfilets entfernen und nach Belieben in dünne Scheiben schneiden.

Vorbereitungszeit: 20 Minuten
Zubereitungszeit: 15 Minuten
Beizzeit: 6 Stunden

Apfelmeerrettich

ZUTATEN

350 g Äpfel (Granny, Cox Orange
oder Jonathan)
etwas Apfelsaft
80 g frischer Meerrettich
30 g Zucker
1/4 l süße Sahne
etwas Zitronensaft
2 EL milder Apfelessig

ZUBEREITUNG

1 Alle Äpfel schälen, Kerngehäuse entfernen. 1 Apfel grob raspeln, mit Zitronensaft beträufeln und zur Seite stellen.

2 Ein Apfelmus herstellen und auskühlen lassen.

3 Den Meerrettich schälen und mit der feinen Reibe reiben. Danach unter das Apfelmus geben.

4 Die Sahne steifschlagen und anschließend unter die Apfel-Meerrettichmasse geben. Alles mit etwas Zucker, Essig, Zitronensaft und Apfelsaft abschmecken.

5 Zum Schluß den grob geraspelten Apfel unterheben.

Zubereitungszeit: 20 Minuten

Meerrettich-mayonnaise

ZUTATEN
(für ca. 500 ml)

200 g Mayonnaise
250 g Sahne
50 g Joghurt
3 TL Meerrettich, frisch gerieben
Salz, weißer Pfeffer, Zucker
Zitronensaft

Zubereitungszeit: 10 Minuten

ZUBEREITUNG

1 Mayonnaise mit Joghurt und geriebenem Meerrettich mischen.

2 Mit Salz, weißem Pfeffer, Zucker und Zitronensaft abschmecken.

3 Sahne schlagen und unterheben.

Rote Bete-Sauce

ZUTATEN
(für ca. 500 ml)

180 g Rote Bete
80 g Apfel
40 g Zwiebel
180 g Joghurt
Salz, Pfeffer
Meerrettich

Vorbereitungszeit: 45 Minuten
Zubereitungszeit: 20 Minuten

ZUBEREITUNG

1 Die Rote Bete mit Schale in Salzwasser garen (Farberhaltung).

2 In kaltem Wasser abschrecken und abziehen.

3 Apfel schälen, kurz in kochendes Wasser geben, damit er nicht braun wird.

4 Apfel, Zwiebel und Rote Bete in kleine Würfel schneiden und mit Joghurt mischen.

5 Mit Salz, Pfeffer und Meerrettich abschmecken.

TIP

Um diese Sauce pikanter im Geschmack zu erhalten, können Sie grüne Pfefferkörner zugeben.

Zum Auflockern der Sauce kurz vor dem Anrichten geschlagene Sahne unterarbeiten.

Zuckerschoten-Matjes-Salat

ZUTATEN
(für ca. 4 Portionen)

350 g Zuckerschoten
Salz, Zucker, Pfeffer
Traubenkernöl, Traubenessig
100 g rote Zwiebeln
200 g Matjesfilets
100 g Staudensellerie
glatte Petersilie
Garnitur:
Tomaten, Paprika

ZUBEREITUNG

1 Aus Essig, Pfeffer, Salz und Zucker eine Vinaigrette rühren.

2 Matjes und Zwiebeln in Streifen schneiden.

3 Staudensellerie von außen schälen, in feine Scheiben schneiden.

4 Petersilienblätter grob zerpflücken.

5 Zuckerschoten blanchieren, in Rauten schneiden.

6 Alle Zutaten in der Vinaigrette wenden und gut durchziehen lassen.

7 Eventuell nachsalzen.

Vorbereitungszeit: 15 Minuten
Zubereitungszeit: 15 Minuten

Fenchel-Orangen-Salat

ZUTATEN
(für ca. 6 Portionen)

4 Orangen
50 ml Olivenöl, vergine extra
1 mittelgroße rote Zwiebel
1 Radicchio
3 Fenchelknollen
1 Bd. Petersilie
2 Scheiben Weißbrot
Knoblauch
Salz

ZUBEREITUNG

1 Orangen mit einem Messer schälen und in dünne Scheiben schneiden oder filetieren.

2 Radicchio mundgerecht zerteilen.

3 Fenchel und die rote Zwiebel halbieren, in Streifen schneiden und blanchieren.

4 Fenchelkraut und Petersilie fein hacken.

5 Orangenfleisch mit Salz bestreuen und mit Olivenöl begießen.

6 Weißbrotwürfel mit Knoblauch in Olivenöl rösten.

7 Orangen mit Radicchio, Fenchel und roter Zwiebel mischen, mit feingehackter Petersilie, Fenchelkraut und Weißbrotwürfeln bestreuen.

Vorbereitungszeit: 20 Minuten
Zubereitungszeit: 10 Minuten

Spargel-Artischocken-Salat

ZUTATEN

250 g frischer Spargel, grün und weiß
60 g Kenia-Bohnen
80 g kleine Champignons
2 St. Frühlingslauch
2 St. Artischockenherzen
3 EL Olivenöl
Paprikapulver, Salz
1 Knoblauchzehe

MARINADE

3 EL Zitronensaft
Salz
schwarzer Pfeffer, frisch gemahlen
3 EL Olivenöl

ZUBEREITUNG

1 Spargel schälen, bißfest garen, Bohnen putzen und blanchieren, in Eiswasser abkühlen und beides in mundgerechte Stücke schneiden.

2 Champignons säubern, vierteln und in Olivenöl mit gehacktem Knoblauch anschwitzen, mit Paprikapulver bestreuen.

3 Aus Öl, Zitronensaft und Pfeffer eine Marinade herstellen.

4 Frühlingslauch in feine Streifen schneiden, Artischockenherzen achteln.

5 Alle Zutaten in eine Schüssel geben und mit der Salatsauce mischen.

Vorbereitungszeit: 25 Minuten
Zubereitungszeit: 15 Minuten

Orangen-Pfeffer-Butter

ZUTATEN

250 g weiche Butter
10 ml Orangensaft
(oder Orangenkonzentrat)
1 Orange, unbehandelt
20 g grüne eingelegte Pfefferkörner
Salz

ZUBEREITUNG

1 Von der Orangenschale mit einem Zestenreißer feine Streifen abziehen, in etwas Orangensaft garen und fein hacken.

2 Pfefferkörner abspülen.

3 Mit der Butter und den übrigen Zutaten mischen.

Zubereitungszeit: 15 Minuten

Bleichselleriecreme mit Räucherfischnocken

ZUTATEN

(für ca. 4 Portionen)

400 g	Bleichsellerie
40 g	Butter
50 g	Schalotten
50 g	Lauch
40 g	Mehl
700 ml	Gemüsebrühe
100 ml	Sahne
	Wermut
	Salz, Pfeffer
1 EL	Crème fraîche
	einige Spritzer Zitrone

GARNITUR

frische Sellerieblätter

Vorbereitungszeit: 15 Minuten
Zubereitungszeit: 30 Minuten

ZUBEREITUNG

1 Die gewürfelten Schalotten und den geschnittenen Lauch sowie den Bleichsellerie in Butter dünsten. Mit Mehl abstäuben und durchschwitzen.

2 Mit 100 ml kalter Gemüsebrühe glattrühren und mit der restlichen heißen Brühe auffüllen.

3 Etwa 10 Minuten reduzieren lassen, mit Sahne vollenden, mit Gewürzen und Wermut abschmecken.

WUSSTEN SIE SCHON?

Bleichsellerie ist ein Staudengemüse. Bekannt ist er auch unter den Namen Stauden- und Stangensellerie oder als englischer Sellerie.

Künstliche Hüllen schützen die Stauden vor Lichteinwirkung und lassen sie dadurch zart und hell werden.

Räucherfischnocken

ZUTATEN

100 g Hechtfilet
80 g Räucherfisch (Wels, Lachs)
200 ml Sahne
Kerbel, Dill

Vorbereitungszeit: 10 Minuten
Zubereitungszeit: 15 Minuten

ZUBEREITUNG

1 Das Hechtfilet zerkleinern, mit etwas Salz in einer Mixmaschine pürieren. Die Sahne nach und nach zugeben.

2 Die entstandene Farce entnehmen, auf Eis setzen und den fein gewürfelten Räucherfisch unterheben.

3 Kräuter und Gewürze zugeben und die Farce abschmecken.

4 Mit Hilfe von zwei Teelöffeln kleine Nocken formen und in Fischfond ziehen lassen.

5 Die Räucherfischnocken als Einlage in die Creme geben.

Schweinefiletscheiben in der Spargelhülle, Sauerampferbuttersauce, neue Kartoffeln

ZUTATEN
(für ca. 4 Portionen)

300 g Schweinefilet
600 g Spargel
150 ml Sahne
50 g Mehl
1 Ei
Butterschmalz
Salz, Pfeffer
Sauerampfer
Butter
500 g Kartoffeln

Vorbereitungszeit: 20 Minuten
Zubereitungszeit: 20 Minuten

ZUBEREITUNG SCHWEINEFILET

1 Das Schweinefilet in dünne Scheiben schneiden, würzen und in Butterschmalz kurz anbraten, dann auskühlen lassen.

2 Vom geschälten Spargel die Spitzen abschneiden und beiseitelegen.

3 Den Spargel grob raspeln und mit etwas Salz 5 Minuten ziehen lassen, anschließend mit Hilfe eines Tuchs auspressen.

4 Aus Mehl, Sahne und Ei einen Teig herstellen, den geraspelten Spargel unterheben und mit den Gewürzen abschmecken.

5 Einen Eßlöffel Teig in eine Pfanne mit heißem Butterschmalz geben und eine Filetscheibe darauf legen. Mit Spargelteig bedecken und von beiden Seiten braun braten.

6 Die Spargelspitzen garen und beim Anrichten verwenden.

Sauerampferbuttersauce

ZUTATEN

3 Eier
250 g Butter
50 g Schalotten
60 g Sauerampfer
Pfefferkörner
20 ml Weißwein
1 Limone

ZUBEREITUNG

1 Aus dem Weißwein, etwas Wasser, der Schalotte, den Stielen des Sauerampfers und den Gewürzen eine Gewürzreduktion herstellen.

2 Die Butter klären.

3 Die Eigelbe mit der ausgekühlten Reduktion auf einem 80 Grad C heißen Wasserbad bis zur Rose aufschlagen.

4 Die geklärte Butter zunächst tropfenweise, später im Faden unter die Eigelbmasse rühren.

5 Die Sauerampferblätter blanchieren, pürieren und unter die Buttersauce rühren. Mit Salz, Pfeffer und Limonensaft abschmecken.

Vorbereitungszeit: 15 Minuten
Zubereitungszeit: 15 Minuten

Moorlammrückenfilet mit Zucchinipiccata, geschmelzten Tomaten und Kartoffelnudeln

ZUTATEN
(für ca. 4 Portionen)

600 g	Lammrückenfilet
350 g	Zucchini
2	Eier
60 g	Parmesan
30 g	Mehl
300 g	Strauchtomaten
80 g	Schalotten
30 g	Butter
2 EL	Dijon-Senf
	Kerbel, Basilikum, Rosmarin, Salbei
50 g	Butterschmalz
	Knoblauch
	Salz, Pfeffer

Vorbereitungszeit: 20 Minuten
Zubereitungszeit: 20 Minuten

WUSSTEN SIE SCHON?

Moorlämmer werden in Flachmoorgebieten gezüchtet. Sie erhalten ihren typischen leicht salzigen Geschmack durch ihre Umgebung.

ZUBEREITUNG LAMMFILET

1 Tomaten einschneiden, blanchieren, abschrecken, abziehen, entkernen und in Würfel schneiden.

2 Die gewürfelten Schalotten in Butter anschwitzen, die Tomatenwürfel zugeben und mit den Kräutern und Gewürzen abschmecken.

3 Eier und Parmesan vermengen und 10 Minuten quellen lassen.

4 Die Zucchini in 1/2 cm dicke Scheiben schneiden, mehlieren, durch die Parmesanmasse ziehen und in Butterschmalz goldbraun braten.

5 Das Lammrückenfilet parieren und kurz im Bratfett anbraten. Danach mit einem Gemisch aus Dijon-Senf und gehacktem Rosmarin einstreichen.

6 Anschließend im Backofen bei 160 Grad C etwa 10 Minuten garen, entspannen lassen, tranchieren und mit Zucchinipiccata, geschmelzten Tomaten und Kartoffelnudeln anrichten.

Kartoffelnudeln

ZUTATEN

300 g	Kartoffeln, mehligkochend
120 g	Mehl
1	Eigelb
15 g	Butter
	Salz, Muskat
40 g	Semmelbrösel
	Butterschmalz

ZUBEREITUNG

1 Die Kartoffeln in der Schale kochen, pellen und durch eine Kartoffelpresse drücken. Mit Salz und Muskat würzen und mit Butter, Eigelb und Mehl rasch zu einem Teig verarbeiten.

2 Diesen auf einem gut gemehlten Tisch zu einer Rolle formen, in gleichmäßige Stücke schneiden und zu fingerlangen Nudeln formen.

3 In siedendem Salzwasser garen, anschließend in Butterschmalz anschwenken und mit Semmelbröseln bestreuen.

Vorbereitungszeit: 10 Minuten
Zubereitungszeit: 40 Minuten

Marinierte Erdbeeren in Florentinerschalen mit einer Cognac-Vanillecreme

ZUTATEN
(für ca. 6 Portionen)

500 g Erdbeeren
40 g Vanillezucker
ca. 150 g geraspelte Kuvertüre
gehobelte Mandelspäne nach Bedarf
4-5 gleichmäßig große Minzblätter zum Garnieren
200 ml Sahne
Zucker und Vanillezucker nach Geschmack für die Creme
2 cl Cognac
2 cl Grand Marnier
1 Blatt Gelatine

Zubereitungszeit: 20 Minuten

ZUBEREITUNG DER ERDBEEREN

1 350 g Erdbeeren halbieren oder vierteln, mit etwas Vanillezucker bestreuen und mit einigen Spritzern Grand Marnier aromatisieren.

2 Die restlichen Erdbeeren mit dem Küchenmixstab zu einem Püree verarbeiten.

3 Beide Komponenten kurz mischen und eventuell mit etwas Zucker nachschmecken.

4 Die flüssige, vorgekühlte Schlagsahne mit Zucker und etwas Vanillezucker steif schlagen.

5 Die eingeweichte Gelatine in den erwärmten Grand Marnier und dem Cognac auflösen und kurz vor dem Stocken unter die Sahne arbeiten. Hierbei empfiehlt es sich, vorher etwas geschlagene Sahne aus der Gesamtmenge mit der Gelatine anzugleichen und dann erst unter die gesamte Masse zugeben. Die Konsistenz der Creme sollte halbflüssig sein.

6 Die Erdbeeren in die Schalen einfüllen, mit der Creme überziehen und mit geraspelten Kuvertürespänen, gebräunten Mandeln und dem Minzblatt ausgarnieren.

TIP

Durch das Ausstreichen der Schalen mit der Schokolade sind diese sehr feuchtigkeitsresistent. Sie können das Ganze deshalb ruhig einige Zeit vorher anrichten und auf Ihr Buffet stellen.

ZUTATEN

150 g Butter
150 g Zucker
45 g Bienenhonig
5 cl flüssige Sahne
70 g gehobelte Mandeln
50 g gehackte Mandeln
45 g gestiftelte Mandeln
35 g Orangeat
25 g Zitronat
20 g Mehl
1/2 Stange Vanille
Kuvertüre zum Auspinseln der Schalen
Förmchen zum Formen
Öl

ZUBEREITUNG DER FLORENTINERSCHALEN

1 Butter, Zucker und Honig sowie die Sahne in einem Kessel oder Topf unter ständigem Rühren goldgelb kochen.

2 Nun die restlichen Zutaten zugeben und wie beim Herstellen von Brandmasse alles solange rösten, bis sich ein Klumpen bildet.

3 Die fertige Masse rasch in geölte Auflaufförmchen drücken und mit einem ebenfalls geölten Eßlöffel (Rückseite) oder einer kleinen Saucenkelle halbrunde Hohlkörper formen. Zur Stabilisierung der Masse in den Förmchen empfiehlt es sich, Rohmarzipan-Kugeln hineinzulegen.

4 Die gefüllten Förmchen bei ca. 200 Grad C fertig backen.

5 Kurz auskühlen lassen und die Marzipankugeln entfernen. Die Hohlkörper mit der Messerspitze vorsichtig lösen und mit der offenen Seite nach unten ganz auskühlen lassen.

6 Anschließend mit temperierter Kuvertüre (37 Grad C) sorgfältig von innen ausstreichen und nochmals erkalten lassen.

Vorbereitungszeit: 1 Stunde
Zubereitungszeit: ca. 3 Stunden mit Auskühlen

Grießplätzchen in einer Haselnußkruste mit Rhabarber-Apfel-Grütze

ZUTATEN

FÜR DIE GRIESSPLÄTZCHEN

(für ca. 10 Portionen)

375 ml Milch
1/2 Vanilleschote
20 g Zucker
65 g Grieß
1 Eigelb, 1 Eiklar
20 g Butter
Salz
Puderzucker

ZUTATEN

FÜR DIE HASELNUSSKRUSTE

150 g gehackte Haselnüsse
2 Eier
50 g Mehl
50 g Butterschmalz

ZUBEREITUNG

1 Die längs halbierte und ausgekratzte Vanilleschote mit Milch, Zucker und etwas Salz zum Kochen bringen.

2 Die Vanilleschote entnehmen und den Grieß unter ständigem Rühren einrieseln und 5 Minuten kochen lassen.

3 Nun die Grießmasse ca. 1,5 cm dick auf ein gefettetes Blech streichen.

4 Nach dem Auskühlen mit einem runden Ausstecher von 7 cm Durchmesser kleine Plätzchen erstellen.

5 Etwas Eiweiß und Puderzucker anrühren und damit die Plätzchen bestreichen.

6 Die Plätzchen mit gehackten Haselnüssen locker bestreuen und auf ein Backblech mit Backpapier legen.

7 Alles für ca. 5 Minuten bei 160-170 Grad C auf der mittleren Schiene im Backofen goldbraun bräunen.

Vorbereitungszeit: 10 Minuten
Zubereitungszeit: 25 Minuten

WUSSTEN SIE SCHON?

Rhabarber wird wie Obst behandelt, ist aber botanisch gesehen ein Staudengemüse.

Vor etwa 5000 Jahren wurde Rhabarber bereits in China als Heilpflanze genutzt.

Die Haupterntezeit für Rhabarber ist April bis Juli.

Rhabarber-Apfel-Grütze

ZUTATEN

300 g Rhabarber
300 g Äpfel
120 g Zucker
1 Limette
250 ml trockener Weißwein
20 g Speisestärke
2 cl Grand Marnier

**Vorbereitungszeit:
10 Minuten
Zubereitungszeit:
25 Minuten**

ZUBEREITUNG

1 Weißwein mit Zucker und etwas Limettensaft aufkochen.

2 Rhabarber und Äpfel putzen, in Stücke schneiden und nacheinander im Weißweinsud weich dünsten.

3 Die Gemüse- und Fruchtstücke entnehmen, Stärke mit Grand Marnier anrühren und, den Sud binden und klar kochen lassen.

4 Rhabarber- und Apfelstücke wieder einlegen und auskühlen lassen.

Frischkäse im Pumpernickelmantel

ZUTATEN
(für ca. 6 Portionen)
100 g Doppelrahmfrischkäse
125 g Speisequark
Salz, Pfeffer
1 rote Paprikaschote
40 g Pinienkerne
1 kl. Bd. Schnittlauch
1 kl. Bd. Petersilie
70 g Pumpernickel
2 cl Korn
1 cl Weinbrand

ZUBEREITUNG

1 Doppelrahmfrischkäse mit dem Speisequark, der gehackten Petersilie und dem geschnittenen Schnittlauch sowie mit Salz und Pfeffer vermischen.

2 Paprikaschote halbieren, waschen und in feine Würfel schneiden.

3 Pinienkerne hacken und rösten.

4 Zutaten unter die Käsemasse geben.

5 Pumpernickel kleinbröseln, mit Korn und Weinbrand mischen und durchziehen lassen.

6 Die eingeweichten Brösel zwischen Klarsichtfolie legen und mit einem Rollholz 0,5 cm dick ausrollen.

7 Die Käsemasse aufstreichen und mit Hilfe der Klarsichtfolie alles zu einer Rolle formen.

8 Die Rolle in Folie einpacken und 2 Stunden kühlen.

9 Danach aufschneiden und mit anderen Käsesorten servieren.

Vorbereitungszeit: 30 Minuten
Zubereitungszeit: 15 Minuten

Vorschlag für ein Sommer-/Herbstbuffet

Terrine mit Rotzungenfilets und Lachsforellen

Spargelkohl und eine leichte Limettencreme

Gemüsegelee mit gepökelter Schweineschulter im geriebenen Teig

Putenvögerl in Tomaten-Kräuter-Püree mit einer Geflügelterrine im Linsenmantel

Eingelegter Tafelspitz mit saurem Paprikagemüse

Fenchel-Honig-Sauce

Brunnenkresse-Sauce

Käse-Obst-Salat

Lauch-Mais-Salat

Käsebutter

Räucherfisch-Butter

Partybrötchen und Laugenstangen

Kalte Kartoffelrahmsuppe

Warmer tannenhonig-gebeizter Lachs
auf Knisterfinken mit Gemüse-Kartoffel-Törtchen

Sauerländer Seildrehermahl

Erdbeer-Riesling-Gelee mit Zitronenjoghurt und Eierlikörsauce

Pistazien-Quarktaschen mit Pflaumen-Mirabellen-Kompott

Terrine mit Rotzungenfilets und Lachsforellen Spargelkohl und eine leichte Limettencreme

ZUTATEN
(für ca. 10 Portionen)

400 g Zanderfilet
150 g Rotzungenfilet
20 g Butter
300 g Lachsforellenfilet
evtl. 1 Eiklar
200 ml Sahne (bei sehr fettem Fischfleisch etwas weniger)
150 g Brokkoli
Salz, Pfeffer Zitronensaft
etwas Cayennepfeffer
evtl. einige Pfefferkörner
50 g klein geschnittene Karotten
20 g grüne Bohnen
10 g Gartenkräuter der Saison

Vorbereitungszeit: 40 Minuten
Zubereitungszeit: 60 Minuten

ZUBEREITUNG

1 Terrinenform mit Klarsichtfolie auslegen.

2 Karotten und Bohnen in feine Stücke schneiden, die Kräuter hacken. Brokkoli in Röschen schneiden und alles (außer den Kräutern) getrennt blanchieren. Kalt abschrecken und auf Küchenkrepp abtrocknen. Der Brokkoli sollte etwas Biß haben.

3 Aus den Zanderfilets und der Sahne (und evtl. 1 Eiklar) in einer Küchenmaschine eine Farce herstellen.

4 Gemüse, gehackte Kräuter und gewürfeltes Rotzungenfilet unter die Farce arbeiten.

5 Das Lachsforellenfilet in dünne Scheiben schneiden, wenn nötig, zwischen Klarsichtfolie plattieren und damit die vorbereitete Terrinenform auslegen.

6 Die Farce in die Terrinenform geben, mit den überlappenden Lachsforellenscheiben bedecken, verschließen und bei 70 Grad C ca. 45 Minuten im Wasserbad garen.

7 Die Terrine mindestens 6 bis 8 Stunden auskühlen lassen, anschließend von außen mit einem Fischgelee bestreichen und die Seiten in gebräunten Mandelscheiben drehen, so daß diese eine Umhüllung bilden.

8 Anschließend nochmals leicht kühlen und danach aufschneiden.

TIP
Als Vorspeise oder Zwischengericht schmecken Terrinen lauwarm serviert besonders gut.

WUSSTEN SIE SCHON?
Spargelkohl ist in Deutschland unter dem Namen Brokkoli bekannt. Brokkoli hat einen um 60 Prozent höheren Vitamin-C-Gehalt als Blumenkohl und das 60fache an Carotin. Violetter Brokkoli ist in Italien sehr beliebt.

Limettencreme

ZUTATEN
40 g Crème fraîche
60 ml Sahne
100 ml Fischfond
Saft von einer Limette
1 Msp. Safran
1 Msp. Cayenne
etwas Arrowroot (Reformhaus)
Salz, Pfeffer, Zucker

ZUBEREITUNG

1 Fischfond mit Safran aufkochen, die Sahne zugeben und leicht mit Salz und Pfeffer würzen.

2 Den Saft der Limette zugeben und das Ganze mit Arrowroot (Pfeilwurzmehl) binden.

3 Auskühlen lassen und alles mit Crème fraîche vollenden.

4 Zum Abrunden evtl. 1 Messerspitze Zucker, Salz und Pfeffer.

Zubereitungszeit: 10 Minuten

WUSSTEN SIE SCHON?

Limetten sind grüne, zitronenähnliche Früchte. Die Form einer Limette ist länglich oval. Die Schale sollte gleichmäßig glänzend sein und ist in der Regel unbehandelt. Eine Frucht enthält 6 bis 7 Prozent Zitronensäure.

TIP

Genau wie beim Backen eine Prise Salz dazugehört, ist bei der Herstellung der Saucen etwas Zucker zum Abrunden nötig.

Gemüsegelee mit gepökelter Schweineschulter im geriebenen Teig

ZUTATEN
(für ca. 10 Portionen)

700 g Schweineschulter gepökelt (vom Fleischer)	
100 g Kochschinken	
100 g durchwachsener Speck	
100 g Karotten	
80 g Brokkoli	
80 g Lauch	
1/2 l Rinderbrühe	
11 Blatt Gelatine	
20 g Butter	
1 Ei	
20 ml Sahne	

ZUTATEN
FÜR GEMÜSEBÜNDEL

50 g Sellerie	
50 g Lauch	
50 g Möhre	
50 g Zwiebel	
30 g Petersilienstengel	

ZUBEREITUNG

1 Die Schweineschulter und den durchwachsenen Speck in Brühe garen. Die Kochzeit beträgt etwa 50 Minuten.

2 Eine halbe Stunde vor Garende das Gemüsebündel dazugeben, anschließend das Fleisch auskühlen lassen und beschweren.

3 Die Karotten waschen, schälen und in kleine Würfel schneiden.

4 Die restlichen Gemüse – außer Lauch – in der Gemüsebrühe blanchieren.

5 Fleisch und Lauch in Würfel schneiden und gut trocknen, danach mit den Gemüsen mischen. Alles vor dem Einfüllen nochmals mit Küchenkrepp gut abtrocknen.

6 Eine gebutterte Pastetenform mit Pastetenteig auskleiden, mit dem Fleisch-Gemüse-Gemisch füllen, mit einer Teigplatte abdecken und gut verschließen.

7 Die Oberfläche mit Teigresten ausgarnieren und zwei Öffnungen ausstechen.

8 Eigelb mit Sahne vermischen und damit den Teig bestreichen.

9 Bei 220 Grad C ca. 30 Minuten backen und auskühlen lassen.

10 Die Gelatine einweichen, in etwas heißem Fond auflösen und zur Rinderbrühe geben.

11 Die Pastete durch die Öffnungen auf dem Teigdeckel mit dem Fond nach und nach auffüllen und erkalten lassen.

TIP

Sollten im Teig Löcher vorhanden sein, diese mit kalter Butter verschließen.

Vorbereitungszeit: 2 Stunden
Zubereitungszeit: 1,5 Stunden

Geriebener Pastetenteig

ZUTATEN

400 g Mehl
2 Eiklar
200 g weiche Butter
20 ml Wasser
1 Eigelb
10 ml Sahne
Salz

ZUBEREITUNG

1 Das Mehl auf den Arbeitstisch sieben.

2 Die Butter zerstückelt hinzugeben und mit den Händen verreiben, so daß Mehl und Butter sich grob mischen.

3 Eine Mulde bilden und alle übrigen Zutaten hineingeben und zu einem glatten Teig verkneten.

4 Teig zu einer Kugel formen, in Klarsichtfolie packen und 1 Stunde kühl stellen.

Zubereitungszeit: 10 Minuten
Zeit des Kühlens: 1 Stunde

Putenvögerl in Tomaten-Kräuter-Püree mit einer Geflügelterrine im Linsenmantel

ZUTATEN
(für ca. 6 Portionen)

- 1 Bd. Basilikum
- 1 Knoblauchzehe
- 60 ml Olivenöl
- schwarzer Pfeffer, Salz, Zucker
- 2 Putenschnitzel (je ca. 125 g)
- 2 dünne Scheiben Schinkenspeck
- 80 g Zwiebel
- 1 kleine Dose geschälte Tomaten
- Balsamico
- Kerbel, Petersilie, Basilikum

Vorbereitungszeit: 15 Minuten
Zubereitungszeit: 25 Minuten

ZUBEREITUNG

1 Basilikumblätter und Knoblauch pürieren. Dabei langsam 30 ml Öl einrühren, pfeffern.

2 Die Schnitzel der Länge nach, Speckscheiben quer halbieren.

3 Die Schnitzel zwischen Klarsichtfolie legen und plattieren, mit Salz und Pfeffer würzen.

4 Das Fleisch mit der Basilikumpaste bestreichen, Speckscheiben einlegen, mit Spießchen feststecken und anbraten.

5 Die Zwiebel schälen, würfeln und im übrigen Olivenöl glasig dünsten.

6 Die Tomaten mit wenig Saft dazugeben, etwas zerdrücken und mit Salz, Pfeffer und Zucker abschmecken.

7 Backofen auf 225 Grad C vorheizen. Die Tomaten in eine feuerfeste Form füllen und die Rouladen hineinsetzen.

8 Auf der Mittelschiene des Ofens 10 bis 15 Minuten garen.

9 Die Vögerl auskühlen lassen.

10 Das erkaltete Tomaten-Kräuterpüree mit Balsamico und Kräutern abschmecken (schmeckt auch lauwarm).

TIP

Rohstoffe wie zartes Fleisch, die plattiert werden, sollten zwischen Folie gelegt werden, damit das Gewebe nicht zu stark zerstört wird.

Geflügelterrine im Linsenmantel

ZUTATEN
(für ca. 6 Portionen)
150 g Geflügelbrustfleisch
170 ml Sahne
50 g Möhren
Kerbel und Kresse je nach Belieben
1 TL rote Pfefferkörner
ca. 70-100 g rote Linsen, gekocht
ca. 50 g dunkelbraune oder gelbe Linsen, gekocht
1/4 l Aspik (Fleischgelee)
Salz, Pfeffer

Vorbereitungszeit: ca. 30 Miuten
Zubereitungszeit: ca. 2 Stunden

ZUBEREITUNG

1 Stellen Sie eine Geflügelfarce her *(siehe Seite 120)*.

2 Die Möhren sehr fein würfeln, die Kräuter hacken und alles zusammen mit den Pfefferkörnern unter die Farce mischen.

3 Eine dreieckige Terrinenform mit Klarsichtfolie auslegen und die Masse einfüllen. Alles bei ca. 70 Grad C im Wasserbad 45-50 Minuten garen.

4 Nach dem Auskühlen die Terrine mit Aspik bestreichen und in den Linsen drehen, bis diese die zwei oberen Seiten voll einhüllen. Nochmals mit Aspik beträufeln und kaltstellen.

Eingelegter Tafelspitz mit saurem Paprikagemüse

ZUTATEN
(für ca. 6 Portionen)

800 g	Tafelspitz (Rinderhüftspitze)
100 g	Lauch
100 g	Möhre
1	Zwiebel
1	Petersilienwurzel
100 g	Sellerie
	Lorbeerblatt, Nelken
	Wacholderbeere, Thymian
1 TL	Bockshornkleesaat

ZUTATEN
FÜR DIE MARINADE

60 ml	Essig
30 ml	Öl
1/2 l	Fleischbrühe
160 g	Gewürzgurken
2	Paprikaschoten, rot/grün
160 g	Tomaten
120 g	Zwiebeln
	Salz, Pfeffer
	eventuell Knoblauch
	Petersilie, Schnittlauch

Vorbereitungszeit: 15 Minuten
Zubereitungszeit: 80 Minuten

TIP

Verwenden Sie für dieses Gericht grobes Salz aus der Salzmühle.

ZUBEREITUNG

1 Den Tafelspitz in Wasser kurz blanchieren.

2 Erneut in heißem Salzwasser ansetzen und leicht köchelnd garen.

3 Lorbeer mit Nelken auf der Zwiebel festspicken, Thymian, Wacholderbeere und geröstete Bockshornkleesaat zu der Bouillon hinzugeben.

4 Eine halbe Stunde vor Garende das zusammengebundene Gemüse (Lauch, Sellerie, Möhre, Petersilienwurzel) zugeben, damit das Aroma erhalten bleibt.

ZUBEREITUNG DER MARINADE

1 Die ausgekühlte Brühe vom Tafelspitz mit Essig mischen.

2 Zwiebeln, Paprika, Gewürzgurken in etwa 1 cm große Würfel schneiden.

3 Die Tomaten abziehen, entkernen und in Würfel schneiden.

4 Die Kräuter waschen und zerkleinern.

5 Alle Zutaten zur Essig-Brühe geben und Öl unterrühren.

6 Mit Salz, Pfeffer und eventuell Knoblauch abschmecken.

7 Den Tafelspitz in dünne, kleine Scheiben schneiden, anrichten, die Marinade darüber geben und über Nacht ziehen lassen.

Fenchel-Honig-Sauce

ZUTATEN
(für ca. 500 ml)

- 300 ml Mayonnaise
- 60 g Crème double oder Crème fraîche
- 70 ml Orangensaft
- (nach Geschmack) 30 ml Grapefruitsaft
- 30 g Honig
- 120 g Fenchel
- Salz, Cayennepfeffer, Zucker
- Orangenlikör
- abgeriebene Schale von Zitronen und Orangen

ZUBEREITUNG

1 Mayonnaise mit Crème fraîche und flüssigem Honig verrühren.

2 Nach und nach Orangen- und Grapefruitsaft dazugeben.

3 Mit den Gewürzen, geriebener Zitronen- und Orangenschale und Orangenlikör abschmecken.

4 Fenchel putzen, schälen, in gleichmäßige Würfel schneiden, blanchieren und unter die Sauce geben.

Zubereitungszeit: 20 Minuten

TIP

Mit blanchierten Orangen- und Zitronenzesten ausgarnieren.

Brunnenkresse-Sauce

ZUTATEN
(für ca. 500 ml)

- 2 Schalotten
- 60 ml Rotweinessig
- 50 ml Limetten- oder Zitronensaft
- 1 TL Dijon-Senf
- 150 ml Sonnenblumenöl
- 100 ml Olivenöl
- 2 Bd. Brunnenkresse
- Salz, Pfeffer, Zucker

ZUBEREITUNG

1 Brunnenkresse wenige Sekunden blanchieren und sofort in Eiswasser geben.

2 Vorsichtig abtropfen lassen und grob wiegen.

3 Schalotten und Knoblauch fein hacken.

4 Essig, Limettensaft und Dijon-Senf verrühren, das Öl dazugeben.

5 Gehackte Brunnenkresse und Schalotten unterrühren und abschmecken.

Zubereitungszeit: 15 Minuten

TIP

Kann auch im Mixer püriert werden, dann erhält man eine grüne Sauce.

Käse-Obst-Salat

ZUTATEN

250 g Gouda
1 Orange
75 g Ananas
1/2 Apfel
75 g blaue Weintrauben
1/2 Banane
125 g Joghurt
etwas Weißwein
125 ml Sahne
Salz, Pfeffer

ZUBEREITUNG

1 Käse und Ananas in 1,5 cm große Würfel schneiden.

2 Orangen filetieren, Weintrauben waschen, halbieren und entkernen.

3 Die Banane pürieren.

4 Aus Joghurt, Weißwein, Bananenpüree, Salz und Pfeffer eine Sauce zubereiten.

5 Käsewürfel und Obst untermengen.

6 Kurz vor dem Servieren die geschlagene Sahne unterheben.

Vorbereitungszeit: 20 Minuten
Zubereitungszeit: 15 Minuten

Lauch-Mais-Salat

ZUTATEN

250 g Lauch, dünne Stangen
150 g Mais
1 Apfel
150 g Kasseler (fertig)
1/4 l Brühe
75 g Schmand
Zitronensaft
Salz, Pfeffer, Zucker

Vorbereitungszeit: 30 Minuten
Zubereitungszeit: 15 Minuten

ZUBEREITUNG

1 Kasseler in Brühe garen, auskühlen lassen und in kleine Würfel schneiden.

2 Lauch putzen, waschen und in halbe, dünne Ringe schneiden.

3 Mais in ein Sieb geben, Maissaft dabei auffangen.

4 Schmand und Maissaft bis zur gewünschten Konsistenz verrühren und mit Salz, Pfeffer und Zucker abschmecken.

5 Äpfel schälen, entkernen, raffeln, mit Zitronensaft beträufeln und unter die Salatsauce mischen.

6 Lauch, Mais und Kasseler dazugeben, gut durchrühren und den Salat im Kühlschrank 24 Stunden lang ziehen lassen.

Käse-butter

ZUTATEN
250 g weiche Butter
150 g Appenzeller
1 Msp. Paprikapulver

ZUBEREITUNG

1 Butter schaumig rühren und mit dem fein geriebenen Appenzeller vermischen.

2 Mit Paprikapulver abschmecken.

Zubereitungszeit: 10 Minuten

Räucherfisch-Butter

ZUTATEN
250 g weiche Butter
100 g Räucherfisch
50 g Forellenfilet (geräuchert)
1 kl. Bd. Dill
Zitrone

ZUBEREITUNG

1 Butter mit dem Räucherfisch und den Forellenfilets in einer Küchenmaschine verarbeiten.

2 Dill zupfen, schneiden und unter die Buttermasse mengen.

3 Mit Zitronensaft abschmecken.

> **TIP**
>
> Lachsabschnitte lassen sich auf diese Weise wirtschaftlich verarbeiten.

Kalte Kartoffelrahmsuppe

ZUTATEN
(für ca. 8 Portionen)

150 g	Staudensellerie
200 g	weißer Lauch
300 g	Kartoffeln
750 ml	Fleischbrühe
100 ml	Sahne
1 Bd.	Schnittlauch
	Salz, Pfeffer, Cayennepfeffer
50 ml	Schmand
	frischer Kerbel
	frische Liebstöckelblätter

Vorbereitungszeit: 20 Minuten
Zubereitungszeit: 40 Minuten

ZUBEREITUNG

1 Staudensellerie, Lauch und Kartoffeln in Würfel schneiden und mit etwas frischem Kerbel, einigen Liebstöckelblättern (vorsichtig) sowie einer Prise Cayennepfeffer in der Fleischbrühe ca. 25 Minuten am Siedepunkt garen.

2 Danach die Suppe mit einem Pürierstab zerkleinern und kalt stellen.

3 Die Sahne und den Schmand in die kalte Suppe rühren und mit etwas grobem Salz aus der Mühle und gemahlenem Pfeffer vollenden.

4 In gekühlte Tassen einfüllen und mit Schnittlauch bestreuen.

5 Bei dieser Art der Herstellung kann die Suppe eine lindgrüne Farbe erhalten.

TIP
An kühleren Tagen kann die Suppe auch warm serviert werden.

Warmer tannenhoniggebeizter Lachs auf Knisterfinken mit Gemüse-Kartoffel-Törtchen

ZUTATEN
(für ca. 12 Portionen)

2 kg	Lachsfilet
300 g	Lauch
200 g	Karotten
200 g	Sellerieknolle
2 kl. Bd.	Petersilie
1 kl. Bd.	Borretsch
4 kl. Bd.	Dill
1 kl. Bd.	Pimpernelle
1 kl. Bd.	Kerbel
300 g	grobes Salz
200 g	Tannenhonig
50 g	Butter

Vorbereitungszeit: 13 Stunden
Zubereitungszeit: 15 Minuten
Backzeit: ca. 4-5 Minuten auf mittlerer Schiene

ZUBEREITUNG

1 Karotten und Sellerie schälen und in feine Würfel schneiden.

2 Den Lauch in feine Streifen schneiden.

3 Das geschnittene Gemüse mit Tannenhonig, gehackten Kräutern und Salz vermengen und auf den Lachsfilets verteilen.

4 Den vorbereiteten Fisch in Klarsichtfolie einschlagen und 12 Stunden ziehen lassen.

5 Die Kräutermasse entfernen und den gebeizten Lachs in Tranchen schneiden.

6 Geklärte Butter mit etwas Honig mischen, die Lachstranchen bestreichen und im Backofen bei 160 Grad C leicht Farbe geben.

Knisterfinken

ZUTATEN

600 g	Stielmus
50 g	Schalotten
30 g	Butter
100 ml	Kalbsfond
50 ml	Sahne
	Salz, Pfeffer, Glutamat

WUSSTEN SIE SCHON?

Knisterfinken, besser bekannt unter dem Namen Stielmus oder Rübstiel, ist ein Stengelgemüse, das gern in Westfalen und im Rheinland gegessen wird. Es werden nur die zarten Blattstiele und kleinste Blätter verarbeitet.

ZUBEREITUNG

1 Die Blätter werden von den Stielen gestreift, Stiele waschen und fein schneiden.

2 Die Schalotten in feine Würfel schneiden.

3 Schalottenwürfel in Butter anschwitzen, Stielmus hinzugeben, anschwitzen, mit Brühe angießen und bei geschlossenem Deckel kurz garen.

4 Sahne angießen und einkochen lassen.

5 Mit Salz und Pfeffer nachschmecken.

Vorbereitungszeit: 15 Minuten
Zubereitungszeit: 10 Minuten

Gemüse-Kartoffel-Törtchen

ZUTATEN
(für ca. 12 Portionen)

800 g Kartoffeln, mehligkochend	
50 g Möhren	
50 g Sellerie	
50 g Lauchzwiebeln	
4 Eigelb	
30 ml Sahne	
30 g Butter	
50 ml Gemüsebrühe	
Salz, Muskat	

ZUBEREITUNG

1 Das Gemüse putzen, schälen und in feine Würfel schneiden.

2 Das Wurzelgemüse in Butter anschwitzen, das Zwiebelgemüse zugeben, mit Gemüsebrühe ablöschen und garziehen lassen.

3 Die geschälten Kartoffeln kochen, abdämpfen und durch eine Kartoffelpresse drücken, mit 2 Eigelben und Gemüsewürfeln mischen und mit Salz und Muskat abschmecken.

4 Die Masse mit Hilfe eines Spritzbeutels mit einer großen Sterntülle auf ein gebuttertes Backblech portionsweise aufspritzen.

5 Eigelb mit Sahne mischen, die Kartoffelrosetten damit bestreichen und im Backofen bei 180 Grad C bräunen lassen.

Vorbereitungszeit: 30 Minuten
Zubereitungszeit: 20 Minuten

Sauerländer Seildrehermahl

ZUTATEN
FÜR DIE FARCE
100 g Geflügelfleisch
125 ml Sahne
Salz, Pfeffer weiß

ZUTATEN
(für ca. 12 Portionen)
750 g Schweinenacken
100 g Kasseler
80 g Geflügelfleisch
100 ml Sahne
50 g Trockenobst,
Pflaumen, Aprikosen, Apfel
Salz, Pfeffer

TIP

Die Farce darf bei der Herstellung nicht zu warm werden, sonst gerinnt das fleischeigene Eiweiß.

Um eine geschmeidige, feine Farce zu erhalten, sollte man die Masse durch ein feines Küchensieb streichen, damit Sehnen und Häute entfernt werden.

Die durchgestrichene Fleischfarce immer kühl halten, auf Eis stellen.

HERSTELLUNG DER GEFLÜGELFARCE

1 Das gekühlte Geflügelfleisch in Stücke schneiden, würzen, durch den Fleischwolf drehen und kühl stellen.

2 Geflügelfleisch in einer Küchenmaschine zerkleinern, anschließend die gut gekühlte Sahne unterarbeiten.

3 Die Geflügelfarce bis zum Gebrauch kalt stellen.

ZUBEREITUNG SEILDREHERMAHL

1 Den Schweinenacken spiralförmig aufschneiden.

2 Das Schweinefleisch ausbreiten, plattieren, mit Salz und Pfeffer würzen.

3 Das Trockenobst in kleine Stücke schneiden und unter die Geflügelfarce mischen. Diese Mischung etwa 1/2 cm dick auf dem Fleisch verstreichen.

4 Das Kasseler in Streifen schneiden, auf der Geflügelfarce verteilen und das Schweinefleisch in die ursprüngliche Form zusammenlegen. Den Braten mit Küchengarn binden und von außen würzen.

5 Den gefüllten Schweinenacken anbraten, anschließend bei 180 Grad C im vorgeheizten Backofen 60 Minuten garen.

6 Hierzu reichen Sie Knisterfinken *(siehe Seite 118)* und Gemüse-Kartoffel-Törtchen *(siehe Seite 119)*.

Vorbereitungszeit: 40 Minuten
Zubereitungszeit: 70 Minuten

Erdbeer-Riesling-Gelee mit Zitronenjoghurt und Eierlikörsauce

ZUTATEN

FÜR ROTES GELEE

(für ca. 8 Portionen)

200 ml Riesling

200 ml Erdbeerwein

8 Blatt Gelatine

(im Sommer 12 bis 14 Blatt)

60 g Zucker

1 Zitrone

150 g Erdbeeren

ZITRONENJOGHURT

300 g Joghurt

80 g Zucker

Zitronenmelisse

etwas Vanillemark

(nach Geschmack)

6 Blatt Gelatine

30 ml Milch

1 Limette

ZUBEREITUNG

1 Riesling und Erdbeerwein mit Zucker erhitzen und mit der eingeweichten, ausgedrückten Gelatine verrühren, anschließend mit Zitronensaft abschmecken. Zwei Drittel der Flüssigkeit in die mit Klarsichtfolie ausgelegte Terrinenform geben und kühlen.

2 Nach 20 Minuten Auskühlzeit die gewürfelten Erdbeeren einsetzen und mit dem Rest des fast kalten, roten Gelees anbinden und erneut kühlen.

3 Für den Zitronenjoghurt die Milch erhitzen, Zucker und die eingeweichte, ausgedrückte Gelatine darin auflösen. Mit etwas Joghurt mischen und zum Rest des Joghurts geben. Die Masse mit Limettensaft abschmecken. Nach Belieben in feine Streifen geschnittene Melisseblätter zugeben.

4 Zitronenjoghurt kurz vor dem Stocken auf den kalten, roten Gelee gießen und erneut mindestens 6 Stunden auskühlen lassen.

Vorbereitungszeit: 30 Minuten
Zubereitungszeit: 60 Minuten

TIP

Gelees lassen sich gut mit einem erhitzten, trockenen Messer schneiden.

Eierlikör-sauce

ZUTATEN

3 Eigelb

40 g Zucker

150 ml Milch

50 ml Sahne

30 ml Eierlikör

1/2 Vanilleschote

Vorbereitungszeit: 10 Minuten
Zubereitungszeit: 30 Minuten

ZUBEREITUNG

1 Die Vanilleschote halbieren, das Vanillemark herauskratzen, mit der Schote zur Milch geben und erhitzen.

2 Eigelbe und Zucker mit dem Schneebesen cremig rühren und rasch die erhitzte Milch unterrühren.

3 Die Mischung auf dem 80 Grad C heißen Wasserbad bis zur Rose abziehen, abkühlen lassen und Eierlikör unterrühren.

4 Kurz vor dem Servieren die geschlagene Sahne unterarbeiten.

TIP

Für eine schnelle Variante der Eierlikörsauce vermengen Sie 2 Teile Crème fraîche mit 1 Teil geschlagene Sahne und 1 Teil Eierlikör. Zur Vollendung 15 g Puderzucker unterheben.

Pistazien-Quarktaschen mit Pflaumen-Mirabellen-Kompott

ZUTATEN
für die Grießgrundmasse
250 ml Milch
25 g Butter
etwas Zitronenabrieb
75 g Grieß
30 g Zucker

ZUBEREITUNG

1 Die Milch mit der Butter, dem Zitronenabrieb und dem Zucker aufkochen. Danach schubweise den Weizengrieß unterrühren und solange auf dem Feuer rühren, bis sich die Masse vom Topfboden löst.

2 Anschließend kaltstellen.

ZUTATEN
für die Quarktaschen
(für ca. 8 Portionen)
250 g Speisequark
60 g Weizenmehl
3 Eier
60 g abgerührte Grießgrundmasse (siehe oben)
etwas Zitrus- oder Vanillearoma
60 g Zucker
40-60 g Krokant und gehackte Pistazien, gemischt
1 cl Mirabellen- oder Pflaumengeist
Butterfett
150 g Rohmarzipan

Vorbereitungszeit: 20 Minuten
Zubereitungszeit: 30 Minuten

ZUBEREITUNG

1 Quark und Mehl mit den Eiern vermischen und gut verrühren, bis eine lockere Masse entsteht.

2 Die Grießmasse unterarbeiten und alles mit den Aromastoffen abschmecken. Sollte die Masse zu fest erscheinen, noch ein Eigelb unterarbeiten.

3 Die Rohmarzipanmasse mit etwas Pflaumen- oder Mirabellengeist kneten, bis sie geschmeidig ist und sich formen läßt.

4 Die Quarkteigmasse ca. 1/2 cm dick ausrollen und rund ausstechen. Nun jeden dieser runden Teigböden mit dem Marzipan füllen und halbmondförmig wie kleine Apfeltaschen einschlagen. Am Rand gut andrücken. Den Rand der Taschen mit Eigelb und Sahne einstreichen.

5 Die Taschen nochmals überpinseln und bei 160-170 Grad C auf mittlerer Schiene im Backofen ca. 10 Minuten backen. Verwenden Sie Backpapier auf dem Ofenblech.

6 Nach dem Backen die Teilchen mit etwas Eiklar am Rand abpinseln und mit der Verschlußseite kurz in die gehackten Krokant-Pistazien tupfen.

Pflaumen-Mirabellen-Kompott

ZUTATEN

150 g entsteinte Pflaumen
150 g entsteinte Mirabellen
80 g Zucker
1-2 EL Pflaumenmus
40 g Gelierzucker
1 cl Rum, Pflaumengeist oder Mirabellenliköre nach Belieben
1 Stück Sternanis
1/4 Zimtstange
150 ml Portwein
Zitronensaft

ZUBEREITUNG

1 Aus Portwein, Zucker und Gewürzen einen Sud bereiten, in den man die Früchte gibt. Danach abgedeckt bei niedriger Temperatur leicht kochen lassen.

2 Sind die Früchte weich, aber mit leichtem Biß, nimmt man sie mit einem Schaumlöffel vorsichtig aus dem Sud.

3 Der Sud wird nun nochmals um die Hälfte eingekocht und mit 1-2 Eßlöffeln fertigem Pflaumenmus leicht gebunden.

4 Die Früchte wieder hinzugeben. Vor dem Servieren den Anisstern und den Zimt entfernen. Mit einigen Spritzern Zitronensaft abrunden.

Vorbereitungszeit: 10 Minuten
Zubereitungszeit: 15 Minuten

Vorschlag für ein Winter-/Weihnachtsbuffet

Sauerländer Bauernpastete und Leberkranz mit einer Sauce von Wiesenchampignons und frischem Estragon auf Linsensalat

Rehrückenfilet mit einer Kaninchen-Pfifferling-Sülze und Schlehensauce

Gefüllte Kalbsröllchen mit Herbsttrompeten, mariniertem Fenchel und Winterlauch

Kalte Hagebuttensauce

Buttermilch-Estragon-Sauce

Roquefortbutter

Petersilien-Schnittlauch-Butter

Wirsingsalat

Salat von Fisch und winterlichen Gemüsen

Rotkohl-Johannisbeeren-Suppe mit Stutenklößchen

Frico von Kaninchen und Schwein im Mangoldblatt serviert, Sherry-Gemüse-Sauce und Kartoffel-Möhren-Hucke

Perlhuhnbrust im Rohschinkenmantel mit gerösteten Nüssen, Apfel-Essig-Sauce und Sauerländer Nudelpickert

Geeister Altenaer Weihnachtskuchen mit eingelegten Kornbirnen und Punschsauce

Mandelcreme mit Weißwein-Zimt-Apfel und Zitronenmelissenschaum

Herzhafter Käserettich

ZUTATEN
FÜR PASTETENTEIG
(siehe Seite 109)

ZUTATEN
FÜR BAUERNPASTETE
(für ca. 10 Portionen)

500 g Schweinefleisch
180 g grüner Speck
200 g Kochschinken
150 g Blutwurst
1 cl Cognac oder Weinbrand
1 cl Madeira
Gewürze: 2 Nelken, 1 Lorbeerblatt, Majoran, Thymian, Piment, Pfefferkörner
2 Wacholderbeeren
Pastetengewürz
2 Eier
50 ml Sahne

**Vorbereitungszeit: 12 Stunden (mit Marinierzeit über Nacht)
Zubereitungszeit: 70 Minuten**

TIP

Je nach Geschmack kann die Blutwurst durch Bauchfleisch oder Kaminrauchwurst ersetzt werden.

Sauerländer Bauernpastete und Leberkranz mit einer Sauce von Wiesenchampignons und frischem Estragon auf Linsensalat

ZUBEREITUNG

1 Pastetenteig herstellen und auskühlen lassen *(siehe Seite 109)*.

2 Schweinefleisch und grünen Speck in 1 cm große Würfel schneiden.

3 Nelken, Lorbeerblatt, Piment, Wacholderbeeren und die Pfefferkörner in einen Gewürzbeutel geben. So können sie bei Bedarf problemlos wieder entnommen werden.

4 Die Majoranblättchen und Thymian mit Cognac und Madeira unter die Fleischstücke mischen. Den Gewürzbeutel einlegen und über Nacht im Kühlhaus marinieren.

5 Nach Entnahme des Gewürzbeutels das Fleisch nach und nach in einer Küchenmaschine grob zerkleinern.

6 Anschließend die Masse gut kühlen.

7 Kochschinken und Blutwurst in Würfel schneiden.

8 Alles gut mischen und – wenn nötig – mit Pastetengewürz nachwürzen.

9 Den Pastetenteig 4 mm dick ausrollen, die Masse brotförmig darauf verteilen und in den Pastetenteig einschlagen.

10 Die Bauernpastete auf ein mit Backpapier belegtes Blech legen, mit Eistreiche (Eigelb und Sahne) einpinseln und bei 200 Grad C im Backofen auf mittlerer Schiene anbacken.

11 Nach 10 Minuten Backzeit abermals einstreichen und bei 160 Grad C 50 bis 60 Minuten fertig backen.

12 Nach dem Auskühlen aufschneiden und mit Sauce und Linsensalat servieren.

Leberkranz

ZUTATEN

(für ca. 18 Portionen)

500 g Schweineleber
600 g grüner Speck
10 Eier
4 Boskopäpfel
4 mittlere Zwiebeln
1 Msp. Pökelsalz
15 g Knoblauch
1 Msp. Thymian
1 Msp. Majoran
1 Msp. Koriander
Pfeffer, Salz
etwas Vanillemark (1/8 Stange)
etwas Zimt
1 cl gute Fleischbrühe
1 cl Cognac
etwas Madeira
etwas Portwein
1-2 Lorbeerblätter
Abrieb 1 Zitrone
300 g Speck
zum Auslegen der Form

ZUBEREITUNG

1 Die Zwiebel, den Knoblauch, die Äpfel schälen und alles in grobe Stücke schneiden. Mit den Kräutern in der Pfanne, ohne Farbe zu nehmen, anschwitzen. Mit etwas Fleischbrühe ablöschen, den Koriander zugeben und vorsichtig einkochen, auskühlen lassen.

2 Die Leber, den in Würfel geschnittenen Speck (ohne Schwarte) und die Apfelmasse durch die mittlere Scheibe des Fleischwolfs geben.

3 Die Masse in einer Küchenmaschine zusammen mit den Eiern nochmals ca. 3 Minuten bearbeiten. Mit etwas Pökelsalz, Salz und dem Vanillemark abschmecken.

4 Den Speck leicht anfrieren lassen und mit einer Aufschnittmaschine in dünne Scheiben schneiden.

5 Die Kranzform mit Speck auslegen, die Farce einfüllen und mit Speck verschließen und im Ofen im Wasserbad ca. 2 Stunden langsam bei 180 Grad C garen. Es empfiehlt sich, unter die Speckscheiben die Lorbeerblätter zu legen, da diese sonst verbrennen.

6 Nach der Garzeit (Kontrolle – klarer Saft auf der Oberfläche der Terrine) diese langsam auskühlen lassen und während dieses Vorgangs mit den Spirituosen beträufeln, so daß das Aroma in den Leberkranz einzieht. Anschließend das Ganze 24 Stunden durchkühlen und bei Gebrauch stürzen und aufschneiden.

Vorbereitungszeit: 50 Minuten
Zeit des Kühlens: 24 Stunden
Zubereitungszeit: 150 Minuten

TIP

Der Leberkranz kann auch mit Gelee überzogen werden.

Sauce von Wiesenchampignons und frischem Estragon

ZUTATEN

30 g Schalotten
20 g Butter
100 g Zuchtchampignons
oder im Sommer
Wiesenchampignons
Thymian nach Bedarf
1/4 Lorbeerblatt
150 ml trockener Weißwein
4 Stengel Estragon
Blattpetersilie
Salz, Pfeffer, Zucker
Zitronensaft
Estragonessig
Geflügelfond
1/4 l Kalbfleischsauce
200 g Mascarpone

TIP

Man kann die Blätter des Estragons und der Petersilie ganz als Garnitur verwenden oder sie vorher fein schneiden und unter die Sauce geben.

Vorbereitungszeit: 20 Minuten
Zubereitungszeit: 30 Minuten

ZUBEREITUNG

1 Die Schalotten in feine Würfel schneiden.

2 Die Champignons putzen, die Blätter vom Estragon und von der Blattpetersilie abzupfen.

3 Aus den Champignon-, Estragon- und Petersilienstielen mit Weißwein, Geflügelbrühe, Zucker und Lorbeerblatt einen Fond kochen und durch ein Sieb seihen.

4 Schalottenwürfel und die geputzten, fein geschnittenen Champignons kurz anschwitzen und mit dem Sud auffüllen, die Kalbfleischsauce zugeben und alles um die Hälfte einkochen.

5 Nach dem Auskühlen mit Estragonessig, Zitronensaft, Salz, Pfeffer und Zucker abschmecken und mit Mascarpone vollenden.

Linsensalat

ZUTATEN

400 ml Gemüsefond
350 g rote Linsen
Salz, Pfeffer
100 g geräucherter Speck
8 EL Öl
250 g rote Zwiebeln
5 EL Obstessig
50 g Walnüsse
oder Haselnüsse

Vorbereitungszeit: 15 Minuten
Zubereitungszeit: 30 Minuten

ZUBEREITUNG

1 Den Fond aufkochen, die Linsen hineingeben und bei milder Hitze im offenen Topf garziehen lassen.

2 Mit Salz und Pfeffer würzen.

3 Speckwürfel braten und abtropfen lassen.

4 Essig mit Salz, Pfeffer und Öl verrühren und die in feine Würfel geschnittenen Zwiebeln zufügen.

5 Die Linsen in einem Durchschlag abtropfen lassen und noch warm unter die Salatsauce rühren.

6 Mit Speckwürfeln und gehackten Nüssen bestreuen.

Rehrückenfilet mit einer Kaninchen-Pfifferling-Sülze und Schlehensauce

ZUTATEN

250 g Kaninchenrückenfilet
150 g Rehrückenfilet (pariert)
30 ml Weißwein
150 g kleine Pfifferlinge
50 g Schalotten
300 ml geklärte Wildbrühe
8-10 Blatt Gelatine
Salz, Pfeffer
einige Salbeiblätter
Bratfett

Vorbereitungszeit: 30 Minuten
Zubereitungszeit: 30 Minuten
Zeit des Kühlens: 6 Stunden

ZUBEREITUNG

1 Eine Kastenform mit Klarsichtfolie auslegen.

2 Das Kaninchenfleisch würfeln, würzen und kurz anbraten, mit Weißwein ablöschen und mit Salbeiblättern aromatisieren. Das Fleisch garziehen und auskühlen lassen.

3 Die Pfifferlinge säubern, kurz mit den Schalottenwürfeln in der Pfanne anbraten und mit etwas Wildbrühe ablöschen.

4 Die Pfifferlinge nach dem Auskühlen mit dem Kaninchenfleisch mischen.

5 Gelatine in etwas kalter Wildbrühe quellen lassen, den restlichen Wildfond erhitzen und zur eingeweichten Gelatine geben.

6 Um einen Geliermantel zu gießen, setzt man die Kastenform in gestoßenes Eis, gibt die Flüssigkeit hinein, läßt diese leicht anziehen und gießt die überschüssige Wildbrühe wieder ab.

7 Wenn der Gelee fest ist, gibt man das Fleisch-Pilz-Gemisch in den inneren Teil des Geleemantels und gießt nach und nach unter zwischenzeitlichem Kühlen die Kastenform auf.

8 Den Gelee je nach Größe der Kastenform bis zu 6 Stunden durchkühlen lassen.

9 Das Rehrückenfilet würzen, rosa braten und auskühlen und auskühlen lassen.

10 Anschließend in Tranchen schneiden auf einem vorbereiteten Sockel anrichten und ausgarnieren.

TIP

Die Kaninchen-Pfifferling-Sülze kann auch in kleine Portionsförmchen gefüllt werden.

Herstellung von Wildbrühe für Wildgelee

ZUTATEN

500 g	Wildknochen
500 g	Fleischabschnitte vom Reh oder Hirsch
80 g	Bratfett
50 g	Möhre
50 g	Sellerie
50 g	Lauch
80 g	Zwiebel
150 ml	trockener Weißwein
2 l	Wasser
50 ml	Madeira
50 ml	Sherry, trocken

Gewürze für den Gewürzbeutel:

- 5 zerdrückte Wacholderbeeren
- 5 g weißer, geschroteter Pfeffer
- 1 Lorbeerblatt
- 2 Pimentkörner
- 1/4 Salbeiblatt
- 1/2 Zweig Rosmarin
- etwas gerösteter Koriander
- Zesten von einer unbehandelten Orange

Herstellungszeit: 3 Stunden

ZUBEREITUNG

1 Die Wildknochen hacken und zusammen mit den Fleischabschnitten bei 180 Grad C in der Bratröhre braun rösten.

2 Nun das geschälte, klein geschnittene Wurzelgemüse dazugeben, mitrösten und ebenfalls Farbe nehmen lassen.

3 Das Zwiebelgemüse zugeben, nur kurz durchschwitzen (damit es nicht bitter wird), mit etwas Weißwein ablöschen und einkochen lassen. Diesen Ablöschvorgang dreimal wiederholen.

4 Den Ansatz mit Wasser auffüllen und den Gewürzbeutel hinzugeben.

5 Etwas über dem Siedepunkt halten (starkes Kochen würde trüben), anschließend entfetten. Die Brühe um die Hälfte einkochen.

6 Danach durch ein Sieb mit einem Seihtuch oder großen Kaffeefilter geben und auskühlen lassen.

7 Den kalten Fond nochmals durch ein Tuch geben (kaltes Fett wird so völlig entfernt), anschließend mit Madeira und Sherry abschmecken.

ZUTATEN

für das Klären von 1 l Wildbrühe

200 g	Wildfleisch (Hesse)
1 l	Wildbrühe
2	Eiklar
50 ml	Wasser
35 g	Sellerie
35 g	Möhren
25 g	Lauch
	wenn nötig, etwas Salz und typische Wildgewürze

Herstellungszeit: 3 Stunden

ZUBEREITUNG

1 Das Wildfleisch wird durch die grobe Scheibe des Fleischwolfs gegeben.

2 Das Gemüse waschen und in etwa 5 mm große Würfel schneiden.

3 Eiklar und Wasser werden mit einem Schneebesen gut verrührt.

4 Nun alle Zutaten vermengen und für 20 Minuten in den Kühlschrank stellen.

5 Die kalte, entfettete Brühe mit dem Klärfleisch vermengen und auf dem Ofen langsam unter zeitweiligem Rühren aufkochen und das aufsteigende Eiweiß mit Hilfe eines Löffels entfernen.

6 Diese Brühe nun noch 1 1/2 Stunden ziehen lassen, um den Geschmack zu stärken.

7 Anschließend wird die Brühe durch ein Passiertuch gegeben. Man sollte dieses vorsichtig mit Hilfe einer Schöpfkelle ausführen und dabei darauf achten, daß die gebundenen Trübstoffe nicht wieder in die Brühe gelangen.

8 Nach dem Klären wird die benötigte Menge Aspik zugegeben, um einen schnittfesten Wildaspik zu bekommen.

Schlehensauce

ZUTATEN

80 g Crème fraîche
60 g Schlehen
200 g Pfifferlingsabschnitte oder andere Pilzreste der Jahreszeit
Öl zum Anbraten
20 g Schalottenwürfel
1/8 l braune Wildsauce
Cassislikör
Salz, Pfeffer
2 cl Schlehenfeuer

Vorbereitungszeit: 15 Minuten
Zubereitungszeit: 20 Minuten

ZUBEREITUNG

1 Pfifferlinge und Pilzabschnitte mit den Schalotten anbraten und mit der Wildsauce ablöschen.

2 Alles bis zur Hälfte einkochen, anschließend mit dem Mixstab pürieren.

3 Mit Crème fraîche auffüllen, nochmals einkochen und mit etwas Cassislikör und Schlehenfeuer abschmecken.

4 Auskühlen lassen und vor Gebrauch mit einem kleinen Schuß Brühe in die nötige Konsistenz bringen. Schlehen unterziehen und servieren.

TIP

Im Winter können Sie eingeweichte Trockenpilze verwenden.

Gefüllte Kalbsröllchen mit Herbsttrompeten, mariniertem Fenchel und Winterlauch

ZUTATEN
FÜR DIE KALBSRÖLLCHEN
(für ca. 6 Portionen)

500 g	Kalbfleisch (Nuß oder Oberschale)
125 g	Schweinemett
80 g	Herbsttrompeten
30 g	Zwiebeln
50 g	Karotten
1/2 Bd.	Schnittlauch
	etwas Knoblauch
	Pastetengewürz
150 g	Blattspinat oder Wirsingblätter
50 ml	Weißwein
100 ml	Kalbsbrühe
1 Zweig	Thymian
	Salz, Pfeffer
	Öl zum Braten
15 g	Aspik oder Gelatine
100 g	Sesamsamen, hell

Vorbereitungszeit: 60 Minuten
Zubereitungszeit: 45-50 Minuten

WUSSTEN SIE SCHON?

Die Herbsttrompete nennt man auch Kraterpilz oder Totentrompete. Sie ist sehr sandig und sollte deshalb immer halbiert gewaschen werden. Der Fruchtkörper ist 4 bis 10 cm hoch und wächst vor allem in Buchenwäldern. Der würzig schmeckende Pilz ist ab August bis Oktober zu finden.

ZUBEREITUNG

1 Aus dem Fleisch 6 Schnitzel schneiden und diese zwischen Klarsichtfolie auf die gewünschte Stärke klopfen, mit wenig Salz und Pfeffer würzen, da das Fleisch noch gefüllt wird.

2 Zwiebeln mit Herbsttrompeten in heißem Fett anbraten und mit gegarten Karottenwürfeln, fein geschnittenem Schnittlauch und nach Geschmack mit etwas fein gewürfeltem Knoblauch vermengen und unter das Schweinemett geben. Die Masse gut durchmengen und mit Salz und Pastetengewürz abschmecken.

3 Danach die Wirsing- oder Spinatblätter ca. 15 Sekunden blanchieren und in Eiswasser abschrecken, auf Küchenkrepp abtrocknen.

4 Die Gemüseblätter auf das vorbereitete Kalbfleisch legen und das Schweinemett gleichmäßig mit einer Palette aufstreichen, vorsichtig aufrollen und die Nahtstelle jeder Roulade mit einem Zahnstocher verschließen.

5 Die Kalbsröllchen von außen mit Salz und Pfeffer würzen, kurz in Fett anbraten, mit Weißwein ablöschen, Thymian hinzugeben, mit Kalbsbrühe angießen und zugedeckt bei 180 Grad C ca. 20 Minuten garen.

6 Die Kalbsröllchen gut durchkühlen. Die eingeweichte, ausgedrückte Gelatine in die warme Kalbsbrühe geben, etwas auskühlen lassen und damit die Kalbsröllchen einstreichen.

7 Sesamsamen ohne Fett hellbraun rösten und die Kalbsröllchen darin wälzen. Die obere und untere Kante der Rouladen abschneiden, Kalbsröllchen halbieren und anrichten.

TIP

Servieren Sie beide Hälften des Röllchens aufrechtstehend, damit die Füllung gut sichtbar ist.

Marinierter Fenchel

ZUTATEN

4 Fenchelknollen
100 ml Gemüsebrühe
100 ml trockener Weißwein
2 Strauchtomaten
2 Lorbeerblätter
60 ml Olivenöl
15 ml Kräuteressig (mild)
Salz, Pfeffer
Zucker
1-2 EL Pernod

Vorbereitungszeit: 20 Minuten
Zubereitungszeit: 30 Minuten

ZUBEREITUNG

1 Fenchel putzen und vierteln, das Fenchelgrün aufbewahren und mit Brühe, Wein und Lorbeerblatt in einen flachen Kochtopf geben.

2 Aufkochen und etwa 10 bis 15 Minuten ohne Deckel köcheln lassen, bis die Flüssigkeit zur Hälfte eingekocht ist. Danach den Fenchel bis zum Fertiggaren in der restlichen Brühe auskühlen lassen.

3 Die Tomaten blanchieren, abziehen und das Tomatenfleisch in 1 cm große Stücke schneiden.

4 Aus Essig, etwas Fenchelfond, Salz, Pfeffer, Zucker, Pernod und Olivenöl eine Marinade herstellen, mit dem Fenchel und den Tomatenwürfeln mischen und ziehen lassen.

5 Das Fenchelgrün grob schneiden und die Marinade damit vollenden.

HANDBOOK OF POLYMER CRYSTALLIZATION

Edited by

EWA PIORKOWSKA
Centre of Molecular and Macromolecular Studies
Polish Academy of Sciences
Lodz, Poland

GREGORY C. RUTLEDGE
Department of Chemical Engineering
Massachusetts Institute of Technology
Cambridge, MA

Copyright © 2013 by John Wiley & Sons, Inc. All rights reserved.

Published by John Wiley & Sons, Inc., Hoboken, New Jersey.
Published simultaneously in Canada.

No part of this publication may be reproduced, stored in a retrieval system, or transmitted in any form or by any means, electronic, mechanical, photocopying, recording, scanning, or otherwise, except as permitted under Section 107 or 108 of the 1976 United States Copyright Act, without either the prior written permission of the Publisher, or authorization through payment of the appropriate per-copy fee to the Copyright Clearance Center, Inc., 222 Rosewood Drive, Danvers, MA 01923, (978) 750-8400, fax (978) 750-4470, or on the web at www.copyright.com. Requests to the Publisher for permission should be addressed to the Permissions Department, John Wiley & Sons, Inc., 111 River Street, Hoboken, NJ 07030, (201) 748-6011, fax (201) 748-6008, or online at http://www.wiley.com/go/permissions.

Limit of Liability/Disclaimer of Warranty: While the publisher and author have used their best efforts in preparing this book, they make no representations or warranties with respect to the accuracy or completeness of the contents of this book and specifically disclaim any implied warranties of merchantability or fitness for a particular purpose. No warranty may be created or extended by sales representatives or written sales materials. The advice and strategies contained herein may not be suitable for your situation. You should consult with a professional where appropriate. Neither the publisher nor author shall be liable for any loss of profit or any other commercial damages, including but not limited to special, incidental, consequential, or other damages.

For general information on our other products and services or for technical support, please contact our Customer Care Department within the United States at (800) 762-2974, outside the United States at (317) 572-3993 or fax (317) 572-4002.

Wiley also publishes its books in a variety of electronic formats. Some content that appears in print may not be available in electronic formats. For more information about Wiley products, visit our web site at www.wiley.com.

Library of Congress Cataloging-in-Publication Data:

Handbook of polymer crystallization / edited by Ewa Piorkowska, Polish Academy of Sciences, Centre of Molecular and Macromolecular Studies, Lodz, Poland and Gregory C. Rutledge, Massachusetts Institute of Technology, Department of Chemical Engineering, Cambridge, MA, USA.
    pages cm
  Includes index.
  ISBN 978-0-470-38023-9 (cloth)
1. Crystalline polymers. I. Piorkowska, Ewa, editor of compilation. II. Rutledge, Gregory Charles, editor of compilation.
  QD382.C78H36 2013
  547′.7–dc23
                    2012037881

Printed in the United States of America.

10 9 8 7 6 5 4 3 2 1

CONTENTS

Preface xiii

Contributors xv

1 Experimental Techniques 1
Benjamin S. Hsiao, Feng Zuo, and Yimin Mao, Christoph Schick

  1.1 Introduction, 1
  1.2 Optical Microscopy, 2
    1.2.1 Reflection and Transmission Microscopy, 2
    1.2.2 Contrast Modes, 2
    1.2.3 Selected Applications, 3
  1.3 Electron Microscopy, 5
    1.3.1 Imaging Principle, 5
    1.3.2 Sample Preparation, 6
    1.3.3 Relevant Experimental Techniques, 7
    1.3.4 Selected Applications, 8
  1.4 Atomic Force Microscopy, 9
    1.4.1 Imaging Principle, 9
    1.4.2 Scanning Modes, 9
    1.4.3 Comparison between AFM and EM, 10
    1.4.4 Recent Development: Video AFM, 10
    1.4.5 Selected Applications, 10
  1.5 Nuclear Magnetic Resonance, 12
    1.5.1 Chemical Shift, 13
    1.5.2 Relevant Techniques, 13
    1.5.3 Recent Development: Multidimensional NMR, 14
    1.5.4 Selected Applications, 14
  1.6 Scattering Techniques: X-Ray, Light, and Neutron, 15
    1.6.1 Wide-Angle X-Ray Diffraction, 15
    1.6.2 Small-Angle X-Ray Scattering, 17
    1.6.3 Small-Angle Light Scattering, 19
    1.6.4 Small-Angle Neutron Scattering, 21
  1.7 Differential Scanning Calorimetry, 22
    1.7.1 Modes of Operation, 22
    1.7.2 Determination of Degree of Crystallinity, 25

1.8 Summary, 25
Acknowledgments, 26
References, 26

2 Crystal Structures of Polymers 31
Claudio De Rosa and Finizia Auriemma

2.1 Constitution and Configuration of Polymer Chains, 31
2.2 Conformation of Polymer Chains in Crystals and Conformational Polymorphism, 33
2.3 Packing of Macromolecules in Polymer Crystals, 43
2.4 Symmetry Breaking, 49
2.5 Packing Effects on the Conformation of Polymer Chains in the Crystals: The Case of Aliphatic Polyamides, 50
2.6 Defects and Disorder in Polymer Crystals, 55
    2.6.1 Substitutional Isomorphism of Different Chains, 56
    2.6.2 Substitutional Isomorphism of Different Monomeric Units, 57
    2.6.3 Conformational Isomorphism, 58
    2.6.4 Disorder in the Stacking of Ordered Layers (Stacking Fault Disorder), 58
2.7 Crystal Habits, 60
    2.7.1 Rounded Lateral Habits, 66
Acknowledgments, 67
References, 67

3 Structure of Polycrystalline Aggregates 73
Buckley Crist

3.1 Introduction, 73
3.2 Crystals Grown from Solution, 75
    3.2.1 Facetted Monolayer Crystals from Dilute Solution, 75
    3.2.2 Dendritic Crystals from Dilute Solution, 81
    3.2.3 Growth Spirals in Dilute Solution, 85
    3.2.4 Concentrated Solutions, 92
3.3 Crystals and Aggregates Grown from Molten Films, 94
    3.3.1 Structures in Thin Films, 94
    3.3.2 Structures in Ultrathin Films, 98
    3.3.3 Edge-On Lamellae in Molten Films, 102
3.4 Spherulitic Aggregates, 104
    3.4.1 Optical Properties of Spherulites, 105
    3.4.2 Occurrence of Spherulites, 108
    3.4.3 Development of Spherulites, 110
    3.4.4 Banded Spherulites and Lamellar Twist, 116
Acknowledgments, 121
References, 121

4 Polymer Nucleation 125
Kiyoka N. Okada and Masamichi Hikosaka

4.1 Introduction, 126
4.2 Classical Nucleation Theory, 126
    4.2.1 Nucleation Rate (I), 126
    4.2.2 Free Energy for Formation of a Nucleus $\Delta G(N)$, 127

4.2.3 Free Energy for Formation of a Critical Nucleus (ΔG^*), 127
4.2.4 Shape of a Nucleus Is Related to Kinetic Parameters, 128
4.2.5 Diffusion, 128
4.3 Direct Observation of Nano-Nucleation by Synchrotron Radiation, 128
4.3.1 Introduction and Experimental Procedure, 128
4.3.2 Observation of Nano-Nucleation by SAXS, 128
4.3.3 Extended Guinier Plot Method and Iteration Method, 129
4.3.4 Kinetic Parameters and Size Distribution of the Nano-Nucleus, 130
4.3.5 Real Image of Nano-Nucleation, 131
4.3.6 Supercooling Dependence of Nano-nucleation, 133
4.3.7 Relationship between Nano-Nucleation and Macro-Crystallization, 133
4.4 Improvement of Nucleation Theory, 135
4.4.1 Introduction, 135
4.4.2 Nucleation Theory Based on Direct Observation of Nucleation, 135
4.4.3 Confirmation of the Theory by Overall Crystallinity, 137
4.5 Homogeneous Nucleation from the Bulk Melt under Elongational Flow, 139
4.5.1 Introduction and Case Study, 139
4.5.2 Formulation of Elongational Strain Rate $\dot{\varepsilon}$, 139
4.5.3 Nano-Oriented Crystals, 140
4.5.4 Evidence of Homogeneous Nucleation, 144
4.5.5 Nano-Nucleation Results in Ultrahigh Performance, 147
4.6 Heterogeneous Nucleation, 148
4.6.1 Introduction, 148
4.6.2 Experimental, 149
4.6.3 Role of Epitaxy in Heterogeneous Nucleation, 150
4.6.4 Acceleration Mechanism of Nucleation of Polymers by Nano-Sizing of Nucleating Agent, 153
4.7 Effect of Entanglement Density on the Nucleation Rate, 156
4.7.1 Introduction and Experimental, 156
4.7.2 Increase of v_e Leads to a Decrease of I, 157
4.7.3 Change of v_e with Δt, 158
4.7.4 Two-Step Entangling Model, 159
4.8 Conclusion, 160
Acknowledgments, 161
References, 161

5 Growth of Polymer Crystals   165

Kohji Tashiro

5.1 Introduction, 165
5.1.1 Complex Behavior of Polymers, 165
5.2 Growth of Polymer Crystals from Solutions, 167
5.2.1 Single Crystals, 167
5.2.2 Crystallization from Solution under Shear, 168
5.2.3 Solution Casting Method, 168
5.3 Growth of Polymer Crystals from Melt, 169
5.3.1 Positive and Negative Spherulites, 169
5.3.2 Spherulite Morphology and Crystalline Modification, 170
5.3.3 Spherulite Patterns of Blend Samples, 172

- 5.4 Crystallization Mechanism of Polymer, 173
  - 5.4.1 Basic Theory of Crystallization of Polymer, 173
  - 5.4.2 Growth Rate of Spherulites, 177
- 5.5 Microscopically Viewed Structural Evolution in the Growing Polymer Crystals, 178
  - 5.5.1 Experimental Techniques, 178
  - 5.5.2 Structural Evolution in Isothermal Crystallization, 179
  - 5.5.3 Shear-Induced Crystallization of the Melt, 186
- 5.6 Crystallization upon Heating from the Glassy State, 189
  - 5.6.1 Cold Crystallization, 189
  - 5.6.2 Solvent-Induced Crystallization of Polymer Glass, 189
- 5.7 Crystallization Phenomenon Induced by Tensile Force, 191
- 5.8 Photoinduced Formation and Growth of Polymer Crystals, 191
- 5.9 Conclusion, 192
- References, 193

6 Computer Modeling of Polymer Crystallization 197
Gregory C. Rutledge

- 6.1 Introduction, 197
- 6.2 Methods, 198
  - 6.2.1 Molecular Dynamics, 199
  - 6.2.2 Langevin Dynamics, 200
  - 6.2.3 Monte Carlo, 200
  - 6.2.4 Kinetic Monte Carlo, 201
- 6.3 Single-Chain Behavior in Crystallization, 202
  - 6.3.1 Solid-on-Solid Models, 202
  - 6.3.2 Molecular and Langevin Dynamics, 203
- 6.4 Crystallization from the Melt, 204
  - 6.4.1 Lattice Monte Carlo Simulations, 205
  - 6.4.2 Molecular Dynamics Using Coarse-Grained Models, 206
  - 6.4.3 Molecular Dynamics Using Atomistic Models, 207
- 6.5 Crystallization under Deformation or Flow, 208
- 6.6 Concluding Remarks, 210
- References, 211

7 Overall Crystallization Kinetics 215
Ewa Piorkowska and Andrzej Galeski

- 7.1 Introduction, 215
- 7.2 Measurements, 216
- 7.3 Simulation, 217
- 7.4 Theories: Isothermal and Nonisothermal Crystallization, 218
  - 7.4.1 Introductory Remarks, 218
  - 7.4.2 Extended Volume Approach, 218
  - 7.4.3 Probabilistic Approaches, 220
  - 7.4.4 Isokinetic Model, 223
  - 7.4.5 Rate Equations, 223
- 7.5 Complex Crystallization Conditions: General Models, 224
- 7.6 Factors Influencing the Overall Crystallization Kinetics, 224
  - 7.6.1 Crystallization in a Uniform Temperature Field, 224
  - 7.6.2 Crystallization in a Temperature Gradient, 225
  - 7.6.3 Crystallization in a Confined Space, 226
  - 7.6.4 Flow-Induced Crystallization, 228

7.7 Analysis of Crystallization Data, 230
    7.7.1 Isothermal Crystallization, 230
    7.7.2 Nonisothermal Crystallization, 231
7.8 Conclusions, 233
References, 234

8 Epitaxial Crystallization of Polymers: Means and Issues   237
Annette Thierry and Bernard A. Lotz

8.1 Introduction and History, 237
8.2 Means of Investigation of Epitaxial Crystallization, 239
    8.2.1 Global Techniques, 239
    8.2.2 Thin Film Techniques, 239
    8.2.3 Sample Preparation Techniques, 240
    8.2.4 Other Samples and Investigation Procedures, 241
8.3 Epitaxial Crystallization of Polymers, 241
    8.3.1 General Principles, 241
    8.3.2 Epitaxial Crystallization of "Linear" Polymers, 243
    8.3.3 Epitaxy of Helical Polymers, 245
    8.3.4 Polymer/Polymer Epitaxy, 250
8.4 Epitaxial Crystallization: Further Issues and Examples, 252
    8.4.1 Topographic versus Lattice Matching, 252
    8.4.2 Epitaxy of Isotactic Polypropylene on Isotactic Polyvinylcyclohexane, 254
    8.4.3 Epitaxy Involving Fold Surfaces of Polymer Crystals, 254
8.5 Epitaxial Crystallization: Some Issues and Applications, 256
    8.5.1 Epitaxial Crystallization and the Design of New Nucleating Agents, 256
    8.5.2 Epitaxial Crystallization and the Design of Composite Materials, 257
    8.5.3 Conformational and Packing Energy Analysis of Polymer Epitaxy, 258
    8.5.4 Epitaxy as a Means to Generate Oriented Opto- or Electroactive Materials, 259
8.6 Conclusions, 260
References, 262

9 Melting   265
Marek Pyda

9.1 Introduction to the Melting of Polymer Crystals, 265
9.2 Parameters of the Melting Process, 267
9.3 Change of Conformation, 268
9.4 Heat of Fusion and Degree of Crystallinity, 270
    9.4.1 Heat of Fusion, 270
    9.4.2 Degree of Crystallinity, 272
9.5 Equilibrium Melting, 274
    9.5.1 The Equilibrium Melting Temperature, 274
    9.5.2 The Equilibrium Thermodynamic Functions, 275
9.6 Other Factors Affecting the Melting Process of Polymer Crystals, 277
    9.6.1 The Influence of the Polymer's Chemical Structure on the Melting Process, 277
    9.6.2 The Effect of Polymer Molar Mass on the Melting Behavior, 277
    9.6.3 Influence of Heating Rate on the Melting, 278

9.6.4 Multiple Melting Peaks of Polymers, 279
9.6.5 Influence of Pressure on the Melting Process, 281
9.6.6 The Melting Process by Other Methods, 281
9.6.7 Diluents Effect: The Influence of Small Diluents on the Melting Process, 282
9.7 Irreversible and Reversible Melting, 282
9.8 Conclusions, 284
References, 285

10 Crystallization of Polymer Blends   287
Mariano Pracella

10.1 General Introduction, 287
10.2 Thermodynamics of Polymer Blends, 288
    10.2.1 General Principles, 288
10.3 Miscible Polymer Blends, 290
    10.3.1 Introduction, 290
    10.3.2 Phase Morphology, 291
    10.3.3 Crystal Growth Rate, 292
    10.3.4 Overall Crystallization Kinetics, 294
    10.3.5 Melting Behavior, 295
    10.3.6 Blends with Partial Miscibility, 296
    10.3.7 Crystallization Behavior of Amorphous/Crystalline Blends, 297
    10.3.8 Crystallization Behavior of Crystalline/Crystalline Blends, 298
10.4 Immiscible Polymer Blends, 303
    10.4.1 Introduction, 303
    10.4.2 Morphology and Crystal Nucleation, 303
    10.4.3 Crystal Growth Rate, 304
    10.4.4 Crystallization Behavior of Immiscible Blends, 305
10.5 Compatibilized Polymer Blends, 307
    10.5.1 Compatibilization Methods, 307
    10.5.2 Morphology and Phase Interactions, 308
    10.5.3 Crystallization Behavior of Compatibilized Blends, 311
10.6 Polymer Blends with Liquid-Crystalline Components, 314
    10.6.1 Introduction, 314
    10.6.2 Mesomorphism and Phase Transition Behavior of Liquid Crystals and Liquid Crystal Polymers, 314
    10.6.3 Crystallization Behavior of Polymer/LC Blends, 316
    10.6.4 Crystallization Behavior of Polymer/LCP Blends, 317
10.7 Concluding Remarks, 320
Abbreviations, 321
References, 322

11 Crystallization in Copolymers   327
Sheng Li and Richard A. Register

11.1 Introduction, 327
11.2 Crystallization in Statistical Copolymers, 328
    11.2.1 Flory's Model, 328
    11.2.2 Solid-State Morphology, 330
    11.2.3 Mechanical Properties, 334
    11.2.4 Crystallization Kinetics, 335
    11.2.5 Statistical Copolymers with Two Crystallizable Units, 337
    11.2.6 Crystallization Thermodynamics, 337

11.3 Crystallization of Block Copolymers from Homogeneous or Weakly Segregated Melts, 340
    11.3.1 Solid-State Morphology, 340
    11.3.2 Crystallization-Driven Structure Formation, 342
11.4 Summary, 343
References, 344

12 Crystallization in Nano-Confined Polymeric Systems   347

Alejandro J. Müller, Maria Luisa Arnal, and Arnaldo T. Lorenzo

12.1 Introduction, 347
12.2 Confined Crystallization in Block Copolymers, 348
    12.2.1 Crystallization within Diblock Copolymers that are Strongly Segregated or Miscible and Contain only One Crystallizable Component, 351
    12.2.2 Crystallization within Strongly Segregated Double-Crystalline Diblock Copolymers and Triblock Copolymers, 355
12.3 Crystallization of Droplet Dispersions and Polymer Layers, 361
12.4 Polymer Blends, 368
    12.4.1 Immiscible Polymer Blends, 368
    12.4.2 Melt Miscible Blends, 371
12.5 Modeling of Confined Crystallization of Macromolecules, 371
12.6 Conclusions, 372
References, 372

13 Crystallization in Polymer Composites and Nanocomposites   379

Ewa Piorkowska

13.1 Introduction, 379
13.2 Microcomposites with Particulate Fillers, 380
13.3 Fiber-Reinforced Composites, 382
13.4 Modeling of Crystallization in Fiber-Reinforced Composites, 385
13.5 Nanocomposites, 388
13.6 Conclusions, 393
Appendix, 393
References, 394

14 Flow-Induced Crystallization   399

Gerrit W.M. Peters, Luigi Balzano, and Rudi J.A. Steenbakkers

14.1 Introduction, 399
14.2 Shear-Induced Crystallization, 401
    14.2.1 Nature of Crystallization Precursors, 405
14.3 Crystallization during Drawing, 407
    14.3.1 Spinning, 408
    14.3.2 Elongation-Induced Crystallization; Lab Conditions, 409
14.4 Models of Flow-Induced Crystallization, 410
    14.4.1 Flow-Enhanced Nucleation, 411
    14.4.2 Flow-Induced Shish Formation, 419
    14.4.3 Application to Injection Molding, 421
14.5 Concluding Remarks, 426
References, 427

15 Crystallization in Processing Conditions 433
Jean-Marc Haudin

- 15.1 Introduction, 433
- 15.2 General Effects of Processing Conditions on Crystallization, 433
    - 15.2.1 Effects of Flow, 433
    - 15.2.2 Effects of Pressure, 435
    - 15.2.3 Effects of Cooling Rate, 436
    - 15.2.4 Effects of a Temperature Gradient, 437
    - 15.2.5 Effects of Surfaces, 439
- 15.3 Modeling, 440
    - 15.3.1 General Framework, 440
    - 15.3.2 Simplified Expressions, 441
    - 15.3.3 General Systems of Differential Equations, 441
- 15.4 Crystallization in Some Selected Processes, 442
    - 15.4.1 Cast Film Extrusion, 442
    - 15.4.2 Fiber Spinning, 445
    - 15.4.3 Film Blowing, 448
    - 15.4.4 Injection Molding, 454
- 15.5 Conclusion, 458
- References, 459

Index 463

PREFACE

Synthetic thermoplastic polymers form an important class of materials that has expanded dramatically over the past half century, finding utility in a variety of end-use applications. Thermoplastics comprise amorphous polymers that are unable to crystallize and polymers that are crystallizable. Since the melting temperatures of crystallizable polymers tend to be approximately 50% higher than their glass transition temperatures, the polymers that crystallize generally find use over a broader temperature range. Crystallization in polymers is a complex phenomenon that differs significantly from the crystallization of low molecular weight substances.

To crystallize, long polymer chains must partially disentangle from other chains and forego conformational entropy to fit into a crystal phase. As a consequence, polymers crystallize from the molten state at temperatures that can be up to several tens of degrees below their thermodynamic melting temperatures. This large supercooling is one of the easiest observed differences that distinguish polymers from other substances. The slow kinetics of crystallization allow for many polymers to be cooled into the glassy state, only to crystallize later when heated back above their glass transition temperatures. During crystallization, flexible polymer chains fold upon themselves to form a crystal. In melt-crystallized structures, thin lamellar polymer crystals form that are interspersed with noncrystalline layers in which fragments of polymer chains are still entangled, giving rise to the semicrystalline state of polymers. The noncrystalline layers include also chain ends, loops, and tie molecules that connect adjacent crystals. The prevalence of the semicrystalline state is another important feature that distinguishes crystallizable polymers from other solids. Frequently, lamellae form polycrystalline aggregates that grow outwards from common nucleation sites. Thus, the overall crystallization kinetics is determined by both the nucleation rate and the growth rate of crystals. In addition, polymers are able to solidify in the form of mesophases that exhibit various degrees of order, although less perfect than that of the crystalline phase.

Usually, the thicknesses of the lamellar polymer crystals and intercrystalline amorphous zones do not exceed a few tens of nanometers. Semicrystalline polymers are in fact "Nature's nanocomposites": self-assembled nanocomposite materials in which a combination of crystals and rubbery amorphous phase may coexist, resulting in the remarkable ductility and toughness of these materials. Another consequence of the relatively small thickness of polymer crystals and the high surface energy of their basal surfaces is a strong dependence of melting temperature on the crystal thickness.

The relatively slow crystallization kinetics of polymers at small supercooling make it possible to control, to some extent, the temperature of crystallization. This enables researchers to study solidification at predetermined isothermal conditions and to link the crystallization and emerging structure with temperature. The temperature at which crystallization occurs influences not only the nucleation and growth of crystals but also the sizes and shapes of the crystals and the overall degree of crystallinity.

In industrial processing, polymeric materials usually crystallize during cooling. Their low thermal conductivity and diffusivity can result in temperature gradients across the product thickness, especially when the release of latent heat of fusion contributes to development of the temperature gradient. Moreover, during processing steps such as extrusion, injection molding, film blowing, or fiber spinning, the flow of material can lead to orientation of the polymer chains, which in turn affects both the crystallization kinetics and the emerging morphology. Depending on the processing conditions and molecular characteristics of a polymer, different structures are observed, from spherulites to shish–kebabs. Crystallization and resulting morphology are strongly related to the temperature, applied shear rate (or strain rate), and total strain achieved during flow. Complex thermomechanical conditions determine the supermolecular structure of polymeric materials and, as a consequence, their properties. The understanding of how the polymer morphology develops during processing is a key issue to linking the processing conditions with final properties of the product.

Different monomers may be copolymerized to modify the properties of thermoplastics. For the same purpose, homo- and copolymers are frequently mixed with other substances, including other polymers, various fillers, and nanofillers. The presence of comonomers in macromolecules, as well as interactions between macromolecules in miscible blends, can affect both crystallization and morphology of the polymeric material. Interfaces and the confinement of polymer chains within a finite volume influence the solidification and morphology of immiscible polymer blends and polymer-based composites. They are also of special importance in ultrathin polymer layers where the thickness is comparable to or smaller than the lamellar crystal thickness itself.

The complexity of polymer crystallization has posed a long-standing challenge to the analytical chemistry community, demanding the development and application of a variety of microscopic, calorimetric, and spectroscopic experimental methods. Among the new techniques emerging over the last decade or two is molecular simulation, which provides unique insight into molecular ordering during polymer crystallization.

The crystallization of polymers has been a subject of ongoing investigations for nearly a century. Although our understanding of this complex subject is far from complete, recent decades have witnessed significant progress, for instance in the understanding of the effects of polymer flow or formation of mesophases. Development of nanoscience and nanotechnology was associated with studies of the crystallization of polymer-based nanocomposites and ultrathin polymer layers.

In light of the recent substantial progress in understanding polymer crystallization, we believe that the subject deserves a comprehensive and updated handbook, consisting of chapters written by renowned specialists in their respective fields. Our aim is to review thoroughly the state of knowledge in the field and to cover numerous important aspects of polymer crystallization, including both past and current developments.

Chapter 1 covers experimental techniques widely used in studies of polymer crystallization. Chapter 2, Chapter 3, Chapter 4, and Chapter 5 are devoted to the structure of crystalline polymers and also to the kinetics of nucleation and growth of the crystalline phase. Chapter 6 is focused on molecular modeling of polymer crystallization, whereas Chapter 7 describes overall crystallization kinetics, with special reference to the theories widely used in practice. Chapter 8 covers the subject of epitaxy. Chapter 9 is dedicated to melting of polymer crystals. Chapter 10, Chapter 11, and Chapter 13 describe the crystallization in copolymers, miscible and immiscible polymer blends, and also polymer composites. Chapter 12 is focused on phenomena related to the confinement of polymer chains. Chapter 14 describes the effect of flow on crystallization, and finally Chapter 15 covers the crystallization in processing conditions.

We are thankful to all of the contributors to this project, for their high quality work that has made this book possible. We hope that the readers, both experts and novices alike, working in the broad field of thermoplastic polymers, may find this handbook a valuable resource.

EWA PIORKOWSKA
GREGORY C. RUTLEDGE

CONTRIBUTORS

Maria Luisa Arnal, Departamento de Ciencia de los Materiales, Universidad Simon Bolivar, Caracas, Venezuela

Finizia Auriemma, Dipartimento di Chimica "Paolo Corradini," Università di Napoli "Federico II," Complesso Monte S.Angelo, Napoli, Italy

Luigi Balzano, Department of Mechanical Engineering, Eindhoven University of Technology, Eindhoven, The Netherlands

Buckley Crist, Department of Materials Science and Engineering, Northwestern University, Evanston, IL

Claudio De Rosa, Dipartimento di Scienze Chimiche, Università di Napoli "Federico II," Complesso Monte S.Angelo, Napoli, Italy

Andrzej Galeski, Centre of Molecular and Macromolecular Studies, Polish Academy of Sciences, Lodz, Poland

Jean-Marc Haudin, MINES ParisTech, Centre de Mise en Forme des Matériaux (CEMEF), Sophia Antipolis, France

Masamichi Hikosaka, Graduate School of Integrated Arts and Sciences, Hiroshima University, Hiroshima, Japan

Benjamin S. Hsiao, Department of Chemistry, SUNY Stony Brook, Stony Brook, NY

Sheng Li, Department of Chemical and Biological Engineering, Princeton University, Princeton, NJ

Arnaldo T. Lorenzo, Departamento de Ciencia de los Materiales, Universidad Simón Bolívar, Caracas Venezuela

Bernard A. Lotz, Institute Charles Sadron, CNRS, University of Strasbourg, Strasbourg, France

Yimin Mao, Department of Chemistry, SUNY Stony Brook, Stony Brook, NY

Alejandro J. Müller, Departamento de Ciencia de los Materiales, Universidad Simón Bolívar, Caracas, Venezuela

Kiyoka N. Okada, Graduate School of Integrated Arts and Sciences, Hiroshima University, Hiroshima, Japan

Gerrit W.M. Peters, Department of Mechanical Engineering, Eindhoven University of Technology, Eindhoven, The Netherlands

Ewa Piorkowska, Centre of Molecular and Macromolecular Studies, Polish Academy of Sciences, Lodz, Poland

Mariano Pracella, Institute of Composite and Biomedical Materials, CNR, National Research Council; Department of Chemical Engineering and Materials Science, University of Pisa, Pisa, Italy

Marek Pyda, Department of Chemistry, Rzeszow University of Technology, Rzeszow, Poland; Department of Pharmacy, Poznan University of Medical Sciences, Poznan, Poland; ATHAS-MP Company, Knoxville, TN

Richard A. Register, Department of Chemical and Biological Engineering, Princeton University, Princeton, NJ

Gregory C. Rutledge, Department of Chemical Engineering, Massachusetts Institute of Technology, Cambridge, MA

Christoph Schick, Institute of Physics, University of Rostock, Rostock, Germany

Rudi J.A. Steenbakkers, Department of Mechanical Engineering, Eindhoven University of Technology, Eindhoven, The Netherlands

Kohji Tashiro, Department of Future Industry-Oriented Basic Science and Materials, Toyota Technological Institute, Nagoya, Japan

Annette Thierry, Institute Charles Sadron, CNRS, University of Strasbourg, Strasbourg, France

Feng Zuo, Department of Chemistry, SUNY Stony Brook, Stony Brook, NY

1

EXPERIMENTAL TECHNIQUES

BENJAMIN S. HSIAO, FENG ZUO, AND YIMIN MAO
Department of Chemistry, Stony Brook University, Stony Brook, New York

CHRISTOPH SCHICK
University of Rostock, Institute of Physics, Rostock, Germany

1.1 Introduction, 1
1.2 Optical Microscopy, 2
    1.2.1 Reflection and Transmission Microscopy, 2
    1.2.2 Contrast Modes, 2
    1.2.3 Selected Applications, 3
1.3 Electron Microscopy, 5
    1.3.1 Imaging Principle, 5
    1.3.2 Sample Preparation, 6
    1.3.3 Relevant Experimental Techniques, 7
    1.3.4 Selected Applications, 8
1.4 Atomic Force Microscopy, 9
    1.4.1 Imaging Principle, 9
    1.4.2 Scanning Modes, 9
    1.4.3 Comparison between AFM and EM, 10
    1.4.4 Recent Development: Video AFM, 10
    1.4.5 Selected Applications, 10
1.5 Nuclear Magnetic Resonance, 12
    1.5.1 Chemical Shift, 13
    1.5.2 Relevant Techniques, 13
    1.5.3 Recent Development: Multidimensional NMR, 14
    1.5.4 Selected Applications, 14
1.6 Scattering Techniques: X-Ray, Light, and Neutron, 15
    1.6.1 Wide-Angle X-Ray Diffraction, 15
    1.6.2 Small-Angle X-Ray Scattering, 17
    1.6.3 Small-Angle Light Scattering, 19
    1.6.4 Small-Angle Neutron Scattering, 21
1.7 Differential Scanning Calorimetry, 22
    1.7.1 Modes of Operation, 22
    1.7.2 Determination of Degree of Crystallinity, 25
1.8 Summary, 26
Acknowledgments, 26
References, 26

1.1 INTRODUCTION

In this chapter, the principle, recent developments, and selected applications of some commonly used experimental techniques for characterizing semicrystalline polymers are described. These techniques include optical microscopy, electron microscopy (transmission and scanning), atomic force microscopy, nuclear magnetic resonance, diffraction and scattering (X-ray, neutron, and light), as well as differential scanning calorimetry. This list represents some of the most commonly used methods of obtaining relevant structure and property information of semicrystalline polymers. Other useful techniques, including spectroscopic methods, such as Fourier transform infrared (FTIR) and Raman spectroscopy, as well as mechanical testing methods (e.g., thermal, tensile, and compression), are not described here but are introduced within context of their use in subsequent chapters.

Handbook of Polymer Crystallization, First Edition. Edited by Ewa Piorkowska and Gregory C. Rutledge.
© 2013 John Wiley & Sons, Inc. Published 2013 by John Wiley & Sons, Inc.

1.2 OPTICAL MICROSCOPY

Optical microscopy (OM), also termed light microscopy, is one of the most commonly used characterization techniques for investigating the morphology (down to submicron scale) of semicrystalline polymers utilizing visible light as a structure probe [1–4]. A conventional optical microscope system consists of two lenses. The first lens, called the objective lens, is a highly powered magnifying glass having a short focal length that creates an enlarged but inverted image of the object on the intermediate image plane. This image is then viewed through another lens called the eyepiece, which provides further enlargement. The total magnification is the product of the two, and it can be up to about 2000 times.

1.2.1 Reflection and Transmission Microscopy

There are two types of optical microscopy, designed based on different collection principles. The first is reflection optical microscopy, in which the observation is made by collecting the light reflected from the surface of the viewing object. The second is transmission optical microscopy, in which the transmitted light passing through the body of the viewing object is collected. Reflection microscopy provides the surface topography of the sample. Since most polymer materials have low surface reflectivity, the incident light can penetrate into the sample, causing scattering and/or refraction at the interface between the sample and the substrate. In this case, the resolution and clarity of the reflected image may be low. This limits the application of reflection microscopy to the study of polymer materials. Nevertheless, reflection optical microscopy is generally useful for characterizing the surface of opaque metal or ceramic samples.

For transmission optical microscopy, samples need to be thin enough for light to pass through. Usually, the sample thickness is about a few microns. The sample preparation schemes include microtoming a bulk sample, solution casting, or melt pressing a thin film. The images can be obtained through bright field or dark field, in which the directly transmitted or scattered light is collected to form the image, respectively. For unstained polymer materials, there is usually only a small difference in the absorption of different species/phases, so the contrast is always low in a bright field. The dark field mode can improve the image contrast, as the light collected is scattered by the sample, showing a bright object in the dark background, but the light intensity can be low. Since contrast is based on the absorption of the viewing area, and for a semicrystalline polymer system (e.g., having spherulitic morphology) there is not much difference in light absorption, the spherulites can be hard to distinguish from melt or from each other. Selective techniques that can enhance the sample contrast are summarized as follows.

1.2.2 Contrast Modes

The common contrast modes include polarized light, phase contrast, differential interference contrast, and Hoffman modulation contrast [5]. Depending on the nature of the polymer, such as refraction index, sample thickness, and optical anisotropies in the materials, different modes of transmission optical microscopy can be employed by mounting special accessories in a classic optical microscope to overcome different problems. For example, a polarizer and analyzer can be mounted before and after the sample to construct a polarized light microscope, commonly used for semicrystalline polymers; a phase plate and phase ring can be added to construct a phase contrast optical microscopy, which is common for studying a noncrystalline multiphase polymer system.

1.2.2.1 Polarized Optical Microscopy
Polarized optical microscopy consists of a typical microscope stage combined with two additional polarizing filters, one (polarizer) before the condenser lens and one (analyzer) after the objective lens [6, 7]. The polarizing filter only allows light that is polarized in one specific plane, which is parallel to the polarization plane of the filter, to go through, while blocking other light with different polarization planes. The polarization planes of the two added polarizing filters are set perpendicular to each other, so that when polarized light from the polarizer pass through the sample without changes in the direction of polarization plane, they cannot pass through the analyzer. As a result, the obtained image will be completely dark. This is the case when isotropic amorphous polymer solids or melts are viewed, as they are optically isotropic. However, if the sample consists of optically anisotropic crystals or an orientated amorphous phase, there will be a strong contrast in these species. Polymer crystals are highly anisotropic in electron density because they have strong covalent bonds along the chain axis, whereas the cohesion along the lateral direction is achieved by much weaker bonding, such as van der Waals forces or hydrogen bonds. When light enters polymer crystals along the nonequivalent axis, it is decomposed into two rays, extraordinary and ordinary rays, with their vibrating directions parallel or perpendicular to the crystallographic axes, respectively. The extraordinary ray travels at a slower velocity, while the ordinary ray maintains the original velocity in the sample, which implies the existence of two refractive indices. This phenomenon is called birefraction, and the difference between two

refractive indices is called birefringence, which can be measured quantitatively and is related to the degree of polymer chain orientation. After polarized lights pass through the sample and the objective lens, two rays emerge together, but they are still vibrating perpendicularly with respect to each other. Only the component that vibrates parallel to the polarization plane of the analyzer can pass through and reach the eyepiece. Polarized optical microscopy is very common for studying semicrystalline polymers since only the crystal phase can be observed, while the amorphous matrix appears as a dark background.

1.2.2.2 Phase Contrast Optical Microscopy Phase contrast optical microscopy converts the phase difference in light to light intensity [8]. Thus, the technique offers better resolution for colorless and transparent thin specimens, in which the contrast may be too low for conventional optical microscopy. The phase difference in the sample arises from the occurrence of scattering and diffraction from different parts of the sample, which slightly alter the phase of light. Phase contrast optical microscopy usually contains a phase ring located under the condenser lens and an objective lens equipped with a phase plate. When light passes through the phase ring, it forms a hollow cone. After passing through the sample, the undeviated light remains in the shape of a hollow cone, but the deviated light is spread out within the cone. Undeviated light and deviated light are thus separated by the phase ring, whereby the deviated light is slowed down by about $1/4\ \lambda$ (wavelength) with respect to the undeviated light, because of the refractive index of the sample. The phase plate further changes the phase of the undeviated light, which can be $1/4\ \lambda$ faster or slower, by adjusting the thickness of the phase shifter in the viewing region where the undeviated light passes through. If undeviated light and deviated light are in the same phase, they result in constructive interference and form a bright image of the samples with dark background. If the undeviated light is $1/2\ \lambda$ ahead of the deviated light, it results in destructive interference and forms dark images of the sample with a bright background.

This technique can be modified in a different way, that is, by changing the amplitude rather than the phase of transmitted and scattered light, using an asymmetric modulator plate, which has dark, gray, and transparent zones, at the rear focal plane. In this case, the incident light passes through a slit plate rather than the phase ring, as in phase contrast microscopy. This is called Hoffman modulation contrast optical microscopy. It can also be combined with polarized light, including a polarizer before the slit. There are also other optical microscopes, such as the differential interference microscope and fluorescence microscope, which we do not discuss here, as they are not so frequently used in the study of semicrystalline polymers.

1.2.2.3 Near-Field Scanning Optical Microscopy The spatial resolution of conventional optical microscopy is limited by the wavelength of the light (the maximum resolution is about 200 nm) due to the far-field effect of light diffraction. However, near-field scanning optical microscopy (NSOM) breaks this limitation by exploiting the properties of evanescent waves, which decay exponentially with the distance from the sample surface [9, 10]. In NSOM, a spatial resolution less than 50 nm can be achieved. This is accomplished by forcing the light to go through a subwavelength diameter aperture, which can be a tapered optical fiber or an AFM cantilever having a hole in the center of the tip, where the probe is at a very short distance, much shorter than the wavelength of the light, near the sample surface. In this case, the resolution in NSOM is not limited by the diffraction but by the aperture diameter in the near-field configuration. The aperture diameter is often 50–100 nm, and the distance is even smaller, about a few nanometers. This short distance is controlled by a feedback mechanism. The probe is then scanned over the surface of the sample without touching it. Thus, it can also be classified as scanning probe microscopy. The light passing through the sample and collected by the scanning probe aperture can be incident light, transmitted light, reflected light, or a combination of these, which represents different modes of operation. The choice of the mode depends on the sample characteristics, which can be transparent or opaque. The signals can be detected by various devices and reconstructed into an optical image. All contrast mechanisms in conventional optical microscopy are also applied in NSOM, such as sample thickness, reflectivity, polarized light, and phase contrast. Although the NSOM can increase the resolution and yield topographic images, it still has some disadvantages over conventional optical microscopy. The disadvantages include low depth of field, poor collection efficiency, and common drawbacks in the operation of mechanical scanning.

1.2.3 Selected Applications

The spatial resolution of conventional optical microscopy is about 1 µm; thus, it becomes an adequate tool for investigating the formation of crystal structure with length scale larger than that [11–31]. Most semicrystalline polymers form spherulites in the order of 100 µm when crystallized from melts or concentrated solutions. The shape of spherulites can be observed directly by using polarized optical microscopy, but the branched lamella, whose thickness is around tens of nanometers,

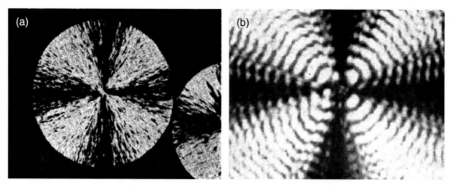

Figure 1.1 Optical microscopy images of spherulites of isotactic polypropylene (a) and polyethylene (b), where magnifications are 240× and 675×, respectively [32, 33].

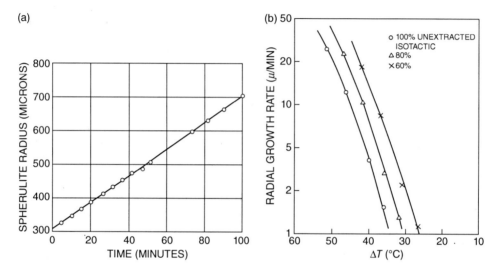

Figure 1.2 (a) Spherulite radius as a function of time during isothermal crystallization at 125°C in 20 wt% iPP and 80 wt% aPP (M_w = 2.6 kg/mol, 100% atacticity) blend. (b) The radial growth rate of spherulites at different degrees of supercooling and iPP content in iPP and aPP (M_w = 87 kg/mol, 95% atacticity) blend [34].

are not resolvable. Optical microscopy can be combined with hot-stage, a special specimen holder in which the temperature can be varied. Thus, the temperature- and time-dependent spherulitic growth in a thin film can be studied by measuring the average diameter of spherulites as a function of time, which yields the growth rate of spherulites. The information on the nucleation kinetics of polymer spherulites can also be obtained. Figure 1.1 shows two representative polarized optical microscopic images of spherulites in isotactic polypropylene (iPP) and polyethylene (PE), respectively [32, 33]. In the iPP spherulite (Fig. 1.1a), a cross-like extinction occurs along the polarization axes, which is usually termed "Maltese cross." When the specimen is rotated, the cross remains stationary, which indicates that the entire spherulite is crystalline within the resolution employed. However, in some other spherulites, another type of extinction pattern, which consists in radial banding, can also be observed under the same experimental conditions. They are called "ringed (or banded) spherulites," such as the case of PE spherulites in Figure 1.1b. It is a zero birefringence phenomenon due to the lamellar twisting along the radical direction during crystallization, where extinction occurs when a polymer chain (the c-axis) is parallel to the polarized axis.

Keith et al. [34] studied the growth of spherulites of iPP (M_w = 178 kg/mol, with 80% isotacticity) at different conditions, including temperature, time, and various iPP/atactic polypropylene (aPP) blends. As shown in Figure 1.2a, when the radii of iPP spherulites are plotted against isothermal crystallization time in a 20/80 (w/w) iPP/aPP blend at 125°C, the growth rate is constant (i.e., 7 μm/min). The effects of supercooling and iPP content on the crystallization rate are shown in Figure 1.2b (we note that the aPP used here is different from that in Fig. 1.2a). A high degree of supercooling or low content of

Figure 1.3 Different types of iPP spherulites. (a) Type I, crystallized at 128°C, (b) Type II, crystallized at 138°C, (c) Type III, crystallized at 125°C, and (d) Type IV, crystallized at 130°C [36]. Scale bar is 200 µm.

aPP matrix can enhance the crystallization rate of iPP spherulites.

In the same polymer, different types of spherulites can be observed. For example, Padden et al. and Keller et al. [35, 36] reported that there are at least four types of spherulites for iPP (Fig. 1.3). Two of them, Types I and II, consist of monoclinic (α) crystal modification, while Types III and IV are crystallized with hexagonal (β) crystal structure. Types I and II are different in birefringence; Type I is slightly positive and Type II is slightly negative. When Type I is heated up, it will change to negative birefringence, similar to Type II; it diminishes slowly and melts away at higher temperatures. Types III and IV are less often observed. They occur sporadically and appear to form within certain constraints of isothermal crystallization. Both Types III and IV have a much greater negative birefringence than Types I and II. In the bulk sample, there is usually a mixture of different types of spherulites. The use of optical microscopy for the analysis of crystalline aggregates is discussed further in Chapter 4.

1.3 ELECTRON MICROSCOPY

1.3.1 Imaging Principle

Electron microscopy (EM) has advantages in both magnification and resolution over optical microscopy [3, 37]. Thus, electron microscopy is a very powerful tool in studying the microstructure of polymers and yielding direct images. Electron microscopy usually consists of three major components: the electron beam source, the illumination system, and the imaging system. The electron beam is analogous to visible light in optical microscopy, while the electromagnetic lens (for manipulating electron beams through electromagnetic interactions) is analogous to the optical lens (for focusing the visible light). High vacuum is needed in electron microscopy, allowing incident electrons and signal electrons to reach the sample and detector, respectively, without being scattered by air and small dust particles. The key parameter in determining the resolution is the wavelength of the incident beam. Theoretical resolution of a microscope can be calculated based on Abbe's equation ($d = 0.61\lambda/(n \sin \theta)$, where d is the smallest distance that can be distinguished, that is, resolution, λ is the wavelength, n is the reflective index that is 1 in the vacuum of electron microscopy, and θ is the collection semiangle of the magnifying lens). Thus, the microscope resolution is proportional to the wavelength of the electron beam; the shorter the wavelength, the higher the resolution. Visible light has a wavelength around 380 to 790 nm, and thus the resolution of the conventional optical microscopy is in the order of 1 µm. Ultraviolet (UV) has a shorter wavelength, and thus the resolution can go below 100 nm. For electron microscopy, the wavelength of the electron beam is much shorter than visible light, so a much higher resolution can be achieved. The wavelength of electron beam is related to the accelerating voltage ($\lambda = h/[2m_0 eV(1 + eV/2m_0 c^2)]^{1/2}$); a higher voltage can result in a shorter wavelength, leading to a better resolution. For instance, with a voltage of 100 kV, the wavelength of the electron beam is 0.0037 nm, yielding a theoretical resolution of 0.005 nm. However, because of the limitation of many other factors, such as monochromation and focusing, the theoretical resolution cannot be obtained. A typical practical limit of resolution for electron microscopy is in the order of 1 nm.

1.3.1.1 Transmission Electron Microscopy

When light goes through a thin sample, a different thickness or different density component in the sample would lead to different absorption of light, thus forming an optical image. However, the image formation in transmission electron microscopy (TEM) is due to scattering of electrons rather than absorption of light [38, 39]. Thicker regions or regions with a higher atomic mass would result in stronger scattering, enabling the region to appear darker in the reconstructed image (this is because more incident electrons are scattered to larger angles). Based on this principle, there are two basic modes in TEM operation: bright-field mode and dark-field mode. In the bright-field mode, the direct transmitted electron beam is collected to construct the image; in the dark-field mode, the diffracted electron beam is used. Such an operation is accomplished by inserting an aperture into the back focal plane of the objective lens and moving the aperture around to let the relative electron beam, that is, transmitted beam or scattered beam, pass through. Since diffracted beams can strongly interact with samples possessing planar defects, stacking faults or particles, the operation of dark-field mode is preferred. In contrast, when interactions between the electron beam and sample are relatively weak, the sample thickness and atomic mass and crystalline region will be more relevant to construct the image using the bright-field mode.

1.3.1.2 Scanning Electron Microscopy

The major difference between scanning electron microscopy (SEM) and TEM is that in the former, electron beams are scanned over a region of the sample surface. When electron beams interact with the sample in a depth of a few to hundreds of nanometers, a variety of backward detectable signals can be collected, including secondary electrons, backscattered electrons, X-rays, and so on. [40, 41]. Each of them can be used to characterize the sample with respect to different properties. The backscattered electrons result from the collision of incident electrons and the atoms in the sample, where coherent backward scattered (about 180°) electrons are formed. Their intensity is thus related to the atomic number—higher mass atom leads to more backscattered electrons and brighter appearance in the image. The secondary electrons result from the electrons that gain energy by inelastic collision between the sample and the incident beam. Due to the restriction of low energy (usually below 50 eV), only secondary electrons escaping near the surface can be detected. Thus, these signals can provide information on the surface topology. After the emission of secondary electrons, higher energy electrons within the atoms can fall into the vacant orbital at the lower energy level, thus generating characteristic X-rays that can also be collected to determine the surface composition. The modern SEM technique can be combined with *in situ* sample stages to investigate real-time behavior of a sample under micro-mechanical and electrically stimulated environments.

1.3.2 Sample Preparation

1.3.2.1 Thin-Film Preparation

SEM requires relatively simple procedures for sample preparation. The samples can be in the form of fiber, film, or bulk, as long as they can be mounted on the sample stub (e.g., using the double-sided carbon tape). However, TEM requires the sample to be ultrathin, usually less than 100 nm, which allows electron beams to go through. For large samples, ultra-microtomy can be used to yield an ultrathin film. For solution and particles, dispersion, casting, and disintegration onto the metal grid with an electron transparent support film are good choices. In addition, sample replication (an indirect method) can also be used to prepare ultrathin specimens. This method involves the evaporation of replicating media, such as carbon or metals, on the sample surface in vacuum to form an ultrathin film. The original sample is subsequently removed (dissolved chemically or physically), leaving the replica with the same surface characteristic and topography of the original sample. For samples that cannot be easily removed, two-stage replication can be used. The first step involves the use an easily removable material, such as poly(acrylic acid) (PAA), followed by the conventional replication step to fabricate the ultrathin specimen for TEM observation.

1.3.2.2 Conducting Problem

Since most polymers are nonconductive, when high energy electron beams are illuminated on the sample surface, the surface charge will accumulate and damage the sample. To prevent the accumulation of electrostatic charge on the surface, it is necessary to coat the sample with electron-conducting materials, such as gold. But it has to be sufficiently thin without disturbing the surface structure of the sample. The common coating techniques include sputter coating and vacuum evaporation. Sputter coating is fast and convenient, but it is usually used for low magnification. The vacuum evaporation method gives finer grains and thinner conductive coating, which is more suitable for high resolution imaging. For TEM observation, samples are usually metal shadowed at an oblique angle (20° to 45°). Since the heavy atoms have strong scattering ability, regions without these metal coatings appear darker in the image. Thus, it can be used to highlight the surface topology and enhance the electron contrast.

1.3.2.3 Contrast Problem The contrast formation in TEM arises from interactions between incident electrons and atoms. The contrast of a polymer sample is often low. This is because polymers usually consist of light atoms such as C, O, and H with only small variations in electron density. To increase the contrast, chemical staining or etching can be applied. Chemical staining involves the incorporation of heavy elements into the sample by chemical reaction. Physical staining is used relatively less often, as it is often not stable in the vacuum environment. Several staining agents (e.g., osmium tetroxide, ruthenium tetroxide, and chlorosulfonic acid, phosphotungstic acid) have been demonstrated, depending on the structure of the sample (especially the functional group). Shadowing with heavy metal atoms can also enhance the contrast. Chemical or physical etching methods are other ways to enhance the surface structure. Chemical etching involves the use of chemical solvent (e.g., acid) to etch away some nonessential part of the sample surface (e.g., amorphous region) to enhance the essential part of the structure (e.g., crystalline region), followed by making replicas or conductive coatings. Physical etching involves the use of plasma or ion beam to etch the sample surface; however, the technique is known to produce artifacts in semicrystalline polymers.

1.3.3 Relevant Experimental Techniques

1.3.3.1 Environmental SEM In conventional SEM, nonconductive polymer samples need be surface coated, whereby the original surface morphology can be damaged or distorted. Environmental SEM (ESEM) is a new technique that allows wet or insulating samples, such as polymers, biological cells, and plants without any pretreatment, to be studied under low pressure and high humidity environments. The charge accumulation problem is resolved by neutralizing negative charges on the sample surface with positively charged ions generated by the interaction between electron beams and surrounding gas molecules (a gas pressure on the order of 10 torr is maintained in the sample chamber). The incident electron beam still passes through a high vacuum column along most of its path, maintained by using pressure-limiting apertures and separating pumps. The distance between the final aperture and the sample surface is around a few millimeters, allowing the reduction of scattering by gas molecules and yielding a high resolution image. The detector is also modified to collect signals under mild environment in the sample chamber. Since ESEM can be operated without coating and under gas environment, many other applications for semicrystalline polymers can be carried out, for example, the melt processing of polymers and liquid–solid interface reaction.

1.3.3.2 High Resolution SEM High resolution SEM is developed by exchanging the regular tungsten filament electron gun with a field-emission gun [42]. The rationale is as follows. It is known that the percentage of SE1 (the direct emitted secondary electrons closed to the sample surface) in the total secondary electrons, including SE2, SE3 (from backscattered electrons, which lose most of their energy when they escape from the sample or hit the wall of the chamber), and SE4 (produced in the electron column), determines the spatial resolution of the image, whereby this percentage is limited by the diameter of the electron probe. The field-emission gun is suitable for high resolution purposes because its probe size is very small (about 1 nm). In addition, the working distance can be short (e.g., a few millimeters), which can enhance the spatial resolution due to low spherical and chromatic aberration.

High resolution TEM (HRTEM) lattice images can be obtained by collecting both transmitted and scattered beams using a large objective aperture. Images are formed from the interference between the beams, giving information regarding lattice parameters, defects and orientation, and so on. In order to achieve high resolution, both high image contrast and high instrumental resolution power are needed. Usually, this requires that the spherical and chromatic aberration and electron wavelength to be as small as possible. Thus, high voltage is needed to generate incident electron beams with high energy and short wavelength. Advanced HRTEM is usually operated at 300 kV and above. Best resolution in the range of 0.5 Å can be achieved. Chromatic aberration can be improved by applying electron velocity filters, in which the electrons with different energies are sorted out, leaving only monochromatic electrons; spherical aberration can be minimized by changing the setup of the lens design. Additionally, other instrumentation parameters, such as beam divergence, magnification, and radiation sensitivity (especially for polymers), also need to be optimized to achieve high resolution.

1.3.3.3 Electron Diffraction Similar to X-ray diffraction, when electron beams interact with atoms in the sample (especially in the crystalline regions), electron diffraction (ED) can occur. The ED measurement can be easily accomplished by changing the strength of the intermediate lens, thus enabling the diffraction pattern to be projected on the viewing screen. Typically, a series of dots are seen in the diffraction pattern from single crystals, and a series of rings are seen from polycrystalline samples. As the wavelength of the electron beam is much shorter than that of an X-ray, the corresponding radius of the Ewald sphere is much larger than the size of the crystal lattice in reciprocal space. Thus, more reflection points can be seen in ED than in X-ray diffraction. There are two advantages of ED over X-ray diffraction: (1) tiny crystals can be examined, and (2) tilting of the crystal orientation can be achieved, allowing the parameters of crystal lattice in reciprocal spacing to be mapped easily. ED can be used to determine the crystal structure, symmetry, and orientation of semicrystalline polymers. However, some limitations are also noted, including the requirement of ultrathin samples, possibility of radiation damage, and general difficulty of analyzing and interpreting the data.

1.3.4 Selected Applications

It is generally difficult to study polymer crystallization under *in situ* conditions by SEM and TEM, but they are extremely useful for investigating polymer structures *ex situ* [11–16, 42–56]. For example, the structure and morphology of PE, one of the most broadly used semicrystalline polymers, has been studied quite extensively using SEM and TEM techniques. To study the structure and morphology of single crystals, PE can be dissolved in solvents such as xylene to form a dilute solution, and then subsequently crystallized. The effects of molecular weight, crystallization temperature, and solution concentration on the crystal morphology have been studied. Figure 1.4 shows the TEM images of solution-crystallized PE at 40°C (a) and 80°C (b) (by Holland and Lindenmeyer [57]), and 90°C (c) (by Bassett and Keller [58]). Three different morphologies, dendrites, diamond, and truncated diamond, were found as the crystallization temperature increased.

Wittmann and Lotz [59] studied PE single crystals grown from dilute solutions using a decoration technique with a low molecular weight component (Fig. 1.5a) (cf. Chapter 9.4). It is seen that different sectors

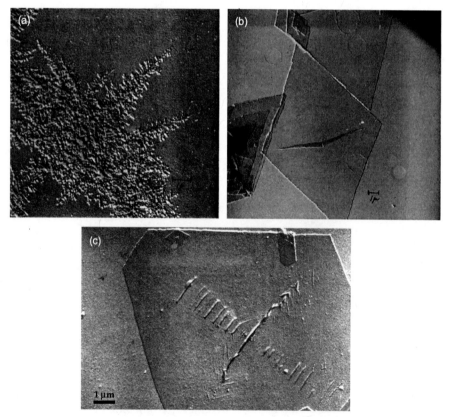

Figure 1.4 TEM images of polyethylene grown from 0.01% xylene solution at (a) 40°C, (b) 80°C, and (c) 90°C [57, 58].

ATOMIC FORCE MICROSCOPY

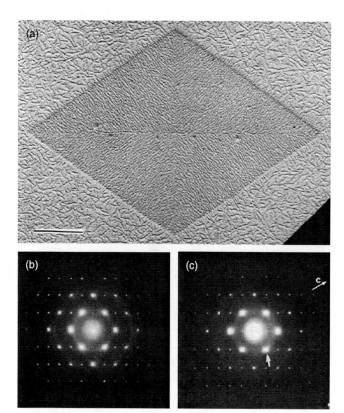

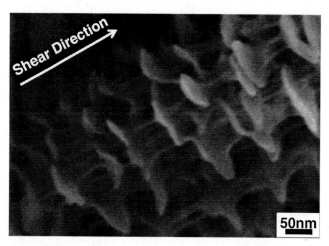

Figure 1.6 SEM image of toluene-extracted UHMWPE crystallites with a shish–kebab structure having multiple shish [60].

Figure 1.5 (a) TEM image of polyethylene single crystal, decorated by vacuum deposition of low molecular weight polyethylene, grown from dilute solution. Scale bar = 1 μm. Electron diffraction patterns of a single polyethylene crystal from an area encompassing (b) all four and (c) only one (lower right or upper left region in (a)) growth sector [59].

have different preferred orientations. Two ED patterns taken on regions encompassing all four sectors and only one sector (lower right or upper left of Fig. 1.5a) are illustrated in Figure 1.5b,c, respectively. In Figure 1.5c, the c-axis orientation of the decorating chains is parallel to the growth face in the selected area (the arrow indicates the 110 spot). The orientations of the lamellar rods and polymer chains are thus confirmed to be perpendicular and parallel, respectively, to the growth front of the corresponding sector.

It is well known that flow-induced crystallization of polymers can lead to shish–kebab structure. Hsiao et al. [60] extracted the ultrahigh molecular weight PE (UHMWPE) shish–kebab entities crystallized after shear cession from the low molecular weight PE matrix at a temperature between the melting points of the two. The shish–kebab crystals were examined with a field-emission SEM at the accelerating voltage of 2 kV. Figure 1.6 shows that multiple shish are formed, where each shish has a diameter of a few nanometers and connects

the adjacent lamellar kebabs of similar size and crystal habit (Fig. 1.6). This phenomenon is discussed further in Chapter 15.

1.4 ATOMIC FORCE MICROSCOPY

1.4.1 Imaging Principle

Atomic force microscopy (AFM) works by scanning the sample surface using a sharp and tiny probe, which is mounted at the end of a cantilever [61, 62]. When the AFM probe scans the sample surface, the interaction forces (including mechanical contact force, electrostatic force, and van der Waals force) between the probe and the sample induce deflection of the cantilever. This deflection can be detected by the change of position of a laser beam reflected on the back of a cantilever and into a position-sensitive detector. Based on this principle, an image of sample surface can be generated. The cantilever is several hundred micrometers long, while the radius of the probe tip is from a few to tens of nanometers. The sharpness, aspect ratio, and the shape of the probe are the most critical parameters to the resolution of AFM. Generally, the sharper probe leads to higher resolution in the image.

1.4.2 Scanning Modes

There are two major scanning modes in AFM: contact mode and vibration mode. In the contact mode, the probe is in contact with the sample surface, where an interaction force is generated. This mode is usually used when the sample surface is hard. To protect the probe and cantilever from colliding with the sample, the cantilever deflection is controlled and adjusted to a fixed value, or a constant force is maintained using the feedback control. Very often, the electrostatic, adhesive, and friction force may pull the probe toward the surface and damage the sample/probe and distort the image (especially when soft polymer samples are studied, where the frictional force is very high). In such a case, the vibration mode is used to minimize the interaction force between the probe and sample surface (the force in the vibration mode is 1–10% of that in the contact mode). The vibration of the cantilever is achieved by using a piezoelectric ceramic. Changes in the vibration amplitude and phase shift between oscillating cantilever and the initial driving signal are measured. The vibration amplitude can be used to depict the topological features of the surface, while the phase shift is related to the intrinsic property, such as adhesion and viscoelastic properties, of the surface chemical composition. In the vibration mode, the amplitude can be small, so that the probe is close to but does not touch the surface (noncontact mode), or the amplitude can be large, so that the probe taps the surface once every oscillating cycle (tapping mode or intermittent contact mode). The tapping mode can provide a better resolution without inducing a strong frictional force; it is the most popular mode in polymer studies.

1.4.3 Comparison between AFM and EM

Compared with the stringent sample requirements of SEM and TEM, AFM requires only a simple sample preparation procedure, which is a major advantage. The other advantages include the following: (1) measurements can be carried out *in situ* or in real time, and (2) measurements can also be carried out in ambient air or in liquid environment. For example, Minko and coworkers [63] obtained the image of adsorbed poly(2-vinylpyridine) single chains (as thin as 0.4 nm) in aqueous solution under different pH values. The chain conformation changes from a two-dimensional (2D) random coil to a strongly compressed three-dimensional (3D) coil at a critical pH of 4.0. In this study, SEM and TEM can only give 2D images, but AFM provides true 3D surface profiles with similar resolution to that of TEM. However, there are also disadvantages in AFM. One is that the field of view in AFM is about 100 µm, which is not as large as SEM (its field of view can reach the order of 1 mm). Another disadvantage is that artifacts in AFM imaging need to be considered carefully; these can arise from the probe, scanning method, image process, and environmental vibration.

1.4.4 Recent Development: Video AFM

One shortcoming in conventional AFM is that it takes a relatively long time (e.g., about a minute) to scan the sample surface and obtain an image. The scanning time is simply not fast enough to yield real-time information about polymer crystallization or melting processes, whose rate is about 1–2 orders of magnitude faster than the imaging speed. A new video AFM [64] technique has been developed, where the imaging speed is in the range of tens of milliseconds. This technique is ideal for studying many kinetics/dynamics behaviors of crystalline polymers in real time. The principle of this technique is that when a force is applied to the end of the tip, the responding resonance of the cantilever (the source of limitation in the scanning rate) is changed. As a result, the imaging rate is significantly improved.

1.4.5 Selected Applications

In polymer crystallization studies, AFM has been successfully used to observe the crystal growth in real time [11–16, 65–72]. For example, Chan, Li, and coworkers synthesized a series of polymers (BA–Cn) by phase transfer-catalyzed polyetherification of 1,n-dibromoalkane (Cn) with bisphenol A (BA). These polymers crystallize slowly near room temperature, and thus are ideal for *in situ* AFM study under the ambient environment [73–75]. The authors reported the nucleation process as well as the growth process of lamella and spherulites (Fig. 1.7). It was seen that the original embryo could either disappear or grow into a stable founding lamella (when the size became larger than the critical value). After it reached about 1 µm in length, lamellar branching (e.g., the occurrence of lamella 2 in Fig. 1.7) was observed. As the growth continued, more branching and splaying took place. Figure 1.8 shows the temperature dependence of lamellar growth rate for BA–C10 (the maximum rate is at 55°C). At the later stage of the lamellar growth, a spherulitic structure was seen. Figure 1.9 shows the images of spherulites developed from homogeneous nucleation (left) and heterogeneous nucleation (right).

Hobbs and coworkers were the first group to demonstrate the use of *in situ* AFM technique to study flow-induced polymer crystallization [76]. For example, their results on the formation of shish–kebab structure in deformed PE melts (deformation was induced by dragging the glass or razor blade across the surface) shown in Figure 1.10a–d were taken at 132, 131.5, 131, and 130.5°C, respectively, during cooling at 0.5°C/min. The perpendicular growth of folded-chain kebab crystals, which were initiated from the shish surface, was clearly observed,. It was interesting to find that some adjacent kebabs from different shish grew toward each other and connected themselves (e.g., A in Fig. 1.10c) or changed their directions to avoid joining (B in Fig. 1.10b). In Figure 1.10d, the arrow represents a newly formed kebab nucleated from a shish, while the dotted lines

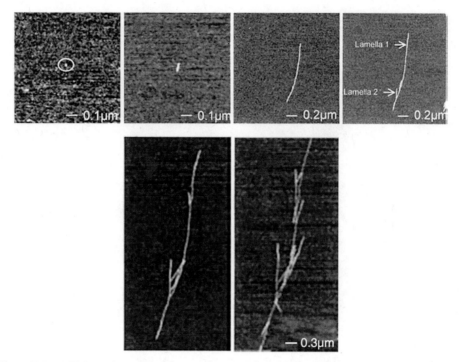

Figure 1.7 AFM tapping mode images of BA-C8 during crystallization at room temperature. One embryo developed into a straight founding lamella; later the branching and splaying occurred [73–75].

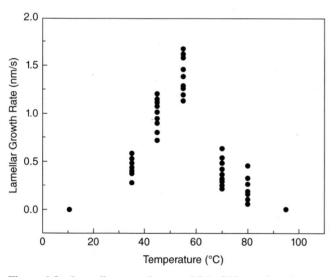

Figure 1.8 Lamellar growth rate of BA-C10 as a function of crystallization temperature [73–75].

Figure 1.9 AFM images of homogeneously nucleated (left) and heterogeneously nucleated (right) BA-C8 spherulites crystallized at 30°C [73–75].

indicate the distorting effect of drift. The authors also measured the growth rate of individual lamellae (numbers 1–7 in Fig. 1.11) under isothermal conditions. They found that the growth rate of a chosen lamella varied significantly at different times, and they also varied for different lamellae at a specific time. This indicates that the constant growth rate of spherulites observed by optical microscopy was not the case for lamellar structures at nanoscale. Further illustrations of this technique are discussed in Chapter 15.

Sophisticated numerical analysis on AFM images can be used to obtain lamellar information. Figure 1.12a–c represents AFM phase images showing the evolution of crystalline structure of PCL/PVC 75/25 (wt/wt) blend at 40°C by Ivanov et al. [77, 78]. Since the boundary between crystal and amorphous phases was defined more clearly in phase image than height image, they chose a critical value in phase image, which was obtained by optimizing the contour line fuzziness, to represent

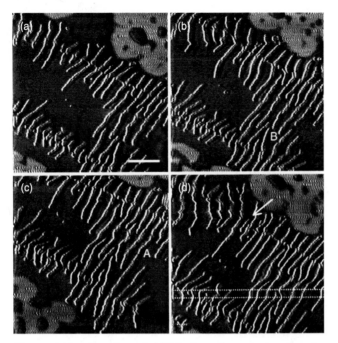

Figure 1.10 A series of AFM phase images showing the growth of shish–kebab structure in deformed PE melts during cooling. The gray scale represents a change in the phase angle of 60°. The scale bar represents 300 nm [76].

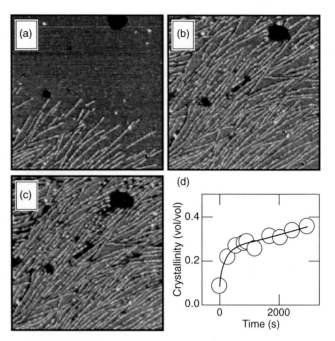

Figure 1.12 (a), (b), (c) are 1 × 1 μm² AFM phase images recorded during isothermal melt crystallization of a PCL/PVC 75/25 (wt/wt) blend at 40°C. Elapsed times are 0 s (a), 541 s (b), and 2931 s (c). The full gray scale is 16°. (d) Volume crystallinity estimated from the images taken at the session [77, 78].

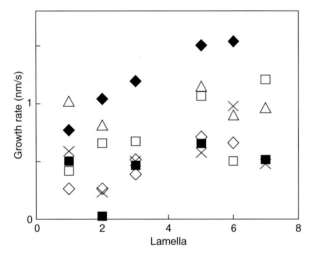

Figure 1.11 The growth rate of seven individual lamella (numbers 1–7) from isothermal crystallization of PE at various times [76].

the intensity envelope of the boundary. So the phase image can be converted to binary format containing only crystal pixels and amorphous pixels, which were above or below the critical value, respectively. The volume crystallinity was estimated by the fraction of crystal pixels, and the results are illustrated in Figure 1.12d. They also obtained the crystal thickness of poly(ethylene terephthalate) (PET) and its distribution during crystallization at 233°C, as shown in Figure 1.13. The thickness of the PET lamella was quite uniform, about 10 nm, without much variation as the time elapsed during isothermal crystallization.

1.5 NUCLEAR MAGNETIC RESONANCE

Nuclear magnetic resonance (NMR) is a powerful spectroscopic technique for studying semicrystalline polymers [79, 80]. The principle of NMR is based on the transition between quantized energy levels caused by the interactions between the material and electromagnetic radiation. There are some prerequisites for the materials suitable for NMR study. First, the nuclei should have a spin angular momentum with an associated magnetic moment, which means the spin quantum number (I) of the nuclei cannot be zero. This requires an odd number of protons or neutrons in the nuclei. Nuclei like ^{16}O or ^{12}C are thus not applicable in NMR spectroscopy. Second, an external magnetic field B_0 is needed to induce the split of the energy levels, depending on the direction of spin component: parallel or antiparallel to B_0. The number of energy levels is given by $2I + 1$. Thus, nuclei like ^1H and ^{13}C (whose I is 1/2) have two energy levels; for other nuclei with I value of 1 or

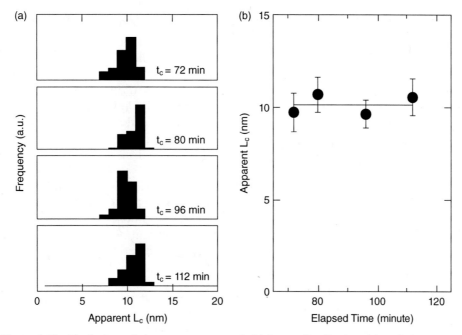

Figure 1.13 Evolution of the apparent crystal thickness distribution (a) and the average crystal thickness (b) computed from the AFM phase images of PET at 233°C. The error bars in (b) indicate the standard deviations of the distributions [77, 78].

3/2, there are 3 or 4 split energy levels—such a situation is too complicated when the transition takes place and is difficult to use in practice. Finally, when an electromagnetic field, perpendicular to the magnetic field, is applied to the sample, the transition can occur at a specific frequency when the energy of the electromagnetic waves is equal to the energy difference between two levels, and this frequency is proportional to the strength of applied external magnetic field. In NMR, the applied frequency is usually between 60 and 600 MHz (they are classified as radio frequency), a higher frequency of up to 900 MHz is also available today, and the magnetic field can be up to about 20 T.

1.5.1 Chemical Shift

If the nuclei are in an isolated environment, their NMR spectrum is a sharp line. However, in reality, nuclei are surrounded by high-velocity electrons, forming an additional magnetic field, which can decrease or increase the effects of external magnetic fields. This behavior is termed "shielding" or "de-shielding," respectively. The nearby atoms can also affect the local magnetic environment and cause the splitting, broadening, and shifting of the lines in the spectrum. The shifting of the lines is called "chemical shift." The NMR spectrum is obtained by plotting absorption versus the chemical shift. Chemical shift is a very sensitive way to characterize the chemical environment. The peak broadening in an NMR spectrum can occur under many circumstances, including anisotropic magnetic shielding, interactions with the surrounding nuclear spin dipoles, and disorder of the structure.

1.5.2 Relevant Techniques

1.5.2.1 Pulsed Fourier Transform NMR Pulsed Fourier transform (FT) NMR represents a breakthrough technique in NMR. Different from conventional NMR, which employs the continuous wave method (i.e., a small amplitude radio frequency wave is applied to the sample continuously, where the frequency or the strength of the magnetic field is varied), pulsed FT NMR utilizes a short and high-power radio frequency pulse that actually contains many frequencies in a broad band and thus can excite the resonances of all spins at the same time. The information collected by this method is the free induction decay of the nuclei, which can be converted into an ordinary NMR spectrum by Fourier transformation. There are many advantages in pulsed FT NMR, including the increase of signal-to-noise ratio, short experimental duration, and easy analysis of the signals.

1.5.2.2 Dipolar Decoupling As the natural abundance of ^{13}C is low, the spins between ^{13}C nuclei are well separated from each other. But the large number of nearby ^{1}H can interfere with the decay of ^{13}C nuclei through a collection of weak interactions (so-called hetero-nuclear dipolar coupling). In solution NMR, dipolar coupling averages to zero due to the thermal motion and fast reorientation of molecules. But it becomes the dominant broadening factor in solid-state NMR (the broadening may be of the order of 20 kHz). In principle, the sample can be spun at a high speed to suppress dipolar couplings, thus reducing line broadening. But this is not practical because mechanical challenges of spinning the sample at high speeds cannot be resolved easily. One effective method to suppress dipolar coupling is to irradiate the sample with a strong radio frequency signal at the proton resonance frequency to hold ^{1}H nuclei in a highly resonating state so that they are not capable of absorbing resonance from ^{13}C.

1.5.2.3 Magic Angle Spinning In solid-state NMR, the chemical shift anisotropy also has a profound effect on the spectrum in peak broadening and absorption. This is because the molecular orientation in the solid cannot be averaged out as in solution and thus the surrounding electron density is asymmetric. The higher the restriction of polymer chains, the more severe the problem is. The chemical shift anisotropy is related to the geometric factor $3\cos^2\theta - 1$. This term becomes zero if θ is equal to 54.7°, which is called the "magic angle." So by spinning the solid sample at the magic angle with respect to the external magnetic field, the effect due to chemical shift anisotropy and dipolar coupling are both minimized. In a way, magic angle spinning in the solid state has the same benefit as the thermal motion in the solution.

1.5.2.4 Cross Polarization While the combination of dipolar decoupling and magic angle spinning provides a way to yield high resolution solid-state NMR spectrum, the problem of low sensitivity still exists due to the low natural abundance of ^{13}C and their long spin-lattice relaxation times in the solid samples. To overcome this problem, cross polarization, a method involving the excitation of ^{1}H spins and then transfer of the excitation to ^{13}C, can be applied. Specifically, ^{1}H magnetization is built up first along the magnetic field and then a 90° pulse rotates the net ^{1}H magnetic moment to the x-axis in the rotating frame. Immediately after the 90° pulse, the ^{1}H irradiation field is shifted from the x-axis to the y-axis by a 90° phase shift in the ^{1}H irradiation, resulting in a spin-lock condition. The transfer of magnetization from ^{1}H spins to ^{13}C spins occurs when the Hartmann–Hahn condition is fulfilled, that is, ^{1}H and ^{13}C resonate at the same frequency. Cross polarization and magic angle spinning is now often combined (CP-MAS NMR) to remove the anisotropic effects, which becomes the most useful technique in solid-state NMR.

1.5.3 Recent Development: Multidimensional NMR

The NMR techniques discussed thus far are all conventional one-dimensional (1D) methods with the aim of reducing dipolar interactions and chemical shift anisotropy. However, the line broadening factors in fact contain useful information related to structure and motion. The extension of NMR spectroscopy to two or more dimensions makes it possible to study the broadening mechanisms and other molecular information. 2D NMR experiments can be divided into four time periods that follow each other, including a preparation period, an evolution period, a mixing period, and a detection period. The preparation and detection periods are the same as excitation and detection in 1D NMR. But in 2D NMR, the spins are allowed to evolve freely in a given time frame under the influence of relevant spin interactions after the preparation period. During the mixing period, changes can occur in the system, such as molecular motion, spin interaction, relaxation, and manipulation. A 3D NMR can be constructed easily from a 2D NMR by inserting an additional indirect evolution time and a second mixing period between the first mixing period and the detection period. Based on the same principle, multidimensional NMR can also be obtained [81].

1.5.4 Selected Applications

In polymer crystallization studies, NMR can be used to obtain information related to structure, chain relaxation, and crystallinity [82–84]. For example, two types of crystal structure, orthorhombic and monoclinic, are available in PE. The orthorhombic crystal structure is formed under normal conditions, while the monoclinic crystal structure can be formed under high pressure, deformed conditions, or in copolymers under normal crystallization conditions.

For example, Hu et al. [85] investigated the monoclinic phase in ethylene copolymers by solid-state NMR. Figure 1.14 shows three CP-MAS ^{13}C NMR spectra of an ethylene copolymer containing 12 mol% butene comonomers crystallized under different thermal conditions. The peak at 34 ppm was assigned to the monoclinic phase, whereas the peak at lower chemical shift was from the orthorhombic phase. The ratios of monoclinic phase to orthorhombic phase were found to be similar in as-received and quenched extrudate samples. The lower intensity in the quenched sample indicates that the size of the crystal was relatively small. In slowly cooled samples, a larger fraction of monoclinic phase was found, which was attributed to increase of crystalline–amorphous interface, which enhanced the stability of the monoclinic phase.

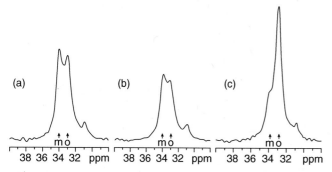

Figure 1.14 Solid-state CP-MAS ^{13}C NMR spectra of ethylene–butene copolymer: (a) as-received, (b) melted and quenched in iced water, and (c) melted and slowly cooled [85].

1.6 SCATTERING TECHNIQUES: X-RAY, LIGHT, AND NEUTRON

When radiation interacts with matter, it can be absorbed or scattered. In the scattering process, if the scattered beam has the same wavelength as the incident beam, the phenomenon is called elastic scattering. Analysis of the time-averaged intensity distribution in this type of measurement will yield geometric information about the scatterers. On the other hand, the wavelength of the scattered beam can be varied by the internal motion of scatterers, which results in a frequency shift depending on the type of motion. Quasi-elastic scattering such as photon correlation spectroscopy and inelastic scattering such as Raman scattering fall into this category. In this case, analysis of intensity fluctuation in time space or line shift/broadening in frequency space can yield information on the dynamic properties of the system. This section will focus on the elastic scattering phenomenon, which is most relevant to semicrystalline polymers.

The principles of X-ray, light, and neutron scattering are essentially the same. The correlations between the measured intensity distribution in reciprocal space and the structure analysis in real space can be made mathematically by Fourier transformation. However, depending on the details of the interaction between radiation and matter, the data analysis techniques may be quite different. Light has the longest wavelength among the three radiation sources; it can only interact with outer-shell electrons of an atom. Therefore, the scattered intensity from light is mainly determined by the fluctuations of polarization. X-rays also interact with electrons, but it has a much higher energy than light; its scattered intensity is related to the fluctuations of electronic density. A neutron beam can penetrate the electron shell and interact with the nucleus. Thus, its scattered intensity is profoundly influenced by the type of atom. The detecting range of these techniques is from angstroms (wide-angle X-ray diffraction [WAXD]) to micrometers (small-angle light scattering [SALS]), which makes them complementary tools to study hierarchical structures on the length scale from crystal lattice to supramolecular structure. In the following subsections, basic principles of scattering from all three sources, and their applications in polymer crystallization, are discussed.

1.6.1 Wide-Angle X-Ray Diffraction

WAXD is a powerful technique to examine the crystal structure at the atomic level and corresponding properties of semicrystalline polymers. A major application of WAXD is to determine material's 3D crystal structures. The protocol follows conventional routine: growing high-quality single crystal, performing diffraction measurements, indexing reflective peaks, and reconstructing the density map by properly solving the phase problem. In this case, the general principles are the same for inorganic, organic, polymeric, and biomacromolecules, which will not be discussed in this section. It belongs to a mature subject called X-ray crystallography. The readers are referred to some excellent monographs [86–89] dealing with this area, as well as the prestigious handbook of *International Table of Crystallography*. Examples of the use of WAXD for this purpose are described in Chapter 3 on the crystal structure of polymers.

This section will focus, from a practically point of view, on how to derive structural parameters that are closely related to characteristics of semicrystalline polymers, such as crystallinity, crystal orientation, and crystal size. The principle of WAXD can be understood by using the concept of the Ewald sphere and reciprocal lattice. Based on this concept, the correlation between the unit cell parameters in real space and the scattering vectors in reciprocal space can be established [90]. In the scattering measurements (including WAXD), the acquired results are either a 1D profile, that is, intensity change as a function of s (s is the scattering vector and is equal to $(2/\lambda)\sin(\theta/2)$, where λ is the wavelength and θ is the scattering angle), or 2D pattern, which is the intensity distribution as a function of both s and ϕ (the polar angle). The latter is most common in the study of anisotropic systems, such as polymer fibers or films. The data analysis scheme is the key to extracting desired structure information for varying applications, which are briefly described as follows.

1.6.1.1 Determination of Crystallinity WAXD has been routinely used to determine the degree of crystallinity in semicrystalline polymers. The method usually involves one assumption, that is, the system is considered as an ideal two-phase model containing only crystalline and amorphous phases. In this system, the scattered intensities from crystalline and amorphous phases can be separated and the degree of crystallinity X_c can be calculated as:

$$X_c = \frac{\sum_{hkl} I_{hkl}(s)}{\sum_{hkl} I_{hkl}(s) + I_a} = \frac{\int_V \bar{I}_{hkl}(\mathbf{s})d\mathbf{s}}{\int_V \bar{I}_{hkl}(\mathbf{s})d\mathbf{s} + \int_V \bar{I}_a(\mathbf{s})d\mathbf{s}} \quad (1.1)$$

where I_{hkl} represented the intensity of the diffraction peak with the index of hkl, the denominator represents the total scattered intensity, and I_a represents the intensity scattered by the amorphous fraction. The volume integration of any scattering point can expressed as

$$\int_V \bar{I}(\mathbf{s})d\mathbf{s} = \int_0^{2\pi} d\psi \int_0^{\pi} \sin\phi d\phi \int_0^{\infty} I(s,\phi,\psi)s^2 ds \quad (1.2)$$

where ψ and ϕ represent the azimuthal angle and polar angle, respectively, and $I(s,\phi,\psi)$ represents the scattered intensity of a point on the surface of the pole figure. In practice, it is difficult to collect the entire 3D scattered intensity distribution in reciprocal space. Usually a 1D or 2D detector is used and information obtained is $I(s)$ or $I(s,\phi)$, respectively. Therefore, the volume integration must be carried out by making certain assumptions. Powder diffraction from the isotropic system illustrates the simplest example. In this case, the scattered intensity is only dependent on s (not ϕ and ψ). The expression of crystallinity can thus be simplified by the integration of $I(s)s^2$ [91].

If crystals show orientation preference, the data obtained from a 1D detector cannot give complete information since the scattered intensity is not evenly distributed on the Ewald sphere, but has some preferred distribution as a function of ϕ and ψ. A simple case to deal with this situation can be found in the system with simple fiber (or cylindrical) symmetry, which means that the scattered intensity is only a function of s and ϕ, but not ψ. Therefore, the triple integration in Equation (1.2) becomes a double one (the integration over ψ angle simply leads to a factor of 2π). Without this assumption, the evaluation of Equation (1.2) can be complicated [92].

1.6.1.2 Degree of Orientation Orientation is an important characteristic in deformed crystalline polymers. In practice, polymers are often oriented by processes such as stretching, injection molding, and extrusion. Polymer crystals formed under these conditions have preferred orientation and thus yield an anisotropic scattering pattern. Examples of this are discussed at length in Chapter 16 in the context of crystallization under processing conditions. By analyzing the scattered intensity distribution associated with certain reflection planes, it is possible to quantitatively evaluate the condition of crystalline orientation. The orientation of a certain reflection plane can be characterized by the angle between its normal and the reference axis. The orientation condition of polymer crystals with fiber symmetry can be described by the Hermans' orientation function (f) defined as [93]

$$f = \frac{1}{2}(3\langle\cos^2\phi\rangle - 1) \quad (1.3)$$

where the term $\langle\cos^2\phi\rangle$ represents the mean square of $\cos\phi$, having the following form

$$\langle\cos^2\phi\rangle = \frac{\int_0^{2\pi} d\psi \int_0^{\pi/2} I(\phi,\psi)\cos^2\phi\sin\phi d\phi}{\int_0^{2\pi} d\psi \int_0^{\pi/2} I(\phi,\psi)\sin\phi d\phi}. \quad (1.4)$$

Equation (1.4) gives the full expression, in which intensity varies with both polar angle ϕ and azimuthal angle ψ. If fiber symmetry is assumed, the intensity will be the same with given ϕ and s and the integration of ψ yields a constant 2π. Usually, a flat 2D detector is used to record the scattering pattern, which is a stereo-projection of 3D scattering intensity distribution. In this case, Fraser correction is needed to correct the distortion due to the stereo-projection [94]. The Hermans' orientation function varies between -0.5 and 1. When $f = -0.5$, the normal and the reference axes are perpendicular to each other; when $f = 1$, the normal is in parallel to the reference axis; when $f = 0$, the system has random orientation.

A more advanced approach to analyzing crystal orientation distribution is to compute the entire 2D diffraction pattern and then compare simulated intensity with experimental data. In this case, it is possible to derive the complete orientation distribution of crystals in real space, and the Hermans' orientation function can be analytically or numerically given, depending on integration kernel used for simulation. Details of 2D pattern computation and mathematical treatment of orientation distribution function was reviewed by Burger [92]. Examples can be found in References [95, 96].

1.6.1.3 Determination of Crystal Size For perfect and infinitely large crystals, the diffraction intensity distribution in reciprocal space is a set of triple periodic impulses. If crystals are restricted in given boundaries, that is, they have finite sizes, the impulse will broaden into certain intensity distributions centered on each node. Therefore, it is possible to estimate the information of crystal size from line broadening intensity around each node in reciprocal space. Mathematically, this is achieved by introducing a form factor into the expression of density distribution and analyzing properties of its Fourier transform. Equation (1.5) gives the general expression of deriving the crystal size from an experimentally obtained scattering profile [90].

$$\frac{\int i(s_0)ds_0}{i^{\max}(s_0)} = 1/L \quad (1.5)$$

where L is the crystal's length in the direction perpendicular to the hkl plane, $i(s_0)$ is proportional to the measured intensity and $i^{\max}(s_0)$ is the maximum of $i(s_0)$ located at $s_0 = 0$ (thus it has a fixed value for a given hkl plane). Equation (1.5) is derived from simple assumptions that the crystal is cubic in shape and the crystal sizes are uniform. In practice, these two requirements are rarely satisfied. However, it still gives a good approximation that the obtained length L can be viewed as a statistical average value. A numerical analysis leads to Scherrer's equation [97]:

$$\beta = \frac{0.9}{L\cos(\theta/2)} \quad (1.6)$$

where β is the full width of half maximum of the line in radian, and θ and λ are the scattering angle and wavelength, respectively. The coefficient 0.9 is a numerical fitting parameter. To obtain a more precise value, appropriate corrections need to be made to the measured diffraction profile [97].

1.6.2 Small-Angle X-Ray Scattering

In principle, the analysis of small-angle X-ray scattering (SAXS) data has no difference from that of WAXD. However, as SAXS measurement mainly focuses on structures on the length scale of nanometers, the usually strict periodicity of scattering unit disappears. In other words, one cannot predict the scatterers' spatial position precisely with some pre-knowledge as in WAXD (i.e., the crystallographic analysis). Thus, it is necessary to establish the relationships between the scattered intensity and structure by a statistical approach [98]. One such relationship is the correlation function, which is mathematically identical to the Patterson function when dealing with the crystal structure using WAXD. For semicrystalline polymers, one basic scattering unit in SAXS is the lamellar crystal, which is a building block for large aggregates or superstructures, such as spherulites. Although the size of lamellae is not uniform, their spatial arrangement often shows a certain degree of long-range correlation. For such a system, an intensity maximum will appear in the scattering profile. The position of the scattering intensity maximum s_m determines the so-called long period L, which is equal to $1/s_m$. The long period is the most direct information one can obtain from the SAXS profile. It represents a statistical average of the interlamellar distance. More advanced analysis can yield the information of lamellar thickness and other structural information, which is however not straightforward. In the following subsections, two standard ways of obtaining the lamellar thickness, based on a 1D stacking model, are discussed. In addition, a qualitative analysis of anisotropic patterns is also demonstrated.

1.6.2.1 Correlation Function Consider an ideal two-phase system. Imagine a chord with two ends A and B separated by a distance r, orienting perpendicular to layers. The 1D correlation function $\gamma_1(x)$ can be written based on density deviations of each phase from the average density [98–100]:

$$\gamma_1(x) = \frac{\langle \eta_A \eta_B \rangle_r}{\langle \eta_A^2 \rangle} \quad (1.7)$$

where η stands for the difference between the local densities and the averaged value; η_A and η_B are values at two ends of the chord. The numerator in Equation (1.7) is an average over all possible multiplications of η_A and η_B separated by distance r. The denominator is an average of η^2 over all points in the system. If the SAXS pattern is isotropic, indicating that each lamella orients independently, $\gamma_1(x)$ can be derived from the scattering curve using

$$\gamma_1(x) = \frac{\int_0^\infty I(s)s^2 \cdot \cos 2\pi sx\, ds}{\int_0^\infty I(s)s^2\, ds}. \quad (1.8)$$

If the thicknesses of lamellar and amorphous layers are monodispersed, $\gamma_1(x)$ will have the maximum value at the origin and will decrease linearly to a given minimum value, corresponding to the minimum overlap between the density distribution function and its autocorrelation counterpart. The minimum value will stay for a given distance and will then increase with x linearly until reaching another maximum location at $x = L$, indicating the first superposition of the density distribution function and its autocorrelation counterpart. The profile of $\gamma_1(x)$ versus x/L for a two-phase model is shown in Figure 1.15.

Once the thickness distribution of lamellar or amorphous domains becomes broader, the minimum horizontal line in Figure 1.15 becomes shorter. From Figure 1.15,

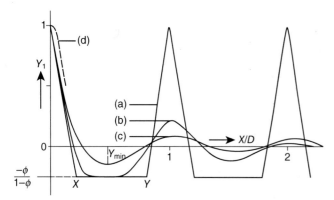

Figure 1.15 Illustration of 1D correlation function $\gamma_1(x)$ as a function of x/L. Curves (a), (b), and (c) represent the systems with different layer distance distribution. From (a) to (c), the distribution becomes broader. Curve (a) represents the system with monodispersed layer distance distribution. Curve (d) is for the system with a transition layer [98].

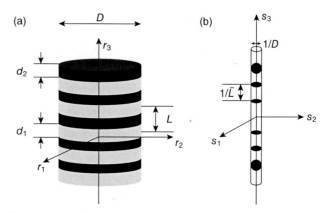

Figure 1.16 Illustration of lamellar stack (a) and its Fourier transformation (b) [106].

which can be obtained directly from experimental data, information on the fraction of crystalline and lamella thicknesses can be determined. The horizontal region of $\gamma_1(x)$ in Figure 1.15 corresponds to the value of $-\phi/(1-\phi)$ (where ϕ represents the volume fraction of crystalline phase). In addition, the slope of the initial part of the correlation function can be expressed as

$$\left(\frac{d\gamma_1(x)}{dx}\right)_{x=0} = \frac{-S/V}{2\phi(1-\phi)} \quad (1.9)$$

where S and V stand for specific surface area and volume, respectively. For an ideal two-phase lamella system, $S/V = 2/L$. Thus, the intercept of initial linearly decayed curve of $\gamma_1(x)$ on the x-axis is equal to $\phi(1-\phi)/L$, where the product ϕL represents the lamellar thickness [101–103].

1.6.2.2 Interface Distribution

Ruland approached the analysis of the alternating two-phase system in a different fashion [104]. He assumed that the system contains randomly oriented stacks with cylindrical symmetry, where each stack is composed of alternating phases with different density ρ_1 and ρ_2. The schematics of one single stack and its Fourier transformation in reciprocal space are shown in Figure 1.16.

In Figure 1.16, the orthogonal coordinates s_1, s_2, and s_3 in reciprocal space are correlated with r_1, r_2, and r_3 in real space (r_3 is the direction in which the density of stack alternates). The interface distribution function $g_1(r)$ can be obtained by the following expression:

$$\frac{1}{t}g_1(r) = \frac{16\pi^3}{V}\int_0^\infty \left(\lim_{x\to\infty} s^4 I(s) - s^4 I(s)\right)\cos(2\pi rs)\,ds. \quad (1.10)$$

Since the 1D density distribution in the r_3 direction is the combination of a set of step functions, their first derivatives are a set of delta functions. Autocorrelation of a set of delta functions is much easier to calculate when compared to operations on a set of step functions. In a typical interface distribution function $g_1(r)$ profile, the length distributions of the first and second phases, as well as the distance distributions between the second nearest interface, can be obtained. Equation (1.10) possesses a negative sign with respect to Equation (1.8), thus the shape of $g_1(r)$ has the reverse trend of Figure 1.15. Once the $g_1(r)$ profile is obtained directly from scattering curve, one can immediately determine the average thickness of each phase and its distribution.

The main operation in the correlation function and interface distribution function method is inverse Fourier transformation of the experimental scattering curve. The correctness in both methods depends very much on the quality of original data and careful extrapolations of scattering data to both zero and large angle. The extrapolation toward zero angle can be done in accordance with the method of Ruland [105]. An alternative approach is to keep the scattering profile as is and fit the curve with a relevant model. In this case error due to extrapolation and Fourier transform of noise data can be avoided. Examples can be found in References [106, 107].

1.6.2.3 Interpretation of Anisotropic 2D Scattering Pattern

Polymer crystallization under external fields (e.g., shear or extensional flows, stretching of polymer solids) usually exhibits preferred orientation, which results in anisotropic scattering patterns. For example, a four-point SAXS pattern was seen during solid-state uniaxial deformation of an ethylene–propylene copolymer (both experimental data and fitted 3D plot are shown in Fig. 1.17) [108].

Figure 1.17 can be explained by the following data analysis schemes. Figure 1.18a demonstrates the corresponding orientation geometry of a lamellar crystal in real space and reciprocal space. The scattered intensity localized between 0° and 90° (polar angle) can be attributed to lamellar tilting in the ϕ angle as shown in Figure 1.18a. Other localized intensity in symmetrical position can be explained based on the same argument. Depending on the tilt angle, the SAXS pattern can vary from four-point to two-point as systematically shown in Figure 1.18b, which was the primary reason for the explanation of Figure 1.17.

1.6.3 Small-Angle Light Scattering

Small-angle light scattering (SALS) is a useful tool for characterizing the crystalline structure on the micrometer scale [109]. It has been pointed out that the intensity in SALS is mainly due to the polarizability of scattering entities. This makes SALS particularly suitable for the investigation of lamellar structure (e.g., spherulite), which is optically anisotropic. In a SALS setup, a polarizer and an analyzer are inserted before and after the sample to control the polarization of the incident beam and the scattered beam. There are two important arrangements of polarizer and analyzer; that is, their polarization directions can be arranged parallel or perpendicular to each other. The corresponding scattering intensity profiles obtained under these geometries are denoted as I_{VV} and I_{HV} (V and H are abbreviations for "vertical" and "horizontal," respectively), where the first letter of the subscripts stands for the direction of analyzer and the second for the polarizer. A schematic of a typical SALS setup is shown in Figure 1.19.

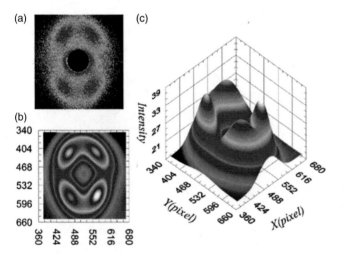

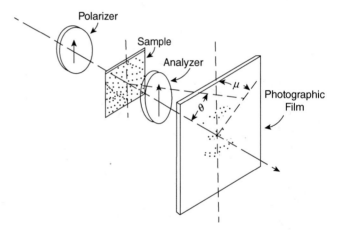

Figure 1.19 Schematic of typical SALS setup [109].

Figure 1.17 Experimental and fitted data of an ethylene–propylene copolymer after stretching: (a) experimental pattern, (b) fitted 3D plot, and (c) contour plot of (b) [108].

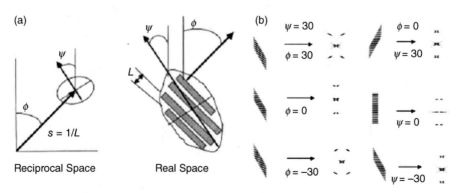

Figure 1.18 Illustration of orientation geometry in real space and reciprocal space (a) and scattering pattern corresponding to different orientation conditions (b) [108].

1.6.3.1 Spherulite Radius

Stein made a series of pioneering SALS studies on polymer crystallization involving spherulitic growth. Suppose lamellar crystals grow in the radial direction of the spherulite, each of which is characterized by two parameters, α_t and α_r, which represent polarizabilities in tangential and radial directions, respectively. I_{HV} can be written as [109, 110]:

$$I_{HV} = KV_s^2\left[\left(\frac{3}{U^3}\right)(\alpha_t - \alpha_r)\sin\mu\cos\mu \right.\\ \left. \cos^2\frac{\theta}{2}\cdot(4\sin U - U\cos U - 3Si)\right]^2 \quad (1.11)$$

where K is a constant; V_s is the volume of the spherulite; θ is the scattering angle; μ is the azimuth angle; $U = qR_s$, where R_s is the radius of the spherulite and q is the scattering vector ($q = 2\pi s$); and Si represents the expression $\int_0^U (\sin x)/(x)\,dx$. In Equation (1.11), I_{HV} depends on both μ and q. The maximum intensity appears along $\pm 45°$. In vertical and horizontal directions, I_{HV} equals zero. Therefore, Equation (1.11) explains the clover-leaf-type pattern frequently obtained under the HV mode. Furthermore, an intensity maximum should be found along $\pm 45°$, where the size of the spherulite can be determined as $R_s = 4.1/q$. Equation (1.11) was derived without the consideration of multiple scattering. For a polydisperse system, the scattering pattern is more diffuse. The obtained spherulite radius is a statistical average over all spherulites with different sizes in the illuminated region.

1.6.3.2 Optical Sign of Spherulite

The optical sign of a spherulite can be obtained from the expression of I_{VV} [110].

$$I_{VV} = KV_s^2\left(\frac{3}{U^3}\right)^2\left[(\alpha_t - \alpha_s)(2\sin U - U\cos U - Si)\right.\\ + (\alpha_r - \alpha_s)(Si - \sin U) \\ \left. + (\alpha_r - \alpha_t)\cos^2\left(\frac{\theta}{2}\right)\cos^2\mu(4\sin U - U\cos U - 3Si)\right]^2. \quad (1.12)$$

Differing from the formula of I_{HV}, I_{VV} depends not only on the difference between α_t and α_r but on their difference with α_s, the polarizability of surrounding. In most cases, α_s is smaller than α_t and α_r. According to Equation (1.12), the I_{VV} scattering pattern should exhibit two lobes located along the vertical or horizontal direction, depending on the optical sign of spherulite. When $\alpha_t > \alpha_r$, the spherulite has negative birefringence; when $\alpha_t < \alpha_r$, the spherulite has positive birefringence.

1.6.3.3 Ring-Banded Spherulite

Ring-banded spherulites are also frequently observed under certain conditions due to periodic twisting of lamellae along the radial direction. Under a microscope, the spherulite image will show a series of alternate dark and light concentric rings. Theoretical calculation of SALS patterns from ring-banded spherulites has been carried out by Stein et al. [111, 112]. If the twisting angle grows linearly in the radial direction, the following relationship between the twisting period and scattering maxima can be given:

$$\lambda = 2\rho\sin(\theta_m/2). \quad (1.13)$$

Equation (1.13) is analogous to Bragg's relation of diffraction where λ is the wavelength, ρ is the spacing of one twisting period, and θ_m is the scattering angle corresponding to the intensity maxima along q.

1.6.3.4 Deformed Spherulite

Theory and experiment on deformed spherulites have also been developed [113]. When a tensile force is applied to semicrystalline polymers, the typical spherulite can be deformed into a prolate spheroid. Equations (1.11) and Equation (1.12) still provide the framework of intensity calculation under HV and VV modes. Assuming the applied force is uniform and uniaxial, the shape factor U in the above expressions will change into

$$U = qR_0\lambda_s^{-1/2}[1 + (\lambda_s^3 - 1)\cos^2(\theta/2)\cos^2\mu]^{1/2} \quad (1.14)$$

where R_0 is the original radius of the undeformed spherulite and λ_s is the ratio of deformation. The deformed spherulite has a length of $\lambda_s R_0$ in the direction of stretching and of $\lambda_s^{-1/2}R_0$ in the direction perpendicular to it.

1.6.3.5 Anisotropic Fluctuation Approach

The above formula of scattered intensity under HV and VV modes are based on a model. The method requires a presumption of the structure from a given supramolecular aggregate composed of unit scatterers. The scattered intensity can also be derived from the fluctuation point of view using a statistical method as demonstrated by Stein et al. [114]. The authors derived the intensity formula based on anisotropic fluctuations, which also confirmed that the Deybe–Beche equation is a special case when no optical anisotropy is present in the scatterers [115]. The invariants of orientation fluctuation and density fluctuation can be obtained as:

$$Q_\delta = \int_0^\infty I_{HV}(q)q^2\,dq \propto \langle\delta^2\rangle \quad (1.15)$$

$$Q_\eta = \int_0^\infty \left[I_{VV} - \frac{4}{3}I_{HV}(q)\right]q^2\,dq \propto \langle\eta^2\rangle \quad (1.16)$$

where Q_δ and Q_η represent two invariants characterizing the magnitude of the system's fluctuations due to orientation (δ) and density (η) variation, respectively.

They can be directly obtained from the scattering curve, disregarding the detailed structure. Thus, they are very useful in the study of crystallization kinetics. Figure 1.20 gives an example of the change in Q_δ and Q_η during isothermal crystallization of i-PP [116]. Q_η shows a maximum, depending on the filling of crystals into the amorphous matrix, while Q_δ increases monotonically with time, indicating the growth and perfection of crystals. It can also be seen that the absolute value of Q_η occurs early as compared with that of Q_δ, which might be caused by some kind of precursors with no anisotropy before crystallization. These results shed light on the mechanism of polymer crystallization.

1.6.4 Small-Angle Neutron Scattering

From the viewpoint of scattering theory, neutron scattering and X-ray scattering can be interpreted with the same framework. However, unlike X-ray scattering experiments, in which the X-ray beam is scattered by electrons, the neutron beam is scattered by nuclei. Despite this difference, the data analysis part of both experiments is similar. One major advantage of the neutron scattering measurement is the deuterium labeling technique, which allows selective "labeling" of part of the sample under the neutron beam. This is particularly useful for obtaining the geometric information about a specific component in the specimen. Therefore, small-angle neutron scattering (SANS) can be a complimentary tool to SAXS. A detailed description of methodology, including the deuterium procedure, can be found elsewhere [100]. This section mainly deals with some of the applications of SANS in polymer crystallization.

One chosen example is about the investigation of the location of chain ends in the lamellar crystal. By selective deuterium labeling on several segments of both ends of an alkene, Ungar et al. were able to identify the locations of chain ends during crystallization [117, 118]. Figure 1.21 shows SANS curves during isothermal

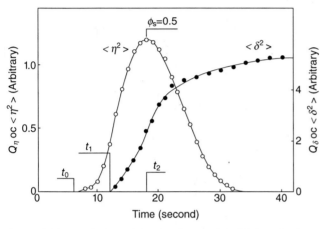

Figure 1.20 Variation of density fluctuation (Q_η) and orientation fluctuation (Q_δ) with time during isothermal crystallization of iPP [116].

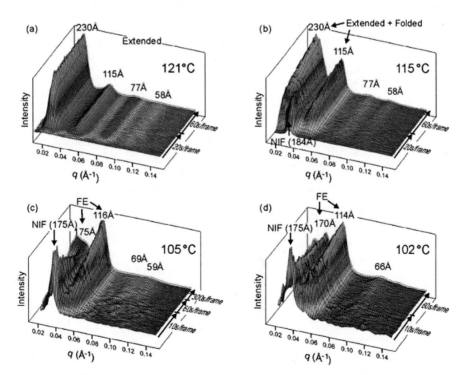

Figure 1.21 Time-resolved SANS study on isothermal crystallization process of C12D25C192H384DC11D23 at (a)121, (b)115, (c)107, and (d)102°C [117, 118].

crystallization of custom-synthesized alkane C216D (abbreviated for $C_{12}D_{25}C_{192}H_{384}DC_{11}D_{23}$) under four different temperatures. This polymer is composed of 216 carbon atoms with the last 12 –CH_2 groups on both ends being deuterated. For crystallizable short chain polymers such as n-alkanes, a very high crystallinity, close to 100%, can be achieved. If the system is monodisperse, the interpretation of the position of the scattering maximum (similar to the long period in SAXS) is very straightforward; it corresponds to the lamellar thickness, because the amorphous layer in this extreme case can be omitted. At high temperatures (e.g., 121°C), the polymer crystallizes into extended-chain crystals since the lamellar thickness calculated from the long period is 230 Å, close to the contour length of the chain when the chain is fully extended. Three high-order scattering maxima are also found at expected positions; that is, their q values are integer multiples of the main peak. As temperature decreases, the polymer first forms unstable transient, noninteger folded chain crystals, which then change into stable, integer folded chain crystals. The peak position associated with noninteger folded chain crystals is located between those of once-folded and twice-folded chain crystals. Furthermore, since only chain ends are labeled, it suggests that chain ends are located in the interfaces between the amorphous and crystalline layers. By imposing Fourier transformation upon the scattering curve, the authors also mapped out the density distribution of the sample, and the tilt angle of the chain within the lamella [117].

1.7 DIFFERENTIAL SCANNING CALORIMETRY

Differential scanning calorimetry (DSC) is an effective analytical tool for characterizing the physical properties of a polymer. DSC allows determination of melting, crystallization, and mesomorphic transition temperatures and the corresponding enthalpy and entropy changes, as well as characterization of the glass transition and other effects that show changes either in heat capacity or in a latent heat. Calorimetry takes a special place among other methods. In addition to calorimetry's simplicity and universality, the energetic characteristics (heat capacity C_P and its integral over temperature T—enthalpy H), measured via DSC, have a clear physical meaning, even though sometimes interpretation may be difficult. For characterization of semicrystalline polymers using DSC, the readers are encouraged to refer to a review of this subject [119].

1.7.1 Modes of Operation

Differential scanning calorimeters consist commonly of two sample positions—one for the sample under investigation and the other for a reference sample, which is often an empty crucible or one filled with an inert material. The principle of operation of a DSC, data treatment, and calibration are described in great detail in several monographs [120–123] and will not be repeated here.

1.7.1.1 Thermal Scan The most common mode of operation of a DSC is heating or cooling at a constant rate. The primary outcome of such an experiment is heat flow rate as a function of time. If the temperature of the sample position is known, data can also be represented as heat flow rate versus temperature. Figure 1.22 shows a typical example. From the heat flow rate curves (Fig. 1.22a), heat capacity, C_p, and with known sample mass, specific heat capacity, c_p, can be obtained. Isotherms at the beginning and at the end of the scan are commonly used to correct for small changes in heat losses between empty, sapphire, and sample measurements by aligning these parts of the curves. Small changes in losses are unavoidable because the thermal properties, such as thermal conductivity, of the samples are changing. On the other hand, inspection of the heat flow rate at the isotherms allows for a check of correct placement and thermal contacts of the parts of the measuring system moved during sample replacement.

In Figure 1.22, comparison of measured specific heat capacity with the reference data from Advanced Thermal Analysis System Data Bank (ATHAS-DB) provides more detailed information about crystallization and melting ranges than is available from the peaks alone [124]. Most of the cold crystallization takes place between 165°C and 200°C. But up to about 230°C, specific heat capacity is very close to the crystalline reference line because an overall exothermic crystallization process is superimposed on base line heat capacity of the semicrystalline polymer. Without such an exothermic contribution, specific heat capacity should be somewhere in between the liquid and the solid reference lines. The measured signal becomes larger than the liquid reference line only at temperatures above 250°C, indicating an overall endothermic melting process. It is known that melting and recrystallization is a continuous process in this temperature region and the sign of the latent heat depends on the imbalance of the two processes, which will be discussed later.

Examples of the use of thermal scanning DSC in the context of polymer melting behavior are discussed further in Chapter 10, and for confined crystallization in Chapter 12.

In addition to scan measurements on heating, DSC allows for cooling in a wide range of cooling rates too. Depending on the instrument and temperature range of interest, cooling rates of up to 500 K/min may be reached

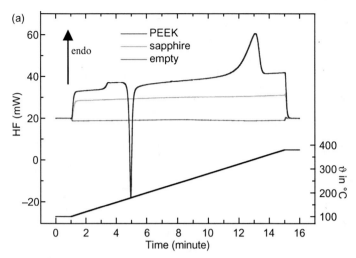
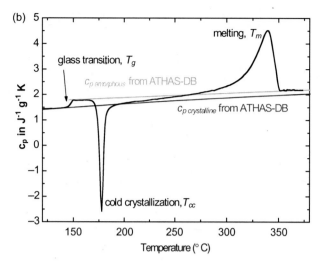

Figure 1.22 (a) Temperature profile and measured heat flow rate for empty pans, sapphire calibration standard (34 mg), and initially amorphous PEEK (29 mg), Heating rate $\beta = 20$ K/min, Perkin Elmer Pyris Diamond DSC. (b) Specific heat capacity versus temperature. Reference data (straight lines) for the fully amorphous (liquid) and crystalline (solid) PEEK from ATHAS-DB [124].

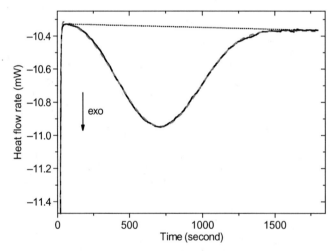

Figure 1.23 Isothermal crystallization experiment on 5 mg of isotactic polypropylene (iPP) at 122°C after cooling from 180°C at 20 K/min. The dotted line is the base line for peak integration and the dashed line is a fit of the KJMA equation to the data.

[125]. However, generally the temperature range for controlled cooling at the highest rates is limited. The possibility of cooling a sample reasonably fast allows studying of structure formation in far-from-equilibrium situations like "quasi" isothermal crystallization at deep undercooling.

1.7.1.2 Isothermal Heat Flow Rate Measurements

A typical "quasi" isothermal crystallization experiment is shown in Figure 1.23. In a first step, the previous crystallization history is erased by annealing at a temperature above the melting temperature of the most stable polymer crystals or, as another possibility, by keeping some crystal nuclei by partial melting (self-nucleation). Next, the sample is cooled to the crystallization temperature. Cooling must be fast enough to avoid crystallization on cooling. If all nuclei were removed, often an induction time is observed and after that crystallization occurs, yielding an exothermic heat flow rate.

After switching from fast cooling to isothermal conditions at time zero, the measured heat flow rate exponentially approaches a constant value (−10.3 mW) with a time constant of about 3 seconds for this DSC. The observed crystallization peak is often symmetric, and then the time of the peak maximum (minimum) is a measure of crystallization half time. Integration of the peak yields the enthalpy change, which can be transformed into relative crystallinity by dividing by the limiting value at infinite time. To obtain development of absolute crystallinity (mass fraction) the curve has to be divided by the enthalpy difference between crystal and liquid at the crystallization temperature, which is available from ATHAS-DB [124]. The commonly applied Kolmogorov–Johnson–Mehl–Avrami (KJMA) model for the kinetic analysis of isothermal crystallization data is based on volume fractions. Therefore, the mass fraction crystallinity, W_c, as always obtained from DSC, should be transformed into volume crystallinity.

1.7.1.3 Temperature Modulation
The first direct measurement of the frequency dependent complex heat

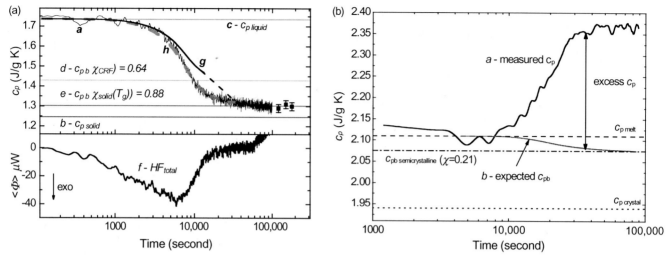

Figure 1.24 Time evolution of heat capacity during quasi-isothermal crystallization of (a) PHB at 296 K, $A_T = 0.4$ K, $t_p = 100$ s, Curve a; Curves b and c correspond to solid and liquid heat capacities from ATHAS-DB, respectively; Curve d was estimated from a two-phase model and Curve e, from a three-phase model; Curve f shows the exothermal effect in the total heat flow; Curves g and h are the expected values from model calculations. (b) PEEK at 306 K, $A_T = 0.5$ K, $t_p = 2400$ s [128].

capacity was performed in 1971 by Hamann et al. [126] at the glass transition of an inorganic polymer. The idea of combining DSC and periodic temperature perturbations (e.g., sinusoidal heating rate profiles) was reconsidered in 1992 due to improvements in computer technology [127], and the technology is termed temperature-modulated DSC (TMDSC). Since then, TMDSC has become a standard tool in thermal analysis and is widely used in polymer characterization.

One should keep in mind that heating (cooling) rate and not temperature is the perturbation in TMDSC. A calorimetric signal can be obtained only if temperature changes (i.e., scan rate ≠ 0). A heating rate perturbation may be added on top of any temperature–time profile, like scan or isothermal. In most cases, a linear underlying heating (cooling) rate or constant mean temperature is used. The (complex) amplitudes, as needed for heat capacity determination, can be obtained with high accuracy and sensitivity by frequency-selective techniques such as Fourier analysis or lock-in amplifiers. In this way, small changes in heat capacity, for example, due to crystallization, can be detected as a function of temperature or time. If baseline heat capacity, namely, heat capacity without any contribution from latent heat, is measured this way, the progress in crystallinity is monitored by the changes in heat capacity. Figure 1.24 shows quasi-isothermal TMDSC measurements during crystallization of polyhydroxybutyrate (PHB) and poly(ether ether ketone) (PEEK).

As shown in Figure 1.24a, baseline heat capacity for PHB was measured as a function of time and compared with the predictions for two- and three-phase models [128]. Such measurements not only allowed studying crystallization kinetics on very long time scales, but also provided information about the development of a rigid amorphous fraction (RAF). The RAF in PHB is established during the quasi-isothermal crystallization, as can be seen from the agreement of curve e with the measured heat capacity at the end of the crystallization process. This example is given here because it demonstrates the power of heat capacity measurements and shows the possibility of studying morphologically induced (isothermal) vitrification of the RAF during crystallization by TMDSC. Further illustrations of this technique are described in Chapter 10. In isothermal TMDSC measurements of polymers such as PEEK (Fig. 1.24B, at common low frequencies), latent heat may contribute to the measured reversing heat capacity. In this case, recrystallization processes appear as an exothermic peak in the nonreversing heat flow rate or heat capacity curves. As a general rule, we can argue that all processes, which are reversed on the time scale of the temperature modulation, contribute to the measured signals. Therefore, the concept of separating reversing and nonreversing events by subtracting the reversing heat flow rate from the total heat flow rate can be applied generally neither to crystallization nor to melting and recrystallization of polymers [129].

1.7.1.4 Fast Scanning Calorimetry

Another promising addition to conventional DSC is fast scanning DSC. By going to the limits of conventional DSCs, heating and cooling rates of up to 500 K/min (8 K/s) can be achieved [125]. At such high rates, care must be taken to avoid smearing of the DSC curves by thermal lag effects. One example study using this technique to characterize semicrystalline polymers is as follows. In melting curves of polymers, often multiple melting peaks are observed. The reason for this observation is still under debate, as either melting-recrystallization mechanisms, or the occurrence of at least two distinct crystal populations, can be considered. Scanning at different heating rates after isothermal crystallization is a powerful tool for distinguishing between those two explanations. In Figure 1.25, heating scans at different heating rates are shown for isothermally crystallized iPS [130].

In Figure 1.25, the high temperature melting peak moves to lower temperatures and decreases in size with increasing heating rate. This behavior is not a consequence of any thermal lag and provides evidence that this peak originates from a melting-recrystallization process on heating. The other peaks move to higher temperatures and increase in size. As long as two or more peaks are distinguishable, it is not possible to assign these peaks to melting-recrystallization or crystal populations of different stability. In the case shown in Figure 1.25, the situation becomes clear at very high rates only. At a heating rate of 500 K/min and more definitely at 30,000 K/min, only one melting peak remains. Clearly, there is only one population of crystals that melts between 200°C and 240°C. All other melting peaks seen at lower heating rates are due to melting-recrystallization. At a heating rate of 10 K/min, melting starts already at about 175°C, only 5 K above the crystallization temperature. As soon as some crystals are molten, the still oriented polymer melt recrystallizes immediately to form slightly more stable (thicker) lamellae. This process continues until there is no possibility to gain further stability on recrystallization within the existing lamellae stack. Then the whole stack has to melt to allow further recrystallization. This can explain the second melting peak seen at 10 K/min above 200°C. The small exothermic effect after this melting peak supports the view of immediate recrystallization. Then the continuous melting-recrystallization process proceeds until, according to the time determined by the heating rate, no recrystallization is possible anymore and the crystals finally melt. Final melting moves therefore to lower temperatures at higher heating rates, and at intermediate heating rates additional peaks may appear, depending on the recrystallization rate and possible gain in stability [131].

1.7.2 Determination of Degree of Crystallinity

DSC in scan mode is frequently used to determine heat of fusion, and from that, the degree of crystallinity of semicrystalline materials. In order to do so, the melting peak has to be integrated and the obtained heat of fusion has to be compared to the heat of fusion of a perfect crystal (100% crystallinity). For polymers, unfortunately, both tasks are not easy to solve. The melting region of polymers is often very broad, and multiple melting peaks may appear. Then construction of the "peak baseline" needed for the integration is not a simple task. The problem becomes even more complex if not only crystalline and liquid amorphous fractions coexist. For most semicrystalline polymers, a rigid amorphous fraction (RAF) coexists with the mobile amorphous fraction (MAF) and its devitrification (vitrification on cooling) has to be taken into account for the construction of the peak baseline too. Heat of fusion of the 100% crystalline material is commonly given for the equilibrium melting temperature, which may be significantly higher than the temperature of the observed melting range. Because of the width of the transition the temperature dependence of the heat of fusion of the 100% crystalline material has to be taken into account.

In Figure 1.26, heating scans of semicrystalline iPS are shown. Finding the right baseline for integration is the more serious problem for the determination of heat of fusion and degree of crystallinity of polymers. Assuming a simple two-phase system consisting of a crystalline

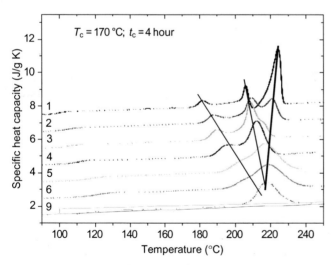

Figure 1.25 Temperature dependences of the specific heat capacity of iPS samples at the following heating rates: 1–10 K/min, 2–50 K/min, 3–100 K/min, 4–200 K/min, 5–400 K/min, 6–500 K/min, 7–30,000 K/min. The samples were crystallized at 170°C for 4 hours. The curves are vertically shifted and the straight lines are guides to the eyes only [130].

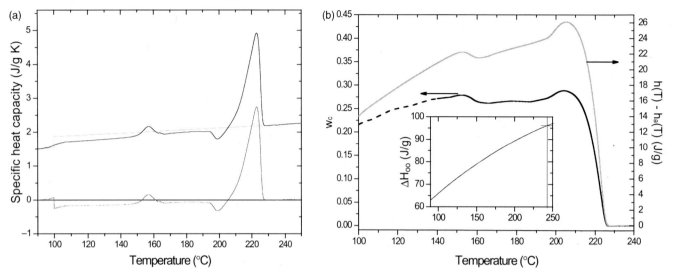

Figure 1.26 (a) Temperature dependences of the specific heat capacity of 4 mg semicrystalline iPS crystallized at 140°C for 12 hours at a heating rate of 10 K/min [133]. Upper curve: The straight line is the specific heat capacity for amorphous iPS from ATHAS-DB [124]. Lower curve: Difference of sample heat capacity and heat capacity of the amorphous PS as needed for integration according to Reference [132]. (b) Top curve; right axis: enthalpy change determined from the bottom curve in Figure 1.25a. Bottom curve: Degree of crystallinity according to Reference [132]. The inset shows the temperature-dependent heat of fusion (crystallization). Equilibrium melting temperature and the corresponding heat of fusion are indicated by the vertical and horizontal thin lines, respectively.

phase and an amorphous phase, which is always in the liquid state above its glass transition temperature, an enthalpy-based procedure could be suggested [130, 132].

The above procedure yields a basically constant degree of crystallinity between 160°C and 200°C, even though the enthalpy change is continuously increasing in this temperature range. This is the temperature range where continuous melting–recrystallization is expected from fast scanning calorimetry. However, below 140°C, the temperature of isothermal crystallization, degree of crystallinity decreases remarkably. The reason for this is the deviation of the real polymer morphology from the assumed two-phase morphology.

1.8 SUMMARY

This chapter describes the basic principle, recent developments, and selected applications of some commonly used experimental techniques (i.e., optical microscopy, electron microscopy, atomic force microscopy, nuclear magnetic resonance, diffraction and scattering (X-ray, neutron, and light), and differential scanning calorimetry) for characterization of semicrystalline polymers. Many excellent reviews for each technique and their usage exist, and the listed references only represent the exemplary ones. More applications of these techniques for some specific and advanced studies can be found in subsequent chapters, where the readers are encouraged to consider their respective references for further information.

ACKNOWLEDGMENTS

BH acknowledges the financial support of this work by the National Science Foundation in the United States and his coworkers B. Chu, C. Burger, R. Somani, L Zhu, and J. Keum. CS acknowledges the valuable contributions of his coworkers, especially A. Minakov, M. Merzlyakov, A. Wurm, H. Huth, S. Adamovsky, and E. Zhuravlev.

REFERENCES

[1] Hemsley, D.A. *Applied Polymer Light Microscopy*, Elsevier Applied Science, London, New York, 1989.

[2] Rawlins, D.J. *Light Microscopy*, Bios Scientific Publishers, Oxford, 1992.

[3] Sawyer, L., Grubb, D.T., Meyers, G.F. *Polymer Microscopy: Characterization and Evaluation of Materials*, 3rd ed. Springer, New York, 2008.

[4] Spencer, M. *Fundamentals of Light Microscopy*, Cambridge University Press, Cambridge, New York, 1982.

[5] Bradbury, S., Evennett, P. *Contrast Techniques in Light Microscopy*, Bios Scientific Publishers, Oxford, 1996.

[6] Hallimond, A.F. *The Polarizing Microscope*, Vickers, New York, 1970.

[7] Robinson, P.C. *Qualitative Polarized-Light Microscopy*, Oxford University Press, New York, 1992.

[8] Bennett, A.H. *Phase Microscopy: Principles and Applications*, Wiley, New York, 1951.

[9] Paesler, M.A., Moyer, P.J. *Near-field Optics: Theory, Instrumentation, and Applications*, Wiley, New York, 1996.

[10] Zayats, A., Richards, D. *Nano-Optics and Near-Field Optical Microscopy*, Artech House, London, 2008.

[11] Geil, P.H. *Polymer Single Crystals*, Krieger, New York, 1973.

[12] Bassett, D.C. *Principles of Polymer Morphology*, Cambridge University Press, Cambridge, UK, 1981.

[13] Strobl, G. *European Physical Journal E* **2000**, *3*(2), 165–183.

[14] Strobl, G. *Progress in Polymer Science* **2006**, *31*(4), 398–442.

[15] Bassett, D.C. *Journal of Macromolecular Science-Physics* **2003**, *B42*(2), 227–256.

[16] Keller, A., Cheng, S.Z.D. *Polymer* **1998**, *39*(19), 4461–4487.

[17] Sun, X., Li, H., Wang, J., Yan, S. *Macromolecules* **2006**, *39*(25), 8720–8726.

[18] Nishida, K., Kaji, K., Kanaya, T., Matsuba, G., Konishi, T. *Journal of Polymer Science Part B-Polymer Physics* **2004**, *42*, 1817–1822.

[19] Hamley, I.W., Castelletto, V., Castillo, R.V., Muller, A.J., Martin, C.M., Pollet, E., Dubois, P. *Macromolecules* **2005**, *38*(2), 463–472.

[20] Albuerne, J., Marquez, L., Muller, A.J., Raquez, J.M., Degee, P., Dubois, P., Castelletto, V., Hamley, I.W. *Macromolecules* **2003**, *36*(5), 1633–1644.

[21] He, C., Sun, J., Zhao, T., Hong, Z., Zhuang, X., Chen, X., Jing, X. *Biomacromolecules* **2005**, *7*(1), 252–258.

[22] Ebert, F., Thurn-Albrecht, T. *Macromolecules* **2003**, *36*(23), 8685–8694.

[23] Hafele, A., Heck, B., Kawai, T., Kohn, P., Strobl, G. *European Physical Journal E* **2005**, *16*(2), 207–216.

[24] Sabino, M.A., Feijoo, J.L., Muller, A.J. *Macromolecular Chemistry and Physics* **2000**, *201*(18), 2687–2698.

[25] Zhang, C.G., Hu, H.Q., Wang, D.J., Yan, S., Han, C.C. *Polymer* **2005**, *46*(19), 8157–8161.

[26] Mamun, A., Umemoto, S., Okui, N., Ishihara, N. *Macromolecules* **2007**, *40*(17), 6296–6303.

[27] Nakamura, H., Miyata, T., Yonetake, K., Masuko, T., Kojima, M. *Macromolecular Rapid Communications* **1995**, *16*(3), 189–196.

[28] Tsuji, H., Ikada, Y. *Polymer* **1995**, *36*(14), 2709–2716.

[29] Rastogi, S., Hikosaka, M., Kawabata, H., Keller, A. *Macromolecules* **1991**, *24*(24), 6384–6391.

[30] Liu, J.P., Jungnickel, B.J. *Journal of Polymer Science Part B-Polymer Physics* **2003**, *41*(9), 873–882.

[31] Hayashi, Y., Matsuba, G., Zhao, Y.F., Nishida, K., Kanaya, T. *Polymer* **2009**, *50*(9), 2095–2103.

[32] Keith, H.D., Padden, F.J. *Journal of Polymer Science* **1959**, *39*(135), 123–138.

[33] Keith, H.D., Padden, F.J. *Journal of Applied Physics* **1964**, *35*(4), 1270–1285.

[34] Keith, H.D., Padden, F.J. *Journal of Applied Physics* **1964**, *35*(4), 1286–1296.

[35] Padden, F.J., Keith, H.D. *Journal of Applied Physics* **1959**, *30*(10), 1479–1484.

[36] Norton, D.R., Keller, A. *Polymer* **1985**, *26*(5), 704–716.

[37] Michler, G.H. *Electron Microscopy of Polymers*, Springer, Berlin, 2008.

[38] Williams, D.B., Carter, C.B., eds. *Transmission Electron Microscopy*, 2nd ed. Springer, New York, 2009.

[39] Reimer, L., Kohl, H. *Transmission Electron Microscopy: Physics of Image Formation*, 5th ed. Springer, New York, 2008.

[40] Reimer, L. *Scanning Electron Microscopy: Physics of Image Formation and Microanalysis*, 2nd ed. Springer, New York, 1998.

[41] Goldstein, J., Newbury, D., Joy, D., Lyman, C., Echlin, P., Lifshin, E., Sawyer, L., Michael, J. *Scanning Electron Microscopy and X-Ray Microanalysis*, 3rd ed. Springer, New York, 2003.

[42] Spence, J.C.H. *High-Resolution Electron Microscopy*, 3rd ed. Oxford University Press, New York, 2009.

[43] Liu, T.X., Petermann, J., He, C.B., Liu, Z.H., Chung, T.S. *Macromolecules* **2001**, *34*(13), 4305–4307.

[44] Kanig, G. *Colloid and Polymer Science* **1983**, *261*(4), 373–374.

[45] Rastogi, S., Newman, M., Keller, A. *Nature* **1991**, *353*(6339), 55–57.

[46] Rastogi, S., Kurelec, L., Lemstra, P.J. *Macromolecules* **1998**, *31*(15), 5022–5031.

[47] Varga, J. *Journal of Macromolecular Science-Physics* **2002**, *B41*(4–6), 1121–1171.

[48] Bassett, D.C., Olley, R.H. *Polymer* **1984**, *25*(7), 935–943.

[49] Olley, R.H., Bassett, D.C. *Polymer* **1989**, *30*(3), 399–409.

[50] Bassett, D.C., Olley, R.H., Alraheil, I.A.M. *Polymer* **1988**, *29*(10), 1745–1754.

[51] Loo, Y.L., Register, R.A., Ryan, A.J. *Physical Review Letters* **2000**, *84*(18), 4120–4123.

[52] Loo, Y.L., Register, R.A., Ryan, A.J. *Macromolecules* **2002**, *35*(6), 2365–2374.

[53] Loo, Y.L., Register, R.A., Ryan, A.J., Dee, G.T. *Macromolecules* **2001**, *34*(26), 8968–8977.

[54] Zhu, L., Calhoun, B.H., Ge, Q., Quirk, R.P., Cheng, S.Z.D., Thomas, E.L., Hsiao, B.S., Yeh, F., Liu, L.Z., Lotz, B. *Macromolecules* **2001**, *34*(5), 1244–1251.

[55] Hamley, I.W., Fairclough, J.P.A., Terrill, N.J., Ryan, A.J., Lipic, P.M., Bates, F.S., TownsAndrews, E. *Macromolecules* **1996**, *29*(27), 8835–8843.

[56] De Rosa, C., Auriemma, F. *Progress in Polymer Science* **2006**, *31*, 145–237.

[57] Holland, V.F., Lindenmeyer, P.H. *Journal of Polymer Science* **1962**, *57*(165), 589–608.

[58] Bassett, D.C., Keller, A. *Philosophical Magazine* **1961**, *6*(63), 345–358.

[59] Wittmann, J.C., Lotz, B. *Journal of Polymer Science Part B-Polymer Physics* **1985**, *23*(1), 205–226.

[60] Hsiao, B.S., Yang, L., Somani, R.H., Avila-Orta, C.A., Zhu, L. *Physical Review Letters* **2005**, *94*(11), 117802/1–117802/4.

[61] Cohen, S.H., Lightbody, M.L. *Atomic Force Microscopy/Scanning Tunneling Microscopy*, Kluwer Academy, New York, 1999.

[62] Ratner, B.D., Tsukruk, V.V. *Scanning Probe Microscopy of Polymers*, American Chemical Society, Washington, DC, 1998.

[63] Roiter, Y., Minko, S. *Journal of the American Chemical Society* **2005**, *127*(45), 15688–15689.

[64] Humphris, A.D.L., Miles, M.J., Hobbs, J.K. *Applied Physics Letters* **2005**, *86*(3), 034106/1–034106/3.

[65] Pearce, R., Vancso, G.J. *Macromolecules* **1997**, *30*(19), 5843–5848.

[66] Hobbs, J.K., McMaster, T.J., Miles, M.J., Barham, P.J. *Polymer* **1998**, *39*(12), 2437–2446.

[67] Taguchi, K., Miyaji, H., Izumi, K., Hoshino, A., Miyamoto, Y., Kokawa, R. *Polymer* **2001**, *42*(17), 7443–7447.

[68] Reiter, G., Sommer, J.U. *Physical Review Letters* **1998**, *80*(17), 3771–3774.

[69] Reiter, G., Castelein, G., Sommer, J.U., Rottele, A., Thurn-Albrecht, T. *Physical Review Letters* **2001**, *87*(22), 226101/1–226101/4.

[70] Tracz, A., Jeszka, J.K., Kucinska, I., Chapel, J.P., Boiteux, G., Kryszewski, M. *Journal of Applied Polymer Science* **2002**, *86*(6), 1329–1336.

[71] Hugel, T., Strobl, G., Thomann, R. *Acta Polymerica* **1999**, *50*(5–6), 214–217.

[72] Loos, J., Thune, P.C., Niemantsverdriet, J.W., Lemstra, P.J. *Macromolecules* **1999**, *32*(26), 8910–8913.

[73] Lei, Y.G., Chan, C.M., Li, J.X., Ng, K.M., Wang, Y., Jiang, Y., Li, L. *Macromolecules* **2002**, *35*(18), 6751–6753.

[74] Jiang, Y., Yan, D.D., Gao, X., Han, C.C., Jin, X.G., Li, L., Wang, Y., Chan, C.M. *Macromolecules* **2003**, *36*(10), 3652–3655.

[75] Lei, Y.G., Chan, C.M., Wang, Y., Ng, K.M., Jiang, Y., Lin, L. *Polymer* **2003**, *44*(16), 4673–4679.

[76] Hobbs, J.K., Humphris, A.D.L., Miles, M.J. *Macromolecules* **2001**, *34*(16), 5508–5519.

[77] Basire, C., Ivanov, D.A. *Physical Review Letters* **2000**, *85*(26), 5587–5590.

[78] Ivanov, D.A., Amalou, Z., Magonov, S.N. *Macromolecules* **2001**, *34*(26), 8944–8952.

[79] Kitayama, T., Hatada, K. *NMR Spectroscopy of Polymers*, Springer, Berlin, 2004.

[80] Mirau, P.A. *A Practical Guide to Understanding the NMR of Polymers*, Wiley, Hoboken, 2005.

[81] Schmidt-Rohr, K., Spiess, H.W. *Multidimensional Solid-State NMR and Polymers*, Academic Press, London, San Diego, 1994.

[82] Sozzani, P., Simonutti, R., Galimberti, M. *Macromolecules* **1993**, *26*(21), 5782–5789.

[83] Mathias, L.J., Davis, R.D., Jarrett, W.L. *Macromolecules* **1999**, *32*(23), 7958–7960.

[84] Hu, W.G., Schmidt-Rohr, K. *Polymer* **2000**, *41*(8), 2979–2987.

[85] Hu, W.G., Sirota, E.B. *Macromolecules* **2003**, *36*(14), 5144–5149.

[86] Buerger, M.J. *X-Ray Crystallography: An Introduction to the Investigation of Crystals by Their Diffraction of Monochromatic X-Radiation*, John Wiley & Sons, 1942.

[87] Massa, W., Robert, O.G. *Crystal Structure Determination*, 4th ed. Springer, 2010.

[88] Giacovazzo, C., Monaco, H.L., Artioli, G., Viterbo, D., Ferraris, G., Gilli, G., Zanotti, G., Catti, M. *Fundamentals of Crystallography*, 2nd ed. Oxford University Press, 2002.

[89] Drenth, J. *Principles of Protein X-Ray Crystallography*, 2nd ed. Springer, 2002.

[90] Guinier, A. *X-Ray Diffraction: In Crystals, Imperfect Crystals, and Amorphous Bodies*, Dover Publications, 1994.

[91] Ruland, W. *Acta Crystallographica* **1961**, *14*(11), 1180.

[92] Burger, C., Hsiao, B.S., Chu, B. *Polymer Reviews* **2010**, *50*(1), 91–111.

[93] Alexander, L.E. *X-ray Diffraction Methods in Polymer Science*, Wiley-Interscience, New York, 1969.

[94] Fraser, R.D.B., Macrae, T.P., Miller, A., Rowlands, R.J. *Journal of Applied Crystallography* **1976**, *9*(APR1), 81–94.

[95] Mao, Y.M., Burger, C., Zuo, F., Hsiao, B.S., Mehta, A., Mitchell, C., Tsou, A.H. *Macromolecules* **2011**, *44*(3), 558–565.

[96] Burger, C., Zhou, H.W., Sics, I., Hsiao, B.S., Chu, B., Graham, L., Glimcher, M.J. *Journal of Applied Crystallography* **2008**, *41*, 252–261.

[97] Warren, B.E. *X-Ray Diffraction*, Dover Publications, 1990.

[98] Glatter, O., Kratky, O. *Small-Angle X-Ray Scattering*, Academic Press, New York, 1982.

[99] Balta-Calleja, F.J., Vonk, C.G. *X Ray Scattering of Synthetic Polymers*, Elsevier Science, 1989.

[100] Roe, R.J. *Methods of X-Ray and Neutron Scattering in Polymer Science*, Oxford University Press, 2000.

[101] Vonk, C.G. *Journal of Applied Crystallography* **1973**, *6*(APR1), 81–86.

[102] Vonk, C.G. *Journal of Applied Crystallography* **1978**, *11*(OCT), 541–546.

[103] Vonk, C.G., Kortleve, G. *Kolloid-Zeitschrift and Zeitschrift Fur Polymere* **1967**, *220*(1), 19.

[104] Ruland, W. *Colloid and Polymer Science* **1977**, *255*(5), 417–427.

[105] Ruland, W. *Journal of Applied Crystallography* **1971**, *4*(FEB1), 70.

[106] Ruland, W., Smarsly, B. *Journal of Applied Crystallography* **2004**, *37*, 575–584.

[107] Burger, C., Zhou, H.W., Wang, H., Sics, I., Hsiao, B.S., Chu, B., Graham, L., Glimcher, M.J. *Biophysical Journal* **2008**, *95*(4), 1985–1992.

[108] Toki, S., Sics, I., Burger, C., Fang, D.F., Liu, L.Z., Hsiao, B.S., Datta, S., Tsou, A.H. *Macromolecules* **2006**, *39*(10), 3588–3597.

[109] Stein, R.S., Rhodes, M.B. *Journal of Applied Physics* **1960**, *31*(11), 1873–1884.

[110] Samuels, R.J. *Journal of Polymer Science Part a-2-Polymer Physics* **1971**, *9*(12), 2165.

[111] Clough, S., Vanaarts, J., Stein, R.S. *Journal of Applied Physics* **1965**, *36*(10), 3072.

[112] Clough, S.B., Stein, R.S. *Journal of Applied Physics* **1967**, *38*(11), 4446.

[113] Samuels, R.J. *Journal of Polymer Science Part C-Polymer Symposium* **1966**, 13PC, 37.

[114] Stein, R.S., Wilson, P.R. *Journal of Applied Physics* **1962**, *33*(6), 1914.

[115] Debye, P., Bueche, A.M. *Journal of Applied Physics* **1949**, *20*(6), 518–525.

[116] Okada, T., Saito, H., Inoue, T. *Macromolecules* **1992**, *25*(7), 1908–1911.

[117] Zeng, X.B., Ungar, G., Spells, S.J., Brooke, G.M., Farren, C., Harden, A. *Physical Review Letters* **2003**, *90*(15), 155508-1–4.

[118] Zeng, Y.B., Ungar, G., Spells, S.J., King, S.M. *Macromolecules* **2005**, *38*(17), 7201–7204.

[119] Schick, C. *Analytical and Bioanalytical Chemistry* **2009**, *395*(6), 1589–1611.

[120] Wunderlich, B., *Thermal Analysis of Polymeric Materials*. 2005; p. 894.

[121] Höhne, G.W.H., Hemminger, W., Flammersheim, H.-J. *Differential Scanning Calorimetry*, 2nd ed. Springer, Berlin, 2003.

[122] Cheng, S.Z.D. *Handbook of Thermal Analysis and Calorimetry*, Vol. 3. Elsevier B. V., New York, 2002.

[123] Mathot, V.B.F. *Calorimetry and Thermal Analysis of Polymers*, Hanser Publishers, München, 1994.

[124] Wunderlich, B. *Pure and Applied Chemistry* **1995**, *67*(6), 1019–1026.

[125] Pijpers, T.F.J., Mathot, V.B.F., Goderis, B., Scherrenberg, R.L., van der Vegte, E.W. *Macromolecules* **2002**, *35*(9), 3601–3613.

[126] Gobrecht, H., Hamann, K., Willers, G. *Journal of Physics E-Scientific Instruments* **1971**, *4*(1), 21–23.

[127] Sauerbrunn, S., Crowe, B., Reading, M. *American Laboratory* **1992**, *24*(12), 44–47.

[128] Schick, C., Wurm, A., Mohammed, A. *Thermochimica Acta* **2003**, *396*(1–2), 119–132.

[129] Schick, C. Temperature modulated differential scanning calorimetry (TMDSC)-Basics and applications to polymers. In *Handbook of Thermal Analysis and Calorimetry*, Vol. 3, Gallagher, P.K., ed. Elsevier, Amsterdam, New York, Tokyo, 2002.

[130] Gray, A.P. *Thermochimica Acta* **1970**, *1*(6), 563–579.

[131] Zhuravlev, E., Schmelzer, J.W.P., Wunderlich, B., Schick, C. *Polymer* **2011**, *52*, 1983–1997.

[132] Mathot, V.B.F., Pijpers, M.F.J. *Journal of Thermal Analysis* **1983**, *28*(2), 349–358.

[133] Minakov, A.A., Mordvintsev, D.A., Tol, R., Schick, C. *Thermochimica Acta* **2006**, *442*(1–2), 25–30.

2

CRYSTAL STRUCTURES OF POLYMERS

CLAUDIO DE ROSA AND FINIZIA AURIEMMA

Dipartimento di Scienze Chimiche, Università di Napoli "Federico II," Complesso Monte S. Angelo, Napoli, Italy

2.1 Constitution and Configuration of Polymer Chains, 31
2.2 Conformation of Polymer Chains in Crystals and Conformational Polymorphism, 33
2.3 Packing of Macromolecules in Polymer Crystals, 43
2.4 Symmetry Breaking, 49
2.5 Packing Effects on the Conformation of Polymer Chains in the Crystals: The case of Aliphatic Polyamides, 50
2.6 Defects and Disorder in Polymer Crystals, 55
    2.6.1 Substitutional Isomorphism of Different Chains, 56
    2.6.2 Substitutional Isomorphism of Different Monomeric units, 57
    2.6.3 Conformational Isomorphism, 58
    2.6.4 Disorder in the Stacking of Ordered Layers (Stacking Fault Disorder), 58
2.7 Crystal Habits, 60
    2.7.1 Rounded Lateral Habits, 66
Acknowledgments, 67
References, 67

2.1 CONSTITUTION AND CONFIGURATION OF POLYMER CHAINS

The crystalline state is characterized by the presence of three-dimensional positional and orientational order. In crystals of polymers the macromolecules are longer than the unit cell parameters and each chain passes through many unit cells. Accordingly, the concept of an ideal crystal of polymers requires infinite molecular mass, completely regular constitution of the macromolecules, completely regular configuration of the units in the macromolecules, and completely regular conformation of the chains. Therefore, general requirements for the crystallizability of polymers are the regularity in the chemical constitution and in the configuration of long sequences of monomeric units [1, 2]. This implies that, for long sequences of polymerized monomers, all the repeating units have the same chemical structure. In addition, whenever a monomeric unit may assume different configurations, the succession of configurations must be regular. The regularity in the succession of configurations of the stereoisomeric centers present along the chains implies, as a direct consequence, that the conformations assumed by macromolecules in the crystals are regular, and can be described by a well-defined symmetry [1].

In vinyl polymers, where the two terminals of the monomeric units are not equivalent and a head and a tail can be distinguished (for instance, the case of propylene), the regularity in the chemical constitution implies a regular enchainment of consecutive monomeric units always head to tail. Defects in the regular constitution may arise from the presence of enchainment of consecutive units via head to head or tail to tail.

Copolymers of different monomeric units that are able to co-crystallize in the same lattice may be considered as possible exceptions to the need of the regularity in the chemical constitution. For instance, in the case of

---

Handbook of Polymer Crystallization, First Edition. Edited by Ewa Piorkowska and Gregory C. Rutledge.
© 2013 John Wiley & Sons, Inc. Published 2013 by John Wiley & Sons, Inc.

vinyl polymers, it is possible to accommodate into the crystalline lattice different comonomeric units having lateral groups with different shape and dimensions. Isotactic copolymers of butene and 3-methylbutene [3], or isotactic copolymers of styrene and o-fluorostyrene [4] are crystalline in the whole range of composition, whereas propene and 1-butene comonomeric units are able to co-crystallize at any composition in both isotactic [5–8] and syndiotactic copolymers [9, 10]. Isomorphism of comonomeric units also occurs in copolymers of acetaldehyde and n-butyraldehyde, which are crystalline over the whole range of composition [11]. Analogous isomorphism of comonomeric units has been observed in trans-1,4-copolymers of butadiene and 1,3-pentadiene [12], or in copolymers of vinylidenefluoride and vinylfluoride [13].

The possible presence of stereoisomeric centers along the chains, as asymmetric atoms in vinyl polymers or double bonds in polydienes, introduces the problem of the possible regularity in the succession of configurations of monomeric units (stereoregularity). According to Corradini [1], in the case of tetrahedral stereoisomeric centers, that is carbon atoms along a chain bonded to two different substituents R_1 and R_2, the possible configurations of monomeric units can be classified in terms of the inherent asymmetry of the chemical bonds rather than that of the atoms. Let l_1 and l_2 be two bonds adjacent to the carbon atom C_i, which carries two different substituents R_1 and R_2 (Fig. 2.1). The two bonds, l_1 and l_2, are chiral, even though the carbon atom C_i is not asymmetric [1, 14], and can be distinguished from a configurational point of view as (+) or (−) bonds [1]. The inherent asymmetry of a bond adjacent to a stereoisomeric center C_i along a chain C_{i-1}–C_i–C_{i+1} is defined using a (+) sign when, looking along the C_{i-1}–C_i (l_1) or C_{i+1}–C_i (l_2) bond, we see the substituents R_1, R_2, C_{i+1} or R_1, R_2, C_{i-1} succeeding each other clockwise [1], with the convention that R_1 is bulkier than R_2 [15] (Fig. 2.1). If these substituents succeed each other counterclockwise, the bond is defined with the (−) sign [1]. It is apparent from Figure 2.1 that if the bond l_1 has a (+) character with respect to the stereoisomeric center C_i, l_2 must have a (−) character and vice versa. Bonds astride a tetrahedral stereoisomeric center are always opposite in sign. Two monomeric units have the same configuration if the bonds adjacent to the tetrahedral stereoisomeric centers are characterized by the same (+) and (−) characters; they are enantiomorphous if the signs (+) and (−) are reversed [1] (Fig. 2.2a).

A pair of consecutive, but not necessarily contiguous, tetrahedral stereoisomeric centers defines a diad [16]. Stereosequences terminating in tetrahedral stereoisomeric centers at both ends, and which comprise two, three, four, five, and so on, consecutive centers of that type, may be called diads, triads, tetrads, pentads, and so on, respectively. If the two units belonging to a diad have the same configuration, the diad is defined *meso* (*m*) and is characterized by a mirror plane of symmetry; if the two units are enantiomorphous, the diad is defined *racemo* (*r*) and is characterized by a twofold rotation axis of symmetry (Fig. 2.2b).

The stereoregularity of a polymer chain implies a regular succession of couples of (+) and (−) bonds. Isotactic polymers are characterized by a regular enchainment of monomeric units having the same configuration, hence by a regular succession of (+) and (−) bonds [1], or a regular succession of *meso* diads [16] (Fig. 2.2c). Syndiotactic polymers are characterized by a regular enchainment of monomeric units having alternatively enantiomorphous configurations, which produces couples of adjacent bonds having the same sign [1] and a regular succession of *racemic* diads [16] (Fig. 2.2d). Although the definition of isotactic and syndiotactic polymers according to the International Union of Pure and Applied Chemistry (IUPAC) rules is well established in terms of succession of *meso* or *racemic* diads [16], the definition of (+) and (−) bonds is useful because it allows the easy treatment of possible configurations in cases of any complexity [1]. Moreover, the (+) and (−) characters of the bonds are strictly related to the accessibility of *gauche*$^+$ or *gauche*$^-$ conformations of the bonds and therefore to the formation of right-handed or left-handed helical conformations [1] (see Section 2.2).

When a monomeric unit contains more than one tetrahedral stereoisomeric center, the relative configuration of the centers has to be defined. In the case of two adjacent stereoisomeric centers, for instance –CHA–CHB–, with A ≠ B, two configurational signs can be assigned to the bonds connecting the centers (Fig. 2.3). The pairs (+, +) and (−, −) define a relative *threo* configuration, whereas the pairs (−, +) and (+, −) define a relative *erythro* configuration [1] (Fig. 2.3). Stereoregu-

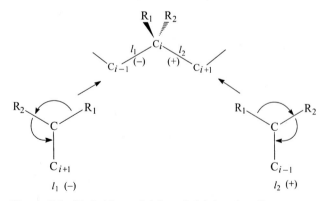

Figure 2.1 Definition of (−) and (+) bonds adjacent to a tetrahedral stereoisomeric center [1]. The substituent R_1 is bulkier than R_2 [15].

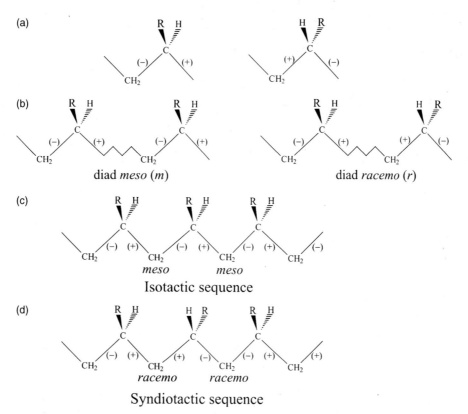

Figure 2.2 Vinyl units with enantiomorphous configurations (a), *meso* and *racemic* diads (b) and sequences of (+) and (−) bonds in isotactic (c) and syndiotactic (d) polymers. The symbol ⋀ represents a symmetrically constituted connecting group, such as –CH$_2$–, –CH$_2$–CH$_2$–, or –CR$_2$–CH$_2$–CR$_2$–.

lar polymers of the kind –(CHA–CHB)$_n$– may be ditactic [17]. A regular alternating succession of (+, +) and (−, −) bonds corresponds to a *threo* diisotactic polymer, the regular succession of (+, −) bonds corresponds to the *erythro* diisotactic polymer, and the succession ... (−, −)(+, −)(+, +)(−, +) ..., corresponds to the disyndiotactic polymer [16, 17] (Fig. 2.3). When the two substituents A and B bonded to the asymmetric carbon atoms are equal, as in –CHA–CHA–, the possible configurations must be defined *racemo*-isotactic and syndiotactic, and *meso*-isotactic and syndiotactic [16] (Fig. 2.3), rather than *threo* and *erhytro*, respectively.

Double bonds present along the chains of polymers of 1,3-dienes with 1,4 additions of the monomeric units are stereoisomeric centers that may assume *cis* or *trans* configurations. Polidienes may also contain up to two stereoisomeric tetrahedral centers. Stereoregular polydienes can be *cis* or *trans* tactic, isotactic or syndiotactic, and diisotactic or disyndiotactic if two stereoisomeric tetrahedral centers are present. In the latter case, *erythro* and *threo* structures are defined depending on the relative configurations of two carbon atoms [1].

The requirement concerning the regularity in the configuration (stereoregularity) is more stringent than that concerning the regularity in the chemical constitution in order for a polymer to be crystalline [1]. This is clearly indicated by the frequent co-crystallization of different comonomers in random copolymers of poly(α-olefins) [3–13]. However, it has been recently clarified that in some cases the presence of defects of stereoregularity, even at high concentrations, does not prevent the crystallization. In the case of isotactic [18, 19] and syndiotactic polypropylene [20–22] the controlled introduction of defects of stereoregularity, through synthesis with single-center organometallic catalysts, has been used to tailor the physical properties of the materials by controlling the crystallization behavior [18–22].

2.2 CONFORMATION OF POLYMER CHAINS IN CRYSTALS AND CONFORMATIONAL POLYMORPHISM

The conformation assumed by polymer chains in the crystalline state depends on the configuration of the stereoisomeric centers present along the chains, and is defined by two basic principles [1, 2, 23–25].

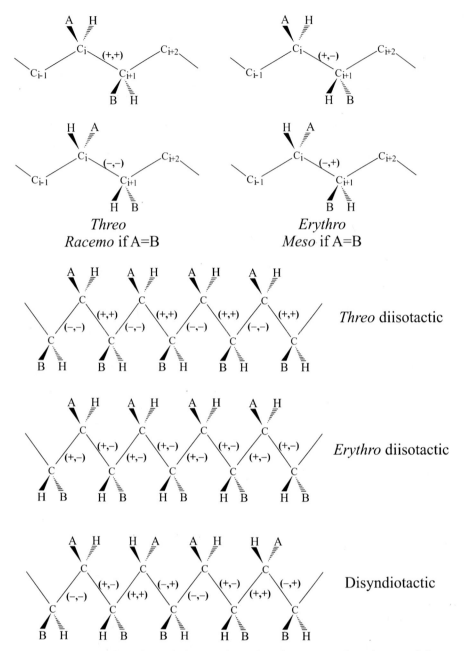

Figure 2.3 *Threo* and *erythro* relative configurations in monomeric units containing two adjacent tetrahedral stereoisomeric centers and two different substituents A ≠ B, and succession of (+) and (−) bonds in *threo*-diisotactic, *erythro*-diisotactic, and disyndiotactic polymers. When A = B the relative configurations are defined *racemo* and *meso*.

1. **The equivalence principle.** The conformation of a polymer chain in the crystalline state is defined by a succession of equivalent structural units, which occupy geometrically (not necessarily crystallographically) equivalent positions with respect to the chain axis. The chain axis is parallel to a crystallographic axis of the crystal.

2. **Principle of minimum internal conformational energy.** The conformation of a polymer chain in a crystal approaches one of the minima of the internal conformational energy, which would be taken by an isolated chain subjected to the restrictions imposed by the equivalence principle.

The necessary geometrical equivalence of structural units along an axis allows defining the possible types of geometrical symmetry that a linear macromolecule may achieve in the crystalline state. The structural unit is in general a fraction of the repeating unit and often corresponds, but not necessarily, to a single monomeric unit. The conformation of a macromolecule is generally defined in terms of its symmetry. The only symmetry operators having a translational component and compatible with a chain repetition are:

- **t** translation c along the chain axis z;
- **c** reflection through a mirror glide plane containing z, plus a translation of $c/2$ along z;
- **s** screw (helical) repetition of M units in N turns; rotation of $2\pi N/M$ around z plus translation of c/M along z. For the helical symmetry the unit twist t is the rotation $t = 2\pi N/M$, the unit height h or p is the translation c/M, the ratio $n = M/N$ is the number of residues per turn and the helical pitch is the ratio $P = c/N$.

Other symmetry operators compatible with a chain repetition are:

- r_n $2\pi/n$ rotation around the chain axis;
- **i** center of symmetry;
- **m** plane of symmetry perpendicular to the chain axis;
- **d** plane of symmetry parallel to the chain axis;
- **2** twofold rotation perpendicular to z-axis.

These symmetry elements may be combined into the chain repetition symmetry groups. Thirteen chain repetition groups, indicated in Table 2.1, have been defined [1] and the conformation of a macromolecule is generally defined in terms of its chain repetition symmetry group [1, 16, 26].

The possible symmetry elements for a chain conformation must be compatible with the chemical constitution and configuration. For instance, whenever the monomeric unit has a directional character, as for instance nylon 6, symmetry elements such as 2, m, and i are ruled out automatically. Rotations r_n around the chain axis for a single chain may be consistent only for very particular constitutional repeating units and very particular values of $2\pi/n$. Moreover, the screw symmetry and the glide plane, corresponding to the line repetition groups **s**(M/N), **s**(M/N)2, **tc** and **tcm**, are the only possible ones for a vinyl polymer [27]. The chain symmetry **s**(M/N) is compatible only with an isotactic configuration, whereas the line repetition symmetries **s**(M/N)2, **tc** and **tcm** are compatible only with a syndiotactic configuration [1].

TABLE 2.1 Possible Chain Repetition Symmetry Groups

s(M/N)1	Isotactic Polypropylene	**s**(3/1)1
Particular case **t**1	*Trans*-1,4-poly(isoprene) (β form)	**s**(1/1) ≡ **t**1
s(M/N)2	Syndiotactic polypropylene	**s**(2/1)2
Particular case **t**2	Syndiotactic polypropylene (form IV) ($T_6G_2T_2G_2$ conformation)	
tm	Nylon 7,7	
td		
tc	*cis*-1,4-Poly(isoprene), *trans*-1,4-poly(isoprene) (α form)	
ti	Isotactic *meso*-ethylene-*cis*-2-butene alternating copolymer, *trans*-1,4-poly(1,3-butadiene) (form I)	
s(2/1)m	*Trans*-polypentenamer	
s(2/1)d	Nylon 6 (planar chain conformation)	
td*m*		
ti*d*	Nylon 6,6 (planar chain conformation)	
tc*m*	1,2-Syndiotactic poly(butadiene), syndiotactic polypropylene (form III)	
tc*i*	*cis*-1,4-Poly(1,3-butadiene)	
s(2/1)d*m*	Polyethylene	

In the case of syndiotactic polymers with chains in helical conformation, as for sPP, the symbol **s**(2/1)2 indicates that neighboring structural units are repeated through the operation of twofold axes perpendicular to the chain axis and each pair of units is repeated according to a helix containing two pairs of monomeric units in one pitch. A line repetition group for sPP in the fully extended *trans*-planar conformation is **tcm**. In this case the repeating unit comprises two monomeric units [20].

Once the symmetry of the chain of a crystalline polymer having a given regular configuration has been assigned using the equivalence principle, the actual conformation assumed by the chain is determined by energetic factors, as defined by the principle of the minimum internal conformational energy. In saturated molecules, the bond orientation effect favors staggered conformations of the bonds (*trans* and *gauche*) [28]. Deviations from staggered conformations can be induced by intramolecular interactions between neighboring atoms, such as in isotactic polymers with bulky side groups. Packing effects generally do not influence the conformation of the chains as long as the conformational

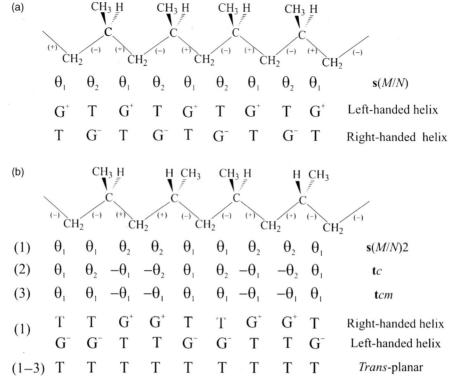

Figure 2.4 Line repetition symmetries, according to the equivalence principle, and corresponding possible conformations, according to the minimum conformational energy, for isotactic (a) and syndiotactic (b) polypropylene. T, *trans*; G, *gauche*.

energy of the isolated chain corresponds to a deep energy minimum. When the energy differences between different conformations of an isolated chain are low, the intermolecular interactions may influence the choice of the conformation in the crystal.

The helical conformations found in the crystals of isotactic polymers may be easily justified by the application of these principles. In the case of isotactic polypropylene (iPP), the configuration corresponds to an alternating succession of (+) and (−) bonds (Fig. 2.4a). If θ_1 and θ_2 are the torsion angles of two successive bonds of the chain, the equivalence principle imposes that successive monomeric units take equivalent conformations in the crystalline state and hence successive bonds assume the same torsion angles θ_1 and θ_2. According to the principle of the staggered bonds, the torsion angles θ_1 and θ_2 tend to be *trans* (T) or *gauche* (G). Intramolecular interactions impose some well-established constraints [1]; in particular, (+) bonds tend to assume only G^+ or T conformations, whereas (−) bonds tend to assume only G^- or T conformations [1]. Moreover, G^+ bonds cannot be followed by G^- bonds, and the pair of torsion angles θ_1 and θ_2 adjacent to a methylene carbon atom cannot be TT for an isotactic polymer and cannot be TG or GT for a syndiotactic polymer. These conditions impose that the only possible conformations for iPP are $(TG^-)_n$ and $(G^+T)_n$, corresponding to a right-handed and left-handed threefold helical conformation, respectively [29].

In the case of sPP, the configuration corresponds to an alternating succession of couples of (+),(+) and (−),(−) bonds (Fig. 2.4b). If θ_1 and θ_2 are the torsion angles of two successive bonds of the chain, the equivalence principle imposes that the only possible successions of torsion angles are those shown in Figure 2.4b:

... $\theta_1\theta_1|\theta_2\theta_2|\theta_1\theta_1|\theta_2\theta_2$ ..., corresponding to the **s(M/N)2** symmetry;

... $\theta_1\theta_2|-\theta_1-\theta_2|\theta_1\theta_2|-\theta_1-\theta_2$ ..., corresponding to the **tc** symmetry;

... $\theta_1\theta_1|-\theta_1-\theta_1|\theta_1\theta_1|-\theta_1-\theta_1$ ..., corresponding to the **tcm** symmetry.

In the **s(M/N)2** symmetry, two successive monomeric units are related by a twofold rotation axis perpendicular to the chain axis centered on the methylene carbon atoms. According to the principle of the minimum conformational energy, the possible conformations are

$(TTG^+G^+)_n$ and $(G^-G^-TT)_n$, corresponding to right-handed and left-handed twofold helical conformations, respectively, found in the crystals of the most stable polymorphic forms of sPP [20, 30–32], and $(TTTT)_n$, corresponding to the *trans*-planar conformation [20, 33, 34]. In the **tc** and **tcm** symmetries, two successive monomeric units are related by a glide plane parallel to the chain axis, so that the torsion angles θ_1 and θ_2 in two successive monomeric units have opposite values. When a mirror plane perpendicular to the chain axis, crossing the methine carbon atom, is also present (**tcm** symmetry), $\theta_2 = \theta_1$. Since G^+G^- and TG successions are forbidden, the minimum conformational energy principle imposes that, for the **tc** and **tcm** symmetries, the only possible conformation is $(TTTT)_n$, corresponding to the fully extended *trans*-planar conformation (Fig. 2.4b).

The 3/1 and 2/1 helical conformations of chains of iPP and sPP, respectively, are the reference conformations for the more general cases of the conformations of isotactic and syndiotactic poly(α-olefins) of the kind $-(CH_2-CH(R))_n-$. The conformation of chains of isotactic poly(α-olefins) in the crystalline state is, indeed, generally helical and corresponds to a succession of nearly *trans* and *gauche* torsion angles, $-(T'G')_n-$, the exact values depending on the bulkiness of the side groups R. The presence of side groups R bulkier than the methyl group (for instance, in isotactic poly[1-butene]) induces slight distortions of the torsion angles θ_1 and θ_2 from the exact *trans* (180°) and *gauche* (60°) values typical of the 3/1 helix of iPP, due to the steric interaction between the bulkier side groups [35]. These interactions induce a similar distortion of the two backbone torsion angles [35], $\theta_1 = 180° + \delta_1$, $\theta_2 = 60° + \delta_2$ for a left-handed helix, and $\theta_1 = -60° - \delta_1$, $\theta_2 = 180° - \delta_2$ for a right-handed helix, with $\delta_1 \approx \delta_2$. These distorted helices have **s**(M/N) symmetries with noninteger values of the ratio M/N.

In all the observed isotactic polymers, the torsion angles do not deviate more than 20° from the staggered (60° and 180°) values and the number of monomeric units per turn M/N ranges between 3 and 4. Chains of 3-substituted polyolefins, such as isotactic poly(3-methyl-1-butene) (iP3MB), assume a 4_1 helical conformation $(T'G')_4$ [36, 37], while 4-substituted polyolefins, such as isotactic poly(4-methyl-1-pentene) (iP4MP), have less distorted helices with 7/2 symmetry $(T'G')_{3.5}$ [38]. When the substituent on the side group is far from the chain atoms, such as in poly(5-methyl-1-hexene), the polymer crystallizes again with a threefold helical conformation [1]. Data concerning the chain conformations and the crystal structures of isotactic polymers are reported in Table 2.2. Models of the chain conformations found for the polymorphic forms of various isotactic polymers are reported in Figure 2.5.

It is apparent from Table 2.2 that most of the isotactic polymers show conformational polymorphism. The crystallization of isotactic polymers in different polymorphic forms having different chain conformations is easily predicted by calculations of the conformational energy under the constraints imposed by the equivalence principle, hence assuming a succession of backbone torsion angles $\ldots \theta_1\theta_2\theta_1\theta_2\theta_1\theta_2 \ldots$ [39]. In the case of iPP, these calculations give only one energy minimum at pairs of torsion angles ($\theta_1 = -60°$, $\theta_2 = 180°$), or ($\theta_1 = 180°$, $\theta_2 = 60°$), corresponding to the right-handed $(G^-T)_n$ and left-handed $(TG^+)_n$, respectively, threefold helical conformation [27], in agreement with the experimental observation that all the crystalline polymorphic forms of iPP are characterized by the same stable 3/1 helical conformation [29]. In the case of isotactic polystyrene (iPS), besides the two absolute minima corresponding to the threefold helical conformation found in the most stable crystalline form of iPS [40], a minimum of higher energy has also been found in the region of the *trans*-planar conformation [41]. This is due to the planarity of the benzene rings, which makes the *trans*-planar conformation energetically feasible. This is in agreement with the disordered conformation found in crystalline gels of iPS [42], characterized by a succession along the chain of sequences in 3_1 helical conformation of opposite hands (right-handed and left handed) connected by short sequences in *trans*-planar conformation [42]. This energy minimum is absent for iPP or for isotactic polybutene (iPB) [41, 43] and other higher poly(α-olefins), such as iP4MP [44], because of the greater repulsions between the nonplanar side groups.

In the case of iPB two minima of the conformational energy have been found in the region of the helical conformation (TG) [41, 43]. The absolute minimum corresponds to the 3/1 helix, found in the form I of iPB [45]. The second relative minimum corresponds to the helical conformation $(T'G')_n$ with values of the torsion angles θ_1 and θ_2 slightly deviated from the exact *trans* (180°) and *gauche* (60°) values typical of the 3/1 helix, due to the steric interaction between the bulkier side groups, and is in agreement with the experimental observation of the 11/3 and 4/1 helical conformations found in the polymorphic forms II and III of iPB, respectively [39, 43, 46, 47]. The helical conformations of the chains of the different polymorphic forms of iPB are shown in Figure 2.6.

In the case of iP4MP, the increased bulkiness of the side groups makes the distorted helical conformations $(T'G')_n$, corresponding to the 7/2 and 4/1 symmetries, more stable than the 3/1 helix. The absolute energy minimum is at values of torsion angles close to the 7/2 helical conformation, found in the form I of iP4MP [38, 48] and 4/1 helix, found in form II [49–51] and form III

TABLE 2.2 Structural Data of Isotactic (*it*) and Syndiotactic (*st*) Polymers

Polymer	Chain Axis (Å)	Chain Symmetry	Unit-Cell Parameters	Space Group	Reference
it-Polypropylene α form	6.5	s(3/1)	$a = 6.65$ Å, $b = 20.96$ Å $c = 6.50$ Å, $\beta = 99.3°$	$P2_1/c - C2/c$	[29, 101, 102]
it-Polypropylene β form	6.5	s(3/1)	$a = b = 11.03$ Å, $c = 6.5$ Å.	$P3$	[114a, 193, 194]
it-Polypropylene γ form	6.5	s(3/1)	$a = 8.54$ Å, $b = 9.93$ Å $c = 42.41$ Å	$Fddd$	[108, 109]
it-Polypropylene trigonal form, in *it*-Poly(proylene-*co*-pentene)	6.5	s(3/1)	$a = b = 17.1$ Å $c = 6.5$ Å, 30 mol% pentene	$R3c - R\bar{3}c$	[105]
it-Polypropylene trigonal form, in *it*-Poly(proylene-*co*-hexene)	6.5	s(3/1)	$a = b = 17.5$ Å $c = 6.5$ Å 26 mol% hexene	$R3c - R\bar{3}c$	[103, 104, 106a]
it-Polybutene form I	6.5	s(3/1)	$a = b = 17.7$ Å, $c = 6.5$ Å	$R3c - R\bar{3}c$	[45]
it-Polybutene form II	21.05	s(11/3)	$a = b = 15.42$ Å, $c = 21.05$ Å	$P\bar{4}$	[43, 46]
it-Polybutene form III	7.56	s(4/1)	$a = 12.38$ Å, $b = 8.88$ Å, $c = 7.56$ Å	$P2_12_12_1$	[47]
it-Poly(3-methyl-1-butene)	6.8	s(4/1)	$a = 9.55$ Å, $b = 17.08$ Å, $c = 6.8$ Å, $\gamma = 116.5°$	$P2_1/b$	[36a, 37, 110]
it-Poly(1-pentene)	6.6	s(3/1)	–	–	[199]
it-Poly((S)-3-methyl-1-pentene)	6.80	s(4/1)	$a = b = 13.25$ Å, $c = 6.80$ Å	$I4_1$	[93]
it-Poly(4-methyl-1-pentene) form I	13.8	s(7/2)	$a = b = 18.66$ Å, $c = 13.80$ Å	$P\bar{4}, P\bar{4}b2$	[38, 48]
it-Poly(4-methyl-1-pentene) form II	7.12	s(4/1)	$a = 10.49$ Å, $b = 18.89$ Å, $c = 7.13$ Å, $\gamma = 113.7°$	$P2_1/b, P2_1$	[49–51]
it-Poly(4-methyl-1-pentene) form III	7.02	s(4/1)	$a = b = 19.46$ Å, $c = 7.02$ Å	$I4_1$	[44, 52]
it-Poly(4-methyl-1-pentene) form IV	6.5	s(3/1)	$a = 22.17$ Å, $c = 6.69$ Å.	–	[53c, 55]
it-Poly(1-hexene)	13.7	s(7/2)	–	–	[200]
it-Poly((S)-4-methyl-1-hexene) form I	13.5	s(7/2)	$a = b = 19.85$ Å, $c = 13.5$ Å	$P\bar{4} - P1$	[38a]
it-Poly((S)-4-methyl-1-hexene) form II	–	–	–	–	[38a]
it-Poly((R),(S)-4-methyl-1-hexene)	13.5	s(7/2)	$a = b = 19.85$ Å, $c = 13.5$ Å	$P\bar{4}$	[38a]
it-Poly(5-methyl-1-hexene)	6.33	s(3/1)	$a = 17.62$ Å, $b = 10.17$ Å, $c = 6.33$ Å	$P2_1$	[94]
it-Poly((S)-5-methyl-1-heptene)	6.36	s(3/1)	$a = 18.40$ Å, $b = 10.62$ Å, $c = 6.36$ Å	$P2_1$	[92, 94b,c]
it-Poly((R),(S)-5-methyl-1-heptene)	38.76	s(19/6)	$a = b = 20.0$ Å, $c = 38.76$ Å	$P\bar{4}$	[94b,c]
it-Polystyrene	6.65	s(3/1)	$a = b = 21.9$ Å, $c = 6.65$ Å	$R3c - R\bar{3}c$	[40]
it-Poly(*o*-methylstyrene)	8.1	s(4/1)	$a = b = 19.01$ Å, $c = 8.1$ Å	$I4_1cd$	[36a, 87]
it-Poly(*m*-methylstyrene)	21.7	s(11/3)	$a = b = 19.81$ Å, $c = 21.74$ Å	$P\bar{4}$	[86]
it-Poly(*o*-fluorostyrene)	6.63	s(3/1)	$a = b = 22.15$ Å, $c = 6.63$ Å	$R3c$	[85]
it-Poly(*p*-fluorostyrene)	8.25	s(4/1)	$a = 17.6$ Å, $b = 12.1$ Å, $c = 8.25$ Å	$P2_12_12_1$	[36, 112]
it-Poly(vinylcyclohexane) form I	6.5	s(4/1)	$a = b = 21.9$ Å, $c = 6.5$ Å	$I4_1/a$	[89, 90]
it-Poly(vinylcyclohexane) form II	44.6	s(24/7)	$a = b = 20.48$ Å, $c = 44.6$ Å	$I\bar{4}$	[201]
it-Poly(α-vinylnaphtalene)	8.1	s(4/1)	$a = b = 21.20$ Å, $c = 8.1$ Å	$I4_1cd$	[88]
it-Poly(vinyl methyl ether)	6.5	s(3/1)	$a = b = 16.25$ Å, $c = 6.5$ Å	$R\bar{3}$	[83]
it-Poly(vinyl isopropyl ether)	35.5	s(17/5)	$a = b = 17.2$ Å, $c = 35.5$ Å	Tetragonal	[202a–c]
it-Poly(vinyl *sec*-butyl ether)	35.5	s(17/5)	$a = b = 18.25$ Å, $c = 35.5$ Å	Tetragonal	[202d]
it-Poly(vinyl isobutyl ether)	6.5	s(3/1)	$a = b\sqrt{3} = 16.8$ Å , $c = 6.5$ Å	Orthorhombic	[202, 203]
it-Poly(vinyl neopentyl ether)	6.5	s(3/1)	$a = b\sqrt{3} = 18.2$ Å , $c = 6.5$ Å	Orthorhombic	[202]
it-Poly(*t*-butylacrylate)	6.5	s(3/1)	–	$P3_1$	[95]
it-1,2-Poly(1,3-butadiene)	6.5	s(3/1)	$a = b = 17.3$ Å, $c = 6.5$ Å	$R3c - R\bar{3}c$	[84]

TABLE 2.2 (*Continued*)

Polymer	Chain Axis (Å)	Chain Symmetry	Unit-Cell Parameters	Space Group	Reference
it-1,2-Poly(4-methyl-1,3-pentadiene)	36.5	s(18/5)	$a = b = 17.80$ Å, $c = 36.5$ Å	$I\bar{4}c2$	[204]
it-Poly(1-oxo-2-phenyltrimethylene) it-Poly(styrene-*alt*-CO)	7.57	s(2/1)	$a = 8.367$ Å, $b = 7.574$ Å, $c = 5.47$ Å, $\beta = 110°$	$P2_1$	[205, 206]
st-Polypropylene form I	7.4	s(2/1)2	$a = 14.5$ Å, $b = 11.2$ Å $c = 7.4$ Å	$Ibca, P2_1/a$	[32, 148]
st-Polypropylene form II	7.4	s(2/1)2	$a = 14.5$ Å, $b = 5.6$ Å, $c = 7.4$ Å	$C222_1$	[31]
st-Polypropylene form III	5.06	t*c*	$a = 5.22$ Å, $b = 11.17$ Å, $c = 5.06$ Å	$P2_1cn$	[33, 34]
st-Polypropylene form IV	11.6	t2 ($T_6G_2T_2G_2$)	$a = 14.17$ Å, $b = 5.72$ Å, $c = 11.6$ Å, $\beta = 108.8°$	$P1, C2$	[67]
st-Polybutene form I	7.73	s(2/1)2	$a = 16.81$ Å, $b = 6.06$ Å, $c = 7.73$ Å	$C222_1$	[68, 70]
st-Polybutene form II	20.0	s(5/3)2	$a = 15.45$ Å, $b = 14.36$ Å, $c = 20$ Å, $\gamma = 116°$	$P2_1/a$	[68, 71]
st-Poly(4-methyl-1-pentene)	46.9	s(12/7)2	$a = b = 18.03$ Å, $c = 46.9$ Å	$P\bar{4}$	[69, 72]
st-Polystyrene α form	5.04	t*c*	$a = b = 26.26$ Å, $c = 5.04$ Å	$P3$	[62, 113]
st-Polystyrene β form	5.1	t*c*	$a = 8.81$ Å, $b = 28.82$ Å $c = 5.1$ Å	$P2_12_12_1\ Cmcm$	[63, 64]
st-Polystyrene γ form	7.7	s(2/1)2	–	–	[59]
st-Polystyrene (nanoporous) δ form	7.7	s(2/1)2	$a = 17.4$ Å, $b = 11.85$ Å, $c = 7.70$ Å, $\gamma = 117°$	$P2_1/a$	[66]
st-Polystyrene (nanoporous) ε form	7.9	s(2/1)2	$a = 16.2$ Å, $b = 22.0$ Å, $c = 7.9$ Å	$Pbcn$	[207]
st-Polystyrene δ form (clathrate forms)	7.7	s(2/1)2	Depend on the guest: $a = 17.58$ Å, $b = 13.26$ Å, $c = 7.71$ Å, $\gamma = 121.2°$ (complex with toluene).	$P2_1/a$	[65]
st-Polystyrene δ form (intercalate forms)	7.8	s(2/1)2	Depend on the guest: $a = 17.5$ Å, $b = 14.5$ Å, $c = 7.8$ Å, $\gamma = 107.8°$ (complex with norbornadiene).	$P2_1/a$	[208]
st-Poly(*p*-methylstyrene) form I	8.1	s(2/1)2	$a = 24.5$ Å, $b = 12.4$ Å, $c = 8.1$ Å, $\gamma = 143.5°$	$P2_1/a$	[209]
st-Poly(*p*-methylstyrene) form II	7.8	s(2/1)2	–	–	[209]
st-Poly(*p*-methylstyrene) form III	5.12	t*cm*	$a = 13.36$ Å, $b = 23.21$ Å, $c = 5.12$ Å	$Pnam$	[210]
st-Poly(*p*-methylstyrene) β class clathrate forms	7.7	s(2/1)2	Depend on the guest: $a = 18.8$ Å, $b = 12.7$ Å, $c = 7.7$ Å, $\gamma = 100°$ (complex with tetrahydrofuran).	$P2_1/a$	[211a,d–g]
st-Poly(*p*-methylstyrene) α class clathrate forms	7.7	s(2/1)2	Depend on the guest: $a = 23.4$ Å, $b = 11.8$ Å, $c = 7.7$ Å, $\gamma = 115°$ (complex with *o*-dichlorobenzene).	$P2_1/a$	[211b,c,f,g]
st-Poly(*p*-methylstyrene) γ class clathrate forms	11.7	t2 ($T_6G_2T_2G_2$)	–	–	[212]
st-Poly(*m*-methylstyrene) form I	7.9	s(2/1)2	–	–	[213]

(*Continued*)

TABLE 2.2 (*Continued*)

Polymer	Chain Axis (Å)	Chain Symmetry	Unit-Cell Parameters	Space Group	Reference
st-Poly(*m*-methylstyrene) form II	–	–	–	–	[213]
st-Poly(*m*-methylstyrene) form III	5.1	**t**c*m*	Mesomorphic form	–	[213]
st-Poly(*m*-methylstyrene) β class clathrate forms	7.8	**s**(2/1)2	$a = 17.8$ Å, $b = 13.1$ Å, and $c = 7.8$ Å.	*Pcaa*	[213, 214]
st-1,2-Poly(1,3-butadiene)	5.1	**t**c*m*	$a = 10.98$ Å, $b = 6.60$ Å, $c = 5.1$ Å	*Pcam*	[100]
st-1,2-Poly(4-methyl-1,3-pentadiene) form I	11.73	**t**2 ($T_6G_2T_2G_2$)	$a = 17.51$ Å, $b = 9.12$ Å, $c = 11.25$ Å, $\alpha = 95.2°$, $\beta = 98.0°$, $\gamma = 92.7°$	$P\bar{1}$	[215, 216]
st-1,2-Poly(4-methyl-1,3-pentadiene) form II	5.05	**t**c	–	–	[215]
st-Poly(1-oxo-2-phenyltrimethylene) *st*-Poly(styrene-*alt*-CO)	7.5	**t**c	$a = 15.5$ Å, $b = 6.15$ Å, $c = 7.56$ Å, $\beta = 105°$	$P2_1/c$	[217–219]

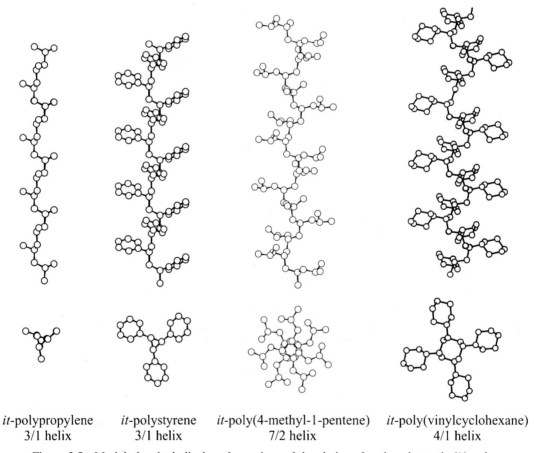

it-polypropylene   *it*-polystyrene   *it*-poly(4-methyl-1-pentene)   *it*-poly(vinylcyclohexane)
3/1 helix   3/1 helix   7/2 helix   4/1 helix

Figure 2.5 Models for the helical conformations of the chains of various isotactic (*it*) polymers as examples of 3/1 and 4/1 symmetries and of complex helices with fractional values of *M/N* intermediate between 3 and 4.

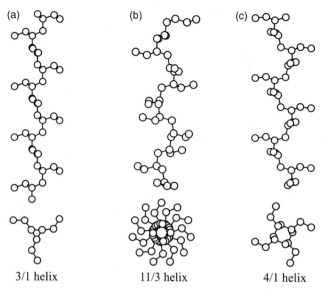

Figure 2.6 Chains of iPB in 3/1 (a), 11/3 (b), and 4/1 (c) helical conformations that crystallize in the forms I [45], II [43, 46], and III [47] of iPB, respectively.

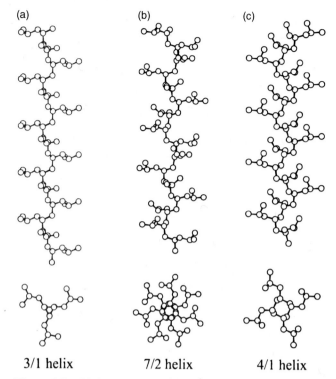

Figure 2.7 Chains of iP4MP in 3/1 (a), 7/2 (b), and 4/1 (c) helical conformations that crystallize in the form IV (a) [55], form I (b) [38, 48], and forms II [49, 50] and III [44, 52] (c) of iP4MP, respectively.

of iP4MP [44, 52, 53]. The relative minimum of higher energy corresponds to the 3/1 helical conformation, found in the less stable form IV of iP4MP [53c–55]. The helical conformations of the chains of the polymorphic forms of iP4MP are shown in Figure 2.7.

The principle of the similar distortions of the torsion angles of the main chain from the staggered values 180° and 60°, due to the bulkiness of the side groups [35], is also valid for the chain conformations of syndiotactic polymers [56]. While the isodistortion gives rise to a shortening of the unit height for isotactic polymers, it induces an increase of the unit height for syndiotactic polymers [56] and produces helical conformations (T'T'G'G')$_n$ with symmetries s(M/N)2 where the number of structural units per turn M/N is generally noninteger. Data concerning the chain conformations and the structure of syndiotactic polymers are also reported in Table 2.2. Models of the chain conformations found in the various polymorphic forms of syndiotactic polymers are reported in Figure 2.8.

Syndiotactic polymers also show polymorphism due to the fact that the chains may assume different low energy conformations that crystallize in different polymorphic forms. Calculations of the conformational energy under the constraints of the equivalence principle and, hence, assuming a sequence of the backbone torsion angles … $\theta_1, \theta_1, \theta_2, \theta_2, \ldots$, allow for an easy interpretation of the conformation polymorphism [56].

In the cases of syndiotactic polystyrene (sPS) [57] and sPP [58], minima of the conformational energy have been found in the regions corresponding to the highly extended *trans* planar ($\theta_1 \approx \theta_2 \approx T = 180°$) and helical conformations ($\theta_1 \approx 60°$ and $\theta_2 \approx 180°$ or $\theta_1 \approx 180°$ and $\theta_2 \approx -60°$). For sPS, the absolute minimum corresponds to the *trans*-planar conformation, in agreement with the fact that the most stable α and β forms of sPS present chains in *trans*-planar conformation [59–64]. A relative energy minimum corresponds, instead, to the twofold helical conformation (TTGG)$_2$, with s(2/1)2 symmetry, ($\theta_1 \approx 60°$, $\theta_2 \approx 180°$ or $\theta_1 \approx 180°$, $\theta_2 \approx -60°$), in agreement with the helical conformation found in the less stable γ and δ forms of sPS [59, 65, 66]. In the case of sPP, the absolute minimum corresponds to the twofold helical conformation, found in the stable forms I and II [30–32], and the relative minimum to the *trans*-planar conformation, found in the metastable form III of sPP [33, 34]. A helical conformation of sPP with sequence (T$_2$G$_2$T$_6$G$_2$)$_n$, made of portions of chain in the regular 2/1 helical T$_2$G$_2$ conformation, and portions in *trans*-planar conformation T$_6$ has been found in the metastable form IV of sPP [67]. The conformations of the chains of the different

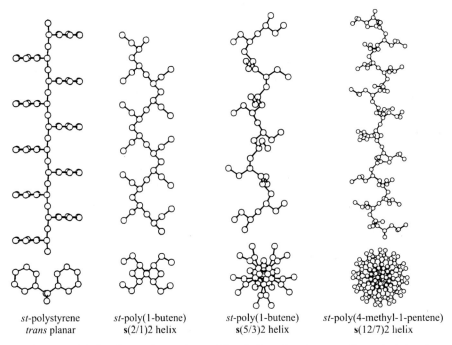

Figure 2.8 Models for the conformations of the chains of various syndiotactic (*st*) polymers as examples of *trans*-planar conformation, twofold **s**(2/1)2 helical conformation, and of complex helices with fractional values of the ratio *M/N*.

polymorphic forms of sPP and sPS are shown in Figure 2.9 and Figure 2.10, respectively.

In the case of syndiotactic polybutene (sPB) and poly(4-methyl-1-pentene) (sP4MP), which have bulkier side groups, deep energy minima are present only in the region of the helical conformation, the minimum in the *trans*-planar region being of higher energy [68, 69]. According to these calculations, no crystalline forms with chains in *trans*-planar conformation have been observed for sPB [68] and sP4MP [69]. For both sPB and sP4MP, two minima of nearly equal energy have been found in the region of the helical conformation. The first minimum corresponds to the twofold (TTGG)$_n$ helical conformation of **s**(2/1)2 symmetry, characterized by staggered values for the torsion angles $\theta_1 \approx 60°$ and $\theta_2 \approx 180°$. The second minimum corresponds to distorted helical conformations (T'T'G'G')$_n$, characterized by values of the torsion angles deviated from the staggered values $\theta_1 = G' = 60° + \delta$; $\theta_2 = T' = 180° + \delta$.

According to these calculations, two crystalline forms of sPB have been found [68, 70, 71]: the most stable form I with chains in the **s**(2/1)2 helical conformation [68, 70] and the metastable form II characterized by chains in the helical conformation with **s**(5/3)2 symmetry [68, 71]. For sP4MP, only one crystalline form with chains in the distorted helical conformation with **s**(12/7)2 symmetry has been found [69, 72], which corresponds to the absolute energy minimum [69]. The helical conformations of

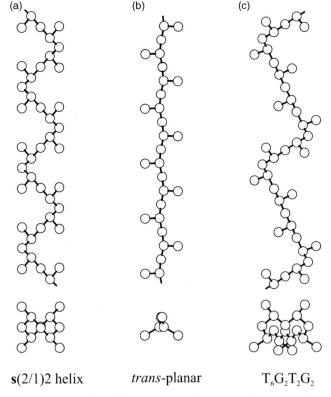

Figure 2.9 Chains of sPP in **s**(2/1)2 helical conformation (a), *trans*-planar conformation (b), and T$_6$G$_2$T$_2$G$_2$ helical conformation (c) that crystallize in forms I and II (a) [30–32], form III (b) [33, 34], and form IV (c) [67] of sPP, respectively.

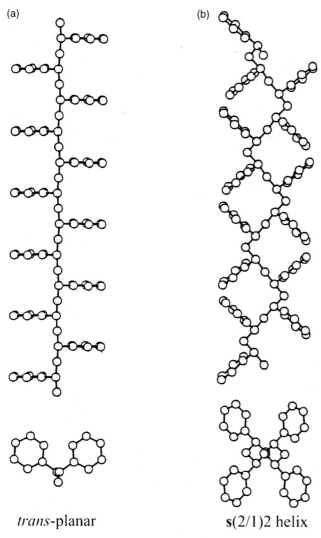

trans-planar   s(2/1)2 helix

Figure 2.10 Chains of sPS in *trans*-planar conformation (a) and s(2/1)2 helical conformation (b) that crystallize in α and β forms (a) [59–64] and in γ and δ forms (b) [59, 65, 66] of sPS, respectively.

the chains of forms I and II of sPB and of sP4MP are shown in Figure 2.8.

2.3 PACKING OF MACROMOLECULES IN POLYMER CRYSTALS

The principles of equivalence and of minumum internal conformational energy allow establishing the conformation assumed by a stereoregular polymer chain in the crystalline state. General rules concerning the mode of packing of polymers in the crystals have also been described by Corradini [1]. When no strong electrostatic interactions are present, polymer crystals are generally built up according to the principle of *close-packing* [73], which establishes that the *packing of molecules in crystals is dominated by the condition that the closest distance between nonbonded atoms is defined by their van der Waals radii*. Kitajgorodskij [73] has shown that, for low molecular weight organic compounds, the close-packing corresponds to the free energy minimum; that is, the crystal structure of a molecule corresponds to one of the minima of the multidimensional energy surface. The close-packing principle implies that the energy minima correspond to packing model structures of minimum occupied volume; that is, the energy minima are close to the minima of the multidimensional volume surface, provided that the distances between neighboring atoms of different molecules are not lower than the sum of their van der Waals radii [73].

Besides the energy factors, defined by the close-packing principle, entropic factors guide the mode of packing of molecules. *A molecule in a crystal tends to maintain part of its symmetry elements, provided that this does not cause a serious loss of density.* As outlined by Kitajgorodskij, in a more symmetric position a molecule has a greater freedom of vibrations; that is, the structure is more probable (entropy factor) because it occupies a wider potential well on the multidimensional energy surface [73].

In the case of polymers, the application of the principle of close-packing is easier than in the case of low molecular weight compounds because the chain conformation of the polymer chains can be established in a separate step, allowing for the determination of the structure along the direction corresponding to the chain axis [1]. Moreover, if the elements of symmetry of the chains are compatible with the crystal, they are generally maintained in the crystal lattice, so that the problem is further simplified. In this case, indeed, geometrically equivalent atoms, belonging to different structural units of the same chain, can assume equivalent positions with respect to the corresponding atoms of neighboring chains; that is, they become crystallographically equivalent [1]. The criterion of close-packing and the entropic factor may serve as a general guideline in crystal modeling. On the basis of these principles, starting from the configuration and the conformation of the chains, it is possible to predict theoretically the mode of packing of most polymers [1].

Corradini has shown that almost all the known crystal structures of polymers are easily rationalizable in terms of these principles [1]. In particular, he suggested that the mode of packing of polymer chains first depends on the outside envelope of the chains [1]. Depending on the conformation, the form of a polymer chain may be approximated by a cylinder of radius r, corresponding to the outside envelope of the atoms of the main chain, bearing a periodic helical relief of radius R, corresponding to the atoms of the lateral groups [1]. Two classes of polymers can be basically distinguished: (1) polymers for which the form of the chain is, in a first approximation, a cylinder of uniform radius, and the ratio r/R is close to 1, such as in polyethylene (PE) [74], *trans*-1,4-poly(1,3-butadiene) [75, 76], and polytetrafuoroethylene [77, 78], and (2) polymers such as many vinyl polymers characterized by helices with a fractional ratio M/N that have an encumbrance similar to that of a screw (Fig. 2.11a).

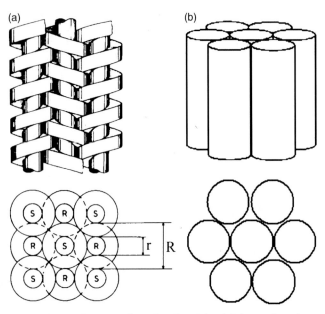

Figure 2.11 Tetragonal mode of packing of skews that simulate helices s(M/N) with fractional ratio M/N (a) and hexagonal mode of packing of cylinders that simulate helices with an uniform radius (b).

In the case of chains having a form of uniform cylinder and the ratio r/R is close to 1, the best mode of packing is the hexagonal arrangement of the chains with coordination number equal to 6 (Fig. 2.11b). For instance, *trans*-1,4-polybutadiene is characterized in the crystalline polymorph stable at low temperatures by an orthorhombic unit cell with a/b in the approximate ratio equal to $\sqrt{3}/2$, which is consistent with a pseudohexagonal close-packing [2, 75, 76, 79], and in the disordered polymorphic form stable at high temperatures by a hexagonal unit cell [2, 79–82].

When the ratio r/R is different from 1 the form of the chains may be approximated by a cylinder in which hollows and bulges are periodically repeated; that is, the chains have an outside envelope similar to a screw [1] (Fig. 2.11a). If the ratio r/R is very small, close to 0.1–0.2, such as for chains in threefold helical conformation, a trigonal packing of enantiomorphous chains may arise. Each 3_1 right-handed chain is surrounded by three left-handed isoclined or anticlined chains, and vice versa (space group $R3c$ or $R\bar{3}$, respectively), such as in iPS (Fig. 2.12a) [40], form I of iPB (Fig. 2.12b) [45], poly(vinyl methyl ether) [83], isotactic 1,2-poly(1,3-butadiene) [84], and isotactic poly(*o*-fluorostyrene) [85].

Higher values of the ratio r/R, close to $\sqrt{2}-1$ (similar to the situation stabilizing NaCl), are obtained in the cases of many vinyl polymers with chains in complex helical conformation s(M/N) with a fractional ratio M/N, ranging between 3 and 4, such as form I of isotactic poly(4-methyl-1-pentene) (7/2 helix) [38], form II of isotactic poly(1-butene) (11/3 helix) [46], isotactic poly(*m*-methylstyrene) (11/3 helix) [86], and syndiotactic poly(4-methyl-1-pentene) (12/7 helix) [72]. In these cases, a tetragonal packing of enantiomorphous chains,

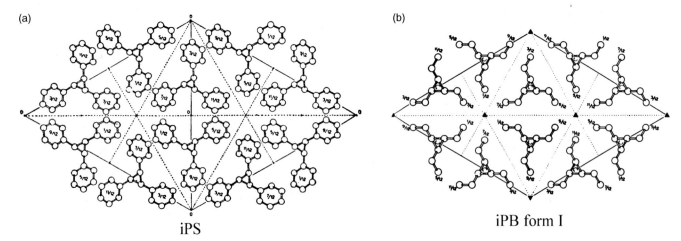

Figure 2.12 Models of packing of the stable form of iPS (a) [40] and form I of iPB (b) [45], with chains in 3/1 helical conformation packed in trigonal lattices according to the space groups $R3c$ or $R\bar{3}c$. Some crystallographic elements of symmetry for the space groups $R3c$ or $R\bar{3}c$ are also indicated.

with coordination number equal to 4, is favored (Fig. 2.11a). Each right-handed chain is surrounded by four left-handed chains and vice versa, and a tight fitting of threads into grooves is achieved [1]. The structures of form I of isotactic poly(4-methyl-1-pentene) and of form II of isotactic poly(1-butene) are shown in Figure 2.13. All the polymers of this class, for which the ratio r/R lies in the range 0.3–0.8, crystallize in a tetragonal lattice with space group $P\bar{4}$.

Similar packing in tetragonal lattices is obtained with chains in 4/1 helical conformation ($M/N = 4$) with possible space groups $I4_1cd$ or $I4_1/a$, with each right-handed chain surrounded by four left-handed isoclined or anticlined chains, respectively, and vice versa [1]. Structures with $I4_1cd$ symmetry have been found for isotactic poly(o-methylstyrene) (Fig. 2.14a) [87] and poly(α-vinylnaphthalene) [88], while the $I4_1/a$ space group has been found for isotactic poly(vinylcyclohexane) (Fig. 2.14b) [89, 90] and almost all the polyaldehydes [91].

In the case of optically active poly(α-olefins) containing a chiral side group, the chirality of the monomeric units favors the formation of helices of one specific chirality (right- or left-handed) [38a, 39, 92, 93]. This is, for instance, the case of poly((S)-3-methyl-1-pentene) (iP(S)3MP), where only 4/1 left-handed helical chains are present in the tetragonal unit cell according to the space group $I4_1$ [93]. Because of the chirality of the lateral group, right-handed and left-handed helices of iP(S)3MP are not equivalent. Two low energy conformations of

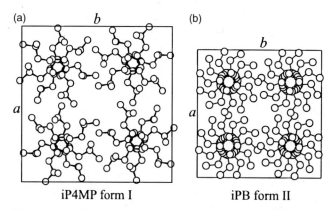

Figure 2.13 Models of packing of form I of iP4MP with chains in 7/2 helical conformation (a) [38] and of form II of iPB with chains in 11/3 helical conformation (b) [46], as examples of packing mode of chains with complex s(M/N) helical conformation with fractional M/N ratio in tetragonal lattices according to the space group $P\bar{4}$.

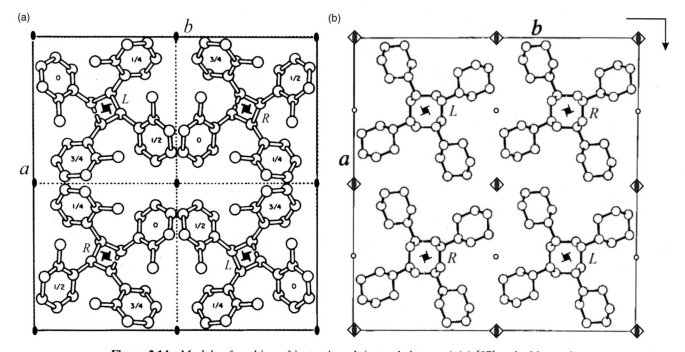

Figure 2.14 Models of packing of isotactic poly(o-methylstyrene) (a) [87] and of isotactic poly(vinylcyclohexane) (b) [89, 90] with chains in 4/1 helical conformation, as examples of packing mode of chains with s(4/1) helical conformation in tetragonal lattices according to the space groups $I4_1cd$ (a) and $I4_1/a$ (b), respectively, where the 4/1 local symmetry of the chains is maintained in the lattice as crystallographic symmetry. R and L indicate right-handed and left-handed helices, respectively. Some crystallographic elements of symmetry for the space groups $I4_1cd$ (a) and $I4_1/a$ (b) are also indicated.

the chiral lateral group are possible for the left-handed helix, while only one low energy conformation is possible for the right-handed helix. The left-handed helix of iP(S)3MS is, therefore, favored over the right-handed one. In the crystal structure, the chains of iP(S)3MP assume a 4/1 helical conformation and only left-handed helices are included in the tetragonal unit cell, with the lateral groups which may take statistically both conformations of minimum energy [93].

In other optically active polymers, as well as in some polymers from achiral monomers, chiral structures, characterized by all isomorphous helical chains in the unit cell, have been found. For instance, in isotactic poly(5-methyl-1-hexene) [94], isotactic poly(t-butylacrylate) [95], and optically active isotactic poly((S)-5-methyl-1-heptene) [94b,c], chiral pseudo-hexagonal or tetragonal packing with isomorphous 3/1 or 4/1 helical chains have been found.

However, the driving force toward the antichiral packing of the type of Figure 2.13 and Figure 2.14 is so high that even in the case of optically active isotactic poly((S)-4-methyl-1-hexene), where the chiral side group stabilizes one of the two possible senses of the helix [38a, 39, 92, 93], it has been found that both right- and left-handed 7/2 helical chains are present in the tetragonal unit cell [38a].

The crystallization of most of the mentioned structures of isotactic and syndiotactic poly(α-olefins) and of stereoregular polydienes is also guided by the entropic principle, which establishes that the symmetry of the isolated chains is generally maintained in the lattice [1]. For instance, in almost all the known structures of polymers having chain conformations with a glide plane, this symmetry element is maintained in the lattice because it allows a good distribution of bulky substituents of different chains between themselves (for instance, cis-1,4-poly(1,3-butadiene) [96], cis-1,4-poly(isoprene) [96–99], syndiotactic 1,2-poly(1,3-butadiene) [100], and form III of sPP [34]) In some cases, the complete chain symmetry is preserved in the crystal lattice; for instance, in cis-1,4-poly(1,3-butadiene) the binary axes perpendicular to the chain axes crossing the double bonds as well as the inversion centers located on the central single bonds (**tci** symmetry) are maintained in the lattice (space group $C2/c$) [96]; in syndiotactic 1,2-poly(1,3-butadiene), the binary axes centered on the CH_2 groups and the symmetry planes perpendicular to the chain axis are also preserved [100].

The most straightforward application of the entropic principle is the driving force that induces crystallization of polymers with chains in **s**(M/N) helical conformation in crystalline lattices containing the screw M/N operator, so that the local helical symmetry of the chains becomes a crystallographic symmetry. According to this principle, almost all isotactic polymers with chains in 3_1 helical conformation crystallize in trigonal lattice (space groups $R3c$, $R\bar{3}$, or $R\bar{3}c$), as shown in Figure 2.12 for iPS [40] and iPB [45]. The local threefold helical symmetry axes of the molecules are maintained in the crystal lattice and coincide with the crystallographic threefold axes. The crystal structure of form I of iPB (Fig. 2.12b) is a prototype of this class of polymer crystals. Chains in 3_1 helical conformation are packed in the trigonal unit cell with axes $a = b = 17.7$ Å and $c = 6.5$ Å, according to the space group $R3c$ or $R\bar{3}c$ [45]. The unit cell houses six chains; each 3_1 right-handed helical chain is surrounded by three left-handed helical chains and vice versa. The density of crystals is high, $\rho_c = 0.95$ g/cm^3, due to the close-packing of helices bearing bulky lateral groups.

It is also well known that the famous crystal structure of the stable form of iPP, found by Natta and Corradini [29], is the exception to the rule of maintaining the threefold helical symmetry of the chains in the crystal lattice. In fact, chains of iPP assume the stable 3/1 helical conformation, but they are not packed in trigonal or hexagonal unit cells, maintaining the crystallographic threefold symmetry, because this would produce a crystal lattice with very low density due to the too small side groups (the methyl groups), compared with the ethyl or phenyl groups in iPB or iPS, respectively. The threefold helical chains are instead packed in a monoclinic unit cell, according to the space group $C2/c$ or $P2_1/c$ [29, 101, 102], so that the local symmetry of the chain conformation is lost in the lattice, allowing for denser packing (Fig. 2.15, $\rho_c = 0.936$ g/cm^3).

However, it has been recently shown [103, 104] that if polypropylene macromolecules are modified, for

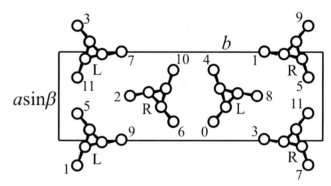

Figure 2.15 Model of packing of α form of iPP with chains in 3_1 helical conformation packed in a monoclinic unit cell according to the space group $C2/c$ or $P2_1/c$ [29, 101, 102]. The heights of the carbon atoms of the methyl groups are indicated in $c/12$ units. R and L indicate right-handed and left-handed helices, respectively.

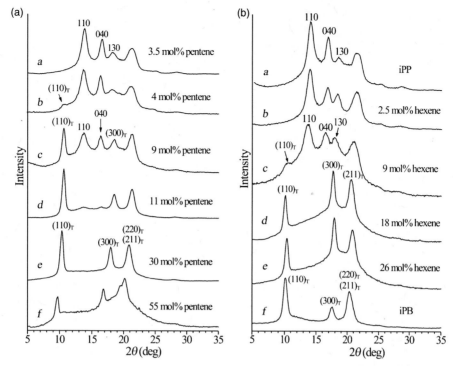

Figure 2.16 X-ray powder diffraction profiles of samples of isotactic propylene–pentene (a) [105] and propylene–hexene (b) [103, 104] random copolymers with the indicated concentration of comonomeric units in comparison with those of the α form of iPP and form I of iPB. The 110, 040, and 130 reflection of the α form of iPP and the $(110)_I$, $(300)_I$, and $(220 + 211)_I$ reflections of the form I of iPB are indicated. Reproduced from References [105] (a) and [103] (b) with permission from American Chemical Society, Copyright 2007 (a) and 2006 (b).

instance by incorporating bulky comonomeric units, such as pentene or hexene, the inclusion of the comonomeric units in the crystals increases the density, and the random copolymers crystallize in a new form characterized by a trigonal unit cell, and the threefold helical symmetry of the chains is maintained in the crystal lattice [103–105]. The structure of isotactic propylene–pentene (iPPe) [105] and propylene–hexene (iPPHe) [103, 104, 106a] random copolymers best demonstrates the general principle of *entropy-driven phase formation in polymers* [103–105].

The X-ray powder diffraction profiles of some samples of iPPe [105] and iPPHe [103, 104] copolymers prepared with metallocene catalysts are reported in Figure 2.16 and compared with those of samples of iPP and iPB homopolymers.

It is apparent that the copolymers crystallize in the α form of iPP up to a concentration of comonomeric units (pentene or hexene) of nearly 10 mol% (profiles a–c of Fig. 2.16a and b,c of Fig. 2.16b). The Bragg distance of 110 and 040 reflections (at $2\theta = 14$ and 16.8°, respectively in the α form of iPP) slightly increase with increasing comonomer concentration, indicating increase of a- and b-axes of the unit cell and inclusion of pentene or hexene units in the crystals of the α form. At comonomer concentrations of 9–10 mol% an additional reflection at $2\theta = 10.2°$ appears, and for higher comonomer contents the X-ray diffraction profile totally changes, the main reflections being at $2\theta \approx 10°$, $17°$, and $20°$ (profiles d–f of Fig. 2.16a and d,e of Fig. 2.16b), and becomes equal to the diffraction profile of form I of iPB (profile f of Fig. 2.16b). This indicates that for these pentene or hexene concentrations the copolymer samples crystallize in a new crystalline form similar to the structure of form I of iPB (Fig. 2.12b). The modified chains of iPP in 3_1 helical conformation, incorporating pentene or hexene comonomeric units, are packed in a trigonal unit cell according to the space group $R3c$ or $R\overline{3}c$ [103–105], as in the cases of iPB [45] and iPS [40] (Fig. 2.12). Pentene and hexene units are included in the crystals of the trigonal form and, in particular, the change of the crystallization habit at comonomer contents higher than 10 mol% allows a nearly complete accommodation of pentene and hexene units in the crystal lattice, with increase of the crystal density that approaches to that of crystals of form I of iPB [45].

Therefore, when propene and pentene units or propene and hexene units are randomly blended along the same macromolecules and the average overall composition of the two comonomers approaches that of butene ($\approx 50\% C_3H_6 + \approx 50\% C_5H_{10} = C_4H_8$), copolymer chains behave as poly(butene) macromolecules and crystallize into the stable form I of iPB, provided that the distribution of the comonomer is random [103, 104]. A model of the crystal structure of the trigonal form that crystallize in iPPe and iPPHe copolymers, with disorder in the positioning of the lateral groups, according to the space group $R3c$, is shown in Figure 2.17. The increase of density allows crystallization of threefold helical chains of iPP in a trigonal unit cell, where the helical symmetry of the chains is maintained in the crystal lattice and coincides with the crystallographic threefold axes, as predicted by principles of polymer crystallography [1]. This form does not crystallize and has never been observed so far for the iPP homopolymer because, in the absence of bulky side groups, it would have a density that is too low [1, 2, 29, 95]. Almost 50 years after the resolution of the crystal structure of the α form of iPP and the enunciation of general principles of polymer crystallography [1, 2], it has been shown that iPP is no longer an exception but the structure of propylene–pentene and propene–hexene copolymers represents the fulfillment of these principles and indicates that the packing of polymer molecules is mainly driven by density and guided by the principle of entropy-driven phase formation in polymers [103–105].

Recently, new interesting phenomena that control the mode of packing of polymers have been found, and it has been shown that the basic principles of polymer crystallography are, in some cases, violated. In particular, (1) an atactic polymer can crystallize; this is, for instance, the case of polyacrylonitrile [107]; (2) in a crystalline polymer the chains can be nonparallel; for instance, the structure of the γ form of iPP is characterized by the packing of nearly perpendicular chains [108, 109]; (3) the principle of entropy-driven phase formation may be violated and the high local symmetry of the chains is lost in the limit-ordered crystalline lattice of polymers (*symmetry breaking*).

The observation of the lack of symmetry in the ordered structures of polymers is strictly related to the possibility of the direct observation of the local arrangements of chains in the crystals using methods of electron diffraction and solid-state ^{13}C nuclear magnetic resonance (NMR) spectroscopy. The study of the crystal structure of polymers, performed with the traditional X-ray diffraction, generally leads to models of packing that describe the order in the long range.

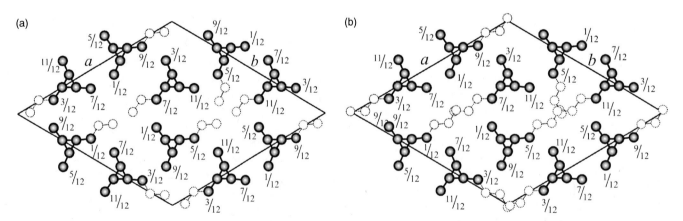

Figure 2.17 Models of the crystal structures of the trigonal form of iPP in the space groups $R3c$ found in propylene–pentene (a) [105] and propene-hexene (b) [103, 104] copolymers. The atoms of ethyl and propyl side groups of pentene and hexene comonomeric units, randomly distributed along each iPP chain, are shown as thin dotted lines. Reproduced from Reference [105] (A) and Reference [103] (b) with permission from American Chemical Society, Copyright 2007 (a) and 2006 (b).

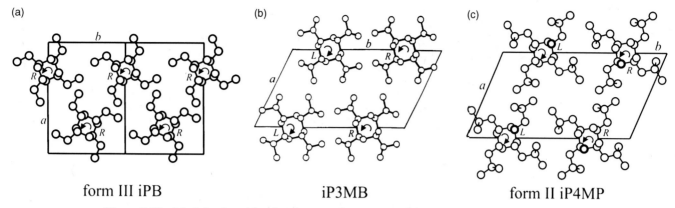

form III iPB   iP3MB   form II iP4MP

Figure 2.18 Models of packing for the crystal structures of form III of iPB (a) [47], iP3MB (b) [37, 110], and form II of iP4MP (c) [49, 50], as examples of symmetry breaking, where chains in 4_1 helical conformation are not packed in tetragonal lattices maintaining the 4_1 symmetry, but are packed in less symmetric orthorhombic ([a] space group $P2_12_12_1$) and monoclinic ([b, c] space group $P2_1/b$ or $P2_1$) unit cells. R and L indicate right-handed and left-handed helices, respectively.

2.4 SYMMETRY BREAKING

The crystal structures of form III of iPB [47], of iP3MB [36, 37, 110], and of form II of iP4MP [49, 50] are typical examples of symmetry breaking. The models of packing are shown in Figure 2.18. In these three examples, the chains are in the 4_1 helical conformation and should be packed in a tetragonal lattice, according to the principle of entropy-driven phase formation, so that the 4_1 helical symmetry of the chains is maintained in the crystals. Typical space groups for isotactic polymers with chains in 4_1 helical conformation are, indeed, $I4_1cd$ and $I4_1/a$ (Fig. 2.14) [87–91]. In the structure of Figure 2.18, the 4_1 helical chains are instead packed in less symmetric orthorhombic (form III of iPB) and monoclinic (iP3MB and form II of iP4MP) unit cells, according to space groups $P2_12_12_1$ for form III of iPB [47] and $P2_1/b$ for iP3MB [37, 110] and form II of iP4MP [49] (or $P2_1$ for form II of iP4MP [50]), so that the 4_1 helical symmetry of the chains is lost in the crystals. In these structures the low symmetry of the lattices has been evidenced by the X-ray [37, 47, 49] and electron [50] diffraction data and, in the case of iP3MB and form II of iP4MP, by splittings of resonances of methyl carbon atoms in the solid-state ^{13}C NMR spectra [49, 110, 111], indicating that methyl carbons of different chains in the unit cells are not equivalent, that is, they have different crystallographic environments, as expected for a monoclinic lattice. Low symmetry orthorhombic lattice, with the $P2_12_12_1$ space group, has also been found for isotactic poly(p-fluorostyrene) having chains in 4_1 helical conformation [36, 112].

Symmetry breaking has also been found in the structure of the α form of sPS. Various models of packing have been proposed for this structure [60–62, 113]. The most important feature is that the trans-planar chains are organized in triplets [60]. The X-ray powder and fiber diffraction patterns [61, 62], as well as the electron diffraction pattern [60, 113] are basically accounted for by a trigonal packing of triplets of trans-planar chains, according to space groups $P3c1$ or $P3$ [61, 62]. Three independent triplets (not related by any element of symmetry) are included in the unit cell. The space group of highest symmetry for the ordered structure would be $P3c1$ if the local glide plane of the trans-planar chains was maintained in the lattice as crystallographic symmetry [61] (Fig. 2.19a). The analysis of the electron diffraction pattern of single crystals [60, 113] shows that the intensities of $hk0$ and $kh0$ reflections are different. This indicates that the symmetry of the space group should be lower than $P3c1$ [62, 113]. These data show that *low symmetries of the unit cell are revealed even for symmetric single crystals, by the asymmetries of the electron diffraction patterns.* The α form of sPS forms, indeed, standard hexagonal single crystals [60, 113] but with a low unit cell symmetry [62]. The removal of the crystallographic glide plane symmetry produces a lowering of the space group symmetry from $P3c1$ to $P3$ [62]. In the space group $P3$ the triplets of chains may rotate around the threefold axes [62] and, in a refined model, the azimuthal orientations of the three independent triplets are found to be different [113]. The crystallographic glide planes are lost because of this rotation and the symmetry is broken (Fig. 2.19b). This low symmetry model describes a local ordered arrangement of the chains, that is, the order at very short distance, which can be detected only by a direct observation of very small

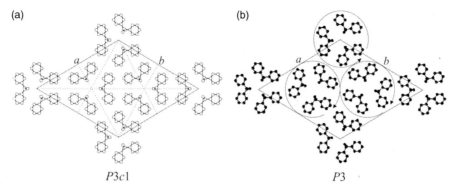

Figure 2.19 Models of packing of the chains in the α form of sPS according to the space group P3c1 [61] (a) and P3 [62, 113] (b). (a) The dotted lines indicate the crystallographic glide planes coincident with the local glide planes of the chains. (b) The triplets of chains are rotated around the threefold axes by three different angles (indicated by the arrowed circles) and the crystallographic glide planes are lost.

area of the diffracting crystals, and accounts for the different intensities of the $hk0$ and $kh0$ reflections observed in the electron diffraction pattern [60, 113]. Disorder in the setting angles of the triplets, or opposite values of the setting angles of the triplets in different domains of the crystal, may produce packing modes with a higher symmetry (Fig. 2.19a), which can describe the order in the long range [62].

The less symmetric model of the structure of sPS of Figure 2.19b is also an example of frustrated crystal structure of polymer [113]. The characteristic feature of frustrated structures is that two motifs maximize their interactions at the expense of the third motif. As a consequence, the third motif is frustrated since it is not in its ideal environment [114]. In the model of Figure 2.19b, the structural motif is the triplet of *trans*-planar chains. The different orientations of the three triplets of chains included in the unit cell are such that two triplets maximize their interactions at the expense of the third triplet [113].

2.5 PACKING EFFECTS ON THE CONFORMATION OF POLYMER CHAINS IN THE CRYSTALS: THE CASE OF ALIPHATIC POLYAMIDES

The general consideration that packing effects have little or no influence on the conformation of the polymer chains in the crystals as long as the conformational energy of the isolated chain corresponds to a deep energy minimum is a working hypothesis useful for explaining the crystal structure and polymorphism phenomena in the majority of cases. Important exceptions to this "rule" may be envisaged in the cases of polyisobutylene [115], poly(ethylene oxide) [115], and poly(*cis*-1,4-butadiene) [116], where calculations of both conformational and packing energy have shown that significant deviations from the minimum energy conformation of isolated chain evaluated under the geometrical restrains imposed by the equivalence postulate may be induced by the crystal field. An important class of synthetic polymers where the crystal field may strongly influence the conformation of chains in the crystals and the corresponding polymorphism phenomena are represented by aliphatic polyamides (PA) or nylons [117], where hydrogen bonds play a key role in the determination of the conformation of the chains in the crystalline domains.

The basic rules that govern the conformation and packing mode of nylon chains in the crystals were already identified by Bunn and Garner [118], who performed the first detailed investigation of the crystal structure of poly(hexamethylene adipamide) and poly(hexamethylene sebacamide). Resorting to the common name of aliphatic PA, that is, nylons, poly(hexamethylene adipamide) and poly(hexamethylene sebacamide) correspond to the nylon 6,6 and nylon 6,10, respectively. In general, there are two groups of aliphatic PA, those indicated as "nylon n," which are synthesized from ω-aminoacids $NH_2(CH_2)_{n-1}COOH$ and/or corresponding cyclic lactams, with n equal to the number of carbon atoms in the monomeric unit (Fig. 2.20a), and PAs indicated as "nylon n m," which are prepared from diamines $NH_2(CH_2)_nNH_2$ and dicarboxylic acids $HOOC(CH_2)_{m-2}COOH$ (or corresponding derivates) with n and m carbon atoms, respectively (Fig. 2.20b). An intrinsic feature related to the constitution of chains of nylons n is that they have a directional property related to the possibility that (C=O)---N bonds may be directed either toward a positive or a

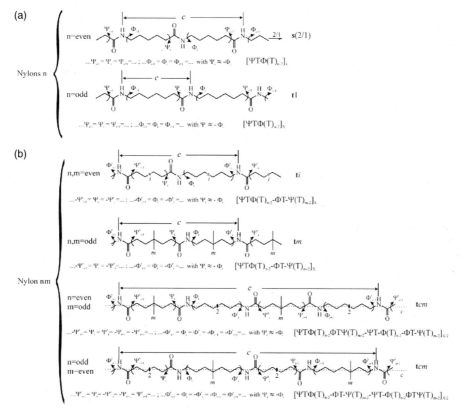

Figure 2.20 Minimum energy conformations of chains of nylon n (a) and nylon n,m in the crystals under the geometrical constraints imposed by the indicated line repetition groups. The identity period c includes two constitutional repeating units for even nylons (a) and even–odd and odd–even nylons (b), and a single constitutional repeating unit for odd nylons (a) and even–even and odd–odd nylons (b).

negative chain axis directions [16] (see Fig. 2.20a). According to the standard nomenclature [16], couples of chains with the same directionality are isoclined or parallel, whereas chains with (C=O)---N bonds directed toward opposite directions are anticlined or antiparallel.

Regardless of the kind of nylon, the main structural features of the polymer chains in the crystals are: (1) the tendency of amide groups of adjacent chains to form 100% hydrogen bonds [118]; (2) the *trans*-planar conformation of the aliphatic portions of chains [118]; (3) the planar conformation of -CH$_2$-CO-NH amide groups [119]; and (4) a nearly linear geometry for hydrogen bonds with angles close to 180° for N-H·····O and H·····O=C interactions [118]. Furthermore, nylons normally crystallize with chains in nearly extended conformations; small contractions of chain periodicity from the value of the fully extended chain may be allowed in order to accomplish the stringent requirement that 100% hydrogen bonds are always formed. As suggested by Natta and Corradini [119a] and Corradini et al. [119b], such deviations are in all cases associated with the chain twisting occurring at amide groups, rather than at the methylene units [120].

Minimum energy conformations of nylon chains in the crystals with indication of some possible line repetition groups compatible with their constitution are shown in Figure 2.20. These conformations may be described, at least to a first approximation, by assuming all torsion angles in *trans*-planar conformation, with the exception of torsion angles adjacent to amide bonds, that is, Ψ = -CH$_2$CH$_2$-CONH- and Φ = -CONH-CH$_2$CH$_2$-, which can deviate from the *trans*-planar conformation of a small or large amount [119] at a low cost of conformational energy [121], depending on the chemical constitution of nylon chains and, for any given nylon chain, on the kind of crystalline polymorph that is obtained.

It is worth noting that in order to preserve the extended and straight conformation of the chains, for each couple of torsion angles Ψ and Φ adjacent to the same amide bond, deviations δ from 180° should be nearly identical but of opposite sign [120]. The values of Ψ and Φ adjacent to the same amide bond are, therefore,

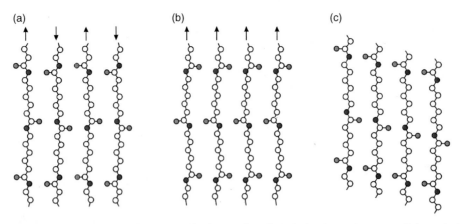

Figure 2.21 Projections of sheets of hydrogen bonded chains in a plane parallel to chain axes of even nylons (a, b) and even–even nylons (c) in the α form with chains in a zigzag planar conformation [122] (a, c) and in the γ form with chains in a twisted less extended conformation [122] (b). The cases of α and γ forms of nylon 6 are shown in (a) and (b) respectively, whereas the case of the α form of nylon 66 is shown in (c). The unit cell is monoclinic for nylon 6 with $a = 9.56$ Å, b (chain axis) = 17.24 Å, $c = 8.01$ Å, and $\beta = 67.5°$ for the α form [123] and $a = 9.33$ Å, b (chain axis) = 16.88 Å, $c = 4.78$ nm, and $\beta = 121°$ for the γ form [123] and triclinic for the α form of nylon 66 with $a = 4.9$ Å, $b = 5.4$ Å, c (chain axis) = 17.2 Å, $\alpha = 48.5°$, and $\beta = 77°$, $\gamma = 63.5°$ [118]. The distance of chain axes in the sheets (a – c) is ≈4.8 Å regardless of crystalline polymorph (α or γ forms) and the numbers n and/or m of carbon atoms per constitutional unit in the chains of nylon n and nylon n,m. The directionality of the chains of nylon 6 in (a) and (b) is indicated by arrows pointing up or down according to the direction of ⋯N–C(=O)⋯ bonds along the chains. Adjacent chains are anticlined in (a) and isoclined in (b). (See color insert.)

generally related each other by the relationship $\Psi \approx 180° + \delta$ and $\Phi \approx 180 - \delta$, so that $\Psi \approx -\Phi$ (Fig. 2.20). As shown in Figure 2.20a, the conformation of the chains of nylons n can be described by a succession of torsion angles $[\Psi T\Phi(T)_{n-2}]_x$, corresponding to the possible line repetition groups $s(2/1)$ for n even, and **t1** for n odd. In the case of nylons n,m the conformation of the chains can be described by a succession of torsion angles $[\Psi T\Phi(T)_{n-2}\Phi T\text{-}\Psi(T)_{m-2}]_x$, for even–even and odd–odd nylons, corresponding to the line repetition groups **ti** and **tm**, respectively, and by the successions $[\Psi T\Phi(T)_{n-2}\Phi T\Psi(T)_{m-2}\text{-}\Psi T\text{-}\Phi(T)_{n-2}\text{-}\Phi T\text{-}\Psi(T)_{m-2}]_{x/2}$ for even–odd nylons, and $[\Psi T\Phi(T)_{n-2}\Phi T\text{-}\Psi(T)_{m-2}\text{-}\Psi T\text{-}\Phi(T)_{n-2}\Phi T\Psi(T)_{m-2}]_{x/2}$ for odd–even nylons, corresponding in both cases to the line repetition group **tcm** (Fig. 2.20b).

In practice, at least to a first approximation, the chains of nylons adapt their own conformation in the crystals in order to maximize the number of hydrogen bonds between amide groups of adjacent chains at a low cost of conformational energy by simply changing the values of Ψ and Φ, and with monomeric units following each other along the chain according to the geometrical restrain imposed by the line repetition group, even though the symmetry elements of the chain are not necessarily retained by the symmetry of the space group of the crystals.

In general, the crystal structure of a large number of nylons basically consists in the presence of two-dimensional arrays of chains linked by hydrogen bonds forming sheets [122]. Examples of these sheets are shown in Figure 2.21 and Figure 2.22. The interchain hydrogen bonds are confined within the planes of these sheets, no intersheet hydrogen bonds exist, and the relative arrangement of sheets in the crystals is controlled by van der Waals interactions. As an example, the packing mode of hydrogen bonded sheets in the α form of nylon 66 is shown in Figure 2.23a. In the α form of nylons, the chains preserve a nearly zigzag planar conformation, show only small deviations of $|\Psi|$ and $|\Phi|$ from 180°, and form sheets of hydrogen bonds where the planes containing the amide groups and the aliphatic residues are only slightly twisted with respect to the plane containing the chain axes (Fig. 2.21a,c and Fig. 2.22a,a′). These sheets are packed in triclinic (Fig. 2.23a) and/or monoclic unit cells [122] and show X-ray fiber diffraction patterns characterized by the presence of two strong equatorial reflections with spacings of ≈4.4 and 3.4 Å, related to the distance of close neighboring

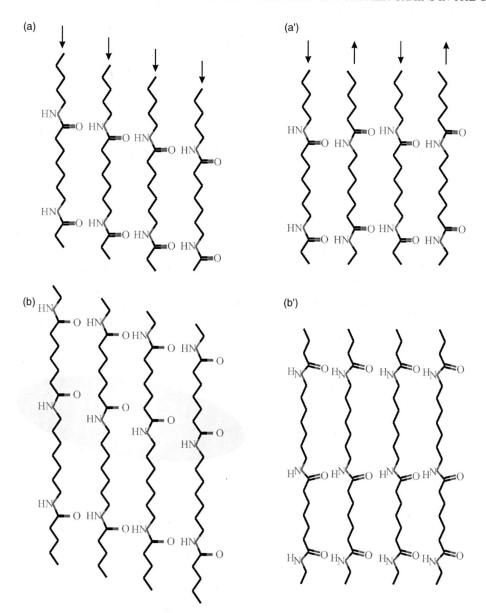

Figure 2.22 Projections of sheets of hydrogen bonded chains in a plane parallel to chain axes of in odd nylons (a, a') and odd–odd nylons (b, b') in the α form with chains in a zigzag planar conformation [122] (a, a') and in the γ form with chains in a twisted less extended conformation [122] (b'). The case of nylon 7 is reported in (a) and (a') showing that in odd nylons sheets with chains in *trans*-planar conformation form 100% hydrogen bonds either between isoclined chains (a) or anticlined chains (a'). The case of nylon 77 is reported in (b, b'), showing that chains in zigzag planar conformation would form sheets deficient in hydrogen bonds in the shadowed region (b), whereas 100% hydrogen bonds are formed within sheets for less extended conformations (b'). (See color insert.)

chains in the sheets and the distance of close neighboring sheets. In the γ form of nylons, the chains are in less extended conformations, the values of $|\Psi|$ and $|\Phi|$ are close to 120°, and the chains form pleated sheets of hydrogen bonds where the planes defined by the aliphatic residues and amide groups are twisted by ≈60° each other (Fig. 2.21b and Fig. 2.22b'). These sheets are stacked in monoclinic unit cells with a nearly pseudohexagonal arrangement of chain axes as indicated by the X-ray fiber diffraction patterns that present a single strong reflection at ≈4.3 Å.

As shown in Figure 2.21a, in the case of nylon 6, even nylons with n less than 8 normally crystallize in the α form [122]. The chains are in a zigzag planar conformation,

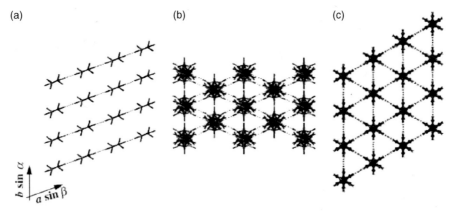

Figure 2.23 Projections parallel to the chain axis for different nylon structures, illustrating hydrogen-bonding schemes. Hydrogen bonds are represented by dashed lines. (a) α form of nylon 66 with interchain hydrogen bonds confined to the ac plane (Figure 2.21C) [118]. (b) Structure of nylon 65 [127c] with interchain hydrogen bonds occurring in two directions. (c) Pseudohexagonal structures of disordered forms of nylons with hydrogen bonds occurring in all three principal directions of a pseudohexagonal lattice [100], [010] and [$\bar{1}\bar{1}$0] [123, 128].

the amide groups in consecutive monomeric units are nearly coplanar with C=O bonds pointing toward two opposite directions, and hydrogen bonds occur between anticlined chains. On the other hand, under special conditions (e.g iodine treatments or by annealing oriented specimens at high temperatures), nylon 6 as well as even nylons with n ≥ 8, tend to crystallize in the γ form [122–125], characterized by chains with a twisted conformation (Fig. 2.21b). The chains in these less extended confomations maintain the coplanarity of amide groups and form pleated sheets where hydrogen bonds occur between isoclined chains (Fig. 2.21b). Finally, as indicated in Figure 2.22a,a′, the case of odd nylons is special because chains in a zigzag planar conformation form sheets where hydrogen bonds may occur either between couples of isoclined chains (Fig. 2.22a) or between couples of anticlined chains (Fig. 2.22b). Odd nylons generally crystallize in the α form.

Even–even nylons generally crystallize in the α form with chains in a zigzag planar conformation (Fig. 2.21c) [118, 122, 125], whereas odd–odd nylons do not crystallize in the α form because *trans*-planar chains are not able to form 100% bonds (Fig. 2.22b). Odd–odd nylons, instead, tend to crystallize in the γ form with chains in twisted conformation forming pleated sheets and 100% hydrogen bonds (Fig. 2.22b′) [122].

Odd–even and even–odd nylons with chains in *trans*-planar conformation would also form deficient hydrogen bonds sheets in two dimensions [126, 127]. These chains adopt a less extended conformation in the crystals with non-negligible deviations of the values of |Ψ| and |Φ| from 180°, and are packed according to a packing mode completely different from the conventional mode of nylons n and nylons nm of Figure 2.21, Figure 2.22, and Figure 2.23a, where interchain hydrogen bonds are confined in two-dimensional sheets. Odd–even [126] and even–odd [127] nylons, indeed, crystallize at room temperature in monoclinic unit cells, where interchain hydrogen bonds are established in two different directions at ≈60° relative to each other as shown in Figure 2.23b. Such structures have been observed in both stretched fibers and single crystals obtained from dilute solutions [126, 127] at room temperature. Oriented fibers show X-ray fiber diffraction patterns characterized by two strong equatorial reflections at ≈4.3 Å and 3.8 Å, reminiscent of those observed in the case of conventional α form of nylons; however, contrary to the α form, odd–even and even–odd nylons chains may not maximize the number of hydrogen bonds while maintaining a zigzag planar conformation. The conformation of chains in the crystals, indeed, is twisted, as in the case of the γ form, with aliphatic residues in a nearly zigzag planar conformation and the torsion angles of |Ψ| and |Φ| deviating from 180° toward values of ≈150°. These twisted conformation causes amide groups of the odd unit to rotate in opposite senses from the plane defined by methylene carbon atoms, and hydrogen bonds along two directions are formed between neighboring chains as shown in the structural model of Figure 2.23b.

It is worth mentioning that the crystalline polymorphic modification of nylons are not restricted to the α and γ forms. Several other crystalline modifications have been described for nylons such as the metastble β form of nylon 6 [123, 128] and nylon 66 [118], which is obtained often in mixture with the α form, the α' form that corresponds to a disordered modification of the α form obtained at high temperatures [129], and the λ form observed for nylon 6 oligomers [130]. For the β form of nylons, as well as for the disordered modifications obtained at high temperatures [131], a third scheme of interchain hydrogen bonds has been proposed with chains characterized by high degree of conformational disorder packed in a pseudo-hexagonal arrangement, forming hydrogen bonds along the three principal directions at 0°, 120°, and 240°, as illustrated in Figure 2.23c.

2.6 DEFECTS AND DISORDER IN POLYMER CRYSTALS

According to a popular definition, a *crystal* is a portion of solid matter, in which some kind of long-range *positional* order exists on the level of atomic dimensions in three-dimensional space [132, 133]. This definition corresponds to a reasonable and generally valid working hypothesis, implying complete long-range positional order of (most of) atoms. However, in polymer crystals the three-dimensional long-range order is never present and the structural disorder inside crystals is a rule rather than an exception. For this reason the concepts of *crystal* and *crystallinity* in polymeric materials are complex and very far from the ideality. First of all, at variance with other crystalline materials, such as metals, polymeric materials are never completely crystalline. They are *semicrystalline* and are generally composed of crystals (lamellae) embedded into an amorphous phase, producing a highly interconnected network [134].

In a slightly enlarged recent definition, a crystal is "any solid having an essentially discrete diffraction diagram" [135]. This definition implies the presence of some kind of long-range three-dimensional periodicity, but not necessarily a complete three-dimensional order of atoms. The requirement of three-dimensional long-range order may appear to be violated in polymer crystals, unless it is considered as a limit, mainly for the following reasons: (1) the macromolecules of a polymer are not uniform; that is, they have different molecular masses, a distribution of molecular masses being always present [136]; (2) constitutional, configurational, and conformational disorders along the polymer chains are always present [137]; and (3) the dimensions of the crystals are very small, mostly in the nanometer range (they are often indicated as crystallites) [134].

Moreover, even in the case of regular constitution, configuration, and conformation, disorder may be present in the crystals because of the presence of defects in the mode of packing. Disorder in the packing may occur while some structural feature, for instance, some atoms or the axes of helical macromolecules, maintain *periodic positions* [137]. The degree of disorder in the packing or in the single macromolecules is sometimes so high that it is difficult to define this state as *crystalline*, even though crystalline entities with a regular shape can still be observed by optical or electronic microscopy. This state can be more properly indicated as intermediate between amorphous phase and ordered crystals [137–139]. These *crystalline* forms that present large amounts of disorder with lacking of periodicities in one or two dimensions (e.g., along or normal to the chain axes) are common in solid *semicrystalline* polymers and are generally indicated as *solid mesophases* [137–142]. In *solid mesophases* the presence of a high amount of disorder frequently prevents the definition of a unit cell and only average periodicities along some lattice directions may be defined [139].

Particularly interesting cases of structural disorder in polymer crystals are those where, even in the presence of a high amount of disorder, a unit cell may be still defined [137, 143]. In this class of disordered crystals (*class i* in References [137, 143]), *the long-range three-dimensional periodicity is maintained only for some characterizing points of the structure. In these cases there is only a partial three-dimensional order and the X-ray diffraction patterns present sharp reflections and diffuse halos.* In these structures the disorder has to be considered as a structural feature and can be studied with modern methods of diffraction [143]. This description of the structural disorder allows introducing a modern view of crystallinity and crystalline orders in polymers, as compatible with the presence of a high degree of disorder and the absence, in many cases, of long-range three-dimensional order [143].

The crystal structures of polymeric materials belonging to this class may be conveniently described by adopting the concepts of *limit ordered* and *limit disordered* model structures [137, 138]. A limit ordered model is an idealized description of the structure in a given space group, resulting in a fixed position of all atoms in the crystal with a perfect three-dimensional order. A limit disordered model is an idealized description in a space group, with statistical occupancy of some or all of the equivalent positions [137, 138]. Structural disorder may arise indeed, while the same unit cell is maintained, for instance, whenever polymer chains, or even layers of chains, may assume different and equivalent positions in the unit cell, without changing the steric interactions with the neighboring chains. In these cases the substitution of chains, or layers of chains, does not produce large disturbance of the packing, so that the crystallinity and the same lattice geometry are preserved. An ideal fully disordered structure characterized by disorder corresponding to the statistical substitution of chains, or layer of chains, can be described by a limit disordered model, which actually may describe the relative position of atoms in the long range. A limit ordered model may be, instead, appropriate for the description of the relative positions of atoms in the short range. The real crystalline forms are, generally, intermediate between limit ordered and limit disordered models, the amount of disorder being dependent on the condition of crystallization and thermal and mechanical treatments of the samples. Disordered structures belonging to this class arise, for instance, from substitutional isomorphism of different chains (Section 2.6.1) or different monomeric units (Section 2.6.2), or conformational isomorphism (Section 2.6.3), or from the presence of stacking faults (Section 2.6.4).

2.6.1 Substitutional Isomorphism of Different Chains

The most stable form of sPP with chains in 2_1 helical conformation (form I) provides an example of substitutional isomorphim of different chains. The structure of form I of sPP has been described in terms of ideal limit ordered and limit disordered models (Fig. 2.24) [32, 144–149]. In the limit ordered model right-handed and left-handed twofold helical chains alternate along the a- and b-axes of the orthorhombic unit cell (space group *Ibca* or *P2$_1$/a*) (Fig. 2.24a) [32, 144–146, 148]. The limit disordered model is characterized by statistical disorder in the positioning of enantiomorphous helices and can be described by the statistical space group *Bmcm* (Fig. 2.24b) [147, 149]. In each site of the lattice right-handed and left-handed chains can be found with the same probability owing to the similar steric hindrance of enantiomorphous helices. The real crystalline forms are generally intermediate between the limit ordered and disordered models, the amount of disorder in the alternation of enantiomorphous helices being dependent on the condition of crystallization [149].

Experimental evidence of the presence of disorder in the positioning of right- and left-handed chains in the structure of form I of sPP comes from the electron diffraction patterns of single crystals [32, 144–146] and the X-ray diffraction patterns of melt-crystallized samples [147–149]. Only at high crystallization temperatures is the 211 reflection present with high intensity in both electron [32, 144–146] and X-ray diffraction patterns [148, 149], indicating a perfect alternation of enantiomorphous helices along both axes of the unit cell and crystallization of a modification of form I very close to the limit ordered model of Figure 2.24a [32]. At lower crystallization temperatures, the 211 reflection presents lower intensities [149] and shows streaks in the electron diffraction patterns of single crystals [146], or is completely absent, indicating disorder in the regular alternation of left- and right-handed helices and crystallization in disordered modifications close to the limit disordered model of Figure 2.24b [149].

Another example of crystal lattice affected by disorder due to isomorphic substitution of different chains is provided by the α form of iPP (Fig. 2.15) [29, 101, 102]. As shown in Figure 2.25a, in the crystal the threefold helical chains of iPP of a given chirality may be up or down depending on the orientation of the bond vector **b** that connects the backbone methine carbon atoms to the lateral methyl carbon atoms, with respect to the c-axis. Isomorphous up and down (anticlined) [16] chains have a similar external steric hindrance because the methyl groups may assume the same position (Fig. 2.25b). Therefore, disorder in the positioning of up and down chains may be present in the crystals of the α form because if isomorphic and anticlined helices of iPP substitute each other in the same site of the lattice, the same steric interactions with neighboring chains are involved.

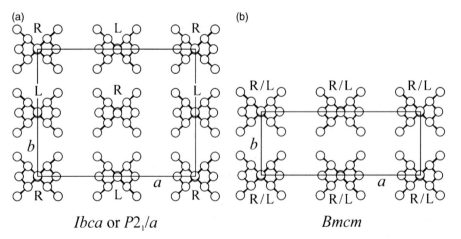

Figure 2.24 Limit-ordered model (space group *Ibca* or *P2$_1$/a*) [32] (a) and limit-disordered model (space group *Bmcm*) [149] (b) for the crystal structure of the form I of sPP. R, right-handed helix; L, left-handed helix.

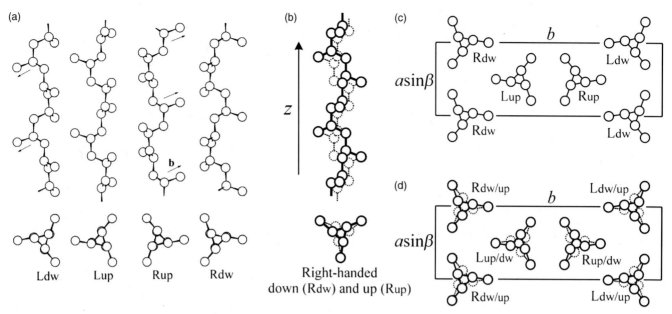

Figure 2.25 (a) Chains of isotactic polypropylene in 3_1 helical conformation, left-handed (L) and right-handed (R), up and down (dw). (b) Right-handed down (continuous lines) and up (dashed lines) chains have the same steric hindrance since the side methyl groups may assume the same positions. (c) Limit-ordered model structure (space group $P2_1/c$) [102] and (d) limit-disordered model structure (space group $C2/c$) [29] of the α form of iPP. (b–d) Reprinted from Reference [143] with permission from American Chemical Society, Copyright 2006.

In the limit ordered model proposed for the α form of iPP (Fig. 2.25c) "up" and "down" chains follow each other according to a well-defined pattern [101, 102]. The limit disordered model (Fig. 2.25d) corresponds to a statistical substitution of up and down isomorphic helices in each site of the lattice [29]. The real crystalline modifications of the α form of iPP are intermediate between the limit ordered and limit disordered models of Figure 2.25, the degree of disorder in the positioning of up and down chains being dependent on the thermal and mechanical history of the sample [150].

2.6.2 Substitutional Isomorphism of Different Monomeric Units

Copolymers of different monomeric units that are able to co-crystallize in the same lattice are classic examples of polymer crystals including disorder due to isomorphic substitution of monomeric units in the crystal lattices. This occurs for instance for isotactic butene-3-methylbutene [3] or styrene-o-fluorostyrene [4] copolymers and isotactic [5–8] and syndiotactic [9, 10] propene-butene copolymers, which are crystalline in the whole range of compositions. In these cases the constitutional disorder due to the presence of monomeric units of different chemical structure, statistically distributed along the polymer chains, does not prevent the crystallization of the resulting copolymers. Co-crystallization of different comonomeric units occurs if the shape of the backbone chain and, therefore, the chain conformation are not affected by the constitutional disorder [1]. In vinyl copolymers this requires a regular configuration of the monomeric units with different constitutions.

In the case of propylene-butene copolymers the presence of constitutional defects (propene or butene monomeric units) does not affect the regular 3_1 and the 2_1 helical conformations of the chains of the isotactic [5–8] and syndiotactic copolymers [10], respectively. The co-crystallization of comonomers of different size produces continuous and regular variations of the crystal lattice parameters with changes in the copolymer composition. For syndiotactic propylene–butene copolymers the dimension of the orthorhombic unit cell changes from that of sPP [31, 32, 147] to that of sPB [70], with increasing concentration of butene comonomeric units [10] (Fig. 2.26a). The gradual variation of the unit cell parameters induces gradual changes of other physical properties, for example, solubility in various solvents or melting temperature. For syndiotactic propylene–butene copolymers

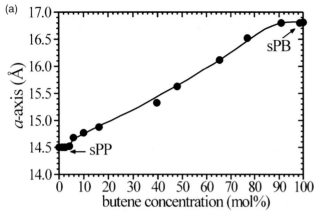

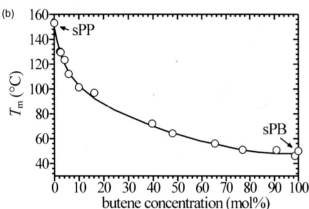

Figure 2.26 Values of the a-axis of the unit cell (a) and melting temperature (b) of syndiotactic propene–butene copolymers as a function of the butene concentration [10]. (A) Reproduced from Reference [10a] with permission from American Chemical Society, Copyright 1998.

the melting temperatures gradually change (Fig. 2.26b) [10] from the values of nearly 150°C typical of sPP [20] to about 50°C typical of sPB [68, 70].

2.6.3 Conformational Isomorphism

For polymers with a regular constitution and configuration, the conformation adopted by the chains in the crystalline state is generally regular (equivalence principle). However, three-dimensional long-range crystalline order may be maintained even when the conformation of the macromolecules is disordered [151]. The term conformational isomorphism refers to the more or less random occurrence in the same lattice site of different, but almost isoenergetic, conformers of the same portion of a molecule [151]. *Conformationally disordered crystals*, that is, structures characterized by disorder in the conformation of molecules, have also been defined as *condis crystals* [141]. Condition for the formation of *condis crystals* is that the macromolecules exist in different conformational isomers of low energy, which

Figure 2.27 Models of the chain conformation of *cis*-1,4-polyisoprene in the crystalline state. The models indicated with solid and dashed lines correspond to a different succession of conformations of the monomeric units, and present similar lateral encumbrance. Reprinted from Reference [143] with permission from American Chemical Society, Copyright 2006.

leave the macromolecules largely in extended conformations so that the parallelism of chain axes is mantained. A classic example of conformational isomorphim in the crystals is provided by *cis*-1,4-polyisoprene (natural rubber), studied by Nyburg [97], and by Natta and Corradini [96]. The X-ray diffraction data of natural rubber are accounted for by disordered models of the chain conformation [99], characterized by a statistical sequence of monomeric units having successive bonds in the conformations A^+TA^-(*cis*) or A^-TA^+(*cis*), such as those shown in Figure 2.27 (A^+, A^-, and T standing for torsion angles close to +120°, −120°, and 180°, respectively).

The disordered models of Figure 2.27 have energy not far from minima of the internal energy of isolated chains of *cis*-1,4-polyisoprene [152], produce an average identity period close to the experimental value of the chain axis of 8.23 Å, and account for the low temperature diffraction patterns of stretched fibers of natural rubber [153]. This model provides an example of the possibility to keep a chain straight, even with a statistical succession of structural units having widely different internal rotation angles, so that a certain short-range order is preserved, allowing crystallization [1].

2.6.4 Disorder in the Stacking of Ordered Layers (Stacking Fault Disorder)

Stacking fault disorder in polymers arises from defects in the stacking of ordered layers of macromolecules along one lattice direction. It originates whenever first neighboring chains are tightly interlocked with bulges and grooves along one lattice direction, forming rows of parallel chains (layers), and more loosely packed along the direction normal to the layers [137]. Along the latter direction different modes of packing of first neighboring chains are feasible at a low cost of free energy. This kind of disorder produces the broadening of reflections in the X-ray diffraction patterns and streaks in the electron diffraction patterns of single crystals [137].

Disorder in the stacking of ordered layers of chains along one crystallographic direction is present in the β

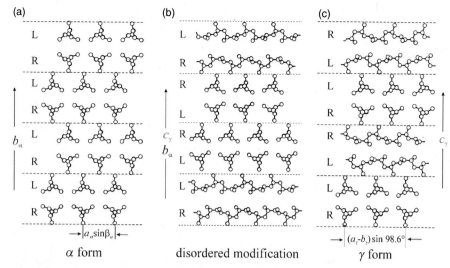

Figure 2.28 Limit-ordered models of the α [29] (a) and γ [108, 109] (c) forms of iPP and disordered succession of bilayers of chains [18, 19, 156–163] (b). The dashed horizontal lines delimit bilayers of chains in the 3/1 helical conformation. R and L indicate right-handed and left-handed helices, respectively. Reproduced from Reference [159] with permission from American Chemical Society, Copyright 2004.

form of sPS [63], in form I and form II of sPP [20, 31, 32, 146, 147, 149, 154, 155], in the α and γ forms of iPP [18, 19, 156–163] and in many other cases [137].

The case of α and γ forms of iPP is interesting because of the unusual nonparallel packing mode of the γ form [108, 109]. The models of packing of the 3_1 helical chains of iPP in the α and γ forms are reported in Figure 2.28a and c, respectively. The packing scheme is similar but, while in the α form the chains are parallel along the c-axis (Fig. 2.28a) [29], the γ form is characterized by a packing of nonparallel chain axes (Fig. 2.28c) [108, 109]. Ordered bilayers of 3_1 helical chains, typical of the α form (Fig. 2.28a), are packed along the c_γ-axis with the chain axis tilted by 81° (Fig. 2.28c). iPP samples prepared with the traditional Ziegler–Natta catalysts generally crystallize in the stable α form, whereas iPP samples prepared with the homogeneous metallocene catalysts crystallize more easily in the γ form and in disordered modifications (Fig. 2.28b) intermediate between α and γ forms [18, 19, 156–163]. The disorder corresponds to the statistical succession along the b_α (c_γ)-axis direction of double layers of chains with the chain axes either parallel (such as in the α form) or nearly perpendicular (such as in the γ form). Inside the same crystalline domain local arrangements of the double layers of chains, piled along the b_α (c_γ)-axis, typical of the α form (with parallel chains) and typical of the γ form (with chains nearly perpendicular) are present (Fig. 2.28b) [18, 19, 156–163].

The amount of γ form obtained by melt crystallizations of metallocene-made iPPs and the degree of disorder depend on the microstructure of chains, and, in particular, on the amount, combination, and distribution of defects of stereoregularity and regioregularity [18, 19, 156–163] and of constitutional defects, as comonomeric units [8, 164–167]. The crystallization of the γ form as disordered modifications of the type of Figure 2.28b explains the lower melting temperature of the γ form crystals than that of the α form [158, 162]. The polymorphic behavior and the order–disorder phenomena in iPP can be described by a *continuum* of disordered modifications intermediate between α and γ forms [18, 19, 156–163].

A particular kind of stacking fault disorder, typical of polymeric materials, is the kink-band disorder. It occurs when, inside crystals of macromolecules having a given conformation, portions of the chains assume a different conformation. These portions of chains are clustered in planes so that the parallelism of the chains is preserved [137]. The defective conformation involves all the molecules in the crystallite, at the same level, forming kink-bands. There are at least three examples of important crystalline polymers presenting kink-band disorder: PE obtained by crystallization under pressure [168], poly(vinylidene fluoride) in forms I and II [169], and sPP in the form II [154, 155] (Fig. 2.29). Kink-band disorder in the form II of sPP (Fig. 2.29) occurs in samples having a relatively low degree of stereoregularity, quench-precipitated from solution [154, 155] or in copolymers of sPP with ethylene [170]. In this case kink-band defects originates from the presence of portions of chains in *trans*-planar conformation in chains having

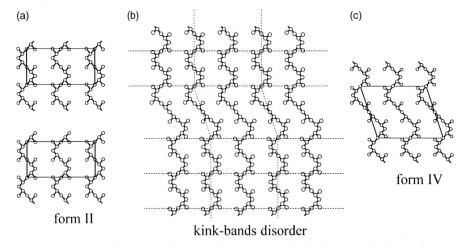

Figure 2.29 Limit-ordered models of packing of forms II [31] (a) and IV [67] (c) of sPP and model of a conformationally disordered modification, presenting kink-bands (b), intermediate between forms II and IV. A kink-band in the form II of sPP, with $(T_2G_2)_n$ helices, is characterized by a defective region with $(T_2G_2T_6G_2)_n$ conformational sequence, as in form IV [154, 155]. Reprinted from Reference [143] with permission from American Chemical Society, Copyright 2006.

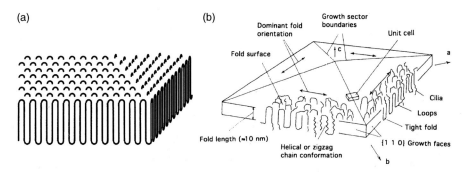

Figure 2.30 (a, b) Models of a polymer single crystal, including (a) only tight folds (i.e., folds characterized by adjacent reentry of the chain inside the lamella) and (b) tight folds, loops (i.e., folds characterized by nonadjacent reentry) and cilia (i.e., dangling chain ends). Sectors may be identified as the portions of a crystal in which the folds have a common orientation. High resolution image (b) kindly supplied by Bernard Lotz [171].

a prevailing twofold helical conformation (Fig. 2.29). The kink-band disordered modifications [154, 155] appear as intermediate structures between the limit ordered model structures of forms II [31] and form IV of sPP [67].

2.7 CRYSTAL HABITS

Polymers with flexible chains crystallize, forming thin lamellae, in which the chains run across the thin dimension, and are perpendicular or inclined at some angle to the basal planes (Fig. 2.30). The thickness of the lamellae is small (10–20 nm) in comparison with the transverse size, which may reach up to several tens of micrometers. In polymers, the usual length of the macromolecular chains is far greater than the thickness of the lamellae [171]. Therefore, in single crystals, each chain is considered to fold back and forth repetitively as the molecule reaches each basal surface of the lamella. Chain folding is a characteristic that mainly distinguishes the single crystals of polymers from those of low molecular weight compounds, and lamellae are the basic morphological units that give rise to larger structures such as spherulites, row-nucleated structures, and transcrystalline structures.

The fact that polymer crystals are thin and do not correspond to crystals including chains in their fully extended form has been attributed to kinetic origins [134, 172]. According to the kinetic theory of secondary nucleation, crystals growing at a given crystallization temperature T_c have to be thicker than the crystals which at this temperature are in equilibrium with the melt. The most probable crystal thickness corresponds to the thickness for which the crystallization rate reaches a maximum. Since the maximum of growth rate is shifted toward higher thickness values with increasing temperature, this theory correctly predicts that the thickness of lamellae increases with increasing temperature. Therefore, at any T_c, if sufficient time were granted for the lamellae, the thickness would progressively grow to the extended chain value [134, 172]. Recently, it has been shown that this point of view might not be correct in general and that the equilibrium thickness can be finite and much smaller than the extended chain value [173].

Independent of the preparation method, polymer single crystals obtained from both melt and solution possess different habits, ranging from ribbon-like elongated entities, to square or hexagonal single crystals [174, 175]. The type of crystal habit formed depends on the symmetry of the crystal unit cell. For unit cells characterized by a low rotational symmetry, single crystals with low symmetry are formed. For example, PE in the orthorhombic form [74, 174], sPP in the orthorhombic form I [32, 144–147, 176], and poly(vinylidene fluoride) in the monoclinic α form [177, 178] show anisotropic elongated single crystals (Fig. 2.31). The asymmetric shape of the single crystals reflects the presence of only twofold axes of symmetry in the unit cell (space groups

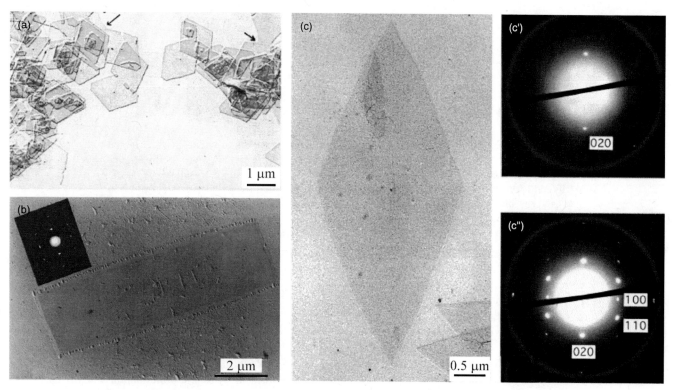

Figure 2.31 Electron micrograph of single crystals of (a) polyethylene (PE) in the orthorhombic form [175], (b) sPP in the orthorhombic form I with chains in helical conformation [32, 144–146, 176], and (c) of poly(vinylidene fluoride) (PVDF) in the monoclinic α form with chain in TGTḠ conformation [177, 178]. The single crystals have been obtained from solution in (a), and by melt crystallization of thin films at 125°C in (b), and 150°C in (c). The crystals are lozenge-shaped in (a) and (c), and lath-shaped in (b), in agreement with the low (rotational) symmetry of the unit cell. Electron diffraction pattern of the single crystals in the proper crystallographic orientation are also shown for sPP (inset) and PVDF (c', c") with specimen rotated around an axis nearly parallel to the b-axis (long axis of the crystals) by 0° (inset in b, and c') and 25–27° (c"). The appearance of 100 and 110 equatorial reflections, beside the 020 reflection in (c") indicates that the PVDF chains are tilted (25–27°) with respect to the fold surface around the long axis of the lamella. (a) Reprinted with permission from Reference [175], Copyright 1981 by Cambridge University Press. (b) Reprinted with permission from Reference [176], Copyright 1996 by American Chemical Society. (c–c") Reprinted with permission from Reference [177], Copyright 2001 by Elsevier.

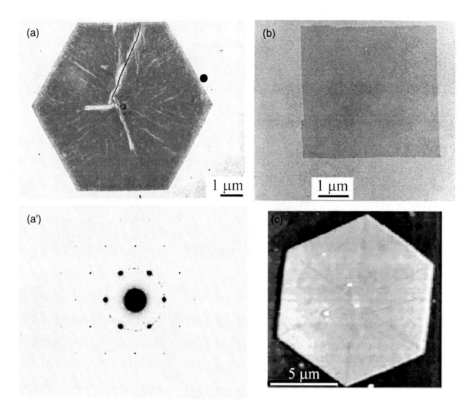

Figure 2.32 Electron micrographs of single crystals of polyoxymethylene in the trigonal form (a), and corresponding electron diffraction pattern (a') [175], of poly(4-methyl-1-pentene) in the tetragonal form III (b) [180] and AFM image of a single crystal of iSP in the trigonal form (c) [179]. The single crystals have been obtained by solution crystallization in (a) and (b) and by isothermal crystallization of an amorphous thin film in (c). (a, a') Reprinted with permission from Reference [175], Copyright 1981 by Cambridge University Press. (b) Reprinted with permission from Reference [180], Copyright 1988 by American Chemical Society. (c) Reprinted with permission from Reference [179], Copyright 2001 by Elsevier.

Pnam for PE [74], *Ibca* for form I of sPP [32], and $P2_1/c$ for the α form of poly(vinylidene fluoride) (PVDF) [178]) and the different growth rates along different crystallographic directions [174, 175].

For crystalline polymorphs with higher rotational symmetries, instead, more symmetric single crystals are formed, such as in the case of the trigonal forms of poly(oxymethylene) [175] and iPS [179], or the tetragonal form III of poly(4-methyl-1-pentene) [44, 52, 53, 180] (Fig. 2.32). The presence of threefold axes of rotational (or helical) symmetry in the unit cell and the hexagonal geometry of the unit cells in the structures of iPS (space group $R\bar{3}c$ [40]) and poly(oxymethylene) (space group $P3_1$ [181]) reflect the hexagonal shape of the single crystals (Fig. 2.32a,c). The presence of fourfold axes of rotational (or helical) symmetry in the unit cell of form III of iP4MP (space group $I4_1$ [44, 52]), which, in turn, depends on the 4_1 helical conformation of the chains, reflects the formation of the square single crystals (Fig. 2.32b).

In all cases, the length of the molecules, the different nature of interactions along the chains (covalent bonds) and in the perpendicular directions (i.e., van der Waals forces, hydrogen bonds, etc.), and especially the presence of folds with the resulting noncrystalline state of the two basal faces of the lamellae, have a strong influence on the shape of the crystals.

When a polymer is crystallized from dilute solutions (polymer concentration lower than 0.1 wt%) a number of different habits may be obtained, even using a single solvent, whose exact shape depends on the temperature and crystallizing conditions (cooling rate, concentration of the solution, presence of impurities, etc.) [174, 175]. However, all habits tend to be variants of a simple shape, generally dictated by the crystallography of interchain packing. This general trend is illustrated in Figure 2.33 in the case of PE. For PE the basic habit is the lozenge-shaped single crystal of Figure 2.33a, with edges delimited by {110} planes, and the *a*- and *b*-axes of the orthorhombic unit cell parallel to the long and

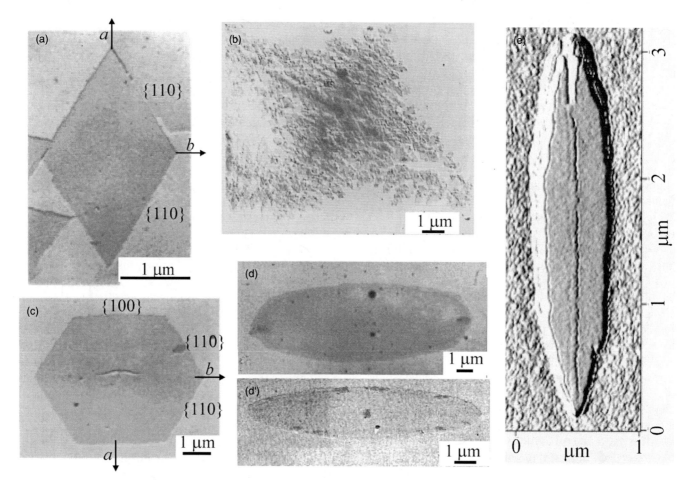

Figure 2.33 Electron micrographs of single crystals of polyethylene [184] (mass average molecular mass $M_w = 1.1\ 10^4$, $M_w/M_n = 1.16$) grown from $2.7\ 10^{-4}$ wt% tetrachloroethylene solution at 71.8°C (a), 0.01 wt% octane solution at 98.0°C (c), 0.02 wt% diphenyl ether solution at 114°C (d), and 0.1 wt. % n-ditriacontane at 110°C (d'). Dentritic structures (b) are obtained for crystallization temperatures lower than 65°C [175]. (e) AFM image of a lenticular single crystal of polyethylene ($M_w = 32100$, $M_w/M_n = 1.11$) grown from the melt at 128°C for 10 minutes [185]. The b-axis of the orthorhombic unit cell of polyethylene is horizontal in (a), (c), and (d) and vertical in (e). (a, c, d, d') Reprinted with permission from Reference [184], Copyright 1991 by Elsevier. (b) Reprinted with permission from Reference [175], Copyright 1981 by Cambridge University Press. (e) Reprinted with permission from Reference [185], Copyright 2005 by Elsevier.

short diagonals of the lozenge, respectively [182]. The lozenge habit is generally obtained at relatively low crystallization temperatures of 65–80°C [174, 175], whereas at lower temperatures dendritic structures are obtained, which are consistent with the basic lozenge-like habit (Fig. 2.33b) [174]. The reason that the lozenges of Figure 2.33a are bounded by flat {110} faces is that the {110} planes are those of closest packing of the orthorhombic form of PE and correspond to the planes of slowest growth rate at temperatures of 65–80°C [174, 175, 182].

At slightly higher crystallization temperatures (>80°C) the single crystal habit changes and truncated lozenges with {110} and {100} growth faces are obtained [174, 175, 182] (Fig. 2.33c). The relative length of {100} facets with respect to the length of the {110} faces gradually increases with increasing temperature, and is associated with an increase of the ratio of the growth rates in the directions normal to the {110} and {100} planes [175, 182].

At crystallization temperatures higher than 100°C the profile of the growth front delimited by the {100} planes becomes rounded and the truncation becomes larger (Fig. 2.33d,d') [183]. Leaf-shaped crystals bound solely by {100} faces or crystals of lenticular shape with {100} faces curved in the middle and straight tangents converging to pointed ends (Fig. 2.33d,e) may be obtained [183–185]. It is worth noting that curved crystal habits of Figure 2.33c,d have also been observed in single crystals of poly(vinylidene fluoride) [177, 186], poly(oxymethylene) [187], and PE crystallized from the melt [188] (Fig. 2.33e). In addition, it has been shown that in melt-crystallized PE [189] a morphological change from the lenticular shape (Fig. 2.33e) into the truncated lozenge habit with curved {100} faces (Fig. 2.33c) is accompanied by a transition of the growth from regime I into regime II (cf. Chapter 6).

Less conventional habits may arise from the imbalance of deposition rates of the chains on opposite sites of the growth planes, as for instance in the case of triangular or truncated triangular crystals of Figure 2.34 [190]. The triangular habit of isotactic poly(tert-butylethylene sulfide) [191] (Fig. 2.34a) and the truncated triangular crystals of isotactic poly(2-vinylpyridine) [190, 192] (Fig. 2.34b) are obtained for frustrated structures [114]. Triangular crystals have, indeed, been observed for several polymers for which three isochiral chains in threefold helical conformation are assembled in a unit cell with trigonal $P3_1$ or $P3_2$ symmetry, producing frustration [114]. However, frustrated structures have also been observed in polymer crystals with chains in different conformations. For instance, as discussed in the Section 2.4, in the case of the α form of sPS frustration results from the different azimuthal settings of three structural motifs included in the unit cell (e.g., triplets of chains in *trans*-planar conformation in Fig. 2.19b). In the structures of Figure 2.34a',b' frustration comes from the different rotational orientations of three threefold helices in the unit cell. Similar frustrated structure has also been found for other polymers, as for instance the β form of iPP [114a, 193, 194].

The characteristic feature of frustrated structures is that two motifs maximize their interactions at the expense of the third motif. As a consequence, the third motif is frustrated since it is not in its ideal environment. In the crystal structures of isotactic poly(tert-butylethylene sulfide) (Fig. 2.34a') and poly(2-vinylpyridine) (Fig. 2.34b'), three isochiral threefold helices are assembled in a unit cell with a trigonal $P3_1$ or $P3_2$ symmetry. The asymmetry of the packing mode stems from the different azimuthal settings of the three helices that build up the unit cell, resulting in different nucleation sites on opposite sides of any given growth plane of the crystal. Present evidence suggests that most of the frustrated polymer crystals are bounded by {100} growth faces, which grow at a slower rate than the more densely packed {110} faces [190, 191].

A second cause of triangular morphology rests again on a trigonal crystal structures with a $R3c$ or $R\bar{3}c$ symmetry, and these structures are, this time, not frustrated. This case is illustrated for the chiral nonracemic poly(L-lactide) (PLLA)/poly(D-lactide) (PDLA) 50/50 mixture in Figure 2.34c. As shown in Reference [190], equimolar mixtures of the two enantiomers PLLA and PDLA with the same molecular mass normally crystallize, forming hexagonal crystals. The origin of the triangular shape of single crystals of Figure 2.34c may be traced back to the fact that this crystal was obtained by crystallization for 3 hours at 200°C after deposition of a single crystal of the racemic mixture of hexagonal shape on a thin film of PLLA, and successive melting of both the crystal and the substrate at 250°C [190], and therefore in the presence of slight excess of PLLA enantiomer. As shown in the model of Figure 2.34c', when the stereocomplexes crystallize, the helices of opposite chirality (represented by the shaded and nonshaded triangular stems) are arranged alternatively along the growth direction normal to the {110} planes. This growth surface is not equivalent with respect to the azimuthal setting of the incoming helical stems. In one growth plane the incoming helix is deposited with one of its corners oriented away from the crystal center. In the next layer it is deposited with one of its corners oriented toward the crystal center. As a consequence the rate of deposition of alternate layers must be significantly different. In addition, the {110} planes are "polar" since right- and left-handed helices have their corners oriented in opposite sense relative to the growth plane. Therefore, four deposition rates must be defined to describe the two oppositely oriented growth rates of such crystals, resulting in an imbalance of deposition rates of PLLA and PDLA helices on opposite sides of the growth plane. Since the slowest growth rate determines the overall growth rate of the crystal face, the overall morphology is determined by the ratio of the slowest growth rates on opposite sites of the growth planes (e.g. (110) vs. ($\bar{1}\bar{1}0$), ($\bar{1}20$) vs. ($1\bar{2}0$), ($2\bar{1}0$) vs. ($\bar{2}10$)). It is worth noting that in the case of achiral polymers such as iPS (Fig. 2.12a [62, 113]) and iPB (Fig. 2.12b [45]), which crystallize in the same space group symmetry of the PLLA/PDLA stereocomplexes, the rate of deposition of right- $(TG^-)_n$ and left-handed $(TG^+)_n$ helices on opposite growth directions of the crystals are identical since each chain can adopt both the conformations, and the shape of crystals is normally hexagonal [190]. However, in the case of PLLA/PDLA stereocomplexes, the situation is different since the chirality of each chain dictates the chirality of helical hand, and also produces limitations in the relative deposition rate of each stereoisomer on the opposite directions of {110} planes. Only for equimolar mixtures of the two enantiomers of identical

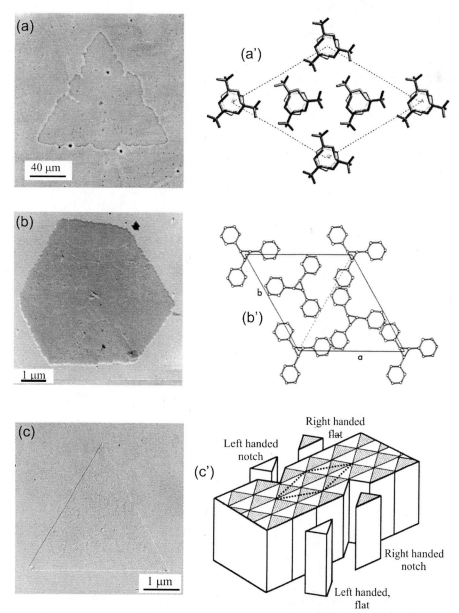

Figure 2.34 (a) Phase contrast optical micrograph of a single crystal of isotactic poly(*tert*-buthylethylene sulfide) formed by thin film growth at 130°C and (a′) corresponding molecular model (in chain axis projection) [191a]. (b) Electron micrograph of a single crystal of isotactic poly(2-vinylpyridine) formed by thin film growth for 15 hours at 200°C and (b′) corresponding molecular model (in chain axis projection) [190, 192]. In A up and down chains are represented as dark and light lines, respectively. (c) Transmission electron micrograph (replica) of a single crystal of the poly(L-lactide) (PLLA)/poly(D-lactide) (PDLA) stereocomplex grown after deposition of a single crystal on a thin film of PLLA, and then melted at 250°C and crystallized for 3 hours at 200°C [190]. (c′) Representation of the arrangement of PLLA and PDLA helices (schematized as triangular rods) in a trigonal unit cell with $R3c$ or $R\bar{3}c$ symmetry (*ab* plane of the unit cell shown by dashed lines). Note the four deposition possibilities for right- or left-handed helices (two for each helix chirality) and the resulting *polar* nature of the crystal with respect to the chirality of deposition sites. The growth faces of crystals in (a), (b), and (c) are delimited by {100} planes of the trigonal unit cells. The trigonal unit cells in (a′) and (b′) contain three identical (isochiral) chains and are examples of frustrated structures. The orientation of the chains on their axis differs significantly, which creates different environments for the different chains. This frustrated packing mode is preferred over a simpler one chain/unit cell in which all the helices would have similar orientation and, therefore, environment. The trigonal unit cell (dashed lines) in (c′) contains six chains, three PDLA and three PLLA helices, of opposite handedness. (a, b) Original figures kindly supplied by Bernard Lotz. (a′) Reprinted with permission from Reference [191a], Copyright 1998 by American Chemical Society. (b′) Redrawn with permission from Reference [192b], Copyright 1977 by Wiley. (c, c′) Reprinted with permission from Reference [190], Copyright 1997 by American Chemical Society).

molecular mass and degree of stereorgularity, do these rates become equivalent and the single crystals of hexagonal shape may be formed [190]. Quite often, the constituents of PLLA/PDLA mixtures may easily show differences in molecular constitution (i.e., molecular mass, molecular mass distribution, degree of stereoregularity) and/or the mixtures may also deviate in the composition from the equimolar one, resulting in differences in the deposition rate of the two stereoisomers on the crystal growth faces. Since the differences in growth rate occurs on opposite sides of {110} growth planes, any departure from the perfect nonracemic mixture of the two enantiomers gives rise to departures from the hexagonal geometry of crystals toward the triangular one [190].

2.7.1 Rounded Lateral Habits

The cause of the formation of rounded lateral habits in PE (Fig. 2.33c–e) and in polymer single crystals in general is unknown, and several mechanisms have been proposed. In the earliest approach proposed by Sadler [195], rounded surfaces occur at high temperatures and corresponds to a zero free energy of a step deposition on a crystal growth front (Fig. 2.35a) so that steps can be generated without the activated state of secondary nucleation. Under such a condition, crystal growth becomes isotropic (Fig. 2.35c) and the profile of the growth front becomes rounded. However, this idea is incompatible with the standard models of polymer crystallization in which the limiting process is surface nucle-

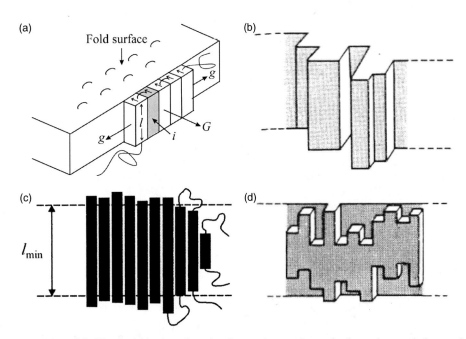

Figure 2.35 (a) Classical picture of nucleation and growth on the lateral growth faces of a polymer crystal, according to Hoffman and Lauritzen. After deposition of the first stem (in gray) at crystal growth front with nucleation rate i, successive stems deposit, up to substrate completion, with rate g; the crystal growth rate G perpendicular to the growth front is proportional to i for g higher or lower than i and to $(ig)^{1/2}$ for i and g almost identical [172]. (b–d) Schematic representations of three different types of roughness that might cause a curved profile of the growth surface. (b) After a new stem appears on a flat substrate at nucleation rate i, subsequent stems lay down laterally next to the first stem at rate g. Accumulation of steps on the growth face may occur because of retardation in advance of steps g. (c) Possible instantaneous configuration of a row of stems of varying length perpendicular to the crystal surface. According to the Sadler's model [195], such a configuration may be obtained by negating the need for nucleation and splitting stems into segments; this causes immobilization (pinning) of segments covered by stems with length $l < l_{min}$, even if this attachment is temporary. (d) Possible instantaneous configuration of a layer of stems of varying lengths depositing onto the crystal surface and parallel to it. The concept of self-poisoning would correspond to the retarding effect on layer spreading rate g because of attachment of stems with $l < l_{min}$ [198f,g].

ation [172]. Successive studies have shown that the curvature of {100} faces in PE may also be explained within the standard hypothesis of nonzero surface nucleation, applying Frank and Seto's model [196, 197]. Accordingly, it is assumed that as a new stem deposits on a one-dimensional growth front (nucleation rate i) it forms a pair of steps facing in opposite directions on the substrate. Subsequent stems lay down laterally to the first stem, propagating the steps at rate g (Fig. 2.35a). Rounded surfaces occur, assuming a retardation of steps movements, with consequent accumulation of steps on the growth face [196d] (Fig. 2.35b). Therefore, according to this model, the growth of crystals remains nucleation controlled as in the classic kinetic theory of polymer crystallization of Hoffmann–Lauritzen [172]. It has been argued that mechanisms inducing such retardation in g may be caused by impurities [196a] or lattice strains [196b].

More recently, the important role played by the self-poisoning effect, especially at high temperatures, in determining the curved habits of polymer crystals has been pointed out [198]. Self-poisoning was discovered by Ungar and Keller in 1987 as the major cause of anomalous minima in the temperature dependence of crystallization rate of long-chain monodisperse n-alkanes [198a] and arises from incorrect but nearly stable stem attachments, which obstruct productive growth. These systems, indeed, depending on the temperature, crystallize either forming extended chain crystals or chain folded crystals characterized by integer folding, that is, in conformations that ensure the location of chain ends at the crystal surface. Crystallization rate minima may typically occur when step propagation of a growth face of an extended-chain crystal is hindered by transient folded-chain deposition, due to the impossibility of extended chains growing on a folded chain substrate. This blocking or "pinning" effect also produces formation of rounded lateral habits, especially at low temperatures [198h]. However, as pointed out in recent works by Ungar [198f,g], whereas in monodisperse oligomers the "pinning" effect is very pronounced due to the quantized nature of lamellar thickness, in polymers the same effect may be overlooked since lamellar thickness does not change with crystallization temperature T_c in a discrete fashion as for oligomers, but rather continuously, and thus no rate minima can be expected. Self-poisoning is envisaged to affect, instead, the shape of lateral faces of the polymers crystals through the following mechanism. At any T_c there is a minimum fold length below which attachments are more likely to melt than be built into the crystal. However, chain segments that are only slightly shorter than this value will have a reasonably long lifetime to cause self-poisoning. This situation is the same as envisaged by Sadler [195] in Figure 2.35c, except that this time a layer of stems is attached parallel to the surface, causing a retardation in g, a case not considered by Sadler [198]. These and other features of crystal habit in solution- and melt-grown polymer crystals are discussed in Chapter 4.

ACKNOWLEDGMENTS

Dr. Bernard Lotz is gratefully acknowledged for the useful discussions and for kindly supplying high resolution images of Figure 2.30b and Figure 2.34a,b.

REFERENCES

[1] Corradini, P. Chain conformation and crystallinity. In *The Stereochemistry of Macromolecules*, Vol. 3, Ketley, A.D., ed. Marcel Dekker, Inc., New York, 1968, p. 1.

[2] Natta, G., Corradini, P. *Nuovo Cimento Suppl.* **1960**, *15*, 9.

[3] Turner Jones, A. *Polymer* **1965**, *6*, 249.

[4] Natta, G., Corradini, P., Sianesi, D., Morero, D. *J. Polym. Sci.* **1961**, *51*, 527.

[5] (a) Cimmino, S., Martuscelli, E., Nicolais, L., Silvestre, C. *Polymer* **1978**, *19*, 1222; (b) Crispino, L., Martuscelli, E., Pracella, M. *Makromol. Chem.* **1980**, *181*, 1747; (c) Cavallo, P., Martuscelli, E., Pracella, M. *Polymer* **1997**, *18*, 891.

[6] Arnold, M., Henschke, O., Knorr, J. *Macromol. Chem. Phys.* **1996**, *197*, 563.

[7] Abiru, T., Mizuno, A., Weigand, F. *J. Appl. Polym. Sci.* **1998**, *68*, 1493.

[8] De Rosa, C., Auriemma, F., Ruiz de Ballesteros, O., Resconi, L., Camurati, I. *Macromolecules* **2007**, *40*, 6600.

[9] (a) Kakugo, M. *Macromol. Symp.* **1995**, *89*, 545; (b) Naga, N., Mizunuma, K., Sadatoshi, H., Kakugo, M. *Macromolecules* **1997**, *30*, 2197; (c) Naga, N., Mizunuma, K., Sadatoshi, H., Kakugo, M. *Polymer* **2000**, *41*, 203.

[10] (a) De Rosa, C., Talarico, G., Caporaso, L., Auriemma, F., Galimberti, M., Fusco, O. *Macromolecules* **1998**, *31*, 9109; (b) De Rosa, C., Auriemma, F., Orlando, I., Talarico, G., Caporaso, L. *Macromolecules* **2001**, *34*, 1663.

[11] Tanaka, A., Hozumi, Y., Hatada, K., Endo, S., Fujishige, S. *J. Polym. Sci.* **1964**, *B2*, 181.

[12] Natta, G., Porri, L., Carbonaro, A., Lugli, G. *Makromol. Chem.* **1962**, *53*, 52.

[13] Guerra, G., Di Dino, G., Centore, R., Petraccone, V., Obrzut, J., Karasz, F.E., MacKnight, W.J. *Makromol. Chem.* **1989**, *190*, 2203.

[14] Flory, P.J., Sundararajan, P.R., DeBolt, L.C. *J. Am. Chem. Soc.* **1974**, *96*, 5015.

[15] Cahn, R.S., Ingold, C.K., Prelog, V. *Experientia* **1956**, *12*, 93.

[16] IUPAC Commission on Macromolecules Nomenclature. *Pure Appl. Chem.* **1979**, *51*, 1101; *Pure Appl. Chem.* **1981**, *53*, 733.

[17] Natta, G., Farina, M., Peraldo, M., Corradini, P., Bressan, G., Ganis, P. *Rend. Fis. Acc. Lincei* **1960**, *28*, 422.

[18] De Rosa, C., Auriemma, F., Di Capua, A., Resconi, L., Guidotti, S., Camurati, I., Nifant'ev, I.E., Laishevtsev, I.P. *J. Am. Chem. Soc.* **2004**, *126*, 17040; De Rosa, C., Auriemma, F., De Lucia, G., Resconi, L. *Polymer* **2005**, *46*, 9461.

[19] De Rosa, C., Auriemma, F. *J. Am. Chem. Soc.* **2006**, *128*, 11024; De Rosa, C., Auriemma, F. *Lect. Notes Phys.* **2007**, *714*, 345.

[20] De Rosa, C., Auriemma, F. *Prog. Polym. Sci.* **2006**, *31*, 145.

[21] De Rosa, C., Auriemma, F., Ruiz de Ballesteros, O. *Chem. Mat.* **2006**, *18*, 3523.

[22] De Rosa, C., Auriemma, F., Ruiz de Ballesteros, O. *Phys. Rev. Lett.* **2006**, *96*, 167801.

[23] Huggins, M.L. *J. Chem. Phys.* **1945**, *13*, 37.

[24] Bunn, C.W. *Proc. Roy. Soc. (London)* **1942**, *A180*, 67.

[25] Pauling, L., Corey, R.B., Branson, H.R. *Proc. Natl. Acad. Sci. U. S. A.* **1951**, *37*, 205.

[26] Corradini, P. *Rend. Fis. Acc. Lincei* **1960**, *28*, 1.

[27] Natta, G., Corradini, P., Ganis, P. *J. Polym. Sci.* **1962**, *58*, 1191.

[28] Bunn, C.W., Holmes, D.R. *Discuss. Faraday Soc.* **1958**, *25*, 95.

[29] Natta, G., Corradini, P. *Nuovo Cimento Suppl.* **1960**, *15*, 40.

[30] Natta, G., Pasquon, I., Corradini, P., Peraldo, M., Pegoraro, M., Zambelli, A. *Rend. Fis. Acc. Lincei* **1960**, *28*, 539.

[31] Corradini, P., Natta, G., Ganis, P., Temussi, P.A. *J. Polym. Sci., C* **1967**, *16*, 2477.

[32] Lotz, B., Lovinger, A.J., Cais, R.E. *Macromolecules* **1988**, *21*, 2375.

[33] Natta, G., Peraldo, M., Allegra, G. *Makromol. Chem.* **1964**, *75*, 215.

[34] Chatani, Y., Maruyama, H., Noguchi, K., Asanuma, T., Shiomura, T. *J. Polym. Sci. C* **1990**, *28*, 393.

[35] Corradini, P., Pasquon, I. *Rend. Fis. Acc. Lincei* **1955**, *19*, 453.

[36] Natta, G., Corradini, P., Bassi, I.W. *Gazz. Chim. It.* **1959**, *89*, 784; *Angew. Chem.* **1958**, *70*, 598.

[37] Corradini, P., Ganis, P., Petraccone, V. *Eur. Polym. J.* **1970**, *6*, 281.

[38] (a) Bassi, I.W., Bonsignori, O., Lorenzi, G.P., Pino, P., Corradini, P., Temussi, P.A. *J. Polym. Sci. Polym. Phys. Ed.* **1971**, *9*, 193; (b) Frank, F.C., Keller, A., O'Connor, A. *Phylos. Mag.* **1959**, *8*, 200.

[39] Corradini, P., Petraccone, V., Pirozzi, B. *Eur. Polym. J.* **1976**, *12*, 831.

[40] Natta, G., Corradini, P. *Makromol. Chem.* **1955**, *16*, 77; Natta, G., Corradini, P., Bassi, I.W. *Nuovo Cimento Suppl.* **1960**, *15*, 68.

[41] Corradini, P., De Rosa, C., Zhi, G., Napolitano, R., Pirozzi, B. *Eur. Polym. J.* **1985**, *21*, 635.

[42] Auriemma, F., De Rosa, C., Corradini, P. *Macromol. Chem. Phys.* **2004**, *205*, 390.

[43] Petraccone, V., Pirozzi, B., Frasci, A., Corradini, P. *Eur. Polym. J.* **1976**, *12*, 323.

[44] De Rosa, C., Borriello, A., Venditto, V., Corradini, P. *Macromolecules* **1994**, *27*, 3864.

[45] Natta, G., Corradini, P., Bassi, I.W. *Nuovo Cimento Suppl.* **1960**, *15*, 52.

[46] Turner Jones, A. *J. Polym. Sci.* **1963**, *B1*, 455; *Polymer* **1966**, *7*, 23.

[47] Cojazzi, G., Malta, V., Celotti, G., Zannetti, R. *Makromol. Chem.* **1976**, *177*, 915.

[48] Kusanagi, H., Takase, M., Chatani, Y., Tadokoro, H. *J. Polym. Sci. Polym. Phys. Ed.* **1978**, *16*, 131.

[49] De Rosa, C. *Macromolecules* **2003**, *36*, 6087.

[50] Ruan, J., Thierry, A., Lotz, B. *Polymer* **2006**, *47*, 5478.

[51] Takayanagi, M., Kawasaki, N. *J. Macromol. Sci.- Phys.* **1967**, *B1*, 741.

[52] De Rosa, C., Auriemma, F., Borriello, A., Corradini, P. *Polymer* **1995**, *36*, 4723.

[53] (a) Charlet, G., Delmas, G., Revol, F.J., Manley, R.St.J. *Polymer* **1984**, *25*, 1613; (b) Charlet, G., Delmas, G. *Polymer* **1984**, *25*, 1619; (c) Charlet, G., Delmas, G. *Polym. Bull.* **1982**, *6*, 367.

[54] Rastogi, S., Newman, M., Keller, A. *Nature* **1991**, *353*, 55; *J. Polym. Sci. Polym. Phys. Ed.* **1993**, *31*, 125.

[55] De Rosa, C. *Macromolecules* **1999**, *32*, 935.

[56] Corradini, P., De Rosa, C., Guerra, G., Pirozzi, B., Venditto, V. *Gazz. Chim. It.* **1992**, *122*, 305.

[57] Corradini, P., Napolitano, R., Pirozzi, B. *Eur. Polym. J.* **1990**, *26*, 157; Napolitano, R., Pirozzi, B. *Macromol. Theory Simul.* **1999**, *8*, 15.

[58] Pirozzi, B., Napolitano, R. *Eur. Polym. J.* **1992**, *28*, 703; Corradini, P., Napolitano, R., Petraccone, V., Pirozzi, B., Tuzi, A. *Macromolecules* **1982**, *15*, 1207.

[59] Guerra, G., Vitagliano, V.M., De Rosa, C., Petraccone, V., Corradini, P. *Macromolecules* **1990**, *23*, 1539.

[60] Greis, O., Xu, Y., Asano, T., Petermann, J. *Polymer* **1989**, *30*, 590.

[61] De Rosa, C., Guerra, G., Petraccone, V., Corradini, P. *Polym. J.* **1991**, *23*, 1435.

[62] De Rosa, C. *Macromolecules* **1996**, *29*, 8460.

[63] De Rosa, C., Rapacciuolo, M., Guerra, G., Petraccone, V., Corradini, P. *Polymer* **1992**, *33*, 1423.

[64] Chatani, Y., Shimane, Y., Ijitsu, T., Yukinari, T. *Polymer* **1993**, *34*, 1625.

[65] (a) Chatani, Y., Shimane, Y., Inagaki, T., Ijitsu, T., Yukinari, T., Shikuma, H. *Polymer* **1993**, *34*, 1620; (b) Chatani, Y., Inagaki, T., Shimane, Y., Shikuma, H. *Polymer* **1993**, *34*, 4841; (c) De Rosa, C., Rizzo, P., Ruiz de Ballesteros, O., Petraccone, V., Guerra, G. *Polymer* **1999**, *40*, 2103.

[66] De Rosa, C., Guerra, G., Petraccone, V., Pirozzi, B. *Macromolecules* **1997**, *30*, 4147.

[67] (a) Chatani, Y., Maruyama, H., Asanuma, T., Shiomura, T. *J. Polym. Sci. Polym. Phys.* **1991**, *29*, 1649; (b) Auriemma, F., De Rosa, C., Ruiz de Ballesteros, O.,

Vinti, V., Corradini, P. *J. Polym. Sci., Polym. Phys.* **1998**, *36*, 395.

[68] De Rosa, C., Venditto, V., Guerra, G., Pirozzi, B., Corradini, P. *Macromolecules* **1991**, *24*, 5645.

[69] De Rosa, C., Venditto, V., Guerra, G., Corradini, P. *Macromolecules* **1992**, *25*, 6938.

[70] De Rosa, C., Venditto, V., Guerra, G., Corradini, P. *Makromol. Chem.* **1992**, *193*, 1351.

[71] De Rosa, C., Scaldarella, D. *Macromolecules* **1997**, *30*, 4153.

[72] De Rosa, C., Venditto, V., Guerra, G., Corradini, P. *Polymer* **1995**, *36*, 3619.

[73] Kitajgorodskij, A.I. *Acta Cryst.* **1965**, *18*, 585; Molecular Crystals and Molecules Academic Press, Inc., New York, 1973.

[74] Bunn, C.W. *Trans. Faraday Soc.* **1939**, *35*, 482.

[75] Natta, G., Corradini, P., Porri, L. *Rend. Fis. Acc. Lincei* **1956**, *20*, 728.

[76] Iwayanagi, S., Sakurai, I., Sakurai, T., Seto, T.J. *J. Macromol. Sci., Phys.* **1970**, *B2*(2), 163.

[77] Bunn, C.W., Howells, E.R. *Nature* **1954**, *174*, 549.

[78] (a) Clark, E.S., Muus, L.T. *Z. Kristallogr.* **1962**, *117*, 119; (b) Sperati, C.A., Starkweather, H.W., Jr. *Adv. Polym. Sci.* **1961**, *2*, 465; (c) Kilian, H.G. *Kolloid Z. Z. Polym.* **1962**, *185*, 13; (d) Weeks, J.J., Clark, E.S., Eby, R.K. *Polymer* **1981**, *22*, 1480; (e) Farmer, B.L., Eby, R.K. *Polymer* **1985**, *26*, 1944; (f) Yamamoto, T., Hara, T. *Polymer* **1982**, *23*, 521.

[79] Natta, G., Porri, L., Corradini, P., Morero, D. *Chim. Ind.* **1958**, *40*, 362.

[80] De Rosa, C., Napolitano, R., Pirozzi, B. *Polymer* **1985**, *26*, 2039.

[81] Corradini, P. *J. Polym. Sci. Polym. Lett. Ed.* **1969**, *7*, 211.

[82] Suehiro, K., Takayanagi, M.J. *J. Macromol. Sci., Phys.* **1970**, *B4*(1), 39.

[83] Corradini, P., Bassi, I.W. *J. Polym. Sci. C* **1968**, *16*, 3233.

[84] Natta, G., Corradini, P., Bassi, I.W. *Rend. Fis. Accad. Lincei* **1957**, *23*, 363.

[85] Natta, G., Corradini, P., Bassi, I.W. *Nuovo Cimento Suppl.* **1960**, *15*, 83.

[86] Corradini, P., Ganis, P. *J. Polym. Sci.* **1960**, *43*, 311.

[87] Corradini, P., Ganis, P. *Nuovo Cimento Suppl.* **1960**, *15*, 96.

[88] Corradini, P., Ganis, P. *Nuovo Cimento Suppl.* **1960**, *15*, 104.

[89] Natta, G., Corradini, P., Bassi, I.W. *Makromol. Chem.* **1959**, *33*, 247.

[90] De Rosa, C., Borriello, A., Corradini, P. *Macromolecules* **1996**, *29*, 6323.

[91] Natta, G., Corradini, P., Bassi, I.W. *J. Polym. Sci.* **1961**, *51*, 505.

[92] Pino, P., Ciardelli, F., Lorenzi, G.P., Montagnoli, G. *Makromol. Chem.* **1963**, *61*, 207; Pino, P. *Adv. Polym. Sci.* **1965**, *4*, 393; Pino, P., Lorenzi, G.P. *J. Am. Chem. Soc.* **1960**, *82*, 4745; Luisi, P.L., Pino, P. *J. Phys. Chem.* **1968**, *72*, 2400.

[93] Petraccone, V., Ganis, P., Corradini, P., Montagnoli, G. *Eur. Polym. J.* **1972**, *8*, 99.

[94] (a) Natta, G., Corradini, P., Bassi, I.W. *Rend. Fis. Accad. Lincei* **1955**, *19*, 404; (b) Natta, G. *Makromol. Chem.* **1960**, *35*, 94; (c) Corradini, P., Martuscelli, E., Montagnoli, E., Petraccone, V. *Eur. Polym. J.* **1970**, *6*, 1201.

[95] Natta, G., Corradini, P. *Chim. Ind. (Milano)* **1963**, *45*, 299.

[96] Natta, G., Corradini, P. *Angew. Chem.* **1956**, *68*, 615; Natta, G., Corradini, P. *Nuovo Cimento Suppl.* **1960**, *15*, 111.

[97] Nyburg, S.C. *Acta Crystallogr.* **1954**, *7*, 385.

[98] Bunn, C.W. *Proc. Roy. Soc.* **1942**, *A180*, 40.

[99] Benedetti, E., Corradini, P., Pedone, C. *Eur. Polym. J.* **1975**, *11*, 585.

[100] Natta, G., Corradini, P. *J. Polym. Sci.* **1956**, *20*, 251.

[101] Mencik, Z. *J. Macromol. Sci. Phys.* **1972**, *6*, 101.

[102] Hikosaka, M., Seto, T. *Polym. J.* **1973**, *5*, 111.

[103] De Rosa, C., Auriemma, F., Corradini, P., Tarallo, O., Dello Iacono, S., Ciaccia, E., Resconi, L. *J. Am. Chem. Soc.* **2006**, *128*, 80.

[104] De Rosa, C., Dello Iacono, S., Auriemma, F., Ciaccia, E., Resconi, L. *Macromolecules* **2006**, *39*, 6098.

[105] De Rosa, C., Auriemma, F., Talarico, G., Ruiz de Ballesteros, O. *Macromolecules* **2007**, *40*, 8531.

[106] (a) Lotz, B., Ruan, J., Thierry, A., Alfonso, G.C., Hiltner, A., Baer, E., Piorkowska, E., Galeski, A. *Macromolecules* **2006**, *39*, 5777; (b) Poon, B., Rogunova, M., Hiltner, A., Baer, E., Chum, S.P., Galeski, A., Piorkowska, E. *Macromolecules* **2005**, *38*, 1232.

[107] Rizzo, P., Auriemma, F., Guerra, G., Petraccone, V., Corradini, P. *Macromolecules* **1996**, *29*, 8852.

[108] Bruckner, S., Meille, S.V. *Nature* **1989**, *340*, 455.

[109] Meille, S.V., Bruckner, S., Porzio, W. *Macromolecules* **1990**, *23*, 4114.

[110] Borriello, A., Busico, V., De Rosa, C., Schulze, D. *Macromolecules* **1995**, *28*, 5679.

[111] De Rosa, C., Capitani, D., Cosco, S. *Macromolecules* **1997**, *30*, 8322.

[112] Farmer, B.L., Lando, J.B. *J. Macromol. Sci. Phys.* **1974**, *10*, 403.

[113] Cartier, L., Okihara, T., Lotz, B. *Macromolecules* **1998**, *31*, 3303.

[114] (a) Lotz, B., Kopp, S., Dorset, D.L. *C. R. Acad. Sci. Paris* **1994**, *319*, 187; (b) Cartier, L., Spassky, N., Lotz, B. *C. R. Acad. Sci. Paris* **1996**, *322*, 429; (c) Lotz, B. *Polym. Prepr., Am. Chem. Soc. Div. Polym. Chem.* **1996**, *37*, 430.

[115] Kusanagi, H., Tadokoro, H., Chatani, Y. *Polymer J.* **1977**, *9*, 181.

[116] Corradini, P., Napolitano, R., Petraccone, V., Pirozzi, B., Tuzi, A. *Eur. Polym. J.* **1981**, *17*, 1217.

[117] Dasgupta, S., Hammond, W.B., Goddard, W.A., III *J. Am. Chem. Soc.* **1996**, *118*, 12291.

[118] Bunn, C.W., Garner, E.V. *Proc. R. Soc. Lond. A* **1947**, *189*, 39.

[119] (a) Natta, G., Corradini, P. *Nuovo Cimento Suppl.* **1960**, *15*, 9; (b) Ciajolo, M.R., Corradini, P., Lepore, U., Petraccone, V. *Gazz.Chim. Ital.* **1972**, *102*, 1091.

[120] Ito, T. *Jpn. J. Appl. Phys.* **1976**, *15*, 2295.

[121] Chakrabarti, P., Dunitz, J.D. *Helv. Chim. Acta* **1982**, *65*, 1555; Flory, P.J. *Statistical Mechanics of Chain Molecules*, John Wiley & Sons, New York, 1969.

[122] Kinoshita, Y. *Makromol. Chem.* **1959**, *33*, 1.

[123] Holmes, D.R., Bunn, C.W., Smith, D.J. *J. Polym. Sci.* **1955**, *17*, 159.

[124] Arimoto, H., Ishibashi, M., Hirai, M., Chatani, Y. *J. Polym. Sci. A* **1964**, *2*, 2283.

[125] For a recent general review see for instance Murthy, N.S. *J. Polym. Sci. B Polym. Phys. Ed.* **2006**, *44*, 1763.

[126] (a) Puiggalí, J., Franco, L., Alemán, C., Subirana, J.A. *Macromolecules* **1998**, *31*, 8540; (b) Franco, L., Subirana, J.A., Puiggalí, J. *Macromolecules* **1998**, *31*, 3912; (c) Villaseñor, P., Franco, L., Subirana, J.A., Puiggali, J. *J. Polym. Sci. B Polym. Phys. Ed.* **1999**, *37*, 2383.

[127] (a) Navarro, E., Franco, L., Subirana, J.A., Puiggalí, J. *Macromolecules* **1995**, *28*, 8742; (b) Franco, L., Cooper, S.J., Atkins, A.D.T., Hill, M., Jones, N.A. *J. Polym. Sci. B Polym. Phys. Ed.* **1998**, *36*, 1153; (c) Navarro, E., Franco, L., Subirana, J.A., Puiggali, J. *Macromolecules* **1996**, *28*, 8742.

[128] Ziabicki, A. *Collect. Czech. Chem. Commun.* **1957**, *22*, 64; Ziabicki, A. *Kolloid-Z.* **1959**, *167*, 132; Auriemma, F., Petraccone, V., Parravicini, L., Corradini, P. *Macromolecules* **1997**, *30*, 7554.

[129] Ramesh, C., Gowd, E.B. *Macromolecules* **2001**, *34*, 3308; Murthy, N.S., Curran, S.A., Aharoni, S.M., Minor, H. *Macromolecules* **2000**, *33*, 5754.

[130] Sikorski, P., Atkins, E.D.T. *Macromolecules* **2001**, *34*, 4788.

[131] Brill, R. *Ztg. Phys. Chem.* **1943**, *61*, 1353; Jones, N.A., Atkins, E.D.T., Hill, M.J., Cooper, S.J., Franco, L. *Macromolecules* **1996**, *29*, 6011; Jones, N.A., Atkins, E.D.T., Hill, M.J., Cooper, S.J., Franco, L. *Polymer* **1997**, *38*, 2689; Jones, N.A., Cooper, S.J., Atkins, E.D.T., Hill, M.J., Franco, L. *J. Polym. Sci. Polym. Phys.* **1997**, *35*, 675; Jones, N.A., Atkins, E.D.T., Hill, M.J., Cooper, S.J., Franco, L. *Macromolecules* **1997**, *30*, 3569; Atkins, E.D.T. *Macromolecules '92: Functional Polymers and Biopolymers*, Canterbury, U.K., Sept. 1992, Abstracts, p. 10; Atkins, E.D.T. *Macromol. Rep.* **1994**, *A31*(Suppls. 6 & 7), 691.

[132] Bragg, W.L. *The Crystalline State. A General Survey*, G. Bell and Sons, London, 1966.

[133] Clegg, W., Blake, A.J., Gould, R.O., Main, P. *Crystal Structure Analysis: Principles and Practice*, Oxford University Press, Oxford, 2002.

[134] Wunderlich, B. *Macromolecular Physics*, Vol. 1, *Crystal Structure, Morphology, Defects*. Academic Press, New York, 1973.

[135] IUCr Commission. *Acta Cryst.* **1992**, *A48*, 922.

[136] IUPAC Commission on Macromolecular Nomenclature. *Pure Appl. Chem.* **1989**, *61*, 211.

[137] De Rosa, C. *Top. Stereochem.* **2003**, *24*, 71.

[138] Corradini, P., Guerra, G. *Adv. Polym. Sci.* **1992**, *100*, 182.

[139] Auriemma, F., Corradini, P., De Rosa, C. *Adv. Polym. Sci.* **2005**, *181*, 1.

[140] Ungar, G. *Polymer* **1993**, *34*, 2050.

[141] Wunderlich, B., Grebowicz, J. *Adv. Polym. Sci.* **1984**, *60/61*, 1.

[142] Allegra, G., Meille, S.V. *Macromolecules* **2004**, *37*, 3487.

[143] Corradini, P., Auriemma, F., De Rosa, C. *Acc. Chem. Res.* **2006**, *39*, 314.

[144] Lovinger, A.J., Lotz, B., Davis, D.D. *Polymer* **1990**, *31*, 2253.

[145] Lovinger, A.J., Davis, D.D., Lotz, B. *Macromolecules* **1991**, *24*, 552.

[146] Lovinger, A.J., Lotz, B., Davis, D.D., Padden, F.J. *Macromolecules* **1993**, *26*, 3494.

[147] De Rosa, C., Corradini, P. *Macromolecules* **1993**, *26*, 5711.

[148] De Rosa, C., Auriemma, F., Corradini, P. *Macromolecules* **1996**, *29*, 7452.

[149] De Rosa, C., Auriemma, F., Vinti, V. *Macromolecules* **1997**, *30*, 4137.

[150] (a) Guerra, G., Petraccone, V., Corradini, P., De Rosa, C., Napolitano, R., Pirozzi, B., Giunchi, G. *J. Polym. Sci. Polym. Phys. Ed.* **1984**, *22*, 1029; (b) De Rosa, C., Guerra, G., Napolitano, R., Petraccone, V., Pirozzi, B. *Eur. Polym. J.* **1984**, *20*, 937; (c) Auriemma, F., Ruiz de Ballesteros, O., De Rosa, C., Corradini, P. *Macromolecules* **2000**, *33*, 8764.

[151] Corradini, P. *J. Polym. Sci. Polym. Symp.* **1975**, *51*, 1.

[152] Napolitano, R., Pirozzi, B. *Gazz. Chim. It.* **1986**, *116*, 323.

[153] Immirzi, A., Tedesco, C., Monaco, G., Tonelli, A.E. *Macromolecules* **2005**, *38*, 1223.

[154] Auriemma, F., Born, R., Spiess, H.W., De Rosa, C., Corradini, P. *Macromolecules* **1995**, *28*, 6902; Auriemma, F., Lewis, R.H., Spiess, H.W., De Rosa, C. *Macromol. Chem. Phys.* **1995**, *196*, 4011.

[155] Auriemma, F., De Rosa, C., Ruiz de Ballesteros, O., Corradini, P. *Macromolecules* **1997**, *30*, 6586.

[156] Auriemma, F., De Rosa, C., Boscato, T., Corradini, P. *Macromolecules* **2001**, *34*, 4815.

[157] De Rosa, C., Auriemma, F., Circelli, T., Waymouth, R.M. *Macromolecules* **2002**, *35*, 3622.

[158] Auriemma, F., De Rosa, C. *Macromolecules* **2002**, *35*, 9057.

[159] De Rosa, C., Auriemma, F., Perretta, C. *Macromolecules* **2004**, *37*, 6843.

[160] De Rosa, C., Auriemma, F., Spera, C., Talarico, G., Tarallo, O. *Macromolecules* **2004**, *37*, 1441.

[161] De Rosa, C., Auriemma, F., Paolillo, M., Resconi, L., Camurati, I. *Macromolecules* **2005**, *38*, 9143.

[162] De Rosa, C., Auriemma, F., Resconi, L. *Macromolecules* **2005**, *38*, 10080.

[163] Auriemma, F., De Rosa, C. *Macromolecules* **2006**, *39*, 7635; Auriemma, F., De Rosa, C., Corradi, M. *Adv. Mater.* **2007**, *19*, 871.

[164] De Rosa, C., Auriemma, F., Vollaro, P., Resconi, L., Guidotti, S., Camurati, I. *Macromolecules* **2011**, *44*, 540.

[165] De Rosa, C., Auriemma, F., Ruiz de Ballesteros, O., De Luca, D., Resconi, L. *Macromolecules* **2008**, *41*, 2172; De Rosa, C., Auriemma, F., Ruiz de Ballesteros, O., Dello Iacono, S., De Luca, D., Resconi, L. *Cryst. Growth Des.* **2009**, *9*, 165.

[166] Hosier, I.L., Alamo, R.G., Esteso, P., Isasi, G.R., Mandelkern, L. *Macromolecules* **2003**, *36*, 5623.

[167] Hosoda, S., Hori, H., Yada, K., Tsuji, M., Nakahara, S. *Polymer* **2002**, *43*, 7451.

[168] Attenburrow, G.E., Bassett, D.C. *J. Mat. Sci.* **1979**, *14*, 2679.

[169] Takahashi, Y., Tadokoro, H., Odajima, A. *Macromolecules* **1980**, *13*, 1318; Takahashi, Y., Kohyama, M., Tadokoro, H. *Macromolecules* **1976**, *9*, 870.

[170] (a) De Rosa, C., Auriemma, F., Vinti, V., Grassi, A., Galimberti, M. *Polymer* **1998**, *39*, 6219; (b) De Rosa, C., Auriemma, F., Talarico, G., Busico, V., Caporaso, L., Capitani, D. *Macromolecules* **2002**, *35*, 1314; (c) De Rosa, C., Auriemma, F., Fanelli, E., Talarico, G., Capitani, D. *Macromolecules* **2003**, *36*, 1850.

[171] Lotz, B., Wittmann, J.C. Structure of polymer single crystals. In *Materials Science and Technology: A Comprehensive Treatment*, Vol. 12, Cahn, R.W., Haasen, P., Kramer, E.J., eds. Wiley-VCH, Weinheim, 1993, pp. 79–151.

[172] Armitstead, K., Golbeck-Wood, G. *Adv. Polym. Sci.* **1993**, *100*, 219; Hoffman, J.D., Miller, R.L. *Polymer* **1997**, *38*, 3151.

[173] Muthukumar, M. *Phil. Trans. R. Soc. Lond.* **2003**, *A361*, 539.

[174] Geil, P.H. *Polymer Single Crystals*, R.E. Krieger, Huntington, 1973.

[175] Bassett, D.C. *Principles of Polymer Morphology*, Cambridge University Press, Cambridge, 1981.

[176] Bu, Z., Yoon, Y., Ho, R.-M., Zhou, W., Jangchud, I., Eby, R.K., Cheng, S.Z.D., Hsieh, E.T., Johnson, T.W., Geerts, R.G., Palackal, S.J., Hawley, G.R., Welch, M.B. *Macromolecules* **1996**, *29*, 6575.

[177] Toda, A., Arita, T., Hikosaka, M. *Polymer* **2001**, *42*, 2223.

[178] Hasegawa, R., Takahashi, Y., Chatani, Y., Tadokoro, H. *Polymer J.* **1972**, *3*, 600.

[179] Taguchi, K., Miyaji, H., Izumi, K., Hoshino, A., Miyamoto, Y., Kokawa, R. *Polymer* **2001**, *42*, 7443.

[180] Pradere, P., Revol, J.F., St. John Manley, R. *Macromolecules* **1988**, *21*, 2747.

[181] Tadokoro, H., Yasumoto, T., Murahashi, S., Nitta, I. *J. Polym. Sci.* **1960**, *44*, 266; Uchida, T., Tadokoro, H. *J. Polym. Sci. Polym. Phys. Ed.* **1967**, *5*, 63.

[182] Bassett, D.C., Frank, F.C., Keller, A. *Philos. Mag.* **1963**, *8*, 1753.

[183] Keith, H.D. *J. Appl. Phys.* **1964**, *35*, 3115; Khoury, F.E. *Faraday Discuss. Chem. Soc.* **1979**, *68*, 404; Khoury, F.E. *Polym. Prep. Japan* **1982**, *31*, 5.

[184] Toda, A. *Polymer* **1991**, *32*, 771.

[185] Toda, A., Okamura, M., Hikosaka, M., Nakagawa, Y. *Polymer* **2005**, *46*, 8708.

[186] Lovinger, A.J., Keith, H.D. *Macromolecules* **1996**, *29*, 8541.

[187] Kovacs, A.J., Gonthier, A. *Kolloid. Z. Z. Polym.* **1972**, *250*, 530; Kovacs, A.J., Gonthier, A., Straupe, C. *J. Polym. Sci. Polym. Symp.* **1975**, *50*, 283; Kovacs, A.J., Gonthier, A., Straupe, C. *J. Polym. Sci. Polym. Symp.* **1977**, *59*, 31; Cheng, S.Z.D., Chen, J. *J. Polym. Sci. B Polym. Phys.* **1991**, *29*, 311.

[188] Hikosaka, M., Seto, T. *Jpn. J. Appl. Phys.* **1982**, *21*, L332; Bassett, D.C., Holley, R.H., Al Raheil, I.A.M. *Polymer* **1988**, *29*, 1539; Keith, H.D., Padden, F.J., Jr., Lotz, B., Wittmann, J.C. *Macromolecules* **1989**, *22*, 2230.

[189] Toda, A. *Colloid Polym. Sci.* **1992**, *270*, 667; Toda, A., Keller, A. *Colloid Polym. Sci.* **1993**, *271*, 328; Toda, A. *Faraday Discuss. Chem. Soc.* **1993**, *95*, 129.

[190] Cartier, L., Okihara, T., Lotz, B. *Macromolecules* **1997**, *30*, 6313.

[191] (a) Cartier, L., Spassky, N., Lotz, B. *Macromolecules* **1998**, *31*, 3040; (b) Matsubayashi, H., Chatani, Y., Tadokoro, H., Dumas, P., Spassky, N., Sigwalt, P. *Macromolecules* **1977**, *10*, 996.

[192] (a) Okihara, T., Cartier, L., Alberda van Ekenstein, G.O.R., Lotz, B. *Polymer* **1998**, *40*, 1; (b) Puterman, M., Kolpak, F.J., Blackwell, J., Lando, J.B. *J. Polym. Sci. Polym. Phys. Ed.* **1977**, *15*, 805.

[193] Dorset, D.L., McCourt, M.P., Kopp, S., Schumacher, M., Okihara, T., Lotz, B. *Polymer* **1998**, *39*, 6331; Stocker, W., Schumacher, M., Graff, S., Thierry, A., Wittmann, J.-C., Lotz, B. *Macromolecules* **1998**, *31*, 807.

[194] Meille, S.V., Ferro, D.R., Bruckner, S., Lovinger, A., Padden, F.J. *Macromolecules* **1994**, *27*, 2615.

[195] Sadler, D.M. *Polymer* **1983**, *24*, 1401; Sadler, D.M. *J. Polym. Sci. Polym. Phys. Ed.* **1985**, *23*, 1533; Sadler, D.M., Gilmer, G.H. *Polym. Commun.* **1987**, *28*, 243.

[196] (a) Toda, A. *J. Phys. Soc. Japan* **1986**, *55*, 3419; (b) Mansfield, M.L. *Polymer* **1988**, *29*, 1755; (c) Hoffman, J.D., Miller, R.L. *Macromolecules* **1989**, *22*, 3038; (d) Toda, A. *Polymer* **1991**, *32*, 771.

[197] Seto, T. *Rep. Progr. Polym. Phys. Jpn.* **1964**, *7*, 67; Frank, F.C. *J. Cryst. Growth* **1974**, *22*, 233.

[198] (a) Ungar, G., Keller, A. *Polymer* **1987**, *28*, 1899; (b) Organ, S.J., Ungar, G., Keller, A. *Macromolecules* **1989**, *22*, 1995; (c) Organ, S.J., Keller, A., Hikosaka, M., Ungar, G. *Polymer* **1996**, *37*, 2517; (d) Ungar, G., Mandal, P.K., Higgs, P.G., de Silva, D.S.M., Boda, E., Chen, C.M. *Phys. Rev. Lett.* **2000**, *85*, 4397; (e) Organ, S.J., Ungar, G. *Macromolecules* **2003**, *36*, 5214; (f) Ungar, G., Zeng, X. *Chem. Rev.* **2001**, *101*, 4157; (g) Ungar, G., Putra, E.G.R., de Silva, D.S.M., Shcherbina, M.A., Waddon, A.J. *Adv. Polym. Sci.* **2005**, *180*, 45; (h) Ungar, G. Self-Poisoning of Crystal Growth Faces in Long Alkanes and Poly(ethylene oxide) Fractions. In *Polymer Crystallization*, Dosiere, M., ed. *NATO ASI Series*. Kluwer, Dordrecht, 1993, p. 63; (i) Putra, E.G.R., Ungar, G. *Macromolecules* **2003**, *36*, 5214.

[199] Natta, G. *Makromol. Chem.* **1955**, *16*, 213; Turner-Jones, A., Aizlewood, J.M. *J. Polym. Sci.* **1963**, *B1*, 471.

[200] Turner-Jones, A. *Makromol. Chem.* **1964**, *71*, 1.

[201] Noether, H.D. *J. Polym. Sci. C* **1967**, *16*, 725.

[202] (a) Dall'Asta, G., Otto, N. *Chim. Ind. (Milan)* **1960**, *42*, 1234; (b) Bassi, I.W. *Rend. Fis. Acc. Naz. Lincei* **1960**, *29*, 193; (c) Natta, G., Allegra, G., Bassi, I.W., Carlini, C., Chiellini, E., Montagnoli, G. *Macromolecules* **1969**, *2*, 311; (d) Natta, G., Bassi, I.W., Allegra, G. *Makromol. Chem.* **1965**, *89*, 81.

[203] Natta, G., Bassi, I.W., Corradini, P. *Makromol. Chem.* **1956**, *18–19*, 455.

[204] Natta, G., Corradini, P., Bassi, I.W., Fagherazzi, G. *Eur. Polym. J.* **1968**, *4*, 297.

[205] Bruckner, S., De Rosa, C., Corradini, P., Porzio, W., Musco, A. *Macromolecules* **1996**, *29*, 1535.

[206] De Rosa, C. *Macromolecules* **1997**, *30*, 5494.

[207] Petraccone, V., Ruiz de Ballesteros, O., Tarallo, O., Rizzo, P., Guerra, G. *Chem. Mater.* **2008**, *20*, 3663.

[208] (a) Petraccone, V., Tarallo, O., Venditto, V., Guerra, G. *Macromolecules* **2005**, *38*, 6965; (b) Tarallo, O., Petraccone, V., Venditto, V., Guerra, G. *Polymer* **2006**, *47*, 2402.

[209] (a) De Rosa, C., Petraccone, V., Guerra, G., Manfredi, C. *Polymer* **1996**, *37*, 5247; (b) Esposito, G., Tarallo, O., Petraccone, V. *Macromolecules* **2006**, *39*, 5037.

[210] De Rosa, C., Petraccone, V., Dal Poggetto, F., Guerra, G., Pirozzi, B., De Lorenzo, M.L., Corradini, P. *Macromolecules* **1995**, *28*, 5507.

[211] (a) Petraccone, V., La Camera, D., Pirozzi, B., Rizzo, P., De Rosa, C. *Macromolecules* **1998**, *31*, 5830; (b) Petraccone, V., La Camera, D., Caporaso, L., De Rosa, C. *Macromolecules* **2000**, *33*, 2610; (c) Rizzo, P., Ruiz De Ballesteros, O., Auriemma, F., De Rosa, C., La Camera, D., Petraccone, V., Lotz, B. *Polymer* **2000**, *41*, 3745; (d) La Camera, D., Petraccone, V., Artimagnella, S., Ruiz de Ballesteros, O. *Macromolecules* **2001**, *34*, 7762; (e) Petraccone, V., Tarallo, O. *Macromol. Symp.* **2004**, *213*, 385; (f) Esposito, G., Tarallo, O., Petraccone, V. *Eur. Polym. J.* **2007**, *43*, 1278; (g) Tarallo, O., Esposito, G., Passarelli, U., Petraccone, V. *Macromolecules* **2007**, *40*, 5471.

[212] Petraccone, V., Esposito, G., Tarallo, O., Caporaso, L. *Macromolecules* **2005**, *38*, 5668.

[213] De Rosa, C., Buono, A., Caporaso, L., Petraccone, V. *Macromolecules* **2001**, *34*, 7349; De Rosa, C., Esposito, S., Buono, A., Auriemma, F. *Polymer* **2003**, *44*, 1655.

[214] (a) Petraccone, V., Tarallo, O., Califano, V. *Macromolecules* **2003**, *36*, 685; (b) Tarallo, O., Buono, A., Califano, V., Petraccone, V. *Macromol. Symp.* **2003**, *203*, 123.

[215] Meille, S.V., Capelli, S., Ricci, G. *Makromol. Chem. Rapid Commun.* **1995**, *16*, 891.

[216] Immirzi, A., Tedesco, C., Meille, S.V., Famulari, A., van Smaalen, S. *Macromolecules* **2003**, *36*, 3666.

[217] Corradini, P., De Rosa, C., Panunzi, A., Petrucci, G., Pino, P. *Chimia* **1990**, *44*, 52.

[218] De Rosa, C., Corradini, P. *Eur. Polym. J.* **1993**, *29*, 163.

[219] Trifuoggi, M., De Rosa, C., Auriemma, F., Corradini, P. *Macromolecules* **1994**, *27*, 3553.

3

STRUCTURE OF POLYCRYSTALLINE AGGREGATES

BUCKLEY CRIST

Department of Materials Science and Engineering, Northwestern University, Evanston, Illinois

3.1 Introduction, 73
3.2 Crystals Grown from Solution, 75
    3.2.1 Facetted Monolayer Crystals from Dilute Solution, 75
    3.2.2 Dendritic Crystals from Dilute Solution, 81
    3.2.3 Growth Spirals in Dilute Solution, 85
    3.2.4 Concentrated Solutions, 92
3.3 Crystals and Aggregates Grown from Molten Films, 94
    3.3.1 Structures in Thin Films, 94
    3.3.2 Structures in Ultrathin Films, 98
    3.3.3 Edge-On Lamellae in Molten Films, 102
3.4 Spherulitic Aggregates, 104
    3.4.1 Optical Properties of Spherulites, 105
    3.4.2 Occurrence of Spherulites, 108
    3.4.3 Development of Spherulites, 110
    3.4.4 Banded Spherulites and Lamellar Twist, 116
Acknowledgments, 121
References, 121

3.1 INTRODUCTION

Under virtually all quiescent conditions, structurally regular, flexible polymer molecules crystallize as thin platelets wherein the chains are nearly perpendicular to the basal or lamellar surface. It is well established that the limited size of crystals in the molecular chain direction is caused by kinetic factors and that some sort of chain folding occurs on the large basal surfaces [1]. We consider first crystallization from very dilute solutions. When conducted at small undercooling ($\Delta T = T_d - T_c$, the difference between dissolution and crystallization temperatures), well-defined *monolayer crystals*, sometimes called single crystals, are formed. These crystals have low-index lateral growth surfaces and the overall shape may be nonplanar to facilitate regular folding on the basal surfaces. An example is provided in Figure 3.1 for polyethylene; the ridges or pleats were formed when the hollow pyramidal crystals collapsed during sedimentation onto the substrate [2]. Note also *spiral growth* on the largest crystal; this structure is commonly observed after crystallization from either solutions or melts, and is frequently invoked as an important mechanism by which new lamellar crystals are formed.

Lowering the temperature of the solution increases the undercooling ΔT and the rate of crystal growth. When the growth rate is elevated to the point where diffusion affects the crystal shape, *dendrites* having regular branches appear as in Figure 3.2 [3]. It is clear that the growth arms are oriented along either the *b*-axis (primary arms) or the *a*-axis (secondary arms); in a dendrite the branching is crystallographic, the structure being a single crystal in which all parts conform to a lattice with a common orientation. Keeping T_c constant, more concentrated solutions give rise to complex aggregates of multiple lamellar crystals such as *axialites* that are described later. The particular solvent can have a pronounced effect on morphology.

Solvent-free liquids (melts) give rise to similar structures and aggregates for polymer crystals, although they are more difficult to study than their solution-crystallized counterparts because separation from

---

Handbook of Polymer Crystallization, First Edition. Edited by Ewa Piorkowska and Gregory C. Rutledge.
© 2013 John Wiley & Sons, Inc. Published 2013 by John Wiley & Sons, Inc.

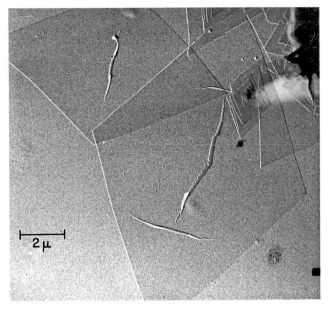

Figure 3.1 Monolayer crystals of polyethylene grown from 0.1% tetrachloroethylene solution by free cooling from about 120°C. The pleats were formed when the hollow pyramid shape crystals collapsed. A small spiral growth is evident on the largest crystal. Transmission electron micrograph from Reneker and Geil [2] with permission from the American Institute of Physics.

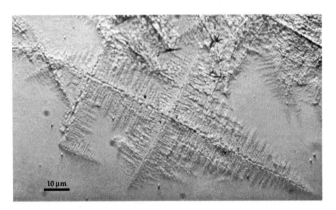

Figure 3.2 Polyethylene dendrite formed on cooling a 0.1% xylene solution. The large primary growth arms are along the crystallographic *a* direction (10 o'clock) and *b* direction (1 o'clock). Secondary growth arms are along *b* and *a*, respectively. There is faint evidence of tertiary arms growing from the secondary arms. Optical micrograph from Geil and Reneker [3] with permission from John Wiley & Sons, Inc.

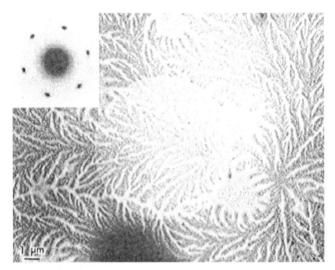

Figure 3.3 Fractal seaweed aggregate from an ultrathin molten film of poly(trifluoroethylene) crystallized at 140°C. The insert is an electron diffraction pattern demonstrating that the selected area of ca. 10 μm diameter is a single crystal. From Lovinger and Cais [4] with permission from the American Chemical Society.

neighboring crystals and/or amorphous regions is challenging. In films with thickness $d < 100$ nm or so, the lamellar crystals are formed most often with their large basal surfaces parallel to the substrate, simplifying the observation of morphologies. Systematically reducing melt thickness d at constant T_c results first in stacked lamellae with faceted growth fronts (*hedrites*), then less facetted single lamellae (perhaps with spiral overgrowths), and finally branched or dendrite-like structures with different degrees of regularity. Figure 3.3 presents the first example of what is now termed *seaweed* structure grown from a very thin film of poly(trifluoroethylene) [4]. While the curved branches appear to lack crystallographic registration with one other, the electron diffraction (ED) pattern demonstrates unambiguously that the seaweed structure is a single crystal, just as is the structurally more regular dendrite in Figure 3.2.

Growth from ultrathin films described above leads to two-dimensional structures because the lamellar thickness of ca. 10 nm is comparable to that of the melt thickness d. This geometric constraint is removed for thicker films or "bulk" melts in which structures may develop in three dimensions. For instance, growth arms such as those in Figure 3.3 may twist or branch to advance out of the plane of the image. Very slow crystallization from the bulk melt at small undercooling $\Delta T = T_m - T_c$ (the difference between melting and crystallization temperatures) generally leads to single crystals, perhaps with growth spirals. These structures are separated from one another not because of dilution, as with solutions, but because the primary nucleation density is small. Reducing the melt crystallization temperature somewhat leads to more primary nucleation sites and to faster growth. Here one observes hedritic stacks of lamellae of a height approaching the film

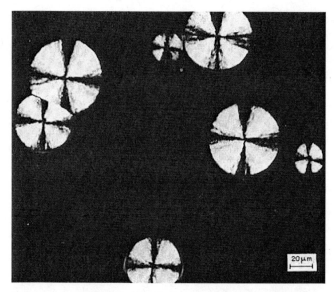

Figure 3.4 Polarized optical micrograph of growing spherulites of nylon 6.6 in a ca. 5-μm-thick film. The dark arms of the Maltese cross pattern are in the directions of the polarizer and analyzer, while the nonbirefringent melt is uniformly dark. From Khoury and Passalgia [5] with kind permission from Springer Science+Business Media B.V.

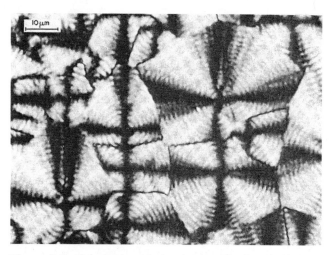

Figure 3.5 Polarized optical micrograph of polyethylene spherulites that have grown to impingement. The ringed appearance or banding is the subject of discussion in Section 3.4.4. From Khoury and Passalgia [5] with kind permission from Springer Science+Business Media B.V.

thickness of, for example, 10 μm. At still larger undercoolings the most common melt-crystallized aggregate is the spherulite, shown for example, in Figure 2.1. Given that a spherulite radius R is generally about 5 μm or greater, it is apparent that structure will be altered when the thickness of the molten film is less than this. In fact, most "spherulites" are intentionally grown from films with thickness $d < R$ in order to facilitate optical microscopic imaging of a single structure. Such disc-like aggregates of thickness $d \approx 1$ μm–10 μm are thought to represent accurately diametrical sections of fully three-dimensional spherulites. As already mentioned, the morphology is genuinely modified when film thickness d is reduced to the range of ca. 100 nm or less. Two examples of spherulites examined by the common method of polarized optical microscopy are presented above. Figure 3.4 captures incomplete spherulite growth in a $d \approx 5$ μm film of nylon 6.10 [5]. The characteristic Maltese cross results from the pattern of optical polarizability that is described in Sections 1.1.2.1 and 5.3.1, and is discussed in Section 3.4.1 of this chapter. The polyethylene spherulites in Figure 3.5 have grown to full impingement and further display concentric light–dark rings that derive from a coherent, periodic twisting of the ribbon-like crystals that constitute the structure [5]. *Banded spherulites* in polyethylene and other polymers is a topic of ongoing interest that is addressed in Section 3.4.4.

This chapter addresses the various polycrystalline structures formed by crystallizing polymers from solutions and from melts as outlined earlier. The goal is to focus on the principles that govern polycrystalline morphology, rather than to catalogue observations for a myriad of polymers and conditions. Mechanisms by which plate-like crystals can be distorted are of interest for the creation of more complex structures. Considerable attention is given to *giant screw dislocations* that are characteristic of spiral growth and, more importantly, are associated with the generation of new lamellae during the crystallization process. Without apology there is an emphasis on polyethylene, by far the most studied crystalline polymer, even though some aspects of its morphology are rather specialized. Spherulites receive major discussion, in part because they are so common and in part because certain aspects (e.g., lamellar twisting) remain unresolved. We attempt to give adequate presentations of alternate explanations where consensus is lacking. It is acknowledged that the level of discussion is occasionally advanced and perhaps challenging to those with limited background in the subject matter. Readers are encouraged to skip those parts that seem too detailed.

3.2 CRYSTALS GROWN FROM SOLUTION

3.2.1 Facetted Monolayer Crystals from Dilute Solution

Well-defined lamellar crystals are formed when the solution is appropriately dilute in polymer (typically

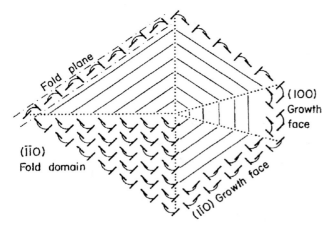

Figure 3.6 Sketch of top views of lozenge-shaped (left, as in Fig. 3.1) and truncated lozenge-shaped (right, as in Fig. 3.16) crystals of polyethylene. The crystallographic **a**-axis it to the right and **b**-axis is vertical up. Adjacent reentry folding is assumed along each growth face. Solid lines represent successive fold planes, while dotted lines indicate sector boundaries that separate distinct fold domains. From Wunderlich [6] with kind permission from the author.

less than 0.1 wt%) and the crystallization temperature T_c is close enough to T_d to insure slow growth. As covered in Reference [1] and in Section 5.4.1, the small thickness dimension of the crystal, $l_c \approx 10\text{–}20$ nm, is established by kinetic barriers and accommodated by folding the polymer chains normal to the large basal surfaces. Plate-like monolayer crystals grow by accretion of chains at the lateral surfaces. A unique feature of lamellar polymer crystals is sectorization that is imparted by chain folding. Because folding is preferentially in the direction parallel to a growth face, the symmetry-related sectors are characterized by different fold directions as illustrated in Figure 3.6 for the case of polyethylene [6]. The left side of Figure 3.6 applies to the lozenge-shaped crystals in Figure 3.1. It should be emphasized that the crystal structure (unit cell orientation) is uniform throughout the object, and only the basal surfaces manifest the distinctions associated with sectors.

The lateral shape of a faceted polymer crystal is governed by two related factors: the symmetry of the crystal structure and the slowest growing planes, the latter having low Miller indices and large interplanar spacings nearly commensurate with the distance between nearest neighbor chains. Again the polyethylene crystals in Figure 3.1 provide an illustrative example, with the growth faces being {110}. Orthorhombic symmetry is manifested in the perpendicular mirror planes connecting the vertices, being normal to the **a**- and **b**-axes. A similar example is provided by poly(4-methylpentene-1) that crystallizes with a tetragonal

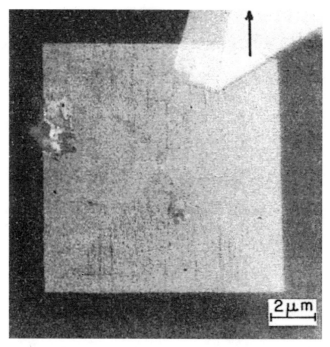

Figure 3.7 Dark-field electron micrograph of a monolayer crystal of poly(4-methylpentene-1) grown from a 0.1% solution in equivolume xylene and amyl acetate solution at 90°C. Each of the four sectors has a {100} growth face; contrast is described in the text. From Khoury and Barnes [7]; contribution of the National Institute of Standards and Technology.

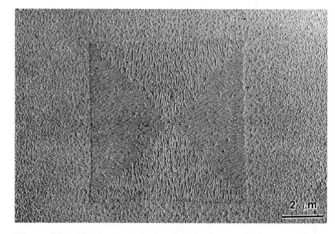

Figure 3.8 Single crystal of poly(ethylene oxide) grown from 0.01% toluene solution at 25°C. Sectors are revealed by decorating the basal surface with short polyethylene crystals as described in the text. While the crystal appears to be square, growth faces are {120} in a monoclinic system. From Chen et al. [8] with permission from John Wiley & Sons, Inc.

symmetry. The crystal shape is square with {100} growth faces as evidenced in Figure 3.7 [7]. Four sectors corresponding to distinct fold domains are revealed by the slight contrast in the dark-field electron micrograph as discussed later. Interesting variations can be observed, particularly in crystals with a lower symmetry. Figure 3.8

is an electron micrograph of a crystal of poly(ethylene oxide) that has a monoclinic symmetry (chain axes lie along c, which is rotated by $\beta = 125°$ from a) [8]. The crystal grows, however, with a square habit defined by {120} growth faces; by happenstance $2a\sin\beta = b$ in this crystal, and the square lateral shape does not convey the true lower structural symmetry. That the chains are predominantly folded in the growth planes is indicated by the direction of the polyethylene rod-like crystal decoration in each sector. Other examples of this decoration technique to reveal preferred folding directions in polyethylene, polyoxymethylene, and isotactic polypropylene crystals are given by Wittmann and Lotz [9]. Sectors in hexagonal polyoxymethylene crystals, where the shape reflects the true (trigonal) structural symmetry, are revealed by dark-field electron microscopy in Figure 3.9 [10]; the growth faces are {10$\bar{1}$0}. In fairly rare instances, polymer crystals grown from dilute solution are lath-like and do not grow with constant shape. Monoclinic α-isotactic polypropylene monolayers in Figure 3.10 grow preferentially along the a^* direction [9]. When cracked perpendicular to a^*, fibrils are pulled out to reveal that folding is within the long (010) planes, not in the narrower (100) growth faces [11]. Polyethylene decoration in Figure 3.10 supports this inference of (010) fold planes. Other examples of lath-like morphology, wherein the fold plane contains the growth direction, are provided by triclinic nylon 6.6 [12] and nylon 10.10 [13]. This brief discussion of lateral shape is closed by noting that clearly single crystalline poly(chlorotriflurouroethylene) grows from dilute solution as essentially circular monolayers with edges that appear be irregularly faceted on the size scale of 100 nm; large planar growth faces are never observed [14]. It is possible that this morphological irregularity results from the fact that the chains are atactic.

While the majority of monolayer polymer crystals grown in dilute solution are planar or nearly so, some three-dimensional aspects are worthy of mention. Sectorization that accompanies the growth of facets can lead to modest departures from planarity as follows. Bassett [15] first noticed that folding leads to subtly different interplanar spacings in different sectors. Consider

Figure 3.9 Dark-field TEM image of a polyoxymethylene crystal grown from 0.02% solution in ortho-dichlorobenzene at 140°C. See text for the origin of contrast that reveals the sectors, each with a {11$\bar{2}$0} growth face about 11 μm long. From Khoury and Barnes [10]; contribution of the National Institute of Standards and Technology.

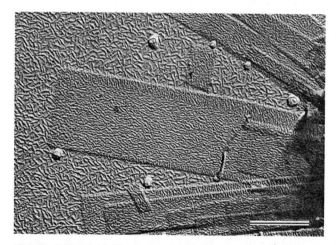

Figure 3.10 Lath-like crystals of isotactic polypropylene grown at 110°C from a 0.01% solution in α-chloronaphthalene. The crystal structure is monoclinic, with b (parallel to the short dimension of the lath) being the unique axis. The crystals have been decorated with polyethylene rods that indicate sectorization. Scale bar is 1 μm. From Wittmann and Lotz [9] with permission from John Wiley & Sons, Inc.

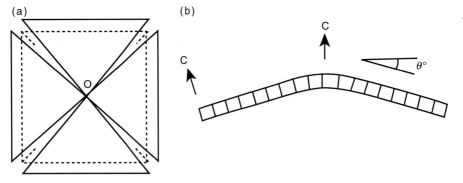

Figure 3.11 (a) Sketch illustrating distortions of a square poly(4-methlypentene-1) crystal through different spacings of {100} planes resulting from folding parallel to growth faces. The dashed line is the undistorted shape, and the solid lines are for the distorted case (exaggerated; see text) that results in mismatch at the sector boundaries. (b) Sketch of sectors that are tilted to relieve the sector boundary mismatch in (a). The chain axis direction is given by C, and the tilt angle θ is about 2° in poly(4-methylpentene-1). From Khoury and Barnes [7]; contribution of the National Institute of Standards and Technology.

for example, the vertical (100) planes in poly(4-methylpentene-1) of Figure 3.7; in the quadrants at 3 o'clock and 9 o'clock these are fold planes, parallel to the vertical growth faces. In the two orthogonal sectors at 12 o'clock and at 6 o'clock, the (100) planes are not fold planes; indeed they intersect the (010) growth planes at 90°. Bassett has ascribed the slight relative difference in interplanar spacings (a strain of ca. 10^{-3}) to folding in preferential directions. Assuming that the growth planes have the larger interplanar spacing, the ideal tetrahedral symmetry would be modified as shown in Figure 3.11a, and the mismatch at sector boundaries could be accommodated by tilting the four segments into the shallow pyramid indicated in Figure 3.11b. This shape grows in solution before collapse onto a substrate. The slant angle θ is predicted to be a few degrees at most, and the crystals readily flatten upon sedimentation with no creases, tears, and so on. The dark-field image in Figure 3.7 was created with the horizontal (200) diffraction spot from a planar (collapsed) crystal lying on the substrate. The slightly different {200} spacings from the two sets of sectors give the contrast, which is reversed if the image is formed with vertical (020) intensity. Precisely the same effect is seen in Figure 3.9 for polyoxymethylene that has been collapsed on the substrate. Again the dark-field image has been created with the horizontal (10$\bar{1}$0) diffraction spot, leading to contrast that includes radial streaks in the four nonhorizontal sectors. While it is not known with certainty how general is this modest nonplanarity resulting from small fold-induced strains, the effect should be present in almost all polymer crystals in which well-defined sectors are observed; exceptions would include, for instance, lath-like crystals as in Figure 3.10.

The extensive morphology studies on polyethylene have revealed interesting effects not reported for other polymers save one. Figure 3.12a shows that low molar mass chains (10 kDa) crystallize into the familiar lozenge shape that gives no ridges, pleats, or tears on sedimentation, suggesting essentially planar lamellae like those discussed in the preceding paragraph. Under identical conditions, high molar mass chains (120 kDa) form crystals that collapse with a pleat, suggesting a conspicuously hollow pyramid; see Figure 3.12b [16]. A thorough discussion of early work to estimate the shape of polyethylene crystals before collapse is presented in section II. 4 of Geil's classic monograph [17]; experimental techniques included optical microscopy, transmission electron microscopy (TEM), and ED. The best evidence points to the large basal fold surfaces of lozenge-shaped crystals such as those in Figure 3.1 and Figure 3.12b having been {314} before collapse [18]. More recently, a very compliant substrate and atomic force microscopy (AFM) were employed to examine the three-dimensional shapes of polyethylene (molar mass 32 kDa) crystals grown from dilute xylene solution. Figure 3.13 presents the hollow pyramid and the related chair shapes in stunning perspective [19]; Miller indices of the fold surfaces are {314} from the ca. 15° tilt angles of the sectors. In this case there is no doubt that staggering of fold planes accompanies sectorization in order to increase the volume available for presumably regular folds. It should be remembered that substantially tilted sectors are not observed in lozenge-shaped crystals composed of low

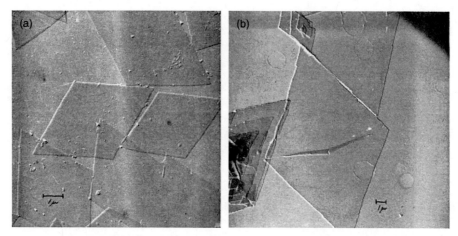

Figure 3.12 (a) TEM of monolayer crystals of polyethylene, M = 10 kDa, grown at 80°C from 0.01% xylene solution. There are no pleats or creases that indicate a nonplanar shape. (b) Exactly as in (a), except that the polyethylene has M = 120 kDa. The pleat along the **b**-axis (small diagonal) indicates that the crystal was a hollow pyramid in solution. Note also the spiral growths. From Holland and Lindenmeyer [16] with permission from John Wiley & Sons, Inc.

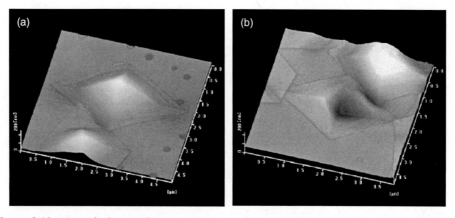

Figure 3.13 Atomic force microscopy images of M = 32 kDa polyethylene crystals grown from 0.01% solution in xylene at 83°C and sedimented onto a compliant substrate made of 7% poly(vinyl alcohol) dissolved in water. Both (a) hollow pyramid and (b) chair crystals retain their shapes. From Toda et al. [19] with permission from Elsevier.

molar mass polyethylene chains (Fig. 3.12a); fold surface crowding effects that result in pronounced chain tilt occur only with long chains. Whether this is caused by more chain ends (fewer folds) with low molar mass, or from bulkier folds with high molar mass is not yet decided. Similar tilting is operative for lozenge-shaped poly(vinylidene fluoride) crystals grown from poly(ethyl acrylate) solution, provided again that the solute molar mass is large enough. In this instance a chain tilt angle of ca. 26° with respect to the (collapsed) basal surface was confirmed by ED [20]. It is interesting to note that the same microscopy-diffraction experiments with the same solvent and temperature show no chain tilt when the poly(vinylidene fluoride) has a lower molar mass of 29 kDa [21]. Beyond these two examples there are few, if any, instances of sectored basal surfaces being tilted with respect to the chain axis better to accommodate folding. Recall that sectorization from folding-driven microstrains (not from tilt as with polyethylene and poly(vinylidene fluoride)) is relatively common.

A different sort of three-dimensional structure may arise from chain folding, however. Should the folds on one side of a monolayer crystal be bulkier than those on the other side, the resultant strain can cause the lamella to curve to the point where it is best described as a scroll. Nylon 6.6 crystallized under conditions that give amine folds on one basal surface and acid folds on the other surface is shown in Figure 3.14 [22]. The

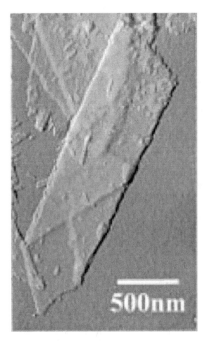

Figure 3.14 AFM image of a collapsed scroll crystal of nylon 6.6 grown from ca. 0.05% solution in glycerine at 172°C. See text for description. From Cai et al. [22] with permission from John Wiley & Sons, Inc.

Figure 3.15 TEM image of polyethylene crystallized from xylene at 90°C. There are six growth faces as sketched in Figure 3.6, right. Still higher T_c leads to even more prominent {100} growth faces. Creases along **b** are from collapse of the hollow pyramid-like crystal on sedimentation. From Bassett and Keller [24] with permission of Taylor & Francis Group, http://www.informaworld.com.

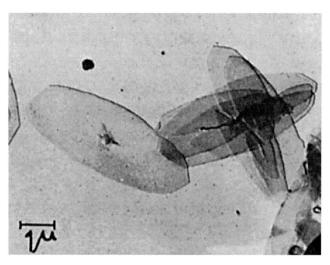

Figure 3.16 Polyethylene crystals grown from tetradecanol at $T_c = 118$°C. The short axis of the crystal is the **a**-axis, and the prominent {100} growth faces are curved. From Organ and Keller [26] with permission of John Wiley & Sons, Inc.

unscrolled crystal has a width of ca. 550 nm and length of ca. 1500 nm; it has rolled about the long axis into of diameter 350 nm in solution and collapsed on sedimentation. While the crystal structure is presumably triclinic, the growth faces were not indexed. The collapsed structure in Figure 3.14 has portions that are one, two, and three lamellar layers thick. A few other instances of scrolled crystals are reviewed by Lotz and Cheng [23].

The shape of polyethylene monolayer crystals is clearly influenced by the crystallization temperature and to a lesser extent by molar mass and concentration. The lozenges in Figure 3.1 and Figure 3.12 have an aspect ratio $AR = l_b/l_a = b/a = 0.66$, which is invariant with size. When the crystallization temperature T_c is raised beyond a certain value (that is greater for lower polymer concentration) the lozenge shape is replaced by a six-sided crystal having both {110} and {100} growth faces. An example is shown in Figure 3.15 for crystallization at 90°C [24]; see Figure 3.6 for the orientation of unit cell axes and fold planes. Folds and pleats in the collapsed crystal indicate a three-dimensional structure that was confirmed by optical micrographs of suspended crystals [17]. The fold surfaces are again {314} for the four {110} sectors, and {201} for the two smaller {100} sectors. The aspect ratio $AR = l_b/l_a$ is increased at higher T_c when the {100} faces become more prominent. Higher temperature slows the overall growth rate, but it decreases {100} growth more than {110} growth, leading to the truncated lozenge shape in Figure 3.15. Passaglia and Khoury analyzed thoroughly the temperature dependence of AR in terms of secondary nucleation theory and the temperature dependence of $\sigma\sigma_e$ (σ is the surface energy for a lateral surface; σ_e is that for a basal surface) for the {100} and {110} growth faces [25]. At still higher temperatures, achieved with poor solvents, the aspect ratio AR continues to increase, but growth faces become noticeably curved and sectorization is less pronounced as seen in Figure 3.16 [26]. The crystals are flat (no pleats or creases on sedimentation) and all chains in the crystal are inclined in the *same* direction about **b** by ca. 35° to the (201) fold surface [27]. Both pronounced **b**-axis growth and a single direction of chain tilt are characteristic of polyethylene melt crystallization as will be described later. Similar changes in shape from lozenge to truncated lozenge have been reported for alkyl polyesters that have crystal structures similar to that of polyethylene [28].

3.2.2 Dendritic Crystals from Dilute Solution

Lowering the crystallization temperature has the predictable effects of increasing the lateral growth rate G and decreasing crystal thickness l_c (see Reference [1]). In some instances (e.g., polyethylene in Section 3.2.1) the lateral habit may change with T_c as well. A far more general effect is the formation of serrated growth fronts below a certain T_c, with the size scale of these serrations or growth arms becoming smaller at lower temperatures. The resulting structure with many growth arms as in Figure 3.2 loosely resembles a tree, hence the term *dendrite*. Systematically lowering T_c reveals the origin of such structures. The polyoxymethylene crystal in Figure 3.17 was grown at 120°C [10], as opposed to $T_c = 140°C$ for the smoothly faceted crystal in Figure 3.9; all other experimental conditions were unchanged.

Notice that the apparent growth faces are no longer straight, but each has a noticeable depression in the center that creates a shallow reentrant corner. Figure 3.18 illustrates that the actual growth faces are still $\{10\bar{1}0\}$, but they are short and discontinuous with steps too small to be observed in the electron micrograph [2]. This change in lateral shape is a consequence of diffusion affecting the growth process as described here.

Return for a moment to the regularly faceted crystal in Figure 3.9 grown more slowly at 140°C; the lateral growth rate G is constant at the value established by undercooling $\Delta T = T_d - T_c$ (see Section 5.4.1 and Reference [16]). Solvent must be expelled from the region that is converted to crystal and polymer must diffuse toward the advancing interface. We consider first the low ΔT condition where G is small and diffusion is fast enough not to influence the crystal growth process. Matching the rate at which solvent is removed by diffusion to that excluded by crystal advance, the steady-state concentration profile of solvent (or "impurity") in front of the advancing interface is given by [29]

$$s(n) = (s_e - s_\infty)\exp[-n/(D/G)] + s_\infty. \quad (3.1)$$

Here s is the solvent concentration and n the (normal) distance from the advancing interface. The far field (bulk) solvent concentration is s_∞, and for convenience the concentration of solvent at the crystal–solution interface is assigned the equilibrium value s_e; these can be described equivalently in terms of the polymer concentrations if desired. The interdiffusion coefficient

Figure 3.17 Transmission electron micrograph of a polyoxymethylene crystal grown from 0.02% solution in ortho-dichlorobenzene at 120°C; compare with Figure 3.9. Limited diffusion to and from the growth faces has resulted in more rapid crystallization near the leading corners, which are 12 μm apart. From Khoury and Barnes [10]; contribution of the National Institute of Standards and Technology.

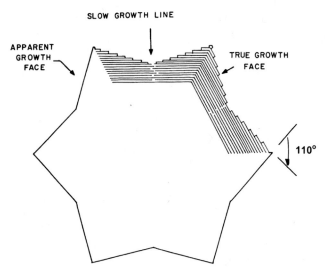

Figure 3.18 Sketch of star-shaped polyoxymethylene crystal in Figure 3.17. From Reneker and Geil [2] with permission from the American Institute of Physics.

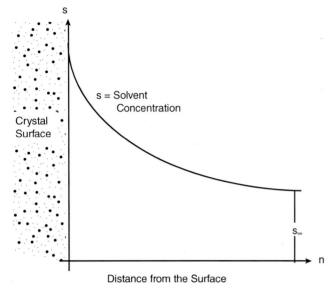

Figure 3.19 Schematic representation of solvent (impurity) concentration in front of the advancing interface as expressed by Equation (3.1). From Wunderlich [6] with kind permission from the author.

D is assumed to be independent of concentration (s), and the quotient $D/G = \delta$ is the diffusion length that indicates the distance over which the concentrations of solvent and polymer return to their far field values. The exponential profile $s(n)$ in Equation (3.1) is illustrated in Figure 3.19 [6]. Slow crystal growth at small undercooling leads to a large value of $\delta = D/G$; the concentration profile has a modest gradient, down which the diffusive flux of solvent away from the interface region is small. When T_c is lowered, G will increase (undercooling) and D will decrease (mobility), both changes leading to a smaller δ and a steeper steady-state profile $s(n)$ needed to remove solvent from the more rapidly advancing interface. At this point it should be recognized that the actual solvent concentration at the advancing interface s_i is less than the equilibrium value s_e because the growth rate would be zero if the free energies of the crystal and solution were equal [30]. When T_c is lowered the more rapid crystal growth raises s_i toward s_e, generating two effects. The larger solvent concentration at the interface leads to a steeper gradient ds/dn and hence faster diffusive transport. The same larger solvent concentration corresponds to a *lower* polymer concentration at the interface, reducing G. In this manner the mass transport rates by diffusion and crystallization remain equal to one another at the lower crystallization temperature. Be reminded that the growth rate G and the concentration profile ds/dn are independent of time in this part of the discussion.

The situation just described pertains to all crystals shown in Section 3.2.1 with well-developed, straight facets whose intersections have created leading corners or vertices. One measure of crystal size is the distance L between leading corners, which increases linearly with time. The star-shaped crystal in Figure 3.18 results when diffusion first exerts control over certain aspects of crystal growth. Diffusive transport to and from the leading corners or vertices of a growing crystal is more facile because the diffusion field is nearly three-dimensional near the tips [30]. Additionally, less solvent is expelled when advancing a vertex because less crystal volume is involved for an advance by a unit length [6]. For these reasons the concentration profiles at leading corners are steeper than that given by Equation (3.1), causing a slightly enhanced local G that is represented by additional nucleated layers near the tips in Figure 3.18. This geometrical enhancement of diffusion and growth rate decays away from the leading corners, and the local G approaches that for a planar interface. Systematically decreasing the local growth rate in this manner converts an originally straight facet into a shallow "V" with the reentrant corner midway between the leading corners. For the same reason that diffusion is enhanced at a leading corner it is retarded at a reentrant corner and the star shape in Figure 3.17 becomes more conspicuous during growth. Additionally, the decrease of the angle of the protruding corners, for example, from 120° to 110° in Figure 3.18, is evidence that diffusion influences the morphology through non-uniformity of the growth rate along the interface. Wunderlich et al. used this sharpening of the leading corners of lozenge-shaped polyethylene crystals grown from solution to define the temperature for the onset of diffusion effects on crystal growth [31]. Dimensional arguments show that this diffusion control of morphology occurs when the crystal size indicated by L approaches the diffusion length δ; small crystals with $L < \delta$ grow with straight facets.

It is important to emphasize that the isothermal growth rate G for a faceted crystal of fixed shape is constant. The subtle geometry changes described earlier for leading and reentrant corners do result in small time dependences of G that are usually ignored. One should recall that two sizes are pertinent to crystal growth, the crystal size, as indicated by, for example, L, and the diffusion length $\delta = D/G$. For slow (nucleation controlled) growth at small undercoolings, $L \ll \delta$ and diffusion serves only the secondary function of removing solvent at the required rate. When the crystal size and diffusion length are comparable ($L \sim \delta$), tip sharpening and reentrant corners appear, as described earlier, as the consequences of subtle diffusion effects on local growth rates. This condition may be brought about by lowering T_c (decreasing δ) or by waiting long enough at any T_c for L to grow to the size of δ. Further increase of L or reduction of δ leads to the condition where diffusion is locally one dimensional, normal to the interface, everywhere of interest. Stated somewhat differently, $L \gg \delta$ and vertices with enhanced mass transport are no longer significant. Rejected solvent accumulates ahead of the growth face, reducing the gradient ds/dn and the rates of both solvent (impurity) removal and interface advance. This is classical diffusion-controlled growth or parabolic growth in which both crystal size L and diffusion length δ increase with time $t^{1/2}$ [32]. The concentration profile remains exponential as in Equation (3.1), but the growth rate G is now proportional to $t^{-1/2}$. The growth of polymer crystals or aggregates discussed in this chapter is almost always with a constant linear growth rate G. When the *shape* of the growing crystal is affected by diffusion, we will use the term *diffusion-controlled morphology*, which should not be confused with diffusion-controlled growth.

Returning to polyoxymethylene solutions, the still faster growth achieved by lowering T_c from 120°C to 114°C creates the more complex structure in Figure 3.20. Given that δ is smaller at lower T_c, we expect tip sharpening and reentrant corners to be observed for crystals of smaller L. More apparent is that each ca. 8 μm-long growth face of the star is decorated by serrations with a spacing of slightly less than 1 μm. Additional features, which are of secondary interest here, are pleats indicating nonplanarity in solution before collapse, and spiral growths that are located preferentially near reentrant corners midway between the leading corners. The serrations are observed under conditions of fast growth and small $\delta = D/G$ where the concentration gradient ahead of the interface is steep. Any smooth interface is unstable to outward directed growth fluctuations as illustrated in Figure 3.21. It is easy to see that such a protrusion forces the concentration profile near the tip to become steeper, leading to faster diffusion and faster tip growth that render the planar interface inherently unstable. One might suppose that a sharper (smaller wavelength) distortion would create steeper gradients and hence grow faster than less sharp (longer wavelength) fluctuations. While correct in principle, this transition to what would be unstable growth is opposed

Figure 3.20 Transmission electron micrograph of a polyoxymethylene crystal grown from 0.02% solution in ortho-dichlorobenzene at 114°C. Faster growth has further sharpened the leading corners; also seen are serrations that are the beginnings of secondary growth arms. The reentrant corners midway between the leading corners have also sharpened, and spiral growths are located near these features. Dark pleats indicate that the crystal had curvature before collapse. From Khoury and Barnes [10]; contribution of the National Institute of Standards and Technology.

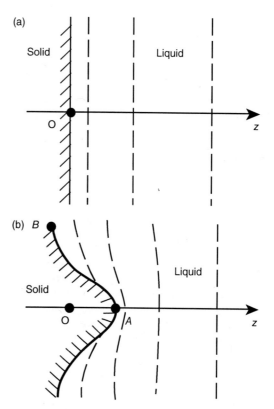

Figure 3.21 Sketch illustrating the instability of a planar interface (a) during growth. Dashed lines represent contours of constant solvent concentration. The outwardly directed part of the fluctuation in part (b) has increased the gradient in the z direction, leading to faster growth at point A than at point B. Inclusion of interfacial energy further modifies the gradient as discussed in the text. From Langer [34] with kind permission from the author and the American Physical Society.

by the lateral surface energy σ between the crystal and the solution. Surface energy increases the free energy of the solid phase where the surface to volume ratio is large, a manifestation of the Gibbs–Thomson effect (see Section 5.4.1.5). In the tip region the curvature of the crystal is large and positive, which decreases both T_m and the equilibrium solvent concentration s_e at the interface in that region. Turning to point B, where the curvature is smaller or negative, the local s_e is greater than that at the tip A. Hence, there is solvent transport parallel to the interface from B to A, reducing the magnitude of the gradient normal to the tip and slowing the tip growth rate G. Not surprisingly, this surface energy effect is most important for sharp distortions with large curvatures. While a planar interface is thus inherently unstable to a fluctuation with a large wavelength, such a distortion grows very slowly because the local gradient is not much changed. Sharper protrusions grow faster until the wavelength is so small that surface energy reduces the effective undercooling toward zero. The Mullins–Sekerka stability analysis of these competing effects shows that the maximum tip growth rate G occurs for interface fluctuations separated by a distance slightly greater than [33, 34]

$$\lambda_D \approx 2\pi(d_o\delta)^{1/2}. \quad (3.2)$$

The relation between interface curvature and local s_e is captured by what is termed the capillary length:

$$d_o = \frac{\sigma V s_e}{(s_e - s_c)k_B T} \quad (3.3)$$

where V is the atomic volume, s_c is the equilibrium concentration of solvent/impurity in the bulk of the crystal, and k_B is Boltzmann's constant. Letting $s_c = 0$, $\sigma = 10$ mJ/m², $V = 1$ nm³ and $T = 350$ K, typical of polyethylene solutions in xylene, and so on, one concludes that $d_o \approx 2$ nm, a molecular scale dimension that is rather insensitive to temperature. Note that Equation (3.2) predicts that growth arm spacing λ_D will be much smaller than the diffusion length δ and that it will scale as $\delta^{1/2}$. Reducing the crystallization temperature decreases $\delta = D/G$; protrusions that become growth arms are more closely spaced at smaller T_c.

The preceding paragraph outlines the reason for the shift from faceted growth (Fig. 3.1) to needle-like growth (Fig. 3.2) as either ΔT (greater G) or molar mass (lower D) are increased. The reader will recognize that vertices or leading corners of faceted crystals constitute pre-existing sites where stable accelerated growth of slender features will occur. Another aspect of dendritic crystallization is the shape of the nonplanar growth front. Considering growth in the absence of surface energy (Gibbs–Thomson) effects, it can be shown that a three-dimensional interface adopts a paraboloidal shape that advances with a constant velocity $G \sim 1/\rho$, where ρ is the radius of curvature [30, 34]. While the interface is nonplanar, its shape is invariant with time as are the stationary concentration profiles that lead to a constant one-dimensional growth rate G for the tip. The important result here is that needle-like crystals grow with a constant tip shape at a constant rate; a large G is accommodated by a more slender needle (smaller ρ) to and from which diffusive transport is more rapid. Inclusion of a surface energy σ appears not to perturb the paraboloid shape significantly, but it establishes one tip radius ρ^* at which G is a maximum; very small ρ grow more slowly because of the Gibbs–Thomson effect. Current theory does not establish which of the manifold of constant growth rates $G(\rho)$ is observed [30, 34].

What distinguishes a dendritic crystal from a needle crystal is branching. A growing dendrite is not a smooth rod with a paraboloidal surface near its extremity, but it has protrusions of spacing $\sim \rho$ that develop a few ρ behind the head of the tip. This "bumpy" tip advances with constant shape at constant G, and the protrusions develop into branches (secondary growth arms) as the tip grows away from them. The underlying reason for protrusions from the lateral tip surface is undoubtedly a dynamic instability like that for a planar growth front, but the formal requirements of the theory in three dimensions are challenging. Progress is easier in two dimensions, where an anisotropic surface energy is shown to give rise to crystallographically oriented, regularly spaced protrusions some distance back from the primary tip, whose overall paraboloidal shape is essentially preserved [35]. Phase-field modeling also captures the nature of such a classical (two-dimensional) dendrite as illustrated in Figure 3.22a [36]. The primary growth arms (diagonal) resemble those along the *a* and *b* directions in the polyethylene dendrite in Figure 3.2. Secondary growth arms, in these cases orthogonal to the primary ones, are conspicuous in both polyethylene and the calculated dendrites. Tip morphologies differ, however. Rather than a paraboloid, the terminal regions of growth arms in a real polymer dendrite are tapering lamellae that are clearly faceted as shown in Figure 3.23 [3]. The two growth faces terminating the primary arm along *b* define an angle of 90°, which is noticeably smaller than 112° between (110) and ($1\bar{1}0$), as in the lozenge crystals of Figure 3.1 and Figure 3.13; this sharpening is like that discussed earlier for polyoxymethylene. Serrations behind the tip are secondary growth arms directed along *a* that are faceted as well. Here the 45° angle defined by the growth faces is less than the 67° expected for (110) and ($\bar{1}10$) fold surfaces. Immature tertiary growth arms are abundant on the second-

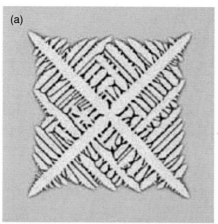 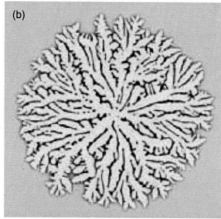

Figure 3.22 Two-dimensional structures calculated by phase-field modeling for crystallization in the presence of impurities. (a) The classic dendrite results from fourfold anisotropy of the crystallization kinetics that assures orthogonal growth of secondary and tertiary arms in this case. The growth tips are parabolic. (b) The dense branched morphology (DBM) is formed when growth rate anisotropy is reduced by 70%. From Granasy et al. [36] with permission from Macmillan Publishers Ltd. (See color insert.)

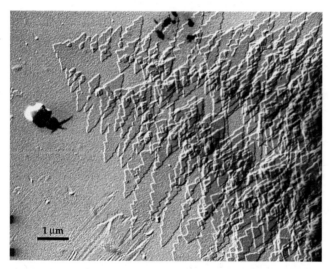

Figure 3.23 Transmission electron micrograph of the tip region of a primary growth arm along **b** for a polyethylene dendrite similar to that in Figure 3.2. Note the faceting at the end of the primary growth arm and at the end of the more mature secondary arms growing along **a**. Also apparent are two rows of dense growth spirals that have formed at reentrant corners between secondary arms. From Geil and Renker [3] with permission from John Wiley & Sons, Inc.

ary arms. One knows that chain folding leads to plate-like crystals that differ in tip shape from the three-dimensional paraboloids in classic dendrites. It is not known if the restriction of this smallest tip dimension is related to the presence of facetted tips in polymer dendrites grown from solution. Note furthermore that growth spirals occur near the reentrant corners between serrations, an effect that is discussed in the following section.

To summarize, diffusion controlled morphology results from the presence of a concentration field characterized by the diffusion length $\delta = D/G$ ahead of the interface. Any faceted crystal has leading corners separated by a distance L, which increases as the crystal grows. The first effect of diffusion is to sharpen these leading corners and to create a reentrant corner for crystals having L of order δ; the shape of small crystals is not affected until L approaches δ. A different diffusion effect, observed when $L \gg \delta$, results from the instability of any planar growth face to outwardly directed fluctuations of the interface. Consideration of both the diffusion field (δ) and lateral surface energy (σ expressed as d_o) establishes the separation or width of the fastest growing instabilities to be $\lambda_D \sim (d_o \delta)^{1/2}$. Steady-state growth rate G of such needle-like crystals is possible with tip shapes that are paraboloidal. But this tip surface itself is subject to instabilities that generate protrusions behind the growing extremity and develop into secondary growth arms of dendrites. A special feature of polymer dendrites is that primary and secondary growth arm tips are faceted, not paraboloidal. Dendritic growth of polymer crystals is revisited for melt crystallization in Section 3.3.

3.2.3 Growth Spirals in Dilute Solution

It is universally agreed that chain folded lamellae only very rarely, if ever, trigger conventional secondary nucleation and growth of additional layers on the basal

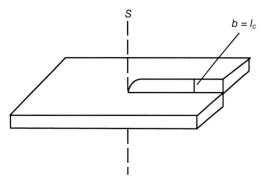

Figure 3.24 Giant screw dislocation characterized by Burgers vector of length b equal to the crystal thickness l_c. The dislocation is a linear defect parallel to S that marks the boundary between slipped and unslipped portions of the crystal. Two steps of height l_c are formed that are the loci for further crystallization. In this example the dislocation is left handed (advancing with counterclockwise rotation).

fold surfaces. Instead, polymer lamellae grown in dilute solution commonly create new lateral layers by a spiral growth mechanism as mentioned in connection with the dendrites in Figure 3.20 and Figure 3.23. Structures of this sort were originally proposed to account for rapid growth of atomic crystals; the basis for spiral growth is the screw dislocation that presents two steps, one on each side of the crystal, to which atoms or molecules may add without creating new surface nuclei [37]. A sketch of what is termed a *giant screw dislocation* in a lamellar crystal, wherein the magnitude of the Burgers vector **b** is equal to the crystal thickness l_c, is presented in Figure 3.24. Chain molecules can add to the exposed steps, just as they would add to the lateral surfaces of an undislocated lamellar crystal, and spiraling ramps grow up and down from the dislocated parent layer as illustrated in Figure 3.25 The advancing steps adopt a spiral geometry because a constant growth velocity normal to the local surface causes the inner part of the step to lead the outer part. Once a steady-state spiral shape has been achieved, growth is propagated by adding molecules to all vertical steps. When all steps have advanced by the terrace width y_0 the spiral has rotated by 2π radians and grown in height by one lamellar thickness l_c; this process can be repeated *ad infinitum*. From the classic analysis of Burton et al., the terrace width y_0 is given by $y_0 \approx 2\pi x_{cr}$ [38]. Here $x_{cr} \sim \sigma/\Delta T$ is the width of the critical two-dimensional nucleus (the smallest surface structure that can exist at T_c) that establishes the shape of the steady-state spiral. At low crystallization temperatures preferred growth directions lead to polygonized spirals that reflect crystal symmetry as in Figure 3.25. When $W/k_B T$ is less than 2 (W is the energy of attachment of a unit, in our case, a stem)

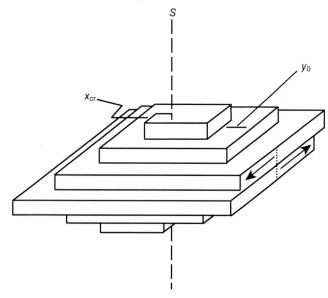

Figure 3.25 Polygonal spiral growth from the giant screw dislocation in Figure 3.24. Arrows on the side surface indicate the initial advance directions of the two steps. Each layer of the spiral has a thickness $b = l_c$. Other dimensions are the terrace width y_0 and the size of the smallest surface nucleus x_{cr}.

the advance rate of a step becomes essentially isotropic and the resulting spiral is circular [39].

Barnes and Price appear to be the only ones to investigate quantitatively the nature of spiral growth in polymer crystals [40]. They observed polygonized terraces with width $y_0 \sim 1/\Delta T$ for polyethylene, polyoxymethylene, and poly(ethylene oxide) crystals grown in dilute solution, but the implied x_{cr} were too large by factors of 3–10. It was proposed that the dimension defining the spiral is not x_c but the dislocation core diameter, which is on the order of $b = l_c$, which also scales with $1/\Delta T$. No better alternative has been put forth for more than 40 years. They also noted that in polyoxymethylene the hexagonal terrace width is much smaller near the center (newest layers) and that each layer is rotated slightly with respect to its neighbors, as is evident in Figure 3.26. The systematic variation in y_0 between layers is consistent with the theory for spiral growth [38], while the relative rotation of layers appears unique to polymer crystals. The left and center features in Figure 3.26 are left-handed and right-handed growth spirals, respectively, with centers (dislocations) spaced about 5 μm apart. If the two sets of oppositely rotating spirals have terraces at the same height (which is the case if grown from a common substrate), they can merge to form nonspiraling terraces. Note that the two lowest (largest) pairs of terraces have combined to form paral-

Figure 3.26 Two spiral growths (left and center) and one terrace growth (right) on a crystal of polyoxymethylene grown from 0.05% xylene solution near room temperature. The three structures have joined to form parallel layers as described in the text. Transmission electron micrograph of unknown magnification (likely about 5000×) from Barnes and Price [40] with permission from Elsevier.

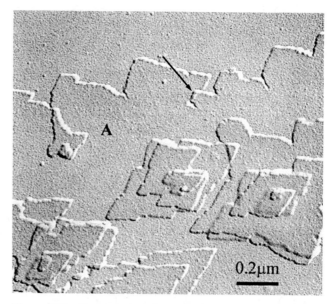

Figure 3.27 Transmission electron micrograph of the edge of a polyethylene dendrite grown at 67°C from 0.01% xylene solution. Notice the channels or slits leading inward from reentrant corners. At two of these (A and arrow) giant screw dislocations have formed. Three other rather irregular growth spirals are evident. From Keith and Chen [43] with permission from Elsevier.

lel layers, not spiraling ramps, and subsequent lateral growth would bring more spiral layers into the terrace mode. The rightmost feature in Figure 3.26 is a not a spiral but a complete *growth terrace* formed from two dislocations of opposite hand that are spaced closer than the width of the topmost layer, ca. 0.5 µm. Note that the lowest levels of this structure have joined with those of the left/right spiral pair as well. Frank predicted growth terraces as well as growth spirals in the seminal proposal for dislocation-assisted crystallization [37].

While the general appearance of growth spirals and growth terraces in polymer crystals is reasonably well accounted for in terms of giant screw dislocations, some clarifications are in order. First, the Burgers vector or dislocation strength **b** is the temperature-dependent crystal thickness l_c, not a constant interatomic distance as in atomic or ionic crystals. Axial displacements of $b \approx 10$ nm in the dislocation core are almost certainly achieved by plastic shear deformation in the chain axis direction. Axial shear strains $\varepsilon = b/r$ outside the core at a distance r from the dislocation line are more problematic. For $r < 100$ nm, the strain $\varepsilon > 0.1$ is almost certainly accommodated by coarse shear (local plastic strain $\varepsilon_p \sim 1$ in the chain direction on every tenth interchain plane, for instance). Only for relatively large $r > 300$ nm does the strain drop into the range $\varepsilon < 0.03$, where linear elasticity can be applied with confidence. The elastic strain energy W_{el} of a screw dislocation of strength b in a plate of thickness l_c and radius r_o was calculated by Eshelby and Stroh to help account for spiral growth. For the case of interest here, where the radius at which plastic deformation ceases, r_p, is larger than $l_c/2$ (the dislocation core is wider than the plate thickness), the result is [41]

$$W_{el} = \frac{\mu b^2}{4\pi} l_c \frac{2}{3}\left(\frac{l_c}{2r_p}\right)^2. \qquad (3.4)$$

Letting $b = l_c = 10$ nm, $r_p = 100$ nm, and shear modulus $\mu = 3$ GPa [42], Equation (3.4) gives $W_{el} = 4 \times 10^{-19}$ J; hence, the ratio $W_{el}/k_B T = 100$ for crystallization at 90°C (363 K). Notice that W_{el} is independent of the overall width of the plate $2r_o$. The proximity of stress-free basal surfaces reduces the magnitude of internal shear stresses and further restricts their distribution to the region near the dislocation core. (For these reasons Eq. [3.4] gives a value about 10^{-3} of the energy calculated for a slab of thickness l_c and width $2r_o$ in an effectively infinite dislocated crystal, for which the factor to the right of l_c is replaced by the familiar $\ln[r_o/r_p] \approx 5$.) At this point it is useful to turn to experimental studies of immature growth spirals such as those near the reentrant corners of polyethylene dendrites in Figure 3.23 and in the higher magnification view of similar features in Figure 3.27 [43]. Note that there are channels extending into the crystal from the reentrant corners at the top of

Figure 3.27. The arrow indicates where a screw dislocation has just been initiated by mutual displacement of the lateral surfaces on either side of a channel; the structure corresponds to Figure 3.24, where the width of the top step is 50 nm and that of the bottom step is 200 nm. As the crystal thickness $l_c = b$ is approximately 11 nm, the axial shear strains associated with the overlapped layers must be greater than 11/75 = 0.15, that is, well within the plastic deformation range. Following this reasoning, the *elastic* strain energy W_{el} of the incipient growth spiral near the arrow in Figure 3.27 is zero, because the lateral dimensions are below r_p in Equation (3.4). Subsequent crystallization leads to wider and multiple layers as seen in the structure to the left of A and in the three and four layer spirals that are further back from the dendrite edge. Lateral growth to mature layers with $r > r_p$ is accompanied by elastic strains that result in the energy W_{el} of Equation (3.4) per layer, an amount that is readily supplied by the much larger free energy of crystallization [44]. Geil [17] and others have observed that neighboring growth spirals often have opposite hands as in Figure 3.26. This pairing could indeed occur to reduce elastic strain energy, provided the size of the spirals was large enough. But elastic strain energy is absent from the energy of *formation* of a small growth spiral with dimensions $r_o < r_p \approx 100$ nm.

There is another component of the energy of an incipient spiral, that associated with the two lateral surfaces of height $b = l_c$ and width r_o. Should these surfaces be created in a perfect crystal, the additional energy would be $W_{sur} = 2br_o\sigma = 10 \times 10^{-18}$ J for $b = 10$ nm, $r_o = 50$ nm, and $\sigma = 10$ mJ/m^2. Hence, $W_{sur}/k_BT = 2000$, and this surface energy penalty renders essentially zero the probability for forming by thermal fluctuations an embryonic screw dislocation as in Figure 3.26. Nevertheless, it is clear from Figure 3.20, Figure 3.23, Figure 3.27 and numerous other micrographs not shown here that spiral growths and hence giant screw dislocations are formed at or near at least 10% of the reentrant corners in polymer dendrites. Reneker and Geil proposed in 1960 that imperfect crystallization during the advance of a reentrant corner led to mechanical weakness and tearing along the "slow growth lines" illustrated in Figure 3.18 [2]. Confirmation of this idea was provided some 40 years later by the slits or channels seen trailing from the reentrant corners of polyethylene dendrites in Figure 3.27. Keith and Chen argued convincingly on morphological grounds that chain folded growth is frustrated near kinetically established reentrant corners [43]. Growth of a dendritic monolayer creates narrow regions where the stem density is low (think of strips with a high concentration of row vacancies) trailing the reentrant corners. These defect areas are clearly the source of giant screw dislocations, and they explain in a qualitative way the abundance and location of spiral growths in dendrites. Remaining to be clarified is the mechanism that shears the opposing surfaces of the slit. Suggestions include hydrodynamic forces on suspended crystals [17] and fold-induced basal surface stresses [43]. Regardless of details, it appears that defect morphology, not a nucleation barrier, controls the creation of spiral growth centers in polymer dendrites grown from solution.

When crystallizing from solution at higher temperatures where faceted, not dendritic, growth prevails, the majority of crystals have spiral overgrowths; monolayers such as those in Figure 3.1 are the exception rather than the rule. Numerous possible giant screw dislocation sources, most sharing a furrow or slit defect, have been proposed. Figure 3.28 presents some examples. The large spiral in the upper left-hand corner is centered on the **b**-axis of the substrate crystal. It is possible that mismatch at a sector boundary, in this case a (100) plane, can lead to a mechanically weakened slit-like region that becomes a giant screw dislocation. Geil posited that the small spiral at the top center came from a tear in the growth face of the pyramidal polyethylene crystal [17]. A variation on mechanical tearing has been demonstrated by Hirai in a much overlooked paper [45]. He documented that two crystals may intersect during

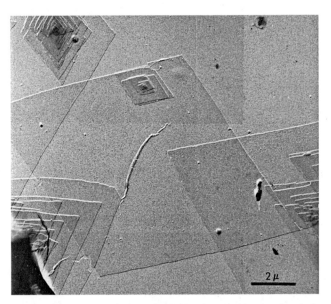

Figure 3.28 Transmission electron micrograph of polyethylene crystals grown from dilute tetrachloroethylene solution. The spiral growth in the upper part of the central crystal is believed to have originated from a tear at the growth face. The larger spiral in the top left of the figure is centered on a sector boundary. Reproduced from Geil [1] with kind permission from the author.

Figure 3.29 Two intersecting crystals of polyethylene grown at 80°C from 0.05% xylene solution. The "top" crystal has the longer *a*-axis pointing to about 10 o'clock, while the "bottom" crystal has the *b*-axis oriented at 4 o'clock. Two oppositely directed steps of thickness l_c are evident on a line near 11 o'clock. Two coincident giant screw dislocations, each left handed, have been created at common the tip of the notches. Transmission electron micrograph of unspecified magnification by Hirai [45] with permission from John Wiley & Sons, Inc.

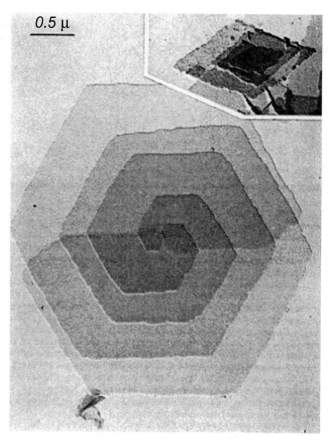

Figure 3.30 Double growth spiral formed from two coincident giant screw dislocations. Isotactic polystyrene grown at 190°C in a 10% atactic polystyrene solution. Growth faces are $\{11\bar{2}0\}$. The small lonzenge-shaped crystal in the insert, which formed in the same preparation, can be ignored. From Keith et al. [46] with permission from John Wiley & Sons, Inc.

growth to create two obvious dislocation steps upon sedimentation as in Figure 3.29. This is an example of *two* coincident (left-handed) screw dislocations for which the other two steps below the intersecting crystals are not visible. Growth from such a dislocation pair will form an up/down set of double spirals—two sets of two identical spirals that differ in rotation angle by π radians. A double spiral can be confirmed only by examining the center where features are smallest, making characterization of these structures a challenge. Figure 3.30 illustrates an unusually favorable case [46] that is discussed below. The reader is referred to reports by Gupta et al. [47] and Lotz et al. [48] of intersecting crystals in polyoxymethylene and poly(ethylene oxide-*b*-styrene), respectively. While such structures, be they caused by crystal–crystal collisions [45], collisions that are coupled with pre-existing crevices [47], or interlocking growth of orthogonal lamellae [48], may seem improbable, Geil has stated that they are in fact rather common [17].

The foregoing discussion does not address spiral growths that emanate from the center of a crystal as illustrated in Figure 3.25. In such cases it is natural to suspect that primary nucleation may be responsible. Proposed mechanisms for a heterogeneous nucleus leading to a giant screw dislocation include epitaxial growth on, or edge impingement with, the particle [49]. Keith has asserted that fortuitous intersection of two lamellae growing from a common nucleating particle led to the remarkable double spiral in Figure 3.30 [43], where the large feature sizes permit clear observation of two spirals offset by π radians at the center. The downward double spiral did not grow because of proximity to the mica substrate. A more specific explanation for such a double spiral is borrowed from poly(ethylene oxide-*b*-styrene) as illustrated in Figure 3.31. Orthogonal pairs of centrally interlocked crystals indeed exist in dilute solutions, and are ascribed to primary nucleation [48]. Rotation about the intersection line to bring the basal surfaces into contact creates two colinear giant screw dislocations and sets up a double spiral like that in Figure 3.30.

In at least one situation, the genesis of giant screw dislocations can be attributed to internal stresses associated with nonplanar crystals. Reference was made in Section 3.1 to the chair form of polyethylene crystals

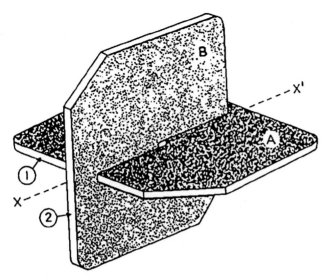

Figure 3.31 Sketch of interlocking crystals growing in dilute solution. Should the lamellae rotate about x-x' to bring the basal surfaces of crystals A and B together, two giant screw dislocations with four steps are formed. These giant screws will lead to double growth spirals as in Figure 3.30. From Lotz et al. [48] with permission from John Wiley & Sons, Inc.

that grows in dilute solution just as frequently as the hollow pyramid [18]; see Figure 3.13. Sketches of these two crystal shapes are presented in Figure 3.32 from which it is obvious that distortions accompany the convex–concave sector boundary that is parallel to the small diagonal (*b*-axis) in the chair form. The mutual displacements required to create the chair may be accommodated in part by screw dislocations that give rise to growth spirals of opposite hand shown in Figure 3.32c and in the AFM images in Figure 3.33. Spiral growths are observed only in larger chair crystals and always with the senses in Figure 3.32 and Figure 3.33. It is clear that the distortion in the "seat" of the chair has moved the left side of the crystal upward and the right side downward, with displacements increasing toward the center along the small diagonal (*b*-axis). Restricting our attention to the top half of the distorted crystal (above the long diagonal), the spiral is based on a right-handed giant screw dislocation. Initiating this feature requires forming a slit along *b* and displacing the cut surfaces up on the left and down on the right, conforming exactly to distortions that are present in the chair form. Anticipating the discussion of melt crystallization to follow, note that the upper part of the crystal with the right handed screw has a left handed twist along the *b* direction. Such dislocations in chair-shaped crystals are restricted to polyethylene and perhaps poly(vinylidene fluoride) [20].

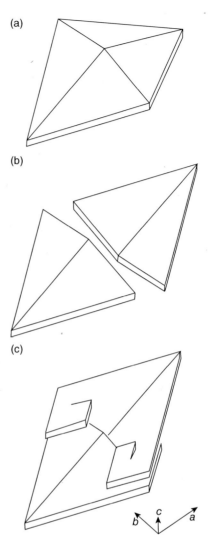

Figure 3.32 Sketches of polyethylene crystals in (a) hollow pyramid shape; (b) chair shape (schematic); (c) chair shape with two spiral growths of opposite hand centered on the short *b*-axis of the crystal. From Toda et al. [19] with permission from Elsevier.

One additional feature of spiral growths is the interaction, or lack thereof, between layers or terraces. In contrast to atomic or ionic crystals, an advancing terrace in a growth spiral of a polymer crystal does not bond in any specific manner to the layer below it. This lack of registration is thought to permit spiral rotations slightly different from 2π radians as in Figure 3.26; the driving force is proposed to be relaxation of stresses in the basal fold surface during spiral growth [50, 51]. More significantly, weak interlamellar bonding allows the spiral layers to splay or to diverge from one another, thereby creating effectively separate lamellae (or lamellar bundles) from what would otherwise be a monolithic

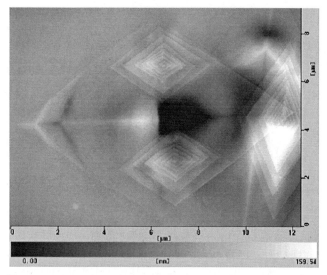

Figure 3.33 AFM image of a polyethylene chair crystal similar to that in Figure 3.13b, but viewed directly from above. Note the right-handed spiral growth on the upper half, and the left-handed spiral on the lower half. A lozenge-shaped crystal with a centrally located spiral growth is on the far right. From Toda et al. [19] with permission from Elsevier.

structure. Micrographs of sedimented or collapsed crystals provide no information on this, but images of crystals suspended in solution do. Figure 3.34 is a phase contrast image of a very large lozenge-shaped polyethylene crystal with substantial spiral growth [52]; when viewed from the top (not shown) it is similar to the sedimented hollow pyramid at the right of Figure 3.33. The edge view along the short **b**-axis diagonal of the crystal in Figure 3.34 confirms that individual layers, or perhaps bundles of layers, are splayed from each other. This splaying in the direction of the long lozenge diagonal (**a**) is obvious, and the outer layers are shortest as expected for spiral growth. The apparent thickness near the center of the crystal (ca. 15 μm) is misleading due to additional splay along the short diagonal. Geometric requirements for the advance of a step as in Figure 3.25 assure that terrace layers cannot separate near the axis of the screw dislocation. Hence, the spiral layers are effectively pinned to one another along the center line of the spiral, but the terraces obviously bend and splay from one another at larger distances. While facilitated by hydrodynamics in dilute solution, this deformation disappears when the solvent is removed, and the terraces "restack" to present the orderly spiral as in the right side of Figure 3.33.

Please note that spiral growth does not lead to multiple lamellae in a formal sense. The structure is better described as a single crystal that adopts the shape of a helicoidal ribbon of tapering width in which the turns

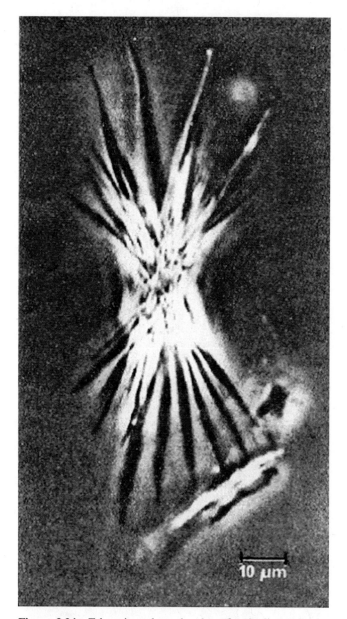

Figure 3.34 Edge view along the short **b**-axis diagonal of a lozenge-shaped polyethylene crystal suspended in solution. The spiral growth layers are clearly splayed from one another. See text for more discussion. Phase contrast optical micrograph from Mitsuhashi and Keller [52] with permission from Elsevier.

are pinned tightly along the helix/spiral axis. The splayed layers apparently grow into the solution at similar rates in similar directions, so a spiral appears to be regular when it is subsequently collapsed by sedimentation. While *terrace growth* gives rise to layers that might appear to be independent of one another (Fig. 3.26, right), these too are pinned along the two dislocation lines of opposite hand that are always present near the center of a terrace. Giant screw dislocations are immobile and cannot mutually annihilate their cores as do their glissile counterparts in atomic and ionic crystals. As will be discussed later, giant screw dislocations are frequently invoked as the source of new lamellar layers in melt crystallization.

3.2.4 Concentrated Solutions

With increasing polymer concentration, the number and structural complexity of crystals and their aggregates increase; hence, optical microscopy is often more useful than TEM. Of general interest is the progression toward spherulitic morphology; most research with solutions of intermediate and high concentrations has been carried out with polyethylene.

Wunderlich and Sullivan [53] investigated polyethylene dendrites formed below 80°C by cooling toluene solutions at a rate of ca. 5°C/min. The most dilute solutions gave dendrites with primary growth arms along a and b having limited spiral growths as in Figure 3.23 and Figure 3.27. Interferometry showed that the longer a arms are about three times thicker than the b arms. For concentrations above 0.02% the overall shape evolved from four-arm to six-arm as shown in Figure 3.35. Be reminded that the structure is macroscopic, with the largest lateral dimension approaching 200 µm. The two primary vertical arms in the a-axis direction are as usual, while the remaining four arms indicate branching in directions different from the b-axis. Each dark interference fringe corresponds to a thickness of 1 µm, so the vertical arms are about 2 µm thick, while the remaining four are 4 µm thick. It was suggested that the nearly horizontal arms grow along a-axes related to the vertical arms by {110} twin planes [6, 53]. From these optical studies the mode of growth arm thickening cannot be determined, but spiral growths are almost certainly involved. In this connection it is instructive that the sideview of a six-arm dendrite in Figure 3.36 shows splaying and curving of growth arms and perhaps layers therein in a manner reminiscent of the spiral growth crystal in Figure 3.34. This image somewhat resembles the "sheaf" structure of nascent spherulites described in Section 3.4.2. Similar experiments with fractionated

Figure 3.35 Interference optical micrograph of polyethylene crystallized from 1.2% toluene by cooling; vertical dimension of the structure is about 200 µm. The six-arm dendrite has been collapsed on a glass slide; vertical arms are about half as thick as the nearly horizontal ones (fewer black interference fringes) as described in the text. From Wunderlich and Sullivan [53] with permission from John Wiley & Sons, Inc.

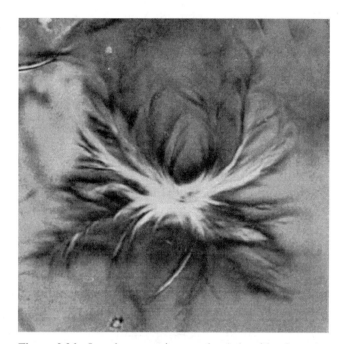

Figure 3.36 Interference micrograph of the side view of a six-arm polyethylene dendrite similar to that in Figure 3.35, but suspended in a mounting medium to prevent collapse. The width of the micrograph is 155 µm. Note the pronounced splaying of the primary growth arms. The feathery features are secondary arms. From Wunderlich and Sullivan [53] with permission from John Wiley & Sons, Inc.

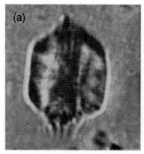 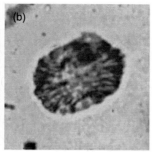 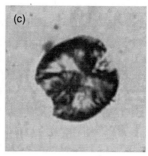

Figure 3.37 Optical micrographs of single compact polyethylene axialite grown from a 1% solution in xylene at ca. 86°C. View (a) is nearly normal to the truncated lonzenge lamellar surfaces, (b) is 90° away, showing the edges of lamellae/lamellar bundles, and (c) is along the axis of the symmetry axis or spine. The width of each optical micrograph is 60 μm. From Bassett et al. [54] with permission of John Wiley & Sons, Inc.

polyethylenes crystallized from xylene solutions demonstrated that branching becomes more frequent and apparently noncrystallographic for molecular weights in excess of 400 kDa [31]. Also observed for all molecular weights were extremely irregular multiarm "hedgehog dendrites" that were associated with certain heterogeneous primary nuclei. These have possible implications for spherulites that are discussed in Section 3.4.3.

A subsequent study by Bassett et al. employed higher crystallization temperatures at which dendrites did not form. For concentrations of up to about 0.3% in xylene and $T_c < 75°C$, the crystals were said to be ordinary multilayers with spiral growths. For higher concentrations and temperatures, quite different compact structures were grown. Three orthogonal views of a single suspended object grown at ca. 86°C from 1% xylene are shown in Figure 3.37 [54]. Figure 3.37a resembles a truncated lozenge that is consistent with crystallization of polyethylene at higher temperatures; the largest dimension of the structure is in the nearly vertical **b**-axis direction. The same object observed from the side (rotated 90° about **b**) shows edges of lamellae or lamellar bundles in Figure 3.37b. The final view from the top (along **b**) can be described by two books placed spine to spine with the pages open or splayed. This structure was termed an *axialite*; note that the symmetry (rotation) axis is in the plane of the faceted crystals. Increased molar mass led to more physically inseparable lamellae, suggesting *tie molecule* segments that are thought to be crucial for mechanical integrity in melt-crystallized polymers. While some rather indirect evidence of spiral growth was presented, these axialites do not possess the characteristic spiral ramps or terrace morphologies ascribed to giant screw dislocations. Lotz et al. [48] have reported poly(ethylene oxide-*b*-styrene) aggregates resembling those in Figure 3.37, which clearly originate from interlocking crystals, not screw dislocations. The

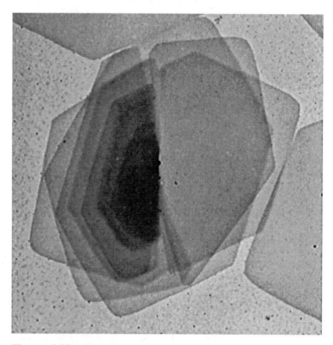

Figure 3.38 Transmission electron micrograph of a sedimented axialite of poly(ethylene oxide-*b*-styrene) grown from 1% solution in xylene at room temperature. This aggregate is a less dense analog of that in Figure 3.37. The height of the vertical spine is about 15 μm. From Lotz et al. [48] with permission from John Wiley & Sons, Inc.

spine corresponds to the direction x-x′ in Figure 3.31, and the leaves of the books are composed largely of half-crystals that nucleate along the spine in Figure 3.38. While this is a plausible explanation for polyethylene axialites as well, it is not known why such a structure would dominate at higher crystallization temperatures over spiral growth.

The transition from solution crystallization to melt crystallization was followed by Keith in a revealing

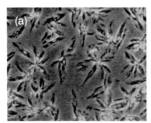  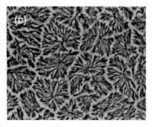

Figure 3.39 (a) M = 4.5 kDa polyethylene aggregates crystallized from 10% n-$C_{36}H_{60}$ solution at 90°C; micrograph width is 280 μm. (b) M = 4.5 kDa polyethylene crystallized from 30% n-$C_{36}H_{60}$ solution at 105°C; micrograph width is 125 μm. (c) M = 168 kDa polyethylene crystallized from 10% n-$C_{36}H_{60}$ solution at 90°C; micrograph width is 280 μm. From Keith [55] with permission of John Wiley & Sons, Inc.

series of experiments that utilized normal paraffins as solvents for polyethylene crystallization [55, 56]. Following isothermal crystallization at an appropriate T_c, the paraffin solvent could be extracted after cooling to room temperature, leaving the polyethylene crystal aggregates for examination by microscopy. The most significant finding was that increasing chain length of the solvent, from n-C_6H_{14} to n-$C_{32}H_{66}$, caused polyethylene to crystallize with enhanced growth in the ***b***-axis direction. The usual increase in aspect ratio AR achieved with higher T_c (see Section 3.2.1) was maintained as well; the greatest ***b***-axis growth was achieved with the largest solvent molecule and the highest crystallization temperature, both conditions approaching those found in melt crystallization. Figure 3.39 illustrates the effect of both T_c and concentration when crystallizing low molar mass polyethylene (M = 4.5 kDa) from n-$C_{32}H_{66}$. Figure 3.39a shows interesting radiating aggregates formed from 10% solution at 90°C. The nature of the nucleus for the aggregates is not known, but the rotations of the crystals do not seem crystallographic. The crystals here are lenticular rather than truncated lozenge-shaped, lacking the {110} facets that define growth in the ***b*** direction in Figure 3.16. Increasing the concentration to 30% and T_c to 110°C gives rise to the structure in Figure 3.39b, which has many aspects of a spherulite. The radial array is quite dense, and the crystals lack smooth growth faces. Molar mass was the final parameter considered by Keith. A fraction with M = 168 kDa crystallized in structures that were more complex and had smaller features than those from the M = 4.5 kDa polyethylene. An example is provided by the "seaweed" structure in Figure 3.39c, which resembles the aggregate in Figure 3.3. Note the frequent noncrystallographic branching on the scale of 10 μm; this is neither a dendtrite nor a spherulite. By contrast, crystallization of the low M = 4.5 kDa polyethylene under the same conditions generates the radial aggregates of lenticular crystals in Figure 3.39a. Keith's experiments

demonstrated that more compact and less regular polycrystalline structures are formed when a larger concentration and/or larger molar mass of the crystallizing polymer is employed. These trends were discussed in terms of feature size being dependent on the diffusion length $\delta = D/G$, which characterizes dendritic growth (Section 3.2.2) [56]. Regardless of details, the diffusion length concept is useful for tracking the evolution from clearly faceted lamellar crystals to the narrow ribbon-like crystals that characterize spherulites.

3.3 CRYSTALS AND AGGREGATES GROWN FROM MOLTEN FILMS

It was seen in the preceding section that microscopy becomes more challenging as the polymer concentration is increased. In the limit of crystallization from the undiluted melt, one must employ sectioning or fracture to reveal structures formed within large volumes. A common alternative is to reduce the amount of crystallizing material by using thin specimens, with the realization that film thickness may affect the results. Most obvious is that growth in the direction of the film normal will be influenced when the structure size approaches the film thickness d. There are two length scales for thickness effects, the larger for aggregates (thin films) and the smaller influencing the growth of monolayer crystals (ultrathin films). Spherulites are deferred for the most part to Section 3.4.

3.3.1 Structures in Thin Films

In situ observation of monolayer polymer crystals with thickness $l_c \approx 10$–50 nm growing in a molten film of thickness $d \approx 10$ μm is generally unrewarding because the optical contrast is very small. One method to overcome this challenge is "self-decoration" as first carried out by Kovacs and Gonthier [57]. A poly(ethylene oxide) fraction, M = 3 kDa, was slowly crystallized as

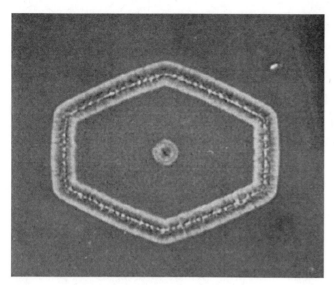

Figure 3.40 Phase contrast optical image of a monolayer crystal of poly(ethylene oxide) grown at 55°C in a 10 μm molten film. Edges of the 22 nm thick lamella are revealed by self-decoration after quenching. The **b**-axis is vertical and the **a***-axis is horizontal; this shape may be compared with that in Figure 3.9. Width of the micrograph is 150 μm. From Kovacs and Gonthier [57] with kind permission from Springer Science+Business Media B.V.

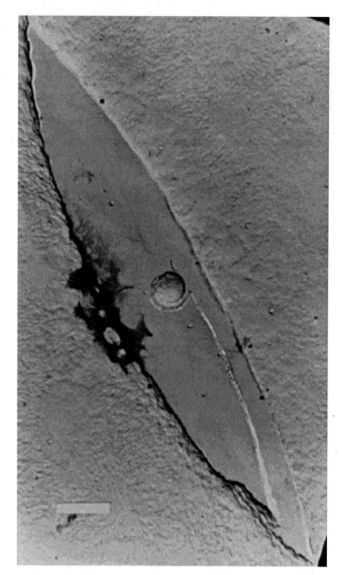

Figure 3.41 Transmission electron micrograph of a polyethylene crystal grown at 130°C from a molten film. A screw dislocation was centered in the etched hole about which spiral growth has started. Scale bar is 2 μm. From Al-Raheil and Al-Share' [58] with permission from John Wiley & Sons, Inc.

extended-chain lamellae at $T_c = 55°C$. Quenching to about −50°C had two effects shown in Figure 3.40. Almost all the originally uncrystallized polymer forms small aggregates with relatively low birefringence, permitting optical images to be transmitted through the crystallized/quenched film. More importantly, the growth faces of a monolayer crystal nucleate local overgrowths that define clearly the lateral shape. The truncated lozenge habit in Figure 3.40 has the same orthorhombic unit cell as the square crystal in Figure 3.8, but melt growth in the **b** direction is with {140} facets rather than {120} facets from dilute solution.

A related approach was taken by Al-Raheil and Al-Share' for polyethylene; again, slow melt crystallization at low ΔT was followed by rapid quenching [58]. Permanganic acid etching selectively removed the matrix spherulites, leaving the interesting structure presented in the electron micrograph of Figure 3.41. The crystal shape is lenticular, like those reported by Keith in *n*-alkane solvents [56]. Quite prominent is the beginning of spiral growth around a hole that has a radius of ca. 500 nm, where a giant screw dislocation had been located. This feature is an extreme "etch pit" of the sort used to reveal dislocations at the surface of atomic and ionic crystals [59]. Estimating the lamellar thickness in Figure 3.41 as 50 nm, shear strains within the missing portion of the spiral where in excess of 0.1, clearly rendering that region susceptible to increased chemical attack by the etchant.

Reducing the crystallization temperature even slightly has pronounced effects in this region of small undercooling. Growth rate and nucleation rate increase, and lamellar thickness decreases, leading to more multilayers from spiral growth about giant screw dislocations that are easier to form in thinner, less perfect crystals. Figure 3.42 provides an excellent example of spiral growth in the melt, here for poly(ethylene oxide), M = 10 kDa, grown at 62°C. The layer thickness is about 40 nm (once-folded chains), and the image is formed by interference microscopy with no self-decoration [57]. In this instance the molten film was thin enough ($d < 100$ nm) to be depleted where the multilayer spiral crystals did not grow, exposing the stepped free surface of the structure, which could be examined after cooling from T_c.

For reasons that are not fully understood, melt crystallization at still lower T_c gives rise to faceted multilayers that lack the spiral ramps of Figure 3.42. Optical microscopy with crossed polars as in Figure 3.43 reveals large *polyhedral* aggregates of low birefringence termed *hedrites* by Geil in 1958 [60]. Presented here are examples from the trigonal β-polymorph of isotactic polypropylene formed with a specific nucleating agent [61, 62]. Crystallization at 135°C creates objects with unlike appearances labeled 1–4, which are different views of growing hedrites. The darkish object 5 in Figure 3.43 is a spherulite of monoclinic α-isotactic polypropylene crystals that exhibit the interesting but complicating cross-hatched morphology discussed in Section 8.3.3.2. Anticipating the discussion to follow, α crystals have a higher T_m than β crystals, hence a larger undercooling at $T_c = 135$°C. This larger undercooling led to the formation of a spherulite, not a hedrite, for α crystals.

Interpretation of Figure 3.43 is assisted with higher resolution AFM images like those in Figure 3.44. Crystallization was again of β-nucleated isotropic polypropylene, this time at $T_c = 140$°C in 100-μm-thick films between glass plates. Following quenching, the films were acid etched before imaging the surface with AFM [62]. The flat-on and edge-on structures in Figure 3.44 establish that a mature hedrite is a stack of faceted lamellar crystals that extends for tens of micometers in all directions. Edge-on (presumably faceted) lamellae in Figure 3.44b grew away from the glass substrate into the melt, and lamellar bundles are seen to curve in a cooperative manner away from the center plane that runs from 5 o'clock to 11 o'clock. The smallest "waist" portion is more than 10 μm in height, implying a core composed of at least 50 lamellae. Additional crystal layers are repeatedly spawned by new screw dislocations formed near advancing growth faces, forcing initially neighboring lamellae further and further apart as lateral growth proceeds. The etched surface of the flat-on view in Figure 3.44a contains hexagonal etch pits (ca. 1–3 μm

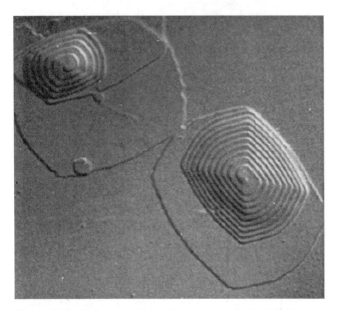

Figure 3.42 Spiral growth multilayer crystals of poly(ethylene oxide) grown at 62°C from a thin molten film. Note that the growth spirals do not emanate from the center of the substrate crystal. Lamellar layer thickness is ca. 40 nm, so the height of the right-most spiral is about 500 nm. The optical micrograph was formed with interference contrast (no self-decoration) based on melt depletion in the thin film. Image width is 100 μm. From Kovacs and Gonthier [57] with kind permission from Springer Science+Business Media B.V.

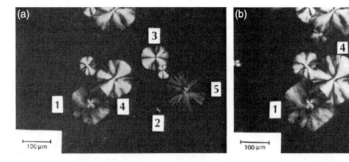

Figure 3.43 Polarized light micrographs of isotractic polypropylene crystallized at 135°C for 50 minutes (a) and 62 minutes (b) in a ca. 25-μm-thick film. The weakly birefringent object 5 is based on monoclinic α crystals and is not of interest here. All other objects have the trigonal β crystal structure. Object 1 is a flat-on view of a hedrite. Objects 2, 3, and 4 are other views of hedrites, subject to possible growth restrictions. Note particularly the evolution of the small plate-like aggregate 2 into an oval shape 3. From Varga and Ehrenstein [61] with kind permission from Springer Science+Business Media B.V.

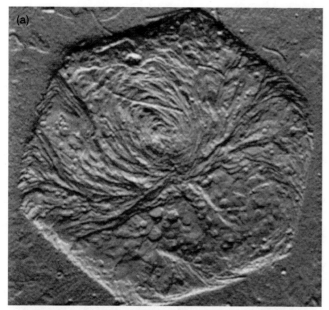

Figure 3.44 AFM images of β isotactic polypropylene crystallized at 140°C. Note the multiple hexagonal etch pits, lower right and the swirled feature, upper left of center in the flat-on view (a). The viewing plane in (b) was against the glass substrate. Each image width is approximately 70 μm. From Vancso et al. [62] with permission from John Wiley & Sons, Inc.

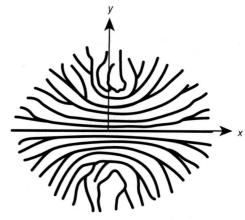

Figure 3.45 Sketch of the center section through the side view of a hedrite; compare with Figure 3.43, objects 3 and 4, or Figure 3.44b. The three dimensional structure has approximate rotational symmetry about the polar axis (y), and approximate mirror symmetry about the equatorial plane (xz). From Vancso et al. [62] with permission from John Wiley & Sons, Inc.

deep) that reveal dozens of screw dislocations. It should be obvious that terrace spreading is here nonuniform, being more rapid in the less constrained directions away from the hedrite center [63].

Another morphological element of the hedrite is lamellae that appear flat-on (not edge-on) in the polar regions of the sideview in Figure 3.44b. The swirled portion in Figure 3.44a is the same feature viewed from (nearly) the top; that hedrite is slightly tilted into page. Combining the two views, we come to the following picture of the development of a hedrite. The structure starts as a core stack of lamellae that most likely developed by spiral growth that maintains the rotational orientation of the faceted layers. Lateral edges of this core are free to grow into the undercooled melt, and multiple screw dislocations near advancing growth faces cause proliferation, bending, and splaying, which were described in the preceding paragraph. This distortion is transversely isotropic; that is, the lamellar bundles resemble two inverted sets of nested bowls, with the polar, flat-on lamellae in Figure 3.44b being formed last. Throughout growth the general shape evolves from a planar stack to an oval aggregate that approaches a sphere as suggested by the sketch in Figure 3.45.

At this point some discussion of terminology is appropriate. A *hedrite*, in which the platelets are stacked in one direction, is clearly distinct from an *axialite* (Fig. 3.37 and Fig. 3.39), wherein the faceted lamellae are rotated with respect to one another about the spine of the structure. From images like Figure 3.44b, some have concluded that bending occurs about one axis only (z in Fig. 3.45), and hence believe that the term *axialite* is appropriate. This is wrong because the distortion clearly has rotational symmetry about the polar axis (y), giving rise to the circular nature of the swirled portion in the center of the flat-on view of the hedrite (Fig. 3.44a). Edge-on or sideviews of a hedrite may be oval, but what has been called an *oval structure* or *ovalite* is actually a hedrite, subject perhaps to growth restraints within the film.

The images in the optical micrographs of Figure 3.43 can now be understood. Consider first object 2 in Figure 3.43a, which is a small but highly birefringent stack of lamellae about 2 μm high and 10 μm wide viewed from the side. Growth of this structure leads to the oval birefringent object labeled 3 in Figure 3.43b, which is clearly equivalent to the edge-on AFM image in Figure 3.44b. Still further growth of the oval shape generates the nearly circular but irregularly birefringent objects 3 and 4. When viewed from the top these look like object 1 in Figure 3.43, where increased birefringence toward the edges reflects the lamellar bending that is so obvious in the AFM image in Figure 3.44b. The birefringent "X" in the center is from those swirled lamellae near the pole that grow nearly in the viewing direction. The hexagonal appearance of object 1 is established by the planar lamellae in the middle of the stack that extend beyond those that bend; the same applies to the flat-on AFM image in Figure 3.44a. These flat-on views in either optical microscopy or AFM suggest improperly that a hedrite is a regularly faceted polyhedron, a hexagonal cylinder in the present case. Absent growth restrictions along the stacking direction, top and bottom shoulders must be rounded as in Figure 3.45.

There is a tendency to classify any circular or nearly circular aggregate as a "spherulite." If a disk-like structure has complete rotational symmetry about the disk axis, then this term is appropriate. Stated in practical terms, the polarized optical image of a spherulite is invariant on rotation, although this simple test is seldom applied [64]. Objects labeled 3 and 4 in Figure 3.43 are not spherulites, even though some are circular, as can be appreciated with the help of Figure 3.45. Regardless of external shape, the internal structure of a hedrite does not have the circular symmetry of a spherulite. One optical characteristic of a spherulite is the dark Maltese cross exhibited in polarized optical micrographs (see Fig. 3.4), which is discussed more fully in Section 3.4.1. Object 3 in Figure 3.43a has four dark arms, but they are for a hedrite oriented as in Figure 3.45, not a spherulite. Flat-on lamellae in the polar regions cause extinction by zero birefringence, while the equatorial region is dark from zero amplitude extinction. The circular object 3 would change appearance if the sample were rotated with respect to the polarizers, while the Maltese cross in Figure 3.4 would not.

With decreasing T_c, the faceting of hedrites becomes less evident, evolving to near circular flat-on lamellae [65, 66]. We return to hedrites in Section 3.4.3 when describing the evolution to coarse and then fine-textured spherulites at still lower crystallization temperatures where the diffusion length $\delta = D/G$ decreases further.

3.3.2 Structures in Ultrathin Films

Mention was made of polycrystalline aggregate growth near free surfaces (Fig. 3.42) or confined surfaces (Fig. 3.44). When the melt film thickness d is of the order of the crystal thickness l_c a number of interesting effects occur. Among the myriad of studies of this sort we focus on the comprehensive work of Taguchi et al. with isotactic polystyrene, M_w = 590 kDa, M_w/M_n = 3.4 [65, 66]. Films with one free surface were spun cast on carbon or glass substrates and self-seeded before isothermal crystallization at selected temperatures, then quenched below T_g = 90°C to permit microscopy at room temperature. AFM images in Figure 3.46 are of structures formed between 210°C and 180°C in ultrathin films of d = 11 nm, which require the growth of single flat-on lamellae of estimated thickness l_c that varies from 13 nm to 7 nm. At the highest T_c = 210°C the hexagonal single crystal is clearly faceted with $\{11\bar{2}0\}$ growth faces that reflect the symmetry of the trigonal unit cell (see Table 2.1 of Chapter 2). Reducing the crystallization temperature to 205°C gives rise to a reentrant corner midway along each $\{11\bar{2}0\}$ face as discussed for solution-grown monolayers in Section 3.2.1. At a still lower T_c regular dendrites with smaller branch separations are observed (Fig. 3.46c,d), then irregular branching and a loss of overall hexagonal shape (Fig. 3.46e,f). This progression confirms the correlation of feature size with $\delta = D/G$ seen in dilute solution crystallization; diffusion-controlled morphology in ultrathin melt films parallels that in solution. We reserve the term dendrite for structures with regular branching, which is almost always in crystallographic directions (Fig. 3.46c–e). The densely branched object grown at 180°C has only the faintest vestiges of crystallographic ordering, and might logically be termed a two-dimensional spherulite on the basis of its appearance. However, ED (see Fig. 3.49 below) clearly confirms it to be a single crystal with chain axes normal to the substrate. All the irregularly branched arms have the same crystallographic orientation, just as with the even more disordered appearing poly(trifluoroethylene) seaweed structure in Figure 3.3.

Varying film thickness in the ultrathin region gives effects that are illustrated by the AFM images in Figure 3.47. Isothermal crystallization at T_c = 180°C establishes the isotactic polystyrene folded chain crystal thickness at $l_c \approx 10$ nm. The systematic change from a dense branched (Fig. 3.47a) to an open structure (Fig. 3.47d) for $d < l_c$ is dictated by conservation of mass. Assume for illustration that $d = 0.5\, l_c$; no more than about 50% of the film area can be occupied by flat-on crystals that are coated by very thin (ca. 2 nm) layers of amorphous polymer. More generally, reducing film thickness from 17 nm to 6 nm results in structures that are progressively better faceted and more regularly branched with larger feature sizes (branch spacing, crystal width). All of these morphology changes are consistent with *larger* diffusion length $\delta = D/G$ at smaller film thickness d.

Figure 3.46 AFM images of isotactic polystryrene crystallized in ultrathin films of $d = 11$ nm. (a) $T_c = 210°C$, 4 hours; (b) $T_c = 205°C$, 4 hours; (c) $T_c = 200°C$, 4 hours; (d) $T_c = 195°C$, 3 hours; (e) $T_c = 190°C$, 1 hour; (f) $T_c = 180°C$, 1 hour. Scale bars are 5 μm. From Taguchi et al. [65] with permission from Elsevier.

From nominal growth rates obtained from Figure 3.47 we see that G is indeed reduced by a factor of 15 when d shrinks from 17 nm to 6 nm. Furthermore, it is well established that chain mobility is enhanced near a free surface; Ellison and Torkelson [67] have established conclusively that T_g in a 14-nm surface layer of (atactic) polystyrene is some 35°C lower than that in bulk, implying that D is greater in thin films at a fixed $T_c = 180°C$. Hence the ratio $\delta = D/G$ increases with smaller d, demonstrating once again the qualitative

Figure 3.47 AFM images of isotactic polystyrene crystallized at $T_c = 180°C$ in ultrathin films of decreasing thickness: (a) $d = 17$ nm, 0.5 hours; (b) $d = 14$ nm, 1 hour; (c) $d = 11$ nm, 1.5 hours; (d) $d = 9.7$ nm, 3.3 hours; (e) $d = 8.7$ nm, 3.3 hours; (f) 6.1 nm, 14 hours. All scale bars are 5 μm. From Taguchi et al. [66] with permission from Taylor & Francis Group, http://www.informaworld.com.

correspondence between diffusion length δ and the crystal morphology.

A discussion of linear growth rates is the subject of Chapter 6; nevertheless, one is struck here by the reduction of G that sets in when the thickness d of the free surface film is about 100 nm. For the best documented case of isotactic polystyrene the data can be represented by $G(d) = G(\infty)(1-p/d)$ [68], where film thickness was varied between 300 nm and 22 nm and $G(\infty)$ is the growth rate in bulk that depends on T_c and molar mass.

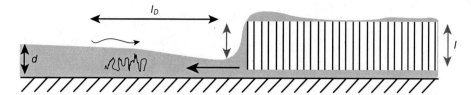

Figure 3.48 Sketch of a crystal of thickness l growing in an ultrathin film of thickness $d < l$. Amorphous polymer must be transported vertically up the height indicated by the vertical double headed arrow. The molten film thickness is depleted over a distance l_D from the interface. From Taguchi et al. [66] with permission from Taylor & Francis Group, http://www.informaworld.com.

The parameter $p \approx 6$ nm was found to be independent of T_c, molar mass, and substrate. Its size suggests a fairly local interaction, but we are unaware of a theory to account for these observations. It has often been asserted that confinement in thin films leads to reduced molecular mobility, but Ellison and Torkelson have shown that this is not the case for polystyrene films on glass with a free surface [67]. It is acknowledged, on the other hand, that strong attractive interactions between a polymer such as poly(ethylene oxide) and a substrate such as oxidized silicon lead to reduced mobility in thin and ultrathin films [69]. Regardless of the presence or absence of interface effects, the behavior of $G(d)$ is altered in ultrathin films where $d \leq l_c$ and the structure shifts to open seaweeds or dendrites. In such circumstances the melt is severely depleted near advancing interfaces, requiring vertical transport of molten polymer to sustain crystal growth as indicated in Figure 3.48. The isothermal growth rate may slow or even stop as amorphous polymer is consumed, particularly if many objects are growing near one another [70]. Schultz et al. [71] attribute the driving force for transporting liquid *uphill* in this manner to capillarity, that is, to lower surface energy when the crystal surfaces are covered by molten polymer. It may be that similar effects operate in films well beyond the ultrathin range. Geil [60] reported in 1958 that the melt thickness around growing polyoxymethylene hedrites was depleted by as much as 30 μm, more than 1000 times the height of ultrathin films. To summarize, reduced crystal growth rates in thin melt films are well documented but not fully understood at present.

Selected area ED results are surprising as well. The $d = 11$ nm structure in Figure 3.47c, which has dense radial fibrils that branch with no obvious regularity, is a single crystal by ED. The same is true of the more open seaweed aggregate for $d = 8$ nm as shown in Figure 3.49b. Referring back to Figure 3.3, we already demonstrated that the irregular seaweed structure of poly(trifluroethylene) is a single crystal [4]. Similar findings with poly(ε-caprolactone) have been published by

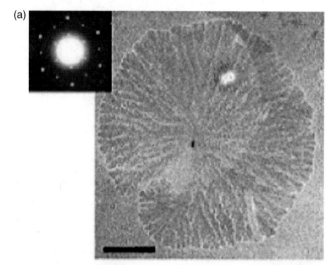

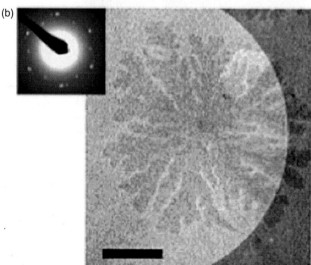

Figure 3.49 Bright field TEM images and electron diffraction patterns of isotactic polystyrene crystallized at $T_c = 180°C$ in films of thickness $d = 11$ nm (a) and 8 nm (b). These are very similar to the AFM images in films of the same thickness on different substrates in Figure 3.47c,e. Scale bars are 2 μm. From Taguch et al. [66] with permission from Taylor & Francis Group, http://www.informaworld.com.

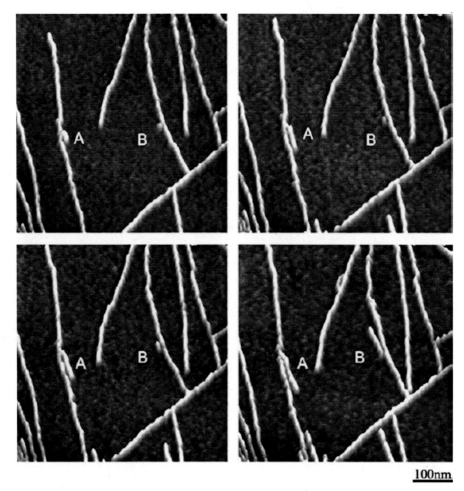

Figure 3.50 AFM images of PBA-C8 crystallizing at room temperature with edge-on lamellae. The time interval between images is approximately 6 minutes. Note particularly the growth of additional edge-on lamella from the "induced nucleation" points A and B. From Li et al. [72a] with permission from the American Chemical Society.

Mareau and Prud'homme. Multilayer structures grown at room temperature in films with $d > 100$ nm, best described as poorly faceted hedrites, exhibit single crystal texture by ED [70]. The inescapable conclusion is that, at least in thin and ultrathin films, the growth direction of, or within, a *single crystal* can occur in a manner that bears no relation to crystal symmetry.

3.3.3 Edge-On Lamellae in Molten Films

In thicker films there is an increased probability of growing edge-on lamellae, an example of which is shown in Figure 3.44b. Under conditions of very slow growth one can observe separate edge-on lamellae that branch and splay, providing information not available from compact structures such as mature hedrites. As introduced in Section 1.3.5, Chan and coworkers have followed the crystallization of poly(bisphenol A octane ether) or PBA-C8 by AFM at room temperature; film thickness was 100–200 nm [72]. In the time-lapse series of Figure 3.50, ca. 10-nm nodules, termed *induced nuclei*, clearly give rise to additional lamellae. There is near universal agreement that the fold surface of a lamella cannot generate a new crystal by secondary nucleation or by growth instabilities of the sort that give rise to dendritic branches. The sketch in Figure 3.51 illustrates how stable folded chain nuclei might be formed from cilia or loose loops near the basal surface of the parent lamella. This proliferation mechanism, which does not involve giant screw dislocations, can account for multilayer faceted crystals that lack growth spirals (see for instance fig. 3 of Reference [70]). The onset of a screw dislocation during melt crystallization was recently imaged with AFM by Franke and Rehse [73] in polypropylene of low isotacticity crystallizing slowly at room temperature in a film of $d \approx 1$ μm. The remarkable sequence in Figure 3.52 is of one edge-on crystal, presumably lath-like with the monoclinic α-phase, creating the two steps of a screw dislocation having a Burgers vector of ca. 20 nm. The dislocation is located near the edge of the crystal closest to the (top) free surface of the film, and there is no information on possible structural defects that could assist in the formation of the dislocation. In the same publication another sequence (not shown) of what appears to be induced nucleation is presented; hence, two proliferation mechanisms were operative.

Wunderlich et al. [74] heated an extended-chain crystal of high molar mass polyethylene to 115°C, melting a thin layer of lateral surface chains that recrystallized epitaxially as edge-on lamellae of thickness l_c = 12 nm. Approximately 25-nm gaps between the lamellae in Figure 3.53 are regions where the melt was depleted. Each lamella splits in a characteristic manner, bifurcating with a pair of oppositely directed kinks that displace the crystal up and down (in the *c*-axis direction of the substrate) by about one lamellar thickness over a distance of ca. 20 nm. The kink angles are typically near 30°. The mechanism for this interesting method for creating additional lamellar crystals is not known, but the geometry of branching in Figure 3.53 is not consistent with either giant screw dislocations or induced nuclei; perhaps tip-splitting, described in Section 3.4, is involved. It is conceivable that some of the junctions in the image result from neighboring parallel lamellae joining together during growth. With this reservation in mind, Figure 3.53 demonstrates that polyethylene

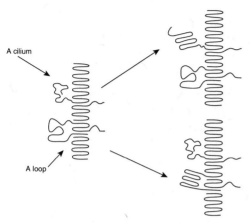

Figure 3.51 Illustration of induced nucleation of a crystal from either cilia or loose folds in the parent lamella. From Chan and Li [72b] with kind permission from Springer Science+Business Media B.V.

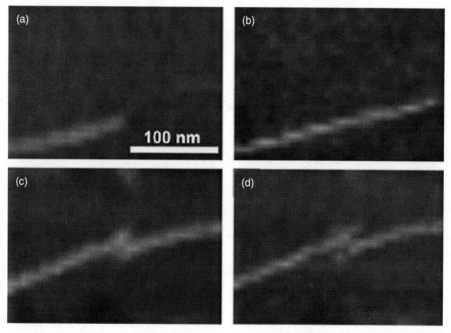

Figure 3.52 AFM images of an edge-on lamella of imperfectly isotactic polypropylene growing at room temperature. Overall crystallization times are 55 minutes, 73 minutes, 169 minutes, and 190 minutes. The first two images show that the growth rate is about 6 nm/min. In frames (c) and (d) the formation of a screw dislocation with its axis in the plane of the image can be seen. From Franke and Rehse [73] with permission from the American Chemical Society.

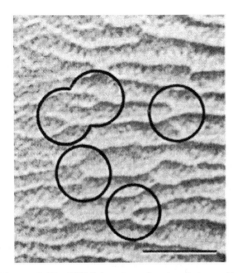 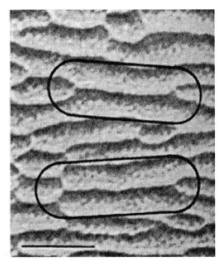

Figure 3.53 TEM images of polyethylene (M_w = 80 kDa, M_w/M_n = 10) edge-on lamellae grown epitaxially at 115°C on the surface of an extended-chain crystal of the same polyethylene. The dominant growth direction is perpendicular to the (vertical) *c*-axis of the substrate. Outlined regions highlight branches that are discussed in the text. The scale bars are 100 nm. From Wunderlich et al. [74] with permission of Taylor & Francis Group, http://www.informaworld.com.

crystals growing in the melt state are able to bifurcate and to generate additional lamellae. For these unique crystallization conditions it is also clear that epitaxy dictates the spreading of lamellae perpendicular to the *c*-axis direction of the polyethylene substrate and that the spacing between lamellae results from depletion of the initial liquid film of unknown thickness.

Anticipating the discussion of spherulites in Section 3.4, an edge-on TEM image of polyethylene (M_w = 30.6 kDa, M_w/M_n = 1.2) crystallized in bulk at 125°C is shown in Figure 3.54. Staining the 60-nm-thick microtomed section created the dark amorphous lines that delineate the ~24-nm-thick lamellar crystals [75]. Lamellar ends around which two other lamellae have grown as in a Voltera edge dislocation (E) can be seen. Other lamellae appear to have nucleated (or terminated) at the basal surface of another crystal (N). The zig-zag portion (ZZ) is attributed by the authors to a giant screw dislocation in which sets of lamellae tilt in opposite directions on either side of the dislocation line (like the projection of front and back threads of a threaded rod viewed sideways). Of primary interest is the large number of bifurcations (B) that are similar to those in the epitaxially grown thin film in Figure 3.53. The parent lamella splits into two daughter lamellae with no visible boundary at the bifurcation. The salient point is that new lamellae can be formed in this manner, without the agency of screw dislocations or induced nuclei, during conventional crystallization from the melt.

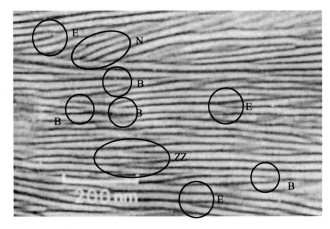

Figure 3.54 TEM of a microtomed and stained section of polyethylene that had been crystallized in bulk at 125°C for 3 hours. Light portions are lamellar crystals viewed edge-on, while dark traces are the amorphous intercrystalline layers. Outlined are examples of branches (B), lamellar ends (E), nucleation sites (N), and a zigzag region (ZZ). After Grubb and Keller [75] with permission from John Wiley and Sons, Inc.

3.4 SPHERULITIC AGGREGATES

Spherulites are polycrystalline aggregates with spherical symmetry. For more than a century it has been known that spherulites are favored by crystallization from impure, viscous media [5]. While polymer spherulites can be grown from solution under certain conditions, the vast majority of studies are for spherulites developed from the molten state. Three-dimensional spherulites are readily formed in a polymer melt at moderate or large undercoolings, that is, at growth rates larger than those used to generate monolayers or hedrites. Another obvious requirement is that the film be thick enough to permit unrestricted growth of a sphere of radius R in all directions. The structure of such bulk crystallized spherulites can be revealed with microscopy of free surfaces, exposed surfaces, or microtomed thin sections. Small-angle light scattering is also used to obtain certain information about spherulites and related structures.

Far more common are studies of two-dimensional spherulites typically grown in films of thickness $d < 10$ μm to avoid multiple aggregates being superimposed on one another in the thickness direction. When viewed from above in an optical microscope, such polycrystalline structures are circular in outline and have full rotational symmetry about the disk axis before impingement (see Fig. 3.4). Other microscopies and microdiffraction can be brought to bear to elucidate the fine-scale structure within the spherulite. With only minor qualifications, two-dimensional spherulites are equivalent to diametral sections of three-dimensional spherulites [76]. The adjective *two-dimensional* is technically incorrect, as mature spherulites such as those in Figure 3.5 have a disk thickness of about 5–10 μm (the assumed thickness of the molten film). Nevertheless, growth is two-dimensional after the spherulite diameter exceeds the film thickness.

All spherulites, either two-dimensional or three-dimensional, have certain structural characteristics. Equivalency in all radial directions requires that the crystals be fibrillar or ribbon-like as opposed to the large, symmetrically faceted lamellae found in hedrites. A second requirement is that additional crystals are formed during radial growth to maintain the same crystalline fraction throughout the spherulite, as illustrated by the isotactic polypropylene structure in Figure 3.55. In this instance crystallization at high T_c created an open spherulite with large features easily observed by optical microscopy. Keith and Padden noted that branching in spherulites is noncrystallographic, with the branching angle being smaller in more compact structures that have smaller amorphous regions adjacent to growing crystals [77]. These new crystals may be formed by screw dislocations, intrinsic nucleation, dendrite-like branching or bifurcation of existing ribbons, or primary nucleation within amorphous regions of the growing spherulite. Twisting of ribbon-like crystals during radial growth, when coupled with proliferation, facilitates the development of fully three-dimensional spherulites or disks with micrometer thickness, but it is not required.

Figure 3.55 Polarized optical micrograph of istotactic polypropylene crystallized at an unspecified but small undercooling; width of the micrograph is 1500 μm. The coarse open structure is a consequence of the large diffusion length $\delta = D/G$. Radially directed features are lamellar bundles of dominant lamellae as wide as 50 μm in tangential directions. Branching maintains an approximately constant proportion of crystals at increasing distances from the center. Note that the orientation of crystals is not strictly radial. From Keith and Padden [91] with permission from the American Institute of Physics.

As might be expected, real spherulites have structural defects that cause departures from the ideal spherical (three-dimensional) or circular (two-dimensional) symmetry. What might not be anticipated is that ideal spherulites are most closely approached by rapid crystallization at large undercoolings. In the following sections we discuss characterization of spherulites with polarized light, the conditions under which polymer spherulites are formed, the radial growth of spherulites, and the twisting of lamellae that leads to "banded spherulites" as in Figure 3.5.

3.4.1 Optical Properties of Spherulites

Polymer spherulites are most frequently studied by polarized optical microscopy because the method is fast, simple, and relatively inexpensive (see Section 1.1.2.1). The remarkable contrast in Figure 3.4 is provided by the birefringent nature of polymer crystals, in which the polarization, expressed as the dimensionless dielectric constant K, and the refractive index $n = K^{1/2}$ are direction dependent. This anisotropy is represented by the indicatrix, an ellipsoid with semi-axes equal in length to the three principal values of n. Isotropic liquids and glasses are nonbirefringent. Cubic crystals, which are not relevant to polymers, are also optically isotropic and nonbirefringent (spherical indicatrix). For tetragonal, hexagonal, or trigonal crystals, the indicatrix is an ellipsoid of revolution with equal values of n perpendicular to the symmetry axis. Such crystals are termed *uniaxial* because there is only one optic axis (the symmetry axis) normal to which the refractive index is transversely isotropic; when viewed along the optic axis the projected indicatrix is circular, and birefringence is not manifested. Crystals of lower symmetry (orthorhombic, monoclinic, and triclinic) have three unequal principal values of n and a fully elliptical indicatrix. There are two directions normal to which the indicatrix has circular sections and hence exhibit no birefringence. These directions define the two optic axes of *biaxial* crystals, which are considered only briefly in this chapter. Polyethylene has an orthorhombic unit cell and is formally biaxial. Because its crystal structure is close to hexagonal, the refractive index perpendicular to the *c*-axis is practically constant. Polyethylene is treated as uniaxial without observable error: $n_c = 1.58$ and $n_{tr} = 1.52$ parallel and transverse to the *c*-axis, respectively [6], and the indicatrix is a prolate ellipsoid of revolution (similar to a rugby ball).

At this point we can interpret the dark Maltese cross (Fig. 3.5) seen in polymer spherulites by referring to Figure 3.56. Absent any birefringent matter in the light path, no intensity is passed by orthogonal (crossed) polarizer P and analyzer A. When birefringent material is present, the transmitted intensity is also zero wherever the polarization direction P is coincident with a semiaxis of the indicatrix. This condition is referred to as zero amplitude extinction; a brief but excellent presentation of birefringence is presented by Wunderlich in Reference [6], pp. 325–329. In spherulites one always has zero amplitude extinction (no transmitted intensity) along radii for which the azimuthal angle μ is equal to 0°/180° or 90°/270° is always zero. For other radii that are inclined to the polarization direction, the brightness becomes maximum at $\mu = \pm 45°$ as expressed by the transmitted intensity ratio [78]

$$I_T / I_o = \sin^2(2\mu)\sin^2\left(\frac{\pi t}{\lambda}\frac{n_{max} - n_{min}}{n_{min}}\right). \quad (3.5)$$

Here t is the optical path length through the spherulite, λ is the average wavelength of light in the crystal, and n_{max} and n_{min} are the largest and smallest refractive indices of the indicatrix associated with each radius in Figure 3.56. Azimuthal dark–light intensity modulation in Figure 3.4 is described by the first factor containing μ. The second factor with refractive indices and specimen thickness t accounts for the amount by which incident polarized light is rotated on passing through the material. For very thin films ($\lambda \ll t$) the argument in large parentheses is small and the spherulite will appear nearly uniformly dark because the transmitted light is scarcely rotated. With usual specimen thickness the

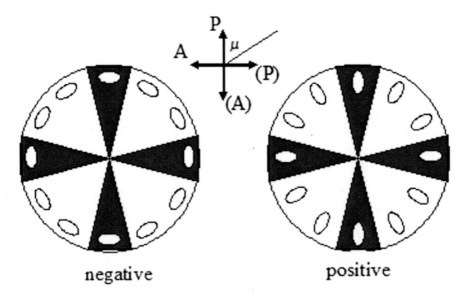

Figure 3.56 Maltese cross pattern exhibited by negatively birefringent and positively birefringent polymer spherulites viewed through crossed polarizer P and analyzer A. For negative spherulites the indicatrix has the largest semiaxis in the tangential direction, while the largest n is radial in a positive spherulite. Directions of radii with respect to the polarization direction are given by μ. The pattern is unchanged by rotating the spherulites about the viewing direction or by interchanging the directions of polarizer (P) and analyzer (A).

dark arms often appear to be relatively narrow with sharp boundaries as sketched in Figure 3.56, a condition that results from nonlinear recording of greatly differing luminosities.

Observation of the Maltese cross pattern in polymer spherulites signifies only that the anisotropic crystals are arranged in such a way as to conform to one of the two possibilities in Figure 3.56. By methods that are not described here [79, 80] one can determine if the largest refractive index is tangential (Fig. 3.56, left) or radial (Fig. 3.56, right). Positive spherulites with n_{max} radial are seldom found in polymers, being confined for the most part to those with biaxial crystals. The large majority of polymer spherulites are negatively birefringent with n_{max} in the tangential direction, a condition consistent with radial growth of chain-folded crystals. Using polyethylene as the classic example, crystal growth along the *b*-axis establishes that $n_{min} = 1.52$ is radial. Depending on the setting of the ribbon-like crystal around the radius, the tangential refractive index may vary from 1.58 (*c*-axis tangential) to 1.52 (*a*-axis tangential). One limiting case assumes rotational symmetry of *a*- and *c*-axes about each spherulite radius, giving the *average* indicatrix of a crystal in the polyethylene spherulite with $n_{max} = 1.55$ (tangential) and $n_{min} = 1.52$ (radial). This indicatrix is an oblate ellipsoid that resembles a pincushion. It should be apparent that such averaging about the *b*-axis requires that many ribbon-like crystals be sampled by light rays passing through the thickness *t*. As will be seen in Section 3.4.3, this condition is not met when broad ribbons are formed at large T_c, and radial streaking is superimposed on the light–dark Maltese cross pattern. Some instances of such coarseness can be seen in the nylon 6.6 spherulites of Figure 3.4.

A different manner of radial growth is manifested as concentric light–dark rings in polarized optical micrographs, such as Figure 3.5, for what are called ringed or banded spherulites. In this case the ribbon-like crystals are not rotationally averaged at each point along each radius, but they grow as coherently twisted ribbons and the projected indicatrix varies continuously along each radius. The period of this twist is constant for isothermal growth and, most remarkably, essentially in phase for all radial directions as discussed in Section 3.4.4. The source of the light–dark bands can be appreciated with the aid of Figure 3.57. Crystal twist is indicated by the periodic change in orientation of the indicatrix along any radius. This example is for a uniaxial polymer crystal in which the indicatrix is a prolate ellipsoid, largest along the chain or *c*-axis direction. Only those settings viewed along the optic axis (parallel to *c*) or viewed along the minor axis (parallel to *a*) are indicated for simplicity. The Maltese cross centered at μ equal to even multiples of 45° is unaffected by this twist because the (vertical)

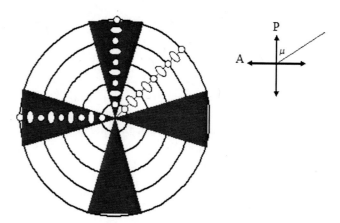

Figure 3.57 A negatively birefringent spherulite displaying the Maltese cross plus concentric light–dark rings when viewed with crossed polarizer and analyzer. The crystal orientation and indicatrix twist continuously about any radius, although only two twist settings 90° apart are indicated. See text for further explanation of the banded spherulite.

polarization direction is always parallel to a semiaxis of the indicatrix as discussed above for zero amplitude extinction. The situation is changed in the "bright" regions of the image centered on μ equal to odd multiples of 45°. It is easy to see that when twist aligns the crystal with the optic axis in the viewing direction, the projected indicatrix is a circle and there is zero birefringence extinction (no transmitted light). This orientation corresponds to each dark circumferential band that runs between the arms of the Maltese cross in Figure 3.57. For $\mu \approx 45°$ the birefringence and transmitted intensity are greatest when the indicatrix is viewed along a minor axis, accounting for the bright bands between the dark ones. The spacing between two neighboring dark bands is one-half the period of twist (rotation is by π radians). A polymer crystal of lower symmetry (orthorhombic, monoclinic, triclinic) has an indicatrix with three unequal semi-axes and two optic axes normal to circular sections. Radial twist in this case results in two dark bands, one for each optic axis, per half-twist, in what is termed a double ringed or double banded spherulite. This case is easily recognized because the radial spacing between rings alternates regularly [76]. It should be recognized that Equation (3.5) does not account for banded spherulites; the more complex expression that incorporates twist of the crystal/indicatrix may be found in Reference [78].

Another manifestation of optical anisotropy is light scattering (Section 1.5.3); the cloudy appearance of most thermoplastic films and molded pieces results from the scattering of incident light by spherulites. Quite generally, light scattering is caused by fluctuations in optical polarizability or refractive index from point to point within the material. For birefringent materials, depolarized (H_V) and polarized (V_V) light scattering can provide information on the shape, size, and perfection of aggregates such as spherulites. The characteristic four-lobed cloverleaf H_V pattern is often used to establish the presence, size, and perfection of spherulites. However, ambiguities inherent in the interpretation of scattering patterns and occasional misunderstanding of often complex scattering theory render many conclusions from such experiments unreliable. The interested reader may consult publications that review the subject [80, 81] or present representative results [82, 83].

3.4.2 Occurrence of Spherulites

Crystallization temperature and molecular weight are the major parameters for controlling the development of polymer spherulites. Other factors such as molecular weight distribution and/or impurities exert lesser effects. As described in Section 3.3.1, melt crystallization at successively lower temperatures gives monolayer crystals, multilayer spiral growth crystals (although both are formed simultaneously), and then hedrites. Hedrites are replaced by spherulites with a further reduction in T_c as illustrated in Figure 3.58 for poly(1-butene). The crystal structure is tetragonal in both morphologies [84]. It should be remembered that the hedrite, being nonbirefringent when viewed flat-on, is scarcely visible when surrounded by molten polymer; quenching provides a suitably birefringent background. Changes occurring within the range of spherulite morphologies are illustrated for a polyethylene fraction, M_w = 30.6 kDa, in Figure 3.59 [85]. Crystallization at higher T_c leads to a systematic coarsening of spherulitic texture, as expected from diffusion length $\delta = D/G$ increasing with temperature (G becomes smaller, D becomes larger). Recall that

δ was shown to be useful for organizing feature sizes in crystals formed from solution and in ultrathin melt films; it applies to spherulites and similar aggregates as well. Coarseness in spherulites is revealed by the radial streaks that disrupt the Maltese cross pattern and the bright regions between. Wider ribbon-like crystals grown at higher T_c are less likely to be orientationally averaged about radii than finer scale ribbons. Consulting Equation (3.5), the effective difference $n_{max} - n_{min}$ may vary from point to point in an irregular way, leading to streaks of higher or lower transmitted brightness. Note that the "textbook" image with the clearly defined Maltese cross is obtained for polyethylene cooled rapidly to room temperature, for which the birefringence properties of the spherulites appear to be uniform. In contrast to poly(1-butene), there is no abrupt transition to or from faceted aggregates with polyethylene, but the morphology changes conspicuously in the range from T_c = 125°C to T_c = 130°C. Those aggregates formed at the highest temperatures resemble sheaves that are described in the following paragraph.

Molecular weight effects have been studied most thoroughly for polyethylene. Isothermal crystallization in the normally accessible range of T_c = 120°C–130°C yields morphologies that vary substantially for low, medium, high, and highest molecular weight polymers [85]. Those fractions with M_w < 18 kDa invariably grow as open, nonspherical sheaf-like structures as seen in the left panel of Figure 3.60. Here again the ratio $\delta = D/G$ is large for small chainlike molecules crystallized at small undercoolings. Lamellae in polyethylene hedrites are not faceted polyhedra as those in poly(1-butene), and so on, but are lenticular like the crystal in Figure 3.41. A stack of platelets with this shape splays predominately about the **a**-axis, which is parallel to the small crystal width. When viewed along the **a** direction this aggregate resembles a sheaf of wheat, which is often

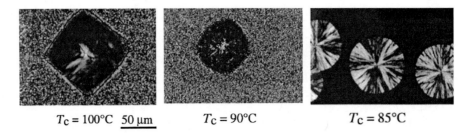

Figure 3.58 Polarized optical micrographs of isotactic poly(1-butene), M_w = 141 kDa. Hedrites were crystallized at high temperatures and quenched to room temperature, creating the light birefringent background of very small spherulites. The spherulite image on the right was taken at T_c = 85°C where the background is molten polymer. The transition from hedrite to spherulite is unambiguous. Scale marker applies to all images. From Fu et al. [84] with permission from the American Chemical Society.

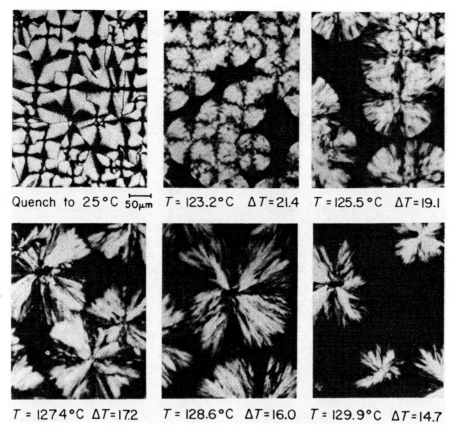

Figure 3.59 Polarized optical micrographs of polyethylene, M_w = 30.6 kDa, as a function of crystallization temperature. There is an evolution to coarser and less geometrically complete spherulites with increasing T_c. From Hoffman et al. [85]; contribution of the National Institute of Standards and Technology.

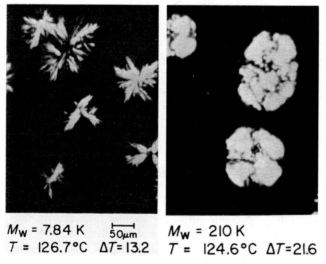

Figure 3.60 Polarized optical micrographs of nonspherulitic crystalline structures formed by low molar mass and high molar mass polyethylene. Low M aggregates are hedrites as discussed in the text. The same scale bar applies to both images. From Hoffman et al. [85]; contribution of the National Institute of Standards and Technology.

described as an axialite because the splay/bending is preferentially about one axis. The bright, birefringent "X-shaped" objects in Figure 3.60 are such polyethylene hedrites viewed along a. (As discussed in Section 3.3.1, immature hedrites grown edge-on near an interface appear to be sheaf-like and have been termed axialites. In that case the apparent splay/bending about only one axis is an artifact of restricted growth, contributed to the confusion between hedrites and axialites.) Polyethylenes with 18 kDa < M_w < 100 kDa form coarse spherulites like those in Figure 3.59, with some tendency for finer texture at larger M. Polyethylenes with 100 kDa < M_w < 900 kDa crystallize as compact, irregular birefringent particles with extremely narrow (or no) extinction bands parallel and perpendicular to the polarization direction P in the right panel of Figure 3.60. Aside from a roughly circular profile (actually more like cauliflower), these bear little resemblance to spherulites. The ability to organize into a spherical structure with the requisite internal symmetry is compromised by large chains, presumably because of reduced molecular mobility. Finally, polyethylene with M_w > 1000 kDa remains birefringent for hours in the melt state at temperatures as high as 190°C. It was impossible to image any structures with optical microscopy, although calorimetry indicated that crystallization occurred on cooling. The inability of very high molar mass polyethylene to organize into polycrystalline aggregates with dimensions of micrometers was confirmed in a later study by Bassett et al., although some groups of lamellar crystals were seen by TEM [86]. One can conjecture that the molten state of ultra-high molecular weight polyethylene is so viscous and heterogeneous that coherent structures with dimensions of micrometers cannot be formed. These microscopy results were generally supported by depolarized (H_V) light scattering experiments on polyethylene fractions examined at room temperature after isothermal crystallization, although the claim for "isolated lamellae" in fractions with M > 2000 kDa is suspect [82]. It is noteworthy that quench crystallization formed spherulites with good optical quality (like in the upper left of Fig. 3.59) for all polyethylene fractions with M < 80 kDa, that is, those with low and medium molar mass. Poly (ethylene oxide) fractions were investigated by microscopy and H_V light scattering [87]; nonspherulitic aggregates were found for lower M and higher T_c, as with polyethylene.

While impurities have been historically linked with spherulite formation [5], Bassett et al. grew large (50 μm) spherulites from the melt of rigorously monodisperse $C_{294}H_{590}$ (M = 4118 Da), but only with once-folded crystals grown at low temperatures [88]. These formed banded spherulites when quenched (like Fig. 3.59, upper left), and coarse open structures (like Fig. 3.59, lower right) at T_c = 118°C. Extended chain lamellae grown at T_c = 127°C organize as simple stacks with little or no radial character. The significance of these important observations is considered in the following section.

3.4.3 Development of Spherulites

What defines a spherulite is its shape and structural symmetry. All radii of an ideal spherulite are equivalent, at least at lengths greater than the 0.1-μm resolution of optical microscopy. The spherical (or circular) envelope of growth fronts is established by advance at rate G of separate fibrillar crystals into the melt from a common nucleus. This ideal shape is altered by growth restrictions presented by other spherulites (impingement/truncation) or by melt interfaces (two-dimensional spherulites).

Polymer spherulites have two additional features. The radially growing crystals are not fibrillar, but ribbon-like, with chain folding establishing the smallest dimension l_c, which is itself an inverse function of undercooling. While difficult to establish with certainty, the internal structure of a polymer spherulite appears to be independent of radial position (at sufficient distance from the center), meaning that the shape and packing of ribbon-like crystals remains substantially unchanged during growth. Additional crystals are required at larger radii to maintain crystal–crystal correlations in tangential directions. These new crystals grow in the gaps between already established radially directed crystals in order to reduce the free energy of the system. Such additional crystals may be formed by primary nucleation or by proliferation from existing crystals. Establishment of fully three-dimensional spherical symmetry is facilitated if polymer lamellae can establish new growth both within the plane of its basal surface (like dendritic branching or spiral growth) and in planes that contain the basal surface normal (like induced nucleation or bifurcation). Finally, such thin ribbon-like crystals are compliant and expected to bend and twist in response to forces present during growth. Such distortions also contribute to achieving spherical symmetry.

This section discusses the primary nucleation and subsequent radial growth of spherulites. The latter concentrates on mechanisms by which an increasing number of ribbon-like crystals appear at larger distances from the spherulite center. The intriguing topic of lamellar twist is deferred to Section 3.4.4.

Primary nucleation of polymer crystals from the melt at usual undercoolings occurs through the agency of heterogeneous solid particles. Heterogeneous nuclei are usually unknown impurities [85], but they may be stable (thick) polymer crystals that are generated by self-seeding [57]. The number density of effective primary nuclei is evaluated directly from the number of spherulites per unit volume; fewer nuclei lead to fewer spherulites that grow to larger dimensions before impingement. The structure of the nucleus in a mature spherulite is difficult to examine, as the region of interest is concealed by crystals that have grown from it. Discussed below are AFM images of PBA-C8, the same polymer for which proliferation by induced nucleation was illustrated in Figure 3.50. Edge-on lamellae were grown at room temperature in 300-nm-thick films on silicon. Growth is slow because of proximity to T_g = 11°C; the crystallization temperature T_c = 22°C is some 60°C below T_m = 83°C [89]. Acknowledging possible effects associated with thin films, this system provides uncommonly useful information on spherulite formation.

One form of spherulite nucleation is illustrated in Figure 3.61. The single lamella in the first image (a) contains an induced nucleus that appears as a barely visible dot slightly below the midpoint. From this grow two lamellae in panel (b). As these new lamellae are on the same side of the parent lamella, they do not correspond to a screw dislocation. Additional induced nuclei

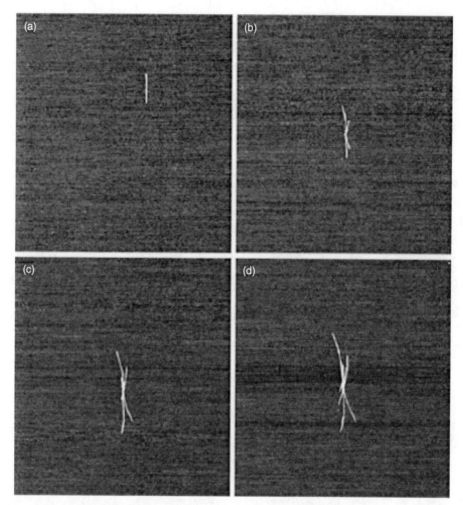

Figure 3.61 Formation of a small lamellar stack in PBA-C8 at room temperature. AFM images are at time intervals of 10.6 minutes. New lamellae are formed by induced nuclei that are just visible as dots at this resolution in panels (a) and (c). Each image is 3 μm wide. From Lei et al. [89] with permission of Elsevier.

appear in panel (c) and grow into still more lamellae in panel (d). Figure 3.62 shows the evolution of such a lamellar stack into a hedrite. Similarity to the isotactic polypropylene hedrite in Figure 3.44b is obvious, but some differences are noteworthy. The smooth curvature of polypropylene lamellae is replaced by abrupt direction changes at each end of the waist in panel (d). All lamellae in PBA-C8 are fairly straight, and dominant lamellae are clearly seen to grow into the melt ahead of others. Bassett was the first to identify dominant lamellae that establish the framework for spherulite development [90].

The aggregate in Figure 3.62i would become the center of a larger spherulite if growth were continued. The hedrite in question has a radius of about 2 μm, which would not be significant in a spherulite of radius $R > 15$ μm. So any polymer spherulite that develops in this manner is nonspherical at the core. We now have a better appreciation of the relation between a hedrite and a spherulite: if a hedrite continues to grow beyond the point at which its envelope becomes spherical (or circular), a spherulite develops around it. When crystallizing at very small undercoolings, the growth rate is so small that hedritic characteristics remain apparent for hours. At lower T_c, the growth rate is larger and all feature sizes are reduced. These two effects combine to surround a smaller hedrite core with radially symmetric overgrowth, that is, a spherulite. Be reminded that the hedrite core of a spherulite will remain apparent until the spherulite becomes much larger than the nonspherical structure at the center. An example of this two-element morphology can be seen for isotactic polystyrene in figure 8 of Reference [64].

It is also possible to grow a spherulite from a set of radially directed lamellae such as those in Figure 3.63.

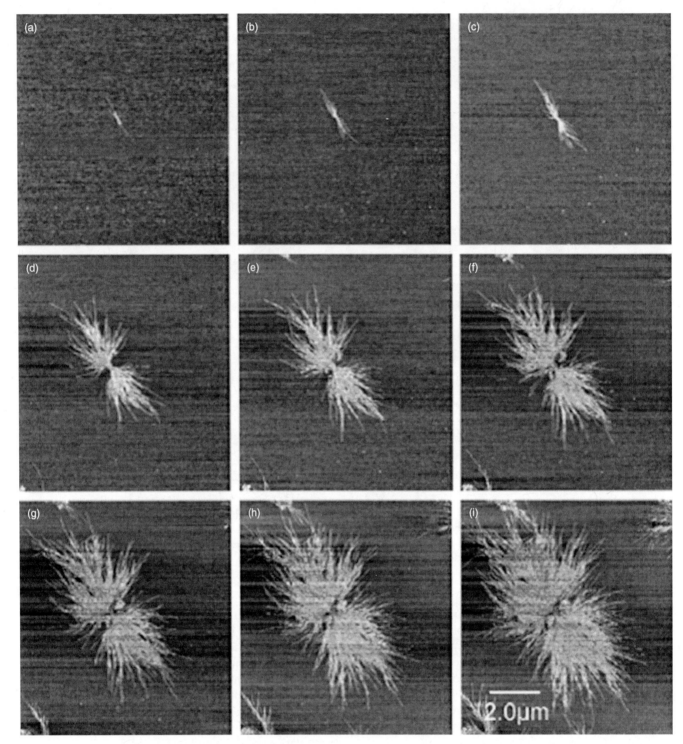

Figure 3.62 Growth at room temperature of PBA-C8 from a small lamellar stack into a hedrite that would constitute the central region of an even larger spherulite. In panel (g) forward, flat-on lamellae can be seen in the polar regions. Note also the dominant lamellae that extend beyond the envelope. Time increments of the AFM images are 14.2 minutes, except 53 minutes between (c) and (d). From Lei et al. [89] with permission from Elsevier.

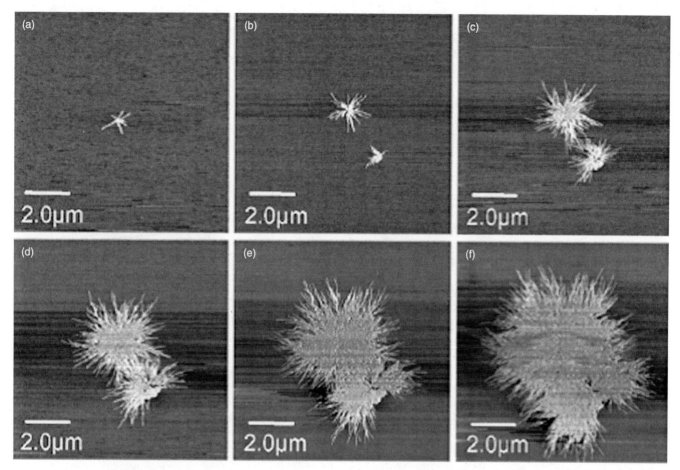

Figure 3.63 AFM images of the growth of a spherulite of PBA-C8 at room temperature. The first structure is a heterogeneous nucleus composed of multiple radially directed lamellae. The second object appearing in panel (b) is a hedrite. Time increments are 14.8 minutes. From Lei et al. [89] with permission from Elsevier.

The first-formed aggregate is based on an adventitious solid, hence the term *heterogeneous nucleation* [89]. In this case the structure has spherulitic symmetry at the earliest stages of growth, and it is similar to hedgehog dendrites found in some concentrated polyethylene solutions [31]. The second, smaller aggregate in this example is a hedrite like that in Figure 3.62, because a polar region is visible in Figure 3.63c–e. It is not known how often this sort of heterogeneous nucleation occurs. One suspects it would be more common at large undercoolings where more heterogeneous nuclei are effective and where hedrites are not favored.

As described briefly in the introduction to this section, spherulite growth requires approximately radially directed fibrillar or ribbon-like crystals and the creation of more crystals at larger distances from the center. Any new crystals spawned from existing ones must splay from the parent lamella or from one another in order to fill the gaps between diverging dominant lamellae. Keith and Padden in 1963 attributed what they termed fibrillar crystals of spherulites to the instability of planar interface growth [91]. For melt crystallization, rejected impurities such as low molar mass chains create a field characterized by $\delta = D/G$ as in Figure 3.19. As described in Section 3.2.2, a planar interface is unstable to outwardly directed fluctuations, but interfacial energy σ was not considered by Keith and Padden. Their analysis predicts that elongated fibrillar crystals with a spacing of about δ will grow into the melt or solution, with rejected impurities being concentrated between the fingerlike entities. This process, sometimes called cellular crystallization or cellulation, is well documented in metal alloys in the presence of a large temperature gradient [92]. Returning to polymers, we recall that the ratio $\delta = D/G$ has been found to account, in a *qualitative* manner, for feature sizes in thin films and for textural coarseness in spherulites crystallized at different T_c (G) or from melts of different viscosity (D). Keith and Padden further coupled cellulation to branching by assuming orientation defects at the tip of growing fibrils.

Neighboring fingers with differently oriented defects were posited to grow in different directions, giving rise to noncrystallographic low-angle branching.

Bassett and coworkers have concluded, on the other hand, that diffusion control of morphology is not responsible for the internal structure of polymer spherulites. They contend that dominant lamellae grow radially with occasional branching to establish the skeletal outline of a spherulite, with subsidiary lamellae filling in the amorphous regions between dominant lamellae [93]. This two-stage process has been confirmed directly by AFM on a number of slowly crystallizing systems [94]. The temperature dependence of texture in polycrystalline aggregates, as for example, in Figure 3.59, is attributed to smaller branching angles at higher T_c [90]. Giant screw dislocations are proposed for branching, wherein adjacent terraces are envisioned to splay from one another in response to repulsion of uncrystallized chain ends (cilia) and/or rough basal surfaces. This latter assertion is supported by texture and splaying observed in monodisperse n-alkanes having chain folded lamellae.

Returning to the diffusion control of morphology, Goldenfeld reviewed the subject with respect to spherulite structure [95]. His contention that the diffusion length $\delta = D/G$ describes large-scale variations in the shape of the spherulite envelope has been confirmed by experiments on random copolymers with many noncrystallizable sequences [96]. More importantly, he identified the lamellar width W with the Mullins–Sekerka instability size $\lambda_D \sim \delta^{1/2} \ll \delta$. When crystals grow radially they also grow in width until W approaches λ_D and the lamellae experience another interface instability and branch by a form of tip-splitting. This repeated noncrystallographic branching generates what is called a dense branch morphology (DBM) that resembles a spherulite as shown for the two-dimensional structure in Figure 3.22b.

These concepts are supported by recent studies by Kajioka et al. on unbanded isotactic poly(1-butene) [97] and isotactic polystyrene [98] spherulites. The basic idea is conveyed in Figure 3.64, where the planar growth fronts at the leading edge of a ribbon-like crystal widen to the point at which they become unstable and undergo fingering or tip-splitting. Another feature is the creation of incipient screw dislocations at the reentrant corners between the newly formed protrusions; recall that these are common in polymer dendrites grown from solution as discussed in Section 3.2.2. Interlamellar repulsion of overlapping basal surfaces, as suggested by Bassett, can lead to splaying and branching through an angle $\Delta\theta$. Characterization of nonbanded spherulites involved estimating the maximum lamellar λ_m width from AFM and TEM images taken near the edge of spherulites grown at different T_c (Fig. 3.65). Polarized optical

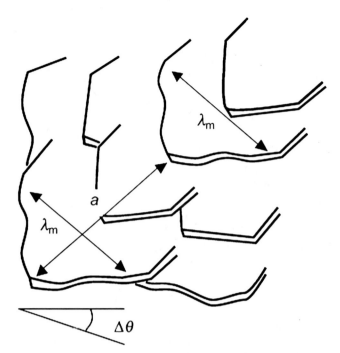

Figure 3.64 Schematic of a radially growing lamella that experiences instabilities of the growth faces at width $W = \lambda_m$. The new lamellae grow with a splay of $\Delta\theta$ that can be in either direction. The instability and splitting recur when the new lamellae grow to $W = \lambda_m$ again. From Kajioka et al. [97] with permission of Elsevier.

microscopy employed superimposed images with the polarization direction P offset by 45° to eliminate the Maltese cross. Resultant micrographs like that in Figure 3.66 were scanned radially to establish L, a quantitative measure of textural coarseness manifested as radial streaking. Finally, the radial growth rate $G(T_c)$ was measured and the results were found to be related according to

$$L \approx 3\lambda_m \propto \left(\frac{D(T)}{G(T)}\right)^{1/2} = \delta^{1/2}(T). \qquad (3.6)$$

Here $D(T)$ is a diffusivity with the appropriate non-Arrhenius temperature dependence. Most significant is that the maximum lamellar width λ_m is proportional to $\delta^{1/2}$, firmly establishing the relevance of interface instability to important elements of spherulite structure. This model has the Mullins–Sekerka instability of width λ_D forming when the interface width has grown to a somewhat larger $W = \lambda_m$. Branching occurs at each instability site, repeating when W has grown from λ_D back to λ_m over the persistence length L. L is a statistical correlation length in the model, so branching does not occur at strictly regular intervals along the radius. In nonbanded

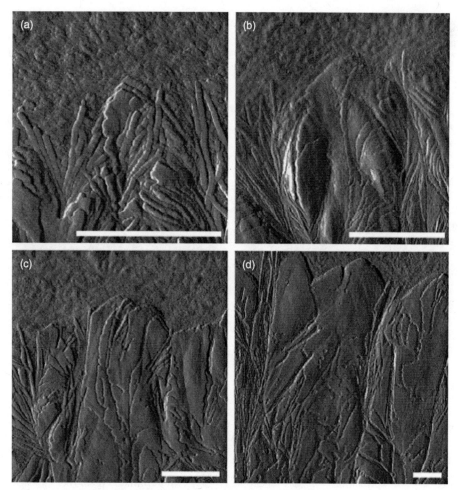

Figure 3.65 AFM images of lamellar crystals at the edge of poly(butene-1) spherulites crystallized at different temperatures. The growth faces are {100} for the tetragonal crystals; compare with the hedrite in Figure 3.58. Note that magnifications are different; each scale bar is 2 μm. The maximum lamellar width λ_m clearly increases with T_c. (a) $T_c = 86.8°C$, $\lambda_m = 0.9$ μm; (b) $T_c = 91.5°C$, $\lambda_m = 1.5$ μm; (c) $T_c = 96.5°C$, $\lambda_m = 2.2$ μm; (d) $T_c = 101.5°C$, $\lambda_m = 5.0$ μm. From Kajioka et al. [97] with permission from Elsevier. (See color insert.)

spherulites branching is assumed to occur by splay displacements in uncorrelated directions. Correlated displacements can lead to banded spherulites discussed in the following section.

The Toda model described in the preceding paragraph nicely supports Goldenfeld's hypotheses [95] with experiments. What has not been clarified to this point is what sort of diffusion is responsible for the field that generates the instability. Schultz has reviewed thoroughly the possibilities in his recent book [30]. Temperature can be dismissed because the thermal diffusivity is high and the corresponding diffusion length is macroscopic, approaching meters. Concentration fields, suggested originally by Keith and Padden [91], are plausible, but the observation of spherulites in impurity-free n-alkanes raises questions about this basis for diffusivity D. A less obvious field is pressure that derives from the volume contraction upon crystallization. Toda et al. [99] developed an analysis akin to Mullins–Sekerka in which negative hydrostatic pressure develops at the interface because mass density increases on crystallization. This hydrostatic tension lowers T_m through the Claussius–Clapeyron relation in a manner analogous to increased impurity concentration. Pressure is relieved by viscous flow from the far field atmospheric pressure region toward the interface, creating a positive pressure gradient (outward from the interface) that leads to instability to outward fluctuations of the planar interface. The result is that the diffusion length is $\delta \sim (1/\eta G)$, where the viscosity $\eta \sim 1/D$ by the Stokes–Einstein relation. At this time it is useful to recall Bassett's demonstration that spherulites form in pure n-alkanes [90], an observation consistent with pressure, not impurities, being responsible for this morphology. Toda et al. have found

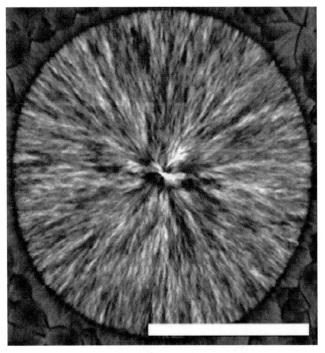

Figure 3.66 Poly(butene-1) spherulite image created by superimposing two polarized optical micrographs with the polarizer offset by 45° to eliminate the Maltese cross. Radial streaking was analyzed to establish a persistence length L. Scale bar is 100 μm. From Kajioka et al. [97] with permission from Elsevier.

that structural feature sizes in spherulites of polyethylene of different molar mass are in fact consistent with viscous flow in a pressure field [99, 100].

In summary, Keith and Padden's concept that ribbon-like crystals and branching in spherulites originate from planar interface instability has evolved over 45 years to the current Goldenfeld/Toda model that accounts in a quantitative manner for the temperature and molar mass dependence of spherulite structure. The best evidence that a pressure gradient drives the instability is consistent with early suggestions that high viscosity is essential to spherulite development [101]. Perhaps future experiments will pursue the combined effects of pressure and concentration gradients. Branching mechanisms include Bassett's repulsion of nearby basal surfaces and Lei's induced nucleation, although others may be operative.

3.4.4 Banded Spherulites and Lamellar Twist

Polarized optical micrographs of spherulites often reveal circumferential dark rings (Fig. 3.5, Fig. 2.1b) that manifest coherent twisting of the indicatrix about different radii as outlined in Section 3.4.1. An example of a doubly banded spherulite is provided in Figure 3.67.

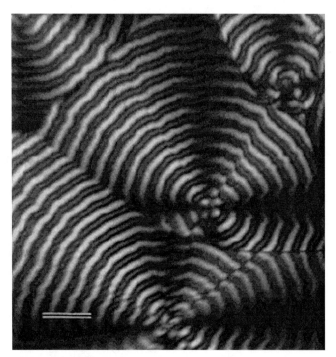

Figure 3.67 Polarized optical micrograph of a doubly banded spherulite in the chiral polymer poly(R-3-hydroxybutyrate). Two closely spaced extinction bands are separated by a wider light region; the crystal structure is orthorhombic and the indicatrix is an ellipsoid with two optic axes. Close inspection of the vertical arms of the Maltese cross reveals dark bands crossing the light regions from left to right, indicating that the twist is left handed. Scale bar is 25 mm. From Saracovan et al. [102] with permission from the American Chemical Society.

The twist period is the same in all radial directions, and there is no decay of coherence with either radial or circumferential separation. At the micrometer size scale observed by optical microscopy, the radial growth rate G is constant in both time and azimuthal angle, accounting for the spherical/circular envelope of spherulites. This radial growth in many instances occurs with a structural period, manifested as bands, that is also constant. It was established in Section 3.2.1 that lamellar crystals of chain folded polymers are compliant and readily adopt nonplanar shapes. The questions addressed here are why crystal distortion is of the twisting type and why it appears to be cooperative over 10s of micrometers. Despite fairly continuous research activity since the 1950s, the reason or reasons for this remarkable twisting remains unsettled to the present time. In this final section we summarize the experimental findings and discuss what is known or thought about lamellar twisting in chiral and achiral polymers.

Experiments have been almost exclusively on two-dimensional spherulites probed with polarized optical microscopy, TEM, or AFM. The following is largely a paraphrase from the excellent review of Keith and Padden [44]. The band spacing S, typically between 1 and 10 µm for conventionally sized spherulites, is constant for fixed T_c and increases when T_c is raised. Banding is more difficult to observe at high T_c because of textural coarseness and because S may approach or exceed the spherulite radius. Banding is observed all the way to the circular growth envelope, that is, it does not develop at a perceptible distance behind the growth front. At fixed ΔT the band spacing S increases with larger molar mass, provided M is not so great as to interfere with spherulite formation. Similarly, S is reduced by lower blend viscosity. Single enantiomers of all chiral polymers display banding; many (but not all) achiral polymers display banding.

In rare instances, crystallization in ultrathin films generates concentric banding by a form of rhythmic growth that causes periodic thickness variations [71]. It is universally agreed, however, that banding in ordinary two-dimensional polymer spherulites results from twisting of lamellar crystals during radial growth. The mechanisms for such twisting are considered in the succeeding discussion. A key aspect of twist is its direction or hand, which, like the thread on a rod, does not change when viewed from either direction. If one tilts a two-dimensional banded spherulite on an optical microscope stage, the banding changes in ways that permit the direction of twist to be determined; the interested reader is referred to Saracovan et al. for a good description of these methods [102]. Direct observation by electron or AFM can be employed as well. One such technique relies on the intersection of a banded spherulite with a free surface, where the twisted lamellae appear as normal or inverted "Cs" as in Figure 3.68 [23]. In this example the polyethylene spherulite has two well defined sectors in which lamellae twist with opposite hands. Polyethylene, being an achiral molecule, is expected to display right handed and left handed twists with equal frequency.

Such is not the case with chiral polymers that have an asymmetric carbon atom in the main chain. These molecules cannot be superimposed on their mirror images and are termed enantiomers designated by R or S (chemists) or by D or L (biologists). Consider the repeat structure of poly(3-hydroxybutyrate):

$$-O-\underset{\underset{CH_3}{|}}{\overset{\overset{H}{|}}{C^*}}-\underset{\underset{H}{|}}{\overset{\overset{H}{|}}{C}}-C-$$

When synthesized with the aid of microorganisms, this polyester is expressed exclusively as the R enantiomer that crystallizes with left-handed helices in an orthorhombic unit cell. Lamellae of these crystals invariably have

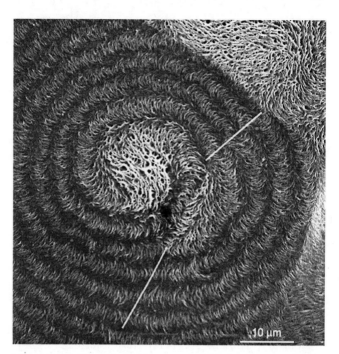

Figure 3.68 Scanning electron microscope image of a polyethylene spherulite emerging from the free surface of a molten film; the spherulite center is below the surface. Clearly evident is the band spacing S = 4.5 µm. Furthermore, the lamellae exhibit a "C" shape that reflects the direction of twist. The lower right sector has a right-hand twist, while the larger upper left portion has left twisting lamellae. From Lotz and Cheng [23] with permission from Elsevier.

a left-handed twist in banded spheruites. The closely related poly(R-3-hydroxyvalerate) has an ethyl group in place of the methyl substituent on C*; this polymer also crystallizes as left-handed helices in an orthorhombic unit cell, but the lamellae have a right-handed twist [102]. While the helices of these two chiral chains are expected to be similar, they do differ in detail as reflected in dissimilar unit cell parameters. Surprisingly, a random copolymer of R-3-hydroxybutyrate with 17 mole% R-3-hydroxyhexanoate gave right-handed twisting lamellae (see Fig. 3.71) [103], not left twisting as in the homopolymer. Other informative examples are provided by polyethers from epoxides. Both poly(epichlorohydrin) and its derivative poly(propylene oxide) can be synthesized as nearly pure R or S enantiomers that in spherulites give right-handed and left-handed twisting lamellae, respectively. Also noteworthy is the absence of lamellar twist in spherulites crystallized from a 50:50 blend of R and S enantiomers [104].

It is clear that uncompensated chemical (configurational) chirality causes lamellar twist manifested as banded polymer spherulites. A particular enantiomer of a particular chiral polymer almost always has lamellar twist of one hand only, but R enantiomers of different polymers may give either right- or left-handed twisted lamellae, and so on. This connection is for melt crystallization only; crystallization of either enantiomer of poly(epichlorohydrin) from dilute solution generates flat lamellae in which the helical chain stems are perpendicular to the basal (001) surface [105]. These observations can be rationalized by a small but systematic cholesteric-like rotation of helices attaching to the growing crystal–melt interface [44]. An alternative explanation is that chirality causes unbalanced surface stresses that in turn cause the lamellae to twist, a mechanism that is explained more fully in the following discussion. Guo et al. applied this surface stress concept to an unusual case where poly(R-3-hydroxyvalerate) exhibits lamellar twist of both hands in different parts of a single spherulite [106]. This heterogeneity was shown to correlate with radial growth along the orthorhombic *b*-axis (right-handed twist) or the orthorhombic *a*-axis (left-handed twist). A qualitative surface stress model based on folding in {110} planes is plausible.

Achiral polymers are a different matter, as they possess no chemical asymmetry upon which to base morphological asymmetry, that is, lamellar twist. Proposed mechanisms for banding in spherulites of achiral polymers are presented in approximate chronological order, with some attempt to counter the heavy emphasis on polyethylene. Schultz and Kinloch analyzed the effect of isochiral screw dislocations situated along a lamellar ribbon as illustrated in Figure 3.69 [107]. There are two contributions to lamellar twist. The major one, due to the topological nature of the dislocation of strength $b = l_c$, creates a twist of the same hand as the screw as is evident in Figure 3.69. When the screw axis is in the center of a ribbon of width W, the tilt angle is $\phi_t = \tan^{-1}(2l_c/W) \approx 11°–33°$ for W/l_c in the range of 10 to 3. Furthermore, the internal elastic stress field of the dislocation vanishes at the lateral free surfaces of the ribbon, which are at distances of order $W/2$ from the dislocation axis. This creates a distortion of the ribbon that is a twist of hand opposite to that of the dislocation. The rather formidable quantitative analysis was carried out by Schultz and Kinloch, who found this angle ϕ to be less than 2° per dislocation for $W/l_c = 3–10$, so this contribution can be safely neglected when compared with the topological ϕ_t. For a typical band spacing $S = 5$ μm, there should be about 10 dislocations each with $\phi_t \approx 18°$, or a dislocation spacing of 0.5 μm. If, however, the lamellar width increases to $W \approx 1$ μm, then $\phi_t \approx 2°$ and the required dislocation spacing is reduced to 50 nm, an unlikely value that is about the same as the dislocation core size. Larger S at larger T_c was attributed to fewer dislocations being formed in thicker crystals. Schultz and Kinloch further suggested that the isochiral hand of the dislocation queue could be established by chain tilt within the lamella, a concept that continues in modified form to this day.

In the 1980s Keith and Padden proposed that chain tilt itself (not screw dislocations) results in axial twisting of growing lamellae that is manifested as banded spherulites. The reviews of Keith and Padden [44] and Lotz and Cheng [23] may be consulted for original references. Chain tilt is almost always found for chains crystallized in an extended (not helical) conformation. For orthorhombic polyethylene and α-poly(vinylidene fluoride), the chains are inclined to the basal lamellar surfaces to provide more volume for chain folding (Section 3.2.1). On the other hand, those aliphatic polyamides (nylons) and polyesters that crystallize with monoclinic

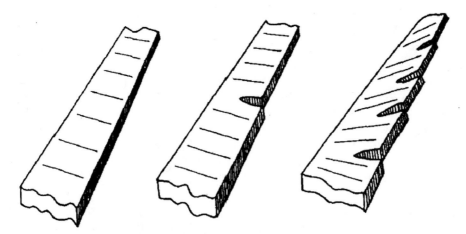

Figure 3.69 Sketch of an undislocated lamellar ribbon (left), a lamella with one left-handed topological screw dislocation of strength $b = l_c$ (center) and a lamella with four left-handed topological giant screw dislocations of the same strength (right). As illustrated, the dislocations have generated a left-hand twist, but no spiral growth. From Schultz and Kinloch [107] with permission from Elsevier.

or triclinic unit cells have chains inclined to (001) because of crystal symmetry. Banded spherulites are found in all such instances. Achiral polymers that pack as helices in the crystalline state rarely exhibit chain tilt or banded spherulites; occasionally S greater than 50 µm is seen, indicating a weak tendency for twisting. The model to account for the robust correlation between chain tilt and banding is presented in Figure 3.70. In essence, chain tilt provides the asymmetry that leads to lamellar twisting. Chain folding is proposed to be different on the top and bottom lamellar surfaces in response to acute or obtuse corners as sketched, creating moments that lead to twisting about the growth axis. There are numerous issues about an initial elastic surface stress imbalance resulting in a permanent (plastic) distortion of the crystal, and so on, but this model seems the most popular at this time [23]. It not only correlates with the presence or absence of banding, but an analysis of twisting of ribbons of different thickness can account for the positive dependence of S on T_c [44].

In 1988 Bassett et al. reported that polyethylene crystals grown from the melt at 130°C had screw dislocations with a hand that correlated with the direction of chain tilt in the parent lamellae [108]. It had been observed earlier that the twist of polyethylene lamellae in banded spherulites correlated with the direction of chain tilt, an observation that inspired the model of Keith and Padden. Since the hands of twist and screw dislocations were linked through chain tilt, Bassett then reasoned that lamellar twist was augmented, if not controlled, by isochiral screw dislocations, but in a manner different from that described by Schultz and Kinloch. He proposed that the spiral growth layers in the melt are not parallel to each other but that they splay apart more like the solution-grown spiral in Figure 3.34. This splaying is exactly that described in Section 3.4.3 for branching of dominant lamellae, but now with the condition of isochirality to achieve a persistent sense of twist. In this case the amorphous surface layer creates forces between adjacent layers, rather than within the plane of the basal layers. Larger band spacing S can be attributed to less frequent dislocations at larger T_c.

The "surface stress" and "isochiral dislocation" schools have maintained their independence over the decades. An enlightening exchange of fairly current ideas, largely focused on polyethylene, has been published by Bassett [109] and by Lotz and Cheng [110]. To this author it is evident that both approaches rely on the pre-existence of chain tilt. In one case the tilt results in nonuniform surface stresses during growth, and in the other case the tilt directs the hand of giant screw dislocations. In both cases, lamellar twist of the same hand results. For achiral polymers the probability of right- and left-handed twist should be equal.

The most recent approach to lamellar twist is due to Schultz in 2003 [111]. This model does not involve chain tilt in any way, but it invokes the concentration (or pressure) field that is perpendicular to the growth direction, not that in the growth direction used for treating instabilities in Section 3.2.2. Untwisted growth of a lamella in this field is unstable since a fortuitous incremental rotation will direct the edges into regions of lower impurity concentration and hence faster growth. The accompanying twist creates elastic strains that raise the free energy of the crystal, lower T_m and hence reduce the undercooling ΔT at the growth face to stabilize the twisting growth. This approach is broadly similar to the Mullins–Sekerka analysis [33] of instabilities of a planar interface outlined in Section 3.2.2. When the diffusion length $\delta = D/G$ is increased by raising T_c or molar mass, simulations show that the twist period (or band spacing S)

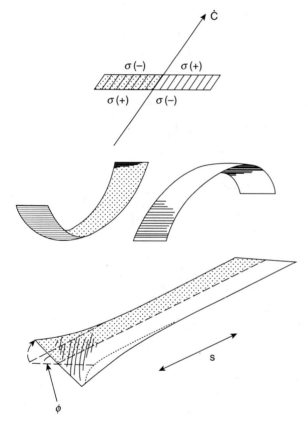

Figure 3.70 The relation between chain tilt and lamellar twist as proposed by Keith and Padden. The top sketch is a view toward advancing growth front that has asymmetry imposed by chain tilt. More compressive stress associated with looser chain folding is indicated by $\sigma(+)$, resulting in transverse torsions that would bend each ribbon half, if free, as in the middle figure. Because the two halves are connected, the end of the ribbon acquires a left handed twist as in the lower figure. From Lotz and Cheng [23] with permission from Elsevier.

increases as observed. While this novel approach seems to predict certain features of twisting, it cannot capture the strong correlation between twisted lamella and chain tilt in achiral polymers. Furthermore, it would improperly predict right- and left-hand twists with equal frequency in a chiral polymer. It appears that Shultz's field-based model does not account for the twisting observed in banded polymer spherulites.

This section is concluded with selected experimental findings that shed some light on banding in polymer spherulites. Returning to chiral polymers, Xu et al. observed twisted lamellar growth in poly(R-3-hydroxybutyrate-co-R-3-hydroxyhexanoate) by time-lapse AFM [103]. Figure 3.71 shows unambiguously the development of uniform right-hand twist during crystallization at $T_c = 85°C$, about 15°C below the experimental T_m. As no

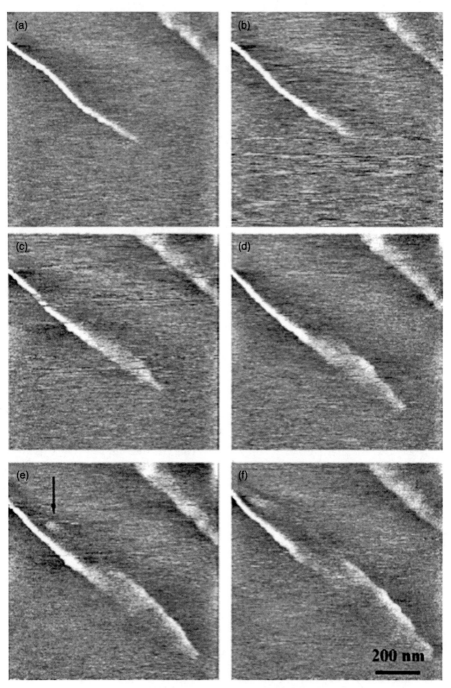

Figure 3.71 AFM phase images at 6-minute intervals of lamellar growth of poly(R-3-hydroxybutryrate-co-R-3-hydroxyhexanoate) at 85°C. A uniform right-handed twist is evident. From Xu et al. [103] with permission from the American Chemical Society.

dislocations are present, either cholesteric-like displacements or surface stresses could cause the twist. For faster growth at $T_c = 75°C$, there appear small spiral growths that are left handed, that is, opposite the hand of the crystal twist. This observation (not shown) seems to be unprecedented. Lamellar twist appears somewhat enhanced at the locations of these screw dislocations, but without any perceptible splay as proposed by Bassett. With the prospect of higher acquisition rate AFM [94], it is likely that this technique can provide much-needed direct information on the development of banded spherulites.

Toda et al. recently reported quite interesting results for the achiral polymers polyethylene [99, 100] and poly(vinylidene fluoride) [112]. Special crystallization cells enabled the determination of growth rate G for banded spherulites at large undercoolings. In addition to G, the maximum lamellar width λ_m and the band spacing S were measured as a function of T_c. As in the analysis of unbanded spherulites described in Section 3.4.3, it was found that the morphological sizes scaled with the square root of the diffusion length:

$$S \propto \lambda_m \propto \left(\frac{D(T)}{G(T)}\right)^{1/2} = \delta(T)^{1/2}. \quad (3.7)$$

Molar mass effects in polyethylene suggested that the diffusivity $D \sim 1/\eta$, implying that the Mullins–Sekerka instability that drives tip-splitting results from a pressure field. Comparison with Equation (3.6) shows that the band spacing S is equivalent to the radial correlation length L, but the dislocations that cause branching are here isochiral as illustrated in Figure 3.72. Chain tilt is responsible for the screw dislocations being isochiral in polyethylene and poly(vinylidine fluoride); in these crystals branching and twist are intimately linked. The temperature dependence of S was found to be consistent with more dislocations in thinner crystals growing at lower T_c, although the implied strain energy of a dislocation was much too small (because the incorrect expression for W_{el} was used). If branching by screw dislocations preserves the direction of chain tilt, then the large sectors of a polyethylene-banded spherulite having the same twist is understandable. We close by restating that this Goldenfeld–Toda approach includes concepts of planar instability from Keith and Padden, isochiral screw dislocations from Schultz and Kinloch, and the coupling of branching and twist as proposed by Bassett. This is currently the best way to think about banded spherulites in achiral polymers.

ACKNOWLEDGMENTS

The author is grateful to P.H. Geil, F. Khoury, B. Lotz, and J.M. Shultz for valuable advice on polymer morphology.

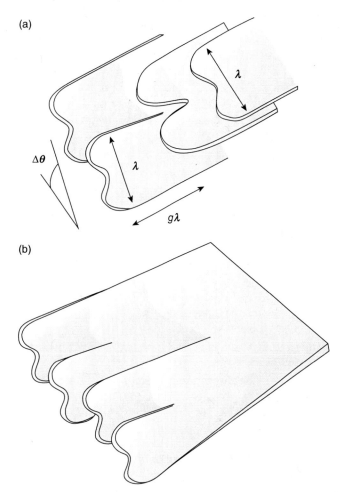

Figure 3.72 Depiction of lamellar growth to width $W = \lambda$ at which size the Mullins–Sekerka instability causes tip splitting that results in isochiral topological screw dislocations. Branching and twisting recur after radial growth by $g\lambda$. From Toda et al. [99] with permission from the American Chemical Society. (See color insert.)

REFERENCES

[1] Hoffman, J.D., Davis, T., Lauritzen, J.I., Jr. The rate of crystallization of linear polymers with chain folding. In *Treatise on Solid State Chemistry*, Vol. 3, Hannay, N.B., ed. Plenum Press, New York, 1976, Chapter 7.

[2] Reneker, D.H., Geil, P.H. *J. Appl. Phys.* **1960**, *31*, 1916–1925.

[3] Geil, P.H., Reneker, D.H. *J. Polym. Sci.* **1961**, *51*, 569–582.

[4] Lovinger, A.J., Cais, R.E. *Macromolecules* **1984**, *17*, 1939–1945.

[5] Khoury, F., Passaglia, E. The morphology of synthetic polymers. In *Treatise on Solid State Chemistry*, Vol. 3, Hannay, N.B., ed. Plenum Press, New York, 1976, Chapter 6.

[6] Wunderlich, B. *Macromolecular Physics*, Vol. 1, Academic Press, New York, 1973. Chapter 3.

[7] Khoury, F., Barnes, J.D. *J. Res. Nat. Bur. Stand.* **1972**, *76A*, 225–252.

[8] Chen, J., Cheng, S.Z.D., Wu, S.S., Lotz, B., Wittmann, J.C. *J. Polym. Sci. B Polym. Phys.* **1995**, *33*, 1861–1855.

[9] Wittmann, J.C., Lotz, B. *J. Polym. Sci. Polym. Phys. Edn.* **1985**, *23*, 205–226.

[10] Khoury, F., Barnes, J.D. *J. Res. Nat. Bur. Stand.* **1974**, *78A*, 95–127.

[11] Morrow, D.R., Sauer, J.A., Woodward, A.E. *J. Polym. Sci.* **1968**, *C16*, 3401–3411.

[12] Dreyfuss, P., Keller, A. *J. Macromol. Sci.-Phys* **1970**, *B4*, 811–836.

[13] Yang, X., Tan, S., Li, G., Zhou, E. *J. Polym. Sci. B Polym. Phys.* **2001**, *39*, 729–735.

[14] Barnes, J.D., Khoury, F. *J. Res. Nat. Bur. Stand.* **1974**, *78A*, 363–373.

[15] Bassett, D.C., Dammont, F.R., Solovey, R. *Polymer* **1964**, *5*, 579–588.

[16] Holland, V.F., Lindenmeyer, P.H. *J. Polym. Sci.* **1962**, *57*, 589–608.

[17] Geil, P.H. *Polymer Single Crystals*, Wiley Interscience, New York, 1963.

[18] Bassett, D.C., Keller, A., Frank, F.C. *Phil. Mag.* **1963**, *8*, 1753–1587.

[19] Toda, A., Okamura, M., Hikosaka, M., Nakagawa, Y. *Polymer* **2003**, *44*, 1635–1638.

[20] Toda, A., Arita, T., Hikosaka, M. *Polymer* **2001**, *42*, 2223–2233.

[21] Briber, R.M., Khoury, F. *J. Polym. Sci. B Polym. Phys.* **1993**, *31*, 1253–1272.

[22] Cai, W., Li, C.Y., Li, L., Lotz, B., Keating, M., Marks, D. *Adv. Mater.* **2004**, *16*, 600–605.

[23] Lotz, B., Cheng, S.Z.D. *Polymer* **2005**, *46*, 577–610.

[24] Bassett, D.C., Keller, A. *Phil. Mag.* **1961**, *6*, 345–358.

[25] Passaglia, E., Khoury, F. *Polymer* **1984**, *25*, 631–644.

[26] Organ, S.J., Keller, A. *J. Polym. Sci. B Polym. Phys.* **1986**, *24*, 2319–2335.

[27] Keith, H.D., Patten, F.J., Jr., Lotz, B., Wittmann, J.C. *Macromolecules* **1989**, *22*, 2230–2238.

[28] Gesti, S., Casas, M.T., Puiggali, J. *Eur. Polym. J.* **2008**, *44*, 2295–2307.

[29] Tiller, W.A., Jackson, K.A., Rutter, J.W., Chalmers, B. *Acta Metall.* **1953**, *1*, 428–437.

[30] Schultz, J.M. *Polymer Crystallization*, American Chemical Society, Washington, DC, 2001. Chapter 10.

[31] Wunderlich, B., James, E.A., Shu, T.-W. *J. Polym. Sci. A* **1964**, *2*, 2759–2769.

[32] Zener, C. *J. Appl. Phys.* **1949**, *40*, 950–953.

[33] Mullins, W.W., Sekerka, R.F. *J. Appl. Phys.* **1963**, *34*, 323–329.

[34] Langer, J.S. *Rev. Mod. Phys.* **1980**, *52*, 1–28.

[35] Brener, E.A., Mel'nikov, V.I. *Adv. Phys.* **1991**, *40*, 53–97.

[36] Granasy, L., Pusztai, T., Börzönyi, T., Warren, J.A., Douglas, J.F. *Nat. Mater.* **2004**, *3*, 645–650.

[37] Frank, F.C. *Discuss. Faraday Soc.* **1949**, *5*, 48–54.

[38] Burton, W.K., Cabrera, N., Frank, F.C. *Philos. Trans. R. Soc. (London)* **1951**, *243*, 299–358.

[39] Müller-Krumbhaar, H., Burkhardt, T.W., Kroll, D.M. *J. Cryst. Growth* **1977**, *38*, 13–22.

[40] Barnes, W.J., Price, F.P. *Polymer* **1964**, *5*, 283–292.

[41] Eshelby, J.D., Stroh, A.N. *Philos. Mag.* **1951**, *42*, 1401–1405.

[42] Kawasara, N., Dasgupta, S., Goddard, W.A. *J. Phys. Chem.* **1991**, *95*, 2260–2272.

[43] Keith, H.D., Chen, W.Y. *Polymer* **2002**, *43*, 6263–6272.

[44] Keith, H.D., Padden, F.J., Jr. *Macromolecules* **1996**, *29*, 7776–7796.

[45] Hirai, N. *J. Polym. Sci.* **1962**, *59*, 321–328.

[46] Keith, H.D., Vadimski, R.G., Padden, F.J., Jr. *J. Polym. Sci. A-2* **1970**, *8*, 1687–1696.

[47] Gohil, R.M., Patel, C.K., Patel, K.C., Patel, R.D. *Eur. Polym. J.* **1973**, *9*, 153–155.

[48] Lotz, B., Kovacs, A.J., Wittmann, J.C. *J. Polym. Sci. Polym. Phys. Edn.* **1975**, *13*, 909–927.

[49] Vand, V., Hanoko, J.I. *Mater. Res. Bull.* **1967**, *2*, 241–251.

[50] Keller, A. *Kolloid- Z.. u. Z. Polymere* **1967**, *219*, 118–131.

[51] Rault, J. *Solid State Comm.* **1975**, *16*, 201–205.

[52] Mitsuhashi, S., Keller, A. *Polymer* **1961**, *2*, 109–112.

[53] Wunderlich, B., Sullivan, .P. *J. Polym. Sci.* **1962**, *61*, 195–221.

[54] Bassett, D.C., Keller, A., Mitsuhashi, S. *J. Polym. Sci. A* **1963**, *1*, 763–788.

[55] Keith, H.D. *J. Polym. Sci. A* **1964**, *2*, 4339–4360.

[56] Keith, H.D. *J. Appl. Phys.* **1964**, *35*, 3115–3126.

[57] Kovacs, A.J., Gonthier, A. *Kolloid. Z. Z. Polym.* **1972**, *250*, 530–551.

[58] Al-Raheil, I.A., Al-Share', M. *J. Appl. Polym. Sci.* **1999**, *72*, 1125–1129.

[59] Friedel, J. *Dislocations*, Pergamon Press, New York, 1964, p. 12.

[60] Geil, P.H. Polyhedral structures in polymers grown from the melt. In *Growth and Perfection of Crystals*, Doremus, R.H., Roberts, B.W., Turnbull, D., eds. Chapman & Hall, New York, 1958, pp. 579–585.

[61] Varga, J., Ehrenstein, G.W. *Colloid Polym. Sci.* **1997**, *275*, 511–519.

[62] Trifonova-van Haerigan, D., Varga, J., Ehrenstein, G.W., Vancso, G.J. *J. Polym. Sci. B Polym. Phys.* **2000**, *38*, 672–681.

[63] Keith, H.D., Padden, F.J., Jr. *J. Polym. Sci. B Polym. Phys.* **1987**, *25*, 2371–2392.

[64] Hashimoto, M. *Polym. J.* **2004**, *36*, 594–599.

[65] Taguchi, K., Miyaji, H., Izumi, K., Hoshino, A., Miyamoto, Y., Kokawa, R. *Polymer* **2001**, *42*, 7443–7447.

[66] Taguchi, K., Miyaji, H., Izumi, K., Hoshino, A., Miyamoto, Y., Kokawa, R. *J. Macromol. Sci. - Phys.* **2002**, *B41*, 1033–1042.

[67] Ellison, C.J., Torkelson, J.M. *Nat. Mater.* **2003**, *2*, 695–700.

[68] Sawamura, S., Miyaji, H., Izumi, K., Sutton, S.J., Miyamatu, Y. *J. Phys. Soc. Jpn.* **1998**, *67*, 3338–3341.

[69] Schönherr, H., Frank, C.W. *Macromolecules* **2003**, *36*, 1199–1208.

[70] Mareau, V.H., Prud'homme, R.E. *Macromolecules* **2005**, *38*, 398–408.

[71] Duan, Y., Zhang, Y., Yan, S., Schultz, J.M. *Polymer* **2005**, *46*, 9015–9021.

[72] (a) Lie, Y.-G., Chan, C.-M., Li, J.-X., Ng, K.M., Wong, Y. *Macromolecules* **2002**, *35*, 6751–6753; (b) Chan, C.-M., Li, L. *Adv. Polym. Sci.* **2005**, *188*, 1–41.

[73] Franke, M., Rehse, N. *Macromolecules* **2008**, *41*, 163–166.

[74] Wunderlich, B., Melillo, L., Cormier, C.M., Davidson, T., Snyder, G. *J. Macromol. Sci.-Phys. B* **1967**, *1*, 485–516.

[75] Grubb, D.T., Keller, A. *J. Polym. Sci. Polym. Sci. Edn.* **1980**, *18*, 207–216.

[76] Keith, H.D., Padden, F.J., Jr. *J. Polym. Sci.* **1959**, *39*, 123–138.

[77] Keith, H.D., Padden, F.J., Jr. *J. Appl. Phys.* **1964**, *35*, 1270–1284.

[78] Price, F.P. *J. Polym. Sci.* **1959**, *37*, 71–89.

[79] Bassett, D.C. *Principles of Polymer Morphology*, Cambridge University Press, New York, 1981, p. 16.

[80] Haudin, J.M. Optical studies of polymer morphology. In *Optical Properties of Polymers*, Meeten, G.H., ed. Elsevier Applied Science Publishers, New York, 1986, Chapter 4.

[81] Stein, R.S., Misra, A., Yuasa, T., Khambatta, F. *Pure Appl. Chem.* **1977**, *49*, 915–928.

[82] Maxfield, J., Mandlelkern, L. *Macromolecules* **1977**, *10*, 1141–1153.

[83] Baert, J., Van Puyvelde, P. *Macromol. Mater. Eng.* **2008**, *293*, 255–273.

[84] Fu, Q., Heck, B., Strobl, G., Thomann, Y. *Macromolecules* **2001**, *34*, 2502–2511.

[85] Hoffman, J.D., Frolen, L.J., Ross, G.S., Lauritzen, J.I., Jr. *J. Res. Nat. Bur. Stand. (U. S.)* **1975**, *79A*, 671–699.

[86] Bassett, D.C., Hodge, A.M., Olley, R.H. *Proc. R. Soc. Lond. A* **1981**, *377*, 39–60.

[87] Allen, R.C., Mandelkern, L. *J. Polym. Sci. Polym. Phys. Edn.* **1982**, *20*, 1465–1484.

[88] Bassett, D.C., Olley, R.H., Sutton, S.J., Vaughan, A.S. *Macromolecules* **1996**, *29*, 1852–1853.

[89] Lei, Y.G., Chan, C.M., Wang, Y., Ng, K.M., Jaing, Y., Lin, L. *Polymer* **2003**, *44*, 4673–4679.

[90] Bassett, D.C. *J. Macromol. Sci.-Phys.* **2003**, *B42*, 227–256.

[91] Keith, H.D., Padden, F.J., Jr. *J. Appl. Phys.* **1963**, *34*, 2409–2421.

[92] Porter, D.A., Easterling, K.E. *Phase Transformations in Metals and Alloys*, 2nd ed. Chapman & Hall, New York, 1992. Chapter 4.

[93] Vaughan, A.S., Bassett, D.C. Crystallization and morphology. In *Comprehensive Polymer Science*, Vol. 2, Allan, G., Bevington, J.C., eds. Pergamon Press, New York, 1989, Chapter 12, pp. 415–457.

[94] Hobbs, J.K., Farrance, O.E., Kailas, L. *Polymer* **2009**, *50*, 4281–4292.

[95] Goldenfeld, N. *J. Cryst. Growth* **1987**, *84*, 601–608.

[96] Abo el Maaty, M.I., Hosier, I.L., Bassett, D.C. *Macromolecules* **1998**, *31*, 153–157.

[97] Kajioka, H., Hikosaka, M., Taguchi, K., Toda, A. *Polymer* **2008**, *49*, 1685–1692.

[98] Kajioka, H., Yoshimoto, S., Taguchi, K., Toda, A. *Macromolecules* **2010**, *43*, 3837–3843.

[99] Toda, A., Okamura, M., Taguchi, K., Hikosaka, M., Kajioka, H. *Macromolecules* **2008**, *41*, 2484–2493.

[100] Toda, A., Taguchi, K., Kajioka, H. *Macromolecules* **2008**, *41*, 7505–7512.

[101] Magill, J.H. Spherulites: a personal perspective. *J. Mater. Sci.* **2001**, *36*, 3143–3164.

[102] Saracovan, I., Keith, H.D., Manley, R.St.J., Brown, G.R. *Macromolecules* **1999**, *32*, 8918–8922.

[103] Xu, J., Guo, B.-G., Zhang, Z.-M., Xhou, J.J., Jiang, Y., Yan, S., Li, L., Schultz, J.M. *Macromolecules* **2004**, *37*, 4118–4123.

[104] Singfield, K.L., Klass, K.M., Brown, G.R. *Macromolecules* **1995**, *28*, 8006–8015.

[105] Saracovan, I., Cox, J.K., Revol, J.-F., Manley, R.St.J., Brown, G.R. *Macromolecules* **1999**, *32*, 717–725.

[106] Ye, H.M., Xu, J., Guo, B.-H., Iwata, T. *Macromolecules* **2009**, *42*, 694–701.

[107] Schultz, J.M., Kinloch, D.R. *Polymer* **1969**, *10*, 271–278.

[108] Bassett, D.C., Olley, R.H., Al Raheil, A.M. *Polymer* **1988**, *29*, 1539–1543.

[109] Bassett, D.C. *Polymer* **2006**, *47*, 3263–3266.

[110] Lotz, B., Cheng, S.Z.D., Bassett, D.C. *Polymer* **2006**, *47*, 3267–3270.

[111] Schultz, J.M. *Polymer* **2003**, *44*, 433–431.

[112] Toda, A., Taguchi, K., Hikosaka, M., Kajioka, H. *Polymer J.* **2008**, *40*, 905–909.

4

POLYMER NUCLEATION

KIYOKA N. OKADA AND MASAMICHI HIKOSAKA
Graduate School of Integrated Arts and Sciences, Hiroshima University, Higashi-Hiroshima City, Hiroshima, Japan

4.1 Introduction, 126
4.2 Classical Nucleation Theory, 126
    4.2.1 Nucleation Rate (I), 126
    4.2.2 Free Energy for Formation of a Nucleus $\Delta G(N)$, 127
    4.2.3 Free Energy for Formation of a Critical Nucleus (ΔG^*), 127
    4.2.4 Shape of a Nucleus Is Related to Kinetic Parameters, 128
    4.2.5 Diffusion, 128
4.3 Direct Observation of Nano-Nucleation by Synchrotron Radiation, 128
    4.3.1 Introduction and Experimental Procedure, 128
    4.3.2 Observation of Nano-Nucleation by SAXS, 128
    4.3.3 Extended Guinier Plot Method and Iteration Method, 129
    4.3.4 Kinetic Parameters and Size Distribution of the Nano-Nucleus, 130
    4.3.5 Real Image of Nano-Nucleation, 131
    4.3.6 Supercooling Dependence of Nano-nucleation, 133
    4.3.7 Relationship between Nano-Nucleation and Macro-Crystallization, 133
4.4 Improvement of Nucleation Theory, 135
    4.4.1 Introduction, 135
    4.4.2 Nucleation Theory Based on Direct Observation of Nucleation, 135
    4.4.3 Confirmation of the Theory by Overall Crystallinity, 137
4.5 Homogeneous Nucleation from the Bulk Melt under Elongational Flow, 139
    4.5.1 Introduction and Case Study, 139
    4.5.2 Formulation of Elongational Strain Rate $\dot{\varepsilon}$, 139
    4.5.3 Nano-Oriented Crystals, 140
    4.5.4 Evidence of Homogeneous Nucleation, 144
    4.5.5 Nano-Nucleation Results in Ultrahigh Performance, 147
4.6 Heterogeneous Nucleation, 148
    4.6.1 Introduction, 148
    4.6.2 Experimental, 149
    4.6.3 Role of Epitaxy in Heterogeneous Nucleation, 150
    4.6.4 Acceleration Mechanism of Nucleation of Polymers by Nano-Sizing of Nucleating Agent, 153
4.7 Effect of Entanglement Density on the Nucleation Rate, 156
    4.7.1 Introduction and Experimental, 156
    4.7.2 Increase of v_e Leads to a Decrease of I, 157
    4.7.3 Change of v_e with Δt, 158
    4.7.4 Two-Step Entangling Model, 159
4.8 Conclusion, 160
Acknowledgments, 161
References, 161

Handbook of Polymer Crystallization, First Edition. Edited by Ewa Piorkowska and Gregory C. Rutledge.
© 2013 John Wiley & Sons, Inc. Published 2013 by John Wiley & Sons, Inc.

4.1 INTRODUCTION

Crystallization from the melt (or gas) is one of the most predominant and well-known phenomena in any material. Nucleation is the early stage of crystallization and significantly controls the structure and physical properties of materials. Described by the classical nucleation theory (CNT) proposed by Becker and Döring, Turnbull and Fisher, and Frenkel in the 1930s [1–3], nucleation has an "induction" and a "steady" period. The induction period leads to the steady period when the nuclei are steadily generated.

Solving the nucleation mechanism is important to understand structures and physical properties of any materials. To our best knowledge, no one has succeeded in observing directly the nucleation from the melt, because the number density of small nuclei on the order of nanometers (which we will henceforth call a "nano-nucleus") is too small to detect [4, 5]. Hence, only alternative experimental studies have been performed on macroscopic crystals (macro-crystals) by means of optical microscopy (OM) or bubble chamber [2]. Recent simulation studies performed on colloid systems [6, 7] also fail to provide a direct observation of nano-nucleation because the thermal fluctuation of nano-nuclei should be much more significant than that of macro-crystals or macro-colloids. This chapter introduces CNT, describes experimental approaches, and discusses the results of direct observation of nano-nucleation.

From the analysis of nano-nucleation, we could obtain kinetic parameters, such as surface free energies of nano-nucleus. Kinetic parameters, which are the surface free energies of a nano-nucleus, are the most important factor in qualitative predictions of the nucleation rate. These kinetic parameters are obtained by solving the simultaneous equations obtained from the degree of supercooling (ΔT) dependences of the nucleation rate (I) or induction time (τ_i) and growth rate (V) in the steady state [8, 9], and from the size dependence of the melting temperature (T_m) of macro-crystals by using the Gibbs–Thomson plot [10].

The scientific goal of nucleation study is to obtain an experimental real image of nano-nucleation and to propose a correct nucleation theory that can explain and predict the nucleation. We have to approach the scientific goal from two different angles, one experimental and the other theoretical.

Two approaches can explain and predict nucleation. The experimental approach tries to clarify the real image of nucleation: how the size, shape, and number of nuclei evolve with the increase of crystallization time (t), that is, to make clear the size distribution $f(N, t)$, where N is the number of particles within a nucleus that indicate atoms, molecules, or sometimes repeating units. It has been impossible to observe $f(N, t)$ directly for a long time.

The theoretical approach constructs a basic equation to explain the observed $f(N, t)$. CNT proposes a fundamental kinetic equation as a basic equation of nucleation by using $f(N, t)$ [3]. However, the kinetic equation of CNT (as presented below) does not satisfy the fundamental mass conservation law, which means that the kinetic equation cannot be regarded as a basic equation. Any basic equation includes parameters (the so-called kinetic parameters determined experimentally) that give actual information about nucleus, nucleation, and so on. It remains an important problem to obtain correct kinetic parameters of nano-nucleation.

4.2 CLASSICAL NUCLEATION THEORY

4.2.1 Nucleation Rate (I)

CNT assumes that the nucleation process is approximated by a linear sequential rate process, as illustrated in Figure 4.1 [1, 2]. N indicates the N-th stage in a nucleation process where a nucleus includes N particles. During the nucleation process, one particle frequently repeats attachment and detachment on the surface of a nucleus. Here, we assume a huge closed system, including a huge total number of particles. The nuclei are generated from the supercooled melt (or supersaturated gas), and finally the system transforms into a single crystal or polycrystals.

The fundamental kinetic equation is as follows:

$$\partial f(N,t)/\partial t \equiv I(N-1,t) - I(N,t), \qquad (4.1)$$

where $I(N, t)$ is a nucleation rate defined by

$$I(N,t) \equiv \alpha'_N f(N,t) - \beta'_{N+1} f(N+1,t), \qquad (4.2)$$

and where α'_N and β'_{N+1} are the transition probabilities of forward and backward flows between the N-th and $N + 1$-th stages, respectively.

Turnbull and Fisher, and Frank and Tosi formulated the $I(N, t)$ for a steady state (I), assuming $I(N-1, t) = I(N,$

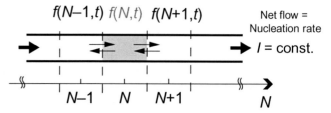

Figure 4.1 Illustration of a linear sequential rate process of the steady state of nucleation for $N \gg N^*$ in CNT.

$t) = \text{const.} \equiv I$ [2, 11]. They obtained the well-known formula,

$$I = I_0 \exp[-\Delta G^*/kT_c], \quad (4.3)$$

where I_0 is the so-called prefactor, ΔG^* is the activation-free energy necessary for formation of a critical nucleus, k is Boltzmann's constant, and T_c is a crystallization temperature. Turnbull and Fisher show that I_0 is given by

$$I_0 = f_0(kT_c/h)\exp[-\Delta E/kT_c], \quad (4.4)$$

where f_0 is f at the zero-th stage, h is Plank's constant, and ΔE is the activation-free energy for the diffusion of particles necessary to join a new lattice moving across an interface. (kT/h) is a frequency factor. Equation (4.4) indicates that two factors—diffusion and the probability of formation of critical nuclei—control the nucleation rate. The first is a function of temperature T, whereas the second is a function of ΔT defined by $\Delta T \equiv T_m^o - T_c$, where T_m^o is the equilibrium melting temperature. Therefore, I is a function of T and ΔT.

There are two kinds of nucleation: heterogeneous and homogeneous. Heterogeneous nucleation is the process of birth of small crystalline regions on or near surfaces of some heterogeneities (impurities) [12], and homogeneous nucleation is the process of birth of small regions of the crystalline phase in the pure supercooled melt. Note that most crystallization from the bulk melt is of the heterogeneous nucleation type and that homogeneous nucleation requires large supercooling, which can be reached in thin films by fast quenching, or in droplets too small to contain the heterogeneities able to nucleate crystallization [13]. See Chapters 11 and 13 for a detailed description of crystallization in polymer droplets.

4.2.2 Free Energy for Formation of a Nucleus $\Delta G(N)$

We consider nucleation from the melt and assume a three-dimensional (3D) rectangular parallelepiped nucleus with sizes of l, m, and n, which are counted by the number of particles or repeating units. l is counted along the polymer chains. N is given by

$$N = lmn \text{ for the 3D nucleus} \quad (4.5a)$$

$$= ln \text{ for the two-dimensional (2D) nucleus.} \quad (4.5b)$$

We assume $m = 1$ for the 2D nucleus. The free energy for formation of a nucleus $(\Delta G(N))$ is defined as

$$\Delta G(N) = G_c(N) - G_m(N), \quad (4.6)$$

where G_c and G_m are the Gibbs's free energy of a crystal and the melt, respectively. $\Delta G(N)$ becomes negative for large N for the supercooled melt, which is the driving force of nucleation.

In the case of heterogeneous nucleation, the $\Delta G(N)$ of the 3D and 2D nuclei are given by

$$\Delta G(N) = -N\Delta g + 2\sigma_e mn + 2\sigma lm + \Delta\sigma nl \text{ for the 3D heterogeneous nucleation} \quad (4.7a)$$

or

$$\Delta G(N) = -N\Delta g + 2\sigma_e n + 2\sigma l + \Delta\sigma nl \text{ for the 2D heterogeneous nucleation,} \quad (4.7b)$$

respectively, where Δg is the free energy of fusion (melting), σ_e and σ are the end and lateral surface free energies, respectively, and $\Delta\sigma$ is defined by

$$\Delta\sigma \equiv \sigma + \sigma_{0s} - \sigma_s, \quad (4.8)$$

where σ_{0s} is the free energy between the heterogeneity crystal and the nucleus, and σ_s is the surface free energy between the heterogeneity and the melt. Here, m is normal to the interface between the nucleus and the heterogeneity and σ, σ_e, $\Delta\sigma$, and Δg are defined per repeating unit. Δg is given approximately by

$$\Delta g = \frac{\Delta h \Delta T}{T_m^o}, \quad (4.9)$$

where Δh is the enthalpy of fusion and also is defined per repeating unit.

In the case of homogeneous nucleation, $\Delta G(N)$ of the 3D nucleus is given by

$$\Delta G(N) = -N\Delta g + 2\sigma_e mn + 2\sigma lm + 2\sigma nl \text{ for the 3D homogeneous nucleation.} \quad (4.10)$$

4.2.3 Free Energy for Formation of a Critical Nucleus (ΔG^*)

Since ΔG^* is the maximum of $\Delta G(N)$, we can formulate ΔG^* by $\partial\Delta G(N)/\partial N = 0$. In the case of heterogeneous nucleation, the ΔG^*s of 3D and 2D nuclei are given by

$$\Delta G^* = \frac{16\sigma\sigma_e\Delta\sigma}{\Delta g^2} \text{ for the 3D corresponding to } \Delta g < 2\Delta\sigma \quad (4.11a)$$

and

$$\Delta G^* = \frac{4\sigma\sigma_e}{\Delta g - \Delta\sigma} \text{ for the 2D corresponding to } \Delta g \geq 2\Delta\sigma, \quad (4.11b)$$

respectively.

In the case of homogeneous nucleation, the ΔG^* is given by

$$\Delta G^* = \frac{32\sigma^2 \sigma_e}{\Delta g^2}. \quad (4.12)$$

4.2.4 Shape of a Nucleus Is Related to Kinetic Parameters

It is reasonable to assume that the shape of the nano-nucleus is similar to that of a critical nucleus with the sizes of l^*, m^*, and n^*, that is:

$$l : m : n = l^* : m^* : n^* \text{ for the 3D nucleus} \quad (4.13a)$$

or

$$l : n = l^* : n^* \text{ for the 2D nucleus.} \quad (4.13b)$$

In the case of heterogeneous nucleation, l^*, m^* and n^* are given by

$$\begin{aligned} l^* &= 4\sigma_e/\Delta g, m^* = 2\Delta\sigma/\Delta g \text{ and} \\ n^* &= 4\sigma/\Delta g \text{ for the 3D nucleus,} \end{aligned} \quad (4.14a)$$

or

$$l^* = 4\sigma_e/\Delta g, m^* = 1 \text{ and } n^* = 4\sigma/\Delta g \text{ for the 2D nucleus.} \quad (4.14b)$$

As m^* is given by Equation (4.14), m^* becomes less than unity ($m^* \leq b1$) with the increase of $\Delta g \propto \Delta T$. In this case we change the critical nucleus from 3D to 2D. As m^* should be an integer, m^* of the 2D nucleus is given by $m^* = 1$ as follows:

$$\begin{aligned} &m^* > 1 \text{ for } \Delta g < 2\Delta\sigma \text{ or } \Delta T < \Delta T^\dagger \\ &\text{(3D critical nucleus) and} \end{aligned} \quad (4.15a)$$

$$m^* = 1 \text{ for } \Delta g \geq 2\Delta\sigma \text{ or } \Delta T \geq \Delta T^\dagger \text{ (2D critical nucleus),} \quad (4.15b)$$

where

$$\Delta T^\dagger = 2T_m^o \Delta\sigma/\Delta h \quad (4.16)$$

from Equation (4.9) and Equation (4.15). When $m^* = 1$ (2D critical nucleus), we assume that m of the nano-nucleus is unity, that is, $m = 1$ for $\Delta g \geq 2\Delta\sigma$ or $\Delta T \geq \Delta T^\dagger$ (2D nucleus).

4.2.5 Diffusion

Frank and Tosi consider three types of diffusion: within the melt, within the interface and within the crystals. Thus, the diffusion process with the highest ΔE should become the main rate determinant in the nucleation process. Diffusion within the crystals is not well known, but it is sometimes important, for example, nucleation in a multicomponent system [11], and the chain sliding diffusion of polymer chains, which mainly controls the formation of folded-chain crystals (FCCs) and extended-chain crystals (ECCs) [14, 15].

CNT shows that the two competing factors controlling the nucleation process, ΔG and ΔE, both correspond to the thermodynamic driving force and kinetic activation barrier in nucleation, respectively.

4.3 DIRECT OBSERVATION OF NANO-NUCLEATION BY SYNCHROTRON RADIATION

4.3.1 Introduction and Experimental Procedure

This section describes two case studies by synchrotron radiation [16, 17]. The first is the small-angle X-ray scattering (SAXS) observation of nano-nucleation of polyethylene (PE). The second is the t revolution of $f(N, t)$.

We observe nano-nucleation directly by adding nucleating agent (NA) to a sample by which the SAXS intensity $I_X(q, t)$ from the nano-nuclei increases as much as 10^4 times, where q is the scattering vector [18, 19]. At the same time, we determine the correct $f(N, t)$ and the 2D shape of the nano-nucleus. In addition, obtaining the ΔT dependence of $f(N, t)$ directly by SAXS shows that nucleation controls the induction period of crystallization, while spinodal decomposition does not [20].

The material is fully fractionated PE (NIST, SRM1483, $M_n = 32 \times 10^3$, $M_w/M_n = 1.1$). We mix PE with NA to increase SAXS intensity from the nano-nuclei, and call it PE+NA [21]. The concentration of NA in a mixture of PE and NA (C_{NA}) is $C_{NA} = 3$ wt%. We melt the sample and then isothermally crystallize it at several T_cs. The ΔT is $\Delta T = 10.5$–13.0 K.

Next, we use another fully fractionated PE ($M_n = 30 \times 10^3$, $M_w/M_n = 1.15$) material for polarizing optical microscopy (POM) observation [8]. We count the number of isolated crystals for which size (a) is $a \geq 1$ µm, where I is defined by

$$I \equiv dv(t)/dt, \quad (4.17)$$

where $v(t)$ is the number density of the nuclei. See References [16] and [17] for the experimental details.

4.3.2 Observation of Nano-Nucleation by SAXS

Figure 4.2 shows the ΔT dependence of $I_X(q, t)$ against q as a function of t, where $I_X(q, t)$ is corrected by sub-

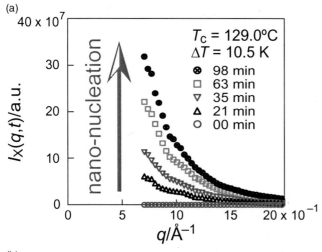

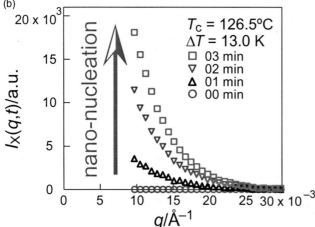

Figure 4.2 ΔT dependence of $I_X(q,t)$ against q as a parameter of t. (a) T_c=129.0°C and ΔT = 10.5 K. (b) T_c = 126.5°C and ΔT = 13.0 K. $I_X(q,t)$ increases with the increase of t, which is the evidence of nano-nucleation. Since $I_X(q,t)$ increases slowly with the decrease of ΔT, it indicates that nano-nucleation becomes difficult with the decrease of ΔT.

tracting the background. $I_X(q, t)$ increases slowly with the increase of t at small ΔT (Fig. 4.2a). At large ΔT, $I_X(q, t)$ increases several orders of magnitude more quickly than for small ΔT, with the increase of t (Fig. 4.2b). In a polymer system, many kinds of fluctuations give $I_X(q,t)$, such as density fluctuations due to nucleation, those due to spinodal decomposition, density fluctuations in amorphous states, density fluctuations in mesophases, and so on. As only the density fluctuations due to nucleation change significantly with the decrease of ΔT and finally diminish in the limit of $\Delta T = 0$, which means $\lim_{\Delta T \to 0} I_X(q,t) = 0$, the observed ΔT dependence of $I_X(q,t)$ clarifies that the increase of $I_X(q,t)$ with the increase of t is evidence of nano-nucleation. Therefore, the induction period, which is an early stage of crystallization by CNT, is due to a nucleation process, and not phase separation, such as spinodal decomposition [20].

4.3.3 Extended Guinier Plot Method and Iteration Method

When nano-nuclei are isolated and dispersed uniformly, $I_X(q,t)$ is given by a summation of the scattering intensities from the isolated nuclei. According to the Guinier plot, $I_X(q, t)$ is approximated by

$$I_X(q,t) = \sum_j I^0_{Xj} \exp\left[-R^2_{gj} q^2 /3\right] \text{ for } R^2_{gj} q^2/3 < 1, \quad (4.18)$$

where

$$I^0_{Xj} = \Delta\rho^2 N^2_j f(N_j, t), \quad (4.19)$$

j indicates the different nuclei of size N_j, $\Delta\rho$ is the difference of the mean electron density between the nucleus and the melt, and R_{gj} is the radius of gyration corresponding to the nuclei of N_j [22, 23]. Finally, we have

$$N_j = \frac{93\sqrt{3}\sigma\sigma_e\Delta\sigma}{(4\sigma^2 + 4\sigma_e^2 + \Delta\sigma^2)^{3/2}}\left(\frac{R_{gj}}{c_0}\right)^3 \text{ for the 3D nucleus} \quad (4.20a)$$

$$= \frac{12\sigma\sigma_e}{\sigma^2 + \sigma_e^2}\left(\frac{R_{gj}}{c_0}\right)^2 \text{ for the 2D nucleus,} \quad (4.20b)$$

where c_0 is the dimension of the repeating units along the molecular chain. In this case study, we use N_j of the 2D nucleus. The combination of Equation (4.19) and Equation (4.20) gives

$$f(N_j,t) = \frac{I^0_{Xj}}{\Delta\rho^2} \frac{(4\sigma^2 + 4\sigma_e^2 + \Delta\sigma^2)^3}{(93\sqrt{3}\sigma\sigma_e\Delta\sigma)^2}\left(\frac{c_0}{R_{gj}}\right)^6 \quad (4.21a)$$

for the 3D nucleus

$$= \frac{I^0_{Xj}}{\Delta\rho^2}\left(\frac{\sigma^2 + \sigma_e^2}{12\sigma\sigma_e}\right)^2\left(\frac{c_0}{R_{gj}}\right)^4 \quad (4.21b)$$

for the 2D nucleus.

Figure 4.3 shows part of the typical result of the extended Guinier plot method for t = 77 minutes, where $\ln I_X(q,t)$ separates into five straight lines of I_{Xj}s. Here I_{X5}, which corresponds to the smallest R_{g5}, is mainly fitted to the $I_X(q,t)$ for the range of $0.01 \leq q^2 \leq 0.015$ Å^{-2}. We obtain R_{gj} and $\ln I^0_{Xj}$ from the slope and vertical intercept of the straight lines, respectively. Note that the slope or R_{gj} increases with the decrease of q^2. We apply the extended Guinier plot method independently for $\ln I_X(q,t)$ against q^2 at each observed t by using Equation (4.18), which also separates them into five straight lines.

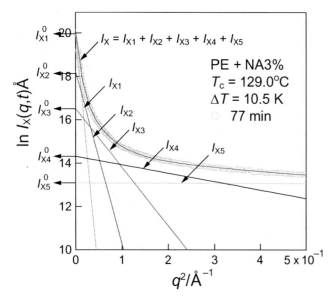

Figure 4.3 Typical result of extended Guinier plot method at $T_c = 129.0°C$. Five straight lines ($I_{X1}, I_{X2}, \ldots I_{X5}$) are separated from $\ln I_X(q, t)$ for $0.05 \times 10^{-3} \leq q^2 \leq 15 \times 10^{-3} \text{Å}^{-2}$. R_{gj} and I^0_{Xj} are obtained from the slope and vertical intercept of the straight lines, respectively. (See color insert.)

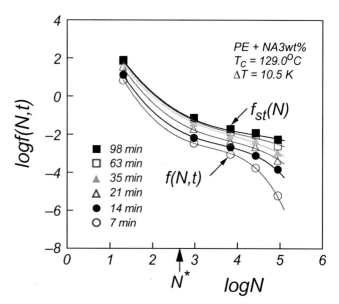

Figure 4.4 Plots of $\log f(N, t)$ against $\log N$ as a function of t at $T_c = 129.0°C$. Five plots of $f(N, t)$ are decomposed by the extended Guinier plot method. $N^* \cong 450$ rep. unit. $f(N,t)$ decreases with the increase of N for any t. This means that a small fraction of nano-nuclei survive and grow up to macro-crystals.

4.3.4 Kinetic Parameters and Size Distribution of the Nano-Nucleus

We determine $f(N, t)$ and the shape of the nano-nucleus as follows. First, we note that $f_{st}(N)$, which is $f(N, t)$ in the steady state, has to be in proportion to the Boltzmann distribution $P_B(N)$ for $N < N^*$, where N^* is N of the critical nucleus [3, 24]. That is,

$$P_B(N) = \exp[-\Delta G(N)/kT] \text{ for } N < N^*. \quad (4.22)$$

$\Delta G(N)$ is given by

$$\Delta G(N) = -\Delta g N + (108\sigma\sigma_e\Delta\sigma)^{1/3} N^{2/3} \text{ for the 3D nucleus} \quad (4.23a)$$

$$= -(\Delta g - \Delta\sigma)N + 4(\sigma\sigma_e)^{1/2} N^{1/2} \text{ for the 2D nucleus [12, 25]}. \quad (4.23b)$$

This allows us to evaluate the kinetic parameters of the nano-nucleus, σ, σ_e, and $\Delta\sigma$, by fitting $P_B(N)$ to the observed $f_{st}(N)$ using the following iteration method, which is one of the technical methods for simultaneously determining $f(N, t)$ and the shape of the nano-nucleus

Step 1: Start from an appropriate set of kinetic parameters (in this study, the kinetic parameters of the macro-crystals in Reference [8]) and calculate $P_B(N)$ using Equation (4.22) and Equation (4.23). Obtain $f_{st}(N)$ using Equation (4.21).

Step 2: Compare the obtained $f_{st}(N)$ with $P_B(N)$. The boundary condition is $f_{st}(0) = P_B(0)$.

Step 3: From the comparison, assume an improved set of kinetic parameters and recalculate $P_B(N)$ and $f_{st}(N)$. Return to Step 2 and trace the loop between Step 3 and Step 2 to obtain the best fit between $f_{st}(N)$ and $P_B(N)$. Thus, we could finally determine correct $f_{st}(N)$ and kinetic parameters.

We can also obtain the correct $f(N_j, t)$ by substituting the parameters, R_{gj} and I^0_{Xj}, into Equation (4.21). Use σ of paraffin as σ(nano), σ(nano) = 7.3×10^{-3} J/m², since the structure of the side surface of the nano-nucleus should be similar to that of paraffin (or n-alkane) [26]. In this case, use Equation (4.16) to obtain $\Delta T^\dagger \cong 7$ K. Since the observed $\Delta T = 10.5$ and 13.0 K satisfy $\Delta T > \Delta T^\dagger$, the shape of nucleus becomes 2D.

We obtain the kinetic parameters σ_e(nano) and $\Delta\sigma$ of the nano-nucleus $\Delta\sigma$(nano). They are σ_e(nano) = 18.5×10^{-3} J/m² and $\Delta\sigma$(nano) = 1.0×10^{-3} J/m². Previously, σ_e(macro) = 88×10^{-3} J/m² was obtained using ΔT dependence of I of the macro-crystals (Gibbs–Thomson plot) by means of OM [8]. Therefore, σ_e(nano) is much smaller than σ_e(macro),

$$\sigma_e(\text{nano}) \cong \frac{1}{5}\sigma_e(\text{macro}) \ll \sigma_e(\text{macro}). \quad (4.24)$$

Figure 4.4 shows the plot obtained for $\log f(N, t)$ against $\log N$ as a function of t. The five plots of $f(N, t)$ are ingredients decomposed by Equation (4.18). $f(N, t)$ decreases with the increase of N for any t. This means that a small number of nano-nuclei survive and grow up to macro-crystals. $f(N, t)$ increases with the increase of t at a fixed N and stops increasing after 100 minutes for $N \leq N^*$. Increasing $f(N, t)$ and constant $f(N, t)$ indicate the induction and steady periods, respectively.

Figure 4.5a shows the t evolution of $f(N, t)$ as a function of N. $f(N, t)$ of smaller N increases significantly and quickly and becomes saturated with the increase of t, whereas $f(N, t)$ of the larger N increases more slowly and becomes saturated with the increase of t. Figure 4.5a shows τ_i after the definition of Andres and Boudart [27]. Figure 4.5b, which illustrates the nano-nucleation, shows that smaller nano-nuclei are generated for $t = 7$ minutes, many nano-nuclei are generated and some grow up to larger ones for $t = 35$ minutes, and many more nano-nuclei and larger ones are generated and grow up for $t \cong 100$ minutes.

4.3.5 Real Image of Nano-Nucleation

We fit the $f_{st}(N)$ obtained in Figure 4.4 against N with $P_B(N)$ (P_B(nano)) for $N < N^*$ using the boundary condition of Step 2, as shown in Figure 4.6a. P_B(nano) fits $f_{st}(N)$ very well for $N < N^*$. For comparison, Figure 4.6a shows the $P_B(N)$ of the macro-crystals (P_B(macro)) using the kinetic parameters of macro-crystals using the

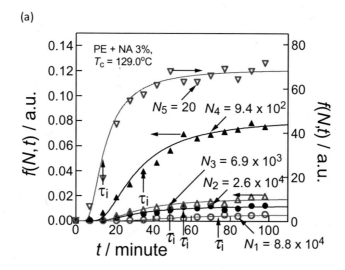

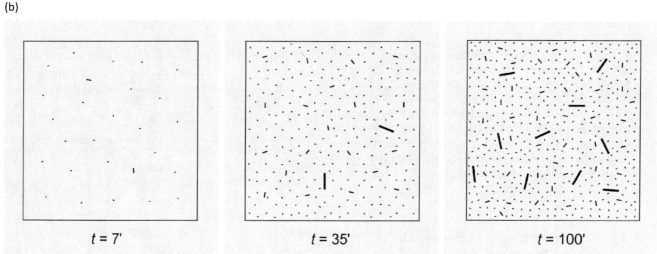

Figure 4.5 Time evolution of $f(N, t)$. (a) Time evolution of $f(N, t)$ as a function of N. Right axis indicates $f(N, t)$ of $N_5 = 20$ rep. unit, and left axis indicates that of the other N_j. $f(N, t)$ of smaller N increased significantly faster and saturated with the increase of t. τ_is are also shown. (b) Illustration of nano-nucleation. Smaller nano-nuclei generated for $t = 7$ min. Many nano-nuclei are generated and a fraction of them grow up to larger ones for $t = 35$ min. Much more nano-nuclei and larger ones were generated and grew up for $t \cong 100$ min.

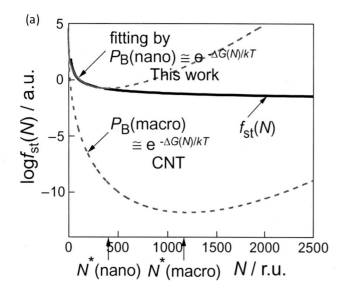

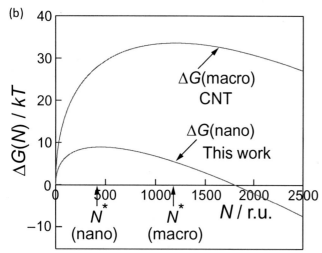

Figure 4.6 (a) Fitting of $\log f_{st}(N)$ with P_B(nano) and P_B(macro). The Boltzmann distributions P_B(nano) and P_B(macro) were calculated by using kinetic parameters of the nano-nucleus and macro-crystal, respectively. P_B(nano) fits $f_{st}(N)$ very well for $N < N^*$, but P_B(macro) does not fit at all. (b) $\Delta G(N)$ against N of nano-nucleus and macro-crystal, which correspond to P_B(nano) and P_B(macro), respectively. $\Delta G_{nano}(N)$, $\Delta G_{macro}(N)$, N^*_{nano}, and N^*_{macro} are $\Delta G(N)$ and N of the critical nucleus calculated using σ_e(nano) and σ_e(macro), respectively. $\Delta G_{nano}(N)$ is much smaller than $\Delta G_{macro}(N)$ for $N \leq N^*$.

boundary condition of Step 2. P_B(macro) does not fit $f_{st}(N)$ at all for $N < N^*$.

If nano-nucleation is a thermal equilibrium phenomenon for all N, we expect that $f_{st}(N)$ should satisfy the Boltzmann distribution. Hence $f_{st}(N)$ should give a minimum at $N = N^*$ and increase significantly for $N > N^*$. However, the observed $f_{st}(N)$ decreases with the increase of N. Therefore P_B(nano) does not fit for $N > N^*$. This means that the nucleation in $N > N^*$ should be a kind of nonequilibrium kinetic phenomenon. To explain this mystery, we propose the nucleation theory described in Section 4.4.

Since Equation (4.24) shows σ_e(nano) $\ll \sigma_e$(macro), $\Delta G_{nano}(N) \ll \Delta G_{macro}(N)$ for $N \leq N^*$ based on Equation (4.23). Figure 4.6b shows the plots of $\Delta G_{nano}(N)$ and $\Delta G_{macro}(N)$. We have

$$\Delta G^*_{nano}(N^*_{nano}) \cong 10kT \ll \Delta G^*_{macro}(N^*_{macro}) \cong 33kT \text{ for } \Delta T = 10.5 \text{ K}, \quad (4.25)$$

where ΔG^*_{nano}, ΔG^*_{macro}, N^*_{nano}, and N^*_{macro} are ΔG^* and N^* using σ_e(nano) and σ_e(macro), respectively. In this case, we also obtain $N^*_{nano} \ll N^*_{macro}$. From the above considerations, we observe large fluctuations of the nano-nucleus with respect to the shape and/or size. Hence, the nano-nucleus can take all possible shapes and has large entropy. The nano-nucleus appears and disappears frequently. In particular, the attachment and detachment of particles or repeating units are very frequent on the interface of the nucleus and there is significant unevenness. Therefore, it is natural that the nano-nucleus is in a quasithermal equilibrium state.

On the other hand, the macro-crystal has less fluctuation with respect to its shape and size. Actually, we can neglect the disappearance of crystal, and $f(N, t)$ cannot decrease with the increase of N for $N \gg N^*$, as optical observation usually shows. Therefore, P_B(macro) cannot fit.

In the case of macro-crystals, it is well known that surface particles are thermodynamically reconstructed into smooth and flat surface by surface diffusion, which is a kind of "Ostwald ripening" and results in large σ_e(macro).

It is interesting to clarify what kind of molecular structure of end surface of polymer crystals corresponds to small and large σ_es of nano-nucleus and macro-crystal of polymers, respectively. However, the size of σ_e also affects the end structures. Figure 4.7 shows that the nano-nucleus will form a loosely folded or bundle nucleus as Price predicted [12]. In the case of a loosely folded or bundle type nano-nucleus (small N), the chain density on the end surface is small and not overcrowded. In the case of a fold type nano-nucleus, the energy required to form sharp folds is very large because one fold of PE has to have three gauche bonds [28]. Therefore, σ_e (loose fold or bundle) is much smaller than σ_e(fold), that is,

$$\sigma_e(\text{loose fold or bundle}) \ll \sigma_e(\text{fold}) \text{ for small } N. \quad (4.26)$$

Macro-crystals tend to form sharp folds [29]. If the nucleus remains bundle-like throughout the construc-

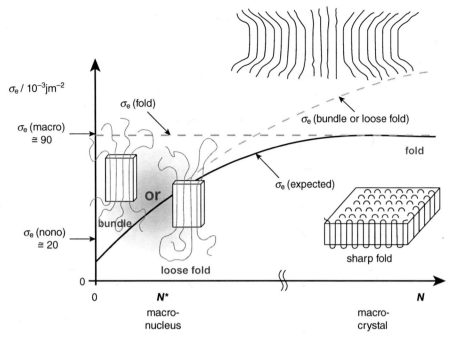

Figure 4.7 Schematic illustration of σ_e against N. The nano-nucleus should form a loose fold or bundle nucleus as Price showed [12] because the energy to form sharp folds is very large. The macro-crystal tends to form sharp folds [29]. Therefore, σ_e(expected) shows the size dependence of expected σ_e. (See color insert.)

tion, the chain density of the end surface increases with the increase of N. Thus, the macro-crystal forms folds to protect against the overcrowded state of chains. The energy needed to form the folds becomes smaller than that needed to form bundles or loose folds. Therefore, it is expected that

$$\sigma_e(\text{loose fold of bundle}) \gg \sigma_e(\text{fold}) \text{ for large } N. \quad (4.27)$$

Figure 4.7 shows the expected size dependence of σ_e as σ_e(expected). We conclude that the molecular structure of the end surface, that is, σ_e, changes with the increase of N.

4.3.6 Supercooling Dependence of Nano-nucleation

Recognizing that the driving force of nucleation and growth is Δg and that $\Delta g \propto \Delta T$ allows us to obtain the ΔT dependence of $f(N, t)$. Figure 4.8a shows $f(N, t)$ against t as a function of ΔT for $N = 2.2 \times 10^4$ repeat units > $N^*(\Delta T = 10.5 \text{ K}) \cong 450$ repeat units, which is the maximum $N^*(\Delta T)$ in this study. $f(N, t)$ begins to increase after a few minutes, increases in proportion to the increase of t and saturated. $f(N, t)$ increases rapidly with the increase of t at large ΔT, while $f(N, t)$ increases slowly at small ΔT. These results confirm that nano-nucleation becomes impossible for smaller ΔT. Note that it is impossible to observe the saturation of $f(N,t)$ for larger ΔT due to the onset of lamellar stacking [18, 19].

We obtain τ_i by Andres and Boudart's method as shown in Figure 4.8a [27] and then $f_{st}^{-1}(N) \cdot \int_0^\infty \{f_{st}(N) - f(N,t)\}dt$ [27] by changing I in Reference [27] to $f(N, t)$. Again, since we cannot observe the saturation of $f(N,t)$ against t at large ΔT, it is impossible to observe τ_i. Therefore, we obtain the onset time $\tau(\Delta T)$, defined as the extrapolated time of the linearly increasing $f(N, t)$. We assume that the $\tau(\Delta T)$ is proportional to τ_i. Figure 4.8b shows how we plot $\tau^{-1}(\Delta T)$ against ΔT^{-1} for $N = 2.2 \times 10^4$ repeat units>$N^*(\Delta T)$, meaning that $\tau^{-1}(\Delta T)$ decreases exponentially with increase of ΔT^{-1}. The empirical formula is

$$\tau^{-1}(\Delta T) \propto \exp[-\gamma/\Delta T], \quad (4.28)$$

where γ is a constant given by $\gamma = 1.8 \times 10^2$ K. Hence, $\lim_{\Delta T \to 0} \tau = \infty$. This means that nucleation becomes impossible when ΔT approaches zero.

4.3.7 Relationship between Nano-Nucleation and Macro-Crystallization

The use of SAXS to clarify a real and exact image of nano-nucleation is not easy, unlike the use of OM, which is both easier and practical. Classical nucleation (CN) studies generally assume that OM can detect the most essential process in nucleation as the zero-th approximation. Suggesting instead that the most essential process in nucleation should be the critical nano-nucleation

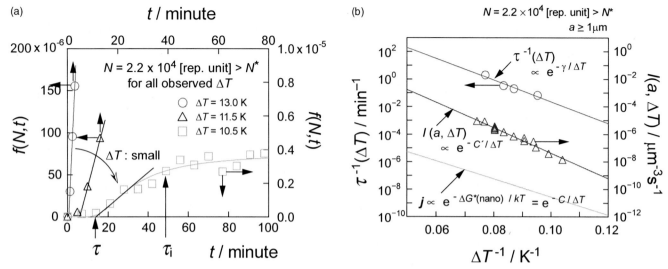

Figure 4.8 ΔT dependence of nano-nucleation and macro-crystallization. (a) Plots of ΔT dependence of $f(N, t)$ against t for $N = 2.2 \times 10^4$ rep. unit $> N^*$. $N^*(\Delta T = 10.5 \text{ K}) \cong 450$ rep. unit, which is the maximum N^* in this study. $f(N, t)$ of $\Delta T = 13.9$ and 11.5 K are shown in the left and top axes. $f(N, t)$ of $\Delta T = 10.5$ K is shown in the right and bottom axes. It was impossible to observe the saturation of $f(N, t)$ for larger ΔT due to onset of lamellar stacking. τ_i of $\Delta T = 10.5$ K and τs for each ΔT are also shown. (b) Plots of τ^{-1}, I, and theoretical j against ΔT^{-1} and comparison of these slopes. The parallel lines confirm the same ΔT dependence.

process, in this section we explain that critical nano-nucleation mainly controls both nano-nucleation and macro-crystallization.

Figure 4.9 illustrates the sequential process of nucleation, which shows $\Delta G(N)$ against N. $\Delta G^*(N^*)$ corresponds to critical nano-nucleation. In the nucleation theory, the so-called net flow of nucleation (j) plays an important role in the nucleation process as illustrated in Figure 4.9 (also see Section 4.4). As the zero-th approximation, critical nano-nucleation should become the main controlling process with an activation barrier in nucleation following Eyring's kinetic theory of absolute reaction rate (theory of absolute reaction rate) [30]. Hence, j can be given by

$$j \propto \exp[-\Delta G^*(N^*)/kT]. \quad (4.29)$$

$\Delta G^*(N^*)$ is given by $\Delta G^*(N^*) \cong 4\sigma\sigma_e/\Delta g$ for $\Delta g \gg \Delta\sigma$, the 2D nucleus [12]. We define them here per one particle or repeating unit. If critical nano-nucleation mainly controls both nano-nucleation and macro-crystallization, j can be rewritten as

$$j \propto \exp[-C/\Delta T], \quad (4.30)$$

where $C = [\Delta G^*(N^*)/kT]\Delta T = 4T_m^\circ \sigma\sigma_e/kT\Delta h$ [12].

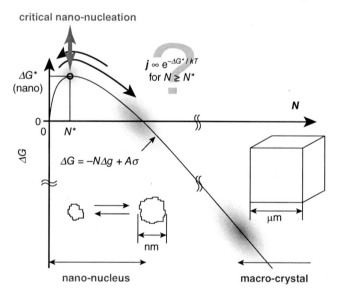

Figure 4.9 Illustration of ΔG against N. A is the surface area of the nucleus. The nano-nucleus shows significant fluctuation with respect to its size and shape. ΔG^*(nano) corresponds to critical nano-nucleation, as shown in Reference [16]. According to Eyring's theory of absolute reaction rate, critical nano-nucleation should become the activation barrier of nucleation. The macro-crystal has smooth and flat surfaces and does not disappear. (See color insert.)

It is impossible to observe j directly, but some observable quantities should correspond to it. The inverse of τ_i in nano-nucleation should be directly related to j, as well as I in macro-crystallization [2]. Equation (4.17) defines I by the rate of macro-crystallization per unit volume and time. If critical nano-nucleation mainly controls nano-nucleation and macro-crystallization, both τ_i^{-1} and I should be proportional to j, respectively, that is, $\tau_i^{-1} \propto I \propto j$. We verify the direct correspondence between nano-nucleation and macro-crystallization by obtaining this proportionality experimentally.

Figure 4.8b also shows $I(\Delta T)$ against ΔT^{-1} for $a \geq 1\,\mu m$. $I(\Delta T)$ decreases exponentially with the increase of ΔT^{-1}. The empirical formula obtained is

$$I(\Delta T) \propto \exp[-C'/\Delta T], \quad (4.31)$$

where C' is a constant given by $C' = 2.1 \times 10^2$ K. Therefore, nucleation becomes significantly difficult when ΔT becomes small.

Figure 4.8b also shows the theoretical j calculated as a function of ΔT by using Equation (4.30). The slope C of Equation (4.30) is given by $C = 1.5 \times 10^2$ K by using σ(nano), σ_e(nano), and $\Delta h = 6.7 \times 10^{-21}$ J/rep. unit [12]. Note that the three straight lines are nearly parallel, that is, their slopes are nearly the same. The slopes of γ, C', and C are given by <Slope> $\pm$ ΔSlope $= (1.8 \pm 0.3) \times 10^2$ K, where <Slope> is the mean slope and ΔSlope is the scatter of the slopes. The relative error ΔSlope/<Slope> is as small as 16%. Thus, we obtain approximately $\gamma \cong C' \cong C$. That is,

$$\tau^{-1} \propto I \propto j, \quad (4.32)$$

which verifies the desired proportionality, that is, they show the same ΔT dependence. In this way, we verify that critical nano-nucleation mainly controls nano-nucleation as well as macro-crystallization experimentally, and we conclude that nano-nucleation directly corresponds to macro-crystallization. We also conclude that nucleation controls the induction period of crystallization and that the spinodal decomposition process proposed by Imai et al. [20] does not, because Equation (4.28) and Equation (4.32) are not expected for the latter process.

4.4 IMPROVEMENT OF NUCLEATION THEORY

4.4.1 Introduction

It should be possible to describe nucleation by using a basic equation of stochastic processes, yet it remains unclear whether or not the so-called fundamental kinetic equation in CNT satisfies the necessary condition of the basic equation, that is, it should satisfy the mass conservation law with respect to a distribution function $y(x, t)$, where x indicates a variable [31]. This is equivalent to saying that $y(x, t)$ should satisfy a normalization condition, that is,

$$\sum_x y(x, t) = 1 \text{ for any } t. \quad (4.33)$$

It has been long believed that a fundamental kinetic equation, Equation (4.1), with respect to $f(N, t)$ proposed by CNT can describe the nucleation process correctly. However, this section explains that $f(N, t)$ and the kinetic equation in CNT do not satisfy the normalized condition and the mass conservation law, respectively. Hence, $f(N, t)$ is not a proper distribution function.

If we regard the nucleation process as the phase transition from 100% supercooled melt to 100% crystal, that is, formation of a single crystal or polycrystal, clearly, $f(N, t)$ should satisfy the following relationship,

$$\sum_{N=1}^{N_{max}} f(N, t) = f(1, 0) \gg 1 \text{ for } t = 0 \text{ (100\% melt)}$$

$$= f(N_{max}, \infty) = 1 \text{ (or a finite small value) for}$$

$$t = \infty \text{ (100\% crystal)}.$$

$$(4.34)$$

Here, N_{max} is a maximum of N. As the $f(N, t)$ does not satisfy the requested normalized conditions of Equation (4.33) for the distribution function of a stochastic process, we cannot consider $f(N, t)$ as a distribution function. Since $f(N, t)$ and $f(N + 1, t)$ do not mean any number of particles, I defined by Equation (4.1) cannot mean net flow in any stochastic process. Hence, the fundamental kinetic equation of CNT given by Equation (4.1) cannot satisfy the mass conservation law. Therefore, the fundamental kinetic equation cannot be a basic equation of a stochastic process [31].

The next section, which introduces a mass distribution function $Q(N, t)$, also describes a new basic equation of the mass conservation law based on the introduction of the net flow $j(N, t)$. We directly observe $Q(N, t)$ and obtain the overall crystallinity during nano-nucleation in the bulk melt, which confirms our proposed nucleation theory.

4.4.2 Nucleation Theory Based on Direct Observation of Nucleation

Figure 4.10 shows a basic equation of nucleation of a stochastic process described by a linear sequential process. Size N corresponds to the N-th stage in the process. We define $Q(N, t)$ by

$$Q(N,t) \equiv Nf(N,t)/v_0. \qquad (4.35)$$

$\sum_{N=1}^{N_{max}} Nf(N,t) = v_0$ is the total number of particles within a closed system. $Q(N, t)$ represents the normalized total number of particles included in the nuclei of size N within a huge closed system. $\oplus$ or $\ominus$ (Fig. 4.10) indicates attachment or detachment of a particle to or from a nucleus, respectively. From the definition of the total number of particles within a closed system, it is obvious that

$$\sum_{N=1}^{N_{max}} Q(N,t) = 1 \text{ for all } t, \qquad (4.36)$$

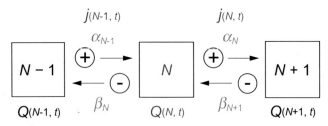

Figure 4.10 Illustration of a linear sequential process defined for $Q(N, t)$. Size N corresponds to the N-th stage in the stochastic process. $\oplus$ and $\ominus$ indicate attachment and detachment of a particle to a nucleus, respectively.

as Figure 4.11 illustrates. Therefore $Q(N, t)$ can be a normalized conserved quantity, that is, it can be a distribution function in the present stochastic process (Fig. 4.10). The normalized net flow $j(N, t)$ with respect to $Q(N, t)$ from the N-th to $N + 1$-th stage is given by

$$j(N,t) \equiv \alpha_N Q(N,t) - \beta_{N+1} Q(N+1,t), \qquad (4.37)$$

where α_N and β_{N+1} are the forward transition probability from the N-th to $N + 1$-th stage and the backward transition probability from the $N + 1$-th to N-th stage per one particle, respectively (Fig. 4.10). Knowing that $Q(N, t)$ means the normalized number of particles, we propose a new basic equation of nucleation by a mass conservation law of $Q(N, t)$,

$$\partial Q(N,t)/\partial t \equiv -\partial j(N,t)/\partial N. \qquad (4.38)$$

Assuming that

$$j(N,t) \equiv -\Gamma \partial Q(N,t)/\partial N, \qquad (4.39)$$

where Γ is a constant gives

$$\partial Q(N,t)/\partial t - \Gamma \partial^2 Q(N,t)/\partial N^2 = 0. \qquad (4.40)$$

This is similar to the well-known basic equation of diffusion processes.

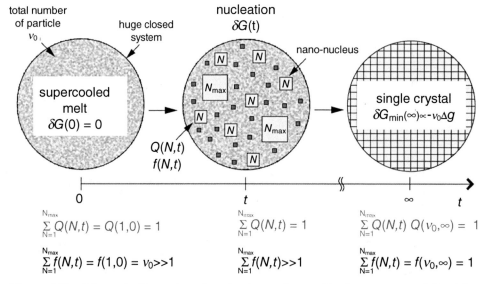

Figure 4.11 Schematic illustration of nucleation and crystallization processes defined for $Q(N, t)$. We consider a huge closed system. Nano-nuclei are generated from the supercooled melt and finally the system transforms into a single crystal. Total free energy of nucleation $\delta G(t)$, $Q(N, t)$, and $f(N, t)$ are also shown. $\delta G(t)$ changes from zero for the supercooled melt to the minimum $\delta G_{min}(t)$ at 100% crystal. Summation of $Q(N, t)$ satisfies unity for all t; however, $f(N, t)$ does not sum to unity. (See color insert.)

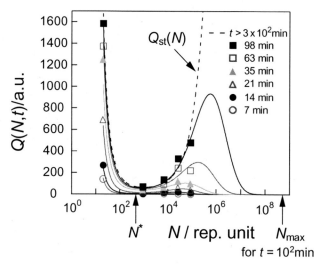

Figure 4.12 Observed $Q(N,t)$ against N as a function of t for $T_c = 129.0°C$ and $\Delta T = 10.5$ K. We plotted $Q(N,t)$ for the range of $N \leq N_{max}$. A typical N_{max} at $t \cong 10^2$ minutes is shown. $Q_{st}(N)$ is a steady state of $Q(N,t)$ for $t \geq 10^2$ min. It is expected that $Q_{st}(N)$ rapidly increases for $N > 10^4$ rep. unit and $t > 3 \times 10^2$ minutes, as shown by the broken curve.

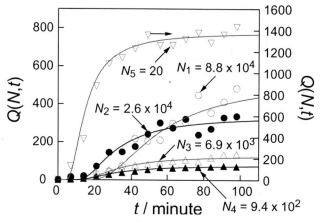

Figure 4.13 $Q(N, t)$ against t as a function of N for $T_c = 129.0°C$ and $\Delta T = 10.5$ K obtained from Figure 4.5. N_1 to N_5 corresponds to five plots of Fig. 4.12. $Q(N, t)$s for N_1, N_2, N_3, and N_4 correspond to the left axis and that for N_5 corresponds to the right axis. $Q(N, t)$ of N_5 increases significantly with the increase of t. $Q(N,t)$ of N_4, which is near the minimum of $Q(N,t)$, increases slowly, and its value at saturation is small. $Q(N, t)$ of N_1 shows late onset time and increases slowly.

4.4.3 Confirmation of the Theory by Overall Crystallinity

Figure 4.12 plots $Q(N, t)$ in linear scale against N as a function of t. With the increase of N, $Q(N, t)$ first decreases for $N \leq N^*$, shows a minimum at $N \cong N^*$ and then it increases. After it passes a maximum at a $N > N^*$, it decreases and becomes zero at $N = N_{max}(t)$. It is natural that $N_{max}(t)$ increases with the increase of t. $Q(N, t)$ at all N increases with the increase of t and attains a steady state (denoted as $Q_{st}(N)$) for $t \geq 10^2$ minutes.

The maximum $Q(N, t)$ is seen at $N \cong 10^6$ repeat units for $t \cong 100$ minutes. We expect that $Q_{st}(N)$ rapidly increases for $N > 10^4$ repeat units and $t \geq 300$ minutes, as shown by the broken curve in Figure 4.12. Note that the U-shaped broken curve of $Q(N, t)$ is essentially similar to that predicted by a Boltzmann distribution, although the increasing rate of the $Q(N, t)$ with the increase of N is much smaller than from a Boltzmann distribution.

From Equation (4.35), we predict that $Q_{st}(N) \propto N$ for large t and N. Figure 4.12 confirms this by showing that $Q_{st}(N) \propto N$ for large $t > 300$ minutes, $N \gg N^*$. We summarize our observations as:

1. The time and N evolution of the observed $Q(N, t)$ in Figure 4.12 confirms that many nano-nuclei appear and disappear frequently for $N < N^*$ and that the increase of mass of larger nuclei ($N > N^*$) will accelerate significantly with the increase of time and N. This acceleration of nucleation gives a natural real image of nucleation as an important cooperative nature of the phase transition from the supercooled melt into crystals, as theoretically expected.

2. The time and N evolutions of the observed $f(N, t)$ confirm that many nano-nuclei appear and disappear frequently for $N < N^*$. It shows that only a very small part of them survive to form larger nuclei and macro-crystals. After growing into larger nuclei and macro-crystals, they do not disappear.

The physical meaning and cause of these characteristic behaviors of $Q(N, t)$ are interesting open questions.

Figure 4.13 shows the time evolution of $Q(N, t)$ as a function of N_p, where p indicates that different sizes of N. $Q(N, t)$ increase significantly with the increase of t with respect to smaller N. $Q(N, t)$ of $N_4 = 9.4 \times 10^2$ repeat units $\cong N^*$, which is near to the minimum, increases slowly, and its quantity of saturation is small. $Q(N, t)$ of $N_1 = 8.8 \times 10^4$ repeat units has a late onset time and increases slowly. The quantity of saturation of N_1 is larger than that of N_2, N_3, and N_4, which corresponds to Figure 4.12.

Figure 4.14, which illustrates the elementary process of nucleation, shows that the increase of net flow $j(N, t)$ for $N \gg N^*$ results from the growth of smaller nuclei by adding particles from the melt (⊕ in the figure). The nuclei grow larger by absorbing particles that come from the melt and also indirectly via the melt from the nuclei that have disappeared. This corresponds to the Ostwald ripening. Figure 4.14 also shows that $j(N, t)$ for $N \gg N^*$ increases with the increase of N at steady state. On the other hand, CNT assumes that the $j(N, t)$ at steady state is constant for N, as illustrated in Figure 4.1.

$Q(N, t)$ is useful for obtaining the time evolution of overall crystallinity $\chi_c(t)$. We define it by

$$\chi_c(t) \equiv \frac{\int_{N'_{min}}^{N_{max}(t)} Q(N,t) dN}{\int_{N'_{min}}^{N_{max}(\infty)} Q_{st}(N) dN} \propto \int_{N'_{min}}^{N_{max}(t)} Q(N,t) dN, \quad (4.41)$$

where $N_{max}(\infty)$ is the final size of a nucleus or crystal after completion of solidification, and N'_{min} is the lower limit of the crystal size of N. As nano-nuclei smaller than the critical nucleus ($N < N^*$) (called -embryos- in CNT) are generated and disappear too frequently, we omit the embryo when evaluating $\chi_c(t)$. Thus,

$$\chi_c(t) \equiv \frac{\int_{N^*}^{N_{max}(t)} Q(N,t) dN}{\int_{N^*}^{N_{max}(\infty)} Q_{st}(N) dN} \propto \int_{N^*}^{N_{max}(t)} Q(N,t) dN. \quad (4.42)$$

In Figure 4.15a, the range N of the integral is pink. Figure 4.15b shows $\chi_c(t)$ against t obtained for $T_c = 129.0°C$ and $\Delta T = 10.5$ K using Equation (4.42). After a short time (only several minutes), at first $\chi_c(t)$ increases slowly, and then faster with the increase of t. We observe steady nucleation for $t \geq 100$ minutes and no depletion of the melt, as shown in Figure 4.13. Therefore, we conclude that the observed $\chi_c(t)$ should be significantly small, meaning $\chi_c(t) \ll 1$. Logically, we expect that $\chi_c(t)$ should finally saturate to unity, corresponding to completion of the melt-solid phase transition from the supercooled melt into (assumed) a single crystal. We can use this result of $\chi_c(t)$ as a test of nucleation theory.

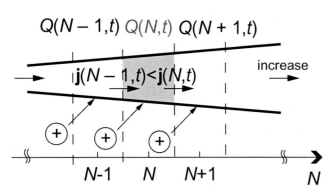

Figure 4.14 Illustration of a new elementary process for $Q(N, t)$ and net flow $j(N, t)$ of nucleation in the steady state for $N \gg N^*$. Direct observation of $Q(N, t)$ indicates that $j(N, t)$ for $N \gg N^*$ increases with the increase of N. ⊕ indicates absorbed particles from the melt.

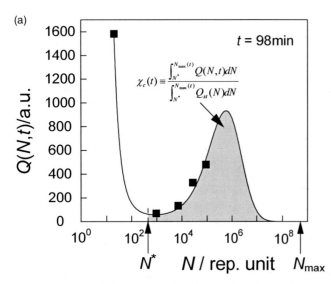
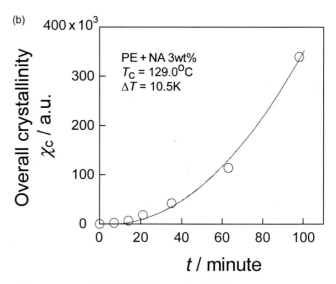

Figure 4.15 (a) Observed $Q(N,t)$ against N for $t = 98$ minutes and $T_c = 129.0°C$ or $\Delta T = 10.5$ K. χ_c is obtained by integrating the pink colored range of N. (b) $\chi_c(t)$ against t for $T_c = 129.0°C$ and $\Delta T = 10.5$ K. $\chi_c(t)$ starts increasing after a rather short time (only several minutes) and increases slowly at first and then faster with increase of t. Steady nucleation is observed for $t \geq 10^2$ minutes, and any "depletion" on the melt was not observed in this study, as shown in Figure 4.13.

4.5 HOMOGENEOUS NUCLEATION FROM THE BULK MELT UNDER ELONGATIONAL FLOW

4.5.1 Introduction and Case Study

This section discusses homogeneous nucleation from the bulk melt [32]. We obtain extreme elongational crystallization of isotactic polypropylene (iPP) by compression of the supercooled melt in an orthogonal direction. We theorize that the melt elongation of polymers should significantly affect the nucleation controlling the structure and properties of solids. Figure 4.16a shows the principle of the melt elongation by the compression method. We compress the supercooled melt sandwiched between two plates. The melt was elongated along a direction perpendicular to the compressed direction. We call the direction of elongation machine direction (MD). We call the perpendicular direction to MD the transverse direction (TD). Figure 4.16b shows a roll type apparatus that can also apply strong compression to the sample. The rapid compression of the melt results in a large elongational strain rate ($\dot{\varepsilon}$).

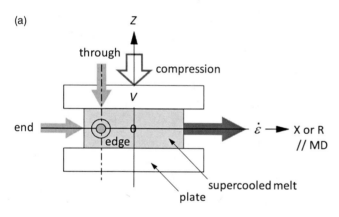

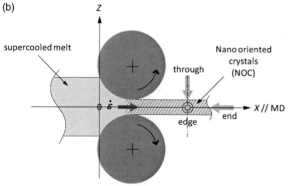

Figure 4.16 Schematic illustration of a cross sectional view of crystallization apparatuses to show the principle of elongational crystallization by the compression method. Z-axis is along the compressed direction. X- or R-axis is parallel to the MD. (a) Compression type apparatus. (b) Roll type apparatus. (See color insert.)

Crystallization without an external field, which is called quiescent, or under a weak external field, has been studied for half a century [33]. It is well known that polymer chains in the melt spontaneously take the shape of a random coil, called the Gaussian chain, due to entropy, and easily entangle with each other. Such a melt is isotropic. In the case of a weak external field, most of the volume of the melt is isotropic [34]. The entangled chains must undergo ordering from the isotropic melt during crystallization [19], but this is difficult because they cannot easily slide along their chain axes and disentangle into an ordered parallel arrangement; therefore, amorphous regions remain in the solid. Hence, conventional polymer solids are composed of both amorphous and crystal, that is, crystallinity (χ_c) is much less than unity [35].

When the elongational strain rate $\dot{\varepsilon}$ becomes larger than a critical value ($\dot{\varepsilon}^*$), the crystallization behavior, structure, and physical properties change discontinuously. In the case of $\dot{\varepsilon}$ larger than $\dot{\varepsilon}^*$, we obtain a morphology we call nano-oriented crystals (NOCs). The NOCs show high crystallinity (nearly equal to unity) and ultrahigh performance.

We use iPP ($M_w = 34 \times 10^4$, $M_w/M_n = 30$, [mmmm] = 98%). We melt the sample at a higher temperature than T_m^o, cool it to a T_c and then elongate into a sheet. The range of $\dot{\varepsilon}$ changes from 0 to 3×10^3 s^{-1}. We observe the crystallization behavior or morphology of the sample by means of POM and transmission electron microscopy (TEM). We observe crystallization along three directions: through (parallel to the compressed direction), edge (perpendicular to through), and end (parallel to the MD) (Fig. 4.16). We observe crystallization by OM along the through direction. Next, we measure compliances.

Compliances by means of a tensile tester. We evaluate toughness semi-quantitatively by repetition of folding along either the MD or TD direction. We perform a thermal resistance by using a hot stage and POM. We observe the lateral length of the sample along the MD and TD, l_{MD} and l_{TD}, respectively. We define the heatproof temperature (T_h) as the temperature where the l/l_0 shrinks or expands more than 3% with the increase of T. We evaluate the transparency by the haze test. We define the haze for sheets of 0.3 mm thickness. See References [32] for the details.

4.5.2 Formulation of Elongational Strain Rate $\dot{\varepsilon}$

We use 1D and 2D compression methods. In the case of 1D compression, we keep the width of the sample constant during compression. In the case of 2D compression, we compress a rod sample into a disk. The degree of melt elongation can be quantitatively expressed by $\dot{\varepsilon}$, which we formulate approximately as follows. We use the relative coordinate system where we take the origin at the center of a sample (Fig. 4.16a and b), where R is the radial direction. The X- and R-axes correspond to the elongational direction and we call them the MD. We denote the initial size of a supercooled molten sample by $(2X_0, 2Y_0, 2Z_0)$ or $(2R_0, 2Z_0)$ for 1D or 2D compression, respectively. We denote the size of the sample at a time (t) during compression by $(2X, 2Y_0, 2Z)$ or $(2R, 2Z)$ for 1D or 2D compression, respectively. We define $\dot{\varepsilon}$ along MD by [36]

$$\dot{\varepsilon} = |\mathring{\mathbf{a}}| \equiv \frac{1}{X} \cdot \frac{dX}{dt} \text{ for the 1D compression} \quad (4.43a)$$

$$\equiv \frac{1}{R} \cdot \frac{dR}{dt} \text{ for the 2D compression.} \quad (4.43b)$$

We define the compression velocity (v) by

$$v = |\mathring{\mathbf{o}}| \equiv -\frac{d(2Z)}{dt}. \quad (4.44)$$

From the mass conservation law, we have

$$X_0 Y_0 Z_0 = X Y_0 Z \text{ for the 1D compression} \quad (4.45a)$$

or

$$\pi R_0^2 (2Z_0) = \pi R^2 (2Z) \text{ for the 2D compression.} \quad (4.45b)$$

Combining Equation (4.43), Equation (4.44), and Equation (4.45) gives

$$\dot{\varepsilon} = \frac{v}{2Z} \text{ for the 1D compression along the } X\text{-axis} \quad (4.46a)$$

$$= \frac{v}{4Z} \text{ for the 2D compression along the } R\text{-axis.} \quad (4.46b)$$

In this study, we approximate v by

$$v \cong \frac{2(Z_0 - Z)}{\Delta t}, \quad (4.47)$$

where Δt is the compressing time. Although $\dot{\varepsilon}$ depends on the thickness of the sample, we simply approximate $\dot{\varepsilon}$ by its average value. We can change $\dot{\varepsilon}$ by changing v and sample thickness. Note that $\dot{\varepsilon}$ for compression of the roll type also can be given by Equation (4.46) in principle.

4.5.3 Nano-Oriented Crystals

4.5.3.1 $\dot{\varepsilon}$ Dependence of the Morphology by OM

Figure 4.17 shows typical polarized optical micrographs of samples after completion of crystallization

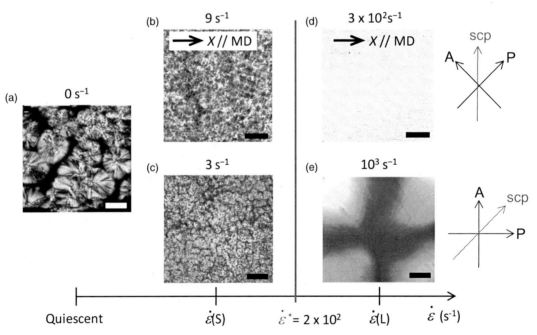

Figure 4.17 Typical polarizing optical morphology of iPP samples crystallized at $T_c=150°C$. (a) Crystallized at quiescent field, $\dot{\varepsilon} = 0 \, s^{-1}$. Scale bar is 200 μm. Thickness of the sample is 70 μm. (b) $\dot{\varepsilon}(S) = 9 \, s^{-1}$. Sample thickness is 0.27 mm. (c) $\dot{\varepsilon}(S) = 3 \, s^{-1}$. Sample thickness is 90 μm. (d) $\dot{\varepsilon}(L) = 3 \times 10^2 \, s^{-1}$. Sample thickness is 0.25 mm. (e) $\dot{\varepsilon}(L) = 10^3 \, s^{-1}$. Sample thickness is 10 μm. (b, d) Crystallized by 1D compression. Scale bar is 50 μm. (c, e) Crystallized by 2D compression. Scale bar is 200 μm. Arrows at the right side indicate the directions of polarizer (P), analyzer (A) and sensitive-color plate. (See color insert.)

at 150°C by 1D ([b] and [d]) and 2D ([a], [c], and [e]) compressions.

We crystallize well-known large spherulites at quiescent field ($\dot{\varepsilon} = 0\,\text{s}^{-1}$) (Fig. 4.17a). The mean diameter (d) of the spherulites is $d \geq 1.5 \times 10^2$ μm. When $\dot{\varepsilon}$ increases, d becomes as small as several tens of μm (Fig. 4.17b,c).

When $\dot{\varepsilon}$ becomes larger than $200\,\text{s}^{-1}$, most morphologies change from spherulites to a new form (Fig. 4.17d and e). The crystal size became too fine to be detected by POM, which suggests that NOCs have been generated. Detailed evidence of formation of the NOCs appears in Section 4.5.3.3. The characteristic colored pattern (corresponding to the retardation [37]) indicates that molecular chains orient along X- and R-axes for the 1D and 2D compressions, respectively. Therefore, the chains orient along MD for both the 1D and 2D compressions. We find that there is a critical elongational strain rate ($\dot{\varepsilon}^*$), whose value we confirm to be $\dot{\varepsilon}^* = 200\,\text{s}^{-1}$ by later X-ray methods. Hereafter, we classify $\dot{\varepsilon}$ into $\dot{\varepsilon}(S)$ and $\dot{\varepsilon}(L)$, where $\dot{\varepsilon}(S) < \dot{\varepsilon}^*$ and $\dot{\varepsilon}(L) \geq \dot{\varepsilon}^*$, respectively. For simplification, we name the samples crystallized at $\dot{\varepsilon}(S)$ and $\dot{\varepsilon}(L)$ by $\dot{\varepsilon}(S)$ and $\dot{\varepsilon}(L)$, respectively.

Although shear should exist in the interface between the sample and plates, we do not detect different morphology, such as skin in the interface of the sample by means of OM, X-ray scattering, or TEM. Figure 4.18 shows typical $\dot{\varepsilon}$ dependence of crystallization behaviors as a function of crystallization time (t) observed by POM. We directly observe the so-called induction time (τ), defined as the onset of crystallization by POM [38]. The T_c is as high as 150°C.

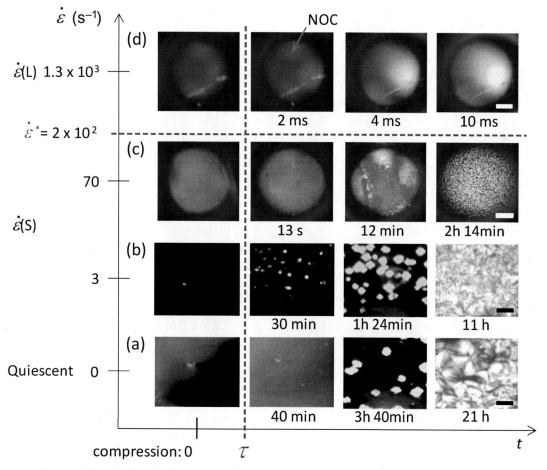

Figure 4.18 Typical $\dot{\varepsilon}$ dependence of the crystallization behavior directly observed by optical microscopy on samples elongationally crystallized by 2D compression at $T_c = 150$°C. t is crystallization time. At $t = 0$, a sample was just compressed. Crystallized at (a) quiescent field, $\dot{\varepsilon} = 0\,\text{s}^{-1}$, (b) $\dot{\varepsilon}(S) = 3\,\text{s}^{-1}$, (c) $\dot{\varepsilon}(S) = 70\,\text{s}^{-1}$, and (d) $\dot{\varepsilon}(L) = 1.3 \times 10^3\,\text{s}^{-1}$. (a, b) Scale bar is 100 μm. (c, d) Scale bar is 500 μm. (See color insert.)

In the crystallization under quiescent field ($\dot{\varepsilon} = 0 \, \text{s}^{-1}$), we observe nuclei at about 40 minutes; crystallization ceases after 21 hours (Fig. 4.18a). Therefore, $\tau = 40$ minutes for $\dot{\varepsilon} = 0$.

For the crystallization at $\dot{\varepsilon} < 60 \, \text{s}^{-1}$, we observe nuclei at $\tau \cong 10$ minutes; crystallization (=formation of spherulites) ceases after 11 hours. Figure 4.18b shows a typical example for $\dot{\varepsilon}(S) = 3 \, \text{s}^{-1}$. Therefore, the crystallization accelerates slightly under a weak elongational field.

When $\dot{\varepsilon}$ becomes larger than $60 \, \text{s}^{-1}$, first, a small fraction of the NOCs crystallize and then small spherulites form gradually. Figure 4.18c shows a typical example for $\dot{\varepsilon}(S) = 70 \, \text{s}^{-1}$. Although we confirm the NOCs generation by retardation, it is difficult to obtain τ of NOCs due to very weak retardation at the early stage. The completion time for solidification is about 2.5 hours.

When $\dot{\varepsilon} \geq 100 \, \text{s}^{-1}$, the fraction of the NOCs significantly increases, and the fraction of the spherulites decreases with the increase of $\dot{\varepsilon}$. The NOCs crystallize within 1 ms. Therefore, we obtain $\tau \cong 1$ ms for the NOCs and $\tau \cong 8$ minutes for the spherulites.

For $\dot{\varepsilon}(L) \geq 300 \, \text{s}^{-1}$, only the NOCs form within 1 ms, and crystallization is completed after 4 ms. Using POM finds no spherulites in the sample. Figure 4.18d shows a typical example for $\dot{\varepsilon}(L) = 1.3 \times 10^3 \, \text{s}^{-1}$. We conclude that the τ of the NOCs for $\dot{\varepsilon}(L)$ is smaller than 1 ms due to the time resolution (about 1 ms) of the high-speed camera.

As the elongation takes about 10 ms in this experiment, crystallization of the NOCs finishes during elongation for $\dot{\varepsilon}(L)$. On the other hand, the spherulites crystallize slowly after elongation ceases.

Figure 4.19 shows a plot of τ against $\dot{\varepsilon}$, where τ is about 40 minutes for the quiescent condition. For comparison, we superimpose a plot of $\dot{\varepsilon} = 0 \, \text{s}^{-1}$ (quiescent) in the left side of Figure 4.19. With the increase of $\dot{\varepsilon}$, τ decreases slightly to 10^3 s for $\dot{\varepsilon}(S)$. In the range of $\dot{\varepsilon}(S)$, τ would be almost constant against $\dot{\varepsilon}$ because the variation of τ is usually large. The two kinds of τ for spherulites and the NOCs overlap at $\dot{\varepsilon} < \dot{\varepsilon}^*$. For $\dot{\varepsilon}(L) \geq \dot{\varepsilon}^*$, τ decreases discontinuously to 1 ms, as large as 10^{-6} times. The significant change of τ is one evidence of the change in the crystallization mechanism from heterogeneous to homogeneous nucleation, as shown in Section 4.5.4.

4.5.3.2 χ_c of the NOC
We obtain χ_c for $\dot{\varepsilon}(L)$ by measuring the density, ρ, of a typical sample. Since $\rho = M/V = 0.94 \, \text{g/cm}^3$, χ_c is obtained by [25]

$$\chi_c = \frac{\rho_c}{\rho}\left(\frac{\rho - \rho_a}{\rho_c - \rho_a}\right) = 0.92 \pm 0.02 \text{ for } \dot{\varepsilon}(L), \quad (4.48)$$

where $\rho_c = 0.946 \, \text{g/cm}^3$ and $\rho_a = 0.852 \, \text{g/cm}^3$ are the density of the α_2 form crystal (as will be shown in Section

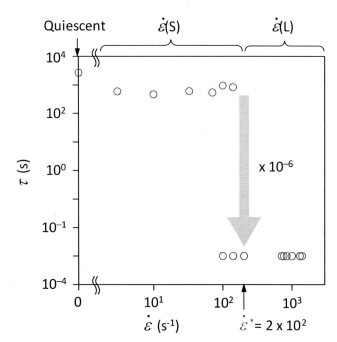

Figure 4.19 Plot of τ against $\dot{\varepsilon}$ at $T_c = 150°C$. Crystallizations by 1D and 2D compression are mixed. The discontinuous decrease of τ indicates existence of $\dot{\varepsilon}^*$ and change in nucleation mechanism.

4.5.3.4) and amorphous iPP at 25°C, respectively [39, 40]. The $\chi_c = 0.94$ is the highest crystallinity for the bulk iPP solid; the usual iPP solid shows $\chi_c < 0.7$ [35].

4.5.3.3 $\dot{\varepsilon}$ Dependence of SAXS Pattern and Verification of the NOCs

SAXS Pattern of $\dot{\varepsilon}(L)$ Figure 4.20a–c shows SAXS patterns of through-, edge-, and end-views for $\dot{\varepsilon}(L)$, respectively. Through and edge patterns for $\dot{\varepsilon}(L)$ show an oriented two-point pattern along the MD as indicated by arrow A. The end pattern shows diffuse scattering. Figure 4.21a shows the scattering intensity (I_X) profile for a typical through pattern. We obtain the I_X by all-around integration along a circular ring. The plot of I_X against the scattering vector (q) shows only one dominant peak, corresponding to the two-point pattern, and a very weak peak at around $q = 0.6 \, \text{nm}^{-1}$. The two-point pattern for through and edge views can be interpreted as being dominated by the first peak of the diffraction pattern of so-called 1D paracrystals [41]. It indicates that the degree of order of paracrystals is significantly low; that is, the disordered structure is roughly close to the one-dimensional liquid-like packing of crystals [42].

As $\chi_c \cong 1$, the particle should be a single crystal-like crystallite that composes the NOCs. Note that we can

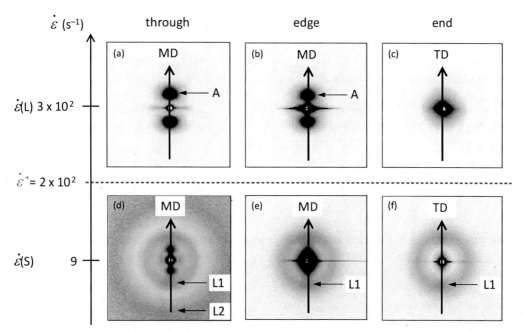

Figure 4.20 $\dot{\varepsilon}$ dependence of SAXS patterns at $T_c = 150°C$. Samples were crystallized by 1D compression. (a–c) $\dot{\varepsilon}(L) = 3 \times 10^2$ s^{-1}. (d–f) $\dot{\varepsilon}(S) = 9$ s^{-1}. (a, d) Through-view. (b, e) Edge-view. (c, f) End-view. (d) The intensity of L2 is increased by 10 times to show the weak ring.

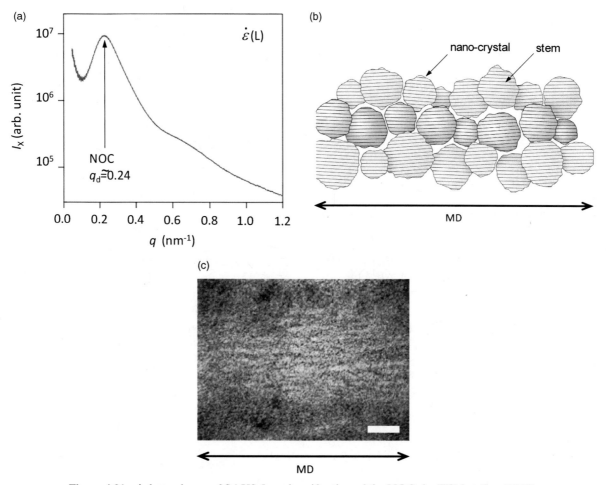

Figure 4.21 $\dot{\varepsilon}$ dependence of SAXS I_X and verification of the NOCs by TEM at $T_c = 150°C$. (a) I_X of through-view against q for $\dot{\varepsilon}(L) = 3 \times 10^2$ s^{-1}. I_X was obtained by all-around integration along a circular ring. The strong peak indicates the formation of NOCs. Crystallized by 1D compression. (b) Schematic illustration of the structure of the NOCs. Connections between nano-crystals are omitted. (c) Transmission electron micrograph of the NOC for edge-view. $\dot{\varepsilon}(L) = 1.25 \times 10^3$ s^{-1}. Scale bar is 100 nm. Crystallized by 2D compression. White dots indicate the formation of NOCs.

approximate the size (d) of a crystal by the distance between the nearest neighbor crystals for $\chi_c \cong 1$. Since we obtain q at the peak (q_d), $q_d = 0.24$ nm^{-1}, we obtain d by $d \cong 2\pi/q_d = 26$ nm for $\dot{\varepsilon}(L)$. The through pattern for $\dot{\varepsilon}(L)$ shows a streak along the equatorial line, which indicates an isolated rod- or string-like structure along the MD by X-ray theory [42]. Based on the observed facts by means of SAXS, WAXS, and TEM (shown later), Figure 4.21b shows a proposed illustration of the structure of the NOCs. In the illustrated model, nano-crystals with mean size 26 nm are linked and oriented along the MD. Because there is significant coherence (with respect to direction and distance) between neighboring nano-crystals along the MD as analyzed above, we regard the train of nano-crystals as a rod or a string along the MD. Because there is very weak coherence between nano-crystals in neighboring rods or strings, we regard the rod or string as an isolated rod that gives the streak.

The end-view is the Fourier transform of the projection along/from the c-axis of the rod or string to the equatorial plane. As the electron density of nano-crystals on the projected plane should smear and become uniform, we observe the shape factor of nano-crystals only, and no unoriented peak like a Debye–Scherrer ring in Figure 4.20c.

Figure 4.21c shows a TEM of the sample for $\dot{\varepsilon}(L)$. The averaged size of crystallites is about 26 nm, and they are oriented along the MD. Therefore, SAXS observes the nature of the NOCs.

SAXS Patterns of $\dot{\varepsilon}(S)$ and Quiescent Figure 4.20d–f shows the SAXS pattern of through-, edge-, and end-views for $\dot{\varepsilon}(S)$, respectively. They are mainly unoriented patterns and weak two-point patterns. The typical I_X for the through pattern obtained by circular integration shows the well-known long period pattern (L1 and L2) in Figure 4.20d. Therefore, the dominant structure of $\dot{\varepsilon}(S)$ is the stacked lamellar one. We obtain the long period (L) from the L1 peak, $L = 2\pi/q_{L1} \cong 15$ nm for $\dot{\varepsilon}(S)$, where q_{L1} is q at the peak of L1. The weak two-point pattern indicates that only tiny amounts of nano-crystals mix at the early stage of crystallization.

The SAXS pattern for the quiescent condition shows the well-known unoriented pattern of the long period. Therefore, the structure is the usual stacked lamellar one. Observed L for the quiescent condition is $L \cong 17$ nm and $L \cong 25$ nm for the 1D and 2D crystallization apparatus, respectively. The latter L value is similar to the usual one crystallized under isothermal conditions [43]. The smaller L in the 1D case is due to the effect of significant melt flow at the die of the extruder.

4.5.3.4 $\dot{\varepsilon}$ Dependence of WAXS Patterns Figure 4.22a–c shows the WAXS patterns of the through-, edge-, and end-views for $\dot{\varepsilon}(L)$, respectively. The through and edge patterns show a highly oriented fiber pattern along the MD, that is, the molecular chains (c-axes) are highly oriented along the MD. This evidence of oriented crystals corresponds to the SAXS result for $\dot{\varepsilon}(L)$. As nano-crystals and c-axes are oriented along the MD, we call the morphology NOCs. The end pattern shows an unoriented pattern. Therefore, we confirm that the NOCs show the typical fiber structure.

We obtain f_c by analyzing the 130 reflection for the through-view pattern (Fig. 4.22a), $f_c \geq 0.9$. This clarifies that molecular chains for $\dot{\varepsilon}(L)$ are highly oriented along the MD.

In the case of $\dot{\varepsilon}(S)$, the through-, edge-, and end-patterns show unoriented Debye–Scherrer rings (Fig. 4.22d–f). The unit cell structure belongs to the α_1 form because there are no $\overline{2}31$ or $\overline{1}61$ reflections.

4.5.3.5 $\dot{\varepsilon}$ Dependence of the NOCs Fraction $f(NOC)$
We obtain the NOCs fraction $f(NOC)$ within the crystalline volume from the analysis of WAXS intensity. We define $f(NOC)$ by

$$f(NOC) \equiv \frac{I_{hkl}(NOC)}{I_{hkl}(unori.) + I_{hkl}(NOC)}, \quad (4.49)$$

where $I_{hkl}(NOC)$ and $I_{hkl}(unori.)$ are the total reflection intensities of an isolated hkl reflection of the NOCs and unoriented crystals, such as spherulites, respectively. We define I_{hkl} by

$$I_{hkl} \equiv \int I_X(\mathbf{q})d\mathbf{q}, \quad (4.50)$$

where $I_X(\mathbf{q})$ is the scattering intensity at $\mathbf{q}(hkl)$, and the integral is carried out within a region in the reciprocal space where scattering spreads from the (hkl) reflection plane. The region depends on scattering from the NOCs or unoriented crystals.

We obtain $f(NOC)$ by analyzing the 130 reflection for the through-view pattern (Fig. 4.23). It is obvious that $f(NOC) = 0$ under the quiescent field. With the increase of $\dot{\varepsilon}$ up to 100 s^{-1}, $f(NOC)$ appears and increases slightly, up to about 0.1. For $\dot{\varepsilon} \geq 1 \times 10^2$ s^{-1}, $f(NOC)$ increases significantly and saturates to $f(NOC) \cong 1$ for $\dot{\varepsilon} \geq 3 \times 10^2$ s^{-1}. Therefore, we define the $\dot{\varepsilon}^*$ as the $\dot{\varepsilon}$ where $f(NOC)$ becomes 0.6. We obtain $\dot{\varepsilon}^* = 2 \times 10^2$ s^{-1} from Figure 4.23.

4.5.4 Evidence of Homogeneous Nucleation

We plot d against $\dot{\varepsilon}$ after completion of solidification in Figure 4.24. We take ds for the quiescent conditions and $\dot{\varepsilon}(S)$ as the diameter of the spherulites obtained by

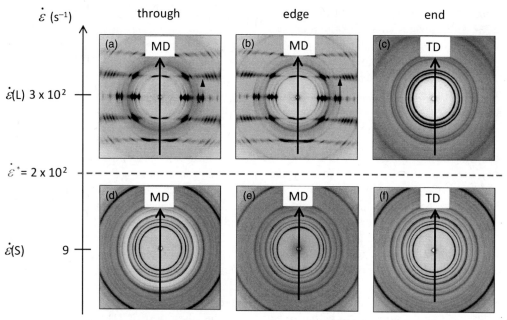

Figure 4.22 $\dot{\varepsilon}$ dependence of WAXS patterns at $T_{cA} = 150°C$. Crystallized by 1D compression. (a–c) $\dot{\varepsilon}(L) = 3 \times 10^2 \ s^{-1}$. (d–f) $\dot{\varepsilon}(S) = 9 \ s^{-1}$. (a, d) Through-view. (b, e) Edge-view. (c, f) End-view. (c–f) The intensity for $q > 16 \ nm^{-1}$ is increased by 10 times to show relatively weak reflections at large q. (a–c) and (d–f) confirm typical fiber and Debye–Scherrer patterns, respectively.

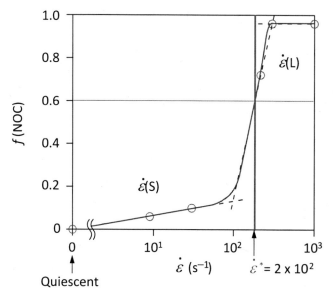

Figure 4.23 $f(NOC)$ against $\dot{\varepsilon}$ at $T_c = 150°C$. Crystallizations by 1D and 2D compression are mixed. Discontinuous increase at $\dot{\varepsilon} > 1 \times 10^2 \ s^{-1}$ is confirmed. From this, $\dot{\varepsilon}^* = 2 \times 10^2 \ s^{-1}$ is obtained.

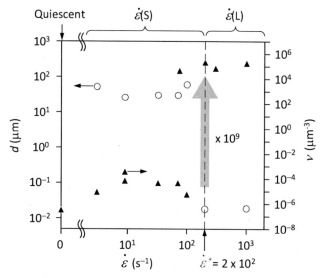

Figure 4.24 $d(\bigcirc)$ and $v(\blacktriangle)$ against $\dot{\varepsilon}$ at $T_c = 150°C$. d and v correspond to left and right axes, respectively. Crystallizations by 1D and 2D compression are mixed.

POM, and these for $\dot\varepsilon(L)$ as the size of the nano-crystal obtained by SAXS. This clarifies that with the increase of $\dot\varepsilon$, d decreases slightly for $\dot\varepsilon(S)$ and decreases discontinuously by as much as about 10^{-3} times for $\dot\varepsilon(L)$. We obtain the number density (v) of spherulites and nano-crystals against $\dot\varepsilon$ by using the approximate equation, $v \cong d^{-3}$ in Figure 4.24. With the increase of $\dot\varepsilon$, the v increases slightly for $\dot\varepsilon(S)$ and increases discontinuously by as much as about 10^9 times for $\dot\varepsilon(L)$.

It is well accepted that a spherulite forms from a nucleus; therefore, the small v of the spherulite indicates that the number density of the nuclei should be small for quiescent conditions and $\dot\varepsilon(S)$. On the other hand, the significant increase of the v for $\dot\varepsilon(L)$ indicates that the number density of nuclei should increase for $\dot\varepsilon \geq \dot\varepsilon^*$. The discontinuous increase of v should be due to the change of nucleation mechanism at $\dot\varepsilon^*$ from heterogeneous nucleation to homogeneous nucleation.

In nature, only a small amount of heterogeneity is essentially included in the melt, and we know that most nucleation from the bulk melt is heterogeneous. The occurrence of homogeneous nucleation is more difficult than heterogeneous nucleation due to the much higher activation barrier of the free energy for formation of a critical nucleus near T_m [12]. We cannot attribute the significant increase of v for $\dot\varepsilon \geq \dot\varepsilon^*$ in this study to the number density of heterogeneities since it is impossible logically that the number of heterogeneities increases discontinuously by 10^9 times only when $\dot\varepsilon$ increases larger than $\dot\varepsilon^*$. Therefore, the increase of v should be evidence that the change takes place from heterogeneous nucleation to homogeneous nucleation and that homogeneous nucleation occurs from the bulk melt for a material near T_m, which results in the NOCs and significant improvement in properties as shown in Section 4.5.5.

Figure 4.25a illustrates the mechanism for homogeneous nucleation by compression. We focus on one Gaussian chain within the bulk melt [44]. The Gaussian chains should be elongated along the MD, that is, elongational direction, when the bulk melt is just compressed at the condition of $\dot\varepsilon(L) \geq \dot\varepsilon^*$. At $\dot\varepsilon(L) \geq \dot\varepsilon^*$, the elongational force overcomes the entropic relaxation of ran-

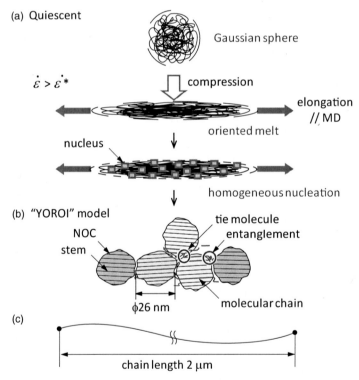

Figure 4.25 Schematic illustration of the NOC nucleation mechanism. (a) A Gaussian sphere within the isotropic melt under quiescent conditions. Compression at $\dot\varepsilon > \dot\varepsilon^*$ induces the "oriented melt" by significant chain elongation, which induces the homogeneous nucleation. (b) Schematic illustration of the "YOROI model" of the NOC structure. (c) Schematic illustration of one molecular chain in the case that we virtually extend its full length. 2 μm is 10^2 times as large as the size of a nano-crystal. (See color insert.)

domization, while at the same time the chains are locally parallel packed. Since the strong elongation can form many parallel packed chains, much of the melted polymer chains are oriented along the elongational direction throughout. Hence, the bulk melt becomes liquid crystal-like, which is the image of the oriented melt. It is natural to imagine that the nucleus nucleates easily within the parallel packed chains. The large number of nuclei generated through the homogeneous nucleation grows up instantaneously into the nano-crystals before the melt structure randomizes due to entropic relaxation (Fig. 4.25b).

Logically speaking, the definition of $\dot{\varepsilon}^*$ is a critical $\dot{\varepsilon}$, where the τ of the homogeneous nucleation becomes shorter than the lifetime of the oriented melt (τ_m). The nucleation depends significantly on ΔT. τ_m corresponds to an entropic relaxation time from the oriented melt to the isotropic one. τ_m depends significantly on M_w and the distribution of molecular weight. Therefore, $\dot{\varepsilon}^*$ depends on ΔT and M_w. It is important to control morphology and structure by changing ΔT, M_w, and M_w distribution. $\dot{\varepsilon}^*$ is a discontinuous point where the morphology, structure, and physical properties (shown in Section 4.5.5) discontinuously change.

Regarding the nucleation for $\dot{\varepsilon}(S) < \dot{\varepsilon}^*$, we note that although elongation induces weak parallel packing of the chains, most of the parallel packing soon relaxes prior to nucleation due to the entropy relaxation. Therefore, it is impossible to create a high enough number density of NOCs in order to observe homogeneous nucleation under these conditions.

During growth, the original molecular entanglements within the melt should be concentrated into the interface between the nano-crystals. Within one nano-crystal, 10^3 stems of molecular chains are parallel packed. When we focus on one chain, it should three dimensionally interpenetrate and connect the nano-crystals more than 100 times, as the mean extended length of one molecular chain is about 2 μm (Fig. 4.25c). Note that one molecule should take an elongated random walk conformation even after suffering critical elongation, that is, the parallel packing is locally realized and the total conformation is an elongated random walk. Therefore, the nano-crystals are tightly connected three dimensionally by carbon–carbon covalent bonds called tie molecules and entanglements. We call this schematic illustration of the NOCs the "YOROI" model, because the structure resembles the ancient armor used by Japanese samurai. We estimate that the mean thickness of the interface between nano-crystals is as narrow as 0.5 nm from the χ_c. A strong SAXS intensity of the two-point pattern of the NOCs should result in a significant difference of electron density between the interior of the NOCs and the interface.

Therefore, we surmise that the electron density of the interface will be less than that of the NOCs because the entanglements need more free volume than the molecular packing within a crystal.

4.5.5 Nano-Nucleation Results in Ultrahigh Performance

Figure 4.26a indicates a typical stress (σ) against strain (ε) for $\dot{\varepsilon}(L)$ and $\dot{\varepsilon}(S)$. The maximum tensile stress (or stress at break, σ_B) is $\sigma_B = 2.1 \times 10^2$ MPa for $\dot{\varepsilon}(L)$. σ_B for $\dot{\varepsilon}(L)$ is about 7 times larger than the conventional sheets for iPP and high density polyethylene (HDPE) [45]. σ_B for $\dot{\varepsilon}(S)$ is $\sigma_B = 32$ MPa, which is comparable to the conventional sheets for iPP and HDPE. We also compare σ_B for $\dot{\varepsilon}(L)$ with other bulk polymer samples thicker than 0.1 mm, for example, $\sigma_B \cong 45$ MPa for polyethylene terephthalate (PET), $\sigma_B \cong 50$ MPa for polystyrene (PS), and $\sigma_B \cong 85$ MPa for nylon66® [45]. We find that σ_B for $\dot{\varepsilon}(L)$ is the highest within conventional polymeric materials, twice as large as that of aluminum and comparable to that of duralumin [46].

We obtain the specific tensile strength, defined by $\sigma_s \equiv \sigma_B/\rho_s$, where ρ_s is the specific gravity. We know that σ_s is a useful index for comparison with different materials, for example, $\sigma_s = 220$ MPa for $\dot{\varepsilon}(L)$ is several times larger than that for the usual steel used for the bodies of cars, $\sigma_s(car) \cong 40$–80 MPa [46]. Thus, the NOCs show specific strength 2–5 times higher than common steel with the same mass.

Young's modulus (E) of the sheet is $E = 4.1$ GPa for $\dot{\varepsilon}(L)$, which is significantly large compared with $E = 1.4$ GPa for $\dot{\varepsilon}(S)$, $E = 1.5$ GPa for conventional iPP, $E = 1.3$ GPa for HDPE, $E = 2.3$ GPa for PET, and $E = 2.6$ GPa for PS and nylon66® [45]. It is well known that σ_B and E of these conventional sheets are much smaller than those of fiber.

We test the thermal resistance of $\dot{\varepsilon}(L)$ by observing the change of the normalized size (l/l_0) with the increase of T, where l is the lateral size of a sample and l_0 is the initial lateral size at room temperature. l/l_0 of the NOCs does not change up to 176°C and then $|l/l_0|$ suddenly changes more than 3%. Therefore, we obtain the heat-proof temperature $T_h = 176$°C for $\dot{\varepsilon}(L)$. We also observe $T_h = 164.1$°C for $\dot{\varepsilon}(S)$ and $T_h \cong 120$°C for commercial biaxially oriented polypropylene. The T_h for $\dot{\varepsilon}(L)$ satisfies the condition for super engineering plastics, that is, $T_h > 150$°C [47]. The high heat resistance of $\dot{\varepsilon}(L)$ should be due to high crystallinity and the high melting temperature of crystals.

We confirm that the NOCs show ultrahigh performance for physical properties, which is analogous to the nano-crystals of inorganic materials showing high

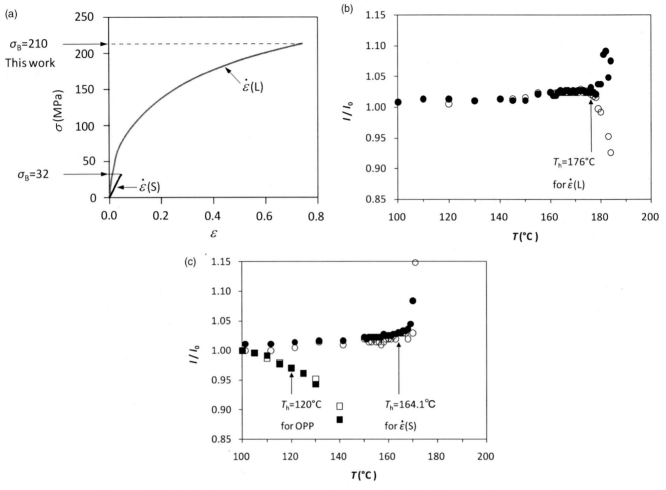

Figure 4.26 Typical example of physical properties. (a) Stress–strain curves for $\dot{\varepsilon}(L) = 3 \times 10^2 \text{ s}^{-1}$ and $\dot{\varepsilon}(S) = 9 \text{ s}^{-1}$. Samples were crystallized by 1D compression at $T_c = 150°C$. The σ_B for $\dot{\varepsilon}(L)$ is about seven times as large as that for $\dot{\varepsilon}(S)$ and/or conventional iPP sheet. (b, c) Thermal resistance test obtained from l/l_0 against T. $\dot{\varepsilon}(L)$ and $\dot{\varepsilon}(S)$ are crystallized by 1D compression.

performance as predicted by Hall-Petch's law [48, 49]. The simultaneous realization of the large tensile strength and large toughness of the NOCs should be due to the 3D connection of the nano-crystals by tie molecules and entanglements as shown by the YOROI model. The molecular connection in the NOCs should correspond to the dislocations in inorganic materials and the high heat resistance of $\dot{\varepsilon}(L)$ should be due to high crystallinity and the high melting temperature of the crystals, which is much higher than the glass transition temperature of the amorphous phase. We might expect NOCs to be used in fields such as industrial supplies where conventional polymers can no longer be used, and to replace the metals or ceramics currently used in products, which will lead us to a sustainable society due to the high possibility of recycling and reuse.

4.6 HETEROGENEOUS NUCLEATION

4.6.1 Introduction

The special materials that have high performance in acceleration of nucleation are called "nucleating agents (NAs)," which play an important role industrially. The polymer industry often uses NA nowadays to improve the performance of polymer materials. Two explanations have been proposed how NA accelerates heterogeneous nucleation. The most popular one suggests that "epitaxy" between NAs and crystals controls the nucleation [50]. The other suggests that suppression of mobility of molecular chains by adding NAs controls the nucleation [51, 52]. Yoshimoto et al. and Lotz et al. showed epitaxy structurally between α form crystals of iPP and NA crystals by means of TEM or atomic force microscope (AFM) [53, 54]. But how epitaxy can control and accelerate heterogeneous nucleation has not been clarified by a kinetic study of nucleation. That is our goal in this section. Epitaxial crystallization is also covered in detail in Chapter 9.

4.6.2 Experimental

We use fully fractionated PE (NIST, SRM1483, $M_w = 32 \times 10^3$, $M_w/M_n = 1.1$) and iPP ($M_n = 15.3 \times 10^3$, $M_w/M_n = 5.6$ and $[mmmm] = 99.5\%$). We use the same NA as in Section 4.3, and $a_{NA} = 0.23 \pm 0.12$ μm. We prepare two samples: polymer mixed with NA, which we call PE + NA or iPP + NA, and polymer only, which we call PE or iPP.

We sandwich a small amount of each sample between two pieces of cover glass. We control the sample for a thickness of 30 μm and put it in a Hot Stage. We count the number density of the nuclei in which lateral size (a) is $a \geq a_{obs} = 1$ μm ($v(t)$). We observe $I(a \geq a_{obs})$ and τ_i from the plot of $v(t)$ against t. We rewrite $I(a \geq a_{obs})$ to $I(a \geq a_{obs}) \equiv dv(t)/dt = I$. C_{NA} of PE+NA is $C_{NA/PE} = 0.4$ wt%. We melt and then crystallize them isothermally at $\Delta T = 12.8$ or 14.9 K. We use samples of iPP + NA to observe C_{NA} dependence of I and τ_i. C_{NA} of iPP + NA is $C_{NA/iPP} = 10^{-4}$–1 wt%. Again, we melt and then crystallize them isothermally at $\Delta T = 39.4$ K.

The unit-cell structure of NA belongs to the monoclinic system which we call the α form [53]. The lattice parameters are $a = 2.6438$ nm, $b = 0.608$ nm, $c = 3.7172$ nm, and $\beta = 93.65$ [53]. As a typical polymer, we use iPP ($M_w = 3.0 \times 10^5$, $M_w/M_n = 4.6$ and $[mmmm] = 97\%$). Table 4.1 shows the parameters for the iPP crystals used in this study [55–59]. We control a_{NA} by applying the following methods.

4.6.2.1 Bottom Up Method 1 (Spray Drying Method) Figure 4.27 is a schematic illustration of the spray drying method. We spray a methanol solution of NA into a tube by a coaxial atomizing nozzle. We maintain the tube's temperature at 70°C to vaporize the droplets. NA crystallizes from the solution during drying due to the increased concentration of NA in the mixture of NA and methanol, MeOH ($C_{NA/MeOH}$). Assuming that one droplet generates one single crystal, a_{NA} is given by

$$a_{NA} = \left(\frac{\rho_{MeOH} C_{NA/MeOH}}{\rho_{NA}} \right)^{\frac{1}{3}} x, \quad (4.51)$$

where ρ_{MeOH}, ρ_{NA} and x represent the densities of MeOH and NA and droplet size, respectively. We can decrease a_{NA} from the order of μm to nm by decreasing $C_{NA/MeOH}$ and/or x. In the coaxial atomizing nozzle system, a droplet size x is known in Reference [60]. Table 4.2 lists the typical $C_{NA/MeOH}$ for the formation of nano NAs (called nano-NA-1 and nano-NA-2) and of macro-NAs (called macro-NA-1 and macro-NA-2).

4.6.2.2 Bottom Up Method 2 (Solution Crystallization Method) We crystallize the NAs from the solution of NA, n-butyl alcohol (n-BuOH) and xylene. The ratio of weight of n-BuOH and xylene is 7:19. We mix xylene to suppress the diffusion of the NA molecules. We control the size by changing the concentration of NA in the solution of NA, n-BuOH, and xylene, $C_{NA/(n-BuOH+xylene)}$.

4.6.2.3 Top Down Method (Mechanical Grinding Method) We crystallize macro-NA (called macro-

TABLE 4.1 Parameters of iPP

$\Delta \sigma$ / J rep. unit^{-1}	1.71×10^{-22} [55]
Δh / J rep. unit^{-1}	1.53×10^{-20} [56]
T_m^o / K	455.8 [57–59]

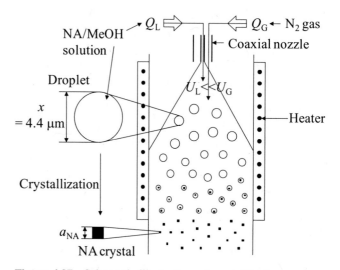

Figure 4.27 Schematic illustration of crystallization process of NA from NA/MeOH solution by spray drying method. $x = 4.4$ μm.

TABLE 4.2 Name and Characteristics of NA Prepared by Various Methods

Method		Name of NA	$\bar{a}_{NA}$/ nm	Comments
Bottom up 1	Spray drying	Nano-NA-1	26^a	$C_{NA/MeOH} = 10^{-5}$ wt%
		Nano-NA-2	53^a	$C_{NA/MeOH} = 10^{-4}$ wt%
		Macro-NA-1	1.5×10^{2a}	$C_{NA/MeOH} = 10^{-2}$ wt%
		Macro-NA-2	4.5×10^{3b}	$C_{NA/MeOH} = 34$ wt%
Bottom up 2	Solution crystallization	Nano-NA-3	5^c	$C_{NA/(n\text{-}BuOH+xylene)} = 0.38$ wt% n-BuOH/xylene = 7/19(w/w)
		Macro-NA-3	4.1×10^{4a}	$C_{NA/(n\text{-}BuOH+xylene)} = 0.61$ wt% n-BuOH/xylene = 7/19(w/w)
Top down	Ball mill	Macro-NA-4	2.3×10^{2a}	
		Macro-NA-5	7.9×10^{2a}	
	Nanomizer	Macro-NA-6	3.9×10^{2a}	
	Jet mill	Macro-NA-7	1.4×10^{3a}	

^{a}Measured by means of SEM.
^{b}Measured by means of OM.
^{c}Measured by WAXS.

NA-3) by grinding the solution using a conventional ball mill, jet mill, or nanomizer. Grinding only obtains macro-NAs (called macro-NA-4–7). We uniformly mix the NA with a solution of iPP and xylene at $T = 130°C$, cool the suspension to room temperature, and dry it. We observe the morphology of NA by OM and SEM. We observe the crystallization behaviors of iPP by OM with a hot stage under nitrogen flow. We melt and crystallize the samples in the range of $T_c = 135$–$158°C$. We evaluate I from the time t dependence of the number density of iPP crystals larger than 2 μm in lateral size. We carry out WAXS measurement by using Cu-Kα radiation ($\lambda = 1.5418$ Å). We measure a_{NA} by SEM, OM, or WAXS. We obtain the mean lateral size ($\overline{a_{NA}}$) by observing the size distribution. We obtain $\overline{a_{NA}}$ of nano-NA-3 by WAXS by using Sherrer's method, as described in Chapter 2:

$$\overline{a_{NA}} = \frac{0.9\lambda}{B\cos\{\sin^{-1}(q\lambda/4\pi)\}}, \quad (4.52)$$

where B is the half width of a reflection. We determine C_{NA} of nano-NA-3 from $I_x(q)$s of NA and iPP crystals. We obtain C_{NA} from the scattering intensities, 110 of iPP and 200 of NA in the mixture of nano-NA-3 and iPP. Details are shown in References [21] and [61].

4.6.3 Role of Epitaxy in Heterogeneous Nucleation [21]

4.6.3.1 Theory For simplicity, we assume that at most one nucleus can nucleate on one NA, that C_{NA} is dilute enough, and that all NA crystals are active. If epitaxy controls the nucleation rate, the prefactor of I (I_0) should be proportional to the surface area of NA (A), that is, $I_0 \propto A$. Also, I_0 should be proportional to the number density of NA (v_{NA}) in the melt, that is, $I_0 \propto v_{NA}$. From these relationships, we obtain that

$$I \propto I_0 \propto v_{NA} A. \quad (4.53)$$

When we assume that all NAs have similar shapes, A is given by $A \propto a_{NA}^2$. The proportionality coefficient will change according to the shape of NA. v_{NA} is defined by the ratio of the total weight of NA per unit volume (M_{NA}) and the weight of one NA (m_{NA}), that is,

$$v_{NA} \equiv M_{NA}/m_{NA}. \quad (4.54)$$

As $M_{NA} \propto C_{NA}$ and $m_{NA} \propto a_{NA}^3$, v_{NA} is given by

$$v_{NA} \propto C_{NA}/a_{NA}^3. \quad (4.55)$$

From Equation (4.53), Equation (4.54), and Equation (4.55), we have the formula,

$$I \propto C_{NA}/a_{NA}. \quad (4.56)$$

Thus, we can demonstrate the important role of epitaxy in nucleation by confirming the behavior of Equation (4.56) experimentally. It is well known that $I(a \geq a_{obs})$ saturates with the increase of C_{NA}; that is, $I(a \geq a_{obs})$ becomes constant for C_{NA} larger than $C_{NA}^\dagger$. For simplicity, we fix a_{obs}, for example, $a_{obs} = 1$ μm. Therefore, a_{obs} does not relate to lateral growth with t or with ΔT. For the sake of simplicity, a_{NA} is fixed. Figure 4.28a illustrates a crystal with size a_{obs} on an NA. C_{NA} is given by

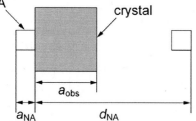
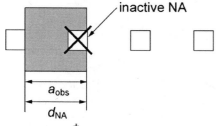
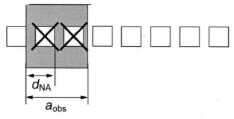

Figure 4.28 Illustration of change of nucleation on a NA with increase of C_{NA}. a_{NA} and a_{obs} are given. (a) $d_{NA} > a_{obs}$. One crystal with size a_{obs} is formed on one NA crystal. (b) $d_{NA} \cong a_{obs}$. One crystal with a_{obs} includes two NA crystals. The newly included NA crystals become "inactive." (c) $d_{NA} < a_{obs}$. Most NAs become inactive.

$$C_{NA} \propto (a_{NA}/d_{NA})^3, \quad (4.57)$$

where d_{NA} is the mean distance between the NAs. When the NA is cubic, C_{NA} is defined by

$$C_{NA} \equiv (a_{NA}/d_{NA})^3. \quad (4.58)$$

In Equation (4.57) and Equation (4.58) d_{NA} decreases with the increase of C_{NA} as shown in Figure 4.28b,c. Therefore, the C_{NA} dependence of $I(a \geq a_{obs})$ depends on the relative relationship between d_{NA} and a_{obs} (Fig. 4.28).

a. $d_{NA} > a_{obs}$

In this condition, one crystal with size a_{obs} forms on one NA crystal. Since it includes only one NA crystal, the other NA crystals can work as fresh NA, which we call active NA crystals. Therefore, we expect a straight line of $I(a \geq a_{obs})$.

b. $d_{NA} \cong a_{obs}$

When $d_{NA} \cong a_{obs}$, the surface of another NA becomes covered by the crystal with a_{obs}. In this case, nucleation cannot happen on the covered NA crystal; that is, the NA crystal cannot work as an NA (we call this an inactive NA crystal) (Fig. 4.28b). When inactive NA crystals start appearing, $I(a \geq a_{obs})$ starts saturating. We define $C_{NA}^\dagger$ by the breaking in $I(a \geq a_{obs})$ versus C_{NA}. Combining Equation (4.58) and the equality of d_{NA} and a_{obs} gives,

$$C_{NA}^\dagger = (a_{NA}/a_{obs})^3. \quad (4.59)$$

c. $d_{NA} < a_{obs}$

Most NAs with the exception of the nucleating NA become inactive (Fig. 4.28c). In this case, $I(a \geq a_{obs})$ saturates. Hence,

$$I(a \geq a_{obs}) \propto C_{NA} \text{ for } C_{NA} < C_{NA}^\dagger, \text{ that is, } d_{NA} > a_{obs}$$
$$\cong \text{const. for } C_{NA} > C_{NA}^\dagger, \text{ that is, } d_{NA} < a_{obs}. \quad (4.60)$$

Equation (4.56) means that $I(a \geq a_{obs})$ increases with the decrease of a_{NA}. For example, when a_{NA} becomes $1/10^2$, $I(a \geq a_{obs})$ should increase 10^2 times.

It is interesting to predict the mean crystal size (a_{max}) after completion of solidification. Since $I(a \geq a_{obs})$ saturates for $C_{NA} > C_{NA}^\dagger$, a_{max} should be proportional to a_{obs}, that is, $a_{max} \propto a_{obs}$. Combining these relationships gives,

$$a_{max} \propto \frac{a_{NA}}{(C_{NA}^\dagger)^{1/3}}. \quad (4.61)$$

Hence,

$$\log a_{max} = \log a_{NA} - \frac{1}{3}\log C_{NA}^\dagger + \text{const.} \quad (4.62)$$

Figure 4.29 illustrates $\log a_{max}$ against $\log C_{NA}^\dagger$ as a parameter of a_{NA} given by Equation (4.62),

$$a_{max} \propto (C_{NA}^\dagger)^{-1/3} \text{ for } a_{NA} = \text{const.} \quad (4.63)$$

For example, we obtain $a_{max}(A)$ at point A when using $C_{NA}^\dagger(A)$ (Fig. 4.29). When we use a smaller a_{NA}, we need less $C_{NA}^\dagger$ for the same $a_{max}(A)$, $C_{NA}^\dagger(B)$ of point B. $a_{max}(A)$ should become smaller, that is, $a_{max}(C)$ of point C when a_{NA} is smaller for the same $C_{NA}^\dagger(A)$. Therefore, we predict that NA will have high performance by breaking

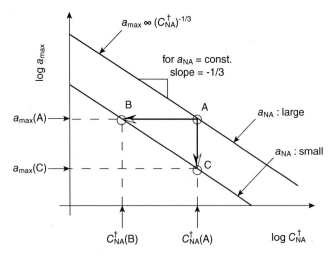

Figure 4.29 Theoretical illustration of $\log a_{max}$ against $\log C_{NA}^{\dagger}$ given by Equation (4.62) as a function of a_{NA}. $A \to B$ indicates that when smaller a_{NA} is used, we need less $C_{NA}^{\dagger}$ for the same a_{max}. $A \to C$ indicates that we can obtain smaller a_{max} when a_{NA} is smaller for the same $C_{NA}^{\dagger}$.

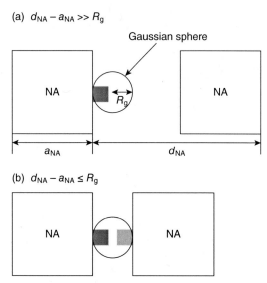

Figure 4.30 Condition that nucleation is a probabilistic phenomenon. (a) $d_{NA} - a_{NA} \gg R_g$. As nuclei on each NA do not interact each other, τ_i is independent from C_{NA}. This is the condition of probabilistic nucleation. (b) $d_{NA} - a_{NA} \leq R_g$. More than two NAs are touched with one Gaussian sphere with R_g. As nucleation competes on two NAs, τ_i should increase with increase of C_{NA}.

up significantly. If we could observe a_{max}, we could obtain the relationship between a_{NA} and $C_{NA}^{\dagger}$; however, we do not observe a_{max}.

As discussed, polymer chains should disentangle and rearrange through chain sliding diffusion during the nucleation process from the melt [14, 19]. As the chains that form a nucleus are included in a Gaussian sphere with a size corresponding to the radius of gyration (R_g) [23], whether nucleation is a probabilistic phenomenon depends on the relative magnitudes of $d_{NA} - a_{NA}$ and R_g (Fig. 4.30).

a. $d_{NA} - a_{NA} \gg R_g$

As one Gaussian sphere touches less than one NA, the nuclei on each NA do not interact with each other, that is, each nuclei should be incoherent (Fig. 4.30a). The probability of nucleation on a NA (P_{NA}) is independent and the same on any NA in the melt. Therefore τ_i should be independent of C_{NA},

$$d\tau_i / dC_{NA} = 0, \quad (4.64)$$

that is, $\tau_i = $ const. This is the condition of probabilistic nucleation.

b. $d_{NA} - a_{NA} \leq R_g$

In this case, we include more than two NAs in one Gaussian sphere with R_g (Fig. 4.30b). The chains would like to nucleate on these NAs in the Gaussian sphere; that is, they compete against each other for one nucleus. Hence, the nucleus becomes coherent, P_{NA} should decrease, and τ_i should increase with the increase of C_{NA}. This case is not the condition of probabilistic nucleation.

4.6.3.2 Results and Discussion Figure 4.31 shows the typical C_{NA} dependence of $v(t)$ against t for iPP + NA at $\Delta T = 39.4$ K. We plot $C_{NA} = 10^{-3}$ wt% on the right axis,

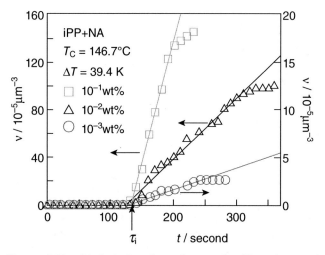

Figure 4.31 Typical C_{NA} dependence of $v(t)$ against t of iPP + NA at $T_c = 146.7$°C and $\Delta T = 39.4$ K. $v(t)$ increased much faster when C_{NA} increased.

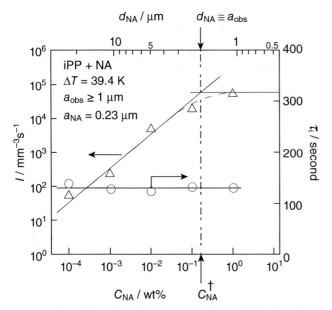

Figure 4.32 Plots of I and τ_i against C_{NA} of iPP + NA for a fixed $a_{NA} = 0.23$ μm at $T_c = 146.7°C$ and $\Delta T = 39.4$ K. Left and right vertical axes indicate I and τ_i, respectively. Upper horizontal axis of top indicates d_{NA}. It verifies that $I \propto C_{NA}$ experimentally, which means that epitaxy controls and accelerates nucleation. $d\tau_i/dC_{NA} = 0$ clarifies that nucleation is a probabilistic phenomenon.

and the other C_{NA}s on the left axis. $v(t)$ increases much faster when C_{NA} increases. This shows that I accelerates with the increase of C_{NA}. On the other hand, τ_i s are almost the same for all C_{NA}, making it clear that τ_i does not depend on C_{NA}.

Figure 4.32 shows the plots of I against C_{NA} of iPP + NA for a fixed a_{NA} (=0.23 μm) at $\Delta T = 39.4$ K. The top horizontal axis is d_{NA} obtained by Equation (4.58). I increases with the increase of C_{NA} and saturates for $C_{NA} \geq 1$ wt%. I increases 10 times when C_{NA} increases 10 times. Thus, we obtain the empirical relationships,

$$I \propto C_{NA} \text{ for } C_{NA} \leq 10^{-2} \text{ wt\%} \quad (4.65)$$

and

$$I \cong \text{const. for } C_{NA} \geq 1 \text{ wt\%.} \quad (4.66)$$

Hence, we have a breaking $C_{NA}(C_{NA}^\dagger)$ at $C_{NA}^\dagger \cong 10^{-1}$ wt%.

These empirical relationships support the theoretical prediction of Equation (4.56) that $I \propto C_{NA}$ for $a_{NA} = $ const. We conclude that the epitaxy of NA controls and accelerates I.

In Figure 4.32, $d_{NA}^\dagger \cong 2$ μm corresponds to $C_{NA}^\dagger \cong 10^{-1}$ wt%, which satisfies the condition of breaking of I. The present range of C_{NA} corresponds to $d_{NA} = 1 \sim 20$ μm.

We obtain plots of τ_i against C_{NA} of iPP + NA for a fixed a_{NA} (=0.23 μm) at $\Delta T = 39.4$ K from Figure 4.31 (Fig. 4.32). τ_i does not depend on all observed C_{NA}. Hence, we obtain

$$d\tau_i/dC_{NA} = 0 \text{ or } \tau_i = \text{const. for all observed } C_{NA}. \quad (4.67)$$

This empirical formula verifies the theoretical prediction of Equation (4.64), from which we conclude that nucleation is a probabilistic phenomenon.

4.6.4 Acceleration Mechanism of Nucleation of Polymers by Nano-Sizing of Nucleating Agent [61]

4.6.4.1 ΔT Dependence of I (Theory)
As mentioned, NA is widely used for improving the performance of semicrystalline polymer materials, such as iPP [62, 63]. NA accelerates I and generally improves the mechanical and optical properties of polymers. Most commercial NAs are made of crystalline materials [64–69]. This section examines the kinetic effect of epitaxy between NA and polymer crystals [53, 70–73].

All interactions, that is, epitaxy, should be reflected in I_0 and ΔG^* in Equation (4.3). $\Delta G^*(\Delta \sigma)$ is related to the efficiency of epitaxy, which is basically controlled by lattice matching of the NA and the polymer crystals. The important role of epitaxy on the ΔG^* dependence of I on iPP with different NAs is reported in Reference [61]. Equation (4.11) indicates that heterogeneous 2D nucleation takes place when ΔT is so large that Δg is much larger than $2\Delta\sigma$. The condition $\Delta g > 2\Delta\sigma$ is usually satisfied since the observed ΔT is several tens of degrees K in most polymer crystallization processes. For example, the usual range of ΔT of iPP is between 30 K and 60 K, so Δg becomes 6 to 12 times larger than $\Delta\sigma$.

When $\Delta g \gg \Delta \sigma$ is satisfied, we can roughly approximate Equation (4.11) by

$$\Delta G^* \cong \frac{4\sigma\sigma_e}{\Delta g} \text{ for } \Delta g \gg \Delta\sigma. \quad (4.68)$$

As the ΔG^* is not a function of $\Delta\sigma$, the epitaxy does not significantly affect the ΔG^*. Therefore, we conclude that the epitaxy of NA affects I_0, and does not significantly affect ΔG^*. In this study, the approximate form of Equation (4.68) is used.

Inserting Equation (4.9) and Equation (4.68) into Equation (4.3) leads to the final formula,

$$I \cong I_0 \exp\left(-\frac{C}{\Delta T}\right), \quad (4.69)$$

where

$$C = \frac{4\sigma\sigma_e T_m^o}{kT\Delta h}. \qquad (4.70)$$

Recall that in Section 4.6.3 we predicted theoretically that $I \propto C_{NA} a_{NA}^{-1}$ (Eq. 4.56). The purpose of Section 4.6.4 is to confirm this relationship by controlling a_{NA} from the order of nm to μm, which clarifies the important role of epitaxy in heterogeneous nucleation.

4.6.4.2 Size and Morphology of NA

Bottom Up Method 1 (Spray Drying Method) The a_{NA} observed by SEM or OM apparently increases from the order of 10 nm to 1 μm with an increase of $C_{NA/MeOH}$ from 10^{-5} to 34 wt%, and shows the formation of nano NA (nano-NA-1) and macro-NA (macro-NA-2) as in Figure 4.33. We plot $\overline{a_{NA}}$ against $C_{NA/MeOH}$ in Figure 4.34 and fit the data by a straight line with a slope of 1/3.

Bottom Up Method 2 (Solution Crystallization Method) When $C_{NA/(n-BuOH+xylene)}$ increases from 0.38 to 0.61 wt%, the formation of nano-NA (nano-NA-3) and macro-NA (macro-NA-3) are confirmed by WAXS and SEM, respectively, as shown below. We obtain $\overline{a_{NA}}$ of nano-NA-3 by WAXS from the half width (B_{obs}) of the 200 reflection. a_{NA} is as small as 5 nm. The morphology of macro-NA resembles a thin, long plate. We obtain $\overline{a_{NA}} = 41$ μm. The aspect ratio between length and width is as large as 20–40.

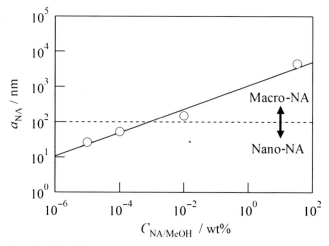

Figure 4.34 Plots of $\overline{a}_{NA}$ of nano- and macro-NAs (nano-NA-1, nano-NA-2, macro-NA-1, and macro-NA-2) crystallized by spray drying method against $C_{NA/MeOH}$. x was 4.4 μm.

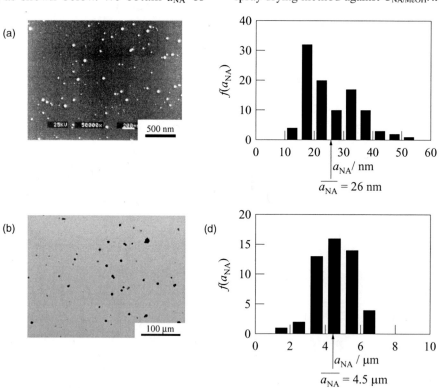

Figure 4.33 Morphology and $f(a_{NA})$ of nano-NA (nano-NA-1) and macro-NA (macro-NA-2) crystallized by spray drying method. $U_G = 340$ m/s, $U_L = 2$ m/s, $Q_G = 3.4 \times 10^{-4}$ m³/s and $Q_L = 3.4 \times 10^{-7}$ m³/s were fixed. Nano-NA and macro-NA were crystallized by controlling $C_{NA/MeOH} = 10^{-5}$ and 34 wt%, respectively. (a) Typical scanning electron micrograph of nano-NA. (b) Typical optical micrograph of macro-NA. (c) $f(a_{NA})$ and $\overline{a}_{NA}$ of nano-NA. (d) $f(a_{NA})$ and $\overline{a}_{NA}$ of macro-NA.

Top Down Method (Mechanical Grinding Method) We obtain only macro-NAs (called macro-NA-4–7) by grinding large macro-NA single crystals (macro-NA-3). Table 4.2 shows the results. $\overline{a_{NA}}$ is on the order of sub-μm to μm. We determine the unit-cell structure of nano-NA (nano-NA-3) as α form by WAXS [53].

4.6.4.3 C_{NA} Dependence of I_0

Figure 4.35 shows how the plot of log$I$ of iPP mixed with nano- or macro-NAs (nano-NA-3 or macro-NA-4, respectively) against ΔT^{-1} as a function of C_{NA}. The upper horizontal axis indicates T_c. All data fit straight lines. Since all slopes of the lines are almost the same, we apply an averaged slope to all of the fitted lines. We obtain I_0 from an intercept of the vertical axis. The lines shift upward at a given ΔT^{-1} with the increase of C_{NA} for a constant $\overline{a_{NA}}$.

Figure 4.36 shows the plot of LogI_0s against C_{NA} for nano- and macro-NAs (nano-NA-3 and macro-NA-4, respectively). Both plots fit well by straight lines with a slope of 1. Therefore, we obtain the empirical formula of $I_0^{exp} \propto C_{NA}$, which satisfies Equation (4.56). I_0 of iPP mixed with nano-NA (I_0(nano-NA-3)) is 50 times larger than that mixed with macro-NA (I_0(macro-NA-4)) for the same C_{NA}. $\overline{a_{NA}}$ of macro-NA ($\overline{a_{NA}}$(macro-NA-4)) is also 50 times larger than that of nano-NA ($\overline{a_{NA}}$(nano-NA-3)), giving

$$I_0(\text{nano-NA-3})/I_0(\text{macro-NA-4})$$
$$= \overline{a_{NA}}(\text{macro-NA-4})/\overline{a_{NA}}(\text{nano-NA-3}) = 50.$$

Thus, experimental relationship $I_0 \propto \overline{a_{NA}}^{-1}$ also satisfies Equation (4.56).

4.6.4.4 $\overline{a_{NA}}$ Dependence of I_0

Figure 4.37 shows the plot of Log$I$ against ΔT^{-1} as a parameter of $\overline{a_{NA}}$ for $C_{NA} = 0.1$ wt%. The upper horizontal axis indicates T_c. The plots fit well by straight lines. As all fitted lines are nearly parallel, we use the averaged slope. We obtain I_0 from an intercept of the vertical axis. As the lines shift upward at a given ΔT^{-1} with the decrease of $\overline{a_{NA}}$ for a constant C_{NA}, I_0 increases with the decrease of $\overline{a_{NA}}$.

Figure 4.38 shows the plot of LogI_0 against $\overline{a_{NA}}$ for $C_{NA} = 0.1$ wt%. The plots fit well by a straight line with a slope of -1. We obtain the empirical formula $I_0^{exp} \propto \overline{a_{NA}}^{-1}$, which satisfies Equation (4.56). A typical example (Fig. 4.38A and B), indicates that I_0(nano-NA-3) ($\overline{a_{NA}} = 5$ nm) is 300 times larger than I_0(macro-NA-7) ($\overline{a_{NA}} = 1.4$ μm).

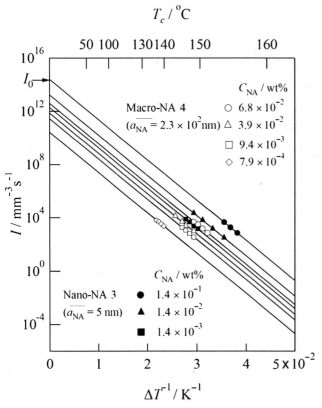

Figure 4.35 Plots of Is against ΔT^{-1} as a parameter of C_{NA} of iPP mixed with nano-NA (nano-NA-3, $\overline{a}_{NA} = 5$ nm) and macro-NA (macro-NA-4, $\overline{a}_{NA} = 2.3 \times 10^2$ nm). Upper axis indicates T_c.

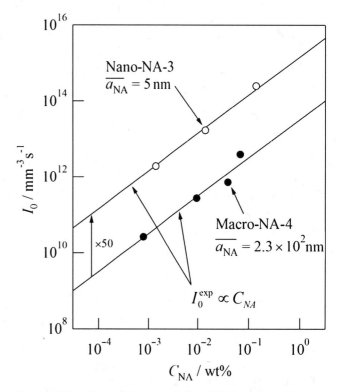

Figure 4.36 Plots of I_0s against C_{NA} of iPP mixed with nano NA (nano NA-3) and macro NA (macro NA-4).

156 POLYMER NUCLEATION

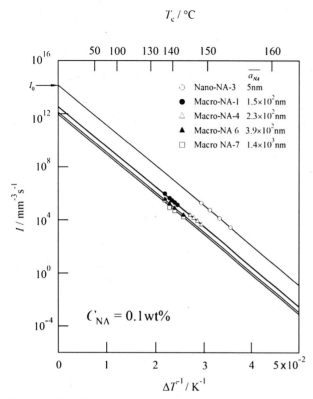

Figure 4.37 Plots of Is against ΔT^{-1} for $C_{NA} = 0.1$ wt% as a function of $\overline{a}_{NA}$. Nano-NA (nano-NA-3) and macro-NAs (macro-NA-1, macro NA-4, macro NA-6 and macro-NA-7) were used. Upper axis indicates T_c.

4.6.4.5 Confirmation of the Prediction
Combination of experimental formulae of $I_0^{exp} \propto C_{NA}$ and $I_0^{exp} \propto \overline{a}_{NA}^{-1}$ gives

$$I_0^{exp} \propto \frac{C_{NA}}{\overline{a}_{NA}}. \tag{4.71}$$

This accords with and serves to confirm the prediction of Equation (4.56). I_0 of iPP mixed with nano-NA ($\overline{a}_{NA} = 5$ nm) is 50 to 10^3 times larger than that mixed with conventional commercial NA ($\overline{a}_{NA} = 0.2 \sim 5$ μm). Therefore, nano-sizing of NA is a significantly effective method to improve the nucleating ability of NA.

4.7 EFFECT OF ENTANGLEMENT DENSITY ON THE NUCLEATION RATE [74]

4.7.1 Introduction and Experimental

This section discusses how entanglements affect I [75]. Since the entanglements cannot be incorporated into the crystal lattice, it is apparent that the entanglements within the melt will suppress nucleation [14, 15]. Figure

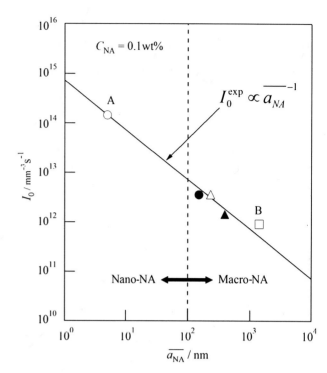

Figure 4.38 Plots of I_0s against $\overline{a}_{NA}$ for $C_{NA}=0.1$ wt%. Nano NA (nano NA-3) and macro NAs (macro NA-1, macro NA-4, macro-NA-6, and macro-NA-7) were used.

4.39 illustrates how the entanglements suppress nucleation. When the nucleus forms from the fully entangled melt, the entanglements within the interface between the melt and nucleus need to be disentangled in order to grow to a larger nucleus. If not disentangled properly, these entanglements cause a pinning effect for the formation and growth of the nucleus. The sliding diffusion of the chain within the nucleus or interface should be suppressed by the entanglements. As a consequence, I should become small. To confirm this, we quantitatively study the entanglement density (ν_e) dependence of I by changing ν_e from 0 to 1 (corresponding to thermal equilibrium melt). We do this by melting a special sample that includes almost no entanglements. After melting, ν_e should increase with the increase of melt-annealing time Δt at a temperature above T_m^o, thereby controlling ν_e within the melt from 0 to 1 by changing Δt. We assume that $\nu_e \cong 0$ for $\Delta t \cong 0$ and $\nu_e \cong 1$ for $\Delta t = \infty$. We prepare the special sample as a nascent polymer (reactor powder) polymerized using the metallocene catalysts at a lower temperature than the crystallization or dissolution temperature [22, 76, 77]. Under this condition, the polymer chain immediately crystallizes during polymerization. Figure 4.40 shows a schematic illustration of a polymer chain formed from a catalyst in solution and the nucleation behavior during the polymerization.

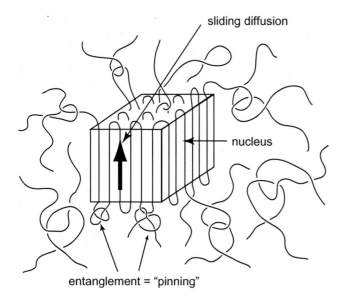

Figure 4.39 Schematic illustration to suggest how nucleation and growth are suppressed by the entanglements. The entanglements on the interface between the nucleus and liquid create a "pinning effect."

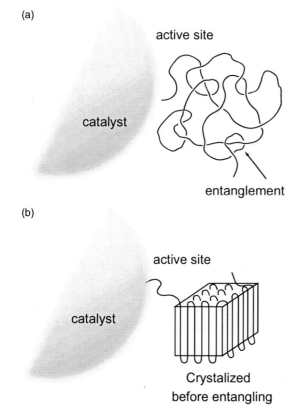

Figure 4.40 (a) Usual polymerization in solution results in the formation of entanglements. (b) No entanglement is included within the reactor powder of PE when it crystallizes during the polymerization.

Note that it is also possible to prepare the melt with different v_e by melting ECCs with different lamellar thicknesses l [75, 78] in order to show that v_e is proportional to $1/l$.

We carry out the polymerization of reactor-PE in the solvent at a low temperature (ca. 70°C). The weight average molecular weight M_w and molecular weight distribution M_w/M_n are 33.1×10^4 and 2.31, respectively. The low temperature (ca. 70°C) corresponds to the crystallization temperature of an n-alkane with ca. 35 carbons (C35). Therefore, the chains should crystallize when the number of carbons of the growing polymer chain increases to more than 35 during polymerization. Since the carbon number (ca. 35) is much smaller than that between entanglements of PE (ca. 100) [79], the crystals should be free from entanglements. We add an NA to reactor-PE in the amount of 0.1 wt% and sandwich the reactor-PE sample between two pieces of cover glass. We observe thermal melt annealing and crystallization by a POM fitted with a hot stage. From the gel permeation chromatography (GPC) measurements, we confirm that the molecular weight of PE does not change during the melt annealing with $\Delta t < 4$ hours. Figure 4.41 is a schematic illustration of a typical crystallization process. We melt the starting sample at a maximum melt-annealing temperature, $T_{max} = 150°C$ for each Δt (from 2 to 180 minutes) and quench it to a T_c ($\Delta T \approx 12°C$). During isothermal crystallization, we determine I by $I \equiv dv/dt$, where v is the number density of crystals within the melt and t is the crystallization time [30].

4.7.2 Increase of v_e Leads to a Decrease of I

Figure 4.42 shows the plot of I of reactor-PE against Δt at the same T_{max} and T_c. I rapidly decreases with the

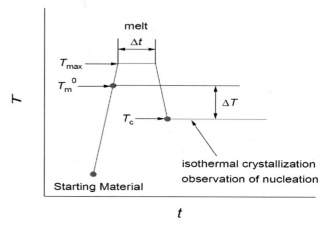

Figure 4.41 Schematic illustration of heating and crystallization processes.

increase of Δt up to $\Delta t \sim 20$ minutes and then slowly decreases. The experimental formula of I as a function of Δt is represented by

$$I(\Delta t) = A\exp(-\Delta t/\tau_f) + B\exp(-\Delta t/\tau_s) + I_\infty, \quad (4.72)$$

where A, B, and I_∞ are the constants and τ_f and τ_s are the relaxation time for formation of fast and slow entanglements, respectively. I_∞ is assumed to be

$$I_\infty = \lim_{\Delta t \to \infty} I(\Delta t). \quad (4.73)$$

Table 4.3 summarizes the fitting parameters. We assume a tentative value of 10^4 for I_∞. Equation (4.72) should be evidence of the two-step increase of v_e against Δt; that is, v_e rapidly increases at first and then slows. This suggests that simple entanglements form within small Δt (<20 minutes) followed by gradual forming of complicated entanglements. This implies that large topological movement, such as disentanglement of complicated entanglements, requires long periods of time.

4.7.3 Change of v_e with Δt

To derive an empirical formula of v_e as a function of Δt, we first assume that Equation (4.72) can be divided into fast and slow entanglements ($I^f(\Delta t)$ and $I^s(\Delta t)$),

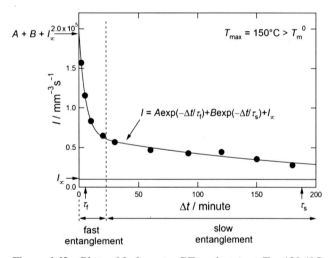

Figure 4.42 Plots of I of reactor-PE against Δt at $T_c = 128.4°C$ and $T_{max} = 150°C$. The experimental data can be divided to two regions that arise from "fast" and "slow" entanglements. Solid curve shows the best fitting with the experimental data.

$$\begin{aligned} I(\Delta t) &= I^f(\Delta t) + I^s(\Delta t) \\ &= \{A\exp(-\Delta t/\tau_f) + I_\infty^f\} + \{B\exp(-\Delta t/\tau_s) + I_\infty^s\}, \end{aligned} \quad (4.74)$$

where $I_\infty = I_\infty^f + I_\infty^s$.

We assume [75, 78] that the following equations apply for each fast and slow entanglement ($I^f(v_e)$ and $I^s(v_e)$),

$$\begin{aligned} I(v_e) &= I^f(v_e) + I^s(v_e) \\ &= I_0^f \exp(-\gamma v_e^f) + I_0^s \exp(-\gamma v_e^s) \end{aligned} \quad (4.75)$$

and

$$v_e = v_e^f + v_e^s, \quad (4.76)$$

where v_e^f and v_e^s are v_e of the fast and slow entanglements, and I_0^f and I_0^s are the constants.

Comparing the first and second terms of Equation (4.74) and Equation (4.75), we obtain the initial conditions

$$\begin{aligned} \lim_{v_e \to 0} I^f(v_e) &= I_0^f = \lim_{\Delta t \to 0} I^f(\Delta t) = A + I_\infty^f \\ \lim_{v_e \to 0} I^s(v_e) &= I_0^s = \lim_{\Delta t \to 0} I^s(\Delta t) = B + I_\infty^s \end{aligned} \quad (4.77)$$

and the boundary conditions

$$\begin{aligned} \lim_{\Delta t \to \infty} I^f(\Delta t) &= I_\infty^f = \lim_{v_e \to \infty} I^f(v_e) = I_0^f e^{-\gamma} \\ \lim_{\Delta t \to \infty} I^s(\Delta t) &= I_\infty^s = \lim_{v_e \to \infty} I^s(v_e) = I_0^s e^{-\gamma}. \end{aligned} \quad (4.78)$$

Finally, we obtain an empirical formula for v_e as a function of Δt,

$$\begin{aligned} v_e(\Delta t) \propto &-\ln\{C\exp(-\Delta t/\tau_f) + D\} \\ &-\ln\{C\exp(-\Delta t/\tau_s) + D\}, \end{aligned} \quad (4.79)$$

where C and D are the constants. Figure 4.43 shows the change of v_e with Δt. For simplicity, we assume

$$v_e^f = v_e^s \text{ for } \Delta t = \infty. \quad (4.80)$$

Table 4.4 summarizes the parameters shown in Figure 4.43. Note that the validity of these assumptions remains to be confirmed.

TABLE 4.3 Fitting Parameters by Equation (5.72)

Parameters	A/mm^{-3} s^{-1}	B/mm^{-3} s^{-1}	τ_f/min	τ_s/min	I_∞/mm^{-3} s^{-1}
Values	1.33×10^5	5.53×10^4	5.4	188	10^4 (Assumed)

4.7.4 Two-Step Entangling Model

Consider a variety of the entanglements that might suppress nucleation and classify them according to variation, such as twist, knot, or loops as shown in Figure 4.44. Accounting for the topological movement, we expect that their formation rates will differ, that is, twists or knots with lower order are easier to form than loops or knots with higher order. Therefore, based on the measurement of I against Δt, estimate which entanglements are constructed initially.

A twist indicates that part of a single chain or multiple chains is twisted. The twist becomes more complicated with an increase in the number of twists, that is, with an increase in the order of twist. We identify the knot by a chain end that passes through a circle of the same chain. The knot becomes high order or complicated the more it passes through the circle. Links, which are similar to knots, consist of multiple chains, and we include them in the class of knots. The conformation of loose folds, called a loop, can form in chain molecules. The loop conformation consists of a bound chain with folding, that is, the tip of the loop. The loop itself can form the twist, knot, or link, as if the loop behaves as a single chain. We call entanglements consisting of loops as Loops in Figure 4.44. Note that no knot or link can form without the chain end or tip of the loop, while a twist can form at any location in the chains.

Simple entanglements form easily without significant topological movement of chains, whereas complicated entanglements form with difficulty due to the large cooperative topological movement required. Here, the topological movement of chains necessarily involves the sliding diffusion along the chain axis. In general, we obtain the molecular weight between entanglements,

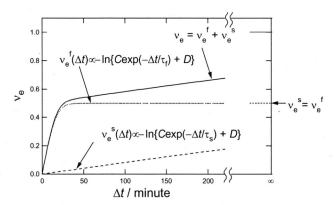

Figure 4.43 Plots of v_e, v_e^f, and v_e^s against Δt given by Equation (4.76). The v_e^f rapidly increases with the increase of Δt, while the v_e^s gradually increases with the increase of Δt. The total v_e (summation of v_e^f and v_e^s) increases by two steps.

TABLE 4.4 Values of Parameters C, D, and γ

	C	D	γ
Values	0.95	0.05	0.17

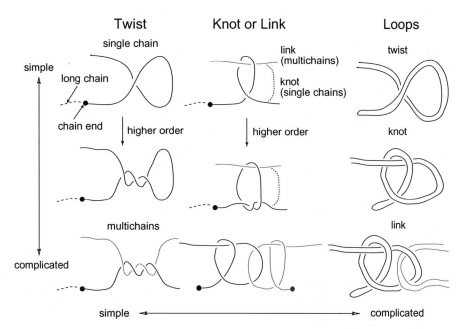

Figure 4.44 Classification of entanglements such as twists, knots, and loops. In this figure, toward the bottom and right sides, entanglements become more "complicated." (See color insert.)

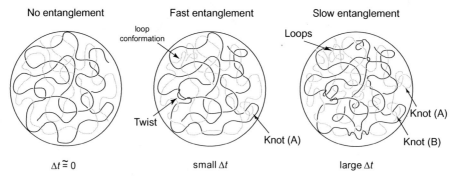

Figure 4.45 Time evolution of entanglements between two random coiled chains. (a) At $\Delta t \cong 0$. Two chains have been not entangled yet. (b) At small Δt. The knot (A) is formed near the chain end. The twist is formed at any place along the chains. The loop conformation is sometimes formed. (c) At large Δt. The knot (A) is transported to the center of chain and a new knot (B) is introduced near the chain end. The loop conformation rarely forms the Loops. (See color insert.)

that is, v_e in the thermal equilibrium state, by rheological measurements [80], but note that the v_e obtained does not coincide necessarily with that evaluated by I in this study because the entanglements that resolve easily, such as twists, are insensitive to rheological measurements.

Figure 4.45 shows a schematic time evolution of entanglements forming between a few chains. At first, the simple entanglements form within a short period. Since a free chain end can easily form the knot, knot (A) forms near the chain end. After a long period, the knot (A) transports to the center of chain, and a new knot (B) forms near the chain end. All the knots in the center of the chain should transport from the chain end. As their number increases, the formation of new knots becomes more difficult due to the decrease in chain mobility, that is, increases in the number of knots in the center of the chain slows. On the other hand, complicated entanglements of loop conformation (Loops in Figure 4.44) may form. Note that the formation of loops requires time, even though the loop conformation can become an entanglement irrespective of the chain ends.

4.8 CONCLUSION

Sections 4.1 and 4.2 introduced nucleation by reviewing CNT. Section 4.3 discussed observation of nano-nucleation by means of SAXS. The correct size distribution $f(N, t)$ and 2D shape (kinetic parameters) of a nano-nucleus are obtained simultaneously by analyzing SAXS intensity $I_X(q, t)$ using the extended Guinier plot method. $f(N, t)$ is shown to decrease with the increase of N for each t. $f(N, t)$ increases with the increase of t and saturates for each N. With the increase of t, $f(N, t)$ of smaller N increases significantly faster and saturates, while $f(N, t)$ of larger N increases more slowly and saturates.

The free energy of the end surface (σ_e) of the nano-nucleus (σ_e(nano)) is much smaller than that of the macro-crystal (σ_e(macro)), that is, σ_e(nano) $\cong$ (1/5) σ_e(macro). Here, macro-crystal means the macroscopic crystal. We conclude that the nano-nucleus shows significant fluctuation with respect to size and shape and repeats frequent generation and disappearance. In the case of macro-crystals, it is well known that surface particles are thermodynamically reconstructed into smooth and flat surfaces by surface diffusion, which is a type of Ostwald ripening that results in large σ_e(macro).

We describe the direct observation of the degree of supercooling (ΔT) dependence of $f(N, t)$ by means of SAXS. $f(N, t)$ increases rapidly with the increase of t at large ΔT, while $f(N, t)$ increases more slowly at small ΔT. We obtain ΔT dependence of the onset time $\tau(\Delta T)$ defined as the extrapolated time of the linearly increasing $f(N, t)$ with t. We describe the empirical formula by $\tau^{-1}(\Delta T) \propto \exp[-\gamma/\Delta T]$, where γ is a constant; that is, nucleation becomes impossible when ΔT approaches 0. We conclude that nucleation controls the induction period of crystallization, rather than the spinodal decomposition process.

The relationship between nano-nucleation and macro-crystallization has been studied. We obtain the ΔT dependence of nucleation rate (I) of a macro-crystal whose size is more than 1 μm by optical microscopy. We describe the empirical formula by $I(\Delta T) \propto \exp[-C'/\Delta T]$, where C' is a constant. We obtain τ^{-1} and I by using the ΔT dependence of $f(N, t)$ proportional to the net flow of nucleation (j), that is, $\tau^{-1} \propto I \propto j$, as the zero-th approximation. This shows that the critical nano-nucleation mainly controls nano-nucleation as well as macro-crystallization experimentally. We conclude that the nano-nucleation directly corresponds to macro-crystallization. This demonstrates that optical microscopy can be used as the zero-th approximation to study nucleation for practical, routine work.

Section 4.4 showed that the $f(N, t)$ and the fundamental kinetic equation in CNT do not satisfy the normalization condition and the mass conservation law, respectively. Hence, the $f(N, t)$ as defined cannot be a correct basic equation in a stochastic process. Instead, we introduce a mass distribution function, $Q(N, t)$, defined by $Q(N, t) Nf(N, t)/v_0$, where v_0 is the total number of particles of a closed system and $Q(N, t)$ satisfies the normalized condition. We arrive at an alternative basic equation, $\partial Q(N, t)/\partial t \equiv -\partial j(N, t)/\partial N$, which satisfies the law of mass conservation. With the increase of N, the observed $Q(N, t)$ first decreases for $N \leq N^*$, shows a minimum at $N \cong N^*$, and then increases. After passing a maximum at $N > N^*$, it then decreases and becomes zero at $N = N_{max}(t)$. This confirms that many nano-nuclei appear and disappear frequently for $N < N^*$ and that the increase of mass of larger nuclei ($N > N^*$) accelerates significantly with the increase of time and N. Nuclei grow to much larger ones by absorbing particles that come both from the melt and from other nuclei indirectly via the melt. This corresponds to Ostwald ripening. The overall crystallinity $\chi_c(t)$ increases after several minutes, then increases slowly, and finally increases more rapidly with the increase of t. We conclude that the observed $\chi_c(t)$ in this study should be significantly small, $\chi_c(t) \ll 1$. Logically, we expect that $\chi_c(t)$ should finally saturate to unity, corresponding to the completion of the melt-solid phase transition from the supercooled melt into the (assumed) single crystal.

Section 4.5 discussed elongational crystallization of iPP by the method of compressing the supercooled melt in the orthogonal direction. When the elongational strain rate ($\dot{\varepsilon}$) becomes larger than a critical one ($\dot{\varepsilon}^*$), the morphology discontinuously changes from the well-known spherulite to (NOCs), with increases in the number density (v) of spherulites and NOCs v by as much as 10^9 times. Therefore, we conclude that the nucleation mechanism discontinuously changes from heterogeneous to elongational flow-induced homogeneous nucleation for $\dot{\varepsilon} \geq \dot{\varepsilon}^*$. The NOCs exhibit ultrahigh performances, such as high tensile stress at break, high Young's modulus, high thermal resistance, and high transparency.

Section 4.6 described the essential role of epitaxy in heterogeneous nucleation by formulating and confirming a relationship, $I \propto I_0 \propto C_{NA}/a_{NA}$, where I is the nucleation rate of polymer crystals, I_0 is a prefactor of I, C_{NA} is the concentration of NA in the mixture of NA and polymers, and a_{NA} is the longest lateral size of the NA crystal. Decreasing a_{NA} from μm to nm is an effective method to develop high-performance NA. Finally, Section 4.7 discussed the important role of entanglement in nucleation by changing the number density of entanglement (v_e) within the supercooled melt. The nucleation rate decreases significantly with the increase of v_e.

ACKNOWLEDGMENTS

The synchrotron radiation experiments were performed at the BL40B2 and FSBL in the SPring-8 with the approval of the Japan Synchrotron Radiation Research Institute (JASRI) (Proposal Nos. 2006A1304, 2006B1185, 2007A1567, 2007B1173, 2008B1611, 2009A1331, 2009B1385 2010A1107, 2010A7228, and 2010B1302). The authors are grateful to J. Washiyama, K. Yamada, and H. Kimura of the Kawasaki Development Center, SunAllomer Ltd.; S. Sasaki and H. Masunaga of JASRI; S. Yamazaki of Okayama University; and T. Urushihara of ADEKA Corporation for their assistance.

REFERENCES

[1] Becker, V.R., Döring, W. *Ann. Phys.* **1935**, *24*, 719.
[2] Turnbull, D., Fisher, J.C. *J. Chem. Phys.* **1949**, *17*, 71.
[3] Frenkel, J. *Kinetic Theory of Liquids*, Dover, New York, 1946.
[4] Akpalu, Y.A., Amis, E.J. *J. Chem. Phys.* **1999**, *111*, 8686.
[5] Akpalu, Y.A., Amis, E.J. *J. Chem. Phys.* **2000**, *113*, 392.
[6] Auer, S., Frenkel, D. *Nature* **2001**, *409*, 1020.
[7] Caccluto, A., Auer, S., Frenkel, D. *Nature* **2004**, *428*, 404.
[8] Ghosh, S.K., Hikosaka, M., Toda, A., Yamazaki, S., Yamada, K. *Macromolecules* **2002**, *35*(18), 6985.
[9] Nishi, M., Hikosaka, M., Toda, A., Takahashi, M. *Polymer* **1998**, *39*, 1592.
[10] Wunderlich, B., Czornyj, G. *Macromolecules* **1977**, *10*, 906.
[11] Frank, F.C., Tosi, M. *Proc. R. Soc. Lond. A* **1961**, *263*, 323.
[12] Price, F.P. Nucleation in polymer crystallization. In *Nucleation*, Zettlemoyer, A.C., ed. Marcel Dekker, New York, 1969, pp. 405–488.
[13] Cormia, R.L., Price, F.P., Turnbull, D. *J. Chem. Phys.* **1962**, *37*, 1333.
[14] Hikosaka, M. *Polymer* **1987**, *28*, 1257.
[15] Hikosaka, M. *Polymer* **1990**, *31*, 458.
[16] Okada, K., Watanabe, K., Wataoka, I., Toda, A., Sasaki, S., Inoue, K., Hikosaka, M. *Polymer* **2007**, *48*, 382.
[17] Okada, K., Watanabe, K., Toda, A., Sasaki, S., Inoue, K., Hikosaka, M. *Polymer* **2007**, *48*, 1116.

[18] Hikosaka, M., Yamazaki, S., Wataoka, I., Das, N.C., Okada, K., Toda, A., Inoue, K. *J. Macromol. Sci. Phys.* **2003**, *B42*, 847.

[19] Hikosaka, M., Watanabe, K., Okada, K., Yamazaki, S. *Adv. Polym. Sci.* **2005**, *191*, 137.

[20] Imai, M., Mori, K., Kizukami, T., Kaji, K., Kanaya, T. *Polymer* **1992**, *33*, 4457.

[21] Okada, K., Watanabe, K., Urushihara, T., Toda, A., Hikosaka, M. *Polymer* **2007**, *48*, 401.

[22] Ottani, S., Ferracini, E., Ferrero, A., Malta, V., Porter, R.S. *Macromolecules* **1995**, *28*, 2411.

[23] Tanaka, H. *Koubunshi no Butsurigaku*, Shokabo, Tokyo, 2001.

[24] Kelton, K.F., Greer, A.L., Thompson, C.V. *J. Chem. Phys.* **1983**, *79*(12), 6261.

[25] Binsbergen, F.L. *J. Polym. Sci.* **1973**, *11*, 117.

[26] Sato, K., Kobayashi, M. *Shishitsu no Kouzou to Dynamics*, Kyoritsu Shuppan, Tokyo, 1992.

[27] Andres, R.P., Boudart, M. *J. Chem. Phys.* **1965**, *42*(5), 2057.

[28] Corradini, P., Petraccone, V., Asslegra, G. *Macromolecules* **1971**, *4*(6), 770.

[29] Keller, A. *Philos. Mag.* **1957**, *2*, 1171.

[30] Nishi, M., Hikosaka, M., Ghosh, S.K., Toda, A., Yamada, K. *Polym. J.* **1999**, *31*, 749.

[31] Okada, M., Nishi, M., Takkashi, M., Matusda, H., Toda, A., Hikosaka, M. *Polymer* **1998**, *39*, 4535.

[32] Okada, K., Washiyama, J., Watanabe, K., Sasaki, S., Masunaga, H., Hikosaka, M. *Polym. J.* **2010**, *42*, 464.

[33] Wunderlich, B. *Macromolecular physics*, Vol. 1, Academic Press, New York and London, 1973.

[34] Yamazaki, S., Watanabe, K., Okada, K., Yamada, K., Tagashira, K., Toda, A., Hikosaka, M. *Polymer* **2005**, *46*, 1675.

[35] Moore, E.P. *Polypropylene Handbook*, Kogyo Chosakai, Tokyo, 1998, Ch. 3.

[36] The Society of Rheology, Japan. *Kohza, Rheology*, Koubunshikankoukai, Kyoto, 1992.

[37] Awaya, Y. *Kobunnshi Sozai no Henko Kenbikyo Nyumon*, Agne Gijutsu Center, Tokyo, 2001.

[38] Frisch, H.L. *J. Chem. Phys.* **1957**, *27*, 90.

[39] Hikosaka, M., Seto, T. *Polym. J.* **1973**, *5*, 111.

[40] Qirk, R.P., Alsamarriaie, M.A.A. *Polymer Handbook*, Awiley-interscience, New York, 1989.

[41] Kakudo, M., Kasai, N. *Koubunshi X-sen Kaisetsu*, Maruzen, Tokyo, 1968, Ch. 5.

[42] Guinier, A. *Theorie et technique de la radiocristallographie*, Dunod, Paris, 1964, Ch. 10–11.

[43] Yamada, K., Hikosaka, M., Toda, A., Yamazaki, S., Tagashira, K. *J. Macromol. Sci. Phys.* **2003**, *B42*, 733.

[44] Tanaka, F. *Koubunshi no Butsurigaku*, Shokabo, Tokyo, 1994.

[45] Kan-no, T. *Plastics Processing Databook*, The Japan Society for Technology of Plasticity; Nikkan Kogyo Shimbun, Tokyo, 2002.

[46] Iida, S. *Butsuri Teisu-hyo*, Asakura Publishing Co., Ltd., Tokyo, 1976.

[47] Kikutani, T., Takemura, K. *Plastic for Processing*, The Japan Society of Polymer Processing; Kogyo Chosakai, Tokyo, 2006.

[48] Eshelby, H.D., Frank, F.C., Nabarro, F.R.N. *Phil. Mag.* **1951**, *42*, 351.

[49] Hall, E.O. *Proc. Phys. Soc.* **1951**, *B64*, 747.

[50] Ide, F. *Plast. Age* **1997**, *43*(4), 163.

[51] Sano, H., Tanaka, K., Nakagawa, H. *Polym. Preprints Jpn.* **1987**, *36*(4), 932.

[52] Kobayashi, T. *Koubunshikakou* **1986**, *35*(1), 30.

[53] Yoshimoto, S., Ueda, T., Yamanaka, K., Kawaguchi, A., Tobita, E., Haruna, T. *Polymer* **2001**, *42*, 9627.

[54] Lotz, B., Wittmann, J.C., Stocker, W., Magonov, S.N., Cantow, H.J. *Polym. Bull. (Berlin, Germany)* **1991**, *26*(2), 209.

[55] Hayashi, K., Hikosaka, M., Toda, A., Maiti, P. *Polym. Preprints Jpn.* **1998**, *47*, 3821.

[56] Brandrup, J., Immergut, E.H., Bloch, D.R., Grulke, E.A. *Polymer Handbook*, 4th ed. John Wiley & Sons, New York, 2003.

[57] Janimak, J.J., Cheng, S.Z.D., Giusti, P.A. *Macromoecules* **1991**, *24*, 2253.

[58] Yamada, K., Hikosaka, M., Toda, A., Yamazaki, S., Tagashira, K. *Macromolecules* **2003**, *36*, 4790.

[59] Yamada, K., Hikosaka, M., Toda, A., Yamazaki, S., Tagashira, K. *Macromolecules* **2003**, *36*, 4802.

[60] Nukiyama, S., Tanasawa, Y. *Nihon Kikaigakkai Ronbunshu* **1939**, *5*, 68.

[61] Urushihara, T., Okada, K., Watanabe, K., Toda, A., Tobita, E., Kawamoto, N., Hikosaka, M. *Polym. J.* **2007**, *39*, 55.

[62] Kurja, J., Mehl, N.A. In *Plastics Additives Handbook*, Zweifel, H., ed. 5th ed. Hanser, Munich, 2001, p. 949.

[63] Fillon, B., Lotz, B., Thierry, A., Wittmann, J.C. *J. Polym. Sci. Polym. Phys.* **1993**, *31*, 1395.

[64] Beck, H.N. *J. Appl. Polym. Sci.* **1967**, *11*, 673.

[65] Binsbergen, F.L. *Polymer* **1970**, *11*, 253.

[66] Ikeda, K. *Koubunnshi Ronbunnshu* **1987**, *44*, 539.

[67] Kobayashi, T., Takemoto, M., Hashimoto, T. *Koubunnshi Ronbunnshu* **1998**, *55*, 613.

[68] Yamasaki, S., Ohashi, Y., Tsutsumi, H., Tsuji, K. *Bull. Chem. Soc. Jpn.* **1995**, *68*, 146.

[69] Watase, M., Itagaki, H. *Bull. Chem. Soc. Jpn.* **1998**, *71*, 1457.

[70] Yan, S., Katzenberg, F., Petermann, J., Yang, D., Shen, Y., Straupe, C., Wittmann, J.C., Lotz, B. *Polymer* **2000**, *41*, 2613.

[71] Wittmann, J.C., Lotz, B. *J. Polym. Sci. Polym. Phys. Ed.* **1981**, *19*, 1837.

[72] Wittmann, J.C., Hodge, A.M., Lotz, B. *J. Polym. Sci. Polym. Phys. Ed.* **1983**, *21*, 2495.

[73] Haubruge, H.G., Daussin, R., Jonas, A.M., Legras, R., Witmann, J.C., Lotz, B. *Macromolecules* **2003**, *36*, 4452.

[74] Yamazaki, S., Gu, F., Watanabe, K., Okada, K., Toda, A., Hikosaka, M. *Polymer* **2006**, *47*, 6422.

[75] Yamazaki, S., Hikosaka, M., Toda, A., Wataoka, I., Gu, F. *Polymer* **2002**, *43*, 6585.

[76] Rastogi, S., Kurelec, L., Cuijpers, J., Lippits, D., Wimmer, M., Lemstra, P.J. *Macromol. Mater. Eng.* **2003**, *288*, 964.

[77] Galland, G.B., Seferin, M., Mauler, R.S., Santos, J.H.Z.D. *Polym. Int.* **1999**, *48*, 660.

[78] Yamazaki, S., Hikosaka, M., Gu, F., Ghosh, S.K., Arakaki, M., Toda, A. *Polym. J.* **2001**, *33*, 906.

[79] Wu, S. *Polym. Eng. Sci.* **1990**, *30*, 753.

[80] Rastogi, S., Lippits, D.R., Peters, G.W.M., Graf, R., Yao, Y., Spiess, H.W. *Nat. Mater.* **2005**, *4*, 635.

5

GROWTH OF POLYMER CRYSTALS

KOHJI TASHIRO

Department of Future Industry-Oriented Basic Science and Materials, Toyota Technological Institute, Nagoya, Japan

5.1 Introduction, 165
    5.1.1 Complex Behavior of Polymers, 165
5.2 Growth of Polymer Crystals from Solutions, 167
    5.2.1 Single Crystals, 167
    5.2.2 Crystallization from Solution under Shear, 168
    5.2.3 Solution Casting Method, 168
5.3 Growth of Polymer Crystals from Melt, 169
    5.3.1 Positive and Negative Spherulites, 169
    5.3.2 Spherulite Morphology and Crystalline Modification, 170
    5.3.3 Spherulite Patterns of Blend Samples, 172
5.4 Crystallization Mechanism of Polymer, 173
    5.4.1 Basic Theory of Crystallization of Polymer, 173
    5.4.2 Growth Rate of Spherulites, 177

5.5 Microscopically Viewed Structural Evolution in the Growing Polymer Crystals, 178
    5.5.1 Experimental Techniques, 178
    5.5.2 Structural Evolution in Isothermal Crystallization, 179
    5.5.3 Shear-Induced Crystallization of the Melt, 186
5.6 Crystallization upon Heating from the Glassy State, 189
    5.6.1 Cold Crystallization, 189
    5.6.2 Solvent-Induced Crystallization of Polymer Glass, 189
5.7 Crystallization Phenomenon Induced by Tensile Force, 191
5.8 Photoinduced Formation and Growth of Polymer Crystals, 191
5.9 Conclusion, 192
References, 193

5.1 INTRODUCTION

The growth of polymer crystals is a complex process, especially when the crystals are subjected to various conditions. This chapter, which focuses on the structural evolution of the growth process, begins by discussing some general features of polymer crystallization. (See Chapter 4 for a description of polymer crystal structures.)

5.1.1 Complex Behavior of Polymers

5.1.1.1 Morphologies As shown in Figure 5.1a, the crystallization of polyoxymethylene (POM) from a dilute solution produces a single crystal when we maintain the solution at a constant temperature; the concepts of lamellae and chain folding were discovered from this morphological process [1]. One sheet of lamella is an aggregation of molecular chains that go out and reenter the plate through the folded structure on the surfaces. This type of crystal morphology is called folded-chain crystal (FCC).

We obtain a bundle of thin fibers by stirring the solution in a circular fashion. Transmission electron microscopy (TEM) observation reveals the morphology to be similar to a necklace, which we call the shish–kebab structure (Fig. 5.1d). The core consists of a bundle of extended-chain crystals (ECC), around which the FCC form at generally regular and repetitive periods along the fiber axis.

Handbook of Polymer Crystallization, First Edition. Edited by Ewa Piorkowska and Gregory C. Rutledge.
© 2013 John Wiley & Sons, Inc. Published 2013 by John Wiley & Sons, Inc.

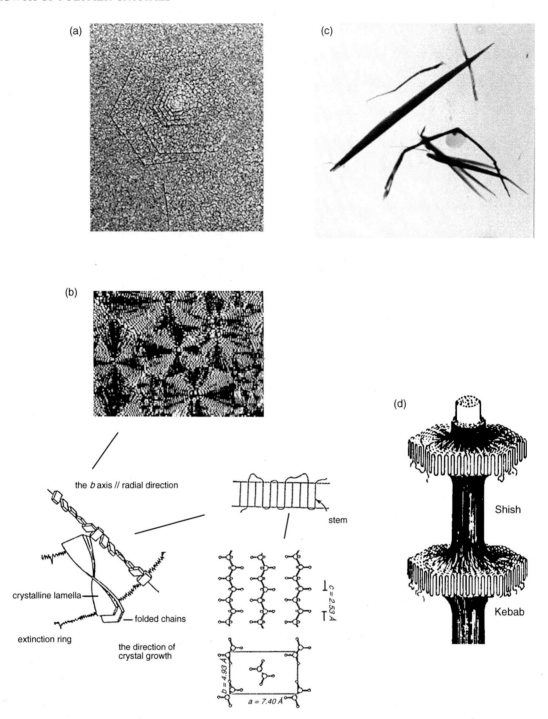

Figure 5.1 (a) The solution-grown polyoxymethylene single crystal, (b) spherulites of melt-cooled polyethylene sample and the hierarchical structure, (c) extended-chain crystals of polyoxymethylene (whisker), and (d) the shish–kebab structure. (See color insert.)

Cooling from the melt produces spherulites in which the lamellae of the FCC morphology stack together (Fig. 5.1b). These lamellae grow radially from the center to form a spherical shape. In the actual experiments, many papers report the two-dimensional (2D) growth of spherulites, which can differ in many points from spherulites grown three-dimensionally (3D). Various conditions, such as the supercooling degree, the cooling of the melt, and the presence of impurities, affect the nucleation and growth of the lamellae. Applying external force (tensile and/or shear stress) to the melt produces the shish–kebab-like structure. ECC crystals form and grow when we anneal the molten samples of polymers like polyethylene (PE) at a high temperature

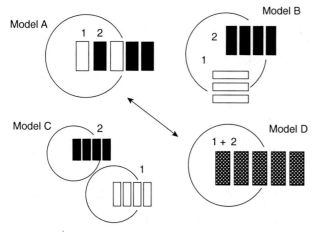

Figure 5.2 Illustration of various lamellar stacking modes in spherulites [4].

under high pressure. The cationic polymerization reaction of trioxane causes POM single crystals of ECC morphology, which we call whiskers, to adhere to the wall of the reaction vessel; Figure 5.1c [2] shows an example.

5.1.1.2 Crystallization of Blend Samples The blend samples of different polymers exhibit other complex crystallization behavior. For example, in the case of blend between a crystalline polymer and an amorphous polymer, the lamellae of crystalline polymer component are surrounded by the amorphous regions built up from these two kinds of polymers. In the amorphous regions, these two polymers might be mixed homogeneously or heterogeneously depending on the miscibility between these two polymers. If both of the two polymer components are crystalline, then the three types of lamellar stacking structure are generated as shown in Figure 5.2 models A, B, and C. In model A, the two kinds of lamellae are stacked in an alternate manner in the same spherulite. In model B, they are spatially separated in the spherulite. In model C, the lamellae of these two polymers are separated in the individual spherulites [3, 4]. As an extreme case, when the two types of polymer are miscible with each other in the crystalline region they are included together in a common lamella and exhibit a co-crystallized morphology (model D). In many cases the crystallization rate of the originally slow polymer component is accelerated remarkably by the coexistence of the other component. (See Chapter 11 for details.)

5.1.1.3 Epitaxial Crystallization An epitaxial crystallization can occur when one polymer component crystallizes on the surface of the film of the uniaxially oriented other polymer component. The polymer chains grow into crystals with their chain axes parallel to the chain direction of the polymer substrate. We observe similar phenomena for nanocomposite material, in which an organic or inorganic low molecular weight compound is contained as a filler in a polymer matrix. When the polymer crystallizes on the surface of the filler, the polymer chains crystallize with their chain axes parallel or perpendicular to the filler axis in an epitaxial mode. The resulting morphology drastically affects the physical property of the bulk sample. Usually, the melting point of the filler is relatively high compared with the polymer crystals. During the subsequent cooling process the filler component crystallizes in a higher temperature region to form a needle shape. Crystallization of the polymer component nucleates heterogeneously on the surface of these needles [5]. Sometimes, the molecular chains crystallize with their chain axes perpendicular to the film surface. Intense nucleation can lead to transcrystallization. (See Chapter 9 for a detailed discussion of epitaxy.)

5.1.1.4 Additional Phase Transitions during Crystallization Many crystalline polymers exhibit polymorphism. The appearance of one particular crystal modification depends on the external conditions: the cooling rate from the melt, the casting condition from the solution, the type of solvent, the external stress, the temperature, and so on. In some cases, the phase transition from one crystallographic modification to another occurs during the crystallization, resulting in more complicated crystallization behavior, resulting in more complicated crystallization behavior. For example, the vinylidene fluoride-trifluoroethylene random copolymer exhibits a ferroelectric phase transition between the low-temperature ferroelectric phase and the high-temperature paraelectric phase at a Curie transition temperature T_c [6]. The low-temperature phase crystallizes naturally when we melt the sample and quickly cool it below T_c. However, before the appearance of the low-temperature ferroelectric phase, the high-temperature phase appears, even though the high-temperature phase is thermodynamically unstable [7]. This is called the Ostwald rule [8], in which the kinetically favorable but thermodynamically unstable phase appears before the thermodynamically stable phase appears. The morphology, crystallization rate, and so on, are influenced by such a complicated crystallization process including the phase transition phenomenon.

5.2 GROWTH OF POLYMER CRYSTALS FROM SOLUTIONS

5.2.1 Single Crystals

To grow a single crystal, we cool a hot dilute solution of POM of 0.1 wt% concentration to a fixed temperature. We then place a drop of the cooled solution on a carbon mesh, and observe the growth of a single crystal by using

TEM (Fig. 5.1a). The width can be several micrometers and the thickness only a few hundred angstroms. The electron diffraction pattern shows that only the $hk0$ reflections are detected in the case of trigonal POM, which indicates that the chain stems stand up in the direction normal to the crystal surface. Stokes is the first to indicate the possibility of chain folding; by measuring the electron diffraction patterns of unoriented *trans*-1,4-polyisoprene, he found that the chain axis is normal to the film plane [9]. Later, Fischer, Till, and Keller made direct observations of polymer single crystals with a chain-folded structure. The concept of chain folding originates from this experimental evidence [10].

A PE single crystal grown from solution does not have the flat plate morphology, but possesses the hollow pyramidal shape as shown in Figure 5.3a [11] (see also Fig. 4.32 and associated discussion). Depending on the preparation condition, the morphology of single crystals is affected sensitively. Normally, the 110 planes appear on the edge of the crystal, but the 100 planes also appear to form the truncated-lozenge-shaped crystal (Fig. 5.3b). The ratio between the short and long axes depends on the crystallization temperature [11, 12]. The molecular chain stems stand up vertically, and the relative height of the neighboring chain stems shifts gradually, relaxing the stress due to the chain fold. This results in the tilt of the folding surfaces and the 3D built-up crystal shape.

5.2.2 Crystallization from Solution under Shear

Crystallization from a solution during stirring produces the shish–kebab-like structure mentioned earlier. As shown in Figure 5.1d, the core shish part is speculated to consist of a bundle of ECC. The kebab parts are built up by an aggregation of FCC. The FCC parts are energetically unstable and can be dissolved into an organic solvent more easily than the core parts, allowing us to produce the bulk fiber of core parts only. This thin fiber possesses a Young's modulus higher than 150 GPa and became a trigger for building up the industry of ultrastrong fibers [13–17].

5.2.3 Solution Casting Method

In the solution casting method, the concentration of the solution becomes higher as the solvent evaporation proceeds and the concentrated solution supersaturates; then the crystallization occurs on the surface of a substrate. Polymer crystals obtained by the solvent casting method are sensitively affected by the evaporation rate of the solvent, the temperature, the polarity of the solvent, and so on. For example, poly(vinylidene fluoride) (PVDF, $-CH_2CF_2-$) shows multiple polymorphic phenomena [6]. We can dissolve PVDF into polar solvents such as acetone, dimethyl foramide (DMF), dimethyl acetamide (DMA), and hexamethyl phosphoric triamide (HMPTA). HMPTA evaporates slowly at room temperature, producing the highly crystalline form I with a polar packing structure of planar-zigzag chains. Increasing the evaporation rate by heating produces the crystalline form III (strictly speaking, disordered III of $T_3GT_3\bar{G}$ chain conformation). DMF and DMA produce the crystalline form III at room temperature. By increasing the evaporation rate, they give the form II of $TGT\bar{G}$ conformation. Acetone gives the crystal form II at room temperature. Therefore, a highly polar solvent, which evaporates slowly at room temperature, gives the crystal form having higher amount of trans sequences (TTTT > $T_3GT_3\bar{G}$ > $TGT\bar{G}$). By increasing the evaporation rate at a high temperature, the chain conformation, including more gauche bonds, crystallizes more easily ($TGT\bar{G}$ > $T_3GT_3\bar{G}$ > TTTT). In fact, even acetone can give the crystal form III when the solution is evaporated slowly at 0°C. We note that crystal form II is kinetically preferable, whereas form I is thermodynamically more stable.

The solvent casting method gives a film with some preferential orientation of the crystallites. We monitor crystal growth during the solvent evaporation process *in situ* by measuring the grazing-incidence small-angle X-ray scattering (GISAXS)/grazing-incidence wide-angle X-ray diffraction (GIWAXD)/Raman data simultaneously. Sasaki et al. observe the crystallization of PE from *p*-xylene solution by dropping some solution onto a silicone wafer and measuring the small- and wide-angle X-ray scatterings by irradiating a highly brilliant syn-

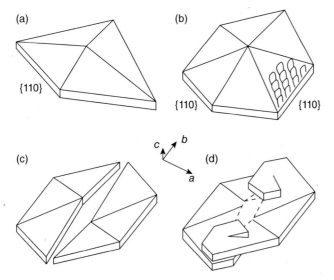

Figure 5.3 Morphologies of polyethylene single crystals: (a) lozenge-shaped tent type, (b) truncated-lozenge-shaped tent type, (c) two halves of truncated lozenge-shaped chair type, and (d) truncated lozenge-shaped chair type with spiral terraces from screw dislocations [11].

5.3 GROWTH OF POLYMER CRYSTALS FROM MELT

5.3.1 Positive and Negative Spherulites

When a crystalline polymer cools from the melt, it shows the aggregation structure of the crystalline and amorphous phases, depending on the crystallization conditions. Quenching the melt to a temperature below the glass transition point (T_g) produces an amorphous sample in which the random coils gather together in the case of flexible linear polymer chains. More detailed study shows, however, that the amorphous phase is not always in a perfectly disordered state, but some degree of orderliness may be existent [19]. Cooling the melt slowly to room temperature or maintaining a constant temperature produces the growth of various types of spherulites. Small nuclei start to appear randomly in the melt and grow quickly or slowly in the radial direction depending on the crystallization temperature, and so on. The growing spherulites impinge upon each other and create the border lines.

We classify these spherulites into negative spherulites and positive spherulites (Fig. 5.5). The difference arises from the anisotropy in the refractive index of crystalline lamellae, as discussed extensively in Section 3.4.1. If the refractive index along the radial direction is larger than that along the tangential direction, the blue color appears in the first and third quadrants (right upward and left lower sections) of the spherulite and the yellow color in the second and fourth quadrants. We call this a positive spherulite. If the refractive index in the radial direction is smaller than that in the tangential direction, the blue color appears in the 2nd and 4th quadrants and the yellow color in the 1st and 3rd quadrants. We call this a negative spherulite. Figure 5.5a is an example of a negative spherulite of poly(ethylene oxide) without concentric rings. High-density PE also is an example of a negative spherulite, but with regularly repeating concentric rings. In the radial growing process, the lamellae twist periodically with the same period as the ring spacing (Fig. 5.1b). The *b*-axis is parallel to the rotation axis and the *a*- and *c*-axes change their orientation periodically [20].

In general, lamellae grow by depositing molecular chains on the front side, as illustrated in Figure 5.6a. In this case, their growth occurs with the chain folding direction perpendicular to the lamellar growing direction. Melt-cooled nylon 66 shows positive spherulites, and the *a*-axis or the hydrogen-bonded sheet planes orient along the radial direction of the lamellae [21, 22]. Assuming that the chain folding direction is always parallel to the hydrogen-bonded sheet plane or the a axis, the chain folding direction becomes parallel to the

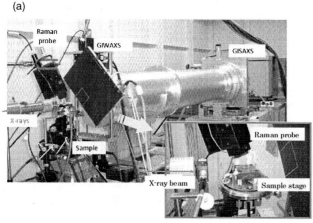

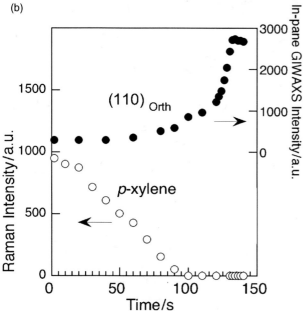

Figure 5.4 (a) Raman, GISAXS, and GIWAXD simultaneous measurement system. The GIWAXD is measured using a flat-panel detector and the GISAXS is measured using a CCD camera. The laser beam is irradiated on the sample surface and the Raman spectrum is measured in the back scattering geometry. (b) The time dependences of the Raman intensity of *p*-xylene band and the intensity of GIWAXD 110 peak [18]. (See color insert.)

chrotron X-ray beam at a very small incident angle from the silicone wafer surface (GISAXS and GIWAXD); see Figure 5.4a and b [18]. The solvent evaporated rapidly and dried up almost perfectly, and orthorhombic PE crystallites began to appear. As the crystallization proceeded, the X-ray scattering patterns showed anisotropy, indicating that the lamellae were preferentially oriented with the chain axis perpendicular to the silicone wafer plate.

(a) Negative Spherulite

(b) Poly(ethylene Adipate)

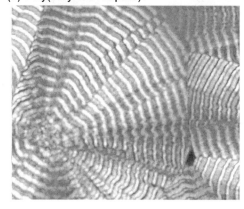

Figure 5.5 (a) A negative spherulite of poly(ethylene oxide) and (b) a spherulite of poly(ethylene adipate). (See color insert.)

folding. According to molecular dynamics (MD) calculation in Reference [24], the relatively weak hydrogen bonds form and break randomly in various directions with a short life-time in the high-temperature pseudohexagonal phase. Once the temperature drops below the Brill transition point, the pseudohexagonal phase transforms to the triclinic phase, in which strong hydrogen bonds form. If the hydrogen bonds form along the radial direction, then the a-axis becomes parallel to the radial direction. If the hydrogen bonds form tangentially or perpendicularly to the radial direction, then the a-axis is also in the same direction. The chain folding direction is perpendicular to the a-axis. Therefore, we do not need to consider that the hydrogen bonding direction is always parallel to the chain folding direction (see Fig. 5.6d).

Occasionally, the positive and negative spherulites can coexist in one sample. For example, syndiotactic polystyrene and its blends with *atactic* polystyrene show the coexistence of the spherulites of the opposite optical properties when cooled from the melt [25].

5.3.2 Spherulite Morphology and Crystalline Modification

The morphology of the spherulites differs depending on the crystal modification. For example, poly(heptamethylene terephthalate) (PHepT, $-[O(CH_2)_7OCO\Phi CO]_n-$) crystallizes into α and β forms from the melt [26, 27]; the melting points are 98°C and 104°C, respectively. Heating the β-form sample to 110°C and cooling to a crystallization temperature T_c of 55–80°C forms small, ring-pattern spherulites in the α form in addition to ringless spherulites, as shown in Figure 5.7. These small ring-pattern spherulites (Ring Type I) disappear at 98°C, or the melting point of the α form. The larger ring-pattern spherulites (Ring Type II) disappear at 104°C, or the melting point of the β form. The double-ring-banded spherulites observed at $T_c = 75$–80°C (Ring Type III) correspond to form α, and Maltese-cross Type 3 spherulites correspond to form β. In addition, α and β form spherulites show different patterns depending on the crystallization temperature.

Poly(ethylene adipate) shows the discontinuous crystallization growth rate at different T_c. For example, the spherulite in Figure 5.5b shows the alternation of yellow and blue colors on the neighboring rings [28, 29]. We note that the mechanism of the multistage change of the spherulite morphology has not yet been clarified. A similar phenomenon is reported for poly(L-lactic acid) [30], where different crystalline forms generate at the different crystallization rate at the different T_cs, for example, the disordered α' form at $T_c < 120$°C and the ordered α form at $T_c > 120$°C [31].

lamellar growth direction, as shown in Figure 5.6b, unlike the normal image in Figure 5.6a. Changing the crystallization condition only slightly produces a negative spherulite, in which the lamellar growth direction and the a axis or the hydrogen bonding direction are perpendicular to each other (Fig. 5.6c). Thus, the positive spherulite of nylon 66 seems unusual as long as the chain fold is assumed to occur in the hydrogen-bonded sheet plane. How can we interpret the sensitive changes of hydrogen bond direction in the spherulites of nylon 66? Nylon 66 shows the Brill transition below the melting point, during which the triclinic crystal lattice transforms from a structure in which conformationally disordered molecular chains or stems are packed in a pseudohexagonal cell [23]. The crystallization behavior has to be considered from the standpoint of this pseudohexagonal structure as long as the crystallization temperature stays in the Brill transition region. The molecular chains reach the front plane of the growing lamellar surface to form the parallel arrangement of the straight stems with the chain

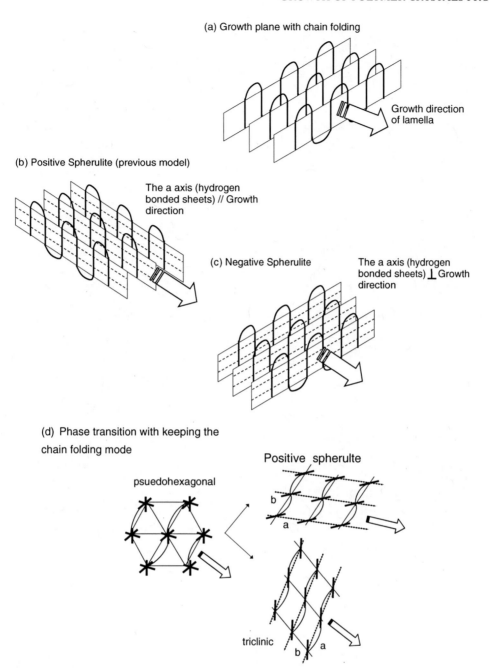

Figure 5.6 Schematic illustration of the lamellar growth process and chain folding in a nylon 6 spherulite. (a) Chain folding occurs in the plane of growing front side, (b) the chain folding plane is parallel to the hydrogen bond plane, (c) the chain folding plane is perpendicular to the hydrogen bond plane, and (d) the transition from the high-temperature pseudohexagonal phase to the low-temperature triclinic phase and the associated formation of the hydrogen-bonded planes.

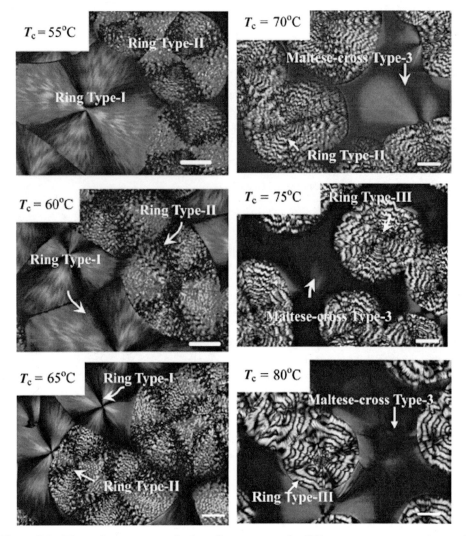

Figure 5.7 The various patterns of spherulites grown at the different temperatures observed for poly(pentamethylene terephthalate) [26]. (See color insert.)

5.3.3 Spherulite Patterns of Blend Samples

Blends of polymers show complicated spherulite patterns. For example, in the blend sample of PVDF with *atactic* poly(methyl methacrylate) (PMMA), PVDF is in the crystalline state and PMMA is in the amorphous state [32]. For polymer-diluent systems, the diluent molecules are expelled out of the lamellae and the spherulite because of their thermal mobility; thus, the diluent concentration in the system changes in front of the growing spherulite. For polymer–polymer blend systems, the thermal mobility of the polymers is not very high; thus, the amorphous polymers remain trapped between the lamellae of the crystalline polymer component. For example, in the crystallization of PVDF70/PMMA30 blend, the core part of the spherulite consists of the stacked lamellae of the PVDF component. As the spherulite grows, it becomes coarse and amorphous pockets of excluded PMMA component appear between the bundles of the stacked lamellae.

The crystallization of poly(L-lactic acid) (PLLA) occurs slowly, and is not very high when crystallized from the melt. We can add nucleating agents such as talc or clay to enhance crystallization. Adding a small amount of poly(glycolic acid) (PGA) enhances crystallization even when the content of PGA is only 0.1 wt%. Figure 5.8 shows POM snapshots taken during crystallization of neat PLLA and a PLLA/PGA blend sample. The presence of PGA increases the number of PLLA spherulites per unit area [33].

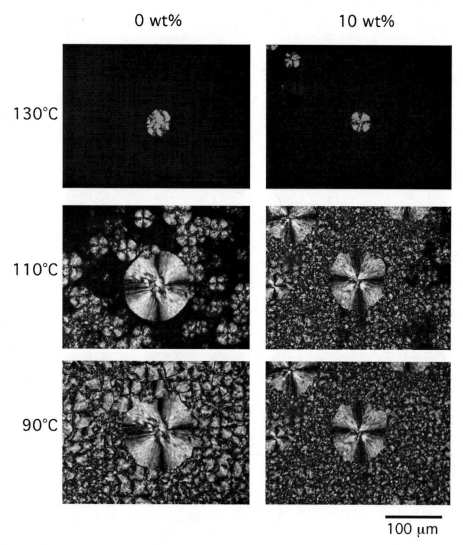

Figure 5.8 Growth of sphetulites in the cooling process from the melt: (left) pure poly(L-lactic acid) and (right) the blend sample of poly(L-lactic acid) and a small amount of poly(glycolic acid) [33].

5.4 CRYSTALLIZATION MECHANISM OF POLYMER

5.4.1 Basic Theory of Crystallization of Polymer

The two stages of nucleation are nucleation of a small seed of crystal (primary nucleation), and growth of the nucleus by attaching the surrounding chains on its surface (secondary nucleation or crystal growth). Primary nucleation occurs *homogeneously* in a solution or in a melt, called the homogeneous nucleation, or *heterogeneously* on the surface of a particle, called the heterogeneous nucleation.

5.4.1.1 Primary Nucleation Homogeneous nucleation requires systems to cross a free energy barrier [34]. For example, crystal nuclei generate sporadically from a supersaturated solution which is energetically metastable and in which density fluctuations occur [35]. A similar situation occurs in the crystallization from the melt.

Following crystal nucleation theory, consider the nucleation of a small crystal from the melt [34, 36]. The random coils in the melt gather to form a small nucleus of a size $a \cdot b \cdot l$, as shown in Figure 5.9. We define the surface energy of the ab plane as σ_e and that of the al plane as σ_s. The change in free energy $\Delta\Phi$ for crystallization from the melt is:

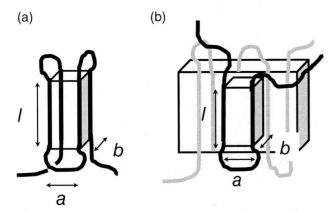

Figure 5.9 Schematic illustration of the primary nucleus.

$\Delta\Phi = \Phi_{\text{nucleus}} - \Phi_{\text{melt}}$ = surface free energy change
 − volume free energy change

$$\begin{aligned}
&= [2 \cdot a \cdot b \cdot \sigma_e + 4 \cdot a \cdot l \cdot \sigma_s] - [a \cdot b \cdot l \cdot (F_{\text{melt}} - F_{\text{crystal}})] \\
&= [2 \cdot a \cdot b \cdot \sigma_e + 4 \cdot a \cdot l \cdot \sigma_s] - [a \cdot b \cdot l \cdot \Delta F_{\text{melt}}] \\
&= [2 \cdot a \cdot b \cdot \sigma_e + 4 \cdot a \cdot l \cdot \sigma_s] - [a \cdot b \cdot l \cdot (\Delta H_{\text{melt}} - T\Delta S_{\text{melt}})]
\end{aligned}$$
(5.1)

where ΔH_{melt} and ΔS_{melt} are the enthalpy and entropy changes, respectively, per volume. The ΔH_{melt} and ΔS_{melt} are weakly dependent on the temperature near the melting point. At $T = T_m^o$, $\Delta H_{\text{melt}} - T_m^o \Delta S_{\text{melt}} = 0$; we can then replace ΔS_{melt}:

$$\begin{aligned}
\Delta\Phi &= [2 \cdot a \cdot b \cdot \sigma_e + 4 \cdot a \cdot l \cdot \sigma_s] - [a \cdot b \cdot l \cdot (\Delta H_{\text{melt}} - T\Delta S_{\text{melt}})] \\
&= [2 \cdot a \cdot b \cdot \sigma_e + 4 \cdot a \cdot l \cdot \sigma_s] \\
&\quad - [a \cdot b \cdot l \cdot (\Delta H_{\text{melt}} - T(\Delta H_{\text{melt}}/T_m^o))] \\
&= [2 \cdot a \cdot b \cdot \sigma_e + 4 \cdot a \cdot l \cdot \sigma_s] - [a \cdot b \cdot l \cdot \Delta H_{\text{melt}} \Delta T/T_m^o].
\end{aligned}$$
(5.2)

where $\Delta T = T_m^o - T$ = the degree of supercooling. The ΔF_{melt} is:

$$\Delta F_{\text{melt}} = \Delta H_{\text{melt}} - T\Delta S_{\text{melt}} = \Delta H_{\text{melt}} \Delta T/T_m^o. \quad (5.3)$$

The first term in Equation (5.2) is positive and the second is negative; hence, the dependence of $\Delta\Phi$ on nucleus sizes passes through a maximum. We obtain parameters a, b, and l under the conditions, $\partial^2 \Delta\Phi/\partial a = 0$, $\partial^2 \Delta\Phi/\partial l = 0$, and so on. For simplicity we assume $a = b$ to obtain the critical values, a^* and l^*, at the maximal point of $\Delta\Phi$:

$$\begin{aligned}
a^* &= 4\sigma_s/\Delta F_{\text{melt}} = (4\sigma_s T_m^o/\Delta H_{\text{melt}})(1/\Delta T) \\
l^* &= 4\sigma_e/\Delta F_{\text{melt}} = (4\sigma_e T_m^o/\Delta H_{\text{melt}})(1/\Delta T). \\
\Delta\Phi^*_{\text{nuclei}} &= 32\sigma_s^2 \sigma_e/(\Delta F_{\text{melt}})^2 = (32\sigma_s^2 \sigma_e T_m^{o2}/\Delta H_{\text{melt}}^2)(1/\Delta T)^2.
\end{aligned}$$
(5.4)

See Chapter 5 for details of the nucleation of polymer crystallites.

5.4.1.2 Growth of Secondary Nuclei The polymer chains migrate in the melt or solution and attach to the surface of the crystal to form secondary (or surface) nuclei with chain folding. The free energy change in this process is:

$$\Delta\Phi = 2 \cdot a \cdot b \cdot \sigma_e + 2 \cdot b \cdot l \cdot \sigma_s - a \cdot b \cdot l \cdot \Delta F_{\text{melt}} \quad (5.5)$$

where b denotes the thickness of the new crystalline layer deposited on the surface of the crystal.

The maximal condition of $\Delta\Phi$ gives:

$$\begin{aligned}
a^* &= 2\sigma_s/\Delta F_{\text{melt}} = (2\sigma_s T_m^o/\Delta H_{\text{melt}})(1/\Delta T) \\
l^* &= 2\sigma_e/\Delta F_{\text{melt}} = (2\sigma_e T_m^o/\Delta H_{\text{melt}})(1/\Delta T) \\
\Delta\Phi^*_{\text{growth}} &= 4 \cdot b \cdot \sigma_s \sigma_e/(\Delta F_{\text{melt}}) \\
&= (4 \cdot b \cdot T_m^o \sigma_s \sigma_e/\Delta H_{\text{melt}})(1/\Delta T).
\end{aligned}$$
(5.6)

Note that the $\Delta\Phi^*$ of the secondary nucleation is lower than that of the primary nucleation; that is, it is easier to generate secondary nuclei.

5.4.1.3 Crystal Growth Rate Two opposing factors govern the growth of crystals [36]: the thermodynamic free energy change necessary for the formation of crystal nuclei, $\Delta\Phi^*$, and the energy barrier that must be crossed so that the molecular chains can move toward the surfae of the crystal, ΔE. The molecular motion includes translational motion, sliding diffusion, and so on. We express the nucleus formation rate I and the crystal growth rate G, respectively, by:

$$\begin{aligned}
I &= I_o \exp[-\Delta E/(RT)] \exp[-\Delta\Phi^*_{\text{nuclei}}/RT] \\
&= I_o \exp[-\Delta E/(RT)] \exp[-K_1 T_m^{o2}/(RT\Delta T^2)]
\end{aligned}$$
(5.7)

$$\begin{aligned}
G &= I_o \exp[-\Delta E/(RT)] \exp[-\Delta\Phi^*_{\text{growth}}/RT] \\
&= G_o \exp[-\Delta E/(RT)] \exp[-K_2 T_m^o/(RT\Delta T)]
\end{aligned}$$
(5.8)

where K_1 and K_2 are constants related to the surface energies and ΔH_{melt}: $K_1 = n_1 \sigma_e \sigma_s^2/\Delta H_{\text{melt}}^2$ and $K_2 = n_2 \sigma_e \sigma_s/\Delta H_{\text{melt}}$. The n_1 and n_2 are constants. As known from these equations, the crystallization rate goes through a maximum at a temperature about halfway between T_g and T_m.

As discussed, $\Delta\Phi^*$ governs the rate of growth. According to the Hoffman–Luritzen (H–L) theory, ΔH_{melt} (and ΔE) determine the potential energy barrier; that is, the potential energy barrier determines the rate of growth, according to Equation (5.7) and Equation (5.8). We apply this principle when there is a smooth interface, for example, a lozenge-type, single crystal of PE. However, sometimes, the single crystal instead shows rounded edges at low supercooling. This rough surface can be explained by assuming that the molecular chains attach randomly to the growing crystallite. They may or may not form the chain folding structure. The lateral correlations are therefore small. According to the kinetic Monte Carlo calculation of Sadler and Gilmer (see Chapter 7), we expect the outer layer of the growing crystal to be thinner than in the bulk part, which results in the rounded crystal profile at the periphery of the crystal that prevents further crystallization [37, 38].

Among the many possible chain configurations, some are not necessarily favorable for the growth of the crystal surface. Once some fluctuation occurs to an entropically disfavored configuration, the growth of a new layer begins. Simply put, the so-called configurational entropy becomes an important contribution to the free energy barrier [37, 38]. As the crystal thickness increases, the required fluctuation is less likely to occur. The entropic barrier to crystallization becomes higher as the crystal thickness increases. The ratio of the rate constants of attaching ($k+$) and detaching ($k-$) chain stems on the surface, based on the Boltzmann weighting factor concept, is:

$$k-/k+ = \exp[2\varepsilon/(kT_m^o)]\exp[-m\varepsilon/(kT_c)] \qquad (5.9)$$

where ε is the interaction energy between the neighboring sites, and m is the number of occupied nearest neighbor sites.

5.4.1.4 Regimes The growth of the secondary nuclei occurs by the adsorption of molecular chains on the crystallite surface, depending on the degree of supercooling ΔT. We classify the growth as shown in Figure 5.10 [34, 36]. We define the generation rate of the surface nuclei as i and the spreading rate of the surface nucleus along the surface as g. According to the H–L theory, i and g can be expressed as:

$$i = i_o \exp[-\Delta E/(RT)]\exp[-K_2 T_m^o/(RT\Delta T)] \qquad (5.10)$$

$$g = g_o \exp[-\Delta E/(RT)]\exp[-2 \cdot a \cdot b_o \cdot \sigma_e/(RT)]. \qquad (5.11)$$

However, since the migration of chain segments to the growth surface should become negligible somewhere near the glass transition temperature (T_g), and not at the absolute zero of temperature, we modify the equations as:

$$i = i_o \exp[-\Delta E/(R(T - T_\infty)) - C^*/(RT\Delta T)] \qquad (5.12)$$

$$g = g_o \exp[-\Delta E/(R(T - T_\infty) - C/(RT)] \qquad (5.13)$$

where i_o, g_o, C^*, and C are constants that are not dependent on the temperature, $T_\infty = T_g + C_1$, where T_g is the glass transition, and C_1 is an empirical constant of about $-30°C$. This applies to Equation (5.7) and Equation (5.8); as known from these equations, rate i is dependent on $\exp[-1/(\Delta T)]$ and rate g is not dependent on ΔT. The regimes are as follows.

I. Regime I: This corresponds to the case of small ΔT, but here, rate i is appreciably smaller than rate g. In other words, rate i, which governs the crystal growth rate G, is:

$$G_I = b_o i L \qquad (5.14)$$

where L is the width of the base crystal plane and b_o is the thickness of one molecular chain stem. The new crystal plane growing from a single nucleus covers the base crystal plane completely.

II. Regime II. This corresponds to the case of relatively large ΔT; rate i is almost equal to rate g, and many nuclei generated on the surface of the base crystal before the whole surface is covered by spreading from the first-generated nucleus. G is:

$$G_{II} = b_o(2ig)^{1/2}. \qquad (5.15)$$

III. Regime III. In the case of even larger ΔT, rate i is overwhelmingly higher than g. The surface of the base crystal is then covered by the many nuclei forming on new layers before the whole surface is covered. G is:

$$G_{III} = \alpha b_o i L (\alpha < 1). \qquad (5.16)$$

We express the logarithms of G in Equation (5.14) and Equation (5.15) as:

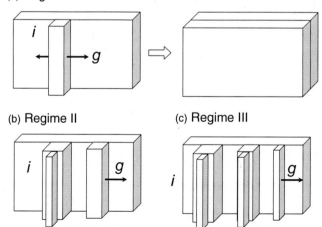

Figure 5.10 Schematic illustration of secondary nucleus formation processes in regimes I, II, and III.

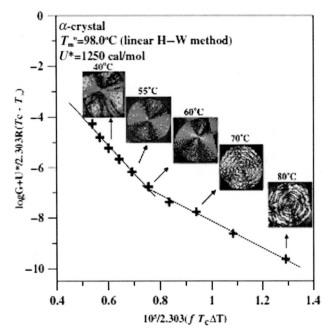

Figure 5.11 Plot of $\ln(G) + \Delta E/(RTc)$ against $1/(Tc\Delta T)$ for the isothermal crystallization of poly(heptamethylene terephthalate), where the ΔE is assumed to be 1250 cal/mol [26]. (See color insert.)

$$\ln(G_I) = \ln(b_oL) - \Delta E/(RT) - (K_2T_m^o/R)(1/(T\Delta T)) \quad (5.17)$$

$$\begin{aligned}\ln(G_{II}) &= \ln(2^{1/2}b_o) - \Delta E/(RT) \\ &\quad - (K_2T_m^o + 2ab_o\sigma_e\Delta T)(1/(2RT\Delta T)) \\ &\sim \ln(2^{1/2}b_o) - \Delta E/(RT) \\ &\quad - (K_2T_m^o/(2R))(1/(T\Delta T)).\end{aligned} \quad (5.18)$$

Therefore, plotting the term $[\ln(G) + \Delta E/(RT)]$ against $1/(T\Delta T)$ means that the slope of the straight line in the temperature region of regime I should be two times larger than the slope in regime II. We predict a similar relationship for regimes II and III. Figure 5.11 shows an example of PHepT, where the ratio of the slopes of the two straight lines is 2.04 [26]. The left side of the plot, for T below $T_c = 60°C$, is for regime III, and the right side, for T above $T_c = 60°C$, is for regime II, where we assume ΔE to be 1250 cal/mol and T_m^o is 98.0°C. Note that the spherulites (α form) generated in these two regimes show different morphologies, that is, a ringless spherulite at 50°C and an irregular ring-banded spherulite at 75°C. The situation can differ depending on the polymers; for example, in the case of poly(L-lactic acid), the axialite crystal is obtained in regime I, whereas the spherulite is obtained in regime II.

The self-diffusion rate of molecular chains in the solution and the reptation motion of entangled chains in the melt also control the rate of growth. As a result, G is inversely proportional to the molecular weight ($G \sim 1/M_w$).

5.4.1.5 Thickening Phenomena of Lamellae
The lamellar thickness l is dependent on the degree of supercooling ΔT.

$$l = u_1/\Delta T + u_2. \quad (5.19)$$

We rewrite Equation (5.6) as:

$$\Delta T = 2\sigma_e T_m^o/(l^*\Delta H_{melt}). \quad (5.20)$$

Since $\Delta T = T_m^o - T_c$, we have:

$$T_c = T_m^o[1 - 2\sigma_e/(l^*\Delta H_{melt})], \quad (5.21)$$

also called the Gibbs–Thomson equation. This relationship is often utilized to estimate the equilibrium temperature T_m^o. The thickness $<l>$ of the lamella formed beyond the critical value l^*, for the condition of relatively small ΔT is:

$$\langle l \rangle = l^* + dl = [2\sigma_e T_m^o/(\Delta H_{melt})](1/\Delta T) + kTc/(b\sigma_s). \quad (5.22)$$

This relationship is observed reasonably for the crystallization of PE from melt and solution at various ΔT. The lamellar thickening occurs through the sliding motion of molecular chains along the chain axis, as observed typically for the annealing process of the single crystal.

The growth of PE crystal from the melt gives the spherulite. The growth of crystals under high pressure of 3000–5000 atm [39] obtains the ECC.

5.4.1.6 Molecular Simulation of Crystallization
More microscopic simulation of crystallization from the solution has been carried out on the basis of Monte Carlo or MD methods. Sundararajan and Kavassalis demonstrate the transformation of fully extended single chain into the folded chain crystal after a long time iteration of MD calculation [40]. Muthukumar et al. assume that the prefolded chains gather to form a seed nucleus with some anisotropy, on the surface of which the polymer chains adsorb and desorb repeatedly, and the crystal grows larger [41]. Yamamoto [42] and Rutledge [43] perform a MD calculation about the crystallization of polymethylene chains. See Chapter 7 for a description of computer simulations of polymer crystallization.

5.4.2 Growth Rate of Spherulites

5.4.2.1 Isothermal Crystallization The growth rate of a spherulite depends on the crystallization temperature T_c. The curve of G versus T_c takes a bell shape, and G is maximal at temperature midway between T_g and T_m. Differentiating Equation (5.8) with respect to T, G_{max} is given by:

$$G_{max} = G_o \exp[-\Delta E/(R^*(2T_{c,max} - T_m^o))] \quad (5.23)$$

$$T_{c,max} = T_m^o C/(C+1) \quad (5.24)$$

$$C = (1 + \Delta E/K)^{1/2}. \quad (5.25)$$

Since the coefficient K is inversely proportional to the melting enthalpy ΔH_m [34, 44], $\Delta E/K$ is approximately constant, with a value of about 23, for a wide variety of polymers. Therefore, the ratio $T_{c,max}/T_m^o$ is ca. 5/6 according to Equation (5.24). In other words, we obtain a universal curve from the curves of G versus, T for the different crystalline polymers. In addition, T_g, $T_{c,max}$, and T_m^o are related by $T_{c,max} \sim (T_g + T_m^o)/2$ [45].

We use differential scanning calorimetry (DSC) thermograms to monitor the crystallization process, for example, isothermal crystallization from the melt. We pack the sample in a DSC pan, heat it, and maintain it at the temperature of the melt for a short time in order to erase the sample preparation history. Then we reduce the temperature to the preset crystallization temperature T_c, and trace the thermal energy change. Figure 5.12a is a schematic illustration of this curve. In many cases the curve follows the Avrami equation:

$$X = X_o\{1 - \exp[-(k(t-t_o))^n]\} \quad (5.26)$$

where X_o is the crystallinity at the end of the primary crystallization stage. We plot the double logarithm of the reduced degree of crystallinity, $\log[-\ln[1-(X/X_o)]]$, against the logarithm of time, $\log(t - t_o)$, giving the rate constant k and the order of crystallization n (Fig. 5.12b). The induction period t_o is the time necessary for the creation of nuclei immediately after the temperature jump. In many cases, we neglect t_o in the analysis since the Avrami curve itself apparently excludes it where the observed X is actually zero. However, t_o is often useful for practical analysis of the data. (See Chapter 8 for details of the Avrami theory, and Reference [46].) The Avrami equation assumes that the crystallinity within the growing spherulite is constant, but does not describe the secondary crystallization observed after the sample is spatially filled by the spherulites in the primary crystallization process. The secondary crystallization is assumed to be an insertion of new, thinner lamellae between the already grown lamellae [47, 48]. A long period detected in the SAXS data becomes a half of

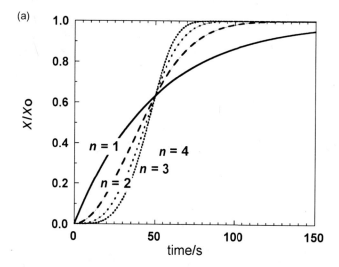

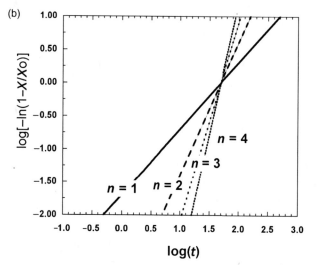

Figure 5.12 (a) Avrami plots for the various n values (the rate constant $k = 0.02$ second^{-1}). (b) Plots of double logarithm of normalized crystallinity X against logarithm of time.

the original value. Some polymers show this lamellar insertion model [49, 50]. In others, the new lamellae grow within the amorphous region of the mature spherulites [51]. We also note that the thickening of lamella is also a form of secondary crystallization.

Various factors affect the growing rate of spherulites. For example, the rate decreases as the molecular weight increases, although the crystallization temperature giving the maximal G is almost the same.

5.4.2.2 Nonisothermal Crystallization The Avrami equation does not apply when we cool the melt from a higher to a lower temperature continuously, or in the nonisothermal crystallization process. We can also use the Ozawa equation or a similar equation [51]:

$$X = X_o\{1 - \exp(-\chi(T)/\beta^n)\} \quad (5.27)$$

where $\chi(T)$ is the crystallization rate constant, and n is the Ozawa exponent, β is the cooling rate, and the temperature, T, is

$$T = T_o - (\Delta T/\Delta t)_o t = T_o - \beta t. \quad (5.28)$$

We estimate the crystallinity X as a function of T at different cooling rates. Plotting the double logarithm of X against the logarithm of β gives the constants $\chi(T)$ and n.

5.5 MICROSCOPICALLY VIEWED STRUCTURAL EVOLUTION IN THE GROWING POLYMER CRYSTALS

5.5.1 Experimental Techniques

Chapter 2 describes the different experimental tools used for microscopic studies of crystallization. WAXD gives information about the crystal structure, including the chain conformation and the chain packing mode as well as the size and orientation of crystallites and defects within the crystallites. SAXS provides information related to the electron density difference between the objects of interest and the surrounding matrix: the shape and size of isolated domains in the melt, the correlation between the aggregated domains, the structure of stacked lamellae, the surface of the lamellae, and so on [52, 53]. In particular, the development of highly sensitive 2D detectors makes it possible to measure the time-dependent changes of SAXS and WAXD in times on the order of microseconds to milliseconds. The GIWAXD and SAXS (GISAXS) are now popular for the study of the surface state of ultra-thin films [54]. The neutron scattering is also useful for the study of crystallization, in particular, by utilizing the blend sample between the deuterated and hydrogenated species, since the scattering cross-sectional area is highly different between them. The most serious problem in the neutron scattering experiment is the weak intensity of neutron beams. This problem is mitigated with the utilization of synchrotron-based spallation neutron sources (where the highly accelerated proton is incident to a mercury tank to generate highly brilliant short-pulse neutron beams) such as the Spallation Neutron Source of the USA [55], ISIS of England [56], and J-PARC of Japan [57]). Small-angle light scattering (SALS) provides information about the formation of spherulites on the submicrometer scale [58, 59]. These scattering methods have been widely used for the study of crystallization of polymers. The recent development of vibrational spectroscopy, that is, the ultra-rapid scanning technique of a Fourier transform-type spectrometer combined with a highly sensitive detector, makes it possible to trace the rapid structural evolution process in a second to millisecond or even microsecond order. The rapid-scanning Fourier transform infrared (FTIR) spectra yield detailed information about the changes in the local chain conformation as well as the intra- and intermolecular interactions during the crystallization process [60, 61].

The problem, however, is that the experimental data collected by one technique may give useful, but nonetheless limited, information. Hence, a combination of the instruments available is indispensable for the overall study of crystallization behavior [62]. For example, we can assemble the usual combination of WAXD and SAXS techniques [13] with the simultaneous measurement of X-ray scattering and dielectric constant to investigate the fluctuation of dipoles in the structural evolution process [63, 64]. The sample cell is useful for the simultaneous measurements, for example, the DSC thermometer, the miniature stretcher, the shearing apparatus, the electrodes, and the sample cell under the application of the strong magnetic field or hydrostatic pressure.

5.5.1.1 Time-Resolved Measurements
We also need to adjust the sample cell to the experimental performance. For example, the experimental apparatus we use for an isothermal crystallization study has to overcome conditions, such as the rapid changes in temperature from that of the melt (T_m) to the pre-scheduled crystallization (T_c). We note that many studies simply transfer the sample cell from the heater set at T_m to the other heater at T_c. Even though the temperature measured at the position of the metal block changes rapidly, at a few hundreds degree/min, the temperature at the sample position does not change so quickly; thus, this is not a true isothermal temperature jump experiment. To solve this problem, the method in Figure 5.13a gives a 600–1000°C/min cooling rate at the sample position (Fig. 5.13b) [62]. The sample cell is melted at the heater A, and while en route to heater B, the sample is stopped for a short time and cooled quickly by blowing cold air or by touching with the cold plate. Immediately after, the sample is moved to heater B, where the temperature fluctuation is within 0.1°C. During this temperature jump process, X-ray scattering and/or infrared/Raman spectra are measured at every millisecond to second.

Melt temperature and melt time are key to successful isothermal crystallization. The sample will decompose thermally [65] if melted for too long a time period and at a temperature far beyond the melting point (T_m). Moreover, shorter melt times may be insufficient to completely erase the crystallites, and the remaining ones

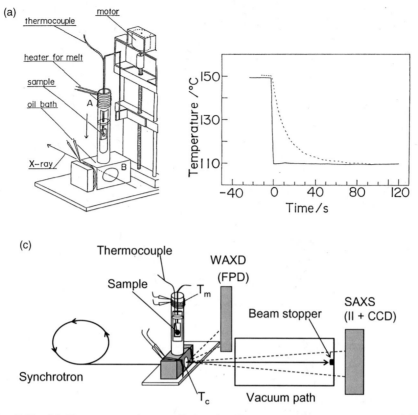

Figure 5.13 (a) Temperature jump cell for the X-ray scattering measurement, (b) time dependence of sample temperature (solid line: 600°C/min, broken line: slow cooling), and (c) simultaneous experimental system of WAXD and SAXS for the isothermal crystallization process [62, 67].

will work as nucleating (the so-called memory effect). The chain orientation might also be maintained [66]. We note that keeping the melt at a temperature near T_m obtains a similar result.

5.5.2 Structural Evolution in Isothermal Crystallization

5.5.2.1 Helical Regularization and Domain Formation of Isotactic Polypropylene

We investigate the structural evolution in isothermal crystallization from the melt by combining the FTIR, WAXD, and SAXS data for isotactic polypropylene (iPP) [67]. We melt the sample at 200°C above the melting point and cooled it steeply at 700°C/min to the crystallization temperature of 140°C ($\Delta T = T_m^o - T_c = 70°C$). Every 1 second, we measured the infrared spectra. We plot the intensities of several crystallization-sensitive bands against time (Fig. 5.14). The difference is observed in the timing of the appearance of these bands. This timing difference comes from the difference in the so-called critical sequence length m^* of each infrared band [68]. We detect the first infrared band when the length of the regular helix or the number of monomeric units included in the regular helix was greater than m^* [69, 70] (m^* can be estimated on the basis of the spectral analysis of a series of random copolymers between the H and D monomeric units [Isotope Dilution Method [68]]). The length of a D (or H) monomer sequence depends statistically on the D/H content, and the total sum of transition dipole moments or the infrared band intensity changes correspondingly. We express the theoretical curves of the infrared intensity plotted against the D/H content by using a critical sequence length m^*. Fitting the observed curve with the theoretical curves of the different m^* allows us to evaluate the m^* for a particular infrared band. The band at 998 cm^{-1} has an m^* value of about 10 monomeric units. For the band at 841 cm^{-1}, $m^* = 14$, and $m^* \gg 15$ for the band at 1221 cm^{-1}. The observed time gaps for these bands indicate that the regular helix grows longer during these gaps.

We also measur the WAXD and SAXS patterns every 1–3 seconds using a synchrotron X-ray beam. In the WAXD pattern we detect the first crystalline peaks at

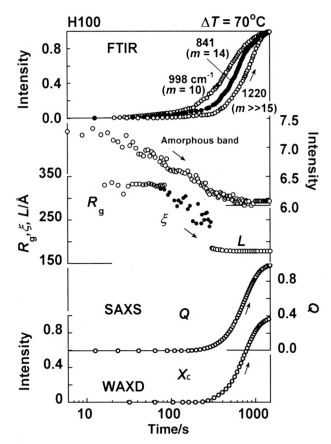

Figure 5.14 Time dependence of the various structural parameters estimated in the isothermal crystallization process of isotactic polypropylene. The FTIR data show the growth of regular helical segments. The R_g, ξ, and L are the radius of gyroid of the higher-density domains, the correlation distance between the neighboring domains, and the long period of the stacked lamellae, respectively, revealed by the SAXS data analysis. The Q is the invariant and is approximately proportional to the degree of crystallinity X_c, which was evaluated also using the WAXD data [67].

around 100 seconds. The invariant Q evaluated from the SAXS pattern also increases, which reflects the degree of crystallinity X (from $Q \propto \int_0^\infty I(q)q^2 dq \propto X(1-X)$).

The SAXS data in the lower scattering angle region are useful in order to know the chain aggregation state in the melt. We assume three stages in the ordering process. In the first stage, the domains created in the melt immediately after the temperature jump have a higher electron density than the surrounding medium, as reflected in the SAXS intensity $I(q)$. Usually we perform a Guinier plot for the evaluation of domain size: $I(q) = I(0)\exp(-R_g^2 q^2/3)$, where $q = (4\pi/\lambda)\sin(\theta)$ (λ is a wavelength of the incident X-ray beam and 2θ is the scattering angle) and R_g is a radius of gyration of the domain [52, 53]. However, this plot is only an approximation of the scattering intensity under the condition of $q \ll 1/R_g$. It is difficult to collect the scattering data in the very small q range satisfying this condition. In order to use the experimental data collected in a higher q range, we therefore return to the original equation. The SAXS intensity $I(q)$ is given by the Fourier transform of the correlation function $\gamma(r)$ corresponding to the electron density function $\rho(r)$:

$$\gamma(r) = \langle (\rho(r) - \langle\rho\rangle)(\rho(r + \Delta r) - \langle\rho\rangle) \rangle_{ensemble} \quad (5.29)$$

where $\langle\rho\rangle$ is the averaged electron density and r and Δr are the distances. Then,

$$I(q) = 4\pi \int_0^\infty \gamma(r)[\sin(qr)/(qr)]r^2 dr. \quad (5.30)$$

Since the term $\sin(qr)/(qr) \approx 1 - (qr)^2/6 + (qr)^4/120$ for $q < 1/R_g$, we approximate Equation (5.30) as:

$$I(q) \approx I(0)[1 - (M_4/6M_2)D^2 q^2 + (M_6/120*M_2)D^4 q^4]. \quad (5.31)$$

where M_k is the k-th moment of the correlation function $\gamma(r)$:

$$M_k = D^{-(k+1)} \int_0^D r^k \gamma(r) dr. \quad (5.32)$$

where D is the longest length of the particle (e.g., D = the radius for a spherical particle). The radius of gyration of the domain is:

$$R_g = (M_4/2M_2)^{1/2} D. \quad (5.33)$$

Figure 5.14 shows the plot of this estimated R_g. In summary, the aggregation of these helical segments detected in the first phase give the domain of size R_g, which remains constant and finally decreases at about 80 seconds.

In the second stage, we assume that the correlation between the neighboring domains increases. We assume the correlation function $\gamma(r)$ is $\gamma(r) = \langle\rho(0)\rangle^2 \exp(-r/\xi)$ following Debye and Bueche [71], where $\langle\rho(0)\rangle$ is the averaged electron density. Substituting this $\gamma(r)$ into Equation (5.32) gives the Debye–Bueche equation:

$$I(q) = A/(1 + \xi^2 q^2)^2 \quad (5.34)$$

where A is a constant. The plot of $I(q)^{-1/2}$ against q^2 gives the correlation length ξ. We note that the value of the decrease in R_g at around 80 seconds is almost the same as the initial ξ value. The decreasing ξ indicates an increase in the correlation strength between the neighboring domains. This time region corresponds to the growth of the long helical segments detected in the infrared spectra. The correlation length deviates from the linear line at around 300 seconds, where we observe the beginning of the long period in the SAXS pattern. This indicates the formation of a stacked lamellar structure consisting of the more highly regularized domains. The correlation function between the regularly stacked lamellae is [52, 53]:

$$K(z) = \langle [\rho(z+z') - \langle \rho \rangle)] * [\rho(z') - \langle \rho \rangle] \rangle \\ = (2/\pi) \int q^2 I(q) \cos(qz) dq. \quad (5.35)$$

Figure 5.15 shows the curve $K(z)$. The several characteristic points on this curve give the parameters of the stacked lamellar structure.

Now we can combine the infrared spectral information with the X-ray scattering data to draw the schematic illustration of the structural evolution process in the isothermal crystallization of iPP from the melt. Immediately after the temperature jump, the short helices form, and these regular parts form domains of ca. $R_g = 33$ nm. As time passes, the helical chain lengths become longer and the domains approach one another, as seen from the shortening correlation length. Finally, the correlation distance changes to the long period of stacked lamellae, where the closely gathered domains form the lamellar structure with long helical segments (see Fig. 5.16).

5.5.2.2 Generation of Disordered Phase in Isothermal Crystallization of Polyethylene
We perform a similar experiment for PE. Figure 5.17 shows the time-resolved measurement of infrared spectra in the isothermal crystallization process from the melt, where we use a linear low-density PE with 17 ethyl branches per

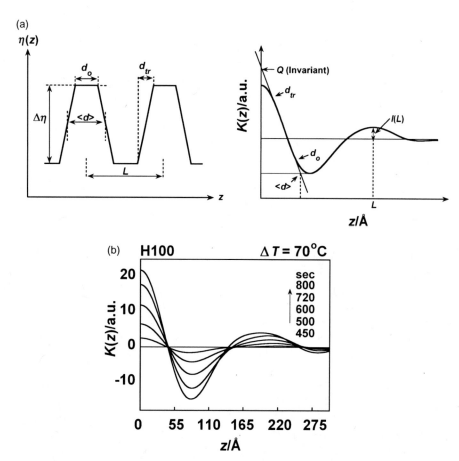

Figure 5.15 (a) Electron density distribution $\rho(z)$ of the stacked lamellar structural model and the corresponding correlation function $K(z)$ and (b) the time dependence of the correlation function evaluated from the SAXS data.

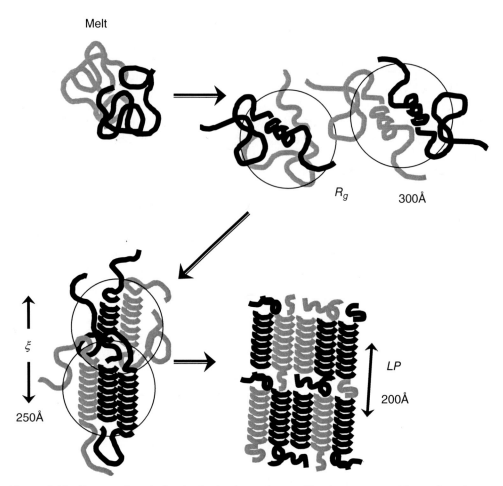

Figure 5.16 Structural evolution in the isothermal crystallization process of isotactic polypropylene revealed by a combination of infrared and WAXD/SAXS data. Parts of random coils in the melt are regularized to short helical segments, which form higher density domains in the melt. These domains approach gradually as shown by a correlation distance ξ and change into stacked lamellar structure [67].

1000 carbon atoms as an example [50]. We observe that the 720 cm^{-1} band increases in intensity. This band (D band) is characteristic of the pseudohexagonal phase and corresponds to the disordered chain conformation built up by the trans and gauche bonds of the methylene sequences [72–75]. In the time region II, this band decreases gradually in intensity, and the infrared bands typical of the orthorhombic crystal lattice appear and increase in intensity. (This process shows for a smaller degree of supercooling (ΔT).) We note that the infrared bands characteristic of the pseudohexagonal and orthorhombic phases coexist for a short period of time. On the other hand, the time-resolved SAXS data measured during this process shows that the long period of the stacked lamellar structure, ca. 800 Å (L_1), appears, and the total amount of stacked lamellae gradually increases. Then, a new SAXS peak appears (L_2), the long period of which is half of the original long period (L_1), corresponding to the secondary crystallization of the amorphous phase sandwiched between the initially existing lamellae. Figure 5.18 shows the structural evolution from the appearance of the conformationally disordered pseudohexagonal phase, and its transformation to the orthorhombic phase and to the growth of stacked lamellar structure. The appearance of the conformationally disordered structure is important in the growing process of PE crystals. Using this model, Strobl assumes that the appearance of the structurally disordered state (or mesomorphic layer) occurs in front of the growing lamella, and regularizes to the orthorhombic crystalline state with the passage of time [76].

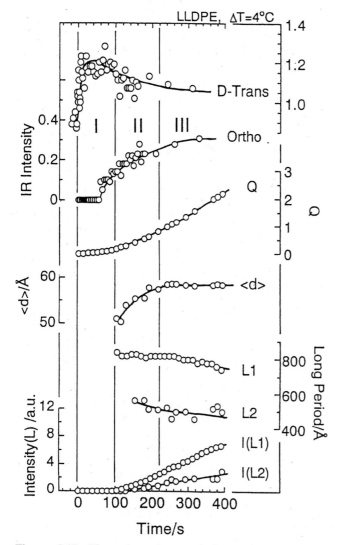

Figure 5.17 Time dependence of the various structural parameters collected by infrared spectra and SAXS measurement in the isothermal crystallization of polyethylene [50, 72]. "D-Trans" indicates the appearance of conformationally disordered trans-type chains in the melt, which decrease in intensity and coexist with the regular trans-zigzag chain segments of the orthorhombic crystal form. The invariant Q increase in parallel. The long period of the stacked lamellae also appears. In other words, the crystalline lamellae consist of the conformationally disordered chain segments of pseudohexagonal packing mode and the regular orthorhombic structure. After 200 seconds, a new lamellar structure (L_2) appeared at the long period almost a half that of the original lamellar structure (L_1), indicating the insertion of new daughter lamellae between the original mother lamellae.

5.5.2.3 Generation of Tie Chains in Isothermal Crystallization of Polyoxymethylene

The infrared spectra of POM is highly sensitive to the aggregation structure of helical chains [77]. Assuming that the crystalline region of POM is a cylindrical shape, the infrared

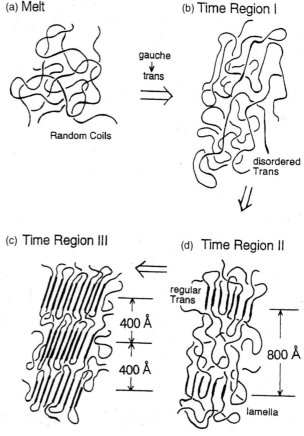

Figure 5.18 Structural evolution in the isothermal crystallization process of polyethylene revealed by a combination of infrared and WAXD/SAXS data. The random coils in the melt are regularized partially to give the pseudohexagonal phase with conformationally disordered chain segments. They develop into the stacked lamellae of regular trans-zigzag chain segments with ca. 800-Å long period. The new lamellae are inserted into the original lamellae and the long period changed to 400 Å [50].

spectral profile changes sensitively, depending on the ratio between the axial length (H) and radius (R) of the cylinder. The extremely high H/R ratio corresponds to the ECC morphology and the zero value to the FCC morphology. For example, the transition dipole moments of the C–O stretching mode are imagined to be arrayed in the cylindrical crystallite. The total sum of long-range interactions between these dipole moments differs depending on the H/R ratio or the morphology. The vibrational frequencies, which are directly related to the total sum of dipole–dipole interactions, shift significantly by changing the H/R ratio [77]. In other words, we can use the infrared bands for the estimation of morphological change in the POM crystallites [78]. Figure 5.19 compares the infrared data and SAXS/WAXD data collected during isothermal crystallization

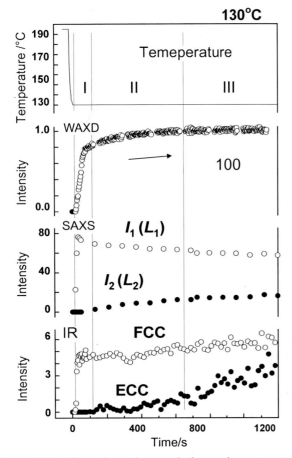

Figure 5.19 Time dependence of the various structural parameters collected by infrared spectra and WAXD/SAXS measurements in the isothermal crystallization of polyoxymethylene. It should be noticed that the appearance of FCC, as known from the infrared spectra, occurs at almost the same time as the appearance of the stacked lamellar structure (L_1) and the 100 WAXD reflection. The ECC infrared band appeared at around 100 seconds, where the generation of new lamellar structure was detected [49, 65].

at 130°C from the melt [65]. In time region I, the FCC bands and the long period of stacked lamellae (L_1) appear. The WAXD data (100 reflection) shows the formation of the normal trigonal crystal. In time region II, the infrared bands of ECC structure appear gradually. The second peak (L_2) appears in the SAXS profile, the long period of which is almost half of the original lamellar stacking period. The creation of the new daughter lamellae between the original lamellae and the appearance of ECC bands occurs at almost the same time. Figure 5.20 shows the situation schematically, where the amorphous molecular chains passing through the neighboring lamellae extend to form the regular helices in the subsequently produced daughter lamellae. Judging from the wavenumber of the observed ECC infrared band,

we estimate these helical chains to form a small, cylindrically shaped bundle 20 nm in length and 2 nm in radius. This bundle, or tie chain, governs the mechanical behavior of the bulk POM sample. Figure 5.20b shows the isothermal crystallization at 150°C. There are no inserted lamellae and extended chains passing through the lamellae, but only the development of the FCC morphology.

5.5.2.4 Role of Hydrogen Bonds in Isothermal Crystallization of Aliphatic Nylons The crystallization behavior of aliphatic nylon differs from that of polyolefins, in which the intermolecular interactions are mainly van der Waals interactions. A balance between the hydrogen bonds and van der Waals forces governs the structure of aliphatic nylon. Figure 5.21 summarizes the time-resolved infrared spectral measurement in the isothermal crystallization process [79]. We detect the NH stretching band of hydrogen-bond-free amide groups at 3400 cm^{-1} in the molten state, as well as the band originating from the hydrogen-bonded amide groups at 3320 cm^{-1}. This means that the hydrogen bonds between the amide groups exist even in the molten state. The hydrogen-bond-free NH band decreases in intensity immediately after the temperature jump, whereas the hydrogen-bonded NH band increases in intensity, becoming sharper, and the peak position shifts to the lower frequency side, which indicates the formation of stronger hydrogen bonds between the regular amide groups (region A). This state continues for a while (region B), and then at around 40 seconds (region C) the hydrogen bonds strengthen further and the amount of the hydrogen-bonded amide groups increases in population at the same time.

We perform time-resolved simultaneous WAXD and SAXS measurements by using synchrotron X-ray radiation, and analyze the data based on the theories described for iPP. We analyze the SAXS by using the Debye–Bueche equation since the hydrogen bonds already exist even in the molten state, and the neighboring domains correlate with each other. The evaluated correlation distance ξ grows shorter with the passage of time and approaches the long period of the stacked lamellae. The infrared bands of the regular methylene segments (the progression bands characteristic of the trans-zigzag conformation of the methylene segments [23]) appear at the same time, and the intensity gradually increases. We use the nylon 1010 sample with the deuterated methylene segments to distinguish the two types of methylene segments –[-NH(CH$_2$)$_{10}$NHCO(CD$_2$)$_8$CO-]$_n$-.

Figure 5.22 illustrates the regularization of chain aggregation state of aliphatic nylon 1010. We note that some portions of the amide groups are hydrogen-

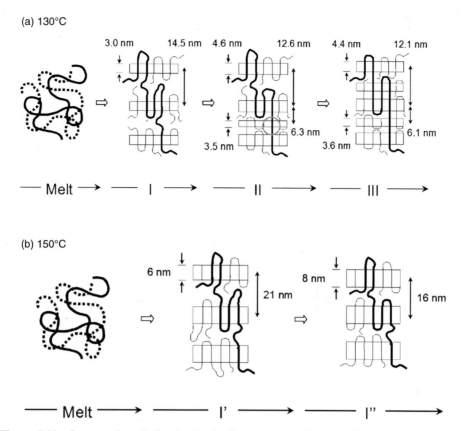

Figure 5.20 Structural evolution in the isothermal crystallization of polyoxymethylene at (a) 130°C and (b) 150°C. The difference between these two processes is seen in the generation of tie chains passing through the neighboring lamellae (ECC) in Figure 5.19 [49, 65].

bonded even in the melt. Once the sample is cooled to the crystallization temperature, the groups increase in population and strength, show the strong correlation detected from the SAXS data, and approach each other. At about 50 seconds, the methylene segments are extended and the crystalline lattices and the stacked lamellar structure are created. Since the crystallization temperature is still in the Brill transition region, the molecular chains are disordered in conformation and packing mode as a whole, although the methylene segments sandwiched between the CO bonds are partially regularized as seen in the increase of infrared trans-zigzag methylene band intensity, and the methylene segments between the NH groups are in the disordered state. The crystallization rate of nylon is higher because of the existence of hydrogen bonds even in the molten state.

5.5.2.5 Crystallization and Chain Folding Mode
One of the most characteristic features of flexible linear polymer chains is their chain folding as part of the crystallization phenomenon. Since many chains are coagulated and entangled in the solid state and they pass through the crystalline and amorphous regions, it is difficult to trace the whole shape of an individual chain separately. One idea is to utilize the small-angle neutron scattering (SANS) technique for the blend sample of fully deuterated polymer species with a low concentration of normal hydrogenated polymer species. By utilizing the high contrast of the neutron scattering power between the D and H atoms, the spatial form of a single chain may be traced clearly. For example, the SANS measurement was performed for a series of *atactic* polystyrene samples with a low concentration of the H species embedded in the D chain matrix [80]. The R_g of an isolated chain evaluated from the SANS data analysis (Gunier plot) was found to change linearly in proportion to the square root of the molecular weight, supporting the concept of the ideal random coil in the amorphous phase, as proposed by Flory [10]. This SANS method was applied to several polymers under the assumption of homogeneous mixing between the D and H polymer chains in the solid state. It is important to confirm the perfect miscibility between them experimentally. If not,

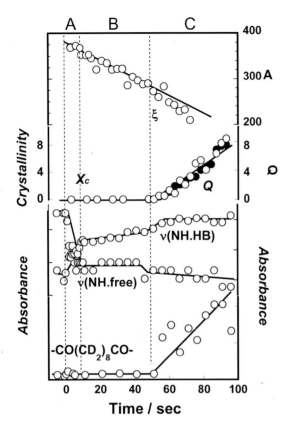

Figure 5.21 Time dependence of the various structural parameters collected by infrared spectra and WAXD/SAXS measurements in the isothermal crystallization of nylon 1010. In the region A, the hydrogen bonds are developed in the melt and the correlation between the higher density domains became stronger. In the region C, the crystal lattice was detected (invariant Q and degree of crystallinity X_c) and the hydrogen bonds became much stronger, as known from the absorbance change of the corresponding infrared bands. The methylene segments became more regularized and the trans-zigzag conformation was detected in this region [79].

shows an almost perfectly homogeneously mixed state at an arbitrary mixing ratio of the D and H chain components [3, 4]. Figure 5.23 shows the infrared spectral change measured for a series of the D/H blend samples prepared by slow cooling from the melt. Similar to the case of D/H blend samples of n-alkanes [85], a pair of bands at 730 and 720 cm^{-1} characteristic of the orthorhombic PE crystal, which originates from the correlation splitting due to the intermolecular interactions between the adjacent H chains [86], changes the splitting width between doublet and singlet depending on the D/H content. This infrared spectral observation indicates that the D and H chain species mix homogeneously in the crystal lattice in a statistically random arrangement. The melting point of the H/D blend sample shifts continuously between the peak positions of the pure H and D components, supporting the infrared spectral data.

We subject these perfectly miscible PE blend samples to the SANS measurement in the crystallization process. We find that the R_g of a D chain has almost the same value before and after crystallization [87]. Figure 5.24 shows this situation schematically. The D chain (H chain) shows the random coil in the molten state. Even after crystallization occurs, the R_g of the D chain is unchanged. This scheme is essentially the same as the Ersterrungs model proposed by Fischer, although his model was for the melt-quenched sample of the D/H blend of high-density PE [88, 89]. Naturally, this structural change results in the random chain folding mode in the crystalline region. The continuous change of the correlation splitting width of infrared bands supports the concept that the D and H stems are statistically and randomly arranged in the crystal lattice [72].

Low molecular weight n-alkanes, such as n-$C_{390}H_{782}$, are also useful for determining the characteristic folding behavior of molecular chains in the crystallization process. According to the time-resolved measurement of the SAXS profiles in the cooling process of long alkane from the melt [90, 91], the crystallization mechanism changes depending on the crystallization temperature T_c. The ECC is formed at a high T_c. A lower T_c gives a disordered packing of loosely folded chains (noninteger folded crystal), which transforms isothermally to the ECC or regularly packed once-folded chains, or the mixture of extended and once-folded molecules depending on the crystallization temperature.

5.5.3 Shear-Induced Crystallization of the Melt

The application of shear stress on the molten polymer results in the elongation flow-induced crystallization [92]. The extension of long chains promotes the formation of long, thread-like structures oriented along the shear direction [93]. The first stage of shear-induced

the D and H species might show more or less the phase separation during the crystallization process. The continuous change in the melting point and the infrared spectral change measured for a series of D/H blend samples with different contents lead us to check the miscibility. iPP [67, 81], PMO [82], and so on, show almost perfect homogeneous mixing or cocrystallization even during slow crystallization. A blend of high-density PE between the D and H species shows the homogeneous mixing when rapidly quenched from the melt, but partial phase separation occurs when they are slowly cooled. The aggregation of the same kind of chains makes it impossible to evaluate the R_g of an isolated D (H) chain [83, 84]. Among the various pairs of D and H PE blends, the blend between a linear low-density PE (LLDPE) with 17 ethyl side chains per 1000 carbon atoms and a high-density deuterated PE (DHDPE)

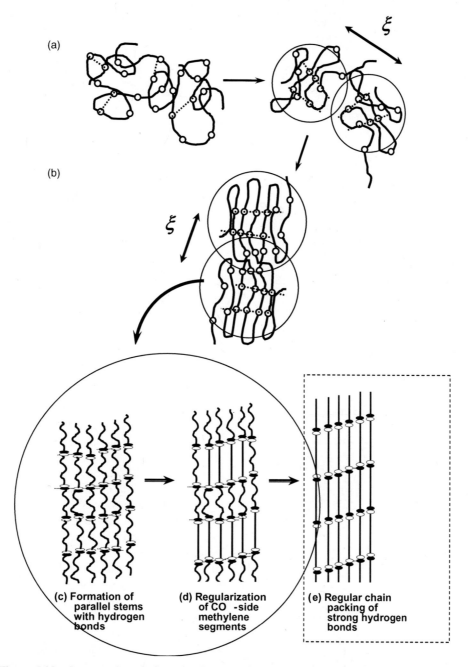

Figure 5.22 Structural evolution of nylon 1010 in isothermal crystallization from the melt. Refer to the experimental data in Figure 5.21 [79].

crystallization is the formation of point-like precursors, which further change to thread-like precursors. These threads have a high aspect ratio and cause the highly oriented lamellar growth or the row-nucleated morphology. On the surface of this row-nucleated morphology, lamellar growth produces the kebab-like structure as mentioned previously [93, 94]. Blending a small portion of high molecular weight component into a normal polymer sample enhances the formation of the row-nucleated morphology. A SANS measurement was performed for a melt-elongated sample of a blend between deuterated low molecular weight PE (97 wt%) and high molecular weight PE (3 wt%) [95]. The SANS pattern shows the streak-like scattering normal to the elongation direction and the two-spots pattern along the elongation direction. The former corresponds to the formation of the shish-like structure and the latter to the kebab-like structure. We note that the SAXS measurement of

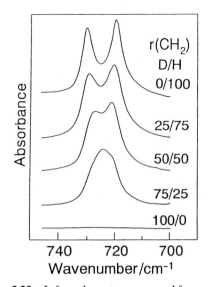
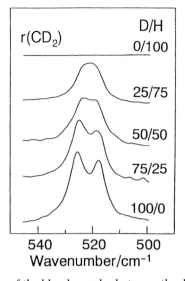

Figure 5.23 Infrared spectra measured for a series of the blend samples between the deuterated high density polyethylene and the linear low density polyethylene. Doublets were observed for D/H = 0/100 and 100/0 samples. As the blending ratio was changed, the splitting width of the bands became smaller and merged into a singlet for the dilute blend samples. These phenomena can be interpreted by assuming that the D and H chain stems are statistically randomly distributed in the crystal lattice [3].

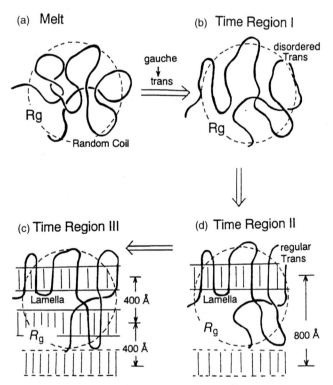

Figure 5.24 Illustration of the structural evolution process in the isothermal crystallization process of polyethylene. The radius of gyration (R_g) was not changed remarkably as known from the SANS data analysis [72] (refer to Fig. 5.18).

the same sample shows only the two-point scattering pattern, corresponding to the kebab-like structure. The difference between the SAXS and SANS data shows that the shish part consists of the high molecular weight component, although the concentration of the high molecular weight component is quite low. A second experiment demonstrates that the polymer chains having molecular weight above a critical orientation molecular weight M^* form the oriented structure at a given shear rate. We consider that the shorter chains do not incorporate into the oriented crystals, as supported by the above-mentioned SANS and SAXS experiments of PE blend [96, 97]. However, a similar experiment obtains a different result for the blend of iPP between the high molecular weight component of normal (hydrogenated) iPP and the low molecular weight component of deuterated iPP [98]. In this experiment the streak scattering was observed for both the high and low molecular weight components, which indicates that both the shish part and the kebab part include these two. A similar experiment was performed also for a D and H blend sample of isotactic polystyrene [99].

We observe the structural evolution during the melt-spinning process by using synchrotron radiation. For example, Murase et al. measure the SAXS and WAXD patterns during melt spinning of PE [100]. Their SAXS data show the formation of stacked lamellae oriented along the flow direction, followed by the insertion of the daughter lamellae between the already existing mother lamellae, consistent with the crystallization study of PE described in the previous section [49, 72].

Another example is the fiber spinning of poly(ethylene terephthalate) (PET) from the melt [101, 102]. In high speed spinning at 6000 m/min, we observe neck formation when the tensile velocity is higher than the inverse reptation time of the melt. At the end of the neck formation, we detect the occurrence of crystallization by using an online X-ray scattering measurement. We detect the generation of mesophase before crystallization [101, 103, 104] when we draw the sample near T_g. We consider that the mesophase is a smectic liquid crystal phase, from which the more regular crystalline phase gradually generates [105].

We can assume the fiber spinning process from the concentrated polymer solution also to be the crystallization phenomenon under shear. Some studies were performed to trace the structural evolution during the solution spinning [106, 107]. (See Chapters 15 and 16 for details.)

5.6 CRYSTALLIZATION UPON HEATING FROM THE GLASSY STATE

Melting a polymer sample and cooling it quickly to a temperature lower than the glass transition point (T_g) produces an amorphous glass sample. The next section describes this cold crystallization process.

5.6.1 Cold Crystallization

Heating a sample of glassy crystallizable polymer above the T_g induces crystallization. The crystalline form obtained sometimes differs from that crystallized from the melt or the solution. We consider that the cold crystallization is induced from a nodule structure existing in the amorphous region and that the nodule consists of a regular chain-folded crystalline-like structure [108]. However, our assumption is inconsistent with Flory's prediction that the amorphous phase contains ideal random coils. Imai et al. proposes the ordering of the amorphous phase through the spinodal decomposition phenomenon [109, 110]. For example, in the case of a melt-quenched PET sample, the time-dependent measurement is made in the annealing process at a temperature 10°C above T_g (80°C). The higher and lower density parts separate gradually and form the continuously distributed parts through the orientation fluctuation of the harder segments of polymer chains. This density fluctuation results in the formation of clusters consisting of nematic-like structure of polymer chains, that is, the nodule structure. Another possible mechanism is that crystallization from the melt occurs by the nucleation mechanism, in which small embryos produced by crossing an energy barrier grow to regular and larger crystalline domains [111]. Panine et al. report the early stage structure formation of PE using time-resolved WAXD and SAXS data and refute the spinodal decomposition mechanism [112]. Olmsted et al. conclude the opposite for the PE sample [113]. They assign the origin of the difference between the nucleation and growth mechanism and the spinodal decomposition mechanism to the metastable amorphous phase and the unstable amorphous phase, respectively. We note the need for more detailed studies of crystalline polymers in addition to PET [114].

5.6.2 Solvent-Induced Crystallization of Polymer Glass

Treating a melt-quenched sample with a solvent vapor can cause solvent-induced crystallization. For example, the chains of the polymer, syndiotactic polystyrene (sPS) [115–117], assume one of two types of molecular conformation. The random coils of the glassy state regularize to the all-trans-planar-zigzag form by annealing (α form), or to a complex $(T_2G_2)_2$ form by absorption of organic solvents (δ form). Heating the δ form obtains the α and β forms. For simplicity, we focus on the formation of the δ form, by comparing the time-resolved infrared, Raman, and WAXD data [116, 117] for the solvent-induced crystallization of sPS glass.

We place the sample into an optical cell with a solvent reservoir. We begin the infrared (or Raman) measurement at the same time we inject the solvent into the reservoir. Figure 5.25 shows the time dependence of the infrared band intensity measured for the sPS–toluene system. The timing of the appearance of the crystallization-sensitive band differs among the bands. Immediately after injecting the solvent, the intensity of the toluene band increases, then the amorphous band intensity decreases, and finally the intensity of the band intrinsic to T_2G_2 increases and forms at 549 cm^{-1}. Next, the intensity of the T_2G_2 bands at 1251, 572 cm^{-1}, and so on, increases. This difference in timing of the appearance of the crystallization-sensitive bands results from the difference in the critical sequence length m^*. The different m^* values of these various bands [116] allow us to describe the evolution of the regular helix conformation. Starting from the random coils in the amorphous region, they are regularized into short helices to produce the band with smaller m^* values. These short helices grow to longer, more regular helical chains as detected by the intensity increment of the bands with higher m^* values. In addition to the information obtained from these infrared (and Raman) bands characteristic of regular helical conformation, the half-width of the amorphous band provides information about the molecular motion of the amorphous chains. The half-width of

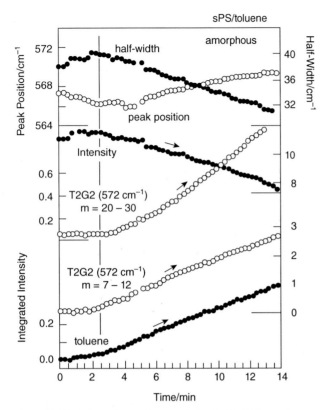

Figure 5.25 Time dependence of the half-width and vibrational frequency of the amorphous infrared band, the integrated intensity of the regular helical bands with the different critical sequence length (m), and the intensity of the toluene band evaluated for the solvent-induced crystallization process of a glassy syndiotactic polystyrene sample. Immediately after the injection of toluene, the half-width of the amorphous band increased, indicating an enhancement of thermal motion in the amorphous chains. This results in the formation and growth of regular helical segments [116, 117].

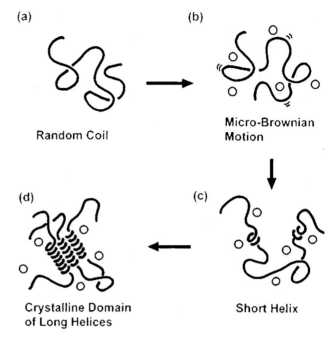

Figure 5.26 Illustration of the structural regularization process of syndiotactic polystyrene derived from Figure 5.25 [118].

a band is inversely proportional to the relaxation time or the measure of thermal mobility. Once we supply toluene to the glassy sample, estimating the half-width of the amorphous band during the crystallization process shows a gradual increase, and at almost the same time we observe the appearance of regular helical bands. These observations indicate that the thermal mobility of the chains in the amorphous region accelerates to induce the transformation from the random coil to the regular helix.

We also perform WAXD measurement as a function of time. We detect X-ray diffractions from the crystalline region at almost the same time as the Raman bands having relatively long m^* values. Since the X-ray diffractions must occur for the first time when the crystalline lattice of helical chains forms, the good correspondence between the Raman (IR) and X-ray data tells us that the formation of crystalline clusters of detectable size start to occur when the helical chains grow long enough, as shown in Figure 5.26.

sPS has a glass transition temperature T_g at ca. 100°C. The solvent-induced crystallization occurs even at room temperatures lower than T_g. We speculate that solvent molecules work as a plasticizer, which lowers the T_g and enhances the thermal motion of polymer chains in the amorphous state. To determine the extent to which T_g lowers by absorbing solvent molecules, we perform a time-dependent measurement of infrared spectra during the solvent-induced crystallization process at various temperatures [116]. We construct an Avrami plot for each crystallization curve, from which we estimate the crystallization rate constant k. We plot the k value against the crystallization temperature, allowing the estimation of T_g by extrapolating the curves to the $k = 0$ point. Toluene lowers the T_g of sPS from 100°C to −30°C, benzene to −70°C, and chloroform to −90°C. MD simulations confirm our speculation [118] that the amorphous chains generate under the 3D periodic condition and some solvent molecules are input into the MD cell. We perform the MD calculation at a constant temperature to estimate the equilibrated specific volume of the cell. The specific volume expands with an increase of temperature and shows a deflection point at a certain temperature, defined as T_g, as shown in Figure 5.27. T_g shifts by ca. 100 and 200°C for toluene and chloroform, respectively, which is consistent with the observed data. We note that solvent-induced crystallization can be observed for other polymers, including PET [119],

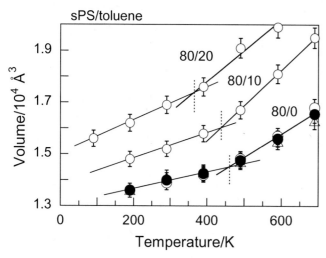

Figure 5.27 Molecular dynamics calculation of the glass transition temperature T_g for the system of syndiotactic polystyrene and toluene. The amorphous chains were generated in the molecular dynamics cell and the trajectory was calculated at the various constant temperatures under constant pressure. The deflection points in the volume–temperature plots show the glass transition points. By increasing the relative content of toluene molecules from 0 to 10 to 20, the T_g was found to shift to lower temperatures [117].

poly(ethylene imine) [120], poly(ether ether ketone) [121] and poly(carbonate bisphenol) [122].

5.7 CRYSTALLIZATION PHENOMENON INDUCED BY TENSILE FORCE

Natural rubber has a melting point at −5°C. By stretching the sample at room temperature, it crystallizes reversibly to a highly-oriented crystalline phase, as evident from the X-ray diffraction pattern [123]. The soft segmental parts of an elastomer show similar crystallization. For example, the multiblock copolymer of poly(tetramethylene terephthalate) and poly(tetramethylene oxide) is an elastomer, which shows remarkable rubber elasticity at room temperature. In the drawn sample of elastomer, the poly(tetramethylene terephthalate) component orients along the draw direction. The soft segmental component of poly(tetramethylene oxide) remains in the amorphous state at ambient temperature. By stretching this oriented sample, the soft segments reversibly crystallize and show a high degree of orientation along the stretching direction [124, 125].

5.8 PHOTOINDUCED FORMATION AND GROWTH OF POLYMER CRYSTALS

Photoinduced solid-state polymerization reaction is useful for producing a single large crystal. Polydiacety-

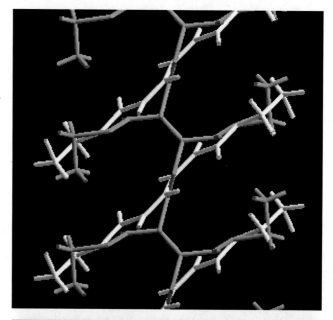
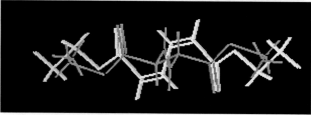

Figure 5.28 Molecular shapes of poly(diethyl *cis,cis*-muconate) and the corresponding monomers in the crystal lattice [130]. The space group symmetry ($P2_1/c$) between them is preserved during the photoinduced solid-state polymerization process. (See color insert.)

lene [126], poly(2,5-di-styryl pyradine) [127], poly(1,4-diethyl *cis,cis*-muconate) [128] are typical examples. Trioxane single crystal gives POM by γ-ray irradiation; the product is not single crystalline but polycrystalline [129].

We show an example of the case of poly(1,4- diethyl *cis,cis*-muconate). We prepare a single crystal of 1,4-diethyl *cis,cis*-muconate from the solution and irradiate with the X-ray beam for the structure analysis of the monomer and the polymer. Since the structural changes occur rapidly during the polymerization reaction, that is, on a time scale of several tens of minutes under the X-ray irradiation, fast acquisition of the X-ray reflections is necessary for accurate structural analysis. A CCD camera makes it possible to collect about 6000 reflections in 13 minutes [130].

Figure 5.28 shows that the monomer and polymer show the same space group symmetry $P2_1/c$, and that molecular symmetry remains throughout the polymerization reaction, with almost no change in the center of gravity

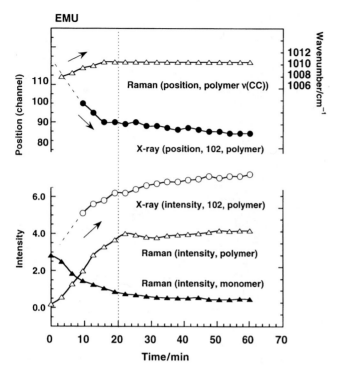

Figure 5.29 Time dependence of Raman and X-ray data measured in the photoinduced solid-state polymerization reaction of diethyl *cis,cis*-muconate single crystal [133].

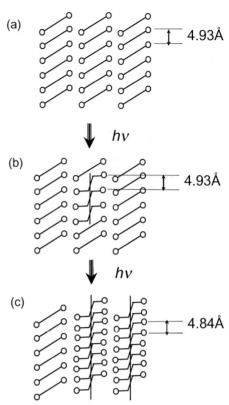

Figure 5.30 Illustration of the structural change in the photoinduced solid-state polymerization reaction of diethyl *cis,cis*-muconate single crystal [133]. The polymer segments generated during the course of the reaction are under tension due to the interactions with the surrounding monomer molecules (b). This tensile stress working on the short polymer chain segments becomes weaker and disappears when the polymer chains become longer and their number is increased in the crystal lattice (c).

viewed along the chain axis. Only the unit cell parameters change slightly. This reaction is called a topotactic reaction, which is a special case of the more general topochemical reactions. We also perform simultaneous measurements of the monomer crystal by WAXD and Raman spectroscopy, and record the Raman spectra during the irradiation of the monomer crystal with the X-ray beam. As shown in Figure 5.29, the X-ray and Raman signals of polymer species increase as the irradiation time increases. We note that the peak positions of X-ray and Raman signals shift in the early stage of the photoinduced polymerization reaction. The X-ray-analyzed repeating period along the chain axis is 4.93 Å (monomer) and 4.84 Å (polymer), a slight, but not negligible, difference. The Raman carbon-carbon (CC) stretching mode of the skeletal chain shows a shift of +2.0 cm^{-1} in total. Independently of these studies, Raman spectral measurements were carried out for the polymer single crystal subjected to tensile stress. The CC stretching band shows a shift of −2.0 cm^{-1}/GPa for an externally applied tensile stress [131, 132]. Based on these experimental data, we consider that the solid-state polymerization reaction generates about 1 GPa *tensile* stress along the chain axis in the early stage of reaction. As shown in Figure 5.30, the neighboring monomer molecules react under the irradiation by X-rays to generate short polymer chains. These polymer chain segments stretch from the regular form by about 1 GPa tensile stress under the interactions with the surrounding monomer molecules. As the polymerization reaction proceeds, the polymer chains grow longer and the number of surrounding polymer components increases. As a result, stress relaxation occurs gradually to produce the stable polymer single crystal [133].

5.9 CONCLUSION

We have reviewed the complex growth of polymer crystals occurring under various conditions by using the data acquired at different levels of structural detail. The mechanism of growth was measured by using a single (or a combination) of the tools available. We suggest that the results of simultaneous measurements clarify the hierarchical structures observed, from the molecular level to the spherulite level.

REFERENCES

[1] Wundelich, B. *Macromolecular Physics*, Academic Press, New York, 1973.

[2] Iguchi, M. *Polymer* **1983**, *24*, 915.

[3] Tashiro, K., Stein, R.S., Hsu, S.L. *Macromolecules* **1992**, *25*, 1801.

[4] Tashiro, K., Satkowski, M.M., Stein, R.S., Li, Y., Chu, B., Hsu, S.L. *Macromolecules* **1992**, *25*, 1809.

[5] Balzano, L., Rastogi, S., Peters, G.W.M. *Macromolecules* **2008**, *41*, 399.

[6] Tashiro, K. Crystal structure and phase transition of PVDF and related copolymers. In *Ferroelectric Polymers: Chemistry, Physics, and Technology*, Nalwa, H.S., ed. Marcel Dekker Inc., New York, 1995, p. 63.

[7] Tashiro, K., Sasaki, S., Saragai, S. *J. Polym. Sci. B Polym. Phys.* **2004**, *42*, 4175.

[8] Ostwald, W.Z. *Phys. Chem.* **1987**, *22*, 286.

[9] Stokes, K.H. *J. Am. Chem. Soc.* **1938**, *60*, 1753.

[10] A special issue on crystallization of polymers. *Faraday Discuss. Chem. Soc.* **1979**, *68*.

[11] Toda, A., Okamura, M., Hikosaka, M., Nakagawa, Y. *Polymer* **2005**, *46*, 8708.

[12] Schultz, J.M. *Polymer Crystallization*, Oxford Univ. Press, New York, 2001.

[13] Gogolewski, S., Pennings, A. *J. Polym.* **1985**, *26*, 1394.

[14] Zwijnenburg, A., Pennings, A.J. *Colloid Polym. Sci.* **1975**, *253*, 452.

[15] Barham, P.J., Keller, A. *J. Mat. Sci.* **1980**, *15*, 2229.

[16] Smith, P., Lemstra, P.J. *J. Mat. Sci.* **1980**, *15*, 505.

[17] Smith, P. *J. Mat. Sci.* **1987**, *22*, 523.

[18] Sasaki, S., Masunaga, H., Itou, K., Tashiro, K., Okuda, H., Takahara, A., Takata, M. *J. Phys. Conf. Ser.* **2009**, *184*, 012015.

[19] Miller, R.L., Boyer, R.F. *J. Polym. Sci. Polym. Phys. Ed.* **1984**, *22*, 2043.

[20] Fujiwara, Y. *J. Appl. Phys.* **1960**, *4*, 10.

[21] Lovinger, A.J. *J. Appl. Phys.* **1978**, *49*, 5003.

[22] Lovinger, A.J. *J. Appl. Phys.* **1978**, *49*, 5014.

[23] Yoshioka, Y., Tashiro, K. *Polymer* **2003**, *44*, 7007.

[24] Tashiro, K., Yoshioka, Y. *Polymer* **2004**, *45*, 4337.

[25] Wang, C., Chen, C.-C., Cheng, Y.-W., Liao, W.-P., Wang, M.-L. *Polymer* **2002**, *43*, 5271.

[26] Yen, K.C., Woo, E.M., Tashiro, K. *Polymer* **2010**, *51*, 5592.

[27] Yen, K.C., Woo, E.M., Tashiro, K. *Macromol. Rapid Comm.* **2010**, *31*, 1343.

[28] Takayanagi, M., Yamashita, T. *J. Polym. Sci.* **1956**, *22*, 552.

[29] Woo, E.M., Wu, P.L., Wu, M.C., Yan, C.C. *Macromol. Chem. Phys.* **2006**, *207*, 2232.

[30] Lorenzo, M.L.D. *Eur. Polym. J.* **2005**, *41*, 569.

[31] Zhang, J., Tashiro, K., Tsuji, H., Domb, A.J. *Macromolecules* **2008**, *41*, 1352.

[32] Okabe, Y., Murakami, H., Osaka, N., Saito, H., Inoue, T. *Polymer* **2010**, *51*, 1494.

[33] Tsuji, H., Tashiro, K., Bouapao, L., Narita, J. *Macromol. Mater. Eng.* **2008**, *293*, 947.

[34] Hoffman, J.D., Miller, R.L. *Polymer* **1997**, *38*, 3151.

[35] Yang, J., McCoy, B.J., Madras, G. *J. Chem. Phys.* **2005**, *122*, 64901.

[36] Lauritzen, J.I., Jr., Hoffman, J.D. *J. Res. Nat. Bur. Std.* **1960**, *64A*, 73; 1961, 65A, 297.

[37] Sadler, D.M., Gilmer, G.H. *Polym. Comm.* **1987**, *28*, 242.

[38] Goldbeck-Wood, G. *Polymer* **1990**, *31*, 586.

[39] Arakawa, T., Wunderlich, B. *J. Polym. Sci. C Polym. Symp.* **1967**, *16*, 653.

[40] Sundararajan, P.R., Kavassalis, T.A. *J. Chem. Soc. Faraday Trans.* **1995**, *91*, 2541.

[41] Zhang, J., Muthukumar, M. *J. Chem. Phys.* **2007**, *126*, 234904.

[42] Yamamoto, T. *Polymer* **2009**, *50*, 1975.

[43] Waheed, N., Ko, M.J., Rutledge, G.C. *Polymer* **2005**, *46*, 4689.

[44] Mandelkern, I., Jain, N.L., Kim, H. *J. Polym. Sci. Part A-2, Polym. Phys.* **1968**, *6*, 165.

[45] Okui, N. *Polymer* **1990**, *31*, 92.

[46] Loreenzo, A.T., Arnal, M.L., Albuerne, J., Muller, A.J. *Polymer* **2007**, *26*, 222.

[47] Kolb, R., Wutz, C., Stribeck, N., von Krosigk, G., Riekel, C. *Polymer* **2001**, *42*, 5257.

[48] Song, H.H., Wu, D.Q., Chu, B., Satokowski, M., Ree, M., Stein, R.S., Phillips, J.C. *Macromolecules* **1990**, *23*, 2380.

[49] Hama, H., Tashiro, K. *Polymer* **2003**, *44*, 2159.

[50] Sasaki, S., Tashiro, K., Kobayashi, M., Izumi, Y., Kobayashi, K. *Polymer* **1999**, *40*, 7125.

[51] Ozawa, T. *Polymer* **1971**, *12*, 150.

[52] Feigin, L.A., Svergun, D.I. *Structure Analysis by Small-Angle X-Ray and Neutron Scattering*, Plenum Press, New York, 1987.

[53] Guinier, A., Fournet, G. *Small Angle Scattering of X-Rays*, John Wiley, New York, 1955.

[54] Busch, P., Rauscher, M., Smilgies, D.-M., Posselt, D., Papadakis, C.M. *J. Appl. Cryst.* **2006**, *39*, 433.

[55] http://neutrons.ornl.gov/facilities/SNS/.

[56] http://www.isis.stfc.ac.uk/science/science.html.

[57] http://j-parc.jp/.

[58] Meeten, G.H., ed. *Optical Properties of Polymers*. Springer, New York, 1986.

[59] Brumberger, H., ed. *Modern Aspects of Small-Angle Scattering, NATO Science Series C*. Springer, New York, 1995.

[60] Chalmers, J.M., Griffiths, P.R., eds. *Handbook of Vibrational Spectroscopy*. John Wiley & Sons, Ltd., New York, 2002.

[61] Everall, J.M., Chalmers, J.M., Griffiths, P.R., eds. *Vibrational Spectroscopy of Polymers*. John Wiley & Sons, Ltd., West Sussex, 2007.

[62] Tashiro, K., Sasaki, S. *Prog. Polym. Sci.* **2003**, *28*, 451.

[63] Fukao, K., Miyamoto, Y. *J. Non-Cryst. Solids* **1998**, *235–237*, 534.

[64] Wurn, A., Minakov, A.A., Schick, C. *Eur. Polym. J.* **2009**, *45*, 3282.

[65] Hama, H., Tashiro, K. *Polymer* **2003**, *44*, 6973.

[66] Mortins, J.A., Chang, W., Brito, A.M. *Polymer* **2010**, *51*, 4185.

[67] Reddy, K.R., Tashiro, K., Sakurai, T., Yamaguchi, N., Sasaki, S., Masunaga, H., Takata, M. *Macromolecules* **2009**, *42*, 4191.

[68] Kobayashi, M., Akita, K., Tadokoro, H. *Makromol. Chem.* **1968**, *118*, 324.

[69] Zhu, X.Y., Yan, D.Y., Fang, Y. *J. Phys. Chem. B* **2001**, *105*, 12461.

[70] Kissin, Y.V., Rishina, L.A. *Eur. Polym. J.* **1976**, *12*, 757.

[71] Debye, P., Bucchc, A.M. *J. Appl. Phys.* **1949**, *20*, 518.

[72] Tashiro, K., Sasaki, S., Gose, N., Kobayashi, M. *Polym. J.* **1998**, *6*, 485.

[73] Snyder, R.G., Maroncelli, M., Qi, S.P., Strauss, H.L. *Science* **1981**, *214*, 188.

[74] Maroncelli, M., Qi, S.P., Strauss, H.L., Snyder, R.G. *J. Am. Chem. Soc.* **1982**, *104*, 6327.

[75] Kim, Y., Strauss, H.L., Snyder, R.G. *J. Phys. Chem.* **1989**, *93*, 7520.

[76] Strobl, G. *Prog. Polym. Sci.* **2006**, *31*, 398.

[77] Kobayashi, M., Sakashita, M. *J. Chem. Phys.* **1992**, *96*, 748.

[78] Hama, H., Tashiro, K. *Polymer* **2003**, *44*, 3107.

[79] Tashiro, K., Nishiyama, A., Tsuji, S., Hashida, T., Hanesaka, M., Takeda, S., Cao, W. Y., C., Reddy, K.R., Masunaga, H., Sasaki, S., Ito, K., Takata, M. *J. Phys. Conf. Ser.* **2009**, *184*, 1071861.

[80] Roe, R.J. *Methods of X-ray and Neutron Scattering in Polymer Science*, Oxford Univ. Press, New York, 2000.

[81] Reddy, K.R., Tashiro, K., Sakurai, T., Yamaguchi, N. *Macromolecules* **2009**, *42*, 1672.

[82] Kongkhlang, T., Reddy, K.R., Kitano, T., Nishu, T., Tashiro, K. *Polym. J.* **2010**, *43*, 66.

[83] Schelten, J., Ballard, D.G.H., Wignall, G.D., Longman, G.W., Schmatz, W. *Polymer* **1976**, *17*, 571.

[84] Schelten, J., Wignall, G.D., Ballard, D.G.H., Longman, G.W. *Polymer* **1977**, *18*, 111.

[85] Cheam, T.C., Krimm, S. *J. Polym. Sci. Polym. Phys.* **1981**, *19*, 423.

[86] Tadokoro, H. *Structure of Crystalline Polymers*, John Wiley and Sons, Inc., New York, 1989.

[87] Tashiro, K., Imanishi, K., Izuchi, M., Kobayashi, M., Itoh, Y., Imai, M., Yamaguchi, Y., Ohashi, M., Stein, R.S. *Macromolecules* **1995**, *28*, 8484.

[88] Fischer, E.W. *Adv. Polym. Sci.* **2005**, *180*, 45.

[89] Fischer, E.W. *Pure Appl. Chem.* **1978**, *50*, 1319.

[90] Ungar, G., Keller, A. *Polymer* **1986**, *27*, 1835.

[91] Unger, G., Putra, E.G.R., de Silva, D.S.M., Schcherbina, M.A., Waddon, A.T. *Adv. Polym. Sci.* **2005**, *180*, 45.

[92] Janeschitz-Kriegl, H. *Crystallization Modalities in Polymer Melt Processing*, Springer, Wien, New York, 2010.

[93] Seki, M., Thurman, D.W., Oberhausen, J.P., Karufield, J.A. *Macromolecules* **2002**, *35*, 2583.

[94] Liedauer, S., Eder, G., Janeschitz-Kriegl, H. *Int. Polym. Process* **1995**, *3*, 243.

[95] Kanaya, T., Matsuba, G., Ogino, Y., Nishida, K., Shimizu, H.M., Shinohara, T., Oku, T., Suzuki, J. *Macromolecules* **2007**, *40*, 3650.

[96] Somani, R.H., Hsiao, B.S., Nogales, A., Srinivas, S., Tsou, A.H., Sics, I., Balta-Calleja, F.J., Ezquerra, T.A. *Macromolecules* **2000**, *33*, 9385.

[97] Nogales, A., Hsiao, B.S., Somani, R.H., Srinivas, S., Tsou, A.H., Bakta-Calleja, F.J., Ezquerra, T.A. *Polymer* **2001**, *42*, 6247.

[98] Kimata, S., Sakurai, T., Nozoe, Y., Kasahara, T., Yamaguchi, N., Karino, T., Shibayama, M., Kornfield, J.A. *Science* **2007**, *36*, 1014.

[99] Hayashi, Y., Matsuba, G., Zhao, Y., Nishida, K., Kanaya, T. *Polymer* **2009**, *50*, 2095.

[100] Murase, H., Kotera, M., Nakamae, K. *Spring-8 Research Frontier*, 2004, 110.

[101] Kolb, R., Seifert, S., Stribeck, N., Zachemann, H.G. *Polymer* **2000**, *41*, 2931.

[102] van Meerveld, J., Hütter, M., Peters, G.W.M. *J. Non-Newtonian Fluid Mech.* **2008**, *150*, 177.

[103] Kawakami, D., Hsiao, B.S., Ran, S., Burger, C., Fu, B., Sies, I., Chu, B., Kikutani, T. *Polymer* **2004**, *45*, 905.

[104] Mahendrasingam, A., Martin, C., Fuller, W., Blundell, D.J., Oldman, R.J., MacKerron, D.H., Harvie, J.L., Riekel, C. *Polymer* **2000**, *41*, 1217.

[105] Li, L., de Jeu, W.H. *Adv. Polym, Sci.* **2005**, *181*, 75.

[106] Ran, S., Burger, C., Fang, D., Cookson, D., Yabuki, K., Teramoto, Y., Cunniff, P.M., Viccaro, P.J., Hsiao, B.S., Chu, B. *NSLS Activity Report*, 2001, 2-147.

[107] Pranzas, P.K., Knochel, A., Kneifel, K., Kamusewitz, H., Weigel, T., Gehrke, R., Funari, S.S., Willumeit, R. *Anal. Bioanal. Chem.* **2003**, *376*, 602.

[108] Geil, P.H. *Faraday Discuss. Chem. Soc.* **1979**, *68*, 141.

[109] Imai, M., Mori, K., Mizuhami, T., Kaji, K., Kanaya, T. *Polymer* **1992**, *33*, 4451.

[110] Imai, M., Kaji, K., Kanaya, T. *Macromolecules* **1994**, *27*, 7103.

[111] Erukhimovitch, V., Baram, J. *Phys. Rev.* **1995**, *B51*, 6221.

[112] Panine, P., Urban, V., Boesecke, P., Narayanan, T. *J. Appl. Cryst.* **2003**, *36*, 991.

[113] Olmsted, P.D., Poon, W.C.K., McLeish, T.C.B., Terrill, N.J., Ryan, A.J. *Phys. Rev. Lett.* **1998**, *81*, 373.

[114] Wang, H. *Polym. Commun.* **2006**, *47*, 4897.

[115] Bhoje Gowd, E., Tashiro, K., Ramesh, C. *Prog. Polym. Sci.* **2009**, *34*, 280.

[116] Tashiro, K., Ueno, Y., Yoshioka, A., Kobayashi, M. *Macromolecules* **2001**, *34*, 310.

[117] Tashiro, K., Yoshioka, A. *Macromolecules* **2002**, *35*, 410.

[118] Yoshioka, A., Tashiro, K. *Macromolecules* **2004**, *36*, 467.

[119] Kulshreshtha, A.K., Khan, A.H., Madan, G.L. *Polymer* **1978**, *19*, 819.

[120] Hashida, T., Tashiro, K., Inaki, Y. *Polymer* **2003**, *44*, 1721.

[121] Mensitieri, G., Nobile, M.A., Apicella, A., Nicolais, L., Garbassi, F. *J. Mater. Sci.* **1990**, *25*, 2963.

[122] Aharoni, S.M., Murthy, N.S. *Int. J. Polym. Mat.* **1998**, *42*, 275.

[123] Tosaka, M. *Polym. J.* **2007**, *39*, 1207.

[124] Tashiro, K., Hiramatsu, M., Ii, T., Kobayashi, M., Tadokoro, H. *Sen-I Gakkaishi* **1986**, *42*, T659.

[125] Tashiro, K., Hiramatsu, M., Ii, T., Kobayashi, M., Tadokoro, H. *Sen-I Gakkaishi* **1986**, *42*, T597.

[126] Enkelmann, V. *Adv. Polym. Sci.* **1984**, *63*, 91.

[127] Hasegawa, M. *Adv. Phys. Org. Chem.* **1995**, *30*, 117.

[128] Matsumoto, A., Yokoi, K., Aoki, S., Tashiro, K., Kamae, T., Kobayashi, M. *Macromolecules* **1998**, *31*, 2129.

[129] Uchida, T., Tadokoro, H. *J. Polym. Sci. Part A-2* **1967**, *5*, 64.

[130] Tashiro, K., Zadorin, A.N., Saragai, S., Kamae, T., Matsumoto, A., Yokoi, K., Aoki, S., Aoki, S. *Macromolecules* **1999**, *32*, 7946.

[131] Nakamoto, S., Tashiro, K., Matsumoto, A. *Macromolecules* **2003**, *36*, 109.

[132] Nakamoto, S., Tashiro, K., Matsumoto, A. *J. Polym. Sci. B Polym. Phys.* **2003**, *41*, 444.

[133] Tashiro, K., Nakamoto, S., Fujii, T., Matsumoto, A. *Polymer* **2003**, *44*, 6043.

6

COMPUTER MODELING OF POLYMER CRYSTALLIZATION

GREGORY C. RUTLEDGE

Department of Chemical Engineering, Massachusetts Institute of Technology, Cambridge, Massachusetts

6.1 Introduction, 197
6.2 Methods, 198
    6.2.1 Molecular Dynamics, 199
    6.2.2 Langevin Dynamics, 200
    6.2.3 Monte Carlo, 200
    6.2.4 Kinetic Monte Carlo, 201
6.3 Single-Chain Behavior in Crystallization, 202
    6.3.1 Solid-on-Solid Models, 202
    6.3.2 Molecular and Langevin Dynamics, 203

6.4 Crystallization from the Melt, 204
    6.4.1 Lattice Monte Carlo Simulations, 205
    6.4.2 Molecular Dynamics Using Coarse-Grained Models, 206
    6.4.3 Molecular Dynamics Using Atomistic Models, 207
6.5 Crystallization under Deformation or Flow, 208
6.6 Concluding Remarks, 210
References, 211

6.1 INTRODUCTION

The crystallization of polymers has been the subject of ongoing investigation for close to a century. The seminal discovery of chain-folded lamellae in the crystallization of polymers is now over 50 years old. Nevertheless, despite decades of experimental and theoretical effort, our understanding of this complex subject remains far from complete. Novel concepts continue to be proposed and evaluated as new methods for the study of crystallization are developed and refined. Among the new techniques of scientific inquiry that have arisen over the past 30 years, computer simulation in particular has enjoyed widespread application to a broad range of problems in polymer science and engineering. With the remarkable doubling of processor speed roughly every 18 months over this period ("Moore's Law"), the reduction in cost per floating point operation and the proliferation of high-performance computing power, computer simulation has risen in prominence to the point where it is often considered a third branch of scientific inquiry, alongside experimentation and theory. The real power of computer simulation, however, has come not only through the increased speed of numerical processing, but through the intellectual development of novel models, algorithms, and problem solving strategies that have generated orders of magnitude improvements in the complexity of problems that can be addressed by computer simulation. This chapter focuses on the developments in molecular simulation to illuminate, and discriminate, the principles and detailed molecular mechanisms that underlie the crystallization of polymers.

Polymer crystallization poses special challenges for investigation by molecular simulation. First, it must be recognized that crystallization is, by it nature, a dynamic process that takes place when a system is driven out of equilibrium. Consider the determination by computer

---

Handbook of Polymer Crystallization, First Edition. Edited by Ewa Piorkowska and Gregory C. Rutledge.
© 2013 John Wiley & Sons, Inc. Published 2013 by John Wiley & Sons, Inc.

simulation of crystal structure and properties, and thermodynamic conditions for melt/crystal or crystal–crystal coexistence; these are problems that are readily handled by equilibrium statistical thermodynamics, and good reviews of these studies are available [1–5]. Similarly, the structure and thermomechanical properties of the intercrystalline domain of semicrystalline polymers have been described using equilibrium statistical thermodynamics, subject to appropriate constraints that characterize the metastable nature of this material [6–13]. Even the dynamics of systems in response to small perturbations from equilibrium can often be characterized adequately by studying dynamic fluctuations at equilibrium [2, 14]. The term "crystallization," on the other hand, indicates a nonequilibrium thermodynamic process that involves the genesis of a new phase and the subsequent metamorphosis of a system, in whole or in part, from the old phase to the new one. It is a process that takes place when the thermodynamic state point of the system, defined by temperature, pressure, concentration, stress, strain, and so on, is changed, giving rise to a first-order transition and the establishment of a new equilibrium, or something approaching it. Second, crystallization, like many phase transformations where nucleation and growth of a new phase may be involved, belongs to a class of rare event processes, in which the processes of interest occur mainly during events of relatively short duration, separated by long waiting periods. Thus, two very disparate time scales are involved and must be resolved. This distinguishes crystallization from the dynamics of systems that are more diffusive in nature, such as the transport of mass, energy, or momentum within a polymer. Such processes are also intrinsically dynamic in nature, but useful information about them can often be obtained even through relatively short trajectories of simulation time; such is not the case with rare event processes unless the initial state of the simulation is carefully prepared. Third, the study of crystallization in polymers, in particular, poses special problems of time and length scale that set it apart from the crystallization of small molecules. The driving force for crystallization is the reduction in free energy that comes with sacrificing the entropy of liquid-like disorder for the enthalpic benefits that accompany the careful packing of molecules into a dense, regular crystalline form; capturing this trade-off accurately demands that both the long chain-like nature of the crystallizing molecule, complete with its multiplicity of conformations that occur in the disordered state, and the short-ranged, intermolecular packing interactions that compound within a regular, ordered crystalline structure, be properly represented. Furthermore, the dynamics of chain-like molecules are complicated by the onset of entangled behavior above a certain chain length or molecular weight, which scales very differently in time than do the dynamics of short sections of the chain on a local scale. The common lamellar crystallites themselves are highly anisotropic, with the thickness of the crystallite being typically an order of magnitude larger than the size of the chemical repeat unit of the polymer, but an order of magnitude smaller than the transverse length of the crystallite.

Despite these challenges, computer simulations were invoked over 25 years ago by Sadler and Gilmer in their efforts to justify an entropic barrier model for polymer crystal growth [15]. Rigby and Roe observed orientational ordering in molecular dynamics (MD) simulations of short n-alkanes, which they described as an isotropic–nematic transition; however, the transition was not immediately reversible upon heating, suggesting that some degree of supercooling and nucleation of a new phase had occurred [16]. However, only in the last decade or so has the power of modern molecular simulation really been brought to bear on the study of crystallization of polymers. The progress made in these years is the focus of this chapter. In the first part of this chapter, we seek to provide some understanding of the methods, their benefits and limitations, as they apply to a dynamic process like crystallization, in much the same way that one must first appreciate the strengths and limitations of any new experimental characterization technique before attempting to use it. In the second part of the chapter, we summarize some of the information that has been gleaned to date from the application of molecular simulations to the study of crystallization of polymers. The brevity of the chapter makes it necessary that only a subset of the results can be discussed, and these only selectively. Several longer review articles are available that summarize in greater detail the activities of particular groups in the field [17–23]; the interested reader is directed to these reviews for further information.

6.2 METHODS

Here we describe simulations of a molecular nature, including atomistic and mesoscale modeling of coarse-grained representations of chains. This is motivated primarily by the long length and time scales of intrinsic interest to the problem of formation of a polymer crystal phase, as suggested in Section 6.1. Problems of an electronic nature may also be important, especially in cases where highly specific, strong interactions such as hydrogen bonds can form to stabilize the ordered crystalline form, but such methods are computationally more intensive, and beyond the current state of the art in simulations of polymer crystallization dynamics. Constitutive equations based on micromechanical models and continuum approaches to model the development of a crystal phase are also available; examples of these are dealt with elsewhere in this handbook (cf. Chapter 7 and Chapter 14). Several excellent texts are available that describe the mechanics of molecular simulation and their applications to problems in polymer science and engineering [24–26]. We merely review them here in enough detail to discuss their utility in studying polymer crystallization.

6.2.1 Molecular Dynamics

By far the most ubiquitous method for the simulation of dynamical processes involving particles and molecules is the MD technique, which dates back to the seminal work of Alder and Wainwright [27]. It is a method based on classical mechanics applied at the atomic, submolecular, or molecular level. The model consists of a structural description of the system, in terms of the coordinates of atoms, groups of atoms, or coarse-grained "beads," and the force field through which these structural components interact. The force field is usually semi-empirical in origin, or it may be derived from quantum mechanical considerations, and is written as an equation for potential energy, usually comprising a summation of two-body interactions between atoms that are not bonded covalently, and two-, three-, and four-body interactions between atoms that are bonded covalently to form a molecular chain. This can be written generically in the form $U(r^N)$, where r^N denotes the vector coordinates of the N atoms or beads comprising the simulation. A number of different force fields have been used in the study of polymer crystallization. The force field embodies the representation of the physical system on the computer, and the results of a simulation are only meaningful to the extent that the force field accurately describes the relevant interactions in real polymer systems. Often, subjective choices are made to improve the speed or scope of a simulation at the expense of resolution or accuracy of representation. Some of these force fields and trade-offs are described in later sections of this chapter, in the context of their use.

From a carefully prepared initial configuration, defined by the position and velocities of the atoms or beads and the size of the box that contains them, the MD simulation then samples the trajectory of configurations prescribed by Newton's Law:

$$F_i = \left(-\partial U(r^N)/\partial r_i\right) = m_i a_i \qquad (6.1)$$

where m_i and a_i are the mass and acceleration, respectively, of atom i. From the known accelerations of each atom, their displacements over a small interval of time are calculated and the new positions are updated numerically, using an algorithm such as the one by Verlet [28]. By its nature, MD is conservative—the total energy, E, is constant throughout the simulation. The total energy is composed of the potential energy, $U(r^N)$, and the kinetic energy, $K(p^N)$, which is a function only of the momenta, p^N. In its most straightforward form, MD samples a system at equilibrium in the microcanonical ensemble (constant number of atoms, N, volume, V, and total energy, E). In order to study the dynamics of a system under conditions more relevant to most experiments, and to impose changes of state in terms of variables under control in the laboratory, thermostats and barostats are often introduced to regulate the temperature and/or state of stress. Such thermostats and barostats can in principle alter the dynamics of the system, and thus must be used with attention to this possibility, but they are important in studies of polymer crystallization in order to accommodate the potentially large heats of fusion and changes in density that accompany phase transformation. MD is remarkable for its efficiency and robustness of implementation to a wide range of systems; as a consequence, MD simulation packages are widely available and in use at the current time [29–32].

A primary limitation of the MD method is the time step. Mathematically, MD is a numerical integration forward in time from an initial condition; the accuracy of the integration is limited by the choice of algorithm and the integration step size. If the step size is too large, energy may not be conserved well over long periods of simulation. Energy conservation requires accurate sampling of the fastest mode of motion in the system. This is usually the bond vibration associated with the lightest atom or bead in the system. For organic polymers involving C–H bonds, a time step of 0.5×10^{-15} second is common; a united atom (UA) force field in which the hydrogen atoms are combined with the carbon atoms to form methyl or methylene beads allows an increase of time step by about a factor of four. Further coarse-graining of the system may permit even larger time steps, but at greater expense in the fidelity of representation of the molecular packing structure and dynamics within the crystal. Indeed, proper use of coarse-graining in dynamic simulations generally involves a temperature-dependent rescaling of time [33], and may even require a change of form of the equations of motion, such as the Langevin dynamics described in the next section, to account for dissipative processes associated with the "lost" degrees of freedom [34]. From these considerations alone, it is apparent that reliable simulations longer than 100 ns (approximately 10^8 time steps), using a UA model, are still relatively rare. Since most phase transformations occur on the time scale of 1 ms, it is not obvious that a naïve application of MD will yield useful information regarding crystallization. To overcome this problem, a number of strategies, some more rigorous than others, have been devised to access longer time scales or to accelerate the dynamics of crystallization; these are outlined in greater detail in the second part of this chapter.

The application of MD to study systems that are undergoing transformation towards a new equilibrium state belongs to the family of methods called nonequilibrium molecular dynamics (NEMD). In implementation, NEMD simulations usually take one of two forms: either a driving force is introduced that maintains the system out of equilibrium at steady state, or else a perturbation is introduced and the system is studied as it relaxes toward equilibrium. The latter is not at steady state, and thus the system is constantly evolving, although not necessarily smoothly in time and/or space. Such unsteady-state NEMD simulations can in some circumstances encounter limitations in their ability to sample adequately some of the dynamics. Nevertheless, most of the MD studies of crystallization for polymers to date are of the unsteady NEMD type.

6.2.2 Langevin Dynamics

Langevin dynamics is closely related to the MD technique [24]. In this method, a separation of time and length scales between the object of interest, the polymer chain(s), and the background environment, usually small solvent molecules or other "fast" degrees of freedom, permits the latter to be approximated in a mean field sense, serving as a thermal bath for the polymer. By doing so, the number of degrees of freedom involved in the numerical integration can be drastically reduced, thus lowering the computational cost per time step and making longer time scale simulations more practical. The forces of interaction between solute particles are augmented by frictional drag and thermal noise terms, characterized by Γ and $W_i(t)$, respectively, that replace the explicit interactions with solvent particles:

$$F_i = -(\partial U/\partial r_i) - \Gamma v_i - W_i(t). \quad (6.2)$$

Γ and $W_i(t)$ in turn are related through the fluctuation–dissipation theorem. v_i is the particle velocity. The hydrodynamic interaction between particles associated with motion of the intervening solvent may also be included, but doing so compromises considerably the computational benefits of the implicit solvent treatment, and has not been considered in the study of polymer crystallization to date. As with the use of the thermostat in MD, the solvent is presumed small enough to pervade the system and interact with all of the polymer particles, including (implicitly) those deeply buried within globules or crystalline aggregates.

6.2.3 Monte Carlo

For the study of systems at equilibrium, Monte Carlo (MC) simulation offers an alternative to MD. MC relies on a Markov chain of configurations created by sampling the phase space using a set of specified "moves" that are "accepted" or "rejected" according to a criterion that ensures convergence of the chain of configurations to their equilibrium distribution. The evolution of a system simulated by the MC method obeys the Master Equation:

$$\frac{\partial P_j(t)}{\partial t} = \sum_i \frac{P_i(t) w_{ij}}{\tau} - \sum_i \frac{P_j(t) w_{ji}}{\tau}. \quad (6.3)$$

where $P_j(t)$ is the probability of being in configuration j at time t, and w_{ji} is the probability to transition from configuration j to configuration i. τ is the characteristic time elapsed per transition [35]. Evolution of the system toward its stationary, equilibrium distribution is ensured by the assumption of detailed balance for all pairs of configurations i and j:

$$P_i(t) w_{ij} = P_j(t) w_{ji}. \quad (6.4)$$

The distribution of configurations at equilibrium is then specified in the usual manner by choosing

$$\frac{w_{ij}}{w_{ji}} = \frac{P_j^{eq}}{P_i^{eq}} \quad (6.5)$$

where $P_j^{eq} = Z^{-1} \exp(-\beta E_j)$ at thermal equilibrium. The partition function, Z, is an unknown but constant quantity that conveniently drops out of Equation (6.5). $\beta = 1/k_B T$, where T is temperature and k_B is Boltzmann's constant. Equation (6.5) does not specify the transition probabilities uniquely; the importance sampling criterion proposed by Metropolis et al. is most common [36]:

$$w_{ij} = \min\left(1, \exp\left(-\beta\left[U\left(r_j^N\right) - U\left(r_i^N\right)\right]\right)\right) \quad (6.6)$$

In writing Equation (6.6), the probability of generating a new trial configuration j is presumed to be a constant, and the kinetic energy is assumed to be the same, on average, for any two configurations i and j.

A real strength of MC simulation is that one is not constrained to transition from one configuration to another through a sequence of physically realistic steps such as those prescribed by Newton's Law. Instead, very unphysical moves can be designed, so long as they preserve the thermodynamic state of the system, defined for example in the canonical ensemble by N, V, and T. Simulations in other ensembles, such as a constant stress ensemble, can be handled through appropriate introduction of a work term to the energy and a MC move that alters the conjugate variable, such as the size and shape of the simulation box. By designing moves that have longer characteristic times, τ, systems that evolve with slower kinetics can be studied within a typical simulation. The sluggish dynamics of long-chain molecules in the melt state, especially beyond the entanglement molecular weight, has made MC very attractive for studying the properties of polymeric systems at equilibrium. However, this efficiency comes at the cost of potentially unphysical dynamical behavior, so that considerable caution must be employed when attempting to interpret the dynamics of systems from an MC simulation. As shown by Kang and Weinberg [35], the popular choices of Metropolis or Kawasaki rules for the transition probabilities w_{ij} leads in general to a configuration-dependent rescaling of time at each step. Assuming that transition state theory can be applied to each transition between configurations i and j, the rescaling of time in the case of Metropolis sampling is simply proportional to $\exp(\beta \varepsilon_{ij})$, where ε_{ij} is the height of the energy barrier, $E^{\ddagger}$, above that of the higher energy configuration, that is, $\varepsilon_{ij} = E^{\ddagger} - \max[E_i, E_j]$. Thus, if ε_{ij} is a constant for all i and j, then the time rescaling associated with each transition is the same, and the time evolved between any two configurations in the Markov chain scales in proportion to the number of MC steps separating them, as often assumed. Otherwise, the time between each transition is rescaled differently for each transition, and transitions that have higher barriers or that require more complex, cooperative events are disproportionately accelerated. When studying dynamical behavior using Metropolis MC, it is important that transitions between configurations be designed with this time rescaling in mind.

If the moves employed are strictly local ones, such as site displacement moves, where the dependence of the barrier height ε_{ij} on configuration is likely to be small, then credible dynamical behavior can often be observed, given a sufficiently large number of individual transitions [37, 38]. The introduction of more efficient moves developed for polymers to sample collective motions, such as cluster moves, pivots, reptation, or rebridging [37, 39–43], to name a few, brings with it a stronger dependence of elapsed time on the configuration involved with a given transition, and potentially unrealistic dynamics. As the system becomes more coarse-grained, even a local MC move represents an increasingly complex set of physical dynamical events; the consequences of this are an increase in the characteristic time τ associated with a move and loss of resolution on shorter time scales. Thus, it is always desirable, where possible, to map the behavior of a system studied by a Markov chain of MC moves to that of the same system using the more realistic Newtonian dynamics before any quantitative conclusions can be drawn regarding the absolute values of rate constants or transport properties.

6.2.4 Kinetic Monte Carlo

The alternative to using the conventional Metropolis MC algorithm to simulate the evolution of a system toward equilibrium is the kinetic Monte Carlo (KMC) method [44–46] (also sometimes called "dynamic" Monte Carlo [47]). In this method, the correct dynamics are ensured by basing the transition probabilities on physical rate processes, usually through invocation of activated state theory to generate the appropriate kinetics:

$$r_{ij} = k_0 \exp\left(-\beta\left(E_{ij}^{\ddagger} - E_i\right)\right) \quad (6.7)$$

where r_{ij} is the rate of transition from configuration i to configuration j. The KMC method relies on the identification of all possible transitions that can occur from a particular configuration and subsequent determination of the rates with which each transition can occur. The transition probabilities can then be computed using

$$w_{ij} = r_{ij} \bigg/ \sum_{m=1}^{n} r_{im}. \quad (6.8)$$

This requires a priori knowledge of the number n of allowed transitions at any step of the simulation, typically prescribed by a set of "rules" for allowed transitions, in order to compute the probability of the next step in the simulation (and the waiting time associated with it). For this reason, early uses of KMC were called the n-Fold Way [44]. The time associated with a given transition out of configuration i at step α is

$$t_\alpha = -\langle t_i \rangle \ln(rn) \quad (6.9)$$

where

$$\langle t_i \rangle = \left[\sum_{m=1}^{n} r_{im}\right]^{-1} \quad (6.10)$$

and rn is a random number drawn uniformly from the interval $(0, 1)$. From Equation (6.8), Equation (6.9), and Equation (6.10), one can see that the moves associated with the largest rates are selected most frequently, and impose the most stringent limitation on the time increment per transition. By coarse-graining (i.e., ignoring, in this case) transitions associated with such fast processes, longer times scales become accessible within a KMC simulation.

In principle, an exhaustive enumeration of allowed transitions would generate not only the correct kinetics, but also the elapsed time associated with each step. This is often feasible for lattice models, but it presupposes some knowledge of the allowed transitions and a good kinetic model to describe the rates r_{ij} associated with each transition. On the other hand, full enumeration of allowed transitions in off-lattice models can be prohibitive, and the n-Fold Way KMC cannot strictly be applied. Importantly, the KMC method reduces to the conventional MC method for special cases where k_0 in Equation (6.7) and the denominator of Equation (6.8) are both constants, independent of configuration. Here again, appropriate selection of moves that satisfy these characteristics in an MC simulation is essential to obtain realistic dynamics. For two recent reviews of these methods, the reader is referred to References [48] and [49].

6.3 SINGLE-CHAIN BEHAVIOR IN CRYSTALLIZATION

6.3.1 Solid-on-Solid Models

Studies involving single (or few) chains organizing at a crystal growth front or into isolated crystallites represent an appropriate starting point for simulations of polymer crystallization since the complicating effects of cooperative behavior involving multiple chains in a dense, viscoelastic liquid are avoided. The earliest applications of computer simulation to crystallization of polymers were KMC simulations on a simple cubic lattice. Among the first of these was the seminal KMC study by Sadler and Gilmer [15]. These simulations were performed by the simple addition or subtraction of "units," each of which corresponds to a coarse-grained chain segment, at the crystal growth front; this was known as the "solid-on-solid" (SOS) model; typical results of this model are illustrated by Figure 6.1. In addition, constraints were introduced to emulate chain connectivity and pinning of chains, attributed to the presence of loops and folds on the lamellar surface. This lattice MC method requires a priori some knowledge of how the kinetic parameters partition into driving force (related to $\Delta E = |E_j - E_i|$) and barrier (related to ε_{ij}) contributions, which decisions must usually be made subjectively. These earliest simulations already offered strong support for "entropic barrier" models of crystal growth, as alternatives to enthalpic barrier models such as the now-classic secondary nucleation model of Lauritzen and Hoffman [50, 51]. By their nature, entropic barrier models require the characterization of one or a few successful crystallizable configurations or crystalli-

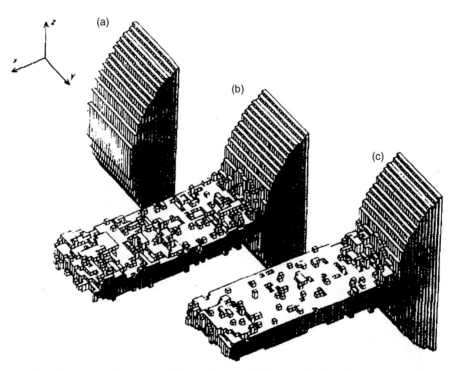

Figure 6.1 Computer drawings of the seed crystal (a) and the lamellar crystals generated by the model of Sadler and Gilmer, using $kT_m^o/\varepsilon = 0.7$ (b) and $kT_m^o/\varepsilon = 0.55$ (c). Reproduced with permission from Reference [15]. Copyright 1984, Elsevier.

zation pathways out of a host of possible configurations or pathways, and thus are particularly suited to study by computer simulations. These early simulations reproduced the experimental observations of curved crystal habits and the linear dependences of $\ln G$ (where G is the crystal growth rate) and lamellar thickness l on the inverse of supercooling, ΔT^{-1}. The supercooling is $\Delta T = T_m - T_c$, where T_m is the thermodynamic melting point and T_c is the temperature at which crystallization occurs. Subsequent simulations of this type were used to identify a kinetic "roughening" of the crystal surface at large supercooling [52], and to study other important situations such as crystallization in the presence of a noncrystallizable comonomer and nonisothermal crystallization [53–55].

Doye and Frenkel advanced this lattice KMC approach by replacing the implicit "pinning" constraints with explicit consideration of chain connectivity and folding as a single polymer chain is reeled into the crystal [56, 57]. In this version of the SOS model, allowed moves consisted of extension of the outermost crystal stem by one unit, reduction by one unit, or introduction of a fold. Only tight (adjacent reentry) folds were allowed. This model was used to test the assumptions of secondary nucleation and entropic barrier theories. A significant outcome of these simulations was evidence for a new mechanism for lamellar thickness selection during polymer crystal growth at sufficiently large supercooling, based on the notion of a fixed point attractor. In this mechanism, all growing lamellae converge towards a common, "dynamically stable" thickness, regardless of their different thicknesses at an initial time t_0. This thickness selection is understood to arise from a dynamical balance between fluctuations that give rise to an unstable crystal stem shorter than the minimum thermodynamically stable length and those that give rise to a stem that substantially "overhangs" the crystal surface. This contrasts with the classical interpretation that lamellae grow at constant thickness, with the fastest growing lamellae merely being most prevalent. At small supercooling, rounding of the growth front was found to terminate crystal growth unless some mechanism for crystal thickening behind the growth front was allowed. Subsequent studies showed this mechanism of thickness selection to accord better with observations of temperature jump experiments, where lamellae having steps in thickness may be found [58]. A review of this work is available in Reference [59].

6.3.2 Molecular and Langevin Dynamics

Among the first studies of polymer crystallization using off-lattice MD techniques was the study of the collapse of single polyethylene (PE) chains in vacuum, corresponding approximately to crystallization from dilute solution in a very poor solvent [60]. The chain was not completely isolated since the use of a thermostat ensured that the otherwise isolated chain could exchange energy with its environment. A UA model for PE was used [61], but this was later shown to be rather too stiff to represent PE accurately [62, 63]; the results are thus more typical of those for a generic, semirigid chain with an ordering transition in excess of 600 K. The smectic droplets, sometimes called "lamellae," that ultimately formed in these simulations can be recognized as a trade-off between the penalties to fold such a chain and the additional surface energy (alternatively, loss of attractive van der Waals energy) that accompanies deviation of the globular shape from one having minimal surface area (maximal attractive van der Waals interactions). The importance of molecular stiffness in the observed behavior was quickly recognized, and the dependence of chain folding on chain rigidity was studied in detail [63]. The mechanism for formation of these ordered globules was attributed to a global collapse, for semirigid chains, or a sequential agglomeration of local collapses, for more flexible ones. Subsequent studies have revisited this model on several occasions [64–66]; for example, at large supercooling, the number and length of stems that formed within an ordered globule were found to be highly metastable [65]. A similar approach was used to study adsorption of a single chain of this type on solid substrates [67]. The method has been extended to the collapse dynamics of poly(ethylene-co-propylene) with various branch distributions [68] and to isotactic polypropylene [69]. Notably, the MD simulation of polypropylene produced chain collapse but without the ordering characteristic of crystallization.

Yamamoto and coworkers studied growth of the polymer crystal by adsorption and ordering of chains from a poor solvent (i.e., vacuum) onto a structured surface using MD [70, 71]. They invoked a coarse-grained, bead-spring model in which flexibility of the chain is controlled by varying the bending stiffness of an otherwise linear, string-like chain; in the absence of the lowest energy zig-zag or helical conformers typical of atomistic models, the dynamics for chain sliding along its contour, both in crystal and melt, are substantially enhanced. In the absence of bending stiffness, the isolated chain undergoes a collapse transition, but no ordering within the globular state was observed using this model. However, in the presence of a corrugated surface, the globule adsorbs strongly and wets the surface; alignment of the segments of the spreading chain is induced by the corrugation of the surface. Simulations using substrates with finite domains of corrugation confirmed that the ordering process is driven by the structure of the substrate. In the strongly absorbed state, the chain is confined to two dimensions in the plane of the substrate, and ordering necessarily occurs through sliding motions of the chain along its contour; from an initial globule configuration in three dimensions, the ordering process was observed to be cooperative in nature, in contrast to the reeling-in process invoked within the KMC model. It proceeds by stages, beginning with the initial adsorption, followed by extension and alignment of segments to form "lamellae," which subsequently "thicken" on a longer time scale. The times reported for these stages should be interpreted with caution because of the coarse-grained nature of the model; nevertheless, the thickening observed in these simulations is still very rapid compared with the thickening of polymer crystals observed on the laboratory time scale. As was the case for the ordered globule configuration in solution, the ordering of the globule on a corrugated substrate was found to exhibit stem lengths that depend sensibly on temperature. This coarse-grained MD approach has also been used to study crystallization from the melt of polymer chains that tend to form helices, either "bare" or with side groups. The neglect of side groups in the "bare" chain model speeds up chain sliding and helix reversals within the collapsed, globular state, but reduces the tendency for chirality selection [72, 73].

Extension of the MD study of single (or few) chains in solution can be found in the Langevin dynamics simulations of Muthukumar and coworkers, in which the solvent is again treated implicitly and serves as a thermal bath for the polymer chain. The polymer chain is also of the UA type with a relatively high stiffness that promotes rapid chain ordering, as evidenced by an ordering transition above 600 K [74–76]. Local collapse processes qualitatively similar to those reported by Kavassalis and Sundararajan [60] were observed, and interpreted as the formation of "baby nuclei" along a single chain; these nuclei were found to coalesce through a reeling in of the strands between them. Upon equilibration of these simulations at small supercooling, the size distribution of nuclei was found to be more or less quantized in stem length (or number of folds per chain), and to predict a global minimum free energy folded chain state, as illustrated in Figure 6.2. This observation led to the proposition of a thermodynamic equilibrium model for crystallization of polymer chains that anticipates a finite lamellar thickness; this model stands in stark contrast to the prevailing kinetic models for lamellar thickness selection. In the equilibrium model, the entropy associated with loops and tails on the crystal surface serves to stabilize the polymer crystallite in a loosely folded structure; the stem lengths of such a folded structure are much smaller than the fully extended chain length, which is usually assumed to be

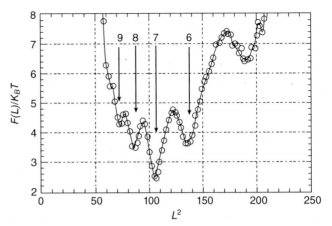

Figure 6.2 Free energy landscape for chains of length $N = 300$ as a function of L, a measure of the thickness of the crystallite. The arrows indicate the number of chain stems in the crystallite. Reproduced with permission from Reference [77]. Copyright 2003, The Royal Society of London.

the global free energy minimum [77]. The dependence of lamellar thickness was again found to vary inversely with the extent of supercooling, ΔT, in accord with experiments. As an aside, it is worth noting that the melting behavior of a single-chain crystallite simulated using the "microrelaxation" model (cf. Section 6.4.1) has also been interpreted as a reversible process, from a folded configuration with a disordered surface layer to a fully disordered droplet [78]. The Langevin dynamics method and histogram reconstruction was also applied to the study of secondary nucleation and the reeling in of chains from solution onto a surface [74, 76]. In this case, the histogram of configurations as a function of the number of segments adsorbed on the surface suggested that no barrier to crystal growth existed; this in turn was interpreted as evidence against the secondary nucleation and entropic barrier models. Subsequently, Sommer reformulated the proposed thermodynamic equilibrium model for many-chain systems (i.e., melts) and recovered the fully extended chain crystallite as the minimum free energy state, in accord with conventional wisdom [79]. The formulation of these models highlights some of the significant differences thermodynamically between polymer crystallization from solution and from melt, differences that too often go underappreciated.

6.4 CRYSTALLIZATION FROM THE MELT

Crystallization from the melt is distinguished by the competitive dynamics between chains or segments of chains at the locus of ordering, and by the slowing down of dynamics due to viscous effects and entanglement. For example, at sufficient supercooling, the peak rate of crystal growth from the melt for several common polymers is on the order of 10^2–10^5 nm/s [80–83], increasing somewhat for low molecular weight chains. This is about one to three orders of magnitude slower than the rates accessible by brute force MD simulations (roughly 10^6 nm/s); thus, under carefully chosen conditions and using modestly coarse-grained models, direct simulation of crystal growth can be possible. Experimental estimates of nucleation rates are less common, and are complicated by size effects and competition between heterogeneous and homogeneous nucleation [80, 82, 84–86], but are invariably many orders of magnitude below those accessible by brute force MD (roughly 10^2/nm^3/s). To overcome this problem, various strategies and approximations have been invoked. The first of these is coarse-graining of the chain representation. Since spatial and temporal scales are coupled, reducing the resolution of the chain model allows access to longer simulation times. This approach comes at the cost of chemical level detail and decreasing accuracy of representation when employed at state points far removed from that at which the "effective potential" was originally developed. A second approach involves simulation of short chains followed by extrapolation of the relevant phenomena observed to longer chains; this approach typically misses important physical behavior, such as entanglements, that are uniquely characteristic of long chains. A third approach employs a preexisting surface or seed, to circumvent the long induction time associated with primary nucleation. Typically, one or more of these simplifying approaches is manifested in the examples that follow.

6.4.1 Lattice Monte Carlo Simulations

Chen and Higgs [87] first approached the problem of crystal growth in the presence of multiple chains, still in dilute solution, using MC simulation with the bond fluctuation model [88]. The bond fluctuation model is a high coordination lattice model that accounts for excluded volume, intersite interactions, and bending stiffness; for purposes of crystallization, the model was further modified to favor energetically the parallel alignment of neighboring bonds from different chains, which helps to stabilize ordered, "crystalline" configurations. The bending stiffness, in particular, was found to be essential in order to observe alignment of chains within the crystal, rather than isotropic aggregation. These simulations are exemplary of the use of the conventional Metropolis algorithm to study kinetics. By restricting the allowed set of transitions in the MC trajectory to local displacements of single sites, the characteristic time τ associated with each move is roughly constant, thereby suggesting a credible mapping of MC steps to real time [37, 88]. The "microrelaxation" MC model [89] may be seen as an evolution of this approach. In this case, the lattice coordination is somewhat less than in the bond fluctuation model, but the interactions terms are essentially the same. In contrast to Chen and Higgs, however, using the microrelaxation model, Hu argues for the parallel packing energy as the primary driving force for formation of an ordered phase [90]. The microrelaxation model is distinguished by the fact that local site displacements are supplemented by nonlocal, sliding moves involving the concerted displacement of some number of beads along the contour of the chain. The sliding move is a form of "generalized reptation," first introduced by Pakula [91, 92]. Because it entails the cooperative motion of several beads, the characteristic time τ associated with the sliding move is expected to be longer than that for single bead moves and dependent on the length of segment that slides; it is instrumental in accelerating the dynamics of the simulation in order to observe polymer crystallization from the melt. The conventional Metropolis algorithm is again used to update the Markov chain; thus, the method is not a dynamic MC algorithm in the sense of Fichthorn and Weinberg [47]. As discussed in Section 6.2, mapping of MC steps to real time is complicated by the introduction of moves with dramatically different characteristic times in the Metropolis algorithm. For sufficiently short physical chains ($N = 16$) and long Markov sampling sequences, Rouse-like scaling is observed with this model. Introduction of a length-dependent friction coefficient to penalize nonlocal sliding moves relative to local bead displacement moves may mitigate the disparity in transition dynamics on shorter times scales in an approximate manner, but a rigorous treatment of the transition kinetics is not yet available. Significantly, varying the friction coefficient alone is sufficient to alter the observed crystal morphology from folded to extended form [93]. Nevertheless, the model has been applied broadly and with some success to a variety of complex polymer systems that have not been otherwise attempted to date. Representative studies include sectorization in a solution-grown single crystal [94], manifestation of the shish–kebab morphology (in dilute solution) [95], the relative stability of liquid–liquid and liquid–solid phase separated states (in solvent-rich systems) [96–98], accelerated recrystallization immediately after melting [99], crystallization under confinement in microphase-separated systems [100–102], and crystallization in thin films [103]. The observations of these works have been interpreted in favor of an "intramolecular" model for nucleation.

6.4.2 Molecular Dynamics Using Coarse-Grained Models

Using the bead-spring model described previously (cf. Section 6.3.2) and a crystal surface to act as the seed, Yamamoto studied the crystal growth of chains of length $N = 100$ from the melt by MD [104–106]. By monitoring trajectories of individual chains during a simulation, he found segregation of beads first into distinct layers, followed by chain sliding motions that reorganize the beads within the layers into crystal-like stems and folds. Figure 6.3 illustrates this process as a function of layer position relative to the crystal. The crystal growth rate was quantified and found to exhibit a maximum as a function of temperature, but to vary considerably from one lamella to another, in accord with recent observations by atomic force microscopy [107]. A tapered growth front with thickening growth behind the front was observed. In contrast to previous entropic arguments for such tapered growth fronts, Yamamoto invoked overcrowding of amorphous loops, which gives rise to tilt of the crystal surface with respect to the crystal stem direction, to explain this observation [106]. The topography of the "fold" surfaces was also characterized; numerous chain loops and folds were observed, with 60–70% connecting first-, second-, or third-nearest neighboring stems in the crystal lattice, substantially in accord with constrained equilibrium MC simulations of the intercrystalline domain of a semicrystalline PE [7, 9]. Radii of gyration of crystallized chains and preordering of chains in the amorphous phase were also investigated. Subsequent attempts to study longer chains of $N = 1000$ beads were complicated by finite size effects. Extension of these studies to melts of helix-forming chains have been limited to short, bare helices, in which chirality selection appears to involve a slow, solid–solid transition from an achiral ordered state [108].

Meyer and coworkers performed conventional MD simulations using a methodically derived coarse-grained model [109] wherein a single bead can be mapped to a monomeric unit of polyvinyl alcohol (PCVA, $-C_2OH_3-$) rather than the single methylene ($-CH_2-$) typical of UA

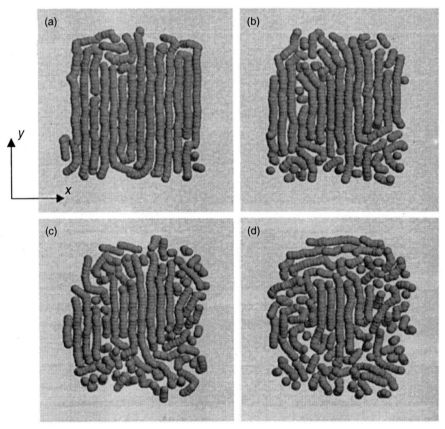

Figure 6.3 Snapshot of UA segments of C100 at 300 K in the (a) first, (b) second, (c) third, and (d) fourth layers in succession, proceeding away from the growth front. This illustrates the in-plane organization of chains close to the crystal surface. Reproduced with permission from Reference [104]. Copyright 2001, American Physical Society.

models [110, 111]. The resulting bending potential exhibits multiple minima, to reflect the several isomeric states of the carbon–carbon bond of the underlying atomistic chain. Like the Yamamoto model, it favors the linear, rod-like chain conformation at low temperatures, but also shows stable configurations with finite bending angles. This model proved sufficient to observe crystallization of chains as long as $N = 100$ directly from the melt, without the benefit of a seed crystal or surface. Chain-folded lamellae were obtained. No attractive ordering interactions were considered, which again supports the idea that chain rigidity is a sufficient, if not necessary, feature of crystallization in polymers. Statistical arguments for ordering of chains in condensed phases driven solely by chain stiffness go as far back as Flory [112]. In this view, crystallization is driven by the combination of an enthalpic tendency toward rod-like conformers at low temperatures, combined with the entropy-driven ordering due to excluded volume interactions in the condensed state. Using a bead-spring model, Miura investigated the effect of rigidity in some detail, and showed that not only does T_m increase with increasing rigidity of the chain, but also the kinetics of crystallization are qualitatively different for semirigid chains versus semiflexible chains, even at the same fractional supercooling. He observed that both local and global order parameters evolve simultaneously for semirigid chains, but that a noticeable waiting time, during which local ordering precedes global ordering, occurs for semiflexible chains [113]. Using mixtures of chains, both the waiting time and the final morphology (global order parameter) were found to be sensitive to the concentration of rigid component. These observations may offer some insight into the relatively high nucleation density and subsequent merging of crystallites observed in simulations of chains with preference for rod-like segments. Using their coarse-grained model, Meyer and coworkers observed hysteresis in the temperature dependence of melting and crystallization behavior. Upon extrapolation of the melting and crystallization lines to the thermodynamic limit of infinite stem length, different temperatures were obtained for these two processes (approximately 580 and 540 K, respectively), consistent with crystallization via an intermediate phase. However, the nature of this intermediate phase remains unclear; different intermediate states have been previously proposed based on experimental evidence [114–116]. Luo and Sommer subsequently used the same coarse-grained model to study crystallization–melting–recrystallization, for the purpose of controlling nucleation through "self-seeding" [117, 118]. During reheating, they observed multiple melting events, giving rise to an Ostwald-like ripening of the most stable crystallite. Then, during the second cooling cycle, they were able to quantify lamellar thickening rates in a single lamellar crystallite.

6.4.3 Molecular Dynamics Using Atomistic Models

Most of the foregoing studies adopt some degree of coarse-graining or intramolecular stiffening within the energy model, both of which have the effect of speeding up crystallization kinetics, at the expense of chemical resolution and detailed treatment of entropy-driven irreversibilities. In a few select instances, however, it is possible to retain greater fidelity of the chemical structure of the hydrocarbon chain and still observe ordering phenomena relevant to polymer crystallization. Using sufficiently short chains (dodecane and smaller), Esselink et al. observed crystallization from the melt in simulations of less than 1-ns duration using a UA model [119]. For chains of length C20 to C100, Waheed et al. introduced seed crystal surfaces and studied the mechanism of crystal growth [120–122]. Propagation of the crystal growth front with time was measured over a range of temperatures, spanning the nucleation- and diffusion-limited regimes. As illustrated by Figure 6.4, the results were found to be qualitatively similar to the experimentally observed behavior for PE at large supercooling [81, 83]. From these observations, Waheed et al. inferred that the growth of chain-extended crystals of short n-alkanes occurs through the relaxation of entire molecules. The growth of chain-folded crystals in PE at large supercooling was then shown to be quantitatively analogous if account is taken for the dynamics of chain segments between entanglements rather than entire molecules. A quantitative, analytical crystal growth rate model encompassing both alkanes and PE was proposed [120, 122], with a molecular weight dependence that is captured by the Rouse time of the relevant chain segment. The growth rate equation is:

$$G(T, N) = G_0 \left(\frac{N_0}{N_1}\right)^{2n} \exp\left[\frac{2.303 n c_1 (T - T_g(N))}{c_2 + (T - T_g(N))}\right]$$
$$\exp\left[-\frac{C}{T} \frac{T_m(N)}{(T_m N) - T}\right]$$

(6.11)

where G_0 is a prefactor for a reference chain of length N_0 at its glass transition, T_m is the equilibrium melting temperature, and C is the ratio of the surface energy to heat of fusion for the crystal nucleus. c_1 and c_2 are the constants of the Williams–Landel–Ferry (WLF) equation [123]. $T_m(N)$ and $T_g(N)$ may be described by the equation of Fox and Loshaek for short alkanes [124]. For chains much shorter than the entanglement length, $N_1 = N$; for longer chains and polymers, $N_1 = N_e$, the

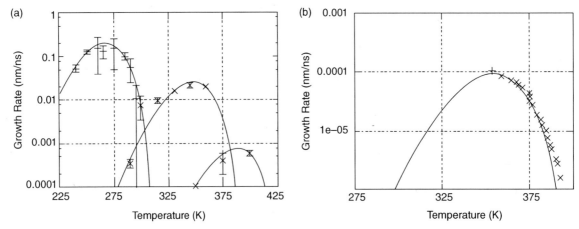

Figure 6.4 Comparison of analytical crystal growth model (solid curves) to simulation data and to experiment, from Waheed and Rutledge [122]. (a) Simulated growth rates of alkanes: C20 (+), C50 (×), C100 (*); (b) Experimental growth rates of polyethylene: Ratajski and Janeschitz-Kriegl [81] (+), Wagner et al. [83, 144] (×). The following parameters were used with Equation (6.11) to generate the solid curves: $\ln(G_0 [m/s]) = -56.9$; $C = 341$ K; $n = 2.04$; $T_m^\infty = 496$ K; $T_g^\infty = 304$ K; $C_m = 5.08 \times 10^3$ K; $C_g = 1.17 \times 10^4$ K. Reproduced with permission from Reference [122]. Copyright 2005, Wiley Interscience.

length of chain between entanglements. For chains of intermediate length comparable to N_e, a crossover behavior not captured by Equation (6.11) should probably be expected. Detailed observations of the forward and reverse propagation of the growth front suggested that crystal growth is best understood as the net result of a dynamic balance between rapid segmental attachment and detachment processes, in accord with entropic barrier models. The formation of an ordered domain comprising 4–5 segments of ~20 carbons each, similar to the observations of Meyer and of Yamamoto, is an important step in stabilizing crystalline order in successive layers.

Gee and Fried [125] observed homogeneous nucleation from the melt using MD of 120-mer chains with a chemically realistic all-atom model of poly(vinylidene fluoride) (PVDF). The crystallization phenomenon and final crystal polymorph were shown to be dependent on the handling of electrostatic interactions. Compared with PE, PVDF is a relatively stiff chain, which probably accounts in part for the enhancement of nucleation rate into the range accessible by simulation. A three-stage nucleation process was proposed, involving first the formation of extended trans conformers, followed by the rate limiting step of clustering of these conformers into aggregates, followed lastly by extension of the stems in the cluster to obtain a final thickness of 25–30 carbons. Massively parallel computation and chains up to C768 with either polar (PVDF) or nonpolar (a "stiffened" UA model for PE with characteristic ratio $C_\infty = 10.7$ at 500 K) potential models were used to follow the ordering stages from the melt in subsequent studies [126, 127]. The prolific formation of independently oriented, block-like smectic clusters as large as 10 nm and the high mobility of chains within such clusters were taken as evidence in support of a prenucleation liquid–liquid demixing phenomenon and progression through an intermediate, nematic or smectic state prior to crystallization. As shown in Figure 6.5, the clusters resemble fringed micelles and are too numerous and mis-oriented to be suggestive of the experimentally observed lamellar morpohology. Subsequent progression from the misaligned, polydomain structure to the familiar lamellar crystalline form, however, was not observed on the time scale of simulation.

6.5 CRYSTALLIZATION UNDER DEFORMATION OR FLOW

While crystallization of polymers in the absence of deformation is conceptually simpler, most polymers in industrial practice are solidified under the influence of deformational flow fields. The consequences of such fields are far from trivial, giving rise to strikingly different crystal sizes, orientations, and semicrystalline morphology; these effects are dealt with in greater detail in Chapter 14 and Chapter 15. The shish–kebab morphology observed during crystallization of PE in uniaxial flow is one such well-known distinction. Another is the amplification of nucleation density, by as much as five orders of magnitude for a modest input of work of

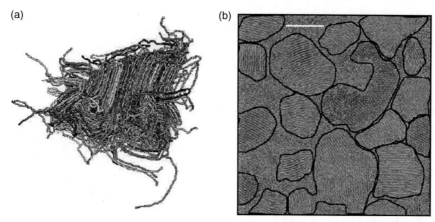

Figure 6.5 (a) A single ordered domain of PVDF shows a fringed-micelle-like morphology for the polar polymer model (similar results are seen for polyethylene). The small portion of the entire polymer ensemble shows both regularly packed and randomly dispersed amorphous regions. The polymer chains show sharp regular folds, long loops, short loops, and cilia. Individual polymers are colored to illustrate polymer chains entering the amorphous region from an ordered region and adjoining two separate adjacent ordered domains (adjacent domains are not shown). (b) A representative ensemble of ordered domains at 600 K showing evidence of the granular morphology of misaligned, block-like clusters. Reproduced with permission from Reference [126]. Copyright 2006, Nature Publishing Group. (See color insert.)

deformation [128]. From the point of view of MD simulation, this amplification is advantageous in that it greatly increases the probability of observing a nucleation event in a conventional MD simulation; however, it brings with it new complications in generating a representative configuration of the polymer as a function of deformation work. In dilute solution, these complications are minor due to the rapid re-equilibration of chains at each stage of deformation. In the melt, however, the deformation rate is more likely to overlap in time scale with important relaxation processes of the system, so that the rate and history of deformation need to be considered carefully.

Crystallization from dilute solution in an elongational flow field has been studied by Langevin dynamics [129]. Chains were observed to undergo a reversible coil-stretch transition at an extension rate that is both temperature- and chain length-dependent. For chains of a given length, shish–kebab-like objects were observed to form at extension rates comparable to those that give rise to coexisting coils and stretched chains; extended chains formed the shish and coiled ones tended to crystallize in the chain-folded configuration (kebabs). Similarly, in studies of bidisperse mixtures undergoing extensional flow, the longer chains were found to extend above a particular elongational flow field while the shorter ones remained coiled; again, extended chain and chain-folded structures were observed to form and subsequently become attached. Some nucleation of the shorter chain crystallites onto the extended chain shish was also observed. This type of simulation is complicated by the number and proximity of chains with respect to the stagnation point of the imposed elongational flow.

Crystallization from an oriented melt, such as would be expected to arise during melt extrusion, has been studied using MD, with chains that are well above the entanglement length. Orientation prior to crystallization was first achieved by imposing a uniaxial deformation, either above T_m [62, 130], typical of a fiber-spinning, or below T_g [131, 132], as might be expected for solid-state drawing followed by annealing and cold crystallization. In contrast to studies of crystallization in amorphous melts, shorter chains are generally detrimental to the study of crystallization from oriented melts. This is because a Weissenberg number (defined as the product of longest relaxation time of the chain and the rate of strain of the system undergoing deformation) on the order of or greater than unity is required to create a state of substantial deformation-induced orientation on the MD time scale. The use of such deformation to induce precrystallization orientation was explored in some depth by Lavine et al. [62] Energy densities on the order of 500–1000 J/cm^3 of irreversible work were employed to generate oriented melts prior to crystallization. By contrast, a recent MC method [133] has shown that comparable levels of orientation can be achieved in a computer simulation with reversible work on the order of 10 J/cm^3, similar to that employed experimentally [128]. This initial state of precrystallization orientation is instrumental in reducing the entropy of the melt state and thereby lowering the free energy barrier to primary homogeneous nucleation. As a consequence, these studies were able to use fairly realistic UA models for PE well above the entanglement molecular weight. The results of the melt quench studies are representative [62, 130]. Systems isothermally crystallized below 325 K were observed to form numerous small, ordered clusters indicative of prolific nucleation, but such clusters did not grow with time. Systems isothermally crystallized above 325 K were observed to form one to three well-defined lamellae with lamellar normals aligned along the flow direction and spanning the simulation cell lateral to the flow direction. The chain stems within these lamellae were tilted with respect to the lamellar normals in a manner consistent with a (201)-oriented crystal–amorphous interface; this chain tilt was argued to be a consequence of crystallographic relaxation processes driven by a lowering of the interfacial energy [7, 130]. The lamellar thicknesses were again found to be inversely proportional to the degree of supercooling. The temperature-dependent morphologies were interpreted in terms of a competition between nucleation and growth processes, which are enhanced by increased molecular orientation, and molecular relaxation, which is accelerated at higher temperatures.

The sensitivity of crystallization behavior to shear rate and total shear strain during a precrystallization steady state NEMD simulation was reported by Jabbarzadeh and Tanner for C162, using the SLLOD equations of motion and Lees-Edwards sliding brick boundary conditions [134]. The system was initially sheared at 393 K, then quenched to 350 K to observe crystallization. For shear rates between 10^8 and 10^{10} s^{-1}, little sensitivity of the crystallization rate was observed; total evolved crystallinity, however, was found to exhibit a maximum at a shear rate corresponding to a Weissenberg number close to unity. Both crystallization rate and total evolved crystallinity were observed to be strong functions of total shear strain, with a critical shear strain of 2–3 being necessary to observe significant enhancements in both quantities.

A novel approach to flow- or deformation-induced crystallization entails the use of MC methods that have been developed to generate nonequilibrium ensembles of polymer melts that are characterized by some degree of anisotropy [133, 135, 136]. Recently, Baig and Edwards employed one of these methods to study crystallization of a UA model of C78 over a range of temperatures from 300 to 450 K, using a uniaxial flow field tensor whose values were estimated to mimic the behavior of the melt under flow conditions with Weissenberg numbers between 0.1 and 200 [137]. Although the kinetics of crystallization are not immediately accessible by this approach, it nevertheless demonstrates that crystallization occurs more readily in such nonequilibrium ensembles as the magnitude of the anisotropy is increased. Below the thermodynamic melting point, the resulting crystals are long-lived. Baig and Edwards go on to show that the so-called configurational temperature is depressed by at least 4–5 degrees in those simulations that crystallize, reminiscent of an effectively greater degree of supercooling.

6.6 CONCLUDING REMARKS

It is apparent that molecular simulations have made significant progress in the study of crystallization of polymers in the past decade. In some sense, it is remarkable that a process as complex and cooperative in nature as the spontaneous organization of chain molecules from an amorphous solution or melt can be studied in such detail with currently available computational resources. Molecular simulations are unparalleled in their ability to test hypotheses, for which purpose experimental methods are too often insufficiently discriminating, and to reveal mechanistic insights with molecular-level resolution. Nevertheless, the application of these modeling tools to the broad field of polymer crystallization is still in its infancy, and it may be premature to draw sweeping conclusions from the study of a few model systems in which crystallization is most readily observed. Much of what has been learned to date has been the result of a gradual progression from fictitious, coarse-grained models of chain-like species to increasingly refined, chemically realistic molecular models. It is not always clear in each case whether the ordered phase formed is actually a solid crystal phase or a liquid crystal phase; the distinction has potentially important ramifications for testing current hypotheses regarding the progression of crystal formation through one or more intermediate phases. The studies reported to date suggest that crystallization of polymers is greatly facilitated by molecular rigidity, which gives rise to a high density of crystallizable chain segments, and by longitudinal mobility of the chain along its contour, which permits the rapid elimination of "mistakes" during formation of a new, ordered phase. Intermolecular packing forces that similarly promote the formation of crystallizable chain segments can be equally effective in promoting ordering. These effects are consistent with entropic barrier models for crystal nucleation and growth, and many simulations have indeed been interpreted as presenting evidence in favor of the entropic, rather than enthalpic, barrier models. However, it remains to be seen whether such conclusions are universal or extensible to slower crystallizing species. The inverse dependence of crystallite thickness on extent of supercooling is also frequently presented as evidence for a common crystallization mechanism in solutions and melts. Indeed, simulations are fairly consistent in their ability to reproduce such a trend, at least qualitatively. However, free energy analyses of smectic droplets in solution phase simulations suggest that the origin of this behavior may be thermodynamic in nature, entirely different from the kinetic origin associated with similarly ordered domains in the melt. Detailed examination of the topology of the ordered phases formed from solutions and melts also reveal qualitative differences between these two cases. Thus, similarities in form at the macroscopic or aggregate scale do not necessarily confer similar coincidences in mechanism or organization at the molecular level.

To facilitate the observation of ordering and crystallization in modeling, most simulations to date have been performed at substantial supercooling. This may be appropriate to industrial processing conditions, but most carefully controlled crystallization experiments have been conducted at fairly modest supercooling, to facilitate measurement. This situation is changing on the experimental front, where efforts are being made to measure crystallization accurately at increasingly large supercooling [138]. This notwithstanding, unless simulation and experimental observations are drawn at comparable temperatures for comparable systems, the different temperature dependences of competing processes, for example, intra- versus intermolecular reorganization, adsorption versus ordering at a surface, and nucleation versus growth, serve as a reminder that caution should be exercised in extrapolating from one to the other. The fine scale of morphology observed in simulations, for example, References [126, 139, 140], remains to be reconciled with the large lateral dimensions of lamellae and the much larger scale of organization into spherulites, observed experimentally.

Development of methodology has been and will continue to be crucial to tackling problems in crystallization. For rare event processes, multiple time scale and accelerated dynamics methods have been developed for simple systems, but remain to be applied in any concerted fashion to chain-like molecules. Similarly, transition path sampling algorithms have progressed significantly in the study of chemical kinetics and in crystallization of small molecules, but remains unexplored in the realm of polymer crystallization. Recent studies of short alkanes using both umbrella sampling MC, for transition path sampling, and mean first passage time analysis of MD trajectories, offers the best examples to date of the application of these methods to chain-like molecules [141, 142]. Simulations of flow-induced crystallization performed to date have tended to be of the class of nonsteady-state dynamics, wherein the kinetics are monitored as a system relaxes from a state of disequilibrium to one of local (or global) equilibrium. Such simulations are inherently limited by the magnitude and disparity of intrinsic relaxation time scales. However, methods now exist to perform steady-state NEMD simulations for systems undergoing shear or planar elongational flows, by which crystallization of polymers in flow can in principle be studied for arbitrarily long periods. As of this writing, results of such simulations for long chains are few, but the precrystallization shear simulation of [134] and a preliminary study of n-eicosane by Ionescu et al. [143] are indicative of this approach.

In the future, refinement of our understanding of crystallization in polymers will likely come through consideration of more realistic, more flexible, and conformationally more interesting chain models. Nonlinear chain topology and the impact of entanglements on crystallization rate and mechanisms remain areas that are largely unexplored by simulation. With a shift from reliance on broad questions of "universal" behavior to increasingly specific and quantitative studies will come increasingly meaningful and discriminating tests against experimental data, quantitative predictions of process–structure–property relationships, and the prospect for computational engineering and design of polymeric materials accounting for crystallization behavior.

REFERENCES

[1] Boyd, R.H. Prediction of polymer crystal-structures and properties. In *Advances in Polymer Science*, Vol. 116, L. Monnerie, U.W. Suter, eds. Springer-Verlag, Berlin, 1994, pp. 1–25.

[2] Rutledge, G.C. Modeling polymer crystals. In *Simulation Methods for Polymers*, Kotelyanskii, M., Theodorou, D.N., eds. Marcel Dekker, New York, 2004.

[3] Tadokoro, H. *Structure of Crystalline Polymers*. Wiley and Sons, New York, 1979.

[4] Tashiro, K. *Progress in Polymer Science* **1993**, *18*(3), 377–435.

[5] Kobayashi, M. *Journal of Chemical Physics* **1979**, *70*(1), 509–518.

[6] Balijepalli, S., Rutledge, G.C. *Journal of Chemical Physics* **1998**, *109*(16), 6523–6526.

[7] Gautam, S., Balijepalli, S., Rutledge, G.C. *Macromolecules* **2000**, *33*(24), 9136–9145.

[8] Hutter, M., in 't Veld, P.J., Rutledge, G.C. *Polymer* **2006**, *47*(15), 5494–5504.

[9] In't Veld, P.J., Hutter, M., Rutledge, G.C. *Macromolecules* **2006**, *39*(1), 439–447.

[10] Kuppa, V.K., in 't Veld, P.J., Rutledge, G.C. *Macromolecules* **2008**, *41*(5), 1896–1896.

[11] Kuppa, V.K., in't Veld, P.J., Rutledge, G.C. *Macromolecules* **2007**, *40*(14), 5187–5195.

[12] Rutledge, G.C. *Journal of Macromolecular Science-Physics* **2002**, *B41*(4–6), 909–922.

[13] Lee, S., Rutledge, G.C. *Macromolecules* **2011**, *44*(8), 3096–3108.

[14] Sumpter, B.G., Noid, D.W., Liang, G.L., Wunderlich, B. Atomistic dynamics of macromolecular crystals. In *Advances in Polymer Science*, Vol. 116, L. Monnerie, UW. Suter, eds., Springer-Verlag, Berlin, 1994, pp. 27–72.

[15] Sadler, D.M., Gilmer, G.H. *Polymer* **1984**, *25*(10), 1446–1452.

[16] Rigby, D., Roe, R.J. *Journal of Chemical Physics* **1988**, *89*(8), 5280–5290.

[17] Hu, W.B. Intramolecular crystal nucleation. In *Lecture Notes in Physics*, Vol. 714, G. Reiter, G.R. Strobl, eds. Springer, Berlin, 2007, pp. 47–64.

[18] Hu, W.B., Frenkel, D. Polymer crystallization driven by anisotropic interactions. In *Advances in Polymer Science*, Vol. 191, G. Allegra, ed., Springer, Berlin, 2005, pp. 1–35.

[19] Muthukumar, M. Modeling polymer crystallization. In *Advances in Polymer Science*, Vol. 191, G. Allegra, ed., Springer, Berlin, 2005, pp. 241–274.

[20] Muthukumar, M. Shifting paradigms in polymer crystallization. In *Progress in Understanding of Polymer Crystallization*, Vol. 714, Reiter, G., Strobl, G.R., eds. Springer, Berlin and Heidelberg, 2007, pp. 1–18.

[21] Waheed, N., Ko, M.J., Rutledge, G.C. Atomistic simulation of polymer melt crystallization by molecular dynamics. In *Progress in Understanding of Polymer Crystallization*, Vol. 714, Reiter, G., Strobl, G.R., eds. Springer, Berlin and Heidelberg, 2007, pp. 457–480.

[22] Yamamoto, T. Molecular dynamics modeling of the crystal-melt interfaces and the growth of chain folded lamellae. In *Advances in Polymer Science*, Vol. 191, G. Allegra, ed., Springer, Berlin, 2005, pp. 37–85.

[23] Yamamoto, T. *Polymer* **2009**, *50*(9), 1975–1985.

[24] Allen, M.P., Tildesley, D.J. *Computer Simulation of Liquids*. Clarendon Press, Oxford, 1987.

[25] Frenkel, D., Smit, B. *Understanding Molecular Simulation: From Algorithms to Applications*, 2nd ed. Academic Press, San Diego, 2002.

[26] Kotelyanskii, M., Theodorou, D.N. *Simulation Methods for Polymers*. Marcel Dekker, New York, 2004.

[27] Alder, B.J., Wainwright, T.E. *Journal of Chemical Physics* **1957**, *27*(5), 1208–1209.

[28] Verlet, L. *Physical Review* **1967**, *159*(1), 98–103.

[29] Berendsen, H.J.C., Vanderspoel, D., Vandrunen, R. *Computer Physics Communications* **1995**, *91*(1–3), 43–56.

[30] Case, D.A., Cheatham, T.E., Darden, T., Gohlke, H., Luo, R., Merz, K.M., Onufriev, A., Simmerling, C., Wang, B., Woods, R.J. *Journal of Computational Chemistry* **2005**, *26*(16), 1668–1688.

[31] Plimpton, S. *Journal of Computational Physics* **1995**, *117*(1), 1–19.

[32] Smith, W., Yong, C.W., Rodger, P.M. *Molecular Simulation* **2002**, *28*(5), 385–471.

[33] Chen, C.X., Depa, P., Maranas, J.K., Sakai, V.G. *Journal of Chemical Physics* **2008**, *128*(12), 12.

[34] Ottinger, H.C. *MRS Bulletin* **2007**, *32*(11), 936–940.

[35] Kang, H.C., Weinberg, W.H. *Journal of Chemical Physics* **1989**, *90*(5), 2824–2830.

[36] Metropolis, N., Rosenbluth, A.W., Rosenbluth, M.N., Teller, A.H., Teller, E. *Journal of Chemical Physics* **1953**, *21*(6), 1087–1092.

[37] Kremer, K., Binder, K., *Computer Physics Reports* **1988**, *7*(6), 259–310.

[38] Paul, W., Binder, K., Heermann, D.W., Kremer, K. *Journal of Chemical Physics* **1991**, *95*(10), 7726–7740.

[39] Depablo, J.J., Laso, M., Siepmann, J.I., Suter, U.W. *Molecular Physics* **1993**, *80*(1), 55–63.

[40] Depablo, J.J., Laso, M., Suter, U.W., Cochran, H.D. *Fluid Phase Equilibria* **1993**, *83*, 323–331.

[41] Escobedo, F.A., Depablo, J.J. *Journal of Chemical Physics* **1995**, *102*(6), 2636–2652.

[42] Karayiannis, N.C., Mavrantzas, V.G., Theodorou, D.N. *Physical Review Letters* **2002**, *88*, 105503.

[43] Pant, P.V.K., Theodorou, D.N. *Macromolecules* **1995**, *28*(21), 7224–7234.

[44] Bortz, A.B., Kalos, M.H., Lebowitz, J.L. *Journal of Computational Physics* **1975**, *17*(1), 10–18.

[45] Gillespie, D.T. *Journal of Computational Physics* **1976**, *22*(4), 403–434.

[46] Gillespie, D.T. *Journal of Physical Chemistry* **1977**, *81*(25), 2340–2361.

[47] Fichthorn, K.A., Weinberg, W.H. *Journal of Chemical Physics* **1991**, *95*(2), 1090–1096.

[48] Battaile, C.C., Srolovitz, D.J. *Annual Review of Materials Research* **2002**, *32*, 297–319.

[49] Voter, A.F., Montalenti, F., Germann, T.C. *Annual Review of Materials Research* **2002**, *32*, 321–346.

[50] Hoffman, J.D., Miller, R.L. *Polymer* **1997**, *38*(13), 3151–3212.

[51] Lauritzen, J.J., Hoffman, J.D. *Journal of Research of the National Bureau of Standards* **1960**, *64A*, 73.

[52] Spinner, M.A., Watkins, R.W., Goldbeckwood, G. *Journal of the Chemical Society-Faraday Transactions* **1995**, *91*(16), 2587–2592.

[53] Goldbeckwood, G. *Polymer* **1990**, *31*(4), 586–592.

[54] Goldbeckwood, G. *Polymer* **1992**, *33*(4), 778–782.

[55] Goldbeckwood, G. *Journal of Polymer Science Part B-Polymer Physics* **1993**, *31*(1), 61–67.

[56] Doye, J.P.K., Frenkel, D. *Journal of Chemical Physics* **1998**, *109*(22), 10033–10041.

[57] Doye, J.P.K., Frenkel, D. *Journal of Chemical Physics* **1999**, *110*(14), 7073–7086.

[58] Doye, J.P.K., Frenkel, D. *Polymer* **2000**, *41*(4), 1519–1528.

[59] Doye, J.P.K. *Polymer* **2000**, *41*(25), 8857–8867.

[60] Kavassalis, T.A., Sundararajan, P.R. *Macromolecules* **1993**, *26*(16), 4144–4150.

[61] Mayo, S.L., Olafson, B.D., Goddard, W.A. *Journal of Physical Chemistry* **1990**, *94*(26), 8897–8909.

[62] Lavine, M.S., Waheed, N., Rutledge, G.C. *Polymer* **2003**, *44*(5), 1771–1779.

[63] Sundararajan, P.R., Kavassalis, T.A. *Journal of the Chemical Society-Faraday Transactions* **1995**, *91*(16), 2541–2549.

[64] Fujiwara, S., Sato, T. *Journal of Chemical Physics* **1997**, *107*(2), 613–622.

[65] Iwata, M., Sato, H. *Physical Chemistry Chemical Physics* **1999**, *1*(10), 2491–2500.

[66] Liao, Q., Jin, X.G. *Journal of Chemical Physics* **1999**, *110*(17), 8835–8841.

[67] Guo, H.X., Yang, X.Z., Li, T. *Physical Review E* **2000**, *61*(4), 4185–4193.

[68] Zhang, X.B., Li, Z.S., Lu, Z.Y., Sun, C.C. *Journal of Chemical Physics* **2001**, *115*(8), 3916–3922.

[69] Choi, P., Blom, H.P., Kavassalis, T.A., Rudin, A. *Macromolecules* **1995**, *28*(24), 8247–8250.

[70] Yamamoto, T. *Journal of Chemical Physics* **1997**, *107*(7), 2653–2663.

[71] Yamamoto, T. *Journal of Chemical Physics* **1998**, *109*(11), 4638–4645.

[72] Yamamoto, T., Sawada, K. *Journal of Chemical Physics* **2005**, *123*(23).

[73] Yamamoto, T., Orimi, N., Urakami, N., Sawada, K. *Faraday Discussions* **2005**, *128*, 75–86.

[74] Liu, C., Muthukumar, M. *Journal of Chemical Physics* **1998**, *109*(6), 2536–2542.

[75] Muthukumar, M., Welch, P. *Polymer* **2000**, *41*(25), 8833–8837.

[76] Welch, P., Muthukumar, M. *Physical Review Letters* **2001**, *87*(21), 218302.

[77] Muthukumar, M. *Philosophical Transactions of the Royal Society A: Physical, Mathematical and Engineering Sciences* **2003**, *361*(1804), 539–554.

[78] Hu, W.B., Frenkel, D., Mathot, V.B.F. *Macromolecules* **2003**, *36*(21), 8178–8183.

[79] Sommer, J.U. Theoretical aspects of the equilibrium state of chain crystals. In *Progress in Understanding of Polymer Crystallization*, Vol. 714, Reiter, G., Strobl, G.R., eds. Springer, Berlin and Heidelberg, 2007, pp. 19–46.

[80] Mamun, A., Umemoto, S., Ishihara, N., Okui, N. *Polymer* **2006**, *47*(15), 5531–5537.

[81] Ratajski, E., Janeschitz-Kriegl, H. *Colloid and Polymer Science* **1996**, *274*(10), 938–951.

[82] Umemoto, S., Hayashi, R., Kawano, R., Kikutani, T., Okui, N. *Journal of Macromolecular Science-Physics* **2003**, *B42*(3–4), 421–430.

[83] Wagner, J., Phillips, P.J. *Polymer* **2001**, *42*(21), 8999–9013.

[84] Barham, P.J. *Journal of Materials Science* **2000**, *35*(20), 5139–5145.

[85] Loo, Y.L., Register, R.A., Ryan, A.J. *Physical Review Letters* **2000**, *84*(18), 4120–4123.

[86] Janeschitz-Kriegl, H., Ratajski, E., Wippel, H. *Colloid and Polymer Science* **1999**, *277*(2–3), 217–226.

[87] Chen, C.M., Higgs, P.G. *Journal of Chemical Physics* **1998**, *108*(10), 4305–4314.

[88] Carmesin, I., Kremer, K. *Macromolecules* **1988**, *21*(9), 2819–2823.

[89] Hu, W.B. *Journal of Chemical Physics* **1998**, *109*(9), 3686–3690.

[90] Hu, W.B. *Journal of Chemical Physics* **2000**, *113*(9), 3901–3908.

[91] Pakula, T. *Macromolecules* **1987**, *20*(3), 679–682.

[92] Nelson, P.H., Hatton, T.A., Rutledge, G.C. *Journal of Chemical Physics* **1997**, *107*(4), 1269–1278.

[93] Hu, W.B. *Journal of Chemical Physics* **2001**, *115*(9), 4395–4401.

[94] Hu, W.B., Frenkel, D., Mathot, V.B.F. *Macromolecules* **2003**, *36*(3), 549–552.

[95] Hu, W.B., Frenkel, D., Mathot, V.B.F. *Macromolecules* **2002**, *35*(19), 7172–7174.

[96] Hu, W.B., Frenkel, D. *Macromolecules* **2004**, *37*(12), 4336–4338.

[97] Hu, W.B., Frenkel, D., Mathot, V.B.F. *Journal of Chemical Physics* **2003**, *118*(22), 10343–10348.

[98] Zha, L.Y., Hu, W.B. *Journal of Physical Chemistry B* **2007**, *111*(39), 11373–11378.

[99] Wang, M.X., Hu, W.B., Ma, Y., Ma, Y.Q. *Macromolecules* **2005**, *38*(7), 2806–2812.

[100] Qian, Y., Cai, T., Hu, W.B. *Macromolecules* **2008**, *41*(20), 7625–7629.

[101] Wang, M.X., Hu, W.B., Ma, Y., Ma, Y.Q. *Journal of Chemical Physics* **2006**, *124*(24), 244901.

[102] Hu, W.B. *Macromolecules* **2005**, *38*(9), 3977–3983.

[103] Ma, Y., Hu, W.B., Reiter, G. *Macromolecules* **2006**, *39*(15), 5159–5164.

[104] Yamamoto, T. *Journal of Chemical Physics* **2001**, *115*(18), 8675–8680.

[105] Yamamoto, T. *Journal of Macromolecular Science-Physics* **2003**, *42*(3–4), 629–640.

[106] Yamamoto, T. *Polymer* **2004**, *45*(4), 1357–1364.

[107] Hobbs, J.K., Miles, M.J. *Macromolecules* **2001**, *34*(3), 353–355.

[108] Yamamoto, T. *Journal of Chemical Physics* **2006**, *125*(6), 064902.

[109] Reith, D., Meyer, H., Muller-Plathe, F. *Macromolecules* **2001**, *34*(7), 2335–2345.

[110] Meyer, H., Muller-Plathe, F. *Journal of Chemical Physics* **2001**, *115*(17), 7807–7810.

[111] Meyer, H., Muller-Plathe, F. *Macromolecules* **2002**, *35*(4), 1241–1252.

[112] Flory, P.J. *Proceedings of the Royal Society of London A* **1956**, *1196*, 60–73.

[113] Miura, T., Kishi, R., Mikami, M., Tanabe, Y. *Physical Review E* **2001**, *63*(6), 061807.

[114] Keller, A., Goldbeckwood, G., Hikosaka, M. *Faraday Discussions* **1993**, *95*, 109–128.

[115] Strobl, G. *European Physical Journal E* **2000**, *3*(2), 165–183.

[116] Olmsted, P.D., Poon, W.C.K., McLeish, T.C.B., Terrrill, N.J., Ryan, A.J. *Physical Review Letters* **1998**, *81*(2), 373–376.

[117] Luo, C.F., Sommer, J.U. *Macromolecules* **2011**, *44*(6), 1523–1529.

[118] Sommer, J.U., Luo, C.F. *Journal of Polymer Science Part B-Polymer Physics* **2010**, *48*(21), 2222–2232.

[119] Esselink, K., Hilbers, P.A.J., Vanbeest, B.W.H. *Journal of Chemical Physics* **1994**, *101*(10), 9033–9041.

[120] Waheed, N., Ko, M.J., Rutledge, G.C. *Polymer* **2005**, *46*(20), 8689–8702.

[121] Waheed, N., Lavine, M.S., Rutledge, G.C. *Journal of Chemical Physics* **2002**, *116*(5), 2301–2309.

[122] Waheed, N., Rutledge, G.C. *Journal of Polymer Science Part B-Polymer Physics* **2005**, *43*(18), 2468–2473.

[123] Williams, M.L., Landel, R.F., Ferry, J.D. *Journal of the American Chemical Society* **1955**, *77*(14), 3701–3707.

[124] Fox, T.G., Loshaek, S. *Journal of Polymer Science* **1955**, *15*, 371–390.

[125] Gee, R.H., Fried, L.E. *Journal of Chemical Physics* **2003**, *118*(8), 3827–3834.

[126] Gee, R.H., Lacevic, N., Fried, L.E. *Nature Materials* **2006**, *5*(1), 39–43.

[127] Lacevic, N., Fried, L.E., Gee, R.H. *Journal of Chemical Physics* **2008**, *128*(1), 014903.

[128] Janeschitz-Kriegl, H., Ratajski, E., Stadlbauer, M. *Rheologica Acta* **2003**, *42*(4), 355–364.

[129] Dukovski, I., Muthukumar, M. *Journal of Chemical Physics* **2003**, *118*(14), 6648–6655.

[130] Ko, M.J., Waheed, N., Lavine, M.S., Rutledge, G.C. *Journal of Chemical Physics* **2004**, *121*(6), 2823–2832.

[131] Koyama, A., Yamamoto, T., Fukao, K., Miyamoto, Y. *Physical Review E* **2002**, *65*(5), 050801.

[132] Koyama, A., Yamamoto, T., Fukao, K., Miyamoto, Y. *Journal of Macromolecular Science-Physics* **2003**, *B42*(3–4), 821–831.

[133] Bernardin, F.E., Rutledge, G.C. *Macromolecules* **2007**, *40*(13), 4691–4702.

[134] Jabbarzadeh, A., Tanner, R.I. *Macromolecules* **2010**, *43*(19), 8136–8142.

[135] Mavrantzas, V.G., Oettinger, H.C. *Macromolecules* **2002**, *35*, 960–975.

[136] Mavrantzas, V.G., Theodorou, D.N. *Macromolecules* **1998**, *31*, 6310–6332.

[137] Baig, C., Edwards, B.J. *Journal of Non-Newtonian Fluid Mechanics* **2010**, *165*(17–18), 992–1004.

[138] Patki, R.P., Phillips, P.J. *European Polymer Journal* **2008**, *44*(2), 534–541.

[139] Takeuchi, H. *Journal of Chemical Physics* **1998**, *109*(13), 5614–5621.

[140] Meyer, H., Baschnagel, J. *European Physical Journal E* **2003**, *12*(1), 147–151.

[141] Yi, P., Rutledge, G.C. *Journal of Chemical Physics* **2009**, *131*, 134902.

[142] Yi, P., Rutledge, G.C. *Journal of Chemical Physics* **2011**, *135*, 024903.

[143] Ionescu, T.C., Baig, C., Edwards, B.J., Keffer, D.J., Habenschuss, A. *Physical Review Letters* **2006**, *96*(3), 037802.

[144] McCoy, J.D., Honnell, K.G., Schweizer, K.S., Curro, J.G. *Journal of Chemical Physics* **1991**, *95*(12), 9348–9366.

7

OVERALL CRYSTALLIZATION KINETICS

Ewa Piorkowska and Andrzej Galeski
Centre of Molecular and Macromolecular Studies, Polish Academy of Sciences, Lodz, Poland

7.1 Introduction, 215
7.2 Measurements, 216
7.3 Simulation, 217
7.4 Theories: Isothermal and Nonisothermal Crystallization, 218
  7.4.1 Introductory Remarks, 218
  7.4.2 Extended Volume Approach, 218
  7.4.3 Probabilistic Approach, 220
  7.4.4 Isokinetic Model, 223
  7.4.5 Rate Equations, 223
7.5 Complex Crystallization Conditions: General Models, 224
7.6 Factors Influencing the Overall Crystallization Kinetics, 224
  7.6.1 Crystallization in a Uniform Temperature Field, 224
  7.6.2 Crystallization in a Temperature Gradient, 225
  7.6.3 Crystallization in a Confined Space, 226
  7.6.4 Flow-induced Crystallization, 228
7.7 Analysis of Crystallization Data, 230
  7.7.1 Isothermal Crystallization, 230
  7.7.2 Nonisothermal Crystallization, 231
7.8 Conclusions, 233
References, 234

7.1 INTRODUCTION

In contrast to majority of low molecular weight substances, polymers are semicrystalline with a significant fraction of the amorphous phase remaining between crystals. Depending on the crystallization conditions and thermomechanical history, polymers crystallize in different forms including single crystals, polycrystalline aggregates, and highly oriented structures.

Primary nuclei, forming when thermal fluctuations overcome a free energy barrier, appear randomly in space and in time, at a rate fluctuating around the momentary mean value, dictated for a given polymer by its thermomechanical history and crystallization conditions. Quiescent crystallization of homopolymers from the melt occurs usually in the form of spherulites growing radially from primary nuclei, as illustrated by Figure 7.1, which shows consecutive stages of spherulitic crystallization at a constant temperature. Impingement of spherulites hinders the growth and leads to the formation of a complex pattern of interspherulitic boundaries. Both the spherulitic pattern and the conversion of melt into spherulites are dominated by the nucleation and growth rate of spherulites. Strong nucleation caused by contact of a polymer with foreign surfaces, filler grains, or fibers leads to transcrystallinity. Flow-induced crystallization leads to morphologies that are strongly related to temperature, applied shear (or elongation) rate, and total strain. Depending on the conditions, different structures are encountered, varying from spherulites to row-nucleated and shish-kebab morphologies. Relationships between influencing factors and crystallization as well as resulting morphologies are reviewed in Chapter 3, Chapter 4, Chapter 5, and Chapter 14.

Handbook of Polymer Crystallization, First Edition. Edited by Ewa Piorkowska and Gregory C. Rutledge.
© 2013 John Wiley & Sons, Inc. Published 2013 by John Wiley & Sons, Inc.

Figure 7.1 Polarized light micrographs of isothermal spherulitic crystallization in iPP thin film at 136°C: (a–d) consecutive stages of crystallization.

Irrespective of structures encountered, the overall crystallization kinetics is characterized by a degree of conversion and a conversion rate.

The conversion of polymer melt into growing entities is described by the conversion degree, which is a ratio of transformed volume or mass to the entire volume or mass of a crystallizing polymer portion, whereas the conversion rate is an increment of the conversion degree in an infinitely small time interval. The theories of overall crystallization kinetics are being applied in numerous papers to analyze the crystallization, especially the nucleation. Those theories are also widely used for predictions of the overall crystallization kinetics during processing, which is very important from the practical point of view.

The first attempts to describe the conversion degree of melt into growing domains concerned the radial growth from nuclei distributed randomly in a material [1–6]. In spite of different reasoning, they led to the equation, best known as the Avrami–Evans equation, which is widely used to analyze the isothermal spherulitic crystallization, which is the crystallization at constant temperature.

However, especially during polymer processing, crystallization occurs in more complex conditions that include a change of temperature with time, temperature gradients, and melt flow. Moreover, limiting surfaces, fillers, and so on also influence the overall conversion rate. Later development of the theory, therefore, focused on the nonisothermal crystallization [7–9], crystallization in a temperature gradient [10, 11] and crystallization in a confined volume [12–18]. Currently, flow-induced crystallization is a subject of intense investigation. To account for the effect of flow on the overall crystallization kinetics, the known theories had to be significantly modified because of a flow-induced change from isotropic spherulites to highly oriented structures [19–21]. However, in many cases complexity of conditions and emerging structures cannot be accounted for properly by analytical models developed so far, and deserves application of computer modeling and/or simplifying assumptions.

In this chapter, we will briefly describe experimental measurements and computer modeling of the overall crystallization kinetics. Furthermore, we will review the overall crystallization theories including the recent developments. Factors influencing the overall crystallization kinetic and reasons for discrepancies between the theories and experimental results will be also addressed.

7.2 MEASUREMENTS

Depending on the experimental method used, to characterize overall crystallization kinetics, either the conversion degree or the conversion rate is measured, while the other is calculated by integration or differentiation with respect to time. The methods used, described in detail in Chapter 1, include differential scanning calorimetry (DSC), microscopy, light depolarization technique, dilatometry, density measurements, wide-angle X-ray scattering (WAXS) and small-angle X-ray scattering (SAXS), laser light scattering, and spectroscopic measurements. It has to be emphasized that measurements of the overall kinetics require collection of a signal from a representative, that is, large enough, portion of a polymer. Otherwise, results of several measurements have to be averaged.

The simplest method, a direct observation of crystallization by means of polarized light microscopy, makes it possible to follow the transformation of a sample volume into a new phase, but it is limited to thin samples in which all growing entities are visible. Other methods allow measurement of the degree of crystallinity, which has to be recalculated to the conversion degree, usually by dividing by the final crystallinity. Depolarized light intensity was recently shown to be a function not only of the degree of crystallinity but also of crystal plate dimensions, even if a correction for scattered light intensity is introduced [22]. However, the light depolarization technique is especially convenient when polycrystalline structure is changing too rapidly to be followed by other experimental techniques. The WAXS integrated intensities for each crystal reflection and amorphous background are used to calculate the mass fraction of the crystalline phase. SAXS technique can be also utilized to follow crystallization, but proper analysis of the SAXS data depends on the state of structure in the materials. One of the methods used is the correlation function analysis, assuming that the peak arises from lamellar stacks. It must be emphasized that the X-ray measurements during crystallization require synchrotron irradiation. Moreover, X-ray scattering profiles are affected by crystalline phase orientation, which might lead to errors in the determination of crystallinity level. The most widely applied method is DSC, which measures the released heat of crystallization. In this case the level of crystallinity is an integral over an appropriate time interval, scaled to the total crystallinity reached at the end of the process. Spectroscopic methods including Fourier transform infrared spectroscopy (FTIR), nuclear magnetic resonance (NMR) and dielectric spectroscopy also allow study of the increase in crystallinity, the latter being applicable to polymer chains, which possess dipole moments.

Independently of the measuring method employed, the overall crystallization kinetics can be characterized by the crystallization induction time and the crystallization half-time. More detailed analysis is frequently performed based on the theories of overall crystallization kinetics. It must be mentioned that in this case the mass crystallinity, measured for instance by the DSC method, should be recalculated to volume crystallinity.

7.3 SIMULATION

Computer models of spherulitic pattern formation were developed in the 1980s [23–25] with the aim of determining the kinetics of the conversion of melt into polycrystalline aggregates and/or parameters of structure. In those models, the positions of nucleation sites are selected by pseudorandom number generators. The easiest way is to generate the positions of nucleation sites in the entire sample and to reject "phantom" nuclei chosen in an already transformed volume, or in a volume inhabited by other entities such as fibers. It is obvious that the nucleation process, for instance, on sample surfaces, requires the generation of additional nuclei. For the nucleation dependent on spatial coordinates or on time, the pseudorandom number generation method of von Neumann [26] can be applied. Radii of spherulites increase in subsequent time intervals according to the assumed growth rate until impingement on neighboring spherulites. It has to be emphasized that the isotropic radial growth is limited to spherulitic crystallization in a uniform temperature field. In a temperature gradient, spherulite shapes are anisotropic and the growth trajectories bend although remain normal to growth fronts [10].

The simplest way of following the overall kinetics of conversion is by monitoring the status of a large number of sampling points selected within a simulated sample. The conversion degree is equal to the fraction of points that are inside the growing domains at a given moment of time. The points can be arranged in a regular array or generated in pseudorandom positions (the Monte Carlo method). The simulation of spherulitic patterns requires computation of positions of interspherulitic boundaries. Points at interspherulitic boundaries are found where the growth trajectories of a given spherulite enter neighboring spherulites. The smaller the subsequent time intervals chosen for the simulation, the better the precision of calculation of the boundary positions. In a uniform temperature field the boundary points are located at intersections of spheres representing spherulites and their positions can be easily computed based on the positions of spherulite centers and the assumed growth rate.

Computer simulation was used in the past either to verify theoretical predictions or to characterize the spherulitic structure development in cases where the theory was insufficient, like the crystallization in fiber-reinforced systems. It can be also applied in those complex cases that cannot be described by relatively simple analytical equations.

Recent efforts have focused on the description of crystallization during industrial processing of polymers, which requires accounting for a complicated thermomechanical history and complex crystallization conditions. The examples of such models are presented in Chapter 15.

7.4 THEORIES: ISOTHERMAL AND NONISOTHERMAL CRYSTALLIZATION

7.4.1 Introductory Remarks

Both the spherulitic pattern and the conversion of melt into spherulites are dominated by the nucleation and the growth rate of spherulites. The models of formation of spherulite structure utilize concepts of instantaneous and spontaneous nucleation, the first occurring simultaneously in the entire sample at the beginning of crystallization and the second being prolonged in time. The models also differentiate between three-dimensional (3D) and two-dimensional (2D) processes, the first occurring in bulk and the second being found in thin films. Instantaneous nucleation is characterized by the nucleation density, D, which is the number of nuclei per unit volume (or surface area) of a polymer. Spontaneous nucleation is described by the nucleation rate, F, which is equal to the number of nuclei appearing in a unit volume (or surface) of an untransformed phase per unit time. In general the nucleation in a given polymer depends on the crystallization temperature, time, and thermal history, whereas the spherulite growth rate, G, depends primarily on the crystallization temperature. However, for given thermal conditions both can be expressed as functions of spatial coordinates and time, $F(x, y, z, t)$ and $G(x, y, z, t)$.

In isothermal conditions the nucleation rate can be described as a function of time only, $F(t)$, whereas the growth rate is a constant. Nonisothermal conditions require accounting for a temperature change. However, for a given cooling or heating procedure, one can easily express the temperature-dependent nucleation rate, $f(T)$, and the growth rate, $g(T)$, as functions of time, $F(t)$ and $G(t)$, respectively. Accordingly, at time t, a radius of a spherulite nucleated at time τ equals

$$r(\tau, t) = \int_\tau^t G(s)ds. \quad (7.1a)$$

For constant G Equation (7.1a) yields:

$$r(\tau, t) = (t - \tau)G. \quad (7.1b)$$

At time t, a volume (or a surface) V of a single unimpinged spherulite nucleated at time τ, equals the volume (or the area) of a sphere (or a circle) having the radius $r(\tau, t)$:

$$V(\tau, t) = 4\pi[r(\tau, t)]^3/3 \quad (7.2a)$$
$$V(\tau, t) = \pi[r(\tau, t)]^2. \quad (7.2b)$$

When neighboring spherulites impinge, the boundary is formed. It can be noticed that for any two spherulites nucleated at τ_1 and τ_2, a difference between their radii, expressed by Equation (7.1a), remains constant during the further growth:

$$\Delta r = \int_{\tau_1}^{\tau_2} G(t)dt. \quad (7.3)$$

The locus of points sharing this property is a branch of a hyperboloid or a plane, the latter being the case when $\tau_1 = \tau_2$. After impingement on neighboring spherulites, the volume of each individual spherulite evolves in a complex way that depends on the nucleation (positions and times) of spherulites involved. All growing entities contribute to the conversion degree. The two best known approaches to the description of overall crystallization kinetics in infinite samples are those of Avrami and Evans, both based on the isovolume assumptions, which enabled to assimilate "volume" and "volume fraction" terms.

7.4.2 Extended Volume Approach

The Avrami model [3–5] utilizes the concept of the so-called extended volume, whereas Evans took advantage of probability theory [2]. Extended volume at time t is equal to the sum of volumes of all domains as if they were growing without impingement from all nucleation attempts occurred up to the time t. In the calculation of the extended volume the impingement of growing domains is not accounted for, as shown in Figure 7.2. Extended volume includes also the "phantom" domains expanding from nucleation attempts in already crystallized regions. An increment of the extended volume fraction dE, occurring in the unconverted region, $1 - \alpha$, results in an increase of real converted volume fraction, $d\alpha$, such as

$$d\alpha/dE = 1 - \alpha. \quad (7.4)$$

Simple transformation and integration leads to the well-known Avrami equation:

$$\alpha = 1 - \exp(-E). \quad (7.5)$$

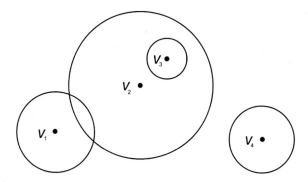

Figure 7.2 Scheme explaining the concept of "extended volume." Extended volume V_{ex} of four domains is equal to the sum of their volumes, $V_1 + V_2 + V_3 + V_4$, and exceeds the transformed volume.

For nonisothermal crystallization, where G is a function of time t, E in Equation (7.5) can be expressed as

$$E(t) = DV(0, t) \qquad (7.6a)$$

$$E(t) = \int_0^t F(\tau) V(\tau, t)\, d\tau. \qquad (7.6b)$$

for the cases of instantaneous and spontaneous nucleation, respectively, where $V(\tau,t)$ is given by Equation (7.2a) and Equation (7.2b) for 3D and 2D crystallization, respectively. Equation (7.6a) can be also obtained from the more general Equation (7.6b) by assuming $F(t) = D\delta(t)$, where $\delta(t)$ is the Dirac delta function. For isothermal crystallization,

$$E(t) = (4\pi G^3/3) \int_0^t F(\tau)(t-\tau)^3\, d\tau \qquad (7.7a)$$

$$E(t) = \pi G^2 \int_0^t F(\tau)(t-\tau)^2\, d\tau \qquad (7.7b)$$

for the 3D and 2D cases, respectively.

The conversion rate, $d\alpha/dt$, is described by the following equation:

$$d\alpha(t)/dt = \exp(-E)\, dE(t)/dt \qquad (7.8)$$

where

$$dE(t)/dt = 4\pi G(t) \int_0^t F(\tau)\left[\int_\tau^t G(s)\, ds\right]^2 d\tau \qquad (7.9a)$$

$$dE(t)/dt = 2\pi G(t) \int_0^t F(\tau)\left[\int_\tau^t G(s)\, ds\right] d\tau \qquad (7.9b)$$

for the 3D and 2D cases, respectively.

For instantaneous nucleation with density D or spontaneous nucleation with a constant rate $F(t) = B$, Equation (7.7a) and Equation (7.7b) assume the well-known form:

$$E = kt^n \qquad (7.10)$$

where k and n depend on the dimensionality of crystallization and on the nucleation mode. For instantaneous nucleation: $k = 4\pi D G^3/3$ and $n = 3$ (3D case) or $k = \pi D G^2$ and $n = 2$ (2D case). For spontaneous nucleation with a constant rate B: $k = \pi B G^3/3$ and $n = 4$ (3D case) or $k = \pi B G^2/3$ and $n = 3$ (2D case). The validity of Equation (7.10) has been verified on numerous occasions through a computer simulation of spherulitic crystallization, for instance in References [24, 25].

When the nucleation of isothermal crystallization consists of both instantaneous and spontaneous processes, the latter with a constant rate, $F(t) = D\delta(t) + B$, Equation (7.7a) and Equation (7.7b) yield:

$$E(t) = 4\pi D G^3 t^3/3 + \pi B G^3 t^4/3 \qquad (7.11a)$$

$$E(t) = \pi D G^2 t^2 + \pi B G^2 t^3/3 \qquad (7.11b)$$

for the 3D and 2D cases, respectively. The first and the second components in the above equations represent contributions to E from the two populations of spherulites, nucleated instantaneously and spontaneously, respectively. Equation (7.10) does not apply in such a case.

In the Avrami derivation the nucleation rate F represents the number of nucleation attempts in a unit volume of a sample per unit time. It is, however, equal to the number of nuclei appearing in a unit volume of an amorphous phase per unit time. If nucleation occurs in the untransformed volume it produces a real spherulite, otherwise a "phantom" spherulite is nucleated. The requirement that an increment of extended volume has to occur in the unconverted region eliminates "phantoms" because the increment of a phantom spherulite volume occurs always in the already transformed fraction of a material. The same condition eliminates spherulites whose growth was earlier stopped by impingement. However, it is possible to derive the Avrami equation neglecting the phantom nuclei by the following reasoning. A volume of average real spherulite nucleated at time τ increases in dt by a fraction proportional to the unconverted area at time t: $dV(\tau, t)[1 - \alpha(t)]$. Considering spherulites nucleated at time τ, we have to scale the untransformed fraction at t to its volume at τ, $[1 - \alpha(\tau)]$. Multiplication by the number of real spherulites nucleated at time τ, $F(\tau)[1 - \alpha(\tau)]$, and integration over $0 < \tau < t$ gives us the following conversion rate:

$$d\alpha(t)/dt = \int_0^t F(\tau)[dV(\tau,t)/dt][1-\alpha(t)]d\tau. \quad (7.12)$$

Dividing both sides by $[1-\alpha(t)]$ and integrating we obtain Equation (7.5) with E expressed by Equation (7.6b).

Similar reasoning, applied by Johnson and Mehl [6] to a problem of nucleation and radial growth of spherical entities, resulted in Equation (7.5), with E expressed by Equation (7.10). The derivations of Tobin [27–29] were also based on a similar principle. However, oversimplified reasoning, for instance, the incorrect assumption of the proportionality of an average spherulite volume (instead of a volume increment) to the unconverted fraction, led Tobin to the erroneous result [30].

The Avrami theory applies to both isothermal and nonisothermal conditions; however, in nonisothermal conditions, Equation (7.6a) and Equation (7.6b), together with Equation (7.2a), Equation (7.2b), and Equation (7.1a), have to be used instead of the simplified Equation (7.7a) and Equation (7.b), or Equation (7.10). The underlying assumption that the growing "extended" grain, which reaches a certain point in the sample as the first one is a real grain, enables elimination of "phantoms" and parts of "extended grains" truncated by the impingement but limits applicability of the theory. For instance, the theory cannot be rigorously applied if two types of domains grow with momentarily different growth rates or if domains grow anisotropically and are randomly oriented in space. In these cases the "extended grain" first arriving to a certain point may not be a real one. Nevertheless, the Avrami theory can be used for the description of the anisotropically growing grains if all of them are identically oriented within the sample.

In the case of instantaneous nucleation, at the beginning of the crystallization, a total number of spherulites in a unit volume, N, equals the nucleation density D.

For the nucleation occurring also during further stages of crystallization the number of spherulites gradually increases in time:

$$N(t) = \int_0^t F(\tau)[1-\alpha(\tau)]d\tau. \quad (7.13)$$

Calculation of the total number of spherulites requires integration over the entire crystallization time: $N_t = N(\infty)$. It is rather obvious that in the case of two samples with the same number of spherulites, the first nucleated instantaneously and the second spontaneously, the crystallization in the first one required a shorter time than in the second one.

7.4.3 Probabilistic Approaches

The derivations based on probability theory utilize the formula that expresses the probability of a number of nucleation events occurring in a finite volume. Consider a volume V_S in which m nucleation events occurred at random positions: $m/V_S = D$. The probability for the event to occur inside a certain finite region of volume V_C is V_C/V_S. The probability that n events out of m occur in this region is expressed by the binomial probability distribution

$$P_n = m![n!(m-n)!]^{-1}(V_C/V_S)^n(1-V_C/V_S)^{m-n} \quad (7.14)$$

When both m and V_S tend to infinity ($m \to \infty$ and $V_S \to \infty$), while maintaining the constant finite ratio D, the binomial distribution transforms into the Poisson probability distribution:

$$P_n = \exp(-E)E^n/n! \quad (7.15)$$

with the expectation value $E = DV_c$.

One notes that the probability that any number of nucleation events occur inside the considered region equals

$$\sum_{n=1}^{\infty} P_n = 1 - P_0. \quad (7.16)$$

Exclusion and inclusion of a point in the transformed fraction are mutually exclusive. Therefore, the probability that an arbitrarily chosen point, denoted here as A, at a given time t will remain outside the growing domains, $P_0(t)$, enables a conversion degree to expressed as

$$\alpha(t) = 1 - P_0(t). \quad (7.17)$$

The known approaches focus on the calculation of $P_0(t)$, that is, on finding the expected value E.

Evans [2] calculated the expectancy of the Poisson probability distribution for the constant propagation rate of domains and two simple nucleation modes: instantaneous and spontaneous with the constant rate, $F(t) = B$. Billon et al. [13] extended this approach to the case of time-dependent nucleation rate. According to the Evans theory, an arbitrarily chosen point A can be reached before time t by growing spheres nucleated around it in a distance r (precisely in a distance within the interval $(r, r+dr)$) before time $t - r/G$; their number is equal to an integral of the nucleation rate $F(\tau)$ over the time interval $(0, t - r/G)$, multiplied by the considered volume, $4\pi r^2 dr$. The total number of spheres occluding the point A until time t is calculated by second integration, over a distance:

$$E(t) = 4\pi \int_0^{Gt}\left[\int_0^{t-r/G} F(s)ds\right]r^2 dr \quad (7.18)$$

Equation (7.18) can be transformed into Equation (7.7a) by integration by parts, followed by the substitution: $r = (t - \tau)G$. The same reasoning applied to the 2D case gives a result equivalent to Equation (7.7b). As in the extended volume approach, instantaneous nucleation can be considered either by neglecting all nucleation events except those occurring exactly at the onset of crystallization or by substituting $D\delta(t)$ for $F(t)$.

The most popular analysis of nonisothermal crystallization data utilizes the Ozawa equation [7], which was derived based on the Evans theory [2] for cooling at a constant rate. The Ozawa equation can be derived assuming that the domains nucleated before time τ around an arbitrary point A in a distance $r(\tau,t)$, as given by Equation (7.1a), will reach the point A before time t. Their number is a product of the integral $_0\int^\tau F(s)ds$ and the volume $4\pi r^2 dr$ or the surface area $2\pi r dr$ in the distance $r(\tau,t)$ from the point A. Calculation of the expectancy E requires integration over a distance, $0 < r < r(0, t)$, which can be substituted by integration over time τ, taking into account Equation (7.1a) and the dependence $dr = -G(\tau)d\tau$. Therefore, the expectancy E is expressed by the following equations:

$$E(t) = 4\pi \int_0^t [r(\tau,t)]^2 G(\tau) \left[\int_0^\tau F(s)ds\right] d\tau \quad (7.19a)$$

$$E(t) = 2\pi \int_0^t r(\tau,t) G(\tau) \left[\int_0^\tau F(s)ds\right] d\tau \quad (7.19b)$$

for 3D and 2D cases, respectively.

It should be noted here that Equation (7.19a) and Equation (7.19b) are readily obtained from the Avrami equation (Eq. 7.6b) by simple integration by parts. Denoting the growth rate and nucleation rate temperature dependencies as $g(T)$ and $f(T)$, respectively, and assuming that the temperature T is a linear function of time t, one obtains the following expressions for expectancy $E(T)$, for the temperature-dependent nucleation rate and for the instantaneous nucleation, respectively:

$$E(T) = p\pi v^{-(m+2)} \int_{Tm}^T \left[\int_{Tm}^{T'} f(z)dz\right] \left[\int_{T'}^T g(z)dz\right]^m g(T')dT' \quad (7.20a)$$

$$E(T) = p\pi v^{-(m+1)} D \int_{Tm}^T \left[\int_{T'}^T g(z)dz\right]^m g(T')dT' \quad (7.20b)$$

where T_m is the temperature beyond which the process cannot proceed and $T' = T(\tau)$. For the 2D case, $m = 1$ and $p = 2$, whereas for the 3D case, $m = 2$ and $p = 4$.

Integration of Equation (7.20b) yields [30]:

$$E(T) = [p/(m+1)]\pi v^{-(m+1)} D \left[\int_{Tm}^T g(z)dz\right]^{m+1}. \quad (7.20c)$$

The Ozawa approach applies to crystallization of polymers during cooling and also to cold crystallization during heating from the glassy state.

General Equation (7.19a) and Equation (7.19b) describing nonisothermal crystallization can be derived based on the probabilistic approach in a simpler way [17, 18]. It is obvious that the point A remains at time t outside of all growing spherulites nucleated instantaneously at zero time, if no nuclei appeared in a sphere around the point A, having a radius equal to $r(0, t)$ and a volume of $V(0, t)$. According to Equation (7.15), the probability of this event is:

$$P_0(t) = \exp[-DV(0, t)]. \quad (7.21)$$

In the case of spontaneous nucleation one has to consider nucleation events occurring in consecutive infinitely small time intervals $(\tau_i; \tau_i + d\tau)$ until time t, where $\tau_1 = 0$ and $\tau_i = i\,d\tau$. The probability that the point A remains at time t beyond the reach of spherulites nucleated during the time interval $(\tau_i, \tau_i + d\tau)$ can be written in the following form:

$$p_0(\tau_i, t) = \exp[-F(\tau_i)d\tau V(\tau_i, t)] \quad (7.22)$$

where $V(\tau_i, t)$ is a spherical volume (or circular area) having the radius that is equal to $r(\tau_i, t)$.

Calculation of the probability that the point A remains at time t outside all spherulites requires multiplication of probabilities:

$$P_0(t) = p_0(\tau_1, t) \ldots p_0(\tau_i, t) \ldots p_0(\tau_n, t) \quad (7.23a)$$

$$P_0(t) = \exp\left[-\int_0^t F(\tau)V(\tau, t)d\tau\right] \quad (7.23b)$$

One notes that $V(\tau,t)$ is equal to the volume of unimpinged spherulite expressed by Equation (7.2a) and Equation (7.2b). In derivations based on probability calculus it is also assumed, as in the extended volume approach, that a growing sphere that passes through an arbitrary point as the first one represents a real spherulite. It appears that the concept of extended volume and probability calculus yield the same result if applied to crystallization in infinite volume with the nucleation and growth rate independent of spatial coordinates.

Calculation of the probability for the point A to be occluded at time t (in time interval from t to $t + dt$) leads directly to the expression for the conversion rate. It is sufficient to consider occlusion of the point A by only one spherulite.

The point A will be occluded at time t by one spherulite nucleated at time $\tau = \tau_i$ if a nucleation site of this spherulite is located in a spherical cup around the point A, $dV(\tau_i, t)$ having the radius $r(\tau_i, t)$ and the thickness $dr = Gdt$. The probability of this event reads:

$$p_1(\tau_i, t) = \exp[-F(\tau_i)d\tau V(\tau_i, t)]F(\tau_i)d\tau dV(\tau_i, t) \quad (7.24)$$

A will be occluded at t only by that one spherulite nucleated at τ_i if in all other consecutive time intervals (τ_j; $\tau_j + d\tau$), where $\tau_j = j\, d\tau$ and $j \neq i$, until time t, no other spherulite is nucleated closer to A than $r(\tau_j, t)$. The probability of that event is expressed by the product: $p_0(\tau_1, t) \ldots p_0(\tau_{i-1}, t)\, p_1(\tau_i, t)\, p_0(\tau_{i+1}, t) \ldots p_0(\tau_n, t)$. The probability that A will be incorporated into any spherulite at time t, regardless of its nucleation time, requires integration over $0 < \tau_i < t$, which leads to the following expression:

$$P_1(t) = \exp\left[-\int_0^t F(\tau)V(\tau, t)d\tau\right]\int_0^t F(\tau)[dV(\tau, t)/dt]d\tau. \quad (7.25)$$

It can be noticed that

$$P_1(t) = \exp[-E(t)][dE(t)/dt]dt = (d\alpha/dt)dt. \quad (7.26)$$

The approach just described can be applied to distinguish contributions to the conversion rate and to the conversion degree from different populations of spherulites, for instance, those nucleated instantaneously (α_{in}) or spontaneously (α_{sp}), in the same 3D sample:

$$d\alpha_{in}(t) = 4\pi D G^3 t^2 \exp(-E)dt \quad (7.27a)$$

$$d\alpha_{sp}(t) = (4/3)\pi B G^3 t^3 \exp(-E)dt \quad (7.27b)$$

and

$$\alpha_{in}(t) = 4\pi D G^3 \int_0^t t^2 \exp(-E)dt \quad (7.28a)$$

$$\alpha_{sp}(t) = (4/3)\pi B G^3 \int_0^t t^3 \exp(-E)dt \quad (7.28b)$$

with E given by Equation (7.11a).

Kolmogoroff [1] also derived Equation (7.5) with E expressed by Equation (7.6b). However, Kolmogoroff's approach is inaccurate, as shown in References [30, 31], although errors made in that derivation cancel out, leading fortuitously to the correct result. Despite the correctness of the final equation, a strict application of Kolmogoroff's reasoning to other crystallization conditions leads to erratic results, which is easily demonstrated by considering crystallization from instantaneous nuclei as an example.

Modification of the previously described probabilistic approach by assuming randomness of nucleation

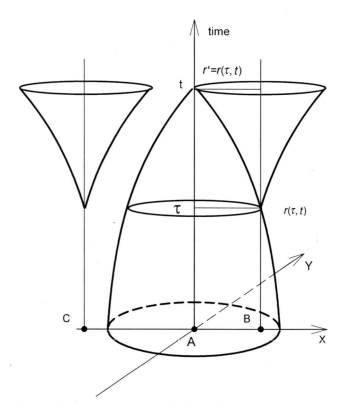

Figure 7.3 Scheme of the conical zone in space and time drawn for 2D crystallization. From two spherulites nucleated at time τ, only one, with a center at point B, that is, at distance $r(\tau, t)$ from A can reach A at time t. Modified from Piorkowska, E., et al. Critical assessment of overall crystallization kinetics theories and predictions. *Prog. Polym. Sci.* **2006**, *31*, 549–575. Copyright 2006, with kind permission from Elsevier.

events not only in space but also in time, with the probability of a nucleation event at time τ related to the momentary nucleation rate, allows simplification of the reasoning and the derivation [17, 18, 32]. The fundamental condition that a spherulite nucleated at τ will reach the point A at time t only if it is nucleated in the distance $r(\tau, t)$ from A, defines a curvilinear conical zone in space and time, shown in Figure 7.3, having the important property that a point A will be occluded at time t only by domains nucleated on the side surface of that cone. Obviously, the point A remains in untransformed fraction of a material under the condition that no nucleation event occurred within the entire conical zone that is in all the "layers" corresponding to consecutive time intervals. Probability of this event is expressed by the Poisson probability distribution with an expected value equal to an integral of the nucleation rate over the conical zone, which leads to the expression identical to Equation (7.23b). For crystallization from instantaneous nuclei, the zone reduces to a sphere in 3D and to a circle in 2D. Moreover, as in all other approaches, general equations derived for the time dependent nucleation rate apply to the instantaneous nucleation when the nucleation rate is expressed as $F(t) = D\delta(t)$, whereas the equations describing the isothermal crystallization are readily obtained by assuming that the growth rate G is a constant.

An important advantage of the approach treating the nucleation process as random also in time is its relatively easy application to more complex crystallization conditions, including spatial confinement, nucleation on sample boundaries, on row nuclei, and in a temperature gradient, described briefly in the next sections. It also makes possible to describe the formation of interspherulite boundaries and characterize spherulite patterns [32].

7.4.4 Isokinetic Model

Additional assumptions about the relation between nucleation and the growth rate as in the Nakamura isokinetic model [8, 9] can simplify the description of overall kinetics. In the Avrami approach [3–5], D_0 nuclei present initially in a unit volume are activated according to the activation frequency $q(t)$:

$$F(t) = D_0 q(t) \exp\left[-\int_0^t q(s)\,ds\right]. \quad (7.29)$$

Substitution of $\xi(t) = \int_0^t q(s)\,ds$, together with the isokinetic assumption that G/q is a constant allows E to be expressed in the following form:

$$E(\xi) = 8\pi N_0 (G/q)^3 [\exp(-\xi) - 1 + \xi - \xi^2/2! + \xi^3/3!]. \quad (7.30)$$

In addition, to account for the density change during crystallization, Nakamura multiplied the right side of Equation (7.30) by an empirical factor, ρ_c/ρ_l, equal to the ratio of semicrystalline phase density to amorphous phase density.

It appears that $E(\xi)$ can be reduced to the form $k_1 \xi^n$ either for instantaneous (ξ very high) or spontaneous (D_0 very large, ξ very low) nucleation. For isothermal conditions, with constant q, $\xi(t) = qt$ and $E = kt^n$, where k is a constant at a given temperature. For nonisothermal conditions, with $k = k(T)$, E assumes the form:

$$E(t) = \left[\int_0^t k(T)^{1/n}\,ds\right]^n = \left[\int_0^t K(T)\,ds\right]^n. \quad (7.31)$$

Equation (7.31) can also be derived assuming that the ratio of spontaneous nucleation rate to spherulite growth rate remains constant during cooling, that is:

$F(t)/G(t) = P$. In the 3D case, for isothermal conditions, with $g(T) = G = \text{const}$:

$$E(t) = \pi P [Gt]^4/3 \quad (7.32)$$

whereas for nonisothermal conditions, for $g(T) = G[t(T)]$ [17, 18]:

$$E(t) = (\pi P/3)\left\{\int_0^t G[t(T)]\,dt\right\}^4. \quad (7.33)$$

Based on Equation (7.33) and assuming that $\pi P\{G[t(T)]\}^4/3 = k(T)$, one can derive Equation (7.31) with $n = 4$. The Nakamura equation (Eq. 7.31) has been widely used in the modeling of crystallization in the injection molding process, for example, References [33–36], because it allows application of the results of isothermal crystallization analysis to the description of nonisothermal crystallization. It can be noticed that in isothermal conditions, for a given temperature T, $k(T) = t_h(T)^{-n} \ln 2$, where t_h is the crystallization half-time. Therefore, for nonisothermal conditions, Equation (7.31) assumes the form:

$$E(t) = \ln 2 \left\{\int_0^t t_h[T(s)]^{-1}\,ds\right\}^n. \quad (7.34)$$

In the view of Equation (7.34), the dependence $t_h(T)$ is sufficient to predict the kinetics of nonisothermal crystallization. Although the formulas were derived for a 3D crystallization process, similar reasoning applies to a 2D process.

7.4.5 Rate Equations

Differentiation of Equation (7.6b) with respect to time [37] leads to a system of differential "rate equations" defining auxiliary interrelated functions $f_i(t)$:

$$f_i(t)G(t) = f'_{i-1}(t). \quad (7.35a)$$

In the 3D case the functions are in the form:

$$f_0(t) = (4\pi/3)\int_{-\infty}^t F(\tau)\left[\int_\tau^t G(s)\,ds\right]^3 d\tau \quad (7.35b)$$

$$f_1(t) = 4\pi \int_{-\infty}^t F(\tau)\left[\int_\tau^t G(s)\,ds\right]^2 d\tau \quad (7.35c)$$

$$f_2(t) = 8\pi \int_{-\infty}^t F(\tau)\left[\int_\tau^t G(s)\,ds\right] d\tau \quad (7.35d)$$

$$f_3(t) = 8\pi \int_{-\infty}^t F(\tau)\,d\tau. \quad (7.35e)$$

The lower limit of integration, $-\infty$, can be replaced by a finite value of time corresponding to the beginning of crystallization. The rate equations are also discussed in Chapter 15. Differentiation of $f_3(t)$ with respect to time permits finding of the nucleation rate in the case of spontaneous nucleation:

$$F(t) = f_3'''(t)/8\pi. \quad (7.36)$$

It can be also noticed that:

$$\alpha(t) = 1 - \exp[-f_o(t)] \quad (7.37a)$$

$$d\alpha(t)/dt = f_1(t)G(t)\exp[-E(t)] = f_1(t)G(t)\exp[-f_o(t)]. \quad (7.37b)$$

For instantaneous nucleation, the functions will have a simpler form, for instance:

$$f_3(t) = 8\pi D. \quad (7.38)$$

The differentiation method was also used by other authors [38, 39] to find sets of equations describing the conversion of melt into spherulites. The relevant equations are listed and discussed in Chapter 15. It has to be mentioned that although Equation (7.36) and Equation (7.38) create potential possibility to determine the nucleation rate or density, the practical use of such approach encounters difficulties because of the necessity of multiple differentiation and knowledge of the growth rate from independent experiments.

7.5 COMPLEX CRYSTALLIZATION CONDITIONS: GENERAL MODELS

The theories and derivations discussed in the preceding sections concerned crystallization where both the nucleation and the spherulite growth depended only on time. In general both of them can depend also on spatial coordinates because of a temperature gradient, orientation, and so on. It must be mentioned that Avrami [5] derived also the expression for E when both G and F depend not only on time but also on spatial coordinates. E was defined as the average number of extended domains that have grown through the point A, leading to the following equation in spherical coordinates r, θ, and φ around the point A as origin:

$$E(t, A) = \int_0^\pi \int_0^{2\pi} \int_0^R \left[\int_0^\tau F(\tau', r, \theta, \varphi) d\tau' \right] r^2 \sin\theta \, dr \, d\varphi \, d\theta \quad (7.39)$$

where τ denotes the nucleation time for the domain nucleated at the position (r, θ, φ) which reaches the point A exactly at time t. Time τ is defined by the differential equation $d\rho = -G(s, \rho, \theta, \varphi)ds$ fulfilling the conditions: $s = t$ at $\rho = 0$ and $s = \tau$ at $\rho = r$; for the domain nucleated at the position (r, θ, φ) at $\tau = 0$ and reaching A at time t, the coordinate r equals the radius of this domain at time t, $R(\theta, \varphi, t)$. At the point A the conversion degree is expressed again by Equation (7.5) with $E(t, A)$ given by Equation (7.39). The conversion degree depends then on time and spatial coordinates.

Generalization of the probabilistic approach described in Section 7.4.3 also permits derivation of an equation for E accounting for spatial dependence of nucleation and growth rate [32]. Again domains growing around the point A are considered. The prerequisite for a domain nucleated at τ to reach the point A exactly at time t is a proper distance, r, of its nucleation site from A. r has to be equal to the radius r' of this domain at time t ($r = r'$ for $t' = t$); the radius r' increases by $dr' = G(t', x, y, z)dt'$ in a time interval dt'; where G is the time and position-dependent growth rate; $r' = 0$ for $\tau = t'$ and $r = 0$ for $\tau = t$. This relationship defines a curvilinear cone in space and time around A. A can be occluded at time t only by domains nucleated on the side surface of that cone. The probability that no domain will be nucleated inside the cone, equal to $1 - \alpha$, is governed by the Poisson distribution, expressed by Equation (7.15) with $n = 0$ and the expectancy E being the integral of nucleation rate F over the volume of the cone around the point A:

$$E(t, A) = \int_\Omega F(t, x, y, z) d\Omega. \quad (7.40)$$

For 3D crystallization from instantaneous nuclei the conical zone in space and time is reduced to a 3D zone.

Both the approaches just described are equivalent. In both cases the number of spherulites nucleated per unit volume around A increases with time:

$$N(t, A) = \int_0^t F(s, A)[1 - \alpha(s, A)]ds. \quad (7.41)$$

Determination of the average number of spherulites in a portion of material requires integrating over spatial coordinates and dividing by an appropriate volume.

In fact, both Equation (7.39) and Equation (7.40) are based on the assumption of radial growth, which is not always true, for instance in a temperature gradient, as will be described in Section 7.6.2.

7.6 FACTORS INFLUENCING THE OVERALL CRYSTALLIZATION KINETICS

7.6.1 Crystallization in a Uniform Temperature Field

Both the experimental results and theories show that the overall crystallization kinetics is governed by the nucleation and the growth rate of spherulites, although more strongly by the latter; for instance, during isothermal 3D crystallization from instantaneous nuclei, t_h depends on a reciprocal of $D^{1/3}G$. Therefore, all factors controlling the nucleation and the growth rate strongly influence the overall crystallization. During quiescent crystallization of a given polymer, the spherulite growth rate and the nucleation depend primarily on crystallization temperature, although the latter is also influenced by the thermal history of the polymer. Polymers crystallize usually from heterogeneous nuclei. Homogeneous nucleation is active at very large supercoolings, which are difficult to reach without first encountering crystallization from heterogeneous nuclei. For the same reason it is impossible to measure the crystal growth rate of many polymers at low temperatures. The nucleation and growth of polymer crystals are discussed in Chapter 4 and Chapter 5. In general, with increasing supercooling, both the nucleation rate and the crystal growth rate increase, pass through maxima, and then decrease. As a consequence, the time required to accomplish the crystallization decreases with increasing supercooling, reaches a minimum value, and increases again. In general, the temperature of nonisothermal crystallization usually depends on the cooling rate; the faster the cooling, the lower the effective crystallization temperature; this is because the formation of nuclei requires time. In Reference [31] the temperature of the beginning of nonisothermal crystallization of isotactic polypropylene (iPP), T_B in degrees Celsius, was described by the experimental dependence, 129.17 exp (–0.00121v), for the cooling rate v below 40°C/min.

The number of nucleation sites can be increased by use of nucleation agents that not only shortens the crystallization time but also causes the elevation of the effective temperature of nonisothermal crystallization during cooling, especially in polyolefins. Addition of 0.2–0.5 wt% of bis(3,4-dimethylbenzylidene) sorbitol to iPP increased its crystallization peak temperature by approximately 18°C [40]. Polymer molecular weight, polymorphism, and application of pressure are other factors that affect nucleation and growth and, hence, the overall crystallization kinetics.

It must be also mentioned that spatial limits and the additional nucleation process on outer surfaces influence the solidification, although the overall effect depends strongly on the relation between the sample size, for instance, thickness, and the spherulite size.

Polymers are poor heat conductors; hence, temperature gradients develop during cooling inside thick-walled products, and they can be further enhanced by the release of heat of crystallization [31, 41]. Flow affects both the structure and the overall crystallization kinetics, as it enforces orientation of polymer chains. The influence of spatial confinement, nucleation on sample boundaries, temperature gradients and flow on overall crystallization kinetics are described in the following sections.

7.6.2 Crystallization in a Temperature Gradient

All the equations derived in the preceding sections, except for Equation (7.39) and Equation (7.40), apply to uniform temperature fields, where temperature is momentarily equal in the entire body. Polymers are poor heat conductors; hence, cooling of thick-walled shapes results in temperature gradients. The gradient can be further enhanced by the release of crystallization enthalpy. The temperature gradient not only differentiates the nucleation and growth rate through the sample, but it also affects the trajectories of growth. In general, the time required for the growth front to travel between points (x_o, y_o, z_o) and (x, y, z) is a functional:

$$t = \int_{x_o}^{x} G^{-1} ds \quad (7.42)$$

where ds is an element of the growth trajectory; $ds = [1 + y'(x)^2 + z'(x)^2]^{1/2} dx$ in 3D. The growth trajectory during crystallization is defined by the requirement that the time t is a minimum; that is, that the variation of the functional (Eq. 7.42) equals zero for G dependent only on spatial coordinates (in a steady state). This leads to a system of differential equations with a solution describing a bunch of trajectories originating from the starting point (x_o, y_o, z_o) with free ends forming the growth front, which is normal to the trajectories. Analytic derivations, computer modeling, and experiments show that in a steady, uniaxial temperature field, the growth trajectories are not straight but bent, although remain normal to the growth front [42–44]. Figure 7.4 shows consecutive stages of crystallization in iPP film in the form of spherulites growing along trajectories that bend toward the higher temperature side and finally become parallel to the temperature gradient. The conversion degree, α, measured on selected isotherms (Fig. 7.5) increased faster with time during gradient crystallization than that during isothermal crystallization of the same iPP at corresponding temperatures; the effect depended on the gradient and temperature increasing with the increase of both. The acceleration of transformation was caused by the invasion of spherulites nucleated in a colder part of a sample, which formed a front advancing toward the high temperature side of a sample.

Derivations of expressions for α are limited to crystallization in a uniaxial temperature gradient [10, 11] and require additional simplifying assumptions, like linear dependence of G on a spatial coordinate and

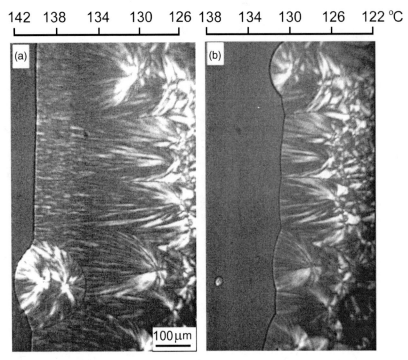

Figure 7.4 Spherulitic crystallization of iPP in the temperature gradient of 35°C/mm: earlier (b) and later (a) stages. Reprinted from Pawlak, A., Piorkowska, E. Crystallization of isotactic polypropylene in a temperature gradient. *Coll. Polym. Sci.* **2001**, *279*, 939–946, fig. 5. Copyright 2001, with kind permission from Springer Science + Business Media.

independence of F of a spatial coordinate [11], or neglecting the bending of growth trajectories [10]. In the latter approach, when T is a function of a spatial coordinate, x, both F and G become x-dependent. A spherulite nucleated at time τ will reach the arbitrarily chosen point $A(x_o, y_o)$, exactly at time t if its nucleation site is located at a distance from A equal to $R(\varphi, \tau, t)$, defined by the equation:

$$t - \tau = (\cos\varphi)^{-1} \int_{x_o}^{x_o + R(\varphi, \tau, t)\cos\varphi} G(x)^{-1} dx \quad (7.43)$$

where φ is an angle with respect to the x-axis. Hence,

$$E(t, x_o) = C \int_0^t \int_{x_o - R(\pi, \tau, t)}^{x_o + R(0, \tau, t)} F(\tau, x)[y(x, \tau, t) - y_o]^n \, dx \, d\tau. \quad (7.44)$$

where for the 2D case C and n are equal to 2 and 1, respectively, whereas for the 3D case they are equal to π and 2, respectively. $R(\pi,\tau,t)$ and $R(0,\tau,t)$ must be found from Equation (7.43) for φ equal to π and 0, respectively. Consequently, α is also a function of time and spatial coordinate. For G = const and F dependent only on time, $F(t)$, Equation (7.44) reduces to Equation (7.7a) and Equation (7.7b) describing E for isothermal crystallization.

In spite of simplifying assumptions, predictions based on Equation (7.44) agree with the experimental results reasonably well, as illustrated in Figure 7.5. Moreover, it appears that the computer simulation of crystallization, with radial growth and also with growth trajectorie normal to growth fronts, gives practically the same results for the conversion of melt into spherulites [10]. Equation (7.44) predicts that the acceleration of crystallization in a temperature gradient depends on nucleation density. More intense nucleation prevents intrusion of spherulites nucleated in a colder part of a sample. Hence, for sufficiently intense nucleation, the influence of a temperature gradient can be neglected, and the overall crystallization kinetics, although depending on the position within a polymer article, will be governed by local conditions.

7.6.3 Crystallization in a Confined Space

The influence of sample thickness on the overall crystallization is best illustrated by the well-known fact that often the spherulitic crystallization in a thin film takes much longer time than that in a polymer bulk under the

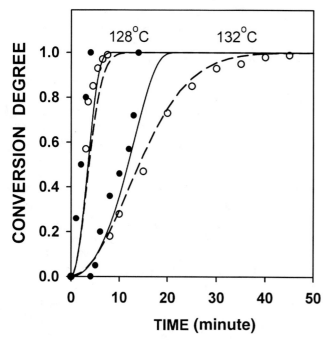

Figure 7.5 Conversion of melt into spherulites measured during crystallization of a thin iPP film in the steady temperature gradient of 35°C/mm determined on isotherms at 128°C and 132°C (filled circles) and in isothermal conditions at corresponding temperature (empty circles) [44]. Dashed and solid lines result from calculations [10] based on Equation (7.7b) and Equation (7.44) for 2D crystallization in isothermal conditions and in a temperature gradient, respectively.

The instantaneous nucleation assumed, with the temperature dependent density $D = 2.308 \times 10^{46} \exp(-0.254\,T)$ (mm^{-2}) (measured experimentally [44] and recalculated for 11-μm-thick film [10]), with temperature T expressed in Kelvin. The spherulitic growth rate temperature dependence according to the Hoffman equation $g = G_0 \exp\{-U[R(T - T_\infty)]^{-1}\}\exp\{-K_g[T(T_m^\circ - T)]^{-1}\}$ with $U = 1500$ cal/mol, $T_\infty = 231.2$ K, $T_m^\circ = 458.2$ K, G_0 and K_g equal 0.3359 cm/s and 1.47×10^5 K^2 in regime II, and 3249 cm/s and 3.30×10^5 K^2 in regime III [10].

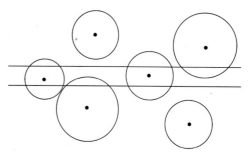

Figure 7.6 Scheme of spherulitic crystallization within a finite volume.

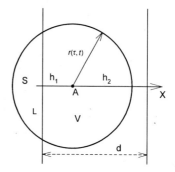

Figure 7.7 Circle with the radius $r(\tau, t)$ around the point A in a finite sample.

same conditions. The reason is explained schematically in Figure 7.6. The conversion of melt into crystalline phase in the confined polymer portion is much slower because of lack of contribution of spherulites, which would have been nucleated in the polymer bulk, beyond the limits indicated in Figure 7.6. However, if additional nucleating sites appeared on the film surfaces, the transformation would instead be accelerated.

Depending on thickness of a polymer layer, d, crystallization is usually treated as a 3D or 2D process; if d is at least several times larger than a spherulite radius, it is treated as 3D, whereas if d is much less than a spherulite size, it is treated as 2D. However, there are intermediate cases when a more complex mathematical description is needed. Development of the theory of overall crystallization kinetics in a limited volume was initiated by Escleine et al. [12] and Billon et al. [13], who derived the respective dependencies for isothermal crystallization in a plate bounded by two parallel planes. Further studies [16–18] were focused on nonisothermal crystallization.

The probabilistic approach allows for relatively simple derivations of the respective formulas. The key points are: (1) to disregard nucleation sites beyond geometrical boundaries of a sample and (2) to account for additional nucleation sites that might appear on sample boundaries, because of contact of a polymer with nucleating surfaces. The condition that the point A is occluded before t only by spherulites nucleated closer than $r(\tau,t)$, given by Equation (7.1a), defines, for each combination of τ and t, a sphere in 3D (or a circle in 2D) around A having the radius $r(\tau, t)$. In the case of a sample of finite thickness, d, we have to consider that, depending on $r(\tau, t)$ and distances from sample boundaries, $h_1 = h$ and $h_2 = d - h$, a part of the sphere may extend beyond one or both boundaries (see Fig. 7.7). Moreover, in such a case the sphere includes fragments of the boundaries where additional nucleation processes might occur. Therefore, A will remain at time t outside of spherulites nucleated at time τ, if none of them is nucleated in this part of the sphere, which is confined between sample boundaries, and if no nucleation event occurs on the fragments of sample surfaces included in the sphere. Integration over the range $0 < \tau < t$ leads to the following expression for E:

$$E(t, h, d-h) = E_\infty(t) + H(t, h) + H(t, d-h) \quad (7.45)$$

where $E_\infty(t)$ is equal to $E(t)$ calculated for an infinite sample, expressed by Equation (7.6b), whereas $H(t, h)$, being nonzero for $r(\tau, t) > h$, describes the influence of a boundary at a distance h from A:

$$H(t, h) = \int_0^{t^*} [F_s(\tau) L(\tau, t, h) - F(\tau) S(\tau, t, h)] d\tau \quad (7.46a)$$

$$r(t^*, t) = h. \quad (7.46b)$$

In Equation (7.46a), $L(\tau, t, s)$ is the surface area (or length) of a boundary included in the considered sphere (or circle), F_s is time-dependent nucleation on this boundary, and $S(\tau, t, h)$ is the volume of a fraction of sphere (or circle) beyond material boundaries. Figure 7.7 shows a relevant scheme, drawn for simplicity, for crystallization in a narrow strip of film. For crystallization in a plate bounded by two parallel planes, S and L are expressed as follows:

$$S(\tau, t, h) = (\pi/3)\{h^3 + 2[r(\tau, t)]^3 - 3h[r(\tau, t)]^2\} \quad (7.47a)$$

$$L(\tau, t, h) = \pi\{[r(\tau, t)]^2 - h^2\} \quad (7.47b)$$

α, which is equal to $1 - \exp[-E(t, h, d-h)]$, depends on time and distances from the polymer boundaries; integration over $0 < h < d$ and division by d is necessary in order to obtain an average value.

Calculation of the probability for A to be occluded at time t by one spherulite nucleated either inside a polymer or on polymer boundaries leads to the equations describing the respective components of conversion rate. Integration over time allows derivation of the separate expressions for two contributions to α: the contribution from spherulites nucleated in the bulk of a polymer, α_i, and the contribution from those nucleated on the sample boundaries, α_s, respectively:

$$\alpha_i(t, h, d-h) = \int_0^t \exp[-E(s, h, d-h)] \int_0^s F(\tau)[V'(\tau, s) - S'(\tau, s, h) - S'(\tau, s, d-h)] d\tau \, ds \quad (7.48a)$$

$$\alpha_s(t, h, d-h) = \int_0^t \exp[-E(s, h, d-h)] \int_0^s F_s(\tau)[L'(\tau, s, h) + L'(\tau, s, d-h)] d\tau \, ds \quad (7.48b)$$

where $V'(\tau, t)$, $S'(\tau, t, h)$, and $L'(\tau, t, h)$ are derivatives of V, S, and L with respect to time t. Setting the upper limit of integration as ∞ allows calculation of the volume fractions occupied by both populations of spherulites in the fully crystallized plate, at distances h and d–h from the plate surfaces.

It should be mentioned that Equation (7.48a) and Equation (7.48b) can be also derived assuming that the increase of volume fraction of one population of spherulites, treated separately, occurs outside spherulites of the other population [11]. Moreover, to describe the conversion of melt into spherulites in a plate of finite thickness the extended volume approach was also utilized [12, 15]. The average volumes of spheres having various radii were calculated, taking into account the truncation of spherulites by plate boundaries, and summed to obtain $E(t)$. The obtained expressions differ from those derived using the probabilistic approach, although the numerical calculations of α gave practically the same results [13]. It seems, however, that the probabilistic approach is the correct one [30] and, in fact, agrees better with the modified extended volume concept developed by Avrami in Reference [5].

It follows from Equation (7.45), Equation (7.46a), and Equation (7.46b) that, in the vicinity of a sample boundary, the conversion of melt into spherulites is slower than that inside an infinite sample, although additional nucleation on the boundaries can accelerate the conversion. The influence of those effects on an average conversion rate and/or conversion degree depends, however, on the relation between the sample thickness and spherulite sizes, the latter being dependent on both the nucleation and growth rate or on nucleation density. Usually, a polymer portion can be treated as infinite if its thickness is several times larger than a spherulte radius, whereas the spatial confinement influences the conversion rate when the sample thickness approaches a spherulite size. Very intense additional nucleation on sample boundaries may lead to transcrystallinity, which results in a shoulder on the ascending slope of the DSC crystallization exotherm [45, 46]. With a decrease in sample thickness, the shoulder develops into the main peak. This is illustrated in Figure 7.8, which compares DSC cooling thermograms and the structure of iPP films of different thicknesses, crystallized in contact with poly(tetrafluoroethylene) foil that nucleated transcrystalline zones.

7.6.4 Flow-Induced Crystallization

In industrial processes such as injection molding, extrusion, fiber spinning, or film blowing, a polymer is subjected to a flow, shear, elongation, or mixed deformation modes. The crystallization occurs either during the flow

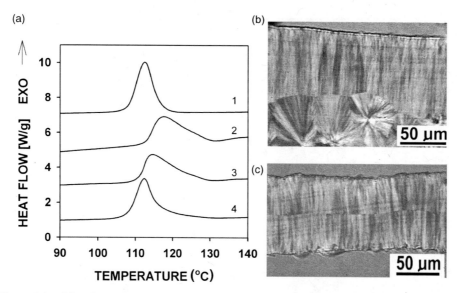

Figure 7.8 (a) DSC crystallization exotherms of iPP recorded during cooling at 10°C/min: 1- 280-μm-thick specimen, 2, 3, and 4- specimens of thickness 45, 90, and 280 μm, respectively, sandwiched between thin poly(tetrafluoroethylene) foils. (b, c) polarized light micrographs of thin sections showing structure of specimens 3 and 4. Reprinted from Gadzinowska, K., Piorkowska, E. Influence of sample thickness and surface nucleation on i-PP crystallization kinetics in DSC measurements. *Polimery* **2003**, *48*, 790–799. Copyright 2003, with kind permission from Polimery.

or soon after the cessation of flow. Similarly, in laboratory conditions, flow-induced crystallization is studied under flow conditions or after the cessation of flow. Depending on the processing conditions and molecular characteristics of a polymer, different morphologies are observed, from spherulites to shish-kebabs. The crystallization process and the resulting structure depend on the orientation effect of the flow, and are strongly related to the temperature, applied shear (or elongation) rate, and total strain. The fundamental processes governing orientation-induced solidification of polymer melts have been studied and discussed by many authors over the last 40 years. The state of knowledge is reviewed in Chapter 14 and Chapter 15.

In general, the induction time for flow-induced crystallization is shorter [47] and the crystallization rate itself is faster [48], as illustrated in Figure 15.1 in Chapter 15.

The apparent effects of flow on spherulitic nucleation include enhancement of nucleation of spherulites [19] and alignment of nuclei parallel to the flow direction. The flow accelerates also the growth rate, but the effect is weaker than that on the nucleation [19, 49]. Anisotropy of the growth, resulting in ellipsoidal shapes of spherulites, was also reported [49]. The observed morphologies include also sheaf-like morphologies, stacks of lamellae, row-nucleated morphologies or cylindrites, and smooth fibrils. The theories developed originally for quiescent crystallization are used also to describe flow-induced crystallization. Recent models consider two types of morphologies: spherulites and shish-kebabs [20, 21]. Others utilize the Avrami–Evans law by modifying k and/or the exponent n [50, 51]; in Reference [51] spherulitic crystallization of iPP followed the Avrami law (Eq. 7.10), with k dependent on a shear rate. To the extent that the crystallization is spherulitic, it is possible to employ directly the expressions derived originally for the quiescent process; in Reference [19], Equation (7.7a) was successfully applied to crystallization with nucleation rate increasing linearly with time during shearing at 140°C at the rates up to 0.3 s^{-1}. It can be noticed that the anisotropy of spherulite growth observed in Reference [49] can be taken into consideration by substituting an extended volume of anisotropic spherulite for $V(\tau,t)$ in Equation (7.6b). To describe the effect of flow on nonisothermal crystallization, the Nakamura equation (Eq. 7.31) is frequently used with k dependent on temperature but also accounting for the effect of flow with an adjustable parameter.

Haudin et al. [21] described shear-induced crystallization, taking into account both spherulites and shish-kebabs. The shish-kebabs were modeled as cylinders with an infinite length. Potential nuclei disappeared by activation and absorption, and new ones were created by flow. The crystallization was described by a set of differential equations, which were solved numerically.

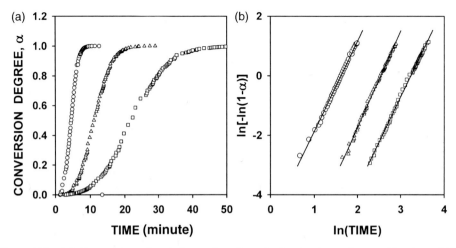

Figure 7.9 (a) Conversion of melt into spherulites during isothermal crystallization of iPP at 128°C (circles), 132°C (triangles), and 135°C (squares) in DSC apparatus. (b) The corresponding Avrami plots for the conversion degree from the range of 0.05 to 0.95, with slopes 3.0, 3.2, and 3.0, respectively; symbols—experimental data; lines—linear regression.

Parameters describing crystallization were optimized using the genetic algorithm inverse method—a stochastic optimization method based on the mechanism of natural selection [52].

It has to be emphasized that the classic Avrami and Evans equations, and consequently the Nakamura approach, were derived by assuming random positions of nuclei in a material; therefore, they do not apply strictly when there is a correlation between positions of nucleation sites. Such nucleation of spherulites is accounted for in the model developed originally for fiber-reinforced polymers [53], described in Chapter 13.

7.7 ANALYSIS OF CRYSTALLIZATION DATA

7.7.1 Isothermal Crystallization

Isothermal crystallization of a polymer is frequently characterized by the induction time and the crystallization half-time. The crystallization induction time is the time that elapses from the moment when the desired crystallization temperature is reached to the onset of crystallization, characterized by the formation of the first nuclei. The crystallization half-time is the time when relative crystallinity reaches 0.5. More detailed analyses of the isothermal crystallization are usually based on the Avrami–Evans theory. Equation (7.10) yields:

$$\ln\{-\ln[1-\alpha(t)]\} = \ln k + n \ln t. \qquad (7.49)$$

Hence, the Avrami plot, which is the plot of $\ln\{-\ln[1-\alpha(t)]\}$ versus $\ln t$, should be in the form of a straight line and enable one to find n and k. The value of n is characteristic of a nucleation mode and dimensionality of the crystallization, whereas k depends on nucleation density, D, or nucleation rate, B, and the growth rate, G, as described in Section 7.4.2. Thus, based on the value of k, it is possible to determine D or B if G is known.

In Figure 7.9a dependencies of conversion degree on time are plotted, having a sigmoidal shape typical of polymer crystallization, calculated for iPP based on DSC measurements. Figure 7.9b shows the corresponding Avrami plots, which, for α in the range of 0.05–0.95, yield n to be about 3, indicating instantaneous nucleation. This value of n is consistent with the straight interspherulitic boundaries found in thin sections of these samples [54].

It is also possible to find the Avrami parameters by fitting the conversion rate curve obtained from DSC data to the first derivative of α expressed by Equation (7.5) with E given by Equation (7.10):

$$d\alpha(t)/dt = nkt^{n-1}\exp(-kt^n). \qquad (7.50)$$

It can be also noticed that at a peak of conversion rate,

$$[dE(t)/dt]_p^2 = [d^2E(t)/dt^2]_p \qquad (7.51)$$

Equation (7.50) and Equation (7.51) yield [55]:

$$1/n = 1 - E(t_p) = 1 + \ln[1-\alpha(t_p)] \qquad (7.52)$$

where the $E(t_p)$ and $\alpha(t_p)$ denote the expectancy and conversion degree at a peak of conversion rate.

The exponent value, n, determined from experimental data for various polymers (mainly based on the

Avrami analysis of DSC measurements) frequently deviates from the theoretically predicted integer numbers. It appears that the Avrami analysis yields:

$$n = d(\ln E)/d(\ln t) = tE^{-1}dE/dt. \quad (7.53)$$

For E expressed by Equation (7.10), n is a constant. However, for more complex nucleation processes, for instance, with nucleation consisting of both instantaneous and spontaneous processes, with E given by Equation (7.11a,b), n depends on time. For example, for the 3D process:

$$n = 3 + [1 + 4D/(Bt)]^{-1}. \quad (7.54)$$

It can be noticed that deviation from $n = 3$ increases in time and depends on the D/B ratio. Although G does not appear explicitly in Equation (7.54), it influences the overall crystallization kinetics and therefore the time needed for crystallization. Thus, the value of n averaged over time depends also on G.

Many reasons for the deviation of n from the predicted constant values are described in the literature, including secondary crystallization, variations in spherulite growth rate, and dependence of nucleation rate on time [56–58]. It was demonstrated by means of computer modeling that nonspherical growth, nonrandom nucleation, or contracting volume produced rather small variations, whereas a time-dependent degree of crystallinity along the spherulite radius can cause large variations in the exponent n [59].

DSC experiments may be also a source of errors in the calculations of conversion degree. Indications concerning the proper protocol for DSC measurements are given in recently published works [30,60] and in Chapter 1. The recommended procedure is to heat up a sample above the equilibrium melting temperature T_m^o to erase history, and then to cool it as fast as possible to the desired temperature of crystallization. The apparatus response should be subtracted from the signal and the baseline correctly determined. The beginning of crystallization may be delayed with respect to time at which the selected temperature was reached by a time called *induction time*. In this case, it is necessary to resolve the onset of crystallization, which is difficult because of negligibly small thermal effects produced by the nucleation. If the assumed onset time of crystallization differs from the true value by t_s, the Avrami analysis yields n_s instead of n:

$$n_s = d(\ln E)/d[\ln(t + t_s)] \quad (7.55a)$$

$$n_s = n(1 + t_s/t). \quad (7.55b)$$

It appears that for nonzero t_s the Avrami plot is nonlinear even for E expressed by Equation (7.10). Moreover, n_s is larger or smaller than n, depending on the sign of t_s, that is, whether the assumed onset of crystallization is too early or too late. This problem is frequently solved by shifting the zero-time to obtain the Avrami plot in the form of a straight line. However, if a source of the nonlinearity is different from the incorrect determination of beginning of crystallization, shifting the onset only increases the error.

It should be noted that DSC measurement delivers the relative mass crystallinity, which can be recalculated to volume degree of crystallinity. Based on the assumption of one crystalline and one amorphous phase, and a constant volume crystallinity inside spherulites, the momentary value of the degree of conversion is calculated by dividing the momentary value of volume degree of crystallinity by the final volume crystallinity obtained after the completion of crystallization.

Moreover, the real temperature of a sample during isothermal crystallization in the DSC might increase above the programmed temperature because of combined effects of the thermal resistance of the sample and the release of the heat of crystallization, especially at a low temperature, promoting fast crystallization and fast release of crystallization heat [61]. As a consequence, the crystallization occurs under nonisothermal conditions. Contrary to this, high crystallization temperature, resulting in low density of nucleation and large spherulites, enhances the influence of sample boundaries on $\alpha(t)$. The volume confinement may decrease the exponent n [30], whereas additional nucleation processes on the sample surfaces might affect not only the exponent n, but even the shape of the conversion rate curve.

It was also demonstrated that in polymer composites, volume inhabited by embedded fibers inaccessible for crystallization and additional nucleation on internal interfaces [53,62,63], can markedly influence the overall crystallization kinetics, as described in Chapter 13. Similar problems might be encountered during crystallization in other polymer systems such as composites with particulate fillers and immiscible polymer blends. Under such conditions, the simplified Avrami equation (Eq. 7.10) does not apply and, as a consequence, the classic Avrami analysis may yield nonlinear plots and/or noninteger n values. It must be emphasized that the problem cannot be solved by application of other, incorrect models, like that of Tobin, which are essentially based on the same assumptions as the Avrami–Evans theory but yield different equations due to incorrect reasoning.

7.7.2 Nonisothermal Crystallization

To characterize nonisothermal crystallization, the crystallization rate peak temperature is frequently used. The more detailed analysis of nonisothermal crystallization is often based on the Ozawa equations, which can be expressed in the following form:

$$\ln\{-\ln[1-\alpha(T)]\} = \ln H(T) - M\ln|v| \quad (7.56)$$

where M equals $m+1$ and $m+2$ for instantaneous nucleation and for nucleation prolonged in time, respectively, m being equal to 1 or 2 for 2D or 3D processes, respectively. The Ozawa analysis utilizes measurements of $\alpha(T)$ at various cooling rates, v. $H(T)$ is independent of v and is called a cooling function.

Equation (7.56) predicts the plots of $\ln\{-\ln[1-\alpha(T)]\}$ versus $\ln|v|$ for a given T in the form of a set of straight lines with a slope of $-M$. Depending on the dimensionality of crystallization and the nucleation mode, M in Equation (7.56) plays a similar role to the Avrami exponent n in Equation (7.10), except that M may equal 3 or 4 for 2D or 3D cases, respectively, for any nucleation process prolonged in time, whereas n assumes these values only for the constant nucleation rate. Intersections of those straight lines with $\ln\{-\ln[1-\alpha(T)]\}$ axis give access to the cooling function $H(T)$. Figure 7.10 illustrates the Ozawa analysis for iPP crystallized at different cooling rates in the range from 0.62 to 40°C/min [30]. Individual plots in Figure 7.10a are composed of linear segments because of the discrete values of cooling rates available in a DSC. The average value of M was 2.85, which is close to 3 and corresponds to 3D growth of instantaneously nucleated spheres. Assuming $M=3$, the cooling function shown in Figure 7.10b was determined, which represents the master curve of the results obtained for the different cooling rates and can be fitted by a polynomial expression.

It must be mentioned that there are many reports on deviation of the Ozawa plots from linearity and also on M values that are different from those predicted theoretically. The analysis of nonisothermal crystallization encounters even more difficulties than that of isothermal crystallization. Additional problems result from the requirement to combine the results of several crystallization experiments performed at different cooling rates. The Ozawa theory is based on the assumption that the nucleation rate dependence on temperature $f(T)$ is unaffected by a cooling rate. As a consequence, the validity of the Ozawa approach is limited to a narrow range of cooling rates that results in the crystallization in similar temperature intervals. Markedly different cooling rates cause variation of M, for instance as shown in Reference [64]. The same applies to other simplified approaches, for example, the Nakamura isokinetic model, in which nonisothermal crystallization is treated as a succession of isothermal processes. The results are reasonable as long as the nucleation process is not influ-

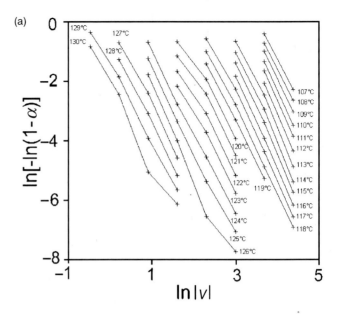

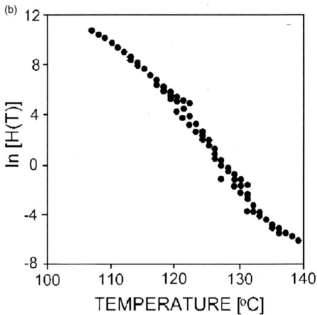

Figure 7.10 The Ozawa plot for iPP crystallized at different cooling rates in the range from 0.62 to 40°C/min; (a) $\ln\{-\ln[1-\alpha(T)]\}$ versus $\ln|v|$ plots, (b) $H(T)$ versus T master curve. Reprinted from Piorkowska, E., et al. Critical assessment of overall crystallization kinetics theories and predictions. *Prog. Polym. Sci.* **2006**, *31*, 549–575. Copyright 2006, with kind permission from Elsevier.

enced markedly by a cooling rate, which is close to reality only for slow cooling rates. Therefore, such approaches cannot be applied to crystallization over wide ranges of temperatures and cooling rates. In addition, the Ozawa equation was derived for a uniform temperature field. Hence, temperature gradients developed within a sample during fast cooling because of poor heat conductivity of polymers, and also by elevation of temperature caused by liberation of heat of crystallization during fast crystallization at large undercooling, may cause additional problems. Contrary to this, low cooling rates promoting slow crystallization at relatively high temperatures can augment the effects of nucleation on sample surfaces, which might affect the shape of the DSC exotherm and might even result in a trans-crystallinity shoulder [16]. It should be noted that the dependence of crystallinity on temperature can be an additional source of errors in calculations of the degree of conversion during nonisothermal crystallization from DSC data.

Similarly, as in the case of the Avrami analysis of isothermal crystallization, the discrepancies between experimentally determined curves and predictions of the Ozawa equation originate mainly from oversimplified assumptions concerning the polymer crystallization. Those discrepancies inspired some authors to search for other equations enabling a better description and analysis of nonisothermal crystallization. For instance, the classic isothermal Avrami analysis based on Equation (7.5) with E expressed by Equation (7.10) was applied to nonisothermal crystallization [65, 66]. Such an approach has no theoretical justification. Even if a straight line Avrami plot is obtained, the parameters k and n are, at best, two adjustable parameters without a clear physical meaning. The Jeziorny method [67] deserves similar criticism. Jeziorny proposed using Equation (7.5) and Equation (7.10) and characterizing the process with the parameter k_c defined as:

$$\log k_c = v^{-1} \log k. \qquad (7.57)$$

In the view of equations describing the nonisothermal crystallization in detail, k_c has no physical meaning. Liu et al. [68] combined isothermal Avrami equation (Eq. 7.10) with the nonisothermal Ozawa equation into a single equation:

$$kt^n = v^{-M} H(T). \qquad (7.58)$$

A plot of log v against log t should give a straight line with the intercept of log $F(T) = \log[H(T)/k]$ and the slope of equal to $-n/M$. In fact, the Ozawa equation and the isothermal Avrami equation (Eq. 7.10) are derived from the same general Equation (7.6a) and Equation (7.6b) but with different assumptions: in the Ozawa equation a constant cooling rate is assumed, while in the Avrami Equation (7.10) the growth rate G is a constant. Therefore, the combination of the equations proposed in References [68] and used by many authors has no justification and is erroneous.

Nonisothermal crystallization is frequently analyzed via calculation of the so-called energy of activation of crystallization according to the Kissinger method [69, 70]. The method is based on the simplifying assumption that a transformation rate during a reaction (crystallization in the present case) is a product of two functions, one depending solely on the transformed fraction, $f(\alpha)$, and the other depending solely on temperature, with an Arrhenius-type dependence:

$$d\alpha/dt = f(\alpha) h_o \exp(-E_a/RT). \qquad (7.59)$$

Transformations of Equation (7.59) yield:

$$\ln(v/T_f^2) = -E_a/RT_f + C_1 \qquad (7.60)$$

where T_f is the temperature at a fixed degree of conversion, and C_1 is a parameter independent of v and T. The data collected during measurements with various cooling rates allow plotting of $\ln(T_f^2/v)$ versus $1/T_f$, which should be in the form of a straight line with a slope equal to E_a/R. In fact, Equation (7.59) does not describe correctly the nonisothermal crystallization of polymers; in addition the activation energy E_a calculated based on Equation (7.60) is often negative. Moreover, it is unclear to which process the single activation energy of crystallization, E_a, should be ascribed: to the nucleation, or to the crystal growth, or to both. The same criticism applies to the determination of the activation energy of crystallization based on isothermal crystallization data.

7.8 CONCLUSIONS

The overall crystallization kinetics of polymers is governed by nucleation and growth of crystalline aggregates, and is influenced by the thermomechanical crystallization conditions and history, including temperature field, pressure, and effects of flow. Also, dimensionality of the process plays an important role. Usually, crystallization in thin films is slower than in polymer bulk, although the nucleation on film surfaces might markedly accelerate the crystallization. In addition, internal interfaces, for instance, in fiber-reinforced composites or in polymer blends, also influence the overall crystallization kinetics.

The known theories dealing with the overall crystallization kinetics assume that the conversion of amorphous phase into crystalline phase occurs via radial growth of domains—spherulites—in the case of polymers. They do not apply to crystallization processes that do not occur via nucleation and radial growth of domains.

Although the general expressions for the degree of conversion account for dependence of nucleation and growth on time and also on spatial coordinates, the number of analytical equations for particular cases is limited.

Although the majority of laboratory experiments are conducted under relatively well-controlled conditions, the classic Avrami plot and the Ozawa plot frequently yield results different from those predicted by the theory, because even under those well-defined conditions the crystallization might be too complex to be analyzed based on those simplified approaches. Industrial processing involves complex thermomechanical pre-crystallization histories and crystallization conditions, including the effects of flow, the time-dependent temperature gradients, and the release of heat of crystallization, the latter additionally modifying the temperature fields. Therefore, to predict correctly the course of crystallization and resulting structures, more realistic crystallization models are necessary and also a coupling with numerical calculations, as demonstrated in Chapter 15.

REFERENCES

[1] Kolmogoroff, A.N. *Izvestiya Akad. Nauk. SSSR Ser. Math.* **1937**, *1*, 355–359.
[2] Evans, U.R. *Trans. Faraday Soc.* **1945**, *41*, 365–374.
[3] Avrami, M. *J. Chem. Phys.* **1939**, *7*, 1103–1112.
[4] Avrami, M. *J. Chem. Phys.* **1940**, *8*, 212–224.
[5] Avrami, M. *J. Chem. Phys.* **1941**, *9*, 177–184.
[6] Johnson, W.A., Mehl, R.F. *Trans. AIME* **1939**, *135*, 416–458.
[7] Ozawa, T. *Polymer* **1971**, *12*, 150–158.
[8] Nakamura, K., Watanabe, T., Katayama, K., Amano, T. *J. Appl. Polym. Sci.* **1972**, *16*, 1077–1091.
[9] Nakamura, K., Katayama, K., Amano, T. *J. Appl. Polym. Sci.* **1973**, *17*, 1031–1041.
[10] Piorkowska, E. *J. Appl. Polym. Sci.* **2002**, *86*, 1351–1362.
[11] Eder, G., Janeschitz-Kriegl, H. Crystallization. In *Materials Science and Technology. A Comprehensive Treatment. Processing of Polymers*, Vol. 18, Meijer, H.E.H., ed. VCH Verlagsgesellschaft GmbH, Weinheim, 1997, pp. 270–341.
[12] Escleine, J.M., Monasse, B., Wey, E., Haudin, J.M. *Colloid Polym. Sci.* **1984**, *262*, 366–373.
[13] Billon, N., Escleine, J.M., Haudin, J.M. *Colloid Polym. Sci.* **1989**, *267*, 668–680.
[14] Billon, N., Haudin, J.M. *Colloid Polym. Sci.* **1989**, *267*, 1064–1076.
[15] Schultz, J.M. *Macromolecules* **1996**, *29*, 3022–3024.
[16] Billon, N., Magnet, C., Haudin, J.M., Lefebvre, D. *Colloid Polym. Sci.* **1994**, *272*, 633–654.
[17] Piorkowska, E. *Colloid Polym. Sci.* **1997**, *275*, 1035–1045.
[18] Piorkowska, E. *Colloid Polym. Sci.* **1997**, *275*, 1046–1059.
[19] Coccorullo, I., Pantani, R., Titomanlio, G. *Macromolecules* **2008**, *41*, 9214–9223.
[20] Zuidema, H., Peters, G.W.M., Meijer, H.E.H. *Macromol. Theory Simul.* **2001**, *10*, 447–460.
[21] Haudin, J.M., Smirnova, J., Silva, L., Monasse, B., Chenot, J.L. *Polym. Sci. Ser. A* **2008**, *50*, 538–549.
[22] Ziabicki, A., Misztal-Faraj, B. *Polymer* **2005**, *46*, 2395–2403.
[23] Tabar, R.J., Wasiak, A., Hong, S.D., Yuasa, T., Stein, R.S. *J. Polym. Sci. Polym. Phys. Ed.* **1981**, *19*, 49–58.
[24] Galeski, A. *J. Polym. Sci. Polym. Phys. Ed.* **1981**, *19*, 721–730.
[25] Galeski, A., Piorkowska, E. *J. Polym. Sci. Polym. Phys. Ed.* **1981**, *19*, 731–741.
[26] von Neumann, J. Various techniques used in connection with random digits. In *Monte Carlo Method*, Householder, A.S., Forsythe, G.E., Germond, H.H., eds. *Natl. Bur. Stand. Appl. Math. Ser. 12*. U.S. Government Printing Office, Washington, DC, 1951, pp. 36–38.
[27] Tobin, M.C. *J. Polym. Sci. Polym. Phys. Ed.* **1974**, *12*, 399–406.
[28] Tobin, M.C. *J. Polym. Sci. Polym. Phys. Ed.* **1976**, *14*, 2253–2257.
[29] Tobin, M.C. *J. Polym. Sci. Polym. Phys. Ed.* **1977**, *15*, 2269–2270.
[30] Piorkowska, E., Galeski, A., Haudin, J.M. *Prog. Polym. Sci.* **2006**, *31*, 549–575.
[31] Piorkowska, E., Galeski, A. *J. Appl. Polym. Sci.* **2002**, *86*, 1363–1372.
[32] Piorkowska, E., Galeski, A. *J. Phys. Chem.* **1985**, *89*, 4700–4703.
[33] Lafleur, P.G., Kamal, M.R. *Polym. Eng. Sci.* **1986**, *26*, 92–102.
[34] Hsiung, C.M., Cakmak, M. *Polym. Eng. Sci.* **1991**, *31*, 1372–1385.
[35] Titomanlio, G., Speranza, V., Brucato, V. *Int. Polym. Process.* **1995**, *10*, 55–61.
[36] Isayev, A.I., Chan, T.W., Gmerek, M., Shimojo, K. *J. Appl. Polym. Sci.* **1995**, *55*, 821–838.
[37] Schneider, W., Koppl, A., Berger, J. *Int. Polym. Process.* **1988**, *2*, 151–154.
[38] Andreucci, D., Fasano, A., Primicerio, M., Paolini, M., Verdi, C. *Math. Models Methods Appl. Sci.* **1994**, *4*, 135–145.
[39] Haudin, J.M., Chenot, J.L. *Int. Polym. Process.* **2004**, *19*, 267–274.
[40] Kristiansen, M., Werner, M., Tervoort, T., Smith, P., Blomenhofer, M., Schmidt, H.W. *Macromolecules* **2003**, *36*, 5150–5156.
[41] Piorkowska, E. *J. Appl. Polym. Sci.* **1997**, *66*, 1015–1028.
[42] Schulze, G.E.W., Naujeck, T.R. *Colloid Polym. Sci.* **1991**, *269*, 689–694.
[43] Schulze, G.E.W., Naujeck, T.R. *Colloid Polym. Sci.* **1991**, *269*, 695–703.

[44] Pawlak, A., Piorkowska, E. *Colloid Polym. Sci.* **2001**, *279*, 939–946.

[45] Gadzinowska, K., Piorkowska, E. *Polimery* **2003**, *48*, 790–799.

[46] Billon, N., Henaff, V., Pelous, E., Haudin, J.M. *J. Appl. Polym. Sci.* **2002**, *86*, 725–733.

[47] Kamal, M.R., Lee, O. *Polym. Eng. Sci.* **1999**, *39*, 236–248.

[48] Devaux, N., Monasse, B., Haudin, J.M., Moldenaers, P., Vermant, J. *Rheol. Acta* **2004**, *43*, 210–222.

[49] Monasse, B. *J. Mater. Sci.* **1995**, *30*, 5002–5012.

[50] Ziabicki, A., Jarecki, L. *J. Appl. Polym. Sci.* **2007**, *105*, 215–223.

[51] Godara, A., Raabe, D., Van Puyvelde, P., Moldenaers, P. *Polym. Test.* **2006**, *25*, 460–469.

[52] Carroll, D.L. *FORTRAN* Genetic Algorithm Front-End Driver Code, http://cuaerospace.com/carroll/ga.html.

[53] Piorkowska, E. *Macromol. Symp.* **2001**, *169*, 143–148.

[54] Gadzinowska, K., Piorkowska, E. *Polimery* **2004**, *49*, 698–705.

[55] Khonakdar, H.A., Shiri, M., Golriz, M., Asadinezhad, A., Jafari, S.H. *E-Polymers* **2008**, no 085.

[56] Price, F.P. *J. Polym. Sci. A* **1965**, *3*, 3079–3086.

[57] Hillier, I.H. *J. Polym. Sci. A* **1965**, *3*, 3067–3078.

[58] Grenier, D., Prudhomme, R.E. *J. Polym. Sci. Polym. Phys. Ed.* **1980**, *18*, 1655–1657.

[59] Hay, J.N., Przekop, Z.J. *J. Polym. Sci. Polym. Phys. Ed.* **1979**, *17*, 951–959.

[60] Lorenzo, A.T., Arnal, M.L., Albuerne, J., Muller, A.J. *Polym. Test.* **2007**, *26*, 222–231.

[61] Martins, J.A., Cruz-Pinto, J.J.C. *J. Appl. Polym. Sci.* **2004**, *91*, 125–131.

[62] Mehl, N.A., Rebenfeld, L. *J. Polym. Sci. B Polym. Phys.* **1993**, *31*, 1677–1686.

[63] Mehl, N.A., Rebenfeld, L. *J. Polym. Sci. B Polym. Phys.* **1993**, *31*, 1687–1693.

[64] Collins, G.L., Menczel, J.D. *Polym. Eng. Sci.* **1992**, *32*, 1270–1277.

[65] de Juana, R., Jauregui, A., Calahorra, E., Cortazar, M. *Polymer* **1996**, *37*, 3339–3345.

[66] Lee, S.W., Ree, M., Park, C.E., Jung, Y.K., Park, C.S., Jin, Y.S., Bae, D.C. *Polymer* **1999**, *40*, 7137–7146.

[67] Jeziorny, A. *Polymer* **1978**, *19*, 1142–1144.

[68] Liu, T., Mo, Z., Wang, S., Zhang, H. *Polym. Eng. Sci.* **1997**, *37*, 568–575.

[69] Kissinger, H.E. *J. Res. Natl. Bur. Stand.* **1956**, *57*, 217–221.

[70] Starink, M.J. *Thermochim. Acta* **2003**, *404*, 163–176.

8

EPITAXIAL CRYSTALLIZATION OF POLYMERS: MEANS AND ISSUES

ANNETTE THIERRY AND BERNARD A. LOTZ

Institut Charles Sadron, CNRS, Université de Strasbourg, Strasbourg, France

8.1 Introduction and History, 237
8.2 Means of Investigation of Epitaxial Crystallization, 239
    8.2.1 Global Techniques, 239
    8.2.2 Thin Film Techniques, 239
    8.2.3 Sample Preparation Techniques, 240
    8.2.4 Other Samples and Investigation Procedures, 241
8.3 Epitaxial Crystallization of Polymers, 241
    8.3.1 General Principles, 241
    8.3.2 Epitaxial Crystallization of "Linear" Polymers, 243
    8.3.3 Epitaxy of Helical Polymers, 245
    8.3.4 Polymer/Polymer Epitaxy, 250
8.4 Epitaxial Crystallization: Further Issues and Examples, 252
    8.4.1 Topographic Versus Lattice Matching, 252
8.4.2 Epitaxy of Isotactic Polypropylene on Isotactic Polyvinylcyclohexane, 254
8.4.3 Epitaxy Involving Fold Surfaces of Polymer Crystals, 254
8.5 Epitaxial Crystallization: Some Issues and Applications, 256
    8.5.1 Epitaxial Crystallization and the Design of New Nucleating Agents, 256
    8.5.2 Epitaxial Crystallization and the Design of Composite Materials, 257
    8.5.3 Conformational and Packing Energy Analysis of Polymer Epitaxy, 258
    8.5.4 Epitaxy as a Means to Generate Oriented Opto- or Electroactive Materials, 259
8.6 Conclusions, 260
References, 262

8.1 INTRODUCTION AND HISTORY

Epitaxial crystallization of materials has been known for a long time. The oriented crystallization of a given crystal (the deposit) on the surface of another crystal (the substrate) has been investigated in quite some detail by Royer in the late 1920s [1]. His work dealt mostly with minerals, for which X-ray investigations had established either the unit-cell geometry and dimensions or even the detailed crystal structure. On the basis of this information and by analyzing the relative orientations of the substrate and deposit, Royer could establish several rules that govern epitaxial crystallization. He pointed out in particular that there must be a dimensional match between the crystal lattices of the substrate and the deposit in the contact plane. This rule of thumb states that the mismatch between the corresponding dimensions must not exceed 15%, or even preferably 10%—a criterion confirmed by and large by all of the more recent studies.

Epitaxial crystallization is still the topic of numerous investigations in the field of materials science, especially in relation with the formation of nanostructured layers in devices. Epitaxial crystallization has comparatively been neglected in the field of crystalline polymers. Early observations on the epitaxial crystallization of polyethylene (PE) on several alkali halide crystals are due to Willems [2, 3] and Fischer [4] in Germany. This line of research was expanded at Case Western Reserve University in the 1960s [5–7]. Of more relevance, however, are investigations of epitaxial crystallization of polymers on organic substrates. Organic substrates offer indeed a much wider range of properties (low unit-cell symmetry, compatibility with the polymer, wide range of cell dimensions, etc.) not to mention the relevance to the design of nucleating agents. An initial study is again due to Case Western. It led to a short note in which the importance of the field was underlined [8], but this line of research was not followed up at Case Western. A later work at McGill University uncovered the role of epitaxy in the eutectic crystallization of some blends of polymer/low molecular weight (Mw) organic or monomer compounds (e.g., poly-ε-caprolactone and trioxane) [9, 10]. More systematic contributions stem from this laboratory, at the initiative of J.C. Wittmann, initially as an extension of the work performed at McGill University. The contributions made use of appropriate sample preparation and experimental investigation techniques, and resulted in the analysis of a number of epitaxies of polymers either on minerals, on low molecular weight organic substrates, or on other polymers [11].

First, however, let us recall the most original features of epitaxial crystallization and its potential as a means of generating oriented morphologies of polymers.

Epitaxial crystallization leads to *oriented* growth of the depositing material. Observation of oriented deposit suggests at once some form of interaction with the substrate. However, the exact nature of these interactions may be difficult to characterize. As a result, several "kinds" of epitaxy can be defined (without however attempting to be exhaustive in the present context). "Graphoepitaxy" defines an orientation induced by the surface topography of the substrate, for instance, the existence of ditches or striations in the substrate induced, for example, by rubbing. No clear-cut lattice match is necessary or involved in this process. "Soft epitaxy" is a more general, or even generic term frequently used to characterize oriented growth on a substrate when no clear lattice matching can be defined or envisaged. By contrast, "hard epitaxy" defines a substrate/deposit relationship that involves clear-cut structural and dimensional match between substrate and deposit. It must be stressed that, frequently, the kind of epitaxy ultimately considered depends on the quality of the experimental/structural information obtained. As seen later on, several epitaxies initially defined as "grapho" or "soft" turned out to be "hard" when the exact relationship (i.e., at the unit cell and, even better, at the molecular level) could be established.

A major characteristic of epitaxial crystallization is that it is a *mild* orienting process. Indeed, the orientation results from a *growth* process directed by, and from, the substrate. As such it departs significantly from all other orienting methods normally used in the processing of crystalline polymers. Such processing typically uses some form of mechanical orientation, such as fiber spinning, and extrusion. Fiber spinning can only produce crystal modifications that are stable to mechanical orientation. By contrast, epitaxial crystallization can be used to orient metastable or unstable crystal modifications—admittedly in relatively thin films and over much shorter distances or areas—determined by the substrate size. It provides invaluable structural information on these crystal modifications. Moreover, and as a fairly general rule, the polymer chains lie parallel to the contact plane of the substrate, with however one major difference from fiber orientation. Epitaxial crystallization selects one specific crystal plane parallel to the chain axis of the polymer as the contact plane; that is, it produces a thin polymer film that has, at least locally, single crystal orientation rather than fiber symmetry. Besides, electron microscopy investigation both of chain folded single crystals (chain axis parallel to the electron beam) and of epitaxially crystallized films (chain axis perpendicular to the beam) makes it possible to perform truly single crystal structural analysis. This is a quite remarkable and unique achievement, considering the intrinsic small size of polymer crystals.

Single crystal orientation can be a major requirement, especially when processing of polymers aims at taking advantage of their anisotropic properties. By analogy, with fiber spinning that enhances uniaxial mechanical properties, it is possible to highlight anisotropic electric, optical, and so on, properties of polymers by generating appropriate uniaxial or even more so, single crystal orientation of these polymers. Epitaxial crystallization may therefore become a major ingredient in generating, for example, thin films used in optoelectronic applications.

Epitaxy also plays a major role in the more traditional field of nucleating agents. The role of epitaxy was recognized only recently, long after the industrial development of this class of additives. As indicated, epitaxy is the result of a mild interaction with a foreign substrate that favors the crystallization, or more exactly its initial nucleation step. Understanding this process therefore becomes an essential ingredient in developing new nucleating agents.

This chapter deals with oriented crystallization induced by a crystalline substrate—orientation of polymer crystals induced by interaction with an amorphous substrate is covered in Chapter 12. It is by no means an exhaustive review of the work on epitaxy of polymers—in this respect relatively recent papers list many references of interest [12, 13]. Rather, this contribution develops in some detail the insights gained on polymer epitaxy, and the means that helped provide these insights. In Section 8.2, the various techniques of investigation are indicated, together with experimental methods of analyzing the detailed interactions between deposit and substrate. Indeed, specific sample preparation and appropriate investigation techniques are crucial in any investigation of epitaxial crystallization. Section 8.3 develops the structural relationships that have been observed in epitaxial crystallization. It details the epitaxial crystallization of "linear" polymers, of which PE is the archetype. It considers the epitaxial crystallization of helical polymers. The more complex molecular architecture of helical polymers generates indeed a couple of further possibilities of epitaxy. Most original among these, epitaxial crystallization can help define the hand (right or left) of the helices in the contact plane—information that cannot be obtained by other means. Section 8.4 includes two more detailed case studies that help reach a submolecular understanding of the topographic interactions underlying the epitaxial relationship. Section 8.5 develops several of the technological applications of epitaxial crystallization mentioned earlier, including the formation of highly ordered functional polymers (e.g., involved in optoelectronic devices) or the important field of artificially enhanced nucleation of crystalline polymers.

8.2 MEANS OF INVESTIGATION OF EPITAXIAL CRYSTALLIZATION

8.2.1 Global Techniques

A favorable interaction between a foreign substance and a polymer results in enhanced nucleation, that is, in faster crystallization rate. Traditionally therefore the enhancement of crystallization rate has been used as an indicator of favorable polymer–foreign particles interactions. Global methods can be used as screening techniques. Historically, such screening techniques have relied on differential scanning calorimetry (DSC) and on the increase of the crystallization temperature of "nucleated" polymers compared with their non-nucleated counterparts. DSC can lead to a crude classification of "favorable" versus less favorable nucleating agents. Binsbergen [14] and Beck [15] investigated by DSC the nucleating activity of thousands of chemicals in PE and in isotactic polypropylene (iPP). A similar classification can be made with a polarizing optical microscope by observing a sample in which particles of different additives have been included: the interactions are manifested by a so-called transcrystallization of the polymer induced by the additive, the "better" ones nucleating at higher temperatures than the poorer ones (cf later, Fig. 8.1a).

This type of information is, however, purely qualitative. It cannot yield any further information on the types of interactions taking place between the polymer and the additive. Actually, when attempting to analyze the observed nucleation efficiency (determined by DSC) in terms of matching of lattice parameters, Binsbergen [14] was led to suggest that only some vague form of orientation and/or matching of polymer chains in ditches of the substrate is at play. This conclusion was later shown to be inadequate, when proper sample preparation and investigation techniques were developed.

8.2.2 Thin Film Techniques

Epitaxial crystallization implies interactions at the interface between the polymer and the foreign particle. These interactions are very short ranged ones—for aliphatic polymers, typically within van der Waals interactions range, that is, mostly within 0.5 to 1 nm. Also, polymer growth tends to introduce orientation disorder: twisting of lamellae (for example, of PE, giving rise to spherulites with concentric extinction bands) has a half period of only a few or even 1 μm. This "morphological" disorder implies that a possible orientation induced by the epitaxial crystallization can no longer be tracked after even only limited growth away from the polymer–additive interface. For this reason, epitaxial crystallization can only be studied on very thin polymer films, investigated in the immediate vicinity of the substrate. In essence, the interface must represent a significant part, or even the major part, of the sample investigated. This in turn limits the type and number of useful investigation techniques. Among scattering techniques, grazing incidence X-ray scattering is most appropriate to investigate thin films deposited on solid thick substrates when investigated by reflection. Reflection high energy electron diffraction (RHEED) is an equivalent technique, suitable for smaller samples.

Conventional transmission electron microscopy is much preferable since it makes it possible to image very small domains and to obtain the corresponding electron diffraction pattern [11].

Ideally, a bilayer less than 20 to 30 nm thick made of the substrate and the deposited polymer film is most suitable. The electron diffraction pattern obtained by transmission through the bilayer is then a composite pattern with combined contributions from the two partners (Fig. 8.1b). Analysis of this single composite pattern provides the full geometrical relationship between the polymer and the substrate. Indeed, the zone axis parallel

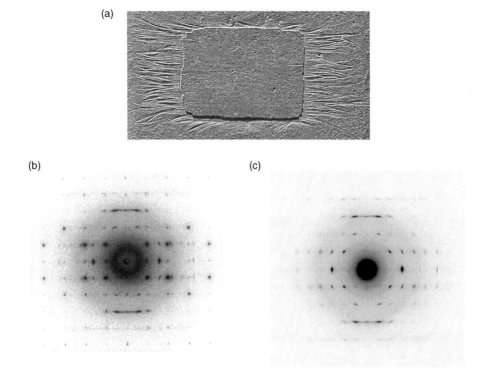

Figure 8.1 (a) Epitaxial crystallization of isotactic polypropylene, β phase, on a single crystal of dicyclohexylterephthalamide (DCHT). The DCHT crystal (≈ 10 µm in length) was deposited on a thin (≈ 20–40 nm) iPP film. After iPP melting followed by partial crystallization at $\approx 130°C$, the sample is quenched and the DCHT single crystal dissolved: the micrograph shows only the imprint left by the DCHT crystal as it sunk in the molten iPP. Initial epitaxial crystallization of iPP lamellae on the nucleating agent surface and further growth into the polymer melt (so-called transcrystallization) is apparent. The smaller spherulites were made during the quenching process. Electron micrograph, Pt/carbon shadowing. (b) Composite diffraction pattern of a sample as shown in part (a) after only partial dissolution of the DCHT. Sharp spots and arced reflections correspond to the DCHT and iPP contributions, respectively. iPP chain axis vertical, (110) contact plane. Note the correspondence of substrate and chain axis periodicities. Parts (a) and (b) reproduced from Reference [39] with permission of the American Chemical Society. (c) Diffraction of the epitaxially crystallized film as shown in part (a) after complete dissolution of the DCHT. The single crystal orientation is indicated by the presence of only one set of reflections (here, 110 and 220) on the equator of the pattern.

to the electron beam (and therefore the contact plane normal to it) can be determined from the observed reflections (and/or the absent ones) in both polymer and substrate diffraction patterns. The relative orientation of the two patterns also provides with exceptional accuracy (within less than one degree) the orientation of the chain axis on the substrate. However, this insight requires careful preparation of appropriate samples.

Atomic force microscopy (AFM) has become a very useful tool for analyzing epitaxially grown thin films. When the polymer contact plane can be exposed (for example, by dissolution of the substrate, or even by physically detaching the polymer overgrowth from, e.g., a mica substrate), AFM makes it possible to image not only the lamellar structure as initiated by that substrate but also, at high resolution, the organization of chains in the contact plane, or, when reaching methyl group resolution, the helical hand of individual stems—a feat not achievable by any other experimental means.

8.2.3 Sample Preparation Techniques

Samples suitable for electron microscopy, electron diffraction, and AFM analysis can be obtained by different means.

When dealing with a substrate that cannot be melted (e.g., talc flakes, salts), a thin film of the polymer is solvent-cast on a glass slide. The crystals of the substrate are deposited on top of the film; the polymer is melted and recrystallized. The substrate is then dissolved with a specific solvent (Fig. 8.1a). If desired, it is dissolved only partly, in order to maintain a thin substrate layer that will diffract (Fig. 8.1b). Further handling of the resulting film rests on standard procedures in electron microscopy: shadowing and/or decoration (optional), backing with a carbon film, floating on water, transfer on electron microscope grids.

In many cases, the organic substrates themselves can be melted and act as a solvent for the polymer, but only in their molten state. In that case, a small amount of the polymer is co-melted with the substrate (e.g., PE and p-terphenyl) between glass slide and cover-slide. (It might be preferable to use two cover-slides in order to minimize thermal inertia during quenching.) On cooling, the substrate crystallizes first—in case of p-terphenyl as large, flat crystals. The molten polymer is rejected near the glass slides and crystallizes later on the fresh, clean surfaces of the substrate. Note that this process is frequently observed when the polymer and substrate have melting temperatures that are close, and form a eutectic, although epitaxial crystallization adds its specific requirements to the process.

Many alternative methods of sample preparation exist. For example, the polymer film can be deposited on the substrate by vaporization. This has been achieved with PE, iPP, poly(vinylidene fluoride), and so on, but does not work with, for example, polyesters or nylons. Vaporization is performed under vacuum, by heating a few milligrams of the polymer deposited on a tungsten wire or in a crucible. This technique produces films of nearly constant thickness and over large areas. The vaporized polymer has of course a lower molecular weight, typically a few thousands of Daltons for PE and iPP. The lower molecular weight is not detrimental to the analysis of the epitaxial relationship. The relationship is defined at the scale of the unit cell, that is, at a length scale significantly smaller than the molecular dimensions. As an illustration, PE and a paraffin (e.g., $C_{36}H_{74}$) deposited on a range of substrates display various kinds of epitaxies (contact planes), but for each of these substrates the paraffin and PE epitaxies are identical [16].

8.2.4 Other Samples and Investigation Procedures

In the bilayer samples mentioned earlier, the chain axis of the polymer lies generally parallel to the contact plane, and the observation is made normal to this plane. It may be useful to examine epitaxies along the chain axis, in particular when investigating polymer/polymer epitaxies. In that case, it is convenient to produce single crystals of the higher melting (or crystallizing) polymer (e.g., in thin films or from dilute solution) and allow the polymer crystallizing at lower temperatures to grow on the lateral edges of the "parent" single crystal. This technique will be illustrated later on, in the specific system of the isotactic polyvinylcyclohexane (iPVCH)/iPP epitaxy (Section 8.4.2).

To conclude this section on the experimental part, complete analysis of the epitaxial relationship between a polymer and a substrate (be it a salt, a low molecular weight organic, or a polymer) is only possible when single crystal orientation of the substrate and associated, specific orientations of the deposit are reached. This requirement indicates that polymer/polymer epitaxies cannot be analyzed properly when the nucleating polymer is in a fiber form since there is no means to establish which of its $hk0$ planes interacts with the deposit. Elaborate orientation means may be needed, such as successive epitaxial crystallizations. In this process, a single crystal orientation of the high melting polymer is first produced by epitaxial crystallization on a higher melting low molecular weight substrate. Subsequent dissolution of the substrate exposes the polymer crystallographic face that was the contact plane in the epitaxy. A second polymer is deposited on that face by various means (solution casting, evaporation, etc.). Melting and recrystallization of the latter polymer yields the epitaxy of interest. It should also be kept in mind that thin films prepared for AFM investigations are usually fully suited for electron microscopy and electron diffraction analysis. In most cases, the latter techniques provide additional, structural information not available through the sole AFM examination, which is thus more limitative.

8.3 EPITAXIAL CRYSTALLIZATION OF POLYMERS

8.3.1 General Principles

As recalled in the introduction, the rules that govern epitaxial crystallization were laid out by Royer back in the late 1920s [1]. In essence, epitaxy rests on favorable *local* interactions between the deposit and the substrate, that is, at the unit-cell scale level. These interactions, typically short range van der Waals, become negligible beyond about 1 nm for, for example, polyolefins, although slightly larger distances need to be considered for longer range interactions (electrostatic, polar, etc.). *Repetition* of these favorable interactions throughout the contact plane must, by necessity, imply some form of lattice matching. This dimensional matching may not be perfect, thus the ±10% leeway between matching periodicities, which is partly compensated by the lattice elasticity and/or generation of local crystallographic defects (point dislocations).

Epitaxial crystallization of polymers conforms to these rules, but adds a number of significant original features. These features stem mostly from the long chain nature of polymers, in which one crystallographic direction (along the chain, with its covalent bonds) differs significantly from the interchain directions.

- Most epitaxies reported so far indicate that the chain axis lies in the contact plane. In essence, all contact planes are of *hk0* type. This has a major morphological consequence: epitaxially crystallized films are made of *edge-on*, chain folded lamellae. The film is thus made of multiple, independent, stacked lamellae. Yet when considering the unit-cell-level organization. The film is *single crystalline* since the specific orientation of each lamella is imposed by the epitaxial relation with the single crystalline substrate. The epitaxial relationship transfers the single crystal character of the substrate to the whole polymer film. When the substrates are low molecular weight materials or minerals, the crystals may be quite large—sometimes several tens of square centimeters. Such large, single crystal domains of polymers are hard to generate by any other means. Of course, single orientation is only reached when, for both the substrate and the polymer, low symmetry contact faces are involved. The polymer may adopt two orientations when similar planes related by symmetry are involved in the epitaxy (e.g., (110) and ($\bar{1}$10) of PE generate two different *a*- and *b*-axes orientations with identical *c*-axis orientation) [17]. High symmetry substrates generate several *chain axis* orientations (e.g., alkali halides generate two polymer chain orientations, while talc usually generates three orientations) [18].
- The local favorable interactions that exist between the depositing chains and the substrate must be repeated in the contact plane. When considering *hk0* contact planes, the distance of interest is *not* therefore the *interplanar* distance associated with these planes, since this distance is normal to the contact plane. Rather, the periodicity of interest is, for example, the *interchain distances within the contact plane*. As an illustration developed in Section 8.3.2, on the (110) interplanar distance in PE is 0.411 nm, but the distance of interest that determines the epitaxy is the 0.445 nm *interchain* distance in that plane (cf Fig. 8.2).
- Since the "quality" of the epitaxy rests in part on the density of favorable interactions between the deposit and the substrate, contact planes are usually densely packed, low index *hk0* planes of the polymer. The matching periodicities are usually

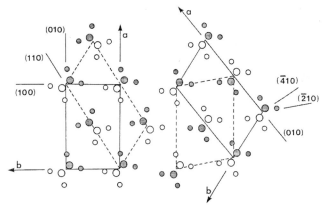

Figure 8.2 The various contact planes obtained so far for the epitaxial crystallization of the orthorhombic and monoclinic phases of polyethylene on substrates with matching periodicities. The corresponding interchain spacings correspond to the first and the second nearest neighbor chains with periodicities of 0.446, 0.494, and 0.744 nm for the orthorhombic (110), (100), and (010) planes and 0.404 nm, 0.523 nm and 0.918 nm for the monoclinic (010), ([$\bar{2}$10]), and ([$\bar{4}$10]) planes, respectively. Reproduced from Reference [11] with permission of Pergamon Press.

short, often the shortest ones in any given contact plane.
- Preservation of a high density of interactions is ideally achieved when the substrate and deposit have identical periodicities. It is therefore of interest to search for substrates that match known periodicities of the polymer, in a one-dimensional or, better, a two-dimensional relationship. Epitaxy may also exist when the corresponding distances are multiple, for example, one substrate periodicity for two deposit periodicities. Larger multiples (1 for 3, or 2 for 3) appear very unlikely, and have been observed only occasionally in polymer epitaxy.
- Matching of polymer periodicities with that of the substrate may be rather complex. The simplest case is of course to match an interchain periodicity, as is the case for PE, considered in the next paragraphs. However, in polymers with a helical conformation, the helix axis is not materialized by a string of atoms. The outer part of the helix interacts more closely with the substrate. In other words, the helical path may be involved in the epitaxy, or more exactly the distance between two successive helical paths, that is between parts of the helix located *on its outer part*. The orientation of the helix path relative to the helix axis differs for right-handed and left-handed helices (cf Fig. 8.9). Therefore, epitaxial deposition of polymers with helical conformation

may (but does not always) help reveal the chirality of the helices located in the polymer contact plane. This possibility is unique to epitaxial crystallization, and occurs only because short-range interactions are involved in epitaxy: for such short ranges, only the helical path "counts."

- As a rule, the epitaxial interactions involve a "foreign" substrate. They are by design less favorable than the interactions of the polymer with itself. Therefore, epitaxial crystallization takes place usually at large supercooling (relatively low temperatures). The actual temperature range is a rough indicator of the "quality" of these interactions.
- The substrates usually have dimensions much larger than the "usual" lamellar thickness of crystalline polymers, typically in the ten or tens of nanometers range. Deposition on such "infinite" substrates (on a molecular scale) allows stem extension during crystallization. For long annealing times, this results in lamellar thicknesses larger, or much larger in and near the contact plane than the "spontaneous" lamellar thickness observed in crystallization from the bulk.

The above general principles constitute the thread of the subsequent chapters. The epitaxy of "simple" polymers is illustrated, with particular emphasis on PE. The epitaxy of several polymers with helical conformation is illustrated next, again with an emphasis on technologically important polymers: iPP and isotactic polybutene. Several more specific examples of epitaxies for which an in-depth analysis could be performed will be considered. In most of these examples, the possibility of playing with the structural polymorphism of polymers is of particular help. It is indeed possible to generate specific crystal modifications of any given polymer. This polymorphism is of course of great technological importance. At the same time, it helps analyze in quite some detail the structural rules that govern epitaxial crystallization.

8.3.2 Epitaxial Crystallization of "Linear" Polymers

Polymers with a simple "shape" are ideally suited to establish the fundamentals of epitaxial crystallization applied to polymers. Most illustrative among these is PE. Its planar zigzag conformation results in a nearly featureless, almost cylindrical chain with a diameter of ≈ 0.5 nm. The small "bumps" aligned along four generatrices of the cylinder correspond to rows of hydrogen atoms, 0.254 nm apart. Similar, relatively simple polymers are the family of polyamides, in which, however, hydrogen bonding generates a strong structural element, namely sheets in which chains are 0.48 nm apart.

Epitaxial crystallization of PE may be considered as a rather academic concern. It is indeed so for most linear PEs produced for example by Ziegler-Natta catalysis, which crystallize "fast," as they have high nucleation and growth rates. However, "modern" PEs, such as the linear low density ones (LLDPE), have much reduced growth rates. It is therefore of technological interest to develop nucleating agents that are efficient for this class of polymers.

Artificially enhanced nucleation of PE was investigated early on by Beck [15] and Binsbergen [14]. Their works are most illustrative. They blended several thousands of different chemicals (minerals, organic solids, and salts, etc.) with PE and attempted to draw conclusions from the observed increase in crystallization temperature (recorded by DSC). In the absence of any detailed structural investigation, and given the wide range of chemical structures and/or unit-cell geometry and cell parameters of the active substrates, they were led to reject epitaxy as a possible mechanism. Rather, they considered some vague form of orientation of polymer chains in "ditches" of the substrate, which amounts to some form of graphoepitaxy.

Later structural data, already described in detail in earlier reviews, led to quite opposite interpretations [11–13, 17]. They revealed that indeed interaction of PE with the substrates follows some strict epitaxy rules. The crux of the analysis lies in two features: (1) use of electron diffraction, often of thin, composite bilayers (substrate and polymer), which helps "see" the interface more clearly, and (2) use of several different substrates with a range of periodicities susceptible to match the PE interchain distances.

PE exits in two crystal modifications, a stable orthorhombic and a metastable monoclinic one. The interchain distances between either nearest neighbors or second nearest neighbors vary from ≈ 0.4 to ≈ 0.9 nm. When substrates with periodicities matching distances found in the stable orthorhombic form are used, this form is produced, and the contact plane with interchain spacing closest to the substrate one is selected. Therefore, three different contact planes could be generated, with interchain periodicities of 0.445 nm [$(110)_{orthoPE}$ contact plane], 0.5 nm [$(100)_{orthoPE}$], and 0.744 nm [$(010)_{orthoPE}$] (Fig. 8.2, left). When the substrates have periodicities differing from these values, but close to interchain distances found in the monoclinic form, this form is produced, as attested by the presence of specific reflections in the diffraction pattern. Thus, three different contact planes of the monoclinic unit cell could be observed, with periodicities of 0.404 nm [$(010)_{monoPE}$], 0.523 nm [$(2\bar{1}0)_{monoPE}$], and 0.918 nm [$(\bar{1}40)_{monoPE}$] (Fig. 8.2, right). Note, however, that this monoclinic phase exists only as a transient layer: a growth transition to the more stable orthorhombic phase takes place shortly away from the interface. Existence of this transient layer came to light only when the specific, thin film technique was used, which revealed the presence of a layer a few nanometers thick of the different, monoclinic phase [11]. It should be noted that Mauritz et al. [7] had made similar observations when investigating the epitaxy of polymers on alkali halides. This monoclinic form is also produced in the epitaxial crystallization of PE on highly ordered pyrolytic graphite (HOPG) [19], although it had been missed in the initial analysis of this epitaxy [20]. This level of structural detail is of course lost when investigating thicker films since this monoclinic form is only a very small part of the film thickness. It is also lost when using more global investigation techniques since it affects only a very small fraction of the total polymer mass.

Similar investigations performed with polyamides are comparatively less telling. Indeed, the hydrogen-bonded sheets are a strong structural feature that does not leave much leeway for diverse epitaxial crystallizations. So far, the only contact plane observed in epitaxial crystallization of polyamides is indeed the hydrogen-bonded sheet [16]. This in turn implies that substrates with a periodicity close to 0.48 to 0.5 nm are most appropriate (provided of course that their compatibility with polyamides is sufficient). In this respect also, investigation of epitaxial crystallization of polyamides teaches us less than that of PE. However, further research is needed to investigate if some less standard crystal modifications of polyamides, such as the γ form of polyamide 6, can be produced by epitaxial crystallization.

A related family of "linear" polymers with zigzag chain conformation is that of aliphatic polyesters. Their interchain distances are frequently comparable to that of PE (with a few exceptions, typically for short aliphatic sequences). These polymers differ by their unit-cell geometry (orthorhombic for poly-ε-caprolactone, monoclinic in other cases). Here again, the interchain distance dominates over the cell geometry in epitaxial crystallization. However, it is possible to obtain (relatively small) truly single crystal domains of, for example PE adipate, in which the β angle of the monoclinic cell is oriented in only one direction: we are then dealing with a multilamellar but, from a crystallographic standpoint, truly single crystalline sample [9, 16].

Among many more "linear" polymers, poly(ethylene terephthalate) (PET) is of particular relevance since its maximum crystal growth rate is slow. The enhanced crystallization of PET has been, and still is, a topic of technological relevance. Following extended work by Legras, Mercier, and Nield [21], the impact of chemical nucleation (as opposed to epitaxial, i.e., physical interactions) has been widely publicized and is indeed observed [22]. For polymers with reactive groups in the main chain (ester, amide, carbonate), these groups are potential sources of chemical reaction with the nucleating agent, especially when high processing temperatures are required.

Most classical nucleating agents of PET (and for that matter, of many other polymers) are based on salts of benzoic acid (Fig. 8.3a). The observations reported by Mercier et al. indicate that PET reacts with these salts. This results in a significant reduction of the polymer molecular weight, together with the formation of "ionic" clusters to which the reacted parts of the chain (i.e., the chain ends) are tethered. Tethering is thought to induce a local orientation of the chain segments, and thus to favor the nucleation step—in effect, the net result is a "chemical nucleation" process [21]. This may be part of the story—a similar analysis is provided to explain the nucleating activity of polymeric ionomers, such as Surlyn®. However, the analysis may not be as simple as it appears. We have observed that the types of nucleating agents used in this study also induce the epitaxial crystallization of PET (Fig. 8.3b). In addition, the type of interaction is as expected from the chemical and crystallographic structure of PET: the contact plane is essentially parallel to the aromatic ring of the chain, which defines the (100) plane as the contact plane. Note that the same contact plane is involved in the epitaxy of PET on talc [23].

Finally, the issue of lamellar thickness at and near the contact plane has been examined more thoroughly with linear polymers. It is therefore fit to report briefly on it. As indicated, the substrate dimensions are much larger than the lamellar thickness characteristic of bulk crystallization. All observations reported so far confirm that the lamellar thickness in the contact plane is larger than the bulk one (sometimes several times larger). Most revealing in this respect are the results obtained by Tracz and coworkers for PE crystallized on HOPG [24, 25], talc or MoS_2 [19]. The lamellar thickness, visualized by AFM, is up to six times larger in a standard cooling procedure, a figure that depends on the substrate nature. Similar observations were made for the crystallization of PET on talc. This substantial increase of the lamellar thickness near the contact face "disappears away from the talc surface where the bulk long period is reached, and the crystallization process has no memory of the fact that it was nucleated by talc" [23]. Note that, in a similar manner, the bulk properties soon take precedence in the growth process away form the contact face. For example, if the epitaxy leads to an "unconventional" growth direction away from the substrate, the fastest growth direction soon takes precedence and becomes the radial growth direction in the developing spherulites.

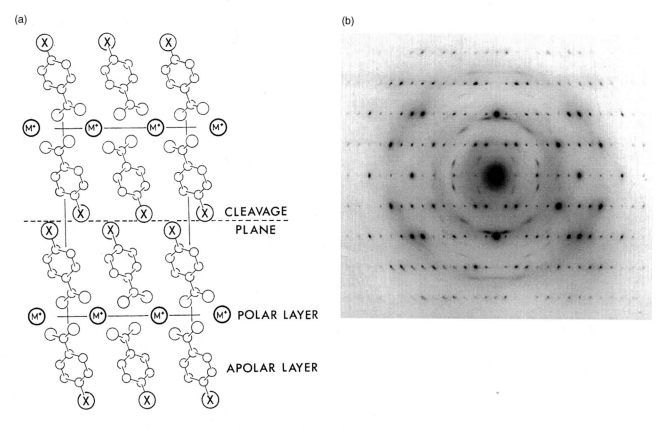

Figure 8.3 (a) The layered structure of aromatic acid salts. The cleavage plane exposes the apolar side of the molecules. The polar parts, with the acid moieties and M⁺ cations, are buried. The cleavage plane properties (e.g., hydrophobicity) and unit-cell parameters can be modulated to some extent by the nature (*t*-butyl, chlorine, etc.) and also by the position (ortho, meta, or para) of the substituent X. Reproduced from Reference [11] with permission of Pergamon Press. (b) Combined diffraction pattern of poly(ethylene terephthalate) and the sodium salt of *p*-chlorobenzoic acid. The salt reflections are sharp spots; the PET reflections are more arced. The contact plane of PET is (100); the chain axis is vertical.

8.3.3 Epitaxy of Helical Polymers

The preceding section has dealt with "linear" polymers. These include of course polymers with essentially a trans–trans conformation, as for PE. However, since in epitaxial crystallization the shape of the polymer is the issue at stake, some polymers that are helical from a crystallographic standpoint behave like the "linear" polymers considered so far. Typically, the polymers have no side chains and are nearly extended, with nevertheless a gently twisted helical conformation. They include, among others, polytetrafluoroethylene (PTFE) with a 15_7 or 13_6 helix, or poly(methylene oxide) and poly(ethylene oxide) with elongated 9_5 and 7_2 helical conformations, respectively. For these polymers, the outer helical path is only slightly tilted to the helix axis, and epitaxial interactions do not differentiate them from "straight" cylinders since the helical grooves are not very prominent. This insensitivity to the details of the conformation may be further enhanced when the helix twist sense (right- or left-handed helices) is not fully determined, for example, in PTFE. Indeed, as seen next for several polyolefins with different side chains, the issue of helical twist sense (or helical hand) becomes a central issue in epitaxial crystallization of helical polymers.

8.3.3.1 Isotactic Polypropylene

Polymers with methyl or more sizeable side chains and a helical conformation have a more complex outer shape than the relatively featureless PE or polymers with a gentle twist just considered. The epitaxial crystallization of iPP has been most thoroughly investigated, if only for its technological interest and industrial relevance. Indeed, iPP has a relatively slow growth rate in the "standard" crystallization temperature range, and enhancement of its nucleation may become necessary under certain processing conditions (e.g., injection molding).

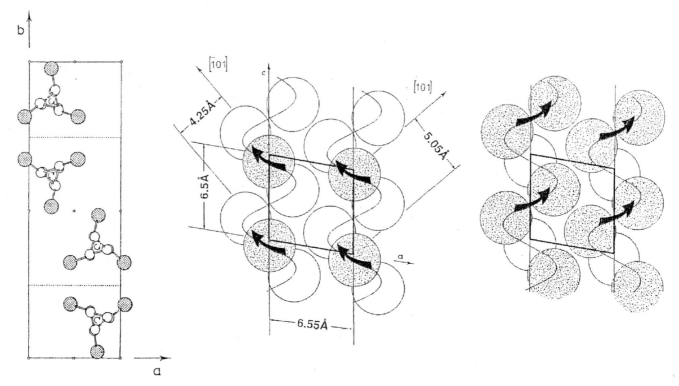

Figure 8.4 The packing of chains in the monoclinic, α phase of isotactic polypropylene (αiPP). Left: as seen in chain axis projection, successive layers parallel to the ac plane (horizontal trace) are made of alternatively right-handed and left-handed helices. Middle and right: the succession of different ac faces of αiPP encountered as one travels along the +b-axis direction. The helical hand (curved arrows) as well as the pattern of methyl groups differs in the two distinct faces. Travelling along the −b-axis direction, the mirror images of these faces would be observed. The less densely populated face (middle) is involved in epitaxial crystallization. Reproduced from Reference [27].

From a structural standpoint, iPP exists in three different crystal modifications that all rest on the same threefold helical chain conformation. Only the packing of helices differs in these three forms [26]. In addition, iPP displays an original self-epitaxy, analyzed later on, which leads to lamellar branching in its stable α phase, and exists as a crystallographic feature in its highly unusual γ phase [27].

The unit cell of αiPP phase is of particular interest. It is monoclinic, with one distinctive and essential feature: its a and c parameters are nearly equal (≈0.65 nm). The threefold helices are organized in isochiral layers in the ac plane, but the helical hand alternates in successive layers, as well as the azimuthal setting of the chains. As a consequence, different ac contact faces exist in the structure [28]. They differ by the density of methyl groups, as illustrated in Figure 8.4.

The ac face that contains only one methyl group is of particular relevance in the context of epitaxial crystallization. Indeed, the methyl groups that line this face generate a lozenge-shaped pattern (as a result of the ≈100° β angle of the cell) of "humps" about 0.4 nm in diameter and spaced 0.65 nm apart. As a consequence, three distinct orientations of methyl rows are materialized: two are parallel to the two diagonals of the face (with inter-row distances of ≈0.5 nm and 0.42 nm), and one is parallel to the a- or c-axes (≈0.65 nm). As for PE, use of substrates that match these periodicities (e.g., sodium benzoate) induces epitaxial crystallization of αiPP [29–31]. In any one of these epitaxies, two different chain orientations are generated. Indeed, the substrate only "feels" the pattern of protruding methyl groups but cannot "identify" the orientation of the chains' axes and their helical hand. In epitaxies that involve the two diagonals of the lozenge, a- and c-axes are thus interchangeable. The same holds true for the epitaxy involving the 0.65-nm periodicity.

To some extent, the epitaxies of the ac face of αiPP are very reminiscent of epitaxies of linear polymers: the "flat" pattern of methyl groups highlights the different distances between rows of methyl groups, which reminds of the varying interchain distances of linear polymers. However, since the αiPP phase has two ac faces differing by the density of methyl groups, the ultimate analy-

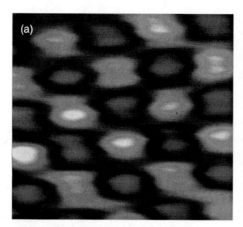 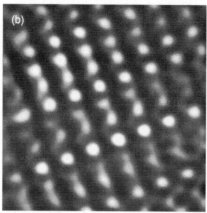

Figure 8.5 (a) The contact face of iPP α phase deposited on benzoic acid. This AFM image shows (in blue) the lozenge-shaped "four" pattern of methyl group 0.65 nm apart (cf Fig. 8.4, middle). Note that the hand of the helices cannot be deduced from this image. It would be right-handed or left-handed if the helix axis were oriented at ≈2 or at ≈10 o'clock, respectively. Reproduced from Reference [32] (Correction) with permission of the American Chemical Society. (b) The (110) contact face of βiPP imaged by AFM. The helix axes are oriented at ≈2 o'clock. The methyl groups (in white), 0.65 nm apart along the chain axis direction (corresponding to one helical turn) are more visible for every *third* chain (i.e., 1.9 nm apart in the 5 o'clock direction), indicating a distinctly different azimuthal setting of one chain out of three in the unit cell. This is a trademark of the frustrated character of the βiPP structure. Reproduced from Reference [57] with permission of the American Chemical Society. (See color insert.)

sis of the epitaxy requires defining which one of these two *ac* faces is the contact plane. This identification cannot come from an analysis of the combined substrate/diffraction pattern alone: they would be identical for the two epitaxies. In order to discriminate between these two possibilities, the exposed pattern of methyl groups must be visualized in real space; that is, the topography of the contact face must be checked by AFM with methyl group resolution. The result is unambiguous, and shows the "four" pattern of methyl groups already discussed [32, 33] (Fig. 8.5a).

One other crystallographic face of αiPP has been observed to be involved in epitaxial crystallization. It is the structurally more complex (110) face. This face involves both right- and left-handed helices. The pattern of methyl side chains exposed in this face generates again a quasi-linear grating, tilted at 57° to the *c*-axis, with an inter-row distance of 0.55 nm. PTFE is most noteworthy among epitaxial substrates that match this 0.55-nm distance [34]. Another, more complex epitaxy with a high melting polyolefin will be discussed later (cf Section 8.4.2).

The β phase of iPP is obtained under normal crystallization conditions as a minor component compared with the α phase. Although the β phase is based on the same threefold helical conformation, it differs significantly from the α phase. The unit cell is trigonal and houses three isochiral helices. These helices have different azimuthal settings in the unit cell, which defines the structure as frustrated [35–37]. From a structural standpoint, the interchain distance and the chain axis repeat distances are nearly equal (0.635 nm and 0.65 nm, respectively). Due to the different azimuthal settings, the methyl side chains do not create a regular, organized pattern, and only the chain axis repeat distance seems to be at play in epitaxial crystallization. Historically, the first substrate found to initiate the β phase is a pigment, γ-chinacridone [38], but many different nucleating agents have been patented, in view of the technological interest in this crystal modification (e.g., better impact strength than the more common α phase). Epitaxial crystallization of the β phase (cf Fig. 8.1) has helped solve its crystal structure and establish its frustrated character [39]. As a result of frustration, the azimuthal settings of the chains in the unit cell are different. Probing the topography of a crystal plane should therefore highlight some helices, but not all helices equally, in that face. Indeed, AFM imaging of the (110) plane of βiPP reveals more clearly the protruding methyl groups of one of the three helices and therefore its different azimuthal setting, which is a real space "signature" of frustration [39] (Fig. 8.5b, c.f. also Chapter 2).

8.3.3.2 A Case of Self-Epitaxy in Polymers: Epitaxy of Isotactic Polypropylene
The stable α phase of iPP displays a highly original morphological feature: the

lamellae branch repeatedly, and moreover at a constant angle between daughter and mother lamellae. Successive generations of lamellar branching generate so-called quadrites in solution crystallization. The same lamellar branching is observed under nearly every crystallization condition: bulk, fibers, and so on [40, 41]. This puzzling feature has been analyzed at a molecular level. It is due to a self-epitaxy [27, 42] that can be described, in crystallographic terms, as a rotation twin.

Analysis of this self-epitaxy starts with the same premises as for the epitaxy on benzoic acid, namely the *ac* crystallographic face with four methyl groups. In the lozenge pattern, the methyl groups are 0.65 nm apart and have a diameter of 0.4 nm. This leaves enough room for the methyl groups of the next layer to penetrate in the "holes" between the methyl groups of the substrate layer. In the crystal structure, the two facing layers are linked by a plane of symmetry (or more exactly a glide plane). This maintains the parallel orientation of the lozenge cell edges, a prerequisite for the interdigitation of methyl groups. It also means that if one layer is made of left-handed helices, the facing layer is made of right-handed helices. An alternative, very favorable packing scheme of interdigitating lozenge patterns of methyl groups can be generated when two layers made of helices *of the same hand* are in contact. This is indeed possible because of the highly unusual lozenge symmetry of the methyl group pattern (Fig. 8.6). However, in that case, one layer must be rotated in such a way as to bring its *a*-axis parallel to the *c*-axis of the substrate layer. Only this operation maintains the parallelism of the two lozenge patterns and allows interdigitation of the methyl groups over the whole contact face.

As indicated, this operation is a rotation twin, with the rotation twin axis parallel to either diagonal of the lozenge, and located half way between the two layers. This operation has an unusual consequence: the helix axes are no longer parallel: they are ≈100° (i.e., the β angle of the unit cell) apart. Generation of this new chain orientation on the lateral *ac* faces of the crystal yields the observed lamellar branching. Repetition of this epitaxy in successive generations yields reversibly either the initial or the daughter orientation of the lamellae—thus the "quadrite" structure characteristic of the α phase of iPP [40]. It should be mentioned that the molecular analysis of this homoepitaxy rests on the combination of crystal structure determination (as was performed by Natta and Corradini [28]) and interpretation of crystal morphology (as observed by, e.g., transmission electron microscopy or AFM). This combination makes it possible to deduce the orientation of the *a*-axis in each of the lamellae and, by a simple reasoning, the helical hand and azimuthal setting (orientation relative

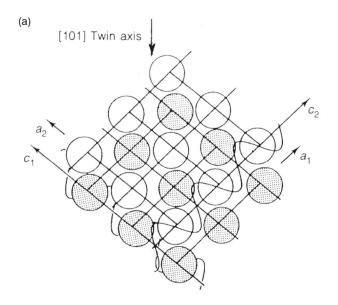

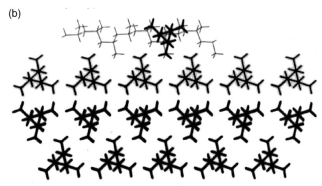

Figure 8.6 (a) Interdigitation of methyl groups in the *ac* face of αiPP that displays one methyl group per cell (cf Fig. 8.4, middle). The substrate layer methyl groups are shaded; the depositing ones are unshaded. The lozenge-shaped pattern of methyl groups allows similar interdigitation for the crystallographic and the self-epitaxial crystallization. The chain orientation of the deposited layer depends on whether the helices in facing planes are antichiral (crystallographic packing) or are isochiral (self-epitaxy leading to lamellar branching). The self-epitaxial deposition is illustrated here. This self-epitaxy is equally described, in crystallographic terms, as a rotation twin ([101] twin axis indicated here). Reproduced from Reference [42] with permission of VCH, Weinheim. (b) Crystallographic and epitaxial deposition of helical stems in the αiPP *ac* growth face, illustrated here in the top layer. The deposition of two helices with different hands is represented. The black helix is antichiral to the nearby substrate (contact) layer helices. It is seen along its *c*-axis, a situation that corresponds to normal, crystallographic deposition. The yellow helix is isochiral to the substrate ones. It is seen nearly horizontal: its chain axis is parallel to the *a*-axis of the substrate (epitaxial deposition). This specific interaction between a chiral helical stem and a substrate layer made of helices with the same chirality corresponds to the initiation of lamellar branching. (Courtesy F. Colonna-Cesari). (See color insert.)

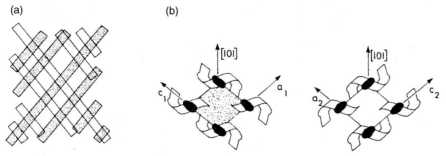

Figure 8.7 Determination of the helical hand of helices in the "quadrites" of isotactic polypropylene. This determination rests on the fact that the epitaxy provides a means of establishing the orientation of the unit-cell axes (a, b, c) in both sets of lamellae. Since the c-axis is normal to the lamellae (left, seen edge-on), the orientations of the a- and c-axes in the two sets of lamellae (differentiated by the shading) can be determined (center and right). This in turn indicates that the shaded lamellae are seen along the $+b$-axis, and the unshaded ones along the $-b$-axis. In addition, the helical path is parallel to the long diagonal of the ac face when one methyl group is exposed (shown here as elongated dark dots, cf also Fig. 8.4). This analysis helps determine the hand and setting of *every* helix in the quadrite. Reproduced from Reference [27].

to the b-axis of the unit cell) of each and every helix involved in the branched lamellae (Fig. 8.7). No other polymer crystal structure allows such a detailed analysis [27]. In turn, it indicates that a stringent selection of helical hands takes place at the growth front [43, 44] or, for that matter, at the contact plane in case of epitaxial crystallization [45].

The lamellar branching as described so far for αiPP corresponds to a "mistake" in the growth process, since it corresponds to the deposition of helices of the "wrong" hand on the lateral face of the growing crystal. However, the same "mistake" becomes the rule and therefore a standard crystallographic feature in the γ phase of iPP determined by Brückner and Meille [46]. In the crystal structure of γiPP indeed, the homoepitaxy or rotation twin is a true ingredient of the *unit-cell* organization. The structure is made of bilayers of helices (one layer made of right-handed helices, one layer made of left-handed helices) (Fig. 8.8). On the outside faces in which the "four" pattern of methyl groups is exposed, the above homoepitaxy takes place: a layer of helices of the same hand as the substrate is deposited, with its chain axis tilted by $\approx 100°$. This leads to the first, and so far the only polymer crystal structure with nonparallel chain axes as also confirmed by electron diffraction of single crystals [47]. It should be noted that the crystallographic analysis of this phase (that took some 30 years to be worked out) helped determine, even prior to the AFM analysis, that the lamellar branching in αiPP takes place when two faces with the "four" pattern of methyl groups are in contact [46].

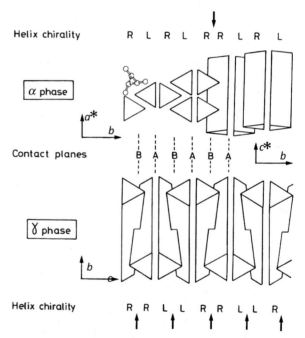

Figure 8.8 Schematic illustration of the γ phase crystal structure of isotactic polypropylene and its structural filiation with the αiPP homoepitaxy. The threefold helices are represented as triangular bars. The systematic repetition of the self-epitaxial packing illustrated in Figure 8.6 (indicated here with arrows) generates the first and so far the only polymer crystal structure with nonparallel chain axes. Reproduced from Reference [47] with permission.

As indicated, the self- or homo-epitaxy observed in the α and γ phases of iPP is the only one recorded so far in polymer crystallography. Its occurrence is undoubtedly related to the very high symmetry of the pattern of "four" methyl groups in its *ac* face. This unusual, more symmetric organization results in some specific properties, such as a reduced birefringence, which is useful in reaching higher transparency of molded pieces. Similar homoepitaxies might exist but with a more limited impact, when the growth faces have a high structural symmetry. Such homoepitaxies might explain the frequent occurrence of lamellar branching in, for example, solution crystallization of nylon 4 (nearly square lateral face with *a*- and *c*-axes ≈0.95 nm). Another potential candidate would be syndiotactic polypropylene (sPP), for which occasional edge-on lamellae nucleate on the lateral (100) growth faces. In its isochiral Form II (or local patches of Form II in an otherwise Form I), the lateral faces display a tilted grating of parallel rows of methyl groups. A "mistake" in helical hand selection would induce, as for αiPP, lamellar branching. However, such possible and limited examples illustrate *a contrario*, that the self-epitaxy of αiPP is indeed exceptional.

8.3.3.3 Epitaxy of Isotactic Poly(1-butene)

Isotactic poly(1-butene) (iPBu1) is an archetypical polymorphic polymer with three different structures that differ by the chain conformation, and thus by the unit-cell geometry and symmetry (cf Chapter 2). The three crystal phases could be obtained by epitaxial crystallization on appropriate substrates [48–50]. Most interesting among them are the epitaxy of Form I (trigonal unit cell, threefold helical conformation, racemic phase) and that of Form III (orthorhombic unit cell, fourfold helical geometry, chiral crystal phase).

Form I is normally obtained by the slow conversion of the kinetically favored Form II. It can be obtained directly by epitaxial crystallization on appropriate substrates [49, 50]. The most original structural feature in this epitaxy stems from the fact that Form I is made, like αiPP, of an antichiral alternation of isochiral layers parallel to the (110) crystal plane. The (110) contact face is therefore made of isochiral helices that may be either right-handed or left-handed. The side chains line up at a small angle relative to the helix axis normal. When a substrate matches this interstrand distance, the helix axis must tilt in order for the side chains to align parallel to the substrate periodicity. This tilt is opposite for right- and left-handed helices since the helical paths are tilted in opposite directions relative to the helix axis (Fig. 8.9a). In other words, the orientation of the helix axis in epitaxial crystallization makes it possible to recognize the actual hand (right or left) of the helices that make up the polymer contact plane [49, 50]. Again, this structural insight is only possible because of the short-range interactions involved in epitaxial crystallization since they highlight the helical path in contact with the substrate.

Form III of iPBu1 had been obtained as solution grown single crystals but never in a fiber-oriented form. Thus, analysis of its structure rested mainly on powder diffraction patterns. Powder patterns display only a limited number of reflections (≈15, with many overlaps). Epitaxial crystallization on 2-quinoxalinol yields a multilamellar, single crystalline Form III with the (110) contact plane [51]. This specific contact plane is of particular interest for the structure determination of this form. Indeed, using a rotation-tilt stage (±60°) in the electron microscope, it is possible to visualize the *ac* as well as the *bc* reciprocal plane—in effect, given the unit-cell symmetry, to cover the whole reciprocal space of this crystal modification. Together with the $hk0$ data obtained from single crystals, this analysis yielded nearly 120 independent reflections. In turn, this enables electron crystallography to be performed when combining these two sets of information. The structure derivation confirmed the essential features determined by the previous analysis based on the X-ray powder pattern, but based on a much more complete set of experimental data [51]. Whereas the additional information provided by this structure derivation is limited in the case of poly(1-butene) Form III, it is clear that structure analysis based on electron crystallography using both single crystals and epitaxially crystallized samples is the method of choice to solve crystal modifications that are metastable or hard to orient. This method should become all the more attractive, as new techniques are developed in electron microscopy (e.g., precession methods) that help overcome the previous uncertainties in the collection of reliable electron diffraction intensity data [52–54].

8.3.4 Polymer/Polymer Epitaxy

Crystalline polymers may be nucleating agents for other crystalline polymers. This holds true of course for polymers that are chemically very similar, for example, high and low density PEs. However, many other examples of polymer/polymer epitaxy are available, even for mildly or incompatible polymer pairs: PE versus aliphatic polyesters, polyamides versus iPP, PE versus iPP and, reciprocally, iPP versus PE, PTFE versus iPP, and so on.

In most of these systems, the issue of compatibility may play a considerable role. However, on a structural basis, the essential rules that govern the epitaxial interactions have been established. In great part, the interactions depend on the linear or helical geometry of the polymer chains.

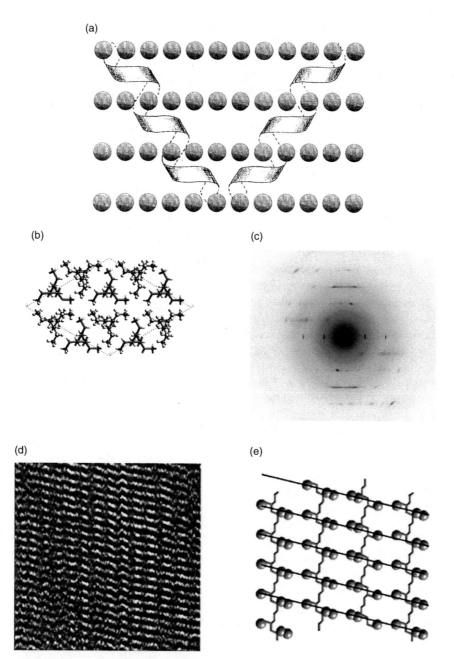

Figure 8.9 Epitaxial crystallization of layers made of isochiral helices: isotactic poly(1-butene) Form I (iPBuI). (a) Illustration of the selection of helical hand in the contact plane when the substrate periodicity matches the interstrand distance. The contact face of the substrate is seen from the substrate interior and is represented as rows of shaded circles. The part of the helical path that interacts with the substrate is shaded. Matching of interstrand distance with the substrate periodicity results in opposite tilts of the polymer helix axes for right- and left-handed helices. The angle between the two c-axes is equal to twice the "tilt angle" (angle between the helix axis normal and the helical path). (b) The crystal structure of iPBuI. The right-handed and left-handed helices are shown in cylinders and balls and sticks, respectively. The trace of the (110) contact face is horizontal. In any (110) face, all helices are isochiral, either right-handed or left-handed. (c) Diffraction pattern of a thin film of iPBuI epitaxially crystallized on 3-fluorobenzoic acid. The chain axis is vertical. Note the asymmetry of this pattern (the right part differs from the left one, cf the strong reflection on the second layer line) indicating that only one (110) contact plane is present in this part of the film and that it contains indeed helices of only one hand (left-handed, judging from the location of the strong spot on the second layer line). Parts (a–c) reproduced from Reference [49] with kind permission of Springer Science + Business Media. (d) Atomic force microscopy of a film as examined in part (c) showing the tilt of the side chains (and thus the orientation of the helical path, corresponding to left-handed helices), as well as the molecular model of the exposed face (only carbon atoms shown in balls). The chain axis is vertical. The limited resolution of the AFM image does not allow differentiation of the exposed "lone" methyl and ethyl parts of the side chains, which precludes observation of the "up" or "down" orientation of helices illustrated in the model (cf. second chain from the right in part (e)). (e) Molecular model of the structure seen in part (d). It highlights the chain axis orientation (vertical) and the CH_2 and CH_3 groups located in the contact face imaged by AFM (shown as balls). Parts (d) and (e) reproduced from Reference [50] by permission of Elsevier. (See color insert.)

8.3.4.1 Epitaxy between Linear Polymers The epitaxy between "linear" polymers usually sums up to the parallel arrangement of molecular chains, evidently more favorable when lattice spacing is comparable. As an illustration, PE and aliphatic polyesters have nearly similar unit-cell parameters (in *c*-axis projection); PE and polyamides have interchain distances that are close to 0.5 nm (0.48 nm for polyamides, 0.5 nm for PE in the *bc* plane) [11].

PTFE is a special case. It has been shown that rubbed PTFE layers induce the oriented crystallization of a number of materials: crystalline and liquid-crystalline polymers as well as low molecular weight liquid-crystalline materials [55]. The underlying orientation process is not elucidated in every case. In many instances, it seems that some form of graphoepitaxy may be involved since no clear-cut structural matching can be defined. Another indicator is the parallel orientation of the deposited chain with the PTFE substrate, which would be compatible with some form of "milder" interaction—but, of course, does not rule out "hard" epitaxy. One example of hard epitaxy, which also results in a tilted orientation of the chain axis relative to the PTFE substrate chain orientation, will be analyzed shortly.

Finally, several liquid-crystalline (LC) polymers have been used as nucleating agents for crystalline polymers that crystallize below the LC transition temperature. As far as the present authors are aware, there have been no detailed reports on the exact structural relationship between these LC polymers and the crystalline polymers, except to mention that the chain axes are parallel, which takes us back to the situation analyzed for PTFE. This limitation also stems from the fact that in the LC state, no clear-cut crystallographic organization in the exposed faces can be defined, which precludes the type of analysis that needs be developed in order to define "hard" epitaxy.

8.3.4.2 Epitaxy between Linear and Helical Polymers Epitaxy between linear and helical polymers may be of particular interest when the contact plane of the helical polymer is build up with isochiral helices, and when the chain axis of the deposited linear polymer is oriented parallel to the helical path. This provides a direct means to determine the exposed helical hand of the substrate polymer. The tilted orientation of chain axes when a helical polymer is involved is therefore an unmistakable indicator of specific interactions, that is, of "hard" epitaxy [11, 29, 30].

Such a situation has been observed again for iPP, this time epitaxially crystallized on PTFE. The contact plane of αiPP is the (110) plane. In this plane, the αiPP methyl groups form rows 0.55 nm apart, and the rows are tilted at 57° to the chain axis. The rows are oriented parallel to the helical path of the helices that have two of their methyl groups exposed in the (110) face, and thus indicate their helical hand. The 0.55-nm distance between rows of methyl groups matches exactly the interchain distance of PTFE. Epitaxy of iPP on a rubbed, oriented PTFE substrate generates indeed two iPP chain orientations that are characteristically 114° apart, twice the 57° tilt angle. This orientation of the deposited chains away from the PTFE chain axis direction rules out any form of graphoepitaxy and demonstrates that the interaction of αiPP and PTFE is truly a "hard" epitaxy [34].

A somewhat similar situation is observed for the αiPP/PE system [11, 29, 30]. Keeping in mind that PE has a 0.5-nm interchain distance in the *bc* plane, and that the *ac* face of iPP also has a 0.5-nm distance between rows of methyl groups tilted by $\beta/2$ to the chain axis, the epitaxy of PE and iPP leads to a composite structure in which the chain axes are ≈50° apart (The monoclinic angle β is ≈100°.) Note that a comparable epitaxy is observed between αiPP and polyamides, with a somewhat shorter interchain distance (≈0.48 nm), but that is still compatible with epitaxial interactions [16].

The latter epitaxies differ in one respect from the iPP/PTFE situation described above, in that the orientation of the linear polymer (PE or polyamide) chain does not correspond to the helical path. This situation is highly exceptional and stems from the topography of the *ac* contact face of αiPP (illustrated in the AFM image of Fig. 8.5a). It is a lozenge pattern of methyl groups under which the helical path is buried. The epitaxial interactions only "feel" this lozenge pattern and highlight the 0.5-nm periodicity. It just happens that this periodicity is oriented along [$\bar{1}$01] (Fig. 8.4), nearly at right angles to the path of the helix that bears the exposed methyl group and that is parallel to [101] direction, that is, to the other diagonal of the lozenge. Were the face with two methyl groups exposed, the orientation of the helical path would indeed be more perceptible, and the epitaxy would lead to parallel orientation of that path and the chain axis of the PE or polyamide chain.

8.4 EPITAXIAL CRYSTALLIZATION: FURTHER ISSUES AND EXAMPLES

8.4.1 Topographic versus Lattice Matching

The first order analysis of epitaxial crystallization usually centers on the standard "lattice matching" criterion, namely near-matching of cell dimensions in corresponding orientations of the contact plane. This is indeed a useful test of any epitaxial crystallization.

However, this dimensional lattice match hides a more complex reality that is at times more difficult to work out. The lattice matching does reflect a *topographic* matching of the contact faces that are partners in the epitaxy. However, establishing the details of the topographic matching suppose having reached a complete knowledge of the two interacting crystal structures, sometimes at a level of detail that requires specific analytical tools. The present section illustrates three examples in which such a detailed level has been reached, and illustrates how specific and even subtle epitaxial interactions may be. They all rest on the submolecular analysis of epitaxies for which the same dimensional match is possible for two distinct contact faces and interactions, but for which the selection of only one contact face is clearly triggered by favorable topographic interactions.

8.4.1.1 The ac Face of Isotactic Polypropylene

The structure of iPP has already been described in earlier sections. Let us recall that two topographically different *ac* faces exist in the unit cell of αiPP. They have the same dimensions, but differ by the density of methyl groups in that face, much like the "four" or the "five" faces of dices (cf Fig. 8.4). Any one of these two faces could be involved in the homoepitaxy leading to lamellar branching in αiPP or leading to the nonparallel chain axes in the γ phase, or also the epitaxy of αiPP on benzoic acid. They would yield strictly similar situations and would be indistinguishable on a structural basis. However, the analysis of the γ phase diffraction pattern made it possible to rule out interactions between the "five" faces and rather favor the "four" face (it leads to significantly better agreement with the diffraction pattern) [46]. This result would suggest that the epitaxy leading to the lamellar branching in the α phase also takes place on the "four" faces. In effect, this epitaxy allows for relatively deep interpenetration of the two-dimensional pattern of methyl groups in the facing contact planes (Fig. 8.6).

The epitaxial crystallization of iPP on benzoic acid is not amenable to the same in-depth analysis using diffraction data only. In that case, it is necessary to resort to AFM analysis of the iPP contact face, after dissolution of the benzoic acid substrate [32, 33]. Here again, the contact face displays the "four" pattern of methyl groups (cf. Fig. 8.5a). It might be questioned whether a substrate that is more "flat" would favor the "five" face of αiPP, that is, also less "bumpy." No experimental evidence has been collected so far on this issue.

8.4.1.2 Forms I and II of Syndiotactic Polypropylene

sPP exists in different crystal modifications. Two of these are of interest in the present context. They are both based on a *ttgg* chain conformation, which generates a helical structure like a rectangular staircase. The helices pack in two different unit cells, both orthorhombic. In the metastable Form II, all helices have the same helical hand. In the stable Form I, the packing of helices is fully antichiral along both *a*- and *b*-axes [56]. (cf. also Chapter 2). The unit-cell parameters are strictly similar (with the proviso of doubling of the *b*-axis in Form I, owing to the existence of alternating, antichiral helices): $a = 1.44$ nm, $b = 0.56$ nm (for Form II, but 1.12 nm for Form I), $c = 0.76$ nm. Form I has been obtained by epitaxial crystallization on *p*-terphenyl, which provides a favorable two-dimensional lattice match. AFM investigation of the contact face made it possible to visualize the alternation of right- and left-handed helices in the *bc* contact face [57].

When sPP crystallizes epitaxially on 2-quinoxalinol (2-Quin) at a low temperature, the metastable Form II is obtained, as evidenced by its different, specific diffraction pattern [58]. Contrary to the monoclinic phase of PE, formation of this metastable phase is not linked with a better dimensional match. Rather, it stems from a much superior topographic match between the polymer and the substrate. The crux of the argument can be summarized in a three-part figure (Fig. 8.10). When seen from the side, the contact face of 2-Quin displays relatively long-range ridges with a periodicity that matches the *c*-axis repeat distance of sPP. The profiles

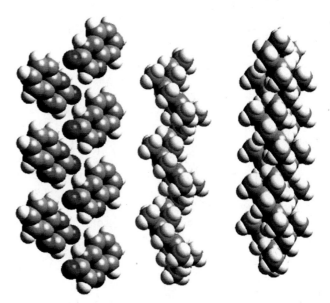

Figure 8.10 Topographic matching between 2-quinoxalinol (left) and syndiotactic polypropylene in its Form II (middle, isochiral helices) and its Form I (right, antichiral helices). Correspondence of the 2-Quin and Form II profiles explains the formation of the latter, metastable structure. Reproduced from Reference [58] with permission of the AmericanChemical Society.

of the sPP contact planes in Form I and in Form II differ significantly. In Form II, all isochiral helices are at the same "height" along the c-axis, which generates also long-range ridges. In Form I on the contrary, right- and left-handed helices are shifted along the c-axis by half the c-axis periodicity. As a result, the profile of the contact plane displays ripples with a shorter periodicity (actually $c/2$). Comparison of the two sPP contact faces profiles with that of 2-Quin indicates at once that the Form II profile matches better that of the 2-Quin substrate—and indeed it is the metastable Form II that is formed on this substrate. Here again, the dimensional matching would not have been discriminative. To the contrary, the topographic matching becomes a clear selection criterion. On a molecular basis, this topographic criterion helps select a unique hand (right or left) of the helices that will be part of the contact face. However, note that 2-Quin is not a superior nucleating agent for sPP. It is not active at high temperatures, and the more stable, antichiral form I is produced "on its own" without any implication of 2-Quin [58].

8.4.2 Epitaxy of Isotactic Polypropylene on Isotactic Polyvinylcyclohexane

It has been observed that the high melting iPVCH is a nucleating agent for αiPP [59–61]. Analysis of the underlying epitaxial relationship illustrates once again the requirements for topographic matching. In addition, it helps illustrate another means of determining the topographic interactions between polymer and substrate.

As for many polyolefins substituted on the α carbon atom of the side chain, iPVCH has a high melting temperature (>300°C). Its crystal structure is tetragonal, the helix has a fourfold symmetry with a repeat distance of 0.65 nm as for the threefold helix of iPP [62, 63]. Therefore, the two chain axis periodicities most likely match in the epitaxy; that is, the chain axes are parallel in the contact plane. Further analysis thus amounts to determining the exact $hk0$ contact planes and the molecular interactions in the contact plane. To this end, αiPP single crystals are grown on the lateral edges of iPVCH single crystals. The resulting morphology and diffraction pattern reveal a very specific interaction [64]. The iPP (110) plane is parallel to the iPVCH (100) plane. The dimensional match is nearly perfect (2.196 nm vs. 2.199 nm, respectively). Moreover, the topographic match is also remarkable. Indeed, the azimuthal setting of the helices in the iPVCH unit cell is at an angle to the a and b cell edges, which generates a corrugated topography in c-axis projection. This same topography characterizes the αiPP (110) plane, which allows for a perfect match (Fig. 8.11). In addition, in the iPP contact plane, the exposed rows of methyl groups are tilted to the chain axis, as are the edges of the exposed cyclohexyl groups of PVCH. The specificity of this topographic match is such that the a-axis of the αiPP unit cell is tilted at some 18°, but in only one direction, relative to the PVCH (100) growth (and contact) face (two orientations would be expected, were the dimensional match only be operative). In turn, this 18° tilt of the iPP epitaxial overgrowth is a morphological marker that helps determine in which way the PVCH helices are rotated within the unit-cell relative to the a- and b-axes, that is, helps "read" the internal structure of the PVCH unit cell [64].

8.4.3 Epitaxy Involving Fold Surfaces of Polymer Crystals

All epitaxial crystallization examples considered so far deal with contact planes that are parallel to the chain axis. They are the most frequent and indeed also the most relevant ones, both scientifically and from a technological viewpoint. However, for the sake of completeness, it is necessary to mention "epitaxies" that involve planes of type hkl, and most prominently the folds planes.

As indicated, epitaxial crystallization implies contact planes of the substrate and deposit that are crystallographic. In polymers, only $hk0$ planes should be considered since they are parallel to the chain axis. By contrast, planes of type hkl "cut" the chain axis, which does not generate an exposed, "free" contact face, since the chains continue on both sides of the plane, possibly with a change in orientation, as in kink-bands. However, "exposed" planes of type hkl exist in polymer crystals, as they are associated with chain folding. This lamellar folds surface is by necessity disordered or, at least, not crystallographically ordered. A priori, the folds surface would not be thought of as a contact plane in any epitaxial crystallization. However, a few examples of epitaxies that involve the end, fold surface of polymer crystals have been reported.

Oriented crystallization of polyoxymethylene (POM) single crystals lying flat on the surface of NaCl and on mica have been reported [65, 66]. Later work dealt with polyphenylene sulfide (PPS), again on a range of inorganic substrates (alkali halides, mica). Both folds plane and folds surface epitaxy (i.e., with the chain lying flat and normal to the substrate surface, respectively) were observed on NaCl. Consistent, rather than random, orientation of the PPS crystals suggests specific interactions involving their folds surfaces. It was observed that "changes in ionic lattice dimensions and ionic nature of the substrate have a substantial effect on the molecular packing of PPS and the resulting orientations," as they

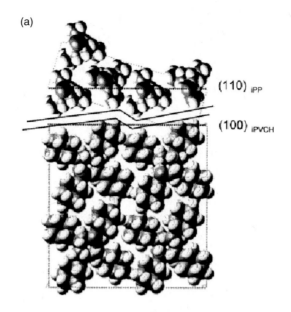

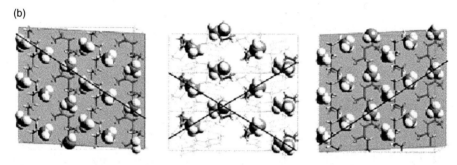

Figure 8.11 Epitaxial crystallization of isotactic polypropylene and its polymeric nucleating agent, isotactic polyvinylcyclohexane. (a) Topographic and dimensional matching of the two contact faces as seen along the chain axes. Corrugations in the $(110)_{iPP}$ and $(100)_{iPVCH}$ planes (underlined) match nearly perfectly. (b) Topographic and dimensional matching as seen normal to the contact plane. The contact faces display rows of methyl groups (iPP, shaded) and edges of cyclohexyl rings (right) that have the same tilt angle and identical spacings. Matching of the two faces can be visualized by "closing the iPP shutters" on the central PVCH "window." Reproduced from Reference [64] with permission of the American Chemical Society. (See color insert.)

define the epitaxy and, also, the polymorphism of the polymer. Moreover, the contact plane of PPS, as well as its orientation, suggests, if nothing else, that the fold surface of the single crystals, produced here in solution, is more ordered than usually assumed [67].

A somewhat similar conclusion can be reached in a different experiment. As indicated earlier, it is possible to vaporize, for example, PE. The vapors condensed and deposited on a cold substrate crystallize under very harsh conditions, well below the temperature of homogeneous nucleation (≈80°C). When the PE vapors are deposited on the fold surface of PE single crystals (or lamellae in spherulites), the chains are oriented by the substrate fold surface, leading to the so-called polymer decoration technique [68]. If the contact plane of the deposit on the fold surface is specific, then this orientation is not a simple orientation induced by ditches; it has at least some characteristics of a "hard" epitaxy, although the substrate has no crystallographic order per se. The most illustrative observation supporting this analysis deals with PE vapors deposited on the surface of POM single crystals (Fig. 8.12). The spacing between planes containing folds in POM is short, that is, 0.386 nm. No such interchain periodicity exists in the stable,

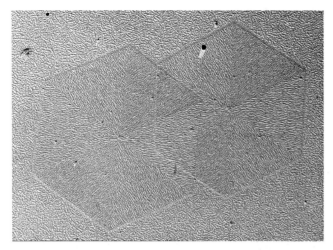

Figure 8.12 Polymer decoration: epitaxial crystallization on the fold surface. Polyethylene vapors were deposited on the surface of single crystals of polyoxymethylene (POM) at room temperature. The resulting PE decoration is made of edge-on lamellae oriented normal to the POM growth faces, with the deposited PE chains parallel to the growth front. The distance between POM fold planes (0.386 nm) imposes the monoclinic (010) PE contact plane, in which chains are separated by ≈0.4 nm [68].

orthorhombic crystal phase of PE. However, it does exist in the monoclinic polymorph. The contact plane of the PE deposit on the fold surface of POM is therefore the (010) plane of the metastable monoclinic crystal modification, for which the interchain distance (0.404 nm) is commensurate with the ditch periodicity of the POM fold surface substrate [68].

Apart from these few examples, no well-documented examples of epitaxy involving the fold surface as a contact plane have been reported. However, the fact that such epitaxies exist indicates that the fold surface of single crystals is sufficiently organized to become involved in, or to induce some form of epitaxial crystallization. Matching of periodicities suggests that the level of interactions goes beyond a simple so-called graphoepitaxy (in which mostly an orientation order of the deposit is generated by interactions with the oriented roughness of the substrate), and could be defined as a "soft" epitaxy. Note however that the nucleation takes place at very low temperatures. A similar nucleation mechanism may be at play at high supercooling, possibly under conditions leading to homogeneous nucleation. It could take place for example in "pockets" of molten polymer trapped and squeezed between the fold surfaces of neighbor, bent lamellae and left-over during the initial spherulite growth.

8.5 EPITAXIAL CRYSTALLIZATION: SOME ISSUES AND APPLICATIONS

8.5.1 Epitaxial Crystallization and the Design of New Nucleating Agents

The issue of nucleating agents has been a recurring one in the previous sections. This industrially important issue is developed in its own right (cf Chapter 4) and only aspects relating to the role of epitaxy will be considered here. Indeed, epitaxy is a physical interaction that helps favor the nucleation of a polymer or any other material for that matter. In polyolefins only weak physical interactions are to be considered, thus the emphasis put so far on an understanding of these interactions, and their structural consequences and manifestations.

Several analyses of polymer/nucleating agent interactions have been performed over the years. As indicated, when the analysis is made at a sufficient level of detail and when the partners in the epitaxy have well-defined crystal structures, (that is, excluding, e.g., liquid-crystalline phases), it appears that most epitaxial interactions belong to the class of "hard" epitaxy. However, a major characteristic of these analyses is that they deal with polymer/nucleating agent systems that have been, for the most part, discovered empirically.

Does the body of knowledge accumulated so far help design new nucleating agents, or at least does it help us screen among potential candidates? It seems that the answer is: not quite or, probably more accurately, not yet. Nucleating agents must fulfill several requirements, which are, at times, contradictory, which are not considered in the epitaxy analysis: compatibility with the (molten) polymer, dispersion, possibly shape of the particles, thermal stability of the agent in the conventional processing window of the polymer, and so on. The so-called clarifying agents must also be very finely dispersed in the polymer, which is usually done by creating a physical gel of the nucleating agent prior to crystallization of the polymer (e.g., sorbitol derivatives) [69, 70].

In the case of clarifying agents, the details (and the quality) of the interactions between the polymer and the nucleating agent may even be relatively secondary. In that case indeed, the main issue is the dispersion. A relatively mild interaction that triggers nucleation of the polymer only slightly above its "conventional" heterogeneous nucleation range would be sufficient to qualify the nucleating agent as a clarifying agent, since nucleation would be initiated on the highly dispersed additive rather than on the "conventional" impurities thought to trigger crystallization. Conversely, however, nucleating agents that trigger nucleation at high temperatures are essential when the issue is speed of processing.

A further difficulty may arise when searching for nucleating agents that are specific for one crystal phase. For example, in the case of iPP, the α and β crystal structures are based on the same helix geometry, which also implies very similar interchain distances in the two structures. It is therefore very difficult—it is actually impossible—to predict which crystal structure will be nucleated by any given nucleating agent. Two observations support this statement: (1) A series of nucleating agents derived from a substituted trisamide have been synthesized recently, and have been tested as nucleating agents for iPP. Depending on the substituent, they induce either the α or the β phase of iPP, with no apparent logic (size of the substituent, differences in packing, crystal structure, or symmetry, etc.) [71]. A detailed structural analysis, as described earlier, is needed to decipher the interactions at play. (2) γ-quinacridone, also known as "permanent red" with code name E3B was patented over 40 years ago and has ever since been considered as a βiPP nucleating agent [38]. It was inferred [72] and shown recently that E3B is actually an αiPP nucleating agent above 140°C, and a βiPP nucleating agent only below 140°C [73]. Since on cooling, the nucleated sample must cross the high temperature region (when E3B is an αiPP nucleating agent), E3B yields consistently lower proportions of βiPP phase than "specific" βiPP nucleating agents. This duality, which is highly unusual, stems again from the fact that the periodicities of iPP involved in the epitaxy are very similar. In the present case, both the 0.65-nm chain axis periodicity of the β phase and the 0.655-nm interchain distance of the α phase in the ac face match a 0.65-nm substrate periodicity [73].

Note that a similar duality of crystal phases is observed when hexamethylbenzene is used as a substrate for the crystallization of poly(L-lactic acid) (PLLA). Two different crystal modifications are produced at ≈120°C and 140°C that differ by the helix conformation (3_2 and 10_7) but have very similar interchain distances [74].

The literature is replete with investigations describing the nucleating activity of a wide range of chemicals (organic, minerals, salts, polymers, etc.) that induce the crystallization of different polymers. It suffices to make an electronic literature and patent search with the proper keywords. Two remarks should be made at this stage: (1) Many patented nucleating agents are not very, or even poorly efficient when this efficiency is evaluated with a reliable "efficiency scale" that uses a self-seeding procedure to generate the "perfectly nucleated" polymer (the crystalline fragments left after partial melting of polymer become, on cooling, perfect initiators of crystallization in terms of compatibility with the molten polymer, dispersion, and crystal structure similarity). [75] (2) Polar polymers and polymers with "loose," irrational helices (e.g., poly(ethylene oxide) with a 7_2 helical conformation, POM with a 9_5 helical conformation) are difficult to nucleate: only few nucleating agents are known for these polymers (cf Chapter 13). The irrational helical conformations are probably to blame since they imply indeed relatively large chain axis repeat distances, thus precluding a high density of any favorable local polymer–substrate interaction.

As a rule, most reports on nucleating agents (industrial and, in most cases, academic) do not detail the structural relationship between the active nucleating agent and the polymer. At present, the search for new nucleating agents remains mostly empirical, or relies on educated guess based on the body of knowledge accumulated so far on the ingredients of a "good" nucleating agent: compatibility, dispersion, epitaxial interactions with the targeted polymer(s). As seen later (cf Section 8.5.3), it appears indeed difficult to make a priori assumptions on the quality of such interactions by conformational and packing energy analysis.

8.5.2 Epitaxial Crystallization and the Design of Composite Materials

Epitaxial crystallization is also an ingredient in the build-up of composite materials. Two examples may be given at this stage, although many more probably exist.

The epitaxial crystallization of PE on iPP has already been analyzed. It leads to a structure in which the αiPP and PE chain axes are not parallel—they are at a 50° angle. Taking advantage of this relative orientation, we can produce a composite structure made of stretched, thin, alternating layers of iPP and PE. Melting of the PE layers and epitaxial recrystallization on the oriented iPP yields a composite in which iPP lamellae, oriented normal to the "fiber" axis, are bridged and connected by tilted PE lamellae, thus ensuring a crystalline and molecular connectivity via the epitaxial relationship. The mechanical and impact properties of this polymer composite (or more precisely, multi-ply composite, mechanically reminiscent of plywood) are improved compared with the initial layered structure, and the adhesive strength is best between layers linked by an epitaxial relationship [76].

Composites that associate various polymers, both crystalline and amorphous, and carbon nanotubes (CNT) are investigated in many laboratories. Improved mechanical and original electric properties have been reported. The interactions between crystalline polymers and CNT are difficult to decipher, given the small size of the latter. Work by Li and coworkers [77], based on electron microscopic observations, indicates that some form of "soft epitaxy" is involved. For CNT with a small diameter (typically single-walled CNT) this epitaxy is only conceivable when the PE chain axis lies nearly parallel to the CNT axis, that is, straight rather than winding around the CNT surface. Indeed, lamellar orientations are normal to the CNT when their diameter is small, indicating that the CNT and PE chain axes are parallel. Different orientations of the lamellae are also observed for thicker, multiwalled CNT, which is reminiscent of the epitaxy of PE on HOPG: the reduced surface curvature no longer hinders the deposition and crystallization of the polymer chains.

8.5.3 Conformational and Packing Energy Analysis of Polymer Epitaxy

The rules that govern polymer epitaxy have been deduced mainly from the analysis of observed epitaxies. The dimensional match at the unit-cell scale merely implies that the local favorable interaction are repeated on a two-dimensional (or at least on a one-dimensional) array in the contact plane. The topographic matching refers to the unit-cell scale interactions. In some instances (illustrated earlier with, e.g., the formation of the sPP Form II on 2-quinoxalinol) the topographic requirements are obvious and indeed intuitively sound.

However, the challenge is to gain a better understanding of the interactions at the interface by resorting to the modern techniques of conformational and packing energy analysis. In essence, the problem is to establish how favorable the "docking" of the polymer on the foreign surface can be and, if possible, evaluate the different docking energies for different contact planes. Ultimately, this approach might help predict or at least screen among different, potential nucleating agents.

Such an approach was developed, initially by Hopfinger and collaborators at Case Western Reserve University [7, 78]. As summarized in the review paper by Hopfinger, they developed the methodology and analyzed mostly the epitaxial crystallization of PE on alkali halide crystals, for which they had ample experimental evidence. In addition, both systems are relatively simple. Mostly the interaction of one chain of PE with the substrate was computed, and few details of the internal energy of the crystal phase formed could be included. Nevertheless, considering the computing limitations of the time, this represents the most constant effort to investigate the energy balance in epitaxial crystallization. In later work by, among others, Ward at the University of Minnesota [79], different strategies have been applied. For example, the energy penalty associated with the lattice expansion or contraction required to achieve dimensional lattice matching was evaluated by computing the packing energy of the polymer and substrate with altered cell dimensions.

In spite of some improvements in insight, it is fair to state that conformational and packing energy analysis has not yet become a standard approach in the deciphering of epitaxial crystallization. The drawbacks are numerous. For example, even when the epitaxy has been established experimentally (contact faces, relative orientation), it is difficult to evaluate over what distance away from the interface the two lattices relieve the surface stresses associated with the dimensional mismatch at the interface, or if local defects (point dislocations, etc.) intervene in the process. Similarly, it is difficult to evaluate the possible impact of steps in the substrate that generate wedges, and possible preferred nucleation sites, although analyses of the "hard" epitaxies described in this contribution do not need to invoke such steps and wedges, which may be operative in "softer" epitaxies.

The technique is even more difficult to use as a predictive tool. Indeed, experimental results show that a given crystal structure may have different contact faces, and furthermore, for any contact face, different relative orientations of the polymer and substrates can be considered. This possible versatility creates a multidimensional space that is difficult to explore systematically. Finally, some epitaxies depend on very subtle energy balances, as illustrated by the versatility of γ-quinacridone towards βiPP, already mentioned in Section 8.5.1 [73]. Whereas the substrate structure does not change, a slight change in the crystallization temperature induces two very different epitaxies, with a 90° change in polymer chain orientation relative to the substrate, and of course a change in the crystal modification that is induced, namely αiPP and βiPP. Even more troublesome, at the transition temperature of 140°C, the two crystal structures are produced simultaneously. Such subtle variations are difficult to pinpoint, and even more so to predict, considering the assumptions that are made in setting up the models, or also the approximations of the possible different sets of potentials that might be used in the calculation.

Perhaps the most noticeable exception to this general statement is the analysis of the self-epitaxy leading to the αiPP lamellar branching or the iPP γ phase. This analysis has been reported by Ferro et al. [80]. However, the system is highly unusual: the two interacting lattices are identical in the underlying self-epitaxy. The analysis thus amounts to determining the details of a *crystal structure* of lowest energy. Furthermore, the structural analysis had indicated all the essential features of the epitaxy (relative orientation, identical hand of the interacting helices). It remains that this analysis confirmed the better interdigitation linked with the self-epitaxy, which in turn is consistent with the fact that the γ phase is the more stable phase under high pressure.

As a rule therefore, conformational and packing energy analysis of epitaxial interactions (at least in the polymer field) must be used, in its present stage of development, mainly as a supporting technique. The core of the investigation of polymer epitaxy should remain the experimental, structural analysis of the interface that rests on diffraction (mostly electron), spectroscopic, and/or (when getting rid of one component) AFM techniques. More direct techniques exist when investigating the epitaxy of inorganic materials and minerals, particularly with electron microscopy. When the interfaces are oriented parallel to the electron beam, direct, high resolution visualization of rows of atoms in the interface becomes possible. Spectacular images of, for example, edge dislocations and local lattice distortions near the interface that help compensate for the lattice mismatch have been produced. It is more than probable that similar dislocations take place in polymer epitaxy. Given the beam sensitivity of polymers to electrons, their direct visualization by high resolution imaging techniques must await further improvements in, for example, digital camera sensitivity.

8.5.4 Epitaxy as a Means to Generate Oriented Opto- or Electroactive Materials

Initiated by the discovery of semiconduction in organic molecules [81] and the report of the first efficient organic device [82], development of highly oriented thin films of semiconducting polymers for organic light emitting diodes has become a highly relevant and timely topic. Epitaxy can be used in this context, and a number of recent studies deal with these aspects. Here again, it should be mentioned that the initial work on epitaxy of the conjugated polymers was performed at Case Western. It dealt with polydiacetylene films with intended applications in the field of nonlinear optics [83].

In the present context, we report only on the elucidation of the epitaxy and its analysis and, in a second part, on the development of elaboration conditions that help produce large size oriented systems.

Unsubstituted conjugated polymers such as polythiophene and poly(*para*-phenylene) cannot be processed in the form of thin films. One means to overcome this difficulty is to use oligomers since they share frequently the properties of their higher molecular weight counterparts (e.g., the electroluminescence of *para*-sexiphenyl [PSP] and poly(*para*-phenylene)). The oligomers are easier to process and, in the context of this chapter, can be oriented by epitaxial crystallization. Deposition techniques are very varied. For PSP, various processing conditions are available: molecular beam epitaxy, hot wall epitaxy, or physical vapor deposition. Substrates and crystallization conditions can be varied almost at will: temperatures range from <100 K to near the desorption temperature (≈430 K), and substrates may be metals, other dielectrics (silicon, TiO_2, alkali halides, etc.), or mica. The epitaxies involved can be analyzed in detail. In all cases, the low temperature β form is produced in which the PSP molecules are arranged in a herringbone fashion and the crystals are flat platelets [84]. At least five different contact planes with the substrates have been identified [85, 86]. For one of them, the PSP molecules are nearly normal to the substrate and the PSP appears as flat platelets. In the other situations, at least one PSP molecule of the unit cell lies flat (or, in some cases, nearly so) on the substrate, giving rise to edge-on platelets that show up as needles (Fig. 8.13) [87]. The different contact planes have been identified, and the major interactions between the deposit and the substrate analyzed. For example, K^+–aromatic ring association seems to be involved in the deposition of PSP on KCl, which reminds of similar analyses for the deposition of PE on NaCl. Moreover, the PSP molecules "feel" and are oriented by a dipole buried in the octogonal site of mica [88]. Kubono and Akiyama used a nucleation theory to interpret the different molecular orientations [89]. In another situation, privileged π–π interactions take place between a diacetylene and the potassium acid phthalate salt substrate, giving rise to a so-called molecular epitaxy [90].

Processability of semiconducting polymers may also be increased by substitution with flexible side chains, such as alkyl moieties that "jacket" the main chain. The properties of interest (e.g., charge mobility or polarized light emission) remain "confined" in the main chain and are highly anisotropic. Epitaxial crystallization becomes a logical tool for structuring and orienting these materials, especially since many of these systems need be used in thin or very thin films (down to a few nanometers); however it should be kept in mind that the more flexible jacket reduces the strength of the interactions with the orienting substrate and leads to a "softer" form of epitaxy, frequently one-dimensional.

Electroactive polymers such as the regioregular poly(3-alkyl-thiophenes) (P3AT) and polyfluorenes (PFO), two polymers used in the fabrication of organic field effect transistors (OFET) and organic solar cells, have been oriented on, for example 1,3,5 trichlorobenzene (TCB). For oligo-3AT, the chains are extended, whereas for higher Mw, the film structure is typically "polymeric" in the sense that it is made of alternating crystalline lamellae (≈20 nm thick) and amorphous, interlamellar regions [91]. Existence, in the latter films, of interlamellar chains ("tie molecules") accounts for the higher charge mobility observed in these systems

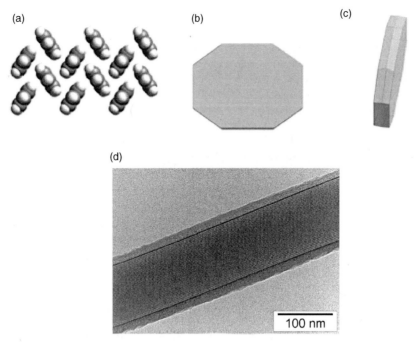

Figure 8.13 (a) Modeling of the molecular organization of the herringbone pattern of *p*-sexiphenyl (PSP) seen along the molecular axis. (b, c) Modeling of the single crystal morphologies of islands (b) and needles (c) generated when the contact planes with the substrate (assumed parallel to the sheet of paper) are (001) and (11$\bar{1}$), respectively. (d) High resolution electron micrograph of a needle showing lattice fringes 2.6 nm apart, which is the length of the PSP molecule. Part (d) reproduced from Reference [87] with permission of the American Chemical Society.

than in the corresponding oligomers, in which such molecular ties between extended chain lamellae are absent. Furthermore, the formation of highly oriented samples makes it possible to perform a structural analysis of the materials investigated by means of electron diffraction and molecular modeling, as illustrated in Figure 8.14 for PFO deposited, again, on TCB.

More interestingly, the lamellar structure characteristic of crystalline polymeric systems provides yet another original tool to generate even more complex nanostructured systems. The epitaxial crystallization of the electron donor P3HT can be made in the presence of an electron acceptor, namely inorganic semiconducting nanoparticles of cadmium selenide (CdSe) surface modified by tri(octyl) phosphine groups. Upon crystallization, the CdSe nanoparticles are rejected to the amorphous interlamellar zones of the P3HT [92]. Furthermore, when the nanoparticles are rod-like, they tend to align preferentially parallel to the P3HT chains [93]. This type of nanoscale hybrid morphology is of particular interest for organic photovoltaic applications: the materials must be made of percolating domains the size of which is commensurate with the diffusion length of the excitons, that is, several tens of nanometers [94].

8.6 CONCLUSIONS

Epitaxial crystallization is one of the few methods that make it possible to control by nonmechanical means and under appropriate processing conditions the morphology and/or structure of crystalline polymers. Furthermore, it may generate single crystalline, although multilamellar, polymer morphologies.

The rules governing epitaxial crystallization had been set up early on for low molecular weight materials. By and large, the same basic rules apply for polymers. However, the structural and conformational diversity of crystalline polymers, and their lamellar structure introduce new and subtle variables in the process.

The correct analysis of epitaxial crystallization of polymers cannot merely rely on global investigation techniques. Whereas the latter are suitable for screening, epitaxy takes place at a very different length scale, namely at the unit-cell level. It is therefore mandatory to use techniques that can "read" the molecular organization at a local scale. Moreover, in case a metastable crystal form is produced, the impact of epitaxy may be lost beyond only a few nanometers away from the interface. This contribution has developed some of

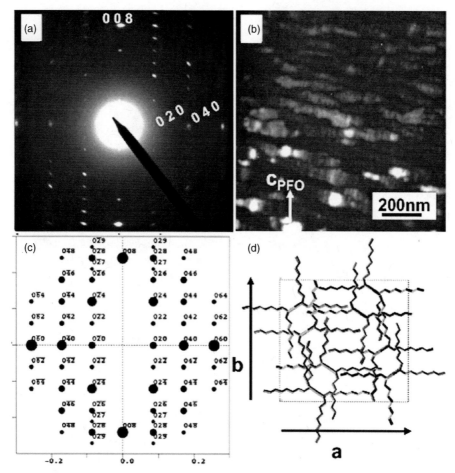

Figure 8.14 (a) Electron diffraction pattern of an oriented film of poly(9,9-di-octyl-2,7-fluorene-diyl) (PFO) produced by directional epitaxy in trichlorobenzene, subsequently annealed at 210°C for 10 minutes and cooled at 0.4°C/min. (b) Dark field of the PFO film, imaged through the 008 reflection. The crystalline lamellae of PFO are separated by narrow grain boundaries (darker lines). (c) Calculated diffraction pattern using the structural model of part (d). Reproduced from Reference [93] with permission of Brinkmann/L'actualité Chimique.

these technical aspects, as they determine the level of insight that can be reached in the analysis of epitaxy. As a rule, it appears that more detailed investigation techniques tend to uncover more specific epitaxial interactions, suggesting "hard" epitaxy rather than "soft" epitaxy. Several examples of "hard" epitaxial interactions in different systems have been provided, drawing in a large part from the present authors' experience. Numerous other examples are available in the literature, although sometimes not analyzed at a sufficient level of detail.

Epitaxy is an original tool in designing polymeric materials. Its role in nucleating agents (especially of nonreactive polymers such as polyolefins) needs not be underlined, even if epitaxy was not recognized immediately when, through trial and error, new nucleating agents were patented. Clearly, however, a whole new field is opening up with the development of devices that build on the anisotropic optoelectronic properties of functional polymers. In many cases, these polymers are in the form of thin films and control of orientation may become of utmost importance. The underlying polymer–substrate interactions may be stronger and more diverse (dipolar, electrostatic, etc.) than the mostly classical van der Waals ones involved for polyolefins. Further work and development of the techniques of polymer epitaxial crystallization will rest on these more technically oriented polymers and applications.

REFERENCES

[1] Royer, L. *Bull. Soc. Fr. Miner. Cristallogr.* **1928**, *51*, 7–159.

[2] Willems, J., Willems, I. *Experientia* **1957**, *13*, 465–465.

[3] Willems, J. *Experientia* **1967**, *23*, 409–504.

[4] Fischer, E.W. *Kolloid Z.Z. Polym.* **1958**, *159*, 108–118.

[5] Koutsky, J.A., Walton, A.G., Baer, E. *J. Polym. Sci. A2* **1966**, *4*, 611–629.

[6] Koutsky, J.A., Walton, A.G., Baer, E. *J. Polym. Sci. B* **1967**, *5*, 177–183.

[7] Mauritz, K.A., Baer, E., Hopfinger, A.J. *J. Polym. Sci. Macromol. Rev.* **1978**, *13*, 1–61.

[8] Walton, A.G., Carr, S.H., Baer, E. *Polymer Prepr.* **1968**, *9*, 603–616.

[9] Wittmann, J.C., St. John Manley, R. *J. Polym. Sci. Polym. Phys. Ed.* **1977**, *15*, 1089–1100.

[10] Wittmann, J.C., St. John Manley, R. *J. Polym. Sci. Polym. Phys. Ed.* **1978**, *16*, 1891–1895.

[11] Wittmann, J.C., Lotz, B. *Prog. Polym. Sci.* **1990**, *15*, 909–948.

[12] Thierry, A. Epitaxial crystallization (of linear polymers). In *Polymeric Materials Encyclopedia*, Vol. 3, Salamone, J.C., ed. CRC Press, Boca Raton, FL, 1996, pp. 2167–2179.

[13] Lotz, B., Thierry, A. Polymer crystals: epitaxial growth. In *Encyclopedia of Materials Science and Technology*, Buschow, K.H.J., Cahn, R.W., Flemings, M.C., Ilschner, B., Kramer, E.J., Mahajan, S., eds. Pergamon, Oxford, UK, 2001, pp. 7267–7272.

[14] Binsbergen, F.L. *Polymer* **1970**, *11*, 253–267.

[15] Beck, H.N. *J. Appl. Polym. Sci.* **1967**, *11*, 673–685.

[16] Wittmann, J.C., Hodge, A.M., Lotz, B. *J. Polym. Sci. Polym. Phys. Ed.* **1983**, *21*, 2495–2509.

[17] Wittmann, J.C., Lotz, B. *J. Polym. Sci. Polym. Phys. Ed.* **1981**, *19*, 1837–1851.

[18] Wittmann, J.C., Lotz, B. *J. Mater. Sci.* **1986**, *21*, 659–668.

[19] Takenaka, Y., Miyaji, H., Hoshino, A., Tracz, A., Jeszka, J.K., Kucinska, I. *Macromolecules* **2004**, *37*, 9667–9669.

[20] Tuinstra, F., Baer, E. *J. Polym. Sci. Polym. Lett.* **1970**, *8*, 861–865.

[21] Legras, R., Mercier, J.P., Nield, E. *Nature (London)* **1983**, *304*, 432–434.

[22] Garcia, D. *J. Polym. Sci. Polym. Phys. Ed.* **1984**, *22*, 2063–2072.

[23] Haubruge, H.G., Daussin, R., Jonas, A.M., Legras, R., Wittmann, J.C., Lotz, B. *Macromolecules* **2003**, *36*, 4452–4456.

[24] Tracz, A., Jeszka, J.K., Kucinska, I., Chapel, J.-P., Boiteux, G., Kryszewski, M. *J. Appl. Polym. Sci.* **2002**, *86*, 1329–1336.

[25] Tracz, A., Kucinska, I., Jeszka, J.K. *Macromolecules* **2003**, *36*, 10130–10132.

[26] Lotz, B., Wittmann, J.C., Lovinger, A.J. *Polymer* **1996**, *37*, 4979–4992.

[27] Lotz, B., Wittmann, J.C. *J. Polym. Sci. B Polym. Phys.* **1986**, *24*, 1541–1558.

[28] Natta, G., Corradini, P. *Nuovo Cimento* **1960**, *15*(Suppl. 1), 40–51.

[29] Lotz, B., Wittmann, J.C. *J. Polym. Sci. B Polym. Phys.* **1986**, *24*, 1559–1575.

[30] Lotz, B., Wittmann, J.C. *J. Polym. Sci. B Polym. Phys.* **1987**, *25*, 1079–1087.

[31] Mathieu, C., Thierry, A., Wittmann, J.C., Lotz, B. *Polymer* **2000**, *41*, 7241–7253.

[32] Stocker, W., Magonov, S.N., Cantow, H.J., Wittmann, J.C., Lotz, B. *Macromolecules* **1993**, *26*, 5915–5923; Correction: **1994**, *27*, 6690–6694.

[33] Stocker, W., Graff, S., Lang, J., Wittmann, J.C., Lotz, B. *Macromolecules* **1994**, *27*, 6677–6678.

[34] Yan, S., Katzenberg, F., Petermann, J., Yang, D., Shen, Y., Straupé, C., Wittmann, J.C., Lotz, B. *Polymer* **2000**, *41*, 2613–2625.

[35] Lotz, B., Kopp, S., Dorset, D.L. *C. R. Acad. Sci.* **1994**, *319*, 187–192.

[36] Meille, S.V., Ferro, D.R., Brückner, S., Lovinger, A.J., Padden, F.J. *Macromolecules* **1994**, *27*, 2615–2622.

[37] Dorset, D.L., McCourt, M.P., Kopp, S., Schumacher, M., Okihara, T., Lotz, B. *Polymer* **1998**, *39*, 6331–6337.

[38] Leugering, H. J. *Makromol. Chem.* **1967**, *109*, 204–216.

[39] Stocker, W., Schumacher, M., Graff, S., Thierry, A., Wittmann, J.C., Lotz, B. *Macromolecules* **1998**, *31*, 807–814.

[40] Khoury, F. *J. Res. Natl. Bur. Stand.* **1966**, *Sect. A 70*, 29–61.

[41] Padden, F.J., Jr., Keith, H.D. *J. Appl. Phys.* **1966**, *37*, 4013–4020.

[42] Lotz, B., Wittmann, J.C. Polymer single crystals. In *Materials Science and Technology*, Vol. 12, *Structure and Properties of Polymers*, Cahn, R.W., Haasen, P., Kramer, E.J., eds. V.C.H., Weinheim, 1993, pp. 79–151. Chap. 3.

[43] Lotz, B. *Eur. Phys. J. E Soft Matter* **2000**, *3*, 185–194.

[44] Cheng, S.Z.D., Lotz, B. *Philos. Trans. R. Soc. Lond.* **2003**, *361*, 517–537.

[45] Lotz, B. *Adv. Polym. Sci.* **2005**, *180*, 17–44.

[46] Brückner, S., Meille, S.V. *Nature (London)* **1989**, *340*, 455–457.

[47] Lotz, B., Graff, S., Straupé, C., Wittmann, J.C. *Polymer* **1991**, *32*, 2902–2910.

[48] Kopp, S., Wittmann, J.C., Lotz, B. *Polymer* **1994**, *35*, 908–915.

[49] Kopp, S., Wittmann, J.C., Lotz, B. *Polymer* **1994**, *35*, 916–924.

[50] Mathieu, C., Stocker, W., Thierry, A., Wittmann, J.C., Lotz, B. *Polymer* **2001**, *42*, 7033–7047.

[51] Dorset, D.L., McCourt, M.P., Kopp, S., Wittmann, J.C., Lotz, B. *Acta Crystallogr.* **1994**, *B50*, 201–208.

[52] Morniroli, J.P., Ji, G., Jacob, D. *Ultramicroscopy* **2012**, *121*, 42–60.

[53] Dorset, D.L., Gilmore, C.J., Jorda, J.L., Nicolopoulos, S. *Ultramicroscopy* **2007**, *107*, 462–473.

[54] McKeown, J.T., Spence, J.C.H. *J. Appl. Phys.* **2009**, *106*(7), 074309/1–074309/8.

[55] Wittmann, J.C., Smith, P. *Nature (London)* **1991**, *352*, 414–417.

[56] Lotz, B., Lovinger, A.J., Cais, R.E. *Macromolecules* **1988**, *21*, 2375–2382.

[57] Stocker, W., Schumacher, M., Graff, S., Lang, J., Wittmann, J.C., Lovinger, A.J., Lotz, B. *Macromolecules* **1994**, *27*, 6948–6955.

[58] Zhang, J., Yang, D., Thierry, A., Wittmann, J.C., Lotz, B. *Macromolecules* **2001**, *34*, 6261–6267.

[59] Kakugo, M., Wakatsuki, K., Wakamatsu, K., Watanabe, K. *Polymer Prepr. (Jpn)* **1990**, *39*, 3884–3887; *Polymer Prepr. (Jpn)* **1991**, *40*, 1145–1145.

[60] Nishikawa, Y., Murakani, S., Kohjiya, S., Kawaguchi, A. *Macromolecules* **1996**, *29*, 5558–5566.

[61] Gahleitner, M., Wolfschwenger, J. Nucleating agents for crystalline polymers. In *Encyclopedia of Materials Science and Technology*, Buschow, K.H.J., Cahn, R.W., Flemings, M.C., Ilschner, B., Kramer, E.J., Mahajan, S., eds. Pergamon, Oxford, UK, 2001, pp. 7239–7244.

[62] De Rosa, C., Borriello, A.M., Corradini, P. *Macromolecules* **1996**, *29*, 6323–6327.

[63] Alcazar, D., Ruan, J., Thierry, A., Kawaguchi, A., Lotz, B. *Macromolecules* **2006**, *39*, 1008–1019.

[64] Alcazar, D., Ruan, J., Thierry, A., Lotz, B. *Macromolecules* **2006**, *39*, 2832–2840.

[65] Kobayashi, K., Takahashi, T. *Kagaku (Tokyo)* **1964**, *34*, 325–328.

[66] Balik, C.M., Hopfinger, A.J. *Macromolecules* **1980**, *13*, 999–1001.

[67] Qian, X.J., Rickert, S.E., Lando, J.B. *J. Mater. Res.* **1989**, *4*, 1005–1017.

[68] Wittmann, J.C., Lotz, B. *J. Polym. Sci. Polym. Phys. Ed.* **1985**, *23*, 205–226.

[69] Thierry, A., Straupé, C., Lotz, B., Wittmann, J.C. *Polym. Commun.* **1990**, *31*, 299–301.

[70] Kristiansen, M., Werner, M., Tervoort, T., Smith, P., Blomenhofer, M., Schmidt, H.-W. *Macromolecules* **2003**, *36*, 5150–5156.

[71] Blomenhofer, M., Ganzleben, S., Hanft, D., Schmidt, H.-W., Kristiansen, M., Werner, M., Smith, P., Stoll, K., Mäder, D., Hoffmann, K. *Macromolecules* **2005**, *38*, 3688–3695.

[72] Jacoby, P., Bersted, B.H., Kissel, W., Smith, C.E. *J. Polym. Sci. B Polym. Phys.* **1986**, *24*, 461–491.

[73] Mathieu, C., Thierry, A., Wittmann, J.C., Lotz, B. *J. Polym. Sci. B Polym. Phys.* **2002**, *40*, 2504–2515.

[74] Cartier, L., Okihara, T., Ikada, Y., Tsuji, H., Puiggali, J., Lotz, B. *Polymer* **2000**, *41*, 8909–8919.

[75] Fillon, B., Lotz, B., Thierry, A., Wittmann, J.C. *J. Polym. Sci. B Polym. Phys.* **1993**, *31*, 1395–1405.

[76] Kestenbach, H.J., Loos, J., Petermann, J. *Polym. Eng. Sci.* **1998**, *38*, 478–484.

[77] Li, L., Li, B., Hood, M.A., Li, C.Y. *Polymer* **2009**, *50*, 953–965.

[78] Hopfinger, A.J. *Plast. Eng.* **1992**, *25*, 439–480.

[79] Hooks, M.D., Fritz, T., Ward, M.D. *Adv. Mater.* **2001**, *13*, 227–241.

[80] Ferro, D.R., Brückner, S., Meille, S.V., Ragazzi, M. *Macromolecules* **1992**, *25*, 5231–5235.

[81] Vartanyan, A.S. *J. Phys. Chem. (USSR)* **1946**, *20*, 1065–1080.

[82] Tang, C.W. *Appl. Phys. Lett.* **1987**, *51*, 913–915.

[83] Rickert, S.E., Lando, J.B., Ching, S. *Mol. Cryst. Liq. Cryst.* **1983**, *93*, 307–314.

[84] Baker, K.N., Fratini, A.V., Resch, T., Knachel, H.C., Adams, W.W., Socci, E.P., Farmer, B.L. *Polymer* **1993**, *34*, 1571–1587.

[85] Mülleger, S., Hlawacek, G., Haber, T., Frank, P., Teichert, C., Resel, R., Winkler, A. *Appl. Phys. A* **2007**, *87*, 103–111.

[86] Haber, T., Andrev, A., Thierry, A., Sitter, H., Oehzelt, M., Resel, R. *J. Cryst. Growth* **2005**, *284*, 209–220.

[87] Haber, T., Oehzelt, M., Resel, R., Andreev, A., Thierry, A., Sitter, H., Smilgies, D.M., Schaffer, B., Grogger, W. *J. Nanosci. Nanotechnol.* **2006**, *6*, 698–703.

[88] Plank, H., Resel, R., Andreev, A., Scariftci, N.S., Hlawacek, G., Teichert, C., Thierry, A., Lotz, B. *Thin Solid Films* **2003**, *443*, 108–114.

[89] Kubono, A., Akiyama, R. *J. Appl. Phys.* **2005**, *98*, 093502/1–093502/6.

[90] Thierry, A., Kajzar, F., Le Moigne, J. *Macromolecules* **1991**, *24*, 2622–2628.

[91] Brinkmann, M., Rannou, P. *Adv. Funct. Mater.* **2007**, *17*, 101–108.

[92] Brinkmann, M., Aldakov, D., Chandezon, F. *Adv. Mater.* **2007**, *19*, 3819–3823.

[93] Brinkmann, M. *Actual. Chim.* **2009**, *326*, 31–34.

[94] Günes, S., Neugebauer, H., Sariciftci, N.S. *Chem. Rev.* **2007**, *107*, 1324–1338.

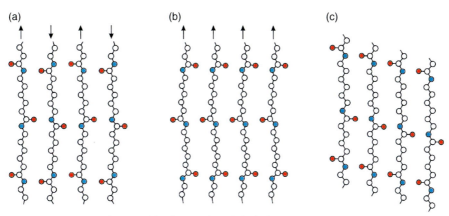

Figure 2.21 Projections of sheets of hydrogen bonded chains in a plane parallel to chain axes of even nylons (a, b) and even–even nylons (c) in the α form with chains in a zigzag planar conformation [122] (a, c) and in the γ form with chains in a twisted less extended conformation [122] (b). (See text for full caption.)

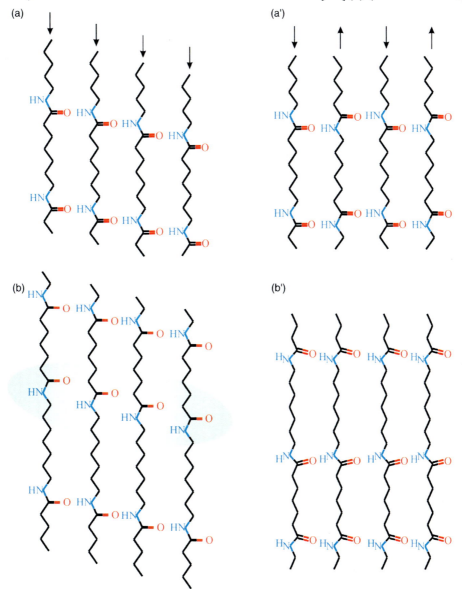

Figure 2.22 Projections of sheets of hydrogen bonded chains in a plane parallel to chain axes of in odd nylons (a, a') and odd–odd nylons (b, b') in the α form with chains in a zigzag planar conformation [122] (a, a') and in the γ form with chains in a twisted less extended conformation [122] (b'). (See text for full caption.)

Handbook of Polymer Crystallization, First Edition. Edited by Ewa Piorkowska and Gregory C. Rutledge.
© 2013 John Wiley & Sons, Inc. Published 2013 by John Wiley & Sons, Inc.

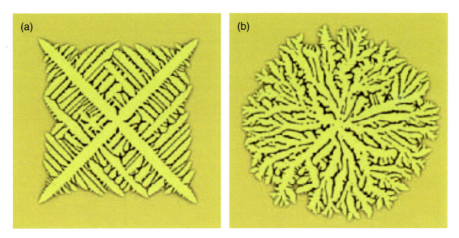

Figure 3.22 Two-dimensional structures calculated by phase-field modeling for crystallization in the presence of impurities. (a) The classic dendrite results from fourfold anisotropy of the crystallization kinetics that assures orthogonal growth of secondary and tertiary arms in this case. The growth tips are parabolic. (b) The dense branched morphology (DBM) is formed when growth rate anisotropy is reduced by 70%. From Granasy et al. [36] with permission from Macmillan Publishers Ltd.

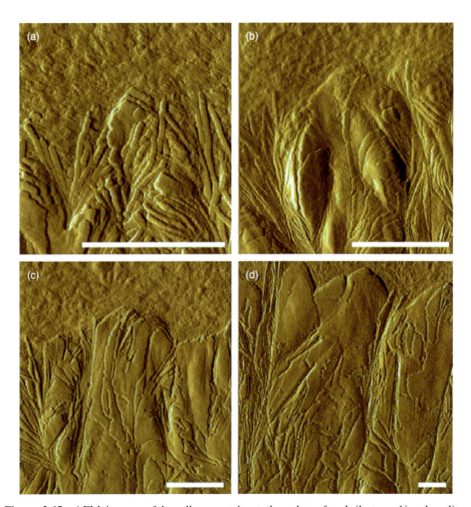

Figure 3.65 AFM images of lamellar crystals at the edge of poly(butene-1) spherulites crystallized at different temperatures. The growth faces are {100} for the tetragonal crystals; compare with the hedrite in Figure 3.58. Note that magnifications are different; each scale bar is 2 μm. The maximum lamellar width λ_m clearly increases with T_c. (a) $T_c = 86.8°C$, $\lambda_m = 0.9$ μm; (b) $T_c = 91.5°C$, $\lambda_m = 1.5$ μm; (c) $T_c = 96.5°C$, $\lambda_m = 2.2$ μm; (d) $T_c = 101.5°C$, $\lambda_m = 5.0$ μm. From Kajioka et al. [97] with permission from Elsevier.

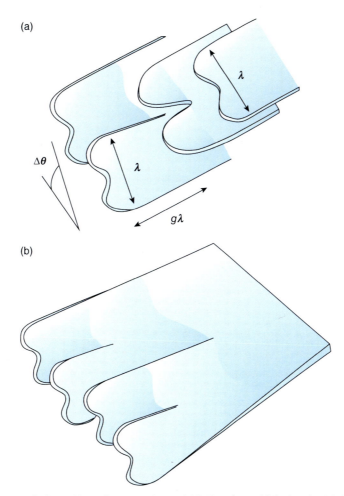

Figure 3.72 Depiction of lamellar growth to width W = λ at which size the Mullins–Sekerka instability causes tip splitting that results in isochiral topological screw dislocations. Branching and twisting recur after radial growth by $g\lambda$. From Toda et al. [99] with permission from the American Chemical Society.

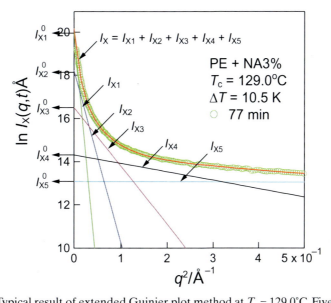

Figure 4.3 Typical result of extended Guinier plot method at $T_c = 129.0°C$. Five straight lines ($I_{X1}, I_{X2}, ... I_{X5}$) are separated from $\ln I_X(q, t)$ for $0.05 \times 10^{-3} \leq q^2 \leq 15 \times 10^{-3}$ Å^{-2}. R_{gj} and I^0_{Xj} are obtained from the slope and vertical intercept of the straight lines, respectively.

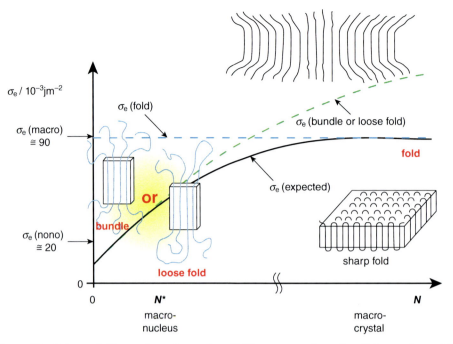

Figure 4.7 Schematic illustration of σ_e against N. The nano-nucleus should form a loose fold or bundle nucleus as Price showed [12] because the energy to form sharp folds is very large. The macro-crystal tends to form sharp folds [29]. Therefore, σ_e(expected) shows the size dependence of expected σ_e.

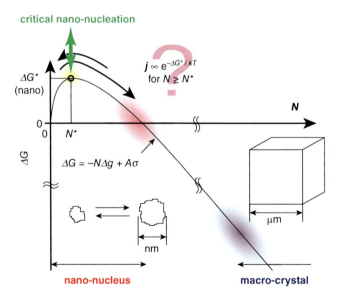

Figure 4.9 Illustration of ΔG against N. A is the surface area of the nucleus. The nano-nucleus shows significant fluctuation with respect to its size and shape. ΔG^*(nano) corresponds to critical nano-nucleation, as shown in Reference [16]. According to Eyring's theory of absolute reaction rate, critical nano-nucleation should become the activation barrier of nucleation. The macro-crystal has smooth and flat surfaces and does not disappear.

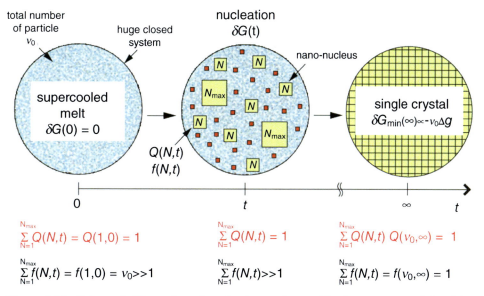

Figure 4.11 Schematic illustration of nucleation and crystallization processes defined for $Q(N, t)$. We consider a huge closed system. Nano-nuclei are generated from the supercooled melt and finally the system transforms into a single crystal. Total free energy of nucleation $\delta G(t)$, $Q(N, t)$, and $f(N, t)$ are also shown. $\delta G(t)$ changes from zero for the supercooled melt to the minimum $\delta G_{min}(t)$ at 100% crystal. Summation of $Q(N, t)$ satisfies unity for all t; however, $f(N, t)$ does not sum to unity.

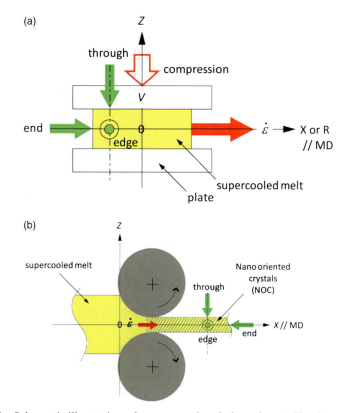

Figure 4.16 Schematic illustration of a cross sectional view of crystallization apparatuses to show the principle of elongational crystallization by the compression method. Z-axis is along the compressed direction. X- or R-axis is parallel to the MD. (a) Compression type apparatus. (b) Roll type apparatus.

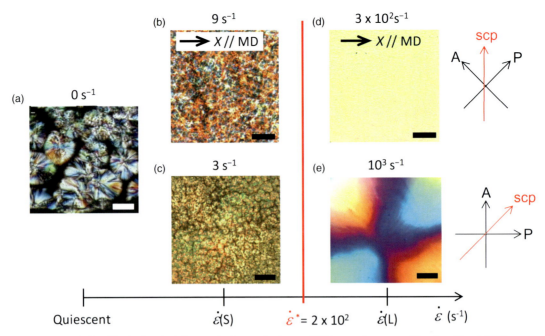

Figure 4.17 Typical polarizing optical morphology of iPP samples crystallized at $T_c = 150°C$. (a) Crystallized at quiescent field, $\dot{\varepsilon} = 0$ s^{-1}. (See text for full caption.)

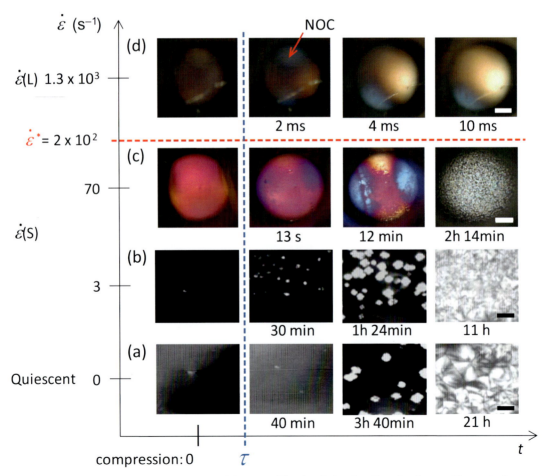

Figure 4.18 Typical $\dot{\varepsilon}$ dependence of the crystallization behavior directly observed by optical microscopy on samples elongationally crystallized by 2D compression at $T_c = 150°C$. (See text for full caption.)

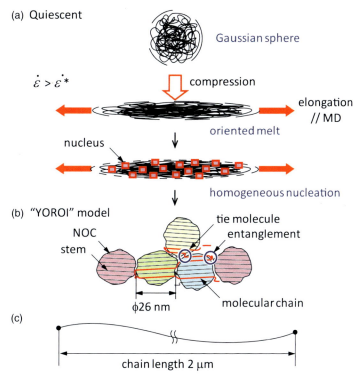

Figure 4.25 Schematic illustration of the NOC nucleation mechanism. (a) A Gaussian sphere within the isotropic melt under quiescent conditions. Compression at $\dot{\varepsilon} > \dot{\varepsilon}^*$ induces the "oriented melt" by significant chain elongation, which induces the homogeneous nucleation. (b) Schematic illustration of the "YOROI model" of the NOC structure. (c) Schematic illustration of one molecular chain in the case that we virtually extend its full length. 2 μm is 10^2 times as large as the size of a nano-crystal.

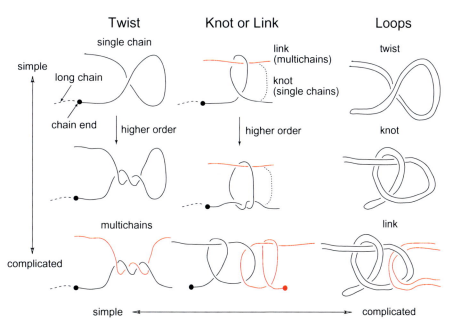

Figure 4.44 Classification of entanglements such as twists, knots, and loops. In this figure, toward the bottom and right sides, entanglements become more "complicated."

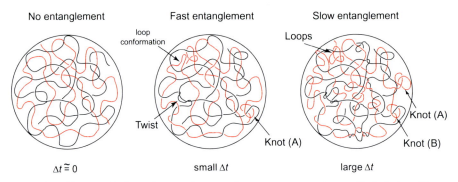

Figure 4.45 Time evolution of entanglements between two random coiled chains. (See text for full caption.)

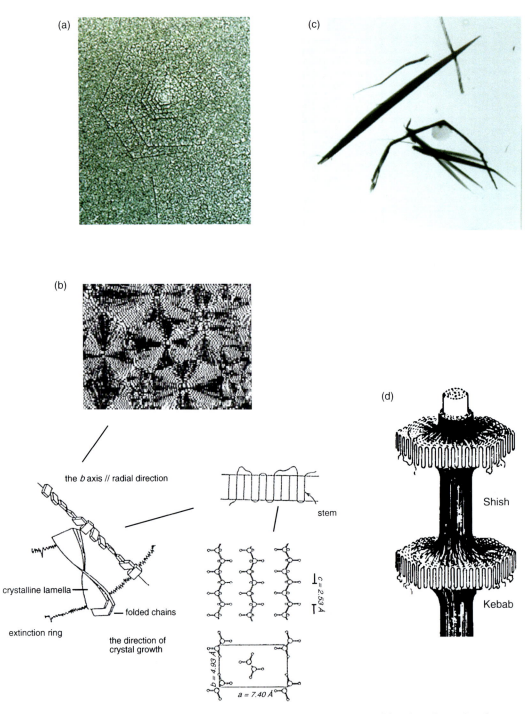

Figure 5.1 (a) The solution-grown polyoxymethylene single crystal, (b) spherulites of melt-cooled polyethylene sample and the hierarchical structure, (c) extended-chain crystals of polyoxymethylene (whisker), and (d) the shish–kebab structure.

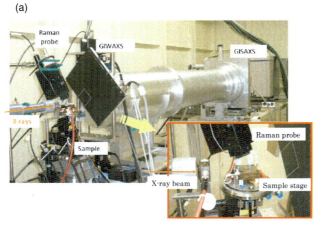

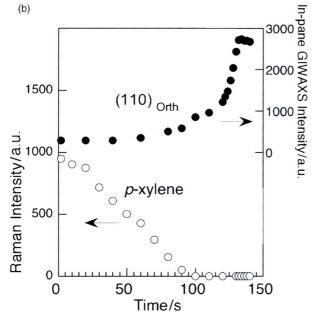

Figure 5.4 (a) Raman, GISAXS, and GIWAXD simultaneous measurement system. The GIWAXD is measured using a flat-panel detector and the GISAXS is measured using a CCD camera. The laser beam is irradiated on the sample surface and the Raman spectrum is measured in the back scattering geometry. (b) The time dependences of the Raman intensity of *p*-xylene band and the intensity of GIWAXD 110 peak [18].

(a) Negative Spherulite

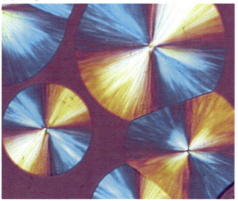

(b) Poly(ethylene Adipate)

Figure 5.5 (a) A negative spherulite of poly(ethylene oxide) and (b) a spherulite of poly(ethylene adipate).

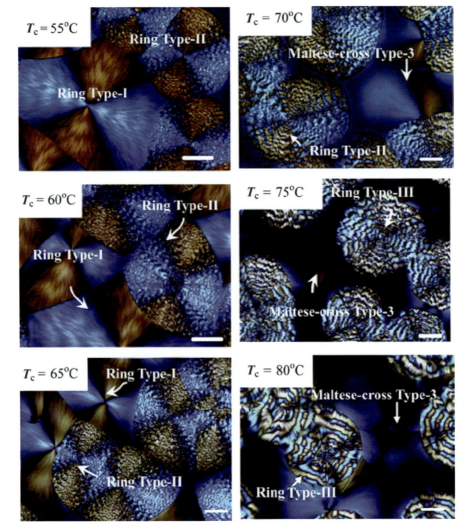

Figure 5.7 The various patterns of spherulites grown at the different temperatures observed for poly(pentamethylene terephthalate) [26].

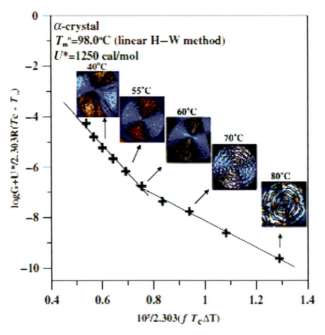

Figure 5.11 Plot of $\ln(G) + \Delta E/(RTc)$ against $1/(Tc\Delta T)$ for the isothermal crystallization of poly(heptamethylene terephthalate), where the ΔE is assumed to be 1250 cal/mol [26].

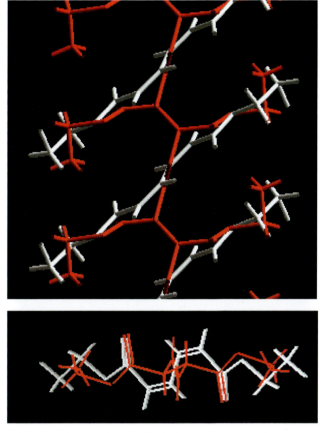

Figure 5.28 Molecular shapes of poly(diethyl *cis,cis*-muconate) and the corresponding monomers in the crystal lattice [130]. (See text for full caption.)

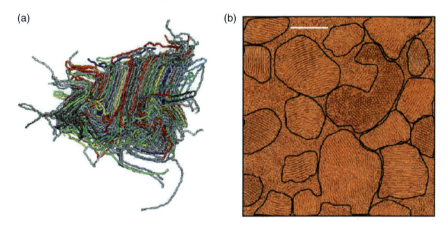

Figure 6.5 (a) A single ordered domain of PVDF shows a fringed-micelle-like morphology for the polar polymer model (similar results are seen for polyethylene). (See text for full caption.)

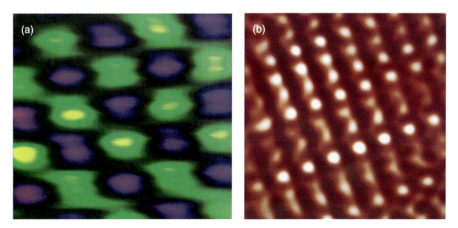

Figure 8.5 (a) The contact face of iPP α phase deposited on benzoic acid. (See text for full caption.)

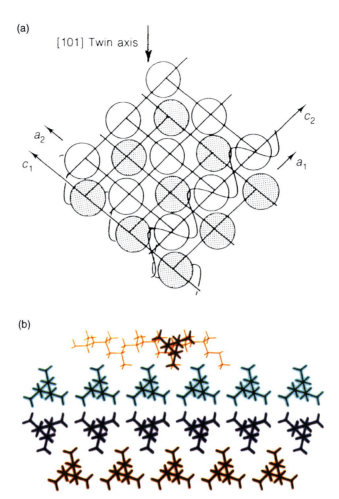

Figure 8.6 (a) Interdigitation of methyl groups in the ac face of αiPP that displays one methyl group per cell (cf Fig. 8.4, middle). The substrate layer methyl groups are shaded; the depositing ones are unshaded. The lozenge-shaped pattern of methyl groups allows similar interdigitation for the crystallographic and the self-epitaxial crystallization. The chain orientation of the deposited layer depends on whether the helices in facing planes are antichiral (crystallographic packing) or are isochiral (self-epitaxy leading to lamellar branching). The self-epitaxial deposition is illustrated here. This self-epitaxy is equally described, in crystallographic terms, as a rotation twin ([101] twin axis indicated here). Reproduced from Reference [42] with permission of VCH, Weinheim. (b) Crystallographic and epitaxial deposition of helical stems in the αiPP ac growth face, illustrated here in the top layer. The deposition of two helices with different hands is represented. The black helix is antichiral to the nearby substrate (contact) layer helices. It is seen along its c-axis, a situation that corresponds to normal, crystallographic deposition. The yellow helix is isochiral to the substrate ones. It is seen nearly horizontal: its chain axis is parallel to the a-axis of the substrate (epitaxial deposition). This specific interaction between a chiral helical stem and a substrate layer made of helices with the same chirality corresponds to the initiation of lamellar branching. (Courtesy F. Colonna-Cesari).

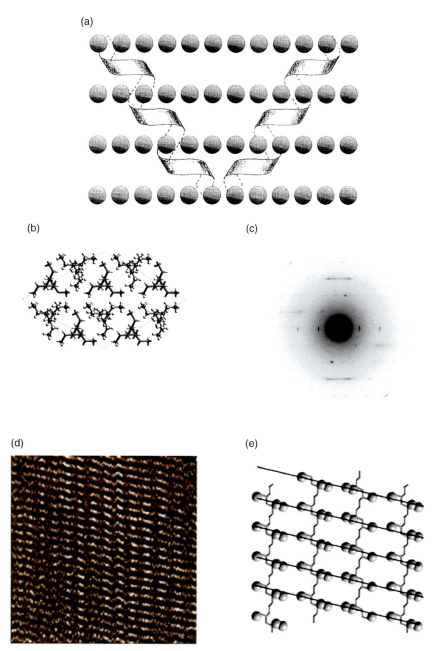

Figure 8.9 Epitaxial crystallization of layers made of isochiral helices: isotactic poly(1-butene) Form I (iPBuI). (See text for full caption.)

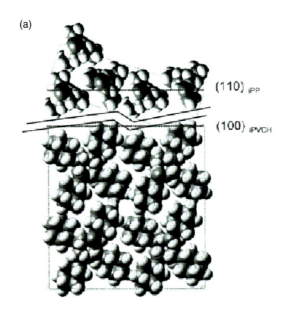

Figure 8.11 Epitaxial crystallization of isotactic polypropylene and its polymeric nucleating agent, isotactic polyvinylcyclohexane. (a) Topographic and dimensional matching of the two contact faces as seen along the chain axes. Corrugations in the $(110)_{iPP}$ and $(100)_{iPVCH}$ planes (underlined) match nearly perfectly. (b) Topographic and dimensional matching as seen normal to the contact plane. The contact faces display rows of methyl groups (iPP, shaded) and edges of cyclohexyl rings (right) that have the same tilt angle and identical spacings. Matching of the two faces can be visualized by "closing the iPP shutters" on the central PVCH "window." Reproduced from Reference [64] with permission of the American Chemical Society.

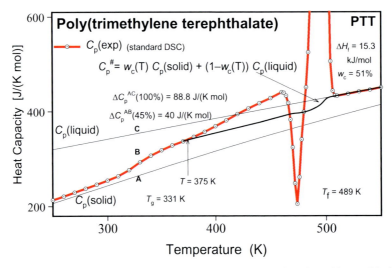

Figure 9.7 Advanced thermal analysis of melting process for estimation of heat of fusion from apparent heat capacity, C_p(exp) of semicrystalline poly(trimethylene teraphthalate) PTT [28].

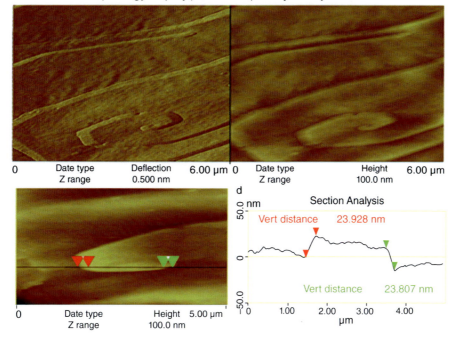

Figure 9.16 (a) Deflection and (b) height images of a flat stack of lamellae of semicrystalline poly(lactic acid) by AFM. (c, d) Details of determination of the lamellar thickness [35].

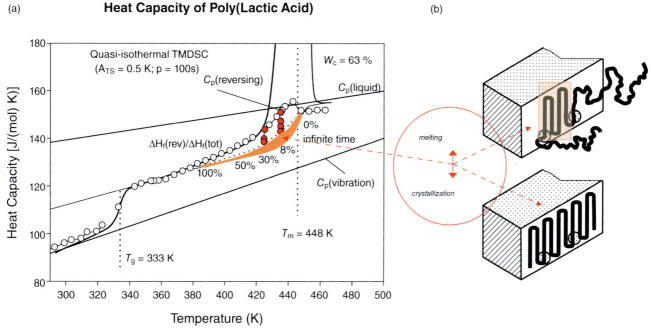

Figure 9.34 (a) The comparison of the reversing heat capacities of poly(lactic acid) (PLA) resulting from different the time domains in the melting region by quasi-isothermal method of temperature-modulated DSC in the frame of vibrational and liquid C_p [55]. (See text for full caption.)

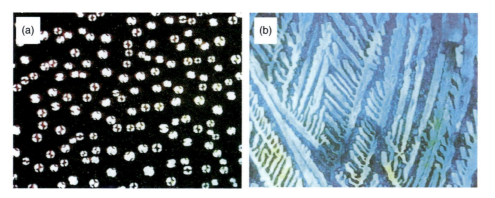

Figure 10.31 Optical micrographs. (See text for full caption.)

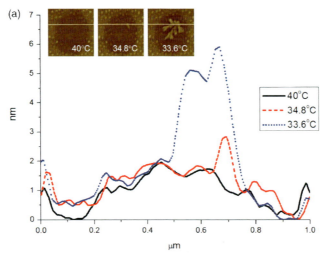

Figure 12.17 (a) Comparison between profiles of an iPP droplet showing the crystallization on cooling.

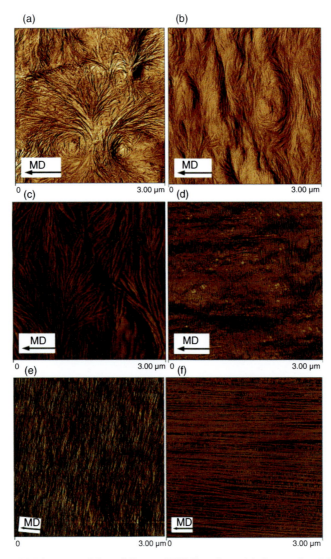

Figure 14.8 AFM images of five different PVDF resins with increasing MW (85–250 kg/mol) exposed to the same flow conditions during film blowing. (a) Resin 1, (b) resin 2, (c) resin 1, higher magnification, (d) resin 3, (e) resin 4, (f) resin 5 [89].

9

MELTING

MAREK PYDA

Department of Chemistry, Rzeszow University of Technology, Rzeszow, Poland
Department of Pharmacy, Poznan University of Medical Sciences, Poznan, Poland
ATHAS-MP Company, Knoxville, Tennessee

9.1 Introduction to the Melting of Polymer Crystals, 265
9.2 Parameters of the Melting Process, 267
9.3 Change of Conformation, 268
9.4 Heat of Fusion and Degree of Crystallinity, 270
　9.4.1 Heat of Fusion, 270
　9.4.2 Degree of Crystallinity, 272
9.5 Equilibrium Melting, 274
　9.5.1 The Equilibrium Melting Temperature, 274
　9.5.2 The Equilibrium Thermodynamic Functions, 275
9.6 Other Factors Affecting the Melting Process of Polymer Crystals, 277
　9.6.1 The Influence of the Polymer's Chemical Structure on the Melting Process, 277
　9.6.2 The Effect of Polymer Molar Mass on the Melting Behavior, 277
　9.6.3 Influence of Heating Rate on the Melting, 278
　9.6.4 Multiple Melting Peaks of Polymers, 279
　9.6.5 Influence of Pressure on the Melting Process, 281
　9.6.6 The Melting Process by Other Methods, 281
　9.6.7 Diluents Effect: The Influence of small Diluents on the Melting Process, 282
9.7 Irreversible and Reversible Melting, 282
9.8 Conclusions, 284
References, 285

9.1 INTRODUCTION TO THE MELTING OF POLYMER CRYSTALS

The melting process of polymers is the reverse of crystallization and occurs during heating when polymers obtain some thermal energy and thus a crystalline phase can pass to the liquid phase. For the crystalline phase of single component polymeric materials the melting process is a first-order phase transition according to equilibrium thermodynamics. At the first-order phase transition temperature, the crystal requires the adsorption of the latent heat of fusion (ΔH_f) to be disordered, the thermodynamic Gibbs free energy (or free enthalpy) (G) is continuous, and its first derivatives, such as volume (V), entropy (S), and thermodynamic function enthalpy (H), and also its second derivatives such as heat capacity (C_p), expansivity (α), and compressibility (β) show discontinuity [1–4]. A scheme of changes of some of these variables is presented in Figure 9.1.

Practically, the experimental results from many studies [1–9] show that the melting of polymers is an irreversible process due to the partial crystalline metastable phase (so-called semicrystalline phase), small crystal size, and crystal defects such as amorphous, mesophases. Generally, the melting process is a function of the thermal history of the crystallization process, the nature of the crystal, and its crystalline state in terms of structure, morphology, and polymer chain macroconformation

Handbook of Polymer Crystallization, First Edition. Edited by Ewa Piorkowska and Gregory C. Rutledge.
© 2013 John Wiley & Sons, Inc. Published 2013 by John Wiley & Sons, Inc.

Melting transition

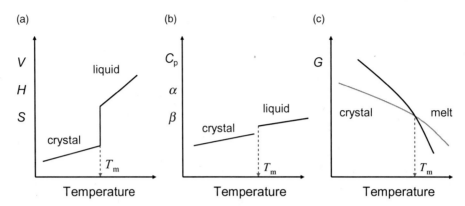

Figure 9.1 Scheme of thermodynamic quantities as functions of temperature at a constant pressure in the melting transition (a) volume (V), enthalpy (H), entropy (S); (b) heat capacity, expansivity (α), compressibility (β); (c) and Gibbs free energy.

[1–9]. On cooling from the melt, the randomly coiled and entangled macromolecules form either crystalline, mobile amorphous, or rigid amorphous phases depending both on kinetics and on the chemical structure of the macromolecules. A typical linear, flexible macromolecule is 100 nm to 1.0 mm in length [1, 3]. In equilibrium, macromolecules in crystals should adopt extended-chain macroconformations. In nonequilibrium, macromolecules crystallize in the form of chain-folded crystals. Depending on the condition of crystallization, the thickness of the chain-folded crystals range from 5 to 50 nm. Polymers are mostly semicrystalline [1, 3] and their crystallinities are typically between 5% and 95%. The melting of polymer crystals usually does not occur at well-defined melting temperatures, but over a melting range. To understand this melting process, it is necessary not only to know the crystal structure and morphology of polymers, but also their connection to the surrounding noncrystalline phase and its properties. The melting behavior is governed by irreversible effects, melting temperature, and heat of fusion, and it should be described in reference to equilibrium [3]. The equilibrium parameters serve as a set of boundaries for the nonequilibrium semicrystalline melting process [1, 3].

The melting process of polymeric systems can be studied utilizing dilatometry, calorimetry with thermal analysis, optical microscopy with hot stage, atomic force microscopy (AFM) with microcalorimetry, X-ray diffraction, and other techniques [1–9]. Special modern calorimetries such as standard differential scanning calorimetry (DSC), temperature-modulated differential scanning calorimetry (TMDSC) [3, 10, 11], and quantitative thermal analysis are very useful for examining the melting behaviors of polymeric system [3, 12–16].

In this chapter, the melting process of polymers is described based on apparent heat capacity and quantitative thermal analysis [3, 17, 18]. Advanced thermal analysis allows the separation of a latent heat from thermodynamic heat capacity for the experimental, apparent heat capacity results, and the separation of the reversible from the irreversible process in the melting region of semicrystalline polymers. Characterization of the pre-melting and melting regions by quantitative thermal analysis permits the identification of the pre-melting transitions within the crystal and the rigid amorphous phases, and also coupling with crystalline and mobile amorphous phases between the melting and glass transition temperatures [19]. The general effects of polymer lamella thickness and perfection, determined by crystallization conditions and post-crystallization thermal history and molar mass, as well as the effects of heating rate, pressure, and diluent characteristics on the melting behavior are also discussed.

Several examples, including polyethylene (PE), poly(trimethylene terephthalate) (PTT), poly(butylene terephthalate) (PBT), poly(lactic acid) (PLA), and others are shown in order to present the rationale behind quantitative thermal analysis of melting in several semicrystalline polymer systems.

The thermal analysis of melting is the primary method in this chapter; however, results obtained by other methods such as dilatometry, X-ray diffraction, AFM, optical microscopy, and neutron scattering are also included.

9.2 PARAMETERS OF THE MELTING PROCESS

The melting process of polymeric materials can be described by a number of parameters and quantities from using different techniques [1–5]. The basic macroscopic parameters measured by calorimetry are melting temperature (T_m), heat of fusion (ΔH_f), and apparent heat capacity (C_p^*). The parameters of dilatometry or X-ray diffractometry techniques are changes of volume (V), thermal expansivity (α), and compressibility (β). The characteristics of equilibrium melting polymers are rarely measured since practically all experimental parameters are measured for nonequilibrium, metastable, semicrystalline polymers. Consequently, the next step is to establish the equilibrium parameters and quantities from different approximations of the experimental data into equilibrium conditions. Thus, the equilibrium melting temperature (T_m^o), heat of fusion for 100% crystal [$\Delta H_f (100\%)$], equilibrium solid and liquid heat capacity, and all thermodynamic functions such as the enthalpy, entropy, and Gibbs free energy (free enthalpy) for equilibrium conditions serve to fully characterize the samples and are used in the analysis of melting polymers. Once the equilibrium characteristics are known, quantitative thermal analysis of the melting process of semicrystalline polymers can be performed in reference to these equilibrium quantities and parameters. All recommended results of equilibrium quantities and parameters, for polymers, are collected and organized as the Advanced Thermal Analysis System (ATHAS) Data Bank [3, 20].

Figure 9.2 shows an example of the changes of specific volume versus temperature during melting of PE by dilatometry [6]. Typically, a big step in volume is observed in over a small range of melting temperature T_m on heating for samples with different density. Also during the melting process, changes in thermal expansivity of PE can be observed, reflected in different slopes of volume versus temperature in solid and liquid states, respectively.

Figure 9.3 shows an example of the melting transition of a semicrystalline polymeric material such as PLA as was obtained by calorimetry from standard DSC. The plot in Figure 9.3 presents the heat flow rate versus temperature with the endothermic peak in the melting region.

In Figure 9.3 an evaluation of all characteristic temperatures of melting and heat of fusion for a semicrystalline polymer (PLA) is illustrated. First, T_b is the beginning of melting temperature, next observed is the extrapolated onset of melting temperature, T_m or T_f, then the peak melting temperature, T_p, and the end of melting temperature, T_e. The heat of fusion, ΔH_f is taken

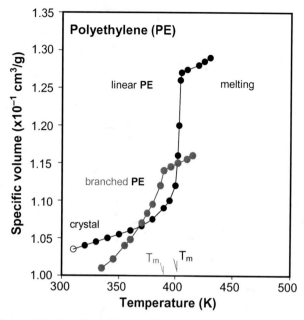

Figure 9.2 Specific volume of linear and branched polyethylene as a function of temperature at a constant pressure in the melting transition range (data from Mandelkern [6]).

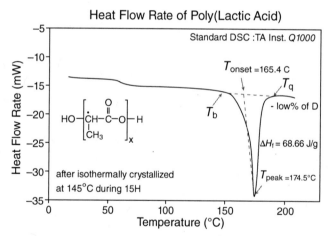

Figure 9.3 Characteristic temperatures of melting transition and heat of fusion from the evaluation of heat flow rate versus temperature for semicrystalline poly(lactic acid) (PLA).

as a peak area between the experimental curve and a straight baseline. The beginning of melting is chosen as a beginning of deviation of the heat flow rate curve from the straight line. This type of analysis is accurate if any changes in the pre-melting region do not appear. It should be noted here that before any analysis of melting results from calorimetry is started, a calibration of temperature, heat of fusion, and heat capacity should be performed with standard, known materials [3].

A quantitative thermal analysis of the melting of semicrystalline polymers should be studied in terms of apparent heat capacity, with their equilibrium solid and liquid heat capacities serving as reference baselines for analysis. Apparent heat capacity, C_p^*, changes during melting can be written as [3]:

$$C_p^* = \frac{dH}{dT} = \left(\frac{\partial H}{\partial T}\right)_{p,n} + \left(\frac{\partial H}{\partial n}\right)_{p,T} \frac{dn}{dT} \quad (9.1a)$$

where

$$C_p = \left(\frac{\partial H}{\partial T}\right)_{p,n} \quad (9.1b)$$

is the thermodynamic heat capacity at constant pressure p and composition n and

$$L = \left(\frac{\partial H}{\partial n}\right)_{p,T} dn \quad (9.1c)$$

is the latent heat (for melting, L is the heat of fusion, $L \equiv \Delta H_f$) at constant pressure p and T is temperature, H is enthalpy, and dT and dn are the changes in temperature and composition, respectively. For the melting process dn/dT equals the derivative of degree of crystallinity with respect to temperature as it is dw_c/dT (where $n \equiv w_c$).

Figure 9.4 presents an example of the quantitative thermal analysis of the melting transition of semicrystalline PLA based on apparent heat capacity, C_p^*. Experimental C_p^* is presented in the frame of two equilibrium baselines: (1) solid (vibrational), and (2) liquid heat capacity of PLA. Onset and peak temperatures were estimated using similar methods to those described for Figure 9.3. The major difference is in the estimation of the beginning of the melting process and heat of fusion. In the case presented in Figure 9.4, the melting process starts in T_{bo}, which is a result of the intersection of experimental heat capacity and semicrystalline baseline, $C_p^\#$(semicrystal). For the calculation of heat of fusion, ΔH_f, of the broad melting endotherm, the baseline heat capacity, $C_p^\#$(semicrystal), should be estimated and used. The corrected value of ΔH_f is the result of the integration of area between the experimental C_p^* and this $C_p^\#$(semicrystal). The heat of fusion of semicrystalline materials is only a fraction of the total heat of fusion of a full crystal polymeric material. In order to estimate the corrected value of crystalline fraction and its change during the broad melting process, the equilibrium parameters are needed. These include, for example, the heat of fusion for 100% crystalline polymeric sample and equilibrium melting temperature as well as equilibrium solid C_p(solid) and liquid C_p(liquid) heat capacity [3, 9, 17, 20].

More details and examples of the quantitative thermal analysis of melting process of several semicrystalline polymer systems such as PE, PTT, PBT, and PLA are presented in the next section. It should be mentioned here that analyses of melting semicrystalline polymers are not possible without taking into account the influence of other phases and mesophases, such as mobile and rigid amorphous phases, characterized by their glass transition temperatures (T_g, T_{RAF}) and ranges [19]. These analyses are governed by their degree of coupling of mobile and rigid amorphous phases to the crystals, and in oriented samples also by some intermediate ordering [3].

9.3 CHANGE OF CONFORMATION

During crystallization, polymer chains incorporated in crystals assume helical conformations [1–3] as described in Chapter 2.

The change in entropy is a key factor influencing melting temperature T_m. The change in Gibbs free energy ($\Delta G_f = \Delta H_f - T_m^\circ \Delta S_f$) on melting should be equal to zero, which leads to the following melting temperature [1, 3]:

$$T_m^\circ = \Delta H_f / \Delta S_f. \quad (9.2)$$

The melting process occurs with an increase in disorder, an increase in entropy ($\Delta S_f = \Delta H_f/T_m$) (7–17 JK^{-1} mol^{-1}), changes of volume (1–20%), and a sigmoidal change of heat capacity under the endothermic peak, which usually for flexible macromolecules depends on the degree of

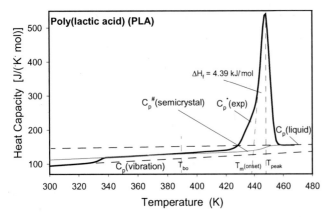

Figure 9.4 Characteristic temperatures of melting and heat of fusion from the evaluation of apparent heat capacity versus temperature for semicrystalline poly(lactic acid) (PLA).

mobile and rigid amorphous phases [3, 12, 17]. The process of melting can be divided into a few steps: the crystal lattice of macromolecules expands to separate segments (motifs) in the melt; the segments disorder, such that translational motion leads to changes of positional entropy, (ΔS_{pos}); rotational motion increases orientational entropy, (ΔS_{or}); and internal rotation motion increases conformational entropy (ΔS_{conf}), for the total entropy of fusion (ΔS_f) (where $\Delta S_f = n\Delta S_{conf} + \Delta S_{pos} + \Delta S_{or}$ and n is number of mobile units in the molecule). In contrast to small molecules, major contributions to the changes in disordering motion for the flexible macromolecule come from changes in conformation on melting; ΔS_{pos} and ΔS_{or} are negligible [1, 3]. The conformational disordering of flexible macromolecules during the melting process can be linked with the changes in the experimental apparent heat capacity. Conformational disordering in the crystal (condis crystal mesophase) is observed in the pre-melting area. It is reflected in changes in heat capacity as was presented in detail by Wunderlich [3]. In both the amorphous and crystalline phases, the microconformation can be described geometrically or energetically. The rotational isomeric states (RIS) model is a common model to discuss the conformational states of single chains of macromolecules [2, 3, 21]. In a general picture of thermal behavior of flexible macromolecules in the melting and liquid areas, for an estimation of apparent heat capacity one should take into account the heat of fusion and contributions to the heat capacity from large-amplitude motions such as conformational and anharmonic motion and normal vibration motion [3, 12, 21]. Heat capacity and heat of transition can be measured as total apparent heat capacity in the melting process by calorimetry [3, 12].

Figure 9.5 shows the experimental apparent heat capacity with all contributions of heat capacity and heat of transition in the melting region of semicrystalline PLA [22]. A major contribution to the thermodynamic heat capacity comes from the vibrational, solid heat capacity, C_p(vibration) (1), which was extended from the low-temperature to the high-temperature data of the melting region. This C_p(vibration) was estimated based on experimental C_p below the glass transition temperature T_g according to the well-established Advanced Thermal Analysis System (ATHAS) used for many polymeric materials [3, 20, 22]. According to the ATHAS approach, the only contribution to the experimental C_p below T_g temperature is from the vibrational motion of the polymer. This solid heat capacity is linked into group vibrational spectra based on experimental infrared and Raman frequencies (normal modes) and skeletal vibrations fitted to the general Tarasov function constructed by the combination of Debye functions [23, 24]. This calculated, solid heat capacity is extended into

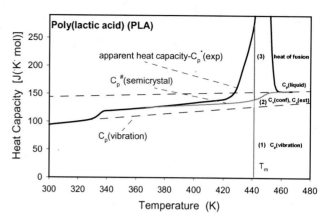

Figure 9.5 Deconvolution of apparent heat capacity of semicrystalline poly(lactic acid) in the melting region based on heat of fusion, conformation, anharmonic, and vibration contributions [22].

the melting region as a reference baseline. Any changes in the apparent heat capacity due to large-amplitude molecular motion (2) including conformational, C_v(conf), anharmonic motion C_p(ext), and latent heat (3) can be judged against this equilibrium baseline heat capacity, C_p(vibration) (1). The total thermodynamic heat capacity under the melting peak presents as semicrystalline heat capacity, $C_p^\#$(semicrystal), as a result of the sum of C_v(conf), C_p(ext), and C_v(vibration). In liquid state, above the melting peak, this sum of heat capacities gives the liquid heat capacity, C_p(liquid). The remaining portion to the total, apparent heat capacity in the melting process is from the latent heat, or endothermic heat of fusion (3). Quantitative thermal analysis allows one to separate all these contributions from the experimental data in the melting region for polymeric materials [2, 3, 22].

The conformational contribution C_v(conf) can be calculated based on the Ising-like model [2, 21] by making use of a previous suggestion by Strobl [2] and applying the derived equation for flexible macromolecules by Wunderlich and Pyda [21].

Figure 9.6 shows a comparison of the experimental and calculated heat capacity with all contributions (C_v(vib), C_v(conf), C_v(ext)) at the liquid-like state of amorphous PE above the glass transition, with good agreement of experimental and calculated C_p [21]. The experimental heat capacities data C_p(exp), in the temperature range from 250 to 600 K above the melting temperature 414 K, also agrees with the calculated C_p [21].

More details on applications of conformation changes to heat capacity for other polymers and polymer–water systems can be found in References [21, 25–27].

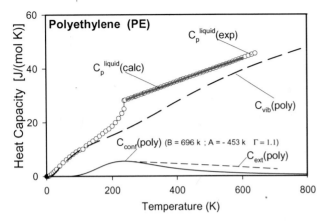

Figure 9.6 Evaluation of liquid heat capacity of polyethylene based on vibration, conformation, and anharmonic contributions [21].

9.4 HEAT OF FUSION AND DEGREE OF CRYSTALLINITY

9.4.1 Heat of Fusion

Heat of fusion is the latent heat, or energy change associated with the melting process from the solid to the liquid state. A typical thermogram of heat flow rate versus temperature for semicrystalline PLA, with the endothermic peak related to the melting of crystal, is presented in Figure 9.3. Heat of fusion of semicrystalline polymers can be estimated, as it was already mentioned, from "zero approximation" as a peak area between experimental data and a straight baseline. A more advanced approach to determine the heat of fusion is illustrated in Figure 9.7, with semicrystalline PTT [28] as an example of finding the apparent heat capacity using quantitative thermal analysis.

Estimation of the heat of fusion is complicated due to reorganization, annealing, and melting of small crystals in the pre-melting region of melting PTT as is presented in Figure 9.7. The calculation of heat of fusion, ΔH_f of broad melting of semicrystalline polymer such as in Figure 9.7, needs first to estimate the baseline $C_p^{\#}$(semicrystal) which separates latent heat from heat capacity. The corrected value of ΔH_f is the result of the integration of the area between the experimental, apparent heat capacity, C_p^*, [C_p(exp)], and this $C_p^{\#}$(semicrystal). Determination of heat of fusion of 100% crystalline polymer is needed in order to estimate the crystalline fraction of polymers and full quantitative analysis of melting.

The equilibrium heat of fusion ΔH_f (100%) can be estimated using a few methods: (a) from the dependence of the heat of fusion on crystallinity; (b) from the measurement of melting temperature in diluent mixture as a function of concentration; (c) by extrapolation from heat of fusion of low molar mass analogs; (d) from the X-ray diffraction method; (e) by infrared spectroscopy; or (f) using the Clausius–Clapeyron equation from measurements of changes of the melting temperature with pressure. All methods were thoroughly presented by Wunderlich and other authors [1, 3, 6, 29–31]. Now, we can look in more detail into the estimation of heat of fusion of 100% crystalline polymeric material from calorimetry by using method (a), using PLA as an example, which is presented in Figure 9.8.

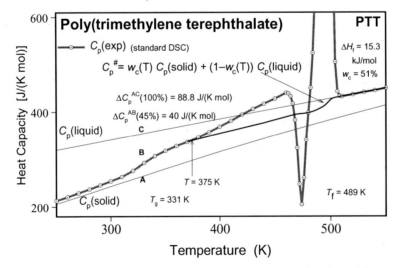

Figure 9.7 Advanced thermal analysis of melting process for estimation of heat of fusion from apparent heat capacity, C_p(exp) of semicrystalline poly(trimethylene teraphthalate) PTT [28]. (See color insert.)

The changes of heat capacity, ΔC_p, at the glass transition temperature, T_g, are plotted versus the measured heats of fusion, ΔH_f, for samples with different thermal histories, and thus with different degrees of crystallinity. The ΔH_f (100%) can be obtained from extrapolation, as is drawn by the solid line from 100% amorphous sample of ΔC_p to 100% crystalline sample of ΔH_f (100%). For PLA, the value of ΔH_f (100%) is equal to 6.554 kJ/mol (91 ± 3 J/g) at the equilibrium melting temperature of $T_m^o = 480$ K [22]. Early results for PE showed estimated heats of fusion ΔH_f for 100% crystalline PE of 4.11 kJ/mol at $T_m^o = 414$ K, as was presented by Wunderlich [1, 3]. Values of the heat of fusion ΔH_f for 100% crystalline PE, PLA, and some other polymeric materials are listed in Table 9.1 according to ATHAS Data Bank [3, 20].

Method (b) for the estimation of the equilibrium heat of fusion is based on melting point depression by a diluent and the Flory–Huggins equation [3, 30]:

$$\frac{1}{T_m} - \frac{1}{T_m^o} = \frac{R}{\Delta H_f} x'((1-\Phi_2) - \chi_c(1-\Phi_2)^2) \quad (9.3)$$

where T_m and T_m^o are the experimental and equilibrium melting temperature, respectively; ΔH_f is heat of fusion per mole of repeating unit; x' is the ratio of partial molar volumes of the polymer repeating unit to the diluent; Φ_2 is the volume fraction of polymer in the mixture; and χ_c is the Flory–Huggins interaction parameter and R is the gas constant

The heat of fusion for 100% crystal ΔH_f can be approximated from the slope of $(1/T_m - 1/T_m^o)/(1-\Phi_2)$ versus $(1-\Phi_2)$. This method was first used by Mandelkern and coworkers [29, 30] for PE, and the heat of fusion of 277–289 J/g was obtained for different diluents. Enthalpies of fusion for a number of different polymers determined through this method are listed in Reference

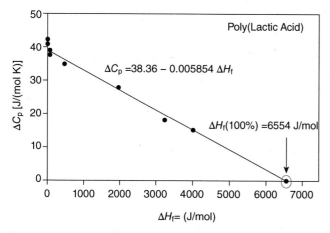

Figure 9.8 Plot of changes in heat capacity at glass transition temperature versus heat of fusion of semicrystalline poly(lactic acid) (PLA) with different thermal history (marked circle shows the estimated heat of fusion for 100% crystal) [22].

Table 9.1 Heat of Fusion, ΔH_f for 100% Crystal and Equilibrium Melting Temperature T_m^o of Some Polymeric Materials according to ATHAS Data Bank [3, 20]

Polymers	Heat of Fusion, ΔH_f for 100% Crystal (kJ/mol)	Equilibrium Melting Temperature T_m^o (K)
Polyethylene (PE) (-CH$_2$)-	4.11	414.6
Polypropylene (PP) (-CH$_2$-CHCH$_3$)-	8.70	460.7
Poly(4-methyl-1-pentene) (P4M1P) [-(CH$_2$)$_3$-CCH$_3$- CH$_3$-]	9.96	523.2
Poly(vinyl alcohol) (PVA) (-CH$_2$-CH(OH)-)	7.11	538.0
Poly(vinyl chloride) (PVCl) (-CH$_2$-CH(Cl)-)	11.0	546.0
Poly(vinyl fluoride) (PVF) (-CH$_2$-CH(F)-)	6.7	483.2
Isotactic-Polystyrene (iPS) (-CH$_2$-CH(C$_6$H$_5$)-)	6.7	483.2
Polyoxymethylene (POM) (-O-CH$_2$-)	9.79	457.2
Polyoxyethylene (POE) (-O-CH$_2$-CH$_2$-)	8.66	342.0
Poly(glycolic acid) (PGA) (-CH$_2$-C(O)O-)	9.74	501.0
Poly(e-caprolactone) (PCL) [(-CH$_2$)$_5$-C(O)O-]	17.9	342.2
Poly(lactic acid) (PLA) -[-CH(CH$_3$)C(O)O-]	5.65	480.0
Poly(hydro butyrate) (PHB) (-CH$_2$CH$_2$-COO-)	12.57	470
Nylon 6 [-CO (-CH$_2$)$_5$-NH-]	26.04	533
Nylon 12 [-CO(-CH$_2$)$_{11}$-NH-]	48.4	500
Nylon 6,6[-CO-(-CH$_2$)$_4$-CO-NH-(-CH$_2$)$_6$-NH-]	57.8	574
Poly(ethylene terephthalate) (PET) -[-C(O)-C$_6$H$_4$-C(O)O-(CH$_2$)$_2$-O-]-	26.9	553
Poly(trimthylene terephthalate) (PTT) -[-C(O)-C$_6$H$_4$-C(O)O-(CH$_2$)$_3$-O-]-	30.0	510
Poly(butylene terephthalate) (PBT) -[-C(O)-C$_6$H$_4$-C(O)O-(CH$_2$)$_4$-O-]-	32.0	518.2
Poly(tetrafluoroethylene) (PTFE) (-CF$_2$-CF$_2$-)	4.1	605

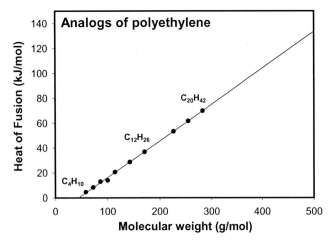

Figure 9.9 Change of heat of fusion with molecular weight for analogs of polyethylene [3, 20].

[5]. Additional discussion of the advantages and disadvantages of this method can be found elsewhere [1].

The method (c) for the estimation of the equilibrium heat of fusion ΔH_f (100%) is based on the determination of low molar mass analog heat of fusion. Figure 9.9 shows the linear increase in heat of fusion with molecular chain length. The typical behavior of analogs of PE [1, 20] is observed, such that bigger heat of fusion ΔH_f corresponds to larger molar mass M_n.

The estimation of the equilibrium heat of fusion ΔH_f (100%) from method (f) is based on using the Clausius–Clapeyron equation [31]:

$$\Delta H_f = \frac{T_m \Delta V_m}{\dfrac{dT_m}{dP}} \qquad (9.4)$$

where $\Delta V_m = V_l - V_c$, and V_l and V_c are the volumes of the liquid and the crystal at the melting point; T_m is the melting temperature in Kelvins; and P is the pressure. All of the quantities, except V_c, are derived from pressure–volume–temperature (*PVT*) relationships measured by dilatometry. The volume of the polymeric crystal can be determined by X-ray diffraction at elevated temperatures. Also the function of $T_m = f(P)$ should be known to calculate the slope dT_m/dP.

Table 9.2 presents an example of data and results of estimation of heat of fusion for polytetrafluoroethylene (PTFE) according to Reference [31].

9.4.2 Degree of Crystallinity

In order to complete the quantitative analysis of the heat of fusion, the crystallinity as a function of tempera-

Table 9.2 Data for the Clausius–Clapeyron Equation (Eq. 9.4) and Resulting Heat of Fusion for Polytetrafluoroethylene Adapted from Reference [31]

Parameters	Virgin Sample	Melted Sample
T_m (°C, $P = 0$)	346.3	328.5
dT_m/dP [°C/(kg/cm^2)]	0.095	0.095
V_l (cm^3/g)	0.6517	0.6349
V_c (cm^3/g)	0.492	0.4855
ΔV_m (cm^3/g)	0.1597	0.1494
ΔH_f (cal/g) or (J/g)	24.4 or 102.1	22.2 or 92.9

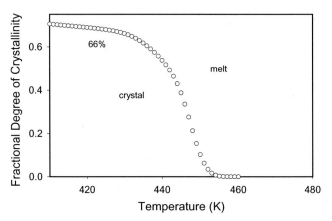

Figure 9.10 The degree of crystallinity $w_c = f(T)$ versus temperature for the semicrystalline PLA resulting from the solution of Equation (9.5) [22].

ture $w_c(T)$ should be determined. To calculate $w_c(T)$, the equation for a two-phase model was used [3, 17, 32]:

$$C_p^*(\exp) = w_c(T)C_p(solid) + (1 - w_c(T))C_p(liquid) \\ - \frac{dw_c}{dT}\Delta H_f(T) \qquad (9.5)$$

where $C_p^*(\exp)$ is the experimental, apparent heat capacity in the melting range; $C_p(solid)$ and $C_p(liquid)$ are the vibrational, solid, and liquid heat capacities, respectively; and $\Delta H_f(T) = H(melt) - H(crystal)$ is also temperature-dependent and is needed for the evaluation of the temperature dependence of the heat of fusion [$d\Delta H_f/dT = C_p(liquid) - C_p(solid)$]. In order to complete the calculation according to Equation (9.5) the enthalpy of fully crystalline $H(crystal)$ and amorphous $H(melt)$ polymers should be known as functions of temperature (see ATHAS Data Bank [20]). Examples of the results of $w_c(T)$ calculated based on Equation (9.5) for semicrystalline PLA [22] and PTT [28] samples are presented in Figure 9.10 and Figure 9.11, respectively.

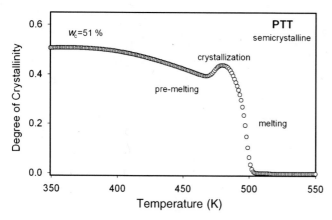

Figure 9.11 Change of degree of crystallinity $w_c = f(T)$ with temperature for the semicrystalline poly(trimethylene terephthalate) (PTT) [28].

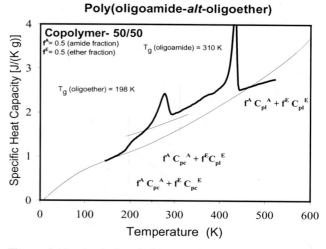

Figure 9.12 Analysis of the experimental apparent heat capacity of copolymer of poly(oligoamide-*alt*-oligoether) (PEBA) in melting areas [33].

The semicrystalline PLA reaches 66% crystallinity around 400 K, and PTT reaches 51% crystallinity around 375 K, then $w_c(T)$ decreases with increasing temperature, and finally drops to zero at the melting temperature. The degree of crystallinity calculated from the "zero approximation," where $w_c = \Delta H_f/\Delta H_f(100\%)$ and with data taken from Figure 9.3 using a straight baseline for calculation of ΔH_f, gives a value of 64%, while advanced approximation gives a 66% value of crystallinity for the examined PLA. Much more useful results can be obtained from the estimation of degree crystallinity resulting from advanced approximation as presented in Figure 9.7 for semicrystalline PTT, where changes in apparent heat capacity during melting are more complicated. In this case, the function, $w_c(T)$, was applied to the analysis of the melting process and the expected baseline semicrystalline heat capacity $C_p^{\#}$(semicrystal) was estimated according to the following expression [3, 17, 22]:

$$C_p^{\#}(\text{semicrystal}) = w_c(T)C_p(\text{solid}) + (1 - w_c(T))C_p(\text{liquid}) \quad (9.6)$$

which can separate the heat of fusion from the true thermodynamic heat capacity in the apparent heat capacity in the melting area (see Fig. 9.7 for PTT and Fig. 9.5 for PLA). Next, with an established $C_p^{\#}$(semicrystal) and baseline, a corrected heat of fusion value, ΔH_f, can be estimated by integration of the area between the experimental heat capacity and the $C_p^{\#}$(semicrystal). For semicrystalline PLA and PTT, the corrected values of heat of fusion are 4.4 kJ/mol and 15.3 kJ/mol, respectively, as is presented in Figure 9.5 and Figure 9.7, respectively. This corrected integration of the melting peak is possible due to the use of direct advanced approximation to obtain the degree of crystallinity resulting from the multistep scheme of the quantitative thermal analysis as used in the ATHAS approach to polymeric materials [3, 22, 28].

The melting transition of copolymers [1, 3] is much more complex due to their type of structure, lengths of segments, and molar masses. Figure 9.12 shows two melting peaks from crystallized ether (E) and amide (A) short sequences of block copolymer of poly[oligoimino(1-oxododecamethylene)-*alt*-oligooxytetramethylene], $\{[-CO(-CH_2)_{11}(-NH-CO(-CH_2)_{11}]_{m-1}-CO[-O(-CH_2)_n]_x$, PEBA, with their weight ratio of 50/50 immiscible components. The first endothermic peak at 278 K is related to the crystal of the ether component $[-O(-CH_2-)]_x$ and the second peak around 410 K is related to the crystal of the amide $[NH-CO(-CH_2)_{m-1}]_x$. In the analyzed copolymer, nanosize crystals are separated by amorphous phase, showing its glass transition temperatures (T_g). Advanced full analysis of PEBA [33] permits the estimation of the crystallinity of both components: 11% for the oligoether blocks and 17% for the oligoamide blocks. The dependence of crystallinity of a 50/50 block poly(oligoamide-*alt*-oligoethers), PEBA, on temperature is presented in Figure 9.13. For melting behavior analysis of such complex block copolymers, the all-equilibrium parameters and quantities of poly(oxytetramethylene) PO4M and nylon 12 were used from the ATHAS Data Bank [3, 20].

In addition to the useful calorimetric methods of determining crystallinity w_c for semicrystalline polymers, other techniques such as X-ray diffraction, dilatometry, and infrared spectroscopy are often applied as is cited in the literature [1–3, 32].

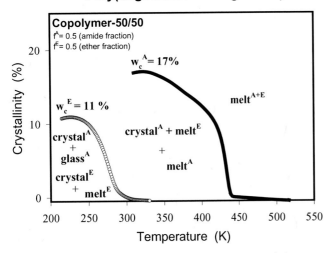

Figure 9.13 Change of degree of crystallnity $w_c = f(T)$ versus temperature of each component for copolymer of poly(oligoamide-*alt*-oligoether) [33].

As already mentioned, the full characterization of the melting process of polymeric materials requires the estimation of the crystalline fraction, which requires knowing not only the heat fusion for 100% crystalline polymer but also the equilibrium melting temperature and all the characteristics of the equilibrium melting.

9.5 EQUILIBRIUM MELTING

9.5.1 The Equilibrium Melting Temperature

For completely crystalline polymers with extended-chain crystals, the melting process on slow heating can occur under equilibrium and stable conditions. Parameters describing this equilibrium first-order melting transition of perfect crystal are the equilibrium melting temperature (T_m^o) and heat of fusion for 100% crystal, ΔH_f (100%). Both parameters are related together by Equation (9.2) ($T_m^o = \Delta H_f / \Delta S_f$). The melting process of macromolecules directly depends on crystal sizes, other parameters of folded chain lamellae structure or fibrillar morphology, and crystal defects. The melting temperature of semicrystalline polymers T_m is a function of lamellae thickness l, heat of fusion ΔH_f, density ρ, and fold surface free energy σ_e. Relations between all quantities can be written using the Gibbs–Thomson equation in the following form [34]:

$$T_m = T_m^o \left(1 - \frac{2\sigma_e}{\rho \Delta H_f l}\right) \quad (9.7)$$

With the help of measurements of the lamellar thickness, l, by dilatometry, AFM or X-ray, and the melting temperature T_m of the nonequilibrium crystal by DSC, it is possible to obtain the equilibrium melting temperature, T_m^o, by extrapolation to infinite lamellar thickness. Next, with Equation (9.7), it is also easy to calculate the fold surface free energy. Usually, the large surface area of the polymer crystal explains irreversibility of the melting process.

In generally accepted descriptions, the equilibrium melting temperature, T_m^o of crystalline polymers corresponds to the melting point of the crystal from which the surface effects can be omitted, and free enthalpy has a minimum at T_m^o. Basically, the above descriptions correspond to an extended-chain crystal with a length of more than 200 nm and approaching infinity. Special pretreatment of semicrystalline flexible macromolecules, such as annealing small size crystals nonisothermally by slow heating or isothermally at a temperature close to the melting temperature usually, does not lead to the equilibrium, extended-chain crystal. A number of extrapolation methods from nonequilibrium to equilibrium properties have been developed, and have been reviewed in the literature [3, 6]. The extrapolation methods are from data of low molar mass such as monomers and oligomers to polymers; from small size crystal to extended-chain crystal; or as a function of crystal perfection. Some of these methods have already been presented; here the extrapolation to obtain the equilibrium melting temperature (T_m^o) is discussed. Figure 9.14 and Figure 9.15 demonstrate two examples of the extrapolation of the T_m^o from measurements of the melting temperatures T_m of small size crystals and the extrapolation to infinite size for PE and PLA, respectively. In the first example, Figure 9.14 shows the estimation of the equilibrium melting temperature from the plot of T_m versus the reciprocal of lamellar thickness $(1/l)$ for semicrystalline PE [1, 3].

In the second example, Figure 9.15 shows a plot of the melting temperatures (T_m) of PLA resulting from different crystallization temperatures as a function of the reciprocal of the lamellar thickness [35]. It is assumed that the melting temperature changes linearly with crystallization temperature, which allows one to employ the Gibbs–Thomson equation to estimate the equilibrium melting temperature (T_m^o) for PLA. The T_m^o should correspond to a length of the extended-chain crystal for $1/l \rightarrow 0$ according to Equation (9.7). The T_m^o of PLA was calculated to be 480 K (207°C), which is close to the value suggested earlier in the literature [36]. Results presented in Figure 9.15 according to Equation (9.7) were already corrected for the presence of amorphous phase in the experimental measurements.

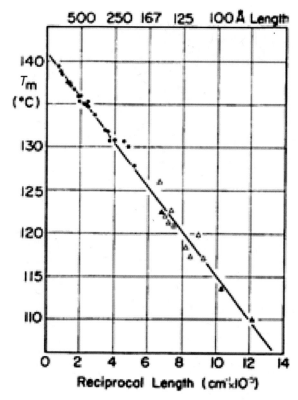

Figure 9.14 The melting temperature of semicrystalline polyethylene as a function of the reciprocal of lamellae thickness [1, 3].

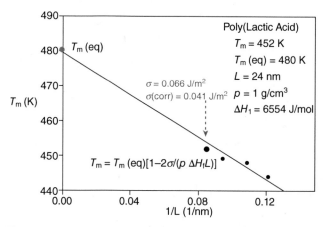

Figure 9.15 The melting temperature of semicrystalline poly(lactic acid) as a function of the reciprocal of lamellae thickness obtained by AFM [35].

The lamellar thicknesses (l) in the semicrystalline PLA was measured by AFM. The micrographs in Figure 9.16 (upper) illustrate an example of typical AFM deflection and height images of the PLA film with a flat stack of lamellae in these images. Figure 9.16 (lower) presents the choice of points of a typical evaluation analysis of one of the lamellar regions. The observed thickness of a layer consisting of the lamellar crystal and the amorphous phase was about 24 nm for the chosen line profile. Thus, the measured thickness must be reduced by the amorphous content. A similar correction can be accomplished by using the measured heat of fusion of the partially crystalline sample as was for the corrected lamellar thickness. In addition, an estimate of the free energy of the fold surface of PLA was obtained from the Gibbs–Thomson equation after correcting for the crystallinity (0.041 J/m²) [35]. Al-Hussein and Strobl [37] used temperature-dependent small-angle X-ray scattering (SAXS) to measure the crystals thickness and equilibrium melting temperature of isotactic polystyrene, and they obtained similar values to those using the Gibbs–Thomson approach.

Figure 9.17 shows the results of the extrapolation of the equilibrium melting temperature T_m^o based on the Hoffman–Weeks extrapolation [38], in which the melting temperature T_m is plotted for various crystallization temperatures T_c for semicrystalline PLA. Data for this method were collected only from calorimetric measurements, and the final result of the value of the T_m^o for PLA is close to 480 K, as obtained from different methods [22, 36]. It should be noted that the above corrected result of the T_m^o for PLA using the Hoffman–Weeks extrapolation was obtained from data for samples crystallized at small supercoolings, at high crystallization temperatures, similar to what was reported for many cases in the literature [3, 39, 40].

The Hoffman–Weeks method is one of the most common approaches in the literature [1, 3, 39, 40] for estimating the equilibrium melting temperature from the experimental data. This frequently used method was often critically assessed as by Hoffman and Miller in Reference [41] and modified as proposed by Phillips and coworkers [39] for iPP to avoid thickening of lamellae.

The equilibrium melting temperatures T_m^o for some other polymeric materials are presented in Table 9.1.

9.5.2 The Equilibrium Thermodynamic Functions

By finding the equilibrium heat capacities of the solid and liquid [C_p(vibration), C_p(liquid)], as well as the equilibrium transition parameters T_m^o, $\Delta H_f(100\%)$, all thermodynamic functions, enthalpy (H), entropy (S), and Gibbs free energy (G), can be calculated as a function of temperature for equilibrium conditions [3]. All recommended results of equilibrium quantities and parameters, for over 200 polymers, have been collected and organized as part of the ATHAS Data Bank, a part of which is available online [20].

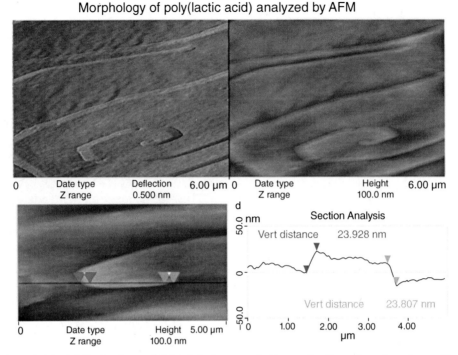

Figure 9.16 (a) Deflection and (b) height images of a flat stack of lamellae of semicrystalline poly(lactic acid) by AFM. (c, d) Details of determination of the lamellar thickness [35]. (See color insert.)

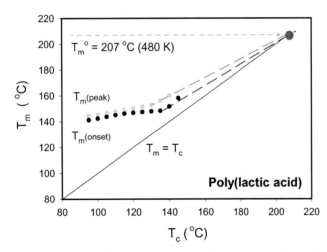

Figure 9.17 Melting temperatures T_m (onset and peak) versus crystallization temperature T_c for semicrystalline poly(lactic acid) (NatureWorks PLA 2002D) [35].

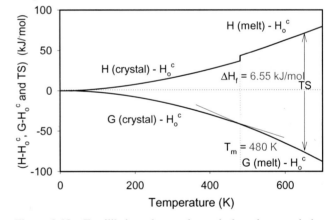

Figure 9.18 Equilibrium thermodynamic functions: enthalpy (H), entropy(S) and Gibbs function (G) versus temperature for poly(lactic acid) (PLA) [22].

Figure 9.18 shows all thermodynamic functions for equilibrium PLA (H_o^c is the reference enthalpy due to integration). The equilibrium melting temperature is taken to be 480 K. At this temperature the enthalpy of the crystal is increased by the heat of fusion of 6.554 kJ/mol to reach the equilibrium enthalpy of melt. The entropy of fusion at T = 480 K is 13.7 J (K/mol). The entropy is plotted in Figure 9.18 as its energy equivalent, TS, the difference between $H - H_o^c$ and $G - H_o^c$ [22].

Characterization and full analysis of the melting of semicrystalline polymers need to take into account the influence of properties of other phases, such as mobile amorphous and interface so-called rigid amorphous, on this nonequilibrium melting process. Modern scanning

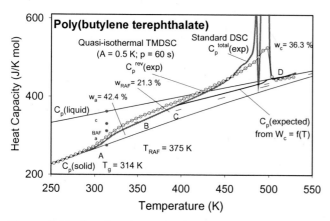

Figure 9.19 Results of quantitative thermal analysis of the experimental, total, and reversing heat capacity of semicrystalline PBT in the melting transition range [12].

calorimetry and advanced thermal analysis are useful for identifying and describing such a dependence. Figure 9.19 shows a full quantitative thermal analysis of melting transition of semicrystalline PBT with consideration of the influence of mobile and rigid amorphous phases on the melting behavior [12].

Figure 9.19 shows the next example of the analysis of the melting process of semicrystalline PBT from the standard DSC and the quasi-isothermal TMDSC [12]. Total and reversing C_p(exp) are analyzed using the two equilibrium baselines of vibrational C_p(solid) and C_p(liquid) in the range of temperatures from 250 K to 550 K with consideration of interface. Quantitative analysis of the broad double melting peak between C and D indicates that the melting starts at around 400 K and ends at around 500 K; a small peak occurs at around 480 K and a big peak around at 497 K. According to the two-phase model, crystallinity was estimated based on Equation (9.5). $W_c = f(T)$ gives the highest value of 36.3%. After establishing a baseline $C_p^\#$(semicrystal), [C_p(expected)] for integration, the corrected value ΔH_f was calculated as 11.6 kJ/mol from standard DSC measurement for semicrystalline PBT. Estimation of the changes in heat capacity (ΔC_p) between the levels of solid and liquid C_p at the glass transition temperature around 314 K gave the value of 42.4% of the mobile amorphous fraction, W_a, of PBT. The remaining fraction in the examined semicrystalline PBT should be related to the rigid amorphous phase (RAF), W_{RAF}, with the value of 21.3% with glass transition at a T_g of 375 K. Agreement of reversing and total heat capacity is observed from start of melting at 400 K until 460 K. The main melting is an irreversible process and only small contributions of reversing C_p are observed without an exothermic peak [12].

The above presented example and also that demonstrated in Figure 9.35 of quantitative thermal analysis of semicrystalline polymers show the significant influence of interfaces present between crystalline phases on the melting process.

9.6 OTHER FACTORS AFFECTING THE MELTING PROCESS OF POLYMER CRYSTALS

9.6.1 The Influence of the Polymer's Chemical Structure on the Melting Process

The polymer's chemical structure has a primary influence on the melting process and there is a direct connection between the melting and crystal structure as described by Ubbelohde [42]. Different chemical compositions of repeating segments of polymers influence their melting behavior. Depending on chemical composition macromolecules can be flexible or rigid. If a polymer chain contains more rigid segments, the melting temperature increases. For example, the melting temperature of PE with the flexible $[-CH_2]_x$ segments is 414.6 K whereas it is 553 K for PET with the segments $-[-C(O)-C_6H_4-C(O)O(CH_2)_2-O-]_{-x}$ being more stiff due to phenyl ring. Table 9.1 presents several examples of melting temperatures of polymers with different chemical structures. Increase in the melting temperature is related to the lowering of changes in entropy during melting of a crystal built of stiff molecules ($T_m = \Delta H_f / \Delta S_f$). The influence of the polymer's chemical structure on the melting process has an important and practical meaning in polymer technology.

9.6.2 The Effect of Polymer Molar Mass on the Melting Behavior

Similar to the chemical structure, the molar mass of macromolecules has a significant impact on the melting process. Generally, for any fully extended-chain crystal, the melting temperature, as well as the heat of fusion, increases with increase in molar mass [1, 3]. Figure 9.20 shows the changes in the melting temperatures of polyoxyethylenes (POE) as a function of molar mass for extended and folded crystals [1, 3].

The melting temperature as a function of molar mass for the most investigated polymer such as PE is presented in Figure 9.21 [1, 3]. The plot shows the equilibrium melting temperatures of PE according to the empirical equation placed inside Figure 9.21. The curves on Figure 9.20 and Figure 9.21 show little changes in melting temperatures for macromolecules with molar mass of around 10,000 g/mol (10 kDa) and higher, whereas for lower mass, the melting temperatures change faster. A similar behavior of linear increase in melting temperatures as shown in Figure 9.21 for PE can be observed for low molar mass analogs of polymers

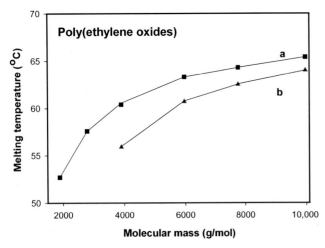

Figure 9.20 Molecular mass dependence of the melting temperatures of poly(ethylene oxides) for extended (a) and folded (b) crystal (based on data from References [1, 3]).

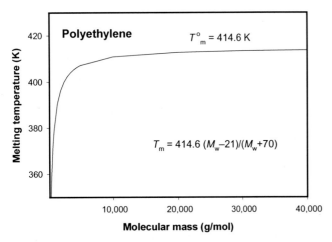

Figure 9.21 Molecular mass dependence of the melting temperatures of polyethylene (see Reference [1, 3]).

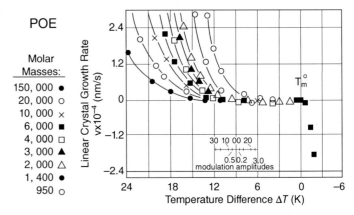

Figure 9.22 The melting and crystallization rates versus difference of temperature for polyoxyethylenes (POEs) with different molar masses [43].

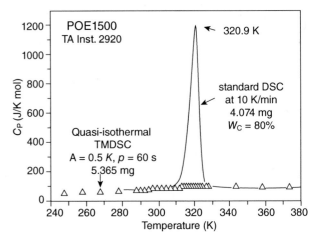

Figure 9.23 A comparison of the apparent heat capacity by standard DSC with the reversing heat capacity by quasi-isothermal temperature-modulated DSC in the melting region of extended-chain crystals of low molar mass (1500 Da) polyoxyethylene (POE) [43].

as is documented in the literature [1]. It can be concluded from the above examples, and can be found for many cases in the literature [1, 3], that the melting temperature for polymeric materials, defined as having a molar mass of more than 10 kDa, remains weakly dependent on molar mass.

As was presented in Figure 9.9, the heat of fusion displays linear dependence on molar mass. Studies of crystallization of polymers with broad distribution of molar mass from the melt indicate a need for a supercooling. Figure 9.22 illustrates the effect of temperature deviation from T_m^o on the crystal growth rate and on the melting rate for POEs of different molar masses [43]. The melting occurs close to equilibrium, whereas crystallization requires considerable supercooling, which is related to a need for nucleation.

Figure 9.23 and Figure 9.24 illustrate that POE with a low molar mass of 1.5 kDa does not show any contribution to reversing the heat capacity, in contrast to POE with a high molar mass of 900 kDa, for which a small but significant reversing component of heat capacity is observed during melting [43].

9.6.3 Influence of Heating Rate on the Melting

The melting process of small metastable, folded polymeric crystals is complicated due to reorganization, annealing, or recrystallization on heating before final melting. For polymers on heating, the crystal phase can be perfected and their lamellae can thicken. Consequently, the measured melting temperature increases with decreasing heating rate. Figure 9.25 illustrates

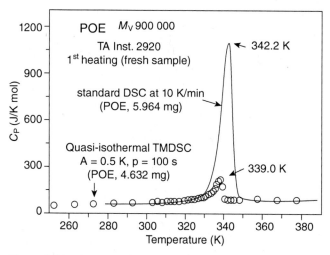

Figure 9.24 A comparison of the apparent heat capacity by standard DSC with the reversing heat capacity by quasi-isothermal temperature-modulated DSC in the melting region of high molar mass (900 kDa) polyoxyethylene (POE) [43].

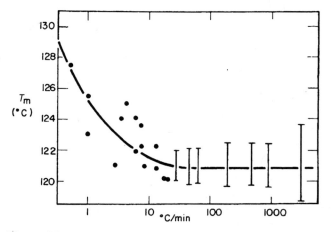

Figure 9.25 Melting temperature as a function of heating rate for semicrystalline polyethylene (PE) according to Wunderlich [1, 3].

changes in melting temperatures as a function of heating rate for semicrystalline PE according to Reference [1, 3]. The melting temperature was measured by interface microscopy. At a lower heating rate, the melting temperature reaches 129°C due to reorganization and thickening of lamellae PE but still remains below the equilibrium melting temperature of 141°C. Figure 9.26 shows pictures of the extended-chain crystal of PE before melting (b) and after melting (a), respectively [1].

Similar dependence of melting temperature on heating rate is demonstrated in Figure 9.27 for a nylon 6 sample with a mixture of dendritic and lamellar crystals 5–6 nm thick, following data presented by Wunderlich [1, 3]. Figure 9.27 shows a typical decrease in the melting peak temperature with increasing heating rate.

In the case of large extended-chain crystal of nylon 6, the measured melting temperature decreased with decreasing heating rate as is presented in Figure 9.28. Such effect is attributed to superheating, as well as to thermal lag during measurement. The melting temperature at zero heating rate was estimated as 225.6°C [1].

Other effects of heating rate on the melting process include multiple melting endotherms of homopolymers.

9.6.4 Multiple Melting Peaks of Polymers

Most polymer crystals are metastable folded chain crystals that can recrystallize and reorganize during heating prior to melting or after initial melting. The result of these effects is an irreversible melting process, which can show multiple melting endotherms of homopolymers by calorimetric measurement. Their origin can be related to different thickness of lamellae, different crystallographic forms, and reorganization phenomena during heating. Generally, irreversible thermodynamic melting can be observed on both examples presented in Figure 9.29 and Figure 9.30 due to time-dependent

Figure 9.26 Melting of extended chain spherulite crystal of PE (a) before melting (b) after melting for 10 hours at 138.3°C (from Wunderlich [1]).

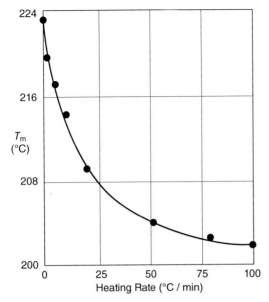

Figure 9.27 Melting temperature as a function of heating rate for semicrystalline nylon 6 according to Wunderlich [1].

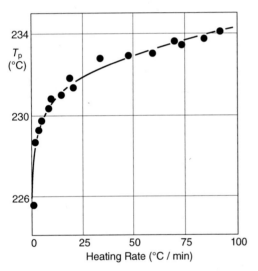

Figure 9.28 Melting temperature of extended chain crystal of nylon 6 as a function of heating rate according to Wunderlich [1].

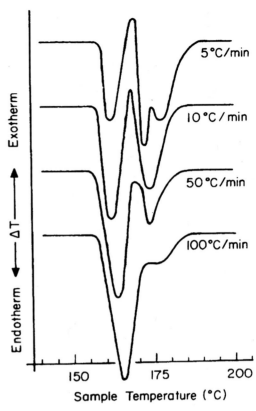

Figure 9.29 Multiple melting peaks of polyoxymethylene hedrites at different heating rates [1, 3].

behaviors of melting multipeaks. Figure 9.29 shows a typical example of the multipeak melting process for hedrites of polyoxymethylene [1, 3]. Three melting peaks are shown for a heating rate of 5°C/min. Between the first two endotherms, an exotherm related to recrystallization occurs after the initial melting. In Figure 9.29, only the first peak remains constant during heating with different rates; the others result from reorganization, perfection, or even recrystallization. As shown in Figure 9.29, the recrystallization can be avoided by heating faster than 100°C/min. According to References [1, 3] the first endotherm corresponds to the melting of lamellae 10–15 nm thick. The full discussion of irreversible thermodynamic melting was presented in Reference [1, 3].

Figure 9.30 shows multiple melting endotherms (curve **a**) recorded during heating (10 K/min) of semicrystalline poly(lactide acid), PLA, resulting from a complex annealing thermal history. Prior to heating, PLA was cooled from the melt to 130°C, isothermally crystallized at 130°C for 5 hours, cooled to room temperature, heated to 120°C, and annealed for 10 hours, heated to 145°C and again annealed for another 10 hours. For comparison curve **b** shows only one endothermic peak for PLA cooled from the melt to 130°C, crystallized isothermally for 5 hours, cooled to room temperature and than heated with the rate of 10 K/min. Higher melting peak temperatures correspond to thicker lamellar crystals of PLA.

Multipeak melting can help to discuss thermal behavior of the entangled and disentangled polymer chains. For example, Galeski and coworkers [44] have found that the extended-chain crystals melted differently, producing melt with lowered chain entanglements. The extended-chain crystals, crystallized under high pres-

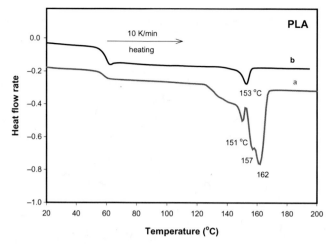

Figure 9.30 Multiple melting peaks of poly(lactide acid) recorded during heating (a) after isothermal crystallization at 130°C for 5 hours followed by annealing at 120°C and 145°C for 10 hours, (b) after isothermal crystallization at 130°C for 5 hours.

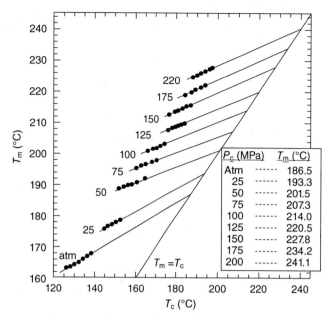

Figure 9.31 The Hoffman–Weeks plot for γ form iPP crystallized under different pressure [47].

sure, and also the chain-folded crystal of high density polyethylene (HDPE) were characterized using DSC, AFM, X-ray diffraction, and light microscopy. Rastogi and coworkers [45, 46] showed a difference in melting behavior between the entangled and disentangled ultra high molecular weight polyethylene (UHMW-PE). At low heating rates, below 1 K/min, the disentangled sample shows two melting endotherms and the entangled PE shows only one melting peak. Complication in the melting process occurs when the chain being detached from crystal surface is shared between different crystals. A higher temperature or longer time is needed if the chain has to overcome topological constraints. Further discussion is given elsewhere [44–46].

9.6.5 Influence of Pressure on the Melting Process

Another important factor of major practical interest is the influence of pressure on the melting of polymeric materials. This dependence has been widely described [3, 44, 47–49]. Generally, for many polymers, melting temperature increases with increasing pressure. Figure 9.31 shows an example of melting temperatures of γ form isotactic polypropylene (iPP) under high pressure from atmospheric to 200 MPa after isothermal crystallization at different crystallization temperatures in the range of 120–200°C [47]. From the Hoffman–Weeks plot of the melting temperature T_m against crystallization temperature T_c, the equilibrium melting temperature T_m^o under different pressure was obtained. The inset in Figure 9.31 shows the changes in T_m^o with pressure, whereas T_m^o is plotted versus pressure in Figure 9.32. It appears that the dependence of T_m^o on pressure is linear. It should also be noted that the high equilibrium melting temperature was obtained for iPP samples crystallized at small supercoolings, similar to other cases [1, 3, 40] where the Hoffman–Weeks method was used.

9.6.6 The Melting Process by Other Methods

The effects of annealing, recrystallization, reorganization, perfection, or crystal thickening by isothermal or nonisothermal treatments of polymeric materials on melting process have been studied by many methods in several laboratories [44, 50–52]. For example, the melting process of PE single crystals was studied by a neutron scattering technique by Barham and Sadler [50]. It was shown that melting of the chain-folded crystal to isotropic random coils takes a short time of around 1–2 seconds to rapidly increase the radius of gyration. The rate of this process remains independent of molar mass for polymeric material defined as having a molar mass of more than 10 kDa. The authors concluded that chain-folded crystals "explode" upon melting and the fold energy is released in an explosive springwise manner. Fragments and ends of chains incorporated in crystals are ejected with a high kinetic energy into the already molten polymer and interlace with other chains rapidly due to entropic force. In contrast, during the melting of highly extended-chain crystals it takes a much longer time to reach the random coil configuration as was shown for PE [50].

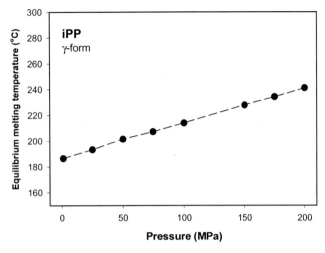

Figure 9.32 The equilibrium melting temperature T_m^o as a function of pressure for γ form iPP based on data in Figure 9.31 [47].

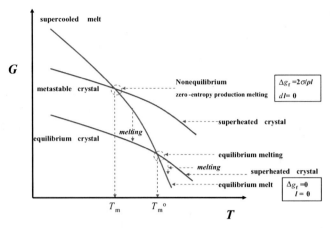

Figure 9.33 Schematic plots of the free enthalpy of equilibrium and metastable polymer phases [1, 53].

Beekmans and coworkers [51] have studied the isothermal melting of POE by AFM and found that lamellar crystals melt at a constant rate in agreement with earlier works by other authors [52]. The constant melting rate indicates that a nucleation-controlled process occurring at the melt front is the rate-controlling step. Essentially, no melting on the fold surfaces was observed. It was proved that the broad melting peak of POE as observed by DSC is related to the distribution of thickness of lamellar crystals formed during the isothermal crystallization.

Estimation of the equilibrium melting point of iPP was conducted in Reference [39] by plotting the melting temperature versus reciprocal lamellar thickness measured by SAXS. The plot was extrapolated to infinite lamellar thickness to obtain the equilibrium melting temperature of 186.1°C, as for PLA in Figure 9.16, although in the latter case the crystal thickness was measured by AFM.

9.6.7 Diluents Effect: The Influence of Small Diluents on the Melting Process

In general, a good solvent introduced to a polymeric system plasticizes the material and on heating the melting of such system occurs at lower melting temperatures than for pure polymer as described by Equation (9.3). A physical reason for the depression of the melting point is the increase in entropy due to the presence of solvent. The depression of melting temperature with respect to that of pure polymer is also observed in miscible blends and in copolymers as is described in Chapter 10 and Chapter 11.

9.7 IRREVERSIBLE AND REVERSIBLE MELTING

Recently, the melting process of semicrystalline polymers was considered as fully irreversible due to small crystal size, entanglements, or crystal defects [1–6]. Discussion of irreversible and reversible thermodynamic melting of polymers can be started from the analysis of the free enthalpy in the melting region as is schematically shown in Figure 9.33.

The equilibrium melting, T_m^o, is marked by the intersection of the free enthalpy plot for equilibrium crystal with that of the lowest free enthalpy melt [1, 3]. The nonequilibrium melting, T_m, corresponds to the intersection of the free enthalpy plot for any metastable crystal with that for supercooled melt, as is presented in Figure 9.33. The metastability originates from a change in the internal free enthalpy $\Delta_i G$ during melting of chain-folded crystal with large surface free energy. The change in the internal free enthalpy consists of changes of the free enthalpy of bulk crystal ($-\Delta g_f \, dm_c$) and the free energy of fold surface ($+2\sigma_e \, dm_c/\rho l$) as well as the annealing or reorganization component ($-2m_c \sigma_e \, dl/\rho l^2$), where m_c is the crystal mass. The process is permitted if [3, 53]:

$$\Delta_i G = -\Delta g_f dm_c + 2\sigma_e dm_c/\rho l - 2m_c\sigma_e dl/\rho l^2 \leq 0. \quad (9.8)$$

Equilibrium is reached for large crystals ($l \to \infty$). The equilibrium melting is characterized by $\Delta_i G = 0$. In the case of metastable crystals, zero entropy production melting occurs when they go to a melt of the same free enthalpy and degree of metastability ($\Delta g_f = 2\sigma_e/\rho l$). Additional information can be obtained from $\Delta g_f = \Delta h_f - T \Delta s_f$, with Δg_f equal to $\Delta h_f \Delta T/T_m^o$, where

$\Delta T = T_m^o - T$ is the deviation from the equilibrium melting temperature. Melting of thin lamellae without reorganization ($dl = 0$) is governed by two terms of the right side of Equation (9.8) written in the form $[\Delta h_f \Delta T / T_m^o - 2\sigma_e/(\rho l)]dm_c$. The melting can occur at a temperature lower than the equilibrium melting temperature. The decrease in melting temperature $\Delta T = 2\sigma_e T_m^o/(\Delta h_f \rho l)$ is related to the surface free energy σ_e and the lamellar thickness l, and causes irreversibility of the melting process. The last expression for ΔT is a different form of the Gibbs–Thomson equation (Eq. 9.7). In the case of melting nanocrystal, where ($l \to 0$), the second term of the right side of Equation (9.8) becomes bigger than the first one, and changes in the free enthalpy of the fold surface dominate over changes in the free enthalpy of bulk crystals in high irreversible melting. Total free enthalpy for a smaller crystal becomes larger and irreversible thermodynamics should be involved for the description of melting nanocrystals.

By introducing TMDSC [10–12, 16] it was possible to examine directly the kinetics and thermodynamics of the reversibility and irreversibility of the latent heat of melting [12–18]. In contrast to small molecules, well-crystallized macromolecules melt irreversibly. The irreversible melting process of low molar mass POE [43] is illustrated in Figure 9.21. Results show lack of reversing heat capacity during melting of a well-crystallized polymeric material. In contrast, a fraction of semicrystalline POE of high molar mass [43] melts reversibly (see Fig. 9.23).

The reversible melting was discovered surprisingly in poly(ethylene terephthalate) (PET) [54] a few years ago, and subsequently this has also been documented for many other semicrystalline polymers [3, 12–19]. Reversible melting basically means that it occurs without changes in all measured parameters in time, in contrast to reversing melting where these parameters change due to the influence of modulation frequency and temperature amplitude on the melting/recrystallization local process. Reversible melting occurs below the equilibrium melting temperature and at a local equilibrium within the globally metastable structure.

It should be remembered here that standard DSC measures the total apparent heat capacity in the melting region, and the quasi-isothermal method of TMDSC measures only the apparent reversing heat capacity. Figure 9.34a shows a comparison of the reversing apparent heat capacity with total apparent heat capacity for semicrystalline PLA. Differences between both heat capacities describe irreversible contributions. Examination of the semicrystalline PLA by quasi-isothermal TMDSC and quantitative thermal analysis allows the separation of any reversible and irreversible processes in the regions between the glass and melting transitions

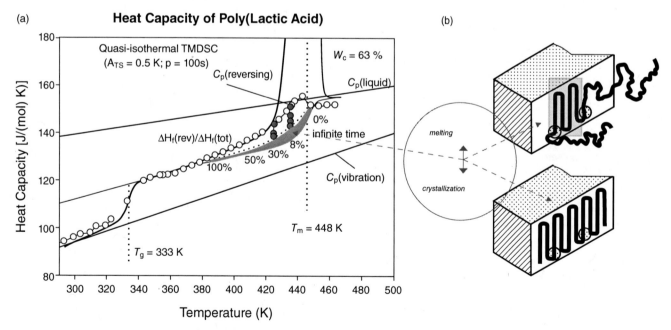

Figure 9.34 (a) The comparison of the reversing heat capacities of poly(lactic acid) (PLA) resulting from different the time domains in the melting region by quasi-isothermal method of temperature-modulated DSC in the frame of vibrational and liquid C_p [55]. (b) Schematic drawing of the mechanism of reversible melting/cystallization of folded chain crystals [53]. (See color insert.)

[55]. Reorganization in the pre-melting region, as well as the major melting, was found to be fully irreversible. Similar to PET [54], only a small contribution from the reversing heat capacity of PLA can be observed within the melting peak [55]. The truly apparent reversible heat capacity was obtained by the infinite time-domain approximation as is shown by shaded area in Figure 9.34a. The reversible melting can be explained based on a decoupling of parts of the molecules from the remaining portion, which must be larger than a molecular nucleus to support recrystallization, as was proposed by Wunderlich [53]. Such a mechanism is presented in Figure 9.34b graphically. The more detailed description of the mechanism of reversible melting is presented in a recently published review [56].

Superheating is a basic phenomenon that needs to be described using irreversible thermodynamics and can be examined by standard and temperature-modulated calorimetry. Superheating of crystals occurs if the heat conduction into or out of a sample is faster than the phase transition.

Figure 9.35 shows a comparison of the apparent heat capacity from standard DSC and reversing C_p by quasi-isothermal TMDSC of poly(oxy-2,6-dimethyl-1,4-phenylene) (PPO) [57]. The semicrystalline PPO with initial 30% crystallinity can serve as an example of superheating of crystal that was enclosed by interface with the glassy, RAF. A reduction of crystallinity during annealing in the melting area was much slower than the decrease in the RAF. Only after mobilization of the RAF phase can the crystal of PPO melt, and for this reason the crystal is superheating around 20 K higher than during heating in a standard DSC.

Fast scanning calorimetry (FSC) is the future method that allows avoiding any crystallization or reorganization of polymeric material between glass and melting transitions, although it does not permit elimination of superheating of crystals. FSC is based on the thermal conductivity in chip calorimetry and can perform cooling and heating of microgram or nanogram film samples with rates of 10–40 kK/s. This allows us to obtain full amorphous compositions for such polymers as iPP, PBT, and others [12, 58]. An application example of the so-called the superfast chip calorimetry (SFCC) has been described earlier and employed in investigating the heat capacity of super-quenched and superheated polymers [58].

9.8 CONCLUSIONS

Experimental and theoretical understanding of the relations between molecular chemical structure and thermal and mechanical properties of semicrystalline polymers is one of the challenges that further work should address. The melting process of polymers is one of the nonequilibrium processes that link experimental data with description on the molecular level. Access to a number of scientific tools provides an excellent opportunity to make significant progress in this important area. Melting behaviors of polymers are usually studied by calorimetry, diffraction, scattering, spectroscopy, and microscopy. Modern calorimetry with advanced thermal analysis can also give some progress in the understanding of the molecular mechanism of melting and crystallization of macromolecules.

In this chapter the analysis of melting of polymers was presented as not only the process of structure changes between the solid and liquid but also as the changes in molecular motions. Modern calorimetry and the quantitative thermal analysis based on heat capacity and interpretation on a molecular motion allows the study of the melting processes in metastable polymers. Thermal analyses of melting are often complicated by irreversible effects, such as broad melting transition, partial crystallinity, reorganization, and reordering and coupling with other phases and mesophases such as mobile amorphous or rigid amorphous. All these nonequilibrium processes and states around and at the melting area need the equilibrium thermodynamic references such as in the case of heat capacity: the solid, vibrational heat capacity, and the liquid heat capacity. Temperature-modulated, standard, and adiabatic calorimetry, together with advanced thermal analysis, permit the separation of reversible from irreversible processes in melting of polymers that contribute to apparent experimental heat capacities of polymeric systems. Development of advanced analysis of the melting process of polymeric materials performed by calorim-

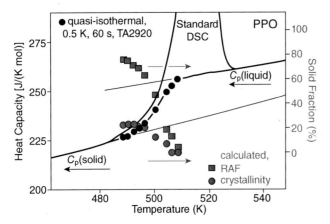

Figure 9.35 Comparison of the reversing (by TMDSC) and apparent heat capacity (by DSC) of semicrystalline poly(oxy-2,6-dimethyl-1,4-phenylene) (PPO) [57].

etry, particularly by FSC, microscopy, especially AFM, diffractometry, spectroscopy, and other techniques can bring a significant progress to our scientific understanding and to practical applications.

REFERENCES

[1] Wunderlich, B. *Macromolecular Physics*, Vol. 1, 2, 3. Academic Press, New York and London, 1973, 1976, 1980.

[2] Strobl, G. *The Physics of Polymers, Concepts for Understanding Their Structures and Behavior*. Springer-Verlag, Berlin, 2007.

[3] Wunderlich, B. *Thermal Analysis of Polymeric Materials*. Springer-Verlag, Berlin, 2005.

[4] Turi, E., ed. *Thermal Characterization of Polymeric Materials*. Academic Press, New York, 1997.

[5] Mandelkern, L., Alamo, R.G. Thermodynamic quantities governing melting. In *Physical Properties of Polymers, Handbook*, Mark, J.E., ed. Springer-Verlag, Berlin, 2007.

[6] Mandelkern, L. *Crystallization of Polymers*. McGraw-Hill, New York, 1964.

[7] Cheng, S.Z.D., ed. *Handbook of Thermal Analysis and Calorimetry*, Vol. 3, *Applications to Polymers and Plastics*. Elsevier Science, Amsterdam, 2002.

[8] Li, C.Y., Cheng, S.Z.D. Semicrystalline polymers. In *Encyclopedia of Polymer Science and Technology*, Kroschwitz, J.I., ed. John Wiley & Sons, New York, 2002.

[9] Wunderlich, B., Pyda, M. Thermodynamic properties of polymers. In *Encyclopedia of Polymer Science and Technology*, 3rd ed., Kroschwitz, J.I., ed. John Wiley & Sons, New York, 2004.

[10] Reading, M. *Trends Polym. Sci.* **1993**, *8*, 248–253.

[11] Boller, A., Wunderlich, B. *J. Therm. Anal.* **1994**, *42*, 307–329.

[12] Pyda, M., Nowak-Pyda, E., Heeg, J., Huth, H., Minakov, A.A., Di Lorenzo, M.L., Schick, C., Wunderlich, B. *J. Polym. Sci. B Polym. Phys.* **2006**, *44*, 1364–1377.

[13] Androsch, R. *Polymer* **2008**, *49*, 4673–4679.

[14] Androsch, R., Wunderlich, B. *J. Polym. Sci. B Polym. Phys.* **2003**, *41*, 2039–2051.

[15] Schick, C., Wurm, A., Mohamed, A. *Colloid Polym. Sci.* **2001**, *297*, 800–806.

[16] Schick, C. Temperature modulated differential calorimetry (TMDSC) and applications to polymers. In *Handbook of Thermal Analysis and Calorimetry*, Vol. 3, *Applications to Polymers and Plastics*, Cheng, S.Z.D., ed. Elsevier Science, Amsterdam, 2002.

[17] Pyda, M., Di Lorenzo, M.L., Pak, J., Kamasa, P., Buzin, A., Grebowicz, J., Wunderlich, B. *J. Polym. Sci. B Polym. Phys.* **2001**, *39*, 1565–1577.

[18] Chen, H., Cebe, P. *Macromolecules* **2009**, *42*, 288–297.

[19] Wunderlich, B. *Prog. Polym. Sci.* **2003**, *28*, 383–450.

[20] Pyda, M., ed. *ATHAS Data Bank*, 2008, http://athas.prz.rzeszow.pl/Default.aspx?op=db.

[21] Pyda, M., Wunderlich, B. *Macromolecules* **1999**, *32*, 2044–2050.

[22] Pyda, M., Bopp, R.C., Wunderlich, B. *J. Chem. Thermodyn.* **2004**, *36*, 731–742.

[23] Debye, P. *Ann. Phys.* **1912**, *344*, 789–839.

[24] Pyda, M., Bartkowiak, M., Wunderlich, B. *J. Therm. Anal.* **1998**, *52*, 631–656.

[25] Pyda, M. *J. Polym. Sci. B Polym. Phys.* **2001**, *39*, 3038–3054.

[26] Pyda, M. *Macromolecules* **2002**, *35*, 4009–4016.

[27] Pyda, M. Quantitative thermal analysis of carbohydrate water systems. In *The Nature of Biological Systems as Revealed by Thermal Methods*, Lorinczy, D., ed. Kluver Academic Publisher, Amsterdam, 2004, pp. 307–333.

[28] Pyda, M., Boller, A., Grebowicz, J., Chuah, H., Lebedev, B.V., Wunderlich, B. *J. Polym. Sci. B Polym. Phys.* **1998**, *36*, 2499–2511.

[29] Quinn, F.A., Jr., Mandelkern, L. *J. Am. Chem. Soc.* **1958**, *80*, 3178–3182.

[30] Flory, P.J. *Principles of Polymer Chemistry*. Cornell Press, Ithaca, 1953.

[31] Starkweather, H.W., Jr., Zoller, P., Jr, Glover, A.J., Vega, A.J. *J. Polym. Sci. B Polym. Phys.* **1982**, *20*, 751–761.

[32] Mathot, V.B.F., ed. *Calorimetry and Thermal Analysis of Polymers*. Hanser Publishers, München, 1994.

[33] Di Lorenzo, M.L., Pyda, M., Wunderlich, B. *J. Polym. Sci. B Polym. Phys.* **2001**, *39*, 1594–1604.

[34] Gibbs, J.W. *The Scientific Work of J.W. Gibbs*. New York, 1906. Thomson, J.J. *Applications of Dynamics*. London, 1888.

[35] Pyda, M., Nowak-Pyda, E., Wunderlich, B. Thermal Analysis and Morphology of Films of Poly(lactic acid) by Calorimetry and AFM. In *Proc. 32nd NATAS Conf.* Williamsburg, VA, Oct. 4–6, Rich, M. J., Ed., CD edition, 32, 2004, p. 10.

[36] Fischer, E.W., Sterzel, H.J., Wegner, G. *Kolloid Z.Z. Polym.* **1973**, *251*, 980–990.

[37] Al-Hussein, M., Strobl, G. *Macromolecules* **2002**, *35*, 1672–1676.

[38] Hoffman, J.D., Weeks, J.J. *J. Res. Natl. Bur. Stand.* **1962**, *66A*, 13–28.

[39] Mezghani, K., Campbell, R.A., Phillips, P.J. *Macromolecules* **1994**, *27*, 997–1002.

[40] Di Lorenzo, M.L. *J. Appl. Polym. Sci.* **2006**, *100*, 3145–3151.

[41] Hoffman, J.D., Miller, R.L. *Polymer* **1997**, *38*, 3151–3212.

[42] Ubbelohde, A.R. Melting and crystal structure. In *Phase Transition, Proc. Chem. Conf, Solvay, 14th, Inst. Univ. Brussels, May 1969*. Wiley, New York, 1971.

[43] Qiu, W., Pyda, M., Nowak-Pyda, E., Habenschuss, A., Wunderlich, B. *J. Polym. Sci. B Polym. Phys.* **2007**, *45*, 475–489.

[44] Psarski, M., Piorkowska, E., Galeski, A. *Macromolecules* **2000**, *33*, 916–932.

[45] Lippits, D.R., Rastogi, S., Hoehne, G.W.H. *Phys. Rev. Lett.* **2006**, *96*, 218303–218307.

[46] Lippits, D.R., Rastogi, S., Talebi, S., Bailly, C. *Macromolecules* **2006**, *39*, 8882–8885.

[47] Mezghani, K., Phillips, P.J. *Polymer* **1998**, *39*, 3735–3744.

[48] Masirek, R., Piorkowska, E., Galeski, A., Hiltner, A., Bear, E. *Macromolecules* **2008**, *41*, 8086–8094.

[49] Kazmierczak, T., Galeski, A. *J. Appl. Polym. Sci.* **2002**, *86*, 1337–1380.

[50] Barham, P.J., Sadler, D.M. *Polymer* **1991**, *32*, 393–395.

[51] Beekmans, L.G.M., van der Meer, D.W., Vancso, G.J. *Polymer* **2002**, *43*, 1887–1895.

[52] Kovacs, A.J., Gonthi, A., Straupe, C.J. *J. Polym. Sci. C Polym. Symp.* **1975**, *50*, 283–325.

[53] Wunderlich, B. *Macromol. Rapid Commun.* **2005**, *26*, 1521–1531.

[54] Okazaki, I., Wunderlich, B. *Macromolecules* **1997**, *30*, 1758–1764.

[55] Pyda, M. Relaxation processes of the amorphous and semicrystalline biodegradable poly(lactic acid) by temperature modulated calorimetry. ACS Spring Meeting, San Diego, CA, March 13–17. *Proc. Polym. Mat. Sci. Eng.*, **2005**, *92*, 570–571.

[56] Wunderlich, B. *J. Therm. Anal.* **2007**, *89*, 321–356.

[57] Pak, J., Pyda, M., Wunderlich, B. *Macromolecules* **2003**, *36*, 495–499.

[58] Minakov, A.A., Moroivintsev, D.A., Schick, C. *Polymer* **2004**, *45*, 3755–3763.

10

CRYSTALLIZATION OF POLYMER BLENDS

Mariano Pracella

Institute of Composite and Biomedical Materials, CNR, National Research Council, Pisa, Italy
Department of Chemical Engineering and Materials Science, University of Pisa, Pisa, Italy

10.1 General Introduction, 287
10.2 Thermodynamics of Polymer Blends, 288
    10.2.1 General Principles, 288
10.3 Miscible Polymer Blends, 290
    10.3.1 Introduction, 290
    10.3.2 Phase Morphology, 291
    10.3.3 Crystal Growth Rate, 292
    10.3.4 Overall Crystallization Kinetics, 294
    10.3.5 Melting Behavior, 295
    10.3.6 Blends with Partial Miscibility, 296
    10.3.7 Crystallization Behavior of Amorphous/Crystalline Blends, 297
    10.3.8 Crystallization Behavior of Crystalline/Crystalline Blends, 298
10.4 Immiscible Polymer Blends, 303
    10.4.1 Introduction, 303
    10.4.2 Morphology and Crystal Nucleation, 303
    10.4.3 Crystal Growth Rate, 304
    10.4.4 Crystallization Behavior of Immiscible Blends, 305

10.5 Compatibilized Polymer Blends, 307
    10.5.1 Compatibilization Methods, 307
    10.5.2 Morphology and Phase Interactions, 308
    10.5.3 Crystallization Behavior of Compatibilized Blends, 311
10.6 Polymer Blends with Liquid-Crystalline Components, 314
    10.6.1 Introduction, 314
    10.6.2 Mesomorphism and Phase Transition Behavior of Liquid Crystals and Liquid Crystal Polymers, 314
    10.6.3 Crystallization Behavior of Polymer/LC Blends, 316
    10.6.4 Crystallization Behavior of Polymer/LCP Blends, 317
10.7 Concluding Remarks, 320
Abbreviations, 321
References, 322

10.1 GENERAL INTRODUCTION

Polymer blends represent one of the most important research topics in the field of macromolecular science. Since the last decades of the 20th century, increasing attention has been given to the study of the structure, properties, and processing of polymer blends from academic, industrial, and governmental institutions. Several thousand of scientific publications and patents are published annually in this field. The main reason for the growing development of polymer blends is their wide application potential in a variety of industrial sectors (packaging, electronics, automotive, aerospace, building, household appliances, biomedical, etc.). As compared to the complex and costly synthesis of new polymers, polymer blending constitutes a very versatile and economically convenient route for producing materials with tailored properties. By varying the composition and blending conditions, as well as by introducing chemical modifications or functional groups along the chains

Handbook of Polymer Crystallization, First Edition. Edited by Ewa Piorkowska and Gregory C. Rutledge.
© 2013 John Wiley & Sons, Inc. Published 2013 by John Wiley & Sons, Inc.

and controlling the phase morphology, it is possible to design materials for specific performances, with optimized rheological, mechanical, and thermal behavior. It has been estimated that polymer blends constitute more than 20% of the total consumption of engineering polymers, and the world market for these materials is expected to increase to over 50 million tons per year.

Blends of macromolecular compounds, such as natural rubber and gutta-percha (cis- and trans-polyisoprene), started to be developed from the first half of the 19th century (first patented blend: 1847) by varying composition and by addition of other components for preparation of various materials. Later on, many synthetic polymers were used in mixtures with high and low molecular weight compounds (plasticizers) in order to improve their properties and applications [1]. Blends of poly(vinyl chloride) (PVC) and butadiene–acrylonitrile copolymers (NBR) have been commercialized since the 1940s. In the same years blends of polystyrene (PS) and polybutadiene (PBD), with the trade name of Styralloy, and mixtures of NBR with styrene–acrylonitrile copolymers (SAN), known as ABS, were introduced, starting a long sequence of products, which together with new families of copolymers (olefin copolymers, block copolymers, polyurethanes, etc.) marked the development of plastic materials.

So far, an extended literature has been published on polymer blends, which includes several reviews and handbooks covering both theoretical and practical aspects [1–6]. A fundamental scientific aspect of polymer blending is that of *miscibility* of the polymer components. Miscibility is the key factor that determines the phase behavior, the superstructure, and thus the properties of the blends. In miscible blends the polymer components give rise to a single phase system, which can combine the properties of plain components displaying characteristics often unique, concerning the morphology, crystallization behavior, thermodynamic, and rheological aspects. However, most polymer blends include immiscible, or at least partially miscible, components, leading to multiphase systems whose properties are generally inferior as compared to those of the single components owing to the lack of interactions between the polymers, low interfacial adhesion, and complex morphological features. The property of these systems can be advantageously improved by suitable chemical and physical *compatibilization* methods, which contribute to reducing the interfacial tension in the molten state and to enhancing the phase dispersion and adhesion at the interface. Addition of block and graft copolymers, as well as introduction of functional reactive groups along the polymer chains and reactive mixing processes, is exploited to obtain controlled and stable morphological characteristics and higher physical or mechanical performance.

A large part of blends is based on crystallizable polymers; therefore, the study of the crystallization processes, crystalline morphologies, and other phase transitions is of great significance for the understanding and the control of the structure–property relationships of these systems. The crystallization behavior and the superstructure of the blend components may be significantly affected by the miscibility phenomena, composition, mixing conditions, as well as interfacial characteristics of the phases in immiscible or compatibilized systems, with consequent effects on the mechanical, thermal, optical, and barrier properties. In this chapter, the basic aspects of crystallization of polymer blends and related topics are presented.

The chapter is divided into five sections. Section 10.2 deals with the thermodynamics of polymer blends: the general principles and the main theories on the phase behavior of polymer mixtures are briefly presented. Section 10.3 deals with the properties of miscible blends with crystallizable components. The phase morphology, crystal growth rate, overall crystallization kinetics, and melting behavior of miscible blends are analyzed. The crystallization phenomena in blends with miscibility gap are also described. Then, examples of miscible systems comprising one or two crystallizable components are reported with particular attention to the thermodynamic and kinetic aspects of the crystallization process.

In Section 10.4 the properties of immiscible blends, and in particular the types of morphology, the nucleation processes, and crystal growth are described. The crystallization behavior of some immiscible systems (with one or two crystallizable components) is reviewed. Section 10.5 deals with compatibilized blends. The main compatibilization methods, including addition of copolymers and reactive mixing methods, are reported. The peculiar crystallization phenomena occurring in compatibilized systems (fractionated crystallization) are examined for blends of polyamides and functionalized polyolefins.

Section 10.6 is dedicated to blends containing liquid-crystalline components. The mesophase behavior of liquid crystals (LCs) and liquid crystal polymers (LCPs), as well as the crystallization processes and the superstructure of blends of crystallizable polymers with LCPs and blends of LCPs, is described.

10.2 THERMODYNAMICS OF POLYMER BLENDS

10.2.1 General Principles

The miscibility and the phase morphology, as well as the physical, rheological, and mechanical properties of multicomponent polymer systems, are determined by the thermodynamic behavior. The thermodynamics of polymer blends aims at developing the theoretical background to establish the conditions of miscibility and thus to predict the phase behavior of polymer pairs—as a function of concentration, temperature, and pressure, depending on the chemical structure, molecular mass, and mass distribution of the macromolecules.

According to the general principles of the thermodynamics, the Gibbs free energy of mixing (ΔG_m) of a binary polymer system is defined as:

$$\Delta G_m = \Delta H_m - T\Delta S_m \quad (10.1)$$

where ΔH_m and ΔS_m are the variations of enthalpy and entropy, respectively, due to the mixing. At constant temperature and pressure, the necessary condition for the system miscibility is that $\Delta G_m < 0$ (Fig. 10.1a), which is fulfilled when $\Delta H_m < 0$ and $\Delta S_m > 0$ (or $|T\Delta S_m| > |\Delta H_m|$, if $\Delta H_m > 0$). If, at a defined temperature, the free energy curve displays a region where ΔG_m is not at a minimum (Fig. 10.1a), phase separation occurs in two mixtures of composition b_1 and b_2 (binodal) located on the tangent to the curve. At compositions intermediate between the inflection points, a_1 and a_2—characterized by the condition that the second derivative of ΔG_m with composition is zero—phase separation proceeds spontaneously from composition fluctuations (spinodal) [2]. Binodal and spinodal curves, defined as a function of temperature, coincide at a critical point, C (Fig. 10.1b), where the third derivative of ΔG_m with composition is zero. At the point C both lower critical solution temperature (LCST) and upper critical solution temperature (UCST) can occur.

On the basis of statistical treatments, for a binary liquid mixture the entropy of mixing can be expressed as:

$$\Delta S_m = R(V_1 + V_2)[(\varphi_1/V_1)\ln\varphi_1 + (\varphi_2/V_2)\ln\varphi_2] \quad (10.2)$$

where φ_i is the volume fraction of each component, V_i is the molar volume of the repeating unit and R the gas constant. Since the contribution of the entropic term ΔS_m is very low for polymers with high molecular mass ($V_i \to \infty$), the miscibility behavior of these systems is mostly determined by the change of enthalpy ΔH_m, which is correlated to the occurrence of molecular interactions between the polymer components.

The basis of the thermodynamics of polymer mixtures were introduced—in around the 1940s—by the mean field lattice model of the Flory–Huggins–Staverman theory on polymer solutions [7, 8]. According to the thermodynamics of regular solutions, Flory and others derived the following equation for the Gibbs free energy of mixing of two polymers A and B:

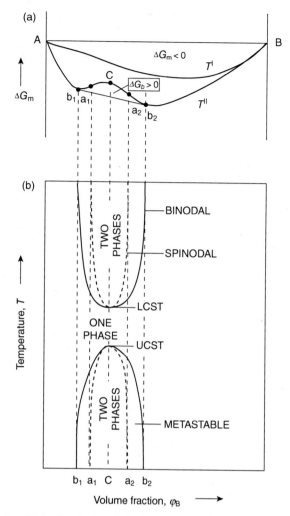

Figure 10.1 Variation of the free energy of mixing (ΔG_m) for a blend of A and B polymer components, as a function of composition (φ). (a) Miscible blend ($\Delta G_m < 0$) at temperature T' and partially miscible blend (miscibility gap: $\Delta G_b > 0$) with spinodal (a_1, a_2) and binodal (b_1, b_2) phase separation, at temperature T''. (b) Temperature–composition plot for a blend exhibiting both LCST and UCST behavior. Redrawn from Vasile et al. [6].

$$\Delta G_m = (RTV/V_r)[(\varphi_A/r_A)\ln\varphi_A + (\varphi_B/r_B)\ln\varphi_B \\ + \chi_{AB}\varphi_A\varphi_B] \quad (10.3)$$

where T is the absolute temperature, V the total volume of the mixture ($V_A + V_B$), V_r is a reference volume (the volume of a segment in the lattice cell, taken equal to the volume of the repeating unit of the polymer chain, assumed the same for both polymers), and φ_i is the volume fraction of each polymer; $r_i = V_i/V_r$ (V_i being the molar volume of component i), thus r_A and r_B represent the number of segments (i.e., the polymerization degree) of the respective polymers. χ_{AB} is the thermodynamic interaction parameter that is related to the intramolecular and intermolecular interaction energy (ε) between segments of polymer chains:

$$\chi_{AB} = (\varepsilon_{AA} + \varepsilon_{BB} - 2\varepsilon_{AB})/k_B T = z\Delta\varepsilon r_i/k_B T V_i \quad (10.4)$$

In Equation (10.4) k_B is the Boltzman constant, z is the coordination number of the lattice, and $\Delta\varepsilon$ is the energy of formation of AB contacts, which can be calculated from the algebraic sum of the interaction energies (= $\varepsilon_{AB} - (\varepsilon_{AA} + \varepsilon_{BB})/2$); the value of ε_{AB} can be assumed equal to the geometrical mean (= $\sqrt{\varepsilon_{AA}\varepsilon_{BB}}$) [9].

Since the contribution to the combinatorial entropy of mixing in Equation (10.3) becomes negligible as the molecular mass of the components increases, the main consequence of the above treatment is that the miscibility of a polymer/polymer mixture is strictly dependent on the Gibbs free energy of interaction, expressed as segmental interaction parameter, which includes various contributions, such as those deriving from specific interactions, dispersive forces, and entropic effects.

When the enthalpic contribution to the Gibbs free energy of mixing is largely determinant, assuming that the combinatorial entropic contribution is negligible, the blend miscibility can be predicted on the basis of the heat of mixing of low molecular weight analogs [10] and the simplified relation may be used:

$$\Delta G_m \approx \Delta H_m = B\varphi_A\varphi_B \quad (10.5)$$

where $B = \chi_{AB}RT(V/V_i)$ is the interaction energy density, and the parameter χ_{AB} contains both an enthalpic and a noncombinatorial entropic contribution.

Values of χ_{AB} and B can be estimated using a semiempirical approach, by a simple method based on Hildebrand solubility parameters [11]:

$$\chi_{AB} = (V_r/RT)(\delta_A - \delta_B)^2. \quad (10.6)$$

The solubility parameter, $\delta = \rho(\sum F_i/M)$, can be calculated from the molar attraction constants, F_i, of all the chemical groups in the repeating unit of the polymer with molecular weight M. This method was successfully used by Krause [12] for an a priori evaluation of the miscibility of polymer blends as a function of temperature, composition, and molecular weight. Coleman et al. [13], using the solubility parameter approach, reported a practical guide for predicting the miscibility of multicomponent polymer systems with calculation of the free energy of mixing, phase diagrams, and miscibility windows.

In addition to the Flory–Huggins rigid-lattice model, the development of the thermodynamics of polymer blends has been signed by the "equation of state" theories. The fluid-lattice model by Sanchez [14] enabled a more quantitative prediction of phase behavior of polymer blends.

Koningsveld and coworkers [15, 16] modified Equation (10.3) by substituting the interaction parameter with a function $\chi_{AB}(\varphi, T) = \chi_H + \chi_S$, containing both an enthalpic (χ_H) and a noncombinatorial entropic (χ_S) contribution to the interaction term (the entropic effect being caused by changes of intersegmental orientation due to the presence of interactions):

$$\chi_{AB}(\varphi, T) = (a_0 + a_1/T + a_2T)(b_0 + b_1\varphi_B + b_2\varphi_B^2) \quad (10.7)$$

where the interaction function χ_{AB} incorporates the composition, temperature, and molecular weight dependence, and $a_0, \ldots a_n$ and $b_0, \ldots b_n$ are constants. Further improvements to the theory have been obtained by taking into account the effect of interacting surface areas of the various segments and coil dimensions as a function of temperature, molar mass, mass distribution, and free volume.

For polymer systems in which strong interactions, such as acid–base or hydrogen bond interactions, are present, either LCST or UCST behavior may be described using the directional-specific model of segmental interactions [17, 18]:

$$\Delta G_m = RTV\varphi_A\varphi_B[(U_2/RT) + \ln(1-\lambda) + (1+q^{-1})] \quad (10.8)$$

where the term between square brackets represents the interaction parameter χ_{AB}, and $\lambda = 1/[(1 + q) \exp\{(U_1 - U_2)/RT\}]$, U_1 and U_2 being the attractive and repulsive interaction energies, respectively, and q the degeneracy number. The interaction parameter contains both an enthalpic and an entropic contribution, and the parameters U_1, U_2, and q are adjustable: depending on the relative values of U_1 and U_2, the temperature dependence of χ_{AB} ($d\chi_{AB}/dT$) can be negative or positive, predicting the UCST or LCST behavior.

10.3 MISCIBLE POLYMER BLENDS

10.3.1 Introduction

In general, the phase behavior and the morphological characteristics, as well as the crystallization process of blends of crystallizable polymers, depend on the composition, the chemical structure of the macromolecules, and their reciprocal interactions, that is, on the miscibility effects (in the melt and the amorphous solid phase).

For miscible blends containing a crystallizable component, the overall Gibbs free energy change of the system, $\Delta G = \Delta G_m + \Delta G_c$, is determined by the contribution of both free energy of mixing ($\Delta G_m \approx B\varphi_A\varphi_B$) and free energy of crystallization at the temperature T: $\Delta G_c \approx -[\Delta H_m^o(1-T/T_m^o)\alpha_c]$, which depends on the enthalpy of fusion of the completely crystalline polymer, ΔH_m^o, the equilibrium melting temperature, T_m^o, and the volumetric crystallinity degree, α_c.

To analyze the crystallization behavior of crystallizable polymer blends, it is suitable to distinguish between systems containing only one crystallizable component (crystalline/amorphous blends) and those containing both crystallizable components (crystalline/crystalline blends). In all cases, the crystallization of a polymer blend will take place in a defined temperature range, between the values of the glass transition temperature, T_g, and the equilibrium melting temperature of the crystallisable polymer, T_m^o; below T_g the chain mobility is inhibited, while at temperatures near T_m^o the crystal nucleation does not occur.

For a binary miscible blend (A: amorphous polymer, B: crystalline polymer) the glass transition is intermediate between those of plain components (T_{gA}, T_{gB}) and thus the crystallization range—and the crystallization behavior—will depend on the glass transition of the amorphous component (T_{gA}) (Fig. 10.2) [19]. In fact, if T_{gA} is lower than T_{gB}, the glass transition of the crystallizable polymer, the "crystallization window" of the blend ($T_m^o - T_g$), where T_m^o represents the equilibrium melting point of B in the blend, is larger than that of the neat crystallizable component ($T_{mB}^o - T_{gB}$), and the ability to crystallize is enhanced. On the contrary, if T_{gA} is higher than T_{gB} ($T_{gA}' > T_{gB}'$), the glass transition of the blend is increased and the crystallization window is reduced. In the extreme case, if $T_g \geq T_m^o$, the crystallization can be completely inhibited, as it can happen in blends with a high content of amorphous component, where the difference ($T_m^o - T_{gA}$) is markedly reduced and the crystallization becomes too slow to be observed. When both the blend components are crystallizable, more complex situations may be observed, depending on either the T_g or the T_m^o value of the two polymers [19].

The effect of the amorphous component on the crystallization ability of the crystallizable polymer has been examined for some miscible blends. An improvement of poly(ε-caprolactone) (PCL) crystallization has been observed in blends with chlorinated polyethylene (CPE) [20], while for poly(ethylene oxide)/poly(ethyl methacrylate) (PEO/PEMA) [21], PCL/SAN [22], and poly(butylene therephthalate)/polyarylate (PBT/PAr) [23] blends, the crystallization ability is markedly reduced.

10.3.2 Phase Morphology

A fundamental aspect of the crystallization behavior of miscible blends is that concerning the morphology development. When crystals grow in the presence of an amorphous component, the morphology is mainly controlled by the phase separation phenomena that occur at the crystal growth front. During the crystallization from the homogeneous melt, the crystallizable component generally solidifies forming spherulitic structures with rejection of the amorphous component at the liquid–crystal interface that increases its concentration in the amorphous phase. The amorphous component can segregate in different modes: it can be rejected in large domains at the spherulite borders (*interspherulitic* zones), or it can be located either between the crystal lamellae (*interlamellar* zones) or between stacks of lamellae (*interfibrillar* zones) [24].

The mode of segregation of the amorphous polymer component is controlled by the chain diffusion. Keith and Padden [25] accounted for the location of the noncrystallizable polymer by the ratio between the diffusion coefficient (D) of the amorphous component into the melt and the growth rate (G) of the crystals. The ratio $\delta = D/G$ has been defined as "segregation distance": when $\delta \gg 1$, the amorphous component moves along with the crystal growth front forming separated domains in interspherulitic zones, or within intraspherulitic regions when $\delta \approx 1$; otherwise, if $\delta \ll 1$, the noncrystallizing molecules can remain trapped into the growing spherulites between the crystalline lamellae ($\delta < 10$ nm) or between the fibrils. In the latter case, which is usually

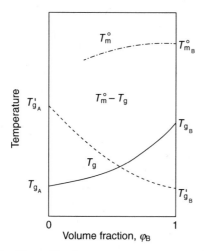

Figure 10.2 Crystallization temperature ranges for crystalline/amorphous miscible polymer blends (A: amorphous polymer, B: crystalline polymer) as a function of volume fraction of the crystalline component. T_g, glass transition temperature of blend: $T_{gA} < T_{gB}$ (solid line), $T_{gA}' > T_{gB}'$ (dashed line). T_m^o, equilibrium melting temperature of polymer B in the blend.

found for melt miscible systems, the amorphous interlamellar regions are constituted by a homogeneous mixture of the two components. In some case, different types of segregation, either interlamellar or interfibrillar, have been observed for the same system, depending on changes of the crystallization conditions, as reported for poly(vinylidene fluoride)/poly(methyl methacrylate) (PVDF/PMMA) blends [26]. For these blends it has been assumed that there exists a "compositional interface": an interfacial region—between the crystalline lamellae and the amorphous layer—with variable polymer composition.

When demixing phenomena are induced by the crystallization of one component, the amorphous component will be removed from the crystallization front and will diffuse away into the melt, while the crystallizing molecules are migrating from the melt to the growth front. Thus, three different regimes can be observed depending on the relative values of G and the diffusion rate of the amorphous component (V_d) within the crystallization temperature range [27], as schematically shown in Figure 10.3.

The rate G has a maximum between the glass transition (T_g) and the equilibrium melting temperature (T_m^o), whereas the diffusion rate V_d increases continuously with temperature. In regime I ($V_d \ll G$), generally observed at low crystallization temperatures, the noncrystallizing component, which separates upon crystallization, remains occluded within the growing crystals and can be incorporated in the interlamellar regions. In regime II ($V_d \approx G$), the noncrystallizing polymer may be in part rejected into the melt and in part incorporated into the growing crystals, depending on the temperature (in this case the local composition of the melt may be very different from the overall concentration since the presence of an excess of noncrystallizing polymer at the growth front changes the composition of the amorphous phase, as compared to that of the initial melt). In regime III ($V_d \gg G$), frequently observed at higher temperatures, the amorphous component, which is released during the crystallization of the crystallizable polymer, diffuses away into the melt, giving rise to a gradual change of the melt composition and reaching a higher content of amorphous polymer with respect to the initial melt composition.

For binary blends with both crystallizable components crystallizing from a homogeneous melt, a *pseudoeutectic* crystallization behavior can be observed [27]. While in the case of blends of low molecular weight materials the melting point depression curves of the two components cross at an intermediate composition and they crystallize simultaneously (*eutectic* crystallization) with formation of finely dispersed crystals of both components, in the case of miscible polymer blends the equilibrium melting point depression of each component—by varying the composition—is generally small and the melt–solid transition curves of the polymers in the phase diagram do not meet. Thus, according to the equilibrium conditions the polymer components would crystallize successively. However, under kinetic conditions (causing larger melting point depression), simultaneous crystallization of the polymers (pseudoeutectic crystallization) may occur, giving rise to mixed crystals, that is, mixed lamellar structures of the components. A model for describing the cooperative crystallization of crystalline/crystalline blends has been presented by Balijepalli and Schultz [28]. The crystallization and the morphology of such systems were reported to be similar to those for eutectic crystallization of small molecules mixtures.

Examples of crystallizable systems with full melt miscibility over the whole composition range have been pointed out for poly(ethylene terephthalate)/poly(butylene terephthalate) (PET/PBT), poly(hydroxy butyrate)/poly(ethylene oxide) (PHB/PEO), and polycarbonate/poly(ε-caprolactone) (PC/PCL) blends [29].

10.3.3 Crystal Growth Rate

According to the kinetic theory, the nucleation controlled growth rate (G) of polymer crystals at the temperature T_c is described by the equation [30, 31]:

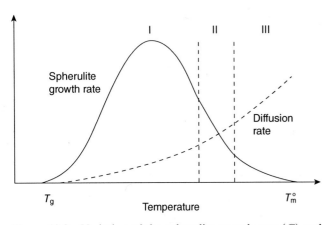

Figure 10.3 Variation of the spherulite growth rate (G) and chain diffusion rate (V_d) in a crystalline/amorphous blend as a function of temperature. Three regimes can occur in the crystallization range depending on temperature. Regime I ($G \gg V_d$): the growing spherulites can incorporate the noncrystallizing polymer into interlamellar or interfibrillar regions. Regime II ($G \approx V_d$): the amorphous component is partially incorporated or rejected at the edges of the spherulites. Regime III ($G \ll V_d$): the noncrystallizing molecules diffuse completely into the melt. Redrawn from Li et al. [27].

$$G = G_0 \exp[-U^*/R(T_c - T_\infty)]\exp[-\Delta\Phi^*/k_B T_c] \quad (10.9)$$

where U^* is the activation energy for the transport of the crystallizing molecules across the liquid–solid interface, T_∞ is the temperature at which the motions for the macromolecular transport cease, $\Delta\Phi^*$ is the Gibbs free energy related to the barrier for nucleation on the substrate, and G_0 is a factor (assumed as a constant) depending on the regime of crystallization and temperature. In Equation (10.9), the transport term is usually evaluated by means of the Williams–Landel–Ferry relation [32] with $U^* = 1500$ cal/mol and $T_\infty = T_g - 30$K. In a more recent version of the theory, the transport term, especially above $T_g + 100$K, is expressed as $\exp(-Q_D^*/RT)$ where Q_D^* denotes the activation energy for reptation. $\Delta\Phi^* = vb\sigma\sigma_e T_m^o/(f\Delta h_u \Delta T)$, where b is the distance between two adjacent folding planes, σ and σ_e are the free energies of the lateral and folding surfaces respectively, Δh_u is the enthalpy of fusion per unit volume of the crystallizable component, $f = 2T/(T_m^o + T_c)$ is a factor that corrects for the change in the enthalpy of fusion with temperature, and v is a constant depending on the regime of growth ($v = 4$ for regime I and III, $v = 2$ for regime II). A more detailed description of the kinetic theory of crystal growth is given in Chapter 5.

When an amorphous polymer is added to a crystallizable polymer, forming a melt miscible system, the thermodynamic and kinetic factors controlling the crystallization process may undergo dramatic changes [33]. First, the chemical potential of the components in the liquid state changes due to occurrence of specific interactions (which are responsible for the miscibility phenomena) between the polymers; this implies changes in the values of the equilibrium melting temperature, T_m^o, and of the energy of nucleation, $\Delta\Phi^*$. Second, the variation of glass transition temperature of the blend, with respect to the neat polymers, influences the activation energy for the transport of the macromolecules in the melt. Further, the crystal growth will be affected by the diffusion of the noncrystallizable component at the growth front, inducing changes in the concentration and transport of the crystallizable polymer at the liquid–solid interface, with consequent effects on the crystal growth. Thus, the crystallization kinetics are determined by the competition between the nucleation/growth process and the rate of segregation of the noncrystallizing component. Taking into account these effects, Alfonso and Russell reported a phenomenological equation of the crystal growth rate (G_m) in a miscible blend [34]:

$$G_m = [\varphi_B k_1 k_2/(k_1 + k_2)]\exp[-\Delta\Phi^*/k_B T_c] \quad (10.10)$$

where φ_B is the volume fraction of the crystallizable component and k_1 is the rate of transport of crystallizing molecules across the liquid–solid interface at T_c: $k_1 = G_0 \exp[-U^*/R(T_c - T_\infty')]$, T_∞' being the value of T_∞ in the blend (see Eq. 10.9). k_2 is the rate at which the amorphous component segregates into the melt: $k_2 = D/d$, where D is the diffusion coefficient and d is the maximum distance over which the amorphous polymer can diffuse away from the growth front ($d = L/2$, with L the lamellar thickness of the crystals). Thus, according to Equation (10.10), the crystal growth rate will be controlled by the relative magnitude of k_1, k_2, and $\Delta\Phi^*$. If $k_1 \gg k_2$, that is, the transport of crystallizable material across liquid–solid interface is fast as compared to the diffusion rate of the noncrystallizing component from the growth front, then Equation (10.10) reduces to $G_m \approx \varphi_B k_2 \exp(-\Delta\Phi^*/k_B T_c)$. On the other hand, if $k_1 \ll k_2$, the rate of transport across the liquid–solid interface becomes the rate-controlling step and Equation (10.10) reduces to: $G_m \approx \varphi_B k_1 \exp(-\Delta\Phi^*/k_B T_c)$.

However, when the contribution of the secondary nucleation term $\Delta\Phi^*$ is dominant (at low undercoolings), the diluent effect of the amorphous component must be taken into account, that is, an additional entropic effect to the nucleation barrier due to the reduced probability of extracting crystalline polymer sequences from the entangled melt at the growth front. Following the treatment of Boon and Azcue for a polymer–diluent mixture [35], the activation energy associated with the secondary nucleation in a miscible blend can be expressed as:

$$\Delta\Phi_{dil}^* = [vb\sigma\sigma_e T_m^o/(f\Delta h_u \Delta T)] \\ - [2\sigma k_B T_m^o T_c \ln\varphi_B/(b\Delta h_u \Delta T)] \quad (10.11)$$

Since the last term on the right is negative, the value of $\Delta\Phi_{dil}^*$ is larger than the corresponding value of the plain crystalline polymer, which implies a decrease of growth rate in the blend, at the same ΔT (Fig. 10.4). Therefore, for a miscible blend, Equation (10.9) can be written in the form:

$$G_m = \varphi_B G_0 \exp[-U^*/R(T_c - T_\infty)]\exp[-\Delta\Phi_{dil}^*/k_B T_c] \quad (10.12)$$

where the pre-exponential factor is multiplied by φ_B as the rate is proportional to the concentration of crystallizable units [36]. By introducing the expression of $\Delta\Phi_{dil}^*$ (Eq. 10.11) and assuming $\sigma = 0.1b\Delta h_u$, it is possible to rearrange Equation (10.12) as [37]:

$$\ln G_m - \ln\varphi_B + U^*/R(T_c - T_\infty) - [(0.2 T_m^o \ln\varphi_B)/\Delta T] = f(G) \\ = \ln G_0 - [0.1vb^2 \sigma_e T_m^o/k_B](1/fT_c\Delta T) \quad (10.13)$$

Plots of the term $f(G)$ versus $1/fT_c\Delta T$ are linear with a slope $0.1vb^2\sigma_e T_m^o/k_B$; thus, by finding the values of b and

294 CRYSTALLIZATION OF POLYMER BLENDS

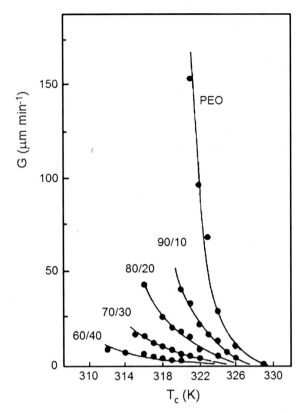

Figure 10.4 Isothermal growth rate of PEO spherulites in miscible PEO/PMMA blends versus T_c for various blend compositions (wt/wt). Reprinted from Martuscelli et al. [37], Copyright 1984, with permission from Elsevier.

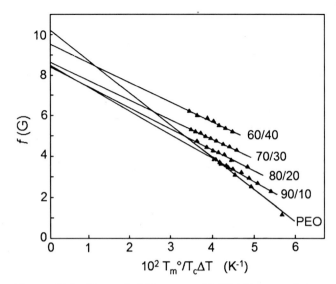

Figure 10.5 Plots of $f(G)$ versus $T_m^o/(T_c\Delta T)$ according to Equation (10.13) for miscible PEO/PMMA blends with various PMMA content (0–40 wt%). Samples isothermally crystallized from the melt. Reprinted from Martuscelli et al. [37], Copyright 1984, with permission from Elsevier.

T_m^o, it is possible to evaluate the change of the surface free energy σ_e of the lamellar crystals in the blend by varying the concentration of noncrystallizing component (Fig. 10.5).

10.3.4 Overall Crystallization Kinetics

The isothermal overall crystallization kinetics of polymer blends from the melt can be analyzed on the basis of the Avrami model [38, 39]:

$$X(t) = 1 - \exp[-K_n t^n] \qquad (10.14)$$

where $X(t)$ is the relative weight fraction of polymer crystallized at time t, K_n the kinetic constant, and n the Avrami exponent, depending on the growth geometry and nucleation type of the crystals. The description of the overall crystallization kinetics is covered in Chapter 7. Values of K_n and n can be calculated at each crystallization temperature, T_c, from the intercepts and slopes, respectively, of the linear regression of $\log\{-\ln[1 - X(t)]\}$ as a function of $\log(t)$. The kinetic constant is related to the crystallization rate of the sample by the relation: $K_n = \ln 2/(t_{1/2})^n$, where $t_{1/2}$ is the half-time of crystallization (which is calculated from plots of $X(t)$ vs. t, for $X(t) = 0.5$). For a crystallization process, which develops through a three-dimensional growth ($n = 3$) of spherulites instantaneously nucleated by N heterogeneous nuclei (per unit volume), at temperature T_c, with radial growth rate G, it is possible to write [38]:

$$K_{(n=3)} = (4\pi\rho_c/3\rho_a)NG^3/(1-\lambda_\infty) \qquad (10.15)$$

where ρ_c and ρ_a are the densities of the crystalline and amorphous phases respectively, and $(1 - \lambda_\infty)$ is the crystalline weight fraction at $t = \infty$. $K_{(n=3)}$ has the dimension of [time]$^{-3}$; for n deviating slightly from 3, the value of the kinetic constant must be recalculated from the experimental value of K_n as: $K_{(n=3)} = (K_n)^{3/n}$. By introducing the expression of G (Eq. 10.9) into Equation (10.15), the following relation is obtained [40]:

$$(1/n)\ln K_n = \ln A_0 - U^*/R(T_c - T_\infty) - \Delta\Phi^*/k_B T_c \qquad (10.16)$$

where A_0 is a parameter including the pre-exponential factor G_0 and the nucleation density N.

For a miscible blend containing a crystallizable component, following the treatment previously described for the spherulite growth rate in a polymer–diluent system (Eq. 10.13), the temperature dependence of the kinetic constant for the overall crystallization rate, under isothermal conditions becomes [37]:

$$(1/n)\ln K_n - \ln\varphi_B + U^*/R(T_c - T_\infty) - [(0.2T_m^o \ln\varphi_B)/\Delta T]$$
$$= f(K_n) = \ln A_0 - (0.1vb^2\sigma_e T_m^o/k_B)/T_c\Delta T. \tag{10.17}$$

From linear plots of the term $f(K_n)$ versus $1/T_c\Delta T$—knowing the value of T_m^o and assuming $\sigma = 0.1b\Delta H_u$—it is possible to evaluate the surface free energy of folding of the lamellar crystals in the blend.

For nonisothermal crystallization processes, the kinetics can be analyzed by taking into account several theoretical models [41–43] including the frequently used Ozawa model [42], as described in Chapter 7.

10.3.5 Melting Behavior

For a crystalline polymer in a blend, the melting behavior is strictly influenced by the miscibility, that is, by the blend composition and thermodynamics, as well as by kinetic factors controlling the growth, structure, geometry, and perfection of the crystals.

According to the kinetic theories, the melting point, T_m, of a polymer crystal with finite size (and in absence of recrystallization phenomena consequent on heating or annealing processes) can be related to the crystallization temperature, T_c, by the Hoffman–Weeks relation [30]:

$$T_m = (1 - 1/\gamma)T_m^o + (1/\gamma)T_c \tag{10.18}$$

where T_m^o is the equilibrium melting temperature for an infinitely thick crystal and γ is the thickening factor, relating the mean lamellar thickness of the crystals to the initial thickness of the growth nuclei at T_c (see Chapter 9). The value of T_m^o can be determined from the linear plot of the experimental melting points T_m as function of T_c, by extrapolation to the line $T_m = T_c$.

For a crystalline polymer in a miscible blend with an amorphous component, the free energy of the crystallizable polymer in the molten blend (G_m^o) is found to be lower than that of the neat polymer in the melt phase (G_{mB}^o), while the free energy of the crystalline phase (G_c) is not affected by mixing. As a consequence, at the equilibrium ($\Delta G = G_m^o - G_c = 0$), the melting temperature of the blend, T_m^o, will be decreased with respect to that of neat polymer, T_{mB}^o (see Fig. 10.2), due to the interactions between the two components. Following the thermodynamic treatment by Scott [44] using the Flory–Huggins approximation [7], Nishi and Wang [45] proposed the following equation for the melting point depression of a miscible polymer blend as function of composition:

$$(1/T_m^o) - (1/T_{mB}^o) = -[V_{Bu}/(\Delta H_u V_{Au})]R\chi_{AB}(1-\varphi_B)^2 \tag{10.19}$$

where V_u is the molar volume of the repeating unit of the two components (A = amorphous, B = crystalline), ΔH_u is the heat of fusion per mol of repeating unit, and φ_B is the volume fraction of crystallisable component. By introducing the interaction energy density $B = RT\chi_{AB}/V_{Au}$, Equation (10.19) can be written as:

$$T_{mB}^o - T_m^o = -T_{mB}^o[V_{Bu}/\Delta H_u]B\varphi_A^2. \tag{10.20}$$

A plot of the melting point difference ($T_{mB}^o - T_m^o$) versus the square of volume fraction of the noncrystallizable component, φ_A, should be linear with an intercept at the origin (if there is no entropic contribution to the melting point depression), and the value of χ_{AB} can be determined from the slope of the linear plot, as shown in Figure 10.6.

A depression of the equilibrium melting temperature implies, for a miscible blend, a negative value of χ_{AB}; in the absence of interactions between the polymer components (when χ_{AB} is zero), no depression of the melting equilibrium temperature is recorded. Values of the interaction parameters and density derived from Equation (10.20) are reported in Table 10.1 for various blend systems.

In many polymer blends, a depression of the experimental melting temperature is observed, which can be ascribed to kinetic and/or morphological effects, different from the thermodynamic effects reported earlier. Kinetic effects may be derived from the growth process of the crystals at large undercoolings and in nonequilibrium

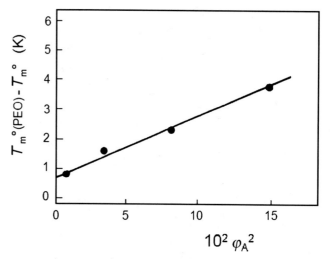

Figure 10.6 Equilibrium melting point difference ($T_m^o(\text{PEO}) - T_m^o$) for miscible PEO-100K/PMMA blends versus the square volume fraction of the noncrystallizable PMMA component, φ_A, according to Equation (10.21). $T_m^o(\text{PEO}) = 74°C$ for PEO-100K. Reprinted from Martuscelli et al. [37], Copyright 1984, with permission from Elsevier.

Table 10.1 Flory Interaction Parameter, χ_{AB}, and Interaction Energy Density, B, for Miscible Binary Blends of Various Polymers

Polymer Blend	χ_{AB}	B (J/cm³)	References
PVDF/PMMA	−0.295	−12.46	Nishi and Wang [45]
PVDF/PEMA	−0.34	−11.95	Kwei et al. [145]
PVDF/PEMA		−13.30	Imken et al. [146]
PEO-20K/PMMA	−1.93	−65.32	Martuscelli and Demma [48]
PEO-100K/PMMA	−0.35	−11.93	Martuscelli et al. [37]
PEO/PVC	−0.094	−6.56	Marco et al. [147]
PCL/PVDF	−1.5		Jo et al. [148]
iPP/iPB	−0.257		Canetti et al. [59]
PEEK/PEI	−0.40	−5.02	Chen and Porter [149]
PI/EVA	−0.02	−7.12	Clough et al. [150]
PVPh/PTT	−0.74	−32.49	Lee and Woo [151]
PVDF/PHB	−0.25		Liu et al. [152]
PBT/PAr	−0.96		Liau et al. [153]

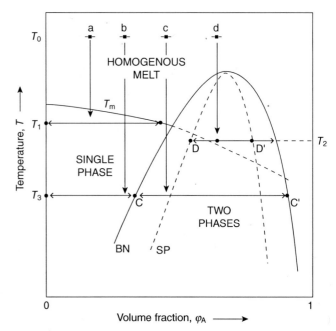

Figure 10.7 Temperature–composition plot of a crystalline/amorphous blend (A: amorphous polymer, B: crystalline polymer) showing partial miscibility (UCST). (a) Crystallization induced by quenching from homogeneous melt (at T_1); (b): demixing induced by crystallization (at T_3); (c) Simultaneous demixing and crystallization (at T_3); (d) Crystallization induced by demixing (at T_2). T_m, melting point curve; BN, binodal; SP, spinodal. Redrawn from Jungnickel [46].

conditions, whereas morphological effects are mainly due to changes in crystal thickness (thickening phenomena), perfection, and size, depending on composition and crystallization conditions. In these cases, to analyze the miscibility behavior, only equilibrium values should be used into the equation of the melting point depression (Eq. 10.20).

10.3.6 Blends with Partial Miscibility

In blends that show a miscibility gap in their composition range, the phase transitions and the superstructure can be markedly affected by the contemporary presence of both crystallization and demixing phenomena, depending on the concentration of the crystallizing component. A competition between the kinetics of the two phenomena can be observed in blends with crystalline and amorphous components when the region of phase separation intersects the crystallization range, as schematically shown in Figure 10.7 for a binary system with a UCST [46].

In case (a), the blend is quenched from the homogeneous melt at temperature T_0 to a temperature T_1 outside the two phase region, where the system crystallizes as a single phase. In case (b), the melt is quenched outside the miscibility gap to a temperature T_3 below the melt–crystallization curve within the single phase region: owing to the crystallization of one component, the concentration of the amorphous polymer in the melt will increase until the binodal curve is reached (point C) and decomposition of the melt into two liquid phases will take place (demixing induced by crystallization). In case (c), the melt is quenched within the biphasic region to a temperature T_3 below the crystallization curve: simultaneous competition between binodal (or spinodal) demixing and crystallization will occur for the coexisting phases (C, C′). Case (d) occurs when the melt is quenched within the miscibility gap to a temperature T_2 above the crystallization curve for that composition, but situated below the crystallization curve for the corresponding spinodal (or binodal) composition; after quenching, demixing will occur, giving rise to two coexisting phases (D, D′) of which only one (D) crystallizes and the other (D′) remains amorphous (crystallization induced by demixing).

Another interesting phenomenon, which can be observed in blends with miscibility gap, is the occurrence of *interface crossing* crystallization [46]. In conditions of phase separation, two phases with different concentrations of the crystallizable component are present and, due to differences in the number density of heterogeneous nuclei, the phase with a higher content of crystalline component will crystallize first. When the crystallizing phase reaches the interface with the other phase, then the crystallization of the second phase will be induced by secondary nucleation phenomena on the same crystals in contact with the melt. The superstructure of the crystals in the two phases that results is quite different owing to the difference in composition and the occurrence of other nucleation processes. An evidence of interface crossing crystallization has been reported for PVDF/PEA blends, which show an LCST behavior [47].

10.3.7 Crystallization Behavior of Amorphous/Crystalline Blends

10.3.7.1 PEO/PMMA Blends

Miscible blends of PEO (M_w = 20 K and 100 K) with amorphous poly(methyl methacrylate) (PMMA, M_w = 110 K) have been studied by microscopic, structural, and thermal analyses, with varying composition and molecular mass of the components [37, 48]. The miscibility of PEO and PMMA was theoretically predicted on the basis of lattice theory and solubility parameter approach. These blends display a single glass transition, composition dependent, at temperature intermediate between those of pure components; moreover, experimental evidence of miscibility in the melt was obtained by ^{13}C nuclear magnetic resonance (NMR) analysis [49]. Films of blends isothermally crystallized from the melt showed (in the composition range from 100% to 60% by weight of PEO) a spherulitic morphology with no segregation phenomena of the amorphous component in interspherulitic zones. With decreasing the PEO content, changes in the spherulite texture and crystal habit have been observed, suggesting the occurrence of phase segregation. In all the examined crystallization range, the spherulite radius increases linearly with time over long crystallization times, indicating that during the growth the concentration of PMMA at the tips of PEO radial lamellae remains constant, and after crystallization the films appear completely filled with impinged spherulites. At constant T_c, the spherulite growth rate drastically decreases with increasing the content of noncrystallizing polymer (see Fig. 10.4), which supports the incorporation of PMMA molecules within the interlamellar regions of the PEO spherulites, in agreement with that reported for miscible PVDF/PMMA blends [50].

Similar effects were found by analyzing the overall crystallization kinetics from the melt: at the same T_c the crystallization half-time ($t_{1/2}$) of the blend increased exponentially with increasing concentration of the amorphous component. The temperature dependence of the spherulite growth rate (G) and kinetic constant (K_n) was then examined according to Equation (10.13)

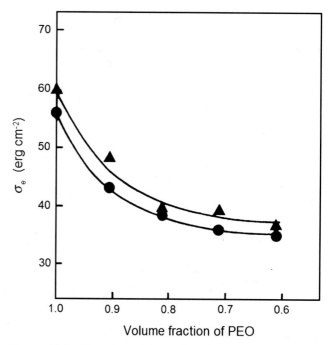

Figure 10.8 Variation of the surface free energy of folding, σ_e with the volume fraction of crystalline component for PEO-100K/PMMA blends. Lower curve: data from spherulite growth rate (Eq. 10.13); upper curve: data from overall crystallization kinetics (Eq. 10.17). Reprinted from Martuscelli et al. [37], Copyright 1984, with permission from Elsevier.

and Equation (10.17) respectively (see Section 10.3.3). Plots of $f(G)$ and $f(K_n)$ as a function of $1/(T_c\Delta T)$ were found to be linear in all the examined T_c ranges (see Fig. 10.5), and from their slopes, values of the free energy associated with secondary nucleation ($\Delta\Phi^*$) and of surface free energy of folding (σ_e) have been calculated at various compositions.

Figure 10.8 shows the marked change of σ_e with increasing fraction of PMMA in the blend, which can be accounted for by the presence of noncrystallizing molecules in the interlamellar regions of PEO crystals causing perturbations in the fold structure (with formation of entanglements and large loops). Thus, the decrease of the surface free energy in the blends could be ascribed to an increase of the entropic contribution to the surface energy, compared with that of (negative) enthalpic contribution. A larger depression of σ_e values was observed with decreasing the molecular weight of PEO (PEO-20K/PMMA blends), suggesting the occurrence of larger intermolecular interactions between PMMA and PEO-20K, and higher entropic effects [48].

A notable composition dependence of the melting parameters and crystallinity degree was reported for all PEO/PMMA blends, with a melting behavior that was affected by the crystallization conditions and molecular weight of each component [34]. A linear variation of T_m versus T_c (see Eq. 10.18) with a constant stability parameter ($1/\gamma$) was recorded for all examined compositions at higher undercoolings, while at low undercoolings nonlinear trends were observed, with values of T_m approaching the melting temperature of pure PEO, likely due to phase separation and annealing phenomena at T_c and/or during the heating of the crystals.

In Figure 10.9 the change in the extrapolated equilibrium melting temperature (T_m^o), determined by different analytical methods, is reported as a function of the weight fraction of PEO. In both cases, a linear decrease in T_m^o was observed on increasing the fraction of PMMA (W_A), according to the expression:

$$T_m^o = T_m^o(\text{PEO}) - \alpha W_A \quad (10.21)$$

where $T_m^o(\text{PEO})$ is the equilibrium melting temperature of pure PEO crystals. Equation (10.21) is analogous to that reported for the composition dependence of T_m^o of random copolymers with variable content of noncrystallizable comonomer units [51]. Following Equation (10.20), the depression of equilibrium melting point ($T_m^o(\text{PEO}) - T_m^o$) was then related to the volume fraction of PMMA, allowing for the evaluation of the Flory interaction parameter χ_{AB} of the blend (see Table 10.1). The observed negative value of χ_{AB} (dependent on the molecular weight of PEO in the blend) supported the miscibility of the two polymers in the examined composition range.

10.3.8 Crystallization Behavior of Crystalline/Crystalline Blends

Miscible blends containing both crystallizable components can crystallize in various modes, following *separate* crystallization, *concurrent* crystallization, or *co-crystallization* of the two polymers. Concurrent (or simultaneous) crystallization can take place when the crystallization temperature range of the components is coincident, whereas co-crystallization is possible if the polymer chains of the polymers are isomorphous, that is, they give rise to a single crystal phase. In the latter case, besides the melt miscibility, a close similarity of chain conformation, crystal lattice symmetry and dimensions are necessary, as in the case of isomorphous poly(vinyl fluoride)/poly(vinylidene fluoride), poly(isopropyl vinyl ether)/poly(sec-butyl-vinyl ether), and isotactic poly(4-methyl pentene)/isotactic poly(4-methyl hexene) blends [3]. In some cases, as reported for miscible blends of PVDF and poly-β-hydroxybutyrate (PHB) [52], a number of peculiar morphological and kinetic features—such as separated spherulitic crystallization, "interpenetrating," or "interfilling" crystallization phenomena—have been observed, depending on thermal treatments. The growth process of interpenetrating spherulites has been examined by Ikehara et al. [53, 54] for miscible blends of poly(butylene adipate-co-butylene succinate) (PBAS) and poly(butylene succinate) (PBSU) with PEO. Spherulites of PBAS and PBSU grow, filling the whole volume before PEO spherulites nucleate and grow inside them. It was reported that PBSU spherulites contain extended amorphous zones and the molecular mobility of PEO molecules inside the spherulites is little hindered, so that the temperature dependence of growth rate of PEO spherulites could be described by the same equation used for crystalline/amorphous blends [54].

Several examples of miscible blends with both crystallizable components have been reported for polyolefins and olefin copolymers, such as high density polyethylene (HDPE)/linear low density polyethylene (LLDPE), HDPE/very low density polyethylene (VLDPE), LDPE/VLDPE, and PP/PB, with the occurrence of concurrent crystallization and/or co-crystallization phenomena [19,

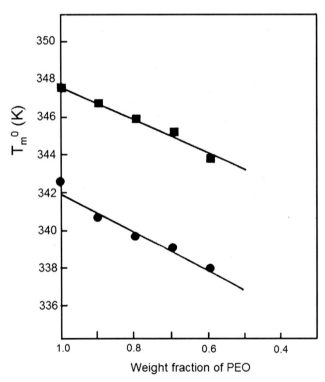

Figure 10.9 Equilibrium melting temperature (T_m^o) of PEO in PEO-100K/PMMA blends as a function of PEO content. Lower line: extrapolated values from optical microscopy observations (heating rate: 1°K/min); upper line: extrapolated values from DSC measurements (heating rate: 20°K/min). Reprinted from Martuscelli et al. [37], Copyright 1984, with permission from Elsevier.

55]. For these systems it is expected that both chemical structure of the components and comonomer content largely affect the miscibility in the melt and the crystallization process.

10.3.8.1 Isotactic Polypropylene/Poly(1-butene) Blends

Blends of iPP with isotactic poly(1-butene) (iPB) were reported to be miscible in any proportion in the melt with a single composition-dependent T_g [56, 57]. In general, iPP and iPB crystallize separately, although the occurrence of partial co-crystallization was observed for blends cooled from the melt at very high cooling rates and iPP can nucleate the growth of iPB crystals [58]. A detailed study of the isothermal crystallization behavior and morphology of iPP/iPB blends at various compositions by Canetti et al. [59] showed that the spherulite growth rate and the overall crystallization rate of iPP in the blends are depressed by the presence of molten iPB (in the range of $T_c = 125–135°C$, where only iPP crystallizes). The spherulite texture of iPP became less regular with a coarse fibrillar structure for iPB content ≥ 30 wt%, without showing phase separation of the noncrystallizing component in interspherulitic zones. Moreover, a significant decrease in the equilibrium melting temperature of iPP (from 183°C to 173°C) was observed with increasing the iPB content. As a consequence, following the Flory–Huggins theory, a negative value of the interaction parameter ($\chi_{AB} = -0.257$) was disclosed, supporting the miscibility of the components in the amorphous state. The isothermal crystallization kinetics of iPP in the blends even displayed a significant dependence of the overall crystallization rate on the iPB concentration. Following the Avrami equation (Eq. 10.14) a value of $n = 3$ was recorded for all examined samples, according to a three-dimensional crystal growth initiated by heterogeneous nucleation. The temperature dependence of the kinetic constant K_n was then analyzed according to Equation (10.17) for a polymer–diluent system: for all blend compositions straight lines were obtained by plotting $f(K_n)$ as a function of $T_m^o/(fT_c\Delta T)$, from which values of σ_e were calculated. A marked decrease of σ_e was found with increasing the iPB amount, indicating that a fraction of the amorphous component had likely segregated in the crystalline regions of iPP spherulites [59].

Further investigations [60] carried out on iPP/iPB blends crystallized either at high ($T_c = 67–82°C$) or low ($T_c = 119–130°C$) undercoolings showed that the two polymer components are miscible in the melt but undergo (partial) phase separation when annealed at a high temperature, giving rise, on the crystallization, to a two-phase morphology with iPB-rich inclusions dispersed within an iPP-rich matrix (Fig. 10.10). The extent of phase separation and the relevant phase composition were dependent on the temperature and time of annealing.

The miscibility of the components also affects the primary nucleation behavior of the crystallizing polymer. In iPP/iPB blends the presence of iPB influences both heterogeneous and homogeneous nucleation of iPP spherulites. The rates of homogeneous nucleation and spherulite growth of iPP were related to the variation of the average spherulite radius as a function of the crystallization temperature [61].

At high crystallization temperatures ($T_c > 119°C$), where iPB does not crystallize, only heterogeneous nucleation is active for iPP crystallization and the number of primary nuclei per unit volume (primary nucleation density) of iPP in the blend decreases with increasing the iPB concentration. In fact the presence of iPB, at least partially miscible with iPP, limits the nucleating activity of the heterogeneities likely due to an increase of the energy barrier for the formation of critical nuclei. At low crystallization temperatures ($T_c < 82°C$) the primary homogeneous nucleation of iPP is active. At intermediate crystallization temperatures both heterogeneous and homogeneous nucleation are operating. The rate of homogeneous nucleation of iPP also decreases as the iPB content increases, as a consequence of the separation process of iPP from the molten blend during its crystallization and the rise of the energy barrier for the secondary nucleation.

At very low crystallization temperatures ($T_c < 75°C$), the growth of iPB crystals in the blends proceeds simultaneously with the crystallization of iPP. The presence of iPB crystals may induce additional nucleation of iPP at the interface between the two polymers; thus, two populations of spherulites can appear in the blends: small iPB spherulites nucleated inside the iPB-rich phase and iPP spherulites nucleated at the interfaces. As a consequence of the above phenomena, the size of iPP spherulites in blends decreases at large undercooling, while it increases at low undercoolings, as compared with plain iPP crystallized at the same T_c [60].

10.3.8.2 Blends of Polypropylene Copolymers

Blends of iPP with random propylene-co-ethylene copolymers have been reported to be miscible and co-crystallizable [62]. In recent years several new copolymers of propylene (PP) with higher α-olefins have been synthesized due to the introduction of new metallocene catalysts. Propylene/1-hexene and propylene/1-octene copolymers have been reported to show thermodynamic properties, storage modulus, and density that decrease in a linear pattern with increasing comonomer content [63, 64]. Blending of copolymers offers the opportunity of designing innovative materials whose properties can be suitably modulated by varying both

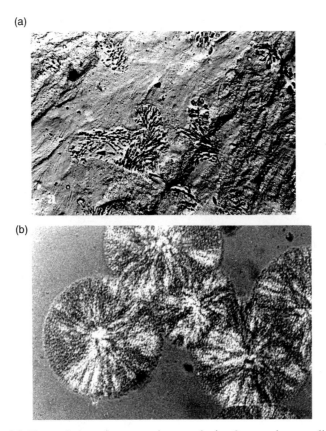

Figure 10.10 (a) Transmission electron micrograph (surface carbon replica) of etched surface of iPP/iPB (70/30) blend crystallized nonisothermally after melting at 190°C, showing lamellar crystals of iPB grown inside the iPP spherulites. (b) Polarizing optical micrograph of iPP spherulites in iPP/iPB (50/50) blend isothermally crystallized at 130°C (320×). The shape and position of iPB inclusions inside the iPP spherulites suggest that phase separation of the two polymers had occurred in the melt before the iPP crystallization. The number and size of iPB inclusions increase with increasing the iPB content [60]. Reprinted from Bartczak et al. [60], Copyright 1984, with permission from John Wiley & Sons, Inc.

blend composition and microstructure of copolymers (structure and amount of comonomer). Miscible blends of propylene-co-ethylene copolymers with different ethylene content were reported to show mixed morphological textures of α-type radial lamellae with γ-type overgrowths and α-crosshatched lamellae, lamellar thickness depending on the copolymer structure and content, and multiple melting behavior that was ascribed to distinct crystal populations [65].

Blends of isotactic propylene-co-ethylene (EP, 3–4.6 mol% ethylene) and propylene-co-1-butene (BP, 7.6 mol% 1-butene) random copolymers were studied by Bartczak et al. [66, 67]. The authors investigated the effect of type, content, and distribution of comonomer units on the miscibility of the components, the crystallization behavior, morphology, and thermal and mechanical properties.

The morphological and structural characteristics of the copolymers and their blends (EP/BP) at various compositions were examined for samples crystallized under different conditions in a wide temperature range—from 60°C to 132°C—by optical microscopy, scanning electron microscopy (SEM), wide-angle X-ray scattering (WAXS), small-angle X-ray scattering (SAXS), and small-angle light scattering (SALS) techniques. In all cases the characteristic spherulitic morphology of isotactic polypropylene (iPP) with α monoclinic crystal structure was found. No change of spherulite morphology was detected with varying the copolymer structure or blend composition, and no phase separation phenomena of the copolymers were observed during the crystallization. For samples crystallized at large undercoolings ($T_c = 60$–$90°C$) with very high crystallization rates, the average radius of the α-type spherulites, determined from SALS patterns, was found to depend on temperature, blend composition and copolymer type [66]. The decrease in the spherulite size with increasing fraction of BP copolymer was associated with

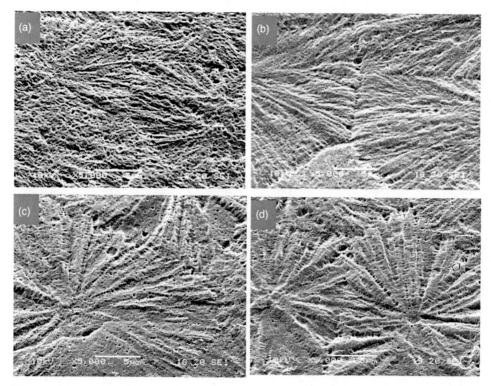

Figure 10.11 SEM micrographs of etched samples of ethylene-propylene copolymer (EPS: 3.0 mol-% ethylene), propylene-(1-butene) copolymer (BPS: 7.6 mol-% 1-butene), and their blends crystallized nonisothermally from the melt. (a): BPS; (b): EPS; (c): BPS/EPS 75/25; (d): BPS/EPS 50/50. Reprinted from Bartczak et al. [66], Copyright 2004, with permission from Elsevier.

a change of primary nucleation, due to activation of the homogeneous nucleation mode (in addition to already active heterogeneous nucleation). WAXS spectra of copolymer blends revealed a shift of the diffraction maxima, which was accounted for by the expansion of the crystal lattice in copolymers, as compared with plain iPP, suggesting that comonomer units must be incorporated in the crystals at least to some extent [68].

The spherulite growth rate, G, of EP and BP copolymers, measured in both isothermal and dynamic conditions, is found to be lower than that of PP homopolymer (BP < EP < PP), and the values of G for the blends are intermediate between those of plain components. Finer details of the spherulitic structure as obtained by scanning electron microscopy (SEM) analysis of plain copolymers and their blends, crystallized from the melt and subjected to permanganic etching, are shown in Figure 10.11. The morphology of α-type spherulites of EPS copolymer (Fig. 10.11b) appears less regular than that of iPP. On the other hand, spherulites of propylene-(1-butene) copolymer (BPS) show a more open and loose texture (Fig. 10.11a) with irregular and diffuse boundaries, resulting from the relatively large amount of noncrystallizable units in this copolymer (9.9 wt% 1-butene), which are most probably rejected into interlamellar layers and trapped here. Micrographs of blends BPS/EPS (Fig. 10.11c,d) reveal a quite open internal structure of spherulites in the blends, depending on the composition. In any of the blends the components did not give rise to separated phases, suggesting that BP copolymer is miscible with the examined EP copolymers in the whole range of composition.

The overall crystallization kinetics of copolymers and their blends have been studied by DSC in the temperature range 100–132°C [69]. For all examined blend compositions a single crystallization exotherm was observed at each T_c, whereas crystallization of mechanical mixtures of the copolymers showed separated exotherms of each component, thus supporting that the crystallization of melt mixed blends occurred from a homogeneous melt. The overall crystallization rate of copolymers was found to be affected by the copolymer structure and lower than that of PP homopolymer (BP < EP < PP), while the crystallization rate of the blends was intermediate between those of pure components (Fig. 10.12). The kinetics were analyzed by means of the Avrami equation (Eq. 10.14); the calculated values of the Avrami exponent for the blends, with average values of n from

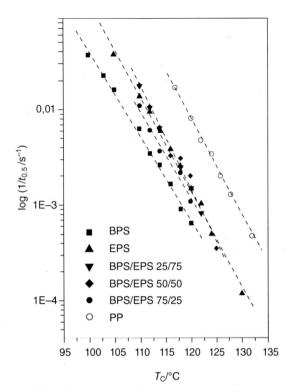

Figure 10.12 Reciprocal of half-time of crystallization, $t_{1/2}$ as a function of crystallization temperature, T_c for isotactic PP, ethylene-propylene copolymer (EPS: 3.0 mol-% ethylene), propylene-(1-butene) copolymer (BPS: 7.6 mol-% 1-butene), and EPS/BPS blends isothermally crystallized from the melt [69].

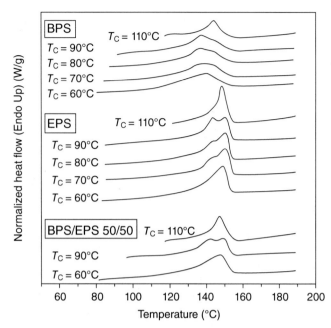

Figure 10.13 DSC melting thermograms of ethylene-propylene copolymer (EPS: 3.0 mol-% ethylene), propylene-(1-butene) copolymer (BPS: 7.6 mol-% 1-butene), and BPS/EPS 50/50 blend after isothermal crystallization in the range of 60–110°C (heating rate: 10°C/min). Reprinted from Bartczak et al. [66], Copyright 2006, with permission from Elsevier.

3.4 to 2.7, were consistent with a spherulitic growth, initiated by heterogeneous nucleation [69].

Melting thermograms of isothermally crystallized samples of pure copolymers and PP are shown in Figure 10.13. For copolymers and blends crystallized at $T_c > 100°C$, multiple melting peaks have been generally observed, whose position and intensity depend on both crystallization temperature and blend composition (type and amount of copolymers). The analysis of melting behavior of the samples using different heating rates indicated the presence of distinct crystal types with different stability and degree of perfection, influenced by the copolymer structure. Linear plots of the observed melting temperature T_m versus T_c were obtained for all blends, with values of the lamellar thickening parameter (γ) slightly higher than 1. The extrapolated equilibrium melting temperatures, T_m^o of BP copolymer (162°C) and EP copolymers (170–173°C), were lower than that of PP (192°C) and the extrapolated T_m^o's of blends were intermediate between those of plain copolymers. Thus, the depression of the temperatures could be accounted for by the occurrence of miscibility phenomena.

The effect of chain irregularities on the depression of the melting point (and heat of fusion) of PP was analyzed using two extreme models, assuming that the defective chain segments are either included into (uniform inclusion model) or rejected completely from the lattice (exclusion model). Equilibrium melting temperatures of BP and EP copolymers were calculated according to the exclusion model based on Flory's equation [70]:

$$1/T_m^o - 1/T_{m\,cop}^o = (R/\Delta H_m^o)\ln(1 - X_{cop}) \quad (10.22)$$

where T_m^o and $T_{m\,cop}^o$ are the equilibrium melting temperatures of homopolymer and copolymer, respectively; ΔH_m^o is the melting entalpy of iPP crystal; and X_{cop} is the mole fraction of comonomer units. The calculated T_m^o's were higher than the experimental ones, indicating that some comonomer inclusion occurs in the crystal structure of the copolymers.

The free energy barrier associated with the secondary nucleation ($\Delta\Phi^*$) and the folding surface free energy of crystals (σ_e) in the blends were then determined on the basis of Equation (10.16) from the slopes of the linear plots. The σ_e values (80–100 × 10^{-3} J/m^2) were consistent with those reported in the literature for PP homopolymer and copolymers (60–120 × 10^{-3} J/m^2) [71].

10.4 IMMISCIBLE POLYMER BLENDS

10.4.1 Introduction

Crystallizable immiscible blends may consist of both crystallizable polymer components (crystalline/crystalline blends), or of one crystalline component (crystalline/amorphous blends), which can be present as matrix phase or as dispersed phase. The crystallization behavior and the structure–properties relationships of immiscible blends of various polymer classes have been investigated by numerous authors; a comprehensive overview of the crystallization phenomena and morphological characteristics of these systems has been reported in References [19, 72].

In general, for immiscible polymer blends the properties are strictly controlled by their phase morphology, depending on the processing conditions, molecular characteristics, and interfacial properties. Although the crystallization of each component takes place in domains separated from the other blend component and with different kinetic conditions, the presence of the second (crystalline or amorphous) polymer can induce marked variations on the primary nucleation phenomena [61], crystal growth, and superstructure, due to effects such as the type and degree of dispersion of the polymers, their chemical structure, and molecular weight, the type of interface, and the crystallization conditions. For blends with crystallizable matrix either nucleating effects or variations of spherulite morphology and growth rate, as compared with plain crystalline polymer, may be observed. Moreover, significant changes in the overall crystallinity, bulk crystallization kinetics, and melting behavior have been reported. On the other hand, important phenomena, such as *fractionated* crystallization may be observed in the crystallization behavior when the crystallizable component constitutes the dispersed phase, depending on its dispersion degree.

10.4.2 Morphology and Crystal Nucleation

The morphological types of immiscible blends can be broadly classified into two main categories: (1) blends with discrete phase structure and (2) blends with bicontinuous phase structure. Other types of morphologies include fibrillar, core-shell, and onion-like structures. In blends with discrete phase structure, such as droplets in a matrix, the morphology development during melt mixing of immiscible polymers involves the formation of ribbons and threads of the dispersed phase in the matrix, breakup of the threads into smaller droplet-like particles, and then coalescence of the droplets into larger ones up to reach the final particle size, as a result of the equilibrium between the breakup and the coalescence of the particles [73]. The parameters that control the process of droplet formation concern the blend composition, melt viscosity ratio, shear rate, and interfacial tension: the dispersion of the minor phase is enhanced for high matrix viscosity, large shear rates, and small values of interfacial tension. According to the empirical relation by Wu [74], the minimum particle size of the dispersed phase is obtained when the viscosities of the components are close each other:

$$\eta_m D \gamma / \Gamma = 4(p)^{\pm 0.84} \quad (10.23)$$

where η_m is the viscosity of the matrix, D is the shear rate during the mixing process, γ is the particle size, Γ is the interfacial tension of the blend, and p the viscosity ratio of dispersed phase to matrix. As the viscosity ratio of the components is higher or lower than 1, the size of the dispersed particles becomes larger. In fact, the deformation and breakup of the liquid threads into droplets is favored when a lower viscosity component is dispersed into a high viscosity matrix (in the opposite case, the dispersed particles tends to retain their size and deformation is reduced) [75].

The formation of "droplet-in-droplet" morphology (or composite droplet morphology) has also been reported for immiscible systems (Fig. 10.14). For binary blends this type of morphology can be spontaneously generated when blending is carried out near the phase inversion region of the two polymer components. The formation of the inclusions is mainly controlled by the value of the interfacial tension.

The presence of co-continuous phase morphology, which consists of at least two coexisting, continuous, and interconnected phases throughout the whole blend volume, is the other important superstructural characteristic

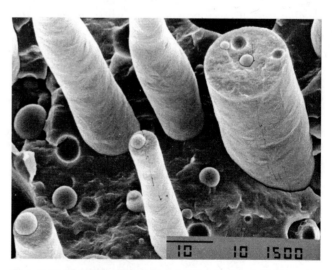

Figure 10.14 SEM micrograph of the fracture surface of a polyamide-6 (PA6)/PP (40/60) blend obtained by extrusion from the melt at 250°C [114].

of immiscible systems. Co-continuous polymer blends have several advantages due to some useful properties (synergistic mechanical properties, selective permeability, etc.) that make them available for various technological applications. Morphologies of co-continuous type can be obtained by freezing from partially miscible blends during the spinodal demixing process, as a consequence of the thermodynamic instability of these systems; co-continuous microphase or macrophase morphologies can be even formed on melt mixing of immiscible polymers under particular conditions, depending on the composition, chemical structure of the components, rheological parameters, or in the presence of phase inversion phenomena [76]. In particular, the development of co-continuous morphologies has been reported for compatibilized immiscible systems with strong interactions at the interfaces, affecting the interfacial tension, droplet formation, and coalescence phenomena.

For immiscible blends with crystallizable matrix and amorphous dispersed phase, the crystal growth and the final morphology can be significantly influenced by the noncrystallizable component, with large changes in the primary nucleation density (number of nuclei per unit volume of crystallisable polymer), as well as in the size, shape, size distribution, texture, and crystallinity degree of the spherulitic superstructures.

The crystal formation, which is controlled by the heterogeneous nucleation under usual crystallization conditions, depends on the number and type of heterogeneities (impurities, catalysts, crystal residues from incomplete melting) present into the melt and characterized by a proper activation energy for the formation of critical sized primary nuclei, at each value of undercooling ($\Delta T = T_m° - T_c$). The number of "active" nuclei for the crystallizable polymer can vary, depending on the thermal history of the sample, melt annealing, and crystallization conditions. Thus, during the cooling at T_c, different types of heterogeneities become active for nucleation and this, consequently, will affect the spherulite size. However, in a blend, the number of heterogeneous nuclei may also change—as compared to the plain polymer in the same crystallization conditions—owing to "migration phenomena" at the interface between the molten phases during the mixing process (see Section 10.4.4.1). The migration of heterogeneities occurs when the interfacial free energy of the impurities within their melt phase is higher than the interfacial energy of those impurities within the other melt phase of the blend [77, 78]. Moreover, changes in the heterogeneous nucleation of a crystallizable component in an immiscible blend may occur due to the effect of surface nucleation at the interface between the phases. This effect will depend on the degree of dispersion, the morphology, and the physical state of the dispersed phase, which in turn are influenced by blend composition, melt viscosity of both phases, and interfacial tension.

When the crystallizable component in the immiscible blend constitutes the dispersed phase and it is finely dispersed as small droplets into the matrix, the crystallization can take place in several steps (fractionated crystallization)—corresponding to different undercoolings larger than the usual undercooling for the crystallization of the neat polymer. DSC cooling thermograms of such systems exibit multiple crystallization exotherms: the lowest temperature exotherm with the largest undercooling is usually associated with homogeneous nucleation. This phenomen is controlled by the distribution and the typology/activity of heterogeneous nuclei present within the droplets, and depends on the droplet size, as it will be more extensively discussed in the Section 10.5.3.1.

10.4.3 Crystal Growth Rate

During the crystallization of the matrix, the droplet-like dispersed amorphous component may be either occluded between the lamellar stacks in intraspherulitic domains, or rejected at the spherulite borders in amorphous interspherulitic zones, or only partially rejected over some distance. In several immiscible systems a partial rejection of small amorphous domains is observed, forming inclusions that can be deformed by the growing front. These phenomena disturb the growth process of the crystals and can cause a change in the growth rate, as a consequence of new energy barriers associated with the rejection and deformation of the amorphous domains. The resulting effect can be expressed by means of a modified equation of the spherulite growth rate [79]:

$$G = G_p \exp[-(E_1 + E_2 + E_3 + E_4)/k_B T_c] \qquad (10.24)$$

where G_p is the growth rate of the plain crystallizable polymer (as described by Eq. 10.9), E_1 is the energy necessary for the rejection of the droplets (proportional to the melt viscosity), E_2 is the energy required to overcome the inertia of the inclusions, E_3 is the energy of formation of new interfaces when the droplets are engulfed, and E_4 is the energy dissipated for the deformation of the engulfed particles. The driving force for the rejection, occlusion, or deformation process is given by the difference existing between the interfacial energy crystal/inclusion (γ_{PS}) and the interfacial energy melt/inclusion (γ_{PL}): when the difference ($\gamma_{PS} - \gamma_{PL}$) is positive, the droplets are rejected, whereas if the difference of interfacial energies is negative the droplets are occluded. For some immiscible blends, it has been calculated that

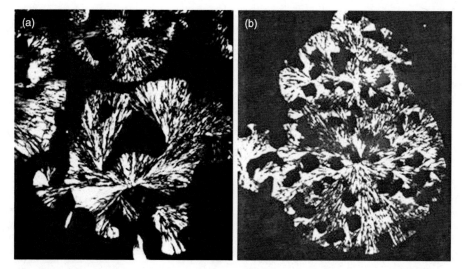

Figure 10.15 Polarizing optical micrographs of iPP spherulites in an iPP/LDPE (50/50) blend during isothermal crystallization at (a) $T_c = 129°C$ and (b) $T_c = 135°C$ (200×). The iPP crystalline lamellae (birefringent zones) surround the molten LDPE occlusions (dark area). Reprinted From Galeski et al. [80], Copyright 1984, with permission from John Wiley & Sons, Inc.

mainly the energy dissipated for the rejection of the inclusions causes a depression of the spherulite growth rate.

Galeski et al. [80] analyzed the morphology and the spherulite growth rate of iPP in blends with LDPE, during isothermal crystallization at T_c's where the LDPE dispersed phase does not crystallize. They found that the shape and orientation of LDPE droplets occluded within the growing spherulites remain undisturbed after the crystallization front had passed, indicating that the same front does not deform the molten droplets, neither does it push them out to the spherulite borders (interspherulitic zones). However, the LDPE droplets do serve as obstacles to the spherulite growth front, causing the formation of concavities (Fig. 10.15) whose shape is due to the non-coincident front of the lamellae surrounding the occlusion from opposite sides and forming a boundary beyond the occlusion.

Based on a simple model shown in Figure 10.16, which describes the effect of retardation (area ACE = ΔS) caused by the occlusion on the growing front, the growth rate G' of the spherulites in the blend was calculated—for a two-dimensional growth—by the relation [80]:

$$G' = G[1 - c(\Delta S/\pi R^2)] \qquad (10.25)$$

where G is the growth rate of iPP spherulites in the neat polymer (at the same T_c), c is the concentration of LDPE in the blend, and R is the average droplet radius. Assuming a monodisperse size distribution of LDPE inclusions, it was estimated that the depression of growth

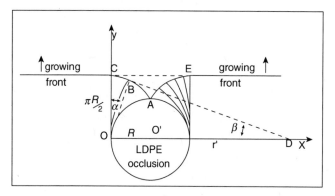

Figure 10.16 Schematic drawing of an iPP spherulite growing around an LDPE dispersed droplet. The profile of growing front beyond the occlusion is described by the equation: $r = (\pi R/2\alpha)\sin\alpha$. Reprinted From Galeski et al. [80], Copyright 1984 with permission from John Wiley & Sons, Inc.

rate in the blend is around 5% for an LDPE content of 50%, independently of the size of LDPE particles, and a similar value was obtained in the case of a three-dimensional growth model. Accordingly, the experimental growth rates of iPP spherulites in the blends, measured at various T_c, were only little affected by the content of the dispersed polymer.

10.4.4 Crystallization Behavior of Immiscible Blends

The properties of these systems depend on the composition and the morphological characteristics, which in turn are affected by the crystallization conditions. Generally, because in the melt the two polymer phases are separated, the crystallization behavior of blends with both crystallizable components follows the same path as for crystalline/amorphous blends. Usually, the two components crystallize separately at temperatures that are almost near the characteristic crystallization temperatures of the neat polymers, but even large changes can be observed, depending on the degree of dispersion of the minor phase into the matrix, with appearance of fractionated or retarded crystallization phenomena. Changes in the primary nucleation density and nucleating activity may be also found due to the occurrence of migration of heterogeneities between the phases in the melt. The two polymers in the blend can crystallize sequentially or even simultaneously (coincident crystallization) [19].

When the crystallization of the matrix polymer takes place in the presence of a molten dispersed phase, the crystallization behavior is comparable to that of crystalline/amorphous blends in which the amorphous component is the dispersed phase. However, a different behavior may be observed when the crystallization of the matrix occurs in the presence of a crystallized dispersed phase. Coincident crystallization of the components has been reported for blends in which the matrix phase has a crystallization temperature lower than that of the dispersed component, and this latter does not crystallize at its usual undercooling, owing to its very fine dispersion into the blend, which causes a lack of heterogeneities that is able to initiate the crystallization of the droplets at their characteristic T_c. In such case, as reported for PVDF/polyamide-6 (PA6) and PVDF/PBT blends [81], on cooling from the melt the molten dispersed phase can crystallize coincidently with the matrix, either at the same T_c of the matrix or at a somewhat higher T_c (intermediate between those of the neat components), acting as nucleating substrate for the matrix polymer.

10.4.4.1 Polyethylene/Polypropylene Blends
Blends of polyolefins represent one of the most studied polymer systems in the field of immiscible blends. Studies on blends of iPP with crystallizable and/or amorphous polyolefins, such as polyethylenes (PEs) of various density (HDPE, LDPE, LLDPE), atactic PP, propylene–etylene elastomers, and polyisobutylene, have shown that their properties depend strongly on the crystalline morphology, crystallization conditions, and composition [82]. In particular, considerable changes have been found in the spherulite nucleation, growth rate, and overall kinetics of crystallization of the blends as compared to pure iPP [83].

Studies on the crystallization kinetics of iPP/HDPE and iPP/LDPE blends showed that the overall crystallization rate of iPP matrix was largely depressed by the presence of the dispersed PE phase [40, 84]. Since the growth rate G of iPP spherulites (in the same T_c range)

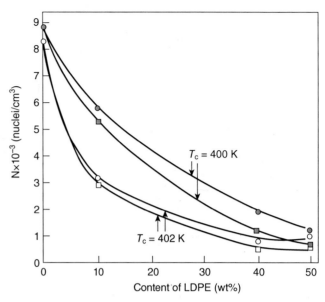

Figure 10.17 Primary nucleation density of iPP crystals in iPP/LDPE blends isothermally crystallized from melt, as a function of LDPE concentration. Values calculated from bulk crystallization kinetics, according to Equation (10.15), per volume of blend (squares) and per volume fraction of iPP in the blend (circles). Reprinted from Galeski et al. [77], Copyright 1984, with permission from Elsevier.

did not significantly change with the blend composition, it followed from the Avrami analysis that the change in crystallization rate from the melt (see Eq. 10.15) depended on changes in the spherulite nucleation density, which is reflected in the number of spherulites per unit volume. In Figure 10.17 the number of primary nuclei active for the growth of iPP spherulites in iPP/LDPE blends is plotted as a function of the LDPE content. It can be noticed that the nucleation density decreases rapidly as the LDPE content increases, in agreement with the observed variation of the number of spherulites in isothermally crystallized bulk samples [77]. As a consequence of the decrease in the nucleation density, the size distribution of the spherulites changed with the addition of LDPE: the average spherulite radius increased with increasing the concentration of the second component (Fig. 10.18). These results indicate that a part of the heterogeneous nuclei active in plain iPP disappears after addition of LDPE, which can be related to the migration of nuclei from the iPP matrix to the PE phase during the melt mixing.

Similar effects were reported for iPP/HDPE blends crystallized at temperatures higher than 127°C [78]. In order to verify the hypothesis of the migration of nuclei and its effect on the primary nucleation of the spherulites, crystallization experiments were carried out on iPP/HDPE blends containing nucleating agents—that is sodium benzoate and magnesium sulphate—active for the crystallization of polypropylene (PP) (at higher T_c)

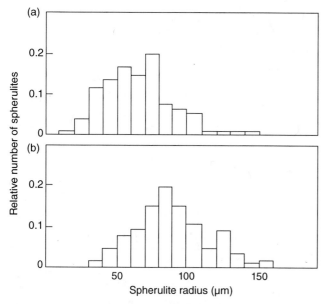

Figure 10.18 Spherulite size distribution for (a) iPP and (b) iPP/LDPE (80/20) blend, measured from thin sections of isothermally crystallized bulk samples ($T_c = 131°C$). Reprinted from Galeski et al. [77], Copyright 1984, with permission from Elsevier.

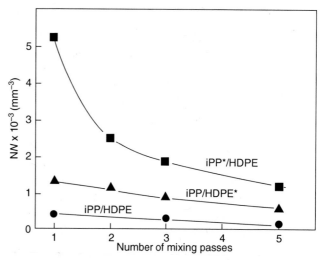

Figure 10.19 Number of primary nuclei per unit volume in iPP/HDPE (80/20) blend films isothermally crystallized at $T_c = 132°C$, containing sodium benzoate as nucleating agent (0.2 wt%), versus the number of mixing passes in extruder. (squares): iPP*/HDPE; (triangles): iPP/HDPE*; (circles): iPP/HDPE (the asterisk indicates the polymer component to which the nucleating agent was initially added). Reprinted from Bartczak et al. [78], Copyright 1986, with permission from Elsevier.

and PE (at lower T_c), respectively. The blends, containing one polymer component with the previously added nucleating agent, were mixed several times in extruder; after each mixing pass, a sample of blend was crystallized isothermally to examine the change of nucleation density as well as the size distribution of spherulites. For comparison, a blend iPP/HDPE obtained with the same mixing process but without nucleating agent was analyzed using the same crystallization conditions. Figure 10.19 shows the values of nucleation density for iPP/HDPE (80/20) blends, as a function of the number of mixing passes.

It can be recognized that when sodium benzoate was initially added to iPP, the number of primary nuclei in the blend with additivated iPP (iPP*/HDPE)—at the first mixing stage—was much larger than that of blend containing additivated HDPE (iPP/HDPE*) and of the reference blend (iPP/HDPE). Then, with increasing number of mixing passes the nucleation density of spherulites in the iPP*/HDPE blend rapidly decreases down to a value near that of nonadditivated iPP, suggesting that most of nucleating particles passed from iPP* to HDPE during the melt mixing. On the contrary, only a few nuclei could move from additivated HDPE* to iPP.

The driving force for the migration of primary nuclei across the interface between the blend components is determined by the difference of interfacial free energy of the nuclei when they are surrounded by molten iPP and by molten HDPE. At crystallization temperatures lower than 127°C a different situation was observed: the nucleation density increased with increasing the HDPE content owing to the formation of PE crystals (able to grow at those T_c) inside the dispersed phase, which can act as heterogeneous nuclei for iPP at the interface in the melt. This caused an increase in the nucleation density of iPP in the blends, as compared to plain iPP crystallized at the same temperature, and consequently, a decrease in the spherulite size.

The analysis of the temperature dependence of growth rate and overall kinetic constant (Eq. 10.9 and Eq. 10.16) for iPP/HDPE and iPP/LDPE blends has shown that the free energy associated with secondary nucleation and the surface free energy of iPP crystals were also influenced by the concentration of noncrystallizing polymer [40, 84]. Linear plots of $(1/n)\ln K_n$ versus $T_m^o/(T_c\Delta T)$, for iPP/LDPE blends, are shown in Figure 10.20. In particular, a decrease of $\Delta\Phi^*$ (at constant undercooling) and σ_e was recorded for the blends with increasing the PE content.

10.5 COMPATIBILIZED POLYMER BLENDS

10.5.1 Compatibilization Methods

In many articles on polymer blends the term "compatibility" is often used with different and, sometimes, controversial meanings: it is frequently used as synonymous with miscibility, referring to systems that are

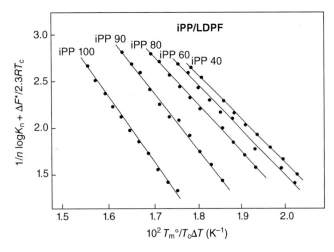

Figure 10.20 Plots of $(1/n)\ln K_n + \Delta F^*/RT_c$ versus $T_m^o/(T_c\Delta T)$ according to Equation (10.16) for iPP/LDPE blends at various compositions (wt% iPP) isothermally crystallized from the melt $[\Delta F^* = 4120\, T_c/(51.6 + T_c - T_g)]$. Reprinted from Martuscelli et al. [84], Copyright 1984, with permission from John Wiley & Sons.

thermodynamically miscible on molecular scale, or more commonly it is applied in a wider sense to immiscible (or partially miscible) blends that do not exhibit large phase separation phenomena and can display a set of useful properties that are more advantageous than those of the single pure components [85]. The latter definition is certainly little scientifically straightforward but offers the opportunity to extend the study of polymer blends properties to a large number of systems (mainly including crystallizable components) that are not miscible from the thermodynamic point of view but can be suitably modified, that is, compatibilized, obtaining improved morphological, physical, and mechanical characteristics that can be modulated by varying composition and processing conditions. In other words, compatibilization may be defined as "a process of modification of interfacial properties of an immiscible polymer blend, leading to creation of a polymer alloy" [86].

Most polymers forming immiscible blends require compatibilization to reach stable and defined properties. According to Utracki [5], compatibilization processes of polymer blends must accomplish three fundamental tasks: (1) reduce the interfacial tension, thus improving the phase dipersion, (2) stabilize the morphology against thermal or shear effects during the melt processing, (3) induce interfacial adhesion in the solid state. The main compatibilization methods—either chemical or physical—include the addition of block or graft copolymers, addition of functionalized polymers and/or copolymers, reactive blending of polymers (reactive compatibilization). The use of each of the above methods depends on various factors, for example, type and amount of polymer, blending process, specific properties and applications.

The compatibilization largely affects the phase morphology of the blends and the interfacial properties, thus it may significantly influence the crystallization behavior of the polymer components and the structure of crystalline phases. In the next paragraphs some examples of blends compatibilized by means of different methods will be presented, with focus on the morphological aspects, phase interaction phenomena, and crystallization behavior.

10.5.2 Morphology and Phase Interactions

10.5.2.1 Blends Compatibilized by Addition of Copolymers

The addition of (nonreactive) block or graft copolymers represents one of the most important approaches to the blend compatibilization. In particular, block (or graft) copolymers containing chain segments with chemical structure similar or identical to the blend components are expected to favor the dispersion and interfacial adhesion between the incompatible polymer components due to the miscibility of the copolymer segments with the corresponding blend components. The requirement that the copolymer should locate preferentially at the interface between the components is strictly related to the molecular weight and chain structure of the copolymer segments [2, 87].

The influence of copolymer structure on the compatibilizing effectiveness has been extensively examined for several blends of polyolefins. Addition of graft (PS-g-LDPE) and block copolymers for the compatibilization of LDPE/PS blends has been reported by various authors, resulting in large improvement of interfacial adhesion and mechanical properties [88, 89]. Ethylene–propylene copolymers (EP) with block and random distribution of units have been used as compatibilizers for blends of PP with HDPE, LDPE, and LLDPE [90, 91], and EPDM-g-PP copolymers were successfully employed for the compatibilization of EP/PP blends [92].

The compatibilizing effect of block copolymers styrene-b-(ethylene-co-butylene)-b-styrene (SEBS) and styrene-b-(ethylene-co-propylene) with two (SEP) and four (SEPSEP) blocks respectively, having different styrene content in the copolymer chain, has been analyzed for blends of poly(ethylene terephthalate) (PET) and iPP [93]. Generally, the addition of any of these copolymers was found to improve the morphology, resulting in increased phase dispersion and reduced coalescence (see Section 10.4.2). The effect of polymer type on the phase morphology of blends with PET matrix is evidenced in the SEM micrographs of Figure

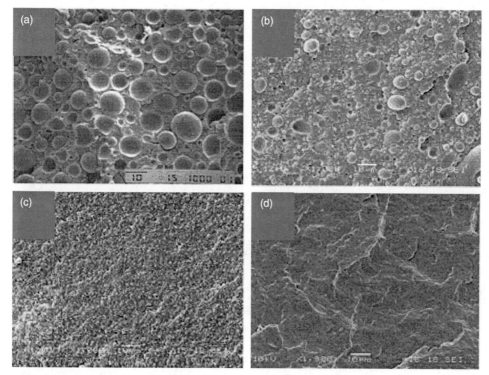

Figure 10.21 SEM micrographs of fracture surfaces of PET/PP blends compatibilized with SEBS, SEP, and SEPSEP block copolymers. (a) PET/PP (75/25), (b) PET/PP/SEBS (75/25/10), (c) PET/PP/SEPSEP (75/25/10), (d) PP/SEBS (75/25) (bar length: 10 μm). The block copolymer content is expressed in part per hundred (phr). Reprinted from Pracella et al. [93], Copyright 2005, with permission from John Wiley & Sons, Inc.

10.21. The noncompatibilized blend PET/PP (75/25) shows a neat phase separation of the components with an average size of PP particles of about 6 μm (Fig. 10.21a). In the compatibilized blends the average size of the minor phase decreased to about 2 μm with addition of SEBS (10 phr) (Fig. 10.21b) and to about 1 μm with SEPSEP (10 phr) (Fig. 10.21c).

The compatibilizing effectiveness of the various block copolymers is related to several aspects, such as the copolymer structure, the molecular weight, the concentration, and the location at the interface [89, 94]. Binary blends of PP and block copolymers were also examined in order to assess the compatibility between the polyolefin components [95]. It was found that binary blends PP/SEP and PP/SEBS (where PP is the major component) showed a finely dispersed copolymer phase with a nearly homogeneous morphology (see Fig. 10.21d).

10.5.2.2 Blends Compatibilized by Addition of Functionalized Polymers

The addition of functional/reactive polymers to immiscible blends is a very versatile method to promote the compatibilization of a large number of heterogeneous polymer systems. Usually, a polymer chemically similar or identical to one of the blend components is modified—by grafting or copolymerization reactions—with functional molecules (i.e., anhydrides, carboxyl acids, epoxides, etc.) that are able to give rise to covalent bonding, polar, or ionic interactions with the second polymer component (reactive compatibilization). Thus, the presence of the modified polymer as third component can promote—through reactions at the interface—the formation of graft or crosslinked copolymers between the polymers, contributing to decrease the interfacial energy between the components and to improve the phase dispersion and interfacial adhesion by chain interpenetration and entanglements.

The addition of functionalized polymers offers the advantage to achieve the blend compatibilization (emulsifying effect) by using a small amount (a few percent) of modified component. This method has found large application, especially for blending of polyolefins with polar polymers, such as polyamides, polyesters, polyethers; moreover, it can be useful in the preparation of polymer composites with various types of fillers [96].

The compatibilization and the properties of blends of poly(ethylene terephthalate) (PET) and polyolefins have been the subject of several studies. PET/HDPE blends have been compatibilized by addition of maleic anhydride grafted polyolefins (HDPE-g-MA, EPR-g-MA, SEBS-g-MA), ethylene-*co*-acrylic acid copolymers (E-AA), ethylene-glycidyl methacrylate copolymers (E-GMA), and polyethylene grafted with glycidyl methacrylate (HDPE-*g*-GMA) [97]. Block copolymers, functionalized with glycidyl methacrylate (SEBS-*g*-GMA, SEP-*g*-GMA, SEPSEP-*g*-GMA), were also employed for the compatibilization of PET/PP blends [93, 98]. The morphological, rheological, and thermodynamic characteristics of the compatibilized blends were found to be strictly influenced by the type of functionalized polyolefin and its concentration, and the mixing procedures [99].

The effect of content of E-GMA copolymer on the average size of PE particles in compatibilized PET/HDPE blends is shown in Figure 10.22. The marked emulsifying effect of E-GMA is accompanied by a strong interfacial adhesion of the dispersed particles to the matrix phase, which can be related to a high reactivity of the GMA groups with PET chain ends at the interface. With increasing compatibilizer content, the average particle size decreases from a value of about 5 μm (for noncompatibilized blends) until an equilibrium value is reached, around 0.5 μm, at a copolymer concentration lower than 10 pph [99]. The equilibrium concentration roughly corresponds to the amount of copolymer necessary to saturate the interface, and in these conditions the particle size reduction is mainly due to suppression of coalescence. The amount of compatibilizer required to saturate the interface (C_{sat}) is a function of the molecular mass of compatibilizer (M), volume fraction of dispersed phase (Φ_d), and average radius of particles (R) [100]:

$$C_{sat} = 3\Phi_d M/(aRN_A) \quad (10.26)$$

where N_A is the Avogadro number. Assuming that all compatibilizer is located at the interface and determining the values of the saturation concentration and equilibrium particle size it is possible to estimate the area, a, occupied by a compatibilizer molecule at the interface, which can be related with the structure of the interphase [101].

Blends of PA6 and LDPE were compatibilized by melt mixing with various polyolefins functionalized with glycidyl methacrylate (LDPE-*g*-GMA, SEBS-*g*-GMA, E-GMA) [102, 103], acrylic acid (EAA), and maleic anhydride (LDPE-*g*-MA, SEBS-*g*-MA) [104, 105]. The compatibilized blends showed a neat improvement of phase dispersion and interfacial adhesion when compared to PA6/LDPE binary blends (Fig. 10.23). The

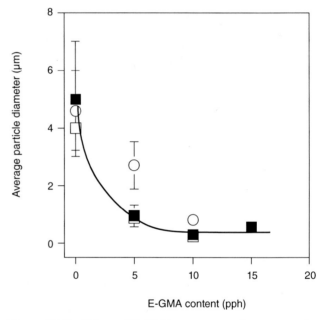

Figure 10.22 Effect of E-GMA content on the average size of HDPE particles in compatibilized PET/HDPE (75/25) blends. Squares: number-average diameter; circles: volume-average diameter. Reprinted from Pracella et al. [99], Copyright 2002, with permission from John Wiley & Sons.

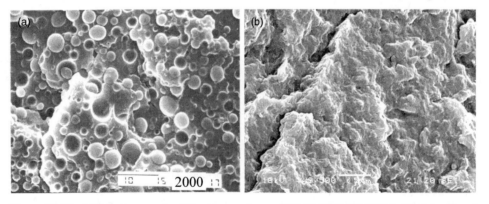

Figure 10.23 SEM micrographs of fracture surfaces of PA6/LDPE (75/25) blends (a) without compatibilizer and (b) compatibilized with 10 phr of LDPE-*g*-GMA (6.8 wt% GMA). Reprinted from Wei et al. [103], Copyright 2005, with permission from John Wiley & Sons.

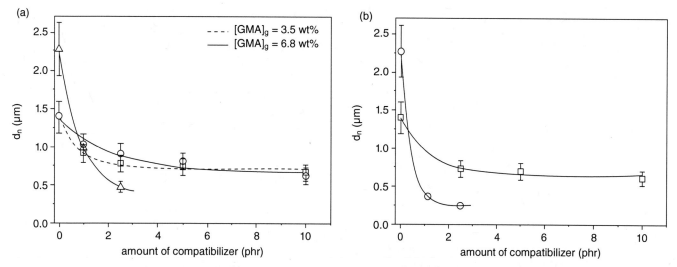

Figure 10.24 Emulsification curves for compatibilized PA6/LDPE blends. (a) PA6/LDPE 25/75 (□, ○) and 75/25 (△) blends compatibilized with LDPE-*g*-GMA; (b) PA6/LDPE 25/75 (□) and 75/25 (○) blends compatibilized with SEBS-*g*-GMA. Reprinted from Wei et al. [103], Copyright 2005, with permission from John Wiley & Sons.

effect of the addition of LDPE-*g*-GMA and SEBS-*g*-GMA copolymers on the phase dispersion in Ny6/LDPE blends, either with polyamide or polyolefin matrix, is shown in Figure 10.24 as a function of compatibilizer content. A very fine dispersion of the LDPE phase (<0.25 μm) in the PA6 matrix was observed on addition of SEBS-*g*-GMA copolymer (Fig. 10.24b). These effects were accounted for by the formation of interchain grafted copolymers at the interface due to the reaction between the epoxide groups of GMA and the carboxyl/amine end-groups of PA6 [102].

10.5.2.3 Blends Compatibilized by Reactive Blending

With respect to the other compatibilization methods, in reactive blending the polymer components containing reactive groups along the chains are processed in proper conditions in order to generate chemical reactions between the components during melt blending, which can give rise to *in situ* formation of (graft, block, or random) *interchain* copolymers acting as compatibilizers, without addition of other polymer components. In some cases, the interchain copolymers are generated during reactive processing in the melt through chain cleavage of polymers followed by recombination, as well as through mechanical scission and recombination under high shear processing. A comprehensive description of the reactive mixing processes is reported in References [86, 106]. In most cases the interchain graft copolymers are formed by reaction at the interface between reactive chain ends and pendant functional groups on the polymer backbone. Commonly, condensation polymers having carboxyl, amino, or hydroxyl end groups are able to form covalent bonds with functional groups, such as cyclic anhydrides, carboxyl acids, epoxides, oxazolines, and isocyanates, inserted along the chain of polyolefins, elastomers, and related copolymers. On the other side, block and random interchain copolymers are mainly formed during interchange reactions in the melt between polycarbonate, polyesters, and polyamides [107].

10.5.3 Crystallization Behavior of Compatibilized Blends

For PET/HDPE blends compatibilized by addition of functionalized polyolefins, the crystallization temperature of PET was found to be shifted to temperatures lower than those observed for plain PET and the noncompatibilized blends [99]. Moreover, the crystallinity degree of the polymers depended on the type and concentration of compatibilizer (Fig. 10.25). The crystallinity of both PET and HDPE phases was markedly depressed upon addition of HDPE-*g*-MA or E-GMA due to the effect of the chemical reactions of functional groups with PET and of the miscibility of the functionalized polyolefins with the HDPE phase. In fact, the crystallization of PET molecules near the interface is affected by the occurrence of interchain grafting reactions, which result in a reduced mobility of the chains and thus depression of crystallization temperature. With decreasing the size of dispersed particles the effect of compatibilizer on the crystallization of PET becomes more pronounced.

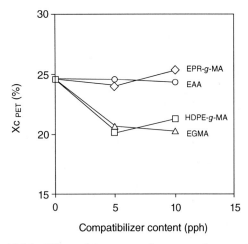

Figure 10.25 Effect of the type and content of compatibilizer (EPR-g-MA, HDPE-g-MA, E-AA, E-GMA) on the crystallinity degree, X_c of PET phase in a PET/HDPE (75/25) blend after crystallization from the melt at cooling rate of 10°C/min. Reprinted from Pracella et al. [99], Copyright 2002, with permission from John Wiley & Sons.

Blends of polyamides and polyolefins modified with functional reactive groups of various types, such as maleic anhydride, acrylic acid, and diethylmaleate, have been intensively investigated by analyzing the effect of the type and content of functional groups and processing conditions [108–110]. A detailed study of the crystallization behavior and crystal structure of blends of nylon 6 (Ny6) both with acrylic acid-modified isotactic polypropylene (PP-AA) and modified polyethylene (PE-AA), as compared to blends of Ny6 with PP and LDPE, was reported by Psarski et al. [111]. Blends with nonfunctionalized polyolefins showed at all compositions the typical features of incompatible systems with no adhesion between the polymer phases and poor dispersion of the minor component (with average sizes from 5 to 15 μm). Otherwise, blends of PA6 with the functionalized polyolefins showed strong interfacial adhesion and high phase dispersion with uniform particle size distribution: for blends with polyolefin matrix, the particle size of the dispersed polyamide phase decreased to about 1 μm (see Fig. 10.27).

These effects, supported by a marked increase of melt viscosity, were related to the occurrence of chemical interactions between the polyamides and functionalized polyolefins at the interface. DSC analysis showed that incompatible Ny6/PP and Ny6/LDPE blends exhibit at all compositions separated crystallization peaks of the two components, whereas the compatibilized blends displayed fractionated and/or coincident crystallization phenomena. For Ny6/PP-AA blends where Ny6 is the matrix, the crystallization of the polyamide phase takes place in a narrow range, close to 190°C, as observed for pure Ny6 (Fig. 10.26a). When Ny6 is the dispersed phase, the crystallization is spread over a wide temperature range and the largest fraction of Ny6 crystallizes at temperatures below 130°C, almost coincidently with the crystallization of the polyolefin matrix—about 60 degrees lower than the usual crystallization temperature of pure Ny6. A similar behavior was observed for Ny6/PE-AA blends (Fig. 10.26b): when Ny6 constitutes the dispersed phase, the largest fraction crystallizes at temperatures below 100°C, close to the crystallization of PE-AA. Such an effect was explained in terms of fractionated crystallization process, which depends on the primary nucleation events of the dispersed polymer particles from the melt. Fractionated crystallization in strongly segregated copolymers and in fine polymers droplets is discussed in Chapter 12.

10.5.3.1 Fractionated Crystallization in Compatibilized Blends
Frensch et al. [112] showed that the crystallization of the dispersed phase in a blend may be shifted to larger undercoolings than that usually observed for the plain component if the number density of dispersed particles exceeds that of heterogeneities (N^*) which normally act as nucleation sites for the component itself. Thus, for a system consisting of dispersed particles with average volume v_d, the minor component crystallizes at its usual temperature when $N^* > 1/v_d$, whereas fractionation of the crystallization occurs if $N^* \leq 1/v_d$. At a very high level of dispersion ($N^* \ll 1/v_d$), the crystallization can occur by homogeneous nucleation, corresponding to the largest attainable undercooling.

In the case of Ny6/PP-AA blends with PP-AA matrix, the number average density of particles was estimated to be more than two orders of magnitude higher than the number density of heterogeneities usually active for the crystallization of bulk Ny6 ($N^* = 3$–$7 \; 10^{-3} \; \mu m^{-3}$). For uncompatibilized Ny6/PP blends, in the same composition range, the average number density of the dispersed Ny6 particles (0.01–0.5 $10^{-3} \; \mu m^{-3}$) was considerably lower than the number density of heterogeneous nuclei of Ny6; thus, the crystallization of the dispersed polyamide could occur at the usual undercooling of the pure polyamide.

At higher temperatures, near 190°C, only a limited number of particles can be nucleated by the heterogeneities usually active for Ny6 crystallization, whereas the others will be nucleated by nuclei active at lower temperatures, until a temperature is reached where homogeneous nucleation occurs. When Ny6 is highly dispersed in the polyolefin matrix the maximum rate of conversion from the melt takes place at a temperature near the crystallization onset of PP-AA. This temperature is higher than the homogeneous nucleation temperature of Ny6 (128°C), suggesting that the coincident crystallization observed for Ny6 and PP-AA is determined by a nucleating interaction between the two components.

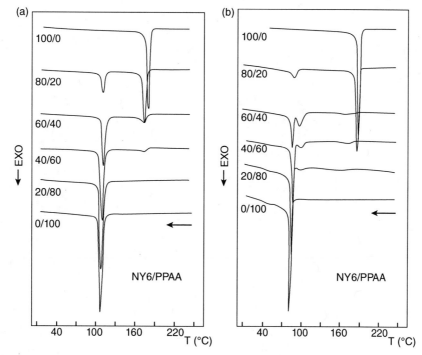

Figure 10.26 DSC thermograms of (a) Ny6/PP-AA and (b) Ny6/PE-AA blends in the composition range 0–100 wt% Ny6, recorded on cooling from the melt at 10°C/min. The high temperature peak corresponds to the crystallization of polyamide phase, the peaks at lower temperature to the crystallization of the polyolefin phases. Reprinted from Psarski et al. [111], Copyright 2000, with permission from Elsevier.

The weight fraction $f(d_n)$ of dispersed Ny6 crystallizing heterogeneously in the blends (at the usual undercooling conditions) was related to the volume of Ny6 particles by the relation:

$$f(d_n) = 1 - \exp\{-N^* \pi d^3 / 6\} \qquad (10.27)$$

where d is the diameter of the particles, N^* is the number density of heterogeneous nuclei in Ny6, and $\pi d^3/6$ is the average volume of the dispersed particles [113]. The plots in Figure 10.27 show the dependence of heterogeneously nucleated fraction of Ny6 droplets on the droplet diameter for two different values of N^*.

Morphological investigations by transmission electron microscopy on ultrathin sections of Ny6/PE-AA blends crystallized from the melt revealed a bimodal size distribution of the dispersed polyamide phase with large (1–3 μm) and small (0.1–1 μm) particles, respectively. In the large particles the lamellar thickness of PA6 crystals was in the range of 3–5 nm, close to that of pure Ny6 (4–5 nm), while in the small particles the crystal thickness was between 1 and 3 nm. The larger particles, which are mainly heterogeneously nucleated, crystallize at lower undercooling (characteristic of pure PA6) with larger lamellar thickness, while the smaller particles crystallize at a higher undercooling, giving rise to thinner lamellae.

The crystallization (and melting) behavior of Ny6/PP-AA and Ny6/PE-AA blends was also analyzed by means of simultaneous WAXS/SAXS real-time analysis (using a synchrotron radiation source), during cooling/heating runs in the temperature range of 80–245°C [114]. For blends with Ny6 as dispersed component, these experiments indicated the appearance of both crystalline peaks of Ny6 and polyolefins in the range of 125–132°C, well below the crystallization temperature of pure Ny6 (190°C). The presence of lamellar-type density fluctuations was pointed out from SAXS patterns at higher temperatures, near 185°C, supporting the presence of an ordering process of the polyamide phase preceding the formation of the real Ny6 crystallites, in accordance with a fractionated crystallization of the dispersed polyamide.

Melting thermograms of Ny6/PP-AA blends with polyamide as dispersed phase, isothermally crystallized from the melt, revealed also the presence of melting peaks of Ny6 at temperatures lower than the usual melting temperature of α form (221°C), indicating the existence of a considerable amount of γ form crystals (215°C). No melting peak of γ phase was observed for Ny6/iPP blends at any Ny6 content.

From the deconvolution analysis of WAXS spectra of the various blends, it was found that in the functionalized

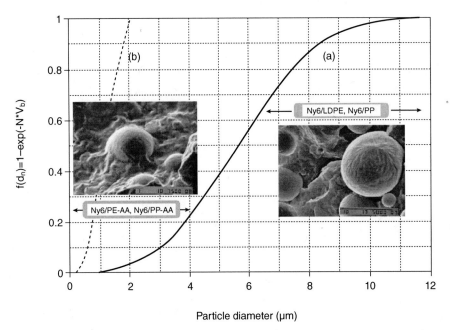

Figure 10.27 Fraction of dispersed Ny6 particles crystallizing heterogeneously in blends of Ny6 with polyolefins (LDPE, PP) and functionalized polyolefins (PE-AA, PP-AA), as a function of particle diameter. Calculated according to Equation (10.27) for $N^* = 7.4 \cdot 10^9$ cm^{-3} (a) and $N^* = 1.0 \cdot 10^{12}$ cm^{-3} (b) SEM micrographs of fracture surfaces of (left) Ny6/PP-AA 40/60 (scale bar: 1 μm) and (right) Ny6/PP 40/60 (scale bar: 10 μm) blends.

blends the weight fraction of γ form crystals monotonically increases with decreasing concentration of Ny6 in the dispersed phase, whereas the fraction of α form crystals decreases [111] (Fig. 10.28). On the contrary, no significant variation of the fraction of the two crystalline modifications was observed for Ny6/PP and Ny6/LDPE blends in the same composition range. Such an effect can be related to the fractionated crystallization behavior of the polyamide: the shift of the crystallization of Ny6 to lower temperatures makes the formation of the γ phase more favored than that of the α phase, which is mainly stable at higher temperatures.

10.6 POLYMER BLENDS WITH LIQUID-CRYSTALLINE COMPONENTS

10.6.1 Introduction

The processability, properties, and performance of conventional polymers can be suitably modified by the addition of both low and high molar weight liquid crystal compounds, making possible the development of new materials for advanced technological applications. In many cases the rheological, thermal, and mechanical behavior of commercial polymers have been reported to be improved by blending with liquid crystal polymers (LCP), with great advantages to the processing conditions and ultimate properties [115]. In parallel, mixtures of polymers with low molar weight liquid crystals (LCs) have assumed an increasing relevance as materials for optic and electro-optic applications, such as polymer dispersed liquid crystal (PDLC) devices [116, 117]. These systems, as compared to the single LC components, can be tailored to meet the requirements of a variety of applications in a broader temperature range and with enhanced orientational effects in electric and magnetic fields.

In this section, the phase behavior, the morphological and thermodynamic characteristics, as well as the crystallization behavior, of some polymer/LC and polymer/LCP binary systems are reported, focusing the attention on the effect of the structural parameters, composition, and miscibility of the components.

10.6.2 Mesomorphism and Phase Transition Behavior of Liquid Crystals and Liquid Crystal Polymers

Liquid crystals, which can be defined as ordered fluids, are characterized by the existence of anisotropy of the molecular structure (rods, discs, planks, helices). They are generally classified according to the type and degree of order (mono- and two-dimensional) into three main

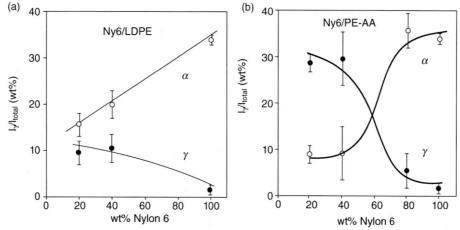

Figure 10.28 Weight fraction of α (○) and γ (●) crystalline phases of Ny6 in (a) Ny6/LDPE and (b) Ny6/PE-AA blends, as a function of Ny6 concentration. $I_{total} = (I_{am} + I_\alpha + I_\gamma)$, where I_{am}, I_α, and I_γ are the integral intensities of Ny6 amorphous halo and the α and γ polymorph reflections, respectively. Reprinted from Psarski et al. [111], Copyright 2000, with permission from Elsevier.

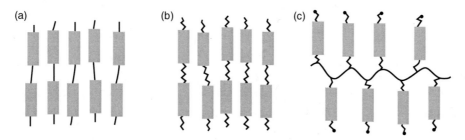

Figure 10.29 Schematic representation of mesophase structure for (a) rigid chain LCPs, (b) main chain LCPs with flexible spacers, and (c) side chain LCPs.

categories: nematic, smectic, and cholesteric (or chiral nematic) mesophases with different orientational and positional anisotropy [118]. In the nematic mesophase the molecules are mostly aligned with their main axis along a prevalent direction without any positional order; the cholesteric phase may be regarded as a particular nematic phase in which the molecules are arranged in twisted parallel planes; in the smectic mesophase the molecules display both an orientational order almost parallel to their axes and some positional order in layers perpendicular to the alignment direction. The mesophases may originate by heating the solid above the melting point (thermotropic LCs), or by dissolution (lyotropic LCs).

Liquid crystal polymer (LCP) mesophases show close analogies with those of low molecular weight LCs. The mesomorphic behavior of polymers depends on the position and distribution of "mesogenic units" along the macromolecular chain: there are two fundamental types of LCPs, those with mesogenic groups in the main chain (*main chain* LCPs) and those with mesogenic groups in the side chains (*side chain* LCPs) (Fig. 10.29). Main chain LCPs with rigid chain structure, as fully aromatic polyesters and polyesteramides, mostly give rise to nematic mesophases, while main chain LCPs with flexible spacers (such as alkyl or oxy-alkyl sequences) between the mesogenic groups can display different mesophases. On the other hand, the mesomorphism of side chain LCPs is more similar to that of low molecular weight LCs, as a consequence of the higher mobility of the mesogenic groups than the constraints existing in main chain LCPs.

The phase behavior of thermotropic LC and LCP compounds is characterized by distinct and reversible isotropic–mesophase and mesophase–crystal transitions, with kinetics of transformation that are largely influenced by the chemical structure and mesophase type. Price and Wendorff [119] showed for a series of LCs that all phase transitions (from isotropic melt to mesophase and to crystal) are controlled by the nucleation and, under isothermal conditions, can be kinetically described by the Avrami equation (Eq. 10.14), where the values of the exponent n are related to the degree of order of the mesophase. This behavior has also been observed for mesomorphous polymers [120]: for nematic LCPs the formation of the mesophase from the isotropic melt has been described on the basis of an instantaneous nucleation process with monodimensional growth ($n = 1$) [121], while for isotropic–smectic transitions, values of $n = 2$–4 have been reported according to two- and three-dimensional growth geometries [122–124]. The crystallization kinetics from the mesophase are generally faster than those observed for the crystallization of conventional polymers from the melt, under comparable undercooling conditions, due to the fact that the LCPs have a considerable degree of order, orientational and/or positional, in the liquid crystal state.

The effect of chain structure and mesophase type on the isothermal crystallization kinetics from the mesophase has been examined for some main chain liquid-crystalline polyesters (derived from 4,4′ terephthaloyldioxydibenzoic acid and aliphatic diols) (HTHm) with different lengths of flexible aliphatic groups along the chain [125]:

$$-[-OC-(C_6H_4)-OOC-(C_6H_4)-COO-(C_6H_4)-COO-(CH_2)_mO-]-$$

where $m = 3$ (HTH3) and $m = 10$ (HTH10). These polyesters displayed mesophases of both nematic and smectic type, with different phase transition temperatures. It was pointed out that the overall crystallization rate from the (smectic) mesophase resulted to be influenced by the length of the aliphatic groups in the chain. The kinetics of phase transition were analyzed according to the Avrami equation, and the temperature dependence of the kinetic constant, K_n, was correlated to the energy of formation of critical nuclei according to Equation (10.16). The results indicated that: (1) the primary nucleation and the growth geometry of the crystals changed with polyester structure ($n \approx 2$ for HTH3, $n = 3$–4 for HTH10); (2) the crystallization from the mesophase was characterized, even at low undercoolings, by relatively low values of $\Delta\Phi^*$ and σ_e (10–18 erg/cm^2) as compared to those observed for polymers crystallized from the isotropic melt (the kinetics of transition from the smectic mesophase are also affected by the type of smectic structure); (3) the energy of formation of crystal nuclei (secondary nucleation) depends on the flexibility of LCP chains; that is, it decreases with increasing the length of the flexible sequences. Thus, at same ΔT, the higher crystallization rate of the HTH10 polyester was mainly accounted for by a lower activation energy of the nucleation process with respect to that of HTH3 polyster.

10.6.3 Crystallization Behavior of Polymer/LC Blends

The thermodynamics of blends of polymers of various flexibility and rigid molecules has been thoroughly treated from the theoretical point of view by Flory and Abe [126], who analyzed the phase equilibria as a function of various parameters, such as molecular structure, molecular mass, temperature, and concentration. The theoretical data indicate that systems constituted by rigid and flexible molecules are mainly heterophasic with limited miscibility effects between the components. In general, it has been observed that the phase behavior of polymer/LC blends is affected by the chemical structure and concentration of the polymer, as well as by the intermolecular interactions with the LC component [127, 128]. Studies on the thermodynamics and kinetics of phase transitions in polymer/LC blends have been reported for a few systems. These studies are of considerable interest due to the possibility of varying the stability range of the mesophase, as a function of composition, or even obtaining the formation of induced mesophases [129].

Blends of PEO with the nematic LC p-azoxyanisole (PAA) [130] and blends of comb-shaped polymers, isotactic poly(octadecylethylene) (POE), and poly(biphenylyloxyexylacrylate) (PBHA), with PAA [131] were analyzed to investigate the effect of polymer structure and composition on the miscibility and the crystallization behavior of the components.

The phase diagram of PEO/PAA blends is reported in Figure 10.30. It may be noticed that the melting temperature of the polymer is almost unaffected by the LC, while the stability of the solid PAA phase and the mesophase transition range are largely changing with the LC content. At temperatures lower than the melting point of PEO (64°C) there are a solid polymer and a solid LC phase (region A); above the melting point of polymer, for PAA content ≥ 20 wt%, a two-phase region (region B) is present: one phase is the molten polymer containing an LC fraction proportional to the saturation concentration of PAA (20 wt%), the other phase is constituted by solid PAA, which can exist with different polymorphic structures. For PAA content ≥ 70 wt%, above the crystal to nematic transition of PAA (region C), there is a nematic PAA phase dispersed as small droplets in a homogeneous polymer/LC liquid mixture (Fig. 10.31a), resembling the structure of PDLC materials obtained by phase separation processes [116, 117]. At temperatures above the melting point of the components (region D), there exists a single phase consisting of a polymer/LC mixture in the isotropic liquid state. On cooling from this phase, the crystallization occurs with formation of PAA dendritic structures, which develop from the whole mass of the molten blend, followed by the crystallization of pure polymer at a lower temperature (Fig. 10.31b). SEM analysis evidenced the presence of platelet-like PAA crystals (about 1 μm thick) homogeneously dispersed in the polymer matrix.

On the other hand, the phase behavior of blends of the polyacrylate PBHA with PAA was markedly dependent on the blend composition [131]. A single isotropic liquid phase existed above the melting temperature of the polymer for PAA content ≤ 20%, while at higher concentrations of LC coexistence of a molten polymer phase and a solid PAA phase was observed (Fig. 10.32).

The formation of nematic droplets dispersed within the isotropic liquid was recorded for blends with PAA content ≥ 70%. On cooling below the nematic to crystal transition, the crystallization of PAA occurred simultaneously from both the nematic and the isotropic liquid phase, giving rise to a grain-like texture. These results were accounted for by a partial miscibility of the components in the PBHA/PAA blends above the melting temperature of the polymer; the miscibility effect could be ascribed to the presence of intermolecular interactions between the aromatic groups of PAA and the biphenylyl groups in the side chain of PBHA. Analogously, the phase behavior of PEO/PPA blends indicated the occurrence of miscibility phenomena in the melt, likely owing to polar interactions between the components.

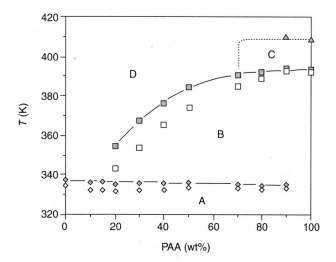

Figure 10.30 Phase transition temperatures of PEO/PAA blends as a function of PAA content. (◊, ♦) melting temperature of PEO; (□, ■) melting temperature of PAA; (▲) isotropization temperature of PAA. Dotted line indicates the nematic to isotropic transition of the LC phase as determined by optical microscopy. A (two phases): solid PEO + solid PAA; B (two phases): molten PEO/PAA blend + solid PAA; C (two phases): molten PEO/PAA blend + nematic PAA phase; D (single phase): isotropic liquid mixture of PEO and PAA. Reprinted from Pracella et al. [130], Copyright 1993, with permission from Taylor & Francis.

10.6.4 Crystallization Behavior of Polymer/LCP Blends

The influence of mesomorphic polymer components on the morphological, physical, and rheological properties of blends with polyester, polyamide, polycarbonate, and polyolefin matrix has been investigated in several cases [115]. Studies on blends of PET, PBT, PC, PS with *main chain* liquid crystal polymers and copolymers of various type (including flexible LC copolyesters and wholly aromatic LC copolyesters) showed that the phase transitions and properties were largely dependent on the chemical structure, molar mass, processing conditions, and concentration of components [132–134]. Generally, these systems displayed phase separation in the molten

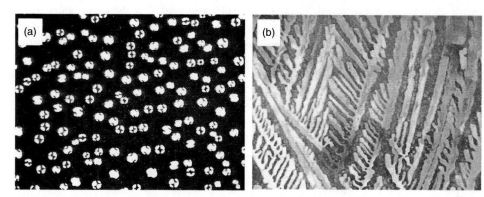

Figure 10.31 Optical micrographs of: (a) PEO/PAA (20/80) blend showing the formation of PAA nematic droplets on cooling from the isotropic melt (region C) at 384 K; (b) PEO/PAA (70/30) blend showing dendritic textures formed on cooling from the isotropic melt (region D) at 303 K (crossed Nicols, ×100). Reprinted from Pracella et al. [130], Copyright 1993, with permission from Taylor & Francis. (See color insert.)

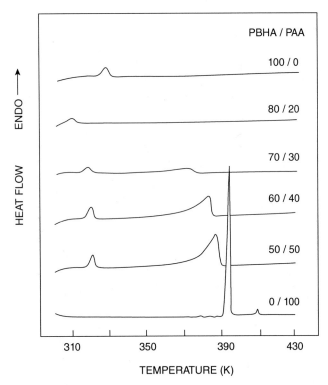

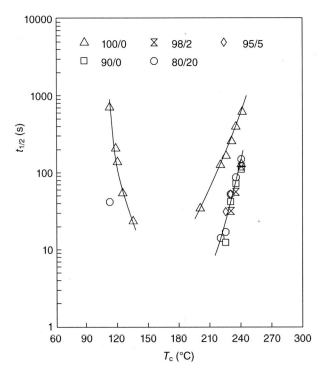

Figure 10.32 DSC heating thermograms of PBHA/PAA blends at various compositions crystallized from the isotropic melt (second run, heating rate: 10 K/min). The traces are normalized to 1 mg samples. Reprinted from Pracella and Bresci [131], Copyright 1995, with permission from Taylor & Francis.

Figure 10.33 Crystallization half-time, $t_{1/2}$, of PPS phase in isothermally crystallized PPS/Vectra-B blends, as a function of the crystallization temperature. Reprinted from Minkova et al. [141], Copyright 1992, with permission from John Wiley & Sons.

state with the coexistence of isotropic and anisotropic phases. In some cases, the occurrence of miscibility phenomena in the melt has been observed, due to the presence of chemical and/or specific interactions between the polymer components [135]. For blends of LCP with polyolefins, such as PE or PP, due to the different chemical nature of these polymers, compatibilization with modified polymers is required to improve the adhesion and mechanical properties. Several functionalized polyolefins and copolymers (PP-g-MA, PP-AA, E-GMA) [136], as well as polyolefin–LCP graft copolymers (PE-g-SBH, PP-g-SBH) synthesized by melt polycondensation, have been used [137, 138].

The presence of a mesomorphic component dispersed in a crystallizable polymer matrix, can induce noteable changes of the crystallization behavior, crystallinity degree, and crystal morphology of the matrix. For blends of PET with liquid-crystalline copolyesters the crystallization rate of PET matrix was found to increase with increasing the LCP content, indicating a nucleating effect of the LCP component [139]. Similar effects have been reported for blends with polyolefin matrix: for blends of iPP with a smectic polyester (PTEB) compatibilized by addition of maleated PP, the crystallization behavior of PP was affected by the LCP and compatibilizer [140]. Minkova et al. observed a strong increase in the crystallization rate of poly(phenylene sulfide) (PPS) in blends of PPS with a nematic, wholly aromatic, copolyesteramide (Vectra-B), independently of the LCP concentration [141] (Fig. 10.33). These blends were biphasic and the presence of Vectra caused a large increase in the crystal nucleation density of PPS, with an appreciable reduction in spherulite size in the blends and without change of the crystallinity degree.

Blends of PBT with the smectic flexible polyester poly(decamethylene 4,4'-terephthaloyldioxydibenzoate) (HTH10) [142–144] were examined in all the composition range in order to assess the occurrence of miscibility phenomena and their effect on the morphological, kinetic, and thermodynamic aspects of the crystallization process. DSC and WAXS analyses indicated the existence of separated crystal phases of the two components for HTH10 contents higher than 30 wt%. On cooling from the isotropic melt a single crystallization peak was observed, and a large depression of the melting temperature of PBT matrix was found with increasing amount of PLC. At higher HTH10 contents

(>50 wt.%), the presence of the smectic mesophase was observed by optical microscopy accompanied by a change of the isotropization temperature range. Samples quenched from the melt exhibited a single glass transition at temperatures intermediate between those of plain polymers, which supported the occurrence of miscibility of the components in the molten state (Fig. 10.34).

The microscopic analysis of blend samples isothermally crystallized from the melt pointed out large changes of the texture, size, and number density of PBT spherulites with varying the composition (Fig. 10.35). A marked decrease of the heterogeneous nucleation density of PBT was recorded with increasing HTH10 content (0–50 wt%), indicating that the activity of primary nuclei was inhibited by the presence of mesomorphic polymer; thus, as the concentration of HTH10 increases, a smaller number of nuclei is effective for the growth of PBT spherulites, causing the formation of larger size spherulite. Moreover, the spherulite radial growth rate of PBT, at constant T_c, decreased with increasing weight fraction of LCP in the blends (Fig. 10.36a), and a minimum of the overall crystallization rate from the melt was found at a concentration of 10 wt% of HTH10 (Fig. 10.36b).

The temperature dependence of K_n was analyzed according to Equation (10.16) and from linear plots of $[(1/n)\ln K_n + U^*/R(T_c - T_\infty)]$ versus $T_m^o/(T_c \Delta T)$ the free energy associated with secondary nucleation, $\Delta \Phi^*$, and the folding surface energy, σ_e, were determined at each examined blend composition [142]. $\Delta \Phi^*$ was found to increase with the HTH10 content, whereas the transport term decreased due to the decrease of T_g in the blends. Thus, the reduction in the overall crystallization rate of PBT in the blends could be accounted for by both kinetics and thermodynamic effects on the nucleation and growth processes of the crystals: the increase in activation energy for the crystal nucleation is justified by the existence of a diluent effect of the LCP component, in contrast with the decrease of transport energy of the macromolecules at the liquid–crystal interface. In accordance with the above effect, a depression of the equilibrium melting temperature of PBT crystals (from 242°C to 235°C) was observed with increasing the content of liquid crystal polyester [142]. The miscibility of the polymer components in the melt, at least for concentrations of HTH $\leq$ 30 wt%, was further supported on the basis of theoretical evaluations [143].

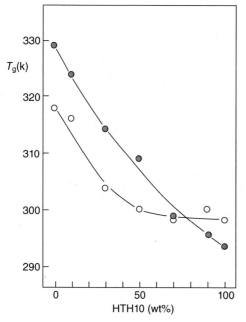

Figure 10.34 Glass transition temperature, T_g, of PBT/HTH10 blends as a function of LCP content. (O) samples quenched from the melt; (●) samples annealed for one hour at 373 K (DSC heating rate: 20 /min). Reprinted from Pracella et al. [143], Copyright 1987, with permission from Taylor & Francis.

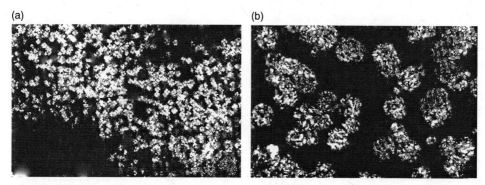

Figure 10.35 Polarizing optical micrographs of (a) plain PBT (235×), and (b) PBT/HTH10 (50/50) blend (130×), crystallizing isothermally from the melt at T_c = 483 K. Reprinted from Pracella et al. [144], Copyright 1989, with permission from John Wiley & Sons.

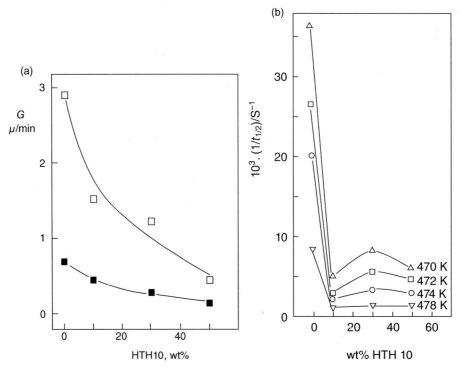

Figure 10.36 (a) Radial growth rate, G, of PBT spherulites in PBT/HTH10 blends isothermally crystallized from the isotropic melt at $T_c = 478$ K (□) and $T_c = 483$ K (■), as a function of HTH10 content. (b) Overall crystallization rate, $1/t_{0.5}$, of PBT in PBT/HTH10 blends crystallized at various T_c, versus HTH10 content. Reprinted from Pracella et al. [144], Copyright 1989, with permission from John Wiley & Sons.

10.7 CONCLUDING REMARKS

In the field of polymer science, the crystallization behavior of polymer blends represents a key issue for the analysis of structure–properties relationships of macromolecular systems. The presence of the second polymer component, either in the melt or in the solid state, can influence the whole crystallization process of the polymer phases, thus the morphology, phase behavior, and physical/mechanical properties. The crystallization processes are controlled by several factors, which are related to equilibrium thermodynamics, kinetic aspects, thermal conditions, melt rheology, as well as chain structure and polymer/polymer interactions. In the present chapter, an overview of the thermodynamic conditions, accompanied by a description of main morphological features of blends containing one or both crystallizable components, is reported.

Crystallization in polymer blends can develop through various types of "solidification paths," resulting in a wide spectrum of morphological textures and crystalline structures. The crystallization path is strictly determined by the miscibility degree of the components. When the polymer components constitute a miscible system, and only one polymer can crystallize (in a defined temperature range), the crystallization is mainly controlled by the phase separation phenomena that occur at the crystal growth front. During the crystallization from the homogeneous melt, the crystallizable polymer generally solidifies with rejection of the amorphous component at the liquid–crystal interface. This latter can be rejected out of the spherulite border (interspherulitic zones), or it can be occluded within intraspherulitic regions (interlamellar and interfibrillar zones) depending on the relative values of crystal growth rate and diffusion rate of the amorphous component. In these conditions the crystal growth is strictly controlled by the changes in the transport energy in the melt and the increase of barrier energy associated with secondary nucleation. Miscible blends containing both crystallizable components can crystallize in various modes, following separate crystallization, concurrent crystallization, or co-crystallization of the two polymers.

Large variations of the thermodynamic parameters, such as surface free energy of crystals and equilibrium melting temperature, and the overall crystallization kinetics (depending on the combined effect of primary nucleation and growth) are generally observed for miscible systems. The crystallization in blends with miscibility gap depends on the contemporary presence of both crystallization and demixing phenomena; thus, by varying the concentration of the crystallizing component, crystallization as a single phase, demixing induced by crystallization, crystallization induced by demixing, and simultaneous demixing/crystallization phenomena can occur.

On the other hand, for immiscible polymer blends, although the crystallization of each component takes place in separated domains and with different kinetic conditions, the presence of the second (crystalline or amorphous) polymer can induce marked alterations of the primary nucleation phenomena, crystal growth, and superstructure. For blends with crystallizable polymer matrix, containing a dispersed component in the molten state, either nucleating effects or variations of spherulite morphology and growth rate may be observed. Migration of nucleating heterogeneities across the interface between the molten polymers can determine important morphological effects, such as those concerning the average spherulite size and relevant distribution in the polymer matrix. However, in the presence of a solidified (or crystallized) dispersed component, even the crystallization of the matrix can be nucleated at the interfaces. Additionally, significant changes in the overall crystallinity, bulk crystallization kinetics, and melting behavior may also be recorded for blends with immiscible components.

The compatibilization of immiscible blends (both by addition of copolymers and by reactive mixing processes) is a very powerful method of controlling the crystalline morphology and improving the properties and applications of these systems. The compatibilizer contributes to decreasing the interfacial energy between the components and to improving the phase dispersion and interfacial adhesion by chain interpenetration and entanglements. Several studies on compatibilized blends demonstrated that the crystallization behavior may undergo notable changes in the presence of a strong emulsifying effect of the compatibilizer at the interface. When the second (crystallizable) component is very finely dispersed in the matrix, peculiar phenomena, such as fractionated or coincident crystallization, may be observed in the crystallization behavior, depending on the primary nucleation events of the dispersed polymer phase.

Finally, polymer blends containing liquid-crystalline components constitute a very interesting research field, whose theoretical aspects and properties need to be developed, especially in view of the wide application potential of these systems in high technology sectors. It has been shown that the crystallization process and the morphology of the polymer matrix can be markedly affected by the mesomorphic behavior of the dispersed LC or LCP component as well as by miscibility effects in the isotropic state. The presence of dispersed nematic and/or smectic mesophases can give rise to an increase in the overall crystallization rate of the matrix from the melt mostly due to nucleating effects of the anisotropic LC phase. For miscible blends containing an LCP as dispersed component, the heterogeneous nucleation density and the spherulite radial growth rate of the crystalline matrix, at constant T_c, can be largely affected by the weight fraction of the LCP component. According to the theoretical models applicable to miscible blends, these effects can be accompanied by a depression of the equilibrium melting point and remarkable changes of crystallization kinetics and morphological characteristics.

ABBREVIATIONS

EAA	ethylene-*co*-acrylic acid copolymer
EGMA	ethylene-*co*-glycidyl methacrylate copolymer
EPR	ethylene-propylene copolymer (elastomer)
EPR-*g*-MA	EPR grafted with maleic anhydride
EVA	ethylene-*co*-vinyl acetate copolymer
HDPE	high density polyethylene
HDPE-*g*-GMA	HDPE grafted with glycidyl methacrylate
HDPE-*g*-MA	HDPE grafted with maleic anhydride
HTH10	poly(decamethylene 4,4′-terephthaloildioxydibenzoate)
iPB	isotactic poly(1-butene)
iPP	isotactic polypropylene
iP4MH	isotactic poly(4-methyl hexane)
iP4MP	isotactic poly(4-methyl pentene)
LCP	liquid crystal polymer
LDPE	low density polyethylene
LLDPE	linear low density polyethylene
NBR	butadiene-acrylonitrile copolymers
PA6 (Ny6)	polyamide-6
PAr	polyarylate
PBAS	poly(butylene adipate-co-butylene succinate)
PBD	polybutadiene
PBSU	poly(butylene succinate)
PBT	poly(butylene terephthalate)
PC	polycarbonate bisphenol-A
PCL	poly(ε-caprolactone)

PE-AA	poly(ethylene-*co*-acrylic acid)
PEEK	poly(ether ether ketone)
PEI	polyetherimide
PEMA	poly(ethyl methacrylate)
PEO	poly(ethylene oxide)
PHB	poly(β-hydroxybutyrate)
PI	poly(isoprene)
PMMA	poly(methyl methacrylate)
PPVE	poly(isopropyl vinyl ether)
PBVE	poly(sec-butyl-vinyl ether)
PP-AA	polypropylene grafted with acrylic acid
PP-*g*-GMA	polypropylene grafted with glycidyl methacrylate
PS	polystyrene
PTT	poly(trimethylene terephthalate)
PVC	poly(vinyl chloride)
PVDF	poly(vinyliden fluoride)
PVF	poly(vinyl fluoride)
PVPh	poly(4-vinyl phenol)
SAN	styrene-acrylonitrile copolymers
SEBS	styrene-*b*-(ethylene-*co*-butylene)-*b*-styrene
SEBS-*g*-GMA	SEBS grafted with glycidyl methacrylate
SEBS-*g*-MA	SEBS grafted with maleic anhydride
SEP	styrene-*b*-(ethylene-*co*-propylene) di-block copolymer
SEPSEP	styrene-*b*-(ethylene-*co*-propylene) tetra-block copolymer
VLDPE	very low density polyethylene

REFERENCES

[1] Utracki, L.A. *Polymer Alloys and Blends*. Hanser Publishers, Munich, 1989.

[2] Paul, D.R., Newman, S., eds. *Polymer Blends*. Academic Press, New York, 1978.

[3] Olabisi, O., Robeson, L.M., Shaw, T. *Polymer-Polymer Miscibility*. Academic Press, New York, 1979.

[4] Folkes, M.J., Hope, P.S., eds. *Polymer Blends and Alloys*. Blackie Academic & Professional, London, 1993.

[5] Utracki, L.A., ed. *Polymer Blends Handbook*, Vol. 1. Kluwer Academic Publishers, Dordrecht, 2002.

[6] Vasile, C., Kulshreshtha, A.K., Bumbu, G.G. Terminology. In *Handbook of Polymer Blends and Composites*, Vol. 3A, Vasile, C., Kulshreshtha, A.K., eds. Rapra Technology Ltd, Shawbury, 2003, Chapter 1.

[7] Flory, P.J. *Principles of Polymer Chemistry*. Cornell University Press, Ithaca, NY, 1953.

[8] Huggins, M.L. *Physical Chemistry of High Polymers*. Wiley Interscience, New York, 1958.

[9] Hildebrand, J.H., Scott, R.L. *The Solubility of Non-Electrolytes*. Dover Publ, New York, 1964.

[10] Cruz, C.A., Paul, D.R., Barlow, J.W. *J. Appl. Polym. Sci.* **1979**, *23*, 589–600.

[11] Krause, S. Polymer-polymer compatibility. In *Polymer Blends*, Paul, D.R., Newmann, S., eds. Academic Press, New York, 1978, Chapter 2.

[12] Krause, S. *J. Macromol. Sci. Rev. Macromol. Chem.* **1972**, C7, 251.

[13] Coleman, M.M., Graf, J.E., Painter, P.C. *Specific Interactions and the Miscibility of Polymer Blends*, Technomic Publisher Co. Inc, Lancaster, 1991.

[14] Sanchez, I.C. Statistical thermodynamics of polymer blends. In *Polymer Blends*, Paul, D.R., Newmann, S., eds. Academic Press, New York, 1978, Chapter 3.

[15] Kleintjens, L.A., Koningsveld, R. *Colloid Polym. Sci.* **1980**, *258*, 711–718.

[16] Koningsveld, R., Onclin, M.H., Kleintjens, L.A. Chapter in *Polymer Compatibility and Incompatibility*, Solc, K., ed. MMI Press, New York, 1982.

[17] Ten Brinke, G., Karasz, F., MacKnight, W.J. *Macromolecules* **1983**, *16*, 1827–1830.

[18] Ten Brinke, G., Karasz, F. *Macromolecules* **1984**, *17*, 815.

[19] Groeninckx, G., Vanneste, M., Everaert, V. Crystallization, morphological structure and melting of polymer blends. In *Polymer Blends Handbook*, Vol. 1, Utracki, L.A., ed. Kluwer Academic Publishers, Dordrecht, 2002, Chapter 3.

[20] Defiew, G., Groeninckx, G., Reynaers, H. *Polymer* **1989**, *30*, 595–601.

[21] Cimmino, S., Martuscelli, E., Silvestre, C., Canetti, M., De Lalla, C., Seves, A. *J. Polym. Sci. Polym. Phys. Ed.* **1989**, B27, 1781.

[22] Defiew, G., Groeninckx, G., Reynaers, H. *Polymer* **1989**, *30*, 2164–2169.

[23] Iruin, J.J., Eguiazabal, J.L., Guzman, G.M. *Eur. Polym. J.* **1989**, *25*, 1169–1172.

[24] Chen, H.L., Wang, S.F. *Polymer* **2000**, *41*, 5157–5164.

[25] Keith, H.D., Padden, F.J. *J. Appl. Phys.* **1964**, *35*, 1270; *J. Appl. Phys.* **1964**, *35*, 1286.

[26] Morra, B.S., Stein, R.S. *J. Polym. Sci. Polym. Phys. Ed.* **1982**, B20, 2261.

[27] Li, Y., Stein, M., Iungnickel, B.J. *Colloid Polym. Sci.* **1991**, *269*, 772.

[28] Balijepalli, S., Schultz, J.M. *Macromolecules* **2006**, *39*, 7407–7414.

[29] Hatzius, K., Li, Y., Werner, M., Jungnickel, B.J. *Angew. Makromol. Chem.* **1996**, *243*, 177.

[30] Hoffman, J.D., Davis, G.T., Lauritzen, J.I. The rate of crystallization of linear polymers with chain folding. In *Treatise on Solid State Chemistry*, Vol. 3, Hannay, N.B., ed. Plenym Press, New York, 1976, Chapter 7.

[31] Hoffman, J.D., Miller, R.L. *Polymer* **1997**, *38*, 3151.

[32] Williams, M.L., Landel, R.F., Ferry, J.D. *J. Am. Chem. Soc.* **1955**, *77*, 3701–3707.

[33] Di Lorenzo, M.L. *Prog. Polym. Sci.* **2005**, *28*, 663–689.

[34] Alfonso, G.C., Russell, T.P. *Macromolecules* **1986**, *19*, 1143–1152.

[35] Boon, J., Azcue, J.M. *J. Polym. Sci. A-2* **1968**, *6*, 885–894.

[36] Vidotto, G., Levy, D.L., Kovacs, A.J. *Kolloid Z.Z. Polym.* **1969**, *230*, 289–305.

[37] Martuscelli, E., Pracella, M., Ping Yue, W. *Polymer* **1984**, *25*, 1097–1106.

[38] Mandelkern, L. *Crystallization of Polymers*. McGraw-Hill, New York, 1964.

[39] Wunderlich, B. *Macromolecular Physics. Crystal Nucleation, Growth, Annealing*, Vol. 2. Academic Press, New York, 1980.

[40] Martuscelli, E., Pracella, M., Avella, M., Greco, R., Ragosta, G. *Makromol. Chem.* **1980**, *181*, 957–967.

[41] Ziabicki, A. *Appl. Polym. Symp.* **1967**, *6*, 1.

[42] Ozawa, T. *Polymer* **1971**, *12*, 150–158.

[43] Nakamura, K., Watanabe, T., Katayama, K., Amano, T. *J. Appl. Polym. Sci.* **1972**, *16*, 1077–1091.

[44] Scott, R.L. *Chem. Phys.* **1949**, *17*, 279.

[45] Nishi, T., Wang, T.T. *Macromolecules* **1975**, *8*, 909–915.

[46] Jungnickel, B.J. Crystallization kinetical peculiarites in polymer blends. In *Polymer Crystallization. Observations, Concepts and Interpretations*, Sommer, J.U., Reiter, G., eds. Springer-Verlag, Berlin, 2003, Chapter 12.

[47] Li, Y., Schneider, L., Jungnickel, B. *Polym. Networks Blends* **1992**, *2*, 135.

[48] Martuscelli, E., Demma, G.B. Morphology, crystallization and melting behavior of poly(ethylene oxide)/poly(methyl methacrylate) blends. In *Polymer Blends. Processing, Morphology and Properties*, Vol. 1, Martuscelli, E., Kryszewski, M., Palumbo, R., eds. Plenum Press, New York, 1980.

[49] Martuscelli, E., Demma, G.B., Rossi, E., Segre, A. *Polym. Commun.* **1983**, *24*, 266–267.

[50] Nishi, T., Wang, T.T. *Macromolecules* **1977**, *10*, 421–425.

[51] Sanchez, I.C., Eby, R.K. *Macromolecules* **1975**, *8*, 638–641.

[52] Liu, J., Jungnickel, B.J. *J. Polym. Sci. B Polym. Phys.* **2007**, *45*, 1917–1931.

[53] Ikehara, T., Kimura, H., Qiu, Z. *Macromolecules* **2005**, *38*, 5104–5108.

[54] Ikehara, T., Urihara, H., Qiu, Z., Nishi, T. *Macromolecules* **2007**, *40*, 8726–8730.

[55] Pracella, M., Benedetti, E., Galleschi, F. *Thermochim. Acta* **1990**, *162*, 163–177.

[56] Piloz, A., Decroix, J.Y., May, J.F. *Angew. Makromol. Chem.* **1976**, *54*, 77.

[57] Siegmann, A. *J. Appl. Polym. Sci.* **1982**, *27*, 1053–1065.

[58] Gohil, R.M., Peterman, J. *J. Macromol. Sci. Phys.* **1980**, *B18*, 217.

[59] Canetti, M., Bonfatti, A.M., Sadocco, P., Seves, A., Pracella, M. *Polym. Networks Blends* **1993**, *3*, 83–88.

[60] Bartczak, Z., Galeski, A., Pracella, M. *J. Appl. Polym. Sci.* **1994**, *54*, 1513–1524.

[61] Bartczak, Z., Galeski, A. *Polymer* **1990**, *31*, 2027–2038.

[62] Wang, D., Gao, J. *J. Appl. Polym. Sci.* **2006**, *99*, 670–678.

[63] Arnold, M., Bornemann, S., Koller, F., Menke, T.J., Kressler, J. *Macromol. Chem. Phys.* **1998**, *199*, 2647–2653.

[64] Lovisi, H., Tavares, M.I.B., Da Silva, N.M., De Menezes, S.M.C., De Santa Maria, L.C., Coutinho, F.M.B. *Polymer* **2001**, *42*, 9791–9799.

[65] Hu, Y.S., Kamdar, A.R., Ansems, P., Chum, P., Hiltner, A.E., Baer, E. *Polymer* **2006**, *47*, 6387–6397.

[66] Bartczak, Z., Chiono, V., Pracella, M. *Polymer* **2004**, *45*, 7549–7561.

[67] Bartczak, Z., Pracella, M. *Eur. Polym. J.* **2006**, *42*, 1819–1829.

[68] Hosoda, S., Hori, H., Yada, K., Nakahara, S., Tsuji, M. *Polymer* **2002**, *43*, 7451–7460.

[69] Chiono, V., Pracella, M. *COST P12 Workshop on Structuring of Polymers*, Capo Miseno (NA), Italy, 2004, Abs. p. 108.

[70] Flory, P.J. *Trans. Faraday Soc.* **1955**, *51*, 848–857.

[71] Crispino, L., Martuscelli, E., Pracella, M. *Makromol. Chem.* **1980**, *181*, 1747–1755.

[72] Tol, R.T., Mathot, V.B.F., Reynaers, H., Groeninckx, G. Relationships between phase morphology, crystallization, and semicrystalline structure in immiscible polymer blends. In *Micro- and Nanostructured Multiphase Polymer Blend Systems*, Harrats, C., Thomas, S., Groeninckx, G., eds. CRC Press, Taylor & Francis, 2006.

[73] Scott, C.E., Macosko, C.W. *Polymer* **1995**, *36*, 461–470.

[74] Wu, S.H. *Polym. Eng. Sci.* **1987**, *27*, 335–343.

[75] Fortelny, I. Theoretical aspects of phase morphology development. In *Micro- and Nanostructured Multiphase Polymer Blend Systems*, Harrats, C., Thomas, S., Groeninckx, G., eds. CRC Press, Taylor & Francis, 2006.

[76] Potschke, P., Paul, D.R. *J. Macromol. Sci. Polym. Rev.* **2003**, *43*, 87–141.

[77] Galeski, A., Bartczak, Z., Pracella, M. *Polymer* **1984**, *25*, 1323–1326.

[78] Bartczak, Z., Galeski, A., Pracella, M. *Polymer* **1986**, *27*, 537–543.

[79] Bartczak, Z., Galeski, A., Martuscelli, E. *Polym. Eng. Sci.* **1984**, *24*, 1155–1165.

[80] Galeski, A., Pracella, M., Martuscelli, E. *J. Polym. Sci. Polym. Phys. Ed.* **1984**, *22*, 739–747.

[81] Frensch, H., Jungnickel, B.J. *Colloid Polym. Sci.* **1989**, *267*, 16–27.

[82] Karger-Kocsis, J., ed. *Polypropylene Structure, Blends and Composites*. Chapman and Hall, London, 1995.

[83] Martuscelli, E. *Polym. Eng. Sci.* **1984**, *24*, 563–586.

[84] Martuscelli, E., Pracella, M., Della Volpe, G., Greco, P. *Makromol. Chem.* **1984**, *185*, 1041–1061.

[85] Bonner, J.G., Hope, P.S. Compatibilisation and reactive blending. Chapter 3. In *Polymer Blends and Alloys*, Folkes, M.J., Hope, P.S., eds. Blackie Academic & Professional, London, 1993.

[86] Brown, S.B. Reactive compatibilization of polymer blends. In *Polymer Blends Handbook*, Vol. 1, Utracki, L.A., ed. Kluwer Academic Publishers, Dordrecht, 2002, Chapter 5.

[87] Noolandi, J. *Polym. Eng. Sci.* **1984**, *24*, 70–78.

[88] Heikens, D., Hoen, N., Barentsen, W., Piet, P., Ladan, H. *J. Polym. Sci. Polym. Symp.* **1978**, *62*, 309.

[89] Fayt, R., Jerome, R., Teyssie, P. *J. Polym. Sci. B Polym. Phys.* **1989**, *27*, 775–793.

[90] Bartlett, D.W., Barlow, J.W., Paul, D.R. *J. Appl. Polym. Sci.* **1982**, *27*, 2351–2360.

[91] Dumoulin, M.M., Farha, C., Utracki, L. *Polym. Eng. Sci.* **1984**, *24*, 1319–1326.

[92] Lohse, D., Datta, S., Kresge, E.N. *Macromolecules* **1991**, *24*, 561–566.

[93] Pracella, M., Chionna, D., Pawlak, A., Galeski, A. *J. Appl. Polym. Sci.* **2005**, *98*, 2201–2211.

[94] Radonjic, G. *J. Appl. Polym. Sci.* **1999**, *72*, 291–307.

[95] Bassani, A., Pessan, L.A., Hage, E. *J. Appl. Polym. Sci.* **2001**, *82*, 2185–2193.

[96] Datta, S., Lohse, D.J. *Polymeric Compatibilizers*, Hanser Publ., Munich, 1996.

[97] Pazzagli, F., Pracella, M. *Macromol. Symp.* **2000**, *149*, 225–230.

[98] Pracella, M., Chionna, D. In *Current Topics in Polymer Science and Technology*, Pracella, M., Galli, G., Giusti, P., eds. *Macromol. Symp.* **2004**, *218*, 173–182.

[99] Pracella, M., Rolla, L., Chionna, D., Galeski, A. *Macromol. Chem. Phys.* **2002**, *203*, 1473–1485.

[100] Ihm, D.J., White, J.L. *J. Appl. Polym. Sci.* **1996**, *60*, 1–7.

[101] Lepers, J.C., Davis, B.D., Tabar, R.J. *J. Polym. Sci. B Polym. Phys.* **1997**, *35*, 2271–2280.

[102] Wei, Q., Chionna, D., Galoppini, E., Pracella, M. *Macromol. Chem. Phys.* **2003**, *204*, 1123–1133.

[103] Wei, Q., Chionna, D., Pracella, M. *Macromol. Chem. Phys.* **2005**, *206*, 777–786.

[104] Scaffaro, R., La Mantia, F.P., Canfora, L., Polacco, G., Filippi, S., Magagnini, P.L. *Polymer* **2003**, *44*, 6951–6957.

[105] Yordanov, C., Minkova, L. *Eur. Polym. J.* **2005**, *41*, 527–534.

[106] Brown, S.B. Reactive extrusion: a survey of chemical reactions of monomers and polymers during extrusion processing. In *Reactive Extrusion, Principles and Practice*, Xanthos, M., ed. Hanser Publ, Munich, 1992, Chapter 4.

[107] Robeson, L.M. *J. Appl. Polym. Sci.* **1985**, *30*, 4081–4098.

[108] Keskkula, H., Paul, D.R. Toughened nylons. In *Nylon Plastics Handbook*, Kohan, M., ed. Carl Hanser, Munich, 1994, Chapter 11.

[109] Lazzeri, A., Malanima, M., Pracella, M. *J. Appl. Polym. Sci.* **1999**, *74*, 3455–3468.

[110] Sanchez, A., Rosales, C., Laredo, E., Muller, A.J., Pracella, M. *Macromol. Chem. Phys.* **2001**, *202*, 2461–2478.

[111] Psarski, M., Pracella, M., Galeski, A. *Polymer* **2000**, *41*, 4923–4932.

[112] Frensch, H., Harnischfeger, P., Jungnickel, B.J. Fractionated crystallization in incompatible polymer blends. In *Multiphase Polymers, Blends, Ionomers and Interpenetrating Networks*, Utracki, L.A., Weiss, R.A., eds. *ACS Symp. Series 395*. Washingthon, DC, 1989.

[113] Tol, R.T., Mathot, V.B.F., Groeninckx, G. *Polymer* **2005**, *46*, 369–382.

[114] Miscenko, N., Groeninckx, G., Reynaers, H., Koch, M., Pracella, M. *4th ATPS Conference on Chemical Modification of Polymers and Reactive Blending*, Gargnano, Italy, 1996, Abs. p. 46.

[115] Brown, C.S., Alder, P.T. Blends containing liquid crystal polymers. In *Polymer Blends and Alloys*, Folkes, M.J., Hope, P.S., eds. Blackie Academic & Professional, London, 1993.

[116] West, J.L. *Mol. Cryst. Liq. Cryst.* **1988**, *157*, 427–441.

[117] Doane, J.W., Golemme, A., West, J.L., Whitehead, J.B., Wu, B.G. *Mol. Cryst. Liq. Cryst.* **1988**, *165*, 511–532.

[118] Demus, D., Richter, L. *Textures of Liquid Crystals*. Verlag Chemie, New York, 1978.

[119] Price, F.P., Wendorff, J.H. *J. Phys. Chem.* **1972**, *76*, 276–280.

[120] Grebowicz, J., Wunderlich, B. *J. Polym. Sci. Polym. Phys. Ed.* **1983**, *21*, 141.

[121] Battacharya, S.K., Misra, A., Stein, R.S., Lenz, R.W., Hahn, P.E. *Polym. Bull.* **1986**, *16*, 465–472.

[122] Pracella, M., De Petris, S., Frosini, V., Magagnini, P.L. *Mol. Cryst. Liq. Cryst.* **1984**, *113*, 225–235.

[123] Yoo, Y.D., Kim, S.C. *Polym. J.* **1988**, *20*, 1117–1124.

[124] Tsai, R.S. *Makromol. Chem.* **1992**, *193*, 2477–2486.

[125] Pracella, M., Frosini, V., Galli, G., Chiellini, E. *Mol. Cryst. Liq. Cryst.* **1984**, *113*, 201–212.

[126] Flory, P.J., Abe, A. *Macromolecules* **1978**, *11*, 1119–1122.

[127] Ballauf, M. *Mol. Cryst. Liq. Cryst.* **1986**, *136*, 175.

[128] Patwardian, A.A., Belfiore, L.A. *Polym. Eng. Sci.* **1988**, *28*, 916–925.

[129] Kelker, H., Hatz, R. *Handbook of Liquid Crystal*. Verlag Chem., Basel, 1980, Chapt. 8.

[130] Pracella, M., Bresci, B., Nicolardi, C. *Liq. Cryst.* **1993**, *14*, 881–888.

[131] Pracella, M., Bresci, B. *Mol. Cryst. Liq. Cryst.* **1995**, *266*, 23–33.

[132] Blizard, K.G., Baird, D.G. *Polym. Eng. Sci.* **1987**, *27*, 653–662.

[133] Ko, C.U., Wilkes, G.L., Wong, C.P. *J. Appl. Polym. Sci.* **1989**, *37*, 3063.

[134] Dutta, D., Fruitwala, H., Kohli, A., Weiss, R.A. *Polym. Eng. Sci.* **1990**, *30*, 1005–1018.

[135] Paci, M., Barone, C., Magagnini, P.L. *J. Polym. Sci. Polym. Phys. Ed.* **1987**, *25*, 1595.

[136] Datta, A., Baird, D.G. *Polymer* **1995**, *36*, 505–514.

[137] La Mantia, F.P., Scaffaro, R., Magagnini, P.L., Paci, M., Sek, D., Minkova, L.I., Miteva, T.S. *Polym. Eng. Sci.* **1997**, *37*, 1164–1170.

[138] Magagnini, P.L., Pracella, M., Minkova, L.I., Miteva, T.S., Sek, D., Grobelny, J., La Mantia, F.P. *J. Appl. Polym. Sci.* **1998**, *69*, 391–403.

[139] Joseph, E.G., Wilkes, G.L., Baird, D.G. Preliminary thermal and structural studies of blends based on a thermotropic liquid crystalline copolyester and polyethylene terephthalate. In *Polymer Liquid Crystals*, Blumstein, A., ed. Plenum Press, New York, 1985.

[140] Alvarez, C., Martinez-Gomez, A., Perez, E., de la Orden, M.U., Martinez-Urreaga, J. *Polymer* **2007**, *48*, 3137–3147.

[141] Minkova, L., Paci, M., Pracella, M., Magagnini, P.L. *Polym. Eng. Sci.* **1992**, *32*, 57–64.

[142] Pracella, M., Dainelli, D., Galli, G., Chiellini, E. *Makromol. Chem.* **1986**, *187*, 2387–2400.

[143] Pracella, M., Chiellini, E., Galli, G., Dainelli, D. *Mol. Cryst. Liq. Cryst.* **1987**, *153*, 525–535.

[144] Pracella, M., Chiellini, E., Dainelli, D. *Makromol. Chem.* **1989**, *190*, 175–189.

[145] Kwei, T.K., Patterson, G.D., Wang, T.T. *Macromolecules* **1976**, *9*, 780–784.

[146] Imken, R.L., Paul, D.R., Barlow, J.W. *Polym. Eng. Sci.* **1976**, *16*, 593–601.

[147] Marco, C., Gomez, M.A., Fatou, J.G., Etxeberria, A., Elorza, M.M., Iruin, J.J. *Eur. Polym. J.* **1993**, *29*, 1477–1481.

[148] Jo, W.H., Park, S.J., Kwon, I.H. *Polym. Int.* **1992**, *29*, 173–178.

[149] Chen, H.L., Porter, R.S. *J. Polym. Sci. Polym. Phys. Ed.* **1993**, *B31*, 1845.

[150] Clough, N.E., Richards, R.W., Ibrahim, T. *Polymer* **1994**, *35*, 1044–1050.

[151] Lee, L.T., Woo, E.M. *Polym. Int.* **2004**, *53*, 1613–1620.

[152] Liu, J., Qiu, Z., Jungnickel, B.J. *J. Polym. Sci. B* **2005**, *43*, 287–295.

[153] Liau, W.B., Tung, S.H., Lai, W.C., Yang, L. *Polymer* **2006**, *47*, 8380–8388.

11

CRYSTALLIZATION IN COPOLYMERS

SHENG LI AND RICHARD A. REGISTER
Department of Chemical and Biological Engineering, Princeton University, Princeton, New Jersey

11.1 Introduction, 327
11.2 Crystallization in Statistical Copolymers, 328
    11.2.1 Flory's Model, 328
    11.2.2 Solid-State Morphology, 330
    11.2.3 Mechanical Properties, 334
    11.2.4 Crystallization Kinetics, 335
    11.2.5 Statistical Copolymers with Two Crystallizable Units, 337
    11.2.6 Crystallization Thermodynamics, 337

11.3 Crystallization of Block Copolymers from Homogeneous or Weakly Segregated Melts, 340
    11.3.1 Solid-State Morphology, 340
    11.3.2 Crystallization-Driven Structure Formation, 342
11.4 Summary, 343
References, 344

11.1 INTRODUCTION

Copolymers are macromolecules composed of two or more chemically distinct monomer units, covalently joined to form a common polymer chain [1, 2]. In these materials, the sequence distribution of the monomer counits plays a critical role in determining the copolymer's crystallization behavior, and consequently influences its solid-state morphology and material properties [1, 2]. At one extreme, different types of monomer units may be randomly incorporated into the polymer chain, resulting in a statistical copolymer. At the other extreme, blocks of homopolymer sequences of different chemical nature and chain length may be joined together to form what is known as a block copolymer. In this chapter, we will review the key effects of comonomer incorporation on the solid-state morphology and crystallization kinetics in both statistical and block copolymers.

On the topic of statistical copolymer crystallization, the scope of the review will be limited to compositionally homogeneous statistical copolymers. In many studies, anionic polymerization of butadiene, followed by hydrogenation, was employed to produce what is often considered a "model" statistically random ethylene–butene copolymer [3, 4]. Other materials considered include compositionally uniform statistical copolymers synthesized via metallocene-type single-site catalysts, compositional fractions of copolymers prepared originally using Ziegler-Natta catalysis, condensation polymers where the sequence distribution can be completely randomized by exchange reactions, and copolymers synthesized via free-radical polymerization in a continuous flow stirred tank reactor under homogeneous conditions.

In semicrystalline block copolymers, the crystallization behavior is often more complex than that observed in statistical copolymers because the solid-state morphology adopted by block copolymers can be driven either by block incompatibility or by crystallization of one or more blocks [5–8]. In this chapter, we will cover only block copolymers with homogeneous or weakly segregated melts, such that crystallization is always the dominant factor in determining solid-state morphology. Crystallization of block copolymers from strongly segregated melts is covered in Chapter 12. Furthermore, the

---

Handbook of Polymer Crystallization, First Edition. Edited by Ewa Piorkowska and Gregory C. Rutledge.
© 2013 John Wiley & Sons, Inc. Published 2013 by John Wiley & Sons, Inc.

block copolymers reviewed here are near-monodisperse in molecular weight; thus, the results shown are not complicated by material polydispersity.

11.2 CRYSTALLIZATION IN STATISTICAL COPOLYMERS

Statistical copolymers refer to a class of copolymers in which the distribution of the monomer counits follows Markovian statistics [1, 2]. In these polymeric materials, since the different chemical units are joined at random, the resulting polymer chains would be expected to encounter difficulties in packing into crystalline structures with long-range order; however, numerous experiments have shown that crystallites can form in statistical copolymers under suitable conditions [2]. In this section, we will discuss the effects of counit incorporation on the solid-state structure and the crystallization kinetics in statistical copolymers. A number of thermodynamic models, which have been proposed to describe the equilibrium crystallization/melting behavior in copolymers, will also be highlighted, and their applicability to describing experimental observations will be discussed.

11.2.1 Flory's Model

The first equilibrium theory of copolymer crystallization was presented by Flory over 50 years ago [9, 10]. The copolymer of interest is composed of crystallizable A units and noncrystallizable B counits. During crystallization, the B counits are assumed to be excluded from the crystalline phase of the copolymer such that the longitudinal growth of the crystallites is determined by the distribution of the B counits along the polymer chain. Furthermore, in his model, Flory considered the case where the A crystallites are in equilibrium with a melt containing mixed A and B units [10]. When crystallites melt, in addition to the entropy increase as a result of the transformation from an ordered crystalline state to a more disordered melt state, there is another positive contribution to the system's entropy because the pure A crystallites melt into a mixed A/B phase. This additional increase in system entropy results in a depression of the copolymer's melting temperature when compared to the melting temperature of a homopolymer of the same crystal thickness.

To account for this additional entropy of mixing, Flory introduced a probability term, P_ζ [10]. It represents the probability that a chosen amorphous unit is a crystallizable A unit, and it belongs to a sequence of at least ζ units long, thus capable of contributing to the growth of crystallites of thickness ζ. Then it follows from equilibrium that the necessary and sufficient condition for crystallization is $P_\zeta^0 > P_\zeta^e$ for at least one value of ζ, where the superscripts 0 and e represent the initial and equilibrium copolymer sequence distributions, respectively [10]. The equilibrium criterion for copolymer crystallization also leads to Equation 11.1, which states that the melting temperature of a copolymer (T_m) depends only on the melting temperature of crystalline homopolymer A (T_m^o), the heat of fusion per mole of A repeat units (ΔH_u), and the sequence propagation probability (p) [10].

$$\frac{1}{T_m} - \frac{1}{T_m^o} = \frac{-R}{\Delta H_u} \ln p. \quad (11.1)$$

The sequence propagation probability, p, is the probability that an A unit is followed by another A unit along a chain. In a truly random copolymer whose comonomer distribution follows zero-order Markovian statistics, p equals X_A, the mole fraction of A units in the polymer; therefore, Equation 11.1 can be rewritten as [10]:

$$\frac{1}{T_m} - \frac{1}{T_m^o} = \frac{-R}{\Delta H_u} \ln X_A. \quad (11.2)$$

A corresponding equation for determining the weight fraction crystallinity, w_c, achievable in a copolymer at a chosen temperature T was also proposed [10]:

$$w_c = (X_A/p)(1-p)^2 p^{\zeta^*}\{p(1-p)^{-2} - e^{-\theta}(1-e^{-\theta})^{-2} + \zeta^*[(1-p)^{-1} - (1-e^{-\theta})^{-1}]\}. \quad (11.3)$$

In Equation 11.3, θ is a dimensionless undercooling defined as

$$\theta = (\Delta H_u/R)(1/T - 1/T_m^o) \quad (11.4)$$

and ζ^* represents the minimum crystal sequence length that may exist at equilibrium, given by:

$$\zeta^* = -\left\{-\frac{2\sigma_e}{RT} + \ln\frac{X_A}{p} + 2\ln[(1-p)(1-e^{-\theta})^{-1}]\right\}(\theta + \ln p)^{-1} \quad (11.5)$$

where σ_e is the surface free energy of the crystal.

Since its introduction, Flory's model has found success at describing the qualitative behavior of copolymer crystallization; however, it typically does not compare well quantitatively to experimental data [11–13]. Richardson et al. [11], then later Alamo et al. [12] examined the melting temperatures of ethylene copolymers with varying counit contents. As illustrated in

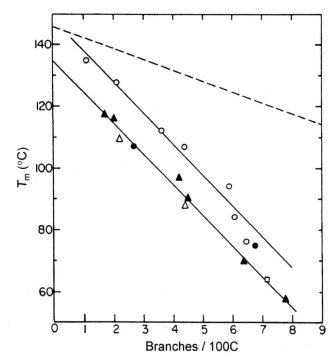

Figure 11.1 Final melting temperatures of ethylene copolymers as a function of branch content: ethylene copolymers containing methyl (open circles), ethyl (open square), and n-propyl (solid triangles) branches; hydrogenated polybutadiene (open triangles); ethylene–vinyl acetate (solid circles). Dashed line represents Flory's equilibrium theory for random copolymers ($p = X_A$), as given in Equation (11.2). Reprinted with permission from Reference [12]. Copyright 1984, American Chemical Society.

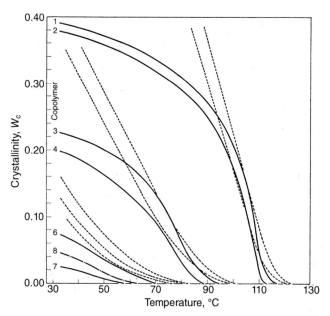

Figure 11.2 Degree of crystallinity (w_c) of statistical ethylene copolymers containing n-propyl or ethyl branches as a function of temperature. Solid lines represent copolymer crystallinity calculated based on measured specific volume: 1 = 1.8 n-propyl branches/100 C; 2 = 2.0 n-propyl branches/100 C; 3 = 4.2 n-propyl branches/100 C; 4 = 4.6 n-propyl branches/100 C; 6 = 6.8 n-propyl branches/100 C; 7 = 7.7 n-propyl branches/100 C; 8 = 7.3 ethyl branches/100 C. Dotted lines represent Flory's equilibrium model for copolymer crystallinity, as given in Equation (11.3). Reprinted from Reference [11]. Copyright 1963, with permission from Elsevier.

Figure 11.1, the experimentally determined copolymer melting temperature decreases with increasing counit content, in agreement with Flory's model; however, the numerical values of the measured melting temperatures are significantly below those calculated from Equation 11.2, and the dependence of T_m on counit content is much stronger.

Although the copolymers shown in Figure 11.1 were crystallized very slowly to allow most favorable conditions for equilibrium crystallization at each temperature, and the reported melting temperatures, measured by dilatometry, were determined by locating the temperatures where the melting curves merged with the liquidus line [11], these conditions were still far removed from the thermodynamic equilibrium upon which the Flory model was built. Furthermore, the formation of thick crystallites that correspond to the equilibrium melting temperature in Flory's model is an extremely rare occurrence. Even if they were present, their minute quantity would make detection difficult. Thus, the experimentally measured copolymer melting temperatures are always lower than those predicted by the equilibrium theory [11, 13, 14].

The degree of crystallinity, calculated based on measured specific volumes, for the same set of statistical ethylene copolymers containing ethyl or n-propyl branches shown in Figure 11.1, are plotted as a function of temperature in Figure 11.2 [11]. When compared to the theoretical w_c, calculated according to Equation 11.3, the experimental values are found to deviate from Flory's prediction at both low and high undercoolings. The observed deviation at shallow undercoolings is due to difficulty in forming thick crystallites at high temperatures, as mentioned in the previous paragraph [11]. The deviation seen at deep undercoolings is attributed to kinetic restrictions imposed on the melt by crystallization that took place at high temperatures: as crystallites begin to form at relatively high temperatures just below the onset of crystallization, they hinder the motion of the remaining molten segments and decrease their likelihood to crystallize as temperature is further reduced [11, 15, 16].

According to Flory's model (see Eq. 11.1 and Eq. 11.2), the melting temperature of a statistical AB copolymer is determined by the concentration of the noncrystallizable B counits and their sequence distribution (through p, if $p \neq X_A$), but is independent of the chemical nature of the counits [10]. Alamo and Mandelkern reported the peak melting temperatures of rapidly crystallized ethylene–alkene copolymers of different short-chain branch length, and concluded that when counits are mainly excluded from the crystalline phase of the copolymer, the measured melting temperatures exhibit a nearly identical dependence on counit concentration, regardless of the chemical nature of the counits [13]. The finding also indicates that minor variations in sequence distribution, such that p does not strictly equal X_A, have an imperceptibly small influence on peak T_m.

In contrast to the observations made by Alamo and Mandelkern, Kale et al. [17] found that at comparable comonomer concentration, ethylene–butene copolymers exhibited higher peak melting temperatures than ethylene–octene copolymers, all synthesized with constrained-geometry single-site catalysts, although the differences in melting temperature between the two types of copolymers were apparent only at higher comonomer contents than Alamo and Mandelkern investigated. Hosoda et al. also reported that in linear low density polyethylene, prepared by Ziegler-Natta catalysis and cross-fractionated to obtain specimens of uniform branch content and comparable molecular weight, the peak melting temperatures of copolymers containing ethyl branches were higher than those of copolymers with isobutyl branches at comparable branch concentrations [18]. It was suggested that the isobutyl branches, being much bulkier than the ethyl branches, may cause more severe crowding at the crystal fold surface, leading to thinner lamellae and lower melting temperatures. The Flory model assumes extended-sequence crystals, where the crystal thickness is equal to the length of the crystallizable sequence, and thus does not properly describe thinner, folded crystals where the fold surface free energy term is important. Thermodynamic models that take into account finite crystal thickness and surface energy are described in Section 11.2.6. Thus, the conflicting reports as to whether comonomer type influences melting temperature could reflect real differences in fold surface free energy, or real differences in comonomer sequence ($p \neq X_A$); they may also reflect the specimens' thermal histories, as often the quantity reported is a peak T_m measured on specimens crystallized during dynamic cooling, rather than the final T_m measured on specimens crystallized very slowly, as would be most appropriate for comparison with the Flory theory (i.e., Fig. 11.1).

In Figure 11.1, although most of the ethylene–alkene copolymers share a common T_m curve, the copolymers with methyl branches exhibit melting temperatures that are distinctly higher than the others [11, 12]. In this case, a substantial fraction of the methyl units are incorporated into the polyethylene crystals, giving rise to melting temperatures that are higher than those observed in analogous copolymers with side groups that are excluded from the crystals. The Flory model also does not consider the possibility of comonomer inclusion; more detailed discussion on branch inclusion in crystals is presented in Section 11.2.2.3 and Section 11.2.5. Thermodynamic models that allow the inclusion of a fraction of counits in the copolymer crystalline phase are presented in Section 11.2.6.

11.2.2 Solid-State Morphology

Similar to semicrystalline homopolymers, statistical copolymers containing crystallizable segments also exhibit structural characteristics on several length scales in the solid state. At the micrometer length scale, despite the presence of comonomer defects, statistical copolymers may still crystallize to form ordered three-dimensional supermolecular structures. At the nanometer length scale, lamellar morphologies are typically observed, while the lamellar size and degree of organization differ depending on the extent of counit incorporation into the copolymer. At the atomic length scale, the crystalline unit-cell structure is also affected by the presence of the noncrystallizable counits. Based on the type and concentration of the counits, they may or may not be included in the crystalline unit cell, and consequently influence the dimensions, symmetry, and stability of the unit cell.

11.2.2.1 Supermolecular Structure Upon crystallization from the melt, homopolymers typically form spherically symmetric aggregates, known as spherulites [19, 20]. Detailed studies on the supermolecular structures of compositionally homogeneous ethylene-1-alkene copolymers [21], fractions of linear low density polyethylenes [22, 23], hydrogenated polybutadienes [21–23], and propylene–alkene copolymers [24, 25] revealed that statistical ethylene- and propylene-based copolymers also exhibit ordered supermolecular structures under suitable crystallization conditions. A schematic morphology map for ethylene copolymers is presented in Figure 11.3 [23]. A dome-shaped region, defined by copolymer molecular weight, crystallization temperature, and counit concentration, is constructed within which spherulites are observed. Overall, the morphology map indicates that the order of the supermolecular structure exhibited by ethylene copolymers worsens as

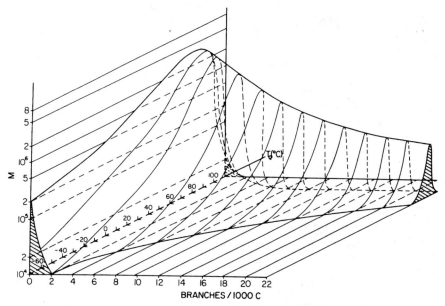

Figure 11.3 Morphology map for nonisothermally crystallized ethylene copolymers, drawn schematically based on experimental data for fractions of linear low density polyethylene and hydrogenated polybutadienes. Spherulitic superstructure is observed within the dome-shaped region defined by the three axes: copolymer molecular weight (M), branch content, and nominal crystallization temperature. Reprinted with permission from Reference [23]. Copyright 1981 American Chemical Society.

molecular weight and counit concentration increase [21–23]. At fixed molecular weight and counit content, the organization of the superstructure may be improved by isothermal crystallization at relatively shallow undercoolings [22, 23].

In addition to counit concentration, the size of the branches also affects the degree of spherulite organization. It was observed that as the alkyl side chains become longer, they exert a greater influence on the interfacial structure of the crystallites. This in turn lowers the organization of the lamellar stacks and leads to less well-developed spherulitic superstructures [21].

11.2.2.2 Lamellar Structure and Crystallite Size
The influence of counit type and concentration on lamellar morphology has been reported for a number of statistical copolymers, including fractions of linear low density polyethylenes [18], compositional fractions of ethylene-1-alkenes [26–28], hydrogenated polybutadienes [26], and compositionally homogeneous ethylene-1-alkene copolymers obtained via single-site metallocene catalysts [29]. Voigt-Martin et al. investigated the morphology of hydrogenated polybutadienes and fractions of ethylene copolymers with vinyl acetate, butene, or octene counits using transmission electron microscopy (TEM) [26]. The lamellar morphologies of the copolymers examined were found to be independent of the chemical nature of the counits. At a low counit concentration, up to about two branches per 100 C atoms, lamellar crystals were typically observed. Both the lateral dimension and the degree of perfection of the lamellae were reduced with increasing counit content. At counit contents above four branches per 100 C atoms, the observed crystallites were found to have lost lamellar characteristics and resembled fringed micelles. An example of this crystallite morphology transition with increasing counit content is illustrated in Figure 11.4 for a series of hydrogenated polybutadienes [26].

Defor et al. studied fractions of ethylene-octene copolymers obtained via preparative temperature-rising elution fractionation [27, 28, 30]. By employing small-angle X-ray scattering (SAXS), the crystal core thickness and the crystalline–amorphous transition layer thickness of the copolymers were examined as functions of branch content. The SAXS data, analyzed using a pseudo-two-phase model, are summarized in Figure 11.5 [28]. They indicate that as the short-chain branching content increases from 2.9 to 28.2 branches per 1000 C atoms, the crystal core thickness decreases from 97 to 18 Å and the transition layer thickness increases from 8 to 21 Å. These results are in qualitative agreement with Flory's prediction that crystal core thickness

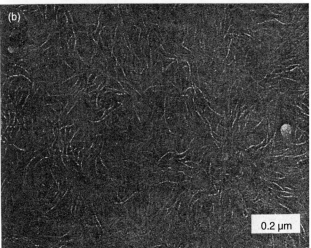

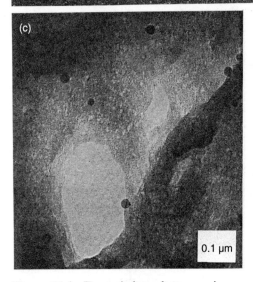

Figure 11.4 Transmission electron micrographs of slowly cooled hydrogenated polybutadienes: (a) 2.2 ethyl branches/100 C; (b) 3.2 ethyl branches/100 C; (c) 4.5 ethyl branches/100 C. From Reference [26]. Copyright (1986 John Wiley & Sons, Inc.). Reprinted with permission of John Wiley & Sons, Inc.

in random copolymers is determined by the concentration of the branches. Furthermore, the observed swelling in transition layer thickness with increasing branching confirms that the short-chain branches, rejected from the crystalline phase, reside preferentially in the crystalline–amorphous transition layer [28].

A shortcoming of Defoor's study is that due to the sample preparation method employed, the copolymer fraction's molecular weight and short-chain branching content are inversely related, thus cannot be treated as independent variables [30]. Consequently, the observations reported regarding copolymer lamellar morphology must be considered as resulting from both factors. Fortunately, similar studies on ethylene copolymer morphology were conducted on compositionally homogeneous ethylene–alkene copolymers with fixed molecular weight, where it was also shown that the transition layer thickness increased with increasing counit concentration but leveled off at high counit contents [29].

11.2.2.3 Crystal Unit-Cell Structure It has been demonstrated repeatedly that in statistical copolymers, the unit cell expands with increasing counit concentration [31, 32]. Howard and Crist studied the unit cell dimensions of a series of hydrogenated polybutadienes containing 0–73 ethyl branches per 1000 C atoms using X-ray diffraction [31]. Both the *a*- and *b*-axes of the unit cell lengthen with increasing counit content but begin to level off above 20 ethyl branches per 1000 C atoms, while the *c*-axis shows a very slight contraction, resulting in a net expansion of the unit-cell volume with increasing counit concentration.

The two most widely accepted mechanisms for this phenomenon are defect inclusion in the crystalline phase and surface stresses related to reduced lamellar thickness [13, 31, 33]. In the second mechanism, defects are mostly rejected from the crystals, but preferentially reside in the interfacial layer, thereby exerting stress on the crystal surface [31, 34, 35]. As the counit concentration increases, the lamellar crystal becomes thinner. This leads to an increase in the crystal's surface-to-volume ratio, which in turn amplifies the magnitude of this stress-induced unit cell deformation.

Rabiej studied the topic of defect location for a series of compositionally homogeneous ethylene–alkene statistical copolymers using small- and wide-angle X-ray scattering (WAXS) [36]. For an ethylene–propylene copolymer, its methyl branches were determined to be partially included in the ethylene unit cell based on the observation that at similar comonomer content, while the lamellar thickness of the ethylene–propylene copolymer was higher than that of copolymers with longer branches, its unit cell was also much bigger than that for unbranched polyethylene. As the length of the branches

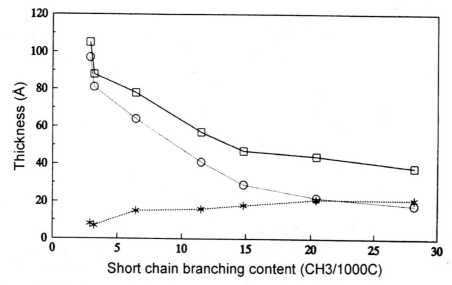

Figure 11.5 SAXS-determined morphology data for compositional fractions of ethylene–octene copolymers: number-averaged lamellar thickness (open squares), crystal core thickness (open circles), transition layer thickness (stars). Reprinted with permission from Reference [28]. Copyright 1993 American Chemical Society.

increased to ethyl and hexyl, the degree of branch inclusion in the crystal unit cell dropped significantly, and unit-cell expansion in these copolymers with longer branches was attributed mainly to surface stresses. In another study involving a series of polyethylenes containing branches ranging from methyl to hexyl, partitioning of short-chain branches between the amorphous and crystalline phases with higher concentration of branches residing in the amorphous phase was also reported, by measuring and modeling changes in X-ray diffraction peak intensity with branch content, rather than through the unit-cell dimensions [37].

Partial inclusion of small branches in the polyethylene unit cell was confirmed by solid-state ^{13}C nuclear magnetic resonance (^{13}C NMR) [38–40]. It was observed that while methyl groups partitioned into the polyethylene unit cell on an equilibrium basis, the composition of the crystalline phase in copolymers containing longer side groups was dependent on crystallization history. Slow-cooled copolymer samples showed lower degrees of defect incorporation because the crystallite was allowed more time to perfect its order [38].

Partitioning of branches in both polyethylene and isotactic polypropylene copolymers was also investigated by Hosoda et al. [41, 42]. Ethylene–alkene and propylene–alkene statistical copolymers were degraded by fuming nitric acid to selectively remove their amorphous phase. The degree of branch inclusion in the residual crystalline phase was then determined by solid-state ^{13}C NMR. For ethylene copolymers, it was confirmed that the ease of branch incorporation into the polyethylene unit cell was inversely related to the bulkiness of the side groups. Specifically, the ratio of the branch content in the crystalline phase to that in the amorphous phase followed the order: methyl (0.22) > ethyl (0.10) > n-butyl (0.07) ≈ n-hexyl (0.06) ≈ n-decyl (0.06) > isobutyl (0.04) [41]. For propylene copolymers, a similar trend was observed, except that more 1-butene counits were found in the crystalline phase than the smaller ethylene counits [42]. This was attributed to the similar helical crystal chain conformation adopted by both polypropylene and polybutene homopolymers.

The distribution of short-chain defects in copolymers was also modeled by Mattice and his colleagues using both two-dimensional and three-dimensional lattices [43–45]. Assuming defects were excluded from the crystalline phase of a copolymer, a nonuniform distribution of branches in the amorphous region between two crystalline lamellae was found. When branches were absent, the anisotropic interfacial region was thin, but it thickened substantially with increases in both branch content and branch size.

Besides its influence on the crystal unit cell dimension, the presence of noncrystallizable counits can also stabilize crystalline phases that are not commonly observed in homopolymers crystallized at atmospheric pressure [46, 47]. X-ray diffraction on a compositionally uniform ethylene statistical copolymer containing

7.3 mol% octene counits showed that in addition to the commonly observed orthorhombic structure, a pseudohexagonal structure was also observed [46, 48]. It was postulated that the pseudohexagonal structure, which is seen in polyethylene homopolymers when crystallized at high temperature and pressure [49, 50], is present in the copolymer because it can better tolerate the noncrystallizable defects than the orthorhombic structure [46, 51].

Similarly, in statistical isotactic polypropylene copolymers containing ethylene or butene counits, a mixture of α monoclinic and γ orthorhombic [52–54] crystal phases was observed, and the proportion of the γ form increased with increasing counit concentration [25, 47, 55, 56]. The γ form is typically observed in propylene homopolymers when crystallized under high pressure [57, 58]. In the case of copolymers, the presence of noncrystallizable counits disrupts the development of polypropylene helices, resulting in an increase in the γ phase content [25, 47, 55, 56]. The γ phase was also observed in isotactic copolymers of propylene and 1-hexene [59]. Additionally, propylene copolymers that contain 10–25 mol% hexene units were found to crystallize in a crystal form having a trigonal unit cell [60, 61]. This structure is isomorphous to that of poly(1-butene), which, in terms of average branch length, is equivalent to a propylene–hexene copolymer with 33 mol% hexene [60].

11.2.3 Mechanical Properties

The mechanical properties of a semicrystalline polymer are intimately related to its morphology. Since counit concentration and size have been shown to affect the morphology of a copolymer, a corresponding influence on its mechanical properties is anticipated. Bensason et al. studied the morphological and mechanical characteristics of compositionally homogeneous ethylene statistical copolymers containing 0–13.6 mol% octene units [62]. At low counit concentration, the copolymers behaved like typical semicrystalline thermoplastics, while at high counit concentration, they behaved more as elastomers. As illustrated schematically in Figure 11.6, this change in mechanical behavior can be correlated to a morphological transition in the copolymers from lamellar to fringed micellar crystals [62]. At high octene content, the fringed micellar crystals act as anchors for the rubbery amorphous chains, allowing the copolymer to behave as an elastomer [62, 63].

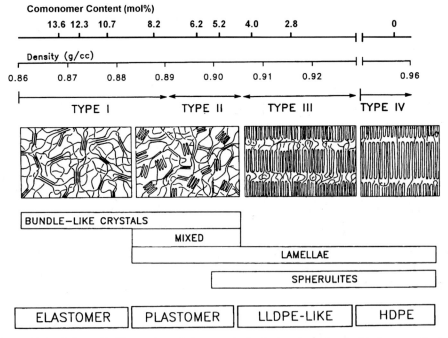

Figure 11.6 Schematic illustration of the morphological and mechanical behavior of ethylene–octene statistical copolymers. With increasing counit content, the copolymer morphology transitions from lamellar crystals to bundle-like crystals, and its mechanical behavior transitions from semicrystalline thermoplastic to elastomeric. Reprinted from Reference [62] with permission of John Wiley & Sons, Inc., Copyright 1996.

The tensile properties of homogeneous ethylene–alkene statistical copolymers were further explored by Kennedy et al. [64]. It has been shown that the yield stress of a semicrystalline polymer is dependent on its crystal thickness [65, 66]. During uniaxial compression, the yield stress of polyethylene was observed to increase with crystal thickness up to 40 nm, whereas for thicker crystals it leveled off [66]. Since the crystal thickness in homogeneous copolymers decreases with increasing counit concentration, not surprisingly, an inverse correlation was also found between yield stress and counit content [64].

The post-yield deformation behavior of a copolymer, on the other hand, depends on both the concentration and size of the counits [64, 67]. Kennedy et al. observed that at elongations beyond the yield point, the deformation characteristics of the copolymers were dominated by strain hardening, and this increase in stress with strain became more prominent as the counit concentration increased [64]. One possible explanation is that at the moderate degree of crystallinity displayed by these copolymers, strain-induced crystallization can take place during deformation, resulting in the observed strain hardening. This post-yield strain hardening behavior was also dependent on counit size: in ethylene–butene copolymers, the increase in stress with strain was much more moderate than that observed in copolymers with longer branches [64]. The difference in the degree of strain hardening observed among copolymers with different counit sizes was attributed to the varying degrees of interaction among branches in the amorphous region.

11.2.4 Crystallization Kinetics

In many ways, crystallization of statistical copolymers resembles that of homopolymers [65, 68–70]. For example, hydrogenated polybutadienes of different branch content and molecular weight show sigmoidal crystallization isotherms, similar to those seen in polyethylene homopolymer crystallization. In addition, at a given isothermal crystallization temperature, the degree of copolymer crystallinity drops above a critical molecular weight, also qualitatively similar to polyethylene homopolymer [69].

However, there are also aspects of the crystallization process that are particular to statistical copolymers [16, 69, 71–76]. In a series of studies on the crystallization and melting behavior of ethylene–butene statistical copolymers, it was observed that after isothermal crystallization, while polyethylene homopolymer exhibited a single-peak melting endotherm, all the copolymers showed bimodal melting behavior [16, 71]. Each melting peak of the copolymer endotherm was determined to represent a distinct crystal population because its shape was unaffected when subjected to crystallization and reheating at different rates. The crystals with higher melting temperature developed from ethylene sequences that were long enough to fold into lamellar crystals. The lower-temperature melting peak corresponded to thinner fringed micellar crystals, formed from segments that were eligible for crystallization at a given isothermal crystallization temperature but too short to fold and thicken. This two-stage crystallization process is unique to copolymers, whereas a perfectly regular homopolymer obviously does not suffer from this crystallizable sequence segregation effect.

In semicrystalline homopolymers, the crystalline lamellar thickness is inversely related to the degree of undercooling below the equilibrium melting temperature [77]. Since the equilibrium melting temperature of a copolymer decreases with increasing counit concentration, one might expect that for a given crystallization temperature, the resulting lamellar thickness of a copolymer would also depend on its counit concentration. Surprisingly, such a correlation between lamellar thickness and counit content is absent in either ethylene–alkene statistical copolymers or syndiotactic poly(propylene-co-octene) statistical copolymers (see Fig. 11.7) [73–75]. This unexpected experimental observation led the authors to conclude that the crystal thickness

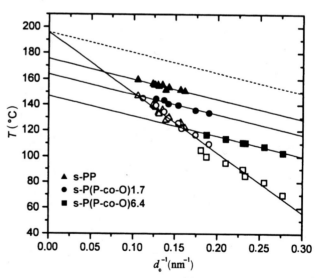

Figure 11.7 SAXS-determined crystal thickness, d_c, as a function of crystallization temperature (open symbols) and melting temperature (filled symbols). The propylene copolymers investigated are: syndiotactic polypropylene with 3% meso diads (s-PP); syndiotactic poly(propylene-co-octene) containing x mol% octene units (s-P(P-co-O)x). Reprinted with permission from Reference [73]. Copyright 1998 American Chemical Society.

in a copolymer is not determined by the degree of undercooling below its equilibrium melting temperature, but instead is relative to that of an intermediate "mesomorphic" phase that forms preceding the appearance of the final lamellar crystal. This mesomorphic phase also has the property that its structure is independent of the noncrystalline counit concentration. The influence of this mesomorphic phase on the crystallization processes in both homopolymers and statistical copolymers was reviewed by Strobl [78].

Another distinguishing aspect of copolymer crystallization is that with increasing counit content, the crystallization isotherms deviate from the Avrami relation, given in Equation 11.6 [79], at progressively lower extents of crystallization [69, 76]

$$1 - f(t) = \exp(-kt^n). \quad (11.6)$$

In Equation 11.6, $f(t)$ is the fraction of the crystallization process that has occurred by time t, and k and n are constants determined by the nature of the crystallization process. At small extents of crystallization (i.e., $f \ll 1$), $\ln(1 - f) \approx -f$, thus Equation 11.6 may be rewritten as:

$$f(t) = kt^n. \quad (11.7)$$

Isothermal crystallization data for ethylene copolymers containing varying amounts of short-chain branches were reported by Alamo and Mandelkern, as shown in Figure 11.8 [69]. In their study, the quantity measured was the weight fraction crystallinity, w_c, determined from specific volume measurements as $w_c(t) = (\overline{v}_a - \overline{v}_t)/(\overline{v}_a - \overline{v}_c)$, where $\overline{v}_a$, $\overline{v}_c$, and $\overline{v}_t$ represent the specific volumes for 100% amorphous and 100% crystalline polyethylene, and for the specimen at time t during the course of crystallization, respectively. Since polymers are never 100% crystalline, w_c is always smaller than f, and w_c does not approach unity at long time (while f does, by definition). But if the proportionality constant between w_c and f (e.g., the degree of crystallinity within the spherulites) is unchanged at short times, then the initial behavior of $\ln w_c$ versus $\ln t$ (or $\log w_c$ vs. $\log t$) should still follow a straight line, with the slope corresponding to the Avrami exponent.

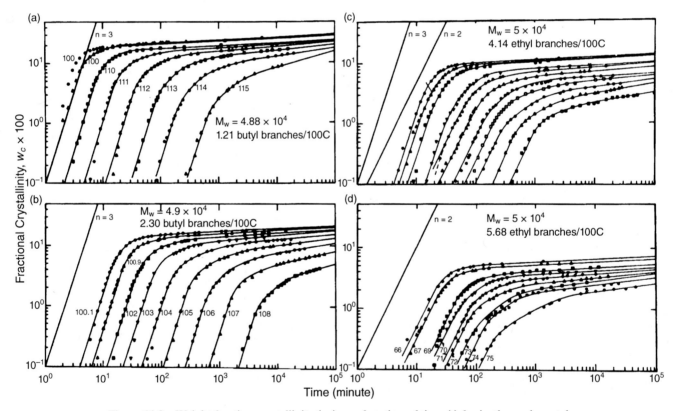

Figure 11.8 Weight fraction crystallinity (w_c) as a function of time (t) for isothermal crystallization at various temperatures indicated (in °C), for an ethylene–hexene statistical copolymer (a), and hydrogenated polybutadienes of varying branch content (b–d). Lines at left in each panel reflect Avrami exponents, $n = 2$ or 3. Reprinted with permission from Reference [69]. Copyright 1991 American Chemical Society.

It is clear from Figure 11.8 that for copolymers with relatively low counit contents (see Fig. 11.8a,b), their isotherms do indeed follow the Avrami relation with $n = 2-3$ at short times. As the counit content increases, the crystallization process becomes more sluggish, and the fraction of the isotherm that follows the Avrami relation drops significantly, as the branches limit the equilibrium crystallinity of the material.

11.2.5 Statistical Copolymers with Two Crystallizable Units

In a copolymer system where both comonomer units are crystallizable, co-crystallization may be observed if the comonomer units are similar in chemical structure, repeat-unit length, and/or crystal chain conformation [80]. Furthermore, a copolymer is said to be isodimorphic if co-crystallization of the different comonomer sequences leads to the observation of two distinct crystalline phases depending on copolymer composition [80].

Both isotactic poly(propylene-co-butene) [81, 82] and syndiotactic poly(propylene-co-butene) [83] statistical copolymers exhibit isodimorphic behavior when crystallized. In isotactic poly(propylene-co-butene), the copolymer was found to crystallize over the entire range of butene content. A transition in crystal unit cell structure was observed at about 50 mol% butene, where below this composition, the crystalline phase resembled that for polypropylene and above this composition, the copolymer was essentially polybutene with propylene defect units [81]. The observed isodimorphic behavior can be explained by the similar helical chain structures exhibited by both polypropylene and polybutene in the crystal, which results in a relatively small free energy penalty for co-crystallization [42, 81–83].

Statistical copolymers of ethylene terephthalate (ET) and 1,4-cyclohexylene dimethylene terephthalate (CT) were also found to co-crystallize over a limited composition range [84, 85]. The copolymers rich in ET were found to form a crystalline phase that contained only ET units, while in the copolymers rich in CT, the crystalline phase contained both ET and CT units. The transition between these two crystal phases, as a function of composition, corresponded to a minimum in both copolymer melting temperature and heat of crystallization. It was speculated that the transition occurs at a composition where the energy difference between the melt and the crystal is identical for the two comonomers [85].

Statistical copolymers of ET and ethylene naphthalene -2,6-dicarboxylate (EN) units present yet another example of isodimorphic crystallization [86]. Both X-ray diffraction and thermal data, shown in Figure 11.9, indicate that as the concentration of ET units increases, the copolymer undergoes a crystal structure transition from a poly(ethylene naphthalate), PEN-type, to a poly(ethylene terephthalate), PET-type, unit cell at approximately 75 mol% ET. Except for the composition where the phase transition occurs, the crystal lattice parameters change continuously with composition, strongly suggesting that the crystal phase contains both ET and EN units.

Other statistical copolymers that have been found to exhibit isodimorphic behavior include poly(β-hydroxybutyrate-co-β-hydroxyvalerate) [87, 88], poly(butylene terephthalate-co-butylene-2,6-naphthalate) [89], poly(butylene terephthalate-co-1,4-cyclohexane dimethylene terephthalate) [90], and poly(butylene terephthalate-co-cyclopentane dimethylene terephthalate) [90]. In all cases, measurable crystallinity was observed over the entire copolymer composition range. An abrupt transition in the crystal structure was detected at some intermediate composition and was correlated with a eutectic-like minimum in the melting temperature [87–90].

11.2.6 Crystallization Thermodynamics

Thus far, we have discussed a number of key experimental observations regarding the effects of counit incorporation on the solid-state structure and the crystallization kinetics in statistical copolymers. In order to better quantify these experimental observations, various thermodynamic models have been proposed. Flory's model, as outlined in Section 11.2.1, correctly describes the equilibrium melting behavior of copolymers in the limit of complete comonomer exclusion; however, it is often found to be inadequate at predicting experimentally accessible copolymer melting temperatures [11–14]. An alternative was proposed by Baur [91], where each polymer sequence is treated as a separate molecule with an average sequence length in the melt given by [91]:

$$\langle \xi \rangle = \frac{1}{2X_B(1-X_B)} \quad (11.8)$$

and X_B is the mole fraction of noncrystallizable B counits in the melt. The melting temperature of the copolymer crystallite in the limit of infinite thickness is then given by [91]:

$$\frac{1}{T_m} - \frac{1}{T_m^o} = \frac{-R}{\Delta H_u}\left[\ln(1-X_B) - \langle \xi \rangle^{-1}\right]. \quad (11.9)$$

Although Baur's copolymer model is built on the rather unrealistic premise that each polymer sequence of average length $\langle \xi \rangle$ in a polymer chain may be treated as a disconnected single molecule, it has been found to match experimental T_m data much better than Flory's

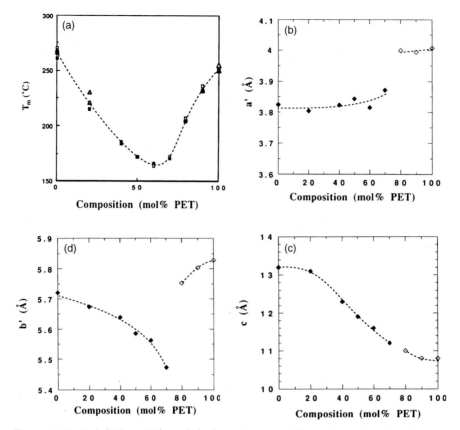

Figure 11.9 Poly(ET-*co*-EN) statistical copolymer melting point and unit-cell data, shown as a function of composition: (a) copolymer melting temperature, T_m; (b) projection of the *a* unit cell length onto the plane normal to the chain axis, a'; (c) projection of the *b* unit cell length onto the plane normal to the chain axis, b'; (d) *c* unit-cell length. In panels (b–d), filled symbols indicate a PEN-like crystal structure, while open symbols correspond to a PET-like structure. Reprinted from Reference [86] with permission of Elsevier, Copyright 1995.

model [85, 92, 93]. In statistical copolymers of poly(L-lactide-*co*-D-lactide) and poly(L-lactide-*co-meso*-lactide) [92, 93], as well as poly(ET-*co*-CT) copolymers of low CT content, where CT is known to be excluded from the PET unit cell during crystallization [85], the experimentally measured melting temperatures were shown to agree well with the predictions of Equation 11.9.

Besides Baur's model, other relationships, both theoretical and empirical, have been proposed to describe the experimentally observed crystallization and melting behavior of statistical copolymers [94–96]. In one study, Pakula presented two models for determining copolymer crystallinity as a function of critical nucleus size [94]. In model one, crystallizable sequences longer than the critical nucleus are allowed to participate in the formation of stable crystallites; however, chain folding is assumed to be absent, so any portion of the crystallizable sequence longer than the critical nucleus size must be rejected to the amorphous phase. In model two, the same criterion for crystallization is applied, except now the crystals are allowed to fold so each sequence can fully contribute to the development of the crystalline lamellae. Pakula then pointed out that any experimental data on copolymer crystallinity should fall between the two model limits. As shown in Figure 11.10, when the model predictions are compared to the crystallinity data for a low density polyethylene containing 35 methyl groups per 1000 C atoms, the experimental values indeed lie between those calculated from the two models.

Burfield proposed an empirical relation between crystallinity and mole fraction of crystallizable units for ethylene copolymers [95, 96]. If the monomer sequence is truly random, then the probability of having *m* ethylene units in an uninterrupted sequence can be expressed as X_E^m. It was then further hypothesized that a correlation between ΔH_m, the melting enthalpy of the copolymer, and X_E^m may be written in the form:

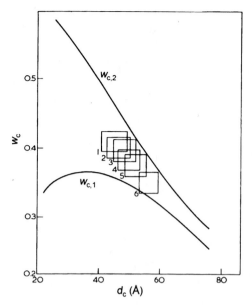

Figure 11.10 Experimentally determined crystallinity (w_c) for a low density polyethylene containing 35 methyl groups per 1000 C atoms (boxes) as a function of lamellar thickness (d_c), in comparison to copolymer crystallinity calculated based on Pakula's model 1 ($w_{c,1}$) and model 2 ($w_{c,2}$). Boxes represent data obtained at different crystallization temperatures, and the edges of the boxes represent estimated measurement errors. Reprinted from Reference [94] with permission of Elsevier, Copyright 1982.

$$\Delta H_m = k' X_E^m \tag{11.10}$$

where k' is a proportionality constant that depends on the preparation and crystallization histories of the copolymer, and m represents the critical ethylene sequence length below which stable crystallites do not form [96].

This relationship was applied to analyze the crystallization data of six different sets of ethylene statistical copolymers [96]. In all cases, a linear relationship between $\log \Delta H_m$ and $\log X_E$ was observed. Furthermore, the values of m determined for ethylene–olefin copolymers were found to be in the range of 6–13, in good agreement with the critical sequence length proposed by Randall and Ruff based on ^{13}C NMR data and modeling considerations [97].

The models presented thus far all implicitly assume that the counits are excluded from the crystalline phase of the copolymer. This assumption is often a very poor description of a real copolymer system. As discussed above, in many copolymers, especially those which are isodimorphic, the crystalline phase contains a mixture of both comonomers. Even in the cases where the counit exclusion assumption is valid under equilibrium conditions, counits may still be found in the crystalline phase

due to kinetic factors [33, 38, 98]. Helfand and Lauritzen pointed out in their analysis of copolymer crystallization that if the crystallite growth rate under an applied crystallization condition is faster than the time required for equilibration of crystal stem attachment/detachment to the growing crystal, then a larger-than-equilibrium amount of counits is expected to be present in the crystalline phase [99].

Sanchez and Eby analyzed the case where an arbitrary amount of the counits, X_{CB}, is included in the copolymer crystalline phase [100]. Changes in the system's bulk free energy were considered, and from that equations for determining copolymer melting temperature were proposed. For crystals of infinite thickness and composition X_{CB}, the copolymer melting temperature is given by [100]:

$$\frac{1}{T_m} - \frac{1}{T_m^o} = \frac{R}{\Delta H_u} \left\{ \frac{\varepsilon X_{CB}}{RT_m} + (1 - X_{CB}) \ln \frac{1 - X_{CB}}{1 - X_B} + X_{CB} \ln \frac{X_{CB}}{X_B} \right\}. \tag{11.11}$$

A new parameter, ε, is introduced, representing the excess free energy for incorporation of a counit into the crystalline phase. When ε is large, counit incorporation is energetically disfavored. In the limit of $\varepsilon \gg 0$, then $X_{CB} = 0$, and Equation 11.11 reduces to that of the comonomer exclusion model proposed by Flory, Equation 11.2.

Sanchez and Eby also considered the case where the crystals have a finite thickness, l, and fold surface free energy, σ_e [100]. Then in place of Equation (11.11), the copolymer melting temperature can be calculated using the following expression:

$$\frac{1}{T_m(l)} - \frac{1}{T_m^o} = \frac{1}{T_m(l)\Delta H_u} \left(\frac{2\sigma_e}{l} + \varepsilon X_{CB} \right)$$
$$+ \frac{R}{\Delta H_u} \left\{ (1 - X_{CB}) \ln \frac{1 - X_{CB}}{1 - X_B} + X_{CB} \ln \frac{X_{CB}}{X_B} \right\}. \tag{11.12}$$

Another model that takes into account the possibility of counit incorporation in the crystalline phase was proposed by Wendling and Suter [101]. In this model, the free energy change associated with defect/counit incorporation into the crystal is treated in a way similar to that used by Sanchez and Eby; however, the model deals with only the limiting case of infinite crystal thickness and adopts Baur's treatment of assuming polymer sequences in a common polymer chain act as separate entities rather than being connected to each other. The melting temperature of the copolymer is then given by

Equation (11.13). In the limit of large defect excess free energy (i.e., $\varepsilon \gg 0$), the Wendling–Suter model (Eq. 11.13) is effectively reduced to the Baur model (Eq. 11.9).

$$\frac{1}{T_m} - \frac{1}{T_m^o} = \frac{R}{\Delta H_u}\left\{\frac{\varepsilon X_{CB}}{RT} + (1-X_{CB})\ln\frac{1-X_{CB}}{1-X_B} + X_{CB}\ln\frac{X_{CB}}{X_B} + \langle\tilde{\xi}\rangle^{-1}\right\}. \quad (11.13)$$

In Equation (11.13), $\langle\tilde{\xi}\rangle$ is analogous to the average sequence length in Baur's model, and it is given by:

$$\langle\tilde{\xi}\rangle = \frac{1}{2(X_B - \tilde{X}_{CB})(1-X_B+\tilde{X}_{CB})}, \text{ for } \tilde{X}_{CB} \leq X_{CB}$$

and

$$\langle\tilde{\xi}\rangle = 0, \text{ for } \tilde{X}_{CB} > X_{CB}, \quad (11.14)$$

where $\tilde{X}_{CB} = \frac{X_{CB}(1-X_B)}{(1-X_{CB})}$.

The Sanchez–Eby and Wendling–Suter models, which differ mainly in the limit of large ε, have been successfully applied to describe experimental copolymer crystallization data, especially when counit inclusion in the crystal unit cell is substantial (i.e., ε is small) [88, 101]. In one such example, Marchessault and colleagues studied the isodimorphic crystallization behavior in poly(β-hydroxybutyrate-co-β-hydroxyvalerate) statistical copolymers [87, 88]. The experimentally measured copolymer melting temperatures were found to be well described by Sanchez and Eby's model with the assumptions that the crystals were of finite thickness (i.e., Eq. 11.12) and defect inclusion was uniform (i.e., $X_{CB} = X_B$) [88].

In another example, the cocrystallization in poly(ET-co-EN) statistical copolymers was modeled using Wendling and Suter's approach [86, 101]. As shown in Figure 11.11, in the context of the model, the free energy associated with incorporating ET units into a PEN-like crystal decreases progressively with increasing ET content [101], most likely due to the progressive change in unit-cell dimensions previously noted in Figure 11.9.

11.3 CRYSTALLIZATION OF BLOCK COPOLYMERS FROM HOMOGENEOUS OR WEAKLY SEGREGATED MELTS

In Section 11.2, we discussed the morphology and crystallization kinetics of statistical copolymers, where the comonomer units are distributed along the polymer

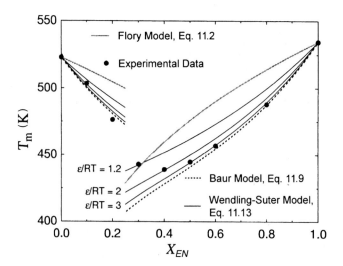

Figure 11.11 Poly(ET-co-EN) statistical copolymer melting temperature (T_m) as a function of EN unit mole fraction (X_{EN}). The experimental data (solid circles) are compared with different theoretical models (Flory model, gray solid line; Baur model, dotted line; Wendling–Suter model, black solid line, calculated with values of ε/RT indicated). Reprinted with permission from Reference [101]. Copyright 1998 American Chemical Society.

backbone following Markovian statistics. In this section, we will focus on the crystallization behavior of block copolymers. Although they differ from statistical copolymers only in the sequence distribution of the counits (e.g., for an ideally random copolymer, $p = X_A$; for a block copolymer, $p = 1$ in the A block), block copolymers exhibit a richer array of potential solid-state morphologies. Structure formation in semicrystalline block copolymers can be driven either by block incompatibility or by crystallization of one or more blocks [5–8]. The crystallization behavior of block copolymers has been an area of active research over the past few decades. In this section, we will restrict our coverage to block copolymers having either a homogeneous or a weakly segregated melt structure, and we will focus on their solid-state morphology and the kinetics of crystallization.

11.3.1 Solid-State Morphology

In contrast to statistical copolymers, whose morphology is determined by the distribution of polymer sequence lengths eligible for crystallization and by kinetic factors, the solid-state morphology of a semicrystalline block copolymer whose melt is homogeneous or at most weakly segregated is ideally governed by an equilibrium process, dependent only on the lengths of the blocks, as proposed by DiMarzio, Guttman, and Hoffman [102].

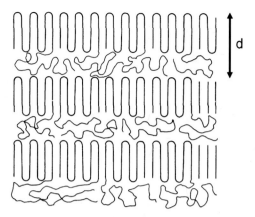

Figure 11.12 Schematic of the equilibrium model for a semicrystalline block copolymer, where d represents the characteristic lamellar microdomain spacing. Reprinted with permission from Reference [102]. Copyright 1980 American Chemical Society.

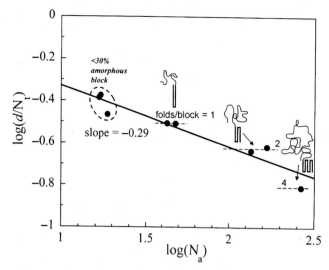

Figure 11.13 Microdomain spacings (d) for hydrogenated poly(norbornene-b-(ethylidene norbornene)) diblock copolymers, plotted in a format consistent with the scaling law $d \propto N_t N_a^v$. Dashed horizontal lines represent hydrogenated polynorbornene block with indicated number of folds per block. Reprinted with permission from Reference [104]. Copyright 2004 American Chemical Society.

Their theory states that for a semicrystalline block copolymer, an equilibrium degree of chain folding is established when a balance is achieved between the fully extended chain configuration preferred by the crystalline block and the random coil configuration preferred by the amorphous block. The resulting minimum free energy state has a characteristic microdomain spacing, d, as illustrated in Figure 11.12, related to the number of segments in the amorphous block, N_a, and the total number of segments in the copolymer, N_t, by the following expression:

$$d \propto N_t N_a^v. \quad (11.15)$$

In DiMarzio, Guttman, and Hoffman's calculation, the exponent $v = -1/3$ [102], while in an alternative model by Whitmore and Noolandi, $v = -5/12$ [103].

Lee and Register examined the microdomain spacing for a series of diblock copolymers of hydrogenated poly(norbornene-b-(ethylidene norbornene)) [104]. The chemistry employed, namely living ring-opening metathesis polymerization, allowed the synthesis of diblocks possessing a high degree of crystallinity with no branching in the crystalline block. Upon crystallization from a disordered melt, the semicrystalline block copolymers were found to adopt lamellar morphologies, with microdomain spacings independent of the crystallization history, consistent with being governed by an equilibrium process. Furthermore, when plotting the copolymers' microdomain spacings according to the scaling law shown in Equation (11.15), a correlation of the form $d \propto N_t N_a^{-0.29}$ was observed, as shown in Figure 11.13, with plateaus in d/N_t evident at each discrete number of folds per block. The experimentally determined scaling exponent, -0.29, is very close to the theoretical value of $-1/3$ calculated by DiMarzio, Guttman, and Hoffman [104].

The crystallization of block copolymers from a homogeneous melt was also investigated by Rangarajan et al. for a series of poly(ethylene-b-(ethylene-alt-propylene)) diblock copolymers [105]. The solid-state morphology was determined to be alternating crystalline/amorphous lamellae with a spherulitic superstructure over the full range of copolymer compositions examined. In that study, the crystallizable polyethylene block was obtained by hydrogenation of an anionically polymerized high 1,4-polybutadiene; thus, the polyethylene block was essentially a statistical copolymer of ethylene and butene containing about 4 mol% butene units. The presence of these randomly distributed ethyl branches along the polyethylene backbone led to the formation of thin crystallites that were unable to span the entire polyethylene domain. Instead of having a solid-state morphology as depicted in Figure 11.12, multiple stacked crystals may exist within a single crystalline-block microdomain, as drawn schematically in Figure 11.14 [105].

When the block copolymer has an ordered yet only weakly segregated melt, crystallization generally disrupts the ordered melt morphology, leading to substantial structural rearrangement, while the extent of reorganization is dependent on the crystallization

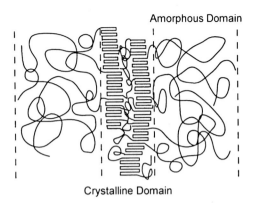

Figure 11.14 Schematic of solid-state morphology for poly(ethylene-*b*-(ethylene-*alt*-propylene)) diblock copolymers crystallized from a homogeneous melt. Presence of ethyl branches within the polyethylene block leads to the formation of short crystal stems, such that several crystals may be accommodated within one crystalline domain. Reprinted with permission from Reference [105]. Copyright 1993 American Chemical Society.

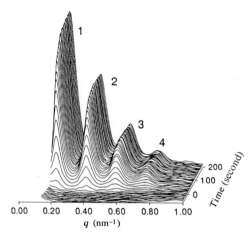

Figure 11.15 Time-resolved small-angle X-ray scattering data for isothermal crystallization of a poly(ethylene-*b*-(ethylene-*alt*-propylene)) diblock copolymer. Each trace represents the intensity integrated over 6 seconds and is q^2 corrected, where $q = (4\pi/\lambda) \sin\theta$, λ is the radiation wavelength, and 2θ is the scattering angle. Reprinted with permission from Reference [115]. Copyright 1995 American Chemical Society.

history [5–8]. Nojima et al. investigated the solid-state morphology and crystallization behavior of poly(ε-caprolactone-*b*-butadiene) diblock copolymers [106–108]. The copolymers were weakly segregated in the melt with order–disorder transition temperatures very close to the melting temperatures of the diblocks. Upon crystallization, the energy gained from crystal formation was found to greatly exceed the energy associated with microphase segregation, and the preexisting order in the melt was replaced by a semicrystalline lamellar morphology much like that observed for diblock copolymers with homogeneous melts.

Similar crystallization behavior, where the ordered melt structure was destroyed upon crystallization and replaced by alternating lamellae with a spherulitic superstructure was also observed in diblock copolymers of poly(ethylene oxide-*b*-(1,2-butylene oxide)) [109], poly(ethylene oxide-*b*-ethylethylene) [110], poly(ethylene oxide-*b*-isoprene) [111], poly(ethylene-*b*-(head-to-head propylene)) [112], poly(ethylene-*b*-ethylethylene) [113] and poly(ethylene-*b*-(ethylene-*alt*-propylene)) [113], and a triblock copolymer of poly(ethylene oxide-*b*-styrene-*b*-ethylene oxide) [114]. In all instances, the solid-state morphology was characterized by a semicrystalline lamellar structure regardless of the initial melt morphology.

In contrast to block copolymers crystallized from homogeneous melts, the domain spacings of block copolymers crystallized from weakly segregated melts depend on both the block lengths and the rate of crystallization [106–108, 112]. In a study on the crystallization of a weakly segregated poly(ethylene-*b*-(head-to-head propylene)), the block copolymer's solid-state microdomain spacing increased progressively from the melt value as the crystallization rate was reduced [112]. This dependence of d on crystallization history clearly indicates the difficulty in achieving the equilibrium crystal thickness when the block copolymer's melt is microphase separated. In a segregated copolymer, the crystallizable block needs to incur an energy penalty for moving from a phase-separated state to an energetically disfavored mixed state before it can diffuse to join a growing crystal, while in the case of a homogeneous copolymer, such an energy barrier is absent [107, 108, 112].

11.3.2 Crystallization-Driven Structure Formation

The dynamics of block copolymer crystallization from a homogenous melt show features of both homopolymer crystallization and microphase separation in amorphous block copolymers [115]. For a poly(ethylene-*b*-(ethylene-*alt*-propylene)) diblock copolymer crystallizing from a homogeneous melt, analysis of its isothermal crystallization revealed that crystal nuclei were generated through heterogeneous nucleation, then grew to form spherulites, as in typical homopolymer crystallization [115]. Furthermore, time-resolved SAXS data obtained during isothermal crystallization, presented in Figure 11.15 [115], clearly show the presence of four peaks at integer q ratios, indicating a well-defined lamellar microdomain morphology. Also shown in Figure 11.15 is that the positions of all four SAXS reflections are nearly constant during the course of isothermal crystallization. Since the period of the lamellar microdomain, d, is determined from the position of the primary SAXS reflection, q^*, via the following equation:

$$d = 2\pi / q^* \qquad (11.16)$$

the microdomain period does not change with time, a feature also commonly observed for microphase separation in amorphous block copolymers.

Since the solid-state structure formed in block copolymers with homogeneous melts is driven by crystallization, the kinetics of lamellar-scale structure formation might be expected to parallel those of crystallization at the unit-cell level. In the same poly(ethylene-b-(ethylene-alt-propylene)) diblock copolymer system, the time evolution of the copolymer crystallinity calculated based on the observed SAXS peaks, as illustrated in Figure 11.16, overlaps with that calculated based on the WAXS data. Since SAXS measures the development of diblock copolymer microstructure on the tens-of-nanometers scale, while WAXS measures polyethylene crystallization on the angstrom scale, the observation that the SAXS data track the WAXS data indicates that the formation of the lamellar microstructure in these diblock copolymers is indeed driven by crystallization, rather than by microphase separation between chemically incompatible blocks [115].

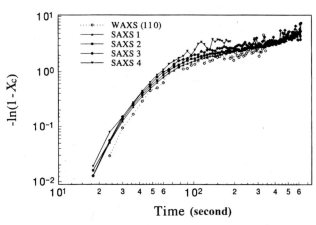

Figure 11.16 Isothermal crystallization of a poly(ethylene-b-(ethylene-alt-propylene)) diblock copolymer, tracked through each of four SAXS reflections from the lamellar domain structure ($q/q^* = 1:2:3:4$, as shown in Figure 11.15), and the orthorhombic polyethylene (110) WAXS peak. X_c is the fraction of the crystallization process completed at time t (analogous to $f(t)$ in Equation 11.6 and Equation 11.7), calculated from the respective X-ray intensity data. Reprinted with permission from Reference [115]. Copyright 1995 American Chemical Society.

The kinetics of block copolymer crystallization from a weakly segregated melt have also been investigated [106–109, 112–114]. In many ways, they are similar to those for crystallization of a block copolymer with a homogeneous melt. The formation of an alternating lamellar microstructure is again driven by crystallization, and isothermal crystallization follows sigmoidal kinetics. In contrast to crystallization of block copolymers with homogeneous melts, the position of the primary SAXS reflection exhibited by block copolymers crystallized from weakly segregated melts is strongly dependent on thermal history, indicating that the formation of an equilibrium semicrystalline lamellar morphology is retarded by the presence of order in the melt [112].

11.4 SUMMARY

In copolymers, the chain architecture, statistical versus blocky, has profound effects on the crystallization behavior. In statistical copolymers containing both crystallizable and noncrystallizable units, it is generally observed that as the concentration of the noncrystallizable counit increases, the resulting crystallite thickness decreases, the lamellar morphology deteriorates, and the supermolecular structure becomes increasingly disordered. In the case of semicrystalline block copolymers, since the crystallizable units are organized in blocks, well-defined lamellae and spherulites are easily formed even when the crystallizable units are in the minority. Furthermore, if the melt is homogeneous or weakly segregated, then the solid-state structure is driven by crystallization.

There is also the special case where two crystallizable units are incorporated into a statistical copolymer. If the two units are structurally similar, in some cases these copolymers can be isodimorphic and show a high degree of crystallinity over the entire range of copolymer compositions. The abrupt transition between the two limiting crystal structures, each characteristic of one of the homopolymers, occurs at a composition that corresponds to a minimum in both melting temperature and heat of fusion.

In order to better quantify the crystallization and melting behavior in copolymers, various models, both empirical and theoretical, have been proposed. The first copolymer melting model was proposed by Flory. Although it correctly describes the equilibrium crystallization/melting behavior in copolymers in the limit of complete counit exclusion, it lacks quantitative accuracy in predicting experimentally accessible copolymer crystallization data. Subsequent models attempt to incorporate crystals of finite thickness and/or allow inclusion of counits in the crystal unit cell. They are generally found to match experimental observations better than Flory's model, and can offer additional insight into the energetics of counit inclusion on copolymer crystallization.

Besides its effects on morphology, comonomer sequence distribution also affects copolymer crystallization kinetics. In statistical copolymers, due to the broad distribution of crystallizable sequence lengths, bimodal melting endotherms are typically observed. In block copolymers, the dynamics of crystallization have features characteristic of both homopolymer crystallization and microphase separation in amorphous block copolymers. In addition, the presence of order in the melt, even if the segregation strength is weak, hinders the development of the equilibrium spacing in the block copolymer solid-state structure.

REFERENCES

[1] Bovey, F.A., Winslow, F.H. The nature of macromolecules. In *Macromolecules, an Introduction to Polymer Science*, Bovey, F.A., Winslow, F.H., eds. Academic Press, New York, 1979, Chapter 1.

[2] Khoury, F., Passaglia, E. The morphology of crystalline synthetic polymers. In *Treatise on Solid State Chemistry*, Vol. 3, Hannay, N.B., ed. Plenum Press, New York, 1976, Chapter 6.

[3] Rachapudy, H., Smith, G.G., Raju, V.R., Graessley, W.W. *J. Polym. Sci., B: Polym. Phys.* **1979**, *17*, 1211–1222.

[4] Krigas, T.M., Carella, J.M., Struglinski, M.J., Crist, B., Graessley, W.W., Schilling, F.C. *J. Polym. Sci., B: Polym. Phys.* **1985**, *23*, 509–520.

[5] Hamley, I.W. *Adv. Polym. Sci.* **1999**, *148*, 113–137.

[6] Loo, Y.L., Register, R.A. Crystallization within block copolymer mesophases. In *Development in Block Copolymer Science and Technology*, Hamley, I.W., ed. John Wiley & Sons, Ltd., Chichester, 2004, Chapter 6.

[7] Muller, A.J., Balsamo, V., Arnal, M.L. *Adv. Polym. Sci.* **2005**, *190*, 1–63.

[8] Register, R.A. Crystallizable block and graft copolymers. In *Encyclopedia of Materials: Science and Technology*, Buschow, K.H.J., Cahn, R.W., Flemings, M.C., Ilschner, B., Kramer, E.J., Mahajan, S., eds. *Elseveier Science*, New York, 2001.

[9] Flory, P.J. *J. Chem. Phys.* **1947**, *15*, 684.

[10] Flory, P.J. *Trans. Faraday Soc.* **1955**, *51*, 848–857.

[11] Richardson, M.J., Flory, P.J., Jackson, J.B. *Polymer* **1963**, *4*, 221–236.

[12] Alamo, R., Domszy, R., Mandelkern, L. *J. Phys. Chem.* **1984**, *88*, 6587–6595.

[13] Alamo, R.G., Mandelkern, L. *Thermochim. Acta* **1994**, *238*, 155–201.

[14] Crist, B. *Polymer* **2003**, *44*, 4563–4572.

[15] Crist, B., Howard, P.R. *Macromolecules* **1999**, *32*, 3057–3067.

[16] Crist, B., Williams, D.N. *J. Macromol. Sci.-Phys.* **2000**, *B39*, 1–13.

[17] Kale, L.T., Plumley, T.A., Patel, R.M., Redwine, O.D., Jain, P. *J. Plast. Film Sheet.* **1996**, *12*, 27–40.

[18] Hosoda, S., Kojima, K., Furuta, M. *Makromol. Chem.* **1986**, *187*, 1501–1514.

[19] Bovey, F.A. Macromolecules in the solid state: Morphology. In *Macromolecules, an Introduction to Polymer Science*, Bovey, F.A., Winslow, F.H., eds. Academic Press, New York, 1979, Chapter 5.

[20] Strobl, G. *The Physics of Polymers: Concepts for Understanding Their Structures and Behavior*, Springer, Berlin and New York, 2007.

[21] Failla, M.D., Lucas, J.C., Mandelkern, L. *Macromolecules* **1994**, *27*, 1334–1337.

[22] Glotin, M., Mandelkern, L. *Macromolecules* **1981**, *14*, 1394–1404.

[23] Mandelkern, L., Glotin, M., Benson, R.A. *Macromolecules* **1981**, *14*, 22–34.

[24] Thomann, R., Kressler, J., Mulhaupt, R. *Polymer* **1998**, *39*, 1907–1915.

[25] Laihonen, S., Gedde, U.W., Werner, P.E., Martinez-Salazar, J. *Polymer* **1997**, *38*, 361–369.

[26] Voigt-Martin, I.G., Alamo, R., Mandelkern, L. *J. Polym. Sci., B: Polym. Phys.* **1986**, *24*, 1283–1302.

[27] Defoor, F., Groeninckx, G., Schouterden, P., Vanderheijden, B. *Polymer* **1992**, *33*, 5186–5190.

[28] Defoor, F., Groeninckx, G., Reynaers, H., Schouterden, P., Vanderheijden, B. *Macromolecules* **1993**, *26*, 2575–2582.

[29] Alamo, R.G., Viers, B.D., Mandelkern, L. *Macromolecules* **1993**, *26*, 5740–5747.

[30] Defoor, F., Groeninckx, G., Schouterden, P., Vanderheijden, B. *Polymer* **1992**, *33*, 3878–3883.

[31] Howard, P.R., Crist, B. *J. Polym. Sci., B: Polym. Phys.* **1989**, *27*, 2269–2282.

[32] Baker, A.M.E., Windle, A.H. *Polymer* **2001**, *42*, 651–665.

[33] Baker, C.H., Mandelkern, L. *Polymer* **1966**, *7*, 71–83.

[34] Bunn, C.W. The structure of polythene. In *Polythene*, 2nd ed., Renfrew, A., Morgan, P., eds. Interscience, New York, 1960, Chapter 5.

[35] Davis, G.T., Weeks, J.J., Martin, G.M., Eby, R.K. *J. Appl. Phys.* **1974**, *45*, 4175–4181.

[36] Rabiej, S. *Eur. Polym. J.* **2005**, *41*, 393–402.

[37] Baker, A.M.E., Windle, A.H. *Polymer* **2001**, *42*, 681–698.

[38] Laupretre, F., Monnerie, L., Barthelemy, L., Vairon, J.P., Sauzeau, A., Roussel, D. *Polym. Bull.* **1986**, *15*, 159–164.

[39] Perez, E., Vanderhart, D.L., Crist, B., Howard, P.R. *Macromolecules* **1987**, *20*, 78–87.

[40] Perez, E., Bello, A., Perena, J.M., Benavente, R., Martinez, M.C., Aguilar, C. *Polymer* **1989**, *30*, 1508–1512.

[41] Hosoda, S., Nomura, H., Gotoh, Y., Kihara, H. *Polymer* **1990**, *31*, 1999–2005.

[42] Hosoda, S., Hori, H., Yada, K., Nakahara, S., Tsuji, M. *Polymer* **2002**, *43*, 7451–7460.

[43] Mathur, S.C., Mattice, W.L. *Macromolecules* **1988**, *21*, 1354–1360.

[44] Mathur, S.C., Rodrigues, K., Mattice, W.L. *Macromolecules* **1989**, *22*, 2781–2785.

[45] Rodrigues, K., Mathur, S.C., Mattice, W.L. *Macromolecules* **1990**, *23*, 2484–2488.

[46] Androsch, R., Blackwell, J., Chvalun, S.N., Wunderlich, B. *Macromolecules* **1999**, *32*, 3735–3740.

[47] Turner-Jones, A. *Polymer* **1971**, *12*, 487–508.

[48] Androsch, R. *Polymer* **1999**, *40*, 2805–2812.

[49] Bassett, D.C., Block, S., Piermari, G.J. *J. Appl. Phys.* **1974**, *45*, 4146–4150.

[50] Yamamoto, T. *J. Macromol. Sci.-Phys.* **1979**, *B16*, 487–509.

[51] de Ballesteros, O.R., Auriemma, F., Guerra, G., Corradini, P. *Macromolecules* **1996**, *29*, 7141–7148.

[52] Bruckner, S., Meille, S.V. *Nature* **1989**, *340*, 455–457.

[53] Meille, S.V., Bruckner, S., Porzio, W. *Macromolecules* **1990**, *23*, 4114–4121.

[54] Lotz, B., Graff, S., Straupe, C., Wittmann, J.C. *Polymer* **1991**, *32*, 2902–2910.

[55] Feng, Y., Jin, X., Hay, J.N. *J. Appl. Polym. Sci.* **1998**, *68*, 381–386.

[56] Laihonen, S., Gedde, U.W., Werner, P.E., Westdahl, M., Jaaskelainen, P., Martinez-Salazar, J. *Polymer* **1997**, *38*, 371–377.

[57] Pae, K.D., Morrow, D.R., Sauer, J.A. *Nature* **1966**, *211*, 514–515.

[58] Campbell, R.A., Phillips, P.J., Lin, J.S. *Polymer* **1993**, *34*, 4809–4816.

[59] Poon, B., Rogunova, M., Hiltner, A., Baer, E., Chum, S.P., Galeski, A., Piorkowska, E. *Macromolecules* **2005**, *38*, 1232–1243.

[60] Lotz, B., Ruan, J., Thierry, A., Alfonso, G.C., Hiltner, A., Baer, E., Piorkowska, E., Galeski, A. *Macromolecules* **2006**, *39*, 5777–5781.

[61] De Rosa, C., Auriemma, F., Corradini, P., Tarallo, O., Dello Iacono, S., Ciaccia, E., Resconi, L. *J. Am. Chem. Soc.* **2006**, *128*, 80–81.

[62] Bensason, S., Minick, J., Moet, A., Chum, S., Hiltner, A., Baer, E. *J. Polym. Sci., B: Polym. Phys.* **1996**, *34*, 1301–1315.

[63] Bensason, S., Stepanov, E.V., Chum, S., Hiltner, A., Baer, E. *Macromolecules* **1997**, *30*, 2436–2444.

[64] Kennedy, M.A., Peacock, A.J., Failla, M.D., Lucas, J.C., Mandelkern, L. *Macromolecules* **1995**, *28*, 1407–1421.

[65] Naga, N., Mizunuma, K., Sadatoshi, H., Kakugo, M. *Polymer* **2000**, *41*, 203–209.

[66] Kazmierczak, T., Galeski, A., Argon, A.S. *Polymer* **2005**, *46*, 8926–8936.

[67] Gupta, P., Wilkes, G.L., Sukhadia, A.M., Krishnaswamy, R.K., Lamborn, M.J., Wharry, S.M., Tso, C.C., DesLauriers, P.J., Mansfield, T., Beyer, F.L. *Polymer* **2005**, *46*, 8819–8837.

[68] Hser, J.C., Carr, S.H. *Polym. Eng. Sci.* **1979**, *19*, 436–440.

[69] Alamo, R.G., Mandelkern, L. *Macromolecules* **1991**, *24*, 6480–6493.

[70] Alamo, R.G., Chan, E.K.M., Mandelkern, L., Voigt-Martin, I.G. *Macromolecules* **1992**, *25*, 6381–6394.

[71] Crist, B., Claudio, E.S. *Macromolecules* **1999**, *32*, 8945–8951.

[72] Alizadeh, A., Richardson, L., Xu, J., McCartney, S., Marand, H., Cheung, Y.W., Chum, S. *Macromolecules* **1999**, *32*, 6221–6235.

[73] Hauser, G., Schmidtke, J., Strobl, G. *Macromolecules* **1998**, *31*, 6250–6258.

[74] Cho, T.Y., Heck, B., Strobl, G. *Colloid Polym. Sci.* **2004**, *282*, 825–832.

[75] Cho, T.Y., Shin, E.J., Jeong, W., Heck, B., Graf, R., Strobl, G., Spiess, H.W., Yoon, D.Y. *Macromol. Rapid Commun.* **2006**, *27*, 322–327.

[76] Gornick, F., Mandelkern, L. *J. Appl. Phys.* **1962**, *33*, 907–913.

[77] Hoffman, J.D., Davis, G.T., Lauritzen, J.I. The rate of crystallization of linear polymers with chain folding. In *Treatise on Solid State Chemistry*, Vol. 3, Hannay, N.B., ed. Plenum Press, New York, 1976, Chapter 7.

[78] Strobl, G. *Rev. Mod. Phys.* **2009**, *81*, 1287–1300.

[79] Avrami, M. *J. Chem. Phys.* **1939**, *7*, 1103–1112.

[80] Allegra, G., Bassi, I.W. *Adv. Polym. Sci.* **1969**, *6*, 549.

[81] Cimmino, S., Martuscelli, E., Nicolais, L., Silvestre, C. *Polymer* **1978**, *19*, 1222–1223.

[82] Crispino, L., Martuscelli, E., Pracella, M. *Makromol. Chem.* **1980**, *181*, 1747–1755.

[83] Naga, N., Mizunuma, K., Sadatoshi, H., Kakugo, M. *Macromolecules* **1997**, *30*, 2197–2200.

[84] Yoshie, N., Inoue, Y., Yoo, H.Y., Okui, N. *Polymer* **1994**, *35*, 1931–1935.

[85] Yoo, H.Y., Umemoto, S., Kikutani, T., Okui, N. *Polymer* **1994**, *35*, 117–122.

[86] Lu, X., Windle, A.H. *Polymer* **1995**, *36*, 451–459.

[87] Bluhm, T.L., Hamer, G.K., Marchessault, R.H., Fyfe, C.A., Veregin, R.P. *Macromolecules* **1986**, *19*, 2871–2876.

[88] Orts, W.J., Marchessault, R.H., Bluhm, T.L. *Macromolecules* **1991**, *24*, 6435–6438.

[89] Jeong, Y.G., Jo, W.H., Lee, S.C. *Macromolecules* **2000**, *33*, 9705–9711.

[90] Sandhya, T.E., Ramesh, C., Sivaram, S. *Macromolecules* **2007**, *40*, 6906–6915.

[91] Baur, H. *Makromol. Chem.* **1966**, *98*, 297–301.

[92] Huang, J., Lisowski, M.S., Runt, J., Hall, E.S., Kean, R.T., Buehler, N., Lin, J.S. *Macromolecules* **1998**, *31*, 2593–2599.

[93] Baratian, S., Hall, E.S., Lin, J.S., Xu, R., Runt, J. *Macromolecules* **2001**, *34*, 4857–4864.

[94] Pakula, T. *Polymer* **1982**, *23*, 1300–1304.

[95] Burfield, D.R., Kashiwa, N. *Makromol. Chem.* **1985**, *186*, 2657–2662.

[96] Burfield, D.R. *Macromolecules* **1987**, *20*, 3020–3023.

[97] Randall, J.C., Ruff, C.J. *Macromolecules* **1988**, *21*, 3446–3454.

[98] Wiberg, G., Werner, P.E., Gedde, U.W. *Mater. Sci. Eng. A* **1993**, *173*, 173–180.

[99] Helfand, E., Lauritzen, J.I. *Macromolecules* **1973**, *6*, 631–638.

[100] Sanchez, I.C., Eby, R.K. *Macromolecules* **1975**, *8*, 638–641.

[101] Wendling, J., Suter, U.W. *Macromolecules* **1998**, *31*, 2516–2520.

[102] DiMarzio, E.A., Guttman, C.M., Hoffman, J.D. *Macromolecules* **1980**, *13*, 1194–1198.

[103] Whitmore, M.D., Noolandi, J. *Macromolecules* **1988**, *21*, 1482–1496.

[104] Lee, L.B.W., Register, R.A. *Macromolecules* **2004**, *37*, 7278–7284.

[105] Rangarajan, P., Register, R.A., Fetters, L.J. *Macromolecules* **1993**, *26*, 4640–4645.

[106] Nojima, S., Kato, K., Yamamoto, S., Ashida, T. *Macromolecules* **1992**, *25*, 2237–2242.

[107] Nojima, S., Nakano, H., Ashida, T. *Polymer* **1993**, *34*, 4168–4170.

[108] Nojima, S., Nakano, H., Takahashi, Y., Ashida, T. *Polymer* **1994**, *35*, 3479–3486.

[109] Yang, Y.W., Tanodekaew, S., Mai, S.M., Booth, C., Ryan, A.J., Bras, W., Viras, K. *Macromolecules* **1995**, *28*, 6029–6041.

[110] Hillmyer, M.A., Bates, F.S., Almdal, K., Mortensen, K., Ryan, A.J., Fairclough, J.P.A. *Science* **1996**, *271*, 976–978.

[111] Floudas, G., Ulrich, R., Wiesner, U. *J. Chem. Phys.* **1999**, *110*, 652–663.

[112] Rangarajan, P., Register, R.A., Fetters, L.J., Bras, W., Naylor, S., Ryan, A.J. *Macromolecules* **1995**, *28*, 4932–4938.

[113] Ryan, A.J., Hamley, I.W., Bras, W., Bates, F.S. *Macromolecules* **1995**, *28*, 3860–3868.

[114] Floudas, G., Tsitsilianis, C. *Macromolecules* **1997**, *30*, 4381–4390.

[115] Rangarajan, P., Register, R.A., Adamson, D.H., Fetters, L.J., Bras, W., Naylor, S., Ryan, A.J. *Macromolecules* **1995**, *28*, 1422–1428.

12

CRYSTALLIZATION IN NANO-CONFINED POLYMERIC SYSTEMS

Alejandro J. Müller, Maria Luisa Arnal, and Arnaldo T. Lorenzo
Grupo de Polímeros USB, Departamento de Ciencia de los Materiales, Universidad Simón Bolívar, Caracas, Venezuela

12.1 Introduction, 347
12.2 Confined Crystallization in Block Copolymers, 348
    12.2.1 Crystallization within Diblock Copolymers that are Strongly Segregated or Miscible and Contain only One Crystallizable Component, 351
    12.2.2 Crystallization within Strongly Segregated Double-Crystalline Diblock Copolymers and Triblock Copolymers, 355
12.3 Crystallization of Droplet Dispersions and Polymer Layers, 361
12.4 Polymer Blends, 368
    12.4.1 Immiscible Polymer Blends, 368
    12.4.2 Melt Miscible Blends, 371
12.5 Modeling of Confined Crystallization of Macromolecules, 371
12.6 Conclusions, 372
References, 372

12.1 INTRODUCTION

Many new materials or devices are produced in the micron or the nano scale. Therefore, if they can crystallize, the materials employed have to nucleate and crystallize within the designed microdomains (MDs). We will refer to isolated crystallizable phases in general terms as MDs even though depending on the material, these phases can have nano-scale confinement in one, two or three dimensions (e.g., lamellae, cylinders, or spheres). Confinement usually implies dispersion of a crystallizable phase into many MDs.

Crystallizable polymers in the bulk generally contain impurities (catalytic debris, nucleating agents, or other impurities of unknown origin) that can cause heterogeneous nucleation, a process that requires a lower free energy than homogeneous nucleation and that typically occurs at lower supercoolings. Therefore, if a dispersion is so well prepared that a large number of MDs results, then the number of MDs may exceed the number of heterogeneities. The usual crystallization of a bulk polymer at low supercoolings can change to a fractionated crystallization process (to be described in detail later; see also Chapter 11) where several crystallization events may be produced at increasing supercoolings. The origin of the several crystallization events that can occur in that case may lie in weakly nucleating heterogeneities, superficial nucleation, or at the largest possible supercooling, homogeneous nucleation. As a consequence, the formation of crystal populations with a wide range of lamellar thicknesses can be obtained. In some specific cases, crystal modifications that are not usually encountered under normal cooling conditions may appear.

Handbook of Polymer Crystallization, First Edition. Edited by Ewa Piorkowska and Gregory C. Rutledge.
© 2013 John Wiley & Sons, Inc. Published 2013 by John Wiley & Sons, Inc.

Taking into account the above considerations, the study of nucleation and crystallization under confined conditions can be regarded as a topic of basic research that may have direct bearing on the morphology and properties of nano-structured materials.

The production of fine dispersions of droplets has been a widely employed experimental strategy to study nucleation and crystallization in metals, organic compounds, and polymers [1–11]. The confinement of the material into droplets of small sizes can lead to changes in the mechanism of nucleation as compared to bulk polymers, if the number of droplets per unit volume is in the same order of magnitude or larger than the number density of heterogeneities originally available in the bulk polymer. If the number of MDs is larger than the number of heterogeneities by several orders of magnitude, exclusive homogeneous nucleation can occur [12].

Confined MDs can be obtained by several strategies:

1. Synthesis of nanostructured materials like block copolymers, where the segregation strength between the blocks produces self-organization through phase separation. In this way lamellae, gyroids, cylinders, and spheres, among other more complicated morphologies, can be obtained.
2. Dispersion of a bulk polymer into droplets or the manufacture of an assembly of finely dispersed droplets. This process can be achieved in different ways: (1) by dispersing the polymer with surfactants in solution or spraying the polymer solution into a nonsolvent; (2) by creating thin films that later can be converted into droplets by dewetting (usually promoted by annealing) from the surface that they are attached to; and (3) by formulating a mini-emulsion.
3. The preparation of immiscible polymer blends with or without compatibilization strategies designed to obtain fine dispersions.

In the following sections, we will discuss the principal aspects and advances of the crystallization within confined geometries. In Table 12.1, we have listed recent works dealing with confined crystallization within block copolymers, polymer droplets, and polymer blends; however, previous references are also discussed in the text below.

12.2 CONFINED CRYSTALLIZATION IN BLOCK COPOLYMERS

Crystallization studies on semicrystalline block copolymer systems have been focused mostly on AB diblock copolymers or ABA triblock copolymers, where one block is amorphous (vitreous or rubbery) and the other semicrystalline (usually, polyethylene [PE], polycaprolactone, [PCL], or poly(ethylene oxide) [POE]) (see References within Table 12.1 [13–148] and also references prior to 2004 [135, 136, 149–263]).

The changes of state that AB or ABA block copolymers (where only one block is capable of crystallization) experience are a direct function of the segregation strength χN of the system (where χ is the Flory–Huggins interaction parameter between A and B, and N, the block copolymer polymerization degree) [259–266] and of three key transition temperatures: the order–disorder transition temperature T_{ODT}, the crystallization temperature (T_c) of the crystallizable block, and the glass transition temperature T_g of the amorphous block. Figure 12.1 presents a scheme that summarizes the relationships between segregation strength and key transition temperatures, for AB and ABA block copolymers.

From Figure 12.1, we have the following possible cases described in the literature. (1) *Homogeneous melt*, $T_{ODT} < T_c > T_g$. In diblock copolymers exhibiting homogeneous melts, microphase separation is driven by crystallization if the T_g of the amorphous block is lower than the T_c of the crystallizable block. This generally results in a lamellar morphology where crystalline lamellae are sandwiched by the amorphous block layers [149–153]. (2) *Weakly segregated systems (low χN values)* and $T_{ODT} > T_c > T_g$. In this case, crystallization often occurs with little morphological constraint, enabling a "breakout" from the ordered melt MDs structure, and the crystallization overwrites any previous structure, usually forming lamellae [149–161]. (3) *Medium segregated systems (intermediate χN value) and $T_{ODT} > T_c > T_g$*. In this case, the final solid-state morphology will depend on the thermal protocol applied; if the cooling from the melt is really fast (quenching), the melt morphology is preserved; otherwise the crystallization of the semicrystalline block can overwhelm the microphase segregation of the *MD* structures and drive the final morphology [149–159]. (4) *Strongly segregated systems (high χN value) and $T_{ODT} > T_c > T_g$*. If the segregation strength is sufficiently strong, the crystallization can be confined within spherical, cylindrical, or lamellar MDs in strongly segregated systems with a rubbery block [158–160, 163–169]. (5) $T_{ODT} > T_g > T_c$. A strictly confined crystallization within MDs has been observed for diblock copolymers with a glassy amorphous block [172–185].

In a previous review [265], examples of all the above cases were discussed in detail. We concentrate in the next sections on the crystallization behavior of strongly segregated block copolymers because it is in these block copolymer systems where we can find most of the crystallization within nano-confined phases. However, we

TABLE 12.1 Recent Works That Report Confined Crystallization (2004–2009)

System	Crystallized Component	Ref.	System	Crystallized Component	Ref.
Polymer blends	PBSU/PVDF	[13]	Block copolymer	PCL	[65]
Polymer blends	PA6	[14]	Droplets	PP	[66]
Polymer blends	PA66	[15]	Droplets	PP	[66]
Block copolymers	PE	[16]	Block copolymer	PMMA	[67]
Block copolymers	PCL	[17]	Droplets	PA6	[68]
Thin film nanolayers	PP	[18]	Droplets	PA6	[69]
Polymer blends	PA6	[19]	Block copolymers	Simulation	[70]
Block copolymers	PEO	[20]	Polymer blends	PPDX	[71]
Polymer blends	Perfluoropolymers	[21]	Polymer blends	PBT	[72]
Polymer blends	PP	[22]	Block copolymer	PE	[73]
Droplets	PEO	[23]	Block copolymer	PEO	[74]
Block copolymers	PLLA	[24]	Droplets	PA6	[75]
Polymer blends	PA6	[25]	Block copolymer	PE	[76]
Block copolymers	PEO	[26]	Polymer blends	PA12	[77]
Polymer blends	PEO	[27]	Block copolymer	PEO	[78]
Block copolymers	Several (review)	[28]	Block copolymer	Several	[79]
Block copolymers	PEO	[29]	Polymer blends	PVDF/PA11	[80]
Miktoarm star copolymer	PCL	[30]	Droplets	PEO	[81]
Block copolymer/polymer blend	PEO	[31]	Block copolymer	PEO	[82]
Block copolymer	PEO	[32]	Block copolymer	PPDX/PEG	[83]
PE nanolayers	PE	[33]	Block copolymer	PEG	[84]
Thin films	PVDF	[34]	Block copolymer	PEO/PCL	[85]
Polymer blends	PET	[35]	Block copolymer	PCL	[86]
Polymer blends	Several	[36]	Polymer blends	PCL	[87]
Polymer blends	PA6	[37]	Polymer blends	PP	[88]
Droplets	PE	[38]	Polymer blends	PA6	[89]
Droplets	PA6	[39]	Block copolymer	PE	[90]
Droplets	PA6	[40]	Polymer blends	PP	[91]
Droplets	PA6	[41]	Polymer blends	PEO	[92]
Droplets	PA6	[42]	Polymer blends	PBT	[93]
Polymer blends	PA6	[43]	Thin film nanolayers	PP	[94]
Polymer blends	PEO	[44]	Thin film nanolayers	PP	[95]
Block copolymers	PEO	[45]	Droplets	PP	[96]
Polymer blends	PA6	[46]	Polymer blends	PEO	[97]
Block copolymers	Several	[47]	Polymer blends	PTT/PP	[98]
Block copolymers	sPP	[48]	Simulation	Several	[99]
Thin film	PET	[49]	Block copolymer	PEO	[100]
Polymer blends	Several	[50]	Block copolymer	PE	[101]
Blends, thin films	PET	[51]	Thin film	PCL	[102]
Polymer blends	PEO	[52]	Polymer blends	PBSA, PLLA	[103]
Block copolymers	PCL	[53]	Droplets	PP	[104]
Thin film	PVDF	[54]	Polymer blends	PEO	[105]
Block copolymer	PODMA	[55]	Thin film	PFO	[106]
Block copolymer	PP	[56]	Thin film	UHMWPE	[107]
Polymer blends	PVDF/PA11	[57]	Thin film/block copolymer	PEO	[108]
Polymer blend	PEO	[58]	Droplets	PnAALAs	[109]
Block copolymer	PE/PEG	[59]	Block copolymer	PEB	[110]
Block copolymer	PEO	[60]	Droplets	PP	[111]
Block copolymer	PE	[61]	Block copolymer	PCL	[112]
Polymer blend	PHB	[62]	Block copolymer/thin film	PLLA	[113]
Block copolymer	Several (Review)	[63]	Block copolymer	PEG	[114]
Block copolymer	PEO	[64]	Block copolymer/polymer blend	PCL	[115]

(*Continued*)

TABLE 12.1 *(Continued)*

System	Crystallized Component	Ref.	System	Crystallized Component	Ref.
Block copolymer	PCL	[116]	Block copolymer/polymer blend	PE	[131]
Block copolymer	PCL/POE	[117]	Block copolymer	PVL	[132]
Block copolymer	PLLA/PEG	[118]	Block copolymer	PLLA/PE	[133]
Block copolymer	PE/PCL	[119]	Block copolymer	PLLA/PE	[134]
Block copolymer	PE/PCL	[120]	Block copolymer	PPDX/PCL	[135]
Block copolymer	PEO	[100]	Block copolymer	PPDX/PCL	[136]
Block copolymer	PE/PCL	[119]	Droplets	Liquid crystal E7	[137]
Block copolymer	PE/PCL	[120]	Droplets	PP-*g*-MA	[138]
Block copolymer	PEO	[121]	Nanoparticles	PE	[139]
Polymer blends	PEO	[122]	Nanoparticles	PE	[140]
Block copolymer	Simulation	[123]	Thin films	PET	[141]
Block copolymer	PEO	[124]	Nanolayers	PEO	[142]
Block copolymer	PEO	[125]	Nanolayers	PEO/EAA	[143]
Polymer blends	PCL	[126]	Nanolayers	PEO	[144]
Polymer blends	PVDF	[127]	Nanopores	sPS	[145]
Block copolymer	PE/P3HT	[128]	Nanopores	POE	[146]
Block copolymer	PE/PCL	[129]	Block copolymer	Simulation	[147]
Block copolymer	PE	[130]	Droplets	Simulation	[148]

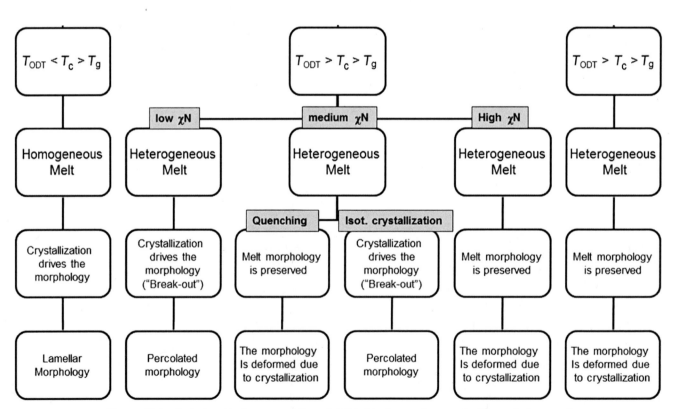

Figure 12.1 Relationship between AB and ABA block copolymers final morphology and the segregation strength and the three critical temperatures.

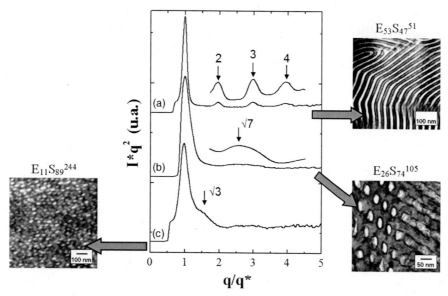

Figure 12.2 SAXS patterns and TEM micrographs of selected PE-b-PS diblock copolymers (white: PE and dark gray: PS): (a) $E_{53}S_{47}^{51}$ (lamellar morphology), (b) $E_{26}S_{74}^{105}$ (PE cylindrical morphology), and (c) $E_{11}S_{89}^{244}$ (PE spherical morphology). Traces have been shifted vertically.

will also consider some special recently reported cases, where fractionated crystallization has been documented in miscible systems. In particular, several reviews have been focused mostly on the phase behavior, crystal structure, morphology, and chain orientation within MD structures [263–267].

12.2.1 Crystallization within Diblock Copolymers that are Strongly Segregated or Miscible and Contain only One Crystallizable Component

Let us consider the crystallization of a model polyethylene phase (PE) that is present in strongly segregated and in miscible diblock copolymers in order to compare two very different cases where confinement or extreme dilution can both induce fractionated crystallization.

The crystallization behavior of PE within polyethylene-*block*-polystyrene (PE-*b*-PS) has been widely investigated [61, 130, 164, 185, 265, 266]. In the recent works of Lorenzo et al. [61, 130], PE-*b*-PS diblock copolymers were analyzed in a wide composition range by differential scanning calorimetry (DSC) and compared with an equivalent homopolymer (PE or hydrogenated polybutadiene). The morphologies of the copolymers in the melt and their changes after crystallization were explored by small-angle X-ray scattering (SAXS) and transmission electron microscopy (TEM) experiments. SAXS experiments demonstrated that PE-*b*-PS formed MD ordered structures in the melt that were not greatly affected by crystallization upon cooling.

Figure 12.2 presents SAXS patterns and TEM micrographs for these PE-*b*-PS diblock copolymers (subscripts indicate the composition in wt% and superscripts the number average molecular weight for the entire diblock copolymer in kg/mol) at room temperature after controlled cooling (10°C/min) from the molten state (150°C). The samples show in their SAXS patterns the characteristic reflections of the different morphologies revealed by TEM.

Confinement effects and topological restrictions on the PE block are enhanced as the PS content in the copolymers increases, causing a decrease in both the crystallization and the melting temperatures of the PE block crystals [61, 130]. DSC cooling scans from the melt and subsequent heating scans are presented in Figure 12.3 for these PE-*b*-PS diblock copolymers and for a comparable neat PE^{25}.

Analysis of the crystallization behavior (see Fig. 12.3) showed a decrease in the crystallization temperature of the PE block (in comparison with the PE homopolymer) as a function of the increasing length of the amorphous PS block. In the case of PE^{25} and $E_{53}S_{47}^{51}$ (where the subscripts indicate the composition in wt% and the superscript the number average molecular weight in kg/mol), the existence of only one main crystallization signal (labeled "1") evidences that the crystallization process started by heterogeneous nucleation [12, 61, 130, 265, 268] from heterogeneities that we shall call type "1" or highly active heterogeneities (this is the typically observed behavior for bulk polymers and for block

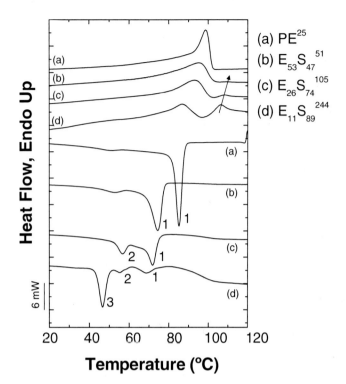

Figure 12.3 DSC cooling and heating scans (10°C/min) for the neat PE homopolymer and for the PE-b-PS diblock copolymers: (a) PE^{25}, (b) $E_{53}S_{47}^{51}$, (c) $E_{26}S_{74}^{105}$, and (d) $E_{11}S_{89}^{244}$. Curves have been shifted vertically. The arrow indicates the PS block glass transition for the PE-b-PS diblock copolymers.

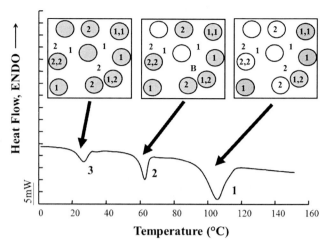

Figure 12.4 A schematic DSC cooling scan exhibiting a typical fractionated crystallization behavior for an ensemble of dispersed droplets in a matrix. The numbers 1 and 2 refer to different types of heterogeneities present in the material (see text).

copolymers where the crystallizable block forms a continuous phase). On the other hand, for $E_{26}S_{74}^{105}$ (PE cylinders in a PS matrix) and $E_{11}S_{89}^{244}$ (PE spheres in a PS matrix) diblock copolymers, multiple crystallization exotherms were observed. This is caused by a *fractionated crystallization* phenomenon [12, 61, 130, 172, 268] arising from the existence of different nucleation events, where each crystallization exotherm (labeled from "1" to "3" in Fig. 12.3c,d) started from a distinct nucleation event (e.g., heterogeneous nucleation from type 1 or type 2 heterogeneities, and at large supercoolings, superficial or homogeneous nucleation, labeled 3). This fractionated crystallization behavior is produced because of the much larger number of isolated MDs (cylindrical or spherical, in these cases) than the number of highly active heterogeneities (type 1) usually present in an equivalent bulk sample of a crystallizable polymer. In order to understand this nucleation change better, we will use the scheme presented in Figure 12.4, which shows a DSC cooling scan where the crystallization does not occur in a single step but in several steps or in a fractionated crystallization fashion. Three crystal-

lization exotherms labeled "1" (higher temperature crystallization exotherm) to "3" (lowest temperature crystallization exotherm) can be observed. When a crystallizable polymer (such as PE, PP, PCL, or PEO) is finely dispersed in a matrix (the number density of the isolated phase must be larger than, or at least of the same order of magnitude as, the concentration of heterogeneities present in the bulk crystallizable polymer), as in blends of immiscible homopolymers (see the section devoted to polymer blends below) or in strongly segregated block copolymers (where the crystallizable polymer is the minority component), the number of heterogeneities present in the bulk crystallizable polymer will be distributed among the isolated phases or migrate to the matrix component. The situation shown in the cartoons of Figure 12.4 may then be envisaged. Starting at high temperature, some MDs with the most effective heterogeneity (type "1") inside them will be able to crystallize at the highest crystallization temperature, T_c, possible. The MDs with the second most active heterogeneity (type "2") will need a larger supercooling in order to nucleate and crystallize. Finally, the lowest temperature exothermic signal is originated by the crystallization of those MDs that do not contain heterogeneities. This particular crystallization exotherm can occur at the lowest possible temperature or maximum supercooling and could be originated from: (1) superficial or interfacial nucleation events (due to the MDs interphase) or (2) from homogeneous nucleation events [12, 172, 265, 268]. In Figure 12.3, for $E_{26}S_{74}^{105}$ and $E_{11}S_{89}^{244}$ the fractionated behavior of the crystallization process is due to the high MD density (according to an estimation from TEM micrographs, about ~10^{12} PE cylinders/cm^3 and 10^{15} PE spheres/cm^3, respectively [61, 130, 172, 265, 268]) in comparison with the heterogeneity concentration usually present in an equivalent bulk sample of the crystallizable polymer (~10^9/cm^3 for the PE) [61, 130, 172, 265, 268].

In the PE-b-PS diblock copolymers under consideration, T_m does not change appreciably if the PE block forms a continuous or percolated phase ($E_{53}S_{47}^{51}$) as can be noted in Figure 12.3. When the morphological confinement increases ($E_{26}S_{74}^{105}$ and $E_{11}S_{89}^{244}$) the T_m value decreases markedly as well as the crystallinity degree (for $E_{11}S_{89}^{244}$ the T_m is 85.2°C, in comparison with 97.1°C for the PE homopolymer).

For this set of PE-b-PS diblock copolymers, several polymer nucleation and growth theories were applied to overall DSC isothermal crystallization rate data [61, 130, 269, 270]. These results indicate that the behavior of the PE-b-PS system is complex. Although the Lauritzen–Hoffman theory was developed for describing crystal growth only, it has been employed to describe overall crystallization data since it is capable of fitting the data remarkably well [269]. In these cases, such as when isothermal crystallization kinetics data obtained by DSC is employed, the energy barrier for crystallization reflected in Kg (denoted by us in this case K_g^τ) contains contribution from both primary nucleation and crystal growth.

If the PE block is well percolated (lamellar morphology), the energy barrier associated with the overall crystallization (i.e., K_g^τ) increases with the increase in PS content. On the other hand, when the PE was isolated within cylinders or spheres MDs, K_g^τ decreased with the degree of confinement since the energy penalty associated with crystal growth decreases as the nucleation becomes the rate-determining step. In such extreme confined cases, for $E_{26}S_{74}^{105}$ and $E_{11}S_{89}^{244}$, it was demonstrated, by applying the kinetic theory of polymer crystallization to data from DSC measurements of isothermal crystallization of previously self-nucleated PE (see Table 12.2), that the crystallization behavior was mostly determined by the nucleation process rather than by crystal growth. These results were in agreement with the low Avrami index values found for these diblock copolymers ($n < 1.5$) [61, 130, 265].

In contrast to the PE-b-PS block copolymers, when PE is covalently bonded to poly(ethylene-alt-propylene) (PEP), a strong diluent effect is observed upon PE crystallization, and in the extreme case of $E_{12}EP_{88}^{238}$, fractionated crystallization was also observed for the PE block. Additionally, the difference between being bonded to a rubbery block or bonded to a glassy block was studied by successive self-nucleation and annealing (SSA). The results showed that the dilution effect of

TABLE 12.2 Values Obtained by Fitting the Lauritzen–Hoffman Theory and the Avrami Equation to DSC Isothermal Experimental Data for the Neat PE and the PE-b-PS Diblock Copolymers [130]

Compolymer	Energy Barrier, Kg (K^2)	Avrami Index Range
PE^{25}	2.27×10^5	$2.8 \to 3.3$
PE^{25} sn at 103°C	1.66×10^5	–
$E_{53}S_{47}^{51}$	4.29×10^5	$2.15 \to 2.31$
$E_{26}S_{74}^{105}$	9.15×10^4	$1.41 \to 1.22$
$E_{11}S_{89}^{244}$	7.04×10^4	$1.06 \to 0.95$
$E_{54}EP_{46}^{53}$	3.05×10^5	$2.55 \to 3.10$
$E_{29}EP_{71}^{99}$	3.14×10^5	$2.30 \to 2.50$
$E_{12}EP_{88}^{238}$	4.96×10^5	$1.55 \to 1.63$

PEP can cause even stronger effects on the depletion of higher melting thermal fractions than the confinement effect of PS [61, 130]. In the case of the PE-b-PEP block copolymers, the results presented in Table 12.2 demonstrate that the energy barrier associated with the overall isothermal crystallization of PE block increases when it is covalently bonded to a PEP miscible block and its value increases with PEP content. Such an energy barrier increase can be physically understood since the availability of chains in the growing front decreases as the system is diluted with miscible PEP chains [130].

Figure 12.5 shows how the Avrami index increases with T_c when the PE content within the diblock copolymers is 50% or higher (also for PE^{25}). This figure also shows how the Avrami index exhibits a decreasing trend as the PE content in the diblock copolymers decreases. In other words, there is a clear correlation between a decrease in the Avrami index and an increase in the degree of restriction (morphological or from dilution) of the PE block within the copolymers. The shift in the crystallization temperature range is another evidence of the restrictions upon PE crystallization as indicated above, since the higher the confinement or dilution degree, the larger the supercooling needed in order to crystallize the PE block.

Loo et al. applied time-resolved SAXS/WAXS to study the crystallization of a range of PE-containing semicrystalline–glassy [185] and semicrystalline–rubbery [164] block copolymers, where the PE block formed spheres or cylinders. For the sphere-forming diblock copolymers, either in a glassy matrix (PE-b-PVCH 5/22, polyethylene-$block$-poly(vinyl cyclohexane)) or in strongly segregated system (PE-b-PSEB 9/55, polyethylene-$block$-poly(styrene-ran-ethylene-ran-butene)), the progress of crystallization resulted in the observation of first-order kinetics (or the equivalent of an Avrami index of $n \sim 1$), therefore confirming confinement of the growing crystals by the isolated MDs. Confined crystallization in cylindrical MDs is also expected to result in first-order crystallization kinetics if these cylinders are not "connected." In those cases, where the cylinders are somewhat connected between them, a sigmoidal crystallization trend is observed, and the overall crystallization rate is faster than for analogous polymers (PE-b-PVCH and PE-b-PSEB) where PE crystallization is completely confined, and therefore each cylinder must be separately nucleated.

From the results given above, three cases can be considered: (1) percolated systems where the crystallizable block is not in isolated MDs as most of the lamellar forming block copolymers (Avrami indices >2); (2) block copolymers that form cylinders within an amorphous matrix, which can be considered an intermediate case since it could contain a fraction of percolated cylinders and a fraction of isolated cylinders; therefore, its fractionated crystallization process will be a reflection of the mixture of these two crystal populations (Avrami indices between 1 and 2); and (3) systems with isolated MDs that can be exemplified by spheres within an amorphous matrix. In this case the overall crystallization kinetics will be dominated by primary nucleation since the growth within such nano-droplets can be considered instantaneous (Avrami indices around 1 or lower). Table 12.3 shows a compilation on the Avrami index values obtained for several systems, and the data on this table are in agreement with the three cases we have just explained.

The Avrami theory was developed for bulk phases that are not interrupted. Therefore, the assumption of free growth in a bulk phase does not strictly apply to the cases where the crystallizing phase has been divided up into many isolated MDs. Nevertheless, as the results discussed previously have shown, several researchers have found a clear correlation between the Avrami

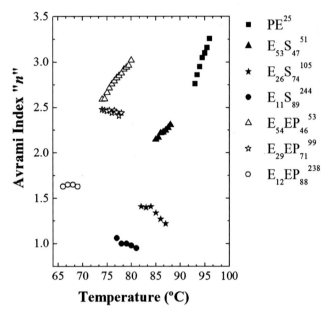

Figure 12.5 Avrami index values as a function of the isothermal crystallization temperature for the indicated PE-b-PS and PE-b-PEP diblock copolymers [130].

TABLE 12.3 Avrami Index Values (n), Isothermal Crystallization Temperature (T_c) Range and Morphology for Different Block Copolymer Systems

Sample	Semicrystalline Block	Morphology	T_c (°C)	n	Ref.
$E_{48}EO_{52}^{1,7}$	POE	Lamellar	11–16	~2.1	[20]
$E_{53}S_{47}^{51}$	PE	Lamellar	82–88	2.12–2.37	[130]
$E_{26}S_{74}^{53}$	PE	Cylinders	82–87	1.20–1.40	[130]
$E_{11}S_{89}^{244}$	PE	Spheres	76–82	0.8–1.1	[130]
$E_{16}S_{84}^{23,4}$	PE	Spheres	53–63	1.1–1.2	[110]
$S_{46}E_{54}^{79,3}$/PS	PE	Lamellar	82–84	1.8–1.9	[131]
$S_{66}E_{34}^{42,5}$/PS	PE	Lamellar/cylinders	102–104	2.4–2.5	[131]
$S_{66}E_{34}^{42,5}$/PS	PE	Lamellar	102–104	2.0	[131]
$V_{13}S_{87}^{0,48}$	PVL	Spheres	−61	1	[132]
$B_{81}EO_{19}^{34}$	POE	Spheres	50	1.29	[125]
$B_{81}EO_{19}^{34}$	POE	Spheres	−18	1.27	[125]
$B_{89}EO_{11}^{102}$	POE	Spheres	0	1.80	[125]
$B_{89}EO_{11}^{102}$	POE	Spheres	−15	1.02	[125]
$E_{82}EO_{18}^{35}$	POE	Spheres	−24	1.23	[125]
$E_{89}EO_{11}^{105}$	POE	Spheres	−16	0.96	[125]

B, butadiene; E, ethylene; EO, Ethylene Oxide; S, Styrene; V, δ-Valerolactone.

exponent and the dimensionality of the crystallizing domains. Also, when isolated clean droplets are produced, the Avrami indices decrease to 1 or lower, an indication that the nucleation becomes the rate-determining step for the overall crystallization kinetics.

In a recent communication, Nojima et al. [132] described the differences found in the crystallization of poly(δ-valerolactone) (PVL) homopolymer and PVL block confined within isolated cylindrical or spherical nanodomains. They proposed a novel way to study the effect of the nanodomain interphase on PVL crystallization. They prepared a set of PVL-*block*-polystyrene (PVL-*b*-PS) diblock copolymers where the PVL component was forming either a cylindrical or a spherical morphology within a PS matrix. Later, these copolymers were treated with high intensity (1000 mW/cm^2) ultraviolet (UV) light in order to cleave the block junction (photo-cleavage). This photo-cleavage process was completely irreversible; that is, the broken PVL segment never recombined to form copolymers again. The procedure is illustrated in Figure 12.6 (taken from Reference [132]). Nojima et al. [132] determined the differences in the crystallization behavior between PVL homopolymer (bulk) (Fig. 12.6c), spatially confined homopolymer (Fig. 12.6b) and spatially confined/chain confined (Fig. 12.6a) PVL block within the PVL-*b*-PS copolymers. They found that the crystallization temperature of the confined homopolymer is much lower than that of bulk homopolymer but higher than the PVL block within the diblock copolymer. These authors concluded that the isolated nanodomains (sphere or cylinder) strongly restrict the crystallization of polymer chains inside them. Also, they found that the melting temperature T_m and heat of fusion ΔH (proportional to the crystallinity) of PVL-confined homopolymer are higher than the PVL block. The authors explained that the crystal orientations are perpendicular to the cylinder axis for tethered blocks while they are parallel for homopolymers, resulting in large differences in the crystal thickness and crystallinity.

Nojima et al. [132], concluded that the crystallization occurs predominantly at the nanodomain interface because the only difference in the crystallization between PVL blocks and PVL homopolymer was whether one end of PVL chains was tethered at the domain interface or not. The effect of chain tethering at domain interfaces is small, but it is not negligible when the crystallization behavior of flexible chains confined within isolated nanodomains is considered.

Recently, Nojima et al. [86] have measured the thermal and dynamic mechanical properties of PCL sphere-forming PCL-*b*-PB diblock copolymers. They found how the dynamic mechanical measurements clearly showed that the crystallization within each PCL sphere domain occurred independently to immediately yield crystallized rigid domains, indicating that crystal nucleation drives the total crystallization in this system.

12.2.2 Crystallization within Strongly Segregated Double-Crystalline Diblock Copolymers and Triblock Copolymers

Polyethylene-*b*-poly(ethylene oxide) diblock copolymers (PE-*b*-PEO) represent an interesting double-crystalline diblock copolymer system since both blocks are strongly segregated and at the same time they have a marked tendency to crystallize in view of their highly flexible linear chains [20]. Hillmyer et al. [271] synthesized PE-*b*-PEO block copolymers of 2.1 and 2.8 kg/mol from hydroxyl terminated poly(1,4-butadiene) catalytically

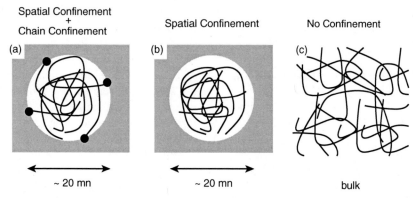

Figure 12.6 Schematic illustration showing crystalline blocks and crystalline homopolymers confined within a spherical nanodomain (a, b) and crystalline homopolymers without any spatial confinement (c). Reprinted from Reference [132] with permission from American Chemical Society. Figure 1 from *Macromolecules* **2008**, 41, 1915–1918.

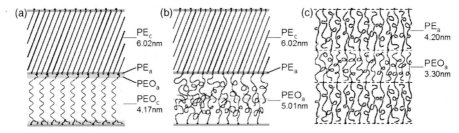

Figure 12.7 Schematic model of $E_{29}EO_{20}$ at different temperatures. (a) Below 28°C: interdigitated, single-crystalline PE, and PEO layers. (b) Between 30°C and 97°C: interdigitated, single-crystalline PE layer, and a double-amorphous PEO layer. (c) Quickly heated to 100°C and held for 4 minutes: interdigitated, single-amorphous PE, and PEO layers. Reprinted from Reference [273] with permission from Elsevier, Copyright 2004.

hydrogenated, employed as a macroinitiator for ethylene oxide (EO) polymerization. They found that the samples formed ordered microstructures in the melt with a T_{ODT} located at experimentally accessible temperatures. These systems have been reported as strongly segregated because of their values of $\chi N > 50$. Sun et al. [20] used DSC, SAXS, and wide-angle X-ray scattering (WAXS) to study a symmetric composition of low molecular weight (~1.7 kg/mol) PE-b-PEO diblock copolymer, and they found that the crystallization of the PEO block was confined between the PE block lamellar crystals, decreasing the crystallization rate of the PEO chains. However, despite the confinement effect, crystallization occurs from heterogeneous nuclei because the lamellar crystals were interconnected [20]. From X-ray and Fourier transform infrared (FTIR) studies they proposed schematic models for the $E_{50}EO_{50}^2$ block copolymer morphology as shown in Figure 12.7. The authors propose that when both PEO and PE blocks are crystalline, the overall lamella contains four components (Fig. 12.7A): crystalline PE, amorphous PE (at both sides of the PE crystals), crystalline PEO, and amorphous PEO (at both sides of the PEO crystals). However, at temperatures above the melting point of the PEO crystals (i.e., 30°C), the overall lamellar structure contains three layers (Fig. 12.7B): crystalline PE, amorphous PE, and amorphous PEO. Above the PE block melting point, the ordered lamellar morphology contains just amorphous PE and PEO layers (Fig. 12.7C).

Higher molecular weights PE-b-PEO diblock copolymers with PEO contents of 11 and 19 wt% were synthesized by Schmalz et al. by sequential living anionic polymerization of butadiene and EO [194, 202]. The PB-b-PEO precursors were hydrogenated employing a Wilkinson catalyst [194, 202]. These systems were studied in detail by Castillo et al. [125] employing TEM, SAXS, and DSC, and they were compared with their respective diblock precursors and equivalent homopolymers. TEM micrographs of $E_{89}EO_{11}^{105}$ and $E_{82}EO_{18}^{35}$ showed a PEO spheres morphology, as expected in view of the strong segregation between the blocks and the composition. The micrographs revealed that in general disordered isolated spheres are present but some percolated MDs could be visualized. This morphology could not be improved by long annealing treatments. However, for the nonhydrogenated systems, a slightly improved morphology was obtained after annealing, revealing more clearly for the $B_{81}EO_{19}^{34}$ block copolymer a pseudo-"hexagonal-packed spheres" pattern. This particular pattern was explained as a coexistence of cylinders and spheres as a consequence of the PEO composition (19 wt% PEO), which is close to the spheres–cylinders domain transitional composition. TEM results were confirmed by SAXS studies [125]. The DSC results showed a marked fractionated crystallization phenomenon of the PEO block for all the copolymers studied [125]. Figure 12.8 and Figure 12.9 present DSC cooling and subsequent heating scans at 10°C/min, respectively, for the BEO and EEO diblock copolymers. For the $B_{81}EO_{19}^{34}$ and $B_{89}EO_{11}^{102}$, three and two crystallization exotherms, respectively, were evident. These crystallization exotherms were explained as a consequence of the confinement of PEO MDs, where most of the spheres are isolated and some are percolated, giving fractionated crystallization. Castillo et al. [125] reported that the observation of different exotherms that were well separated in temperature during cooling scans also allowed the observation for the first time of corresponding multiple fusion endotherms for the PEO block during subsequent heating scans, a novel result that they termed "fractionated melting." These multiple endotherms are a consequence of the formation of lamellar crystals of different thicknesses and thermodynamic stability whose reorganization capacity during the scans is limited as they are strongly confined in their MDs. The correspondence between the different crystallization and fusion processes was carefully demonstrated by performing cumulative isothermal crystallization treat-

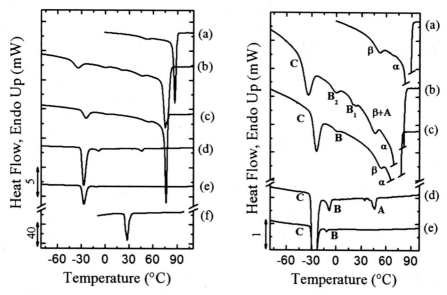

Figure 12.8 DSC cooling scans at 10°C/min after melting at 120°C for: (a) PE[25], (b) $E_{82}EO_{18}^{35}$, (c) $E_{89}EO_{11}^{105}$, (d) $B_{81}EO_{19}^{34}$, (e) $B_{89}EO_{11}^{102}$, and (f) PEO[2]. Right: Close-up of the left side figure. See text for details [125].

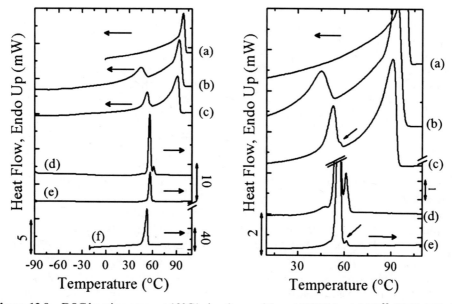

Figure 12.9 DSC heating scans at 10°C/min after melting at 120°C for (a) PE[25], (b) $E_{82}EO_{18}^{35}$, (c) $E_{89}EO_{11}^{105}$, (d) $B_{81}EO_{19}^{34}$, (e) $B_{89}EO_{11}^{102}$, and (f) PEO[2]. Right: Close-up of the left side figure. See text for details [125].

ments on the samples followed by immediate heating scans.

Final heating scans after $B_{81}EO_{19}^{34}$ was crystallized isothermally employing three different thermal treatments can be seen in Figure 12.10. The following describes the thermal treatments applied: (1) One crystallization step. The sample was isothermally crystallized to saturation at 50°C after quenching from the melt. Then, the sample was heated from 50°C to 80°C in order to melt the crystals formed at 50°C, and only one melting peak (labeled A) was obtained as expected. In this case, only the MDs containing the most active heterogeneities (i.e., type A as labeled in Fig. 12.8) crystallized; they correspond to the percolated spheres seen

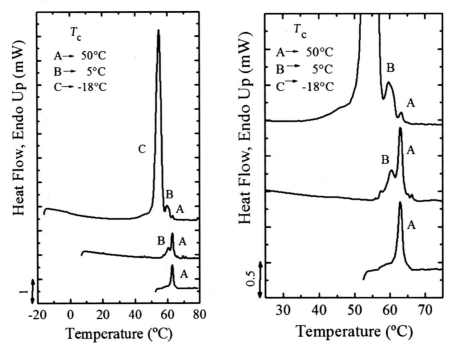

Figure 12.10 Final heating scans after $B_{81}EO_{19}^{34}$ was crystallized isothermally employing three different thermal treatments [125]. See text for details.

by TEM. (2) Two sequential crystallization steps. The sample was first crystallized at 50°C until saturation and then quickly quenched to 5°C where it was left to crystallize for sufficient time to achieve saturation. This second crystallization step was designed to crystallize the PEO spheres that contained type B heterogeneities (see Fig. 12.10). The sample was then heated from 5°C to 80°C in order to record the heating scan shown in Figure 12.10, and a bimodal melting was obtained, reflecting the fusion of the two spheres populations that crystallized at 5°C (endotherm B, Fig. 12.10) and 50°C (endotherm A, Fig. 12.10). (3) Three sequential crystallization steps. The sample was crystallized at 50°C, then at 5°C, and finally at −18°C. The third and final successive crystallization step was chosen to isothermally crystallize the majority of the PEO spheres within $B_{81}EO_{19}^{34}$ that are isolated and do not contain heterogeneities A or B and therefore can only crystallize at very large supercoolings. Figure 12.10 shows that a fractionated melting with three different well-spaced peaks was obtained by Castillo et al. [125] corresponding to the three sequential isothermal crystallization steps. It is noteworthy, as it is in Figure 12.9, that the dominant melting endotherm corresponds to the fusion of superficially or homogeneously nucleated MD (corresponding to exotherm C, Fig. 12.8), or the truly isolated heterogeneity free spheres. The same effect of fractionated melting was obtained by Castillo et al. in $B_{89}EO_{11}^{102}$ and for both hydrogenated copolymers, $E_{82}EO_{18}^{35}$ and $E_{89}EO_{11}^{105}$ [125].

Bailey et al. [203] and Epps et al. [272] reported variations of the melting point of PEO blocks within polyisoprene-b-polystyrene-b-poly(ethylene oxide) (PI-b-PS-b-PEO) and PS-b-PI-b-PEO. For a constant PS/PI ratio, the T_m of the PEO block was lower when it was directly linked to PS instead of to PI. This behavior was attributed to the glassy character of the PS block, while the PI is rubbery at the T_c of PEO. Additionally, reductions in the T_m of the PEO block as the domain spacings of the PEO microphases decrease within the same systems have been reported for PB-b-PI-b-PEO [203], PI-b-PS-b-PEO, and PS-b-PI-b-PEO [272] triblock terpolymers. Also, Guo et al. [101] applied the self-assembly of block copolymers to prepare self-organized organic–inorganic hybrid composites with a low molecular weight PE-b-PEO and a rigid matrix of silica network. They reported that the $E_{50}EO_{50}/SiO_2$ composites went through a series of morphological changes with the decrease in the diblock copolymer concentration, as revealed by TEM. The samples changed from lamellar to hexagonal mesostructures and then to disordered wormlike aggregates. The confined crystallization of PE block within a rigid silica matrix resulted in PE fractionated crystallization with a very

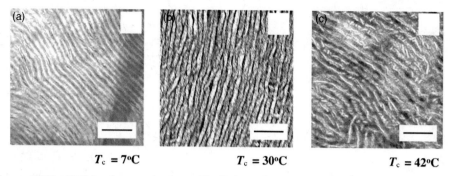

Figure 12.11 TEM micrographs for a 51:49 (vol%) PCL-*b*-PE diblock copolymer (total M_n = 18 Kg/mol) isothermally crystallized at the indicated T_c. The bar represents 100 nm. Reprinted from Reference [20] with permission from Elsevier, Copyright 2004.

low crystallization temperature for the 25/75 $E_{50}EO_{50}$/SiO$_2$ composite material, which the authors interpreted as being due to homogeneously nucleated crystallization, although surface nucleation is also possible for this system.

Nojima et al. have published different reports in which the morphology as well as the PCL block crystallization within melt-quenched PE-*b*-PCL block copolymers of low molecular weight has been studied [119, 273]. Initially, they employed three block copolymers, whose M_n varied between 8 and 18 kg/mol. Using SAXS, they found that the samples were microphase separated in the melt, and in the compositions evaluated, the PE block crystallization destroyed the melt morphology. They isothermally crystallized the copolymers at temperatures within the 5–45°C range. Employing DSC, SAXS, and TEM, they found that the PE block crystallizes during quenching to yield an alternating structure consisting of crystalline lamellar PE and amorphous layers, regardless of whether the MD structure in the melt was cylindrical or lamellar. Later, the PCL block crystallizes starting from this PE lamellar morphology after some induction period. The PCL melting temperature changes considerably with T_c, as expected, but there was no significant difference between the melting temperatures of PCL homopolymer and PCL blocks. Balsamo et al. [191] obtained similar results when they studied PCL crystallization within PS-*b*-PE-*b*-PCL triblock terpolymers. These results indicate that the spatial restriction imposed by the PE lamellar morphology does not work effectively against the subsequent crystallization of the PCL blocks.

The crystallization temperature of the PCL blocks was found to be a determining parameter for the final morphology and thermal behavior of PE-*b*-PCL diblock copolymers [119, 273]. At low T_c, the PCL blocks crystallize within the PE lamellar morphology, and, eventually, this morphology is preserved throughout the crystallization process of the PCL. At high T_c, on the other hand, the crystallization of the PCL blocks destroyed the PE lamellar morphology, resulting in a new lamellar morphology, as can be appreciated in Figure 12.11 and in the SAXS pattern (results not shown). Figure 12.11 shows the morphology of an almost symmetric sample of PCL-*b*-PE, and it is possible to observe that the PE lamellar morphology is destroyed and PE crystals are scattered within the PCL lamellar morphology (Fig. 12.11c). These observations are consistent with the SAXS results, where the diffraction peaks change completely into a diffuse scattering peak located at a lower angle when the sample is quenched to 45°C. This indicates that the MD structure has been transformed from PE lamellar morphology into PCL lamellar morphology. At the same time, the increase of the spacing with increasing T_c suggests that the PCL block crystallizes in a similar way to the PCL homopolymer, with no influence of the previous PE lamellar morphology. DSC results agree with this interpretation.

More recently, Nojima et al. [132, 273] studied in greater detail the crystallization behavior of the PCL within PCL-*b*-PE diblock copolymers and compared it with a PCL-*b*-PB diblock copolymer. They determined the crystallization rate by DSC measurements and showed that the crystallization rate of the PCL block within PCL-*b*-PE diblock copolymers is almost equal to that of the PCL block within PCL-*b*-PB at high T_c. However, upon decreasing T_c a difference arose, and the crystallization rate was higher when the PCL was attached to PE than when it was bonded to PB. For the PE-*b*-PCL diblock copolymer at low T_c, lower Avrami indices (~1.6) were obtained as compared to the crystallization at high T_c, and no macroscopic changes were detected by polarized light optical microscopy (PLOM) during crystallization. These results lead them to postulate that the crystallization of the PCL block at lower T_c produces a morphological transition, even though it

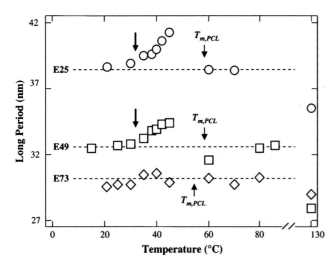

Figure 12.12 The long period plotted against T_c for E73, E49, and E25. Reprinted from Reference [119] with permission from Elsevier, Copyright 2007.

is occurring within the pre-existing PE lamellae, and a kind of confinement effect by PE crystallites may be responsible for the low Avrami index values. The results are in agreement with the findings of Balsamo et al. in PS-b-PB-b-PCL triblock terpolymers [191], when the PCL crystallization kinetics was compared in compositions whose morphological order was changed by annealing the samples in the melt for different times.

Nojima et al. [119, 273] evaluated how the PCL crystallization is affected by the stability of PE lamellar morphology. The stability of the PE lamellar morphology was controlled by the volume fractions or the crystallinity of PE blocks within the block copolymers. The authors evaluated block copolymers with volume fractions of PE between 86% and 25%. Figure 12.12 shows the long period (l) against T_c for three PE-b-PCL diblock copolymers. For PE contents of 73% and 86%, the crystallization of the PCL block was confined within the PE lamellar morphology irrespective of T_c, as revealed by the invariant values of the long period with T_c. On the other hand, when the PE block content was lower than 73%, l changed in a very peculiar manner as can be seen in Figure 12.12. This was explained by the fact that at the crystallization temperatures where l is increasing, the PCL block is able to crystallize and deforms or partially destroys the previously formed PE block lamellae transforming the lamellar structure into thicker lamellae. The effect clearly disappears upon melting the PCL crystals or at large supercoolings where the crystallization of the PCL block is once again confined within the PE lamellae, according to Nojima et al. [119, 273].

Müller et al. [133, 134] have studied double-crystalline PLLA-b-PE and amorphous–crystalline poly(D-lactic acid) (PDLA)-b-PE diblock copolymers by DSC, PLOM, TEM, SAXS, and WAXS. Poly(L-lactic acid) (PLLA) refers to the pure L isomer polymer that can crystallize because of its structural regularity, while PDLA is a random mixture of D and L isomers and therefore cannot crystallize. DSC cooling and subsequent heating scans at 10°C/min are shown in Figure 12.13 for PLLA-b-PE, PLDA-b-PE, and homo-PLLA and PE. The PLLA-b-PE diblock exhibits a single coincident exotherm upon cooling from the melt (as indicated in Fig. 12.13), while during the subsequent heating run, two well-defined fusion endotherms can be seen. Müller et al. demonstrated that the crystallization kinetics of the PLLA block is slowed down because of the covalently bonded and molten PE block, and during cooling from the melt at 10°C/min its delayed crystallization process overlaps with that of the PE block, which starts at lower temperatures. Additionally, the crystallization process of each block can be separated in temperature by employing a slower cooling rate (see Reference [133]) or by self-nucleating the PLLA block in a similar way to that reported previously for PPDX-b-PCL [198].

As expected for a strongly segregated systems, the PLLA block within PLLA-b-PE did not form spherulites at any examined temperature, since the crystallization of each component has to occur in the confined space defined by the MD; that is, no break-out can occur [133, 134].

Figure 12.14 presents the values of the inverse of the half-crystallization time, $1/\tau_{50\%}$, as a function of T_c reported by Müller et al. [133] for a PLLA-b-PE and a corresponding homopolymer. The results clearly indicate that the PLLA block within the copolymer crystallizes at much slower rates than homo-PLLA when similar crystallization temperatures are considered by extrapolation. Such a decrease in the overall crystallization rate of the PLLA block within the copolymer (and the higher supercooling needed for crystallization) is considered responsible for the coincident crystallization effect that can be observed when the PLLA-b-PE diblock copolymer is cooled down from the melt at rates larger than 2°C/min. A similar effect has also been reported by Müller et al. for weakly segregated poly(p-dioxanone)-b-polycaprolactone diblock copolymers [135, 136].

Figure 12.14 also shows crystallization data for the PE block within PLLA-b-PE (after the PLLA block was crystallized until saturation), PDLA-b-PE, and also for a corresponding homo-PE. It can be observed that the crystallization rate of the PE block is reduced, as compared with homo-PE, regardless of whether it is covalently linked to amorphous PLDA or to semicrys-

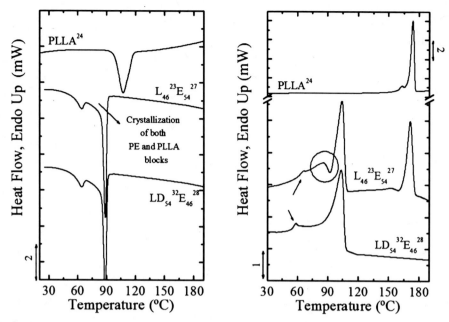

Figure 12.13 Left side: DSC cooling scans at 10°C/min, after melting at 190°C for 3 minutes, for the block copolymers indicated within. Right side: DSC subsequent heating scans (at 10°C/min) to the cooling scans presented on the left side; the circle and the arrows denote the cold crystallization and the T_g temperature of the PLLA block [133].

talline PLLA. In the case of PLLA-b-PE, since the PLLA block was crystallized to saturation first, a nucleation effect of the PLLA crystals on the PE block is now evidenced, if we compared the PE crystallization in both PLDA-b-PE and PLLA-b-PE block copolymers. As a result, even though the crystallization rate of the PE block is depressed in the PLLA-b-PE diblock copolymer, the nucleation effect compensates this rate reduction, and in the end, the PE block attached to the semicrystalline PLLA can crystallize faster than that attached to amorphous PLDA. This result occurs even though one could anticipate a degree of confinement similar or higher (because of the presence of a ~50% of PLLA crystalline phase) in the case of PLLA-b-PE as compared to PLDA-b-PE. The authors concluded that in the double-crystalline PLLA-b-PE, coincident crystallization of PLLA and PE blocks was observed during the cooling process because the crystallization rate of the PLLA block was retarded by the covalent linkage with the PE block. When the PLLA block was self-nucleated, a complete separation of the crystallization process of both blocks was achieved. Also, the authors established that the crystallization of both PE and PLLA blocks were effectively confined within the respective lamellar MDs. There are also several reports in the literature for double-crystalline diblock copolymers, where the first block to crystallize may confine the crystallization of the second block. For reasons of space

these will not be treated here, but the interested reader is referred to a recent review that reports these cases in detail [267].

This section has shown examples of how through MD isolation and confinement, which typically results from the self-assembly of block copolymers, crystalline phases can change their nucleation behavior from heterogeneous to superficial, or homogeneous nucleation and their crystallization kinetics can also change from a complex process to a simple first-order process dominated by nucleation. Intermediate behavior is common, when percolated and isolated phases coexist. In many cases fractionated crystallization can be found as well as fractionated melting (although this last case has only been documented once for nanometric PEO droplets within PB-b-PEO or PE-b-PEO as presented above).

12.3 CRYSTALLIZATION OF DROPLET DISPERSIONS AND POLYMER LAYERS

The study of droplet dispersions is the oldest strategy to study nucleation changes induced by producing isolated clean phases of crystallizable materials. Many of these pioneering studies [1–10] demonstrated that obtaining the homogeneous nucleation temperature of a polymeric material can be very difficult and that the influence of superficial nucleation can be also quite

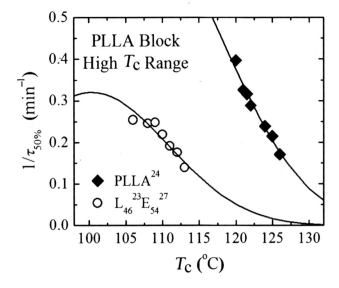

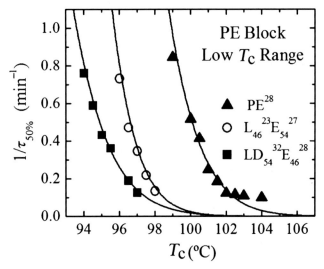

Figure 12.14 Inverse of the half-crystallization time as a function of isothermal crystallization temperature for the PLLA and PE block within the indicated block copolymers and homopolymers [133].

important in many cases. We have previously reviewed in detail the early literature of droplet crystallization in References [265, 268]. In this section we report on the remarkable progress achieved on the subject of droplet nucleation and crystallization by several authors in the past few years.

Also, in recent years, micro- and nanolayers have offered a great opportunity to analyze the influence of film thickness (and the influence of the interface with a foreign material—substrate) on polymer crystallization and final morphology. Generally, the crystallization process is only affected when the film thickness is less than the average spherulitic dimension; in that case the semicrystalline material will crystallize into flattened spherulites or discoids [18, 66, 140].

Dalnoki-Veress et al. [23, 38, 64, 81] have designed a novel method to produce fine droplet dispersions of semicrystalline polymers (PEO and PE) by de-wetting. They first prepared a thin film of, for instance, PEO, by spin coating on an immiscible substrate like polystyrene (PS) (previously deposited on silica). Then they annealed the materials at a temperature just below the glass transition temperature of PS in order to cause de-wetting of the PEO into isolated spheres. The droplet dispersion thus formed can be studied by polarized light optical microscopy (PLOM), atomic force microscopy (AFM), and elipsometry. The nucleation kinetics corresponding to homogeneous and heterogeneous nucleation processes were determined by PLOM and found to be different. Dalnoki-Veress et al. [23, 38, 81] have concluded that for homogeneous nucleation, the kinetic pre-exponential factor divided by the nucleation rate and by the supercooling depends on the volume of the droplets. However, in the case of heterogeneous nucleation, the same quantity depends on the surface of the droplets. In the case of the dewetted PEO droplet population that was heterogeneously nucleated, the PEO nucleation process occurred in a temperature interval in between 56°C and 46°C. Correlation plots of two consecutive experiments on the same sample as a function of crystallization temperature yielded a slope close to one. On the other hand, heterogeneity free droplets crystallized at a temperature of −5.5°C starting from homogeneous nuclei. In this case, the correlation plot for two consecutive experiments did not yield a distribution around a straight line with a slope of 1. This difference is related to the fact that in the case of homogeneous nucleation, the energy barrier for nucleation is a function of the PEO in itself; therefore, if all the droplets have the same size they all have the same nucleation probability. The data dispersion around the crystallization temperature of −5.5°C, in the homogeneous nucleation case, is due to the variation of the droplet dimensions since the droplets area varies between 100 and 300 μm². Dalnoki-Veress et al. have demonstrated that the homogeneous nucleation rate depends on droplet size, specifically on their volume since the time constant for nucleation (τ) varies with R^{-3} (where R is the droplet radius). Furthermore, the temperature dependence of the nucleation rate of the PEO droplets was consistent with the classical nucleation rate since a direct relationship was observed between the time required for the nucleation event (normalized by the volume, i.e., τV) and the inverse of the square of the supercooling required for crystallization (i.e., $[T_c(T_m - T_c)^2]^{-1}$). Based on this work, Müller et al. found an empirical correlation between the crystallization temperature of confined PEO phases and their volume [265].

Recently, Massa et al. [81] studied the effect of droplet volume on the nucleation process using the same de-wetting technique. They prepared different droplet sizes and the smallest ones were in the nanometer range and contained only 10 PEO chains per droplet. Surprisingly, the nucleation was not affected by the extreme degree of confinement in spite of the very large surface to volume ratio of these tiny droplets whose dimensions could be smaller than the radius of gyration of one chain. The authors also found that the homogeneous nucleation process was independent of chain length or molecular weight by employing two different homopolymers and two PS-b-PEO block copolymers. The results obtained suggest that the formation of homogenous nuclei at high supercoolings is only affected by immediate neighboring chain segments and not by the total chain length. These interesting results on the volume and the molecular weight dependence of the PEO droplets nucleation are summarized in Figure 12.15 and Figure 12.16.

Figure 12.15 shows AFM images of PEO droplets on a PS substrate. In Figure 12.15a the droplets are molten and their size distribution can be appreciated. In Figure 12.15b the PEO has crystallized and the crystalline lamellae can be easily identified inside the droplets. Even in the smallest droplets that contain of the order of 10 chains (one is circled in white as an example) crystalline lamellae can be observed in their interior.

Figure 12.16 shows the dependence of the droplet volume on the square of the supercooling required for crystallization. The linear relationship is observed to hold over 9 orders of magnitude (10^3 µm^3 down to 10^{-6} µm^3), for molecular weights differing in two orders of magnitude and for two different polymer architectures (homopolymers and linear diblock copolymers).

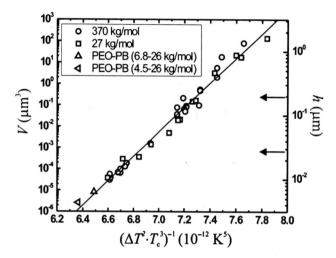

Figure 12.16 Droplet volume as a function $[\Delta T^2 T_c^3]^{-1}$. The average droplet height is indicated on the right axis, with arrows identifying the length scale $2R_G$ for the two homopolymers investigated. Reprinted from Reference [81] with permission from The American Physical Society. Figure 3(b) from *Phys. Rev. Lett.* **2006**, 97, 247802-3.

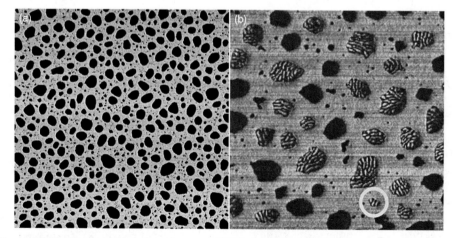

Figure 12.15 Typical AFM phase images of PEO droplets. (a) The difference in the damping associated with the molten PEO and the glassy PS makes it possible to clearly measure the base area of each droplet, in order to obtain the droplet volume (8 µm × 8 µm). (b) The partially crystallized sample clearly shows the lamellar structure within the droplets. Even in droplets which contain ~ 10 chains (shown in the white circle), ordered lamellae are observed (1.25 µm × 1.25 µm). Reprinted from Reference [81] with permission from The American Physical Society. Figure 2 from *Phys. Rev. Lett.* **2006**, 97, 247802-2.

The right axis in Figure 12.16 indicates the mean height of the droplet on the PS substrate and the arrows in the same axis indicate the dimensions of two times the radius of gyration of the studied PEO homopolymers. This shows that for many droplet sizes, the nucleation and crystallization are occurring under extreme confinement conditions. Under extreme confinement, one could speculate that a transition to superficial nucleation could occur; however, this would change the slope in the graph of Figure 12.16, a fact that does not happen. In summary, homogeneous nucleation is a highly localized process and therefore it is not influenced by the molecular weight or by the architecture of the chains (at least when comparing a homopolymer and a strongly segregated linear diblock copolymer). In addition, the temperature dependence of the homogeneous nucleation rate does not change with droplet volume. These results are in disagreement with those of Nojima et al. [132] presented above, where the authors concluded for the evaluated system that the nucleation was predominantly occurring at the block copolymer interphase. The nature of the specific system employed may have a bearing in this matter.

Kailas et al. [96] prepared dispersions of polypropylene nanodroplets, by spin coating and subsequent de-wetting. They studied their crystallization *in situ* by hot-stage AFM employing cooling rates of 60°C/min. The PP droplets are flattened (pancake-like droplets), so that their diameter is much larger than their thickness. The authors found three types of nucleation events and observed that the nucleation depends on the volume and thickness of the droplets, in contrast to the findings of Massa et al. [81]. Kailas et al. [96] explained the difference, arguing that in their work they go down to 2 nm in thickness size, while the minimum thickness employed by Massa et al. is 5 nm, and apparently this difference in size affects the confinement level. The authors reported three types of behavior:

1. Instantaneous nucleation and quick crystal growth in isolated droplets whose thickness is greater or equal to 5 nm. The crystallization temperatures observed were in the range of 38°C to 37°C, and the crystallization temperature has a dependence on droplet volume.
2. Nucleation and slow growth where only one nucleus is formed inside the droplets. This behavior was observed in droplets that had a thickness of between 2 and 3 nm and a diameter of around 700 nm. The crystallization temperature was 34.8°C.
3. Multiple nucleation within the droplets accompanied by slow growth. This behavior was found for thicknesses of 3.5 to 5 nm and a crystallization temperature of 33°C.

The authors proposed that at high degrees of confinement, the thickness and the volume of the droplets influence the nucleation temperature observed and also the way in which the crystalline structure growths. For thicknesses lower than 5 nm exactly this happens. The observed dependency occurs because in droplets whose thickness is very small (lower than 5 nm), the dimensions of the critical nucleus are comparable to the thickness of the droplets. In those cases where at least one dimension is comparable to the thickness of the droplet, the nucleation rate decreases since the nucleation event requires variations that include a droplet thickness increase; therefore, these results are explained in terms of thickness dependence and are not attributable to surface nucleation.

Figure 12.17a shows the increment in thickness during the crystallization of one droplet that occurs at 33.6°C. Figure 12.17b shows the dependence of the crystallization temperature on the thickness of the droplets in a range of 0.5–7 nm. Both results support the hypothesis of the authors. The temperature-dependent AFM studies also showed that during heating scans, reorganization processes occur that transformed the PP from the smectic phase to the α-crystal modification.

One curious result from this study is the fact that the minimum crystallization temperature reported for 0.5 nm thickness PP droplets is 24°C. This temperature presumably corresponds to the crystallization of homogeneously nucleated PP droplets. In other words the homogeneous nucleation temperature for these extremely small nanodroplets is still 24°C above the T_g of PP (whose T_g is approximately 0°C). In the case of PEO and PCL spheres within diblock and triblock copolymers, the homogeneous nucleation observed during DSC cooling scans occurs at temperatures that only differ approximately 1–5°C from their respective T_g values. As expected, the homogeneous nucleation should occur at the maximum available supercooling. It is therefore still unknown why in PP and also in PE, the homogeneous nucleation temperature can occur at such relatively shallow supercoolings [265, 268, 274–279].

Other recent approaches to prepare droplet dispersions to study their crystallization have been reported by Montenegro and Lanfester [280], Tongcher et al. [137], Taden and Lanfester [281] (mini-emulsions), and Ibarretxe et al. [138] (aqueous dispersions of polyolefins).

Montenegro and Lanfester [280], Tongcher et al. [137], and Taden and Lanfester [281] have produced droplet dispersions by preparing a mini-emulsion of diverse substances: alkenes, polymers, and liquid crystals among others. They employed additives to produce but a constant height of about 25 nm. The crystallization of these PEO droplets occurred at −23.3°C. The crystalline structure of the PEO crystals within the droplets was found by WAXS to be the same as that formed by PEO in the bulk. Inside each droplet, 4 or 5 lamellae are formed which are not connected; therefore, the authors claimed that the crystallization of polymers confined in mini-emulsions can be also used to obtain single chain single crystals. Montenegro and Lanfester [280], Tongcher et al. [137], and Taden and Lanfester [281] have found that the crystallization of the PEO droplets produced by mini-emulsion occurs in a single exotherm, as opposed to the case of polyblends where multiple exotherms (i.e., fractionated crystallization) can be found. They attributed this result to the greater homogeneity in droplet size and smaller diameters produced. When the same authors studied the crystallization of alkene droplets, they found for those alkenes with pair number of carbon atoms that their crystalline structure was altered, since it was originally triclinic for the crystals in the bulk material but orthorhombic for that in the droplets.

In order to study the crystallization process of droplets when they are dispersed in an immiscible liquid with no interactions with the crystallizing phase, Ibarretxe et al. [138] prepared aqueous dispersions of polypropylene grafted with maleic anhydride (PP-g-MA) and ethylene-ran-1-octene random copolymers. The dispersions were prepared by stirring mixtures of the polymer with potassium hydroxide and surfactants. The PP-g-MAH dispersions were heated at 5°C/min up to 200°C and then cooled at the same rate to room temperature. Different proportions of polymer and water were prepared as indicated in Table 12.4. In this table, it is shown that the smallest particle sizes were obtained when conditions E were employed. The particle size distributions estimated by light scattering are shown in Figure 12.18, where in the pie charts the clear color areas represent the percentage of particles whose dimensions are lower than 0.04 μm and therefore not resolvable by this technique. In the case of conditions E, 98% of the droplets have sizes lower than 0.04 μm. The DSC cooling scans corresponding to the different samples described in Table 12.4 and Figure 12.18 are shown in Figure 12.19.

Figure 12.19 shows that for the droplets prepared with conditions A, the crystallization occurs in a similar way to that of the bulk polymer since the droplet size is too big and the heterogeneity content is similar to that in the bulk. For droplets dispersions prepared with conditions B, C, and D fractionated crystallization develops and multiple crystallization exotherms can be appreciated. As the proportion of smaller droplets increases, the importance of the lowest temperature exotherm increases. A similar behavior has been reported before

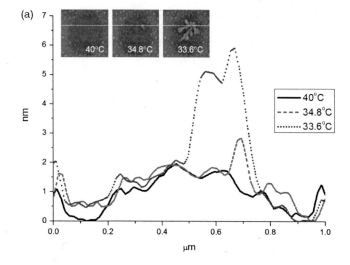

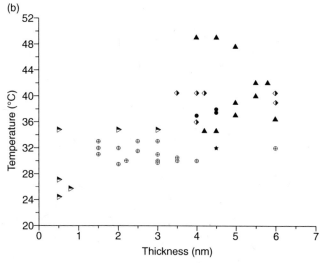

Figure 12.17 (a) Comparison between profiles of an iPP droplet showing the crystallization on cooling. (b) Plot of the crystallization temperature versus the thickness of the droplets obtained from six samples. Reprinted from Reference [96] with permission from American Chemical Society. Figure 7 from *Macromolecules* **2007**, 40, 7223–7230. (See color insert for panel a.)

mini-emulsions, such as surfactants, agents that controlled osmotic pressure, and others. They produced mini-emulsions by high speed stirring, and later they stabilized them by sonication. These authors found depressions on the crystallization temperature of the droplets as compared to the bulk materials for alkenes, liquid crystals, and PEO. In the case of PEO mini-emulsions, they obtained droplets of approximately 100 nm in size; drying of the dispersion leads to a highly ordered arrangement of PEO platelets of different sizes

TABLE 12.4 Formulation Parameters and Characterization Results of the PP-*g*-MA Dispersions Prepared in the Pressure Vessel. Reprinted from Reference [22] with Permission from Elsevier, Copyright 2004

Sample	1	2	3	4	5
Polymer content (%)	24	27	17	23	41
KOH content (%)	1	3	2	2	4
Surfactant content (%)	1	0	3	1	12
Water content (%)	74	70	78	74	43
Emulsification temperature (°C)	185	200	165	190	200
Main stirrer speed (rpm)	300	300	100	300	350
Emulsification time (minute)	30	40	30	40	30
Fraction small particles[a] (mass %)	0	38	40	66	98

[a]Fraction of very small particles (below 0.04 μm) as estimated from turbidity measurements.

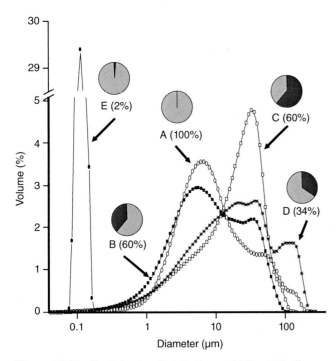

Figure 12.18 Particle size distributions of PP-*g*-MA dispersions in water obtained with the Coulter LS230 and estimation of the amount of solids detected by this instrument (represented by the dark sectors in the pie charts). Material that is not detected by the instrument has probably a particle size of <0.04 μm. Reprinted from Reference [22] with permission from Elsevier, Copyright 2004.

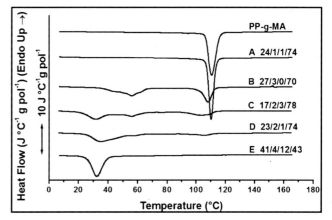

Figure 12.19 DSC cooling scans of bulk PP-*g*-MA and of PP-*g*-MA dispersed samples A to E. Reprinted from Reference [22] with permission from Elsevier, Copyright 2004.

in polymer blends when a compatibilizer is used to control the particle size [39–42, 268, 274–279]. In the case of formulation E, where 98% of the droplets have sizes smaller than 40 nm, the sample crystallizes exclusively at 33°C. The authors interpret correctly this result by explaining that in the absence of any type of heterogeneities, the nucleation of the crystalline phase could only arise from homogeneous nucleation within the droplets or from the nucleation capability of the surface or interphase. Since the PP-*g*-MAH are dispersed only in water, it is unlikely that water plays a role on the nucleation; however, the complex interphase with surfactant molecules within it could perhaps play a role by altering the mobility of the PP chains grafted with maleic anhydride and thereby affecting the nucleation process. If we suppose that the exotherm at 33°C is really caused by the crystallization of homogeneously nucleated droplets, then its different value from other literature reports for PP droplets could be due to the volume dependence of the crystallizing phase on the homogeneous nucleation temperature (see Fig. 12.17b and Reference [157]). Another factor to take into account is the presence of the grafted MAH chains that interrupt linear PP chains and could also cause depression of the crystallization temperature.

Weber et al. [139]. produced a stable dispersion of individual PE nanoparticles synthesized in water at

15°C and 40 atm using a nickel-catalyzed polymerization. Combining cryogenic transmission electron microscopy (cryo-TEM) with X-ray scattering, the authors demonstrate that the PE nanoparticles consist of a single crystalline lamella sandwiched between two thin amorphous polymer layers ("nanohamburgers"). These nanocrystals with only 14 chains are very small single crystals of PE. The small thickness is related to the supercooling (more than 100°C) that is due to the low temperature at which the polymerization takes place. PE nanodispersions may have a high potential for understanding polymer crystallization.

Thin films introduce one-dimensional (1D) spatial confinement of polymers and concomitantly affect their crystallization behavior. When the polymer is confined in a 1D reduced environment, the formation of crystal nuclei will be drastically affected (especially at higher temperatures). Also, the preferential orientation of polymer crystals will also be influenced by confinement, a phenomenon that has been studied [18, 282–298]. In general, experimental observations regarding the effects of film thickness can be classified into several categories:

a. Thickness of several hundred of nanometers: predominantly edge-on lamellar crystals have been found for this condition. Examples can be found for: isotactic polypropylene [283, 284], multilayer coextruded iPP/polystyrene [18], polyamide 6 [285], poly(ethylene oxide) (PEO) [286], poly(ethylene naphthalene) [287], poly(ethylene terephthalate) [288], and PEO in poly(vinyl chloride) blends [289].

b. "Ultrathin films" (thickness <100 nm): in these cases, the films thickness is similar to the polymer coil average size; this characteristic will provoke the formation of flat-on (flattened) lamellar crystals. Examples include poly(vinylidene fluoride) [290], PEO [291], and poly(3-hydroxybutyrate) [292]. However, it has to be noted that several references [18, 33, 140] reported edge-on lamellae in such ultrathin films; this allows the conclusion that the difference in orientation of lamellae with respect to interface (flat-on or edge-on lamellae) depends on the interaction of the crystallizing polymers with the evaluated surface/substrate.

c. "Quasi-two-dimensional" thin films: this category encompasses those thin films where the crystallization becomes diffusion limited, as shown by experiments using PEO [294–296], PE [297], and PET [298].

With the decrease of the film thickness, the morphological transition from edge-on to flat-on (flattened) crystals has been observed in a wide range of semicrystalline polymers [18, 282–298]. It has been assumed that this transition could reflect the influence of the spatial confinement by the film thickness upon the formation of the crystal nuclei. At high temperatures the crystal nuclei dimensions may not be reached (due to the same spatial restriction) and therefore a drastic nucleation change can occur leading to a different flat-on morphology.

Recently, a novel method to prepare multilayers and nanolayers from a sequential coextrusion process has been introduced. In this method, the number of layers can be largely increased at the expense of reducing the thickness of the coextruded layers. It is also possible to obtain nanodroplet dispersions by annealing such multilayer coextruded ensemble. The following systems have been studied employing this method: polyethylene/polystyrene (PE/PS), polypropylene/polystyrene (PP/PS), polycarbonate/poly(ethylene terephtalate) (PC/PET), and poly(ethylene oxide)/ethylene acrilic acid copolymer (PEO/EAA). The crystallization behavior within the nanolayers and within the spheres that are obtained after heating and coalescence of the nanolayers has also been studied [18, 33, 66, 94, 104, 111, 140–143].

Wang et al. [142] and Pethe et al. [143] studied the crystallization of layers of PEO in a multilayer system of PEO co-extruded with an ethylene acrylic acid copolymer. The authors studied the crystallization in layers whose thickness varied between 3.6 μm and 8 nm. The orientation of the lamellae was random for layers of 3.6 μm in thickness. By reducing the thickness of the PEO layers to 20 nm, single lamellae were found in each PEO layer according to AFM, SAXS, and WAXS results. In addition, the oxygen permeability was reduced by two orders of magnitude in the system that has PEO nanolayers with a thickness of 20 nm; each PEO nanolayer contained a single large lateral lamella within it (i.e., a large PEO single crystal). The preparation of controlled thickness multilayer arrangements complements the potential of blends, thin films, and block copolymers for the study of the phenomenon of crystallization in confined conditions. This procedure could yield better performance materials due to the peculiar crystalline morphologies that may be generated, such as single lamella containing layers.

Jin et al. [66, 94, 104, 111] and Bernal-Lara et al. [33] have studied the behavior of nanodroplet dispersions by annealing a multilayer coextruded ensemble of 257 thin layers formed by alternating PE or PP layers with immiscible PS layers. In the PP case, each thin PP film within the ensemble is approximately 12 nm thin. When the multilayer ensemble is annealed, PP nanodroplets of sizes close to 30 nm are formed. The authors found crystallization temperatures of around 40°C and attributed this high supercooling as compared to the bulk polymer to homogeneously nucleated crystal formation. However, no evidence is presented to disregard other possibilities such as superficial nucleation. Their WAXS results indicate that the PP is crystallizing in a smectic phase within the nanodroplets. This type of crystallographic arrangement could be a consequence of the way the nanodroplets are prepared, since they come from the rupture and coalescence of nanolayers and therefore are in agreement with the recent observation of Kailas et al. [96], who found similar results for droplets whose thicknesses were below 5 nm (see above). On the other hand, Arnal et al. [279] have obtained PP droplets in the micron range (1–2 µm) in a PS matrix (by melt blending) and have shown by WAXS that the droplets crystallize in the typical α phase of PP, just as the bulk polymer. Clearly, the size of the droplets has an influence on whether the smectic PP phase develops or not.

In related works, Jin et al. [66, 94, 104, 111] studied the effect of adding nucleating agents to multilayered thin-film ensembles containing PP. After annealing the ensemble to prepare droplets of PP in a PS matrix, the exotherm at 40°C, which was attributed to homogeneously nucleated crystallization, decreased in size when sorbitol was used as a nucleating agent. This corroborates previous findings by Santana and Müller, who reported the complete disappearance of fractionated crystallization of PP droplets in a PS matrix when the nucleating agent phtalocyanine blue was added to the blend [274].

Taking into account all of the results presented above, we can conclude that in order to be sure that homogenous nucleation is indeed present (even when first-order crystallization kinetics is encountered), the crystallization rate must exhibit a dependence on the volume of the droplets or on the cube of the particle diameter. Additionally, even in extremely small droplets comparable to only a few chains in size, the nucleation still occurs within the interior of the droplets. Furthermore, the homogeneous nucleation event is independent of the molecular weight and of the molecular architecture (at least when comparing homopolymers and diblock copolymers). The homogeneous nucleation temperature is a function of the particle size. In certain cases, when the droplets size is nanometric, modifications of the crystal structure of the polymer as compared with that usually observed in the bulk have been reported. The effects of superficial nucleation are important and should be taken into consideration.

12.4 POLYMER BLENDS

Polymer blending represents a well-known strategy for the preparation of novel polymeric materials that could in principle combine desirable properties from the starting homopolymers. Polymer blends can be miscible or immiscible, but in both cases fractionated crystallization of the minor component can occur, as will be shown here.

Since many polymer blends are immiscible, many strategies to compatibilize them have been developed, among them the use of block copolymers as emulsifiers that can migrate to the interphase and reduce the interfacial tension and the size of the dispersed phase. Another possibility is to induce chemical reactions during blending, that is, reactive blending. In many works dealing with polymer blends the phenomenon of fractionated crystallization is observed as a consequence of the dispersion of a crystallizable polymer in a polymeric matrix [12, 268, 274–279, 299]. The term fractionated crystallization was introduced by Frensch et al. [12] after studying several systems: polyethylene/polymethylene oxide (PE/POM), poly(vinylidene fluoride/polyamide-6 (PVDF/PA-6), and poly(vinylidene fluoride)/poly(butylene terephthalate) (PVDF/PBTP). The fractionated crystallization phenomenon depends on the relative number average of particles of dispersed phase in comparison with the number of heterogeneities available (see for instance Reference [268]). In those cases where the dispersed phase size is small enough, so that the number of droplets exceeds the number of usually active heterogeneities, the crystallization is fractionated and occurs in several exotherms. Each exotherm corresponds to a different degree of supercooling associated with a specific nucleation effect. The main effects of fractionated crystallization are: (1) the split of crystallization in several exotherms; (2) the inhibition of the crystallization at the usual temperature can be ocassionally observed; (3) the simultaneous crystallization (where the exotherms are overlapped in the same T_c range) of both blend components (if both components can crystallize); and (4) homogeneous or superficial nucleation may be sometimes observed [12, 61, 130, 172, 265, 268]. Several recent examples are reported in Table 12.1. In this section we will concentrate on some relevant recent studies that have specifically focused on the fractionated crystallization phenomena.

12.4.1 Immiscible Polymer Blends

Many papers have been published in the last 20 years that deal with fractionated crystallization and confined crystallization in polymer blends or in block copolymers blended with homopolymers. Some of these studies are briefly mentioned here while more recent works are treated in more detail.

Many studies have reported the preparation of immiscible polymer blends where at least one component can crystallize in a fractionated fashion. The blends include: polyamide 6/poly(vinylidene fluoride) and poly(butylene terephtalate)/poly(vinylidene fluoride) [300], poly(3-hydroxybutyrate)/poly(ethylene oxide) [301], poly(amide 6)/polypropylene [302], polypropylene/branched PE [276], and polyolefins/poly(amide 6) [303]. Santana and Müller dispersed polypropylene (PP) in an immiscible PS matrix. The authors reported that the nucleation mechanism changed from predominantly heterogeneous to predominantly homogeneous. They also demonstrated using a nucleating agent that the fractionated crystallization exhibited by PP droplets was due to the lack of active nuclei [274]. Arnal et al. prepared PE/PS and PP/PS blends and reported the influence of the particle size distribution on the fractionated crystallization behavior [268, 277, 279]. Dedecker et al. studied the fractionated crystallization of poly(amide 6) (PA6) within polyamide 6/poly(methylmetacrylate) blends compatibilized by a reactive maleated polystyrene with 20% maleic anhydride [304].

Everaert et al. prepared poly (methylene oxide)/polystyrene-poly(2,6-dimethyl-1,4 phenylene ether) (POM/(PS/PPE)) and studied the fractionated crystallization of POM when different glass transition temperature matrices were produced by changing the composition of the PS/PPE phases [305, 306]. Wilkinson et al. produced a series of polypropylene/polyamide 6/SEBS ternary blends. The progressive replacement of SEBS by reactive SEBS-g-MA reduced the interfacial tension between the components and then the blends could exhibit significant variations in mechanical and thermal behavior [307].

Zhu et al. and Huang et al. employed a block copolymer/homopolymer system (poly(ethylene oxide)-b-polystyrene/polystyrene) in order to study the crystallization of PEO under hard and soft confinement [180, 244]. In a related work, Xu et al. prepared blends of poly(oxyethylene)-b-poly(oxybutylene) and polystyrene/poly(oxybutylene) and compared confined versus breakout crystallization [249, 308]. Guo et al. studied a block copolymer/thermoset blend constituted by poly(ethylene)-b-poly(ethylene oxide)/bisphenol A type epoxy resin. The authors reported the nanoconfinement effect on the crystallization kinetics of the PE block [309].

Tol et al. [39–42] have written a review [310] featuring mainly their systematic study on the crystallization behavior of a ternary immiscible blend constituted by atactic polystyrene (PS), poly(phenylene oxide), PPE, and PA6. The first two polymers are miscible with each other, and neither is miscible with PA6. In view of the miscibility between PS and PPE, it is possible to change the morphology of the blends by changing the composition of the matrix without affecting the interfacial tension with the PA6 dispersed phase. Therefore, PA6 dispersions are prepared in PS, in PPE, or in PPE/PS matrices. Because of the differences in T_g of the polymers conforming to the matrix, it is conceivable that PA6 crystallization takes place within a rubbery or a glassy matrix. The authors studied the effects of blend morphology, dispersed phase size and its distribution, and the influence of the different types of matrices on the crystallization of PA6. They employed DSC, WAXS, SEM, and TEM. The main results of the works of Tol et al. [39–42] can be summarized as follows:

a. They corroborated previous findings in several other blends; that is, the fractionated crystallization phenomenon depends on the relative number average of particles of dispersed phase in comparison with the number of heterogeneities available in the bulk (i.e., before dispersion) [12, 172, 268, 274–279]. The fractionated crystallization phenomenon is very sensitive to variations in the thermal history of the sample. Isothermal annealing at high temperature can produce several effects: (1) in cases where co-continuous morphologies exist, they could evolve to dispersed phase morphologies with concomitant fractionated crystallization; (2) in cases where a dispersed phase morphology is present, coalescence could be promoted and the importance of fractionated crystallization may decrease; and (3) the authors corroborate previous findings in relation to the fact that partial melting or self-nucleation can significantly enhance nucleation density and provoke the disappearance or the decrease of fractionated crystallization [12, 172, 268, 274–279].

b. The physical state of the matrix can affect the behavior of the system. In the case where the matrix (i.e., PPE) was in the glassy state before the crystallization of the PA6 droplets, the nucleation density was found to be higher than when the matrix was rubbery or molten (PS matrix).

c. Isothermal crystallization of PA6 droplets (dispersed in polymeric matrices) were performed by previously self-nucleating the material. In those cases where the droplets had smaller sizes (size variation ranged from 7 to 1 μm), the half-crystallization times were longer. This indicates that small droplet sizes can slow down the crystallization kinetics, leading to lower T_c values.

d. The isothermal crystallization study performed with the homopolymer and with the blends in a wide temperature range allowed Tol et al. [39–42] to report that the temperature dependence of the crystallization kinetics is lower for the PA6 homopolymer (whose isothermal crystallization

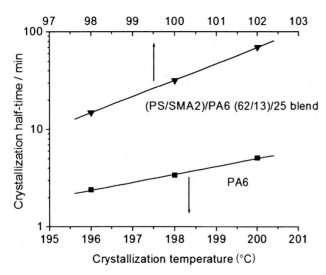

Figure 12.20 Crystallization half-time versus isothermal crystallization temperature for PA6 and a (PS/SMA2)/PA6 (62/13)/25 blend. Reprinted from Reference [41] with permission from Elsevier, Copyright 2005.

was measured in between 190°C and 200°C) than for a compatibilized blend (PS/SMA2)/PA6 (62/13)/25, whose isothermal crystallization was determined at temperatures close to 100°C. Figure 12.20 shows that the crystallization half-time (whose inverse would be proportional to the overall crystallization rate) exhibits a stronger temperature dependence for the PA6 droplets in the blend than for bulk PA6. This variation in the temperature dependence could indicate that the dominating process in the overall crystallization of the PA6 droplets in the blend is the nucleation (occurring at an extremely large supercooling of 110°C) rather than the growth. This result could indicate that the overall crystallization process within the droplets is controlled by the nucleation.

e. Metastability of the crystals produced at large supercoolings. The phenomenon of fractionated crystallization is manifested in the observation of large differences in the cooling scans of a bulk polymer and the same polymer in a fine dispersion, since very large differences could be observed in the crystallization temperatures. However, during the subsequent heating scans, the differences observed in the melting temperatures are not very large in the majority of the cases (an exception to this general trend has been recently found in the case of block copolymers—see Section 12.2—where fractionated crystallization and a corresponding fractionated melting are shown [134]).

Also, many discrepancies can be found in between the enthalpies of crystallization (obtained during cooling scans) and enthalpies of melting (obtained during heating scans). These discrepancies have their origin in the metastability of the crystals generated at large supercoolings, which usually reorganize during the subsequent heating scans. These reorganization processes may include lamellar thickening and lateral growth by additional crystallization. In fact, depending on the polymer, cold crystallization can be observed during the heating scans, as well as double melting peaks.

f. In the particular case of PA6 and the (PS/SMA2)/PA6 (62/13)/25 blend, the reorganization process during the scan was studied by ultrafast calorimetry [75]. Cooling and heating at 500 K/s inhibits the crystallization of both bulk PA6 and the PA6 droplets within the blend. By employing heating rates of 2000 K/s it is possible to obtain the real melting endotherm without any reorganization during the scan after isothermal crystallizations at different temperatures. Tol et al. [39–42, 310] performed isothermal crystallizations with both types of samples at 85°C, 135°C, and 175°C. It was observed that the PA6 droplets in the blend were only able to crystallize at 85°C, while bulk PA6 crystallized at the three temperatures. In the heating scans (see figure 5 in Reference [75]) the melting of bulk PA6 occurs at progressively higher temperatures as T_c increases, as expected. In the case of the 85°C isothermal crystallization temperature, the melting behavior of the PA6 droplets was very similar to that of the PA6 in the bulk, so at least in this case, it seems that the reorganization processes during the scan were very similar in nature and were not affected by the confinement at the scale of those PA6 droplets (around 150 nm).

g. Formation of polymorphic structures. Tol et al. [310] studied by WAXS and DSC the crystalline structure of the following samples: PA6, 75/25 PS/PA6, and (62/13)/25 (PS/SMA2)/PA6. They found that PA6 crystallized preferentially in the α form, while the PA6 droplets (whose size is in the order of microns) within the 75/25 PS/PA6 blend crystallized in the stable γ phase. In those PA6 droplets whose size is smaller than one micron, as in the PA6 within the (62/13)/25 (PS/SMA2)/PA6, they were able to crystallize the droplets at 85°C and they formed the unstable β phase.

h. As can be gathered from the above examples, the crystallization under confined conditions in polymer blends not only modifies the nucleation and the overall crystallization kinetics of a polymer, it can also allow the study of the nucleation processes in detail (homogeneous, heterogeneous, or superficial). Additionally, the isolation of specific crystallographic phases may be achieved and with the appropriate tools the metastability of the crystals can be studied.

i. Among other recent works reporting fractionated crystallization in immiscible blends (see Table 12.1), we can also mention that of Kim et al. [126]. These authors evaluate the efficiency of different compatibilizing agents for blends of atactic PS and PCL. The best dispersion of PCL in PS was obtained by using 5% of a nearly symmetrical polystyrene-b-4-polyhydroxystyrene (S/HS) diblock copolymer in a complex blending procedure involving an initial solution mixing followed by melt blending. Omonov et al. [43] studied ternary blends in which all three components are immiscible: PP, PS, and PA6. They employed PP-g-MAH and PS grafted with maleic anhydride (PS-g-MAH) as compatibilizers. In the compatibilized blends of composition 40/25/5/35/5 PA/PP/PP-g-AM//PS/PS-g-AM the PA6 crystallizes in a fractionated way. Balsamo and Gouveia [88] have reported fractionated crystallization of the PP phase when this is dispersed into a PCL matrix.

12.4.2 Melt Miscible Blends

Even though the fractionated crystallization phenomenon is more frequently reported in immiscible blends, its occurrence is also possible in blends whose amorphous phases are miscible. He et al. [146] have studied blends of poly(butylene succinate) and poly(ethylene oxide) (PBS/PEO) in a wide composition range by DSC, solid-state ^{13}C NMR, and WAXS. The blends exhibit a single T_g whose value is composition dependent. The DSC cooling scans showed multiple crystallization exotherms for the 70/30 PBS/PEO blend. For blends with lower PEO contents, only one crystallization exotherm was observed at –10°C (i.e., 80/20, 85/15, 90/10 PBS/PEO blends). Solid-state NMR indicated that the relaxation processes of the blends can be approximated to a single process. The authors propose that in those blends where PEO is the minor component, this polymer can crystallize in a confined way within the interlamellar regions of the previously crystallized PBS (that crystallizes at higher temperatures). The PBS supercrystalline structures generate confined amorphous regions in which PEO crystallizes. The authors try to generalize the requirements for the observation of fractionated crystallization for miscible blends of two hypothetical polymers A and B:

i. The lamellae, spherulites, or fibrils of polymer B provoke the isolation of polymer A in specific domains.
ii. Polymer B must not induce the crystallization of polymer A.
iii. The concentration of heterogeneities in the system should be low.
iv. The T_g of polymer B should not be too high, so that the crystallization of polymer A would not be inhibited.

12.5 MODELING OF CONFINED CRYSTALLIZATION OF MACROMOLECULES

The present chapter has centered on experimental efforts performed to study confined polymer crystallization. However, molecular dynamics simulations and dynamic Monte Carlo simulations have also been recently employed to study confined nucleation and crystallization of polymeric systems [99, 147]. These methods and their application to polymer crystallization are discussed in detail in Chapter 6. A recent reference by Hu et al. reviews the efforts performed by these researchers in trying to understand the effects of nanoconfinement on polymer crystallization mainly through dynamic Monte Carlo simulations of lattice polymers [147, 311]. The authors have performed such types of simulations in order to study homopolymers confined in ultrathin films [282], nanorods [312] and nanodroplets [147], and crystallizable block components within diblock copolymers confined in lamellar [313, 314], cylindrical [70, 315], and spherical [148] MDs.

Particularly relevant for this chapter are the results obtained by Hu et al. on the confined crystallization of nanodroplets [147] and spherical MDs within block copolymers [148]. The simulated nanodroplets, which could have resulted from a dewetting experiment such as those already explained above, resembled a pancake. Upon decreasing the size of the droplet, both nucleation and crystallization rate became slower. At the interfaces, there was a strong preference for edge-on crystal orientation in concordance with recent experimental observations [81, 96]. Nevertheless, the simulation results indicated that the contribution of interfacial or surface nucleation rate to the overall nucleation rate was equally important to the nucleation of randomly oriented nuclei, which could homogeneously nucleate inside the pancake volume. Therefore, Hu et al. [147] concluded that the nucleation rate of the nanodroplets depends on both the thickness and the volume of the droplets [147].

In a recent article, Cai et al. reported dynamic Monte Carlo simulations of the crystallization of a diblock copolymer component within spherical hard confinement [148]. They compare their results with those of short chains made by breaking the diblock copolymer junctions; in other words they compare the confined crystallization of tethered and nontethered chains of similar sizes in spherical MDs surrounded by a glassy matrix. The simulation results indicate that tethered chains in the diblock copolymer crystallize faster than the free chains but develop lower crystallinity. Similar results were obtained experimentally by Nojima et al. [132]. Cai et al. attribute the faster crystallization for the tethered chains in the diblock copolymer case to the slightly stretched block copolymer chains and explain the lower crystallinity by considering that the chains near the interfaces are prone to remain amorphous.

An interesting result obtained by the simulations is that the hard confined nanospheres nucleate homogeneously and crystallize with a first-order kinetics at high temperatures with an Avrami index close to one. As the crystallization temperature was decreased, the Avrami index dropped to 0.5. Several experimental results on diblock copolymers have reported qualitatively similar trends (see Table 12.3). In more complex systems such as triblock terpolymers with two crystallizing blocks, Avrami indices of 0.5 and lower have also been experimentally determined [316].

12.6 CONCLUSIONS

Confined crystallization is a phenomenon that occurs in droplet dispersions, polymer blends, block copolymers, and thin films. Confinement has many consequences on the nucleation and crystallization behavior. Among the most notorious are the production of fractionated crystallization and the possibility of isolating crystallizable phases whose nucleation may be very different: heterogeneous, superficial, or homogeneous nucleation. In specific cases confinement can also lead to crystal modifications for polymorphic polymers.

Confinement has been used as a tool for studying homogeneous nucleation. Recent studies conclude that the process starts at the interior of the particles (for droplet dispersions) and the temperature at which it appears exhibits volume dependence. In specific block copolymer cases, chain tethering may induce surface nucleation. Homogeneous nucleation has been found to occur in extremely small domains (of the order of 5 nm in thickness or less) and in isolated droplets. In such nanodomains, homogeneous nucleation can continue to be a phenomenon that is intrinsic of the material (with its size dependence) and may not be affected by superficial phenomena in spite of the extremely large surfaces.

In specific block copolymer cases, fractionated crystallization can lead to fractionated melting with little apparent reorganization during the scan. However, most systems exhibit reorganization during heating. The reorganization process during heating scans that may occur in confined MDs are in most cases due to the large supercoolings involved in the production of the crystals rather than to confinement effects.

REFERENCES

[1] Price, F.P. Nucleation in polymer crystallization. In *Nucleation*, Zettlemoyer, A.C., ed. Marcel Dekker, New York, 1969.

[2] Vonnegut, B. *J. Colloid Sci.* **1948**, *3*, 563.

[3] Turnbull, D., Cech, R.E. *J. Appl. Phys.* **1950**, *21*, 804.

[4] Pound, G.M., La Mer, V.K. *J. Am. Chem. Soc.* **1952**, *74*, 2323.

[5] Turnbull, D. *J. Chem. Phys.* **1952**, *20*, 411.

[6] Turnbull, D., Cormia, R.L. *J. Chem. Phys.* **1961**, *34*, 820.

[7] Cormia, R.L., Price, F.P., Turnbull, D. *J. Chem. Phys.* **1962**, *37*, 1333.

[8] Burns, J.R., Turnbull, D. *J. Appl. Phys.* **1966**, *37*, 4021.

[9] Koutsky, J.A., Walton, A.G., Baer, E. *J. Appl. Phys.* **1967**, *38*, 1832.

[10] Gornick, F., Ross, G.S., Frolen, L.J. *J. Polym. Sci.* **1967**, *C18*, 79.

[11] Barham, P.J., Jarvis, D.A., Keller, A. *J. Polym. Sci. Polym. Phys. Ed.* **1982**, *20*, 1733.

[12] Frensch, H., Harnischfeger, P., Jungnickel, B.J. Fractionated crystallization in incompatible polymer blends. In *Multiphase Polymers: Blends and Ionomers*, ACS Symp Series 395, Utracky, L.A., Weiss, R.A., eds. American Chemical Society, Washington, DC, 1989 and references therein.

[13] Li, Y., Kaito, A., Horiuchi, S. *Macromolecules* **2004**, *37*, 2119.

[14] Shi, D., Yin, J., Ke, Z., Gao, Y., Li, R.K.Y. *J. Appl. Polym. Sci.* **2004**, *91*, 3742.

[15] Sacchi, A., Di Landro, L., Pegoraro, M., Severini, F. *Eur. Polym. J.* **2004**, *40*, 1705.

[16] Xu, J.-T., Ding, P.-J., Fu, Z.-S., Fan, Z.-Q. *Polym. Int.* **2004**, *53*, 1314.

[17] Michell, R.M., Müller, A.J., Castelleto, V., Hamley, I., Deshayes, G., Dubois, Ph. *Macromolecules* **2009**, *42*, 6671.

[18] Jin, Y., Rogunova, M., Hiltner, A., Baer, E., Nowacki, R., Galeski, A., Piorkowska, E. *J. Polym. Sci. B Polym. Phys.* **2004**, *42*, 3380.

[19] Zhang, X., Liu, Y., Gao, J., Huang, F., Song, Z., Wei, G., Qiao, J. *Polymer* **2004**, *45*, 6959.

[20] Sun, L., Liu, Y., Zhu, L., Hsiao, B., Avila-Orta, C. *Polymer* **2004**, *45*, 8181.

[21] Apostolo, M., Triulzi, F. *J. Fluor. Chem.* **2004**, *125*, 303.

[22] Uriguen, J., Bremer, L., Mathot, V., Groeninckx, G. *Polymer* **2004**, *45*, 5961.

[23] Massa, M.V., Dalnoki-Veress, K. *Phys. Rev. Lett.* **2004**, *92*, 255509.

[24] Ho, R.-M., Lin, F.-H., Tsai, C.-C., Lin, C.-C., Ko, B.-T., Hsiao, B.S., Sics, I. *Macromolecules* **2004**, *37*, 5985.

[25] Tol, R.T., Groeninckx, G., Vinckier, I., Moldenaers, P., Mewis, J. *Polymer* **2004**, *45*, 2587.

[26] Xu, J.-T., Liang, G.-D., Fan, Z.-Q. *Polymer* **2004**, *45*, 6675.

[27] He, Y., Zhu, B., Kai, W., Inoue, Y. *Macromolecules* **2004**, *37*, 3337.

[28] Loo, Y., Register, R.A. Crystallization within block copolymer mesophases. In *Developments in Block Copolymer Science and Technology*, 1st ed., Hamley, I.W., ed. Wiley, Weinheim, Germany, 2004, Chapter 6.

[29] Sun, L., Zhu, L., Ge, Q., Quirk, R., Xue, C., Cheng, S.Z.D., Hsiao, B.S., Avila-Orta, C.A., Sics, I., Cantino, M.E. *Polymer* **2004**, *45*, 2931.

[30] Lorenzo, A.T., Müller, A.J., Lin, M.-C., Chen, H.-L., Jeng, U.-S., Priftis, D., Pitsikalis, M., Hadjichristidis, N. *Macromolecules* **2009**, *42*, 8353.

[31] Huang, Y.-Y., Yang, C.H., Chen, H.L., Chiu, F.C., Lin, T.-L., Liou, W. *Macromolecules* **2004**, *37*, 486.

[32] Xu, J.-T., Xue, L., Mai, S.-M., Ryan, A.J. *J. Appl. Polym. Sci.* **2004**, *93*, 870.

[33] Bernal-Lara, T.E., Liu, R.Y.F., Hiltner, A., Baer, E. *Polymer* **2005**, *46*, 3043.

[34] Yoo, S., Yun, S.-H., Choi, J.M., Sohn, B.H., Zin, W.-C., Jung, J.C., Lee, K.H., Jo, S.M., Cho, J., Park, C. *Polymer* **2005**, *46*, 3776.

[35] Álvarez, C., Nogales, A., García-Gutíerrez, M.C., Sanz, A., Denchev, Z., Funari, S.S., Bruix, M., Ezquerra, T.A. *Eur. Phys. J. E* **2005**, *18*, 459.

[36] Harrats, C., Thomas, S., Groeninckx, G. *Micro and Nanostructured Multiphase Polymer Blend Systems: Phase Morphology and Interfaces*, 1st ed. CRC Press, Boca Raton, FL, 2005.

[37] Yordanov, C., Minkova, L. *Eur. Polym. J.* **2005**, *41*, 527.

[38] Massa, M.V., Lee, M.S.M., Dalnoki-Veress, K. *J. Polym. Sci. B Polym. Phys.* **2005**, *43*, 3438.

[39] Tol, T., Mathot, V.B.F., Groeninckx, G. *Polymer* **2005**, *46*, 369.

[40] Tol, T., Mathot, V.B.F., Groeninckx, G. *Polymer* **2005**, *46*, 383.

[41] Tol, T., Mathot, V.B.F., Groeninckx, G. *Polymer* **2005**, *46*, 2955.

[42] Tol, T., Mathot, V.B.F., Reynaers, H., Goderis, B., Groeninckx, G. *Polymer* **2005**, *46*, 2966.

[43] Omonov, T.S., Harrats, C., Groeninckx, G. *Polymer* **2005**, *46*, 12322.

[44] Hsu, J.-Y., Nandan, B., Chen, M.-C., Chiu, F.-C., Chen, H.-L. *Polymer* **2005**, *46*, 11837.

[45] Xu, J.-T., Jin, W., Liang, G.-D., Fan, Z.-Q. *Polymer* **2005**, *46*, 1709.

[46] Filippi, S., Minkova, L., Dintcheva, N., Narducci, P., Magagnini, P. *Polymer* **2005**, *46*, 8054.

[47] Segalman, R.A. *Mater. Sci. Eng. R* **2005**, *48*, 191.

[48] Ho, R.-M., Chung, T.-M., Tsai, J.-C., Kuo, J.-C., Hsiao, B.S., Sics, I. *Macromol. Rapid Commun.* **2005**, *26*, 107.

[49] Zhang, Y., Lu, Y.-L., Shen, D.Y. *Chin. Chem. Lett.* **2005**, *16*, 987.

[50] Thomas, S., Harrats, C., Groeninckx, G. *Micro and Nanostructured Polymer Blends: State of the Art, Challenges, and Future Prospects*, 1st ed. CRC Press, Boca Raton, FL, 2005.

[51] Orench, I.P., Stribeck, N., Ania, F., Baer, E., Hiltner, A., Calleja, F.J.B. *Polymer* **2009**, *50*, 2680.

[52] Xu, J.T., Ryan, A.J., Mai, S.M., Yuan, J.J., Cheng, S.Y. *J. Macromol. Sci. B. Phys.* **2005**, *43*, 685.

[53] Zhang, Q., Wang, M., Wooley, K.L. *Curr. Org. Chem.* **2005**, *9*, 1053.

[54] Hu, Z., Baralia, G., Bayot, V., Gohy, J.F., Jonas, A.M. *Nano Lett.* **2005**, *5*, 1738.

[55] Hempel, E., Budde, H., Höring, S., Beiner, M. *Thermochim. Acta* **2005**, *432*, 254.

[56] Ruokolainen, J., Mezzenga, R., Fredrickson, G.H., Kramer, E.J., Hustad, P.D., Coates, G.W. *Macromolecules* **2005**, *38*, 851.

[57] Shimizu, H., Li, Y., Kaito, A., Sano, H. *Macromolecules* **2005**, *38*, 7880.

[58] Zhao, L., Kai, W., He, Y., Zhu, B., Inoue, Y. *J. Polym. Sci. B Polym. Phys.* **2005**, *43*, 2665.

[59] Xu, J.-T., Jin, W., Fan, Z.-Q. *J. Appl. Polym. Sci.* **2005**, *98*, 208.

[60] Ibrahim, K., Starck, P., Löfgren, B., Seppälä, J. *J. Polym. Sci. A Polym. Chem.* **2005**, *43*, 5049.

[61] Lorenzo, A.T., Arnal, M.L., Müller, A.J., Boschetti de Fierro, A., Abetz, V. *Eur. Polym. J.* **2006**, *42*, 516.

[62] Kaito, A. *Polymer* **2006**, *47*, 3548.

[63] Nandan, B., Hsu, Y., Chen, H.-L. *J. Macromol. Sci. C Polym. Rev.* **2006**, *46*, 143.

[64] Carvalho, J.L., Massa, M.V., Dalnoki-Veress, K. *J. Polym. Sci. B Polym. Phys.* **2006**, *44*, 3448.

[65] Meng, F., Zheng, S., Zhang, W., Li, H., Liang, Q. *Macromolecules* **2006**, *39*, 711.

[66] Jin, Y., Hiltner, A., Baer, E., Masirek, R., Piorkowska, E., Galeski, A. *J. Polym. Sci. B Polym. Phys.* **2006**, *44*, 1795.

[67] Lee, J.K., Kim, J.S., Lim, H.J., Lee, K.H., Jo, S.M., Ougizawa, T. *Polymer* **2006**, *47*, 5420.

[68] Salmerón, M., Mathot, V., Poel, G.V., Groeninckx, G., Bruls, W. *J. Polym. Sci. B Polym. Phys.* **2006**, *44*, 815.

[69] Sánchez, M.S., Mathot, V., Groeninckx, G., Bruls, W. *Polymer* **2006**, *47*, 5314.

[70] Wang, M., Hu, W., Ma, Y., Ma, Y.-Q. *J. Chem. Phys.* **2006**, *124*, 244901.

[71] Brito, Y., Sabino, M.A., Ronca, G., Albuerne, J., Müller, A.J. *Rev. LatinAm. Metal. Mater.* **2006**, *26*, 1.

[72] Pillin, I., Feller, J.-F. *Macromol. Mater. Eng.* **2006**, *291*, 1375.

[73] Guo, Q. *Thermochim. Acta* **2006**, *451*, 168.

[74] Huang, P., Guo, Y., Quirk, R.P., Ruan, J., Lotz, B., Thomas, E.L., Hsiao, B.S., Avila-Orta, C., Sics, I., Cheng, S. *Polymer* **2006**, *47*, 5457.

[75] Tol, R.T., Minakov, A.A., Adamovsky, S.A., Mathot, V.B.F., Schick, C. *Polymer* **2006**, *47*, 2172.

[76] Yu, P.-Q., Xie, X.-M., Wang, Z., Li, H.-S., Bates, F.S. *Polymer* **2006**, *47*, 1460.

[77] Wu, Y., Yang, Y., Li, B., Han, Y. *J. Appl. Polym. Sci.* **2006**, *100*, 3187.

[78] Huang, Y., Liu, X.-B., Zhang, H.-L., Zhu, D.-S., Sun, Y.-J., Yan, S.-K., Wang, J., Chen, X.-F., Wan, X.-H., Chen, E.-Q., Zhou, Q.-F. *Polymer* **2006**, *47*, 1217.

[79] Vasilev, C., Reiter, G., Pispas, S., Hadjichristidis, N. *Polymer* **2006**, *47*, 330.

[80] Li, Y., Shimizu, H. *Eur. Polym. J.* **2006**, *42*, 3202.

[81] Massa, M.V., Carvalho, J.L., Dalnoki-Veress, K. *Phys. Rev. Lett.* **2006**, *97*, 247802.

[82] Wang, L., Xu, J.-T., Ding, P.-J., Fan, Z.-Q. *Chin. J. Polym. Sci.* **2006**, *24*, 473.

[83] Yang, K.-K., Zheng, L., Wang, Y.-Z., Zeng, J.-B., Wang, X.-L., Chen, S.-C., Zeng, Q., Li, B. *J. Appl. Polym. Sci.* **2006**, *102*, 1092.

[84] Yang, J., Zhao, T., Cui, J., Liu, L., Zhou, Y., Li, G., Zhou, E., Chen, X. *J. Polym. Sci. B Polym. Phys.* **2006**, *44*, 3215.

[85] He, C., Sun, J., Ma, J., Chen, X., Jing, X. *Biomacromolecules* **2006**, *7*, 3482.

[86] Nojima, S., Inokawa, D., Kawamura, T., Nitta, K.-H. *Polym. J.* **2008**, *40*, 986.

[87] Lovera, D., Márquez, L., Balsamo, V., Taddei, A., Castelli, C., Müller, A.J. *Macromol. Chem. Phys.* **2007**, *208*, 924.

[88] Balsamo, V., Gouveia, L.M. *J. Polym. Sci. B Polym. Phys.* **2007**, *45*, 1365.

[89] Bose, S., Bhattacharyya, A.R., Kodgire, P.V., Misra, A. *Polymer* **2007**, *48*, 356.

[90] Sinturel, C., Vayer, M., Erre, R., Amenitsch, H. *Macromolecules* **2007**, *40*, 2532.

[91] Omonov, T., Harrats, C., Moldenaers, P., Groeninckx, G. *Polymer* **2007**, *48*, 5917.

[92] Ye, H.-M., Peng, M., Xu, J., Guo, B.-H., Chen, Q., Yun, T.-L., Ma, H. *Polymer* **2007**, *48*, 7364.

[93] Huang, J.-W. *Eur. Polym. J.* **2007**, *43*, 4188.

[94] Jin, Y., Hiltner, A., Baer, E. *J. Polym. Sci. B Polym. Phys.* **2007**, *45*, 1138.

[95] Langhe, D., Jin, Y., Hiltner, A., Baer, E. *Antec-Conference Proceedings* 2007, *3*, 1745.

[96] Kailas, L., Vasilev, C., Audinot, J.-N., Migeon, H.-N., Hobbs, J.-K. *Macromolecules* **2007**, *40*, 7223.

[97] Hou, W.-M., Zhou, J.-J., Gan, Z.-H., Shi, A.-C., Chan, C.-M., Li, L. *Polymer* **2007**, *48*, 4926.

[98] Xue, M.-L., Yu, Y.-L., Chuah, H.H. *J. Macromol. Sci. B Phys.* **2007**, *46*, 603.

[99] Miura, T., Mikami, M. *Phys. Rev. E* **2007**, *75*, 031804.

[100] Komura, M., Iyoda, T. *Macromolecules* **2007**, *40*, 4106.

[101] Guo, Q., Thomann, R., Gronski, W. *Polymer* **2007**, *48*, 3925.

[102] Qiao, C., Jiang, S., Ji, X., An, L., Jiang, B. *Front. Chem. China* **2007**, *2*, 343.

[103] Wang, Y., Mano, J.F. *J. Appl. Polym. Sci.* **2007**, *105*, 3204.

[104] Jin, Y., Hiltner, A., Baer, E. *J. Polym. Sci. B Polym. Phys.* **2007**, *45*, 1788.

[105] Gao, Y., Liu, H. *J. Appl. Polym. Sci.* **2007**, *106*, 2718.

[106] Chen, S.H., Wu, Y.H., Su, C.H., Jeng, U., Hsieh, C.C., Su, A.C., Chen, S.A. *Macromolecules* **2007**, *40*, 5353.

[107] Camarillo, A.A., Roth, S.V., Bösecke, P., Buchner, S., Krenn, K., Gehrke, R., Stribeck, N. *J. Mater. Sci.* **2007**, *42*, 6212.

[108] Peng, J., Han, Y., Knoll, W., Kim, D.H. *Macromol. Rapid Commun.* **2007**, *28*, 1422.

[109] Gao, W.-P., Bai, Y., Chen, E.-Q., Zhou, Q.-F. *Chin. J. Polym. Sci.* **2005**, *23*, 275.

[110] Liang, G.D., Xu, J.T., Fan, Z.Q. *Eur. Polym. J.* **2007**, *43*, 3153.

[111] Jin, Y., Hiltner, A., Baer, E. *J. Appl. Polym. Sci.* **2007**, *105*, 3260.

[112] Wang, H., Chen, X., Pan, C.Y. *Eur. Polym. J.* **2007**, *43*, 1905.

[113] Wei, Y., Pan, C., Li, B., Han, Y. *J. Chem. Phys.* **2007**, *126*, 104902.

[114] Chen, Y.-F., Zhang, F.-B., Xie, X.-M., Yuan, J.-Y. *Polymer* **2007**, *48*, 2755.

[115] Hsu, J.-Y., Hsieh, I.-F., Nandan, B., Chiu, F.-C., Chen, J., Jeng, U.-S., Chen, H.-L. *Macromolecules* **2007**, *40*, 5014.

[116] Sun, Y.-S., Chung, T.-M., Li, Y.-J., Ho, R.-M., Ko, B.-T., Jeng, U.-S. *Macromolecules* **2007**, *40*, 6778.

[117] Li, L., Meng, F., Zhong, Z., Byelov, D., De Jeu, W.H., Feijen, J. *J. Chem. Phys.* **2007**, *126*, 024904.

[118] Yang, J., Zhao, T., Zhou, Y., Liu, L., Li, G., Zhou, E., Chen, X. *Macromolecules* **2007**, *40*, 2791.

[119] Nojima, S., Ito, K., Ikeda, H. *Polymer* **2007**, *48*, 3607.

[120] Nojima, M.S., Kiji, T., Ohguma, Y. *Macromolecules* **2007**, *40*, 7566.

[121] Hsiao, M.S., Zheng, J.X., Van Horn, R.M., Quirk, R.P., Cheng, S.Z.D., Lotz, B., Thomas, E.L., Chen, H.L. *American Phys. Soc.* C1. 00082, 2008, APS March Meeting.

[122] Zhu, J., Wang, M. *J. Macromol. Sci. B Phys.* **2008**, *47*, 401.

[123] Pinna, M., Guo, X., Zvelindovsky, A.V. *Polymer* **2008**, *49*, 2797.

[124] Hsiao, M.-S., Chen, W.Y., Zheng, J.X., Van Horn, R.M., Quirk, R.P., Ivanov, D.A., Thomas, E.L., Lotz, B., Cheng, S.Z.D. *Macromolecules* **2008**, *41*, 4794.

[125] Castillo, R.V., Arnal, M.L., Müller, A.J., Hamley, I.W., Castelletto, V., Schmalz, H., Abetz, V. *Macromolecules* **2008**, *41*, 879.

[126] Kim, J., Sandoval, R.W., Dettmer, C.M., Nguyen, S.T., Torkelson, J.M. *Polymer* **2008**, *49*, 2686.

[127] Li, Y., Iwakura, Y., Zhao, L., Shimizu, H. *Macromolecules* **2008**, *41*, 3120.

[128] Müller, C., Radano, C.P., Smith, P., Stingelin-Stutzmann, N. *Polymer* **2008**, *49*, 3973.

[129] Ikeda, H., Ohguma, Y., Nojima, S. *Polym. J.* **2008**, *40*, 241.

[130] Lorenzo, A.T., Arnal, M.L., Müller, A.J., Boschetti-de-Fierro, A., Abetz, V. *Macromolecules* **2007**, *40*, 5023.

[131] Takeshita, H., Gao, Y.-J., Natsui, T., Rodriguez, E., Miya, M., Takenaka, K., Shiomi, T. *Polymer* **2007**, *48*, 7660.

[132] Nojima, S., Ohguma, Y., Namiki, S., Ishizone, T., Yamaguchi, K. *Macromolecules* **2008**, *41*, 1915.

[133] Müller, A.J., Castillo, R.V., Hillmyer, M. *Macromol. Symp.* **2006**, *242*, 174.

[134] Castillo, R.V., Müller, A.J., Lin, M.-C., Chen, H.-L., Jeng, U.-S., Hillmyer, M.A. *Macromolecules* **2008**, *41*, 6154.

[135] Müller, A.J., Albuerne, J., Esteves, L.M., Márquez, L., Raquez, J.-M., Degée, Ph., Dubois, Ph., Collings, S., Hamley, I.W. *Macromol. Symp.* **2004**, *215*, 369.

[136] Müller, A.J., Albuerne, J., Márquez, L., Raquez, J.-M., Degée, Ph., Dubois, Ph., Hobbs, J., Hamley, I.W. *Faraday Discuss.* **2005**, *128*, 231.

[137] Tongcher, O., Sigel, R., Landfester, K. *Langmuir* **2006**, *22*, 4504.

[138] Ibarretxe, J., Groeninckx, G., Bremer, L., Mathot, V.B.F. *Polymer* **2009**, *50*, 4584.

[139] Weber, C.H.M., Chiche, A., Krausch, G., Rosenfeldt, S., Ballauf, M., Harnau, L., Göttker-Schnetmann, I., Tong, Q., Mecking, S. *Nano Lett.* **2007**, *7*, 2024.

[140] Bernal-Lara, T.E., Masirek, R., Hiltner, A., Baer, E., Piorkowska, E., Galeski, A. *J. Appl. Polym. Sci.* **2006**, *99*, 597.

[141] Puente Orench, I., Stribeck, N., Ania, F., Baer, E., Hiltner, A., Baltá Calleja, F.J. *Polymer* **2009**, *50*, 2680.

[142] Wang, H., Keum, J.K., Hiltner, A., Baer, E., Freeman, B., Rozanski, A., Galeski, A. *Science* **2009**, *323*, 757.

[143] Pethe, V.V., Wang, H.P., Hiltner, A., Baer, E., Freeman, B.D. *J. Appl. Polym. Sci.* **2008**, *110*, 1411.

[144] Bishop, C., Teeters, D. *Electrochim. Acta* **2009**, *54*, 4084.

[145] Wu, H., Wang, W., Huang, Y., Wang, C., Su, Z. *Macromolecules* **2008**, *41*, 7755.

[146] He, Y., Weihua, Z., Inoue, Y. *Macromolecules* **2004**, *37*, 3337.

[147] Hu, W., Cai, T., Ma, Y., Hobbs, J.K., Farrance, O., Reiter, G. *Faraday Discuss.* **2009**, *143*, 129.

[148] Cai, T., Qian, Y., Ma, Y., Ren, Y., Hu, W. *Macromolecules* **2009**, *42*, 3381.

[149] Rangarajan, P., Register, R.A., Fetters, L.J. *Macromolecules* **1993**, *26*, 4640.

[150] Rangarajan, P., Register, R.A., Adamson, D.H., Fetters, L.J., Bras, W., Naylor, S., Ryan, A.J. *Macromolecules* **1995**, *28*, 1422.

[151] Ryan, A.J., Hamley, I.W., Bras, W., Bates, F.S. *Macromolecules* **1995**, *28*, 3860.

[152] Richardson, P.H., Richards, R.W., Blundelospprunl, D.J., MacDonald, W.A., Mills, P. *Polymer* **1995**, *36*, 3059.

[153] Quiram, D.J., Register, R.A., Marchand, G.R., Ryan, A.J. *Macromolecules* **1997**, *30*, 8338.

[154] Douzinas, K.C., Cohen, R.E., Halasa, A.F. *Macromolecules* **1991**, *24*, 4457.

[155] Hamley, I.W., Patrick, J., Fairclough, A., Terrill, N.J., Ryan, A.J., Lipic, P.M., Bates, F.S., Towns-Andrews, E. *Macromolecules* **1996**, *29*, 8835.

[156] Rangarajan, P., Register, R.A., Fetters, L.J., Bras, W., Taylor, S., Ryan, A.J. *Macromolecules* **1995**, *28*, 4932.

[157] Nojima, S., Kato, K., Yamamoto, S., Ashida, T. *Macromolecules* **1992**, *25*, 2237.

[158] Quiram, D.J., Register, R.A., Marchand, G.R. *Macromolecules* **1997**, *30*, 4551.

[159] Rohadi, A., Endo, R., Tanimoto, S., Sasaki, S., Nojima, S. *Polym. J.* **2000**, *32*, 602.

[160] Rohadi, A., Tanimoto, S., Sasaki, S., Nojima, S. *Polym. J.* **2000**, *32*, 859.

[161] Ryan, A.J., Fairclough, J.P.A., Hamley, I.W., Mai, S.-M., Booth, C. *Macromolecules* **1997**, *30*, 1723.

[162] Zhang, F., Chen, Y., Huang, H., Hu, Z., He, T. *Langmuir* **2003**, *19*, 5563.

[163] Hillmyer, M.A., Bates, F.S. *Macromol. Symp.* **1997**, *117*, 121.

[164] Loo, Y.-L., Register, R.A., Ryan, A.J. *Macromolecules* **2002**, *35*, 2365.

[165] Nojima, S., Toei, M., Hara, S., Tanimoto, S., Sasaki, S. *Polymer* **2002**, *43*, 4087.

[166] Reiter, G., Castelein, G., Sommer, J.-U., Röttele, A., Thurn-Albrecht, T. *Phys. Rev. Lett.* **2001**, *87*, 226101.

[167] Robitaille, C., Prud'homme, J. *Macromolecules* **1983**, *16*, 665.

[168] Quiram, D.J., Register, R.A., Marchand, G.R., Adamson, D.H. *Macromolecules* **1998**, *31*, 4891.

[169] Ueda, M., Sakurai, K., Okamoto, S., Lohse, D., MacKnight, W.J., Shinkai, S., Sakurai, S., Nomura, S. *Polymer* **2003**, *44*, 6995.

[170] Reiter, G. *J. Polym. Sci. B Polym. Phys.* **2003**, *41*, 1869.

[171] Reiter, G., Castelein, G., Sommer, J.U. Crystallization of polymers in thin films: Model experiments. In *Polymer Crystallization, Observations, Concepts and Interpretations*, Sommer, J.U., Reiter, G., eds. Springer, Berlin, 2003.

[172] Müller, A.J., Balsamo, V., Arnal, M.L., Jakob, T., Schmalz, H., Abetz, V. *Macromolecules* **2002**, *35*, 3048.

[173] Arnal, M.L., Balsamo, V., López-Carrasquero, F., Contreras, J., Carrillo, M., Schmalz, H., Abetz, V., Laredo, E., Müller, A.J. *Macromolecules* **2001**, *34*, 7973.

[174] Floudas, G., Tsitsilianis, C. *Macromolecules* **1997**, *30*, 4381.

[175] Gervais, M., Gallot, B. *Polymer* **1981**, *22*, 1129.

[176] Lotz, B., Kovacs, A.J. *Polym. Prep.* **1969**, *10*, 820.

[177] O'Malley, J.J. *J. Polym. Sci. Polym. Symp.* **1977**, *60*, 151.

[178] Zhu, L., Chen, Y., Zhang, A., Calhoun, B.H., Chun, M., Quirk, R.P., Cheng, S.Z.D., Hsiao, B.S., Yeh, F., Hashimoto, T. *Phys. Rev. B* **1999**, *60*, 10022.

[179] Zhu, L., Cheng, S.Z.D., Calhoun, B.H., Ge, Q., Quirk, R.P., Thomas, E.L., Hsiao, B.S., Yeh, F., Lotz, B. *Polymer* **2001**, *42*, 5829.

[180] Zhu, L., Mimnaugh, B.R., Ge, Q., Quirk, R.P., Cheng, S.Z.D., Thomas, E.L., Lotz, B., Hsiao, B.S., Yeh, F., Liu, L. *Polymer* **2001**, *42*, 9121.

[181] Zhu, L., Cheng, S.Z.D., Huang, P., Ge, Q., Quirk, R.P., Thomas, E.L., Lotz, B., Hsiao, B.S., Yeh, F., Liu, L. *Adv. Mater.* **2002**, *14*, 31.

[182] Zhu, L., Huang, P., Chen, W.Y., Ge, Q., Quirk, R.P., Cheng, S.Z.D., Thomas, E.L., Lotz, B., Hsiao, B.S., Yeh, F., Liu, L. *Macromolecules* **2002**, *35*, 3553.

[183] Xu, J.T., Yuan, J.J., Cheng, S.Y. *Eur. Polym. J.* **2003**, *39*, 2091.

[184] Weimann, P.A., Hajduk, D.A., Chu, C., Chaffin, K.A., Brodil, J.C., Bates, F.S. *J. Polym. Sci. B Polym. Phys.* **1999**, *37*, 2053.

[185] Loo, Y.-L., Register, R.A., Ryan, A.J., Dee, G.T. *Macromolecules* **2001**, *34*, 8968.

[186] Röttele, A., Thurn-Albrecht, T., Sommer, J.U., Reiter, G. *Macromolecules* **2003**, *36*, 1257.

[187] Chen, H.-L., Hsiao, S.-C., Lin, T.-L., Yamauchi, K., Hasegawa, H., Hashimoto, T. *Macromolecules* **2001**, *34*, 671.

[188] Loo, Y.L., Register, R.A., Ryan, A.J. *Phys. Rev. Lett.* **2000**, *84*, 4120.

[189] Chen, H.-L., Wu, J.-C., Lin, T.-L., Lin, J.-S. *Macromolecules* **2001**, *34*, 6936.

[190] Xu, J.T., Fairclough, J.P.A., Mai, S.M., Chaibundit, C., Mingvanish, M., Booth, C., Ryan, A.J. *Polymer* **2003**, *44*, 6843.

[191] Balsamo, V., Müller, A.J., Stadler, R. *Macromolecules* **1998**, *31*, 7756.

[192] Balsamo, V., Paolini, Y., Ronca, G., Müller, A.J. *Macromol. Chem. Phys.* **2000**, *201*, 2711.

[193] Schmalz, H., Abetz, V., Müller, A.J. *Macromol. Symp.* **2002**, *183*, 179.

[194] Schmalz, H., Müller, A.J., Abetz, V. *Macromol. Chem. Phys.* **2003**, *204*, 111.

[195] Choi, Y.K., Bae, Y.H., Kim, S.W. *Macromolecules* **1998**, *31*, 8766.

[196] Bogdanov, B., Vidts, A., Schacht, E., Berghmans, H. *Macromolecules* **1999**, *32*, 726.

[197] Wang, Y., Hillmyer, M.C. *J. Polym. Sci. A Polym. Chem.* **2001**, *39*, 2755.

[198] Albuerne, J., Márquez, L., Müller, A.J., Raquez, J.M., Degée, Ph., Dubois, Ph., Castelletto, V., Hamley, I.W. *Macromolecules* **2003**, *36*, 1633.

[199] Shiomi, T., Takeshita, H., Kawaguchi, H., Nagai, M., Takenaka, K., Miya, M. *Macromolecules* **2002**, *35*, 8056.

[200] Balsamo, V., von Gyldenfeldt, F., Stadler, R. *Macromol. Chem. Phys.* **1996**, *197*, 1159.

[201] Balsamo, V., von Gyldenfeldt, F., Stadler, R. *Macromol. Chem. Phys.* **1996**, *197*, 3317.

[202] Schmalz, H., Knoll, A., Müller, A.J., Abetz, V. *Macromolecules* **2002**, *35*, 10004.

[203] Bailey, T.S., Pham, H.D., Bates, F.S. *Macromolecules* **2001**, *34*, 6994.

[204] Schmalz, H., Böker, A., Lange, R., Krausch, G., Abetz, V. *Macromolecules* **2001**, *34*, 8720.

[205] Balsamo, V., Stadler, R. *Macromol. Symp.* **1997**, *117*, 153.

[206] Floudas, G., Reiter, G., Lambert, O., Dumas, P. *Macromolecules* **1998**, *31*, 7279.

[207] Cohen, R.E., Bellare, A., Drzewinski, M.A. *Macromolecules* **1994**, *27*, 2321.

[208] Xie, R., Sun, G., Yang, B., Jiang, B. *Macromolecules* **1994**, *27*, 3444.

[209] Nojima, S., Takahashi, Y., Ashida, T. *Polymer* **1995**, *36*, 2853.

[210] Nojima, S., Yamamoto, S., Ashida, T. *Polym. J.* **1995**, *27*, 673.

[211] Zhang, R., Luo, X., Ma, D. *Polymer* **1995**, *36*, 4361.

[212] Drzewinski, M.A. *Macromol. Symp.* **1995**, *91*, 107.

[213] Hamley, I.W., Patrick, J., Fairclough, A., Ryan, A.J., Bates, F.S., Towns-Andrews, E. *Polymer* **1996**, *37*, 4425.

[214] Gan, Z., Jiang, B., Zhang, J. *J. Appl. Polym. Sci.* **1996**, *59*, 961.

[215] Gan, Z., Jiang, B., Zhang, J. *J. Appl. Polym. Sci.* **1997**, *63*, 1793.

[216] Mai, S.-M., Fairclough, J.P.A., Viras, K., Gorry, P.A., Hamley, I.W., Ryan, A.J., Booth, C. *Macromolecules* **1997**, *30*, 8392.

[217] Alig, I., Tadjbakhsch, S., Floudas, G., Tsitsilianis, C. *Macromolecules* **1998**, *31*, 6917.

[218] Hamley, I.W., Wallwork, M.L., Smith, D.A., Fairclough, J.P.A., Ryan, A.J., Mai, S.M., Yang, Y.W., Booth, C. *Polymer* **1998**, *39*, 3321.

[219] Nojima, S., Tanaka, H., Rohadi, A., Sasaki, S. *Polymer* **1998**, *39*, 1727.

[220] Balsamo, V., Müller, A.J., Gyldenfeldt, F.V., Stadler, R. *Macromol. Chem. Phys.* **1998**, *199*, 1063.

[221] Reiter, G., Castelein, G., Hoerner, P., Riess, G., Blumen, A., Sommer, J.U. *Phys. Rev. Lett.* **1999**, *83*, 3844.

[222] Nojima, S., Kuroda, M., Sasaki, S. *Polym. J.* **1997**, *29*, 642.

[223] Nojima, S., Kikuchi, N., Rohadi, A., Tanimoto, S., Sasaki, S. *Macromolecules* **1999**, *32*, 3727.

[224] Nojima, N., Kanda, Y., Sasaki, S. *Polym. J.* **1998**, *30*, 628.

[225] Nojima, S., Hashizume, K., Rohadi, A., Sasaki, S. *Polymer* **1997**, *38*, 2711.

[226] Nojima, S., Fujimoto, M., Kakihira, H., Sasaki, S. *Polym. J.* **1998**, *30*, 968.

[227] Nojima, S., Kakihira, H., Tanimoto, S., Nakatani, H., Sasaki, S. *Polym. J.* **2000**, *32*, 75.

[228] Reiter, G., Castelein, G., Hoerner, P., Riess, G., Sommer, J.U., Floudas, G. *Eur. Phys. J. E* **2000**, *2*, 319.

[229] Loo, Y.L., Register, R.A., Adamson, D.H. *J. Polym. Sci. B Polym. Phys.* **2000**, *38*, 2564.

[230] Zhu, L., Cheng, S.Z.D., Calhoun, B.H., Ge, Q., Quirk, R.P., Thomas, E.L., Hsiao, B.S., Ye, F., Lotz, B. *J. Am. Chem. Soc.* **2000**, *122*, 5957.

[231] De Rosa, C., Park, C., Lotz, B., Wittmann, J.C., Fetters, L.J., Thomas, E.L. *Macromolecules* **2000**, *33*, 4871.

[232] Mai, S.-M., Mingvanish, W., Turner, S.C., Chaibundit, C., Fairclough, J.P.A., Heatley, F., Matsen, M.W., Ryan, A.J., Booth, C. *Macromolecules* **2000**, *33*, 5124.

[233] Park, C., De Rosa, C., Fetters, L.J., Thomas, E.L. *Macromolecules* **2000**, *33*, 7931.

[234] Zhu, L., Huang, P., Cheng, S.Z.D., Ge, Q., Quirk, R.P., Thomas, E.L., Lotz, B., Wittmann, J.C., Hsiao, B.S., Fengji, Y., Liu, L. *Phys. Rev. Lett.* **2001**, *86*, 6030.

[235] Zhu, L., Calhoun, B.H., Ge, Q., Quirk, R.P., Cheng, S.Z.D., Thomas, E.L., Hsiao, B.S., Yeh, F., Liu, L., Lotz, B. *Macromolecules* **2001**, *34*, 1244.

[236] Shiomi, T., Tsukada, H., Takeshita, H., Takenaka, K., Tezuka, Y. *Polymer* **2001**, *42*, 4997.

[237] Thünemann, A.F., General, S. *Macromolecules* **2001**, *34*, 6978.

[238] Childs, M.A., Matlock, D.D., Dorgan, J.R., Ohmo, T.R. *Biomacromolecules* **2001**, *2*, 526.

[239] Buzdugan, E., Ghioca, P., Stribeck, N., Beckman, E.J., Serban, S. *Macromol. Mater. Eng.* **2001**, *286*, 497.

[240] Fairclough, J.P.A., Mai, S.M., Matsen, M.W., Bras, W., Messe, L., Turner, S.C., Gleeson, A.J., Booth, C., Hamley, I.W., Ryan, A.J. *J. Chem. Phys.* **2001**, *114*, 5425.

[241] Hong, S., MacKnight, W.J., Russell, T.P., Gido, S.P. *Macromolecules* **2001**, *34*, 2398.

[242] Hong, S., MacKnight, W.J., Russell, T.P., Gido, S.P. *Macromolecules* **2001**, *34*, 2876.

[243] Floudas, G., Vazaiou, B., Shipper, F., Ulrich, R., Wiesner, U., Iatrou, H., Hadjichristidis, N. *Macromolecules* **2001**, *34*, 2947.

[244] Huang, P., Zhu, L., Cheng, S.Z.D., Ge, Q., Quirk, R., Thomas, E.L., Lotz, B., Hsiao, B.S., Liu, L., Yeh, F. *Macromolecules* **2001**, *34*, 6649.

[245] Hong, S., Yang, L., MacKnight, J., Gido, S.P. *Macromolecules* **2001**, *34*, 7009.

[246] Baiardo, M., Alfonso, G.C. *Macromol. Chem. Phys.* **2001**, *202*, 2509.

[247] Hong, S., Bushleman, A.A., MacKnight, W.J., Gido, S.P., Lohse, D.J., Fetters, L.J. *Polymer* **2001**, *42*, 5909.

[248] Reiter, G., Castelein, G., Sommer, J.U. *Macromol. Symp.* **2002**, *183*, 173.

[249] Xu, J.-T., Turner, S.C., Fairclough, J.P.A., Mai, S.-M., Ryan, A.J., Chaibundit, C., Booth, C. *Macromolecules* **2002**, *35*, 3614.

[250] Opitz, R., Lambreva, D.M., De Jeu, W.H. *Macromolecules* **2002**, *35*, 6930.

[251] Hamley, I.W., Castelleto, V., Floudas, G., Schipper, F. *Macromolecules* **2002**, *35*, 8839.

[252] Ruokolainen, J., Fredrickson, G.H., Kramer, E.J., Ryu, C.Y., Hahn, S.F., Magonov, S.N. *Macromolecules* **2002**, *35*, 9391.

[253] Mortensen, K., Brown, W., Almdal, K., Alami, E., Jada, A. *Langmuir* **1997**, *13*, 3635.

[254] Li, L., Séréro, Y., Koch, M.H.J., Jeu, W.H. *Macromolecules* **2003**, *36*, 529.

[255] Schmalz, H., Abetz, V., Lange, R. *Compos. Sci. Technol.* **2003**, *63*, 1179.

[256] Zhang, F., Huang, H., Hu, Z., Chen, Y., He, T. *Langmuir* **2003**, *19*, 10100.

[257] Park, C., De Rosa, C., Lotz, B., Fetters, L.J., Thomas, E.L. *Macromol. Chem. Phys.* **2003**, *204*, 1514.

[258] Chen, H.-L., Li, H.-C., Huang, Y.-Y., Chiu, F.-C. *Macromolecules* **2002**, *35*, 2417.

[259] Brown, R.A., Masters, A.J., Price, C., Yuan, X. Chain segregation in block copolymers. In *Comprehensive Polymer Science—The Synthesis, Characterizations, Reaction & Applications of Polymers*, Vol. 7, 1st ed., Aggarwal, S., ed. Pergamon Press plc., London, 1989.

[260] Hadjichristidis, N., Pispas, S., Floudas, G. *Block Copolymers: Synthetic Strategies, Physical Properties, and Applications*, 1st ed. Wiley-Interscience, Hoboken, NJ, 2003.

[261] Abetz, V. Block copolymers. In *Encyclopedia of Polymer Science and Engineering*, Mark, H.F., ed. John Wiley & Sons, Inc., New York, 2001, I-LV.

[262] Abetz, V. Assemblies in complex block copolymer systems. In *Supramolecular Polymers*, Ciferri, A., ed. Marcel Dekker Inc., New York, 2000, Chapter 6.

[263] Hamley, I.W. *The Physics of Block Copolymers*, Oxford University Press, London, 1998.

[264] Müller, A.J., Balsamo, V., Arnal, M.L. Crystallization in block copolymers with more than one crystallizable block. In *Lecture Notes in Physics: Progress in Understanding of Polymer Crystallization*, Reiter, G., Strobl, G., eds. Springer, Berlin, Germany, 2007.

[265] Müller, A.J., Balsamo, V., Arnal, M.L. *Adv. Polym. Sci.* **2005**, *190*, 1.

[266] Hamley, I.W. *Adv. Polym. Sci.* **1999**, *148*, 113.

[267] Castillo, R.V., Müller, A.J. *Prog. Polym. Sci.* **2009**, *34*, 516.

[268] Arnal, M.L., Matos, M.E., Morales, R.A., Santana, O.O., Müller, A.J. *Macromol. Chem. Phys.* **1998**, *199*, 2275.

[269] Lorenzo, A.T., Müller, A.J. *J. Polym. Sci. B Polym. Phys.* **2008**, *46*, 1478.

[270] Lorenzo, A.T., Arnal, M.L., Albuerne, J., Müller, A.J. *Polym. Test.* **2007**, *26*, 222.

[271] Hillmyer, M.A., Bates, F.S. *Macromolecules* **1996**, *29*, 6994.

[272] Epps, T.H., III, Bailey, T.S., Waletzko, R., Bates, F.S. *Macromolecules* **2003**, *36*, 2873.

[273] Nojima, S., Akutsu, Y., Washino, A., Tanimoto, S. *Polymer* **2004**, *45*, 7317.

[274] Santana, O.O., Müller, A.J. *Polym. Bull.* **1994**, *32*, 471.

[275] Morales, R.A., Arnal, M.L., Müller, A.J. *Polym. Bull.* **1995**, *35*, 379.

[276] Manaure, A.C., Morales, R.A., Sánchez, J.J., Müller, A.J. *J. Appl. Polym. Sci.* **1997**, *66*, 2481.

[277] Arnal, M.L., Müller, A.J. *Macromol. Chem. Phys.* **1999**, *200*, 2559.

[278] Manaure, A., Müller, A.J. *Macromol. Chem. Phys.* **2000**, *201*, 958.

[279] Arnal, M.L., Müller, A.J., Maiti, P., Hikosaka, M. *Macromol. Chem. Phys.* **2000**, *201*, 2493.

[280] Montenegro, R., Landfester, K. *Langmuir* **2003**, *19*, 5996.

[281] Taden, A., Landfester, K. *Macromolecules* **2003**, *36*, 4037.

[282] Ma, Y., Hu, W., Reiter, G. *Macromolecules* **2006**, *39*, 5159.

[283] Padden, F.J., Jr., Keith, H.D. *J. Appl. Phys.* **1966**, *37*, 4013.

[284] Cho, K., Kim, D., Yoon, S. *Macromolecules* **2003**, *36*, 7652.

[285] Muratoglu, O.K., Argon, A.S., Cohen, R.E. *Polymer* **1995**, *36*, 2143.

[286] Pearce, R., Vancso, G.J. *Macromolecules* **1997**, *30*, 5843.

[287] Tsuji, M., Novillo, L.F.A., Fujita, M., Murakami, S., Kohjiya, S. *J. Mater. Res.* **1999**, *14*, 251.

[288] Durell, M., Macdonald, J.E., Trolley, D., Wehrum, A., Jukes, P.C., Jones, R.A.L., Walker, C.J., Brown, S. *Europhys. Lett.* **2002**, *58*, 844.

[289] Basire, C., Ivanov, D.A. *Phys. Rev. Lett.* **2000**, *85*, 5587.

[290] Lovinger, A.J., Keith, H.D. *Macromolecules* **1979**, *12*, 919.

[291] Kovacs, A.J., Straupe, C. *Faraday Discuss.* **1979**, *68*, 225.

[292] Schonherr, H., Frank, C.W. *Macromolecules* **2003**, *36*, 1188.

[293] Abe, H., Kikkawa, Y., Iwata, T., Aoki, H., Akehata, T., Doi, Y. *Polymer* **2000**, *41*, 867.

[294] Reiter, G., Sommer, J. *Phys. Rev. Lett.* **1998**, *80*, 3771.

[295] Reiter, G., Sommer, J. *J. Chem. Phys.* **2000**, *112*, 4376.

[296] Sommer, J., Reiter, G. *J. Chem. Phys.* **2000**, *112*, 4384.

[297] Zhang, F., Liu, J., Huang, H., Du, B., He, T. *Eur. Phys. J. E* **2002**, *8*, 289.

[298] Sakai, Y., Imai, M., Kaji, K., Tsuji, M. *J. Cryst. Growth* **1999**, *203*, 244.

[299] Klemmer, N., Jungnickel, B.J. *Colloid Polym. Sci.* **1984**, *262*, 381.

[300] Frensch, H., Jungnickel, B.J. *Colloid Polym. Sci.* **1989**, *267*, 16.

[301] Avella, M., Martuscelli, E., Raimo, M. *Polymer* **1993**, *34*, 3234.

[302] Ikkala, O.T., Holsti-Miettinen, R.M., Sépala, J. *J. Appl. Polym. Sci.* **1993**, *49*, 1165.

[303] Tang, T., Huang, B. *J. Appl. Polym. Sci.* **1994**, *53*, 355.

[304] Dedecker, K., Groeninckx, G. *Polymer* **1998**, *39*, 4993.

[305] Evereaert, V., Groeninckx, G., Aerts, L. *Polymer* **2000**, *41*, 1409.

[306] Evereaert, V., Groeninckx, G., Koch, M.H.J., Reinares, H. *Polymer* **2003**, *44*, 3491.

[307] Wilkinson, A.N., Clemens, M.L., Harding, V.M. *Polymer* **2004**, *45*, 5239.

[308] Xu, J.T., Fairclough, J.P.A., Mai, S.M., Ryan, A.J., Chaibundit, C. *Macromolecules* **2002**, *35*, 6937.

[309] Guo, Q., Thomann, R., Gronski, W., Staneva, R., Ivanova, R., Stühn, B. *Macromolecules* **2003**, *36*, 3635.

[310] Tol, R.T., Mathot, V.B.F., Reynaers, H., Groeninckx, G. *Micro and Nanostructured Multiphase Polymer Blend Systems: Relationship between Phase Morphology, Crystallization and Semicrystalline Structure in Inmiscible Polymer Blends*, 1st ed. Boca Raton, FL, 2005.

[311] Hu, W., Frenkel, D. *Adv. Polym. Sci.* **2005**, *191*, 1.

[312] Ma, Y., Hu, W., Hobbs, J., Reiter, G. *Soft Matter* **2008**, *4*, 540.

[313] Hu, W., Frenkel, D. *Faraday Discuss.* **2005**, *128*, 253.

[314] Hu, W. *Macromolecules* **2005**, *38*, 3977.

[315] Qian, Y., Cai, T., Hu, W. *Macromolecules* **2008**, *41*, 7625.

[316] Balsamo, V., Urdaneta, N., Pérez, L., Carrizales, P., Abetz, V., Müller, A.J. *Eur. Polym. J.* **2004**, *40*, 1033.

13

CRYSTALLIZATION IN POLYMER COMPOSITES AND NANOCOMPOSITES

EWA PIORKOWSKA

Centre of Molecular and Macromolecular Studies, Polish Academy of Sciences, Lodz, Poland

13.1 Introduction, 379
13.2 Microcomposites with Particulate Fillers, 380
13.3 Fiber-Reinforced Composites, 382
13.4 Modeling of Crystallization in Fiber-Reinforced Composites, 385

13.5 Nanocomposites, 388
13.6 Conclusions, 393
Appendix, 393
References, 394

13.1 INTRODUCTION

The development of polymer composites is driven by increasing demands for improvement of materials properties. Polymer composites are polymer-based materials with at least one functional additive of organic or nonorganic origin [1, 2]. To tailor materials properties for a broad range of applications, various additives are introduced into polymers. They may be natural or synthetic and include many substances in the form of particles of different sizes and shapes, isotropic–spherical, and anisotropic: fibrous, flaky, or disk-like. The filler content can reach 40–50%. Depending on their functions, the additives may be classified as modifiers, property extenders, or processing aids. Glass in the form of fibers or hollow glass bubbles, carbon materials (carbon black, fibers, graphite, nanotubes), calcium carbonate, attapulgite, wollastonite, silica, talc, montmorillonite (MMT), and natural fibers are used, among others. Polymer composites comprise also materials where reinforcement is polymeric. In self-reinforced polymer composites, which are also referred to as single-phase or homocomposites, the same polymer is forming both the reinforcing and matrix phases.

The advantages of filling include improved dimensional stability due to less volume shrinkage during crystallization and/or glass transition, and lower thermal expansion coefficient. Other benefits include lower costs, higher modulus, higher impact resistance, modified barrier properties, reduced flammability, higher swelling resistance, and enhanced ionic conductivity. The use of nanometer-sized particles as fillers makes it possible to improve the properties at very low loading levels, usually a few percent. Polymer composites are also classified according to sizes of filler particles as microcomposites and nanocomposites. Nanoparticles have at least one characteristic size on a nanometer scale; they are in the form of nanopowders, nanofibers, and nanoplatelets. Well-known examples of the last two are carbon nanotubes (CNTs) and exfoliated MMT, respectively. All nanofillers have large surface areas, whereas the layered nanoclays and nanofibers are in addition characterized by high aspect ratios.

The nanofillers gain increasing acceptance and utility. Novel processing methods are developed that allow to improve dispersion and exfoliation of clays, such as the use of supercritical fluids, ultrasound, and solid-state shear processing [2]. Another important trend in

---

Handbook of Polymer Crystallization, First Edition. Edited by Ewa Piorkowska and Gregory C. Rutledge.
© 2013 John Wiley & Sons, Inc. Published 2013 by John Wiley & Sons, Inc.

polymer composites is the use of functional additives such as flame retardants, stabilizers and antioxidants, surface modifiers, and processing aids [2]. Fillers are frequently modified to improve the dispersion, to control adhesion with a polymer matrix, to prevent moisture absorption, and so on. More than one additive can be introduced to a polymer to improve different properties. Moreover, polymer composites may contain not only an additive but also another polymer, acting for instance as a compatibilizer. Another recent trend is the development of so-called green composites, where biodegradable fillers, such as flax, hemp, jute, and wood flour [2, 3], are used. It has to be emphasized that the green composites with biodegradable fillers have many advantages, including recyclability, decreased wear of equipment, low density, and low price of the fillers. Biodegradability is especially important when the fillers are used to reinforce biodegradable polymers like polylactide (PLA).

The presence of internal interfaces frequently affects crystallization of a polymer matrix. Space inhabited by fillers is not accessible for nucleation; hence, quantitatively, similar effects can be expected to those occurring during crystallization in a confined volume. Fillers, including nanofillers, frequently exhibit nucleation activity. Intense nucleation can occur also on reinforcing fibers leading to transcrystalline morphology. The nucleation effect of fillers on mechanical properties is problematic; some authors find better adhesion as a factor improving properties and others evidence diminished properties. In conducting polymer composites, where contacts between filler particles are important, nucleating particles become isolated inside spherulites of matrix and do not contribute to the conductive path [4]. Nevertheless, the filler acting as a nucleating agent shortens the crystallization time and increases the temperature at which the polymer crystallizes during processing, thereby reducing cycle time and increasing productivity. In addition to nucleation, the crystal growth in polymer matrix can also be affected, especially in nanocomposites. It must be mentioned that interactions with fillers can result in a change of polymorphic forms of crystals, for instance, stabilization of the monoclinic γ form of polyamide 6 (PA6) nanocomposites with MMT [5]. The role of epitaxy in the selective nucleation of polymorphic forms is discussed in Chapter 8. Further, the presence of fillers might enhance the effect of flow on crystallization, like it occurs in isotactic polypropylene (iPP) nanocomposites with exfoliated MMT [6] or silver (Ag) nanoparticles [7].

Polymer composites and nanocomposites, as well as additives used, are subjects of numerous books and reviews, for instance, References [1–3, 8–14]. This chapter is therefore focused on typical phenomena caused by the presence of solid additives dispersed in polymer matrices, rather than on a systematic description of known systems. The examples concern the influence of additives on the nucleation of crystallization, on the growth of crystals, and on the morphology of crystalized matrices. The modeling of crystallization in fiber-reinforced composites is also addressed.

13.2 MICROCOMPOSITES WITH PARTICULATE FILLERS

The most common mineral reinforcements that are used in polymers are chalk, talc, mica, silica, and wollastonite, typically in amounts ranging from 10% to 40% by weight. Among fillers for iPP, talc—natural hydrated magnesium silicate—has been used in largest quantities in various applications. It is also used for polyethylene (PE) and polyamides (PAs), but in much smaller quantities. Talc is a layered mineral; its elementary sheet is composed of a layer of magnesium–oxygen/hydroxyl octahedra, sandwiched between two layers of silicon–oxygen tetrahedra; the layers can be superposed indefinitely. Although talc particles can be fibrous, lamellar, needle-shaped, or granular, only the lamellar paticles are used as polymer fillers [13]. Talc is a cost-effective additive that decreases mold shrinkage and, depending on a polymer, can effectively provide antiblocking, reinforcement, and improved barrier properties of thermoplastics. Disadvantages include a decrease in tensile strength, elongation at break, and impact strength. Being a soft mineral, talc minimizes wear of processing equipment. Talc is known for its nucleating activity in many polymers including polyolefins [15–18], poly(oxymethylene) (POM) [19, 20], poly(vinylidene fluoride) (PVDF) [21], PA6 [17], poly(ethylene terephtalate) (PET) [22], poly(hydroxybutyrate) (PHB) [23], and PLA [24].

In iPP talc nucleates the α monoclinic crystallographic form. The content of talc in iPP-based composites reaches 40 wt% but nonisothermal crystallization temperature (T_c) increases by several degrees for the cooling rate of 10°C/min and saturates at the concentration about 2 wt% [25]. Nucleation on talc particles significantly shortens the isothermal crystallization time of the iPP matrix; the crystallization half-time in the composite with 2 wt% of talc is approximately four times shorter than that of neat iPP. Improved nucleation ability of silane-treated talc was also reported [25]. Fine talc particles, with average size of about 1 μm, were found to nucleate iPP crystallization most efficiently [15]. It was also shown in Reference [15] that the (010) crystallographic plane of the iPP α monoclinic lamella matches the talc basal planes, containing oxygen, at the surface of a tetrahedral sheet. The presence of talc was found to affect crystal orientation in injection-molded specimens [18, 26–28]. In both neat and talc-filled iPP the c-axes and a^*-axes of the α crystals were oriented in the flow direction. In addition, in talc-filled iPP the b-axes were oriented toward the thickness direction [18, 26, 27]. However, after melting and recrystallization of the injection-molded composite, the orientation of c- and a^*-axes in a plane parallel to the surface of sample was lost, whereas orientation of b-axis was retained [28]. The crystal orientation in talc-filled injection-molded specimens is then interpreted as a combined result of orientation of talc particles with the cleavage planes parallel to the flow direction in injection molding, on which nucleation is very frequent, and also anisotropy of crystal growth caused by the flow [27]. Moreover, the cleavage planes of talc particles orient parallel to the surface of the thermoformed parts and induce preferential growth of crystals with the b-axis of polymer chains normal to the particle surfaces [29].

Chalk–calcium carbonate ($CaCO_3$), another frequently applied filler, is used mainly in poly(vinyl chloride). However, it is also added to iPP and PE not only to reduce the cost but also to modify their mechanical properties, stability, and flame retardant characteristics. The advantages of chalk include high chemical purity, high degree of whiteness, low abrasiveness, good dispersibility, and approval for food use. Finely ground calcium carbonate particles can have the size of a few micrometers or even submicron size, the latter in the case of so-called ultrafine ground chalk. Precipitated calcium carbonate crystals can have various shapes and sizes ranging down to several tens of nanometers. Calcium carbonate has three polymorphic forms: aragonite, vaterite, and calcite, the first and the second being metastable forms, and the trigonal crystal structure of the calcite being the most common. Calcium carbonate is frequently modified with about 3 wt% of fatty acids, such as stearic acid, for use in nonaqueous systems. In Reference [30] the nucleating effect of unmodified chalk in iPP was examined and found to be very weak; studies of isothermal crystallization led to the conclusion that the addition of 40 wt% of precipitated chalk had similar effect to that of 0.25 wt% of sodium benzoate, a known nucleating agent for iPP. Although the number of nuclei per cube centimeter in the isothermally crystallized composite with 40 wt% of chalk increased by orders of magnitude as compared to neat iPP, it was still about two orders of magnitude lower than the number of chalk particles. The nucleating ability of calcite was, however, higher than that of aragonite. No effect of chalk on crystal growth rate was observed. T_c of nonisothermal crystallization during cooling of the composite with 40 wt% of chalk at 10°C/min increased by 12°C. Modification of chalk with oligomer of ethylene oxide reduced the ability of chalk to nucleate iPP crystallization. Other literature data indicate the importance of both particle size and aggregation; for the filler content of 20 vol%, an increase of specific surface area from 2.2 to 16.5 m^2/g increased the T_c of iPP by about 20°C [31].

Bartczak et al. [32] investigated the mechanical and thermal properties of high density PE (HDPE) filled with different grades of calcium stearate-treated chalk with particles having an average size (by weight) of 3.50, 0.70, and 0.44 μm in various contents ranging up to 30 vol%, that is, 55 wt%. The fillers used had a minor effect on nonisothermal T_c during cooling at the rate 10°C/min; the chalk with the largest particles increased the T_c only by about 2°C, whereas the two others had even less effect, below 0.5°C. The melting endotherms of composites shifted slightly toward lower temperature, demonstrating that the lamellae were thinner than those in neat HDPE while their number increased as the crystallinity degree of HDPE matrix enlarged by up to 8 wt%. Those effects intensified with an increase of the filler content in the composite, particularly with increasing specific surface area of the filler. Changes in the number density and size of lamellar crystallites were attributed to the influence of HDPE–filler interface. Studies of HDPE films with thickness ranging from 15 nm to 1.2 μm, crystallized nonisothermally adjacent to (104) crystallographic planes of calcite, utilizing atomic force microscopy (AFM) and X-ray techniques, demonstrated that lamellar HDPE crystallites preferentially grew "edge-on" on calcite [33] as shown in Figure 13.1. Therefore, it was assumed that in composites the chalk particles were enveloped by 0.3- to 0.4-μm-thick shells of specifically oriented HDPE crystallites and surrounded by crystallographically unoriented HDPE matrix. It was postulated that this morphology was responsible for the dramatic 12-fold increase of toughness of the composites when the mean interparticle ligament thickness of the matrix HDPE decreased to values below 0.6 μm. According to References [32, 33], the source of enhanced toughness and ductility was the anisotropic crystal plasticity in the transcrystalline layers percolating through the material. It has to be mentioned that the same mechanism was proposed to explain increased toughness of HDPE blends with rubber [34] and PA-based blends with rubber [35, 36]; in Reference [36], in thin PA6 films crystallized on thin films of ethylene-propylene-diene rubber, the hydrogen-bonded (002) planes of PA6 α crystals were parallel to the substrate. Prevailing edge-on lamellar–crystal orientation was attributed to crystal nucleation induced by the parallel alignment of coil segments of molten polymer in contact with foreign walls [37]. It has to be mentioned that the impact tests were carried out in

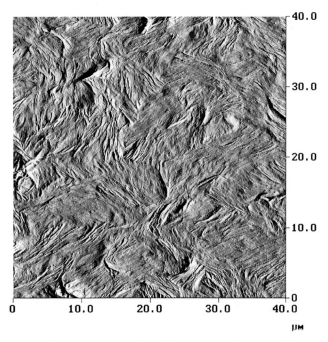

Figure 13.1 Contact mode AFM deflection image of 0.2-μm thin films of HDPE crystallized on calcite surface. Reprinted from Bartczak, Z., et al. The morphology and orientation of polyethylene in films of sub-micron thickness crystallized in contact with calcite and rubber substrates. *Polymer* **1999**, *40*, 2367–2380, with kind permission from Elsevier, Copyright 1999.

Reference [32] on injection molded samples, whereas toughness of compression-molded samples of similar material increased much less [38]. Moreover, flow-induced crystal orientation was proved by transmission electron microscopy (TEM) in injection-molded rubber toughened systems [39, 40] similar to those described in References [34, 35] instead of transcrystalline layers. In addition, the improved toughness was lost in injection-molded specimens after remelting followed by quiescent crystallization. Numerical simulations [41] demonstrated that the presence of rigid particles in sheared polymer melts produced highly oriented molecular stretch regions between two separating particles and near the top and the bottom of neighboring particles. However, the elongational stretch of molecules was nonhomogeneous. Also, regions with a molecular stretch lower than in the neat polymer melt for the same shear flow were found, caused by the "shielding" effect of particles. According to Reference [41], these effects can explain the existence of a critical interparticle ligament thickness for toughening of filled semicrystalline polymers and also semicrystalline polymer blends.

An interesting class of polymer-based materials are conductive polymer composites, which are manufactured by blending semicrystalline polymers with conductive fillers at a concentration above their percolation thresholds [42, 43]. Electrically conductive carbon blacks consist of very fine particles of sizes in the range of 10–50 nm fused to form aggregates. The tendency of carbon blacks to form chain-like aggregates allows the percolation threshold to be reached at a concentration of about 5 vol%, in comparison with the 25 vol% required for metal powders [44]. The percolation threshold is influenced by the type of carbon filler and its physical properties, and also by the polarity and viscosity of the polymer, the latter due to the degrading effect of shear on carbon black aggregates during processing. However, the crystallization of polymer matrix has also a significant effect on the percolation threshold. During crystallization of the polymer matrix, the filler remains in the amorphous phase; a major part of the carbon black aggregates is rejected into interspherulitic boundaries, whereas the rest is trapped in interlamellar amorphous regions within the spherulites. As a consequence, the threshold percolation concentration of carbon blacks in semicrystalline polymers is lower than that in amorphous matrices [42, 44].

13.3 FIBER-REINFORCED COMPOSITES

Reinforcing polymer matrices with fibers can lead to improved stiffness, tensile strength, and impact strength. Reinforcing fibers, in the form of short fibers, long fibers, or mats, include glass fibers, carbon fibers, fibers of other polymers, and natural fibers [1]. Orientation of long fibers in the polymer matrix is required to achieve good properties.

Many researchers reported the nucleation effect of fibers in various composites, which affects the crystallization kinetics and final morphology of fiber-reinforced materials. Figure 13.2 shows a polarized micrograph of iPP composite with 20 wt% of hemp fibers [45]. The micrograph illustrates the nucleation effect of fibers. The addition of fibers resulted in decreased half-time of isothermal crystallization and increased nonisothermal T_c of iPP. Biodegradable composites of PLA with various green fillers, including flax fibers, wood fibers, wood flour, cellulose fibers, cellulose nanowhiskers, and hemp fibers, have been studied recently [46–49]. Nucleation of PLA spherulites by wood flour and hemp [48, 49] was observed, as well as by fillers produced from agricultural by-products [50]. Figure 13.3 illustrates the nucleation effect of hemp fibers in PLA.

Intense nucleation of matrix crystallization on reinforcing fibers leads to transcystallinity. Recently, transcrystallinity in polymer composites has been reviewed by Quan et al. [51]. Transcrystallinity is known to occur in several semicrystalline polymers including iPP, PE, PA, poly (ether ether ketone) (PEEK), and poly(phenylene sulfide) (PPS) in contact with carbon

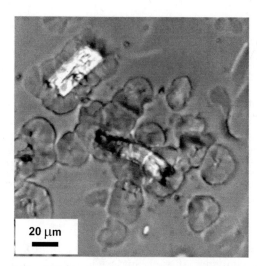

Figure 13.2 Polarized optical micrograph of iPP composite with 20 wt% of hemp fibers during isothermal crystallization at 132°C. Reprinted from Pracella, M., et al. Functionalization, compatibilization and properties of polypropylene composites with Hemp fibres. *Compos. Sci. Technol.* **2006**, *66*, 2218–2230, with permission from Elsevier, Copyright 2005.

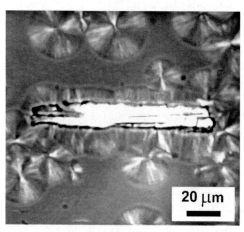

Figure 13.3 Polarized optical micrograph of PLA composite with 5 wt% of hemp fibers during isothermal crystallization at 116°C. Reprinted from Masirek, R., et al. Composites of poly(L-lactide) with hemp fibers: morphology and thermal and mechanical properties. *J. Appl. Polym. Sci.* **2007**, *105*, 255–268, with kind permission from Wiley, Copyright 2007.

fibers, glass fibers, aramid fibers, natural fibers, and so on. The transcrystallinity development is highly specific to the fiber–matrix combination. Different authors indicated the significance of many factors related to fibers, including their chemical composition, surface energy, and topography [51–57]. Owing to the importance of fiber surface properties, the treatment of fibers, including coating, can have a marked effect on their ability to nucleate crystallization of the polymer matrix. The role of epitaxy on fiber surfaces and crystallization behavior of the matrix polymer was also pointed out [51, 58].

Essentially, the development of transcrystallinity is associated with the high density of heterogeneously nucleating sites on the fiber surface, restricting crystal growth to the direction perpendicular to the fiber. However, it was also demonstrated [59, 60] that residual stresses resulting from a mismatch in the thermal expansion coefficients of fiber and matrix, which depend on cooling rate and temperature, play an important role. In Reference [59] crystallization in thin iPP films with various fibers was studied by polarized light microscopy. The ability to nucleate transcrystallization of iPP during isothermal crystallization in samples that were melt annealed at 200°C and cooled at 10°C/min to crystallization temperature depended on the fiber type. In particular, high modulus carbon fibers and aramid fibers induced transcrystallization whereas high-strength and intermediate modulus carbon fibers, glass fibers, and alumina fibers did not. Moreover, there was an upper temperature limit above which the transcrystallinity was not observed, even in the case of high modulus carbon fibers and aramid fibers; this limiting temperature increased with iPP molecular weight, being 138°C and 145°C for iPP with M_w of 270 kg/mol and M_w of 380 kg/mol, respectively. The growth rate of transcrystalline regions was the same as the radial growth rate of spherulites. During further experiments [60] the aramid fibers were pulled through polymer melts with a speed in the range of 5–500 μm/min at various temperatures, and crystallization of iPP at 140°C around the fibers was studied. Pulling at all speeds at 140°C induced transcrystalline morphology around the fibers, whereas only the fastest pre-crystallization pulling at 160°C and 180°C was effective. The studies of influence of cooling rate in the range of 0.2–280°C/min on quiescent crystallization of iPP with embedded glass, carbon, and aramid fibers demonstrated that sufficiently fast cooling induced development of transcrystallinity around the fibers in each case. The minimum cooling rate was 10°C/min in the case of aramid fibers, whereas in the case of high modulus carbon fibers and glass fibers the respective cooling rates were higher, 50°C/min and 100°C/min, respectively. The occurrence of trancrystallinity depended also on fiber length and the position along the fiber. Moreover, it was correlated with the magnitude and sign of the axial thermal expansion coefficient of fibers. These findings allowed the authors to conclude that the trancrystallization induced by the fibers studied was governed by the mismatch in thermal expansion coefficient. During cooling the mismatch caused strain at the fiber–polymer melt interface, which resulted in stresses in the melt at the interface leading to orientation of polymer macromolecules and to formation of row nuclei acting as nucleation sites for further chain-folded overgrowth. Such a scenario explains also the effect of temperature and interactions between a fiber and a matrix.

At high undercooling a small stress is sufficient to induce the orientation since the ability of molecules to relax decreases with decreasing temperature. A high level of interactions between a fiber and a matrix leads to greater adsorption of polymer chains onto the fiber surface, and these anchored molecules are more susceptible to orientation.

The effect of shear flow on development of transcrystallinity around the fibers was studied by a number of authors [54, 60–65]. Experiments with pulling glass fibers in iPP evidenced the formation of row nuclei along the fibers [65]. After pulling, the trigonal β phase transcrystalline zones crystallized around the fibers. The authors took advantage of the melting temperature of the β phase, lower than that of the α phase. Selective melting of the β phase evidenced the presence of α phase row nuclei along the fibers, which were visible in a polarized light microscope. It was also observed that flow-induced enhancement of primary nucleation in the polymer matrix, leading to an increased number of spherulites, could hinder the growth of transcrystalline regions [62].

The role of fiber thermal conductivity was also pointed out [54]; the temperature gradient developing during cooling at the interface between fiber and matrix caused by the mismatch of their thermal conductivity facilitated transcrystallization.

In addition to the heterogeneous nucleation and shear- or strain-induced nucleation on fiber surfaces, the third reason for the development of transcrystallinity was also indicated [51], related to impurities present in the matrix polymer; absorption of the impurities on fiber surfaces can also enhance nucleation and facilitate the transcrystallization.

iPP with poly(tetrafluoroethylene) (PTFE) fibers is an example of an all-polymer composite. PTFE fibers were found to nucleate crystallization of iPP [66, 67], which resulted in transcrystalline zones around the fibers. In Reference [67] a mechanism, based on thermal stress-induced orientation and relaxation of polymer chains, was proposed to account for the nucleation of transcrystallization on PTFE fibers. It was also suggested that small-scale grooves at the fiber surfaces caused the concentration of thermal stresses and enhanced the nucleation process. However, it was found later [68] that the α monoclinic phase of iPP crystallizes epitaxially on PTFE via a contact plane (110). It can be noticed that also PTFE films strongly nucleate iPP crystallization [69] as shown in Figure 7.8 in Chapter 7. Moreover, PTFE particles of submicron size nucleate iPP and also other polymers such as HDPE, PA6, PVDF, PET, and POM [70, 71]. It was also observed [72] that PTFE powders of high molecular weight ($M_n = 2 \times 10^7$ g/mol) underwent fibrillation during mixing with iPP that resulted in the PTFE scaffold of bundles of 20- to 30-nm-thick nanofibrils. Fibrillation of PTFE powders was reported also in Reference [73]. The PTFE nanofibers nucleated crystallization of iPP, POM, HDPE, PET, and polyamide 12 (PA12). The significant increase of nonisothermal T_c of iPP was observed already at low contents of PTFE, 0.001–0.005 wt% [70, 73]. Sufficient shearing of PTFE particles with chain extended crystals and low content of entanglements allows the particles during mixing with iPP to be fibrillated fully [74]. The composite with 5 wt% of nanofibrillated PTFE crystallized during cooling at 10°C/min at T_c by about 10°C higher than neat iPP.

In self-reinforced polymer composites the same polymer forms both the matrix and the reinforcement. The advantages of such materials include favorable performance–cost balance and density lower than that of traditional composites. In addition, self-reinforced polymer composites can be easily recycled. In Reference [75] self-reinforced HDPE was manufactured by enforcing molecular orientation during processing. The oriented molecules acted as row nuclei and promoted formation of cylindritic and shish–kebab-type morphology. The self-reinforced HDPE rod had high stiffness and strength. Moreover, the thermal shrinkage measured in the reinforcing direction was highly reduced. In most cases, self-reinforced polymer composites are obtained through the so-called hot compaction technique [76]. Other processing methods include film stacking, powder impregnation, and solution impregnation [77]. During the hot compaction process an array of oriented fibers and tapes are subjected to suitable temperature and pressure in order to melt selectively a thin skin of each individual fiber or tape [76–78]. This molten material recrystallizes on cooling and binds the entire composite together, ensuring an excellent adhesion between the fibers and matrix. The recrystallization of the molten polymer is facilitated by nucleation on nonmolten fiber cores.

Irrespective of the reasons, the strong nucleation on fibers results in structures consisting of columnar entities with transcrystalline morphology. The content of spherulites nucleated in polymer bulk depends on fiber content and nucleation density on fiber surfaces and also inside a polymer matrix.

It is obvious that the presence of fibers and nucleation on fibers affects the overall crystallization kinetics. The nucleation on fibers accelerates the crystallization. Moreover, the overall crystallization kinetics in fiber-reinforced polymers frequently deviates from predictions by the Avrami–Evans theory because the basic assumption of random positions of nuclei is not fulfilled. For instance, the Avrami exponent, calculated regardless of inapplicability of the theory, is lower (or decreases rapidly with progression of crystallization) than in corresponding unreinforced systems [79–81].

13.4 MODELING OF CRYSTALLIZATION IN FIBER-REINFORCED COMPOSITES

The description of overall kinetics of crystallization in fiber-reinforced systems requires taking into account that the volume inhabited by fibers is not accessible for crystallization. Moreover, spherulites are nucleated not only in polymer bulk but they can also be nucleated on fiber surfaces; the intense nucleation on fiber surfaces leads to development of transcrystallinity. Therefore, the description of overall kinetics in fiber-reinforced systems encounters the same difficulties as that of crystallization in a finite volume, described in Chapter 7. The main difference is that fibers are dispersed within a polymer matrix in a more or less random way.

Computer modeling of isothermal crystallization in fiber-reinforced composites concerned nonoverlapping long fibers aligned parallel in one direction and having equal diameters [82–85]. In References [82, 83, 85] the fibers were dispersed randomly within the polymer matrix, whereas in Reference [84] they were arranged in a hexagonal array. Spherulites were nucleated in the polymer bulk either instantaneously (that is, at the beginning of crystallization) or spontaneously during the entire crystallization process, whereas the nucleation on fiber surfaces was only instantaneous. Once nucleated each spherulite grew, at a constant rate, in all radial directions until impingement with another spherulite, a fiber or a boundary wall of a simulated sample. A more detailed description of computer models of spherulitic crystallization is given in Chapter 7. The two-dimensional case considered in Reference [82] was in fact an assembly of polymer strips with different finite width separated by fibers impenetrable for growing spherulites. However, in the three-dimensional case, impingement with fibers limited the growth of spherulites only in certain directions [83]. The basic conclusion was that the presence of fibers that do not nucleate crystallization slows down the overall crystallization rate in comparison to that of pure polymer, whereas the nucleation on fibers accelerates the crystallization. Moreover, the Avrami plots might have slopes different from those predicted by the Avrami–Evans theory for neat polymers, discussed in Chapter 7, or might even deviate from straight lines. The influence of fibers on overall crystallization rate increases with increasing fiber content and also with decreasing fiber diameter.

To predict the conversion of melt into spherulites during isothermal crystallization of fiber-reinforced composites, the concept of "extended volume" was used [86] in a similar way to what was done in References [87, 88] for crystallization in a finite volume. The probabilistic approach explained in Chapter 7 and References [85, 89, 90] was also applied to bulk crystallization in a composite reinforced with long fibers. As a first approximation fiber volume was neglected; therefore, each fiber was represented by a straight line. It was also assumed that the length of fibers exceeded significantly the spherulite size; therefore, the effect of fiber ends could be neglected.

The key problem in the probabilistic approach is to calculate the probability, $P_0(t)$, that an arbitrarily chosen point will remain in an uncrystallized fraction of material at a certain time t elapsed from the beginning of crystallization, that is, from the moment of nucleation of the first spherulite. In the case of instantaneous nucleation, the point A will remain at time t outside of growing spherulites, if none of them is nucleated within a sphere with the point A at the center and radius of $R(t)$ equal to a spherulite radius at time t:

$$R(t) = \int_0^t G(\tau) d\tau \tag{13.1}$$

where G denotes the time-dependent growth rate of spherulites. In general, G depends on temperature being constant during isothermal crystallization. During non-isothermal crystallization G changes with temperature, although for any cooling protocol the temperature dependence can be easily recalculated for the time dependence.

The probability, $P_0(t)$, that during instantaneous nucleation no spherulite is nucleated in a sphere of radius $R = R(t)$ is a product of two probabilities: the probability that no spherulite is nucleated in polymer bulk, denoted here as $P_B(t)$, and the probability that no spherulite is nucleated on fibers, denoted as $P_f(t)$. $P_B(t)$ is given by the simple expression:

$$P_B(t) = \exp(-4\pi D R^3 / 3) \tag{13.2}$$

where D is the density of instantaneous nucleation equal to a number of nuclei per a volume unit of a polymer. To calculate $P_f(t)$ it is necessary to sum the probability P_{f1} that no fiber crosses the sphere and the probability P_{f2} that no nucleation event occurs on fibers crossing the sphere that is on their fragments embedded in the sphere.

If all fibers are aligned in one direction the fibers crossing the considered sphere have to cross a circle around point A with radius R. The probability that no fiber crosses the circle reads:

$$P_{f1}(t) = \exp(-\pi D_f R^2) \tag{13.3}$$

where D_f is a number of fibers crossing an area unit of a surface normal to the fiber direction. D_f is equal to the total length of fibers in a volume unit of a composite. P_{f2} itself is the sum:

$$P_{f2}(t) = \sum_{n=1}^{\infty} P_{fn}(t) \qquad (13.4)$$

where each component P_{fn} denotes the probability that n fibers enter the sphere and no nucleation event occurs on their fragments included in the sphere.

The probability that a fiber crosses the considered circle in a distance s_i from A equals $\exp(-\pi D_f R^2)$ $(2\pi D_f s_i \, ds_i)$. The length of the fiber section embedded in the sphere equals $2(R^2 - s_i^2)^{1/2}$, whereas the probability that no nucleation event occurs on this section reads: $\exp[-2D_s(R^2 - s_i^2)^{1/2}]$, where D_s denotes nonzero nucleation density on fibers, equal to a number of nuclei per a fiber length unit. To calculate P_{fn} it is necessary to determine at first the probability that n fibers cross the circle at distances $s_i, i = 1\ldots\ldots n$, from the point A, and that no nucleation event occurs on their sections embedded in the sphere:

$$P_n(t) = \exp(-\pi D_f R^2)$$
$$\prod_{i=1}^{n}(2\pi D_f s_i ds_i)\exp[-2D_s(R^2-s_i^2)^{1/2}] \qquad (13.5)$$

Accounting for the possibility that each fiber can cross the sphere in any position requires integration over the ranges $0 < s_i < R$ followed by division by $n!$ to avoid multiple counting of the same events. Finally we have:

$$P_{fn}(t) = \exp(-\pi D_f R^2)\{0.5\pi D_f D_s^{-2} \\ [1-\exp(-2D_s R)(2D_s R+1)]\}^n (n!)^{-1} \qquad (13.6)$$

Equation (13.2), Equation (13.3), Equation (13.4), and Equation (13.6) yield:

$$P_0(t) = \exp\{-(4/3)\pi DR^3 - \pi D_f R^2 \\ - 0.5\pi D_f D_s^{-2}[(2RD_s+1)\exp(-2D_s R) - 1]\} \qquad (13.7)$$

The conversion degree of melt into spherulites, α, equals:

$$\alpha(t) = 1 - P_0(t). \qquad (13.8)$$

It follows from Equation (13.7) and Equation (13.8) that for D_s tending to infinity, α tends to $1-\exp[-(4/3)\pi DR^3 - \pi D_f R^2]$. Moreover, the straight line Avrami plot can be expected only if either D or D_f equals zero.

The above equations were derived assuming that all fibers were aligned in the same direction. Let us assume, however, that there are m populations of fibers differently oriented in a sample, characterized by $D_{fi}, i = 1, \ldots, m$, with $\Sigma D_{fi} = D_f$. The probability P_{f1} will be a product of all $P_{f1i} = \exp(-\pi D_{fi}R^2)$, therefore it will be again expressed by Equation (13.3). The same reasoning applies to P_{f2}. It follows that Equation (13.7) is valid independently of the orientation distribution of fibers.

Moreover, Equation (13.8) with $P_0(t)$ given by Equation (13.7) can be derived based on the concept of "extended volume"; in this case all spherulites nucleated on a fiber have to be treated as a single domain with volume determined by an external envelope; calculations require accounting for randomness of positions of nuclei along a fiber.

Validity of Equation (13.8) was verified by computer simulation of spherulitic crystallization [85]. Figure 13.4a shows plots of conversion degree versus time for the case of isothermal crystallization (G = const) whereas Figure 13.4b illustrates the exemplary computer simulated spherulite pattern. It has to be mentioned that the above described model can be also useful to some extent in the case of flow-induced crystallization with row nuclei.

In order to account for a fiber volume, a different approach has to be used [85]. A portion of a composite is considered that consists of a fiber of radius r_f, surrounded by a polymer cylindrical layer (Fig. 13.5). The layer thickness, $r_g - r_f$, is governed by the total fiber content, $C_f = (r_f/r_g)^2$. The instantaneous nucleation density on fiber surface, equal to a number of nuclei per unit area, is denoted as D_s. Again, the probability has to be calculated that no nucleation event will occur in the sphere around the point A, with the radius R given by Equation (13.1) and volume $V = (4/3)\pi R^3$. This probability, p_0, is a product of two probabilities: (1) that no spherulite will be nucleated in polymer bulk, equal to $\exp[-D(V-V_f)]$, and (2) that no spherulite will be nucleated on a fiber surface, equal to $\exp(-D_s S_f)$, where V_f is a volume of that part of the considered sphere that is embodied by the fiber and S_f is the area of the fiber surface enclosed within the sphere. p_0, depending on s, equals:

$$p_0(s,t) = \exp[-D(V-V_f) - D_s S_f]. \qquad (13.9)$$

It can be noticed that for $s > R$, both V_f and S_f are equal to zero.

For $R > r_g - r_f - s$, when only a part of the sphere V, of volume V_c, is included in the considered portion of the composite, p_0 is approximated by the following formula:

$$p_0(s,t) = \exp\{[-D(V_c - V_f) - D_s S_f]V/V_c\}. \qquad (13.10)$$

The detailed expressions for V_c, V_f, and S_f are given in the Appendix.

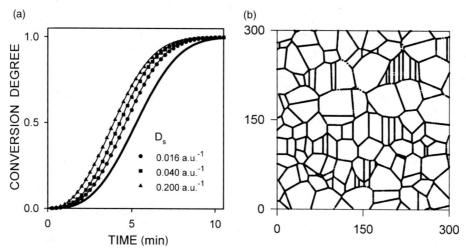

Figure 13.4 (a) Conversion degree dependence on time in neat polymer (thick solid line) and fiber-reinforced composites as obtained from computer simulation (symbols) and predicted by Equation (13.7) and Equation (13.8) (lines): $D = 9 \times 10^{-6}$ a.u.$^{-3}$, $D_f = 3.5 \times 10^{-4}$/a.u.$^{-2}$, $G = 5$ a.u./min, D_s as indicated in the figure. Data from Reference [85]. (b) Cross-section of computer-simulated fiber-reinforced composite. Fibers aligned horizontally. $D_s = 0.04$ a.u.$^{-1}$ D and D_f as in part (a). Reprinted from Piorkowska, E. Modeling of crystallization kinetics in fiber reinforced composites. *Macromol. Symp.* **2001**, *169*, 143–148, with kind permission from Wiley, Copyright 2001.

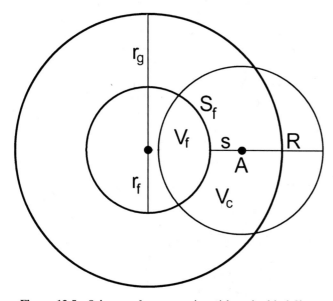

Figure 13.5 Scheme of a composite with embedded fiber.

The conversion degree in distance s from the fiber surface equals $1 - p_0(s, t)$. The average conversion degree in the entire portion of a composite is calculated by integration:

$$\alpha_{av}(t) = 1 - 2\left(r_g^2 - r_f^2\right)^{-1} \int_0^{r_g - r_f} (s + r_f) p_0(s, t) ds. \quad (13.11)$$

Figure 13.6a compares the conversion degree calculated based on Equation (13.11) and obtained via computer simulation, whereas Figure 13.6b shows the computer-simulated structure of fiber-reinforced composite. It follows that Equation (13.11) describes correctly the conversion of melt into spherulites in fiber-reinforced composites, although with some limitations. The used approximation resulted in deviation of the predicted conversion degree from that obtained from the computer simulation after the crystallization half-time in the case of very intense nucleation on fibers.

Both the probabilistic approach and the computer simulation predict that in composites with non-nucleating fibers the conversion of melt into spherulites is slower than that in neat polymer, whereas the nucleation on fibers accelerates the conversion. The overall crystallization kinetics and spherulitic morphology are controlled by a number of factors: bulk nucleation density, nucleation density on the fiber surface, spherulitic growth rate, fiber volume fraction, and fiber diameter. For the same volume content of fibers, stronger effect is observed for thinner fibers, as illustrated in Figure 13.6a.

It is rather clear that the classic Avrami–Evans theory, outlined in Chapter 7, does not permit description of the conversion of polymer melt into spherulites in polymer composites with fibers, even in the simplest case of isothermal crystallization. Therefore, the coefficients calculated based on the Avrami plots are only adjustable parameters and do not have clear meanings in such cases.

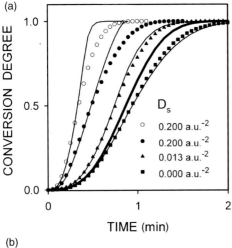

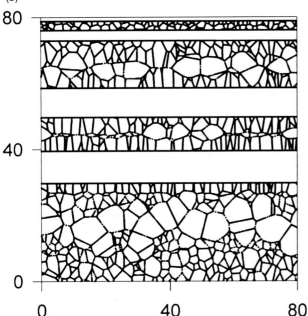

Figure 13.6 (a) Conversion degree dependence on time in neat polymer (thick solid line) and in fiber-reinforced composites with fiber content of 50 vol% as obtained from computer simulation (symbols) and predicted by Equation (13.11) (lines) for $G = 5$ a.u./min and $D = 0.002$ a.u.$^{-3}$. D_s as indicated in the figure. $r_f = 10$ a.u. (full symbols) and $r_f = 5$ a.u. (open symbols). Data from Reference [85]. (b) Cross-section of computer-simulated fiber-reinforced composite with fiber content of 25 vol% for $G = 5$ a.u./min, $D = 0.002$ a.u.$^{-3}$, and $D_s = 0.2$ a.u.$^{-2}$, $r_f = 5$ a.u. Reprinted from Piorkowska, E. Modeling of crystallization kinetics in fiber reinforced composites. *Macromol. Symp.* **2001**, *169*, 143–148, with kind permission from Wiley, Copyright 2001.

13.5 NANOCOMPOSITES

The major advantage of using nanosized fillers is the large surface area of interactions between the filler and the matrix, which allows filler content to decrease to 3–5%. Depending on nanoparticle shape, the nanoplatelets, nanofibers, and nanopowders are classified as one-, two-, or three-dimensional nanofillers, respectively.

A frequently used one-dimensional nanofiller is MMT, which belongs to the smectite family of 2:1 phyllosilicates. The MMT crystal lattice consists of 1-nm-thin layers—platelets, with central octahedral sheet of alumina fused between two external silica tetrahedral sheets. The other two dimensions of MMT platelets are usually larger than 200 nm. The platelets form stacks with van der Waals gaps or galleries between them, about 0.3 nm thin. In the pristine state MMT is only compatible with hydrophilic polymers, such as poly(ethylene oxide) (PEO) and poly(vinyl alcohol) [91]. In order to improve compatibility with other polymers, MMT is organomodified (o-MMT); that is, the alkali cations present in galleries are ion exchanged with organic cations such as alkyl ammonium, which leads to an increase in interlayer spacing. In general, polymer nanocomposites with clay can be prepared via *in situ* intercalative polymerization of monomers inserted into the clay galleries, by polymer intercalation by the solution method or melt intercalation, the latter method being widely used. In the case of nonpolar polymers like polyolefins polymer functionalization by introducing polar or polarizable groups is additionally required. For instance, maleated polyolefins, maleated polyethylene (PE-g-MA) or isotactic polypropylene (PP-g-MA), are used as matrix polymers for nanocomposites with o-MMT but also as compatibilizers for polyolefin-based nanocomposites with o-MMT. Methods of preparation of polymer-clay nanocomposites are widely reviewed in References [8–11, 91].

Polymer nanocomposites with o-MMT are classified as intercalated or exfoliated. In the first type of nanocomposites, polymer chains insert into galleries of o-MMT particles, increasing interlayer spacing, whereas in the second, the clay platelets are separated and dispersed within a polymer matrix. o-MMT dispersed in polymer matrix has a large specific surface area, 750–800 m^2/g, and a high elastic modulus of 170 GPa [92, 93]. Efficient modification of properties requires the clay exfoliation. In practice, especially in polyolefins, full exfoliation is difficult to achieve, and nanocomposites with clay frequently have complex and hierarchical structure, including larger particles in addition to individual silicate platelets [94]. The polymer nanocomposites with exfoliated clay exhibit modified mechanical properties, reduced flammability, improved barrier properties, and so on. Exemplary transmission electron micrograph of iPP nanocomposite with o-MMT is shown in Figure 13.7. It has to be mentioned that the orientation of exfoliated MMT platelets is beneficial for the properties of nanocomposites [95].

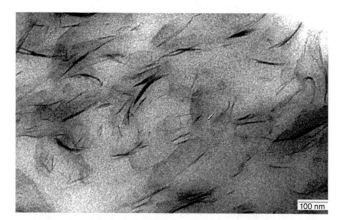

Figure 13.7 Transmission electron micrograph of ultrathin section of iPP based nanocomposite with 5 wt% of exfoliated o-MMT (Cloisite 15A, Southern Clay Products Gonzales, TX, USA) compatibilized with 10 wt% of PP-g-MA.

The dispersed clay particles can nucleate crystallization in a polymer matrix, decreasing considerably spherulite size. However, enhancement of crystallization due to the nucleating effect of nanoclays, if observed, is more pronounced at low contents, in the range of 1–5 wt%, whereas high loading may result in retardation of crystallization. Enhanced crystallization of a polymer matrix in the presence of clay was reported for different polymers including PA [96, 97], iPP [98, 99], PE [100], PET [101], and PVDF [102–104]. In Reference [96] isothermal crystallization of PA6 nanocomposites, prepared by melt blending, with small contents of clay was faster, whereas that of nanocomposites with relatively large filler contents was slower than in neat PA6; the borderline clay content, near 3–4 wt%, depended on PA6 molecular weight. The materials with relatively large clay loading exhibited also lower T_c during cooling from the molten state. Acceleration of isothermal crystallization in PA6 nanocomposites with clay, prepared by both *in situ* polymerization and melt processing, was reported in Reference [97]. Moreover, transcrystalline zones around clay platelets in PA6/o-MMT nanocomposites were also observed [105].

Light microscopy studies of crystallization in intercalated nanocomposites of PEO with Na$^+$ MMT content up to 10 wt% [106] revealed that MMT tactoids or agglomerates delayed the spherulite growth as the lamellae were forced to grow with tortuous paths around these particles. Spherulite size in the nanocomposites decreased if compared with neat PEO because of an increase in the primary nucleation density. At 45°C and 50°C, primary nucleation density increased with increasing clay content; in the nanocomposite with 10 wt% of the clay, nucleation density was an order of magnitude larger than in neat PEO. Isothermal crystallization was faster in the nanocomposites, especially in those with small content of clay, but the nonisothermal T_c decreased with the increasing clay loading, although the overall crystallinity of PEO was not affected.

An increase of nonisothermal T_c was observed for PE-g-MA composites with o-MMT and laponite prepared by melt mixing [100, 107] in which exfoliation of clay was reported. Practically no difference in nonisothermal crystallization of LDPE, LDPE/o-MMT, and LDPE/PE-g-MA/o-MMT nanocomposites was observed [108]. It has to be noted that the exfoliation of clay was achieved only in the nanocomposites compatibilized with PE-g-MA.

The acceleration of crystallization in iPP nanocomposites with clay was reported in many papers. The elevation of the nonisothermal crystallization peak temperature due to the presence of o-MMT was found in composites prepared by melt blending of o-MMT with iPP [109, 110]. The nucleation effect of o-MMT during isothermal crystallization was observed in both PP-g-MA/o-MMT [99, 111] and iPP/PP-g-MA/o-MMT [98] systems and also in iPP/o-MMT nanocomposites synthesized by intercalation polymerization. In Reference [112], an increase of nonisothermal T_c and a decrease of spherulite size in iPP/o-MMT and iPP/PA-g-MA/o-MMT were reported. It has to be noted that X-ray studies [98, 111, 112] indicated the presence of a significant amount of intercalated clay tactoids in the investigated systems. When fine clay dispersion was achieved the nucleating effect of clay was limited, and lower T_c and crystallization rates were observed [112]. In Reference [111], in the nanocomposites crystallized at high temperatures, a higher density of dispersed particles was found around the interspherulitic boundaries and interpreted as a result of the segregation of the clay particles during crystallization. Moreover, extensive intercalation occurred during crystallization, especially at high temperatures, due to the long time required for solidification; the degree of intercalation of PP-g-MA chains in the silicate galleries strongly depended on the elapsed time in the molten state. It was also observed [99] that the d-spacing of (110) and (040) crystallographic planes of the α phase of iPP slightly increased with clay loading. Moreover, the γ orthorhombic phase was detected, and its content increased with the clay content. In Reference [113], the acceleration of isothermal crystallization in iPP/PP-g-MA/o-MMT was reported but only in systems containing the clay tactoids, while no o-MMT nucleation ability was observed in nanocomposites with well-dispersed clay. In addition, a decrease in spherulite growth rate with increasing clay content was also found. In Reference [110] nonisothermal crystallization of iPP composites with two different MMT fillers was studied. It was demonstrated that the ability of MMT to nucleate iPP crystallization depended on clay deposit and the organo-treatment of clay, the latter acting not by the modification of the clay surface tension but by the alteration of interlayer distance. The strongest nucleation effect was shown by the neat, untreated filler. It was concluded then that the nucleation occurred not on the flat surfaces but rather between the galleries of clay particles. The authors attributed the nucleation to the MMT particles with collapsed galleries with periodicity about 1 nm (wide-angle X-ray scattering [WAXS] reflection at $2\theta = 8.8°$).

In References [6, 114, 115] shear-induced crystallization of iPP-based nanocomposites with o-MMT was examined. In Reference [114] early stages of flow-induced isothermal spherulitic crystallization of intercalated iPP/PP-g-MA/o-MMT nanocomposites with 2 wt% of the clay were studied after application of shear flow for a short time of up to 30 seconds. The flow induced enhancement of crystallization was stronger in the nanocomposite than in neat iPP. However, acceleration of crystallization in iPP/PP-g-MA blend was also observed.

In Reference [6] crystallization of iPP/PP-g-MA/o-MMT nanocomposites with the clay content ranging from 3 wt% to 10 wt% was studied in the quiescent state and during shearing. o-MMT exhibited only weak nucleation activity during quiescent crystallization, which was reflected in the shortening of the isothermal crystallization half-time, although less than two times, and a decrease in spherulite size in compatibilized nanocomposites with 6 wt% and 10 wt% of clay as compared to neat iPP and iPP/PP-g-MA blends with corresponding amounts of the compatibilizer. During quiescent isothermal crystallization in nanocomposite films, intense nucleation of iPP spherulites was observed when the polymer was forced to flow to compensate the volume shrinkage due to crystallization, as illustrated in Figure 13.8. Studies of crystallization during shearing demonstrated that slow shearing, at rates less than 1 s^{-1}, tremendously enhanced the nucleation and overall crystallization rate at 135°C and 132°C in all nanocomposites, although it had no marked influence on crystallization of neat iPP and the blends with compatibilizers. For instance, it was estimated that shearing of iPP/PP-g-MA/o-MMT with 3 wt% of clay at the slowest rate of 0.15 s^{-1} caused an increase in nucleation density by two orders of magnitude. In Reference [115] shear-induced isothermal crystallization in iPP/PP-g-MA/o-MMT nanocomposites with 3 wt% of clay was followed by a light depolarization technique. Prior to the crystallization, samples were sheared at 1 or 2 s^{-1} for 10 seconds at a crystallization temperature of 136°C. Enhancement of the nucleation

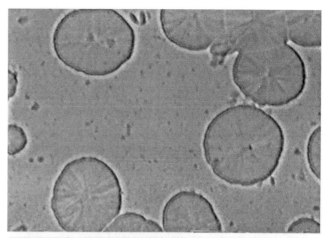

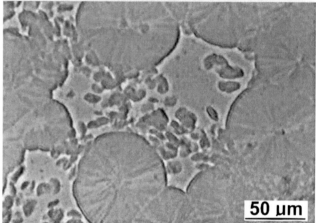

Figure 13.8 Consecutive stages of isothermal crystallization in thin film of nanocomposite iPP/PP-g-MA/o-MMT (87:10:3 by weight), between glass slides, at 128°C. Reprinted from Nowacki, R., et al. Spherulite nucleation in isotactic polypropylene based nanocomposites with montmorillonite under shear. *Polymer* **2004**, *45*, 4877–4892, with kind permission from Elsevier, Copyright 2004.

and acceleration of the crystallization after shearing, observed in the compatibilized nanocomposites, intensified with improvement of clay exfoliation. Figure 13.9 shows the effects of shear on the microstructure of the nanocomposite. The shearing decreased the crystallization half time from 15 minutes at quiescent conditions to approximately 2 minutes. The sheared samples of compatibilized nanocomposites with exfoliated clay exhibited weak orientation of crystals with (040) crystallographic planes parallel to the shearing direction. Most probably, a small population of oriented crystals formed, owing to the shear-induced orientation of iPP chains, and served as nuclei for further, nearly isotropic, growth. The results indicate that the effect of shear is augmented in iPP nanocomposites with exfoliated clay; therefore, even small shear rates can effectively enhance nucleation and accelerate crystallization.

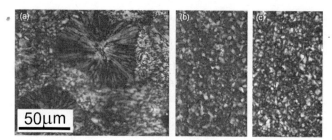

Figure 13.9 Polarized light micrographs of thin sections of films iPP/PP-*g*-MA/o-MMT nanocomposite (87:10:3 by weight) crystallized at 136°C: without shearing (a), after shearing at 1 s^{-1} (b), and at 2 s^{-1} (c) for 10 seconds. Reprinted from Rozanski, A., et al. Shear-induced crystallization of isotactic polypropylene based nanocomposites with montmorillonite. *Eur. Polym. J.* **2009**, *45*, 88–101, with kind permission from Elsevier, Copyright 2008.

The enhancement of polymer orientation in nanocomposites with the clay was also reported by other authors. A high level of orientation of PA6 matrix in injection-molded nanocomposite parts was found [116]. Orientation of iPP crystals was also augmented in iPP/PP-*g*-MA/o-MMT extrudates [117] and injection-molded parts [118], especially those manufactured by dynamic packing injection molding. The reasons pointed out by the authors include shear amplification occurring in spaces between adjacent nanoparticles moving with different velocity during filling of a mold, alignment of clay platelets along the flow direction constraining the growth of iPP crystals and hindered relaxation of macromolecules caused by constraints and interactions with clay particles.

Polymer–silicate interactions can stabilize a polymer metastable phase and induce polymorphism. The examples include PAs and PVDF. The PA6 monoclinic α phase, with shorter hydrogen bonds, is thermodynamically most stable and crystallizes during slow cooling from the melt. The γ crystals can be obtained by high-speed melt spinning or iodine treatment of the α phase [119]. Enhanced crystallization of PA6 in the form of γ phase (indexed as monoclinic or pseudohexagonal) in the presence of the clay platelets was attributed to conformational changes of the chains induced by the proximity of the surface limiting the formation of hydrogen-bonded sheets [9, 97]. The stabilization of the γ phase by silicate platelets and promotion of the molecular orientation due to polymer–silicate interaction in a commercial PA6-based copolymer was also reported [120]. Another example of stabilization of metastable crystallographic form by nanofiller platelets is formation of the orthorhombic β-form crystals in PVDF nanocomposites [102, 103], whereas in the melt-crystallized neat PVDF the monoclinic α polymorph was dominant.

A typical example of two-dimensional nanofillers are CNTs, cylinders built of graphene layers that can be synthesized in arc discharge, by means of laser ablation or by chemical vapor deposition from hydrocarbons. They are either in the form of concentric tubes (multi-wall nanotubes, MWNTs) or individual cylinders (single-wall nanotubes, SWNTs). Their diameters range from about 1 to 100 nm, whereas lengths range from several micrometers to millimeters or even centimeters. Since their discovery, CNTs have attracted worldwide attention because of outstanding properties, both mechanical and electrical. Their elastic moduli exceed 1 TPa, whereas tensile strength reaches tens of GPa [121]. Because of the small diameter and hydrophobicity of the CNT surface, the homogeneous dispersion of CNTs in polymer matrix is difficult. Techniques to improve the CNT dispersion within the polymers are reviewed in References [9, 12, 121, 122] and include solution mixing, sonication, coagulation, melt compounding, *in situ* miniemulsion polymerization, oxidation, or chemical functionalization of the tube surface and use of surfactants. Low CNT content improves the elastic modulus and increases tensile stresses of the polymeric material, whereas ductility is decreased moderately. Orientation of CNTs is beneficial for stiffness and tensile toughness [9]. Addition of CNTs to polymer increases also electrical conductivity and reduces flammability [12, 122]. Similar to the case of polymer nanocomposites with MMT, the influence of CNTs on the overall crystallization kinetics of the polymer matrix depends on their content.

It was found that the crystallization behavior of PA 66 nanocomposites with 0.1–2 wt% of MWNTs depended on filler content [123]. A small loading of MWNTs, 0.1 wt%, accelerated isothermal crystallization, whereas larger contents had an opposite effect. Nonisothermal DSC crystallization peaks of the nanocomposites were shifted toward lower temperatures, while crystallization onset temperature remained similar to that of the neat polymer. Moreover, DSC thermograms recorded during heating of nonisothermaly crystallized specimens showed multiple melting peaks, which were attributed to changes in lamellar thickness upon heating. The crystallite sizes of the triclinic α form also decreased with the increasing content of MWNTs. It was also concluded that MWNTs nucleated the crystallization of PA66 but the tube network hindered the growth of large crystals.

The increase of nonisothermal T_c and shortening of isothermal crystallization by a factor of 6 was reported for HDPE/SWNT nanocomposites with nanofiller content ranging from 0.02 to 8 wt% [124]. Moreover, the enhanced nucleation in nanocomposites changed the spherulitic morphology of HDPE to axialitic-like aggregates of significantly reduced size, while the lamellar characteristics remained unaffected. The increase of T_c during cooling was reported also in References 125 and 126 for HDPE/SWNT nanocomposites. In Reference [126] SWNT bundles templated PE crystallization; lamellae grew perpendicular to the SWNT surface with the PE chains parallel to the SWNT axis.

CNTs were found to nucleate also crystallization of iPP [127]. The increase of T_c and crystallization onset temperature due to strong heterogeneous nucleation was reported for highly dispersed PP-g-MA/CNT composites [128]; the effect of SWNTs was more pronounced than that of MWNTs. Saturation of crystallization onset at temperature by about 15°C higher than that of neat polymer occurred for CNT content above 0.5 wt%. TEM studies confirmed the presence of transcrystalline phase around the CNTs due to their strong nucleating activity. The nanocomposites exhibited also higher melting temperatures, which were attributed to the higher perfection of the transcrystalline phase and related to the temperature at which it was formed during nonisothermal crystallization. The transcrystallinity induced in iPP by nucleation on CNTs was also reported in Reference [129].

Recent progress in nanotechnology resulted in the development of various routes for preparing three-dimensional nanoparticles, including sol–gel, flame spraying, inert gas condensation, chemical vapor deposition, and ball milling [9]. The inorganic particles are added to polymers to modify their, mechanical, electrical, optical, and bacteriostatic properties, and flammability. Filling thermoplastics and elastomers with nanosized silica or calcium carbonate results in improved stiffness and toughness. Inorganic nanoparticles can provide heterogeneous nucleation sites for the polymer crystallization as evidenced by higher nonisothermal T_c and shorter isothermal crystallization [130, 131].

Calcium carbonate is the most frequently used nanoparticulate filler for iPP. It was found that about 5 vol% of chalk particles with sizes ranging from 30 to 90 nm increased nonisothermal T_c by approximately 10°C [132]; however, the increase in the chalk content did not result in further significant changes in T_c. In Reference [133] the authors observed that the addition of $CaCO_3$ particles resulted in small and imperfect iPP spherulites, decreased spherulite growth rate, and induced formation of the β-form iPP.

Surface treatment of $CaCO_3$ can change its nucleating activity in iPP. In Reference [134] iPP composites with nano-$CaCO_3$ were modified with iPP grafted with acrylic acid (PP-g-AA). T_c of iPP in the composites increased with increasing nano-$CaCO_3$ content, and it was further increased by the addition of PP-g-AA. Recently, composites of iPP with 1 wt% and 3 wt% of nanosized calcium carbonate, both calcite and aragonite, coated either with PP-g-MA or fatty acids were studied [135]. All the types of nanosized chalk particles produced only a very minor effect on the growth rate of iPP spherulites. The effect of nanopowders on nucleation depended on coating; only particles coated with PP-g-MA nucleated iPP crystallization, which caused shortening the isothermal crystallization and increasing the onset temperature of nonisothermal crystallization. Fatty acid coating resulted in decreased nucleation density, which was attributed to inefficiency of the particles to nucleate crystallization and possible dissolution of nucleating heterogeneities present in iPP by the fatty acids. Moreover, PP-g-MA-coated particles were better dispersed in the iPP matrix than particles coated with fatty acids.

In iPP with 0.5–1 wt% of SiO_2 particles ranging from 30 to 80 nm in size, T_c increased by 7°C [131]. SiO_2 particles that are 16 nm in size [136] exhibited only weak nucleating activity in iPP. Nanoparticles of ZnO and Al_2O_3 having sizes of several tens of nanometers had only a weak influence on crystallization of iPP matrix [137]. From 0.1 to 1 wt% of Ag nanoparticles dispersed in iPP caused its T_c to increase by 5°C [138]. In Reference [7] a similar effect was observed; 0.1–5 wt% of Ag nanoparicles resulted in an increase of T_c by 7°C. Moreover, the oscillatory shear-induced crystallization of iPP was accelerated with increasing Ag content and imposed frequency of oscillations. In both References [7, 138] an increased content of the β phase was reported.

A new class of polymer nanocomposites comprises those with cage-shaped polyhedral oligomeric silsesquioxanes (POSS), having the general formula $(RSiO_{1.5})_n$, where R is hydrogen or an organic group, such as alkyl, aryl, or any of their derivatives. POSS molecules contain a polyhedral silicon–oxygen nanostructured skeleton. They can be functionalized by attaching organic substituents to corner silicon atoms. Functionalization of the POSS cage through copolymerization or chemical grafting as well as physical mixing allows dispersion of POSS particles in many polymers. The incorporation of POSS particles in polymer matrices results in enhanced mechanical performance, increase of glass transition temperature (T_g), and thermal decomposition temperature [139, 140]. POSS particles forming crystal aggregates in polymer matrices can serve as nucleating agents, whereas molecularly dispersed POSS can retard the crystal growth rate. However, these effects depend on interactions of POSS with polymer chains. It was found that both the glass transition temperature T_g and the crystallization process in mixtures of PEO with octakis-functionalized POSSs depended on their functional groups [141]. The PEO/POSS homogeneous systems exhibited higher T_g and lower melting temperatures than the neat PEO. Moreover, the isothermal crystallization half-time increased, whereas the spherulite growth rate decreased with increasing POSS content.

The effect was more pronounced in the case of stronger hydrogen bonding between the POSS and PEO matrices.

In Reference [142] nanocomposites of iPP with 10–30 wt% of octamethyl POSS ($(RSiO_{1.5})_8$ with R being methyl) were studied. POSS particles nucleated iPP crystallization, which was reflected in an increase of T_c; for example, T_c of the sample with 10 wt% of POSS was higher by 3°C than that of neat iPP. Isothermal crystallization of nanocomposites with 10 wt% of POSS was faster than that of neat iPP, but it slowed down at 130°C and 135°C with increasing POSS content. While crystal aggregates of POSS nucleated the crystallization, the molecularly dispersed POSS hindered the crystal growth, inhibiting the diffusion of iPP chains. In contrast, the molecularly dispersed POSS facilitated crystallization during shear flow. Moreover, higher POSS concentrations resulted in faster crystallization rates during shear. It was inferred that well-dispersed POSS molecules can act as physical crosslinkers and thus hinder the motion and relaxation of polymer molecules after cessation of flow. iPP with 2 wt% and 3 wt% of octamethyl POSS [143] exhibited the multiexotherm isothermal crystallization, which was explained as a combined effect of nucleation of iPP crystals on POSS threads, formed due to POSS crystallization and aggregation, and retardation of nucleation and growth of iPP crystals in the remaining bulk molten iPP regions. In Reference [144] nanocomposites of iPP with 3–10 wt% of POSS having different alkyl substituents (methyl, isobutyl, or isooctyl) were examined. The dispersion of POSS improved with increasing length of substituent chains. In the nanocomposites with more than 3 wt% of octamethyl POSS the iPP crystal growth rate increased, whereas in the other materials it was unaffected by fillers. Octamethyl POSS particles acted as nucleation sites for iPP spherulites, which was mirrored in elevation of nonisothermal T_c of the nanocomposites. The addition of other types of POSS resulted in a decrease of T_c as compared with neat iPP. Isobutyl POSS was found to induce the presence of the trigonal β and orthorhombic γ forms in iPP [139]. In Reference [145] nonisothermal crystallization of HDPE remained unaffected by the presence of up to 5 wt% octamethyl POSS, but at 10 wt% of POSS, the crystallization onset temperature increased by about 3–4°C.

13.6 CONCLUSIONS

The influence of fillers on crystallization behavior of polymer matrix depends on the interaction between filler surface and polymer chains. In numerous cases, fillers act as nucleation sites for polymer crystallization. Intense nucleation on the surfaces of reinforcing fibers leads to the development of transcrystallinity. However, phenomena affecting nucleation of fibers can be more complex than heterogeneous nucleation and include orientation of polymer chains during cooling due to the mismatch in thermal expansion coefficients of fibers and matrix. Nanosized fillers exhibit also nucleating activity in polymer matrices, although again it depends on polymer–filler interactions. Nucleation ability of CNT and o-MMT in different polymers was reported, although many authors observed that o-MMT tactoids nucleated crystallization rather than exfoliated and well-dispersed platelets. Certain nanopowders, including nanochalk and Ag nanoparticles, can also serve as nucleation sites. It has to be pointed out that frequently the surfaces of fillers particles are modified, for instance, coated or grafted with polymer chains to improve dispersion. Compatibilizers are also used for the same purpose. The modification of filler surface and presence of additional components in composites affects polymer–filler interactions, which influence polymer crystallization.

Microfillers and fibers essentially do not affect the spherulite growth rate. However, finely dispersed nanofillers can retard the spherulite growth. POSS crystal aggregates can serve as nucleating sites for polymer crystallization, whereas molecularly dispersed POSS can decrease the crystal growth rate. It has to be noted also that the presence of fillers in polymers, especially of nanofillers, can stabilize metastable crystallographic forms. Moreover, fillers can enhance the effects of flow during processing, leading to stronger crystal orientation. Thus, the final influence of fillers on crystallization and structure of a polymer depends also on the thermomechanical history of a composite.

APPENDIX

Both V_f and S_f in Equation (13.9) and Equation (13.10) are equal to zero for $R \leq s$. V_f and S_f for $R > s$ are expressed by the following formulae [85]:

For $s + 2r_f \geq R > s$:

$$V_f = 2\int_0^g [\beta r_f^2 + \alpha(R^2 - z^2) - W]dz \quad (13.A1)$$

$$S_f = 4\int_0^g r_f \beta dz \quad (13.A2)$$

For $R > s + 2r_f$:

$$V_f = 2\left\{\pi r_f^2 h + \int_h^g [\beta r_f^2 + \alpha(R^2 - z^2) - W]dz\right\} \quad (13.A3)$$

$$S_f = 4r_f\left(\pi h + \int_h^g \beta dz\right) \quad (13.A4)$$

where
$$g = [R^2 - s^2]^{0.5} \quad (13.A5)$$
$$h = [R^2 - (2r_f + s)^2]^{0.5} \quad (13.A6)$$
$$\alpha = \arcsin[W(r_f + s)^{-1}(R^2 - z^2)^{-0.5}] \quad (13.A7)$$
$$\beta = \pi - \arcsin[W(r_f + s)^{-1}r_f^{-1}] \text{ for } z^2 < R^2 - (r_f + s)^2 - r_f^2 \quad (13.A8a)$$
$$\beta = \arcsin[W(r_f + s)^{-1}r_f^{-1}] \text{ for } z^2 \geq R^2 - (r_f + s)^2 - r_f^2 \quad (13.A8b)$$
$$W = 0.5\{(R^2 - z^2 - s^2)[(2r_f + s)^2 - R^2 + z^2]\}^{0.5} \quad (13.A9)$$

V_c in Equation (13.10) is expressed in the following way [85]:

For $r_g + r_f + s \geq R > r_g - r_f - s$:

$$V_c = 2\left\{\int_0^u [\beta_1 r_g^2 + \alpha_1(R^2 - z^2) - W_1]dz + \pi(2R^2/3 - R^2u + u^3/3)\right\} \quad (13.A10)$$

For $R > r_g + r_f + s$:

$$V_c = 2\left\{\pi r_g^2 p + \int_p^u [\beta_1 r_g^2 + \alpha_1(R^2 - z^2) - W_1]dz + \pi(2R^2/3 - R^2u + u^3/3)\right\} \quad (13.A11)$$

where
$$u = [R^2 - (r_g - r_f - s)^2]^{0.5} \quad (13.A12)$$
$$p = [R^2 - (r_g + r_f + s)^2]^{0.5} \quad (13.A13)$$
$$\alpha_1 = \arcsin[W_1(r_f + s)^{-1}(R^2 - z^2)^{-0.5}]$$
$$\text{for } z^2 \leq R^2 - r_g^2 + (r_f + s)^2 \quad (13.A14a)$$
$$\alpha_1 = \pi - \arcsin[W_1(r_f + s)^{-1}(R^2 - z^2)^{-0.5}]$$
$$\text{for } z^2 > R^2 - r_g^2 + (r_f + s)^2 \quad (13.A14b)$$
$$\beta_1 = \pi - \arcsin[W_1(r_f + s)^{-1}r_g^{-1}] \text{ for } z^2 < R^2 - r_g^2 - (r_f + s)^2 \quad (13.A15a)$$
$$\beta_1 = \arcsin[W_1(r_f + s)^{-1}r_g^{-1}] \text{ for } z^2 \geq R^2 - r_g^2 - (r_f + s)^2 \quad (13.A15b)$$
$$W_1 = 0.5\{2r_g^2[(r_f + s)^2 + (R^2 - z^2)] - r_g^4 - [(r_f + s)^2 - (R^2 - z^2)]^2\}^{0.5} \quad (13.A16)$$

It has to be noted that in the derivations of Equation (13.9) and Equation (13.10) radial growth of spherulites was assumed and the curvature of growth trajectories, which had to omit fibers, was neglected.

REFERENCES

[1] Friedrich, K., Fakirov, S., Zhang, Z. *Polymer Composites. From Nano- to Macro-Scale*, Springer, New York, 2005.

[2] Nwabunna, D., Kyu, T., eds. *Polyolefin Composites*. John Wiley and Sons Inc., Hoboken, NJ, 2008.

[3] John, M.J., Thomas, S. *Carbohydr. Polym.* **2008**, *71*, 343–364.

[4] Boiteux, G., Boullanger, Ch., Cassagnau, Ph., Fulchiron, R., Seytre, G. *Macromol. Symp.* **2006**, *233*, 246–253.

[5] Lincoln, D.M., Vaia, R.A., Wang, Z.G., Hsiao, B.S., Krishnamoorti, R. *Polymer* **2001**, *42*, 9975–9985.

[6] Nowacki, R., Monasse, B., Piorkowska, E., Galeski, A., Haudin, J.M. *Polymer* **2004**, *45*, 4877–4892.

[7] Chae, D.W., Kim, B.Ch. *Macromol. Mater. Eng.* **2005**, *290*, 1149–1156.

[8] Utracki, L.A. *Clay-Containing Polymeric Materials Nanocomposites*, Vol. 1, Rapra Technology Ltd., Shawbury, UK, 2004.

[9] Tjong, S.C. *Mater. Sci. Eng.* **2006**, *R53*, 73–197.

[10] Usuki, A., Hasegawa, N., Kato, M. *Adv. Polym. Sci.* **2005**, *179*, 135–195.

[11] Pavlidou, S., Papaspyrides, C.D. *Prog. Polym. Sci.* **2008**, *33*, 1119–1198.

[12] Moniruzzaman, M., Winey, K.I. *Macromolecules* **2006**, *39*, 5194–5205.

[13] Gachtner, R., Muller, H., eds. *Plastic Additives Handbook*. Carl Hanser Verlag, Munich, 1993.

[14] Rothon, R.N. *Adv. Polym. Sci.* **1999**, *139*, 67–107.

[15] Ferrage, E., Martin, F., Boudet, A., Petit, S., Fourty, G., Jouffret, F., Micoud, P., De Parseval, P., Salvi, S., Bourgerette, C., Ferret, J., Saint-Gerard, Y., Burrato, S., Fortune, J.P. *J. Mater. Sci.* **2002**, *37*, 1561–1573.

[16] Choi, W.J., Kim, S.Ch. *Polymer* **2004**, *45*, 2393–2401.

[17] Murthy, N.S., Kotliar, A.M., Sibilia, J.P., Sacks, W. *J. Appl. Polym. Sci.* **1986**, *31*, 2569–2582.

[18] Rybnikar, F. *J. Appl. Polym. Sci.* **1989**, *38*, 1479–1490.

[19] Hechelhammer, W. British Patent 1133490, **1968**.

[20] Hechelhammer, W. German Patent 1247645, **1967**.

[21] Pillin, I., Pimbert, S., Levesque, G. *Polym. Eng. Sci.* **2002**, *42*, 2193–2201.

[22] Haubruge, H.G., Daussin, R., Jonas, A.M., Legras, R., Wittmann, J.C., Lotz, B. *Macromolecules* **2003**, *36*, 4452–4456.

[23] Barham, P.J. *J. Mater. Sci.* **1984**, *19*, 3826–3834.

[24] Kolstad, J.J. *J. Appl. Polym. Sci.* **1996**, *62*, 1079–1091.

[25] Velasco, J.J., De Saja, J.A., Martinez, A.B. *J. Appl. Polym. Sci.* **1996**, *61*, 125–132.

[26] Fujiyama, M., Wakino, T. *J. Appl. Polym. Sci.* **1991**, *42*, 9–20.

[27] Naiki, M., Fukui, Y., Matsumura, T., Nomura, T., Matsuda, M. *J. Appl. Polym. Sci.* **2001**, *79*, 1693–1703.

[28] Fujiyama, M. *Int. Polym. Process.* **1992**, *7*, 165–171.

[29] Suh, Ch.H., White, J.L. *Polym. Eng. Sci.* **1996**, *36*, 2188–2197.

[30] Kowalewski, T., Galeski, A. *J. Appl. Polym. Sci.* **1986**, *32*, 2919–2934.

[31] Karger-Kocsis, J., ed. *Polypropylene: An A–Z Reference*. Kluwer Academic Publishers, Dordrecht, 1999.

[32] Bartczak, Z., Argon, A.S., Cohen, R.E., Weinberg, M. *Polymer* **1999**, *40*, 2347–2365.

[33] Bartczak, Z., Argon, A.S., Cohen, R.E., Kowalewski, T. *Polymer* **1999**, *40*, 2367–2380.

[34] Bartczak, Z., Argon, A.S., Cohen, R.E., Weinberg, M. *Polymer* **1999**, *40*, 2331–2346.

[35] Muratoglu, O.K., Argon, A.S., Cohen, R.E., Weinberg, M. *Polymer* **1995**, *36*, 921–930.

[36] Muratoglu, O.K., Argon, A.S., Cohen, R.E. *Polymer* **1995**, *36*, 2143–2152.

[37] Ma, Y., Hu, W., Reiter, G. *Macromolecules* **2006**, *39*, 5159–5164.

[38] Schrauwen, B.A.G., Govaert, L.E., Peters, G.W.M., Meijer, H.E.H. *Macromol. Symp.* **2002**, *185*, 89–102.

[39] Corte, L., Beaume, F., Leibler, L. *Polymer* **2005**, *46*, 2748–2757.

[40] Corte, L., Leibler, L. *Macromolecules* **2007**, *40*, 5606–5611.

[41] Hwang, W.R., Peters, G.W.M., Hulsen, M.A., Meijer, H.E.H. *Macromolecules* **2006**, *39*, 8389–8398.

[42] Zhang, W., Dehghani-Sanij, A.A., Blackburn, R.S. *J. Mater. Sci.* **2007**, *42*, 3408–3418.

[43] Boiteux, G., Mamunya, Ye.P., Lebedev, E.V., Adamczewski, A., Boullanger, C., Cassagnau, P., Seytre, G. *Synth. Met.* **2007**, *157*, 1071–1073.

[44] Narkis, M., Vaxman, A. *J. Appl. Polym. Sci.* **1984**, *29*, 1639–1652.

[45] Pracella, M., Chionna, D., Anguillesi, I., Kulinski, Z., Piorkowska, E. *Compos. Sci. Technol.* **2006**, *66*, 2218–2230.

[46] Zini, E., Baiardo, M., Armelao, L., Scandola, M. *Macromol. Biosci.* **2004**, *4*, 286–295.

[47] Oksman, K., Skrifvar, M., Selin, J.F. *Compos. Sci. Technol.* **2003**, *63*, 1317–1324.

[48] Mathew, A.P., Oksman, K., Sain, M. *J. Appl. Polym. Sci.* **2006**, *101*, 300–310.

[49] Masirek, R., Kulinski, Z., Chionna, D., Piorkowska, E., Pracella, M. *J. Appl. Polym. Sci.* **2007**, *105*, 255–268.

[50] Lezak, E., Kulinski, Z., Masirek, R., Piorkowska, E., Pracella, M., Gadzinowska, K. *Macromol. Biosci.* **2008**, *8*, 1190–1200.

[51] Quan, H., Li, Z.M., Yang, M.B., Huang, R. *Compos. Sci. Technol.* **2005**, *65*, 999–1021.

[52] Sukhanova, T.E., Lednicky, F., Urban, J., Baklagina, Y.G., Mikhailov, G.M., Kudryavtsev, V.V. *J. Mater. Sci.* **1995**, *30*, 2201–2214.

[53] Wang, C., Liu, C.R. *J. Polym. Sci. B Polym. Phys.* **1998**, *36*, 1361–1370.

[54] Cai, Y.Q., Petermann, J., Wittich, H. *J. Appl. Polym. Sci.* **1997**, *65*, 67–75.

[55] Chen, E.J.H., Hsiao, B.S. *Polym. Eng. Sci.* **1992**, *32*, 280–286.

[56] Schonhorn, H., Ryan, F.W. *J. Polym. Sci.* A2 Polym. Phys. **1968**, *6*, 231–240.

[57] Cho, K.W., Kim, D.W., Yoon, S. *Macromolecules* **2003**, *36*, 7652–7660.

[58] Loos, J., Schimanski, T., Hofman, J., Peijs, T., Lemstra, P.J. *Polymer* **2001**, *42*, 3827–3834.

[59] Thomason, J.L., Van Rooyen, A.A. *J. Mater. Sci.* **1992**, *27*, 889–896.

[60] Thomason, J.L., Van Rooyen, A.A. *J. Mater. Sci.* **1992**, *27*, 897–907.

[61] Misra, A., Deopura, B.L., Xavier, S.F., Hartley, D., Peters, R.H. *Angew. Makromol. Chem.* **1983**, *113*, 113–120.

[62] Lagasse, R.R., Maxwell, B. *Polym. Eng. Sci.* **1976**, *16*, 189–199.

[63] Monasse, B. *J. Mater. Sci.* **1992**, *27*, 6047–6052.

[64] Varga, J., Karger-Kocsis, J. *Compos. Sci. Technol.* **1993**, *48*, 191–198.

[65] Varga, J., Karger-Kocsis, J. *Polym. Bull.* **1993**, *30*, 105–110.

[66] Wang, C., Hwang, L.M. *J. Polym. Sci. B Polym. Phys.* **1996**, *34*, 47–56.

[67] Wang, C., Liu, C.R. *Polymer* **1999**, *40*, 289–298.

[68] Yan, S., Katzenberg, F., Petermann, J., Yang, D., Shen, Y., Straupe, C., Wittmann, J.C., Lotz, B. *Polymer* **2000**, *41*, 2613–2625.

[69] Gadzinowska, K., Piorkowska, E. *Polimery* **2003**, *48*, 790–799.

[70] Masirek, R., Piorkowska, E., Galeski, A. Polish Patent 209925, 2011.

[71] Masirek, R., Piorkowska, E. *Eur. Polym. J.* **2010**, *46*, 1436–1445.

[72] van der Meer, D.W., Milazzo, D., Sanguineti, A., Vansco, G.J. *Polym. Eng. Sci.* **2005**, *45*, 458–468.

[73] Bernland, K., Smith, P. *J. Appl. Polym. Sci.* **2009**, *114*, 281–287.

[74] Jurczuk, K., Galeski, A., Piorkowska, E. European Patent application EP-11460010, 2011.

[75] Prox, M., Pornnimit, B., Varga, J., Ehrenstein, G.W. *J. Therm. Anal.* **1990**, *36*, 1675–1684.

[76] Ward, I.M., Hine, P.J. *Polymer* **2004**, *45*, 1423–1437.

[77] Hine, P.J., Ward, I.M., Jordan, N.D., Olley, R., Bassett, D.C. *Polymer* **2003**, *44*, 1117–1131.

[78] Jordan, N.D., Bassett, D.C., Olley, R.H., Hine, P.J., Ward, I.M. *Polymer* **2003**, *44*, 1133–1143.

[79] Desio, G.P., Rebenfeld, L. *J. Appl. Polym. Sci.* **1990**, *39*, 825–835.

[80] Kenny, J.M., Maffezzoli, A. *Polym. Eng. Sci.* **1991**, *31*, 607–614.

[81] Caramaro, L., Chabert, B., Chauchard, J., Vukhanh, T. *Polym. Eng. Sci.* **1991**, *31*, 1279–1285.

[82] Mehl, N.A., Rebenfeld, L. *J. Polym. Sci. B Polym. Phys.* **1993**, *31*, 1677–1686.

[83] Mehl, N.A., Rebenfeld, L. *J. Polym. Sci. B Polym. Phys.* **1993**, *31*, 1687–1693.

[84] Krause, Th., Kalinka, G., Auer, C., Hinrichsen, G. *J. Appl. Polym. Sci.* **1994**, *51*, 399–406.

[85] Piorkowska, E. *Macromol. Symp.* **2001**, *169*, 143–148.

[86] Benard, A., Advani, S.G. *J. Appl. Polym. Sci.* **1998**, *70*, 1677–1687.

[87] Escleine, J.M., Monasse, B., Wey, E., Haudin, J.M. *Colloid Polym. Sci.* **1984**, *262*, 366–373.

[88] Schultz, J.M. *Macromolecules* **1996**, *29*, 3022–3024.

[89] Piorkowska, E., Galeski, A. *J. Phys. Chem.* **1985**, *89*, 4700–4703.

[90] Piorkowska, E., Galeski, A., Haudin, J.M. *Prog. Polym. Sci.* **2006**, *31*, 549–575.

[91] Manias, E., Touny, A., Wu, L., Strawhecker, K., Lu, B., Chung, T.C. *Chem. Mater.* **2001**, *13*, 3516–3523.

[92] Shia, D., Hui, C.Y., Burnside, S.D., Giannelis, E.P. *Polym. Compos.* **1998**, *19*, 608–617.

[93] Luo, J.J., Daniel, I.M. *Compos. Sci. Technol.* **2003**, *63*, 1607–1616.

[94] Szazdi, L., Pukanszky, B., Jr., Vancso, G.J., Pukanszky, B. *Polymer* **2006**, *47*, 4638–4648.

[95] Golebiewski, J., Rozanski, A., Dzwonkowski, J., Galeski, A. *Eur. Polym. J.* **2008**, *44*, 270–286.

[96] Fornes, T.D., Paul, D.R. *Polymer* **2003**, *44*, 3945–3961.

[97] Lincoln, D.M., Vaia, R.A., Krishnamoorti, R. *Macromolecules* **2004**, *37*, 4554–4561.

[98] Hambir, S., Bulakh, N., Jog, J.P. *Polym. Eng. Sci.* **2002**, *42*, 1800–1807.

[99] Maiti, P., Nam, P.H., Okamoto, M., Kotaka, T., Hasegawa, N., Usuki, A. *Polym. Eng. Sci.* **2002**, *42*, 1864–1871.

[100] Gopakumar, T.G., Lee, J.A., Kontopoulou, M., Parent, J.S. *Polymer* **2002**, *43*, 5483–5491.

[101] Ke, Y., Long, Ch., Qi, Z. *J. Appl. Polym. Sci.* **1999**, *71*, 1139–1146.

[102] Priya, L., Jog, J.P. *J. Polym. Sci. B Polym. Phys.* **2002**, *40*, 1682–1689.

[103] Shah, D., Maiti, P., Gunn, E., Schnidt, D.F., Jiang, D.D., Batt, C.A., Giannelis, E.P. *Adv. Mater.* **2004**, *16*, 1173–1177.

[104] Dillon, D.R., Tenneti, K.K., Li, C.Y., Ko, F.K., Sics, I., Hsiao, B.S. *Polymer* **2006**, *47*, 1678–1688.

[105] Dasari, A., Yu, Z.Z., Mai, Y.W. *Macromolecules* **2007**, *40*, 123–130.

[106] Strawhecker, K.E., Manias, E. *Chem. Mater.* **2003**, *15*, 844–849.

[107] Wang, K.H., Choi, M.H., Koo, C.M., Xu, M.Z., Chung, I.J., Jang, M.C., Choi, S.W., Song, H.H. *J. Polym. Sci. B Polym. Phys.* **2002**, *40*, 1454–1463.

[108] Morawiec, J., Pawlak, A., Slouf, M., Galeski, A., Piorkowska, E., Krasnikowa, N. *Eur. Polym. J.* **2005**, *41*, 1115–1122.

[109] Xu, W., Ge, M., He, P. *J. Polym. Sci. B Polym. Phys.* **2002**, *40*, 408–414.

[110] Pozsgay, A., Frater, T., Papp, L., Sajo, I., Pukanszky, B. *J. Macromol. Sci. B Phys.* **2002**, *41*, 1249–1265.

[111] Maiti, P., Nam, P.H., Okamoto, M., Hasegawa, N., Usuki, A. *Macomolecules* **2002**, *35*, 2042–2049.

[112] Perrin-Sarazin, F., Ton-That, M.T., Bureau, M.N., Denault, J. *Polymer* **2005**, *46*, 11624–11634.

[113] Svoboda, P., Zeng, Ch., Wang, H., Lee, J., Tomasko, D.L. *J. Appl. Polym. Sci.* **2002**, *85*, 1562–1570.

[114] Somwangthanaroj, A., Lee, E.C., Solomon, M.J. *Macromolecules* **2003**, *36*, 2333–2342.

[115] Rozanski, A., Monasse, B., Szkudlarek, E., Pawlak, A., Piorkowska, E., Galeski, A., Haudin, J.M. *Eur. Polym. J.* **2009**, *45*, 88–101.

[116] Yalcin, B., Valladares, D., Cakmak, M. *Polymer* **2003**, *44*, 6913–6925.

[117] Wang, K., Xiao, Y., Na, B., Tan, H., Zhang, Q., Fu, Q. *Polymer* **2005**, *46*, 9022–9032.

[118] Koo, C.M., Kim, J.H., Wang, K.H., Chung, I.J. *J. Polym. Sci. B Polym. Phys.* **2005**, *43*, 158–167.

[119] Arimoto, H., Ishibashi, M., Hirai, M., Chatani, Y. *J. Polym. Sci. A* **1965**, *3*, 317–326.

[120] Incarnato, L., Scarfato, P., Russo, G.M., Di Maio, L., Iannelli, P., Acierno, D. *Polymer* **2003**, *44*, 4625–4634.

[121] Coleman, J.N., Khan, U., Blau, W.J., Gunko, Y.K. *Carbon* **2006**, *44*, 1624–1652.

[122] Bokobza, L. *Polymer* **2007**, *48*, 4907–4920.

[123] Li, L., Li, Ch.Y., Ni, Ch., Rong, L., Hsiao, B. *Polymer* **2007**, *48*, 3452–3460.

[124] Jeon, K., Lumata, L., Tokumoto, T., Steven, E., Brooks, J., Alamo, R.G. *Polymer* **2007**, *48*, 4751–4764.

[125] Trujillo, M., Arnal, M.L., Muller, A.J., Laredo, E., Bredeau, S., Bonduel, D., Dubois, Ph. *Macromolecules* **2007**, *40*, 6268–6276.

[126] Haggenmueller, R., Fischer, J.E., Winey, K.I. *Macromolecules* **2006**, *39*, 2964–2971.

[127] Assouline, E., Lustiger, A., Barber, A.H., Cooper, C.A., Klein, E., Wachtel, E., Wagner, H.D. *J. Polym. Sci. B Polym. Phys.* **2003**, *41*, 520–527.

[128] Miltner, H.E., Grossiord, N., Lu, K., Loos, J., Koning, C.E., Van Mele, B. *Macromolecules* **2008**, *41*, 5753–5762.

[129] Zhang, S., Minus, M.L., Zhu, L., Wong, Ch.P., Kumar, S. *Polymer* **2008**, *49*, 1356–1364.

[130] Saujanya, C., Radhakrishnan, S. *Polymer* **2001**, *42*, 6723–6731.

[131] Jain, S., Goossens, H., van Duin, M., Lemstra, P. *Polymer* **2005**, *46*, 8805–8818.

[132] Chan, C.M., Wu, J.S., Li, J.X., Cheung, Y.K. *Polymer* **2002**, *43*, 2981–2992.

[133] Zhang, Q.X., Yu, Z.Z., Xie, X.L., Mai, Y.W. *Polymer* **2004**, *45*, 5985–5994.

[134] Lin, Z.D., Huang, Z.Z., Zhang, Y., Mai, K.C., Zeng, H.M. *J. Appl. Polym. Sci.* **2004**, *91*, 2443–2453.

[135] Avella, M., Cosco, S., Di Lorenzo, M.L., Di Pace, E., Errico, M.E., Gentile, G. *Eur. Polym. J.* **2006**, *42*, 1548–1557.

[136] Qian, J., He, P., Nie, K. *J. Appl. Polym. Sci.* **2004**, *91*, 1013–1019.

[137] Pawlak, A., Morawiec, J., Piorkowska, E., Galeski, A. *Solid State Phenom.* **2003**, *94*, 335–338.

[138] Tjong, S.C., Bao, S. *E-Polymers*, **2007**, article number 139, http://www.e-polymers.org.

[139] Li, G., Wang, L., Ni, H., Pittman, Ch.U., Jr. *J. Inorg. Organomet. Polym.* **2001**, *11*, 123–154.

[140] Fina, A., Tabuani, D., Frache, A., Camino, G. *Polymer* **2005**, *46*, 7855–7866.

[141] Huang, K.W., Tsai, L.W., Kuo, S.W. *Polymer* **2009**, *50*, 4876–4887.

[142] Fu, B.X., Yang, L., Somani, R.H., Zong, S.X., Hsiao, B.S., Phillips, S., Blanski, R., Ruth, P. *J. Polym. Sci. B Polym. Phys.* **2001**, *39*, 2727–2739.

[143] Chen, J.H., Yao, B.X., Su, W.B., Yang, Y.B. *Polymer* **2007**, *48*, 1756–1769.

[144] Pracella, M., Chionna, D., Fina, A., Tabuani, D., Frache, A., Camino, G. *Macromol. Symp.* **2006**, *234*, 59–67.

[145] Joshi, M., Butola, B.S. *Polymer* **2004**, *45*, 4953–4968.

14

FLOW-INDUCED CRYSTALLIZATION

GERRIT W.M. PETERS, LUIGI BALZANO, AND RUDI J.A. STEENBAKKERS

Eindhoven University of Technology, Department of Mechanical Engineering, Materials Technology, Eindhoven, The Netherlands

14.1 Introduction, 399
14.2 Shear-Induced Crystallization, 401
    14.2.1 Nature of Crystallization Precursors, 405
14.3 Crystallization during Drawing, 407
    14.3.1 Spinning, 408
    14.3.2 Elongation-Induced Crystallization; Lab Conditions, 409
14.4 Models of Flow-Induced Crystallization, 410
    14.4.1 Flow-Enhanced Nucleation, 411
    14.4.2 Flow-Induced Shish Formation, 419
    14.4.3 Application to Injection Molding, 421
14.5 Concluding Remarks, 426
References, 427

14.1 INTRODUCTION

It is well known that flow gradients can have a significant effect on the crystallization of polymers, both with respect to enhanced kinetics and with respect to a change in the type of crystallites that are formed [1–4]. This has important consequences for the processing of polymers. Two extreme examples are injection molding (IM) and fiber spinning (FS). The first one is a typical case where there is hardly any control over the final structure or morphology in a product. Different locations in the product have experienced different thermomechanical histories and therefore can show completely different structural properties (see Fig. 14.1).

This implies also completely different final (mechanical) properties for different locations in a product. Figure 14.2 shows that differences in molecular properties (here the molecular weight) are important but that processing conditions can be even much more important. Notice that even brittle and tough behavior can be observed in the same product.

With FS, crystallization always takes place under the same conditions that can be controlled via the draw down ratio, melt temperature, and so on. In general, there is a radial gradient in properties but no axial gradient and thus the average fiber properties can be controlled [5–8]. Moreover, due to the effect of the (elongational) flow, crystallization kinetics can speed up by a factor of 10^6; that is, for many polymers the whole spinning process would not be feasible without flow.

There is a need for predictive numerical models for process optimization, that is, increasing production speed, improving mechanical properties (FS), and finding indications for bad spots or limited use and, most importantly, long-term dimensional stability (IM). However, although ≈65% of the polymers produced are semicrystalline, process design tools as used for amorphous polymers are hardly available for semicrystalline polymers. The reason for that is the complex interplay between molecular properties and the processing conditions, leading to phenomena taking place on a wide range of time and length scales and for a variety of phases and structures. Molecular properties are reflected in the rheological and crystallization behavior. The first task is to design and use some well-defined experiments that reveal all these features. Second, the experimental

Handbook of Polymer Crystallization, First Edition. Edited by Ewa Piorkowska and Gregory C. Rutledge.
© 2013 John Wiley & Sons, Inc. Published 2013 by John Wiley & Sons, Inc.

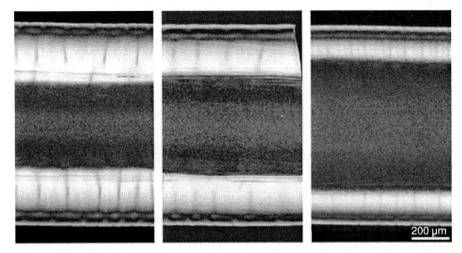

Figure 14.1 Optical micrographs of cross section of an injection-molded PE plate at positions close to the gate (left), the middle (mid) and far from the gate (right) viewed between cross-polars at 45° with flow direction, showing differences in thickness of different layers [175].

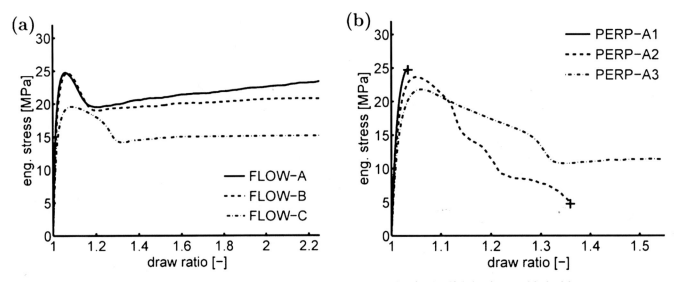

Figure 14.2 Macroscopic tensile behavior of three samples (A, B, C) injection-molded with the same processing conditions but differing in molecular weight (MW): (a) tested in flow direction; and (b) sample A, tested perpendicular to flow direction and at different distances from the gate [175].

findings should be translated into mathematically formulated physical models, suited to be implemented in numerical codes for simulation of polymer shaping processes. Finally, this modeling should be validated for a range of conditions including processing conditions (more on this can be found in Chapter 15); this is one of the most difficult tasks because of the lack of knowledge on the initial conditions and the boundary conditions.

In this chapter attention is paid to all three aspects. Most of the work presented is limited to shear flow since it has received most of the attention in the literature. The general questions that will be addressed here are:

- How do the different structures observed relate to the flow conditions: deformation rates, stress, pressure, thermal conditions, material parameters, additives, and so on?

- How can one model this on a continuum level so it is applicable in numerical codes for process simulation?

The work presented in this chapter is focused on the effect of flow on crystallization of polymer melts; quiescent crystallization is discussed in Chapter 7, and for crystallization of polymer solutions we refer to Chapter 5 and to the literature [2]. The modeling presented is on a continuum level (coarse-grained); molecular modeling is presented in Chapter 6. The backgrounds of the experimental methods applied are discussed in more detail in Chapter 1. This chapter can, of course, not be exhaustive and more background information on specific topics and in-depth discussions can be found in the literature [9–12] and references therein.

14.2 SHEAR-INDUCED CRYSTALLIZATION

The most studied flow type is simple shear flow, which is dominant in all pressure- and drag-driven flows. The strategies adopted, after keeping the material for a sufficient period above the equilibrium melting point in order to erase any history effects, are:

- cooling to a temperature where the flow is applied, followed by cooling to a chosen crystallization temperature, keeping the sample at that temperature until no changes are observed, and cooling to room temperature.
- cooling to the crystallization temperature where the flow is applied, keeping the sample at that temperature until no changes are observed, and then cooling to room temperature.
- cooling to the crystallization temperature where continuous flow is applied until the sample solidifies.

It should be stressed that during this type of flow experiment *the temperature control is crucial* since the crystallization kinetics depend exponentially on the undercooling. A key issue, in that sense, is the dimension of the sample, especially with high cooling rates. A sample that is too thick will lead to large temperature gradients [13] and obscure the results.

The first two protocols are called short-term shear experiments, introduced by the group of Janeschitz-Kriegl and coworkers [14, 15] and adopted by many others. It is important to notice that the group of Janeschitz-Kriegl and, later on, the group of Kornfield [16–18] apply constant pressure in their slit flow experiments, while most groups apply a constant throughput (in case of a slit flow) or a constant shear rate (in case of a drag flow). The idea behind the constant pressure-driven flow is that the material is (nearly) immediately in a stationary state, which makes the interpretation of the results easier, while for a constant shear rate flow, the stress, and thus the molecular state, has to build up, which implies a more complex mechanical history. The original idea of short-term shear experiments was to separate the effects of the flow from the effects of crystallization; crystallization implies nucleation (which can be considered as physical crosslinking [19]) and growth of crystallites (forming a suspension), which will change the rheological behavior of the melt in a complex way [20–23] and this, in turn, will have an effect on the flow. The short-term shear should be short enough to prevent this complex interplay.

Devices used for flow-induced crystallization (FIC) experiments are all types of rheometers: rotational plate/plate, cone/plate, Couette, sliding plates, capillary rheometers, including the multipass rheometer (MPR) [24–26], and shear devices; in-house built [27], Linkam shear cell [28, 29], fiber pull-out [30–34], FS, and complex flows; and contraction/expansion and cross-slot [35–38].

In particular, the experiments on rotational rheometers are limited in the range of shear rates, while most of the other flow devices allow for higher shear rates, up to those typical for industrial processes [39–44].

These shear flow experiments are combined with multiple analytical methods, such as mechanical spectroscopy, optical microscopy, polarimetry and dichroism, infrared and Raman spectroscopy, light scattering, wide-angle X-ray diffraction (WAXD), and small-angle X-ray scattering (SAXS), which can track structural changes on different length and time scales (see Chapter 1). Since a rotational rheometer is both a flow device and a spectrometer, and it can be found in nearly every polymer testing laboratory, it is often used for studying FIC. An often used characteristic measure for quantifying the influences of flow on crystallization is the (half) crystallization time, the time at which half of the maximum of the measured signal (e.g., the modulus, Fig. 14.3), latent heat, viscosity, light intensity, etc.) is reached. Details on the number, size, and orientation of the crystalline structures are left aside when using such a global measure, which is a drawback of such methods.

FIC is strongly affected by the long chain molecules, that is, the high molecular weight (HMW) tail of the molecular weight distribution (MWD) [45–49]. It is thought that, given a shear rate, temperature, and (constant) strain, only polymer chains above a "critical orientation molecular weight" can initiate oriented structures that are stable even at high temperatures, that is, above the nominal melting temperature, to form fibrillar structures [50–55]. These structures are here termed *precursors* and discussed in more detail in the

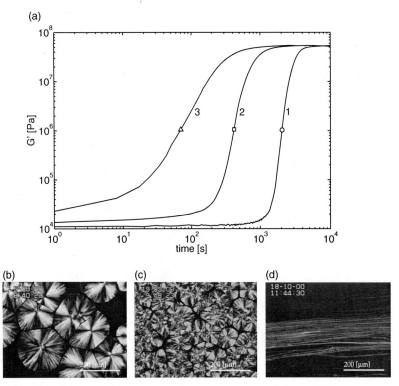

Figure 14.3 Evolution of the storage modulus during crystallization of an iPP grade at $T_{exp} = 135°C$, measured under quiescent conditions (○, 1) and after shearing at $\dot{\gamma} = 60\,(1/s)$ for $t_s = 1\,s$ (□, 2), and $t_s = 6\,s$ (△, 3). Optical micrographs indicate the characteristic morphology for these three crystallization experiments [176].

next section. According to Reference [52], this idea implies that the number of flow-induced nuclei is also limited because the number of molecules above the critical molecular weight can be exhausted. Leveling off of the number of flow-induced point nuclei was observed by Housmans for three different isotactic polypropylene (iPPs) [56].

Seki et al. [48] used bimodal blends of different fractions of low and high molecular weight. It was shown that the quiescent crystallization is not affected by the addition of long chains, while all blends show accelerated kinetics when shear is applied. The role of long chains is thought to be a cooperative rather than a single chain effect, and is due to long chain–long chain entanglements (overlap). This idea is supported by earlier investigations of Keller and Kolnaar [2], who suggest that extension of long chains takes place between constraints imposed by the surrounding molecules.

The development of oriented structures was related to the deformation rate and the (average) molecular weight by Acierno et al. [57] and Elmoumni et al. [49, 58] by using the Weissenberg number $Wi = \tau_d \dot{\gamma}$, where τ_d is the characteristic disentanglement time of the melt, for example the inverse of the frequency of the crossover of the elastic, G', with the loss modulus, G''. A more sophisticated analysis was given by van Meerveld et al. [59]. Depending on the flow strength, expressed in terms of two different characteristic time scales that *correspond to the HMW tail* and the deformation rate, three regimes are identified:

I. For shear rates lower then $1/\tau_d$, where τ_d is the reptation or disengagement time, no noticeable influence of the flow is observed; that is, the crystallization takes place as for quiescent conditions. For this regime the related Weissenberg numbers, defined as $Wi_o = \tau_d \dot{\gamma}$ (related to molecular orientation) and $Wi_s = \tau_R \dot{\gamma}$, where τ_R is the Rouse time (related to molecular stretch), are both smaller than 1, that is, $Wi_o < 1, Wi_s < 1$.

II. For shear rates higher then $1/\tau_d$, but lower then $1/\tau_R$, only orientation effects enhance the point nucleation; that is, on top of the normally observed athermal nucleation, the flow causes an additional sporadic nucleation. The number of extra nuclei depends on the flow strength and the flow duration. For the Weissenberg numbers it now holds: $Wi_o \geq 1, Wi_s < 1$.

III. For shear rates higher then $1/\tau_d$, and $1/\tau_R$, molecular stretch, Λ, occurs and the flow generates fibrillar nuclei, so-called shish, on which lamellae grow laterally, so-called kebabs. The number and length of the shish depend on the flow strength and the flow duration. For the Weissenberg numbers it now holds: $Wi_o \geq 1$, $Wi_s \geq 1$.

The stretch regime can be divided in *two subregimes* depending on the global configuration of the chain and the rotational isomerization (RI). For relatively low chain stretch, Λ, the chain maintains a Gaussian configuration and the amount of RI is small. On the other hand, for high levels of Λ the influence of the finite extensibility of the chain sets in and the chain configuration becomes non-Gaussian and the amount of RI is large. A critical value Λ^* denotes the transition between the two chain stretching regimes. This critical value depends on chain stiffness, expressed by C_∞ (and therefore on the temperature; $C_\infty(T)$), chain length, and the MWD. Typically, $\Lambda^* \approx 0.3 - 0.5\,\Lambda_{max}$, where $\Lambda_{max} = \sqrt{N_e} = b/l\,(C_\infty + 1)$, and N_e the number of Kuhn segments per entanglement, b the tube diameter, and l the bond length. This should be considered as a (semi-) empirical relationship, indicating qualitative trends in the change of the configuration and conformation of the chain upon stretching at a given temperature.

The Rouse time τ_R and the reptation time τ_d can be estimated from the theory for monodisperse melts according to [60, 61]:

$$\tau_R = \tau_e Z^2 \quad (14.1)$$

$$\tau_d = 3_e Z^3 \left[1 - \mu\left(\frac{1}{Z}\right)^{0.5}\right]^2 \quad (14.2)$$

where Z is the number of entanglements defined as $Z = M_w/M_e$, τ_e is the equilibration time of an entanglement segment, and κ is a constant of the order of unity ($\mu = 1.53 \pm 0.05$) [62]. More complex expressions can be found in Likhtman and McLeish [63]. Calculation of these characteristic relaxation times requires the knowledge of τ_e for the material under consideration. Notice that τ_e is temperature dependent $\tau_e(T) = \tau_e(T_{ref})\,a_T$ according to the time temperature shift factor a_T as, for example, determined with rheological dynamic measurements.

The definition of the different regimes in terms of critical Weissenberg numbers can be refined; intermediate regimes should be defined where the flow is strong enough but too short to reach stationary values for the orientation ($Wi_o \geq 1$) or the molecular stretch ($Wi_s \geq 1$) (see Fig. 14.4). When the shear strain level is increased, the two transition points in the curve move to lower

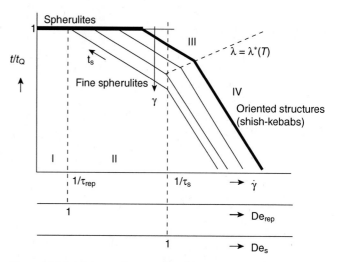

Figure 14.4 Schematic representation of the different flow regimes and morphology types in flow-induced crystallization [176].

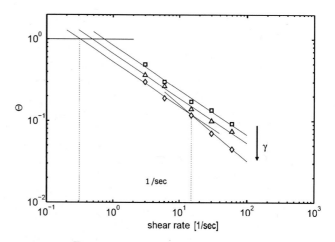

Figure 14.5 Normalized crystallization half-time, Θ, versus shear rate for the three different levels of shear strain: $\gamma = 60$ ($\square$), $\gamma = 120$ ($\triangle$), $\gamma = 240$ ($\bigcirc$) [176].

shear rates and, eventually, coincide with the transitions between the different flow regimes.

Different groups have observed these regimes [64–67] (see also Fig. 14.5). In Figure 14.5 it is demonstrated that, indeed, the total strain plays an important role. If the critical strain is not reached, the stretch regime is not probed. Notice that, for example, Hadinata et al. [66] show similar results but for continuous flow. This is much more complicated than short-term shear (interplay between the nucleation and growth process and the changing rheology). However, three regimes are sometimes seen in their results (cf. fig. 8b in Hadinata et al. [66] and fig. 9 in Hadinata et al. [67]).

Notice that the influence of the temperature on the flow strength is captured by the temperature dependency of the relaxation times.

The previous discussion relates to the initial state of the flow-induced structures, which form the fingerprint for the final structures; enhanced point nucleation creates a more fine-grained structure than the equivalent quiescent structure, mild stretch will lead to internal orientation of the spherulites while higher stretch levels will create fibrils (shish) on which lamellae (kebabs) will grow. The initial nucleated structure is, therefore, of utmost importance for the evolving post-shearing structure.

Another view on the formation of shish is given by Janeschitz-Kriegl and coworkers [4]. They consider the mechanism of shish formation as a convection-induced accumulation process of existing nuclei, whose size can change at the same time, both effects caused by the flow. Due to a change in size, dormant nuclei can become active. The results (nucleation density) are expressed in terms of the work applied. If the work is large enough, that is, as soon as the number of nuclei becomes sufficiently large, an aggregation into shish occurs quite suddenly. Recently, this concept of critical mechanical work was also used by the group of Ryan for the analysis of shear-induced crystallization of model blends of hydrogenated polybutadiene (h-PBD) [28]. It was found that a critical amount of work is required for shish formation and that this critical amount only depends on the chemical structure and the MWD of the polymer and is independent of the shear rate as soon as it exceeds the inverse of the Rouse time. The latter connects again to the classification of van Meerveld [59]. Other groups tested the work concept with varying success [56, 64].

The previous discussion also relates to short-term shearing, that is, the material, and thus rheological, changes during shear are so small that they can be neglected. For long-term shearing the material does change and a time-dependent nonlinear coupling between the crystallization process and the evolving rheological behavior exists. This can be described as a sequence of coupled events:

1. Flow nucleates point- and/or fibrillar nuclei. These nuclei can act as physical crosslinks [19].
2. If the flow is strong enough, and its duration long enough, the nucleation density becomes high enough to give rise to a gel-like behavior [68, 69].
3. Even when no gel-like behavior occurs, that is, the precursor density is too low, the growing crystalline structures will form a mixture of a polymer melt and elastic solid-like particles that can be looked upon as a viscoelastic dispersion (anisotropic, in the case of fibrillar nucleation) [20, 21, 70].
4. The particles will locally modify the flow, more specifically intensify the flow, which leads to stronger flow effects (a locally increased Weissenberg number) [71].
5. This intensified flow will cause an increased flow-induced nucleation and so on.

The situation is even more complex when viscous dissipation and the release of the crystallization enthalpy are taken into account. For pressure-driven flows, where the shear rate varies from the core to the wall of the flow channel, the flow becomes nonisothermal and a locally increased temperature can reduce the flow effects, since the characteristic relaxation times, and thus the Weissenberg number, will decrease. This might lead to cases where a stronger flow has less effect on the formation of oriented crystalline structures. These cases can only be analyzed by using a numerical model, as for example a finite element code, that includes all physical aspects of the problem [11, 72–77].

During processing, things become again more complicated than when examined under ideal, laboratory conditions. Pressure levels easily reach 200 MPa, and cooling rates at mold walls rise to up to 1000 K/s. There are a number of studies that examine the effect of these extreme conditions separately, but only a few studies that consider combined effects, that is, the influence of high cooling rates and pressure [78–80] and, even more complicated, the combined influence of shear, high pressure, and fast cooling [42, 79, 81, 82].

Pressure is often thought to simply shift the melting temperature to higher values. However, the influence of pressure on the nucleation and growth rates is hardly studied. Moreover, pressure also has a marked effect on the relaxation spectrum of the polymer and thus on the Weissenberg number for a given shear rate and temperature. This combined effect was studied systematically by van der Beek et al. [81], who found that, for sufficiently large undercooling (preventing too large effects of molecular relaxation and remelting) the classification as described above still holds when the pressure was taken into account by:

$$Wi = a_T a_p \tau \dot{\gamma} \quad (14.3)$$

where a_T is the temperature shift factor and a_p is the pressure shift factor given by:

$$a_p = \exp(\kappa P/T) \quad (14.4)$$

where κ is a material-specific parameter. A similar study that includes the effect of random copolymers is presented by Housmans et al. [83] (see also Forstner et al. [82]), where, in a clear way, the combined effects of

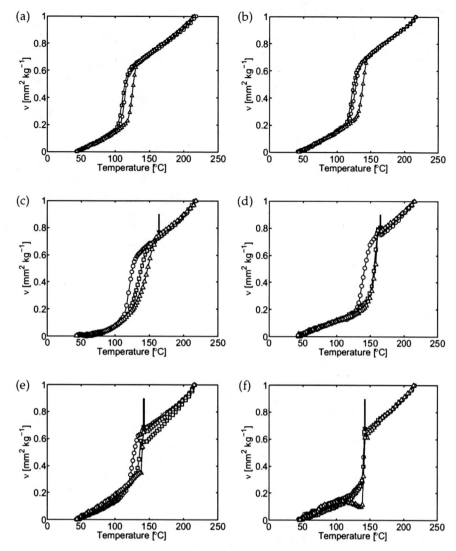

Figure 14.6 Relative specific volume of iPP1 (○), iPP2 (□), and iPP3 (△) samples at a cooling rate of 1.5°C/s at quiescent conditions (a, b) and with a shear step (68 (1/s) for 2 s) applied at $T = 164°C$ (c, d) and $T = 142°C$ (e, f) with a pressure of 100 bar (a, c, e) and 600 bar (b, d, f). Adapted from Reference [82].

molecular weight (i.e., relaxation time), pressure, and shear flow are demonstrated. Figure 14.6 shows the specific volume traces for three different iPPs (M_w = 310, 376, 466 kg/mol, M_w/M_n = 3.4, 6.7, 6.6, respectively) for two different pressures for quiescent crystallization and crystallization after shear applied at two different temperatures.

The main observations are the increasing transition temperatures for an increasing pressure and increasing Weissenberg number, that is, when shear is applied at a lower temperature. Due to the higher polydispersity index of iPP2, that is, a more extended HMW tail while having (nearly) the same molecular weight, the effect of flow on crystallization kinetics increases compared with iPP1. In the case of iPP3 the melt almost immediately starts to crystallize after the application of flow, which supports the idea that HMW and higher polydispersity are most effective in the enhancement of crystallization kinetics in flow experiments. The undershoot in the specific volume for iPP3 in Figure 14.6f is not physical, but an experimental error related to the design of the setup.

14.2.1 Nature of Crystallization Precursors

Mitsuhashi [84] reported for the first time the formation of string-like polyethylene (PE) structures during stirring of a solution. Since then many more observations on such structures, also for other polymers, have been made and the idea of flow-induced oriented precursors has been experimentally well established [28, 29, 54, 85, 86]. An extended review on flow-induced shish–kebab precursors was given by Somani et al. [9] including a historical overview of different views on shish nucleation and growth. These oriented structures might be amorphous, mesomorphic, or crystalline, depending on their evolution. They can be created and survive for a long time at temperatures above the nominal melting temperature, which is typically several tens of degrees lower than the equilibrium or thermodynamic melting temperature, since their relaxation behavior at these temperatures is slow [26, 28, 54, 55, 86, 87]. Their creation is dominated by a small fraction of the longest molecules [29, 47, 48, 55]. Seki et al. [48] demonstrated this for bimodal blends; in a flow field these molecules stretch the most and relax the slowest because of their long relaxation times (Rouse and disengagement time). Orientation on a segmental level enhances the local ordering, and other molecules that are entangled with these long molecules become aligned too. The long molecules initiate the precursors; all the others are equally used to build them, at least in a "normal" polydisperse melt in which all molecules can, potentially, crystallize. This was demonstrated in an experimental study based on neutron scattering and using deuterium labeling of different parts of the MWD of an iPP by Kimata et al. [88]. The long chains "recruit their neighboring chains to join in forming the shish."

Model PE blends consisting of a low molecular weight (LMW) matrix that was kept amorphous by choosing the experimental temperature higher than its melting temperature, that is, acting as a solvent, and a crystallizable HMW minor component were studied by Hsiao and coworkers [85]. Such special blends allow for the examination of the crystallization behavior under flow of the HMW component only. Shish formation was directly observable from SAXS measurements for sufficiently high HMW concentration and indirectly from WAXD (oriented kebab).

Electron micrographs, made after dissolving the LMW component, showed an unexpected shish–kebab structure for these special blends; adjacent kebabs are interconnected by multiple short shish, quite different from the conventional results/view of one shish connecting multiple kebabs (see Fig. 14.7). It is not clear whether this is a result of the special blend or also applies to normal entangled blends. Nevertheless, based on these results Hsiao et al. [85] proposed a model for the shish–kebab formation not discussed in detail here.

A bimodal system with the opposite behavior, namely an HMW atactic polypropylene as the precursor com-

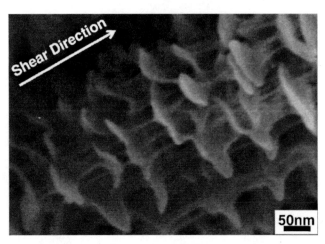

Figure 14.7 SEM image of toluene-extracted UHMWPE crystallites with a shish–kebab structure having multiple shish [85].

ponent blended with a relatively LMW iPP, was studied by the same group. It was found that primary shish kebab nuclei can originate from flow-induced noncrystalline precursor structures; that is, iPP can nucleate from oriented and extended amorphous chains.

The final morphologies/structures that are generated after cooling to room temperature depend on the length of the precursors; when they are (much) shorter than the typical local spherulite size, they will generate spherulites with an oriented core. When they are very long, up to a few micrometers, shish–kebab structures will emerge. For intermediate sizes, elongated/distorted spherulites or row nuclei are observed. These different stages are nicely visualized in a paper of Xu et al. [89], as shown in Figure 14.8.

All structures can also be found over the thickness of a sample from a slit flow (see for example Custódio et al. [74]).

This crucial role of flow-induced precursors (FIPs) in structural and morphological developments during crystallization was studied in detail by Balzano et al. [55]. The metastable FIPs, having very low or no crystallinity and formed at temperatures surprisingly high compared with T_m^o, can grow into crystals or dissolve in the melt, depending on the conditions. FIPs formed at very high temperatures, for instance, 160°C or 200°C for iPP, are undetectable with SAXS and WAXD and yet have a strong influence on the crystallization of the polymer. FIPs increase the temperature at which nucleation sets in upon cooling and promote orientation at both structural and morphological levels.

Not much is known about the very early stages, that is, even during a short flow pulse, of precursor formation

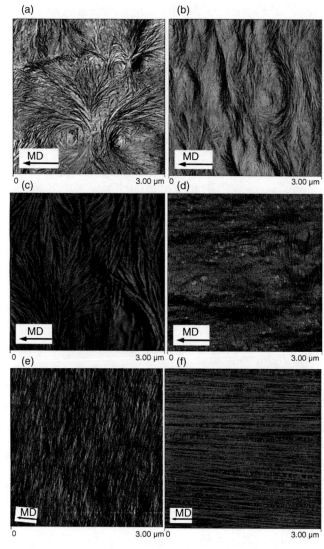

Figure 14.8 AFM images of five different PVDF resins with increasing MW (85–250 kg/mol) exposed to the same flow conditions during film blowing. (a) Resin 1, (b) resin 2, (c) resin 1, higher magnification, (d) resin 3, (e) resin 4, (f) resin 5 [89]. (See color insert.)

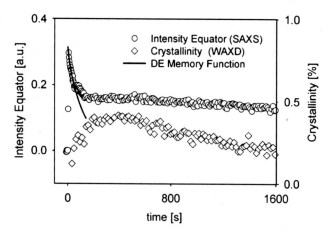

Figure 14.9 Equatorial intensity I_{eq}^{SAXS} and crystallinity χ^{WAXD} as a function of time after step shear at 142°C. The initial drop of I_{eq}^{SAXS} is well captured with the memory function of the Doi-Edwards (DE) model (continuous line) [55].

[90]. An important observation with regard to this, using a bimodal PE, was the initial relaxation of shish, just before crystallization sets in. At 142°C, shear flow induces needle-like FIPs of which many do not meet the necessary size requirements for stability and dissolve back in the melt. Remarkably, the dissolution time scale (measurable with SAXS) matches exactly the time scale for the reptation of HMW molecules (see Fig. 14.9). The relaxation due to melting (crystallinity is slowly going down) after this early stage has a completely different time scale.

This link between dissolution of FIPs and HMW chain dynamics suggests again that the early FIPs are governed by the HMW fraction. Stable FIPs crystallize and form a suspension of crystalline shish only; nucleation of the kebabs is suppressed because of the high temperature. The formation of needle-like FIPs and shish demands shear rates that are high enough for orientation and stretch of HMW chains. But this is not the only requirement. Clearly, a critical total macroscopic strain should also be exceeded; $\gamma = 50 - 100$ for the bimodal blend that Balzano et al. [91] used. This is in line with the classification given by van Meerveld et al. [59]. The needle-like FIPs and shish act as nucleating agents and raise the nucleation temperature and template the morphology of the polymer. With time-resolved SAXS, it is possible to differentiate between the high-temperature epitaxial nucleation of kebabs and the nucleation of lamellae randomly assembled in spherulites, at lower temperatures. It was shown that ~0.5 vol% of shish is sufficient to produce a fully oriented morphology on cooling.

The shear-induced crystallization of heterogeneous systems is a subject that has received much less attention, but there are a few, both experimental [41, 92, 93] and theoretical, studies [71].

14.3 CRYSTALLIZATION DURING DRAWING

Several polymer forming processes are dominated by uni- or biaxial drawing, such as FS and film blowing. These forming processes contrast with IM, where there is hardly any control over the physical and mechanical properties, which will vary over the whole product. With

FS and film blowing, properties can be controlled by varying the process parameters and thus the structure created in the processing step. This shows the importance of such processes.

Roughly two types of experiments are carried out with different goals: (1) experiments in which controlled extensional flow is applied, that is, homogenous and constant deformation rate and constant temperature, in order to gain fundamental understanding of crystallization behavior during such flow and (2) experiments on the drawing process in order to understand and control that process. These two types of elongation-induced crystallization experiments will be discussed separately.

All aspects of crystallization dynamics of polymers, the strong dependence on the temperature, cooling rate, and the application of flow, are of relevance to high-speed FS (uniaxial extensional flow) [1–3, 13] and during biaxial extensional flow, that is, film blowing [28, 93–95].

Pioneering work using online observations was performed by Ziabicki and Kawai [7], Nakamura et al. [97], Spruiell and White [98], Laun and Schuch [99], and Ishizuka and Koyama [100]. During spinning and film blowing the melt is quickly cooled far below the melting temperature and the molecules become stretched and oriented, strongly affecting the (mechanical) properties. The remainder of this section is limited to uniaxial extensional flow.

14.3.1 Spinning

With FS, the crystallization rate increases by several orders of magnitude for relatively large take-up speeds (>4000 m/min for nylon and poly(ethylene terephthalate) [PET]), and this is generally assumed to be connected to flow (or stress)-induced crystallization [101, 102]. A characteristic feature of high-speed FS of crystallizing polymers is the formation of a neck in the filament [103, 104]. The systematic experimental analysis of Haberkorn et al. [101] provides physical insight into the neck formation for nylon 6 and nylon 66. Two observations are of particular importance. First, they showed that only in the neck region the elongation rate, $\dot{\varepsilon}$, exceeds the reciprocal of the characteristic reptation time of the HMW chains in the melt, obtained from Equation (14.2) using $Z = M_w/M_e$. Second, the onset of the crystallization occurs at the end of the neck region, but the majority of the crystallization occurs after the neck is formed. Similar findings are reported for PE [100] and PET [105]. These two experimental findings suggest that only at the end of the neck the chains are sufficiently stretched to enhance the crystallization rate by several orders of magnitude. The necking behavior is complicated by the presence of radial variations of the temperature and stress, which is reflected by the presence of the so-called sheath–core structure of as-spun fibers [106].

A review of simulations of low-speed FS of slowly crystallizing polymers that are not affected by the crystallization dynamics is given by Denn [6]. The models discussed use a Newtonian description of the melt, and consequently neck formation is not predicted. Viscoelasticity is incorporated in the models by Ziabicki et al. [107], Joo et al. [108], Kulkarni and Beris [109], and Doufas et al. [110–112]. Ziabicki et al. and Joo et al. use "single" phase models; only the viscosity (relaxation time) changes with degree of crystallinity. Neck formation is not reported or predicted. A two-phase model where the stress contributions of the amorphous melt and a stiff crystalline phase are weighted by means of the degree of crystallinity was used by Kulkarni et al. [38] and by Kannan and Rajagopal [113]. Doufas et al. [110] used additive stress contributions from amorphous and crystalline phases without an explicit weighting by the crystallinity. These models are able to predict neck formation, suggesting that the stress contributions of the amorphous and crystal phases need to be reflected separately.

FIC models for FS often apply the Nakamura equation [114] to describe the crystallization dynamics (see for example References [115–117]). However, the use of the Nakamura equation is inappropriate because, first, the "isokinetic" assumption is not satisfied during FIC, and, second, a change in the number density of crystals cannot be described [3].

A continuum model, based on a nonequilibrium thermodynamics analysis of the FIC of polymer melts [118], was developed by van Meerveld et al. [8]. The major difference with previous models lies in the description of the crystallization dynamics. Flow-induced nucleation and growth of fibrils occur due to the stretching of the amorphous chains, in addition to the quiescent nucleation and growth of spherulites. This approach uses a set of rate equations that capture the morphology during FS, making it possible to distinguish between nucleation and growth dynamics and the formation of differently shaped crystals. Examples of models that describe enhanced nucleation of spherulites are given in Isayev et al. [75] and Zheng and Kennedy [73], and examples of models that describe the formation of the shish–kebab morphology are discussed in Eder et al. [3], Zuidema et al. [19], and Custódio et al. [74]. The description of the degree of crystallinity by means of a set of rate equations [119–121] is identical to the crystallization theory of Kolmogorov [122] and Avrami [123–125]. In principle, the use of the rate equations is an attractive approach to describe FIC on a continuum level, as changes in the crystallization dynamics under general flow conditions can be incorporated in a more transpar-

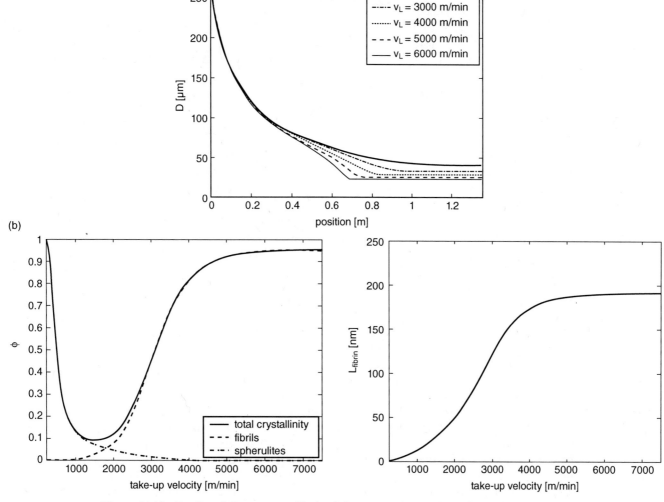

Figure 14.10 Predicted diameter profile (top) for constant mass throughput of $W = 2.492$ g/min and the crystallinity (bottom, left) and average fibril length (bottom, right) at $z = L$ with increasing take-up velocity [8].

ent and considerably more detailed fashion than the Nakamura equation.

An illustrative example from van Meerveld et al. [8] demonstrating the richness of the model is given in Figure 14.10 (top) where the shape of the fiber, including the neck region is shown, while in Figure 14.10 (bottom) the concentration of spherulites and shish–kebab structures and shish length is given, respectively.

14.3.2 Elongation-Induced Crystallization; Lab Conditions

Systematic experimental work on controlled extensional flow was performed by a few groups. A special device (the "Windbix") was designed in the group of Janeschitz-Kriegl [126] that provides uniaxial elongation with a constant stress. The major advantage of this device is the fully controlled, homogeneous deformation field that (nearly) instantaneously reaches a steady state.

Janeschitz-Kriegl and coworkers put forward the hypothesis that the flow improves existing/created precursors, which grow in size (in the flow direction) and therefore become active at higher temperatures and, ultimately, when the length is larger than the typical spherulite size, become shish.

Swartjes et al. [38] used an in-house designed cross-slot flow and analyzed their results experimentally using birefringence and X-ray methods (the cross-slot device was equipped with special diamond windows), showing the existence of a highly oriented narrow region of crystalline fiber-like structures on the outflow center line.

These results were interpreted by means of numerical simulations of the inhomogeneous deformation field, a disadvantage of this approach. However, it allows, in principle, for high deformation rates, and, because the flow is confined, it is thought that flow instabilities are prevented. Only qualitative agreement was obtained.

Okamoto and coworkers [127, 128] designed an extensional flow optometer, based on Meissner's extensional rheometer, and applied it to the study of elongation-induced crystallization of PET in the supercooled (100–130°C) liquid state. The structure evolution was measured using birefringence and light scattering. Depending on the temperature, enhanced nucleation and growth of spherulitic or oriented crystallites were observed. In particular, in the high temperature range, (≈120–130°C) complex phenomena occur: spherulite formation, spherulite deformation/breakup, and reorganization into oriented crystallites. Also two different poly(ethylene naphthalates) were studied in the range of 170–190°C, as well as metallocene-catalyzed syndiotactic polystyrene in the range of 110–140°C using the same experimental methods.

Hadinata et al. [129] recently studied the elongation-induced crystallization of an HMW isotactic polybutene-1 melt and compared the results with shear-induced crystallization. They used an extensional flow fixture, similar to the Sentmanat Extensional Rheometer [130], that can be installed on a standard rotational viscometer and consists of dual wind-up drums. The experiments concerned continuous elongation (in contrast with the short-term shear experiments described previously and the short-term shear experiments by Stadlbauer et al. [126]) for a fixed elongation rate, from which the onset times of crystallization were obtained. Important for the experimental interpretation of the onset time was the prediction, using the molecular stress function (MSF) model [131], of the strain hardening behavior of the noncrystallizing melt so the extra strain hardening due to crystallization could be distinguished. It was shown that extensional flow is more effective than shear flow when compared at the same deformation rates.

Sentmanat et al. [132] applied their rotating clamp device to study the FIC behavior of a metallocene linear low density poly(ethylene) (m-LLDPE) and high density poly(ethylene) (HDPE) over a range of temperatures near the differential scanning calorimetry (DSC) peak melt temperature. Temperature and strain dependence of the FIC behavior was demonstrated. Tensile stress growth and melt flow birefringence measurements revealed the critical FIC behavior of the HDPE over a span of just 1°C. Cessation of elongation experiments very near the peak melt temperature revealed the retardation effect that FIC has on the stress relaxation behavior of the crystallizing melt.

14.4 MODELS OF FLOW-INDUCED CRYSTALLIZATION

In the literature, modeling is done on different levels of molecular and morphological detail. A trade-off between the two is inevitable. For example, simulations on the length and time scales of individual molecules (see Chapter 6) describe the physics of initial nucleation events, but they do not take into account the effect of the developing microstructure on the rheological properties, the flow, and (as a result of both) the nucleation process. Nor do they incorporate the influence of complex thermal and flow conditions. On the other hand, continuum models allow the calculation of variables characterizing the microstructure. The most detailed approaches are based on a set of differential equations for the creation and growth of spheres, representing spherulites [119, 120], with an additional set for the creation and growth of cylinders, representing shish–kebabs [14, 19], or by a single set of differential equations describing both of these morphologies and their intermediates [74, 121]. Continuum models necessarily involve a more coarse-grained description of the molecular aspects of FIC kinetics. A purely empirical approach [14], based on macroscopic flow parameters only, is not generally applicable to different materials or different thermal and flow conditions. Improvements in this respect involve coupling kinetic parameters, which determine the nucleation and growth of different morphologies, with an average measure of the conformation of the (HMW) chains, obtained from a nonlinear viscoelastic model [8, 19, 73, 74, 110, 111, 112, 117, 133–135]. Moreover, the microstructure can be coupled with the rheology, either by an empirical volume-fraction-dependent viscosity multiplier [8, 11, 19, 22, 133, 136] or by a suspension model [20, 21, 23, 70].

It is well known that flow has a great impact on the nucleation rate and, if the strain rate is high enough, the longitudinal growth rate of crystallization precursors. Many examples can be found in the literature cited in the previous sections. Studies of the effect of flow on the lamellar growth rate are far scarcer. The growth rate of spherulites during flow has been reported to increase as a function of the strain rate, in fiber pull-out experiments [30–34] as well as steady shear flows [137–140]. Conflicting results have been obtained for the spherulitic growth rate after flow. Tribout et al. [31] observed an increase after short-term shearing at the temperature at which the material was left to crystallize, whereas Koscher and Fulchiron [140] (in similar experiments) and Huo et al. [141] (who applied the shear above the melting point before cooling down to crystallize) saw no influence of the preceding flow. Huo et al. also found that the spherulitic growth rate was increased after a period of shear that was started at a high temperature and prolonged during cooling. They interpreted this effect in terms of the modified Hoffman–Lauritzen theory proposed by Coppola et al. [142] (see the next section). Following these authors, Huo et al. [141] used the steady-state solution for the flow-induced free energy change of the Doi–Edwards model [143]. As Tavichai et al. [137] pointed out, this approach is not valid for the experiments of Huo et al. because, once the flow has stopped, the flow-induced free energy starts to relax. One might argue that this relaxation is probably very slow at the low temperatures of crystallization, where the increase in the growth rate was mainly observed. Nevertheless, the assumption of steady state remains unrealistic for the complex thermal and mechanical history of the experiments (simultaneous shearing and cooling). The issue of the lamellar growth rate in FIC is not considered further in this chapter. Instead, attention is focused on flow-enhanced nucleation and the transition to oriented growth, both of which depend much more dramatically on flow conditions.

A number of FIC models are discussed in Section 14.4.1. The aim is to give an overview of the most successful approaches, in terms of capturing the phenomena observed in laboratory FIC experiments, and to compare the physical ideas in these models. Flow-enhanced nucleation is the main subject of Section 14.4.1, but some of the models discussed there additionally describe shish growth. A model for shish growth that is in better agreement with detailed experimental observations, developed by Custódio et al. [74], is summarized in Section 14.4.2. Implementation in IM simulations is discussed in Section 14.4.3. Results of such simulations by Custódio et al. are shown as an example of the current state of the art. Their model captures the following phenomena and features of FIC:

- precursor creation rate based on the deformed state (stretch) of the HMW tail;
- anisotropic growth of precursors, leading to nuclei of varying sizes (from spherical to cylindrical);
- critical stress for the initiation of longitudinal growth of point-like precursors into shish;
- morphological details (number, dimensions, surface, volume) of spherulites and shish–kebabs;
- local variations in the morphology (e.g., in finite element method (FEM) simulations);
- changing rheological behavior as a function of the crystalline state, in terms of a changing relaxation spectrum (as shown, for example, by Pogodina et al. [68, 144]) and in terms of suspension behavior [20–23];

- temperature-dependent relaxation behavior of precursors above the nominal melting point, which seems to be governed by the rheological relaxation times when the precursor is noncrystalline and by another (melting) mechanism with a much larger characteristic relaxation time [55].

14.4.1 Flow-Enhanced Nucleation

Since the 1990s, experimental evidence for the importance of subcritical nuclei, which we call precursors, in FIC has accumulated rapidly. Several (more often than not, conflicting) hypotheses have been put forward to explain the physical nature of these precursors and their role in the nucleation process. A review that highlights many of the ideas and controversies was presented by Kumaraswamy [10]. The introduction of Steenbakkers and Peters [135] provides an overview of the main results and interpretations from rheometry and optical microscopy. Their section IV C does the same, but more briefly, for a variety of other techniques. Baert and Van Puyvelde [12] critically reviewed small-angle light scattering studies on the early stage of FIC and their interpretations. Extensive compilations of work from specific research groups are also available [3, 9, 145].

With the advent of sophisticated simulation techniques, the physics of the flow-enhanced nucleation process at the molecular level are gradually being unraveled (see Chapter 6). The results of such investigations can serve to validate and/or improve continuum-level FIC models. Some of the most advanced of these are compared here in terms of the formulation of flow-enhanced nucleation kinetics. A description of flow-induced oriented structure formation and application to IM are discussed in Section 14.4.2 and Section 14.4.3, respectively. We focus on models that calculate the number density and dimensions of nuclei since this is necessary to predict morphological features beyond merely the degree of crystallization or the volume fraction of semicrystalline material. Therefore, approaches based on a (modified) Nakamura equation are left out of consideration.

The models discussed here can be divided into two groups, based on the two main hypotheses concerning the origin of FIPs. The first, which is more widely used, is that precursors are created in the amorphous phase through a sporadic process, driven by thermal fluctuations. Flow presumably lowers the free energy barrier associated with this process and thus accelerates it. As we will see, the specific effect of flow on the creation rate varies among the models developed. The second hypothesis, put forward by Janeschitz-Kriegl and coworkers [146–148], is that the amorphous phase already contains so-called dormant precursors of different sizes, which are unable to nucleate until their size-dependent activation temperature is reached. These precursors are homogeneous, made of the polymer itself, as opposed to nucleating agents or other heterogeneities. Homogeneous precursors are commonly envisioned as (cylindrical) bundles of crystalline or liquid-crystalline stems, with the amorphous portions of the participating chains protruding from the ends (the "fringed micelle" model). According to Janeschitz-Kriegl [148], flow can cause a bundle to grow in length. This decreases the bulk contribution to the driving force for crystallization (the difference in free energy between the precursor and an equal amount of chains in the amorphous phase). The interfacial energy associated with the lateral surface of the bundle increases, but this is a minor effect. The end surfaces are more important; they have a much higher interfacial energy due to the difference in density between the fringes and the crystalline stems. Their relative contribution to the free energy decreases as the precursor grows in length. Thus, fewer stems are necessary for it to become active, or with a given number of stems, it becomes active at a higher temperature. Activation of dormant precursors is thus athermal in nature [149].

The effect of flow on nucleation is usually ascribed exclusively to the creation of new precursors or to the activation of preexisting dormant precursors. However, it is possible that both processes take place. Current experimental capabilities are insufficient to resolve this issue because, unlike shish, point-like precursors cannot be detected. Hence, it is unknown whether FIPs originate from the pure amorphous phase, from preexisting dormant precursors, or from both. Typical continuum-level FIC models lack the level of detail to determine which interpretation is correct. Nevertheless, they can shed some light on the role of molecular deformation and relaxation in flow-enhanced nucleation. The objective of the present work is to provide a theoretical framework, in which models based either on one of the two or on both hypotheses are contained. We depart from the idea that sporadic creation and athermal activation of FIPs take place side by side. Eventually one of the two may be switched off and additional assumptions may be introduced to obtain a range of different models.

The distribution function of precursors per unit volume with the number of stems n and the length l is denoted by $\rho(n, l)$. We introduce $n^*(T, l)$ as the critical number of stems. The number densities of active and dormant precursors are then:

$$N_{pa} = \int_0^\infty \sum_{n=n^*(T,l)}^\infty \rho(n,l) dl \qquad (14.5)$$

and

$$N_{pd} = \int_0^\infty \sum_{n=1}^{n^*(T,l)-1} \rho(n,l) dl, \qquad (14.6)$$

respectively. The total number density of precursors is

$$N_p = N_{pa} + N_{pd}. \qquad (14.7)$$

The number of stems is discrete. However, if the average number of stems per precursor is much greater than 1, n can be approximated as a continuous variable. Thus:

$$N_{pa} = \int_0^\infty \int_{n^*(T,l)}^\infty \rho(n,l) dn dl \qquad (14.8)$$

and

$$N_{pd} = \int_0^\infty \int_0^{n^*(T,l)} \rho(n,l) dn dl. \qquad (14.9)$$

The continuous approximation is used here. Roozemond et al. [150] calculated the critical number of stems for iPP, based on a crude estimate of the typical length of precursors in a quiescent melt, $l_0 = 10$ nm. They found $n^*(T, l_0) > 10$ at temperatures $T > 138°C$.

The material time derivative of the size distribution is

$$\dot{\rho}(n,l) \equiv \frac{\partial \rho}{\partial t} + \vec{\nabla} \cdot (\vec{v}\rho) = \dot{\rho}_c + \dot{\rho}_g + \dot{\rho}_n + \dot{\rho}_d. \qquad (14.10)$$

The first term on the right-hand side is the creation rate. The second term is the rate of change of the size distribution due to lateral and longitudinal growth,

$$\dot{\rho}_g = -\dot{n}(l)\frac{\partial \rho}{\partial n} - \dot{l}(n)\frac{\partial \rho}{\partial l}. \qquad (14.11)$$

The minus signs are due to the fact that the derivatives are taken in an Eulerian sense; an imaginary observer would be located at a fixed position $\{n,l\}$ in the space of precursor dimensions and see the distribution $\rho(n, l)$ flow past. The attachment and detachment of stems and the lengthening and shortening of stems, already incorporated in a precursor, are stochastic processes. Here, however, the time scales of fluctuations in n and l are not resolved. The deterministic growth rates $\dot{n}(l)$ and $\dot{l}(n)$ are ensemble averages over all precursors with the same length and over all precursors with the same number of stems, respectively, which may be provided by molecular-level simulations such as those discussed in Chapter 6. The lateral growth rate, which is determined by the change of the free energy due to the addition of a single stem, is assumed to be independent of n. This assumption seems reasonable except for very small n. (Suppose, for example, that stems are packed in a hexagonal fashion. Then the growth of the lateral interface, and hence the change of the free energy, upon attachment of a stem to a precursor of length l is the same for all $n \geq 2$.) Lengthening of the stems also increases the lateral interface. Since this increase depends on the radius of the precursor, the longitudinal growth rate is expected to depend on n. The lengthening process is assumed to be localized at the ends of the precursor, so it should be independent of l.

The third term on the right-hand side of Equation (14.10) is the nucleation rate,

$$\dot{\rho}_n = -\frac{\rho(n,l)}{\tau_{pn}} H(n - n^*(T,l)), \qquad (14.12)$$

where τ_{pn} is the characteristic time of nucleation. A linear dependence on ρ is chosen because the active precursors are widely separated in space [135, 148], and therefore all nucleation events should be independent. The Heaviside function H ensures that only active precursors nucleate. The last term in Equation (14.10) accounts for dissolution of precursors into the pure amorphous phase,

$$\dot{\rho}_d = -\frac{\rho(n,l)}{\tau_{pd}}, \qquad (14.13)$$

with the characteristic time of dissolution τ_{pd}.

The evolution of the number density of active precursors N_{pa} is obtained by taking the time derivative of Equation (14.8) while substituting Equation (14.10) to Equation (14.13). The lateral growth term in Equation (14.11) is integrated by parts over n,

$$-\int_{n^*(T,l)}^{\infty} \dot{n}(l) \frac{\partial \rho}{\partial n} dn = -\dot{n}(l)\rho(n,l)\big|_{n=n^*(T,l)}^{\infty}$$
$$+ \int_{n^*(T,l)}^{\infty} \frac{\partial \dot{n}}{\partial n} \rho(n,l) dn \qquad (14.14)$$
$$= \dot{n}(l)\rho(n^*(T,l),l),$$

and then integrated over l. Here we have made use of the fact that infinitely thick precursors have a vanishingly small probability, $\rho(n \to \infty, l) = 0$. The longitudinal growth term is first integrated over n and then integrated over l, using Leibniz's rule:

$$-\int_0^{\infty} \int_{n^*(T,l)}^{\infty} \dot{l}(n) \frac{\partial \rho}{\partial l} dn dl = -\int_0^{\infty} \frac{d}{dl}\int_{n^*(T,l)}^{\infty} \dot{l}(n)\rho(n,l) dn dl$$
$$- \int_0^{\infty} \dot{l}(n^*(T,l))\rho(n^*(T,l),l) \frac{\partial n^*}{\partial l} dl$$
$$= -\int_0^{\infty} \dot{l}(n^*(T,l))\rho(n^*(T,l),l) \frac{\partial n^*}{\partial l} dl.$$
$$(14.15)$$

The term involving a double integral over n and l vanishes after carrying out the integration over l because, first, infinitely long precursors have a vanishingly small probability, $\rho(n, l \to \infty) = 0$, and second, the critical number of stems goes to infinity as the precursor length goes to zero, $n^*(T, l \to 0) \to \infty$. It follows that

$$\dot{N}_{pa} = \int_0^{\infty}\int_{n^*(T,l)}^{\infty} \dot{\rho}_c(n,l) dn dl + \int_0^{\infty}\left(\dot{n}(l) - 2\dot{l}(n^*(T,l))\frac{\partial n^*}{\partial l}\right.$$
$$\left.- \dot{T}\frac{\partial n^*}{\partial T}\right)\rho(n^*(T,l),l) dl - \frac{N_{pa}}{\tau_{pn}} - \frac{N_{pa}}{\tau_{pd}}.$$
$$(14.16)$$

The first term on the right-hand side is the rate of creation of active precursors directly from the amorphous phase. The second term is the rate of change of N_{pa} due to activation of dormant precursors, which is caused by changes in the dimensions $\{n, l\}$ and/or the critical number of stems $n^*(T, l)$. The lateral growth contribution and one half of the longitudinal growth contribution follow from integrating Equation (14.11) with the help of Equation (14.14) and Equation (14.15). This part represents the activation of dormant precursors due to changes in their dimensions. The other half of the longitudinal growth contribution and the heating/cooling contribution appear as a result of the lower limit of the integral over n in Equation (14.8), when taking the time derivative according to Leibniz's rule. This part represents the activation of dormant precursors due to changes in the critical number of stems. The third term on the right-hand side of Equation (14.16) is the nucleation rate,

$$\dot{N}_n = \frac{N_{pa}}{\tau_{pn}}, \qquad (14.17)$$

and the fourth is the rate of dissolution of active precursors.

Equation (14.17) was proposed by Avrami [123] and others (see the references in Avrami's paper). They did not consider any processes by which the number density of precursors might change other than nucleation and being swallowed by already growing crystallites. The effect of swallowing can be incorporated by using N_n as input in an integral equation [122–125] or a set of differential equations [14, 119–121] for the evolution of the semicrystalline morphology. This is not discussed here since the focus is on nucleation kinetics in the early stage of crystallization. By definition, only active precursors can nucleate. Whether they will, or end up being swallowed, depends on how the morphology develops, that is, on the complex interplay of cooling and flow, which in general makes the nucleation and growth rates time dependent.

Eder and Janeschitz-Kriegl [3] and Zuidema et al. [19] initially included a dissolution term in the nucleation rate, but then set the associated time constant to infinity. They did this because otherwise the number of crystallites, in their case shish–kebabs, could diminish, which would be unrealistic. Melting (which does make crystallites disappear) was not modeled since it is generally not important in processing. In the coupled rate equations applied by these authors, the length, surface area, and volume of dissolved nuclei remain and continue to grow. Zheng and Kennedy [73] kept the dissolution time of nuclei finite, but set it to a very high value (10^6 s). The inconsistency of having nuclei contribute to crystallization after they disappear is naturally avoided in the present theoretical framework since only precursors can dissolve. Experiments show that the dissolution of FIPs is much slower than typical flow time scales in experimental and industrial conditions [54, 151, 152].

Taking the time derivative of Equation (14.9) and substituting Equation (14.10) to Equation (14.13) results in

$$\dot{N}_{pd} = \int_0^\infty \int_0^{n^*(T,l)} \dot{\rho}_c(n,l)dn dl - \int_0^\infty \left(\dot{n}(l) - 2\dot{l}(n^*(T,l)) \right) \frac{\partial n^*}{\partial l}$$
$$- \dot{T}\frac{\partial n^*}{\partial T} \right) \rho(n^*(T,l),l)dl - \frac{N_{pd}}{\tau_{pd}}.$$

(14.18)

The terms on the right-hand side represent creation, activation, and dissolution of dormant precursors, respectively. The sum of the activation terms in Equation (14.16) and Equation (14.18) is zero; transfer of precursors between the dormant and active states does not change the total number density N_p.

It is important to note that Equation (14.16), Equation (14.17), and Equation (14.18) do not constitute a closed set of equations; the evolution of the size distribution, Equation (14.10), still has to be calculated. For efficient simulations of flow-enhanced nucleation in polymer processing, closure of Equation (14.16), Equation (14.17), and Equation (14.18) is necessary. This is possible by introducing some assumptions. The mathematical structure of many existing flow-enhanced nucleation models, which do not contain all the details considered here, can be reproduced in this way, as shown in Sections 14.4.1.2–14.4.1.4. The influence of flow, for example on the rate of creation of precursors, is subsequently specified for a number of these models. A common assumption is that all FIPs are active, so that their size distribution need not be considered. Quiescent precursors are then treated as a separate species because it is known from experiments that they do have a distribution of sizes or, equivalently, of activation temperatures. This is discussed next.

14.4.1.1 Quiescent Nucleation Well below the nominal melting point, which is the temperature regime relevant for processing, the number density of spherulites in a quiescent melt is a unique function of the temperature [3]. This has been observed even in very pure melts, where the majority of nuclei are homogeneous, that is, made of the polymer itself rather than impurities [50, 153]. The number density versus temperature does not decrease in time, nor is it affected by annealing even above the equilibrium melting point. In our theoretical framework, this behavior is reproduced as follows:

- Precursors do not grow, $\dot{n} = \dot{l} = 0$. Consequently, each precursor becomes active at a fixed temperature T_a and the size distribution can be replaced by an activation temperature distribution $\rho^q(T_a)$.
- There is no sporadic creation process, $\dot{\rho}_c^q = 0$.
- Precursors do not dissolve, $\tau_{pd} \to \infty$, and therefore disappear due to nucleation only.

The number density of active quiescent precursors, whose activation temperatures are higher than the actual temperature, is

$$N_{pa}^q = \int_T^{T_m^o} \rho^q(T_a) dT_a.$$ (14.19)

Here T_m^o is the equilibrium melting temperature, at which the critical number of stems goes to infinity even for a precursor of infinite length. All precursors with activation temperatures below the actual temperature are dormant,

$$N_{pd}^q = \int_{T_g}^T \rho^q(T_a) dT_a,$$ (14.20)

where T_g is the glass transition temperature. The rate of change of the activation temperature distribution is

$$\dot{\rho}^q(T_a) = -\frac{\rho^q(T_a)}{\tau_{pn}} H(T_a - T)$$ (14.21)

and hence taking the time derivative of Equation (14.19),

$$\dot{N}_{pa}^q = -\dot{T}\rho^q(T) - \frac{N_{pa}^q}{\tau_{pn}},$$ (14.22)

and the time derivative of Equation (14.20),

$$\dot{N}_{pd}^q = \dot{T}\rho^q(T).$$ (14.23)

The total number density of quiescent precursors is the sum of the active and dormant ones, as in Equation (14.7).

The nucleation rate is

$$\dot{N}_n^q = \frac{N_{pa}^q}{\tau_{pn}}. \quad (14.24)$$

It is generally observed in isothermal quiescent experiments (after quenching the melt to the desired temperature) that all spherulites have the same diameter. When the measured diameter is extrapolated versus time, it is seen that all spherulites start growing immediately when the experimental temperature is reached. This suggests that $\tau_{pn} = 0$. Equation (14.22) and Equation (14.24) can then be combined and rewritten as

$$\dot{N}_n^q = -\dot{T}\rho^q(T). \quad (14.25)$$

In this case, all activated precursors immediately nucleate. Consequently, the activation temperature distribution becomes

$$\rho^q(T_a) = \rho^q(T_a)\big|_{t=0} H(\min(T_{\exp}) - T_a), \quad (14.26)$$

where $t = 0$ corresponds to the beginning of the experiment and $\min(T_{\exp})$ is the lowest temperature reached during the experiment up to the current time.

In a quiescent melt, the minimum temperature for sporadic creation of precursors (or equivalently, since $\tau_{pn} = 0$, sporadic nucleation) can be estimated based on thermodynamic arguments. For example, for iPP, Janeschitz-Kriegl [148] found that this minimum temperature is close to the nominal melting point (typically between 160°C and 165°C). Since crystallization is very slow in this regime, experiments and manufacturing processes are usually conducted at lower temperatures, where Equation (14.19) is accurate.

14.4.1.2 Simplified Descriptions Most existing continuum-level FIC models make use of the assumption that all FIPs are active, $n^* = 0$. The activation terms in Equation (14.16) and Equation (14.18) then vanish since $\rho^f(n = 0, l) = 0$: infinitely thin precursors are unstable. The superscript f indicates that the distribution contains FIPs only ($\rho^f = \rho - \rho^q$). The rate of change of the number density of FIPs can thus be written as

$$\dot{N}_p^f = I_p^f - \frac{N_p^f}{\tau_{pn}} - \frac{N_p^f}{\tau_{pd}}, \quad (14.27)$$

where

$$I_p^f = \int_0^\infty \int_0^\infty \dot{\rho}_c^f(n,l) dn dl \quad (14.28)$$

is related, usually in a phenomenological way, to the strain rate or some measure of the conformation of the (HMW) chains in the melt. Now the size distribution of FIPs need not be tracked during simulations. The total number density of precursors is

$$N_p = N_p^q + N_p^f. \quad (14.29)$$

The quiescent precursors do have a size distribution, or equivalently an activation temperature distribution, whose initial state can be obtained from quiescent crystallization experiments. The evolution of this distribution and the number density of quiescent precursors can be calculated as explained above.

The assumption that all FIPs are active naturally rules out the hypothesis of Janeschitz-Kriegl that the nucleation density increases as a result of an activation process accelerated by flow. Roozemond et al. [150] developed a model based on this hypothesis. They made the following assumptions:

- Quiescent precursors and FIPs are of the same species. Their initial size distribution is obtained from quiescent crystallization experiments. From these experiments, it is known that dissolution is negligible, $\tau_{pd} \to \infty$.
- There is no sporadic creation process, $\dot{\rho}_c = 0$.
- The number of stems of a precursor is constant, $\dot{n} = 0$.
- Flow increases the longitudinal growth rate $\dot{l}$ and thus enhances the activation of dormant precursors.
- All precursors have the same initial length l_0 and the same $\dot{l}$ (independent of the number of stems).

According to the last assumption, the size distribution has the form

$$\rho(n, l) = \tilde{\rho}(n)\delta(l - l_0 - \Delta l), \quad (14.30)$$

where

$$\Delta l = \int_0^t \dot{l}(t') dt' \quad (14.31)$$

is the increase in length of the precursors since the beginning of the experiment at $t = 0$. The distribution of the number of stems changes due to nucleation,

$$\dot{\tilde{\rho}} = -\frac{\tilde{\rho}(n)}{\tau_{pn}} H(n - n^*(T,l)). \quad (14.32)$$

Substituting Equation (14.30) in Equation (14.16) and applying the other assumptions yields

TABLE 14.1 Form of the Terms in Equation (14.27) for Different Flow-Enhanced Nucleation Models. Symbols Are Explained in the Text

Model	I_p^f	τ_{pn}	τ_{pd}	$\dot{L}$
Coppola et al. [142], Acierno et al. [159], Zheng and Kennedy [73]	$\propto \Delta G e^{-\Delta G^{-n}} - \Delta G^q e^{-\Delta (G^q)^{-n}}$	$=0$	(a)	(b)
Eder and co [3, 14]	$\propto \dot{\gamma}^2$	$=0$	(a)	$\propto \dot{\gamma}^2$
Zuidema et al. [19], Swartjes et al. [38]	$\propto J_2(\boldsymbol{B}_e^d)$	$=0$	(a)	$\propto J_2(\boldsymbol{B}_e^d)$
Koscher and Fulchiron [140]	$\propto N_1$	$=0$	(a)	(b)
Van Meerveld et al. [8]	$\propto J_2(\boldsymbol{A})$ (c)	$=0$	(a)	$\propto J_2(\boldsymbol{A})$ (c)
Custódio et al. [74]	$=g_p(\Lambda^4 - 1)$	$=0$		
Steenbakkers and Peters [135]	$g_p(\Lambda^4-1)$, g_p given by Equation (14.43)	$=\begin{cases}\infty & \dot{\gamma} \neq 0 \\ 0 & \dot{\gamma} = 0\end{cases}$	$\to \infty$	$\propto J_2(\boldsymbol{B}_{e,\text{avg}}^d)$
Graham and Olmsted [166, 167]	$\propto e^{\eta(\Lambda^2-1)}$ (d)	$=0$	(a)	(b)
Roozemond et al. [150]	Equation (14.35), $\dot{\iota} \propto \Lambda^4 - 1$	$=\begin{cases}\infty & \dot{\gamma} \neq 0 \\ 0 & \dot{\gamma} = 0\end{cases}$	$\to \infty$	(b)

(a) The dissolution time is arbitrary when nucleation is instantaneous.
(b) Shish formation was not modeled.
(c) Prefactor dependent on tr($\boldsymbol{A}$).
(d) From molecular-level simulations.

$$\dot{N}_{pa} = I_{pa} - \frac{N_{pa}}{\tau_{pn}} \qquad (14.33)$$

with

$$I_{pa} = \left(-2\dot{l} \left.\frac{\partial n^*}{\partial l}\right|_{l=l_0+\Delta l} - \dot{T} \left.\frac{\partial n^*}{\partial T}\right|_{l=l_0+\Delta l}\right) \tilde{\rho}(n^*(T, l_0 + \Delta l)). \qquad (14.34)$$

Roozemond et al. [150] related the longitudinal growth rate to the average stretch of the HMW chains. We define

$$I_p^f = -2\dot{l} \left.\frac{\partial n^*}{\partial l}\right|_{l=l_0+\Delta l} \tilde{\rho}(n^*(T, l_0 + \Delta l)) \qquad (14.35)$$

to facilitate comparison with models based on the hypothesis of enhanced sporadic creation of precursors. The remaining part of Equation (14.34) is analogous to the activation of dormant quiescent precursors in those models.

14.4.1.3 Models without a Flow-Induced Precursor Phase

Flow-enhanced nucleation is in most cases described by an expression of the form

$$\dot{N}_n^f = I_p^f, \qquad (14.36)$$

which can be obtained by taking the limit $\tau_{pn} \to 0$ of Equation (14.27). Physically, this means that all precursors are active and nucleate instantaneously. Table 14.1 lists I_p^f for a number of models with a flow-enhanced nucleation rate given by Equation (14.36), which are discussed next. Subsequently, some models that describe nucleation via a FIP phase are discussed. These are also included in Table 14.1.

Coppola et al. [142] modified the classical nucleation theory of Hoffman and Lauritzen by adding the flow-induced increase in the Gibbs free energy of the amorphous phase to the Gibbs free energy difference between the quiescent amorphous phase and the crystalline phase. This can be expressed as follows,

$$\Delta G = G_{\text{amorph}} - G_{\text{cryst}} = \Delta G^q + \Delta G^f, \qquad (14.37)$$

where

$$\Delta G^q = G_{\text{amorph}}^q - G_{\text{cryst}} \qquad (14.38)$$

is the Gibbs free energy difference between the phases in the quiescent state and

$$\Delta G^f = G_{\text{amorph}} - G_{\text{amorph}}^q \qquad (14.39)$$

is the contribution due to flow. According to the modified Hoffman–Lauritzen theory, the nucleation rate is an exponential function of ΔG, which cannot be written as the sum of a purely quiescent and a purely flow-induced contribution. In this respect it differs from most of the models discussed later.

Coppola et al. [142] calculated the dimensionless induction time, defined as the ratio of the quiescent nucleation rate over the total nucleation rate, as a function of the strain rate in continuous shear flow. They used ΔG^f according to different rheological models: the Doi–Edwards model with the independent alignment assumption, DE-IAA [143], the linear elastic dumbbell model [154], and the finitely extensible nonlinear elastic dumbbell model with Peterlin's closure approximation, FENE-P [155]. The Doi–Edwards results showed the best agreement with experimental dimensionless induction times, defined as the time at which the viscosity suddenly starts to increase rapidly, normalized by the time at which this happens in quiescent crystallization [156–158].

Acierno et al. [159] applied the modified Hoffman–Lauritzen theory to bidisperse melts, using the DE-IAA model with double reptation [160]. They found excellent agreement with experimental dimensionless induction times, again determined from the viscosity upturn, for bidisperse blends with a range of compositions. Zheng and Kennedy [73] used the modified Hoffman–Lauritzen theory in combination with the FENE-P model. An important difference with the work of the previously mentioned authors is that they made a coupling between rheological properties and the microstructure. The relaxation time of the semicrystalline phase, which was described by a rigid dumbbell model, and the viscosity of the two-phase material both increased as a function of the volume fraction of the semicrystalline phase. Zheng and Kennedy calculated this volume fraction and showed that the time when it reached 0.5 compared reasonably well with the half-crystallization time from DSC measurements by Koscher and Fulchiron [140].

Note that these FIC models have not been validated in terms of morphological features, such as the number density or size distribution of spherulites. One problem is that the classical nucleation theory predicts a sporadic nucleation rate even in quiescent melts, which is not observed experimentally. Zheng and Kennedy [73] calculated the flow-enhanced nucleation rate as $I_p^f = I_p(\Delta G) - I_p(\Delta G^q)$. The last term in this equation is the quiescent sporadic nucleation rate, which is predicted by the modified Hoffman–Lauritzen theory. However, for the quiescent nuclei, Zheng and Kennedy used an activation temperature distribution $\rho^q(T_a)$ whose initial state was determined experimentally, and which changed only due to nucleation; see Equation (14.21). A self-consistent approach to their model would be to include $I_p(\Delta G^q)$ in the quiescent nucleation rate. It can then be checked if this is indeed negligible compared with the athermal part.

A parameter known to influence flow-enhanced nucleation is the strain rate. It is customary to define an effective "shear" rate in terms of the deformation rate tensor D,

$$\dot{\gamma} = \sqrt{2\boldsymbol{D}:\boldsymbol{D}}. \quad (14.40)$$

This definition can be used in all types of flow and produces the actual shear rate in pure shearing flows. Eder and coworkers found that the product $\dot{\gamma}^4 t_s^2$ where t_s denotes the shear time, was approximately constant at the boundary between the fine-grained layer and the oriented skin layer, observed in samples crystallized after pressure-driven flow through a rectangular slit. They devised a model in which the creation rate I_p^f and the growth rate of point-like nuclei into shish are both proportional to the square of the shear rate. This leads to a total length of shish per unit volume $L_{tot} \propto \dot{\gamma}^4 t_s^2$. However, since the shear rate varies linearly across the height of the slit y, the model actually predicts a gradual increase $L_{tot} \propto y^4$ instead of the sharp boundary observed experimentally (also by many other research groups) at a specific y, that is, at a specific shear rate or strain. Kornfield and coworkers [17, 18, 48, 145] suggested that the sudden onset of oriented structure formation is the result of a critical stress to initiate the longitudinal growth of point-like precursors into shish. Custódio et al. [74] accurately characterized this transition based on critical morphological features (see the discussion at the end of this chapter of their IM simulations).

Eder and coworkers also observed that $\dot{\gamma}^2 t_s$ was approximately constant at the transition from the spherulitic core to the fine-grained layer. If this layer is the result of flow-enhanced point-like nucleation, then the (again sharp) transition is not explained by their model with $\dot{N}_n^f \propto \dot{\gamma}^2$, which leads to a number density of nuclei $N_n \propto y^2$.

Zuidema et al. [19] adopted the structure of the FIC model of Eder and coworkers, but replaced the square of the shear rate (in the expressions for I_p^f and the longitudinal growth rate of shish) by the second invariant (J_2) of the deviatoric elastic Finger tensor,

$$\boldsymbol{B}_e^d = \boldsymbol{B}_e - \frac{1}{3} tr(\boldsymbol{B}_e)\boldsymbol{I}, \quad (14.41)$$

corresponding to the slowest mode in a multimode Leonov model. Later, Swartjes et al. [38] used the extended Pompom (XPP) model in the same FIC framework. Thus, these authors made a connection between the nucleation kinetics and the average molecular deformation, instead of just the macroscopic flow, and their approach is readily applicable to different materials and temperatures, contrary to that of Eder and coworkers. Zuidema et al. found that, for the slowest relaxation mode only, the calculated number densities of shish at the boundaries between the morphological layers were independent of the shear rate. This agrees with the now widespread belief that the longest chains in a melt dominate flow-enhanced nucleation, and suggests that a critical amount of threadlike nuclei is required for an observable shish–kebab morphology in the final, fully crystallized state.

An essential part of the work of Peters and coworkers [19, 38, 72, 74, 133] is that the relaxation time of the slowest mode increases linearly with the number density of flow-induced nuclei. Their explanation is that these nuclei act as physical crosslinks, or branch points, on the long molecules. As a result of the slower relaxation of these molecules, the probability of creating new nuclei is locally increased. Based on this hypothesis, one would expect to see nuclei appear in clusters, which is not found experimentally. Steenbakkers and Peters discussed this issue in some detail [135]. The evidence of clusters might be destroyed because they are torn apart by the flow. An alternative explanation is that the increase of the longest relaxation time is the fingerprint of a network of connected dormant and active precursors, rather than local crosslinking. Such a network will stiffen as the number density of FIPs increases. Quiescent cold crystallization experiments, where the temperature is increased from the glassy state, may reveal whether the total number density of precursors (most of which are dormant when crystallizing from the melt) is high enough for them to form a network.

From a phenomenological point of view, the dependence of the relaxation dynamics on the number density of nuclei turned out to be necessary (in this kind of model) to capture the strong effect of flow. It was validated with a large number of different short-term and continuous experiments from the Janeschitz-Kriegl group. Parameters were determined using only one of these experiments, while the results for all the other experiments, namely the position of the transition between the oriented and the fine-grained layer, were predicted [19].

Koscher and Fulchiron [140] assumed I_p^f to be proportional to the first normal stress difference N_1, which they calculated with an upper-convected Maxwell model. Although a larger HMW tail leads to longer time scales in the relaxation spectrum, and therefore enhances the development of the first normal stress difference, this approach does not emphasize the importance of the longest molecules as much as when the nucleation rate is related to the conformation of the slowest relaxation mode only. Furthermore, Koscher and Fulchiron did not make any of the relaxation times dependent on the number density of nuclei. Their reason was that, in the experiments considered in their work, flow took place in the early stage of crystallization without any significant crystallinity. However, according to the physical crosslinking hypothesis, it is not the degree of crystallinity or the semicrystalline volume fraction that slows down the relaxation dynamics, but the connectivity of chains involved in FIPs.

Van Meerveld et al. [8] developed an FIC model consistent with the nonequilibrium thermodynamics framework GENERIC [161, 162, 163]. They used a modified Giesekus model for the conformation of the amorphous part of a crystallizing chain, with a nonlinear spring constant dependent on the crystallized fraction, similar to earlier work by Doufas et al. [95, 110–112]. The nucleation rate and the longitudinal growth rate of shish were both taken proportional to the second invariant of the conformation tensor A of the amorphous part (see Table 14.1). This was inspired by the work of Zuidema et al. [19], but as the authors pointed out, it is also supported by the experimental observation of Mahendrasingam et al. [164] that the crystallization dynamics of PET scale with the fourth power of the Hermans orientation factor.

14.4.1.4 Models with a Flow-Induced Precursor Phase Few FIC models distinguish between precursors and nuclei. One of these was developed by Steenbakkers and Peters [135], based on the hypothesis that flow accelerates the sporadic creation of precursors. These authors found that the increase of the number density of spherulites, after short-term shear flows with different rates and durations, was captured very well by a dependence of I_p^f on the stretch Λ of the HMW fraction of the melt, calculated by the Rolie-Poly model [165]. A power law with exponent 4 was found, as shown in Table 14.1. This is a refinement of the work of Zuidema et al. [19], where I_p^f depended on the second invariant of the deviatoric part of the elastic Finger tensor B_e. Both are related according to

$$J_2(B_e^d) = 9\Lambda^4 J_2(S^d) \tag{14.42}$$

and, for the experiments considered by Steenbakkers and Peters, it turned out that the orientation invariant $J_2(S^d)$ varied only slightly among experiments, because in all cases the steady-state orientation was reached quickly relative to the shear time. As yet unpublished results from the same group, where the shear times were in the transient startup regime of the orientation invariant, showed a *decrease* of the final number density of spherulites with increasing shear rate when the orientation-based creation model $I_p^f \propto J_2(\mathbf{S}^d)$ was used. This is in contradiction with experiments, and hence Steenbakkers and Peters' model strongly suggests that stretch is what drives the creation of FIPs, not orientation.

Graham and Olmsted [166, 167] used coarse-grained kinetic Monte Carlo simulations to simulate anisotropic nucleation based on the chain configurations obtained from a molecular flow model, the Graham–Likhtman and Milner–McLeish (GLaMM) model [168, 169]. These simulations confirm the power law with exponent 4 up to reasonably high shear rates (molecular stretch up to 3 to 4). They actually found an exponential dependence on the square of the molecular stretch. A practical problem of such an expression is that it contains an extra parameter: besides the prefactor for the stretch, there is a prefactor for the exponential function as a whole, which gives the quiescent sporadic creation rate. Since quiescent nucleation is predominantly athermal, this parameter cannot be determined for common melts.

The results of Steenbakkers and Peters [135] critically depend on a few assumptions, based on experimental observations. First of all, Baert et al. [27] and Housmans et al. [56] reported a saturation in the number density of spherulites with increasing shear rate (for a constant strain) and increasing duration of flow (for a constant shear rate), respectively. Therefore, the prefactor of the stretch-dependent term $\Lambda^4 - 1$ in the creation rate I_p^f is written as

$$g_p = \left(1 - \frac{N_p^f + N_n^f}{N_{\max}^f}\right) g_{0p}. \qquad (14.43)$$

Here g_{0p} is a parameter that scales with temperature according to the rheological shift factor $a_T(T, T_{\text{ref}})$.

A general observation is that all spherulites become visible at approximately the same time (within a few seconds after the cessation of flow) and that their diameters are nearly equal. A possible explanation is that flow interferes with the ability of chains to be arranged in folded-chain lamellae. Consequently, during the flow, FIPs are created but are not easily nucleated. This agrees with the experimental results of Blundell et al. [164, 170], which showed that, for strain rates higher than the inverse of the stretch relaxation time, crystallization did not start until after the cessation of flow. Therefore, Steenbakkers and Peters (whose experiments were indeed in the chain stretching regime) implemented a step function to model the effect of flow on the nucleation process, as shown in Table 14.1.

Finally, they adopted the physical crosslinking hypothesis of Zuidema et al. [19], but made the relaxation times of the slowest mode linearly dependent on the number density of FIPs N_p^f rather than the number density of flow-induced nuclei N_n^f. In combination with the strain rate dependence of τ_{pn} shown in Table 14.1, this results in a strong increase of the precursor number density that mainly takes place during flow, followed by instantaneous nucleation after flow, so that the spherulites end up having nearly the same size, in agreement with experiments.

The flow-enhanced nucleation model of Roozemond et al. [150] is described in Equation (14.30), Equation (14.31), Equation (14.32), Equation (14.33), Equation (14.34), and Equation (14.35). Of all the models listed in Table 14.1, it is the only one based on Janeschitz-Kriegl's hypothesis that FIPs originate from the flow-enhanced activation of dormant precursors, which are already present in the quiescent melt. The factor 2 in I_p^f is absent in the work of Roozemond et al. However, this error is absorbed by the prefactor of the stretch-dependent longitudinal growth rate, which is the single adjustable parameter of their model. Number densities of spherulites from short-term shear experiments were reproduced quantitatively by this model as well as that of Steenbakkers and Peters [135]. Roozemond et al. followed these authors' suggestion that the characteristic nucleation time is practically infinite during short-term shear experiments and falls back to zero when the flow is switched off. However, they did not need to assume any slowing down of the (HMW) relaxation dynamics. This would even have been hard to defend since the total number of precursors (dormant and active) does not change other than through nucleation. Finally, the experimentally observed saturation of the nucleation density came out of their model instead of being built in.

14.4.2 Flow-Induced Shish Formation

The mechanism by which shish are formed out of point-like FIPs is still not fully understood. Nevertheless, a few experimental observations can guide the modeling of shish formation. Kornfield and coworkers observed that the transition to oriented crystallization occurs very abruptly when a critical stress is surpassed [17, 18, 145] and that long chains lower this critical stress [48]. Kimata et al. [88] concluded from neutron scattering experiments that, although shish formation is accelerated by long chains, the shish structure does not have a higher content of these chains than the rest of the melt.

The critical stress may be related to a critical stretch or orientation of the HMW chains to initiate the growth of a point-like FIP into a shish. The growth process itself is driven by the conformations of chains at the ends of the shish, which are random members of the MWD. Custódio et al. [74] therefore expressed the growth rate as

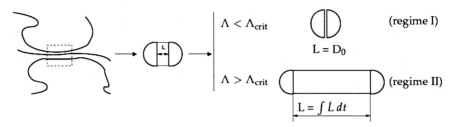

Figure 14.11 Model for the growth of nuclei.

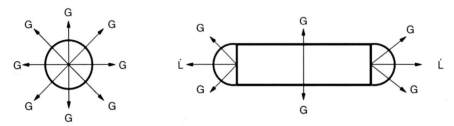

Figure 14.12 Growth of isotropic and oriented crystalline structures. Reprinted from Custódio et al. [74].

$$\dot{L} = \begin{cases} 0 & \Lambda \leq \Lambda_{\text{crit}} \\ g_L J_2(\boldsymbol{B}^d_{e,\text{avg}}) & \Lambda > \Lambda_{\text{crit}} \end{cases} \quad (14.44)$$

in terms of the deviatoric elastic Finger tensor of an "average" mode with reptation time

$$\tau_{d,\text{avg}} = \frac{\sum_i G_i \tau_i^2}{\sum_i G_i \tau_i}, \quad (14.45)$$

and Rouse time $\tau_{R,\text{avg}} = \tau_{d,\text{avg}} M_e/(3 M_w)$. They applied the Rolie-Poly model to this mode as well as the slowest mode in the relaxation spectrum, which was used in a flow-enhanced nucleation model similar to that of Steenbakkers and Peters [135], but with instantaneous nucleation of FIPs even during flow. Some of the FIC models in Table 14.1 also include descriptions of shish growth. These models, which have been discussed in the previous section, do not specify a criterion for initiation of shish growth, and they relate the growth rate either to the macroscopic flow or to the conformation of the HMW chains.

The model of Custódio et al. [74] describes every crystallite as a cylinder with a hemispherical cap at each end. The length of the cylindrical part then determines whether the crystallite will look more like a spherulite or more like a shish–kebab. In Figure 14.11, this concept for the morphological development is illustrated. The growth mechanisms for isotropic (spherulites) and oriented (shish–kebab) crystalline structures are illustrated in Figure 14.12. The cylinder grows in length with the rate $\dot{L}$ given by Equation (14.44). The cylinder and the caps both grow in the radial direction with the lamellar growth rate G.

The parameter g_L is made temperature dependent according to the rheological relaxation time shift factor a_T.

From the undisturbed nucleation rate it is possible to calculate the undisturbed sum of radii, total surface area, and volume of the caps per unit volume, by applying the Schneider rate equations [3, 119]. With the shish growth rate, the undisturbed total length, surface area, and volume of the cylinders per unit volume can be calculated from the Eder rate equations [3, 15]. A correction for swallowing of nuclei by growing crystallites and impingement of these crystallites is made to calculate the real volume fraction of semicrystalline material [122–125]. The undisturbed volume fractions of the caps and cylinders are added up in this correction,

$$\varphi = 1 - e^{-V}, \quad (14.46)$$

where φ is the real volume fraction of capped cylinders and $V = V_{\text{sph}} + V_{\text{cyl}}$ is their undisturbed volume (V_{sph} and V_{cyl} referring to the hemispherical caps and the cylinders, respectively).

The real number of flow-induced nuclei per unit volume N_{real}^f and the real total shish length per unit volume $L_{\text{tot,real}}$ can be found directly with the following expressions:

$$\dot{N}_{\text{real}}^f = \delta g_n \left(1 - \frac{N_n^f}{N_{\text{max}}^f}\right)(\Lambda^4 - 1)(1-\varphi) \quad (14.47)$$

and

$$\dot{L}_{\text{tot,real}} = N_{\text{real}}^f g_L J_2\left(B_{e,\text{avg}}^d\right)(1-\varphi). \quad (14.48)$$

Custódio et al. [74] added the parameter δ to circumvent numerical problems. They did not adopt the dependence of the characteristic nucleation time on the strain rate from Steenbakkers and Peters [135] (see Table 14.1), but instead they took $\tau_{pn} = 0$ under all conditions. The reptation and Rouse times of the HMW fraction were made linearly dependent on the number density of flow-induced nuclei. The parameter δ was set to one for all nonzero strain rates and to zero when the strain rate was zero. Thus, no more nuclei are created after the flow stops, mimicking the model of Steenbakkers and Peters.

Finally, a few important features of the model are stressed:

- The classification scheme as proposed by van Meerveld et al. [59] is implicitly incorporated by the characteristic times in the rheological model.
- The structure of the model gives a clear view where different physical phenomena are described and what the relation is with the rheological behavior. Thus, it is easy to adapt to new physical findings.

14.4.3 Application to Injection Molding

Several groups developed numerical models for the simulation of the IM process. Early works modeled the effect of temperature on the crystallization rate only and included the crystallization heat in the energy equation (see for example Hieber [171]). The effect of shear was taken into account by, for example a modified Nakamura equation where the kinetic parameters were made (shear) stress dependent [22, 76, 77, 116, 172].

Pantani et al. [11] gave an extensive review on available models to predict and characterize the morphology of injection-molded parts. The authors themselves proposed a model to predict the morphology of injection-molded iPP, in which flow kinematics are computed using a lubrication approximation. Polymorphism was accounted for, using the Avrami–Evans–Nakamura equation to describe the crystallization kinetics of the mesomorphic phase, while the evolution of the α phase was modeled using Kolmogorov's model [122].

Isayev and coworkers published a series of papers [75, 76] in which they built up an increasingly advanced model for FIC in IM. Using special extrusion experiments, they parameterized the crystallization model they applied [13] and verified the numerical results by comparing with the thickness of the highly oriented skin layer in injection molded bars. The crystallization model, describing enhanced point nucleation as a function of the shear rate, also allows for relaxation of the generated nuclei. Parameters were taken to be temperature dependent. Process simulations were based on viscous flow simulations; both the filling and packing stage (compressibility) were considered. In a modified model Isayev et al. introduced a molecular deformation factor, mimicking the nonlinear viscoelastic behavior of the polymer that shortened the induction time [173]. Depending on the history of this deformation factor, different types of crystalline structures (highly oriented crystallites, deformed spherulites, or undeformed spherulites) can be generated that will dominate at a specific location in a product. Processing parameters such as injection speed, melt, and wall temperature, and the average molecular weight were shown to have a large influence on the formation of the highly oriented skin layer. The molecular deformation factor was replaced by a multimode Leonov model from which the entropy reduction of the oriented melt was obtained [172]. This entropy reduction leads to an elevated equilibrium melting temperature, included in a modified Nakamura equation, which determines the occurrence of FIC.

A model that predicts in more detail the spatial distribution of different crystalline structures in semicrystalline products was proposed by Zuidema et al. [19]. Zheng and Kennedy [73] followed a similar approach to that taken by Coppola et al. [142] by using the flow-induced free energy change of the amorphous melt, calculated from a FENE-elastic dumbbell model, to modify the nucleation rate expression from Ziabicki [7]. The total stress was taken as the sum of the amorphous phase and the semicrystalline phase contribution. The semicrystalline phase contribution to the stress was described by a rigid dumbbell model, similar to Doufas et al. [117], in which the characteristic time and the modulus were made functions of the relative crystallinity. A special part of their model is the orientation (from the rigid dumbbell model) dependency of the way crystal structures grow; no orientation leads to spherulitic growth while for oriented structures the growth changes toward fibrillar.

Smirnova et al. [174] used a differential set of Avrami equations to predict crystallinity and the average size of spherulites in IM, but in their study only temperature effects were taken into account.

Most of these numerical models give little insight into the morphology developed, failing to provide information about the shape and dimensions of oriented crystalline structures; they lack molecular understanding, and they do not couple FIC with melt rheology.

Moreover, some do not discriminate between nonoriented and oriented crystals, assuming similar growth mechanisms, which is in clear contradiction with experimental evidence that shows the growth kinetics of a spherulite to be profoundly different from that of a shish.

Recently, Custódio et al. [74] used a more detailed FIC model, summarized in the previous section, to simulate a range of well-defined IM experiments on an iPP resin, performed by Housmans et al. [25, 41]. The model was implemented in a finite-element IM code in which the computed flow kinematics were used, in a decoupled fashion, to solve the coupled viscoelastic stress–crystallization problem. A comparison was made between the morphological predictions in terms of number, size, and shape of crystalline structures and polarized optical light microscopy results for two different sets of experiments. Four different isothermal slit flow experiments (6×1.5 mm^2) using an MPR—see Table 14.2 for the flow conditions—and three well-controlled moldings of a rectangular bar ($2 \times 12 \times 135$ mm^3) using a CA, differing in filling time—see Table 14.3—were performed. For the filling experiments the injection and mold temperature were set to 220°C and 80°C, respectively. In all the experiments the same fully characterized iPP was used (HD120MO, Borealis).

Figure 14.13 shows the micrographs and the computed total shish length per unit volume $L_{tot,real}$, the total number density of flow-induced nuclei N_{real}^f and the local average shish length, $\langle L \rangle = L_{tot,real}/N_{real}^f$, across the slit for the four MPR experiments. The values predicted for condition MPR1, one of the two experiments with a clear oriented skin layer, at the transitions between the oriented and fine-grained layer and between the fine-grained and spherulitic core layers (filled circles), were tested if they could be used as critical values ($L_{tot,crit}$, $\langle L \rangle_{crit}$, and $N_{f,ori}$ at the transition of the oriented shear layer and $N_{f,fg}$ at the transition of the fine-grained layer to the spherulitic core) that have to be surpassed for the layers to become visible (open circles).

The computed $L_{tot,real}$ and $\langle L \rangle$ for conditions MPR1 and MPR2 lie within the FIC region (did not cross the fine-grained layer to the spherulitical core), implying that the critical stretch Λ_{crit} was reached only within this region.

When applicable (there is no oriented shear layer for the MPR3 and MPR4 conditions) the critical values from MPR1 agree reasonably well with the predictions for the other experiments (open circles). The criterion based on total shish length, $L_{tot,real}$, seems to give the best agreement. The predicted number of flow-induced nuclei at the fine-grained/spherulitic transition is relatively high for MPR3 and MPR4. Predicted MPR1 values for the fine-grained to oriented transition are given as a reference at the wall when no oriented layer has developed, that is, for MPR3 and MPR4. Such results are clearly important since they imply that a critical, total, or average shish length required for an observable oriented shear layer was not reached.

A more obvious measure for visibility of the oriented layer in particular seems to be the relative total volume, $V_{ori} = V_{cyl}/(V_{sph} + V_{cyl})$, of oriented material. Results are presented in Figure 14.14. The value of V_{ori} computed at the transition from the oriented shear layer to the fine-grained layer in conditions MPR1 and MPR2 is almost the same ≈ 0.025. For flow conditions MPR3 and MPR4, across the sample thickness, V_{ori} is smaller than the critical value $V_{ori,crit}$ defined from flow condition MPR1. This is in agreement with the experimental results that no visible oriented shear layer developed under flow conditions MPR3 and MPR4.

Notice that this analysis is based on a coarse characterization by means of optical light microscopy and thus can give qualitative agreement only. A critical shish length on the order of 1 mm seems rather high, indicating that the model parameters need a further calibration based on better resolved experimental results [43, 55].

The results for the nonisothermal experiments were analyzed in the same way as the MPR results. The micrograph (Fig. 14.15) shows layers different from the MPR results: a thin *skin* layer, a *transition* layer, a *sheared* oriented layer, and the isotropic core. The skin layer originates from the deposition of stretched material in the flow front (fountain flow) that is subsequently quenched at the walls.

The predicted values at the transitions for the MPR1 condition are shown as open circles. The values for $L_{tot,real}$ computed at the transition of the oriented layer are of the same order as the $L_{tot,crit}$ value from MPR1

TABLE 14.2 Flow Conditions for the MPR Experiments

Conditions	t_{flow} (second)	v_{avg} (m/s)	T_{flow} (°C)
MPR1	0.1875	0.2	165
MPR2	0.375	0.1	145
MPR3	0.375	0.1	165
MPR4	3.0	0.0125	145

TABLE 14.3 Flow Conditions for the Injection Molding Experiments

Conditions	v_{avg} (m/s)	t_{flow} (second)
CA1	0.126	2
CA2	0.0662	4
CA3	0.03758	8

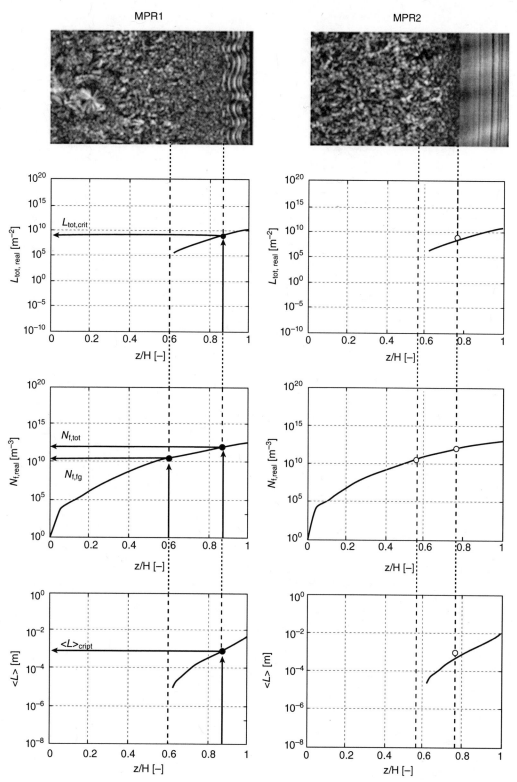

Figure 14.13 Distribution across half of the normalized slit thickness of the total shish length $L_{tot,real}$, the number of flow-induced nuclei per unit volume $N_{f,real}$, and the average shish length $<L>$ for all MPR flow conditions [74].

424 FLOW-INDUCED CRYSTALLIZATION

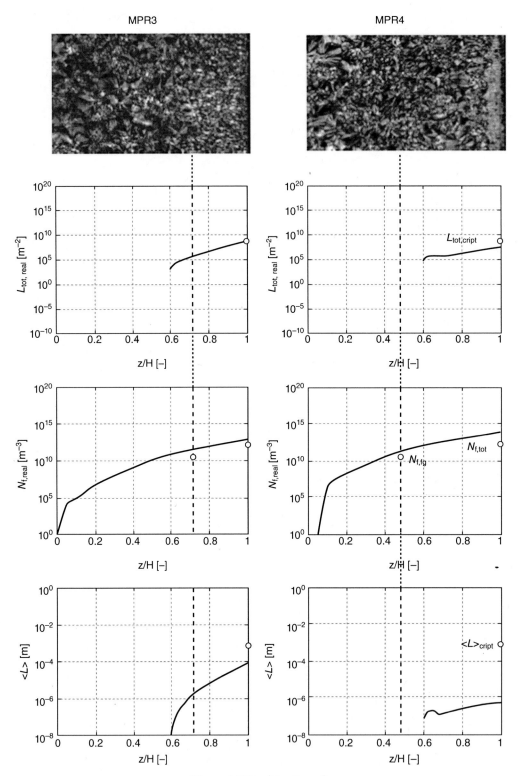

Figure 14.13 (*Continued*)

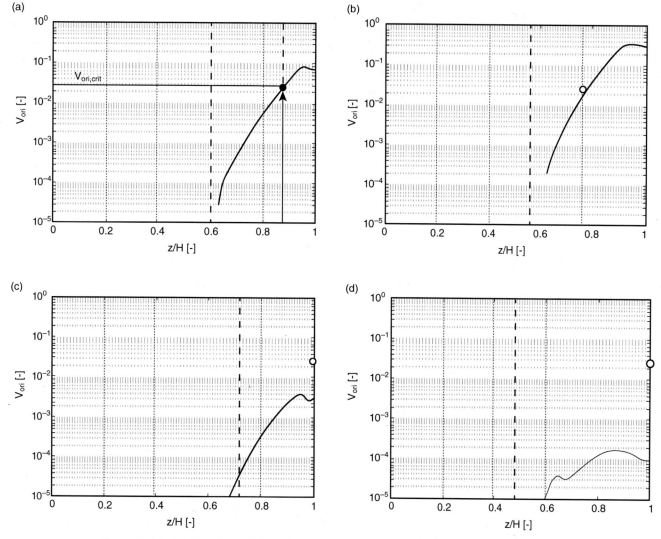

Figure 14.14 Distribution of the relative volume of oriented material across half of the normalized slit thickness: flow condition (a) MPR1, (b) MPR2, (c) MPR3, (d) MPR4 [74].

while, on the other hand, the predicted values for $<L>$ and $N_{f,ori}$ both differ by two to three orders of magnitude from the critical values $<L>_{crit}$ and $N_{f,ori}$. Although the predicted values at the transition positions are the same for all three quantities for these three experiments with completely different filling conditions, they seem not to be the right candidates to predict these transitions. When the volume fraction of oriented crystals is used, results become much better (see Fig. 14.16). Using the critical value $V_{ori,crit}$ from the MPR1 condition (open circles), an excellent agreement is found with the predicted values at the transition position, at least for conditions CA2 and CA3, indicating that a criterion based on the relative volume of oriented crystals is a good predictor for this transition, both for quasi-isothermal (MPR) and nonisothermal (CA) conditions. Due to start-up effects, which become more noticeable at high piston speeds (short flow times), the calculated average velocity in the slit for condition CA1 (see Table 14.3) is overestimated. This could explain the lower predicted thickness of the shear oriented layer for this condition (due to more heat convection and viscous heating).

It is interesting that the model captures the transition between the skin and shear layers quite well. For all the conditions, almost everywhere in this region the critical stretch Λ_{crit} was not reached and no shish–kebabs are thus predicted. This means that the coupling between the fast cooling close to the wall and the transient viscoelastic behavior is captured quite well.

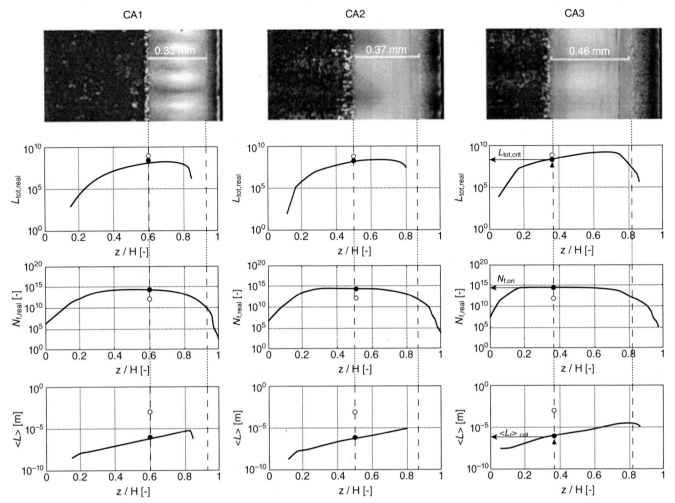

Figure 14.15 Distribution across half of the normalized slit thickness of the total shish length $L_{\text{tot,real}}$, the number of flow-induced nuclei per unit volume $N_{\text{f,real}}$, and the average shish length $\langle L \rangle$ for all three CA flow conditions [74].

Of course, these results need more detailed experimental validation on different length scales. However, they show the potential of the presented approach and give a clear pathway for future work.

14.5 CONCLUDING REMARKS

Most of the basic principles of FIC are reasonably well understood. The effects of a specific thermomechanical history can be anticipated, but quantification of these effects in terms of structural and morphological information, most desirable in terms of a (numerical) model, is often lacking.

There is a need for models that capture the most important phenomena, that is, those that determine the final product properties, and are applicable to realistic processing problems. This requires that these models are parameterized and validated for real (very often extreme) processing conditions. This includes high deformation rates, high cooling rates, and substantial pressure levels, and, important when considering real processing, combinations of these conditions. The required experimental techniques have to be made simple enough to make such an approach acceptable and successful.

Moreover, such models should contain molecular parameters in order to get indications for material modification that lead to desirable behavior. Molecular models can provide detailed physical understanding that will help to implement such molecular modifications aiming at improving or creating specific properties, and give directions on how to formulate (parts of) continuum models.

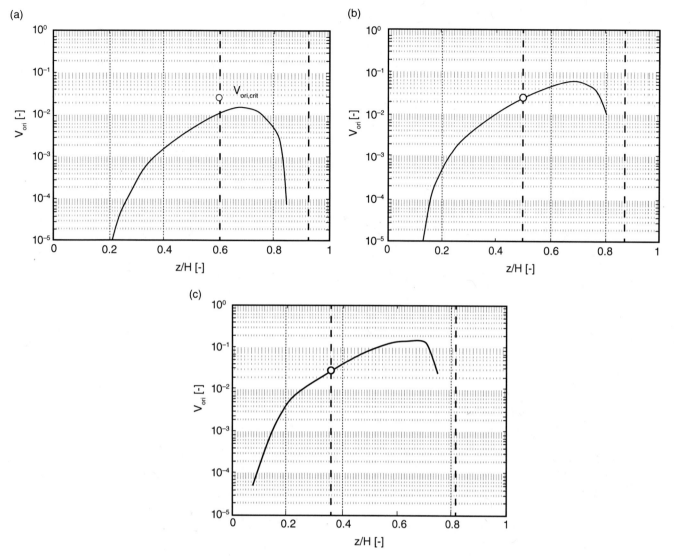

Figure 14.16 Distribution across half of the normalized slit thickness of the relative volume of oriented material for flow condition (a) CA1, (b) CA2, (c) CA3 [74].

REFERENCES

[1] Schultz, J.M. *Polymer Crystallization. The Development of Crystalline Order in Thermoplastic Polymers*, Oxford University Press, Oxford, 2001.

[2] Keller, A., Kolnaar, H.W.H. Flow induced orientation and structure formation. In *Materials Science and Technology: Processing of Polymers*, Vol. 18, Meijer, H.E.H., ed. VCH, New York, 1997.

[3] Eder, G.H., Janeschitz-Kriegl, H. Structure development during processing: Crystallization. In *Materials Science and Technology*, Vol. 18, Meijer, H.E.H., ed. Wiley–VCH, Weinheim, 1997, pp. 269–342.

[4] Janeschitz-Kriegl, H. *Crystallization Modalities in Polymer Melt Processing: Fundamental Aspects of Structure Formation*, Springer, New York, 2009.

[5] Ziabicki, A. *Colloid Polym. Sci.* **1996**, *274*, 209–217.

[6] Denn, M.M. Fibre spinning. In *Computational Analysis in Polymer Processing*, Pearson, J.R.A., Richardson, S.M., eds. Applied Science Publishers, London, 1983, pp. 176–216.

[7] Ziabicki, A., Kawai, H. *High-Speed Fiber Spinning. Science and Engineering Aspects*, John Wiley & Sons, London, 1985.

[8] van Meerveld, J., Hütter, M., Peters, G.W.M. *J. Non-Newton. Fluid Mech.* **2008**, *150*(2–3), 177–195.

[9] Somani, R.H., Yang, L., Zhu, L., Hsiao, B.S. *Polymer* **2005**, *46*(20), 8587–8623.

[10] Kumaraswamy, G. *J. Macromol. Sci. C Polym. Rev.* **2005**, *45*, 375–397.

[11] Pantani, R., Coccorullo, I., Speranza, V., Titomanlio, G. *Prog. Polym. Sci.* **2005**, *30*(12), 1185–1222.

[12] Baert, J., van Puyvelde, P. *Macromol. Mater. Eng.* **2008**, *293*, 255–273.

[13] Eder, G.H., Janeschitz-Kriegl, H., Liedauer, S. *Prog. Polym. Sci.* **1990**, *15*(4), 626–714.

[14] Liedauer, S., Eder, G., Janeschitz-Kriegl, H., Jerschow, P., Geymayer, W., Ingolic, E. *Int. Polym. Process.* **1993**, *8*(3), 236–244.

[15] Liedauer, S., Eder, G., Janeschitz-Kriegl, H. *Int. Polym. Process.* **1995**, *10*(3), 243–250.

[16] Kumaraswamy, G., Verma, R.K., Kornfield, J.A. *Rev. Sci. Instrum.* **1999**, *70*(4), 2097–2104.

[17] Kumaraswamy, G., Issaian, A.M., Kornfield, J.A. *Macromolecules* **1999**, *32*, 7537–7547.

[18] Kumaraswamy, G., Verma, R.K., Issaian, A.M., Wang, P., Kornfield, J.A., Yeh, F., Hsiao, B.S., Olley, R.H. *Polymer* **2000**, *41*, 8931–8940.

[19] Zuidema, H., Peters, G.W.M., Meijer, H.E.H. *Macromol. Theory Simul.* **2001**, *10*(5), 447–460.

[20] Tanner, R.I. *J. Non-Newton. Fluid Mech.* **2002**, *102*, 397–408.

[21] Steenbakkers, R.J.A., Peters, G.W.M. *Rheol. Acta* **2008**, *47*, 643–665.

[22] Lamberti, G., Peters, G.W.M., Titomanlio, G. *Int. Polym. Process.* **2007**, *22*(3), 303–310.

[23] Roozemond, P.C., Janssens, V., van Puyvelde, P., Peters, G.W.M. *Rheol. Acta* **2012**, *51*(2), 97–109.

[24] Scelsi, L., Mackley, M.R. *Rheol. Acta* **2008**, *47*, 895–908.

[25] Housmans, J.W., Balzano, L., Santoro, D., Peters, G.W.M., Meijer, H.E.H. *Int. Polym. Process.* **2009**, *24*(2), 185–197.

[26] Balzano, L., Cavallo, D., van Erp, T.B., Ma, Z., Housmans, J.W., Fernandez-Ballester, L., Peters, G.W.M. *IOP Conf. Ser: Mater. Sci. Eng.* **2010**, *14*, 012005.

[27] Baert, J., Langouche, F., van Puyvelde, P. *Macromolecules* **2006**, *39*, 9215–9222.

[28] Mykhaylyk, O.O., Chambon, P., Graham, R.S., Fairclough, P.J.A., Olmsted, P.D., Ryan, A.J. *Macromolecules* **2008**, *41*(6), 1901–1904.

[29] Yang, L., Somani, R.H., Sics, I., Hsiao, B.S., Kolb, R., Lohse, D. *J. Phys. Condens. Matter* **2006**, *18*, 2421–2436.

[30] Monasse, B. *J. Mater. Sci.* **1992**, *27*, 6047–6052.

[31] Tribout, C., Monasse, B., Haudin, J.M. *Colloid Polym. Sci.* **1996**, *274*, 197–208.

[32] Varga, J., Karger-Kocsis, J. *J. Polym. Sci. B Polym. Phys.* **1996**, *34*, 657–670.

[33] Jay, F., Haudin, J.M., Monasse, B. *J. Mater. Sci.* **1999**, *34*, 2089–2102.

[34] Duplay, C., Monasse, B., Haudin, J.M., Costa, J.L. *J. Mater. Sci.* **2000**, *35*, 6093–6103.

[35] Kolnaar, J.W.H., Keller, A., Seifert, S., Zschunke, C., Zachmann, H.G. *Polym. Commun.* **1955**, *36*, 3969–3974.

[36] Mackley, M.R., Keller, A. *Polymer* **1973**, *14*, 16–20.

[37] Saquet, O., Moggridge, G.D., Mackley, M.R. *J. Mater. Sci.* **2000**, *35*, 1–7.

[38] Swartjes, F.H.M., Peters, G.W.M., Rastogi, S., Meijer, H.E.H. *Int. Polym. Process.* **2003**, *18*(1), 53–66.

[39] van der Beek, M.H.E., Peters, G.W.M., Meijer, H.E.H. *Macromolecules* **2006**, *39*(26), 9278–9284.

[40] Jerschow, P. Crystallization of polypropylene. New experiments, evaluation methods and choice of material compositions. PhD thesis, Johannes Kepler Universität, Linz, Austria, 1994.

[41] Housmans, J.W., Gahleitner, M., Peters, G.W.M., Meijer, H.E.H. *Polymer* **2009**, *50*, 2304–2319.

[42] Luye, J.F., Regine, G., Le Bot, P.H., Delaunay, D., Fulchiron, R. *J. Appl. Polym. Sci.* **2001**, *79*, 302–311.

[43] Balzano, L., Rastogi, S., Peters, G.W.M. *Macromolecules* **2009**, *42*(6), 2088–2092.

[44] Janeschitz-Kriegl, H., Ratajski, E., Stadlbauer, M. *Rheol. Acta* **2003**, *42*, 355–364.

[45] Jerschow, P., Janeschitz-Kriegl, H. *Int. Polym. Process.* **1997**, *12*(1), 72–77.

[46] Vleeshouwers, S., Meijer, H.E.H. *Rheol. Acta* **1996**, *35*, 391–399.

[47] Nogales, A., Hsiao, B.S., Somani, R.H., Srinivas, S., Tsou, A.H., Balta-Calleja, F.J., Ezquerra, T.A. *Polymer* **2001**, *42*, 5247–5256.

[48] Seki, M., Thurman, D.W., Oberhauser, J.P., Kornfield, J.A. *Macromolecules* **2002**, *35*, 2583–2594.

[49] Elmoumni, A., Gonzalez-Ruiz, R.A., Coughlin, E.B., Winter, H.H. *J. Chem. Phys.* **2005**, *206*, 125–134.

[50] Alfonso, G.C., Ziabicki, A. *Colloid Polym. Sci.* **1995**, *273*, 317.

[51] Somani, R.S., Hsiao, B.S., Nogales, A., Srinivas, S., Tsou, A.H., Sics, I., Balta-Calleja, F.J., Ezquerra, T. *Macromolecules* **2000**, *33*, 9385–9394.

[52] Somani, R.H., Yang, L., Hsiao, B.S. *Physica A* **2002**, *304*, 145–157.

[53] Alfonso, G.C., Scardigli, P. *Macromol. Symp.* **1997**, *118*, 323–328.

[54] Azzurri, F., Alfonso, G.C. *Macromolecules* **2005**, *38*, 1723–1728.

[55] Balzano, L., Kukalyekar, N., Rastogi, S., Peters, G.W.M., Chadwick, J.C. *Phys. Rev. Lett.* **2008**, *100*, 048302.

[56] Housmans, J.W., Steenbakkers, R.J.A., Roozemond, P.C., Peters, G.W.M., Meijer, H.E.H. *Macromolecules* **2009**, *42*(15), 5728–5740.

[57] Acierno, S., Palomba, B., Winter, H.H., Grizzuti, N. *Rheol. Acta* **2003**, *42*, 243–250.

[58] Elmoumni, A., Winter, H.H., Waddon, A.J., Fruitwala, H. *Macromolecules* **2003**, *36*, 6453–6461.

[59] van Meerveld, J., Peters, G.W.M., Hütter, M. *Rheol. Acta* **2004**, *44*, 119–134.

[60] Doi, M., Edwards, S.F. *The Theory of Polymer Dynamics*, Clarendon Press, Oxford, 1986.

[61] McLeish, T.C.B., Milner, S.T. *Adv. Polym. Sci.* **1999**, *43*, 195–256.

[62] Ketzmerick, R., Öttinger, H.C. *Continuum Mech. Thermodyn.* **1989**, *1*, 113–124.

[63] Likhtman, A.E., McLeish, T.C.B. *Macromolecules* **2002**, *35*(16), 6332–6343.

[64] Baert, J., Langouche, F., van Puyvelde, P. *Fibres Text. East. Eur.* **2008**, *16*, 73–76.

[65] Vega, J.F., Hristova, D.G., Peters, G.W.M. *J. Therm. Anal. Calorim.* **2009**, *98*(3), 655–666.

[66] Hadinata, C., Gabriel, C., Ruellman, M., Laun, H.M. *J. Rheol.* **2005**, *49*(1), 327–349.

[67] Hadinata, C., Gabriel, C., Ruellman, M., Kao, N., Laun, H.M. *Rheol. Acta* **2006**, *45*(5), 539–546.

[68] Pogodina, N.V., Winter, H.H., Srinivas, S. *J Polym. Sci. B Polym. Phys.* **1999**, *37*(24), 3512–3519.

[69] Coppola, S., Acierno, S., Grizzuti, N., Vlassopoulos, D. *Macromolecules* **2006**, *39*, 1507–1514.

[70] Tanner, R.I., Qi, F. *Korea-Aust. Rheol. J.* **2005**, *17*, 149–156.

[71] Hwang, W.R., Peters, G.W.M., Hulsen, M.A., Meijer, H.E.H. *Macromolecules* **2006**, *39*(24), 8389–8398.

[72] Zuidema, H. Flow induced crystallization of polymers. PhD thesis, Eindhoven, University of Technology, Eindhoven, The Netherlands, 2000.

[73] Zheng, R., Kennedy, P.K. *J. Rheol.* **2004**, *48*, 823–842.

[74] Custódio, F.J.M.F., Steenbakkers, R.J.A., Anderson, P.D., Peters, G.W.M., Meijer, H.E.H. *Macromol. Theory Simul.* **2009**, *18*(9), 469–494.

[75] Isayev, A.I., Chan, T.W., Shimojo, K., Gmerek, M. *J. Appl. Polym. Sci.* **1995**, *55*, 807–819.

[76] Isayev, A.I., Chan, T.W., Gmerek, M., Shimojo, K. *J. Appl. Polym. Sci.* **1995**, *55*, 821–838.

[77] Isayev, A.I., Churdpunt, Y., Guo, X. *Int. Polym. Process.* **2000**, *15*(1), 72–82.

[78] La Carrubba, V., Brucato, V., Piccarolo, S. *Polym. Eng. Sci.* **2000**, *40*(11), 2430–2441.

[79] Brucato, V., Piccarolo, S., La Carrubba, V. *Chem. Eng. Sci.* **2002**, *57*, 4129–4143.

[80] Zuidema, H., Peters, G.W.M., Meijer, H.E.H. *J. Appl. Polym. Sci.* **2001**, *82*, 1170–1186.

[81] van der Beek, M.H.E., Peters, G.W.M., Meijer, H.E.H. *Macromolecules* **2006**, *39*(5), 1805–1814.

[82] Forstner, R., Peters, G.W.M., Rendina, C., Housmans, J.W., Meijer, H.E.H. *J. Therm. Anal. Calorim.* **2009**, *98*, 683–691.

[83] Housmans, J.W., Balzano, L., Adinolfi, M., Peters, G.W.M., Meijer, H.E.H. *Macromol. Mater. Eng.* **2009**, *294*(4), 231–243.

[84] Mitsuhashi, S.S. *Bull. Text. Res. Inst. (J)* **1963**, *66*, 1.

[85] Hsiao, B.S., Yang, L., Somani, R.H., Avila-Orta, C.A., Zhu, L. *Phys. Rev. Lett.* **2005**, *94*, 117802.

[86] Kumaraswamy, G., Kornfield, J.A., Yeh, F., Hsiao, B.S. *Macromolecules* **2002**, *35*, 1762–1769.

[87] Göschel, U., Swartjes, F.H.M., Peters, G.W.M., Meijer, H.E.H. *Polymer* **2000**, *41*, 1541–1550.

[88] Kimata, S., Sakurai, T., Nozue, Y., Kasahara, T., Yamaguchi, N., Karino, T., Shibayama, M., Kornfield, J.A. *Science* **2007**, *316*(5827), 1014–1017.

[89] Xu, J., Johnson, M., Wilkes, G.L. *Polymer* **2004**, *45*, 5327–5340.

[90] Lee, K.G., Schultz, J.M. *Polymer* **1993**, *34*(21), 4455–4470.

[91] Balzano, L., Rastogi, S., Peters, G.W.M. *Macromolecules* **2011**, *44*(8), 2926–2933.

[92] Balzano, L., Rastogi, S., Peters, G.W.M. *Macromolecules* **2008**, *41*, 399–408.

[93] Cakmak, M., Yalcin, B. Evolution of structural hierarchy in injection molded semicrystalline polymers. In *Injection Molding; Technology and Fundamentals*, Kamal, M.R., Isayev, A.I., Liu, S.J., eds. Hanser, Munich, 2009, pp. 687–730.

[94] Doufas, A.K., McHugh, A.J. *J. Rheol.* **2001**, *45*, 1085–1104.

[95] Muslet, I.A., Kamal, M.R. *J. Rheol.* **2004**, *48*, 525.

[96] Sarafrazi, S., Sharif, F. *Int. Polym. Process.* **2008**, *23*(1), 30–37.

[97] Nakamura, K., Watanabe, T., Katayama, K. *J. Appl. Polym. Sci.* **1972**, *16*, 1077–1091.

[98] Spruiell, J.E., White, J.L. *Polym. Eng. Sci.* **1975**, *15*, 660–667.

[99] Laun, H.M., Schuch, H. *J. Rheol.* **1989**, *33*(1), 119–175.

[100] Ishizuka, O., Koyama, K. Rheology and dynamics of melt spinning: viscoelastic polypropylene and polyethylenes. In *High-Speed Fiber Spinning. Science and Engineering Aspects*, Ziabicki, A., Kawai, H., eds. John Wiley & Sons, New York, 1985, pp. 383–429.

[101] Haberkorn, H., Hahn, K., Breuer, H., Dorrer, H.D., Matthies, P. *J. Appl. Polym. Sci.* **1993**, *47*(9), 1551–1579.

[102] Shimiyu, J., Okui, N., Kikutani, T. Fine structure and physical properties of fibers melt spun at high speeds from various polymers. In *High-Speed Fiber Spinning. Science and Engineering Aspects*, Ziabicki, A., Kawai, H., eds. John Wiley & Sons, New York, 1985, pp. 173–201.

[103] Vassilatos, G., Knox, B.H., Frankfort, H.R.E. Dynamics, structure and fiber properties in high-speed spinning of polyethylene terephthalate. In *High-Speed Fiber Spinning. Science and Engineering Aspects*, Ziabicki, A., Kawai, H., eds. John Wiley & Sons, New York, 1985, pp. 383–429.

[104] George, H.H., Holt, A., Buckley, A. *Polym. Eng. Sci.* **1983**, *23*(2), 95–99.

[105] Kolb, R., Seifert, S., Stribeck, N., Zachmann, H.G. *Polymer* **2000**, *41*(8), 2931–2935.

[106] Raghavan, J.S., Cuculo, J.A. *J. Polym. Sci. B Polym. Phys.* **1999**, *379*(14), 1565–1573.

[107] Ziabicki, A., Jarecki, L., Wasiak, A. *Comput. Theor. Polym. Sci.* **1998**, *8*(1/2), 143–157.

[108] Joo, Y.L., Sun, J., Smith, M.D., Armstrong, R.C., Brown, R.A., Ross, R.A. *J. Non-Newton. Fluid Mech.* **2002**, *102*(1), 37–70.

[109] Kulkarni, J.A., Beris, A.N. *J. Rheol.* **1998**, *42*(4), 971–994.

[110] Doufas, A.K., McHugh, A.J., Miller, C. *J. Non-Newton. Fluid Mech.* **2000**, *92*(1), 27–66.

[111] Doufas, A.K., McHugh, A.J., Miller, C., Immameni, A. *J. Non-Newton. Fluid Mech.* **2000**, *92*(1), 81–103.

[112] Doufas, A.K., McHugh, A.J. *J. Rheol.* **2001**, *25*(2), 403–420.

[113] Kannan, K., Rajagopal, K.R. *J. Rheol.* **2005**, *49*(3), 683–703.

[114] Nakamura, K., Katayama, K., Amano, T. *J. Appl. Polym. Sci.* **1973**, *17*(4), 1031–1041.

[115] Zieminski, K.F., Spruiell, J.E. *J. Appl. Polym. Sci.* **1988**, *35*(8), 2223–2245.

[116] Patel, R.M., Bheda, J.H., Spruiell, J.E. *J. Appl. Polym. Sci.* **1991**, *42*(6), 1671–1682.

[117] Doufas, A.K., Dairanieh, I.S., McHugh, A.J. *J. Rheol.* **1999**, *43*(1), 85–109.

[118] van Meerveld, J. Model development and validation of rheological and flow induced crystallization models for entangled polymer melts. PhD thesis, Diss. Nr. 16124, ETH, Zürich, Switzerland, 2005.

[119] Schneider, W., Köppl, A., Berger, J. *Int. Polym. Process.* **1988**, *2*(3–4), 151–154.

[120] Hütter, M. *Phys. Rev. E* **2001**, *64*(1), 011209.

[121] Hütter, M., Rutledge, G.C., Armstrong, R.C. *Phys. Fluids* **2005**, *17*(1), 014107.

[122] Kolmogorov, A.N. *Izv. Akad. Nauk SSSR, Ser. Math.* **1937**, *1*, 355–359.

[123] Avrami, M. *J. Chem. Phys.* **1939**, *7*, 1103–1112.

[124] Avrami, M. *J. Chem. Phys.* **1940**, *8*, 212–224.

[125] Avrami, M. *J. Chem. Phys.* **1941**, *9*, 177–184.

[126] Stadlbauer, M., Janeschitz-Kriegl, H., Eder, G., Ratajski, E. *J. Rheol.* **2004**, *48*(3), 631–639.

[127] Okamoto, M., Kubo, H., Kotaka, T. *Macromolecules* **1998**, *31*(13), 4223–4231.

[128] Okamoto, M., Kubo, H., Kotaka, T. *Macromolecules* **1999**, *32*(19), 6206–6214.

[129] Hadinata, C., Boos, D., Gabriel, C., Wassner, E., Rüllmann, M., Kao, N., Laun, M. *J. Rheol.* **2007**, *51*(2), 195–215.

[130] Sentmanat, M.L. *Rheol. Acta* **2004**, *43*(6), 657–669.

[131] Wagner, M.H., Rubio, P., Bastian, H. *J. Rheol.* **2001**, *45*, 1387–1412.

[132] Sentmanat, M., Delgadillo, O., Hatzikiriakos, S.G. *Proceedings of the 78th Annual Meeting of the Society of Rheology*, Portland, Maine USA, 2006.

[133] Peters, G.W.M., Swartjes, F.H.M., Meijer, H.E.H. *Macromol. Symp.* **2002**, *185*, 277–292.

[134] Swartjes, F.H.M. Stress induced crystallization in elongational flow. PhD thesis, Eindhoven University of Technology, Eindhoven, The Netherlands, 2001.

[135] Steenbakkers, R.J.A., Peters, G.W.M. *J. Rheol.* **2011**, *55*, 401–433.

[136] Titomanlio, G., Lamberti, G. *Rheol. Acta* **2004**, *43*(2), 146–158.

[137] Tavichai, O., Feng, L., Kamal, M.R. *Polym. Eng. Sci.* **2006**, *46*, 1468–1475.

[138] Coccorrullo, R., Pantani, R., Titomanlio, G. *Macromolecules* **2008**, *41*, 9214–9223.

[139] Pantani, R., Coccorrullo, R., Volpe, V., Titomanlio, G. *Macromolecules* **2010**, *43*, 9030–9038.

[140] Koscher, E., Fulchiron, R. *Polymer* **2002**, *43*, 6931–6942.

[141] Huo, H., Meng, Y., Li, H., Jiang, S., An, L. *Eur. Phys. J. E* **2004**, *15*, 167–175.

[142] Coppola, S., Grizzuti, N., Maffettone, P.L. *Macromolecules* **2001**, *34*(14), 5030–5036.

[143] Marrucci, G., Grizzuti, N. *J. Rheol.* **1983**, *27*, 433–450.

[144] Pogodina, N.V., Lavrenko, V.P., Srinivas, S., Winter, H.H. *Polymer* **2001**, *42*, 9031–9043.

[145] Kornfield, J.A., Kumaraswamy, G., Issaian, A.M. *Ind. Eng. Chem. Res.* **2002**, *41*, 6383–6392.

[146] Janeschitz-Kriegl, H. *Colloid Polym. Sci.* **1997**, *275*, 1121–1135.

[147] Janeschitz-Kriegl, H., Ratajski, E., Wippel, H. *Colloid Polym. Sci.* **1999**, *277*, 217–226.

[148] Janeschitz-Kriegl, H., Ratajski, E. *Colloid Polym. Sci.* **2003**, *281*, 1157–1171.

[149] Fischer, J.C., Hollomon, J.H., Turnbull, D. *J. Appl. Phys.* **1948**, *19*, 775–784.

[150] Roozemond, P.C., Steenbakkers, R.J.A., Peters, G.W.M. *Macromol. Theory Simul.* **2011**, *20*, 93–109.

[151] Azzurri, F., Alfonso, G.C. *Macromolecules* **2008**, *41*(4), 1377–1383.

[152] Cavallo, D., Azzurri, F., Balzano, L., Funari, S., Alfonso, G.C. *Macromolecules* **2010**, *43*(22), 9394–9400.

[153] Piccarolo, S., Saiu, M., Brucato, V., Titomanlio, G. *J. Appl. Polym. Sci.* **1992**, *46*, 625–634.

[154] Sarti, G.C., Marrucci, G. *Chem. Eng. Sci.* **1973**, *28*, 1053–1059.

[155] Peterlin, A. *J. Chem. Phys.* **1960**, *33*, 1799–1802.

[156] Lagasse, R.R., Maxwell, B. *Polym. Eng. Sci.* **1976**, *16*(3), 189–199.

[157] Nieh, J.Y., Lee, L.J. *Polym. Eng. Sci.* **1998**, *38*, 1121–1132.

[158] Acierno, S., Coppola, S., Grizzuti, N., Maffettone, P.L. *Macromol. Symp.* **2002**, *185*, 233–241.

[159] Acierno, S., Coppola, S., Grizzuti, N. *J. Rheol.* **2008**, *52*, 551–566.

[160] des Cloizeaux, J.J. *Europhys. Lett.* **1988**, *5*, 437–442.

[161] Öttinger, H.C., Grmela, M. *Phys. Rev. E* **1997**, *56*, 6633–6655.

[162] Grmela, M., Öttinger, H.C. *Phys. Rev. E* **1997**, *56*, 6620–6632.

[163] Öttinger, H.C. *Phys. Rev. E* **1998**, *57*, 1416–1420.

[164] Mahendrasingam, A., Blundell, D.J., Martin, C., Fuller, W., MacKerron, D.H., Harvie, J.L., Oldman, R.J., Riekel, C. *Polymer* **2000**, *41*, 7803–7814.

[165] Likhtman, A.E., Graham, R.S. *J. Non-Newton. Fluid Mech.* **2003**, *114*, 1–12.

[166] Graham, R.S., Olmsted, P.D. *Phys. Rev. Lett.* **2009**, *103*, 115702.

[167] Graham, R.S., Olmsted, P.D. *Faraday Discuss.* **2010**, *144*, 1–22.

[168] Milner, S.T., McLeish, T.C.B., Likhtman, A.E. *J. Rheol.* **2001**, *45*(2), 539–563.

[169] Graham, R.S., Likhtman, A.E., McLeish, T.C.B., Milner, S.T. *J. Rheol.* **2003**, *47*(5), 1171–1200.

[170] Blundell, D.J., Mahendrasingam, A., Martin, C., Fuller, W., MacKerron, D.H., Harvie, J.L., Oldman, R.J., Riekel, C. *Polymer* **2000**, *41*, 7793–7802.

[171] Hieber, C.A. *Polym. Eng. Sci.* **2002**, *42*(7), 1387–1409.

[172] Kim, K.H., Isayev, A.I., Kwon, K. *J. Appl. Polym. Sci.* **2005**, *95*(3), 502–523.

[173] Guo, X., Isayev, A.I., Demiray, M. *Polym. Eng. Sci.* **1999**, *39*, 2132–2149.

[174] Smirnova, J., Silva, L., Monasse, B., Chenot, J.L., Haudin, J.M. *Int. Polym. Process.* **2005**, *20*, 178–185.

[175] Schrauwen, B.A.G., van Breemen, L.C.A., Spoelstra, A.B., Govaert, L.E., Peters, G.W.M., Meijer, H.E.H. *Macromolecules* **2004**, *37*, 8618–8633.

[176] Housmans, J.W., Peters, G.W.M., Meijer, H.E.H. *J. Therm. Anal. Calorim.* **2009**, *98*, 693–705.

15

CRYSTALLIZATION IN PROCESSING CONDITIONS

JEAN-MARC HAUDIN

MINES ParisTech, Centre de Mise en Forme des Matériaux (CEMEF), Sophia Antipolis, France

15.1 Introduction, 433
15.2 General Effects of Processing Conditions on Crystallization, 433
    15.2.1 Effects of Flow, 433
    15.2.2 Effects of Pressure, 435
    15.2.3 Effects of Cooling Rate, 436
    15.2.4 Effects of a Temperature Gradient, 437
    15.2.5 Effects of Surfaces, 439
15.3 Modeling, 440
    15.3.1 General Framework, 440
    15.3.2 Simplified Expressions, 441
    15.3.3 General Systems of Differential Equations, 441
15.4 Crystallization in some Selected Processes, 442
    15.4.1 Cast Film Extrusion, 442
    15.4.2 Fiber Spinning, 445
    15.4.3 Film Blowing, 448
    15.4.4 Injection Molding, 454
15.5 Conclusion, 458
References, 459

15.1 INTRODUCTION

Structure development is becoming a key issue in polymer processing, with a view to mastering the final properties of the products, for instance, their mechanical properties. Among the phenomena involved, crystallization plays a major role. It generally occurs under complex, inhomogeneous, and coupled mechanical (flow, pressure), thermal (cooling rates, temperature gradients), and geometrical (contact with processing tools) conditions. Numerical simulation is a useful tool for understanding and predicting these coupled phenomena. It requires the introduction of a crystallization model into a computer code dedicated to a thermomechanical description of the process.

In this chapter, the general effects of processing conditions (mechanical, thermal, geometrical) on the crystallization phenomena (nucleation, growth, overall kinetics, development of morphologies) will be first discussed. Then, the principles of the modeling of structure development will be presented, with the laws describing overall kinetics.

Finally, four case studies will be presented, which correspond to different influences of the processing conditions on the final microstructures. In cast film extrusion, crystallization occurs after cessation of flow, and the thermal conditions are very important. In fiber spinning and film blowing, it takes place during flow in uniaxial or biaxial conditions, respectively. In injection molding, different situations may be encountered as a function of the location in the part.

15.2 GENERAL EFFECTS OF PROCESSING CONDITIONS ON CRYSTALLIZATION

15.2.1 Effects of Flow

Many papers have been devoted to the relationships between processing conditions, and in particular, flow conditions, microstructure, and properties. In parallel,

---

Handbook of Polymer Crystallization, First Edition. Edited by Ewa Piorkowska and Gregory C. Rutledge.
© 2013 John Wiley & Sons, Inc. Published 2013 by John Wiley & Sons, Inc.

many laboratory experiments have been designed to capture the specific influence of flow under well-defined conditions (for a review see [1] and Chapter 14). From all these data, general rules on the effects of flow can be proposed.

Thermoplastics are composed of flexible macromolecules, which adopt a random-coil conformation at rest, and can be easily deformed by flow. Under flow, they also tend to be oriented along the flow direction. Stretching and orientation of macromolecules in the melt have consequences on crystallization thermodynamics and kinetics, as well as on the subsequent morphologies.

15.2.1.1 Thermodynamics and Kinetics Flow increases the equilibrium melting temperature and enhances all the kinetics (nucleation, growth, overall kinetics). The increase of the equilibrium melting temperature can be explained by a simple model. In quiescent conditions, the equilibrium melting temperature is defined by:

$$T_0 = \frac{\Delta h}{\Delta s} \quad (15.1)$$

where Δh and Δs are the enthalpy and the entropy of fusion per unit volume, respectively. Due to the reduction of the number of conformations, flow mainly affects the entropy of fusion, which decreases. The equilibrium melting temperature becomes:

$$T_0' = \frac{\Delta h}{\Delta s'} > T_0 \quad (15.2)$$

since $\Delta s' < \Delta s$. It means that in isothermal conditions, the undercooling is increased and that during cooling, crystallization occurs at higher temperature, which is observed experimentally. This could simply explain why the nucleation and growth kinetics are enhanced. Nevertheless, the melting point elevation theory cannot predict the rheological behavior of the crystallizing system, due to complex coupling effects. More sophisticated thermodynamic approaches are necessary. For instance, Doufas et al. [2] have proposed a model based on the Hamiltonian–Poisson bracket formalism. The amorphous phase is modeled as a modified Giesekus fluid and the crystalline phase is considered as a collection of multibead rigid rods that grow and orient in the flow field. These two phases are coupled with crystallinity through the dissipative Poisson brackets.

A large number of experimental studies (e.g., [3]) have shown that flow increases both the total number of activated nuclei and the nucleation rate. Concerning the effect of flow on growth rate, there is still some debate. However, Monasse [4] has clearly shown that growth is enhanced in the three directions of space:

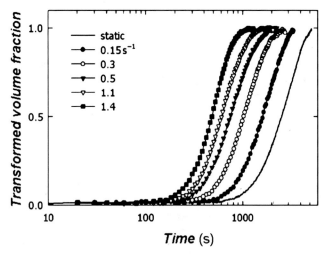

Figure 15.1 Evolution of the transformed volume fraction with shear rate (s^{-1}). Isotactic polypropylene at 136°C [10].

along the shear-flow direction, but much more perpendicularly to it. This anisotropic growth has a direct consequence on morphologies (see Section 15.2.1.2). Furthermore, the flow effect on growth rate is greater when molecular weight increases [5].

The enhancement of overall kinetics can be characterized:

- by the decrease of characteristic times defined experimentally: induction time [6, 7], half-transformation time [8, 9];
- by the evolution of the transformed volume fraction $\alpha(t)$ [10]. Figure 15.1 demonstrates the acceleration of the crystallization kinetics with increasing shear rate. α is deduced from depolarized light intensity measurements.

15.2.1.2 Morphologies The effects of flow on the development of morphologies are to:

- decrease the size of the crystalline entities, which results from the increase of the number of nuclei;
- arrange nuclei in lines parallel to the flow direction (row nucleation). Simultaneously, the shape of the nuclei changes: from point-like to thread-like precursors;
- induce an anisotropic growth of lamellar crystals. As growth proceeds by the deposit of molecular stems on the growth surface, orientation of macromolecules in the melt favors growth in the direction perpendicular to flow.

Taking into account these effects, the morphologies that can be expected by increasing flow intensity are spherulites (Fig. 15.2a), spherulites deformed into ellipsoids (Fig. 15.2b), sheaf-like morphologies (Fig. 15.2c), and stacks of lamellae when the opening of the sheaves tends to zero, row-nucleated morphologies or cylindrites [11, 12]. At low stress (Keller I model, Fig. 15.2d), the columnar morphology can be described as a stack of thin spherulitic slices consisting of twisted radial crystallites. Under higher stress, crystalline lamellae are flat (Keller II model, Fig. 15.2e). It is now acknowledged that the nucleating line forming in the melt can be identified with the fibrous, partly extended-chain backbone of the solution-crystallized shish–kebabs. The latter morphologies consist of a central thread that is covered with folded-chain platelets at regular intervals [13]. At very high stress, smooth fibrils are obtained (Fig. 15.2f). The occurrence of these various morphologies in selected processes will be discussed in Section 15.4.

15.2.2 Effects of Pressure

Pressure may enhance some crystalline modifications. For instance, the crystallization of γ phase is favored in isotactic polypropylene under high pressure [14–18]. Pressure may also induce important morphological changes. It has been known since the 1960s that polyethylene can crystallize from the melt in the form of extended-chain lamellae for pressures higher than 3000 bar [19–21]. This morphology has been related to the existence of a pseudohexagonal *condis* mesophase [22]. Chain straightening in the chain-extended samples occurs under high pressure and temperature through chain slippage (or "sliding diffusion") in the *condis* mesophase [23, 24]. The above-mentioned morphological changes take place in a pressure range beyond the usual processing conditions.

Pressure plays a major role in injection molding. It affects crystallization and conditions shrinkage. The effects of pressure can be studied through pressure, specific volume, temperature (PVT) diagrams, which give the specific volume of the material as a function of temperature and pressure. Figure 15.3 presents the PVT diagram of an isotactic polypropylene obtained during

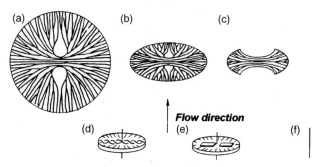

Figure 15.2 Morphological change with increasing flow intensity: (a) spherulite; (b) ellipsoidal spherulite; (c) sheaf-like texture; (d, e) row-nucleated morphologies, (f) smooth fibrils.

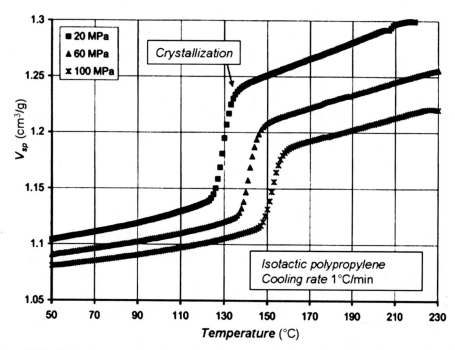

Figure 15.3 PVT diagram of an isotactic polypropylene obtained during isobaric cooling [28].

isobaric cooling. Crystallization induces a sharp decrease of the specific volume. The PVT diagram of a semicrystalline polymer can be described by the following equation:

$$V_{sp} = X_c V_c(P,T) + (1-X_c)V_a(P,T) \qquad (15.3)$$

where X_c is the mass crystallinity, $V_c(P,T)$ and $V_a(P,T)$ are the specific volumes of the amorphous and crystalline phases, respectively. $V_a(P,T)$ can be described by the Tait equation [25], modified by Tamman [26]:

$$V_a(P,T) = V_a(0,T)\left[1 - C\ln\left(1 + \frac{P}{B(T)}\right)\right] \qquad (15.4)$$

where $V_a(0,T)$ and $B(T)$ are temperature functions and C is a constant, generally taken as equal to 0.0894. With respect to amorphous polymers, two additional problems appear. The first one is to know the variations of $V_c(P,T)$ with pressure and temperature. A first approach is to consider it as constant [27] or to assume linear pressure and temperature variations [28]. The second and more important problem concerns the evolution of crystallinity during solidification, which is very sensitive to processing conditions, especially cooling rate. This brings some limitations to the generality of the PVT approach.

The main effect of pressure on crystallization is to shift the equilibrium melting temperature to higher values. It can be explained by Equation (15.1) and Equation (15.2), but here the decrease of the entropy of fusion is due to the reduction of free volume. It means that during cooling, crystallization occurs at higher temperatures, which is observed experimentally (Fig. 15.3). For polypropylene, the increase of the equilibrium melting temperature can be described by the following equation [28]:

$$T_0'(°C) = T_0 + 0.283P(MPa) - 2.08\,10^{-4}P^2. \qquad (15.5)$$

Unfortunately, classical dilatometers cannot be operated at high cooling rates because of the temperature gradient occurring within the sample. This problem can be solved by modeling the dilatometry experiment [28] or by designing novel setups [29, 30]: special injection mold [29], miniaturized dilatometer [30], and so on.

15.2.3 Effects of Cooling Rate

The main effects of the cooling rate $\dot{T} = dT/dt$ can be illustrated thanks to a simple laboratory experiment (Fig. 15.4). A polymer specimen is cooled from the melt at a constant cooling rate in a calorimeter. The apparatus records the heat power dQ/dt liberated by crystal-

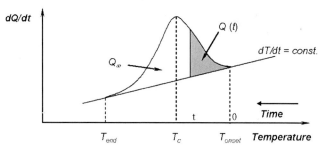

Figure 15.4 DSC trace recorded during the crystallization of a polymer at a constant cooling rate.

lization as a function of time t (or temperature T). Crystallization starts at T_{onset} and is completed at T_{end}; a peak is observed at T_c, which is generally taken as the crystallization temperature. After subtraction of the baseline, the area under the curve gives access to the enthalpy of crystallization per unit mass ΔH, that is, to the final crystallinity. Increasing cooling rate

- shifts the crystallization peak toward lower temperatures: T_{onset}, T_c, T_{end} decrease;
- lowers the enthalpy of crystallization ΔH and, consequently, the crystallinity. The evolutions are highly dependent on the polymer. "Slow crystallizing" polymers like poly(ethylene terephthalate) (PET) can be quenched into the amorphous state: voluminous chemical groups are incorporated in their chains, which slows down their crystallization kinetics. On the contrary, this is practically impossible for polyethylene, which has a very flexible chain. In the case of isotactic polypropylene, rapid quenching generally leads to the disordered smectic phase. Only recently, amorphous isotactic polypropylene was obtained at very high cooling rates in nanocalorimetry experiments [31].

These trends, introduced in a simple case, are general.

Overall crystallization kinetics can be described experimentally by the ratio $Q(t)/Q_\infty$ of the heat $Q(t)$ liberated between the onset of crystallization and time t to the total heat of crystallization Q_∞ (see Fig. 15.4). To a first approximation, this ratio can be assimilated to the volume fraction α transformed into spherulites, and described by the laws for overall crystallization kinetics, for example, Ozawa's equation (see Section 15.3.2). Logically, the $\alpha(T)$ curves are shifted to lower temperatures when the cooling rate increases. Until recently, classical calorimetry allowed us to determine the kinetic law only at low or moderate cooling rates, typically from 0.125 to 40°C/min. This raised questions when these data were used to model crystallization in processes where the cooling rates were much higher. As a result of academic work and industrial development, it is now possible to work confidently with commercial equipment at several hundreds °C/min. Nevertheless, it appears more and more necessary to obtain crystallization data at still higher cooling rates. Different technical solutions are possible: specific hot stages [32, 33], annular mold, and use of an inverse method [34], quenching of thin polymer films [35, 36], and nanocalorimetry [31].

From a morphological point of view, an increase in the cooling rate generally involves a decrease of the spherulite size because of an increase of the nucleation density. The perfection of the crystalline arrangements can be also affected. For instance, in an injection-molded polyamide 12 part, the zone near the surface exhibits a low crystallinity, and crystalline lamellae are poorly organized, in a nonspherulitic manner (see Section 15.4.4.2).

15.2.4 Effects of a Temperature Gradient

15.2.4.1 General Features Temperature gradients induce remarkable changes in the spherulite shape, which usually becomes quasiparabolic (open outline, see Fig. 15.5) [37]. A teardrop shape (closed outline) is observed in isotactic polypropylene for α phase spherulites growing in a β phase matrix, that is, for two phases growing at different rates [38]. Trajectories of spherulite growth are not radial; they change their directions, which, however, remain normal to growth fronts.

Solidification within a temperature gradient can be achieved in two types of experimental setups:

1. a zone solidification apparatus [37–40]: the sample passes slowly through a steep temperature gradient. It melts and crystallizes; the crystallization front is formed and moves along the sample. Thus, the crystallization occurs in a temperature gradient, but at a stable temperature at the front.

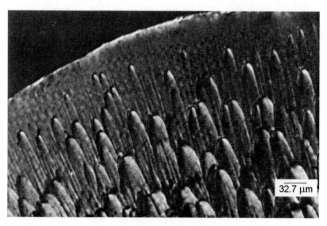

Figure 15.5 Quasiparabolic spherulites observed in the microtomed section of a polyethylene pellet.

2. a device in which a constant temperature gradient is established between two metal blocks at different temperatures [41]. This better corresponds to polymer processing.

In a constant temperature gradient [41], crystallization logically begins on the colder side. Isolated spherulites grow at rates imposed by the local temperatures. Therefore, they are more extended into the direction of decreasing temperature. This growth toward the lower temperature region is stopped by impingement with neighboring spherulites. The spherulites are then forced to propagate into the opposite direction, where nucleation is weaker. A continuous growth front is formed and advances through the hotter part of the film. Boundaries between spherulites are straight lines when they are nucleated simultaneously at the same isotherm. Otherwise, they are curved toward the high temperature region and finally become parallel to the temperature gradient. In zone solidification experiments, straight boundaries are observed when two spherulites are nucleated simultaneously at the same distance from the front. In the case of teardrop shapes this leads to the formation of a cardioid-like twin [38].

The morphological patterns are very sensitive to the nucleation density and to its variation with temperature:

- if the nuclei leading to quasiparabolic spherulites are very close together, their proximity forces the crystalline entities to grow parallel to the direction of the temperature gradient. The final morphology is then similar to transcrystallinity (see Section 15.2.5), despite its different origin. In actual processes, effects of heterogeneous nucleation ("true" transcrystallinity) and temperature gradient are often combined.
- when a steady state with a continuous front is established, new spherulites are nucleated ahead of the front [38]. Therefore, the development of lamellae parallel to the temperature gradient assumes the suppression of nucleation on the high temperature side. In zone solidification experiments, it is possible to obtain "infinitely" extended lamellae from nucleation points at one end of the polymer specimen [39].

15.2.4.2 Physical Models

Lovinger and Gryte's Model Lovinger and Gryte have proposed a simple model that describes the growth of a spherulite nucleated in a temperature gradient ahead of a uniaxially moving crystal front [37]. The gradient is

438 CRYSTALLIZATION IN PROCESSING CONDITIONS

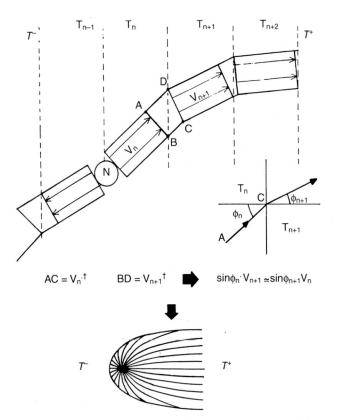

Figure 15.6 Spherulite growth in a temperature gradient. Lovinger and Gryte's model [37].

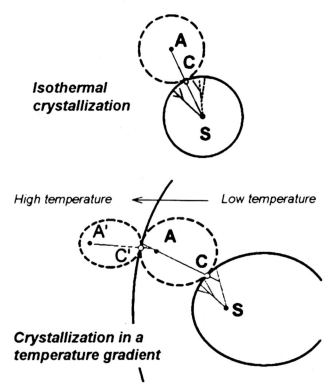

Figure 15.7 Spherulite growth in a temperature gradient. Piorkowska's model [41].

divided into slabs of constant temperature (Fig. 15.6). A stack of lamellae originating from a nucleus N will grow at a constant rate V_n in the slab of temperature T_n, until the growth front reaches the position AB. Then, a side of the lamellar front (B) grows at $T_{n+1} > T_n$, at a lower growth rate V_{n+1}. The other side of the front (A) continues its growth at the original faster rate until it reaches point C. Thus, when one side of the front has grown from A to C, the other one has advanced only from B to D, and the direction of the front has rotated from AB to CD. At this point, the entire front is again in an isothermal region and will grow at a constant rate in the direction perpendicular to CD, until the side (D) reaches the boundary between the T_{n+1} and T_{n+2} slabs, where the same process will be repeated. The rotation of the growth front from AB to CD can be quantified by an approximate equation, analogous to the Snell–Descartes law for light refraction (see Fig. 15.6).

According to foregoing model, all the forward-growing lamellae will exhibit a monotonic curvature and tend to a horizontal asymptote (direction of temperature gradient). The model also predicts that the lamellae growing in the backward direction should tend to a vertical asymptote, which is not observed experimentally.

Piorkowska's Model This morphological model is based on observations by atomic force microscopy (AFM), which show that the growth of lamellae inclined at large angles to the temperature gradient is frequently stopped by less inclined lamellae [41]. Therefore, the change of growth trajectories toward the higher temperature region is assumed to result from the competition between lamellae in space filling. This leads to the mechanism explained in Figure 15.7 [41].

In isothermal conditions, a given point A can be reached simultaneously by growing lamellae, if they pass at the same time the circular dashed line. A spherulite of center S meets this circle at point C belonging to SA. Thus, the radial direction SA indicates the fastest growth path for the spherulite lamellae toward point A. In a uniaxial temperature gradient, both the spherulite outline and the dashed rim are no longer circular and C is outside SA. The lamella propagating in the CA direction will arrive at A before any other, and stop the growth of lamellae inclined at larger angles to the temperature gradient. During a next step, the dashed rim around point A′ meets the spherulite's new outline at C′, and C′A′ indicates the fastest growth path toward A′. Therefore, the paths of fastest growth progressively bend toward the hotter sample side, as observed experimentally.

15.2.4.3 Mathematical Modeling Lovinger and Gryte [37] used their physical model to compute the shape of a spherulite and the paths of its constitutive lamellae. For the same purpose, Schulze and Naujeck developed an analytical model, which considered either a linear field of growth rate [42] or a linear temperature field [43]. This analytical approach and the numerical method of Lovinger and Gryte give the same results [44].

Swaminarayan and Charbon presented two methods of simulating the growth of an isolated spherulite: the arborescent method and the front-tracking method [44]. In a second article [45], the same authors coupled the front-tracking techniques with (1) a stochastic model for spherulite nucleation, (2) a cellular model for spherulite impingement and solid fraction evolution, and (3) a finite difference method for solving the energy equation. This multiscale approach predicts the final microstructure in a macroscopic part.

For a constant temperature gradient, Piorkowska and coworkers [41] conducted a computer simulation of two-dimensional (2D) spherulitic crystallization. The spherulite centers were randomly generated. For each time interval the perimeter of each spherulite was shifted by a distance equal to the product of the time interval by the growth rate at the local temperature. The points of spherulite perimeters that invaded neighboring spherulites were rejected. The version of the model based on a growth perpendicular to the growth front reproduces correctly the features of the spherulitic patterns in a temperature gradient.

15.2.5 Effects of Surfaces

In many cases, polymer crystallization occurs in the presence of well-identified foreign bodies, such as processing tools (molds, calibrators, chill-rolls), laboratory equipment (glass slides, differential scanning calorimetry [DSC] pans), fillers (e.g., $CaCO_3$), reinforcing materials (especially fibers), nodules in blends, or nucleating agents, that is, substances added on purpose to promote intense heterogeneous nucleation. In such cases, the main problem is the competition between heterogeneous nucleation in the bulk polymer and heterogeneous nucleation on the well-identified surfaces. These cases are discussed in further detail in Chapter 8, Chapter 10, Chapter 12, and Chapter 13. Three types of behavior can be distinguished: (1) inactivity of surfaces: spherulites appear only in the polymer volume; (2) medium activity of the surfaces: a few half-spherulites are created from surface nuclei; (3) high activity of the surfaces: if many heterogeneous nuclei are activated at the surfaces, their proximity imposes that entities emanating from these nuclei grow preferentially normal to

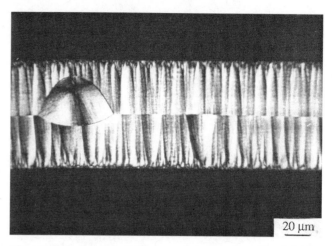

Figure 15.8 Transcrystalline zones in a polyamide 6-6 film. Only one bulk spherulite is visible.

the surface, leading to what is usually called transcrystalline zones (Fig. 15.8). This interpretation of transcrystallinity, due to Fitchmun and Newman [46], is based only on geometrical considerations and does not require the occurrence of flow or temperature gradients.

The competition between surface and bulk nucleation can be studied through crystallizations of thin polymer films in contact with pan-surfaces in a DSC apparatus. A first series of experiments conducted with polyamide 6-6 [47] showed that important transcrystalline regions corresponded to coarse spherulites at the specimen core. Conversely, thin transcrystalline regions were associated with a large number of small spherulites at the core. A second series of experiments was then performed with high density polyethylene (HDPE) films of different thicknesses ranging from 192 to 865 μm [48]. All the samples had important transcrystalline zones at their surfaces. Thin samples were almost completely overlapped by transcrystalline regions. Medium-thickness samples contained more volume spherulites, but one row of spherulites to the maximum appeared in their mid-plane. Thick samples, for their part, contained two larger spherulites in the area of the thickness that was not overlapped by transcrystalline zones. The total thickness of the transcrystalline zones and the maximum diameter of the bulk spherulites both increased up to a maximum value of about 350 μm, which was reached for the same sample thickness (Fig. 15.9). These results show that in thin samples the transcrystalline thickness is mainly limited by the sample thickness and the inner spherulitic morphology is disturbed. The greater the thickness, the more important are the transcrystalline zones up to a certain value. Then, in thick samples, spherulites are more numerous and stop the development of transcrystallinity.

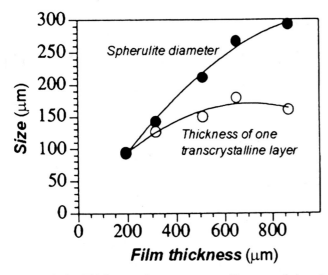

Figure 15.9 Thickness of one transcrystalline zone (○) and maximum diameter of the bulk spherulites (●) as a function of the film thickness [48].

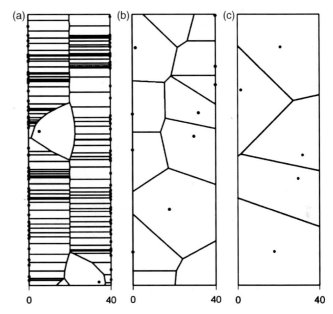

Figure 15.10 Computer-simulated thin polymer films having a width of 40 units: (a) intense surface nucleation; (b) weak surface nucleation; (c) no surface nucleation [51].

In two dimensions, the boundary between a transcrystalline zone and an isolated spherulite in the bulk is a curved line, as seen in Figure 15.8. Devaux et al. [49] calculated this boundary for a 2D crystallization at constant cooling rate. When only one crystalline phase is present, this is a parabola. The spherulite looks like a spherulite crystallized in a gradient temperature, but here the boundary is a true parabola due to a uniform temperature in the specimen, as already mentioned by Lovinger and Gryte [37]. Then, they considered the case of polypropylene with two phases α and β growing at different rates, in two situations: transcrystalline zone β/spherulite α and transcrystalline zone α/spherulite β. In the first one, the α spherulite exhibits a teardrop shape as in a temperature gradient [38].

Transcrystallinity in thin strips of polymer films can be reproduced by 2D or three-dimensional (3D) computer simulations (e.g., [47, 50, 51]). Additional nuclei with a given density are simply added on the borders and the program calculates the actual shapes of semicrystalline entities (Fig. 15.10). This demonstrates the geometrical origin of "pure" transcrystallinity. Computer simulation was also employed to study crystallization at fiber surfaces [52–56].

15.3 MODELING

15.3.1 General Framework

The coupling between the thermomechanical model of the process and the crystallization kinetics is generally achieved through the energy equation, which is modified to take into account the heat released by crystallization:

$$\rho\left(c\frac{dT}{dt} - \Delta H \frac{d\alpha}{dt}\right) = div(k\,\mathbf{grad}\,T) + \dot{w} \quad (15.6)$$

where T is the temperature and t is the time; ρ, c, and k are the density, the mass specific heat, and the thermal conductivity, respectively; $\dot{w}$ is the viscous dissipation term; ΔH is the total heat per unit mass released by the crystallization (see Section 15.2.3); and $\alpha(t)$ is the transformed volume fraction.

$\alpha(t)$ can be described by different mathematical expressions, which have been critically assessed in a recent review by Piorkowska et al. [57] (see also Chapter 7). Most of them derive from the general equation proposed by Avrami [58–60]:

$$\alpha(t) = 1 - \exp[-\tilde{\alpha}(t)] \quad (15.7)$$

$\tilde{\alpha}(t)$ is the "extended" transformed fraction, which is calculated by ignoring the impingement of growing domains and including the "phantom" entities originating from nucleation attempts in already solidified areas. For spheres growing at a radial growth rate $G(t)$, $\tilde{\alpha}(t)$ is given by:

$$\tilde{\alpha}(t) = \frac{4\pi}{3}\int_0^t \left[\int_\tau^t G(u)du\right]^3 \frac{d\tilde{N}_a(\tau)}{d\tau}d\tau \quad (15.8)$$

where $d\tilde{N}_a(t)/dt$ is the "extended" nucleation rate.

15.3.2 Simplified Expressions

In isothermal conditions, $G = const.$, and if the nucleation is either purely instantaneous ($d\tilde{N}_a(\tau)/d\tau = D\delta(\tau)$, δ being the Dirac delta function), or purely sporadic (or "spontaneous" according to Chapter 7) in time ($d\tilde{N}_a(\tau)/d\tau = B$), Equation (15.8) assumes the form:

$$\tilde{\alpha}(t) = kt^n \quad (15.9)$$

where k is a temperature function dependent on the nucleation and growth rates, and n is the Avrami exponent, which assumes integer values depending on the type of nucleation and the dimensionality of the process. Nakamura et al. [61] have extended Equation (15.9) to nonisothermal crystallization:

$$\tilde{\alpha}(t) = \left[\int_0^t k(T)^{1/n} ds\right]^n = \left[\int_0^t K(T) ds\right]^n \quad (15.10)$$

where T is the time-dependent temperature. This approach is very popular in polymer processing.

For cooling at a constant rate $\dot{T}$ and the same types of nucleation as above (instantaneous or sporadic in time), Ozawa [62] has proposed the following expression:

$$\tilde{\alpha}(t) = \frac{\chi(T)}{|\dot{T}^n|} \quad (15.11)$$

generalized by Billon et al. [63] to nonconstant cooling rate in the form:

$$\tilde{\alpha}(t) = \left[\int_0^t -\frac{d\chi^{1/n}(T)}{dT}ds\right]^n \quad (15.12)$$

where n is the Avrami exponent and $\chi(T)$ a temperature function. Ozawa–Billon's approach is formally equivalent to Nakamura's one. It is easy to see that:

$$\frac{d\chi^{1/n}(T)}{dT} = -k^{1/n}(T) = -K(T). \quad (15.13)$$

Nevertheless, from an experimental point of view, Nakamura's approach utilizes results of isothermal crystallization, while Ozawa's involves experiments performed at constant cooling rates. The kinetic parameters $\chi(T)$ and n can be modified to take into account flow effects [64, 65]:

$$\ln \chi(T, \dot{\alpha}) = \ln \chi(T) + f(\dot{\alpha}) \quad (15.14)$$
$$n(\dot{\alpha}) = n + g(\dot{\alpha}) \quad (15.15)$$

where $\dot{\alpha}$ is the strain rate (shear or elongation), and the functions $f(\dot{\alpha})$ and $g(\dot{\alpha})$ are deduced from experiments.

15.3.3 General Systems of Differential Equations

Schneider et al. [66] differentiated Equation (15.8) with respect to time and obtained a system of differential equations, called the rate equations, enabling the creation of auxiliary functions $\phi_i(t)$ interrelated in the following way:

$$\phi_i(t)G(t) = \dot{\phi}_{i-1}(t) \quad (15.16)$$

for $i = 1, 2$, and 3, $\dot{\phi}_{i-1}(t)$ being the time derivative of $\phi_{i-1}(t)$. These functions are in the form:

$$\phi_0(t) = \frac{4\pi}{3}\int_0^t\left[\int_\tau^t G(u)du\right]^3 \frac{d\tilde{N}_a(\tau)}{d\tau}d\tau = \tilde{\alpha}(t) \quad (15.17a)$$

$$\phi_1(t) = 4\pi\int_0^t\left[\int_\tau^t G(u)du\right]^2 \frac{d\tilde{N}_a(\tau)}{d\tau}d\tau \quad (15.17b)$$

$$\phi_2(t) = 8\pi\int_0^t\left[\int_\tau^t G(u)du\right]\frac{d\tilde{N}_a(\tau)}{d\tau}d\tau \quad (15.17c)$$

$$\phi_3(t) = 8\pi\int_0^t \frac{d\tilde{N}_a(\tau)}{d\tau}d\tau = 8\pi\tilde{N}_a(t). \quad (15.17d)$$

The functions ϕ_0 and ϕ_1 describe the total volume and surface of all the spherulites, per unit of volume, neglecting, however, spherulite impingement and truncation while taking into account phantom spherulites. With the same assumptions, $\phi_2/8\pi$ and $\phi_3/8\pi$ represent the sum of radii and the number of spherulites in unit volume.

More recently, Haudin and Chenot [67] also differentiated Equation (15.8), with additional considerations on nucleation based on Avrami's work [58, 59]: active nuclei originate from potential nuclei that are activated at the frequency $q(t)$. These potential nuclei may disappear either by activation or by absorption by a growing entity. Conversely, new potential nuclei may be generated during cooling. In the 3D case, the authors arrive to a nonlinear system of seven differential equations with seven unknown functions:

$$\frac{dN}{dt} = -N\left(q + \frac{1}{1-\alpha}\frac{d\alpha}{dt}\right) + (1-\alpha)\frac{dN_0(T)}{dT}\frac{dT}{dt} \quad (15.18a)$$

$$\frac{d\alpha}{dt} = 4\pi(1-\alpha)G(F^2\tilde{N}_a - 2FP + Q) \quad (15.18b)$$

$$\frac{dN_a}{dt} = qN \tag{15.18c}$$

$$\frac{d\tilde{N}_a}{dt} = \frac{qN}{1-\alpha} \tag{15.18d}$$

$$\frac{dF}{dt} = G \tag{15.18e}$$

$$\frac{dP}{dt} = F\frac{d\tilde{N}_a}{dt} \tag{15.18f}$$

$$\frac{dQ}{dt} = F^2 \frac{d\tilde{N}_a}{dt} \tag{15.18g}$$

with the initial conditions at time $t = 0$:

$$N(0) = N_0, \alpha(0) = N_a(0) = \tilde{N}_a(0) = F(0) = P(0) = Q(0) = 0. \tag{15.19}$$

The main variables are N, α, N_a, $\tilde{N}_a$ and three auxiliary functions F, P and Q are added to get a first-order ordinary differential system. N and N_a are the number of potential and activated nuclei per unit volume at time t, respectively; $\tilde{N}_a$ is the "extended" number of activated nuclei per unit volume. The model predicts crystallization using three physical parameters: the initial density of potential nuclei N_0, the frequency of activation q of these nuclei, and the growth rate G.

A major interest of the differential forms is that they are more suitable for numerical simulation. Both Schneider et al. [66] and Haudin and Chenot [67] approaches have been extended to integrate flow effects [68, 69]. Flow introduces additional nuclei. Two types of morphologies can be considered: spherulites (point-like nuclei) or shish–kebabs (thread-like nuclei). The number density N_f of flow-induced nuclei is given by the following type of equation:

$$\frac{dN_f}{dt} + \frac{1}{\lambda}N_f = f \tag{15.20}$$

where λ is a relaxation time, and f is a function that describes the effect of flow and varies according to the authors.

15.4 CRYSTALLIZATION IN SOME SELECTED PROCESSES

15.4.1 Cast Film Extrusion

15.4.1.1 Presentation of the Process Cast film extrusion is one of the important processes to manufacture plates, sheets, and films of polymer. It is generally pre-

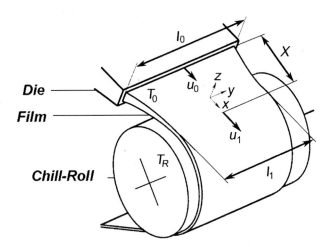

Figure 15.11 Cast film extrusion. Sketch of the process.

ferred to other processes for low viscosity polymers or for technical films requiring, for instance, a constant thickness or a smooth surface. An important application of this technique is to provide primary sheets or films, which can be either uniaxially (polyethylene or polypropylene tapes) or biaxially (PET films for audio or video tapes, polypropylene films for capacitors) stretched. This application has been chosen to illustrate structure development.

In cast film extrusion (Fig. 15.11), the polymer melt is extruded through a slit die, slightly stretched on a short distance in air (air gap X about 10 cm), and cooled on the metallic surface of a thermoregulated chill-roll. Primary polypropylene films for subsequent biaxial stretching will be considered here. Their thickness is in the 300–500 µm range. Experimental studies show that in current industrial practice the polymer cannot crystallize in air and that the film geometry no longer varies as soon as the film is in contact with the roll. Therefore, the process can be divided into two distinct steps: stretching the molten polymer in air and cooling on the roll, where crystallization occurs. Three key parameters for structure development are:

- the temperature T_0 of the polymer at the die exit (extrusion temperature),
- the temperature T_R of the chill roll,
- the average stretching stress $\bar{\sigma}_{xx}$ in air.

The analysis of structure development is based on the combination of a thermomechanical model and of an experimental study of structures and morphologies inside the films.

15.4.1.2 Thermomechanical Model Taking into account the operating conditions, a general model of the process can be divided into two parts: (1) a thermo-mechanical model of stretching the liquid polymer in air and (2) a purely thermal model of cooling on the roll, taking crystallization phenomena into account. Many models have been proposed for stretching in air [70]. They differ by the kinematical assumptions (1D: uniform section reduction; 2D: "dog-bone" section with a membrane approximation, fully 3D), the rheological behaviour (Newtonian, viscoelastic), and the thermal hypotheses (isothermal, nonisothermal).

We consider here the model proposed Cotto et al. [71], which is 1D, Newtonian, and nonisothermal. It provides a correct description of the velocity and the temperature profiles at each step of the path in air. The temperature field $T(x, z)$ is obtained by solving the energy equation with appropriate assumptions and boundary conditions:

$$u(x)\frac{\partial T(x,z)}{\partial x} = \frac{k}{\rho c}\frac{\partial^2 T(x,z)}{\partial z^2} \quad (15.21)$$

where k is the thermal conductivity, assumed to be constant, ρ and c are the density and the mass specific heat, respectively; and $u(x)$ is the velocity component along the flow direction. This equation is valid in air and also on the roll as long as crystallization does not occur (on the roll $u(x) = u_1$). This equation is solved by an explicit finite-difference method, with a 2D mesh along x (i) and z (j).

When crystallization occurs, the energy equation has to be modified to take into account the heat liberated by crystallization:

$$u_1\frac{\partial T(x,z)}{\partial x} = \frac{k}{\rho c}\frac{\partial^2 T(x,z)}{\partial z^2} + u_1\frac{\Delta H}{c}\frac{\partial \alpha(x,z)}{\partial x} \quad (15.22)$$

where ΔH is the actual enthalpy of crystallization per unit mass and $\alpha(x, z)$ is the transformed volume fraction (solidified faction) at point (x, z). For the mathematical treatment of the kinetic law $\alpha(t)$ we used the discretized form of Equation (15.12) [72].

We have also developed a simplified method [71, 72], which is still used in industry to treat practical problems. In this simplified approach, the program directly uses an experimental crystallization curve recorded at an appropriate cooling rate. The gradual release of the latent heat between the onset (T_{onset}) and the end (T_{end}) of crystallization gives rise to an exothermal peak (see Fig. 15.4), which can be approximated by an isosceles triangle with an area equal to the enthalpy of crystallization per unit mass ΔH. The temperature profile at step $i–1$ (along x) and the heat Δh_j already released by the crystallization of a mass element located at node $(i–1, j)$ are supposed to be known. The temperature profile $T'(i, j)$ at step i is first calculated by solving Equation (15.21), that is, without taking crystallization into account. If the temperature $T_j' = T'(i, j)$ of the mass element at node (i, j) is between T_{onset} and T_{end}, this element will crystallize and liberate an additional heat δh_j. The temperature rise δT_j due to δh_j is then calculated, which gives the actual temperature $T_j = T_j' + \delta T_j$, and makes it possible to determine the temperature profile at each step i along the axial direction. As in Section 15.2.3, the transformed fraction α is defined as the ratio of the heat already released to the total heat of crystallization.

15.4.1.3 Results of the Calculations

For small air gaps, there is only a small decrease of the film temperature in air (3–8°C). Therefore, stretching can be considered a quasi-isothermal process and the polymer cannot crystallize in air.

On the roll, the dissymmetrical cooling of the film surfaces induces very different cooling rates (Fig. 15.12) and important temperature gradients in the film thickness (Fig. 15.13). It also explains the shape of the crystallization zone (Fig. 15.14). The lower surface of the film

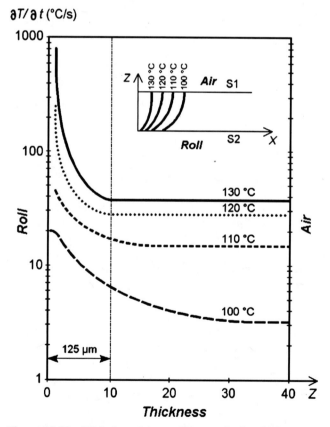

Figure 15.12 Variation of the cooling rate in the thickness of a polypropylene film on the isothermal lines 100°C, 110°C, 120°C, and 130°C, along the run on the roll [71, 72].

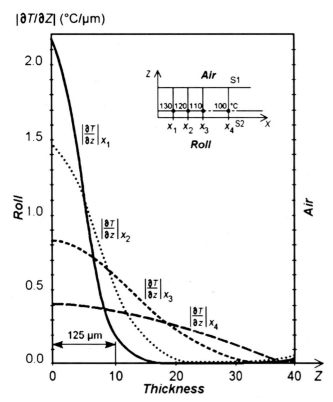

Figure 15.13 Variation of the temperature gradient in the thickness of a polypropylene film at different steps on the roll [71, 72].

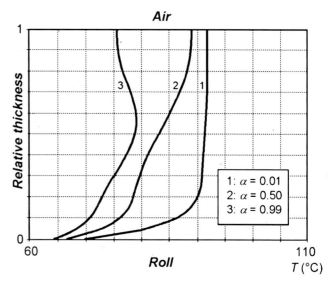

Figure 15.14 Crystallization zone in a polypropylene film. Curves 1, 2, 3 correspond to different values of the transformed volume fraction [72].

begins to crystallize as soon as it is in contact with the roll, at temperatures lower than the rest of the film, which starts crystallizing at the same temperature (curve corresponding to $\alpha = 0.01$). The temperature associated with the half-transformation curve, which can be considered as the local crystallization temperature, increases monotonically from the roll to the air zone. The end of the crystallization occurs at higher temperatures in the median zone ($\alpha = 0.99$).

15.4.1.4 Influence of Processing on Structure Development

Stretching in Air The final orientation in the films is weak. This weak orientation results both from the small values of the elongation rate (a few s^{-1}) and from the relaxation of the molecular orientation in the melt during cooling. Nevertheless, stretching in air can significantly affect the nucleation and growth of crystalline entities. If $\bar{\sigma}_{xx}$ is higher than a critical value, which is about 10 kPa for this type of polypropylene, the average size of the spherulites decreases and their shape is also altered: the spherulites exhibit an ellipsoidal shape with the major axis perpendicular to the stretching direction.

As a consequence, the overall kinetics can be also enhanced, especially at high roll temperature. To establish this point, the kinetic law has been modified to integrate the effect of stretching in air on subsequent crystallization on the roll: n has been kept equal to 3 and $\ln \chi$ has been described by Equation (15.14), where $\dot{\alpha}$ is the elongation rate just before the contact with the roll and the function $f(\dot{\alpha})$ is deduced from laboratory experiments. Figure 15.15 compares the average transformed volume fractions in the thickness of the film, calculated with and without elongation effect [65]. A very important difference is observed between the two curves. This effect has been validated by online measurements of the light backscattered by the film. When crystallization occurs, the light intensity I recorded by the photomonitor increases because of the scattering by the crystallites, and then decreases when the contact between metal and polymer is lost, which can be related to the end of crystallization. Indeed, the experimental curve is close to that calculated with elongation effect (Fig. 15.15).

Cooling on the Roll The microscopic observation of microtomed sections reveals two types of spherulites: a background of positively and weakly birefringent spherulites, crystallized in the α phase, and highly negative spherulites crystallized in the β phase.

In all the films, three zones can be distinguished (Fig. 15.16):

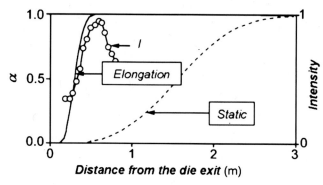

Figure 15.15 Comparison between experimental and calculated transformed volume fractions. The experimental values are deduced from light intensity measurements. The calculations are performed in two cases: without (static) or with elongation effect [65].

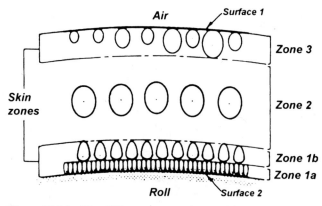

Figure 15.16 The different zones observed in a cross section of a polypropylene film [71, 72].

- a skin zone in contact with the roll (zone 1),
- a median zone (zone 2), which generally represents 50–70% of the thickness,
- a skin zone in contact with air (zone 3).

A careful investigation of zone 1 often allowed us to divide it into (1) a transcrystalline zone 1a, due to the combined effects of surface nucleation and thermal gradient, and (2) a zone 1b presenting a finer microstructure with numerous quasiparabolic spherulites near the end of the transcrystalline region. A complete analysis of some films [71, 72], from a thermomechanical and microstructural point of view, made it possible to correlate the microstructure of zone 1 and its thickness with the cooling rates and the temperature gradients calculated by the model (Fig. 15.12 and Fig. 15.13).

The β phase is in general preferentially located in the skin zones. Its average concentration and its distribution within the films vary considerably with the extrusion

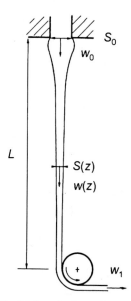

Figure 15.17 Melt spinning of a monofilament.

temperature T_0 and the roll temperature T_R [72]. The quantity of β phase increases when T_0 decreases and when T_R increases. Furthermore:

- for low extrusion temperatures, the β phase distribution is symmetrical in the film, when T_R is high ($T_R \geq 95°C$). Conversely, if T_R is low, the β phase concentration is higher in zone 3 (air) than in zone 1 (roll);
- for high extrusion temperatures ($T_0 > 250°C$), the β phase concentration is higher in zone 1, whatever T_R.

It is then possible, by modifying T_0 and T_R, to obtain quite different microstructures.

15.4.2 Fiber Spinning

15.4.2.1 Presentation of the Process
The melt spinning of fibers is an industrial processing operation of great commercial importance. Its principle is illustrated in Figure 15.17: a molten polymer filament is extruded through an orifice, stretched, and cooled in air until it solidifies. Crystallization occurs under the combined effects of drawing and cooling. It has been characterized by many online measurements. Several pertinent reviews have already been dedicated to structure development in this process [73–77]. Therefore, we will limit ourselves to a synthesis of significant results.

A major structural feature in fibers is the level of orientation. In fiber spinning, the polymer is subjected to a uniaxial stretching, which induces an orientation of macromolecules in the melt. After solidification, this orientation is partly frozen in the amorphous phase. On the other hand, molecular orientation has an influence on nucleation and growth of crystals, if the polymer is semicrystalline. Therefore, a major effect of processing is to create orientation both in the crystalline and amorphous phases. Many studies have been devoted to orientation characterization, especially in the crystalline phase.

15.4.2.2 Characterization of Crystalline Orientation by X-Ray Diffraction

Orientation of the crystalline phase in fibers has been mainly characterized by wide angle X-ray diffraction (WAXD), as described in Chapter 1. The Debye–Scherrer method with a flat-film camera makes it possible to obtain rapidly a first appraisal of the degree of orientation. A monochromatic or quasi-monochromatic (e.g., Ni-filtered Cu Kα radiation) X-ray beam is incident upon parallel polymer fibers perpendicular to their surface. A photographic film records the diffracted beams. They form circular rings, each ring corresponding to a specific hkl crystalline reflection. If the specimen is isotropic, the rings are continuous with a uniform intensity. If the specimen is oriented (or textured), the intensity distribution is generally not uniform. Continuous rings with intensity reinforcement, arcs, and finally isolated spots may be observed for increasing orientation.

The average state of orientation can be described by orientation factors, which are simple functions of the mean-square cosines of the angles ϕ_j between a crystallographic axis j ($j = a, b, c$) and the fiber axis:

$$f_j = \frac{3\langle \cos^2 \phi_j \rangle - 1}{2}. \quad (15.23)$$

Because of the cylindrical symmetry, the $\langle\cos^2\phi_j\rangle$ can be deduced from the intensity distribution on the Debye–Scherrer rings and from more or less complicated geometrical calculations in the crystalline system of the polymer [73, 76, 78].

15.4.2.3 Typical Experimental Results and Morphological Models

Figure 15.18 concerns polyethylene fibers obtained in laboratory experiments [73, 76]. It gives the orientation factors f_a, f_b, f_c defined by Equation (15.23) as a function of the take-up velocity w_1 for a given flow rate. The increase of f_c with w_1 reflects a better orientation of the chains in the crystalline phase. Furthermore, the variations of f_a, f_b, f_c can be interpreted in terms of the morphological models presented in Section 15.2.1.2. At a very low take-up velocity ($w_1 < 10$ m/min), the distribution of the a-, b-, c-axes is quasi-isotropic because the effects of drawing are too weak to modify the spherulitic morphology obtained in

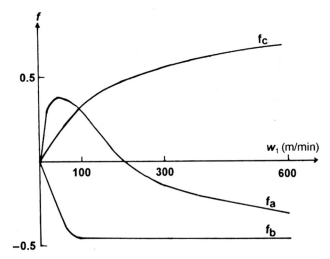

Figure 15.18 Variations of the orientation factors of polyethylene as a function of take-up velocity [73, 76].

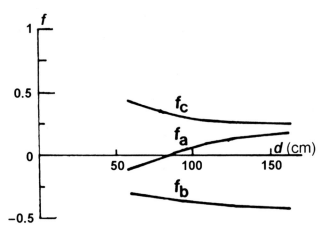

Figure 15.19 Variations of the orientation factors of polyethylene along the spinning line at intermediate take-up velocities (100–200 m/min) [73, 76].

quiescent conditions (Fig. 15.2a and Fig. 15.20a). The domain of intermediate speeds ($w_1 \sim 100$ m/min) is well described by the Keller I model (Fig. 15.2d). At high speed ($w_1 > 300$ m/min), one tends to the Keller II model (Fig. 15.2e), but the maximum orientation of the chain axis is far from the ideal value $f_c = 1$ predicted by the model. The same experiments were performed online. At low (50 m/min) and high (556 m/min) velocity, the orientation measured online is very close to that of the final fiber, and the morphologies can be described by the Keller I and II models, respectively (Fig. 15.20b,d). Conversely, in the intermediate range (100–200 m/min) the orientation of the a- and c-axes varies along the spinning line (Fig. 15.19). When crystallization starts, the orientation is close to that observed at high speed. Then,

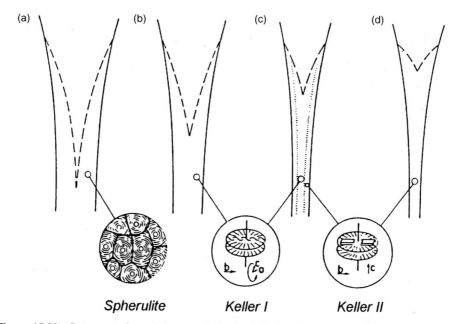

Figure 15.20 Interpretation of the morphologies in polyethylene fibers: (a) very low speeds (<10 m/min): spherulites; (b) low speeds (50 m/min): Keller I model; (c) intermediate speeds (100–200 m/min): skin-core structure; (d) high speed (556 m/min): Keller II model [73, 76].

it tends to the orientation state for low velocity. This suggests that at the fiber surface, crystallization starts with Keller II morphology and continues inside with Keller I morphology (Fig. 15.20c). This leads to a "skin-core" structure.

In isotactic polypropylene [73, 76], the smectic phase or the monoclinic α phase can be obtained according to cooling conditions. Furthermore, the α phase may, in certain conditions, exhibit a bimodal crystalline texture, that is, two populations of crystals with their c or their a^*-axis along the fiber axis, respectively (a^* is the axis of the reciprocal lattice related to a). This is revealed by additional arcs or spots on the 110 and 130 reflections, while the 040 reflections remain unchanged [79] (Fig. 15.21). This can be interpreted in terms of a cylindritic morphology with two types of lamellae: classical radial lamellae and tangential ones obtained by epitaxial growth, which is a particular feature of polypropylene crystallization (see Chapter 8).

A great amount of work has been devoted to high speed spinning of PET because of its industrial importance (for reviews see References [75, 77]). An increase of the take-up velocity first induces an orientation of the macromolecular chains, but the material remains amorphous: no change in density is observed below 3000 m/min. As an intermediate stage, many authors postulate the development of an oriented "mesophase" prior to the crystallization into the usual triclinic phase. Then,

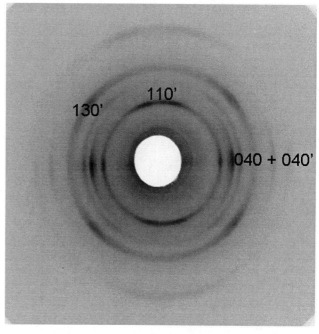

Figure 15.21 X-ray diffraction pattern of a polypropylene sample containing a bimodal texture.

both birefringence and crystallinity increase up to maxima observed in the neighborhood of 6000 m/min. Their decrease at higher speed results from the competition between cooling and drawing, which additionally induces a "skin-core" structure. Another interesting feature is the formation of a neck above 4500 m/min: it corresponds to an abrupt increase of birefringence and is associated with the development of crystallization. The basic crystalline entities are parallelepiped extended-chain crystallites, whose dimensions increase with take-up velocity. Their mutual organization can be studied by small-angle X-ray scattering (SAXS). As crystallinity develops, four-point patterns are observed. For higher speeds, they are changed into distorted two-point meridional patterns, with an equatorial streak indicating void formation along the fiber axis. Both WAXD (wide-angle X-ray diffraction) and SAXS patterns make it possible to propose morphological models like those presented in Figure 15.22. In these models the high speed spun fiber consists of microfibrils containing alternating crystalline blocks and amorphous regions parallel to the fiber axis. Adjacent microfibrils are shifted parallel to each other, constituting a larger region in which the crystals form an angle φ with the normal to the fiber axis.

15.4.2.4 Modeling Since the late sixties, fiber spinning has been the object of many thermomechanical models including crystallization phenomena [74–77]. Most of them are based on the extension of isothermal Avrami's approach (Eq. 15.7 and Eq. 15.9) to nonisothermal crystallization, which is now known as Nakamura's model (Eq. 15.10). In such an approach, the K function depends not only on temperature but also on flow effects. This flow dependence must be established experimentally through a relevant physical parameter such as stress, stored energy, orientation factor, and birefringence. It must be noticed that in some models, Avrami's exponent is taken equal to one. Doufas et al. have applied their two-phase model (see Section 15.2.1.1) to fiber spinning [80] and obtained good comparisons with experiments [81]. This model is interesting since it introduces a coupling between mechanical, thermal, and crystallization parameters. Nevertheless, it must be underlined that the crystallization kinetics is also described by Nakamura's equation, with an additional term that accounts for the effect of flow through an adjustable parameter.

15.4.3 Film Blowing

15.4.3.1 Presentation of the Process Film blowing is the main process to manufacture polymer films. It is essentially dedicated to polyethylene, especially for packaging or agricultural applications. In this process, the polymer melt is extruded through an annular die, and then simultaneously inflated by a certain volume of air entrapped in the bubble and drawn by nip rolls (Fig. 15.23). Cooling is achieved by blowing air through a ring located outside the bubble. In recent technological

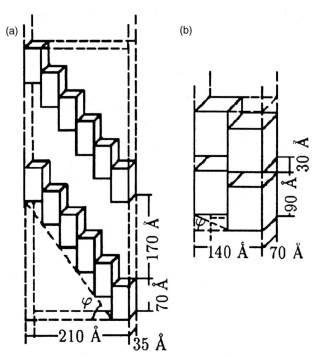

Figure 15.22 Models of microfibrils in high speed spun PET: (a) 5000 m/min; (b) 9000 m/min [77].

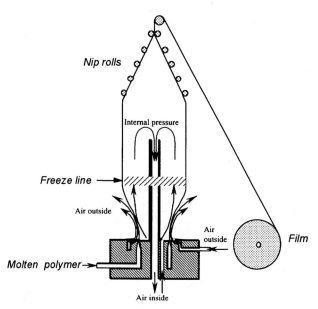

Figure 15.23 Schematic diagram of the film blowing process.

developments, the film can be also cooled from inside with the help of a cooling mandrel, or from outside but with sophisticated double-flux air rings. Once the film is solidified, it is pulled, folded and wound on cylindrical cores. The main technological parameters are then:

- the blow-up ratio Bur, that is, the ratio of the final radius of the bubble to the radius of the die,
- the draw ratio Dr or take-up ratio Tur, that is, the ratio of the take-up velocity to the velocity at the die exit,
- the freeze line height Flh at which the polymer solidifies.

The polymer is subjected to a biaxial stretching, which creates orientation both in the crystalline and in the amorphous phases. As in fiber spinning, many studies have been dedicated to orientation characterization, especially in the crystalline phase, but biaxial orientation requires more sophisticated methods. More recently, much effort has been devoted to the description of the morphology at the lamellar scale, for example, by electron microscopy.

15.4.3.2 Orientation Studies

Experimental Techniques Orientation of the crystalline phase in polyethylene films has been mainly characterized by WAXD [82–98]. In the first studies, the Debye–Scherrer method was employed with a flat-film camera [82–84]. This technique was still used in further work because of its rapidity and its simplicity [87, 88, 93, 95–98].

After the pioneering work of Lindenmeyer and Lustig [85], the use of pole figures has been generalized [86, 89–95]. Pole figures are stereographic projections giving the space distribution of the normals N_{hkl} to the {hkl} crystallographic planes. These projections are plotted in the 1, 2, 3 or OXYZ or (MD, TD, ND) frame of reference where:

- Direction 1 = OX = MD is the vertical direction of longitudinal stretching, also called machine direction,
- Direction 2 = OY = TD is the transverse direction,
- Direction 3 = OZ = ND is the direction of the film normal.

The film plane OXY or (MD, TD) is usually taken as projection plane. If the film is too thin, several layers are stacked. To construct a pole figure, the intensity diffracted by the {hkl} planes is recorded as a function of two angles ρ_Z and β_Z: ρ_Z is the angle between OZ and the normal N_{hkl} to the diffracting plane; β_Z is the angle between OX and the projection of N_{hkl} onto the OXY plane (Fig. 15.24a). After corrections and normalization, this intensity represents the density $q(\rho_Z, \beta_Z)$ of N_{hkl} normals. A Wulff net graduated in ρ_Z and β_Z makes it possible to plot, for each couple (ρ_Z, β_Z), the value of $q(\rho_Z, \beta_Z)$ on the stereographic projection (Fig. 15.24b). Isodensity lines are then drawn, the representative points being also called poles. Level 1 corresponds to a density equal to the average density.

From the approaches of Wilchinsky [78] and of Desper and Stein [99], some authors [86, 93] combined pole figures and calculation of uniaxial orientation factors, given by:

$$f_{j,i} = \frac{3\langle \cos^2 \phi_{j,i}\rangle - 1}{2}. \qquad (15.24)$$

Equation (15.24) is a generalization of Equation (15.23); $\phi_{j,i}$ denotes the angle between a crystallographic axis j ($j = a, b, c$) and a macroscopic axis i (i = MD, TD, ND). Choi et al. [94] and Haudin et al. [97] preferred the

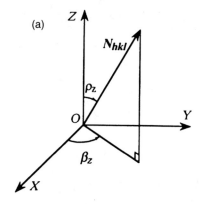
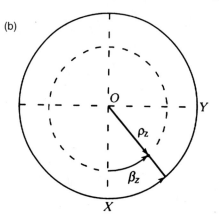

Figure 15.24 Characterization of the orientation of a normal N_{hkl}: (a) in 3D-space; (b) on the stereographic projection.

biaxial orientation factors introduced by White and Spruiell [100]:

$$f_{j,MD}^B = 2\langle\cos^2\phi_{j,MD}\rangle + \langle\cos^2\phi_{j,TD}\rangle - 1 \quad (15.25a)$$

$$f_{j,TD}^B = \langle\cos^2\phi_{j,MD}\rangle + 2\langle\cos^2\phi_{j,TD}\rangle - 1. \quad (15.25b)$$

For polyethylene, the <$\cos^2\phi_{j,i}$> for the a- and b-axes are calculated directly from the pole figures. The values for the c-axis are then deduced from these calculations [93, 94]. The biaxial orientation factors can be expressed in terms of an orientation triangle as shown in Figure 15.25. This triangle is a region in the f_{MD}^B versus f_{TD}^B space set about the origin (0, 0) and with corners at (1, 0), (0, 1), and (−1, −1). The origin represents isotropy, while the points (1, 0), (0, 1) and (−1, −1) correspond to perfect uniaxial orientation in the MD, TD, and ND directions, respectively. The first bisector describes states of perfect biaxial orientation.

Typical Experimental Results The X-ray diffraction patterns of low density polyethylene (LDPE) films show the three main reflections of PE: 110, 200, and 020. The 020 reflection, which is less intense, is not easily visible on the photographic prints. It is the reason why the patterns of Figure 15.26 have been redrawn. For a blow-up ratio (Bur) close to one, the patterns corresponding to the lowest draw ratios exhibit specific features reported in many papers (Fig. 15.26a): the 200 ring is reduced to two arcs along the MD direction; the 110 reflection is in the form of four arcs symmetrical with respect to MD and TD; the 020 reflection is composed of two arcs along TD. When draw ratio (Dr) increases (Fig. 15.26b), each 200 arc is split into two new arcs moving away from MD, whereas the other reflections seem less sensitive to the draw ratio.

Figure 15.27 presents 200 and 020 pole figures of an LDPE [85]. They give direct access to the orientation of the a- and b-axes. Unlike the case of HDPE, there is no 002 reflection, and consequently no direct information on the c-axes. This information cannot be deduced from the qualitative analysis of the 200 and 020 pole figures, and the average orientation of the c-axes can be obtained only through the calculation of orientation factors. The figure, which shows the influence of increasing Bur at constant film thickness, will be discussed later.

Figure 15.28, which displays White–Spruiell triangles, makes a synthesis of results obtained on three series of blown films differing by the nature of the polymer and the processing conditions [101]:

- series A: two LDPE with about the same density, but differing by their average molar masses and relaxation times;
- series B: two LDPE and a linear low-density polyethylene (LLDPE) with about the same density. Extrusion was achieved using either a single-flux air ring or a double-flux air ring;
- series C: seven LLDPE differing by the type of catalysts and the type of branching.

These results will be discussed in the following section.

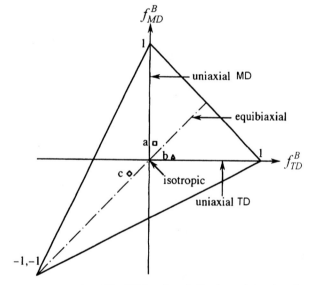

Figure 15.25 The White–Spruiell orientation triangle.

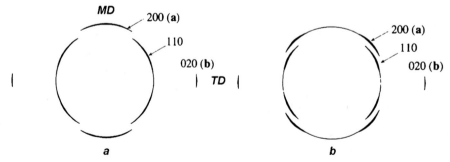

Figure 15.26 Redrawn X-ray diffraction patterns of LDPE films with Bur ~ 1: (a) Dr = 9.8; (b) Dr = 23.8 [97].

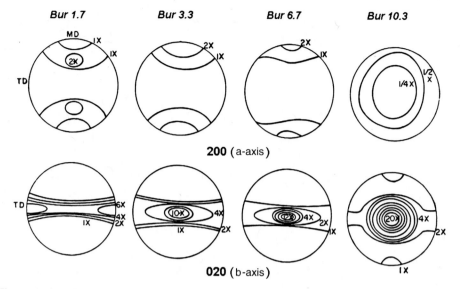

Figure 15.27 200 and 020 pole figures of an LDPE as a function of the blow-up ratio [85].

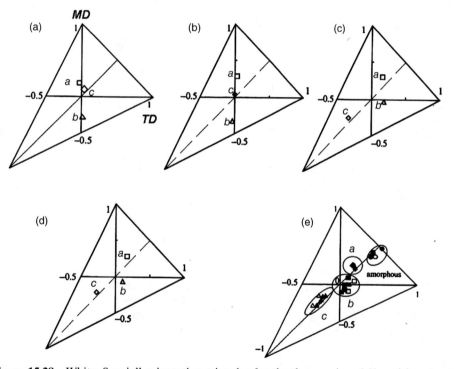

Figure 15.28 White–Spruiell orientation triangles for the three series of films: (a) series A; (b) series B LDPE, single-flux air ring; (c) series B LDPE, double-flux air ring; (d) series B LLDPE, double-flux air ring; (e) series C [101].

Influence of the Polymer and the Processing Conditions The specific effect of drawing is well appreciated in experiments achieved with Bur close to one. The b-axis, which is the growth axis of polyethylene crystals, is perpendicular to MD. A deviation of the perfect cylindrical symmetry around MD is very often observed with a preferred orientation along TD. At low draw ratios, the a-axes are oriented along MD. When Dr increases, they become oriented away from MD, at an angle which tends to 90°. However, this limit value has been obtained only in a few cases, for highly drawn HDPE [96].

The influence of blowing is well described by Figure 15.27. At low blow-up ratio (Bur = 1.7), the distribution of the b-axes is the same as for Bur = 1. When Bur

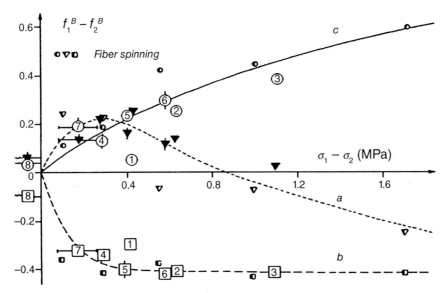

Figure 15.29 Plot of the difference in the biaxial orientation factors as a function of the difference in the final stresses in the longitudinal and transverse directions. Case of HDPE [94].

increases, the *b*-axes remain perpendicular to MD, but a maximum of the pole density appears around ND (Bur = 3.3 and 6.7). At the same time, the *a*-axes density exhibits a maximum at about 45° from the machine direction (Bur = 1.7). For higher Bur (Bur = 6.7), the *a*-axes are preferentially oriented along MD, and the Debye–Scherrer diagram is analogous to the one of Figure 15.26a, although the blowing of the film is important. At very high blow-up ratio, there is an important change in the crystalline texture: a strong orientation of the *b*-axis parallel to the film normal appears, and the *a*-axis is uniformly dispersed in the plane of the film. These results are in agreement with those of other authors, who observed the same general evolution. Nevertheless, the values of Dr and Bur for obtaining a given texture, as well as the exact position and intensity of the maxima, depend on the system under investigation. For instance, the maximum observed for the *a*-axis distribution at Bur = 1.7 may be located between 20° and 50° from MD (see for instance [90–94]).

Many results show that in the crystalline phase the macromolecular chains tend to be oriented along MD, as soon as there is drawing in that direction. As a consequence, the texture remains almost uniaxial even in blown specimens, as shown by Figure 15.28a, where the representative points of the *a*-, *b*-, *c*-axes in the orientation triangle are close to the MD axis. The orientation tends to become equibiaxial when (1) the blow-up ratio is increased, (2) the freeze line height is increased, or (3) the draw ratio is reduced. In industrial practice, the blow-up ratio is often limited to about four. Therefore, it is necessary to decrease Dr to tend toward a biaxial orientation, but in such conditions the level of orientation becomes very weak. Experiments with Bur values of about 10 as in Lindenmeyer and Lustig's work [85] are rare. It must be noticed in this case that the increase in Bur is accompanied by a decrease of Dr since the film thickness is constant. This explains the important effects observed.

To quantitatively express the competition between drawing and blowing in the case of HDPE films, Choi et al. [94] have plotted $f_{j,1}^B - f_{j,2}^B$ for *a*, *b*, and *c* against the difference $\sigma_1-\sigma_2$ of the final stresses in the longitudinal and transverse directions, respectively (Fig. 15.29). They also plotted previous results obtained for HDPE melt-spun fibers. The points for film blowing and fiber spinning are located on the same curves, which suggests the same mechanisms of structure development in both processes. Haudin et al. did the same plot for the two LDPE of series A [97]. Similar results are obtained, but stresses are much lower for LDPE (Fig. 15.30). The right part of Figure 15.30 ($\sigma_1 - \sigma_2 > 0$) concerns films with Bur close to 1. When $\sigma_1 - \sigma_2$ increases with drawing:

- the orientation of the crystalline chains (*c*-axes) in the machine direction increases, but the stress level is too low to induce a high orientation;
- the *b*-axes become very rapidly perpendicular to the machine direction, with an orientation factor difference close to –0.5;
- the *a*-axis first presents an orientation along MD, which is maximum at $\sigma_1 - \sigma_2 = 0.04$ MPa. Then, the orientation factor difference decreases, which reflects a progressive orientation away from MD.

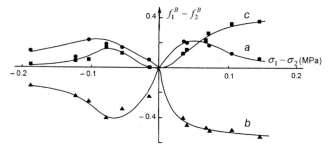

Figure 15.30 Plot of the difference in the biaxial orientation factors as a function of the difference in the final stresses in the longitudinal and transverse directions. Case of LDPE [97].

The left part of Figure 15.30 ($\sigma_1 - \sigma_2 < 0$), which was not explored by Choi et al. except for one condition [94], concerns blown films. When $\sigma_1 - \sigma_2$ varies between 0 and −0.06 MPa, a, b, and c exhibit the same type of behavior as for the specimens with Bur = 1. Then, after their maximum, the curves for the a- and c-axes decrease and seem to tend to zero. At the same time, the orientation factor difference for the b-axis tends to zero by negative values. This demonstrates the progressive influence of blowing, which seems to be efficient only above some critical value of the stress difference.

The experiments of series B lay emphasis on the cooling conditions. With a single-flux air ring, crystalline orientation is of the same type as in the first series, as shown by the orientation triangles. For both types of specimens, White–Spruiell triangles show a nearly uniaxial orientation, with a preferential orientation of the chain axis (c-axis) along DM (Fig. 15.28a,b). When a double-flux air ring is used, a new texture with the c-axis preferentially in the film thickness is revealed by the orientation triangles (Fig. 15.28c). For given processing conditions, the nature of the material is of little influence: the same texture is obtained for an LDPE (Fig. 15.28c) and an LLDPE (Fig. 15.28d).

Series C compares LLDPE with different chemical structures, but transformed in the same processing conditions. Because of these changes in chemical structure, inducing for instance differences in the relaxation times, the quantitative levels of orientation are different from one polymer to another. Nevertheless, they all exhibit the same type of texture, with the same features as in series B for specimens cooled with a double-flux air ring (Fig. 15.28e): almost isotropic distribution of b-axes, and c-axes preferentially in the film thickness. The amorphous chains, for their part, are isotropically located in the film plane (Fig. 15.28e).

15.4.3.3 Morphological Models
X-ray patterns exhibiting a preferential orientation of the a-axis along the machine direction were first interpreted by the a-texture model [102], in which the a-axis lies along MD, whereas b and c are randomly distributed in the perpendicular plane. This model was soon abandoned and replaced by the row-structure model with twisted lamellae (Keller I), described in Figure 15.2d. More recently, the model for high stress (Keller II) was applied to highly drawn HDPE films [96]. To take into account orientation states intermediate between the spherulite and the row-nucleated structures, Haudin and coworkers [93, 97] proposed a sheaf model, in which the crystallites are represented by arcs of circles. This makes it possible to obtain a wide range of morphologies, and to calculate the corresponding orientation factors of the b-axis, for comparison with experimental data. Therefore, the proposed morphologies are fully included in the morphological sequence of Figure 15.2. These models, which assume a cylindrical symmetry around MD, can be modified by introducing an elliptical cross section of the morphologies, which could explain some preferential orientation of the b-axes along TD [88]. The degree of twisting of crystalline lamellae is also an important morphological parameter. Keller considered only two extreme cases [11, 12]: random twisting around the radius and absence of twisting. Nagasawa et al. have improved the model by calculating the evolution of the orientation of the a-axis as a function of the degree of twisting of lamellar crystals [88].

Until recently the row-structure model has been supported by many observations of the surfaces of blown films. Garber and Clark [103] investigated the row structure in polyoxymethylene blown films. They reported, for the first time, direct experimental evidence of fibril nuclei aligned along the extrusion direction, with bundles of twisted lamellae oriented normal to the fibrils. The work of Nagasawa et al. [87, 88] must also be mentioned. The observation of surface replicas by transmission electron microscopy (TEM) revealed, at the surface of the films, stacks of lamellae grown perpendicular to the extrusion direction. By a complementary study combining different experimental techniques, the authors showed that the lamellae were organized into columnar morphologies, which is consistent with the cylindritic model. Concerning the sheaf model, sheaf-like textures were several times detected at the surface of polybutene-1 films [87, 104]. Nowadays, the surface morphology of blown films can be easily investigated by AFM (e.g., [105]).

It is more complicated to explain the crystalline textures where b tends to be oriented along the film normal. Some authors [94] proposed a model consisting of arrays of row-nucleated morphologies randomly distributed in the film plane (Fig. 15.31). Maddams and Preedy [90] suggested the influence of transcrystallinity,

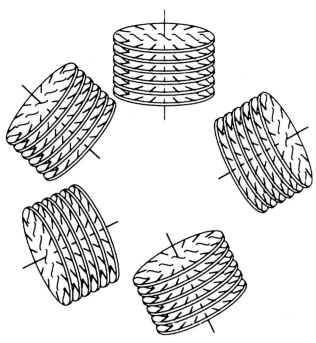

Figure 15.31 Model for the description of crystalline morphologies in a polyethylene film with an equibiaxial texture [94].

whereas Matsumura [89] also assumed a inhomogeneous texture in the film thickness. He considered different layers consisting of cylindrites with a variable elliptical cross-section. This model is able to explain the appearance of a preferred orientation of the b-axis along ND.

Preparation of thin films now allows the authors to visualize by TEM the organization of crystalline lamellae in polyethylene films [96, 98, 106–109]. The morphological features under consideration are generally the growth direction of the lamellae and their degree of twisting. For instance, Tas [106] showed that for blow-up ratios close to one, the lamellae were stacked with their growth axis perpendicular to the extrusion direction. When the blow-up ratio increased, they were more randomly distributed. As a function of the degree of long chain branching, Prasad et al. [108] obtained either well-oriented stacked lamellae with distinguishable fibril nuclei along MD (high LCB), or lamellae randomly oriented with respect to MD (low LCB). Lu et al. [109] observed a structure consisting of two superimposed row-oriented textures, with lamellae stacked along the machine and the transverse directions, respectively. Finally, an interesting contribution of Yu and Wilkes [96] was to make a clear distinction between stacks of lamellae, which can be considered as a limiting case of the sheaf model, and "true" row-nucleated structures with fibril nuclei.

With the development of LLDPE, spherulites are also observed in the films. They can be characterized by small-angle light scattering (SALS) [95]. This technique can be used to follow online structure development [110]. The variation of average scattered intensity with axial position can be described using two Avrami kinetic processes in parallel. The first step accounts for crystal growth and corresponds to the temperature plateau. The later processes start with the impingement of the growing spherulites and reflect secondary crystallization and orientation processes.

All the results reported in this section dealing with film blowing generally support the morphological models described in Figure 15.2a–f, and sometimes bring some subtle refinements. However, the crystalline texture observed in Figure 15.28c–e and characterized by a preferential orientation of the c-axis in the film thickness cannot be accounted for by these models. To gather more information, the surface of the series C films corresponding to Figure 15.28e was observed by SEM [101]. A clear difference was observed between the least and the most oriented films: globular spherulite-like morphologies on one hand, and stacks of lamellae on the other hand, with a progressive variation in-between. The changes in the orientation factors seem relatively weak compared with these drastic morphological changes. Furthermore, the apparent spherulitic texture is not associated with isotropy, and the stacks of twisted lamellae do not correspond to the Keller I model. Consequently, this apparent discrepancy between crystallographic and morphological textures remains an open problem. This discrepancy has been also emphasized in other work [107].

15.4.3.4 Modeling Compared with fiber spinning, film blowing has been the object of few models including crystallization phenomena [111–115]. Most of them are based on Nakamura's model (Eq. 15.10). As for fiber spinning, the variations of K with both temperature and flow are taken into account. The two-phase model of Doufas et al. has been also applied to film blowing [112, 114].

15.4.4 Injection Molding

15.4.4.1 Presentation of the Process Injection molding is a commercially important process for the production of parts with various sizes and shapes in large quantity. The molten polymer is injected under pressure into a cold cavity (Fig. 15.32). During this filling stage, macromolecules in the polymer fluid are oriented and deformed by flow. At the contact with the mold, a polymer layer solidifies rapidly and there is an important temperature gradient in this region. One can also

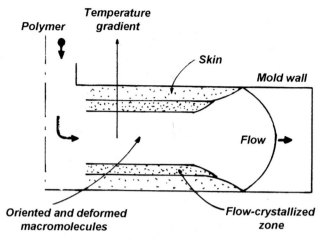

Figure 15.32 The filling stage in injection molding. The shape and the thickness of the solidified layers are schematic.

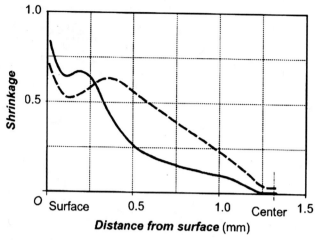

Figure 15.33 Variation of the longitudinal shrinkage in two polystyrene specimens injected at different speeds [134].

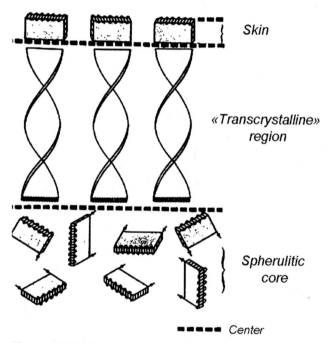

Figure 15.34 Crystalline morphologies in a polyoxymethylene bar [130].

suppose that between this solidified layer and the melt, an additional layer has crystallized under the influence of flow. Once the mold is filled the polymer is maintained under pressure to compensate volume changes during cooling. The polymer continues to crystallize under pressure and under the influence of a much weaker flow, but at a lower temperature. When the gate is sealed, the rest of the crystallization occurs under quiescent conditions with a possible relaxation of the orientation and the deformation of the macromolecules. Therefore, the structure development is very complex and a heterogeneous microstructure is expected both along the flow direction and in the cross section of the parts. This implies that a detailed investigation of the microstructures must be local, and that locally, the final microstructure observed will be the result of a complex thermomechanical history.

Due to the industrial importance of the process, many semicrystalline polymers have been investigated: polyethylene [116–121], isotatic polypropylene [122–127], polybutene-1 [128], polyoxymethylene (or polyacetal) [129–131], polyamide 6 [132], poly(phenylene sulphide) (PPS) [133], and so on.

15.4.4.2 Typical Experimental Results Consider first an amorphous polymer: polystyrene [134]. This first example has been chosen to show the effect of flow on the final orientation. The molecular orientation in the part thickness has been characterized by shrinkage measurements (Fig. 15.33). It is maximum at the surface, decreases, passes through a secondary maximum, and finally tends to zero at the core.

For semicrystalline polymers, the first important study on the microstructure of injected parts is by Clark and concerns polyoxymethylene bars [129, 130]. Three zones are observed by optical microscopy from the surface to the center of the bar (Fig. 15.34). In the first zone beginning at the surface, crystalline lamellae are perpendicular both to the surface and to the flow direction. The morphology consists of stacks of lamellae, as checked by SAXS and SEM. In the second zone, improperly called the "transcrystalline region," lamellae are still perpendicular to the surface but lose their preferred orientation with respect to the flow direction. At the end

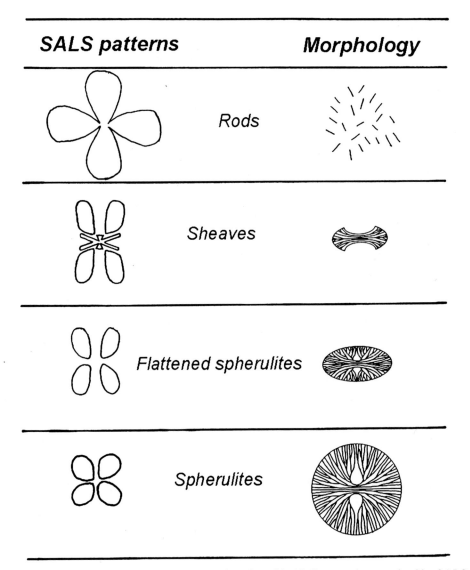

Figure 15.35 The morphological sequence in polyamide 12 discs, as characterized by SALS: from spherulites (core) to rods (skin) (J.M. Escleine and J.M. Haudin, unpublished results).

of this zone, quasiparabolic spherulites can be observed, but they were not identified by Clark. Finally, there is no preferred orientation at the core, and the morphology is spherulitic.

The morphologies in 2-mm-thick polyamide 12 discs have been investigated by SALS (J.M. Escleine and J.M. Haudin, unpublished results). The SALS patterns (Fig. 15.35) have been interpreted using the current models existing in the literature [135]. At about 100 µm from the surface, the pattern is of the rod-like type, which indicates a poor organization of the crystalline lamellae. Furthermore, additional observations indicate a high global orientation. The patterns observed at 200, 300, and 400 µm correspond to sheaf-like morphologies.

Spherulitic patterns appear at 500 µm, with a gradual passage from flattened spherulites to perfect spherulitic morphologies at the core.

From these observations and many others on fast crystallizing polymers, it is possible to draw a number of conclusions. First of all, most of the morphologies discussed in this chapter can be found in injection molding. The microstructure of the parts is multilayered, with the number of layers varying from two to five or more, and some continuous evolution of the morphology can even be observed at some locations in the specimen. Nevertheless, one generally considers that the different layers can be gathered into a skin zone and a core zone, frequently separated by an intermediate or shear zone. Additionally, some authors assume a transition zone between the skin and the shear zones. The core is spherulitic. The microstructure of the shear zone highly depends on the polymer and on the processing conditions. In the skin, no morphology is usually discernible by optical microscopy, but a high birefringence is observed, which is the sign of an important molecular orientation. Different types of morphologies can be generated: poorly organized crystals, stacks of lamellae, and row-nucleated structures.

Slow crystallizing polymers such as PET or PPS have their glass transition temperature T_g above room temperature. They crystallize slowly in quiescent conditions and can be quenched into the amorphous state. Conversely, crystallization can be considerably accelerated by flow. Therefore, the final microstructure results from the competition between thermal and flow conditions. For instance, in the case of PPS [133], one obtains:

- uniformly amorphous parts at low mold temperature (below T_g) and high injection speed;
- three layers at intermediate mold temperature (above T_g) and low injection speed: amorphous skin, flow-crystallized layer, amorphous, or semicrystalline core;
- uniformly semicrystalline parts at high mold temperature (above 170°C).

15.4.4.3 Morphological Models The observed microstructures can be interpreted using the general considerations developed in Section 15.2. First of all, the existence of stacks of lamellae results from the combined effects of surface nucleation and temperature gradient, which lead to a lamellar growth perpendicular to the surface, and also from flow, which favors the crystalline growth perpendicular to the injection direction. Quasiparabolic spherulites are the signature of the temperature gradient. The morphological sequence—spherulites, flattened spherulites, sheaves—correspond to increasing influence of flow. But here, what is actually acting on crystallization is the "residual" effect of flow, that is, the partially or totally relaxed orientation and deformation of macromolecules in the melt. At the core, this relaxation is total or almost total, and the morphology is spherulitic. The flattened spherulites can be associated, as in cast film extrusion, to crystallization after cessation of flow. Sheaf-like morphologies and row-nucleated structures correspond to crystallization during flow.

The specificities of the polymer flow during the filling stage have also to be taken into account. The flow can be divided into two parts [136]:

1. an elongation flow at the flow front called fountain flow,

2. a shear flow behind the front, with a maximum shear rate at a distance from the interface between the solidified layer and the melt.

Tadmor [136] used this description to interpret the orientation profile in amorphous polymers (see Fig. 15.33): the orientation in the skin is due to the fountain flow and the secondary maximum to the shear flow behind the front, with, in both cases, some relaxation of the orientation during cooling. This can be generalized to semicrystalline polymers, where the same type of orientation profile is found for the crystalline phase (e.g. [137]), even if it is sometimes difficult to find an orientation maximum at the surface, perhaps for experimental reasons. Additional effects may be introduced by the packing stage. The packing flow may induce a new secondary maximum in the orientation profile, but lower than the first one [137].

This analysis was also used by Bowman [131] to interpret the layers observed in an acetal copolymer (Fig. 15.36). Layers 1 and 2 constitute the skin and correspond to the crystallization of macromolecules oriented by fountain flow: in layer 1, there is a rapid freezing and the morphology consists of stacks of lamellae, as in Clark's work [129, 130]. In layer 2, there has been some relaxation in the molecular orientation, and quasiparabolic spherulites are also observed as a result of an

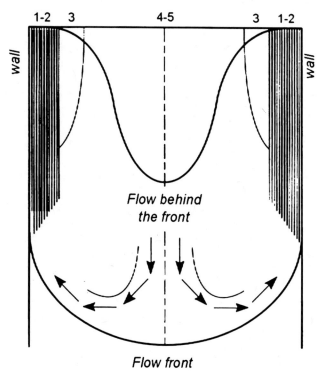

Figure 15.36 Interpretation of the morphological layers and zones in an acetal copolymer [131].

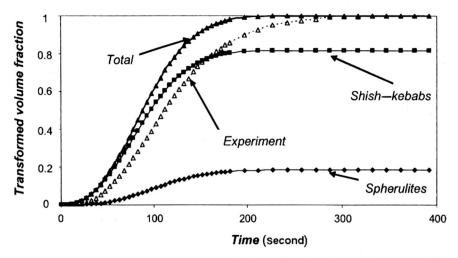

Figure 15.37 Distribution of the transformed volume fractions for a shear rate of 75 s^{-1}: spherulites, shish–kebabs and total. Comparison with experiment. Isotactic polypropylene at 132°C [69].

important temperature gradient. Layer 3 corresponds to the intermediate or shear zone, which has crystallized in the flow behind the front. This justifies our initial assumption in Section 15.4.4.1. Layers 4 and 5 form the core zone, which has crystallized after cessation of flow, in the form of spherulites.

15.4.4.4 Modeling Much work has been devoted to the introduction of crystallization into thermomechanical models of the injection-molding process [64, 68, 69, 138–149]. The conservation equations (mass, momentum, and energy) were first solved by the finite difference method [138–143, 146, 147] for a simplified flow geometry, either 2D [138, 139], or one-dimensional (1D) as a result of the lubrication approximation [140–143, 146, 147]. Then appeared finite element simulations, in 2D [145] or within the frame of the Hele-Shaw approximations [68, 144, 148]. Until now, only few studies concerned the implementation of a crystallization kinetics into 3D codes [149], which do not require any geometrical or kinematic assumption.

Nakamura's Equation (15.10) has been widely used to model crystallization in injection molding [138, 139, 142, 143, 146, 147]. Other authors [64, 140, 141, 145] have based their calculations on Ozawa's equation extended by Billon et al. to nonconstant cooling rates (Eq. 15.12). These kinetic laws have been modified to integrate flow effects. To avoid such simplified approaches, some authors used the most general form of Avrami's theory (Eq. 15.7 and Eq. 15.8), either in its initial form [148] or after the mathematical transformations proposed by Schneider et al. [66] or Haudin and Chenot [67]. Schneider et al. and Haudin and Chenot obtained a set of differential equations (see Section 15.3.3) that is more suitable for numerical simulation and has been applied in finite element models for injection molding [68, 69, 144, 149].

Previous papers focus mainly on the transformed fraction. They often deduce the absolute crystallinity [139, 143, 144], and calculate the solid layer [139], especially at the end of the filling stage [64, 140, 141, 145–147]. They sometimes predict the mean spherulite size [146, 147]. Recently, much more detailed predictions of structure development, including the effects of flow on morphology, have been published [68, 69]. Two types of morphologies are taken into account: spherulites and row-nucleated structures (shish–kebabs). Figure 15.37 shows an example of calculations of the transformed fraction for each type of morphology [69].

15.5 CONCLUSION

Structure development has been followed by numerous experimental techniques, many authors often combining several of them: rheological measurements, optical microscopy, optical measurements (birefringence, dichroism, turbidity, depolarized light intensity [DLI]), SALS, SAXS, WAXD, and so on. These techniques have been used:

- in laboratory experiments with specific devices, to determine the effect of an isolated parameter on crystallization, for example, flow;
- in the analysis of manufactured specimens: fibers, films, moldings;
- in online measurements.

All these experiments have provided a huge amount of data, which makes it possible to establish a general description of crystallization in polymer processing. This has been done in this chapter and applied to typical processes, differing in the severity of mechanical and thermal solicitations.

However, data are still lacking in certain domains. This is the case of crystallization at high cooling rates, in spite of recent efforts. The experimental study of coupled effects, for example, flow and pressure, is just at its beginning. Concerning flow, the basic mechanisms of flow-induced nucleation remain unknown (for a discussion, see Reference [150]). As an interpretation of their results, many authors invoke a prenucleation stage: "aggregates" or "precursors," which become active nuclei by the flow treatment (see Chapter 14). The "aggregates" or "dormant nuclei" could be, at some junctions of the network, detected in rheological measurements. In the same way, the enhancement of growth by flow is still unexplained. This type of study remains of prime importance for deriving pertinent nucleation laws to be introduced in simulation models for polymer processing.

In general Avrami's theory gives a good framework for the treatment of overall crystallization kinetics. Unnecessary assumptions can now be avoided and the equations can be cast into a differential system, suitable for numerical integration. Flow introduces additional nuclei. Two types of morphologies can be now considered: spherulites (point-like nuclei) or shish–kebabs (thread-like nuclei). As indicated above, the problem is to write physically based equations for this generation of nuclei by flow.

From a thermodynamic point of view, the coupling between flow and crystallization should be formally taken into account. This should lead to additional terms in the energy equation. In this field, the approach proposed by McHugh and coworkers [2, 80, 81, 112, 114] is of great interest.

Very often, papers focus mainly on the transformed fraction. In fact, due to their statistical character, overall theories also provide information on morphology, for example, in the 2D case: the number of entities, the length of boundary lines, and the number of triple points. Such an analysis has been applied in Reference [51]. In the same way, an interesting output of Haudin and Chenot's [67] calculations is the average size of morphological entities, and their size distribution, which is more original. Although all the correlations are not yet firmly established, quantitative morphological data are of prime importance for the understanding of properties (mechanical, optical, etc.). Therefore, relevant morphological parameters have to be identified, and a compromise has to be found between the heaviness of the general statistical treatment and the possibility of its incorporation into numerical models for polymer processing.

In conclusion, the future is obviously to develop more rigorous and physically based models, but it must also be conceded that approximate models often give good results, from an engineering and even scientific point of view.

REFERENCES

[1] Haudin, J.M. Flow-induced crystallization in polymer processing. In *Advances in Material Forming. Esaform 10 Years on*, Chinesta, F., Cueto, E., eds. Springer-Verlag France, Paris, 2007, pp. 23–35.

[2] Doufas, A.K., Dairanieh, I.S., McHugh, A.J. *J. Rheol.* **1999**, *43*, 85–109.

[3] Tribout, C., Monasse, B., Haudin, J.M. *Colloid Polym. Sci.* **1996**, *274*, 197–208.

[4] Monasse, B. *J. Mater. Sci.* **1995**, *30*, 5002–5012.

[5] Haudin, J.M., Duplay, C., Monasse, B., Costa, J.L. *Macromol. Symp.* **2002**, *185*, 119–133.

[6] Lagasse, R.R., Maxwell, B. *Polym. Eng. Sci.* **1976**, *16*, 189–199.

[7] Sherwood, C.H., Price, F.P., Stein, R.S. *J. Polym. Sci. Polym. Symp.* **1978**, *63*, 77–94.

[8] Koscher, E., Fulchiron, R. *Polymer* **2002**, *43*, 6931–6942.

[9] Acierno, S., Palomba, B., Winter, H.H., Grizzuti, N. *Rheol. Acta* **2003**, *42*, 243–250.

[10] Devaux, N., Monasse, B., Haudin, J.M., Moldenaers, P., Vermant, J. *Rheol. Acta* **2004**, *43*, 212–222.

[11] Keller, A., Machin, M.J. *J. Macromol. Sci. Phys.* **1967**, *B1*(1), 41–91.

[12] Hill, M.J., Keller, A. *J. Macromol. Sci. Phys.* **1969**, *B3*(1), 153–159.

[13] Pennings, A.J. *J. Polym. Sci. Polym. Symp.* **1977**, *59*, 55–86.

[14] Kardos, J.L., Christiansen, A.W., Baer, E. *J. Polym. Sci. A2* **1966**, *4*, 777–788.

[15] Campbell, R.A., Phillips, P.J. *Polymer* **1993**, *34*, 4809–4816.

[16] Mezghani, K., Phillips, P.J. *Polymer* **1997**, *38*, 5725–5733.

[17] Brückner, S., Phillips, P.J., Mezghani, K., Meille, S.V. *Macromol. Rapid Commun.* **1997**, *18*, 1–7.

[18] Angelloz, C., Fulchiron, R., Douillard, A., Chabert, B., Fillit, R., Vautrin, A., David, L. *Macromolecules* **2000**, *33*, 4138–4145.

[19] Wunderlich, B., Arakawa, T. *J. Polym. Sci. A* **1964**, *2*, 3697–3706.

[20] Geil, P.H., Anderson, F.R., Wunderlich, B., Arakawa, T. *J. Polym. Sci. A* **1964**, *2*, 3707–3720.

[21] Rees, D.V., Bassett, D.C. *Nature* **1968**, *219*, 368–370.

[22] Bassett, D.C., Block, S., Piermani, G.J. *J. Appl. Phys.* **1974**, *45*, 4146–4150.

[23] Hikosawa, M. *Polymer* **1987**, *28*, 1257–1264.

[24] Hikosawa, M. *Polymer* **1990**, *31*, 458–468.

[25] Tait, P.G. *Phys. Chem.* **1888**, *2*, 1.

[26] Tamman, G. *Phys. Chem.* **1895**, *17*, 620.

[27] Hieber, O.A. *Int. Polym. Process.* **1997**, *12*, 249–256.

[28] Fulchiron, R., Koscher, E., Poutot, G., Delaunay, D., Régnier, G. *J. Macromol. Sci. Phys.* **2001**, *B40*, 297–314.

[29] Brucato, V., Piccarolo, S., La Carruba, V. *Int. Polym. Process.* **2000**, *15*, 103–110.

[30] van der Beek, M.H.E., Peters, G.W.M., Meijer, H.E.H. *Macromol. Mater. Eng.* **2005**, *290*, 443–455.

[31] de Santis, F., Adamovsky, S., Titomanlio, G., Schick, C. *Macromolecules* **2006**, *39*, 2562–2567.

[32] Ding, Z., Spruiell, J.E. *J. Polym. Sci. B Polym. Phys.* **1996**, *34*, 2783–2804.

[33] Haudin, J.M., Boyer, S.A.E. *PPS 23 Proceedings*, The Polymer Processing Society 23rd Annual Meeting, Goa, India, 2009.

[34] Poutot, G. Etude des transferts thermiques lors de la cristallisation d'un polymère semi-cristallin. PhD thesis, University of Nantes, 2002.

[35] Brucato, V., De Santis, F., Lamberti, G., Titomanlio, G. *Polym. Bull.* **2002**, *48*, 207–212.

[36] Brucato, V., Piccarolo, S., La Carrubba, V. *Chem. Eng. Sci.* **2002**, *57*, 4129–4143.

[37] Lovinger, A.J., Gryte, C.C. *J. Appl. Phys.* **1976**, *47*, 1999–2004.

[38] Lovinger, A.J., Chua, J.O., Gryte, C.C. *J. Polym. Sci. Polym. Phys. Ed.* **1977**, *15*, 641–656.

[39] Lovinger, A.J., Gryte, C.C. *Macromolecules* **1976**, *9*, 247–253.

[40] Lovinger, A.J., Chua, J.O., Gryte, C.C. *J. Phys. [E]* **1976**, *9*, 927–929.

[41] Piorkowska, E., Pawlak, A., Chapel, J.P., Nowacki, R. *Int. J. Forming Processes* **2004**, *7*, 195–208.

[42] Schulze, G.E.W., Naujeck, T.R. *Colloid Polym. Sci.* **1991**, *269*, 689–694.

[43] Schulze, G.E.W., Naujeck, T.R. *Colloid Polym. Sci.* **1991**, *269*, 695–703.

[44] Swaminarayan, S., Charbon, Ch. *Polym. Eng. Sci.* **1998**, *38*, 634–643.

[45] Charbon, Ch., Swaminarayan, S. *Polym. Eng. Sci.* **1998**, *38*, 644–656.

[46] Fitchmun, D.R., Newman, S. *J. Polym. Sci. A2* **1970**, *8*, 1545–1564.

[47] Billon, N., Magnet, C., Haudin, J.M., Lefebvre, D. *Colloid Polym. Sci.* **1994**, *272*, 633–654.

[48] Billon, N., Henaff, V., Pelous, E., Haudin, J.M. *J. Appl. Polym. Sci.* **2002**, *86*, 725–733.

[49] Devaux, E., Gérard, J.F., Bourgin, P., Chabert, B. *Compos. Sci. Technol.* **1993**, *48*, 199–203.

[50] Billon, N., Escleine, J.M., Haudin, J.M. *Colloid Polym. Sci.* **1989**, *267*, 668–680.

[51] Piorkowska, E., Billon, N., Haudin, J.M., Gadzinowska, K. *J. Appl. Polym. Sci.* **2005**, *97*, 2319–2329.

[52] Billon, N., Monasse, B., Haudin, J.M. *Ann. Compos.* **1989**, *1–2*, 117–124.

[53] Mehl, N.A., Rebenfeld, L. *J. Polym. Sci. B Polym. Phys.* **1993**, *31*, 1677–1686.

[54] Mehl, N.A., Rebenfeld, L. *J. Polym. Sci. B Polym. Phys.* **1993**, *31*, 1687–1693.

[55] Krause, T.H., Kalinka, G., Auer, C., Hinrichsen, G. *J. Appl. Polym. Sci.* **1994**, *51*, 399–406.

[56] Piorkowska, E. *Macromol. Symp.* **2001**, *169*, 143–148.

[57] Piorkowska, E., Galeski, A., Haudin, J.M. *Prog. Polym. Sci.* **2006**, *31*, 549–575.

[58] Avrami, M. *J. Chem. Phys.* **1939**, *7*, 1103–1112.

[59] Avrami, M. *J. Chem. Phys.* **1940**, *8*, 212–224.

[60] Avrami, M. *J. Chem. Phys.* **1941**, *9*, 177–184.

[61] Nakamura, K., Watanabe, T., Katayama, K., Amano, T. *J. Appl. Polym. Sci.* **1972**, *16*, 1077–1091.

[62] Ozawa, T. *Polymer* **1971**, *12*, 150–158.

[63] Billon, N., Barq, P., Haudin, J.M. *Int. Polym. Process.* **1991**, *6*, 348–355.

[64] Haudin, J.M., Billon, N. *Prog. Colloid Polym. Sci.* **1992**, *87*, 132–137.

[65] Jay, F., Monasse, B., Haudin, J.M. *Int. J. Forming Processes* **1998**, *1*, 75–95.

[66] Schneider, W., Koppl, A., Berger, J. *Int. Polym. Process.* **1988**, *2*, 151–154.

[67] Haudin, J.M., Chenot, J.L. *Int. Polym. Process.* **2004**, *19*, 267–274.

[68] Zuidema, H., Peters, G.W.M., Meijer, H.E.H. *Macromol. Theory Simul.* **2001**, *10*, 447–460.

[69] Haudin, J.M., Smirnova, J., Silva, L., Monasse, B., Chenot, J.L. *Polym. Sci. A* **2008**, *50*, 538–549.

[70] Agassant, J.F., Haudin, J.M. Mise en forme des polymères thermoplastiques. In *Matériaux Polymères*, 2nd ed., Carrega, M., ed. Dunod/L'Usine Nouvelle, Paris, 2007, pp. 53–110.

[71] Cotto, D., Duffo, P., Haudin, J.M. *Int. Polym. Process.* **1989**, *4*, 103–113.

[72] Duffo, P., Monasse, B., Haudin, J.M. *J. Polym. Eng.* **1991**, *10*, 151–229.

[73] Spruiell, J.E., White, J.L. *Appl. Polym. Symp.* **1975**, *27*, 121–157.

[74] Ziabicki, A. *Fundamentals of Fiber Formation*, Wiley, New York, 1976.

[75] Ziabicki, A., Kawai, H., eds. *High-Speed Fiber Spinning*, Wiley, New York, 1985.

[76] White, J.L., Cakmak, M. *Adv. Polym. Tech.* **1986**, *6*, 295–338.

[77] Spruiell, J.E. Structure and property development during the melt-spinning of synthetic fibres. In *Structure Development During Polymer Processing*, Cunha, A.M.,

Fakirov, S., eds. Kluwer Academic Press, Dordrecht, 2000, pp. 195–220.

[78] Wilchinsky, Z.W. *J. Appl. Polym. Sci.* **1963**, *7*, 923–933.

[79] Andersen, P.G., Carr, S.H. *J. Mater. Sci.* **1975**, *10*, 870–888.

[80] Doufas, A.K., McHugh, A.J., Miller, C. *J. Non-Newton. Fluid Mech.* **2000**, *92*, 27–66.

[81] Doufas, A.K., McHugh, A.J., Miller, C., Immaneni, A. *J. Non-Newton. Fluid Mech.* **2000**, *92*, 81–103.

[82] Holmes, D.R., Miller, R.G., Palmer, R.P., Bunn, C.W. *Nature* **1953**, *171*, 1104–1106.

[83] Holmes, D.R., Palmer, R.P. *J. Polym. Sci.* **1958**, *31*, 345–358.

[84] Aggarwal, S.L., Tilley, G.P., Sweeting, O.J. *J. Appl. Polym. Sci.* **1959**, *1*, 91–100.

[85] Lindenmeyer, P.H., Lustig, S. *J. Appl. Polym. Sci.* **1965**, *9*, 227–240.

[86] Desper, C.R. *J. Appl. Polym. Sci.* **1969**, *13*, 169–191.

[87] Nagasawa, T., Matsumura, T., Hoshino, S. *Appl. Polym. Symp.* **1973**, *20*, 275–293.

[88] Nagasawa, T., Matsumura, T., Hoshino, S. *Appl. Polym. Symp.* **1973**, *20*, 295–313.

[89] Matsumura, T. *Kobunshi Ronbunshu Eng. Ed.* **1976**, *5*, 529–543.

[90] Maddams, W.F., Preedy, J.E. *J. Appl. Polym. Sci.* **1978**, *22*, 2721–2737.

[91] Maddams, W.F., Preedy, J.E. *J. Appl. Polym. Sci.* **1978**, *22*, 2739–2749.

[92] Maddams, W.F., Preedy, J.E. *J. Appl. Polym. Sci.* **1978**, *22*, 2751–2759.

[93] Haudin, J.M. *Ann. Chimie France* **1980**, *5*, 513–534.

[94] Choi, K.J., Spruiell, J.E., White, J.L. *J. Polym. Sci. Polym Phys. Ed.* **1982**, *20*, 27–47.

[95] Kwack, T.H., Han, C.D., Vickers, M.E. *J. Appl. Polym. Sci.* **1988**, *35*, 363–389.

[96] Yu, T.H., Wilkes, G.L. *Polymer* **1996**, *37*, 4675–4687.

[97] Haudin, J.M., Piana, A., Monasse, B., Monge, G., Gourdon, B. *Ann. Chim. Sci. Mat.* **1999**, *24*, 555–580.

[98] Krishnaswamy, R.K., Sukhadia, A.M. *Polymer* **2000**, *41*, 9205–9217.

[99] Desper, C.R., Stein, R.S. *J. Appl. Phys.* **1966**, *37*, 3990–4002.

[100] White, J.L., Spruiell, J.E. *Polym. Eng. Sci.* **1981**, *21*, 859–868.

[101] Haudin, J.M., André, J.M., Bellet, G., Monasse, B., Navard, P. *La Revue de Métallurgie-CIT/Science et Génie des Matériaux* **2002**, Décembre, 1097–1104.

[102] Judge, J.T., Stein, R.S. *J. Appl. Phys.* **1961**, *32*, 2357–2363.

[103] Garber, C.A., Clark, E.S. *J. Macromol. Sci. Phys.* **1970**, *B4*(3), 499–517.

[104] Hashimoto, T., Todo, A., Murakami, Y., Kawai, H. *J. Polym. Sci. Polym. Phys. Ed.* **1977**, *15*, 501–521.

[105] Fatahi, S., Ajji, A., Lafleur, P.G. *Int. Polym. Process.* **2007**, *22*, 334–345.

[106] Tas, P. Film blowing: from polymer to product. PhD thesis, Eindhoven University of Technology, 1994.

[107] Lu, J., Sue, H.J., Rieker, T.P. *J. Mater. Sci.* **2000**, *35*, 5169–5178.

[108] Prasad, A., Shroff, R., Rane, S., Beaucage, G. *Polymer* **2001**, *42*, 3101–3113.

[109] Lu, J., Sue, H.J., Rieker, T.P. *Polymer* **2001**, *42*, 4635–4646.

[110] Bullwinkel, M.D., Campbell, G.A., Rasmussen, D.H., Krexa, J., Brancewitz, C.J. *Int. Polym. Process.* **2001**, *16*, 41–47.

[111] Ashok, B.K., Campbell, G.A. *Int. Polym. Process.* **1992**, *7*, 240–247.

[112] Doufas, A.K., McHugh, A.J. *J. Rheol.* **2001**, *45*, 1085–1104.

[113] Muslet, I.A., Kamal, M.R. *J. Rheol.* **2004**, *48*, 525–550.

[114] Henrichsen, L.K., McHugh, A.J. *Int. Polym. Process.* **2007**, *22*, 179–189.

[115] Sarafrazi, S., Sharif, F. *Int. Polym. Process.* **2008**, *23*, 30–37.

[116] Bakerdjian, Z., Kamal, M.R. *Polym. Eng. Sci.* **1977**, *17*, 96–100.

[117] Moy, F.H., Kamal, M.R. *Polym. Eng. Sci.* **1980**, *20*, 957–964.

[118] Kamal, M.R., Kalyon, D.M., Dealy, J.M. *Polym. Eng. Sci.* **1980**, *20*, 1117–1125.

[119] Bayer, R.K., Zachmann, H.G., Balta-Calleja, F.J., Umbach, H. *Polym. Eng. Sci.* **1989**, *26*, 186–192.

[120] Lopez Cabarcos, E., Bayer, R.K., Zachmann, H.G., Balta-Calleja, F.J., Meins, W. *Polym. Eng. Sci.* **1989**, *26*, 193–201.

[121] Wu, J.P., White, J.L. *Int. Polym. Process.* **1992**, *7*, 350–357.

[122] Kantz, M.R., Newman, H.D., Jr., Stigale, F.H. *J. Appl. Polym. Sci.* **1972**, *16*, 1249–1260.

[123] Fitchmun, D.R., Mencik, Z. *J. Polym. Sci. Polym. Phys. Ed.* **1973**, *11*, 951–971.

[124] Mencik, Z., Fitchmun, D.R. *J. Polym. Sci. Polym. Phys. Ed.* **1973**, *11*, 973–989.

[125] Trotignon, J.P., Verdu, J. *J. Appl. Polym. Sci.* **1987**, *34*, 1–18.

[126] Fujiyama, M., Wakino, T., Kawasaki, Y. *J. Appl. Polym. Sci.* **1988**, *35*, 29–49.

[127] Saiu, M., Brucato, V., Piccarolo, S., Titomanlio, G. *Int. Polym. Process.* **1992**, *7*, 267–273.

[128] Guo, M., Bowman, J. *J. Appl. Polym. Sci.* **1983**, *28*, 2341–2362.

[129] Clark, E.S. *SPE J.* **1967**, *23*, 46–49.

[130] Clark, E.S. *Appl. Polym. Symp.* **1973**, *20*, 325–332.

[131] Bowman, J. *J. Mater. Sci.* **1981**, *16*, 1151–1166.

[132] Mencik, Z., Chompff, A.J. *J. Polym. Sci. Polym. Phys. Ed.* **1974**, *12*, 977–989.

[133] Hsiung, C.M., Cakmak, M., White, J.L. *Int. Polym. Process.* **1990**, *5*, 109–123.

[134] Menges, G., Wübken, G. *SPE ANTEC Preprints*, 1973, p. 519.

[135] Haudin, J.M. Optical studies of polymer morphology. In *Optical Properties of Polymers*, Meeten, G.H., ed. Elsevier Applied Science, Barking, UK, 1986, pp. 167–264.

[136] Tadmor, Z. *J. Appl. Polym. Sci.* **1974**, *18*, 1753–1772.

[137] Mendoza, R. Morphologies induites dans les pièces en polyoléfines moulées par injection. PhD thesis, Ecole Nationale Supérieure d'Arts et Métiers, Paris, 2005.

[138] Lafleur, P.G., Kamal, M.R. *Polym. Eng. Sci.* **1986**, *26*, 92–102.

[139] Kamal, M.R., Lafleur, P.G. *Polym. Eng. Sci.* **1986**, *26*, 103–110.

[140] Dufossé, C. Modélisation et etude expérimentale de la cristallisation de polyéthylènes au cours du cycle d'injection. PhD thesis, Ecole Nationale Supérieure des Mines de Paris, Sophia Antipolis, 1990.

[141] Tribout, C. Etude expérimentale et théorique de la cristallisation du polypropylène sous cisaillement. Application au procédé d'injection. PhD thesis, Ecole Nationale Supérieure des Mines de Paris, Sophia Antipolis, 1993.

[142] Hsiung, C.M., Cakmak, M., Ulcer, Y. *Polymer* **1996**, *37*, 4455–4471.

[143] Titomanlio, G., Speranza, V., Brucato, V. *Int. Polym. Process.* **1997**, *12*, 45–53.

[144] Verhoyen, O. Etude expérimentale et modélisation de l'influence de l'orientation sur la cristallisation des polymères thermoplastiques en moulage par injection. PhD thesis, Catholic University of Louvain, 1997.

[145] Vintimiglia, A.S. Implémentation d'une cinétique de cristallisation des polymères dans une simulation numérique bidimensionnelle par éléments finis: application à l'injection des thermoplastiques et au procédé push-pull. PhD thesis, Ecole Nationale Supérieure des Mines de Paris, Sophia Antipolis, 1999.

[146] Guo, X., Isayev, A.I., Guo, L. *Polym. Eng. Sci.* **1999**, *39*, 2096–2114.

[147] Guo, X., Isayev, A.I., Demiray, M. *Polym. Eng. Sci.* **1999**, *39*, 2132–2149.

[148] Kennedy, P.K., Zheng, R. *Proceedings of the Conference on Polymer Crystallization and Structure Formation in Processing*, Linz, Austria, 2003.

[149] Smirnova, J., Silva, L., Monasse, B., Chenot, J.L., Haudin, J.M. *Int. Polym. Process.* **2005**, *20*, 178–185.

[150] Janeschitz-Kriegl, H. *Macromolecules* **2006**, *39*, 4448–4454.

INDEX

Note: Page numbers in *italics* refers to figures, **bold** indicates tables.

absolute reaction rate theory   134
acetaldehyde, copolymers of *n*-butyraldehyde and   32
achiral polymers   118
activation energy of crystallization   233
additives   380
advanced thermal analysis   266, 269
Advanced Thermal Analysis System Data Bank
    (ATHAS-DB)   22, 23, 267, 271, 273, 275
aggregates
    edge-on lamellae from molten films   102–104
    grown from molten films   94–104
    grown from thin films   94–98
    grown from ultrathin films   98–102
Ag nanoparticles   392, 393
Al_2O_3 392
aliphatic nylons
    role of hydrogen bonds in isothermal crystallization
        of   184–185
    see also nylons
aliphatic polyamides
    groups of   50
    hydrogen bonded chains in   *52, 53, 54*
    packing effects on the conformation of polymer chains in
        crystals of   50–55
    structural features of the polymer chains in crystals of   51
    see also nylons
aliphatic polyesters   244
alkali halides   244
n-alkanes, low molecular weight   186
amorphous/crystalline blends, crystallization behavior
    of   297–298
amorphous polymers, orientation profile in   457
anisotropic scattering patterns   18–19
apparent heat capacity   267, 268
    see also heat capacity
aragonite   381
aramid fibers   383
aromatic acid salts   *245*
atactic polymers   48
atactic polypropylene   406
    see also polypropylene (PP)
atactic polystyrene   369
    see also polystyrene (PS)
atomic force microscopy (AFM)   9–12, 240
    applications of   10–12
    comparison between electron microscopy and   10
    contact scanning mode   9
    imaging principle   9
    scanning modes   9–10
    tapping mode images of BA-C8 during crystallization   *11*
    vibration scanning mode   9
    video AFM   10
atomistic models   207–208
Avrami equation   177, 218, 219, 230
Avrami–Evans equation   216
Avrami–Evans–Nakamura equation   421
Avrami–Evans theory   230, 384, 387
Avrami exponent *see* Avrami index
Avrami index   232, 294, 334, 336, 353, 354, 372, 381, 384, 441
Avrami model   218, 294
    see also Kolmogorov–Johnson–Mehl–Avrami (KJMA) model
Avrami plot   234

Handbook of Polymer Crystallization, First Edition. Edited by Ewa Piorkowska and Gregory C. Rutledge.
© 2013 John Wiley & Sons, Inc. Published 2013 by John Wiley & Sons, Inc.

Avrami theory 220, 459
axialites 73, 93, 97

$B_{81}EO_{19}$ 356, 357, 358
    DSC cooling scans for *357*
    DSC heating scans for *357, 358*
$B_{89}EO_{11}$ 356, 358
    Avrami index values for **354**
    DSC cooling scans for *357*
    DSC heating scans for *357*
    isothermal crystallization temperature for **354**
    range and morphology for **354**
BA-C8, AFM images of *11*
BA-C10 *11*
ball mill **150**
banded spherulites *see* spherulites
barostats 199
Baur's copolymer model 337
biaxial drawing 407
biodegradable fillers 380
birefraction 2
birefringence 3
bis(3,4-diméthylbenzylidene) sorbitol 225
blend samples
    crystallization of 167
    spherulites of 172
block copolymers 327
    confined crystallization in 348–361
    crystallization from homogeneous or weakly segregated melts 340–343
    diblock copolymers exhibiting homogeneous melts 348
    fractionated crystallization in 372
    literature regarding confined crystallization in 348, **349**, **350**
    medium segregated systems 348
    relationship between AB and ABA block copolymers final morphology and segregation strength and critical temperatures *350*
    solid-state morphology 340–342
    strongly segregated systems 348
    weakly segregated systems 348
    see also copolymers
bond fluctuation model 205
BPS *see* propylene-(1-butene) copolymer (BPS)
bulk melt, homogeneous nucleation under elongational flow from 139–148
Burgers vector **b** 87
butadiene, *trans*-1,4-copolymers of 1,3-pentadiene and 32
butene, isotactic copolymers of 3-methylbutene and 32
n-butyraldehyde, copolymers of acetaldehyde and 32

cadmium selenide 260
calcite 381
calcium carbonate ($CaCO_3$) 380, 381, 392
calorimetry
    differential scanning calorimetry (DSC) *see* differential scanning calorimetry (DSC)
    fast scanning calorimetry (FSC) 284
    parameters of 267
capillary length 84

carbon fibers 383
carbon nanotubes (CNT) 257–258, 379, 391–392
    multi-wall nanotubes (MWNTs) 391
    single-wall nanotubes (SWNTs) 391
cast film extrusion 433
    crystallization in 442–445
    thermomechanical model 442–443
chain tilt 118, 119, 121
chalk 380, 381, 392
chemical etching 7
chemical shift 13
chemical staining 7
chlorinated polyethylene (CPE) 291
cis configurations 33
clarifying agents 256
classical nucleation theory (CNT) 126–128, 160, 161
    diffusion 128
    free energy for formation of a critical nucleus 127–128
    nucleation rate 126–127
    relation of nucleus shape to kinetic parameters 128
clathrate forms
    α class **39**
    β class **39, 40**
    γ class **39**
Clausius–Clapeyron equation 270, 272
close-packing principle 43
CNTs *see* carbon nanotubes (CNT); classical nucleation theory (CNT)
coarse-grained kinetic Monte Carlo simulations 419
coarse-grained models 206–207
co-continuous polymer blends 304
co-crystallization 298
cold crystallization 189
compatibilized polymer blends 307–314, 321
    by addition of copolymers 308–309
    by addition of functionalized polymers 309–311
    compatibilized methods 307–308
    crystallization behavior of 311–314
    fractionated crystallization in 312–314
    morphology and phase interactions of 308–311
    by reactive blending 311
composite materials 380
    epitaxial crystallization and the design of 257–258
    fiber-reinforced composites *see* fiber-reinforced composites
compressibility 265
computer modeling of polymer crystallization 197–214
    applications of 210
    simulations of flow-induced crystallization 211
    and the study of the crystallization of polymers 210
concurrent crystallization 298
condis crystals 58
conductive polymer composites 382
confined crystallization 226–228
    in block copolymers 348–361
    modeling of confined crystallization of macromolecules 371–372
    occurrence of 372
confined microdomains 348
conformational isomorphism 58

conformational polymorphism 33–43
conversion degree 216, 222, 225, 231, 234
   dependence on time in neat polymer and fiber-reinforced composites *388*
   of fiber-reinforced composites 387
conversion rate 216, 219, 222
cooling on the roll 444–445
cooling rate, effects on crystallization 436–437
copolymers 327–346
   co-crystallization of copolymers of different monomeric units 31
   crystallization-driven structure formation 342–343
   crystallization kinetics 344
   lamellar structure and crystalline size of 331–332
   mechanical properties of 334–335
   melting transition of 273
   post-yield deformation behavior of 335
   solid-state morphology of 330–334
   supermolecular structure of 330–331
   see also block copolymers
correlation functions 17–18
coupled effects 459
cross polarization
   and magic angle spinning NMR (CP-MAS NMR) 14
   in NMR 14
crystal growth rate 174–175
crystal habits 60–67
   rounded lateral habits 66–67
crystalline/crystalline blends 298–302
crystalline orientation by X-ray diffraction 446
crystalline polymers, interactions between carbon nanotubes and 257
crystallinity (χ_c)
   degree of 25–26, 272–274, 329
   of nano-oriented crystals 142
   use of WAXD to determine 15–16
crystallization
   in cast film extrusion 442–445
   in a confined space 226–228
   in copolymers 327–346
   under deformation or flow 208–210
   from dilute solution in an elongational flow field 209
   during drawing 407–410
   of droplet dispersions and polymer layers 361–368
   effects of cooling rate on 436–437
   effects of pressure on 435–436
   effects of processing conditions on 433–440
   effects of surfaces on 439–440
   effects of temperature gradients on 437–439
   elongation-induced 409–410
   extended volume approach 218–220
   factors influencing crystallization kinetics 224–230
   in film blowing 448–454
   flow-induced crystallization *see* flow-induced crystallization (FIC)
   general requirements for crystallizability of polymers 31
   growth trajectory during 225
   at high cooling rates 459
   induced by tensile force 191
   and injection molding 454–458
   isothermal and nonisothermal theories 218–224
   isothermal crystallization 230–231
   from the melt 204–208
   modeling of confined crystallization of macromolecules 371–372
   modeling of crystallization in fiber-reinforced composites 385–387
   modeling of crystallization in processing conditions 440–442
   models for complex conditions 224
   molecular simulation of 176
   in nano-confined polymeric systems 347–378
   nonisothermal crystallization 231–233
   observation of 217
   phase transitions during 167
   of polymer blends 287–325
   in polymer composites and nanocomposites 379–397
   in processing conditions 433–462
   sensitivity to shear rate and total shear strain during precrystallization steady state NEMD simulation 210
   shear-induced crystallization 186–189, 229, 401–407
   single-chain behavior in 202–204
   from solution under shear 168
   in statistical copolymers 328–340
   within strongly segregated double-crystalline diblock copolymers and triblock copolymers 355–361
   in strongly segregated or miscible and containing one crystallizable component diblock copolymers 351–355
   in temperature gradients 225–226
   in thin films 233
   in uniform temperature fields 224–225
   upon heating from the glassy state 189–191
crystallization data, analysis of 230–233
crystallization half-time 230
crystallization mechanism 173–178
   basic theory of 173–176
   regimes 175–176
crystallization time 401
crystals
   conformationally disordered crystals 58
   defects and disorder in 55–60
   definition of 55
   dendrite crystals from dilute solutions 81–85
   facetted monolayer crystals grown from dilute solutions 75–81
   grown from concentrated solutions 92–94
   grown from molten films 94–104
   grown from solutions 75–94
   growth fluctuations 83
   growth from melt 169–172
   growth from solutions 167–169
   growth of 165–195
   growth of single crystals from solutions 167–168
   intersection of 89
   lamellae 60–61
   microscopically viewed structural evolution in growing 178–189
   nucleation and growth on the lateral growth faces of 66

crystals (*Continued*)
    packing of macromolecules in   43–48
    photoinduced formation and growth of   191–192
    roughness on the growth surfaces of   66
    spiral growth in   86
    thickness of   60–61
    time-resolved measurements   178–179
    from ultrathin films   98–102
crystal size   16–17, 82
1,4-cyclohexylene dimethylene terephthalate   337

Debye–Bueche equation   180, 184
Debye–Scherrer method   446, 449
deformation rate tensor   417
degree of crystallinity   25–26, 272–274, 329
D enantiomers   117
dendrites   73, 81–85
diads   32
1,n-dibromoalkane (Cn), polyetherification with bisphenol A   10
dielectric spectroscopy   217
1,4-diethyl *cis,cis*-muconate   191
differential scanning calorimetry (DSC)   22–26, 217, 231, 239, 351
    and determination of degree of crystallinity   25–26
    isothermal heat flow rate measurements   23
    modes of operation   22–25
    temperature modulation   23–24
    thermal scan   22–23
diffusion   128
diffusion-controlled morphology   83, 85
diffusion length   82
dilatometry, parameters of   267
diluents, influence on the melting of polymer crystals   282
dislocation strength **b**   87
disorder, in crystals   55–60
disyndiotactic polymer configurations   34
Doi–Edwards model   411, 417
drawing, crystallization during   407–410
droplets
    dispersions and polymer layers, crystallization in   361–368
    literature regarding confined crystallization in   **349, 350**
DSC *see* differential scanning calorimetry (DSC)
dynamic Monte Carlo method *see* kinetic Monte Carlo method
dynamic Monte Carlo simulations *see* kinetic Monte Carlo method

E3B   257
E$_{12}$EP$_{88}$
    Avrami index range   **353**
    energy barrier   **353**
E$_{29}$EO$_{20}$ *356*
E$_{29}$EP$_{71}$
    Avrami index range   **353**
    energy barrier   **353**
E$_{50}$EO$_{50}$ 356
E$_{53}$S$_{47}$
    Avrami index range   **353**
    energy barrier   **353**
E$_{54}$EP$_{46}$
    Avrami index range   **353**
    energy barrier   **353**
E$_{82}$EO$_{18}$
    DSC cooling scans for   *357*
    DSC heating scans for   *357*
E$_{89}$EO$_{11}$ 358
    DSC cooling scans for   *357*
    DSC heating scans for   *357*
Eder equations   420
elastic strain energy   87, 88
electroactive materials   259–260
electron diffraction   8
electron microscopy (EM)   5–9
    applications of   8–9
    comparison between atomic force microscopy and   10
    conducting problems in   6–7
    environmental SEM (ESEM)   7
    imaging principle   5–6
    sample preparation for   6–7
    scanning election microscopy (SEM)   6
elongational strain rate   139–140
    fraction of nano-oriented crystals   144
    SAXS patterns of   142–144
    WAXS patterns   144, *145*
elongation-induced crystallization   409–410
enantiomers   117
energy balances   258
energy conservation   199
energy of activation of crystallization   233
entanglements
    effect on the nucleation rate   156–160, 161
    time and density of   158
    two-step model   159–160
enthalpy   265
entropic barrier models, for crystal nucleation and growth   210
entropic principle   46
entropy   43, 47, 265, 289
environmental SEM (ESEM)   7
epitaxial crystallization   167, 237–264
    analysis of   260
    characteristics of   238
    conformational and packing energy analysis of   258–259
    and the design of composite materials   257–258
    and the design of nucleating agents   256–257
    and the design of polymeric materials   261
    on fiber surfaces   383
    general principles of   241–243
    and generation of oriented opto- or electroactive materials   259–260
    global investigation techniques   239
    of helical polymers   245–250
    investigation of   239–241
    involving polymer crystal fold surfaces   254–256
    of isotactic poly(1-butene)   250
    of isotactic polypropylene   *240*, 245–247
    of isotactic polypropylene on isotactic polyvinylcyclohexane   254, *255*

issues and applications of 256–260
kinetic effect between nucleating agents and polymer crystals 153–154
lattice matching 252–254
   between linear and helical polymers 252
   of linear polymers 243–244, 252
   and nucleating agents 261
   on organic substrates 238
   role in heterogeneous nucleation 150–153, 161
   role in nucleating agents 238
   rules governing 260
   sample preparation techniques for investigation of 240–241
   thin film techniques of investigating 239–240
   topographic versus lattice matching in 252–254
epitaxy *see* epitaxial crystallization
equilibrium heat of fusion 270
equilibrium melting 274–277
equilibrium melting temperature 267, **271**, 274–275, 434
equilibrium thermodynamic functions 275–277
equivalence principle 34, 36
erythro configurations 32, 33, *34*
etching methods 7
ethylene–alkene copolymers 330, 333, 335
ethylene–butene copolymers 327
   crystallization kinetics of 335
   peak melting temperatures 330
   solid-state CP-MAS ^{13}C NMR spectra of 14, *15*
ethylene-*co*-acrylic acid copolymers 310
ethylene copolymers 330
   final melting temperatures of *329*
   isothermal crystallization data for 336
   morphology map for nonisothermally crystallized *331*
ethylene-glycidyl methacrylate copolymers 310
ethylene–hexene statistical copolymer *336*
ethylene naphthalene-2,6-dicarboxylate 337
ethylene–octene copolymers 331
   morphological and mechanical behavior of statistical *334*
   peak melting temperatures 330
ethylene oxide (EO) 356
ethylene–propylene copolymer
   crystallization rate of *302*
   DSC melting thermograms of *302*
   methyl branches 332
ethylene-*ran*-1-octene 365
ethylene statistical copolymers 337
   ethylene naphthalene-2,6-dicarboxylate (EN) and 337
ethylene terephthalate statistical copolymers 337
Evans equation 230
Evans theory 220
exfoliated polymer nanocomposites with o-MMT 388
expansivity 265
experimental techniques 1–29, 458
   atomic force microscopy (AFM) 9–12, 240
   for characterizing semicrystalline polymers 1–29
   differential scanning calorimetry (DSC) 22–26, 217, 239, 351
   electron diffraction (ED) 8
   electron microscopy 5–9, 10
   environmental SEM (ESEM) 7
   high resolution SEM 7
   high resolution TEM (HRTEM) 7
   nuclear magnetic resonance (NMR) 12–14, 217
   optical microscopy 2–5, 133
   scattering techniques 15–21
extended-chain crystals 165
extended Guinier plot method 129, *130*
extended Pompom model 417
extended volume 218–220, 385
extensional flow optometer 410
Eyring's kinetic theory of absolute reaction rate 134

facetted monolayer crystals, grown from dilute solution 75–81
fast scanning calorimetry (FSC) 25, 284
fatty acids 392
FENE-P model 417
fiber-reinforced composites 382–385
   computer-stimulated *387*
   conversion degree in *387*, *388*
   with embedded fibers *387*
   modeling of crystallization in 385–387
fibers 393
   aramid fibers 383
   carbon fibers 383
fiber spinning 238, 399, 408–409, 433, 445–448, 454
   crystalline orientation by X-ray diffraction 446
   experimental results and morphological models 446–448
   FIC models for 408
   modeling of 448
   presentation of 445–446
   simulations of low-speed 408
fiber thermal conductivity 384
fibrils 408
FIC *see* flow-induced crystallization (FIC)
fillers 379, 380
   biodegradable fillers 380
   influence on crystallization behavior of polymer matrices 393
   microcomposites with particulate 380–382
film blowing 408, 433, 448–454
   experimental results 450
   experimental techniques 449–450
   influence of the polymer and the processing conditions 451–453
   modeling 454
   orientation studies 449–453
   parameters of 449
   process 448–449
film stacking 384
film thickness 367
finite difference method 458
FIP *see* flow-induced precursors (FIP)
Flory–Huggins equation 271
Flory–Huggins rigid-lattice model 290
Flory–Huggins–Staverman theory 289
Flory interaction parameter 298
Flory's model 328–330, 337, 343

flow
    effect on development of morphologies 434–435
    effects on crystallization 433–435
    effects on thermodynamics and kinetics 434
    and pressure 459
flow-enhanced nucleation model 411–419
    form of the terms in equation for **416**
    models without a flow-induced precursor phase 416–418
    quiescent nucleation 414–415
    simplified descriptions 415–416
flow-induced crystallization (FIC) 216, 228–230, 399–431
    crystallization rate 229
    devices used for 401
    flow-enhanced nucleation model 411–419
    with a flow-induced precursor phase 418–419
    flow regimes and morphology types in *403*
    induction time 229
    models of 410–426
    phenomena and features of 411
flow-induced nucleation 408
flow-induced precursors (FIP) 406, 407, 411
flow-induced shish formation 419–421
o-fluorostyrene, isotactic copolymers of styrene and 32
folded-chain crystals (FCC) 165
Fourier transform infrared (FTIR) 178, 217
fractionated crystallization 347, 368, 369
    in block copolymers 372
    in compatibilized polymer blends 312–314
    in immiscible blends 371
    main effects of 368
    in melt miscible blends 371
free energy
    for formation of a critical nucleus 127–128
    for formation of a nucleus 127
functional additives 380
functionalized polymers 309–311

gauche (G) torsion angles 36
GENERIC 418
giant screw dislocations 75, 86, *86*, 89, *90*, 91
Gibbs free energy 265, 268, 289
Gibbs–Thomson effect 84
Gibbs–Thomson equation 176, 274
GIWAXD and SAXS (GISAXS) 178
Graham–Likhtman and Milner–McLeish (GLaMM) model 419
graphoepitaxy 238
grazing incidence X-ray scattering 239
green composites 380
growth spirals in dilute solution 85–92
gutta-percha 288

halides *see* alkali halides
Hamiltonian–Poisson bracket formalism 434
hard epitaxy 238, 252, 258, 261
    see also epitaxial crystallization
HDPE *see* high-density polyethylene (HDPE)
heat capacity 265
    see also apparent heat capacity

heat of fusion 267, 270–272
Heaviside function 413
hedrites 96, *97*, 108
    differences between axialites and 97
    relation between spherulites and 111
Hele–Shaw approximations 458
helical polymers
    epitaxy between linear and 252
    epitaxy of 245–250
heterogeneous nucleation 127, 148–156, 173, 372, 437
    bottom up method II (solution crystallization method) 149
    bottom up method I (spray drying method) 149
    free energy for formation of a critical nucleus 127
    free energy for formation of a nucleus 127
    role of epitaxy in 150–153, 161
hexamethylbenzene 257
hexamethyl phosphoric triamide (HMPTA) 168
high-density deuterated PE (DHDPE) 186
high-density polyethylene (HDPE) 169, 281, 439
    drawing and blowing in films of 452
    FIC behavior of 410
    filled with calcium stearate-treated chalk 381
high-density polyethylene/linear low density polyethylene (HDPE/LLDPE) 298
high-density polyethylene/single-wall nanotubes (HDPE/SWNT) nanocomposites 391
high-density polyethylene/very low density polyethylene (HDPE/VLDPE) 298
highly ordered pyrolytic graphite (HOPG) 244
high resolution SEM 7
high resolution TEM (HRTEM) 7
Hildebrand solubility parameters 290
Hoffman modulation contrast optical microscopy 3
Hoffman-Weeks method 275
homocomposites 379
homogeneous melts, crystallization of block copolymers from 340–343
homogeneous nucleation 127, 144–147, 173, 208, 348, 362, 364, 368, 372
    from the bulk melt under elongational flow 139–148, 161
    by compression 146
    free energy for formation of a critical nucleus 128
    free energy for formation of a nucleus 127
homopolymers, quiescent crystallization of 215
HTH10 *see* poly(decamethylene 4,4′-terephthaloyldioxydibenzoate) (HTH10)
hydrated magnesium silicate 380
hydrogenated polybutadienes 330
    shear-induced crystallization of 404
    transmission electron micrographs of *332*
    weight fraction crystallinity of *336*
hydrogen bonds, role in isothermal crystallization of aliphatic nylons 184–185
R-3-hydroxybutyrate 117
R-3-hydroxyhexanoate 117

immiscible polymer blends 303–307, 321, 368–371
    compatibilized polymer blends 321

composite droplet morphology   303
crystal growth rate   304–305
crystallization behavior of   305–307
droplet-in-droplet morphology   303
morphology and crystal nucleation   303–304
impurities, in matrix polymers   384
induced nuclei   102
induction time   230, 231, 417
inelastic scattering   15
injection molding   399, 433, 454–458
   applications of flow-induced crystallization to   421–426
   experimental results   455–457
   flow conditions for experiments   **422**
   macroscopic tensile behavior of injection-molded samples   *400*
   modeling   458
   morphological models   457–458
   optical micrographs of injection-molded PE   *400*
   process   454–455
   role of pressure in   435
instantaneous nucleation   218, 219, 220, 222
   nucleation rate   224
   and quick crystal growth   364
intercalated polymer nanocomposites   388
interface crossing crystallization   296
interface distribution function   18
intermolecular packing forces   210
iPB *see* isotactic polybutene (iPB)
iPP *see* isotactic polypropylene (iPP)
iPS *see* isotactic polystyrene (iPS)
irreversible melting of polymer crystals   282–284
isochiral helices, epitaxial crystallization of   *251*
isokinetic model   223
isotactic-1,2-poly(1,3-butadiene)   **38**
isotactic-1,2-poly(4-methyl-1,3-pentadiene)   **39**
isotactic butene-3-methylbutene   57
isotactic *meso*-ethylene *cis*-2-butene alternating copolymer, *trans*-1,4-poly(1,3-butadiene) (form I)   **35**
isotactic poly((S)5-methyl-1-heptene)   46
isotactic poly(1-hexene)   **38**
isotactic poly(1-oxo-2-phenyltrimethylene)   **39**
isotactic poly(1-pentene)   **38**
isotactic poly(2-vinylpyridine)   64, *65*
isotactic poly(3-methyl-1-butene)   **38**
isotactic poly(4-methyl-1-pentene)   **38**, *40*, 45
isotactic poly(4-methyl pentene)/isotactic poly(4-methyl hexene)   298
isotactic poly(5-methyl-1-hexene)   **38**, 46
isotactic poly(α-olefins)   37
isotactic poly(α-vinylnaphtalene)   **38**
isotactic polybutene (iPB)   37, **38**, *41*, 108, 410
   conformational energy minima   37
   crystal structures of form III of   49
   epitaxial crystallization of   250
   models of packing of   *44, 45*
   structure of form II of   45
   unbanded   114
isotactic poly(*o*-fluorostyrene)   **38**
isotactic poly(*p*-fluorostyrene)   **38**, 49

isotactic polymers   32
   (+) and (−) bonds in   *33*
   helical conformations in crystals of   36
   models for the helical conformations of the chains of various   40
   structural data of   **38–40**
isotactic poly((R),(S)-5-methyl-1-heptene)   **38**
isotactic poly((S)-5-methyl-1-heptene)   **38**
isotactic poly((R),(S)-4-methyl-1-hexene)   **38**
isotactic poly((S)-4-methyl-1-hexene)   **38**, 46
isotactic poly((S)-3-methyl-1-pentene)   **38**
isotactic poly(*m*-methylstyrene)   **38**
isotactic poly(*o*-methylstyrene)   **38**, 45
isotactic poly(octadecylethylene)   316
isotactic polypropylene (iPP)   35, 36, 37, **38**, *40*, 96, 253, 306, 308, 402, 436
   αiPP   246, 257, 258; *see also* monoclinic form
   α and β crystal structures   257
   βiPP   257, 258; *see also* trigonal form
   blends with propylene-*co*-ethylene copolymers   299
   calcium carbonate as a filler   381
   collapse dynamics of   203
   crystallization of β-nucleated   96, *97*
   crystallization of the γ phase   435
   crystallization rate of   *302*
   crystal structure of the stable form of   46
   disorder modification form of   59
   DSC and the nucleating activity of   239
   edge-on lamellae of imperfect   103
   epitaxial crystallization of   240, 245–247
   epitaxial crystallization of iPP on isotactic polyvinylcyclohexane   254, *255*
   epitaxial crystallization of PE on   257
   equilibrium melting point   282
   evolution of the storage modulus during crystallization of   *402*
   evolution of the transformed volume fraction with shear rate   *434*
   γ form of   48
   grafted with acrylic acid (PP-*g*-AA)   392
   hedrites from the trigonal β-polymorph   96
   helical regularization and domain formation of   179–181
   with hemp fibers   382
   iPP crystals in iPP/PP-*g*-MA/o-MMT   391
   iPP-*g*-MA/o-MMT   390, *391*
   isothermal spherulitic crystallization   216
   lattice affected by disorder   56
   limit-ordered models of the α and γ forms of   59, *59*
   line repetition symmetries and corresponding conformations for   36
   minimum temperature for creation of precursors   415
   morphology and spherulite growth rate of iPP in blends with LDPE   305
   morphology of injection-molded   421
   nanocomposites with exfoliated MMT or silver (Ag) nanoparticles   380
   nanocomposites with octamethyl POSS   393
   nanocomposite with exfoliated o-MMT   *389*
   nonisothermal crystallization of   225

isotactic polypropylene (iPP) (*Continued*)
    nucleation transcrystallization of 383
    Ozawa analysis for iPP crystallized at different cooling rates 232
    partitioning of branches in copolymers of 333
    in propylene–pentene and propene–hexene 48
    with PTFE fibers 384
    PVT diagram during isobaric cooling 435
    relative specific volumes of samples of 405
    self-epitaxy of 247–250
    shear-induced crystallization 390
    smectic phase or monoclinic α phase 447
    spherulitic crystallization of 226
    substitutional isomorphism of different chains in 56–57
    talc in 380–381
    temperature gradients 437
    trigonal form **38**, *48*
    see also polypropylene
isotactic poly(propylene-*co*-butene) 337
isotactic poly(propylene-*co*-hexene) **38**
isotactic poly(propylene-*co*-pentene) **38**
isotactic polypropylene/high density polyethylene (iPP/HDPE) blends 306, 307
isotactic polypropylene/isotactic poly(1-butene) (iPP/iPB)
    Flory interaction parameter of miscible blends of **296**
    interaction energy density of miscible blends of **296**
isotactic polypropylene/low density polyethylene (iPP/LDPE) blends 306
isotactic polypropylene/poly(1-butene) blends 299
isotactic polystyrene (iPS) 37, **38**, *40*, 62, 114
    bright-field TEM images and electron diffraction patterns of *101*
    crystallized in ultrathin films *99, 100*
    double growth spiral formed from giant screw dislocations *89*
    equilibrium melting temperature **271**
    film thickness 100
    heating scans of semicrystalline *25, 26*
    heat of fusion **271**
    models of packing of *44*
isotactic poly(styrene-*alt*-CO) **39**
isotactic poly(*t*-butylacrylate) **38**, 46
isotactic poly(*tert*-butylethylene sulfide) *64, 65*
isotactic poly(vinylcyclohexane) (iPVCH) **38**, *40*, 45, 241
    epitaxial crystallization of iPP on *254, 255*
    models of packing of *45*
isotactic poly(vinyl isobutyl ether) **38**
isotactic poly(vinyl isopropyl ether) **38**
isotactic poly(vinyl methyl ether) **38**
isotactic poly(vinyl neopentyl ether) **38**
isotactic poly(vinyl *sec*-butyl ether) **38**
isotactic propylene-*co*-ethylene 300
isotactic propylene–hexene (iPPHe) 47
isotactic propylene–pentene (iPPE) 47
isothermal annealing 369
isothermal crystallization 218–224, 369
    analysis of crystallization data of 230–231
    conversion rate of 219
    in fiber-reinforced composites 385
    nucleation rate of 218
    structural evolution in 179–186
    temperature for block copolymer systems of **354**
isothermal heat flow rate measurements 23
isotropic melt 139
iteration method 129

jet mill **150**
Jeziorny method 233

Kawaski rules 201
Keller II model 446
Keller I model 446
kinetic Monte Carlo method 201–202, 371
kinetics 215–235
    analysis of crystallization data 230–233
    effects on crystallization 434
    factors influencing 224–230, 233
    factors influencing crystallization 224–230
    isothermal and nonisothermal crystallization theories 218–224
    measurements 216–217
    models for complex crystallization conditions 224
    simulation of 217–218
kink-band disorder 59
kink-bands 254
knots, and entanglements 159
Kolmogorov–Johnson–Mehl–Avrami (KJMA) model 23

lamellae 260
    edge-on lamellae from molten films 102–104
    with left-handed topological giant screw dislocations *118*
    radially growing *114*
    thickness of 176, 244
lamellar ribbon *118*
lamellar twists
    banded spherulites and 116–121
    relation between chain tilt and *119*
Langevin dynamics 200, 209
    molecular dynamics and 203–204
latent heat of fusion 265
lattice matching 252–254
lattice Monte Carlo simulations 205
Lauritzen–Hoffman theory 353
Lees-Edwards sliding brick boundary conditions 210
L enantiomers 117
light emitting diodes 259
light microscopy *see* optical microscopy
light scattering 15, 107–108
limit disordered model structures 55–56
limit ordered model structures 55–56
linear elastic dumbbell model 417
linear low density polyethylenes (LLDPE) 243, 330, 410, 454
linear low density polyethylenes/very low density polyethylene (LLDPE/VLDPE) 298
linear polymers
    epitaxial crystallization of 243–244
    epitaxy between 252
    epitaxy between helical and 252

INDEX

links, and entanglements   159
liquid-crystalline components, polymer blends with   314–319
liquid crystal polymers (LCP)   314–316, 321
liquid crystals   314, 321
   cholesteric mesophase   315
   mesomorphism and phase transition behavior of   314–316
   nematic mesophase   315
   smectic mesophase   315
LLDPE *see* linear low density polyethylenes (LLDPE)
loops, and entanglements   159
loose folds   159
Lovinger and Gryte's model   437–438
low density polyethylene (LDPE)
   crystallinity of   *339*
   X-ray diffraction patterns of   450

macro-crystallization, relationship between nano-nucleation and   133–135, 160
macromolecules
   modeling of confined crystallization of   371–372
   packing of macromolecules in polymer crystals   43–48
magic angle spinning   14
maleated isotactic polypropylene (PP-*g*-MA)   388
maleated polyethylene (PE-*g*-MA)   388
maleated polyolefins   388
Maltese cross   4, 75, 98, 106–107, 108, 114, *116*, 170
Master equation   200
mathematical modeling, crystallization in temperature gradients   439
matrix polymers, crystallization behavior of   383
mechanical grinding method (top down method) *see* top down method (mechanical grinding method)
melting, of miscible polymer blends   295–296
melting of polymer crystals   265–286
   influence of heating rate on   278–279
   influence of small diluents on   282
   influence of the polymer's chemical structure on   277
   introduction to   265–266
   irreversible   265, 282–284
   multiple melting peaks of polymers   279–281
   parameters of   267–268
   polymer molar mass and   277–278
   pressure and   281
   reversible   282–284
   study of   266
   thermodynamic quantities   *266*
melting point elevation theory   434
melting temperature   267
melt miscible blends   371
melts
   crystallization from   204–208
   shear-induced crystallization of   186–189
melt temperature   178
melt time   178
meso (m) diads   32, *33*
metastability   370
3-methylbutene, isotactic copolymers of butene and   32
Metropolis Monte Carlo simulation   201, 205
mica   380

microcomposites   379
   with particulate fillers   380–382
microdomains   347
microfillers   393
microrelaxation model   205
miktoarm star copolymer   **349**
mini-emulsions   365
minimum crystallization temperature   364
miscibility   288
miscible polymer blends   290–302, 321
   analysis of the crystallization of   291
   binary   291
   crystal growth in the presence of amorphous components   291
   crystal growth rate   292–294
   crystallization behavior of amorphous/crystalline blends   297–298
   crystallization behavior of crystalline/crystalline blends   298–302
   Flory interaction parameters of binary   **296**
   interaction energy densities of binary   **296**
   melting behavior of   295–296
   overall crystallization kinetics   294–295
   with partial miscibility   296–297
   phase morphology   291–292
MMT *see* montmorillonite (MMT)
mobile amorphous fraction (MAF)   25
modeling
   of crystallization in fiber-reinforced composites   385–387
   of crystallization in processing conditions   440–442
   of fiber spinning   448
   injection molding   458
   mathematical modeling, crystallization in temperature gradients   439
models
   application of FIC models to injection molding   421–426
   a-texture model   453
   atomistic models   207–208
   Baur's copolymer model   337
   bond fluctuation model   205
   coarse-grained   206–207
   for complex crystallization conditions   224
   directional-specific models of segmental interactions   290
   Doi–Edwards model   411, 417
   entropic barrier models   210
   extended Pompom model   417
   FENE-P model   417
   Flory–Huggins rigid-lattice model   290
   Flory's model   328–330, 337, 343
   flow-enhanced nucleation model   411–419
   flow-induced crystallization   410–426
   Graham–Likhtman and Milner–McLeish (GLaMM) model   419
   isokinetic model   223
   isotactic polybutene (iPB)   *44, 45*
   Keller II model   446
   Keller I model   446
   linear elastic dumbbell model   417
   Lovinger and Gryte's model   437–438

models (*Continued*)
  microrelaxation model   205
  modified Giesekus model   418
  Nakamura model   223, 232, 448, 454
  Piorkowska's model   438
  Rolie-Poly model   420
  Sanchez–Eby model   340
  sheaf model   453
  solid-on-solid models   202–203
  Toda model   115
  Wendling–Suter model   340
  YOROI model of nano-oriented crystals (NOCs)   147
modified Hoffman–Lauritzen theory   411, 417
molar mass, and melting of polymer crystals   277–278
molecular deformation factor   421
molecular dynamics   199–200
  and Langevin dynamics   203–204
  using atomistic models   207–208
  using coarse-grained models   206–207
molecular dynamics simulations   371
molecular epitaxy   259
molecular rigidity   210
molecular stress function   410
molten films
  crystals and aggregates grown from   94–104
  edge-on lamellae from   102–104
monoclinic form   447
monolayer crystals   73
  grown from solutions   167–168
  orientation of   238
monomeric units, substitutional isomorphism of   57–58
Monte Carlo simulation   200–201
montmorillonite (MMT)   388
  ability to nucleate iPP crystallization   390
  exfoliated MMT   379
morphology, for complex crystallization conditions   **354**
Mullins–Sekerka stability   84, 121
multipass rheometer (MPR) experiments, flow conditions for   **422**
multipeak melting   280

Nakamura equation   223, 229, 230, 408, 458
Nakamura model   223, 232, 448, 454
nano-$CaCO_3$, iPP composites with, modified with PP-g-AA   392
nanochalk   393
nanoclays   389
nanocomposites, crystallization in polymer composites and   379–397
nano-confined polymeric systems   347–378
nanolayers   **350**
nanometer-sized particles, as fillers   379
nanomizer   **150**
nano-nucleation
  direct observation by synchrotron radiation   128–135
  kinetic parameters of   126, 130–131
  observation by small-angle X-ray scattering (SAXS)   128–129, 160
  real images of   131–133
  relationship between macro-crystallization and   133–135, 160
  size distribution of nano-nuclei   130–131
  supercooling dependence of   133
  and ultrahigh performance   147–148
nano-oriented crystals (NOCs)   139, 140–144, 161
  crystallinity (χ_c) of   142
  elongational strain rate dependence of the morphology by OM   140–142
  elongational strain rate dependence of the NOCs fraction   144
  verification of   142–144
  YOROI model   147
nanoparticles
  literature regarding confined crystallization in   **350**
  preparation of three-dimensional nanoparticles   392
  three-dimensional   392
nanopores   **350**
nanopowders   393
natural rubber (*cis*-1,4-polyisoprene)   58, 191, 288
Near-Field Scanning Optical microscopy (NSOM)   3
neck formation   408
needle crystals   84
negative spherulites   169–170
neutron scattering   15
n-Fold Way Kinetic Monte Carlo   201, 202
nonequilibrium molecular dynamics (NEMD)   200
nonisothermal crystallization   218–224, 389
  analysis of crystallization data   231–233
  Avrami equation   219
  Avrami theory   220
  effect of flow on   229
  in fiber-reinforced composites   385
  nucleation rate   218
  Ozawa equation   221
nonspherulitic crystalline structures   *109*
nuclear magnetic resonance (NMR)   12–14, 217
  applications of   14
  chemical shift   13
  cross polarization in   14
  dipolar decoupling   13–14
  magic angle spinning   14
  multidimensional   14
  pulsed Fourier Transform NMR   13
  solid-state   14
nucleating agents   148–149
  added to multilayered thin-film ensembles   368
  bottom up method I (spray drying method) and   149, **150**, 154
  bottom up method II (solution crystallization) and   149, **150**, 154
  efficiency of   257
  epitaxial crystallization and the design of new   256–257, 261
  epitaxy in   238
  nano-sizing of   153–156
  of poly(ethylene terephthalate) (PET)   244
  size and morphology of   154–155
  top down method (mechanical grinding method)   149–150, **150**, 155

nucleation 125–163, 372
  effect of entanglement density on the rate of 156–160, 161
  flow-induced 408
  free energy for formation of a critical nucleus 127–128
  free energy for formation of a nucleus 127
  goal of study of 126
  heterogeneous nucleation *see* heterogeneous nucleation
  homogeneous nucleation *see* homogeneous nucleation
  induction period 126
  instantaneous nucleation 218, 219, 220, 222, 224, 364
  as a linear sequential process 126
  quiescent nucleation 414–415
  sequential process of 134
  and slow crystal growth 364
  spontaneous nucleation 218, 219, 222, 224
  steady period 126
nucleation density 389
nucleation rate 413, 415
  flow and 410
  and increase of entanglement density 157–158
  instantaneous nucleation 224
  isothermal crystallization 218
  spontaneous nucleation 224
nucleation theory 135–138, 161
  based on direct observation of nucleation 135–136
  confirmation by overall crystallinity 137–138
nucleus
  free energy necessary for formation of a critical nucleus 127–128
  shape related to kinetic parameters 128
numerical simulation 433
Nylon 6 **35**, 54, 408
  equilibrium melting temperature **271**
  heat of fusion **271**
  lamellar growth process and chain folding in spherulites of *171*
  melting temperature as a function of heating rate for semicrystalline *280*
  metastable β form of 54
Nylon 6/PE-AA blends 313
Nylon 6/PP-AA blends 312, 313
Nylon 6.6 **35**, 77, 79–80
  collapsed scroll crystal of *80*
  equilibrium melting temperature **271**
  heat of fusion **271**
  polarized optical micrograph of growing spherulites of *75*
Nylon 7.7 **35**
Nylon 10.10 77
Nylon 12
  equilibrium melting temperature **271**
  heat of fusion **271**
Nylon 65 54, *54*
Nylon 66 *54*, 170, 408
Nylon n, minimum energy conformations of chains of *51*
Nylon n,m, minimum energy conformations of chains of *51*
nylons 50–55
  even-odd 54
  odd-even 54
  odd nylons 54
  odd-odd nylons 54
  see also aliphatic nylons; aliphatic polyamides

olefin copolymers, miscible blends with crystallizable components 298
oligo-3AT 259
cis-1,4-poly(isoprene), *trans*-1,4-poly(isoprene) (α form) **35**
optical microscopy 2–5, 133
  applications of 3–5
  contrast modes 2–3
  Hoffman modulation contrast optical microscopy 3
  Near-Field Scanning Optical microscopy (NSOM) 3
  phase contrast optical microscopy 3
  polarized optical microscopy 2–3
  reflection optical microscopy 2
  transmission optical microscopy 2–5
opto-active materials 259–260
organic field effect transistors (OFET) 259
organic solar cells 259
organo-modified MMT (o-MMT) 388, 389, 393
orientation 16, 446
oriented growth 238
Ostwald ripening 132, 138, 160, 161
Ostwald rule 167
Ozawa equation 177, 221, 232
Ozawa plot 234

P3HT 260
PA6 *see* polyamide 6 (PA6)
particulate fillers, microcomposites with 380–382
PBA-C8 110
  crystals with edge-on lamellae *102*
  formation of a small lamellar stack in *111*
  growth from small lamellar stack into a hedrite *112*
  growth of a spherulite of *113*
PBHA/PAA *318*
PBT *see* poly(butylene terephthalate) (PBT)
PEBA 273
1,3-pentadiene, *trans*-1,4-copolymers of butadiene and 32
PEO *see* poly(ethylene oxide) (PEO)
permanent red 257
PET *see* poly(ethylene terephthalate) (PET)
phase contrast optical microscopy 3
photon correlation spectroscopy 15
physical etching 7
physical staining 7
Piorkowska's model 438
PLDA-*b*-PE 360, 361
PLLA *see* poly(L-lactic acid)
POE *see* poly(oxyethylene)
Poisson probability distribution 222
polarized optical microscopy 2–3, 217
polar polymers 257
pole figures 449
cis-1,4-poly(1,3-butadiene) **35**
poly(1,4-diethyl *cis,cis*-muconate) 191
poly(1-butene) *see* poly(butene-1)
poly(2,5-di-styrl pyradine) 191

poly(2,6-dimethyl-1,4-phenylene ether) (PPE)   369
poly(3-alkyl-thiophenes) (P3AT)   259
poly(3-hydroxybutyrate)   117
poly(3-hydroxybutyrate)/poly(ethylene oxide)   369
poly(3-methyl-1-butene) (iP3MB)   49
poly(4-methyl-1-pentene)   37–41, 62, 78
   crystalline forms of syndiotactic   42
   crystal structures of form II of   49
   distortions of a square crystal of   78
   electron diffraction pattern of   62
   equilibrium melting temperature   271
   grown from dilute solution   76
   heat of fusion   271
   models of packing of form I of   45
poly(4-vinyl phenol)/poly(trimethylene terephthalate) (PVPh/PTT)
   Flory interaction parameter of miscible blends of   296
   interaction energy density of miscible blends of   296
poly(9,9-di-octyl-2,7-fluorene-diyl)   261
polyacrylonitrile   48
polyamide 6 (PA6)   369, 370, 380, 389, 391
   and LDPE blends   310
   nanocomposites with MMT   380
   PA6/poly(methylmetacrylate) blends   369
   PA6/polypropylene   369
   PA6/poly(vinylidene fluoride)   369
   PA6/PP blend   303
polyamide 6.6   439
polyamide 12 disks, morphological sequences in   456
polyamide 66   391
polyamides
   crystallization behavior of compatibilized blends   312
   epitaxial crystallization of   243, 244
   fillers for   380
   packing effects on the conformation of polymer chains in crystals of aliphatic   50–55
poly(α-olefins)   37, 45
poly(α-vinylnaphthalene)   45
poly(β-hydroxybutyrate-co-β-hydroxyvaleate)   340
poly(biphenyloxyexyacrylate) (PBHA)   316
poly(bisphenol A octane ether) (PBA-C8)   102
trans-1,4-polybutadiene   44
polybutadiene (PBD)   288
poly(butene-1)   115, 116, 251
polybutene, PB-b-PI-b-PEO   358
poly(butylene adipate-co-butylene succinate) (PBAS)   298
poly(butylene succinate)   298, 371
   and poly(ethylene oxide) blends   371
poly(butylene terephthalate) (PBT)   266
   blends with poly(decamethylene 4,4'-terephthaloyldioxydibenzoate) (HTH10)   318
   equilibrium melting temperature   271
   heat of fusion   271
   polarizing optical micrographs of   319
   quantitative thermal analysis of the heat capacity of semicrystalline   277
poly(butylene terephthalate) (PBT)/HTH10
   glass transition temperature of   319
   overall crystallization rate of PBT in   320
   polarizing optical micrographs of   319
   radial growth rate of PBT spherulites in   320
poly(butylene terephthalate)/polyarylate (PBT/PAr)   291
   Flory interaction parameter of miscible blends of   296
   interaction energy density of miscible blends of   296
poly(butylene terephthalate)/poly(vinylidene fluoride)   369
poly(ε-caprolactone) (PCL)   291
   equilibrium melting temperature   271
   heat of fusion   271
   interaction energy density of miscible blends of poly(vinylidene fluoride) (PVDF) and   296
   PCL-b-PB diblock copolymers   355, 359
   PCL-b-PE diblock copolymers   359
poly(ε-caprolactone-b-butadiene)   342
poly(ε-caprolactone)/poly(vinylidene fluoride) (PCL/PVDF), Flory interaction parameter of   296
polycarbonate/poly(ε-caprolactone) (PC/PCL)   292
polycarbonate/poly(ethylene terephthalate) (PC/PET)   367
poly(chlorotrifluoroethylene)   77
poly(cis-1,4-butadiene)   50
polycrystalline aggregates   73–123
poly(decamethylene 4,4'-terephthaloyldioxydibenzoate) (HTH10)   319
polydiacetylene   191, 259
polydienes   32, 33
poly(δ-valerolactone)   355
poly(δ-valerolactone)-block-polystyrene (PVL-b-PS) diblock copolymers   355
poly(epichlorhydrin)   117, 118
polyesters see aliphatic polyesters
poly(ET-co-CT)   338
poly(ET-co-EN)   340
poly (ether ether ketone)/polyetherimide (PEEK/PEI)
   Flory interaction parameter of miscible blends of   296
   interaction energy density of miscible blends of   296
poly-ethers   117
polyethylene (PE)   63, 75, 79, 107, 266, 408, 436, 450
   aggregates   94
   anisotropic elongated single crystals in the orthorhombic forms of   61
   atomic force microscopy (AFM) images of crystals of   79
   Avrami index range   353
   blends with a low molecular weight matrix   406
   calcium carbonate as a filler   381
   chair crystal shapes   90, 91
   change of heat of fusion with molecular weight for analogs of   272
   collapse dynamics of   203
   crystal habits   62–63
   crystallization of high molar mass chains   78
   crystallization of low molar mass chains   78
   curved crystal habits   64
   dendrites   73, 74, 87, 88, 92
   DSC and the nucleating activity of   239
   DSC cooling scans for   357
   DSC heating scans for   357
   edge-on lamellae of   104
   edge-on TEM image of   104
   electron micrographs of single crystals of   63

energy barrier **353**
epitaxial crystallization of 238, 243, 257, 258
equilibrium melting temperature **271**
fibers 446
fillers for 380
film blowing 448
generation of disordered phase in isothermal crystallization of 181–182
grafted with glycidyl methacrylate 310
grown from concentrated solutions 92
growth of banded spherulites of 121
growth rate of lamella from isothermal crystallization of 11, *12*
heating rate for semicrystalline 279
heat of fusion **271**
hedrites 109
hollow pyramid crystal shapes *90*
intersecting crystals of *89*
kink-band disorder in 59
lamellar twists 117
liquid heat capacity of *270*
lozenged-shaped crystal of *76, 91*
melting of extended chain spherulite crystal of *279*
melting temperature of semicrystalline 275, 279
metastable monoclinic crystals 243
molecular mass dependence on the melting temperatures of *278*
molecular weight effects 108
monolayer crystals of *73, 74*
morphology of a single crystal grown from solution 168
orthorhombic polyethylene 118
partitioning of branches in copolymers of 333
PE-*b*-PEO diblock copolymers 356
PE-*b*-PEP block copolymers 353
PE-*b*-PEP diblock copolymers *354*
polarized optical micrographs of *109*
polyethylene (PE)-*b*-poly(ε-caprolactone) (PCL) block copolymers 359
production of fine droplet dispersions of 362
rounded lateral habits 66–67
s(2/1)d*m* symmetry group **35**
screw dislocations correlated with chain tilt 119
semicrystalline–glassy and semicrystalline–rubbery block copolymers 353
shape of monolayer crystals of 80
shish-kebab crystals in deformed 10
six-sided crystal of 80
specific volume of linear and branched 267
spherulite emerging from the free surface of a molten film *117*
spherulites of melt-cooled PE sample and the hierarchical structure *166*
spiral growth originating from a tear at the growth face *88*
stable orthorhombic crystals 243
string-like 405
strongly segregated and in miscible diblock copolymers 351
study of the structure and morphology of 8–9
TEM image of *9*
truncated lozenge-shaped crystals of 76
uniaxial 106
see also chlorinated polyethylene (CPE)
poly(ethylene adipate) 170, 244
poly(ethylene-*alt*-propylene) (PEP) 353
poly(ethylene-*b*-(ethylene-*alt*-propylene)) 341, 342, 343
poly(ethylene-*b*-ethylethylene) 342
poly(ethylene-*b*-(head-to-head propylene)) 342
polyethylene-*block*-polystyrene (PE-*b*-PS) 351–353
Avrami index values of *354*
SAXS patterns and TEM micrographs of *351*
polyethylene-*b*-poly(ε-caprolactone) (PE-*b*-PCL) block copolymers 359, 360
poly(ethylene)-*b*-poly(ethylene oxide)/bisphenol A type epoxy resin 369
polyethylene-*b*-poly(ethylene oxide) diblock copolymers (PE-*b*-PEO) 355
poly(ethylene-*co*-propylene) 203
polyethylene (PE) films
 orientation of the crystalline phase in 449
 visualization of the crystalline lamellae in 454
polyethylene (PE) homopolymer, DSC cooling and heating scans for *352*
polyethylene (PE) nanolayers, literature regarding confined crystallization in **349**
poly(ethylene naphthalates) 410
poly(ethylene oxide) (PEO) 50, 245, 298, 371
 blends with nematic LC p-azoxyanisole (PAA) 316
 co-extruded with ethylene acrylic acid copolymer 367
 crystallization under hard and soft confinement 369
 crystals from thin films 94
 DSC cooling scans for *357*
 DSC heating scans for *357*
 mini-emulsions 365
 molecular mass dependence of the melting temperatures of *278*
 monolayer crystals of *95*
 PEO droplets on a PS substrate 363
 production of fine droplet dispersions of 362
 single crystal of *76, 77*
 spiral growth multilayer crystals of *96*
 see also polyoxyethylene (POE)
poly(ethylene oxide-*b*-(1,2-butylene oxide)) 342
poly(ethylene oxide-*b*-ethylethylene) 342
poly(ethylene oxide-*b*-isoprene) 342
poly(ethylene oxide)-*b*-polystyrene/polystyrene 369
poly(ethylene oxide-*b*-styrene) 89, 93
poly(ethylene oxide-*b*-styrene-*b*-ethylene oxide) 342
poly(ethylene oxide)/ethylene acrylic acid copolymer (PEO/EAA) 367
poly(ethylene oxide)/p-azoxyanisole (PEO/PAA) blends *317*
poly(ethylene oxide)/poly(ethyl methacrylate) (PEO/PEMA) 291
poly(ethylene oxide)/poly(methyl methacrylate) (PEO/PMMA) blends
 crystallization behavior of 297–298
 Flory interaction parameter of **296**
 interaction energy density of miscible blends of **296**
 isothermal growth rate of PEO spherulites in miscible *294*

poly(ethylene oxide)/poly(vinyl chloride) (PEO/PVC)
    Flory interaction parameter of **296**
    interaction energy density of miscible blends of **296**
polyethylene/polymethylene oxide (PE/POM) 368
polyethylene/polypropylene blends 306–307
polyethylene/polystyrene (PE/PS) 367
poly(ethylene terephthalate) (PET) 244, 308, 380, 408, 436
    compatibilization and properties of blends of 309
    elongation-induced crystallization of 410
    equilibrium melting temperature **271**
    fiber-spinning of 189
    glass transition temperature of 457
    heat of fusion **271**
    high speed spinning of 447
    reversible melting of polymer crystals 283
poly(ethylene terephthalate)/high density polyethylene (PET/HDPE) 309, 311–314
poly(ethylene terephthalate)/poly(butylene terephthalate) (PET/PBT) 292
poly(ethylene terephthalate)/polypropylene (PET/PP) 309
polyfluorenes (PFO) 259
poly(glycolic acid) (PGA) 172, *173*
    equilibrium melting temperature **271**
    heat of fusion **271**
polygonal spiral growth, from giant screw dislocations 86
polyhedral aggregates 96
polyhedral oligomeric silsesquioxanes (POSS) 392, 393
poly(heptamethylene terephthalate) 170
poly(hexamethylene adipamide) 50
poly(hexamethylene sebacamide) 50
poly(R-3-hydroxybutyrate) *116*
poly(hydroxybutyrate) (PHB) 380
    equilibrium melting temperature **271**
    heat capacity for 24
    heat of fusion **271**
    rigid amorphous fraction (RAF) 24
poly(R-3-hydroxybutyrate-*co*-R-3-hydroxyhexanoate) 120
poly-β-hydroxybutyrate (PHB) 298
poly(hydroxy butyrate)/poly(ethylene oxide) (PHB/PEO) 292
poly(R-3-hydroxyvalerate) 117, 118
polyisobutylene 50
cis-1,4-polyisoprene (natural rubber) 58, *58*
polyisoprene 288
trans-1,4-poly(isoprene) (β form) **35**
polyisoprene-*b*-polystyrene-*b*-poly(ethylene oxide) (PI-*b*-PS-*b*-PEO) 358
polyisoprene/ethylene-*co*-vinyl acetate copolymer (PI/EVA)
    Flory interaction parameter of miscible blends of **296**
    interaction energy density of miscible blends of **296**
poly(isopropyl vinyl ether)/poly(sec-butyl-vinyl ether) 298
poly(lactic acid) (PLA) 266, 267, 268, 273, 380, 382
    apparent heat capacity of *269*
    crystallization temperature for semicrystalline 276
    degree of crystallinity versus temperature for *272*
    enthalpy, entropy and Gibbs function versus temperature for *276*
    equilibrium melting temperature **271**

    heat capacity changes in *271*
    heat of fusion **271**
    lamellae of semicrystalline 276
    lamellar thickness of 275
    melting endotherms of 280, *281*
    melting temperature of semicrystalline 275, 276
    melting transition of 267
    reversing heat capacities of *283*, 284
poly(L-lactic acid) 170, 172, *173*, 257
    PLLA-*b*-PE 360, 361
poly(L-lactide-*co*-D-lactide) 338
poly(L-lactide-*co-meso*-lactide) 338
poly(L-lactide)/poly(D-lactide) (PLLA/PDLA) 64, *65*, 66
polymer blends
    co-continuous polymer blends 304
    compatibilized polymer blends 307–314, 321
    containing liquid-crystalline components 321
    crystallization in nano-confined polymeric systems 368–371
    crystallization of 287–325
    development of 288
    immiscible polymer blends 303–307, 368–371
    introduction to 287–288
    with liquid-crystalline components 314–319
    literature regarding confined crystallization in **349, 350**
    miscibility of 288
    miscible 290–302
    thermodynamics of 288–290
polymer chains
    conformation of 33–43
    constitution and configuration of 31–33
    crystallization and chain folding mode 185–186
    lamellae folding in 60
    repetition symmetry groups **35**
    stereoisomeric centers along 32
    stereoregularity of 32
    symmetry operators 35
    tetrahedral stereoisomeric centers in 32
polymer composites
    additives for 379
    classification of 379
    crystallization in nanocomposites and 379–397
    definition of 379
polymer crystal fold surfaces, epitaxial crystallization involving 254–256
polymer crystallization, computer modeling of 197–214
polymer crystals *see* crystals
polymer decoration technique 255, *256*
polymer dispersed liquid crystal (PDLC) devices 314
polymer epitaxy, conformational and packing energy analysis of 258–259
polymer films, film blowing of 448
polymer glass, solvent-induced crystallization of 189–191
polymeric ionomers 244
polymer/liquid crystal blends 316–317
polymer/liquid crystal polymer blends 317–319
polymer/nucleating agent interactions 256
polymer nucleation 125–163
polymer/polymer epitaxy 250–252

polymers
  changes in conformations of 268–269
  complex behavior of 165–167
  conversion degree dependence on time in neat
    polymers *388*
  crystallization mechanism of 173–178
  crystallization of blend samples 167
  crystal structures of 31–72
  entropy-driven phase formation in 47
  epitaxial crystallization of 167, 237–264
  epitaxial relationship between substrates and 241
  experimental techniques for characterizing
    semicrystalline 1–29
  hexagonal mode of packing of cylinders 44
  loose irrational helices 257
  morphologies 165–167
  tetragonal mode of packing of skews 44
polymer–silicate interactions 391
poly((S)-3-methyl-1-pentene) (iP(S)3MP) 45, 46
poly(methylene oxide)/polystyrene-poly(2,6-dimethyl-1,4
  phenylene ether) (POM/(PS/PPE)) 369
poly(methyl methacrylate), blend sample with
  poly(vinylidene fluoride) (PVDF) 172
polymorphic structures 370
polymorphism 33–43, 421
poly(norbornene-*b*-(ethylidene norbornene)) 341
polyolefins 256
  3-substituted 37
  4-substituted 37
  compatibilization and properties of blends of 309
  crystallization behavior of compatibilized blends 312
  epitaxial crystallization of 241
  miscible blends with crystallizable components 298
  nucleating activity of talc in 380
polyolefins/polyamide 6 369
poly(oligoamide-*alt*-oligoether) *273, 274*
poly[oligoimino(1-oxododecamethylene)-*alt*-
  oligooxytetramethylene] 273
poly(*o*-methylstyrene) 45
poly(oxy-2,6-dimethyl-1,4-phenylene) (PPO) 284
polyoxyethylene (POE)
  apparent and reversing heat capacity of *278, 279*
  equilibrium melting temperature **271**
  heat of fusion **271**
  melting and crystallization rates versus difference of
    temperature for POEs with different molar masses *278*
  melting and crystallization rate versus difference of
    temperature for POE with different molar masses *278*
  see also poly(ethylene oxide) (PEO)
poly(oxyethylene)-*b*-poly(oxybutylene) 369
polyoxymethylene (POM) 78, 81, *83*, 380, 455
  crystallization from a dilute solution 165, *166*
  curved crystal habits 64
  electron micrographs of single crystals in the trigonal form
    of *62*
  equilibrium melting temperature **271**
  extended-chain crystals *166*
  generation of tie chains in isothermal crystallization
    of 183–184

heat of fusion **271**
hexagonal crystals 77
intersecting crystals of 89
multipeak melting process for hedrites of
  280
oriented crystallization of 254
row structure in blown films 453
spiral growths and terrace growths in 87
star-shaped crystal of *81*
poly(pentamethylene terephthalate) *172*
trans-polypentenamer 35
poly(*para*-phenylene) 259
poly(phenylene oxide) 369
polyphenylene sulfide (PPS) 254
  crystallization half-time of PSS phase in PPS/Vectra-B
    blends *318*
  crystallization rate in blends of 318
  glass transition temperature of 457
polypropylene (PP) 440
  dispersal in an immiscible PS matrix 369
  effect of increase of equilibrium melting
    temperature 436
  equilibrium melting temperature **271**
  grafted with maleic anhydride (PP-*g*-MA) 365
  heat of fusion **271**
  monoclinic α-isotactic monolayers 77
  nanodroplets 364
  PP/branched PE 369
  PP-*g*-MA **366**, *366*, 389
  PP-*g*-MAH 366
  PP/PB 298
  see also atactic polypropylene; isotactic polypropylene;
    syndiotactic polypropylene
polypropylene copolymers
  crystallization behavior of blends of 299–302
  crystallization rate of 301
  spherulite growth rate of 301
polypropylene film *444*
poly(propylene oxide) 117
polypropylene/polyamide 6/SEBS ternary blends
  369
polypropylene/polystyrene (PP/PS) 367
polystyrene (PS) 185, 288, 455
  PS-*b*-PB-*b*-PCL 360
  PS-*b*-PE-*b*-PCL 359
  PS-*b*-PI-*b*-PEO 358
  (PS/SMA2)/PA6 blend 370
  see also atactic polystyrene
  see also syndiotactic polystyrene
polystyrene-*b*-4-polyhydroxystyrene 371
polystyrene/poly(oxybutylene) 369
polytetrafluoroethylene (PTFE) 245
  Clausius–Clapeyron equation and heat of fusion for
    272
  epitaxy between layers of 252
  equilibrium melting temperature **271**
  fibers 384
  foil 228, *229*
  heat of fusion **271**

poly(tetramethylene oxide), and poly(tetramethylene terephthalate) copolymer   191
polythiophene   259
poly(trifluoroethylene)   74
poly(trimethylene terephthalate) (PTT)   266
   change of degree of crystallinity with temperature for   273
   equilibrium melting temperature   **271**
   estimated heat of fusion from apparent heat capacity of   270
   heat of fusion   **271**
polyvinyl alcohol (PVA)   206
   equilibrium melting temperature   **271**
   heat of fusion   **271**
poly(vinyl chloride) (PVC)   381
   butadiene-acrylonitrile copolymers (NBR)   288
   equilibrium melting temperature   **271**
   heat of fusion   **271**
poly(vinylcyclohexane)   45
poly(vinyl fluoride) (PVF)
   equilibrium melting temperature   **271**
   heat of fusion   **271**
poly(vinyl fluoride)/poly(vinylidene fluoride)   298
poly(vinylidene fluoride) (PVDF)   79, 118, 168, 208, 298, 380, *407*
   β-form crystals in nanocomposites of   391
   blend sample with atactic poly(methyl methacrylate) (PVDF/PMMA)   172
   curved crystal habits   64
   growth of banded spherulites of   121
   kink-band disorder in   59
   α polymorph in melt-crystallized neat PVDF   391
poly(vinylidene fluoride)/polyamide-6 (PVDF/PA6)   306, 368
poly(vinylidene fluoride)/poly-β-hydroxybutyrate (PVDF/PHB)
   Flory interaction parameter of miscible blends of   296
   interaction energy density of miscible blends of   296
poly(vinylidene fluoride)/poly(butylene terephthalate) (PVDF/PBT)   306, 368
poly(vinylidene fluoride)/poly(ethyl methacrylate) (PVDF/PEMA)
   Flory interaction parameter of   296
   interaction energy density of miscible blends of   296
poly(vinylidene fluoride)/poly(methyl methacrylate) (PVDF/PMMA)   292
   Flory interaction parameter of   296
   interaction energy density of miscible blends of   296
positive spherulites   169–170
POSS (polyhedral oligomeric silsesquioxanes)   392, 393
powder impregnation   384
π–π interactions, between diacetylene and potassium phthalate salt substrate   259
precursors   401, 412
pressure
   effects on crystallization   435–436
   flow and   459
   influence on the melting of polymer crystals   281
   role in injection molding   435
primary nucleation   173–174

primary nuclei   215
primary polypropylene films   442
principle of minimum internal conformational energy   34
principle of the staggered bonds   36
probabilistic approach   385
probability theory   218, 220–223
processing conditions
   cooling on the roll   444–445
   crystalline orientation by X-ray diffraction   446
   crystallization in   433–462
   effects of flow on crystallization   433–435
   effects of thermodynamics and kinetics on crystallization   434
   effects on crystallization   433–440
   fiber spinning   445–448
   influence on structure development   444–445
   modeling of crystallization in   440–442
   stretching in air   444
propene–butene copolymers   57
propene–hexene, trigonal form of iPP in the space groups *R3c* found in copolymers of   48
propylene-(1-butene) copolymer (BPS)
   BPS/EPS blend   *302*
   crystallization rate of   *302*
   DSC melting thermograms of   *302*
   ethylene-propylene copolymer (BPS/EPS) blend   *302*
   spherulites of   301
propylene/1-hexene co-polymers   299
propylene/1-octene co-polymers   299
propylene–alkene copolymers   330, 333
propylene–butene copolymers   57
propylene-*co*-1-butene   300
propylene-*co*-ethylene copolymers   300
propylene copolymers   333, *335*
propylene–pentene, trigonal form of iPP in the space groups *R3c* found in copolymers of   48
pseudoeutectic crystallization   292
pulsed Fourier Transform NMR   13
PVC *see* poly(vinyl chloride) (PVC)

quasi-elastic scattering   15
quiescent nucleation   414–415
quiescent sporadic nucleation rate   417
γ-quinacridone   257, 258
2-quinoxalinol   253

racemic (r) diads   32, *33*
Raman scattering   15
range, for block copolymer systems   **354**
rate equations   223–224, 408, 441
reactive blending   311
reflection high energy electron diffraction (RHEED)   239
reflection optical microscopy   2
relaxation time   418
R enantiomers   117
reptation time   403
reversible melting of polymer crystals   282–284
rigid amorphous fraction (RAF)   25
Rolie-Poly model   420

INDEX

rotational rheometers 401
rounded lateral habits 66–67
Rouse time 403
row-structure model with twisted lamellae 453
rubber *see* natural rubber (*cis*-1,4-polyisoprene)

Sanchez–Eby model 340
SAXS *see* small-angle X-ray scattering (SAXS)
scanning election microscopy (SEM) 6
   high resolution SEM 7
   sample preparation for 6
scattering techniques 15–21
   anisotropic 2D scattering pattern 18–19
   fast scanning calorimetry 25–26
   small-angle light scattering (SALS) 19–20
   small-angle Neutron scattering (SANS) 21–22
   small-angle X-ray scattering (SAXS) 17–19
   wide-angle X-ray diffraction (WAXD) 15–17
Schneider rate equations 420
seaweed structure 74
secondary nuclei 174
segmental interactions, directional-specific model of 290
self-poisoning 67
self-reinforced high density polyethylene (HDPE) 384
self-reinforced polymers 379, 384
semiconducting polymers 259
semicrystalline polymers 55
   block copolymers 327
   experimental techniques for characterizing 1–29
   homopolymers 335
   mechanical properties of 334–335
   PVT diagram of 436
S enantiomers 117
sequential coextrusion process 367
para-sexiphenyl (PSP) 259, *260*
sheaf model 453
shear-induced crystallization 229, 401–407
   constant pressure 401
   of heterogeneous systems 407
   of melts 186–189
   precursors 405–407
   short-term 401, 404
   temperature control in 401
shear strain, crystallization time versus shear rate for *403*
shish formation 404
   flow-induced shish formation 419–421
shish-kebab crystals 9, 165, *166*, 168, 208, 406
   in deformed polyethylene melts 10
   shear-induced crystallization and 229
shish-kebab precursors 406
short-term shearing 404
silica 380
simulations, literature regarding confined crystallization 350
single crystals *see* monolayer crystals
single-phase polymer materials 379
single-wall nanotubes (SWNTs) 391, 392
SLLOD equations of motion 210
slow crystallizing polymers 436, 457

small-angle light scattering (SALS) 19–20, 105, 178, 454
   anisotropic fluctuation approach 20–21
   deformed spherulites 20
   optical sign of spherulites 20
   ring-banded spherulites 20
   spherulite radius 19
small-angle neutron scattering (SANS) 21–22, 185
small-angle X-ray scattering (SAXS) 17–19, 133, 160, 178, 180, 217, 275, 343, 351, 448
   correlation function 17–18
   elongational strain rate dependence of pattern of 142–144
   interface distribution function 18
   observation of nano-nucleation by 128–129
   patterns for quiescent conditions 144
sodium benzoate 307, 381
soft epitaxy 238, 256, 258, 261
solid mesophases 55
solid-on-solid models 202–203
solid-state nuclear magnetic resonance (NMR) 14
solubility parameters 290
solution casting method 168–169
solution crystallization method 149, **150**
solution impregnation 384
solvent-induced crystallization, of polymer glass 189–191
spherulites 104–121, 215, 233
   banded spherulites 75, 105, 107, 116–121
   of blend samples 172
   computer modeling of spherulitic pattern formation 217–218
   deformed spherulites 20
   development of 110–116
   double banded spherulites 107
   double ringed 107
   growth rate of 177–178
   in isotactic polypropylene (iPP) 4
   isothermal crystallization and growth rate of 177
   lamellar twist 116–121
   Maltese cross 106–107
   morphology and crystalline modification 170
   nonisothermal crystallization and growth rate of 177–178
   nucleation 110
   occurrences of 108–110
   optical microscopy to observe 3
   optical properties of 105–108
   optical sign of 20
   polarized optical image of 98
   in polyethylene (PE) 4
   positive and negative spherulites from melt 169–170
   quasiparabolic 457
   radial growth of 110
   radius 20
   relation between hedrites and 111
   ribbon-like crystals and branching in 116
   ring-banded 20
   shear-induced crystallization and 229
   structural characteristics of 105
spinning *see* fiber spinning

spontaneous nucleation 218, 219, 222, 224
spray drying method 149, **150**, 154
sputter coating 7
stacking fault disorder 58–60
   kink-band disorder 59
staining agents 7
statistical copolymers 327
   crystallization in 328–340
   crystallization kinetics of 335–337
   crystallization thermodynamics 337–340
   crystal unit-cell structure 332–334
   with two crystallizable units 337
statistical ethylene copolymers, degree of crystallinity of *329*
statistical isotactic polypropylene copolymers 334
strain rate 417
stretch regimes 403
strongly segregated double-crystalline diblock copolymers and triblock copolymers 355–361
Styralloy 288
styrene–acrylonitrile copolymers (SAN) 288
styrene-*b*-(ethylene-*co*-butylene)-*b*-styrene 308
styrene-*b*-(ethylene-*co*-propylene) 308
styrene, isotactic copolymers of *o*-fluorostyrene and 32
styrene-*o*-fluorostyrene copolymers 57
substitutional isomorphism 56–57
substrates, epitaxial relationship between polymers and 241
supercooling 160, 175, 176
   computer simulations at 211
superfast chip calorimetry (SFCC) 284
superheating 284
surface free energies 126, 295
surfaces, effects on crystallization 439–440
Surlyn® 244
SWNT *see* single-wall nanotubes (SWNTs)
symmetry breaking 49–50
symmetry operators 35
synchrotron radiation, direct observation of nano-nucleation by 128–135
syndiotactic 1,2-poly(1,3-butadiene) **40**
syndiotactic 1,2-poly(4-methyl-1,3-pentadiene) **40**
syndiotactic poly(1-oxo-2-phenyltrimethylene) **40**
syndiotactic poly(4-methyl-1-pentene) **39**
syndiotactic poly(α-olefins) 37
1,2-syndiotactic poly(butadiene) **35**
syndiotactic polybutene (sPB) **39**, 42
syndiotactic polymers 32
   (+) and (−) bonds in *33*
   distortion of torsion angles 41
   polymorphism 41
   s(2/1)2 35
   structural data of **39–40**
syndiotactic poly(*m*-methylstyrene) **39**, 40
syndiotactic poly(*p*-methylstyrene) **39**
syndiotactic polypropylene (sPP) 33, **35**, 36, **39**, *335*
   anisotropic elongated single crystals in the orthorhombic form I of 61
   conformational energy minima 41
   conformations of the different polymorphic forms of 42, *43*

forms I and II 253–254
   kink-band disorder in 59, *60*
   limit-ordered models of packing of forms II and IV of *60*
   line repetition symmetries and corresponding conformations for *36*
   s(2/1)2 helix *42*
   substitutional isomorphism of different chains in 56
   $T_6G_2T_2G_2$ helical conformation *42*
   trans-planar conformation *42*
syndiotactic poly(propylene-*co*-butene) 337
syndiotactic poly(propylene-*co*-octene) *335*
syndiotactic polystyrene (sPS) **39**, 189–191
   conformational energy minima 41
   conformations of the different polymorphic forms of 42, *43*
   models of packing of the chains in the α form of sPS according to the space group P3 50
   models of packing of the chains in the α form of sPS according to the space group P3c1 50
   s(2/1)2 helix conformation *43*
   symmetry breaking in the α form of 49
   trans-planar conformation *43*
syndiotactic poly(styrene-*alt*-CO) **40**
syndiotactic propylene–butene copolymers 57, *58*

talc 380
tcm 35
temperature gradients
   effects on crystallization 437–439
   Lovinger and Gryte's model 437–438
   mathematical modeling 439
   physical models 437–438
   Piorkowska's model 438
temperature-modulated DSC (TMDSC) 23–24, 283
tensile force, crystallization induced by 191
terrace growths 87
theory of absolution reaction rate 134
thermodynamics
   effects on crystallization 434
   of polymer blends 288–290
thermomechanical model, for cast film extrusion 442–443
thermoplastics 434
thermostats 199
thin film nanolayers, literature regarding confined crystallization in **349, 350**
thin films 94–98, 367
   crystallization in 233
   literature regarding confined crystallization in **349, 350**
threo configurations 32, 33, *34*
TMDSC *see* temperature-modulated DSC (TMDSC)
Toda model 115
top down method (mechanical grinding method) 149–150, **150**, 155
topographic matching 252–254, 258
topotactic reactions 192
trans configurations 33
transcrystallinity 382–383, 385, 437, 453
   effect of shear flow on development of 384
   in thin strips of polymer films 440

transmission electron microscopy (TEM) 6, 239, 351
   bright-field mode 6
   contrast problem in 7
   dark-field mode 6
   high resolution TEM (HRTEM) 7
   imaging principle 6
   sample preparation for 6
transmission optical microscopy 2
trans (T) torsion angles 36
1,3,5-trichlorobenzene (TCB) 259
trigonal form **38**, *48*
trioxane 167
twists, and entanglements 159
   see also lamellar twists

ultrathin films 98–102
uniaxial drawings 407
unsubstituted conjugated polymers 259

vacuum evaporation method 7
vaporization 255
   of polymer films on substrates 241
vaterite 381
video AFM 10
vinylfluoride, copolymers of vinylidenefluoride and 32
vinylidene fluoride
   copolymers of trifluoroethylene and 167
   copolymers of vinylfluoride and 32

vinyl polymers 32
   asymmetric atoms in 32
   regularity in the chemical constitution of 31
volume 265

WAXS *see* wide-angle X-ray scattering (WAXS)
weakly segregated melts, crystallization of block copolymers from 340–343
Weissenberg numbers 209, 403, 404
Wendling–Suter model 340
White–Spruiell orientation triangles 450, *451*, 453
wide-angle X-ray diffraction (WAXD) 15–17, 178, 180, 446, 448, 449
wide-angle X-ray scattering (WAXS) 144, *145*, 217, 343
Williams-Landel-Ferry relation 293
wollastonite 380

X-ray diffraction 267, 446
see also wide-angle X-ray diffraction (WAXD)
X-rays 15

YOROI model 148

zero amplitude extinction 106
Ziegler-Natta catalysis 243
ZnO 392

Jakobsmuschel- und Seeteufelspieß, Limetten-Meerrettich-Sauce und Salat von Chayoten

ZUTATEN
FÜR DIE SPIESSE
450 g Seeteufelfilet
oder Seeteufelbäckchen
Tandoori-Gewürzmarinade
8 Stück Jakobsmuscheln
8 Scheiben Frühstücksspeck (Bacon)
200 g Palmherzen
1 rote Paprika
1 gelbe Paprika
Salz, Pfeffer
Zitronensaft
schwarzer und weißer Sesam

TIP

Diese Spieße können warm oder kalt verzehrt werden. Der Seeteufel kann auch durch Rotbarsch oder Thunfisch ersetzt werden.

ZUBEREITUNG

1 Seeteufelfilet oder -bäckchen parieren und in Stücke von etwa 40 Gramm portionieren. Das Portionieren entfällt bei den Seeteufelbäckchen. Der Seeteufel wird für 1 Stunde in einer Tandoori-Gewürzmarinade eingelegt.

2 Die Jakobsmuscheln werden geputzt, der Rogen kann nach Belieben entfernt werden. Anschließend werden die Muscheln mit Speck umwickelt.

3 Die Paprika abziehen und in Stücke schneiden, die Palmenherzen ebenfalls in Stücke schneiden.

4 Die Jakobsmuscheln, den Seeteufel, die Paprika und die Palmenherzen abwechselnd auf Spieße stecken.

5 Die Spieße im Ofen bei 180 Grad C etwa 10-15 Minuten backen. Mit Sesam bestreuen.

Vorbereitungszeit: 60 Minuten
Zubereitungszeit: ca. 30 Minuten

WUSSTEN SIE SCHON?

Palmitos oder Palmherzen sind eine Spezialität aus der Karibik und vor allem aus Südamerika. Dort werden die nußartig schmeckenden Palmherzen am liebsten roh oder in fruchtigen Salaten mit Fisch oder Langusten mit Limonensaft gegessen. Das zarte, weiße, knackige Palmmark ist ausschließlich als Konserve im Handel erhältlich.

Tandoori-Marinade

TANDOORI-MARINADE

150 g Bio-Joghurt

1/2 TL fein gehackter Knoblauch

1-2 EL Tandoori- oder Vindaloo-Paste

Saft einer Limette

1 TL Garam masala

Salz nach Geschmack

ZUBEREITUNG

Alle Zutaten gut verrühren.

Herstellungszeit: ca. 10 Minuten

Tandoori-paste

ZUBEREITUNG

Alle Zutaten gut vermengen.

WUSSTEN SIE SCHON?

Die Tandoori-Gewürzpaste ist eine auch aus Indien stammende rote Gewürzmischung. Sie ist pikant und färbt Fleisch- oder Fischgerichte nach dem Marinieren rot. Für die Marinade wird häufig Naturjoghurt mit Tandoori verrührt.

In indischen oder asiatischen Geschäften ist Tandoori als Paste und als Pulver erhältlich.

Garam masala ist eine aus Indien stammende würzige, aber nicht scharfe Gewürzmischung aus fein im Mörser gestoßenen Gewürzen. Die einzelnen Zutaten können mengenmäßig unterschiedlich kombiniert werden, um den Geschmack zu verändern.

ZUTATEN

4 EL Zitronensaft

3 Knoblauchzehen, gehackt

2 TL frischer Ingwer, gehackt

1/2 TL Cayennepfeffer

2 TL Rosenpaprika, mittelscharf

2 TL Kreuzkümmel, gemahlen

1 TL frisch gemahlener Pfeffer

3 TL Kurkuma

1/2 TL frisch gemahlene Muskatnuß

1/4 TL rote Lebensmittelfarbe

Herstellungszeit: ca. 10 Minuten

Garam masala

ZUBEREITUNG

1 Alles im Mörser fein zerstoßen und nach Belieben 2 Eßlöffel gemahlenen Zimt und etwa 1/2 geriebene Muskatnuß hinzufügen.

2 Fertige Mischungen sind in indischen oder Asia-Läden erhältlich.

ZUTATEN

3 EL Kardamonsamen

1/2 EL Kreuzkümmelsamen

1 TL schwarze Pfefferkörner

1/2 TL Nelken

Herstellungszeit: ca. 10 Minuten

Salat von Chayoten mit Macadamia-Nußöl-Dressing

ZUTATEN

- 2 Chayoten (Christophinen), etwa 300 g
- 150 g Salatgurke
- 150 g Möhren
- 50 g rote Zwiebel
- 50 g weiße Zwiebel
- 150 g Strauchtomaten
- 1 kleiner Romanasalat
- 1 Avocado, nicht zu reif
- Radicchio- und Chicoréeblätter zum Garnieren
- 2 Jalapeño-Chilis, eingelegt aus dem Glas
- Zitronensaft

ZUTATEN FÜR DAS DRESSING

- 125 ml Macadamia- oder Olivenöl
- 60 ml Ananas- oder Apfelessig
- Salz, weißer Pfeffer
- Zucker nach Geschmack

Vorbereitungszeit: 20 Minuten
Zubereitungszeit: 10 Minuten

ZUBEREITUNG

1 Chayoten und Möhren schälen, in Streifen schneiden und in Salzwasser bißfest etwa 5 bis 8 Minuten blanchieren, in kaltem Wasser abschrecken.

2 Salatgurke schälen, halbieren und entkernen, die Hälften in Scheiben schneiden.

3 Rote und weiße Zwiebeln schälen und in nicht zu feine Ringe schneiden und dazugeben.

4 Avocado schälen, entkernen und in große Würfel schneiden, mit Zitronensaft marinieren.

5 Strauchtomaten vierteln, Romanasalat in nicht zu feine Streifen schneiden.

6 Die Zutaten des Dressings gut verrühren.

7 Das Ganze mit dem Macadamia-Dressing mischen und mit Radicchio und Chicorée ausgarnieren.

WUSSTEN SIE SCHON?

Die Chayoten stammen aus Mexiko und Brasilien. Die birnenförmigen Früchte haben einen milden Geschmack und sind dem Kohlrabi sehr ähnlich.

Limetten-Meerrettich-Sauce

ZUTATEN

- 40 g geriebener Meerrettich
- 65 ml Limettensaft
- 65 ml Mayonnaise (Grundrezept)
- 100 ml Joghurt
- Salz, frisch gemahlener Pfeffer
- Zucker nach Geschmack

Herstellungszeit: ca. 15 Minuten

ZUBEREITUNG

Alle Zutaten mischen und kalt stellen, damit sich das Aroma entwikkeln kann.

TIP

Diese Sauce können Sie grün färben, indem Sie einen Eßlöffel fein gehackte oder pürierte Kräuter wie Kerbel und Petersilie zufügen.

Rinderfilet-Garnelen-Spieße mit Guacamole und Reissalat

ZUTATEN
FÜR DIE SPIESSE

500 g	Rinderfilet
12	Garnelen (Black Tiger 20/24 ohne Kopf und Schale)
1 Bd.	Frühlingszwiebeln
8 St.	Minimaiskolben
100 ml	Mais- oder Rapsöl
	Salz, Pfeffer
	Zitronensaft

Vorbereitungszeit: 20 Minuten
Zeit des Marinierens: 1-2 Stunden
Backzeit: ca. 10-15 Minuten

TIP

Rinderfilet und Garnelen – als „Surf and Turf" in der internationalen Küche bekannt – können ohne weiteres durch marinierte Geflügelbrust ersetzt werden.

ZUBEREITUNG

1 Rinderfilet parieren und längs mit der Faser zweimal teilen und anschließend in etwa 40-g-Würfel schneiden.

2 Die Würfel werden 1 bis 2 Stunden mariniert. Hierfür empfiehlt es sich, eine pikante Gewürzmarinade zu verwenden wie zum Beispiel die Mischungen „West Indies", „Rum-Gewürzmischung" oder eine „Teriyaki-Marinade" mit einem fernöstlichen Touch. Man kann auch nur Salz und Pfeffer verwenden.

3 Nach dem Marinieren das Fleisch gut abtropfen lassen und in heißem Fett kurz anbraten. Sofort wenden und aus der Pfanne nehmen.

4 Garnelen, die schon gegart sind, werden in diesem Zustand auf die Spieße gesteckt. Garnelen, die roh verwendet werden, müssen gebraten und mit Salz, Pfeffer und Zitronensaft gewürzt werden.

5 Garnelen, Rinderfilet, Minimaiskolben und Frühlingszwiebeln abwechselnd auf Spieße stecken und im vorgeheizten Backofen bei 160 Grad C etwa 6 Minuten medium grillen.

Guacamole

ZUTATEN

2	reife Avocados
50 g	Zwiebel
2	kleine Knoblauchzehen
2	Frühlingszwiebeln
2	Jalapeño-Chilis, entkernt und fein gehackt
2	Serano-Chilis oder Sambal Oelek
45 ml	Limonensaft
1 1/2 EL	gehackter frischer Koriander
	Salz, Pfeffer

Zubereitungszeit: ca. 15 Minuten

ZUBEREITUNG

1 Avocados halbieren, mit einem Löffel das Fruchtfleisch herausnehmen und zerdrücken oder pürieren.

2 Zwiebeln, Knoblauch, Frühlingszwiebeln, Chilis und Koriander fein hacken, unterheben, mit Salz, Pfeffer und Limonensaft abschmecken.

3 Kalt stellen.

WUSSTEN SIE SCHON?

Guacamole ist eine aus Avocados und Gewürzen hergestellte würzige Paste und kann durch Cocktailsauce, Curry-Mayonnaise und Ananas-Chutney ersetzt werden.

Rum-Gewürzmischung

ZUTATEN
2 EL Knoblauch, fein gehackt
2 TL Ingwer, fein gehackt
2 TL Piment, gemahlen
1/2 TL Zimt, gemahlen
1/2 TL Muskatnuß, gemahlen
2 TL Salz
3 Lorbeerblätter, zerrieben
2 TL Cayennepfeffer
100 ml Limettensaft
1 mittelgroße Zwiebel, fein gehackt

ca. 150 ml brauner Rum
ca. 100 g Rohrzucker
4 EL Öl

Herstellungszeit: ca. 20 Minuten

Teriyaki-Gewürzmischung

ZUTATEN
60 ml Soja-Sauce
3 EL Sake oder Sherry dry
2 EL Öl
1 EL Zitronensaft
1 EL Rohr- oder Palmzucker
1 EL Ingwer, fein gehackt
1-2 Knoblauchzehen, fein gehackt
1/4 TL Sambal Oelek oder feingehackte Chilischoten

> **TIP**
>
> Im Handel gibt es auch fertige Teriyaki-Sauce.

Herstellungszeit: ca. 10 Minuten

»West-Indies«-Gewürzmischung

ZUTATEN
3 TL Currypulver oder 2 TL Currypaste
3 TL Paprikapulver, edelsüß
1 1/2 TL Kreuzkümmel, gemahlen
3/4 TL Piment, gemahlen
1/2 TL Chilipulver
4 EL Öl

Herstellungszeit: ca. 10 Minuten

Reissalat mit Chilis und Ananas

ZUTATEN
(für ca. 8 Portionen)

1 mittelgroße Flugananas
150 g Zucchini
2 rote Paprika
1 Bd. Frühlingszwiebeln
3-4 Jalapeño Chilis
80 g Kasseler
oder gekochter Schinken
3 EL geröstete Pinienkerne
1 rote Zwiebel,
in Würfel geschnitten
2-3 EL gehacktes
Koriandergrün
1 EL Ingwer, gehackt
250 g gekochter Langkornreis
2 EL Walnußöl
2 EL Sonnenblumenöl
Saft von 1-2 Zitronen
Salz, Pfeffer, Zucker

ZUBEREITUNG

1 Ananas schälen und in gleichmäßige, 2 cm große Würfel schneiden.

2 Zucchini und Paprika in 1 cm große Würfel schneiden und mit den Zwiebeln in wenig Öl bißfest dünsten.

3 Frühlingszwiebeln und entkernte Chilis in Ringe schneiden.

4 Zwiebel und Kasseler in feine Würfel schneiden.

5 Alle Zutaten mischen und mit den Gewürzen und dem Zitronensaft abschmecken.

6 Mindestens 1 Stunde marinieren lassen und nochmals abschmecken.

7 In der ausgehöhlten Ananas servieren.

TIP

Dieser Salat bekommt mit gekochtem Wildreis oder Vollkornreis einen besonderen Charakter.

Man kann ihn mit in Rum eingeweichten Rosinen und Currypulver oder Kurkuma zu einem Curryreis verfeinern.

Tandoori-Hähnchen

ZUTATEN
6 Hähnchenkeulen oder -brüste
Tandoori-Marinade

ZUBEREITUNG

1 Von den Hähnchenkeulen oder -brüsten die Haut entfernen.

2 Fleischstücke in der Tandoori-Marinade 4 bis 5 Stunden einlegen, dann herausnehmen und leicht abstreifen.

3 Alle Geflügelteile auf ein Backblech mit Backpapier legen und im Backofen bei 180 Grad C ca. 20 bis 30 Minuten garen.

Jerk Poulardenbrust

ZUTATEN
FÜR DIE POULARDENBRUST
1 kg ausgelöste Poulardenbrüste
3 EL Jerk-Würzmischung

ZUBEREITUNG

1 Poulardenbrüste parieren und für 1 Stunde in beliebiger Jerk-Würzmischung im Kühlschrank marinieren.

2 Auf einem gefetteten Backblech im vorgeheizten Backofen bei 180 bis 200 Grad C etwa 25 Minuten grillen. Nach halber Garzeit wenden.

Vorbereitungszeit: 10 Minuten
Zeit des Marinierens: ca. 1 Stunde
Backzeit: ca. 25 Minuten

TIP
Aus dem entstandenen Bratensaft kann eine Sauce hergestellt werden.

WUSSTEN SIE SCHON?
„Jerk" ist der Oberbegriff für eine pikante, kreolische Würzmischung und ist in türkischen oder Asia-Läden zu erhalten *(siehe Seite 200)*.

Ananas-Chutney

ZUTATEN

500 g	Ananas
1	Frühlingszwiebel
25 g	Kokosflocken
50 g	rote Paprikaschote
50 g	Zwiebeln
15 ml	Chilisauce
15 g	Ingwerwurzel
15 ml	frisch gepreßter Limettensaft
30 ml	Weißweinessig
15 ml	brauner Rum
50 g	Butter
	Salz, weißer Pfeffer
	Zucker
	Kurkuma

ZUBEREITUNG

1 Ananas und Zwiebel würfeln, Frühlingszwiebel in Ringe schneiden.

2 Paprika als Einlage in gleichmäßige kleine Würfel schneiden.

3 Kokosflocken rösten und Ingwer fein hacken.

4 Zwiebeln und zwei Drittel der Ananaswürfel in Butter anschwitzen, mit

5 Essig, Limettensaft und Rum ablöschen, 10 Minuten garen und anschließend pürieren (eventuell noch durch ein Sieb streichen).

6 Ananassauce und die restlichen Zutaten (ohne Frühlingszwiebeln) aufkochen.

7 Zum Schluß die Frühlingszwiebeln dazugeben und mit Salz, Pfeffer und Zucker abschmecken. Kurkuma benötigt man, um die Farbe zu verbessern.

8 Gut gekühlt servieren.

Tomatensalsa

ZUTATEN

200 g reife Tomaten
2 Schalotten
2 Serrano-Chilis oder Sambal Oelek
1 Knoblauchzehe
1 TL Salz
3 EL frischer Koriander, gehackt
2 EL Limonensaft
1/4 Salatgurke
Olivenöl

Herstellungszeit: 10 Minuten

ZUBEREITUNG

1 Tomaten und Salatgurke schälen, entkernen und in Würfel schneiden.

2 Schalotten und Knoblauch fein hacken, Chilis in feine Ringe schneiden.

3 Alle Zutaten gut mischen und 1 Eßlöffel Olivenöl (oder nach Belieben) dazugeben.

4 30 Minuten im Kühlschrank ziehen lassen.

TIP

Abgezogene, rote und gelbe Paprikawürfel eignen sich als Einlage.

Erdnußsauce

ZUTATEN

250 g geröstete Erdnüsse, fein püriert, oder Erdnußbutter
250 ml Sahne oder Milch
2 Chilis
1 Zwiebel
2 Knoblauchzehen
1 cm Ingwer
Saft einer Zitrone
Geflügelbrühe
3 EL Erdnußöl
Salz, Pfeffer

ZUBEREITUNG

1 Zwiebel, Ingwer und Knoblauch schälen, fein hacken und in Erdnußöl anschwitzen.

2 Die fein pürierten Erdnüsse (oder Erdnußbutter) dazugeben und mit Zitronensaft ablöschen.

3 Nach und nach die Sahne unterrühren, die fein gehackten Chilis zufügen und mit Salz, Pfeffer und eventuell etwas Zitronensaft abschmecken.

4 Die gewünschte Konsistenz erhalten Sie durch die Zugabe von Geflügelbrühe.

TIP

Erdnußsauce kann warm oder kalt serviert werden.

Barbarie-Entenbrust mit Palmzucker und »Fünf Gewürzen« karamelisiert, Sansibar-Salat

ZUTATEN

- 4 Barbarie-Entenbrüste
- 2 St. Palmzucker
- 1 TL chinesische »Fünf Gewürze«
- Saft von 1 Zitrone
- 1 TL Sesamsamen
- Salz, Pfeffer
- 2 EL Öl

Vorbereitungszeit: ca. 20 Minuten
Backzeit: ca. 10 Minuten

ZUBEREITUNG DER ENTENBRÜSTE

1 Entenbrüste parieren, das Fett trimmen und kreuzweise einritzen.

2 Palmzucker in 2 Eßlöffeln Wasser auflösen, mit »Fünf Gewürzen« und Zitronensaft abschmecken.

3 Die Entenbrüste zuerst auf der Hautseite, dann auf der Fleischseite in Öl kurz anbraten, anschließend im Ofen bei 180 Grad C ca. 17 bis 20 Minuten (je nach Schwere) braten. Nach ca. 15 Minuten Palmzuckerlösung mit einem Pinsel aufstreichen und nun die Brüste fertiggaren. Unter einem Grill überkrusten, dabei noch mehrmals einstreichen, so daß eine schöne gleichmäßig braune Kruste entsteht. Beim letzten Einstreichen mit Sesamsamen bestreuen.

4 Das Fleisch muß ruhen, damit es zart rosa wird. Anschließend die Entenbrüste schräg aufschneiden und an dem Salat anrichten.

WUSSTEN SIE SCHON?

Palmzucker ist ähnlich wie der Rohrzucker ein brauner, unraffinierter Zucker. Er wird aus dem Saft einer asiatischen Palmenart gewonnen.

Der Palmzucker wird rund geformt und im Palmblatt oder als Sirup in asiatischen Lebensmittelgeschäften angeboten. Er schmilzt besonders gut und gibt den süß-sauren Gerichten der asiatischen Küche eine milde Süße, außerdem karamelisiert er gleichmäßig.

»Fünf Gewürze« – auch »Five Spices« genannt – ist eine asiatische Gewürzkombination, die vor allem von Hindus benutzt wird. Sie kann unterschiedliche Gewürzkomponenten besitzen. In der Regel sind es Sternanis, Fenchelsamen, Nelken, Zimt und Kümmel. Aber auch Pfeffer und Senfsaat können verwendet werden.

Reis- und Fleischgerichte sollten Sie vorsichtig würzen, sonst wird der Geschmack zu intensiv.

Sansibar-Salat

ZUTATEN

(für ca. 8 Portionen)

1 Zucchini
1 Karotte
1 kleine Staudensellerie
50 g Okraschoten
1 rote Paprika
50 g Sojasprossen
50 g Brokkoliröschen
50 g Enoke-Pilze
50 g Kokosnuß, frisch und am Stück
1-2 rote Chilis
1 cm Ingwer, frisch
1-2 Knoblauchzehen
6 Limonenblätter
2 Stangen Zitronengras
100 ml Kokosmilch
Saft von 1 Zitrone
1 EL Koriandergrün, gehackt
Salz
4 EL Erdnußöl

Vorbereitungszeit: ca. 20 Minuten
Zubereitungszeit: ca. 20 Minuten

TIP

Sansibar-Salat am besten lauwarm servieren.

ZUBEREITUNG

1 Zucchini in Stifte von 3 cm Länge und 2 mm Breite schneiden. Karotten und Staudensellerie schälen und ebenfalls in Stifte schneiden.

2 Paprika abziehen, Brokkoliröschen und Okraschoten putzen, kurz in Salzwasser blanchieren und in Eiswasser abschrecken.

3 Knoblauch und Ingwer fein würfeln. Vom Zitronengras nur das weiche Innere in Streifen schneiden.

4 Öl erhitzen (am besten im Wok) und zuerst Knoblauch und Ingwer anschwitzen. Karotten-, Sellerie- und Zucchinistreifen nach dem Garpunkt zugeben und kurz mitschwitzen. Limonenblätter und Zitronengras beigeben.

5 Kokosmilch und die in Ringe geschnittenen, von Kernen befreiten Chilis zufügen. Nach Geschmack Zitronensaft unterrühren. Alles in allem nicht länger als 3 bis 4 Minuten garen.

6 Das restliche Gemüse – Paprika, Okraschoten, Brokkoliröschen und Sojasprossen – unterheben.

7 Kokosnuß in feine Späne schneiden und kurz fritieren, bis sie knusprig sind.

8 Kurz vor dem Servieren Enoke-Pilze und Koriander unterheben, mit gerösteten Kokosnußspänen garnieren und die Limonenblätter entfernen.

WUSSTEN SIE SCHON?

Die Okra ist ein Gemüse, welches schon vor Christi Geburt bekannt war und ursprünglich aus Afrika stammt. Heute ist sie auf der ganzen Welt bekannt und wird vor allem in Asien sehr geschätzt.

Die fingerlange, dunkelgrüne Okra – deshalb auch der Name „Ladyfinger" – bekommt nach dem Garen einen leichten Schleim. Im Inneren besitzt sie wie die Paprikaschote kleine Kerne, die durchaus mitgegessen werden können. Für Salate sollte sie mit Wasser abgespült werden.

Enoke-Pilze, die in Asien und vor allem in den USA sehr beliebt sind, sind 6 bis 7 cm lang und wachsen bündelweise zusammen.

Enoke-Pilze sind weiß und bestehen zu 95 Prozent aus Stielen mit einer kleinen runden Kappe. Sie eignen sich besonders als Rohkost, die nur kurz mariniert wird, oder als Garnitur an Salaten.

Tempura-Garnelen auf Linsen-Ananas-Curry

ZUTATEN
FÜR DIE GARNELEN
(für ca. 4 Portionen)

- 16 Stück Garnelen 16/20
- 250 g Weizenmehl Type 405
- 1 Msp. Backpulver
- 250 ml Wasser
- 1/2 TL Koriandersamen, grob gemahlen
- Salz, weißer Pfeffer, frisch gemahlen
- Saft einer Zitrone

ZUBEREITUNG TEIG

1 Mehl und Backpulver sieben und mit dem kalten Wasser mit einem Schneebesen gut verrühren, so daß keine Klümpchen entstehen.

2 Den Teig mit etwas Salz und dem Koriander abschmecken.

3 Die Garnelen am Schwanzende festhalten und in den Ausbackteig tauchen, anschließend in Fritierfett schwimmend goldgelb ausbacken.

TIP

Wenn der Ausbackteig noch leichter sein soll, benötigt man ein geschlagenes Eiweiß, das unter den Teig gehoben wird.

Auch Kokosflocken oder Vollwertmehle können dem Teig beigemischt werden.

Anstelle von Garnelen können Sie auch Fisch, Geflügel oder Gemüse wie zum Beispiel Champignons, Blumenkohl oder Brokkoli verwenden.

ZUBEREITUNG GARNELEN

1 Garnelen, falls sie nicht geschält sind, bis auf das letzte Panzerelement am Schwanzende schälen und den Darm entfernen.

2 Butterfly einschneiden, das heißt Schmetterlingsschnitt, dabei wird mit einem scharfen Messer die Garnele in der Mitte zwei Drittel längs eingeschnitten.

3 Erst kurz vor dem Ausbacken mit Salz, Pfeffer und Zitronensaft würzen.

Vorbereitungszeit: 10 Minuten
Zubereitungszeit: 10 Minuten

Linsen-Ananas-Curry

ZUTATEN
(für ca. 4 Portionen)

100 g Weizengrieß (Bulgur)
125 g Zwiebeln
2 cm Ingwer, in feine Würfel geschnitten
2 Knoblauchzehen, fein gehackt
3 EL Olivenöl
100 g getrocknete Linsen
1 EL Madras-Curry
400 g frische Ananas
1 EL Sojasauce
50 g Pinienkerne
2 Frühlingszwiebeln
Salz, Pfeffer
Zitronen, Zitronensaft

ZUBEREITUNG

1 Eingeweichte Linsen abtropfen lassen, dabei die Einweichflüssigkeit auffangen und später wieder zugeben.

2 Weizengrieß etwa 15 Minuten in Salzwasser bei kleiner Flamme garen. In einem Sieb abschütten und mit kaltem Wasser abspülen.

3 Zwiebeln in feine Würfel schneiden und mit dem Ingwer und dem Knoblauch in Öl anschwitzen.

4 Die Linsen und die in Würfel geschnittene Ananas in der Einweichflüssigkeit mit dem Currypulver aufkochen und 10 Minuten ziehen lassen.

5 Den Weizengrieß zugeben und mit Sojasauce, Salz und Pfeffer abschmecken.

6 Vor dem Servieren die Frühlingszwiebeln dazugeben und mit den gerösteten Pinienkernen ausgarnieren.

Vorbereitungszeit: ca. 30 Minuten
Zubereitungszeit: ca. 10 Minuten

TIP

Neben den braunen Puy-Linsen können auch gelbe oder rote Linsen verwendet oder kombiniert werden.

Auch rote Paprikawürfel verändern dieses Gericht.

Frisch gepreßter Orangen- oder Zitronensaft gibt eine besondere Note.

Bohnensalat

ZUTATEN

je 150 g weiße, rote und schwarze Bohnen
150 g grüne Keniabohnen
1 rote Paprika
1 feste Mango
2 Stück Zwiebellauch
2 Jalapeño-Chilis
1 cm Ingwer
1/2 TL Zitronenthymian, gehackt
Saft von 1 bis 2 Zitronen
50 ml Olivenöl
Salz, Pfeffer aus der Mühle

Vorbereitungszeit: ca. 30 Minuten
Zubereitungszeit: ca. 15 Minuten

ZUBEREITUNG

1 Die grünen Bohnen waschen, putzen, schräg schneiden, bißfest blanchieren und in Eiswasser abschrecken, damit sie die Farbe behalten.

2 Die weißen, roten und die schwarzen Bohnen getrennt in Salzwasser garen oder abgetropft aus der Konserve verwenden.

3 Paprika würfeln, Mango schälen und auf die gleiche Größe schneiden.

4 Zwiebeln, Zwiebellauch und Chilis in feine Ringe schneiden.

5 Alle Zutaten mischen und kühl durchziehen lassen.

6 Vor dem Servieren nochmals abschmecken.

WUSSTEN SIE SCHON?

Schwarze Bohnen, eine Spezialität aus Kuba, erhalten Sie im Asia-Laden.

TIP

Dieser Salat kann durch Kasselerwürfel oder Thunfisch geschmacklich verändert werden. Koriandergrün gibt einen südamerikanischen Touch.

Zitrusgebeizter Lachs

ZUTATEN

(für ca. 10 Portionen)

1 Seite Lachs (ca. 1,5 kg)
40 g grobes Meersalz
40 g Zucker
2 Limetten
10 St. Kumquats
2 Stangen Zitronengras
50 g Karotten
50 g Zwiebeln
50 g Sellerie
2 cm frischer Ingwer
1 TL grober Zitronenpfeffer
1/2 TL gebrochener Piment
1 Lorbeerblatt
2 EL Koriander
1 EL Epazote oder gehackte Zitronenmelisse

ZUBEREITUNG

1 Die Lachsseite, falls nötig, parieren und von Gräten befreien.

2 Karotten, Zwiebeln, Sellerie und Ingwer schälen und in dünne Scheiben oder Streifen schneiden.

3 Das Zitronengras grob hacken, die Kumquats waschen und in Scheiben schneiden.

4 Limetten waschen und mit einem Sparschäler schälen. Diese Limettenschale in feine Streifen schneiden und darauf achten, daß so wenig wie möglich von dem Weißen unter der Schale mit verarbeitet wird, da es bitter schmeckt.

5 Das Lorbeerblatt zerreiben.

6 Alle Zutaten mit dem Saft einer halben Limette mischen.

7 Die Beize nun gleichmäßig auf der Lachsseite verteilen und für 24 Stunden im Kühlschrank marinieren.

8 Nach der Hälfte der Zeit wenden, einen Teil der Beize auf die Hautseite geben und erneut kühlstellen.

9 Die Beizzutaten mit der Hand abstreifen und gegebenenfalls den Lachs kurz mit kaltem Wasser abspülen.

Vorbereitungszeit: ca. 30 Minuten
Zeit des Marinierens: ca. 24 Stunden

TIP

Zur Präsentation einer zitrusgebeizten Lachsseite verwendet man gehackte Kräuter und feine Limettenstreifen.

Lachs-Frühlingszwiebel-Salat

ZUTATEN

- 250 g zitrusgebeizter Lachs (siehe Seite 210)
- 250 g frische, kleine Spinatblätter
- 150 g kleine Champignons
- 2 St. Frühlingszwiebeln
- 50 g Sojasprossen
- 2 Strauchtomaten
- 1 Bd. roter Basilikum
- 1 TL gerösteter Sesamsamen
- Kresse, Chicorée oder Shiso-Mix zum Garnieren

ZUTATEN FÜR DAS DRESSING

- 25 ml Estragonessig
- 25 ml Weißweinessig
- 100 ml Sonnenblumenöl
- 1/2 TL milder Senf
- Zucker, Salz
- Pfeffer, frisch gemahlen
- Limettensaft

Vorbereitungszeit: 15 Minuten
Zubereitungszeit: 15 Minuten

ZUBEREITUNG

1 Lachs in feine gabellange Streifen schneiden.

2 Spinatblätter putzen, waschen und trockenschleudern.

3 Champignons säubern und vierteln, Frühlingszwiebeln putzen und schräg in Scheiben schneiden.

4 Sojasprossen waschen, wenn nötig, die braunen Wurzeln entfernen.

5 Die Tomaten abziehen und würfeln.

6 Essig mischen, Senf und Öl unterrühren und mit Zucker, Salz, Pfeffer und Limettensaft abschmecken.

7 Alle Zutaten nach Bedarf mit dem Dressing mischen und mit Chicorée und Kresse ausgarnieren.

Glasnudelsalat mit Rinderfiletstreifen

ZUTATEN
(für ca. 10 Portionen)

250 g Rinderfilet
250 g Glasnudeln
100 g Lauch (nur das Grüne)
100 g Karotten
100 g rote Paprika
100 g Bambussprossen
2 cm Ingwer, fein gewürfelt
3 rote Chilis
2 Knoblauchzehen, fein gehackt
30 ml Reisessig
1 TL Sesamöl
40 ml Sojaöl
30 ml Sojasauce
(oder nach Geschmack)
Limettensaft

WUSSTEN SIE SCHON?

Junger Bambus, auch Bambussprossen genannt, kommt frisch oder in feine Streifen geschnitten in Konserven in den Handel.

Glasnudeln werden aus Mungobohnen hergestellt und in heißem Wasser zum Quellen eingeweicht. Sie müssen nicht gekocht werden.

TIP

Anstelle von Rinderfilet können Sie auch Hähnchenbrust oder Garnelen verwenden.

ZUBEREITUNG

1 Glasnudeln mit einem Liter heißes Wasser übergießen, darin 10 Minuten quellen lassen, anschließend in einem Sieb abgießen und mit kaltem Wasser durchspülen.

2 Lauch und Karotten in feine Streifen schneiden, für wenige Sekunden in Salzwasser blanchieren und sofort in Eiswasser abschrecken.

3 Paprika vierteln, entkernen und in feine Streifen schneiden.

4 Die Bambussprossen in einem Sieb abtropfen lassen.

5 Das Rinderfilet parieren, in feine Streifen schneiden und in wenig heißem Sojaöl kurz medium braten und rasch abkühlen.

6 Aus Reisessig, Sesam- und Sojaöl sowie Sojasauce ein Dressing herstellen. Mit Ingwer, Knoblauch und feinen Chiliringen abschmecken.

7 Alle Zutaten mischen, mehrere Stunden gut durchziehen lassen und mit Limettensaft abschmecken.

Vorbereitungszeit: ca. 20 Minuten
Zubereitungszeit: ca. 15 Minuten

Kokosbrioche

ZUTATEN FÜR DEN VORTEIG

70 g Mehl
50 ml Milch
15 g Hefe

ZUTATEN FÜR DEN HAUPTTEIG

120 g Mehl
60 g geröstete Kokosflocken
5 Eigelb
30 g Rohrzucker
50 ml Kokosmilch
80 g Butter

ZUBEREITUNG VORTEIG

1 Das Mehl in eine Schüssel sieben. In die Mitte eine Mulde drücken.

2 Die in lauwarmer Milch aufgelöste Hefe dazugießen und verrühren.

3 Den Vorteig zugedeckt gut temperiert gehen lassen.

ZUBEREITUNG HAUPTTEIG

4 Mehl, Kokosflocken, Eigelbe, Rohrzucker und Kokosmilch unter den Vorteig mengen und nochmals gehen lassen.

5 Die weiche Butter unter den Teig arbeiten und erneut temperiert gehen lassen.

6 Den Teig in eine gefettete Brot- oder Brioche-Form füllen, mit Eigelb bestreichen und 30 Minuten bei 220 Grad C im Ofen ausbacken.

Vorbereitungszeit: ca. 15 Minuten
Zeit zum Gehenlassen: ca. 45 Minuten
Backzeit: ca. 30 Minuten

Erntedank-Brot

ZUTATEN
(für ca. 10 Portionen)

500 g Weizenmehl
42 g Hefe
1/4 l lauwarme Milch
60 g flüssige Butter oder
60 ml Olivenöl
1/4 TL Kardamon, gemahlen
1/4 TL Muskatnuß, frisch gerieben
2 EL Zucker
1 TL Salz
2 EL Grand Marnier
2 Eiweiß
1 EL Wasser
Sesam- und Mohnsamen

Vorbereitungszeit: 15 Minuten
Zeit zum Gehenlassen:
ca. 1 Stunde
Backzeit: ca. 20 Minuten

ZUBEREITUNG

1 Mehl in eine Schüssel sieben und in die Mitte eine Mulde hineindrücken.

2 Die in lauwarmer Milch aufgelöste Hefe und den Zucker dazugeben, verrühren und den Teig zugedeckt gut temperiert gehen lassen.

3 Das flüssige Fett, Grand Marnier und die Gewürze unterarbeiten und den Teig nochmals gehen lassen.

4 Den Teig zu Brötchen oder Stangen formen. Eiweiß und Wasser verrühren, auf das Brot streichen und mit Sesam- oder Mohnsamen bestreuen. Im Backofen je nach Größe des Brotes bei etwa 200 Grad C ca. 20 Minuten ausbacken.

5 Während des Backens 1/4 Liter Wasser verdampfen lassen, so wird das Brot besonders knusprig.

6 Sie können aber auch aus einem Drittel des Teiges ein Blatt, aus dem restlichen Teig kleine Kugeln formen und zu einer Traube zusammensetzen.

Zwiebel-Rosmarin-Brot

ZUTATEN

450 g Mehl
70 g Parmesan
42 g Hefe
80 ml Milch
60 ml Olivenöl
2 Zwiebeln
frischer Rosmarin, grob gehackt
1 TL Salz
1 TL Zucker

Vorbereitungszeit:
ca. 15 Minuten
Zeit zum Gehenlassen:
ca. 1 Stunde
Backzeit: ca. 30 Minuten

ZUBEREITUNG

1 Mehl in eine Schüssel sieben und in die Mitte eine Mulde hineindrücken.

2 Die in lauwarmer Milch aufgelöste Hefe und den Zucker dazugeben und verrühren.

3 Den Teig zugedeckt gut temperiert gehen lassen.

4 Mit Olivenöl und 50 Gramm Parmesan zu einem Teig kneten und nochmals gehen lassen.

5 Den Teig auf 2 Zentimeter Stärke ausrollen und mit etwas Olivenöl einstreichen.

6 Die in Ringe geschnittenen Zwiebeln werden gleichmäßig auf dem Teig verteilt und mit Rosmarin und Parmesankäse bestreut.

7 Im Backofen bei 190 Grad C etwa 20 Minuten hellbraun backen.

Tomatenbutter

ZUTATEN

500 g weiche Butter
2 Schalotten
1 Knoblauchzehe
80 g eingelegte getrocknete Tomaten
1 TL Tomatenmark
1 EL Basilikum, gehackt
Salz, Zucker, Zitronenpfeffer
Saft einer halben Zitrone
einige Tropfen Balsamico-Essig

ZUBEREITUNG

1 Butter schaumig rühren und fein gehackte Schalotten und Knoblauch sowie Tomatenmark unterrühren.

2 Die eingelegten Tomaten abtropfen lassen, fein hacken und mit dem Basilikum dazugeben.

3 Mit Salz, Zucker, Zitronenpfeffer, Zitronensaft und Balsamico-Essig abschmecken.

Herstellungszeit: ca. 30 Minuten

Salak-Zwiebelschmalz

ZUTATEN

500 g fetter Rückenspeck
200 g Salak
200 g Zwiebeln
1/2 TL Majoran
1/2 TL Thymian
Salz
weißer Pfeffer aus der Mühle
Schmalz

Herstellungszeit: ca. 45 Minuten

ZUBEREITUNG

1 Speck durch den Fleischwolf drehen, langsam erhitzen, auslassen und heiß durch ein Metallhaarsieb passieren.

2 Salaks schälen, entkernen, mit den Zwiebeln in kleine Würfel schneiden, in wenig Schmalz anschwitzen und mit dem restlichen Schmalz mischen.

3 Mit Majoran, Thymian, Salz und Pfeffer nach Belieben würzen.

WUSSTEN SIE SCHON?

Salaks sind exotische Früchte, die in Asien sehr bekannt sind. Sie haben eine braune schlangenhautähnliche Schale und besitzen ein festes, fruchtiges Fleisch, das nach saurem Apfel schmeckt.

TIP

Versuchen Sie diese Variante mit Gänseschmalz. Neben Salakwürfeln können auch feste Mango- oder Apfelwürfel verwendet werden.

Quinoa-Plätzchen

ZUTATEN

50 g Quinoa
50 g Weizenmehl
150 ml Vollmilch
1 Ei
1 TL gehackte Petersilie
Salz, weißer Pfeffer, frisch gemahlen
gemahlener Koriander

Vorbereitungszeit: ca. 20 Minuten
Zubereitungszeit: ca. 20 Minuten

ZUBEREITUNG

1 Quinoa in etwa 300 ml Salzwasser aufkochen, bei milder Hitze 15 Minuten garen und in einem Sieb abtropfen lassen.

2 Aus Mehl, Milch und Ei einen Pfannkuchenteig herstellen, mit Salz, Pfeffer und Koriander abschmecken.

3 Quinoa und gehackte Petersilie mit dem Teig verrühren.

4 In einer beschichteten Pfanne in Butter zu einem Pfannkuchen backen, mit einem Ausstecher in die gewünschte Form bringen und auf der Suppe plazieren.

WUSSTEN SIE SCHON?

Quinoa oder das Gold der Inkas ist eine Körnerfrucht und diente als Hauptgrundnahrungsmittel. In Südamerika gilt Quinoa als „Arme-Leute-Essen". Aufgrund der biologischen Ausgewogenheit und des hohen Gehalts an Eiweiß, Vitaminen und Mineralstoffen wird Quinoa in den letzten Jahren in der Vollwerternährung hoch geschätzt.

Quinoa kann wie Reis als Vollkorn gekocht, als Mehl oder Schrot verarbeitet werden. Sie erhalten Quinoa in Bio- oder Reformhäusern.

TIP

Für den Pfannkuchenteig können neben den Quinoa-Körnern auch Wildreis und andere Getreidearten verwendet werden.

Durch Zugabe von blanchierten Gemüsewürfeln verändern Sie die Optik.

TIP

Die Suppen werden mit einer Kelle oder Kanne vorsichtig, damit sie nicht ineinander laufen, separat eingefüllt. Dabei ist darauf zu achten, daß sie die gleiche Konsistenz besitzen.

Quinoa-Plätzchen in die Mitte geben.

Mais- und Paprikacreme

ZUTATEN
FÜR DIE MAISCREME

350 g Maiskörner
300 ml Geflügelbrühe
150 ml Sahne
2 Schalotten
Saft 1/2 Zitrone
1/2 TL Kurkuma
Salz, Zucker,
weißer Pfeffer, frisch gemahlen

ZUBEREITUNG

1 Schalotten in Würfel schneiden und in Butter anschwitzen.

2 Den abgetropften Mais zugeben und mit der Geflügelbrühe 15 Minuten kochen.

3 Mit einem Mixer wird die Suppe püriert, anschließend durch ein Sieb passiert.

4 Danach mit Sahne verfeinern und mit den Gewürzen und dem Zitronensaft abschmecken.

ZUTATEN
FÜR DIE PAPRIKACREME

400 g rote Paprika
300 ml Geflügelfond
150 ml Sahne
1 EL Tomatenmark
2 Schalotten
3 EL Olivenöl
Salz, Zucker,
weißer Pfeffer, frisch gemahlen
etwas Balsamico-Essig

ZUBEREITUNG

1 Paprika in grobe, Schalotten in feine Würfel schneiden.

2 Beides in Olivenöl anschwitzen, bis es etwas Farbe bekommt, Tomatenmark zugeben und mit Geflügelfond auffüllen.

3 Etwa 15 Minuten kochen, danach in einem Mixer pürieren und durch ein Sieb passieren.

4 Mit Sahne verfeinern und mit den Gewürzen und dem Essig abschmecken.

Vorbereitungszeit: ca. 40 Minuten
Zubereitungszeit: ca. 20 Minuten

Spare-ribs

ZUTATEN

1 kg Schälrippchen

ZUTATEN FÜR DIE MARINADE

1 EL fein gehackter Knoblauch
1,5 EL fein gehackter Ingwer
1 EL Honig
1 EL Hoi Sin Sauce
2 EL helle Sojasauce
1/4 TL Five Spices Powder (Fünf Gewürze)
2 EL Ketchup
1 EL Balsamico-Essig
2 EL Pflaumenwein
1 EL Sesamöl
2 EL Sojaöl
1/2 TL Sambal Oelek

Vorbereitungszeit: ca. 15 Minuten
Zeit des Marinierens: mind. 2 Stunden
Backzeit: ca. 35 Minuten

ZUBEREITUNG

1 Alle Zutaten der Marinade verrühren und abschmecken.

2 Die Schälrippen portionieren und je nach Geschmack für mindestens 2 Stunden in der Würzmarinade einlegen.

3 Im Ofen bei 160 Grad C 35 Minuten knusprig garen, dabei mehrmals mit Marinade einstreichen.

TIP

Spare-ribs können sowohl vom Rind als auch vom Schwein hergestellt werden.

Um den gewünschten Barbecue-Geschmack zu bekommen, können sie auch gegrillt werden.

Man kann sie auch mit gehackten Erdnüssen oder gerösteten Kokosflocken bestreuen.

Curry-Brätlinge

ZUTATEN

600 g kleine Kartoffeln
100 g Zwiebelwürfel
1 EL Knoblauch, fein gehackt
1 EL Ingwer, fein gehackt
1 TL Zucker
1/2 TL Kurkuma
1/2 TL Chilipulver
150 ml Geflügelbrühe
50 ml Erdnußöl
1/2 TL Garam masala (siehe Seite 197)
Salz nach Geschmack

ZUBEREITUNG

1 Kartoffeln waschen, in der Schale garen und pellen.

2 Zwiebel, Ingwer und Knoblauch in Öl anschwitzen.

3 Zucker, Kurkuma und Chilipulver dazugeben und mitschwitzen.

4 Brätlinge (Kartoffeln) beigeben und mit Brühe ablöschen.

5 So lange durchschwenken, bis nur noch wenig Flüssigkeit vorhanden ist und die Brätlinge eine gleichmäßige gold-gelbe Farbe angenommen haben.

6 Kurz vor dem Servieren die Garam-masala-Mischung zufügen.

Gemüse aus dem Wok

ZUTATEN

1 EL Knoblauch, fein gehackt	
50 g Zwiebeln	
100 g Romanesco-Röschen	
100 g Spargel	
80 g Schlangenbohnen	
80 g Lotuswurzeln	
80 g Karotten	
80 g Minimaiskolben	
80 g rote Paprika	
50 g Sojasprossen	
100 ml Geflügelbrühe	
2 EL Thai-Fischsauce	
3 EL süße Chilisauce	
2 EL Oystersauce (Austernsauce)	
2 EL Zitronensaft	
Sojaöl zum Braten	
Pfeffer, frisch gemahlen oder 1 fein gehackte Chilischote	

ZUBEREITUNG

1 Spargel schälen, längs halbieren und mit Minimais auf Stücke von etwa 4 cm schneiden.

2 Lotuswurzeln schälen und in Scheiben schneiden.

3 Paprika halbieren, entkernen und mit Schlangenbohnen auf gleiche Größe schneiden.

4 Karotten schälen und in Stäbchen schneiden.

5 Zwiebeln schälen, vierteln und in zentimeterdicke Streifen schneiden.

6 In einem Wok das Öl erhitzen, den Knoblauch und die Zwiebelstreifen anschwitzen. Das Gemüse nach dem Garpunkt in der Zutatenreihenfolge dazugeben und unter mehrmaligem Rühren bißfest anbraten.

7 Mit Saucen, Geflügelbrühe und Zitronensaft abschmecken und mit geschlossenem Deckel wenige Minuten nachziehen lassen.

TIP

Pfannenrühren ist eine asiatische Garmethode. Hierbei wird jedes Gemüse besonders knackig und schmackhaft.

Rinderfilet im griechischen Blätterteig, schwarze Bohnensauce

ZUTATEN

800 g	Rinderfilet, Mittelstück
250 g	Korallenpilze
150 g	Pak-choi
100 g	Knoblauchsprossen
50 g	Schalotten
100 ml	Sojaöl
1/4 TL	grüne Currypaste
	Saft einer halben Limette
	Salz, Zitronenpfeffer
500 g	griechischer Blätterteig (Phyllo-Teig)
2	Eier
1 EL	Sesam

ZUBEREITUNG

1 Rinderfilet parieren und in Stücke von etwa 150 g portionieren.

2 Pak-choi waschen und in feine Streifen schneiden.

3 Korallenpilze vierteln und in feine Scheiben schneiden.

4 Die Knoblauchsprossen in Ringe schneiden, Schalotten fein würfeln.

5 In der einen Hälfte des Sojaöls die mit Salz und Zitronenpfeffer gewürzten Rinderfilets von beiden Seiten und rundherum anbraten, damit beim späteren Garen kein Fleischsaft austreten kann. Anschließend zum Abtropfen auf ein Küchengitter legen.

6 Das restliche Öl in die Pfanne geben und die Schalottenwürfel anschwitzen, dann nach und nach erst Pak-choi, anschließend die Pilze und zum Schluß die Knoblauchsprossen mitdünsten.

7 Mit Currypaste und etwas Limettensaft abschmecken.

8 Den Phyllo-Teig auslegen, mit einem scharfen Messer zurechtschneiden und an den Rändern mit aufgeschlagenem Ei einstreichen.

9 Das Rinderfilet auf den Teig setzen, mit 2 Eßlöffeln des Gemüses bedecken und den Teig um das Filet schlagen.

10 Das Eiklar mit etwas Wasser verdünnen und den Teig von außen leicht einstreichen, dann mit Sesam bestreuen.

11 Im vorgeheizten Backofen bei 180 Grad C 12 bis 15 Minuten backen. Die Garzeit richtet sich nach der Kerntemperatur des Rinderfilets.

WUSSTEN SIE SCHON?

Der Korallenpilz oder Pom Pom blanc ist ein aus Asien stammender, nach Kokos und Limonen schmeckender, delikater und vor allem bißfester Pilz.

Er besitzt einen außergewöhnlich hohen Gehalt an Aminosäuren und Mineralstoffen, deshalb wird er in seiner Heimat auch als Heilmittel verwendet.

Noch wird er in kleinen Mengen im süddeutschen Raum gezüchtet und ist über den Feinkosthandel erhältlich.

Pak-choi, auch Senfkohl genannt, ist eines der beliebtesten Gemüse Asiens.

Nach kurzer Garzeit bleibt Pak-choi wunderbar bißfest.

Er besteht zu zwei Dritteln aus weißen knackigen Stielen, an deren Ende sich ein Blatt befindet, das dem Mangold ähnelt.

Die Stiele benötigen beim Garen etwas mehr Zeit als die Blätter.

Sie erhalten Pak-choi in Asia-Läden.

TIP

Jedes Kurzbratfleisch kann in diesem Teig gebacken werden. Anstelle von Phyllo-Teig können Sie auch Blätterteig verwenden.

Bohnensauce

ZUTATEN

80 g Schalotten
5 Knoblauchzehen (nach Geschmack)
100 ml Sake
100 ml Rindfleisch- oder Kalbfleischfond
2 EL Mirin
2-3 EL Bohnensauce
etwas Mondamin zum Binden
40 g kalte Butterwürfel
1 EL Sojaöl
Sichuan-Pfeffer
einige Spritzer Zitrone

ZUBEREITUNG

1 Schalotten und Knoblauchwürfel in Öl anschwitzen, mit Sake ablöschen und die Brühe dazugießen.

2 Bohnensauce nach Geschmack unterrühren. Die Sauce darf nicht zu salzig werden, auf gewünschten Geschmack reduzieren.

3 Falls Fleischsaft vom Filet vorhanden ist, dazugießen und mit Mirin und Pfeffer abschmecken.

4 Mondamin und Butter zum Binden der Sauce verwenden und zum Schluß noch mit Zitronensaft abschmecken.

Bonito im Bananenblatt

ZUTATEN

800 g	Thunfischfilet (Bonito)
1	halbfeste Papaya
3	rote Zwiebeln
3	Knoblauchzehen, fein gehackt
3	Frühlingszwiebeln
	Saft einer Limette
2 EL	helle Sojasauce
1 EL	Fischsauce
1 EL	gehackter Koriander
1-2	Chilis (nach Geschmack)
4 St.	Limonenblätter
1-2	Bananenblätter
	Zahnstocher

Vorbereitungszeit: 20 Minuten
Zubereitungszeit: 20 Minuten

ZUBEREITUNG

1 Thunfisch parieren und in vier gleichmäßige Scheiben quer zur Faser hin schneiden.

2 Aus Limettensaft, Soja- und Fischsauce, Koriander, Knoblauch und Chilis eine Marinade herstellen.

3 Die Papaya schälen, entkernen und in Scheiben schneiden.

4 Frühlingszwiebeln putzen und schräg in Scheiben schneiden.

5 Zum Portionieren der Bananenblätter die Stiele aus der Mitte herausschneiden und die Blätter längs halbieren.

6 Den Thunfisch mit der Würzmarinade einstreichen und auf die Bananenblätter setzen.

7 Mit Papayascheiben, roten Zwiebelringen und Frühlingszwiebelscheiben belegen.

8 Die restliche Marinade darüber verteilen und in die Bananenblätter einwickeln.

9 Die Blätter mit Zahnstochern oder Küchengarn schließen und im Backofen bei 180 Grad C etwa 15 Minuten backen.

10 Dieses Gericht kann im Bananenblatt serviert werden, welches jedoch nicht zum Verzehr geeignet ist.

WUSSTEN SIE SCHON?

Der Bonito ist ein kleiner bis mittelgroßer Thunfisch. Als besonderes Merkmal besitzt er dunkle Längsstreifen auf der silbrig schimmernden Bauchseite.

Bonito wird in runden Scheiben oder als Filet ganzjährig angeboten.

Bananenblätter erhalten Sie frisch oder gefroren in Asia-Läden. Sie eignen sich besonders für die Präsentation exotischer Speisen.

Papayas wachsen in unterschiedlichen Formen von rund bis oval überall in den Tropen.

Die empfindlichen Früchte sind im ausgereiften Zustand mit einigen Tropfen Zitronensaft eine Spezialität. Zum Kochen dürfen sie jedoch grün und noch halbfest sein. Gern werden sie als „Zartmacher" für Fleischgerichte verwendet, da sie ein eiweißspaltendes Enzym besitzen.

Die aus fermentierten Sojabohnen hergestellte Sojasauce wird in allen asiatischen Ländern zum Würzen verwendet.

Neben der hellen Sojasauce gibt es auch eine dunkle, die für Schmorgerichte verwendet wird.

Außerdem werden auch leicht gesalzene, pikante oder nach Pilzen schmeckende Sojasaucen angeboten.

Paprika-Ananas-Gemüse

ZUTATEN

100 g rote Paprika
100 g gelbe Paprika
100 g Staudensellerie
150 g Sojasprossen
100 g Gemüsezwiebeln
2 Stangen Zwiebellauch
150 g reife Ananas
2 Knoblauchzehen, fein gehackt
Saft einer Limette
80 g Butter
2 Tomaten
1 EL Tomatenmark
Salz, Palmzucker
frische Chilis nach Geschmack
2 EL geröstete Kokosflocken

ZUBEREITUNG

1 Paprika waschen, vierteln und entkernen.

2 Staudensellerie schälen und mit den Paprikavierteln in gleiche Streifen schneiden.

3 Zwiebeln und Ananas schälen und mit den abgezogenen Tomaten in 1 cm große Würfel schneiden.

4 Den fein gehackten Knoblauch mit den Zwiebeln in einer Pfanne anschwitzen, das Gemüse je nach Garpunkt nach und nach zugeben, das heißt erst den Staudensellerie kurz dünsten und dann die Paprikastreifen mit den Ananaswürfeln dazugeben und mit Deckel weiterdünsten.

5 Nach wenigen Minuten die Sojasprossen und den in Ringe geschnittenen Zwiebellauch wenige Minuten mit anziehen lassen.

6 Eventuell etwas Wasser und Tomatenmark hinzugeben und durchrühren.

7 Zum Schluß die Tomatenwürfel so zugeben, daß sie nur warm werden. Mit Salz, Chilis, Palmzucker und Limettensaft abschmecken.

8 Beim Anrichten mit Kokosflocken bestreuen.

Maisfritter

ZUTATEN

60 g Butter
100 ml Wasser
150 g Weizenmehl Type 405
2 Eier
100 g pürierter Mais
100 g Mais (Körner)
2 EL frisch geriebener Parmesan
2 EL Schnittlauchröllchen
Salz, Pfeffer nach Geschmack
Zum Ausbacken:
1 kg Kokosfett oder 1 l Öl

ZUBEREITUNG

1 Wie beim Brandteig Butter und Wasser aufkochen. Das Mehl unterrühren, bis sich ein Kloß bildet *(siehe Seite 62)*.

2 Den Teig anschließend in eine Schüssel geben und etwas abkühlen lassen.

3 Die verquirlten Eier unterheben, bis sich ein glatter Teig bildet.

4 Nach und nach die restlichen Zutaten unterrühren und mit Salz und Pfeffer abschmecken.

5 Den Teig mit einem geölten Löffel abstechen und in Fett schwimmend ausbacken.

Vorbereitungs- und Ausbackzeit: je ca. 20 Minuten

Kokos-Maispudding mit Tamarillosauce

ZUTATEN

FÜR DEN PUDDING

250 ml Vollmilch
300 ml Kokosmilch
250 ml süße Sahne
100 ml Batida de Coco
80 g Butter
300 g Zucker
200 g Maisgrieß
2 EL Rum
1 1/2 Vanilleschoten
60 g geröstete Kokosflocken

Zubereitungszeit: ca. 2 Stunden

TIP

Zu diesem Pudding schmecken auch andere Fruchtsaucen, zum Beispiel Mango- oder Kiwisauce sowie ein frischer Obstsalat.

Anstelle von Maisgrieß können Sie Hartweizengrieß oder Milchreis verwenden.

ZUBEREITUNG

1 Vanilleschoten längs halbieren, das Vanillemark herausschaben, mit Milch, Kokosmilch und süßer Sahne aufkochen.

2 50 Gramm Butter und den Zucker zufügen, Vanilleschoten entfernen.

3 Den Maisgrieß in die kochende Milch einrühren, etwa 3 Minuten unter Rühren köcheln und mit Batida de Coco und Rum abschmecken.

4 Den heißen Grieß in eine gebutterte Form geben und glattstreichen.

5 Im Kühlschrank abkühlen lassen, danach stürzen, portionieren und mit Kokosflocken bestreuen.

Tamarillosauce

ZUTATEN

5 reife Tamarillos
40 ml trockener Weißwein
40 ml roter Portwein
2 EL Grenadine Sirup
Saft einer Limette
100 g Puderzucker
Grand Marnier

Zubereitungszeit: ca. 30 Minuten

ZUBEREITUNG

1 Tamarillos halbieren, mit einem Eßlöffel das Fruchtfleisch herausnehmen, dieses mit Weiß-, Portwein und Puderzucker aufkochen und anschließend pürieren.

2 Nach dem Abkühlen mit Grenadine Sirup, Limettensaft und Grand Marnier abschmecken.

WUSSTEN SIE SCHON?

Die Tamarillo – auch Baumtomate genannt – kommt aus dem südamerikanischen Hochland, Afrika und Australien.

Obwohl sie dem Aussehen nach einer Tomate ähnelt, ist ihr Geschmack außerordentlich fruchtig, säuerlich und exotisch. Sie ist reich an Vitaminen und Mineralstoffen.

Bananen-Rum-Parfait

ZUTATEN

350 g reife Bananen
130 g Puderzucker
Saft einer Zitrone
20 ml dunkler Rum
100 g Zucker
4 Eigelb
1 Ei
30 ml Eierlikör
800 ml geschlagene Sahne
Schokoladenspäne

Vorbereitungszeit: 40 Minuten
Kühlzeit: 4-5 Stunden

ZUBEREITUNG

1 Bananen mit Puderzucker, Zitronensaft und Rum pürieren.

2 Zucker, Eigelb und das Ei im Wasserbad erst warm, dann kalt schlagen, bis die Masse weiß und cremig ist.

3 Die Hälfte der geschlagenen Sahne und das Bananenmus vorsichtig unter die Eimasse rühren.

4 Zum Schluß die restliche Sahne, Eierlikör und Schokoladenspäne unterheben.

5 Die Masse in eine Parfait-Form füllen und frieren.

Mozzarella-Cheddar-Wonton

ZUTATEN

150 g Mozzarella
150 g Cheddar
1 Frühlingszwiebel
1 TL gehackter grüner Pfeffer
1 Paket Wonton-Teig
2 Eigelb
Fett zum Fritieren

TIP

Wonton-Teig wird für Frühlingsrollen, Snacks und Dim-Sums fritiert oder gedämpft verwendet. Dieser Teig ist in zwei Größen im Asia-Laden erhältlich.

ZUBEREITUNG

1 Mozzarella und Cheddar fein würfeln, mit Frühlingszwiebelringen und grünem Pfeffer mischen.

2 Wonton-Blätter auslegen und mit je einem Teelöffel Käsemischung belegen.

3 Die Teigränder mit verquirltem Ei einstreichen. Den Teig einschlagen und gut andrücken.

4 In Fett schwimmend ausbacken und heiß servieren.

Vorbereitungszeit: ca. 15 Minuten
Zubereitungszeit: ca. 15 Minuten

Nashibirne mit Gorgonzola

ZUTATEN

(für ca. 10 Portionen)
150 g Gorgonzola
50 g Hüttenkäse
50 g Quark
Limettensaft
1 Jalapeño-Chili, fein gehackt
2 EL rote Paprikawürfel
Koriandergrün
Salz
4 Nashibirnen
Zitronensaft
2 St. Limonenblätter
100 ml halbtrockener Weißwein
50 ml Zimtblütenwein
Zucker nach Geschmack

ZUBEREITUNG

1 Weißwein, Zimtblütenwein, Zitronensaft, Limonenblätter und Zucker aufkochen.

2 Nashibirnen halbieren, entkernen, 5 Minuten darin auf den Punkt garen und in dem Fond erkalten lassen.

3 Gorgonzola, Quark und Limettensaft pürieren. Hüttenkäse, gehackte Chilis und Paprikawürfel unterheben und mit Salz abschmekken.

4 Mit einem Dressierbeutel und großer Sterntülle auf die Birnenhälften spritzen und mit Koriandergrün ausgarnieren.

Vorbereitungszeit: ca. 30 Minuten
Zubereitungszeit: ca. 15 Minuten

TIP

Zimtblütenwein erhalten Sie in asiatischen Lebensmittelgeschäften.

Er kann ersetzt werden, indem man 1 bis 2 Zimtstangen beim Garen dazugibt und nur Weißwein verwendet.

Register

A

Ahornsirup, -dip 32, 57

Ananas 203, 208, 224

Äpfel 53, 103, 148, 153, 170, 182

Apfel-Essig-Sauce 148

Aprikosen 30, 54

Artischocken 41, 94

Auberginen 50, 66, 69

Avocadomus 63

B

Bachforellenfilets 90

Baguettes 23

Bananen 192, 222, 227

Barbarie-Entenbrust 205

Birnen 63, 151, 185

Blaubeermark (Stippmilch) 184

Bleichsellerie 53, 95

Blüten 30, 58

Blutwurstscheiben (Arm und Reich) 170

Bohnensalat 209

Bohnensauce 221

Bonito 222

Brätlinge, Curry- 218

Braunbiersauce 172

Brombeerschmand 185

Brot, Zwiebel-Rosmarin- 214

Brunnenkresse-Sauce 113

Buttermilch 138, 182

Butterzubereitungen 94, 115, 139, 215

C

Cabua-Kakao (Kuchen) 80

Champagnertörtchen 55

Champignons 44, 129

Chayoten 198

Cheddar 64, 228

Crêpes 52

D

Datteln 81

Dinkelbratlinge 27

Döbel 163

E

Ebereschenbeeren 76

Eier 21, 49

Eierlikörsauce 123

Entenbrust 158, 205

Erdbeeren 31, 100, 122

Erdnußsauce 204

Estragon (Saucen) 129, 138

F

Feigen (Törtchen) 55

Fenchel 43, 93, 113, 136

Fisch 87, 141

Flugananas 201

Forellen 87, 90

Frischkäse 16, 39, 46, 104

Früchte 32, 191

Frühlingssalat 15

Frühlingszwiebeln 176, 211

Fünf Gewürze 205

G

Gänseblumen-Vinaigrette 17

Garam masala 197

Garnelen 199, 207

Gartengurken 48

Geflügel 111, 120

Geflügelbrustfleisch 111

Gemüse 20, 36, 65, 66, 89, 119, 145, 194, 219, 224

Glasnudeln 212

Gorgonzola 25, 39, 228

Gouda 114

Gratin, Kartoffel- 78

Greyerzer 27

Grießplätzchen 102

Grüne-Kräutersauce 164

Grütze 103

H

Hagebuttensauce 138, 185

Hähnchen 202

Halbgefrorenes 57

Hase, Falscher 75

Hechtfilet 160

Herbsttrompeten 134

Hirschmedaillons 159

Holunderblüten 30

Honig (Fenchel-Honig-Sauce) 113

J

Jakobsmuscheln 196

Jerk-Poulardenbrust 202

Johannisbeeren 142, 184

K

Kalb 134, 170

Kaninchen 131, 144

Karotten 176

Karpfenfilet 168

Kartoffeln 98, 116, 146, 162, 169

Käse 33, 82, 114, 154

Kasseler 120

Kichererbsen-Crêpes 52

Kirschdöbel 163

Knisterfinken 118

Knoblauchcreme 19

Kokosbrioche 213

Kokosmilch 213, 225

Korianderkompott 160

Kornbirnen 151

Kräuterbutter 45

Kräutersauce 77, 164, 173

Krebse 162

Kuchen, Weihnachts- 150

Kürbiskern-Dip 19

Kürbis-Korianderkompott 160

Kürbisse, Zwerg- 39

L

Lachs 106, 118, 141, 210, 211

Lammrücken 98, 178

Lauch 25, 114, 137

Leber (Schwein) 128

Limettencreme, -sauce 107, 198

Linsen 63, 68, 111, 130, 208

M

Macadamia 198

Mais 77, 114, 217, 224, 225

Mandelbrot 46

Mandelcreme 152

Mandelkuchen 80

Mango 70

Matjesfilets 93

Mayonnaise 41, 92

Meerrettich 90, 92, 165, 170, 198

Minimozzarella, eingelegt 56

Mirabellen-Kompott 125

Möhren 70, 146

Mozzarella-Cheddar-Wonton 228

N

Nashibirne 228

Nudelpickert 149

O

Ochse (Frico) 176

Orange 93, 94

P

Papayasauce 192

Paprika 28, 44, 112, 217, 224

Pastete 109, 127

Pastinaken 24

Perlhuhnbrust 147

Pflaumen 124, 125, 182

Pilze 51

Pistazien-Quarktaschen 124

Plätzchen 83, 88

Poulardenbrüste 202

Preiselbeermarinade 159

Pudding 225

Pumpernickel 104, 172

Punschsauce 151

Pute 110

Q

Quark 89, 124, 184

Quinoa-Plätzchen 216

R

Räucherfisch 96, 115

Rauke 22, 163

Reh 131

Reibekuchen 180

Reissalat 201

Renke 163

Rettich, Käse- 154

Rhabarber 103

Ricotta 25, 31, 79

Rinderfilet 176, 199, 212, 220

Rosmarinbrot 214

Rote Bete 92, 141

Rote Linsen 27, 63

Rotkohl 142, 161

Rotzungenfilet 106

Rum (Gewürzmischung) 200

S

Salak-Zwiebelschmalz 215

Salat 15, 69, 70, 206, 209

Sandmöhren 26

Sauerkraut (Rieslingkraut) 167

Schafskäsecreme 46

Schälrippchen 218

Schinkenpfannkuchen 172

Schlehensauce 133

Schmand-Brötchen 47

Schwarzbrot-Struwen 171

Schwarzwurzelgemüse 77

Schwedenmilch 48

Schweinefilet 96, 144, 172

Schweinenacken 120

Schweineschulter 108

Seeteufelbäckchen 196

Seeteufelfilet 196

Seildrehermahl 120

Sellerie 64, 95

Sesam 23, 53, 72

Sherry-Gemüse-Sauce 145

Sojabohnen 67

Sojasprossen 77

Spare-ribs 218

Spargel 94, 96

Stiltoncreme 81

Stippmilch 184

Strauchtomaten 98

Stubenküken 174

Stutenklößchen 142

Süppchen, kalt 48

Suppen 74, 116, 142, 166

Sushi 194

T

Tafelspitz 112

Tamarillosauce 226

Tandoori 197, 202

Teriyaki 200

Thübingerle, G'rissene 73

Tofu 40, 41, 67, 68

Tomaten 87, 204, 215

Tomatenmark 215

Tomatensauce 42

Topinambur 159

Traubenkompott 56

V

Vinaigrette 17

Vollkorn-Croissants (versch.) 45, 62, 73, 82

W

Walnußbaguette 19, 23

Weißkohlsalat 70

Welfenhut 186

Welsfilet 87

West-Indies 200

Wildbrühe 132

Williams-Christ-Birnen 151

Winterendivien 159

Wirsingsalat 140

Wonton 228

Wurzelrübencreme 24

Z

Zanderfilet 106, 167

Zitrone (Zutat) 122, 153

Zucchini 69, 88, 98

Zuckerschoten 93

Zwergkürbisse 39

Hinweise zu den Rezepten

MENGEN

Die angegebenen Mengen in den Zutatenlisten beziehen sich auf 4 Portionen, soweit nicht anders angegeben. Bei Eßlöffel und Teelöffelangaben wurde von gestrichenen Maßen ausgegangen.

ZEITEN

Alle Zeiten sind Richtwerte, die nach individueller Fähigkeit kürzer oder länger sein können.

BACKZEITEN

Sie beziehen sich auf Elektroherd mit Ober- und Unterhitze. Bei einem Umluftherd reduzieren sich die Temperaturangaben um ca. 25 Prozent.

ABKÜRZUNGEN

EL   Eßlöffel
TL   Teelöffel
mg   Milligramm
g   Gramm   (1000 mg = 1 g)
kg   Kilogramm (1000 g = 1 kg)
ml   Milliliter   (1000 ml = 1 l)
cl   Zentiliter   (10 ml = 1 cl)
l   Liter   (1000 ml/100 cl = 1 l)
Msp.   Messerspitze
Prise   die Menge, die zwischen zwei Fingerspitzen zu fassen ist

Umrechnung für Flüssigkeiten

1/8 l	125 ml	1	l	1000 ml
1/4 l	250 ml	0,1	l	100 ml
1/2 l	500 ml	1	cl	10 ml

RICHTWERTE

Maß für einen normalen Eßlöffel oder Teelöffel, gestrichen voll:

Lebensmittel	EL	TL
Mehl	10 g	3 g
Speisestärke	10 g	5 g
Zucker	15 g	5 g
Salz	10 g	5 g
Fett	15 g	5 g
Öl	10 g	5 g
Puderzucker	10 g	3 g

Edition cuisine
im Verlag Glückauf

L'Art Gourmand

Stilleben für Auge, Kochkunst und Gourmets von Aertsen bis Van Gogh

Herausgegeben von Paul Beusen, Sybille Ebert-Schifferer und Ekkehard Mai

Leineneinband mit Schutzumschlag im Format 25 cm x 30,5 cm. 1997. 382 Seiten mit meist farbigen Abbildungen

Preis 138 DM (1008 öS/138 sFr)
ISBN 3-7739-0675-7

Der Untertitel verrät das Besondere dieses einzigartigen Kunstbuchs: Das kulinarische Europa stellt sich dar in einem Stilleben für Auge, Kochkunst und Gourmets. Ausgehend von dem Plan, die gleichnamige Kunstausstellung mit einem attraktiven Katalog aufzuwerten, ist dieses faszinierende und außergewöhnliche Buch entstanden.

VGE cuisine

Seit 1996 bietet die VGE-Versandbuchhandlung unter diesem Label ein spezielles Leistungsbündel für Hoteliers, Gastronomen und Küchenpraktiker an.

Fordern sie unseren Prospekt an oder bestellen Sie direkt:

Verlag Glückauf GmbH
Montebruchstraße 2
D-45219 Essen
Telefon   (0 20 54) 9 24-201
Telefax   (0 20 54) 9 24-209
E-Mail   vge-cuisine@t-online.de
Internet www.vge.de